Trade and Markets in Byzantium

DUMBARTON OAKS BYZANTINE SYMPOSIA AND COLLOQUIA

Series Editor
Margaret Mullett

Editorial Board
John Duffy
John Haldon
Ioli Kalavrezou

Trade and Markets in Byzantium

Edited by
CÉCILE MORRISSON

Dumbarton Oaks Research Library and Collection

Copyright © 2012 by Dumbarton Oaks Research Library and Collection
Trustees for Harvard University, Washington, D.C.
All rights reserved
Printed in the United States of America

Library of Congress Cataloging-in-Publication Data

Trade and markets in Byzantium / edited by Cécile Morrisson.
   p. cm. — (Dumbarton Oaks Byzantine symposia and colloquia)
   Includes index.
   ISBN 978-0-88402-377-7 (hbk. : alk. paper)
 1. Byzantine Empire—Commerce—History. 2. Byzantine Empire—Economic conditions.
   I. Morrisson, Cécile.
   HF405.T73 2012
   381.09495—dc23
                       2011046482

www.doaks/org/publications

Designed and typeset by Barbara Haines

Cover image: Amphora with Confronted Hybrid Figures, polychrome glazed and incised ceramic.
Antioch, 13th century. Washington, D.C., Dumbarton Oaks, BZ.1967.8.

To the memory of Angeliki Laiou—

pathbreaking leader in the study of the Byzantine economy,

inspiring and irreplaceable friend and colleague

χάρις

CONTENTS

Foreword ix

Introduction 1
CÉCILE MORRISSON

Late Antiquity and the Early Middle Ages

ONE • Were Late Roman and Byzantine Economies Market Economies?
A Comparative Look at Historiography 13
JEAN-MICHEL CARRIÉ

TWO • Regional and Interregional Exchanges in the Eastern
Mediterranean during the Early Byzantine Period
The Evidence of Amphorae 27
DOMINIQUE PIERI

THREE • Movements and Markets in the First Millennium
Information, Containers, and Shipwrecks 51
MICHAEL MCCORMICK

FOUR • Commerce and Exchange in the Seventh and Eighth Centuries
Regional Trade and the Movement of Goods 99
JOHN F. HALDON

The Middle and Late Byzantine Periods

FIVE • Regional Networks in the Balkans in the Middle and Late Byzantine Periods 125
ANGELIKI E. LAIOU†

SIX • Regional Networks in Asia Minor during the Middle Byzantine Period,
Seventh–Eleventh Centuries
An Approach 147
JOHANNES KODER

SEVEN • Business as Usual?
Archaeological Evidence for Byzantine Commercial Enterprise
at Amorium in the Seventh to Eleventh Centuries 177
CHRISTOPHER LIGHTFOOT

EIGHT • Byzantine Glazed Ceramics on the Market
An Approach 193
DEMETRA PAPANIKOLA-BAKIRTZI

West and East: Local Exchanges in Neighboring Worlds

NINE • Local and Interregional Exchanges in the Lower Po Valley, Eighth–Ninth Centuries 219
SAURO GELICHI

TEN • Adriatic Trade Networks in the Twelfth and Early Thirteenth Centuries 235
ROWAN W. DORIN

ELEVEN • Annual Fairs, Regional Networks, and Trade Routes in Syria, Sixth–Tenth Centuries 281
ANDRÉ BINGGELI

TWELVE • Trade and Economy in Antioch and Cilicia in the Twelfth and Thirteenth Centuries 297
SCOTT REDFORD

THIRTEEN • Regional Exchange and the Role of the Shop in Byzantine and Early Islamic Syria-Palestine
An Archaeological View 311
ALAN WALMSLEY

Markets and the Marketplace

FOURTEEN • From *polis* to *emporion*?
Retail and Regulation in the Late Antique City 333
LUKE LAVAN

FIFTEEN • Weighing, Measuring, Paying
Exchanges in the Market and the Marketplace 379
CÉCILE MORRISSON

SIXTEEN • Daily Life at the Marketplace in Late Antiquity and Byzantium 399
BRIGITTE PITARAKIS

Conclusion

SEVENTEEN • Byzantine Trade
Summary and Prospect 429
PETER TEMIN

Abbreviations 437
About the Authors 441
Index 445

FOREWORD

This book emerged from the 2008 Spring Symposium held at Dumbarton Oaks 2–4 May. For their help in organizing the meeting, blessed by clement weather that enabled participants to fully enjoy all the graces of the gardens, I am most grateful to Polly Evans, Danica Kane, Mario Garcia, and Joe Mills, who looked to its smooth running and recording. My warm thanks to Jan Ziołkowski, Director of Dumbarton Oaks, who hosted and welcomed his first Symposium of Byzantine Studies with his characteristic elegance and openness. My special gratitude to the then Director of Byzantine Studies, Alice-Mary Talbot, who directed so graciously and efficiently this thirteenth and last Symposium of her tenure. I also thank the contributors who have taken time out of their busy schedules to participate in the colloquium, to discuss reciprocally their respective papers, and then to create this book.

After the Symposium, it was decided to include two studies of great relevance to our topic: that of Rowan Dorin, doctoral student of Angeliki Laiou, on Adriatic trade networks in the twelfth and early thirteenth centuries and that of Luke Lavan on retail and regulation in the late antique city.

This is the fourth volume in the series Dumbarton Oaks Byzantine Symposia and Colloquia: it was preceded by *Becoming Byzantine: Children and Childhood in Byzantium,* edited by Alice-Mary Talbot and Arietta Papaconstantinou (2009); *The Old Testament in Byzantium,* edited by Paul Magdalino and Robert Nelson (2010); and *San Marco, Byzantium, and the Myths of Venice,* edited by Henry Maguire and Robert Nelson (2010). Editing and producing this book proved to be a longer process than some impatient authors would have liked. The result will, I hope, compensate for their regrets. Alice-Mary Talbot and her successor, Margaret Mullett, were instrumental in preparing the papers for publication, and the Director of Publications, Kathy Sparkes, brought her special skills to the quality of illustrations and her stamina to set the book on track. Joel Kalvesmaki scrutinized the manuscript with his usual acumen. Alice Falk copyedited the mass of papers with great patience. To all, I extend special gratefulness.

Early in the preparation of this publication, the untimely and shocking death of Angeliki Laiou, an immense loss to the whole world of Byzantine studies, stirred particular grief among all participants in the Symposium, speakers and listeners alike. This had been the last occasion on which she met her colleagues in community and delivered a paper, and the last time she attended a symposium at Dumbarton Oaks, the institution and place to which she had devoted such passionate and clear-minded energy during the years of her directorship (1989–98) and well beyond. There was not a hint of her impending illness; her presence was as imposing and her interventions as sharp and appropriate as ever.

It is just and meet that this book be dedicated to her memory as a modest token of our debt to a great historian. Without her pioneering work on the Byzantine economy, the present studies would probably not have been written or assembled.

Cécile Morrisson

Introduction

Although trade is often featured in Byzantine archaeological meetings or in those offering a regional perspective, it is rarely the center of them. The symposium that took place in Dumbarton Oaks on 2–4 May 2008 and gave rise to this book was entirely devoted to trade and markets in Byzantium. It was not, however, the first colloquium with Byzantine trade as its main subject. The Oxford conference held at Somerville College on 29 May 1999 (later edited and published by Sean Kingsley and Michael Decker as *Economy and Exchange in the East Mediterranean during Late Antiquity*) may have been the first to set forth down this path—if "late antiquity" is taken as coterminous with "Byzantine"—and to signal the revived attention spurred by the accumulating wealth of new archaeological material.[1] Because of its wider chronological range, the British 38th Spring Symposium of Byzantine Studies titled "Byzantine Trade (4th–12th c.): Recent Archaeological Work," held in Oxford in March 2004, was advertised as the first symposium directly focused on Byzantine trade.[2] Finally, another conference held in Vienna in October 2005, codirected and just published by one of our speakers, Johannes Koder—"Handelsgüter und Verkehrswege: Aspekte der Warenversorgung im östlichen Mittelmeerraum (4. bis 15. Jahrhundert)"—underscored the growing interest in the subject.[3]

Trade deserves special attention because, as many economic historians have shown, it plays an essential role in the economy and particularly in economic development; the famous slogan "Trade Not Aid" embraced by African leaders and Western economists nicely encapsulates the idea that growth results not from massive aid but from an increase in exports, which—as the examples of Japan, Korea, Taiwan, and now China demonstrate—leads underdeveloped economies out of poverty.[4] All things being equal, the evolution of the Byzantine economy from the ninth to the twelfth century and, later, from small-scale trade to far-flung involvement in international exchanges clearly illustrates the correlation between the expansion of trade and that of the economy in general. However they interpret its

---

1 S. Kingsley and M. Decker, eds., *Economy and Exchange in the East Mediterranean during Late Antiquity: Proceedings of a Conference at Somerville College, Oxford, 29th May, 1999* (Oxford, 2001).
2 M. Mundell Mango, ed., *Byzantine Trade, 4th–12th Centuries: The Archaeology of Local, Regional and International Exchange,* Papers of the Thirty-eighth Spring Symposium of Byzantine Studies, St John's College, University of Oxford, March 2004, Society for the Promotion of Byzantine Studies 14 (Aldershot, 2009); review by J.-P. Sodini and me in *The Medieval Review* 10.03.04 (March 2009), at http://hdl.handle.net/2022/6770 (accessed August 2010).

3 E. Kislinger, J. Koder, and A. Künzler, *Handelsgüter und Verkehrswege/Aspekte der Warenversorgung im östlichen Mittelmeerraum (4. bis 15. Jahrhundert),* Österreichische Akademie der Wissenschaften, Veröffentlichungen zur Byzanzforschung 18 (Vienna, 2010). This volume appeared too late for its contents to be taken into account here.
4 World Bank, "Industrialization and Foreign Trade," in *World Development Report 1987* (New York, 1987), 38–170, available at http://go.worldbank.org/6DBKU5WP10 (accessed August 2010); S. Edwards, "Openness, Trade Liberalization, and Growth in Developing Countries," *Journal of Economic Literature* 31 (1993): 1358–93.

causes and context, this expansion is now generally recognized by historians. An expanding trade relies on an efficient division of labor, about which Adam Smith said, with typical Scottish humor: "Man has almost constant occasion for the help of his brethren, and it is in vain for him to expect it from their benevolence only."[5]

Indeed, the permanence of interregional and international relations, defined as the exchange of commodities, information, and population at all levels, which Peregrine Horden and Nicholas Purcell labeled "connectivity," is a primary concern of their *Corrupting Sea* and of another magisterial book, Michael McCormick's *Origins of the European Economy*,[6] while receiving due consideration in the *Economic History of Byzantium*, edited by Angeliki Laiou. In her final overview, she pointed to the parallels she had drawn between the West and the Byzantine economy as supporting her "insistence on trade as a dynamic element in the medieval economy, especially in the eleventh and twelfth centuries."[7] In his no less monumental *Framing the Early Middle Ages*, Chris Wickham proclaimed that his final chapter, "Systems of Exchange," was "in many ways the core of the book."[8] Although it may have been a later addition and a shift of thinking by an author who has reflected for many years on the transformation of the Roman world, it marks a welcome recognition of the importance of trade. The recent assessment of early and mid-Byzantine trade at the regional and international levels provided by the contributions to the Oxford 2004 symposium clearly recognized its vitality and role, even in the dark eighth century, in comparison with "non-economic exchange."

"Trade and Markets" versus the Byzantine Market Economy

The invitation letter stated that the Symposium would "focus equally on markets and the market place." Because of the polysemy of the term "market," this phrase requires qualification. The Dumbarton Oaks meeting did not consider the concept of *the* Byzantine market, defined as an economic system of transactions to exchange goods and services, nor did it formally assess different models of the extension of the Byzantine market economy, whether constituted in a comprehensive network of relatively independent markets or in fragmented, unconnected markets within the more restrictive frame of a tributary state.

But that long-debated topic could not be passed over entirely; it is treated in the first and last chapters of this volume. In the latter, Peter Temin analyzes the Polanyian concepts of reciprocity, redistribution, and exchange and Frederic Pryor's differentiation of exchanges and transfers, before stating the conditions in prices and individual behavior that are characteristic of a market economy. The skeptics who deny the existence of a Byzantine "market" should take note that a market economy is one in which market exchanges are the most common type of interaction—other forms of exchanges, whether reciprocal or redistributive, may take place as well, as indeed was the case in Byzantium. In the first chapter, Jean-Michel Carrié recalls the shifting fortunes of the "traditional, innocently modernist" model of late antiquity in the early twentieth century and the "primitivist" one, before offering his own characterization of the late Roman market economy. He concurs with Peter Temin in defining it as a "conglomeration of interdependent markets."[9] And this notion of the Byzantine economy as a network of interconnected relatively "free" markets[10] implicitly lies behind most of the chapters in this volume.

Trade in the Debate Regarding the Ancient Economy

A short account of the various schools of thought may be of use. Broadly speaking, the "modernists" view the ancient economy as functioning, all things being equal, in ways comparable to the modern one, with differences in quantity and not quality; this idea was maintained by both Michael Rostovtzeff

---

5 A. Smith, *An Inquiry into the Nature and Causes of the Wealth of Nations* (1776), book I, chap. 2.2.
6 P. Horden and N. Purcell, *The Corrupting Sea: A Study of Mediterranean History* (Oxford, 2000); review by M. Whittow in *English Historical Review* 116 (2001): 900–2; M. McCormick, *Origins of the European Economy: Communications and Commerce, A.D. 300–900* (Cambridge, 2001).
7 A. E. Laiou, "The Byzantine Economy: An Overview," in *EHB* 3:1148.
8 C. Wickham, *Framing the Early Middle Ages: Europe and the Mediterranean, 400–800* (Oxford, 2005), 693.

9 J.-M. Carrié, "Market Economies? Links between Late Roman and Byzantine Economic Historiography," below, 13.
10 P. Temin, "A Market Economy in the Early Roman Empire," *JRS* 91 (2001): 169–81.

and Henri Pirenne.[11] The "primitivists," on the other hand, insist, as did Moses Finley in several influential essays, that modern analysts cannot approach the ancient economy using economic concepts ignored by its actors and that it was essentially driven by social forces rather than a desire for profit.[12] The ideal of self-sufficiency (*autarkeia*) prevailed; there was hardly any division of labor, regional specialization, or technical innovation; goods were traded or rather redistributed mainly for social or political reasons; and trade played a negligible role in the economy. This "academic battleground," to use Keith Hopkins's phrase,[13] involved mainly historians of the early and late Roman economy, as Rostovtzeff's views opposed those of Hugo Jones, but it did not leave Byzantinists untouched. Michael Hendy, who acknowledged his intellectual debt to Finley, Jones, and Philip Grierson,[14] brilliantly took sides with them in his great book and other studies in which he contended that the role of the state in the "Byzantine monetary economy" was paramount: trade, in his view, played no part at all in the state's monetary policy nor in its resources and only a limited one in monetary distribution and circulation.[15] Evelyne Patlagean also upheld the approach of "primitivists," relying on the perspectives of Karl Polanyi, Moses Finley, and Marcel Mauss (notably in her paper delivered at Spoleto in 1992).[16]

In contrast, Angeliki Laiou was well aware of the developments of contemporary economic analysis and modern economic history and did not shy from employing their categories in her reasoning. Therefore Patlagean implicitly considered her a "modernist," in her long, nuanced review of *The Economic History of Byzantium* in 2004.[17] Yet Laiou's conception of the Byzantine economy was quite balanced, and she did not belong among those whom Carrié calls the traditional, innocent modernists. Before outlining Byzantine trade in the middle Byzantine period,[18] she devoted an entire chapter to the noneconomic forms of exchange as defined by Mauss and Polanyi,[19] which Grierson highlighted in his pioneering and famous article, "Commerce in the Dark Ages."[20] For the late Roman period, readers should consult the seminal article by Richard Whittaker and his analysis of its "tied trade," as well as the more recent assessment offered in the introduction to the *Cambridge Economic History of Greco-Roman Antiquity*.[21]

In that authoritative volume, distribution in the early Roman Empire is viewed from a more balanced perspective, which signals that the debate has subsided and a new consensus has been reached. Neville Morley, among others, recognizes that the Roman economy was "organized through market incentives or directed through requisition and compulsion" and knew a "degree of integration, of the movement of goods, people, and ideas."[22] In spite of the revival

---

11 M. I. Rostovtzeff, *A History of the Ancient World*, vol. 1 (Oxford, 1926), 10; H. Pirenne, *Mahomet et Charlemagne*, 2nd ed. (Paris, 1937), 219.
12 M. I. Finley, *The Ancient Economy*, 3rd ed. (Berkeley, 1999). See also the account of M. M. Austin and P. Vidal-Naquet, *Economic and Social History of Ancient Greece: An Introduction*, trans. and rev. M. M. Austin (London, 1977); originally published as *Économies et sociétés en Grèce ancienne* (Paris, 1972).
13 K. Hopkins, introduction to *Trade in the Ancient Economy*, ed. P. Garnsey, K. Hopkins, and C. R. Whittaker (London, 1983), ix.
14 M. F. Hendy, *The Economy, Fiscal Administration and Coinage of Byzantium* (Northampton, 1989), x.
15 Idem, *Studies in the Byzantine Monetary Economy, c. 300–1450* (Cambridge, 1985). He strongly opposed attempts to apply economic reasoning to the interpretation of monetary developments, as in the case of the eleventh-century debasement (25).
16 É. Patlagean, "Byzance et les marchés du grand commerce vers 830–vers 1030: Entre Pirenne et Polanyi," in *Mercati e mercanti nell'alto medioevo: L'area Euroasiatica e l'area Mediterranea*, Settimane di studi del Centro italiano di studi sull'alto medioevo 40 (Spoleto, 1993), 587–632.

17 É. Patlagean, "Écrire l'histoire économique de Byzance: À propos d'un ouvrage récent," *Le Moyen Age* 110 (2004): 659–69. She used the metaphor "mise à proximité" to mean "modernism."
18 A. E. Laiou, "Economic and Noneconomic Exchange," in *EHB* 2:681–96.
19 Eadem, "Exchange and Trade, Seventh–Twelfth Centuries," in *EHB* 2:697–770.
20 P. Grierson, "Commerce in the Dark Ages: A Critique of the Evidence," *Transactions of the Royal Historical Society*, 5th ser., 9 (1959): 123–40 (repr. in idem, *Dark Age Numismatics* [London, 1979], art. II).
21 C. R. Whittaker, "Late Roman Trade and Traders," in Garnsey, Hopkins, and Whittaker, eds., *Trade in the Ancient Economy*, 163–80; I. Morris, R. P. Saller, and W. Scheidel, introduction to *Cambridge Economic History of Greco-Roman Antiquity*, ed. I. Morris, R. P. Saller, and W. Scheidel (Cambridge, 2007), 1–7. See also W. Scheidel and S. von Reden, eds., *The Ancient Economy* (Edinburgh, 2002), which offers a collection of reprinted articles on the subject with their own comments, and J. Manning and I. Morris, eds., *The Ancient Economy: Evidence and Models* (Stanford, 2005), which collects original essays attempting to frame the enlarged available evidence in new models that incorporate basic economics and abandon the Finleyan orthodoxy.
22 N. Morley, "The Early Roman Empire: Distribution," in Morris, Saller, and Scheidel, eds., *Cambridge Economic History of Greco-Roman Antiquity*, 570–91, at 591; and idem, *Trade in Classical Antiquity* (Cambridge, 2007).

of the old polemic provoked by Peter Bang's recent book,[23] the debate has progressed to the point that all participants are at least more aware of the importance for current and future investigations of two elements: on the one hand, quantification of the "performance" of the Roman economy (production, input-output, costs and benefits, population and standards of living, prices, sales, and exports),[24] and, on the other hand, the role of structures such as institutions, technology, ecology, demography, and ideology. Though not put in the same terms, such an approach was by and large that of the *Economic History of Byzantium,* which provided the framework for this Symposium; we thus did not take up the debate again.

Local, Regional, and Interregional Exchanges: The Evidence

The purpose of bringing together historians and archaeologists was to gather further evidence and present the state of the art of research on the movement of goods—"things that travelled" in the words of David Whitehouse[25]—within the Byzantine world on markets at various levels, especially at the regional scale. Regional trade was rather neglected in previous research, which had long been more interested in interregional and long-distance trade and the mostly prestige or luxury items it carried than in smaller regional and local markets and marketplaces. The numerous markets that make up the Byzantine market economy imply a chain of transactions in which trade takes place on varied tiers. How to classify these markets is an issue considered by several chapters.[26] Various criteria can be used for this purpose, most notably those offered by Luuk de Ligt in his *Fairs and Markets in the Roman Empire:*[27] type of transaction, duration, and distance. A combination of the last two, duration and distance—the latter reflecting the constraints on human travel in an ancient or medieval context—seems relatively free from dispute and has been used in this book.

The Three Levels of Trade

Agreement emerged in the Symposium on the following rough limits of the three tiers:

ONE Local, defined as a one-day transit time, or within a radius of less than about 50 kilometers (31 miles) by land or the distance of one day's sailing,[28] to a maximum of two or three days' travel on foot.[29] This is the smallest and the most difficult level to apprehend. But the diffusion of the most ordinary cooking ware generally constitutes a good proxy of a network with a 50-kilometer radius, as shown by Alan Walmsley, who uses as a marker Jerash Bowls, Palestinian Fine Ware from Jerusalem, and Red Painted Ware of Jordanian origin (possibly from ʿAmmān).[30] Archaeology is now fortunately devoting greater attention to this kind of ordinary ceramics—witness the now regular meetings on Late Roman Coarse Wares (LRCW), published in three volumes to date—and this area of research,

---

23 P. F. Bang, *The Roman Bazaar: A Comparative Study of Trade and Markets in a Tributary Empire* (Cambridge, 2008). P. Temin published a critical review in *Journal of Economic History* 69 (2009): 1165–66; for more positive remarks from a historian, see B. Shaw in *Journal of Interdisciplinary History* 41 (2010): 126–27.
24 A. Bowman and A. Wilson, eds., *Quantifying the Roman Economy: Methods and Problems* (Oxford, 2009), particularly A. Wilson's "Approaches to Quantifying Roman Trade," 210–49; M. Fulford's "Response" to this chapter, 250–65; and W. Harris's "Comment," 259–65. See also the contribution to the proceedings of the Brussels Francqui Conference (2009): "Long-term Quantification in Ancient Mediterranean History," *Quantifying Monetary Supplies in Greco-Roman Times,* ed. F. de Callataÿ, Pragmateiai 19 (Bari, 2011).
25 D. Whitehouse, "'Things that Travelled': The Surprising Case of Raw Glass," *Early Medieval Europe* 12 (2003): 301–5.
26 See A. E. Laiou, "Regional Networks in the Balkans in the Middle and Late Byzantine Periods"; S. Redford, "Trade and Economy in Antioch Cilicia in the Twelfth and Thirteenth Centuries"; and J. Koder, "Regional Networks in Asia Minor during the Middle Byzantine Period (Seventh–Eleventh Centuries): An Approach."
27 L. de Ligt, *Fairs and Markets in the Roman Empire: Economic and Social Aspects of Periodic Trade in a Pre-industrial Society,* Dutch Monographs on Ancient History and Archaeology 11 (Amsterdam, 1993), 1, 79–81.
28 Laiou, "Regional Networks in the Balkans," 126 n. 5; M. McCormick, "Byzantium on the Move: Imagining a Communications History," in *Travel in the Byzantine World: Papers from the Thirty-fourth Spring Symposium of Byzantine Studies, Birmingham, April 2000,* ed. R. Macrides, Society for the Promotion of Byzantine Studies 10 (Aldershot, 2000), 3–29; Koder, "Regional Networks in Asia Minor," 147.
29 J. Haldon, "Commerce and Exchange in the Seventh and Eighth Centuries: Regional Trade and the Movement of Goods," 99.
30 See in this volume A. Walmsley, "Regional Exchange and the Role of the Shop in Byzantine and Early Islamic Syria-Palestine: An Archaeological View," 311–30.

though not systematized, is also being explored in the Byzantine period.

TWO Above this limit and below ten days' travel is the regional level;[31] in terms of distance, it corresponds to a radius of 100 to 300 kilometers. Regional travel also involves professional traders, whereas local trade is still partly or mostly in the hands of the local producers themselves.[32] For this tier, the ongoing study of unglazed coarse pottery is a promising line of research that is beginning to be investigated—for instance, in Amorion by Chris Lightfoot and his team[33]—and still has much to tell us. In defining regional networks, we are also aided by the study of ecological conditions for agricultural and other production. As Johannes Koder highlights, the supply radius from the hinterland to urban settlements varied according to the agrarian productivity of their respective landscapes. All things being equal, local and regional trade mostly concerned everyday staples (foodstuffs) and pottery, but it also handled raw material and energy sources for crafts such as hemp, flax, leather, iron, wood, charcoal, and so on.[34]

THREE Interregional trade connects two different regions that each have a radius of 100 to 300 kilometers. It is not necessarily carried over a long distance, but that is most frequently the case, for the two regions are not systematically coterminous. It is often but not always international; conversely, regional exchanges might cross over political boundaries in the middle Byzantine period, as between Byzantium and the Bulgars, or in the later period, as Scott Redford describes, between Armenian Cilicia and the Principality of Antioch, and as was the rule in the "small states" of the fragmented Byzantine world after 1204.

It should be pointed out that for maritime commerce, the distinction between the regional and interregional is more blurred, since the lower cost of transportation does not limit quantities as much as it does in terrestrial trade. Moreover, the two levels often intermingle, since commodities that travel long distances often end up in regional exchanges and vice versa, as the "intra-Adriatic port-hopping" described by Rowan Dorin illustrates.[35]

Sources: Archaeology, Numismatics, Texts, and Documents

Another obvious area of agreement pertains to our various sources, and the need to combine and cross-check them. The seminal contribution of archaeology is now fully and universally recognized. In many instances, as will be seen below, it opens entirely new avenues; in others, as in the case of Comacchio described by Sauro Gelichi,[36] it offers a welcome confirmation of the trends suggested by the study of written sources. The abundance of the material yielded by archaeology over the past fifty years, its context, and its wide distribution in themselves argue for a movement that, in the late Roman world as well as in the twelfth century and later, involved trade in a wide range of goods, from luxury items to more common commodities. Ceramics feature in many contributions of this volume: on the one hand, high-value glazed ceramics enable scholars to trace regional and interregional commerce and are a main focus of Demetra Papanikola-Bakirtzi's and Scott Redford's chapters; on the other hand, unpretentious and cheaper unglazed or even coarse pottery points to geographically smaller networks with a larger clientele.

The enormous progress made in the classification of amphorae and the location of their production centers, together with the analyses of their contents, enables Dominique Pieri, by plotting the varied provenances against the distribution of finds, not only to outline in detail the long-distance export and distribution of Gaza wine through the Mediterranean and to the West but also to highlight the regional imports in Beirut of Acre amphorae and Bag amphorae, as well as the local distribution of North Syrian ones, attested in Zeugma, Ruṣāfa, Apameia, and villages in the Limestone massif. "Operational" approaches to amphorae can lead to economic inferences: the implicit relation between the heavy Late Roman African amphorae of some 80 kilograms each and

---

31 Koder, "Regional Networks in Asia Minor," 147 and n. 3.
32 Laiou, "Regional Networks in the Balkans," 126.
33 C. Lightfoot, "Business as Usual? Archaeological Evidence for Byzantine Commercial Enterprise in Amorium in the Seventh to Eleventh Centuries," 190.
34 Koder, "Regional Networks in Asia Minor," 155–58.

35 In this volume, R. Dorin, "Adriatic Trade Networks in the Twelfth and Early Thirteenth Centuries," 264.
36 See in this volume S. Gelichi, "Local and Interregional Exchanges in the Lower Po Valley (Eighth–Ninth Centuries)."

elaborate port facilities; the ergonomic explanation of the curious shape of Aegean Kapitän 2 or Pieri's Late Roman 9, which was easier for a single stevedore to grasp and carry; and the lightness and thinness of the walls of sixth-century globular amphorae, which made it possible to transport more content for the same tare and were better adapted to beachside or smaller-scale landings as well as to reuse.[37]

Although ceramics evidence has brought a revolutionary change in our perception and even has enabled us to quantify Roman and Byzantine exchanges, as Pieri emphasizes, the bias resulting from the "invisibility" of commodities transported in perishable packing (bags, skins, or textiles) or simply as a loose cargo, such as grain, lentils and other pulses, textiles, spices, furs, and the like, seems nearly insuperable for archaeological investigation, where they hardly leave any trace. The problem is addressed at length in Michael McCormick's chapter below. The solution is often to turn to indirect evidence—primarily written documents; for example, their frequent mention of *cupae* in the West and βουττία in the East points to the key role of wooden containers in transportation.

Some contributors to the Symposium included numismatics—an approach rarely taken before, which bears tribute to the efforts of researchers in that discipline to make its material available to and usable by nonspecialists—even if its evidence, not yet included in a geodatabase, is difficult to interpret because coins change hands so much more easily than do other materials.[38] Nevertheless, when considered in aggregate and in relation to other material, whether archaeological or documentary, coin circulation can help define chronological patterns or spatial distribution, as the chapters by Lightfoot, John Haldon, and Laiou show. The latter two authors saw as paradoxical the lack of precious metal coin finds from large and active production and trade centers such as Corinth or Athens, but this phenomenon should not be surprising; indeed, it is common throughout the Byzantine world, due to the higher rate of loss of petty coinage (one is much more likely to expend effort to recover a gold or silver coin than a small one of little value). The coexistence in some particular areas of coins from various political entities sometimes points to a "currency community," as in the case of the Antioch region and Cilicia in the thirteenth century—a community that is also made visible in a community of taste, as expressed by the motifs of the Port Saint Symeon Ware or its imitations and their standardization.

The testimony of texts on trade have been used ever since Wilhelm Heyd's *Histoire du commerce du Levant au Moyen Âge* (1885–86) or Henri Pirenne's famous *Mahomet et Charlemagne* (posthumously published in 1937) for their meaningful and picturesque anecdotes, but not until Michael McCormick's *Origins of the European Economy* (2001) was the potential of all written sources and documents for statistical analysis fully recognized and exploited. The rich western archives, even when already the object of numerous studies, can provide new perspectives when approached from new angles, as Rowan Dorin does in his study of the regional Adriatic networks in the twelfth and early thirteenth centuries, before Venice had fully established her dominance of the region's sea-lanes.

More obliquely, literary or religious texts can also yield details in the many metaphors related to commercial practice, the good and evil deeds or the risks incurred as found in Church teachings on virtuous trading, and all the allusions to market-conditioned behavior. Such metaphors also tell us that trade and markets were so common that the many topoi based on them were readily understood by churchgoers.[39] Previously neglected texts, such as the Arab

---

37 See in this volume D. Pieri, "Regional and Interregional Exchanges in the Eastern Mediterranean in the Early Byzantine Period: The Evidence of Amphorae," and M. McCormick, "Movements and Markets in the First Millennium: Information, Containers, and Shipwrecks," as well as E. Zanini, "Forma delle anfore e forme del commercio tardoantico: Spunti per una riflessione," in *LRCW 3, Third International Conference on Late Roman Coarse Wares, Cooking Wares and Amphorae in the Mediterranean: Archaeology and Archaeometry, Comparison between Western and Eastern Mediterranean* (forthcoming).

38 C. Morrisson, "La monnaie sur les routes fluviales et maritimes des échanges dans le monde méditerranéen (VIe–IXe siècle)," in *L'acqua nei secoli altomedievali (Spoleto, 12–17 aprile 2007)*, Settimane di studio della Fondazione Centro italiano di studi sull'alto Medioevo 55 (Spoleto, 2008), 631–70. See the cautionary observations on the value of coins as evidence in A. Stahl, "Coinage," *Early Medieval Europe* 12 (2003): 293–99.

39 McCormick, "Movements and Markets in the First Millennium," analyzes several metaphors on trade, risk, profit, etc. 78–79; C. Morrisson, "Weighing, Measuring, Paying: Exchanges in the Market and the Marketplace," analyzes cases (legal or literary) of defrauders and swindlers, 387–88, 389–90]; L. Lavan, "From *polis* to *emporion*? Retail and Regulation in the Late Antique City," 333–77, examines shops and daily exchanges in late antiquity, passim.

almanacs and chronological treatises examined by André Binggeli, yield precious information on Bilād al-Shām's fairs (the regular intervals at which they were held and the area from which they drew attendees); those in Filasṭīn; those on the Damascus–Mecca route, which existed in the preceding period under Byzantine rule; and the later ones established in the Jazīra on the Euphrates axis.

Relying on this combined evidence, the essays in the first three sections of the book concur in depicting and analyzing the dynamics of local, regional, and interregional trade and that of the artisanal or manufactured products which were exchanged. The last section is devoted to the practical functioning and environment of the Byzantine marketplace.

Marketplace and Shops

The final chapters in this volume consider regulation and control of measures, weights, and payments—an essential institutional condition of the functioning of market exchange generally,[40] and specifically an important foundation of the Byzantine economy[41]—together with indirect taxes from the fifth to the fifteenth century. The unified system inherited from Rome, which was of great benefit in supporting market exchanges and lowering transaction costs, never disappeared even when Byzantium had to agree, from the twelfth century onward, that the privileged Italian merchant communities could use their own measures in their colonies.[42] Brigitte Pitarakis provides a material perspective on this legal and documentary survey by bringing together representations in various media of everyday transactions and installations and the widely attested archaeological remains of measuring and weighing instruments.

Markets as physical spaces have received scarcely any attention, except in the recent studies by Luke Lavan.[43] He offers here an in-depth and innovative study of archaeological evidence for shops and markets in late antiquity, combined with many references to the abundant literary sources. He presents an almost exhaustive survey of present knowledge of material environment for transactions, including market stalls (tables) revealed by slits cut in front of porticoes; wooden tables revealed by postholes and *topos* inscriptions; cellular shops, often grouped according to their trade and equipped with shelves for the display of goods, counters, and, in the case of taverns, benches or couches for customers; and specialized market buildings, whether tetragonal agorai and *macella* or sigma shopping plazas. In addition, he proposes a new interpretation of the legal texts (especially *CTh* 15) that have long been taken as a proof of the encroachment of streets and the transformation of the late antique city into a *medina*. The overall picture clearly supports his main argument that the "commercialization" of city centers was a sign not of urban decay but of a conscious evolution toward a new monumentality, accepted and even fostered by urban elites in the sixth century. This new urban environment obviously matched the active exchanges inferred elsewhere in the book from other sources.

The subject of shops and markets is also considered by Alan Walmsley in the last section of his chapter, which partly overlaps with Lavan's observations and complements them: in Byzantine and early Islamic Syria and Palestine, excavations of many secondary urban centers and even big villages (Ruṣāfa, Palmyra, Pella, Jarash, Skythopolis, Arsūf, Umm al-Raṣāṣ, Subaytah/Shivta) provide evidence from the sixth through the eighth century for market streets and agglomerated courtyard units, often located near the church or the mosque. The continuity, renovation, and even new construction of these facilities offer yet more proof of the vigorous functioning of local exchange.

* * * * * * * *

Though it may be bold to generalize, we may draw some conclusions about points of agreement between the contributors: a widely shared focus on

---

40 World Bank, *World Development Report 2002: Building Institutions for Markets* (New York, 2002), available at http://go.worldbank.org/YGBBFHL1Y0 (accessed August 2010).
41 On the importance of legal and social institutions and intangible resources for economic stability and growth in Byzantium, see A. E. Laiou and C. Morrisson, *The Byzantine Economy* (Cambridge, 2007), 17–22.
42 Morrisson, "Weighing, Measuring, Paying," 392–93.
43 L. Lavan, "Fora and Agorai in Mediterranean Cities: Fourth and Fifth Centuries A.D.," in *Social and Political Life in Late Antiquity*, ed. W. Bowden, C. Machado, and A. Gutteridge, Late Antique Archaeology 3.1 (Leiden, 2006), 195–249; T. Putzeys and L. Lavan, "Commercial Space in Late Antiquity," in *Objects in Context, Objects in Use: Material Spatiality in Late Antiquity*, ed. L. Lavan, E. Swift, and T. Putzeys, Late Antique Archaeology 5 (Leiden, 2007), 81–109.

geographical and ecological constraints to explain the formation and limitations of regional or local markets supplying an urban center, as well as close attention to the division of labor conducive to interregional exchanges. Relying on such analysis, many essays explore the correlation between trade and urbanization, an element most typically at work in the expansion of long-distance and interregional trade in the Adriatic and the Aegean beginning in the twelfth century or even earlier, since larger cities such as Venice or Constantinople could no longer rely on their medium-range hinterland to feed their inhabitants. Whereas the growth of urban centers was both a cause and a precondition for the emergence of interregional networks, the development of rural centers (e.g., in Boeotia) entailed the expansion of regional and local networks as analyzed by Laiou and Papanikola-Bakirtzi and in other studies. When examined over the course of centuries, most regions displayed common trends, though the mid-Byzantine decline did not occur at the same date everywhere, and the subsequent recovery started in some places as early as the late eighth or early ninth century, at others only in the late tenth century.

The most striking commonality is a new vision of the so-called dark age (the long eighth century, broadly speaking). It is true that increased localization and decreased quality of production in this period cannot be doubted, as exemplified inter alia by the restricted diffusion of Sagalassos local semi-fine and coarse kitchen wares; but contributors with different emphases and approaches converged in insisting on the continuity of general settlement and economic activity in Asia Minor. They also concurred in describing the resilience of some coastal areas or islands, like Cyprus, due to the survival of long-distance trade. However limited, these long-distance relations can be traced—for example, in the wide diffusion of Crimean transport amphorae as far as Butrint and in the new centers of trade in northern Italian sites like Comacchio. Resilience also characterized certain areas of inland Anatolia, where the decline of long-distance trade, the plague, and other factors had less effect and where the presence of the army stimulated agricultural and artisanal production aimed at satisfying its needs.

At the same time, weight was given to the analysis of regional diversity and to the changing patterns of networks, such as the growing importance of the Black Sea north–south route between Amastris, Paphlagonia, and Cherson; the shift of the Adriatic trade from a north–south to a west–east emphasis; the reorientation of Halmyros trade from its earlier destination, Thessalonike, to its western hinterland; and so on. Better knowledge of common wares or new approaches to documentary analysis enabled several contributors to look for the structure of local or regional networks, stressing the role of secondary distribution centers[44] or differentiating between regular and occasional markets.[45] New aspects or contexts of exchanges were brought to light for the first time, such as informal markets on the beachside and retail sales on board the tramp ships themselves, probably aimed at dodging imperial taxes.

Not all topics or aspects could be addressed, and regional trade in the late Byzantine period, for which contemporaneous documents can certainly yield more information than has already been retrieved,[46] was not thoroughly treated. Few attempts at quantification were made, despite their necessity for valid economic analysis (admittedly, their dependence on ancient and medieval documents obviously limits the precision of such efforts). One of the possible approaches to the subject suggested here relies on a renewed survey of shipwrecks, a much greater number of which are known now (ca. 309 for the Mediterranean, AD 300 to 1500) than in 1992, when Anthony Parker published his pioneering book on the subject.[47] Michael McCormick is aware of the imperfection of this proxy measure of seaborne traffic, due to the influence of such other factors as decline in population and demand, difference in ship sizes and the cargoes transported, variations in the sinking rate caused by different knowledge and conditions of navigation, and the age of the vessel.[48] Yet all these biases can be taken

---

44 Walmsley, "Regional Exchange and the Role of the Shop," below, 315, and Dorin, "Adriatic Trade Networks," below, 271, etc.
45 A. Bingelli, "Annual Fairs, Regional Networks, and Trade Routes in Bilād al-Shām (Sixth–Tenth Centuries)."
46 E.g., by K.-P. Matschke, "Commerce, Trade, Markets and Money: Thirteenth–Fifteenth Centuries," in *EHB* 2:771–806, who deals with "regional economic zones" at 782–89.
47 A. J. Parker, *Ancient Shipwrecks of the Mediterranean and the Roman Provinces*, BAR International Series 580 (Oxford, 1992).
48 McCormick, "Movements and Markets in the First Millennium," 89–98. See also Wilson's review of Parker's data in "Approaches to Quantifying Roman Trade," 219–29, who likewise both emphasizes an increase in the use of barrels rather than amphorae as perhaps leading to the decline in the number of perceived shipwrecks in late antiquity from its peak in the second

into account to qualify the present picture—a lower number of datable wrecks from the ninth to the fifteenth century than from antiquity, though other sources point to considerable numbers of bigger ships in the late medieval Mediterranean. Another task will be to compare assemblages of pottery production or usage, following on the pioneering attempts to quantify the frequency of late Roman sherds of a defined form (ARS) over time.[49] Similarly, the already well-known comparisons of find patterns from late antique Mediterranean sites published by Michael Fulford and Clementina Panella[50] could be extended to the Byzantine period, when more progress has been made in identifying ceramics and publishing sites—provided that there is enough consistency in how finds are recorded, classified, and published that the necessary geodatabases can be built. A number of hurdles, both methodological and practical (notably, unequal distribution of information) are still in the way, but a consensus on what we know, at least qualitatively, and what we do not has been achieved, and several lines of research have been proposed.

From my standpoint as the editor and a historian, such are the main points that I encourage the reader of this book to bear in mind. A genuine economic perspective is offered in Peter Temin's assessment at the end of this book. The variety and complexity of the exchange networks analyzed by the essays in this volume, the ubiquity of coins or at least the role of money as measure of exchange, the persistence of local exchanges throughout the designated period, and the recovery of long-distance trade from its eighth-century nadir, which signals the return to economic prosperity in the eleventh and twelfth centuries—all characterize the Byzantine markets as free but regulated. It now remains to follow the paths that have been opened in the various chapters of this volume.

Cécile Morrisson, August 2010

---

century AD and examines the influence of the size of ships on their sinking rate.

49 Wilson, "Approaches to Quantifying Roman Trade," 237–43.
50 M. G. Fulford, "To East and West: The Mediterranean Trade of Cyrenaica and Tripolitania in Antiquity," in *Libya: Research in Archaeology, Environment, History and Society, 1969–1989*, ed. D. J. Mattingly and J. A. Lloyd, Libyan Studies 20 (London, 1989), 169–91; C. Panella, "Gli scambi nel Mediterraneo Occidentale dal IV al VII secolo dal punto di vista di alcune 'merci,'" in *Hommes et richesses dans l'empire byzantin*, vol. 1, IVe–VIIe *siècle*, Réalités byzantines 1 (Paris, 1989), 129–41; eadem, "Merci e scambi nel Mediterraneo tardoantico," in *Storia di Roma*, ed. A. Carandini, L. Cracco Ruggini, and A. Giardina, vol. 3.2, *L'età tardoantico: I luoghi e le culture* (Turin, 1993), 613–97.

Late Antiquity and the Early Middle Ages

• ONE •

Were Late Roman and Byzantine Economies Market Economies?

A Comparative Look at Historiography

JEAN-MICHEL CARRIÉ

Economic history, a relatively recent branch of Byzantine studies,[1] has been tempted to convert itself from a traditional, innocently modernist approach to one that embraces the so-called primitivist paradigm.[2] Reacting against this tendency, *The Economic History of Byzantium,* edited by Angeliki Laiou, fortunately dissociated itself from the Polanyian and Finleyan models, sometimes at the risk of exposing itself to the kind of criticism addressed to the nineteenth-century "modernists" that precisely aroused, initially with good reasons and praiseworthy intents, the "primitivist" reaction.[3]

Roman economic history has a longer experience of debate between modernists and primitivists,[4] which has recently been reshaped in a persistently bitter controversy between primitivists and anti-primitivists, whom the former try to dismiss by labeling them "neo-modernists."[5] It suffices here to recall how swiftly the position favoring a market economy under the Roman Empire recently expressed by Peter Temin aroused an indignant reply from Peter Bang.[6] I myself am inclined to accept Temin's argument, except for the very last words of his article. Here his obvious pleasure in turning upside down Finley's formula that "ancient society did not have an economic system which was an enormous conglomeration of interdependent markets" perhaps led him to go beyond what his own argument permitted. Personally, I could even agree with his conclusion that "ancient Rome had an economic system that was an enormous conglomeration of interdependent markets," merely removing the adjective "enormous," though my chapter will revise upward the quantitative levels of production, consumption, and exchange of the Roman world. So the first part of my paper will be devoted to legitimizing the application of the word "market" to the Roman Empire. But independently of the position adopted in the confrontation between "primitivists"

---

1 The belatedness of Byzantine economic history should be connected with the same delay in studying the late Roman Orient, which is lamented by S. Kingsley and M. Decker, "New Rome, New Theories on Inter-regional Exchange: An Introduction to the East Mediterranean Economy in Late Antiquity," in *Economy and Exchange in the East Mediterranean during Late Antiquity: Proceedings of a Conference at Somerville College, Oxford, 29th May, 1999,* ed. S. Kingsley and M. Decker (Oxford, 2001), 1–27.
2 Especially M. F. Hendy, *Studies in the Byzantine Monetary Economy, c. 300–1450* (Cambridge, 1985).
3 See J.-M. Carrié in J.-M. Carrié and A. Rousselle, *L'Empire romain en mutation: Des Sévères à Constantin 192–337,* Points Histoire, Nouvelle Histoire de l'Antiquité 10 (Paris, 1999), 513–19, for a brief summary and essential bibliographical references.
4 The debate can even be traced back to the dissent between Karl Bücher and Eduard Meyer: see *The Bücher-Meyer Controversy,* ed. M. I. Finley (New York, 1979). Immanuel Wallerstein's theoretical analysis of precapitalistic societies remains embedded in a primitivist view of ancient economies—as noted by Gregg Woolf, who examines whether Wallerstein's economic models are applicable to the Roman world; see G. Woolf, "World-Systems Analysis and the Roman Empire," *JRA* 3 (1990): 44–58.
5 As has happened to me: J. Maucourant, "Le 'marché' est-il un 'signifiant vide'?" in *L'économie antique: Une économie de marché?,* ed. Y. Roman and J. Dalaison (Paris, 2008), 17–47, at 38.
6 P. Temin, "A Market Economy in the Early Roman Empire," *JRS* 91 (2001): 169–81; P. F. Bang, "Trade and Empire: In Search of Organizing Concepts for the Roman Economy," *Past and Present* 195 (2007): 3–54.

and "anti-primitivists," my impression is that Byzantinists, who have often turned to economic history from other backgrounds—the study of texts, artifacts, and immaterial civilization—could take advantage of the secular, rich, vivid, contradictory debate among historians of antiquity, in which the two camps abundantly developed their arguments. Because I, as an anti-primitivist, do not feel myself a neo-modernist, I must confess to often feeling ill at ease and bewildered at some enthusiastic descriptions of Byzantine economic life, as a whole or in some of its particular aspects, in terms of astounding intensity, productivity, and, most upsetting to me, striking "modernity." I wonder if those using such terms are completely aware of their import in any historiographic discourse. While I resolutely reject the primitivist views when applied to the increasingly evolved economic life of the Roman world, especially in its last centuries, which continue to manifest new technological advances, I am at least grateful to primitivists for having cleared Roman economic historiography of its former propensity to anachronistic assessments of ancient economic performance. I here hope to contribute to better communication between Roman and Byzantine historiographic experiences and historical realities, taking into account as well the unsatisfactory contact between those still separate fields of historiography, "oriental Byzantine" and "occidental early medieval."[7]

Second, I will briefly update the main characteristics of the late antique economy that were most redrawn by recent research, offering now a corrected ground on which we could better appreciate the degree of continuity and change in economic structures, evolutions, and models between the later fourth and ninth centuries. Finally, I will examine the respective functions of city and countryside in the network of exchanges, their complementary interplay in a market economy.

The Criteria for a Market Economy

An essential proviso for a trading economy to be described as a market economy consists in the level of impersonality reached by regulating elements such as supply and demand, the fixing of prices, and the freedom of economic actors. Using the word "market" is nonsense if the ideological and social system imposes constraints on the free functioning of the economic factors, or if non-economic elements interfere with the economic forces: for instance, giving weight to the social position of the parties involved in the exchange.[8] In this respect, I am convinced that the late Roman imperial state mainly retained the previous stance: the central power should not interfere in the free functioning of the private sphere. Indeed, the cities, by virtue of their autonomy, were responsible for more restrictions, especially insofar as the regulation of the marketplace, the imposition of municipal duties, and the control of the prices of staples were concerned.[9]

Another criterion of a market economy is the geographical range, though such range does not guarantee that a given economy will qualify. In this regard, a most useful distinction between "world-empire" and "world-economy" has been highlighted by Greg Woolf, following Wallerstein: "World-empires were basically redistributive in economic form. No doubt they bred clusters of merchants who engaged in economic exchange (primarily long distance trade) but such clusters, however large, were a minor part of the total economy and not fundamentally determinative of its fate."[10] I will return to this point later.

On the other hand, we may speak of a market economy even where there is no unique, self-

---

7 I make no effort to conceal the fact that the present chapter expresses positions that are a reaction against the contemporary mainstream, or rather give voice to an anti-consensus that is beginning to develop: I do not feel isolated at all. Even the recently published vol. 12 of the *Cambridge Economic History of the Greco-Roman World* (ed. W. Scheidel, I. Morris, and R. Saller [Cambridge, 2007]), to which I refer for information on different views, is frequently reluctant to abandon the prevailing consensus that minimizes the performance levels reached by the ancient economy even in its later phases. The case made here brings together massive evidence in support of a nonminimalist description and theorization of the late Roman economy; it in no way demonstrates the "optimistic disposition" generally adduced by mainstream historiography, which seeks to discredit "heterodox" views on the subject by shifting the disagreement from the arena of scientific debate into that of individual psychology.

8 See, e.g., M. Martinat, "L'économie moderne entre justice et marché," in Roman and Dalaison, eds., *L'économie antique*, 253–62.
9 J.-M. Carrié, "Les échanges commerciaux et l'État antique tardif," in *Les échanges dans l'Antiquité: Le rôle de l'État*, Entretiens d'Archéologie et d'Histoire 1 (Saint-Bertrand-de-Comminges, 1994), 175–211, and idem, in Carrié and Rousselle, *L'Empire romain en mutation*, 679–96.
10 Woolf, "World-Systems Analysis," 47.

governing market,[11] letting aside the fact that this pattern may never reach integral fulfilment, and will never be anything more than an abstract explanatory principle.[12] It is enough that partial markets be interconnected by their more-or-less close integration into a network or system of markets. Therefore the historian of the Roman economy should have the courage to consider his subject in terms of a market economy even when the market lacks its unifying function at the world level. Some fundamentalist economists voice their most inflammatory criticism against those historians of ancient economy who dare use the word "market" even when they apply it to the evolved economy of the last centuries of the Roman Empire.[13] Such behavior shows their complete indifference to or, more accurately, ignorance of the fact that, ironically enough, the concept itself, albeit in practical phrases, did exist in Roman language and thought.

Market Prices, Information, and Currency

Our habit of theorizing about economic processes leads us to deny to the ancients any concept that they did not formalize in some treatise. Yet, we repeatedly find in Roman practical documentation behaviors and devices that strongly imply some underlying conceptualization. This is true of the concept of "market," which was not the object of any theoretical treatment, but appears in some Latin texts in connection with market prices: *pretia in foro rerum venalium*. The phrase is used in imperial edicts that regulate the conversion from commodities into cash of some military officers' fees (*adaeratio*). For an exceptional concession of *adaeratio* of the military *annona*, we can turn to the provisions of Arcadius, Honorius, and Theodosius in a constitution issued in Constantinople in 406, stipulating that gratuities in kind called *stillaturae* should be converted into cash only according to the selling prices *in foro rerum venalium*,[14] with the obvious intent of preventing the military officers from extorting arbitrary amounts. A regulation issued in 424 by Honorius and Theodosius for the East even refers both to the market prices for converting the supply of military commodities from in-kind payment to cash (in the case of regular *annonae*) and to the official rate of conversion in copper, not gold, of fiscal military supplies (in the case of legitimate supplementary supplies for military officers' own needs), with the presumed intention of protecting the taxpayers from undue conversion from copper to gold coinage at the market price, which was higher than the official tariffication.[15]

The same phrase is used in defining the rate of reimbursement of refunded requisitions. For instance, in an edict of 384 for the Eastern provinces, which makes the process of refunding (*comparatio*) requisitions of extra supplies for military *annona* independent of the allotment of fiscal levy by appealing to the producers' free will in selling their products to the state (*usibus publicis distrahere fruges*), such refunds are calculated at the market price.[16] Likewise, citizens of Rome and later Constantinople who benefited from the *annona civica*, in addition to their free grain allocation, enjoyed the privilege of a special, reduced price for paying such foodstuffs as wine, oil, and meat: in 365 the political price for the *vinum populi Romani* was fixed by Valentinian and Valens at the value of three-quarters of the prevailing market price for each quality level,[17] the difference being paid by the imperial treasury.

---

11 Even today it can be said that "a market economy is primarily a markets economy"; R. Guesnerie, *L'économie de marché* (Paris 1996), 17.
12 See A. Guéry, "Les historiens, les marchés et le marché," in *Histoire des représentations du marché*, ed. G. Bensimon (Paris, 2005), 786–802.
13 Maucourant, "Le 'marché' est-il un 'signifiant vide'?" 38.
14 *CTh* 7.4.28: "Hoc quoque legis auctoritate complexo, ut semper dierum, per quas resistentes tribuni emolumenti gratia sollemniter stillaturae nomine consecuntur species, non aliter adaerentur, nisi ut in foro rerum venalium distrahuntur." The text, slightly modified, recurs in *CI* 12.37.12.5.
15 *CTh* 7.4.36: "Si quando tribuni sive comites vel praepositi numerorum per provincias annonas voluerint, hoc est quas pro dignitate sua consequuntur, in aere percipere, non aliis eas pretiis, nisi quae in foro rerum venalium habeantur, adaerandas esse cognoscant. Si alias annonas, quae non suae dignitatis erunt, sed alio modo, dum tamen licito, suis commodis adquisitas in auro sibi dari duces sive tribuni voluerint, illis pretiis contenti sint, quae in forma aerariarum annonarum universis militibus sollemni observatione praebentur."
16 *CTh* 11.15.2 (Gratian, Valentinian, and Theodosius, Beirut, 384): "Cunctos formari plenius conveniet, ut in speciebus etiam annonariis, quae a provincialibus sub transactione comparationis pretio expeti solent, sciant nullam sibi necessitatem indictionis imponi, sed huius adscriptionis necessitatem sublatam.... Unusquisque provincialium nostrorum arbitratu proprio et mente devota species petitas isdem pretiis, quae in foro rerum venalium habeantur, libens praestet ac distrahat[.]"
17 *CTh* 11.2.2 (Valentinian and Valens, Milan, 365): "In tantumque populi usibus profutura provisionis nostrae emolumenta porreximus, ut etiam pretio laxamenta tribuantur. Sanximus

Moreover, some business letters in the papyri provide direct evidence that market prices existed and information about them circulated. We can begin with the correspondence between two brothers datable to the mid-350s (i.e., during the last outburst of nominal inflation in the fourth century, when the flow of gold was still insufficient), which directly testifies to seasonal stress in the supply of gold currency even at a time when the order to levy the tax on recruits (*aurum tironicum*) was only a rumor insistently reported throughout the province, but not yet in force.[18] This papyrus shows the price of the *solidus* on the market literally rising daily,[19] owing to the competition between tax collectors: many taxpayers, indeed, who owed less than one solidus, paid in copper currency, which the collector had to exchange for gold coins, the only coinage accepted by the state tax office. It is no surprise that the informant on monetary matters and provider of cash to those brothers dwelling in Oxyrhynchos is himself in the Egyptian metropolis, Alexandria, 500 kilometers distant. We have here a vivid glimpse into the existence of an integrated monetary and financial market functioning at a provincial level.

The unity of the fourth-century Roman monetary system has long been called into question, and even denied, simply because the expression of prices in East and West has been misunderstood. That the system was unified, as in previous centuries, is now irrefutably confirmed thanks to graffiti indicating the value of a western gold multiple in terms of denarii as accounting units, giving a number quite consonant with what we know of the exchange price of the aureus in the Orient in the same period, around 309.[20]

Such a unified currency market is accompanied by at least regionally integrated commercial markets. That markets function to unify supply and demand has been strongly denied, as far as the ancient economy is concerned, by the Polanyian and Finleyan schools. But at the opposite extreme from any philosophical theorization of economics, another papyrus, *P.Oxy.* xxxiv.2729, which can be dated ca. 352–54, brings us face to face with the realities of market opportunities and speculations. From his retail and wholesale store (ἀποθήκη), a man named Dioscorides is writing to his brother Achilles, upriver and far away. Concerned about restocking the family store, he has just sent Achilles, by boat, two pigs of raw iron, each weighing 100 pounds, and a large sum of money—6700 myriads of denarii weighing between 8.5 and 14.7 kilograms—bulky enough to fill two big ceramic containers (we are still in the peak of inflation, but those disadvantages do not in the least discourage business enterprise) so that Achilles and his connections—relatives or partners—can buy the greatest possible quantities of copper containers for resale. Knowing that prices are rising, and fearing that high prices will deter his associates from buying, Dioscorides indicates a list of current prices for a range of articles and ends by indicating "the price of the day for the solidus" (730 myriads of denarii). Dioscorides' implicit reasoning is that in time of continual inflation liquid assets should be exchanged as quickly as possible for goods whose price will immediately rise. What information relevant to our present investigation can we draw from this exceptionally rich document?[21] This trader is sending raw iron to a place where it can be sold at a profit, a place from which, conversely, copper artifacts may be imported to be resold at a profit. It is clear that he is empirically observing market prices, paying particularly close attention because the situation is evolving rapidly. Knowing prices and how they compare in two different places is essential and indispensable to ensuring that transactions between them are profitable; and the fact that the two places are separated by some hundreds of kilometers, as is possible here, or even thousands, makes no difference. Here we see unambiguous evidence for the existence and knowledge of the market: but should it have come as a revelation?

It has been repeatedly observed that the ancient world nowhere records the publication of market price lists like modern French *mercuriales*. In my view, this absence is a sign of the low level of public interference in the free play of economic agents

---

quippe, ut per vini singulas qualitates detracta quarta pretiorum, quae habentur in foro rerum venalium, eadem species a mercantibus comparetur."

18 *P.Oxy.* xxxviii.3401. See J.-M. Carrié, "Aspects concrets de la vie monétaire en province," *RN* 159 (2003): 175–203, at 187.

19 καθ' ἡμέραν ἀναβένι (= ἀναβαίνει). The value of the solidus suggests a date around 357.

20 A. Hostein, "Le préfet du prétoire Vitalianus et le tarif de la livre d'or," *AnTard* 15 (2008): 251–57.

21 The other aspects have been exhaustively developed in J.-M. Carrié, "Papyrologica numismatica (1)," *Aegyptus* 64 (1984): 203–27, with special attention to the numismatic and monetary issues.

rather than a sign of the market's nonexistence. Dioscorides himself seems to be a walking market price list. And numerous texts bear witness that people everywhere had a notion of the normal average price for basic goods, especially foodstuffs, both at a level of common knowledge and, in some cases, at a subtler level of professional specialization.

We should also note that the reference to the *forum rerum venalium* as a natural arbitrator of exchange, endowed with a sort of empirical legitimacy, is radically antithetical to the medieval and modern ideology of the *iustum pretium*, which was developed in conjunction with the Christian moral condemnation of the loan at interest and, more generally, of the commercial benefit.[22] In the previous Roman tradition, loans at interest were never reproved, while commercial benefit was an object not of moral censure but of sociological scorn in the context of the ideal of the *homo liberalis*.[23] However effective those moral restrictions may actually have been, they clearly constituted long-lasting obstacles to a market economy in the lands of western Europe for many centuries. In this respect, the Roman economy was much less restrained than its historical successors.

At this point we can all recognize that awareness of "the market" and its role in economic reasoning and practice is not in itself proof of the existence of a world-sized, self-governing market. Depending on the commodities and salable goods involved, unified markets could be of very different scales, from local to universal.

Technological and Management Innovation

I will introduce now some considerations on the quantitative levels reached by the evolved economy of late antiquity, a necessary—though not sufficient—requirement for it to be characterized as a market economy. A rigorous, judicious refutation of Finley's surmise that the ancients lacked interest in technological innovation and, consequently, had a primitive level of technology and low productivity, has been provided by Kevin Greene,[24] following the revolutionary studies by Örjan Wikander and Claude Domergue on the use of water power by the Romans in such varied contexts as grinding mills, artificial erosion of ore-containing mountains (flushing, sluicing, *ruina montis*), mechanical camshafts to set in motion hammers for crushing metallic ore, and so on.[25] Recently the credit of many technical inventions previously attributed to the Middle Ages was restored to antiquity, especially late antiquity. In 1994 Kevin Greene published a decisive article on this topic.[26] All these techniques and all this equipment necessitated financial investment and economic calculation.

Recent advances in archaeological research have definitely cleared away the old myth that long-distance trading carried only high-value artifacts for the wealthiest, an assumption that dramatically reduced the extent and significance of such trade. Archaeologists have recently discovered a specific method of glass processing in antiquity by use of Egyptian niter (the medieval process, in contrast, used ashes). Such a technique would necessitate transporting over long distances massive quantities of glass cullets—the raw material required for the production of glass artifacts—from eastern parts of the Roman Empire to western secondary workshops. Given the wide dispersal of those workshops, a high organizational level was needed to ship this material over sea and land, together with methods to identify markets and assess their profitability. The production of primary glass was highly concentrated, as proved by cargoes found in shipwrecks and by the characteristics of excavated ovens: they were capable of producing castings weighing up to 16 tons, which were later broken into pieces for easier transport.[27]

22 See G. Todeschini, *I mercanti e il tempio: La società cristiana e il circolo virtuoso della ricchezza fra medioevo ed Età moderna* (Bologna, 2002); M. Martinat, *Le "juste marché": Le système annonaire romain aux XVIe et XVIIe siècles* (Rome, 2004).
23 Cicero, *De officiis* 1.42.150–51. On this topic in late antiquity, see S. MacCormack, "The Virtue of Work: An Augustinian Transformation," *AnTard* 9 (2001): 219–37.

24 M. I. Finley, *The Ancient Economy*, 2nd ed. (London, 1985); K. Greene, "Technological Innovation and Economic Progress in the Ancient World: M. I. Finley Reconsidered," *EHR* 53 (2000): 29–59.
25 O. Wikander, *Handbook of Ancient Water Technology* (Leiden, 2000); C. Domergue, *Les mines de la péninsule ibérique dans l'antiquité romaine* (Rome, 1990); for a synthesis with bibliography see A. Wilson, "Machines, Power and the Ancient Economy," *JRS* 92 (2002): 1–32.
26 See K. Greene, "Technology and Innovation in Context: The Roman Background to Mediaeval and Later Developments," *JRA* 7 (1994): 22–33; Wilson, "Machines."
27 For the capacity of glass production in primary workshops, see D. Foy and M. D. Nenna, "L'Orient des origines: Les ateliers primaires," in *Tout feu, tout sable: Mille ans de verre antique dans le Midi de la France*, ed. M. D. Nenna (Marseille, 2001), 35–38,

Those commercial exchanges of heavy raw material were accompanied from the start by a strategically planned transfer and the creation of local agencies where specialized workers sere sent to transform the raw glass into retail artifacts. They remained until skilled manpower was available locally.

The impressive quantities in which a range of other common articles were produced for trade and widely consumed are now under everybody's eyes: they decisively refute the assertions of Finley. According to Maurice Picon, the striking archaeological void that Aldo Schiavone supposed to be proof of the rather narrow basis of Roman manufacture disappears as soon as the usual limitations of urban archaeology can be surpassed: such was the case at Autun (Augustodunum), where excavations in various parts of the site brought to light extended areas dedicated to intensive artisanal activities.[28] Even the international diffusion of given types of ceramics has been denied any economic significance by some ingenious theories. Jean-Paul Morel, after assembling a sampling of reductive views on ancient ceramic production, concludes that "Il y a là je ne dis pas toute une école, mais toute une tendance lourde refusant de prendre en considération les exploits commerciaux de certaines céramiques italiennes (et autres), toute une pente à remonter."[29] The archaeological evidence is becoming ever more eloquent.[30] For example, for the South Gallic sigillata of the early empire, the technical data provided by the ovens excavated at la Graufesenque, which suggest average castings of thirty thousand pieces for every firing, permit a reasonable estimate of the total yearly production as nearly one million vessels.[31] Furthermore, Jean-Paul Morel demonstrates how the systematic study of a given kind of ceramic, including minor sites of production and commercialization, opens new avenues to acknowledge otherwise unsuspected commercial and marketing capabilities in the classical world. More thorough identifications of places of production and areas of exportation lead to a new vision of the ancient commercial economy, one that makes it impossible to continue to ignore the role of human initiative and abilities and the existence of diversified strategies, such as spreading and relocation, in the conquest of markets.[32] In some better-documented cases at least, the role of the customers' taste has come to the fore, as it has been recently shown that some manufacturing centers could adapt their production to the cultural habits of geographically or ethnically specific markets.[33] Morel concludes by stressing the "complexité et diversité des systèmes productifs et commerciaux."[34]

In his article cited above, Picon observes that the production of sigillata ceramic exhibits a wide array of rather modern characteristics: "more than likely intervention of various financial investors, entanglement of technical and commercial factors in the productive process, command and valorization of new expertise, the setting up of "original modes of production and distribution."[35] An instructive example of such interconnections is the way in which the abandonment of black glaze ceramic in favor of sigillata implied that wood consumption multiplied by four or five times, requiring in turn a higher level of investment, which should have led to a greater concentration of firms in order to limit the effects of the higher production price to be competitive in export markets.[36]

These are the very conclusions to which I was independently led when bringing together fresh information—archaeological, technological, and textual—related to textile and clothing production.[37] It is hardly comprehensible why the impor-

---

39–66; M. Picon, "Production artisanale et manufacturière à l'époque romaine: À propos de *L'Histoire brisée* d'Aldo Schiavone*,*" in Roman and Dalaison, eds., *L'économie antique*, 191–214, at 204–9.

28 Picon, "Production artisanale et manufacturière," 191–95, 204.

29 J.-P. Morel, "Les céramiques hellénistiques et romaines et les problèmes de 'marché,'" in Roman and Dalaison, eds., *L'économie antique,* 161–89, at 171–72.

30 For African sigillata, a worldwide exported ceramic, see S. Tortorella, "La ceramica africana: Un bilancio dell'ultimo decennio di ricerche," in *Productions et exportations africaines: Actualités archéologiques, Afrique du Nord antique et médiévale,* ed. P. Trousset, VIᵉ Colloque international sur l'histoire et l'archéologie de l'Afrique du Nord, Pau, octobre 1993 (Paris, 1995), 79–102.

31 Picon, "Production artisanale et manufacturière," 198–201.

32 Morel, "Les céramiques hellénistiques et romaines," 175–79.

33 Ibid., 180–83.

34 Ibid., 197.

35 Picon, "Production artisanale et manufacturière," 209.

36 Ibid., 202–3.

37 J.-M. Carrié, "Vitalité de l'industrie textile à la fin de l'Antiquité: Considérations économiques et technologiques," *AnTard* 12 (2004): 13–43; idem, "Tissus et vêtements dans l'Antiquité tardive, Bibliographie raisonnée," ibid., 45–54. Both articles are part of a collection of articles related to textiles: *Tissus et vêtements dans l'Antiquité tardive,* ed. J.-M. Carrié, Actes du Colloque de Lyon, Musée Historique des Tissus, 18–19 janvier 2003.

tance of textile production, from the point of view of its impact on economy and manpower, has been undervalued and neglected, or even simply ignored. Though late antiquity was not the major turning point in the history of fabric and dress as has long been claimed—the horizontal drawloom with treadles is a far later invention—the large-scale diffusion of innovations, most of which had appeared in the first and second centuries of the Roman Empire, together with new and improved expertise, enabled products to become more diverse and complex. Since professional expertise was then required to weave those fabrics that were increasingly requested for everyday use, there was a considerable decline in the use of homemade fabrics, which were now competing with the output of town- or village-dwelling specialists who targeted specific markets. As the wide diffusion of ceramics also demonstrates, there was an interaction between innovative techniques, the immediate appeal to consumers of new products, and eventually the organizational patterns of production. On the other hand, the political and cultural unification of the ancient world favored exchanges between different weaving traditions and attitudes toward dress—inside and outside the Mediterranean world—which encouraged a process of integration. No wonder, then, that the textile sector knew some forms of outstanding concentration. A decisive reappraisal of the volume of textile manufacture production was forced on us by *P.Oxy.Hels.* 40 (second half of the third century AD) as excellently reinterpreted and commented on by Peter Van Minnen, and other pieces of evidence point in the same direction.[38] In quantity, such production bears comparison with that of medieval Europe and suggests the existence of a very large regional and international market for textiles.

These success stories reflect the conjunction of a number of conditions: a large production capacity, technological innovation, availability of investment, geographic concentration of the firms, a highly organized commercial network, and in particular the formation of a wide market of Mediterranean consumers whose tastes and expectations were becoming standardized. More and more shipwrecks bear testimony to this long-distance transfer of low-cost artifacts and heavy raw materials. The lesson to be learned here is that only recently, and only for the better-known varieties of ceramics, have specialists in Roman crafts become able to draw on a deeper knowledge of the typology, chronology, geographic areas of production, and commercial diffusion of some artifacts to persuasively reconstruct the market controlled by the firms that exported those artifacts.[39] It took no less than a half century to acquire sufficient knowledge of those ceramic materials to enable such comprehensive and detailed conclusions to be reached. Because the study of eastern artifacts has lagged behind that of western crafts, attempts to describe the markets for one or another eastern trade article would be premature. At least the study of eastern amphorae: Late Roman 4 (Palestinian and Cyprus wines), Late Roman 1 (wine and oil from North Syria, Cilicia and Cyprus) Late Roman 2 (Aegean oil)—the most widely distributed types in all the Mediterranean area and especially in the Danubian area in the fourth to seventh centuries—has made great strides in the past twenty years.[40] At the same time, the experience of western archaeology in this field could be highly useful for specialists in eastern materials, offering them methodological models and conceptual patterns.

Continuity and Change in Economic Structures and Models from the Later Fourth through the Ninth Century

The persistent separation and mutual isolation of the two academic fields that are ancient and Byzantine history have blurred the question of continuity and change from the end of the Western Roman Empire through the shaping of a Byzantine identity. As too easily happens when we look for information in areas of history that are not ours, we tend to draw from mainstream historiography, whose accepted creed is generally out of date, having been superseded by the constant renewal of fresh research. There is thus a risk that any comparison which we venture between

---

38 P. van Minnen, "The Volume of the Oxyrhynchite Textile Trade," *Münstersche Beiträge zur antike Handelsgeschichte* 5.2 (1986): 88–95, and Carrié, "Vitalité de l'industrie textile."

39 As exemplified by Morel, "Les céramiques hellénistiques et romaines."
40 See, in Kingsley and Decker, eds., *Economy and Exchange*, S. Kingsley, "The Economic Impact of the Palestinian Wine Trade in Late Antiquity," 44–68; M. Decker, "Food for an Empire: Wine and Oil Production in North Syria," 69–86; and O. Karagiorgou, "LR2: A Container for the Military Annona on the Danubian Border?" 129–66.

late Roman Empire (fourth–fifth centuries) and proto-Byzantine realities (sixth–seventh centuries) are based on obsolete historiographic topoi. Here I will simply point out the recent developments that affect some of the major characteristics to be taken into account when attempting comparisons between late Roman and proto-Byzantine economies.

Intervention of the State in the Economy

The state interfered more as itself an economic actor than as a regulatory power hindering the free initiative of the private sector. Except for occasional embargoes on exports, directed at hostile nations, the state's legislative focus in the economic was exclusively on its own fields of economic activity: that is, modes of acquisition, management, and sale or donation of imperial property (lands, quarries and mines, state manufactures, and monopolies); the contribution of revenues from imperial property to the public finances; and the system of food allowances to the capitals, to the military, and to professional groups in the service of the state.

The standard view of the economic impact of the state factories should be revised downward. Their production exclusively filled the needs of the state (*vestis militaris*, weapons for the imperial army, silver plate and jewelry for official rewards and presents). The state factories neither drained the free productive sector nor competed with it. The imperial lands, for all their wide extent, were managed no differently than the private large estates. Rather than being viewed a state property, the imperial domain should be seen as the largest private property in the Roman Empire.[41]

The importance of the annona foodstuffs in proportion to the general bulk of long-distance trade has also been overstated, as illustrated by the primitivist assertion that such transfers to Rome and Constantinople represent the only sector of large-quantity trade in the ancient world. It can be demonstrated that the civic annona was strictly designed for public distributions (*frumentationes*) and was limited to a fixed number of recipients, constituting a minority of the population.[42] In the absence of any official sale of staples at a reduced "political price," as Domenico Vera has shown,[43] most inhabitants of the capitals depended on the free market. That entity, whose existence Jean Durliat arbitrarily denied,[44] was in the hands partly of independent traders, and partly of the so-called *navicularii*, those ship providers who were linked to the remunerated transfer of grain for public distribution, but who in addition could trade freely, with the benefit of the fiscal exemptions they enjoyed. The free food market in Rome and Constantinople was supplied by private producers and also, as I hope to have elsewhere demonstrated, by the large amount of fiscal grain which was sold from the imperial public property to private traders or to the *navicularii*, thus contributing to the general commercial life.[45] The other large cities in the Mediterranean world mainly depended on imported staples; the urban free market of foodstuffs was an indispensable outlet for the great landowners, whose estates were directed to produce the largest possible agricultural surplus. Generally speaking, local markets were far less strictly regulated under the Roman Empire than in western Europe from the twelfth through eighteenth centuries, and also less than in medieval Byzantium.

For all those reasons, I find totally exaggerated and inappropriate the definition of the Roman economy as a "tributary mode of production," which has recently become the fashionable consensus.[46] Even Greg Woolf, in his remarkably intelligent and far

41 See Carrié, "Les échanges commerciaux," 177–78 and, ultimately, D. Vera, "Fisco, annona e commercio nel Mediterraneo tardoantico: destini incrociati o vite parallele?" in *LRCW3 Late Roman Coarse Wares, Cooking Wares and Amphorae in the Mediterranean: Archaeology and Archaeometry; Comparison between Western and Eastern Mediterranean*, ed. S. Menchelli, S. Santoro, M. Pasquinucci, and G. Guiducci, BAR Int. Series 2185 (Oxford, 2010), 1:1–18.

42 See J.-M. Carrié, "L'institution annonaire de la première à la deuxième Rome: Continuité et innovation," in *Nourrir les cités du bassin méditerranéen: Antiquité–temps modernes,* ed. B. Marin and C. Virlouvet (Paris, 2003), 153–211.

43 D. Vera, "*Panis Ostiensis atque fiscalis*: Vecchie e nuove questioni di storia annonaria romana," in *"Humana sapit": Études d'Antiquité tardive offertes à Lellia Cracco Ruggini*, ed. J.-M. Carrié and R. Lizzi Testa (Turnhout, 2002), 341–56.

44 J. Durliat, *De la ville antique à la ville byzantine: Le problème des subsistances*, Collection de l'E.F.R. 136 (Rome, 1990); see my review in *AnnalesESC* (1993): 1145–50.

45 Carrié, "L'institution annonaire," 177.

46 Here I simply refer the reader to its emphatic presentation by Chris Wickham in his modeling of the transition from antiquity to the early Middle Ages, beginning with his 1984 milestone article, "The Other Transition: From the Ancient World to Feudalism," *Past and Present* 103: 3–36, through his 2005 masterpiece, *Framing the Early Middle Ages: Europe and the Mediterranean, 400–800* (Oxford).

from primitivistic article, while rightly proclaiming it "necessary to examine the exchange systems of the Roman Mediterranean, first of all, in terms of its incorporation in a world-empire," still sticks to the view that "the economy of the Mediterranean was dominated by the demands of the Roman world-empire." The only point which I feel reluctantly obliged to disagree with is his assertion that "World-systems analysis contributes to the consensus that the ancient economy was dominated by political and military forces."[47] Such an idea rests on the common overvaluation of the state-controlled economic sector, which is supposed to have stifled the free market economy by depriving it of most of the productive surplus. That widely shared view mainly reflects the overrepresentation of this sector in surviving documents—let us consider just the legal sources!

The Professional Organization of Handicraft

Eighty years ago, some modern commentators convincingly argued that the medieval corporatist system had no connection to any hypothetical Roman origin.[48] Nevertheless, descriptions of the late Roman *collegia* in traditionalist historiography have quite often merely projected onto them the model of the medieval corporatist system. Such a view is contradicted by the juridical and papyrological evidence[49] and received its final death blow from the recent revision of the Sardis inscription.[50] It thus should be indisputable that even in late antiquity the Roman professional associations never regulated and controlled working conditions, apprenticeship, salaries and prices, and quality control; they never agreed between themselves on market sharing; and so on. Roman collegia fulfilled their public service obligations (*ministeria*, *munia*, etc.), if any, to the cities, while being subject neither to state control nor to requests for production. The theory of the authoritarian submission of craft associations to an overall state corporatism arises from a misunderstanding of legal restraints on persons and patrimonies: their application is mistakenly extended to the whole range of Roman professional collegia, though they, actually, concerned only those *corpora* that were contractually committed to the imperial state in order to secure the public annona. As a direct result of the tetrarchic tax reform the professional collegia, initially religious institutions aimed at conviviality, self-representation, and social mediation within the framework of the city's relational system, were turned into associations responsible for the allocation and levy of their own professional tax (the *chrysargyron*). We should note that the *Book of the Prefect* ascribed to Emperor Leo the Wise, an essential tenth-century source for understanding the Byzantine professional collegia, does not seem to have introduced inner regulation and control, except in the specific case of notaries (an exception easy to understand). For that reason, my impression is that if any continuity obtained between Roman and Byzantine professional associations, it need not be viewed as a sign of their shared relationship with the Western medieval corporative system, as Speros Vryonis maintained.[51] The consequence, for our current theme, is that in late antiquity as well as in previous centuries, neither the imperial state nor corporative restrictions hindered the economic actors and the free play of market rules, except in the case of the food supply within the framework of the cities.

The Large Estate and the Market

The ancient estate economy necessarily had to develop two sectors, one that produced for monetary sale and the other focused on self-sufficiency, to meet its own consumption needs and to reduce its running costs, through mechanisms of internal barter or balancing operations. It would be enough to record how the interpretation of what was formerly called the "Heroninos archive" has been turned upside down by Dominic Rathbone in his reconstruction

---

47 Woolf, "World-Systems Analysis," 53.
48 J. Kulischer, *Allgemeine Wirtschaftsgeschichte des Mittelalters und der Neuzeit*, vol. 1 (Munich, 1928), 181–92. A few years later G. Mickwitz also denounced such a connection as anachronistic: see "Un problème d'influence: Byzance et l'économie de l'Occident médiéval," *Annales d'histoire économique et sociale* 8 (1936): 21–28. More recently, see G. Dagron, "The Urban Economy, Seventh–Twelfth Centuries," in *EHB*, 2:385–453, here 405–10.
49 See J.-M. Carrié, "Les associations professionnelles à l'époque tardive, entre *munus* et convivialité," in Carrié and Lizzi Testa, eds., *"Humana sapit,"* 309–32.
50 See M. di Branco, "Lavoro e conflittualità in una città tardoantica d'Asia Minore: Una rilettura dell'epigrafe di Sardi CIG 3467 (= Le Bas-Waddington 628 = Sardis VII, 1, n. 18)," *AnTard* 8 (2000): 181–208.
51 S. Vryonis Jr., "Byzantine Δημοκρατία and the Guilds in the Eleventh Century," *DOP* 17 (1963): 289–314.

and analysis of the "Appianus archive."[52] So, even if part of the entries of the estates' archive reflected mere bookkeeping devices rather than transactions, the economic model to which such a form of large landownership conformed undoubtedly was looking for the profits that were allowed by the market through monetized transactions, currency being the unavoidable and necessary mean of fixing the exchange value.

Such evidence and the model that can be deduced from it have made obsolete the enduring surmise that the ancient economy had an autarkic character, another good example of how ancient practice, in so many fields of human experience, could do without dogmatic theory. It has been abundantly demonstrated how hypocritical—and misleading for the modern historian—was the senatorial discourse on trading activity and how multifarious were the methods used to evade the socioideological taboo to which senators were theoretically subject: the ruling ideology was in some way inconsistent with how they actually behaved. We similarly risk being misled, in my opinion, when we take at face value such texts that, repeating over and over the topos of an attack on luxury, induced the primitivists to adopt their central conviction that the ancient economy did not seek to optimize gain and win marginal profit.

A question still remains largely open: is there any chance of estimating and comparing the expanse and possible extension of the large estate from the late Roman period through the Byzantine age?

The Extent of Private Financial Life

Although the republican system of adjudication to *publicani* was abandoned totally for the exaction of *tributum* and to a lesser extent for the levy of customs and management of mines, quarries, and public works, the tax levy still made its contribution to the intensity of financial life. Since the state had few civil officials it was necessary to involve the municipal class (*bouleutai/curiales*) through the system of *leitourgeiai/munera*. Actually, those private collectors had to borrow the funds which they were obliged to deposit as security in advance of the future proceeds of the tax levied by them.[53] Here also, the decline in urban populations, in the vitality of towns and in civic institutions that occurred in the East from the sixth century onward caused changes in the system of tax levying and, consequently, in the general financial life of the provinces.

The High Level of Monetization of the Economy in the Fourth Century

Ironically enough, the thesis of a reversion to a "natural economy" founded on barter and transactions in kind because of shortages and loss of credibility of the currency has been applied to the very period of antiquity when coinage was most abundant. The recently unearthed and edited archives from Kellis, a village in the most remote part of the isolated Great Western Oasis (nowadays the Dakhla oasis), documenting the life of a family over several generations,[54] affords us the liveliest snapshot of the many uses of currency in a rural sphere through the fourth century: even large expenses were paid in much-debased currency during the period of severest lack of high-value coinage. The idea still prevailing in the secondary literature that monetary disturbances and nominal inflation from the seventies of the third century through the sixties of the fourth century caused a general spread of transactions in kind (for rents, salaries, loans, purchases and sales, and so on), which superseded cash payments, should definitely be discarded. It is worth noting here that after Federico Morelli's reconsideration and systematic study, the gratuities in oil and wine granted to the workers of the episcopal church at Arsinoe in the sixth century can no longer be interpreted as a salary in kind; they instead represented daily rations by right of *trophē* (food allowance), a standard clause of work contracts that sometimes constrained the employer to buy these foodstuffs outside the estate.[55] And even a quick skimming of the pages of the Vienna accounting papyri of the sixth century makes obvious that payments in coins largely predominate over

---

52 D. Rathbone, *Economic Rationalism and Rural Society in Third-Century A.D. Egypt: The Heroninos Archive and the Appianus Estate* (Cambridge, 1991).

53 *P.Oxy.* xlviii.3419, line 9.

54 *The Kellis Agricultural Account Book: P.Kell. IV Gr. 96*, ed. R. S. Bagnall, with contributions from C. A. Hope, R. G. Jenkins, A. J. Mills, J. L. Sharpe III, U. Thanheiser, and G. Wagner, Dakhleh Oasis Project 7, Oxbow 92 (Oxford, 1997).

55 F. Morelli, *Olio e retribuzioni nell'Egitto tardo (V–VIII d. C.)* (Florence, 1996), 28–41, 176–77.

those in kind,⁵⁶ confirming that the historiographic myth of a late antique barter economy is completely untenable.

The view that the late antique economy reverted to premonetary forms of exchange has been fostered among modern historians by many misunderstandings of the late Roman tax system, in which annona taxes (levied in kind) were merely a single element—already existing under the early Empire—and were prominent only in some provinces or even parts of provinces.⁵⁷

Money and prices are two inseparable aspects of the same reality. Although admitting that the monetization of a given economy, by itself, gives no indication as to whether it is a market economy,⁵⁸ I am convinced that from the end of the third century at least, currency was functioning in the empire as an element helping to integrate the market. The famous Edict on Prices issued by Diocletian and his colleague Maximian is generally adduced as proof that a price control policy was instituted by the late empire rulers. But the edict's intention becomes clearer when connected with the simultaneous nominal inflation, never mentioned by the text (for obvious political reasons), since the problem of prices was a direct consequence of Diocletian's monetary policy: that is, the overvaluation of the exchange ratio of the debased "silver" currency to gold currency arbitrarily imposed by the state. That the real problem lay in the monetary situation is betrayed by the description of the rise in prices "from day to day and almost from moment to moment,"⁵⁹ which echoes the perception of the rise in market price of the gold coins expressed in papyri. The crime against the state denounced here is actually the behavior of tradesmen who treat currency not at its face value, which the emperors try to enforce, but at the debased value constantly and universally redetermined by the market. The emperors openly refrain from fixing prices, being content to set maximum prices that are never and nowhere to be infringed.⁶⁰ On the other hand, the rulers cannot be unaware of the integrating function of currency when they designate as the main targets of their measure "venditores emptoresque, quibus consuetudo est adire portus et peregrinas obire provincias."⁶¹

The official Roman attempts at a price control system, isolated and intended to address temporary situations even when long lasting, were primarily aimed not at regulating the economic market but at ruling the monetary market. Inasmuch as they claimed to institute maximum prices, they have nothing to do with a definition of a "fair price." More accurately: they had the effect of causing a true market and even a kind of auto-regulation, since the users automatically adjusted the current rate of exchange between gold currency and the debased, fiduciary one, to the actual value of the metals.

I suspect that the dispositions of an edict of 454 (*CTh* 9.23.1), which strangely limits to a very modest amount the copper cash allowed on board ship, were motivated by a wish to thwart the opportunity for professional seaborne traders to speculate on the varying rates of change of copper to gold among the different provinces of the empire. Bringing together those pieces of evidence enables us, in my opinion, to infer at the same time the existence of market phenomena, the opportunities offered by a genuine integrated market, and the actual limitation of the market to the provincial and even regional dimension. Those potentialities were severely restricted both by the paucity of economic actors in a position to take advantage of a unified, integrated market and by the obstacles raised to such unification by the state which, especially in currency matters, tried to create regional compartments and actually succeeded in imposing such a rigid system from the fifth century onward with the local *stathmoi*.

The Complementary Interplay of Town and Country in the Network of Exchanges, and the Question of the Consumer City

On the one hand, cities apparently concentrated what can be described as "the market." On the other hand, as generally happens in traditional preindustrial societies, the difference in socioeconomic level between city and countryside was a powerful factor limiting the market. Essential to the theoretical

---

56 *P.Kl. Form.* I and II (*Stud. Pal. III* and *VIII*), passim.
57 J.-M. Carrié, "Dioclétien et la fiscalité," *AnTard* 2 (1994): 33–64, and idem, in Carrié and Rousselle, *L'Empire romain en mutation,* 593–609.
58 Martinat, "L'économie moderne," 256–57.
59 *P.Oxy.* xlviii.3419, line 9, quoted above, note 19.
60 *Edictum Diocletiani et collegarum de pretiis rerum venalium,* proem. (ed. M. Giacchero [Genoa, 1974]): "non pretia venalium rerum— neque enim id fieri iustum putatur ... sed modum statuendum esse censuimus...."
61 Ibid.

conceptualization of exchanges and trade in the Roman Empire and central in the debate between economic historians has been the antithesis "consumer city" and "producer city," which Finley allegedly exhumed from the economic reflections of Max Weber. On the one hand, we should be grateful to Finley for having acquainted the ancient historians with Weberian categories that they had overlooked. On the other hand, Finley's employment of Weber's thought is unfaithful to the original and misleading, as has been authoritatively shown by Hinnerk Bruhns, first because in Weber the opposition "consumer" versus "producer" is related not to town and countryside but concerns the "consumer city" and the "producer city" and, more seriously, because Finley never took into account the heuristic and categorical status of the Weberian *Idealtypus*.[62] Somewhat ironically, Paul Erdkamp, while recently trying to defend Weber's concepts against Finley's criticism, did not challenge Finley's insensitivity to the very nature of the Weberian *Idealtypus*, but built his defense on Finley's alteration of Weber's thought.[63] Moreover, Bruhns rightly restored the paternity of the concept "consumer city" (*Konsumptionsstadt*) to Werner Sombart, who introduced it in *Der moderne Kapitalismus*. According to Sombart, the "consumer city" is "a city which does not pay for the agricultural products which feed her with products of her own as counterpart, because the city need not pay for them, but mostly receives them for free through an entitlement (*auf Grund irgendeines Rechtstitel*) (tax, rent, or something similar), without any counter-value being delivered."[64] Later Max Weber, in *Agrarverhältnisse im Altertum* (1909) and again in *Der Stadt* (published posthumously in 1921), borrowed from Sombart the concept of a "consumer city," but applied it to only a few of the ancient cities—not, as Finley would have it, generalizing to all of them. In addition Weber used this classification not to contrast the ancient cities with their hinterland, but to contrast the ancient town, which was concerned about the consumer's interests, and the medieval city, which was concerned about the producer's interests. Even in the late stages of his reflection, Weber kept on using the *Idealtypus* as an analytical and not a descriptive intellectual tool.

I will use the terminology "consumer city" and "producing hinterland" with the meanings attributed to them by Finley, which have shaped the debate on this ground among historians of antiquity. The contrast thus commonly maintained leads to a denial of any reciprocity in the relations between urban and rural economies. But the natural impulse, on the contrary, is to suppose the existence of some reciprocity that enables a circuit of mutual exchange. Two ways of escaping this dilemma have been favored by the primitivists. The first one is to reduce the urban productive activities to the manufacture of luxury items—unnecessary, ostentatious, and exclusively for the use of the urban ruling class. Erdkamp, on this point, does not diverge from the Finleyans when he provocatively jokes about "bronze and marble statues."[65] This obviously ignores the fact that modern archaeology no longer looks for artistic masterpieces but has by now accumulated tons and tons of low-cost, widely diffused items that could be acquired even by the rural population. These archaeological investigations have upended the traditional vision still prevailing in Finley (and even more dominant in Weber's time) of a contrast between opulent cities and miserable autarkic countrysides. Ancient texts and documents share responsibility for such a vision, because the ruling ideology of the landowning class, with few exceptions, obliterated the socioeconomic importance and sheer numbers of craftsmen and salesmen. But there should be added a demographic argument: the proportion of the urban population in the Roman Empire reached levels not again matched in Europe before the eighteenth century. Clearly most of this urban population could not remain idle—people had to earn their living. And if the urban craftsmen had worked only to provide for the needs of the city-dwelling landowners, cities could never have grown so large.

---

62 H. Bruhns, "De Werner Sombart à Max Weber et Moses I. Finley: La typologie de la ville antique et la question de la ville de consommation," in *L'origine des richesses dépensées dans la ville antique,* ed. P. Leveau (Aix-en-Provence and Marseille, 1985), 255–73.

63 D. Erdkamp, "Beyond the Limits of the 'Consumer City': A Model of the Urban and Rural Economy in the Roman World," *Historia* 50 (2001): 332–56.

64 W. Sombart, *Der moderne Kapitalismus*, 2nd edition (Munich–Leipzig, 1916), 1:142: "Eine Konsumptionsstadt nenne ich diejenige Stadt, die ihren Lebensunterhalt . . . nicht mit eigenen Produkten bezahlt, weil sie es nicht nötig hat. Sie bezieht vielmehr diesen Lebensunterhalt auf Grund irgendeines Rechtstitels (Steuern, Rente oder dergleichen) ohne Gegenwerte leisten zu müssen."

65 Erdkamp, "Beyond the Limits of the 'Consumer City,'" 339.

The second way to deny the existence of a reciprocal exchange between cities and countryside, a way that is too easy, asserts that craftsmanship was concentrated in a minority of productive centers that depended exclusively on exporting goods to the nonindustrial cities. Archaeological research now makes it clear, however, that alongside a few highly specialized cities that were famous for their export activities existed hundreds of cities that produced only for the local and regional markets. As fascinating as they may be, imported ceramics should not monopolize the interest of historians, nor should the consideration of productive and commercial activities be restricted to the ceramic evidence. We should also take into account all those excavated artifacts which are just beginning to be preserved, analyzed, scientifically studied, and published: metallic objects, bone, leather, ropes, rush, and especially textiles. Textiles are preserved only under special conditions of soil and climate, but even where they could still be found, they were not kept for study by archaeologists until recently, being, more often than not, simply thrown out in the rubble. Last but not least, we should add all the nonmaterial activities of the "service sector" whose actual importance, though it can be easily deduced from literary, juridical, and documentary texts, has been generally ignored in reference works on economy and manpower in antiquity.

Elsewhere I have argued, on archaeological and technological grounds, that an ever-increasing proportion of textile and garment production took place in urban professional workshops, owing to the expanding market for more elaborate fabrics that demanded more sophisticated know-how.[66] I also argued that under these new conditions, domestic production of textiles could exceed a given range only with difficulty; above that upper limit, it might have competed in harmful ways with agricultural activities—and in fact professional weavers are also to be found in rural areas. With regard to the connections between technological improvements, patterns of productive and commercial organization, consumers' changing tastes, and diversified standards of living, in a context of increasing circulation of goods and integration of markets, I was led to conclusions very similar to those of Jean-Paul Morel and Maurice Picon as expressed in two Lyons colloquia recently published in one volume, already abundantly quoted in this chapter.[67] Among many other conclusions, this study enabled me to differentiate more precisely two main patterns of relationship between the productive branch and the commercial one: one tying the two branches together and the other keeping them separate, according to the type of target market.

But returning now to the problem of whether there is reciprocity in economic exchange between the city and the countryside, which here interests us as either a positive or negative factor in the development of a market economy, I find it difficult to avoid the conclusion that once the reassessed volume of urban production has risen so high that it must be recognized by anybody who is not blinded by theoretical prejudice, we can no longer maintain the position that the urban population, mainly engaged in artisanal activities, could simply feed themselves and get the raw materials needed for transformation outside a circuit of commercial exchange between the town and the countryside. The amount and range of such an exchange largely exceeded, we can be sure, the so-called city entitlements (the rentals levied by the city's resident landowners); free peasants—who existed in great numbers, even if our documents overrepresent the large estates—needed the city outlet for their commercial surplus. Conversely, urban products also needed the rural outlet, and archaeological surveys are beginning to dispel the old view of the countryside as a monetary desert. This pattern is absolutely consistent with the existence and increasing importance of periodic markets, as exemplified especially in Italy and Africa.[68]

For all those reasons, I am convinced that instead of nonreciprocity, we should argue for unevenness in the exchange relation between town and country, due to the added value generated by city-made artifacts with respect to the raw materials and staples that city-dwellers extract from or buy in the countryside. I tentatively calculated an approximate level in the case of wool and common wool garments, which gave me an indicative order of 2.66 times for the rate

---

66   Carrié, "Vitalité de l'industrie textile," esp. 23–36.

67   Roman and Dalaison, eds., *L'économie antique: Une économie de marché?*; see Morel, "Les céramiques hellénistiques et romaines"; Picon, "Production artisanale et manufacturière."

68   See *Mercati permanenti e mercati periodici nel mondo romano,* ed. E. Lo Cascio, Atti degli incontri capresi di storia dell'economia antica, Capri 13–15 ottobre 1997, Pragmateiai 2 (Bari, 2000), esp. Y. Zelener, "Market Dynamics in Roman North Africa," 223–35.

of the added value.⁶⁹ This kind of inquiry could also be of interest for Byzantine economic history, taking into account the sharp drop of the urban population, which created completely new conditions for economic life.

Concluding Remarks

When adopting commercial transfers as a vantage point, I could agree with Peter Temin in defining the Roman economy as a conglomerate of separate markets. It is what Léopold Migeotte, referring to the Hellenistic economy, has called "une économie à marchés" (an economy "with markets"), slightly modifying the phrase coined by Alain Bresson to describe the economy of classical Greece: "une économie à marché,"⁷⁰ an economy "with a market," differentiating it from a modern "market economy."⁷¹

When adopting monetary functioning as a vantage point, I would be tempted to define the late Roman economy as a unified economic space divided into compartments. Perhaps those slight variations in phraseology reflect the actual evolution and progress toward an always incomplete but always increasing integration of the ancient Mediterranean world into a world economy. As shown by Federico Morelli's surveys, the monetary form spread without stop in Egypt from the Ptolemaic age through the sixth century C.E., when it was the predominant form of payment for rents, loans, and wages: some texts provide a most explicit "expression of an economy definitely bound to the use of currency and in which monetized exchange was perceived as the normal form of exchange."⁷²

In order not to wander outside my own field of supposed expertise, I leave it to the Byzantinists to characterize, with regard to the market, the economy that adapted itself to changing contexts and scales during the centuries that constitute their own field. Conservatively, it may at least be suggested that the fading of the classical city and its socioeconomic functions, central to the structuring of the Roman market economy, together with the reduced scale of the Byzantine "world-empire" and economic space, acted as major drivers of change and rupture in the economic fate of the middle Byzantine period.

---

69 Carrié, "Vitalité de l'industrie textile," 42 with n. 151, where a regrettable mathematical error gave a wrong number (subsequently corrected in *AnTard* 13 [2005]: Errata, 8).

70 L. Migeotte, *L'économie des cités grecques de l'archaïsme au Haut-Empire romain*, 2nd ed. (Paris, 2007); see also idem in Roman and Dalaison, eds., *L'économie antique,* 81; A. Bresson, *La cité marchande* (Bordeaux-Paris, 2000), 304.

71 For a comparative/contrastive analysis of ancient and modern (sixteenth through eighteenth centuries) economies, see J.-Y. Grenier, "Économie de surplus, économie du circuit: Les prix et les échanges dans l'Antiquité gréco-romaine et dans l'Ancien Régime," in *Prix et formation des prix dans les économies antiques*, Entretiens d'Archéologie et d'Histoire 3 (Saint-Bertrand-de-Comminges, 1997), 385–405.

72 Morelli, *Olio e retribuzioni*, 174.

• TWO •

Regional and Interregional Exchanges in the Eastern Mediterranean during the Early Byzantine Period

The Evidence of Amphorae

DOMINIQUE PIERI

OVER THE COURSE OF ONLY A FEW YEARS, our knowledge of late antique amphorae from the eastern Mediterranean has advanced so spectacularly that these objects have become particularly reliable evidence in establishing the chronology and stratigraphy of many sites in the Mediterranean basin. The emergence of new amphora types revealed by recent excavations, as well as their integration into increasingly complex typological classifications, brings into focus the dynamic character of manufacturing in the East, especially the Near East (Cilicia, Syria, Phoenicia, and Palestine). The commercial success of several eastern commodities from the beginning of the fifth century onward—particularly wine, which was widely distributed in large-scale trade during the late period—attests to a reorientation of production methods and a notably successful transformation of commerce.

Treating the question of commercial exchanges in the eastern Mediterranean basin during late antiquity requires a synthesis of available historical and archaeological data. Even today, however, significant unknowns, such as how production was organized, are thwarted by disparities and (especially) asymmetries in the data available. With the exception of juridical texts on the regulation of certain economic activities, there is little textual evidence that would enable us to arrive at a broad understanding of how trade was organized, and it is often difficult to distinguish the effects of larger economic trends from those of microeconomies. Certainly, research has sought to emphasize the importance of specific agents in the production process, but these studies remain narrow or limited in scope.[1] Many of the economic models regarding commercial exchanges recently postulated for late antiquity rely in part on data collected through archaeology, which can complement textual evidence. These models are based on the analysis of archaeological remains originating in material culture (ceramics, coins, glass, metals, and organic matter).[2]

---

1   J.-P. Rey-Coquais, "Fortune et rang social des gens de métiers de Tyr au Bas-Empire," *Ktèma* 4 (1979): 281–92; J.-P. Sodini, "L'artisanat urbain à l'époque paléochrétienne (IVe–VIIe s.)," *Ktèma* 4 (1979): 71–118; G. Tate, "Les métiers dans les villages de la Syrie du Nord," *Ktèma* 16 (1991): 73–78; C. R. Whittaker, "Late Roman Trade and Traders," in *Trade in the Ancient Economy,* ed. P. Garnsey, K. Hopkins, and C. R. Whittaker (London, 1983), 163–80; M. Mundell Mango, "The Commercial Map of Constantinople," *DOP* 54 (2000): 189–207; M. Decker, "The Wine Trade of Cilicia in Late Antiquity," *Aram* 17 (2005): 51–59; E. Zanini, "Artisans and Traders in Late Antiquity: Exploring the Limits of Archaeological Evidence," in *Social and Political Life in Late Antiquity,* ed. W. Bowden, A. Gutteridge, and C. Machado, Late Antique Archaeology 3.1 (Leiden, 2006), 373–411.

2   J.-P. Sodini, "Productions et échanges dans le monde protobyzantin (IVe–VIIe s.): Le cas de la céramique," in *Byzanz als Raum: Zu Methoden und Inhalten der historischen Geographie des Östlichen Mittelmeerraumes,* ed. K. Belke, F. Hild, J. Koder, and P. Soustal (Vienna, 2000), 181–96; C. Morrisson and J.-P. Sodini, "The Sixth-Century Economy," in *EHB* 1:171–220; M. McCormick, *Origins of the European Economy: Communications and Commerce, A.D. 300–900* (Cambridge, 2001); C. Wickham, *Framing the Early Middle Ages: Europe and the Mediterranean, 400–800* (Oxford, 2005); A. E. Laiou and C. Morrisson, *The Byzantine Economy* (Cambridge, 2007). More recently, see M. Decker, *Tilling the Hateful Earth: Agricultural Production and Trade in the Late Antique East* (Oxford, 2009); M. Mundell Mango, ed., *Byzantine Trade, 4th–12th Centuries: The Archaeology of Local, Regional and International Exchange,*

Ceramics constitute one of the most important tools available for understanding the mechanism of trade between the fourth and seventh centuries. The archaeology of the past twenty years has entirely revitalized our understanding of the history, particularly the economic history, of the Mediterranean in late antiquity and the early Middle Ages. Much attention has focused on amphorae, the packaging of choice for commercial products during the Roman period and late antiquity; as such, they are particularly useful for adducing information about exchanges. They carried wine, olive oil, and garum, essential products in the Mediterranean way of life. Indeed, the study of amphorae—the veritable time capsules of antiquity—has facilitated some of the most remarkable developments in the analysis of specific economic exchanges.[3]

In addition to the significant recent advances in our knowledge of ceramics (establishing the typologies of amphorae; mapping distribution and quantitative data; specifying origins, contents, and dating, etc.), we have increasingly come to understand the broader mechanisms of the trade in amphorae. We thus are in a position to survey both the significance and limitations of evidence derived from amphorae.

Amphorae: Attesting to the Dynamism of the East

Archaeological activity has advanced significantly in the eastern Mediterranean during the past several years, thanks in particular to rescue and salvage archaeology undertaken in Istanbul, Athens, Alexandria, Beirut, Caesarea Maritima, and Gaza. These recent finds have enriched our knowledge of amphorae, and we have come a long way from the famous typological diagram of John A. Riley, who in 1982 classified, for the first time, seven international amphora types known collectively under the rubric "Late Roman Amphorae" (fig. 2.1).[4]

Over the course of twenty years, these seven late period eastern amphora types have multiplied to more than a hundred—not just attesting to great progress in typological classification but also providing evidence of the economic and commercial vitality of the eastern Mediterranean basin. Archaeology regularly reveals new amphora types that enable us to further refine these classifications, emphasizing a manufacture based largely in the major eastern urban centers, but supplemented as well by a multitude of secondary workshops spread over a vast geographic area (Jal'ad, Galilee, the Negev, the environs of Lake Mareotis, and the middle Nile Valley). Among the most recently recognized types, by way of example, are amphorae made at Sinope on the Black Sea, Beirut, Tyre, and Aqaba (fig. 2.2). The science of dating these amphorae has advanced to such an extent that they now constitute exceptionally reliable chronological markers.[5] To gain an idea of the

---

Papers of the Thirty-eighth Spring Symposium of Byzantine Studies, St John's College, University of Oxford, March 2004, Society for the Promotion of Byzantine Studies 14 (Aldershot, 2009).

3 The extent of these advances may be gauged from conference proceedings of the past several years: *La céramique byzantine et proto-islamique en Syrie-Jordanie, IVe–VIIIe siècles apr. J.-C.,* ed. E. Villeneuve and P. Watson (Beirut, 2001); *La céramique médiévale en Méditerranée,* ed. G. Démians d'Archimbaud, Actes du VIe congrès international sur la céramique médiévale (Aix-en-Provence, 1997); *Ceramica in Italia: VI–VII secolo,* ed. L. Saguì, Atti del Convegno in onore di John W. Hayes (Florence, 1998); *Contenitori da trasporto tra Tardo Antico e Basso Medioevo,* Actes du XXXe colloque international sur la céramique, Albisola, 16–18 mai 1997 (Florence, 1999); *Contextos ceràmics d'època romana tardana i de l'alta edat mitjana (segles IV–X),* ed. M. Comes i Solà and J. M. Gurt Esparraguera, actes, taula rodono, Badalona 6, 7 i 8 novembre de 1996 (Barcelona, 1997); *VIIe Congrès international sur la céramique médiévale en Méditerranée, Thessalonique, 11–16 octobre 1999: Actes,* ed. Ch. Bakirtzis (Athens, 2003); *Transport Amphorae and Trade in the Eastern Mediterranean: Acts of the International Colloquium at the Danish Institute at Athens, September 26–29, 2002,* ed. J. Eiring and J. Lund, Monographs of the Danish Institute at Athens 5 (Athens, 2004); *LRCW 1: Late Roman Coarse Wares, Cooking Wares and Amphorae in the Mediterranean: Archaeology and Archaeometry,* ed. J. M. Gurt Esparraguera, J. Buxeda i Garrigós, and M. A. Cau Ontiveros, BAR International Series 1340 (Oxford, 2005); *LRCW 2: Late Roman Coarse Wares, Cooking Wares and Amphorae in the Mediterranean: Archaeology and Archaeometry,* ed. M. Bonifay and J.-C. Tréglia, BAR International Series 1662 (Oxford, 2007); *Çanak: Late Antique and Medieval Pottery and Tiles in Mediterranean Archaeological Contexts,* ed. B. Böhlendorf-Arslan, A. Osman Uysal, and J. Witte-Orr, Proceedings of the First International Symposium on Late Antique, Byzantine, Seljuk, and Ottoman Pottery and Tiles in Archaeological Contexts (Çanakkale, 1–3 June 2005), Byzas 7 (Istanbul, 2007).

4 J. A. Riley, "New Light on Relations between the Eastern Mediterranean and Carthage in the Vandal and Byzantine Periods: The Evidence from University of Michigan Excavations," in *Actes du Colloque sur la céramique antique de Carthage* (Tunis, 1982), 111–22.

5 Among recent publications, see J. Herrin and A. Toydemir, "Byzantine Pottery," in *Kalenderhane in Istanbul,* vol. 2, *The Excavations: Final Reports on the Archaeological Exploration and Restoration at Kalenderhane Camii, 1966–1978,* ed. C. L. Striker and Y. Doğan Kuban (Mainz, 2007), 69–122; B. L. Johnson, *Ashkelon 2: Imported Pottery of the Roman and Late Roman Periods*

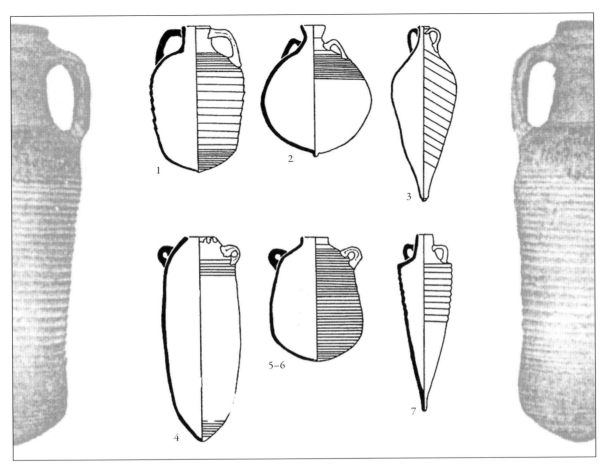

Figure 2.1. First typological diagram of Late Roman Eastern Amphorae by J. A. Riley ("The Pottery from Cisterns 1977.1, 1977.2 and 1977.3," in *Excavations at Carthage, 1977,* ed. J. H. Humphrey, vol. 6 [Ann Arbor, 1981], fig. 2)

progress that has been achieved in typological classification, consider the most famous of the eastern amphora types—Late Roman Amphora (LR) 1, which was so commercially successful that it penetrated the farthest-flung regions: Great Britain, the southern Egyptian oases, and the Far East. It is probably to be identified with the famous *seriola* described at the beginning of the seventh century by Isidore of Seville.[6] The changes in the form of amphorae over time are noteworthy, as is the existence of subtypes—a phenomenon recently attested and applicable to late eastern amphorae in their entirety (fig. 2.3).[7] One of the most remarkable phenomena is the abundance from the beginning of the fifth century onward—even the dominance—of amphorae originating in the eastern Mediterranean; they are ubiquitous at all the major Mediterranean consumption sites, both eastern and western. To fully understand the significance of eastern manufacture and its impact on the Mediterranean's entire commercial network, it is enough to observe the statistical totals in the major western cities (Rome, Naples, Narbonne, Marseille,

---

(Winona Lake, [Ind.], 2008); idem, "The Pottery," in J. Patrich, *Archaeological Excavations at Caesarea Maritima, Areas CC, KK and NN, Final Reports,* vol. 1, *The Objects* (Jerusalem, 2008), 12–208.

6   Isidore, *Etymologiae sive Origines* 20.6.6: "Seriola est orcarum ordo directus vel vas fictile vini apud Syriam primum excogitatum; sicut Cilicises a Cilicia nuncupati, unde [et] primum advectae sunt" (A *seriola* is a straight-sided type of *tun*, or a ceramic wine vessel first invented in Syria; just as Cilicises are named from Cilicia, from where they were [also] first imported) (W. M. Lindsay, *Isidori Hispalensis Episcopi Etymologiarum sive*

Originum Libri XX [Oxford, 1911]; *The Etymologies of Isidore of Seville,* trans. S. A. Barney et al. [Cambridge, 2006]).

7   D. Pieri, *Le commerce du vin oriental à l'époque byzantine, V^e–VIIe siècles: Le témoignage des amphores en Gaule,* Bibliothèque archéologique et historique 174 (Beirut, 2005).

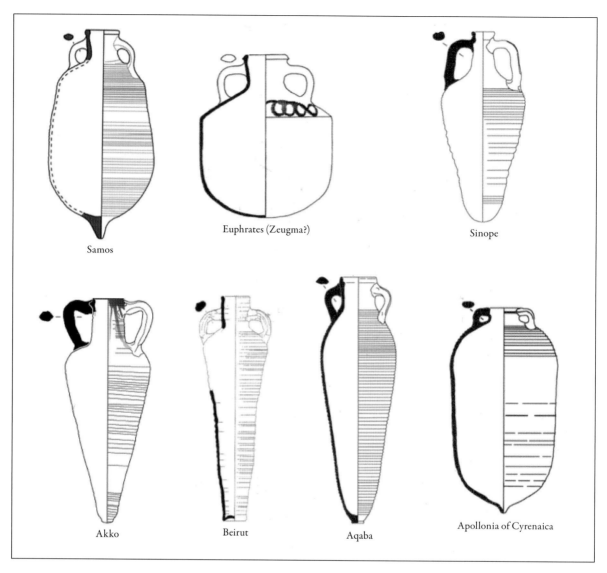

Figure 2.2. An evolution in classification: new amphorae of the past decade (drawing by author)

Tarragon, and Carthage) attributable to the various regions that produced transport containers. In southern Gaul, for example, the entry of eastern imports is reflected in their very high numbers for much of the fifth century, averaging 30 to 45 percent of all the amphorae recovered in the deposits at Narbonne, Arles, and Marseille. More specifically, the census of archaeological contexts at Marseille—one of the most important of the Mediterranean ports in late antiquity— clearly demonstrates a very marked presence of products from the eastern Mediterranean.[8]

They date largely to the fifth century but remain a substantial presence throughout the sixth. Analysis of the distribution of amphorae found at Marseille according to their place of origin reveals the significant presence of eastern imports. A sudden and massive increase beginning in the second quarter of the

---

[8] M. Bonifay and D. Pieri, "Amphores du Ve au VIIe s. à Marseille: Nouvelles données sur la typologie et le contenu," *JRA* 8 (1995): 94–120; D. Pieri, "Les amphores des sondages 6 et 7 de la Bourse," "Les amphores tardives du puits 225 du quartier du Bon-Jésus," and "Les amphores du puits du cap Titol," in *Fouilles à Marseille: Les mobiliers (Ier–VIIe s. ap. J.-C.)*, ed. M. Bonifay, M.-B. Carre, and Y. Rigoir (Aix-en-Provence, 1998), 108–27, 231–42, and 260–64. D. Pieri, "Béryte dans le grand commerce méditerranéen (V^e–VIIe s. apr. J.-C.)," in *Productions et échanges dans la Syrie gréco-romaine*, ed. M. Sartre, supp. Topoï 8 (Lyon, 2007), 297–327.

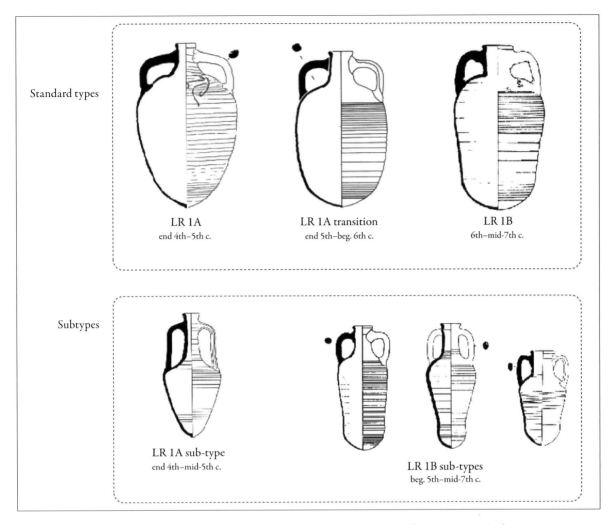

Figure 2.3. Examples of typological evolution of the type LR 1B, 6th–7th c. AD (drawing by author)

fifth century is noteworthy: the years 420–30 in fact mark the beginning of the penetration of eastern products in the West, and similar results have been found in Rome and Carthage. The imports of these wares are constant until the first half of the seventh century, when a precipitous drop is evident—clearly the result of the catastrophic events in the East associated with the war against the Persian Sasanids and the subsequent Arab-Muslim conquest. Elsewhere in the West—whether Rome, Tarragon, or Carthage—imports consistently seem to follow the same trajectory, with similar orders of magnitude (table 2.1).

The decline of western centers of production from the middle of the third century, marked by the gradual disappearance of Roman merchant guilds and the decline of Iberian and Gallic amphora workshops, as well as by the exceptional commercial draw that Constantinople exerted in the East beginning in the mid-fourth century, prompted the emergence of new regional areas of production that had previously been largely dormant. Certain areas in the eastern Mediterranean rose to prominence as a result of their specialized production of goods intended for export: continental Greece (the Peloponnese), particular islands in the Aegean Sea (Samos, Chios, and Thasos), Crete, Cyprus, the western and southern fringes of Asia Minor, the southern shores of the Black Sea, the Levant, and Egypt (fig. 2.4). The commercial success of the East is evident in the rise in production resulting from strong local demand, as well as demand from distant provinces. Two distinguishing examples are noteworthy: the increase in the size of certain eastern amphorae, such as the LR 4, from the fifth to seventh centuries (fig. 2.5)

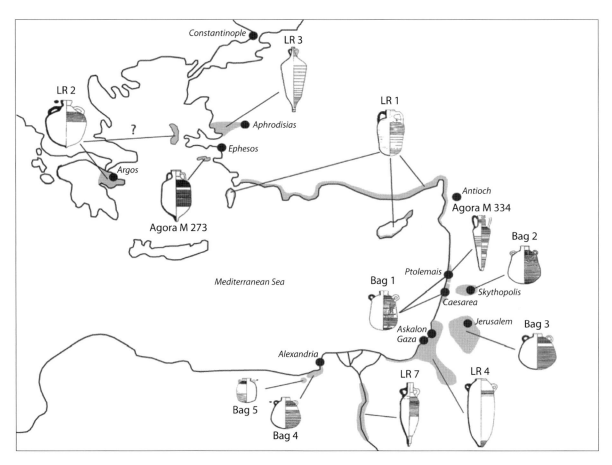

Figure 2.4. Main types of eastern late Roman amphorae and their production areas (after Pieri, *Le commerce du vin oriental*, fig. 107)

and the growth in both the size and the productivity of manufacturing sites (fig. 2.6).

In the East itself, the quantitative data available remain sparse. Beirut, for example, has yielded nearly all the major products associated with the eastern Mediterranean (fig. 2.7).⁹ All the major amphora types are present, in proportions that vary according to type and period. Four distinct regions clearly exported provisions to Beirut as a favored trading partner: Isauria-Cilicia, Cyprus, Palestine, and the Black Sea. Beirut also maintained ties with the Aegean, Asia Minor, and Egypt. Although it imported goods from all of the eastern regions, the city nonetheless tended to favor southern markets situated between the river Jordan and the Mediterranean, extending even as far as the Negev. The diversity of amphora types, their varied origins, and their noticeable presence until the middle of the seventh century might indicate that the famous earthquake of 551 did not harm Beirut's commercial vitality to the extent that is often claimed: from the amphorae, in fact, no decrease in the volume of trade is observable. By contrast, a very distinct diminution in the volume of trade evidently accompanied the political change brought about by the Arab conquest of the region. Producing regions contracted, and under the Byzantine organizational model only Egypt and Transjordan continued to engage in manufacturing.

At other sites, in central or eastern Europe (Istanbul, Thasos, Samos, Butrint, Argos, Anemourion, and Alexandria), the dominance of LR 1 is incontrovertible,¹⁰ with the exception of military

---

9 D. Pieri, "Béryte dans le grand commerce méditerranéen (Vᶜ–VIIᶜ s. apr. J.-C.)," in *Productions et échanges dans la Syrie gréco-romaine*, ed. M. Sartre, supp. Topoï 8 (Lyon, 2007), 297–327.

10 J. W. Hayes, "Amphorae," in *Excavations at Saraçhane in Istanbul*, vol. 2, *The Pottery* (Princeton, N.J., 1992), 61–79; Herrin and Toydemir, "Byzantine Pottery"; C. Abadie-Reynal and

Table 2.1 Comparative data on amphorae from several areas of the western Mediterranean

	Amphora type		
Site and date	Eastern	African	Unclassified
Rome Crypta Balbi, sond. IIIEX 410–480	14.5% NMI	52.0% NMI	
Rome Magna Mater, sond. I–L 420–440	20.0% NMI	40.0% NMI	
Tarragona Vila-Roma 425–450	26.0% NMI	24.5% NMI	
Rome Schola Praeconum I 430–450	46.4% sherds	42.5% sherds	
Rome Magna Mater, sond. P 440–480	27.0% NMI	32.5% NMI	
Naples Carminiello ai Mannesi 430–450	10.1% sherds	44.4% sherds	45.4% sherds
Naples Carminiello ai Mannesi 490–510	16.5% sherds	21.0% sherds	52.8% sherds
Rome Schola Praeconum II 500–530	40.7% sherds	40.4% sherds	
Carthage Michigan Excavations, "deposit" XV 550	68.8% sherds	12.0% sherds	
Naples Carminiello ai Mannesi late 6th–early 7th c.	34.6% sherds	18.8% sherds	46.8% sherds

SOURCE: Pieri, *Le commerce du vin oriental*, 167.
NMI = minimum number of vessels present.

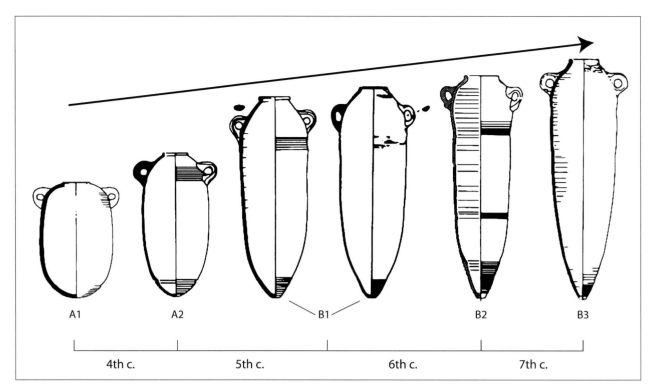

Figure 2.5. An example of the increasing capacity of eastern Mediterranean amphorae: LR 4, produced in the Gaza district of Palestine and widely distributed around the Mediterranean during the 4th to 7th centuries (drawing by author)

positions on the Danubian *limes*. There the type was supplanted by LR 2, which figured more prominently in the provisioning of frontier troops.[11] One must nonetheless guard against too simplistic a conception of the manufacture of amphorae in the East, for many recent studies now suggest more complex models. The number of centers of manufacture seems to have increased, and a regional character becomes evident, with the appearance of atypical forms among the major types.[12] These forms do not extend beyond the regional context, and some output is distributed over limited geographic areas. For example, the recently recognized North Syrian Amphora (NSA) 1, manufactured on the Euphrates River, has been found at only a few sites, in a narrow area from the Euphrates to northern Syria.[13]

J.-P. Sodini, *La céramique paléochrétienne de Thasos (Aliki, Delkos, Fouilles anciennes)* (Paris, 1992); C. Steckner, "Les amphores LR 1 et LR 2 en relation avec le pressoir du complexe ecclésiastique des thermes de Samos," in *Recherches sur la céramique byzantine,* ed. V. Déroche and J.-M. Spieser (Athens, 1989), 57–71; P. Reynolds, "The Roman Pottery from the Triconch Palace," in *Byzantine Butrint: Excavations and Survey, 1994–1999,* ed. R. Hodges, W. Bowden, and K. Lako (Oxford, 2004), 224–69; C. Abadie-Reynal, "Céramique et commerce dans le bassin égéen du IVe au VIIe siècle," in *Hommes et richesses dans l'Empire byzantin,* vol. 1, *IVe–VIIe siècles* (Paris, 1989), 143–59; eadem, "Les amphores protobyzantines d'Argos (IVe–VIe siècles)," in Déroche and Spieser, eds., *Recherches sur la céramique byzantine,* 47–56; eadem, "Les importations moyen-orientales à Argos (IVe–VIIe siècles)," in Villeneuve and Watson, eds., *La céramique byzantine et protoislamique en Syrie-Jordanie,* 283–87; C. K. Williams, *Anemurium: The Roman and Early Byzantine Pottery* (Wetteren, 1989); M. Bonifay, R. Leffy, C. Capelli, and D. Pieri, "Les céramiques du remplissage de la citerne du Sérapéum à Alexandrie," *Alexandrina* 2 (2002): 39–84.

11 O. Karagiorgou, "Mapping Trade by the Amphora," in Mango, ed., *Byzantine Trade, 4th–12th Centuries,* 37–58; eadem, "LR2: A Container for the Military *annona* on the Danubian Border?" in *Economy and Exchange in the East Mediterranean during Late Antiquity,* ed. S. Kingsley and M. Decker (Oxford, 2001), 129–66.

12 Such is the case for the amphora associated with the LR 3 group, especially on the evidence of its morphology, since it has but a single handle. This amphora, documented only at Sardis in the sixth century, had very limited geographic distribution over a short period. M. Rautman, "Two Late Roman Wells at Sardis," *AASOR* 53 (1995): 37–84.

13 D. Pieri, "Nouvelles productions d'amphores de Syrie du Nord aux époques protobyzantine et omeyyade," *Mélanges*

Figure 2.6. Late Roman refuse heaps; Antinoopolis, Egypt (photo by author)

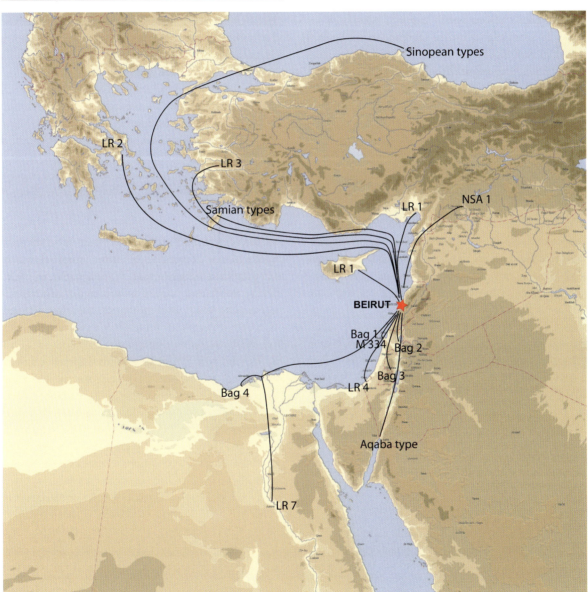

Figure 2.7. Origins of amphorae found in Beirut, 5th–7th c. AD (Pieri, "Béryte dans le grand commerce méditerranéen," 327, fig. 16)

Differences are discernible when the manufactured goods were intended for short- or middle-distance commerce. Moreover, we need to be able to distinguish manufacturing centers that produced containers intended for long-distance trade from those whose products were intended for more local markets.[14] In addition, the uncertainty regarding the true proportions of local manufacture and regional imports, as well as the presence of workshops that could imitate "international" forms, further complicates our understanding of the manufacture of amphorae in the East.

The Transport of Goods by Amphora: A Lucrative Trade

The progress in identifying their contents has also made it possible to understand a new aspect of how these containers functioned in regional and interregional markets, and to correct misinformation about maritime trade in late antiquity.

There is no longer any doubt that the vast majority of amphorae from the eastern Mediterranean contained wine. This finding is based in part on the character of the inscriptions painted on amphorae; it also relies on the presence of pitch on the vessels' inner surfaces, as has often been noted in archaeological studies of the ports at Carthage, Marseille, Port-Vendres, and Fos, as well as of seabed shipwrecks, such as those of Yassı Ada, the Palud, the Dramont E, the Saint-Gervais 2, Dor D, and Giglio Porto. Literary testimony, moreover, describes the great majority of eastern regions as essentially producers and above all as exporters of wine. The texts provide information in two areas: the reputation of specific eastern wines and the locations of vineyards as well as the names of the estates. Eastern wines were in fact highly esteemed and widely celebrated in the West by such illustrious writers as Sidonius Apollinaris, Gregory of Tours, and Isidore of Seville.

While the eastern trade in ivory, precious stones, perfumes, papyrus, spices, and textiles was very lucrative, wine seems to have been one of the most profitable commodities of the *pars orientis*. Wine was produced throughout the East, in great quantity and of excellent quality, but often also at great cost. Ancient authors describe celebrated estates throughout the eastern Mediterranean basin, whose wines were valued not only for their fine taste but also for their curative powers. Several recipes prescribed by eminent physicians of the period, such as Alexander of Tralles and Paul of Aegina, describe eastern wines, especially those of Gaza and Askalon, as essential in treating a variety of afflictions. Sidonius Apollinaris, in a text composed around AD 460, apologizes for not being able to offer wines from Italy, Greece, and the East to his guest, the senator Ommatius:

> Vina mihi non sunt Gazetica, Chia, Falerna.
> Quaeque Sarepteno palmite missa bibas.
>
> As for wines, I have none of Gaza, no Chian or Falernian,
> none sent by the vines of Sarepta for you to drink.
>
> (trans. W. B. Anderson)[15]

In late antiquity, the prosperity of southern Palestine depended on its agriculture and more specifically on viticulture, which several texts describe as widespread, sometimes even in areas that did not readily support the cultivation of grapes, such as the sand dunes at the southern end of Gaza or the desert areas of the Negev.

The example of Gaza shows that specific regions specialized in viticulture, which constituted a large proportion of their agriculture, in order above all to export a commodity that was renowned throughout the empire and in every corner of the Mediterranean. Gaza apparently gave its name to wines produced in part outside of its territory, including those of the Negev. The name was probably applied to several regional estates under the broad rubric "wine of Gaza" (*vinum Gazetum, Gazetina, Gazeticum*), somewhat as is done in the present day for

---

Jean-Pierre Sodini, *TM* 15 (2005): 583–96; C. Abadie-Reynal, A.-S. Martz, and A. Kador, "Late Roman and Byzantine Pottery in Zeugma: Groups of the Beginning of the Fifth Century," in Böhlendorf-Arslan, Osman Uysal, and Witte-Orr, eds., *Çanak: Late Antique and Medieval Pottery and Tiles*, 181–94.

14 S. Demesticha, "The Seventh-Century Cypriot Amphora Types: Regional or International?" in *Tradition and Transition: Maritime Studies in the Wake of the Byzantine Shipwreck at Yassıada, Turkey* (College Station, Tex., forthcoming).

15 Sidonius Apollinaris, *Carmina* 17.15–16; Sidoine Apollinaire, *Poèmes*, vol. 3, ed. and trans. A. Loyen (Paris, 1970); *Poems and Letters*, trans. W. B. Anderson (Cambridge, Mass., and London, 1936).

Bordeaux wines. Archaeological evidence, moreover, tends to confirm this hypothesis, for the same kinds of containers were apparently used indiscriminately to transport wine from Gaza, Askalon, and the Negev. Wine from southern Palestine, shipped through Gaza, might have acquired an international reputation. Beginning in the fourth century, abundant literary evidence attests to the fame of the estates at Gaza and Askalon, prized even in the West—in Gaul, especially, but in Africa, Italy, and Spain as well. Ancient authors lay particular emphasis on the wines of Palestine, and in particular those from the region of Gaza and the Negev.

With respect to Gaul, several texts make specific reference to wine "from Gaza." At Tours, an individual named Eberulf, seeking to please his friend Claudius, gave him strong wines from Laodikeia and Gaza: "Misitque pueros unum post alium ad requerenda potenciora vina, Laticina videlicet adque Gazitina" (He sent his servants, one after another, to find the strongest wines, that is, from Laodikeia and Gaza).[16] Venantius Fortunatus (ca. 530–ca. 600), who was a contemporary of Gregory of Tours, enumerated the best wines of the period: "Falerna, Gazaque, Creta, Samus, Cypros, Colofona, Seraptis, lucida perspicuis certantia vina lapillis vix discernendis crystallina pocula potis" (Falerna and Gaza, Crete, Samos, Cyprus, Colophona, Serepta, bright wine vying with translucent gems, crystal goblets with the drafts they contain that can scarcely be distinguished from them [trans. M. Roberts]).[17]

For regions outside of Gaul, other texts provide information on a number of topics. For example, Flavius Cresconius Corippus, in the second half of the sixth century, composed a list of the wines served by Justin II at Justinian's funerary banquet. He identifies the best wines as being those from Palestine, and we learn that they are white wines (*alba colore*): "dulcia Bacchi | munera, quae Sarepta ferax, quae Gaza crearet, | Ascalon et laetis dederat quae grata colonis . . . prisca Palaestini miscentur dona Lyaei, | alba colore nivis blandoque levissima gusto" (the sweet gifts of Bacchus, which wild Sarepta and Gaza had created, and which lovely Ashkelon had given to her happy colonists[.] . . . The ancient gifts of the Palestinian Laeus were mingled in, white with the color of snow, and light with bland taste [trans. Av. Cameron]).[18]

These texts indicate, moreover, that the popularity of wines from southern Palestine derived not only from their taste but also from their medicinal properties. Several medical treatises composed between the fourth and the seventh century record that southern Palestinian wine, particularly that from Askalon, was a common medicinal ingredient. In the second half of the fourth century, Oribasius, the personal physician of the Julian the Apostate, recommended a mixture called *anisatum*, made of twenty-one bowls of wine from Askalon, seven bowls of honey, and two hundred anise seeds, for the treatment of various illnesses—particularly stomach ailments.[19] In addition to wine's being a luxury beverage or as a remedy, ancient texts record an altogether different function, in which it figures as an element of the liturgy. Gaza wine, according to several sources, thus seems to have had a cultural use. In fact, it is specifically mentioned by ecclesiastical authors when they refer to the wine used in the Mass. In emphasizing the quality of wine from Gaza, Gregory of Tours records that it had been acquired not to end up in the gullet of a subdeacon but to fill the chalice.[20] John the Almsgiver, at the beginning of the seventh century, refused to perform the Eucharist with a wine from Palestine because of its exorbitant cost, preferring an Egyptian wine whose taste and price were less extravagant.[21] Archaeology confirms the high cost of wine from Gaza and its use in the liturgy, for amphorae from Gaza are sometimes the only containers of eastern provenience found in western sites associated with religious vocations. In the West, Gaza amphorae are most often found in large redistribution centers, as well as in districts inhabited by the

---

16 Gregory of Tours, *Historia Francorum* 7.29; Grégoire de Tours, *Histoire des Francs*, trans. R. Latouche, 3rd ed. (Paris, 1995).

17 Venantius Fortunatus, *De Vita S. Martini* 2; Venance Fortunat, *Œuvres*, vol. 4, *La vie de saint Martin*, ed. and trans. S. Quesnel (Paris, 1996); M. Roberts, "Venantius Fortunatus' Life of St. Martin," *Traditio* 57 (2002): 129–87.

18 Corippus, *In laudem Iustini Augusti minoris* 3.85–97; Corippe, *Éloge de l'empereur Justin II*, ed. and trans. S. Antès (Paris, 1981); *In laudem Iustini Augusti minoris*, trans. Av. Cameron (London, 1976).

19 Oribasius, *Collectionum Medicarum Reliquiae, CMG* 6:1–2.

20 Gregory of Tours, *De gloria confessorum* 65.

21 A.-J. Festugière, *Léontios de Néapolis: Vie de Syméon le Fou et Vie de Jean de Chypre* (Paris, 1974), 327.

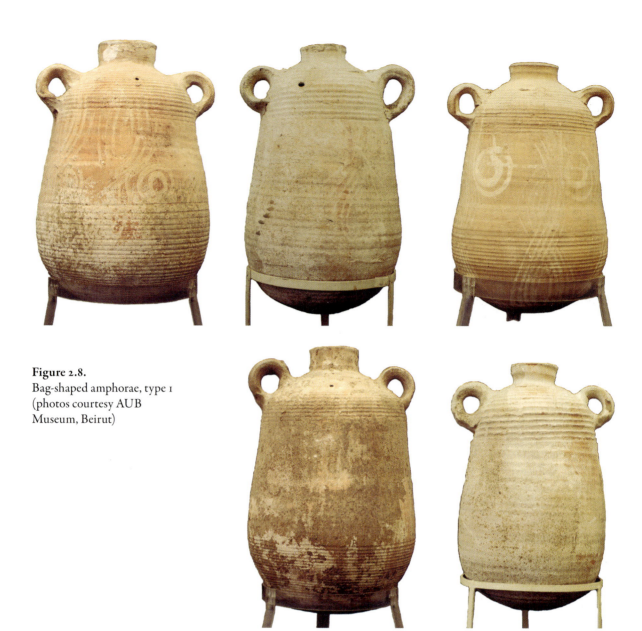

Figure 2.8.
Bag-shaped amphorae, type 1 (photos courtesy AUB Museum, Beirut)

aristocracy.[22] Nor can the possibility be ruled out that this wine, highly valued as it was, had symbolic connotations for certain wealthy individuals in the wake of its promotion by the many pilgrims returning from the Holy Land.

Equally interesting are Type 1 Bag-shaped Amphorae, originating in the region of Ptolemais, which also likely transported a specific kind of wine (fig. 2.8). The consistent presence on their bellies of a stylized painted decoration, sometimes depicting a menorah, suggests that these containers held wine intended (whether exclusively or not) for Jewish communities, whose trade in such wine is amply attested in the records of ancient authors.[23]

22 See, for example, C. Amiel and F. Berthault, "Les amphores du Bas-Empire et de l'Antiquité tardive dans le Sud-Ouest de la France: Apport à l'étude du commerce à grande distance pendant l'Antiquité," in *La civilisation urbaine de l'Antiquité tardive dans le Sud-Ouest de la Gaule,* ed. L. Maurin and J.-M. Pailler, Actes du IIIe colloque Aquitania et des XVIes journées d'archéologie mérovingienne, Toulouse, 23–24 juin 1995, *Aquitania* 14 (1996): 255–63.

23 S. Dar, *Sumaqa: A Roman and Byzantine Jewish Village on Mount Carmel, Israel* (Oxford, 1999); S. A. Kingsley, "The Economic Impact of the Palestinian Wine Trade in Late Antiquity,"

It thus seems clear that the main consumers of wine in the West were members of lay and religious elites. As texts show, only privileged individuals of high social rank could have afforded such costly purchases. The best wines of the period came from the East, and, held in high esteem by local elites (extending even to the courts of kings and emperors), they were essential to setting a fine table. The list of wines served at the banquet celebrating the accession of Justin II clearly bears witness to the preeminence of eastern wines. In the East itself, however, the consumption of wine was an altogether different matter, for proximity to the sites of production made wine accessible to a larger number of people. Indeed, the containers are found as often in rural as in urban locations, and in extremely diverse archaeological layers (habitats of every sort, refuse dumps, small forts, etc.). Wine thus seems to have been consumed more democratically in the East, by all ranks of society, and do not appear have been reserved for the upper classes.

Exchanges: Means and Agents

The differences observed in the clientele might be explained by the various ways in which commodities were distributed. Eastern products, and wine in particular, could have crossed the Mediterranean only through organized commercial enterprises specializing in large-scale trade. Throughout late antiquity, the Mediterranean remained the sole true link between East and West, and the means of trade had changed little since the Roman imperial period. Transportation costs, particularly costs associated with maritime transport, seem to have had a greater impact than before on the price of products involved in long-distance trade. The development of an increasingly onerous fiscal system—as much in the West as in the East—might have been one of the more obvious reasons for the prohibitive cost of certain commodities,[24] but it was surely not the only one. A strong demand in the West for luxury products from the East probably also stimulated trade, whose participants appear to have been limited to a few essentially independent producers, merchants, and freight carriers.[25] The apparent drop in the number of ships traveling the Mediterranean, now attested for late antiquity by submarine archaeology, might have been an equally significant factor. According to data gathered and presented by J. A. Parker, only 206 of more than 1,200 Mediterranean shipwrecks can be ascribed to the late Roman Empire and the early Middle Ages.[26]

Several conclusions can be drawn from these observations. First, in diachronic terms, it is striking that between the sixth century BC and the tenth century AD, the number of shipwrecks that can be associated with late antiquity constitutes a very small proportion of the total: barely a tenth of the total number of documented shipwrecks, or 120 for the entire Mediterranean basin (fig. 2.9). Second, if we take only the data from the third century AD forward, a precipitous drop in shipwrecks is evident—a trajectory that concludes in a single instance of a shipwreck in the eighth century (fig. 2.10). The decline is even clearer when we consider the nature of these ships and their cargo. Only fifty or so of the wrecks dating between the fourth and seventh centuries carried amphorae. Among these fifty, only eight had a cargo of eastern amphorae; a mere ten or so were traveling east.[27] The conclusions that we can draw from this remarkable study should nonetheless be interpreted with some caution, since more recent studies tend to moderate this picture of a drastic decline in maritime trade.[28]

---

in Kingsley and Decker, eds., *Economy and Exchange in the East Mediterranean during Late Antiquity*, 44–68.

24 P. Garnsey and C. R. Whittaker, "Trade, Industry and the Urban Economy," in *The Cambridge Ancient History*, 3rd ed., vol. 13, *The Late Empire, A.D. 337–425*, ed. Av. Cameron and P. Garnsey (Cambridge, 1998), 312–35; J.-M. Carrié, "Les échanges commerciaux et l'État antique tardif," in *Les échanges dans l'Antiquité: Le rôle de l'État*, Entretiens d'Archéologie et d'Histoire 1 (Saint-Bertrand-de-Comminges, 1994), 175–211.

25 Whittaker, "Late Roman Trade and Traders"; B. Sirks, "The Importation and Distribution of Olive Oil and Wine in Rome and Constantinople," in *Food for Rome: The Legal Structure of the Transportation and Processing of Supplies for the Imperial Distributions in Rome and Constantinople*, ed. idem (Amsterdam, 1991), 388–94; A. Carandini, "Il mondo della tarda antichità visto attraverso le merci," in A. Giardina, *Società romana e impero tardo antico*, vol. 3 (Rome, 1986), 3–19.

26 A. J. Parker, *Ancient Shipwrecks of the Mediterranean and the Roman Provinces*, BAR International Series 580 (Oxford, 1992).

27 G. Volpe, "Archeologia subacquea e commerci in età tardoantica," in *Archeologia subacquea: Come opera l'archeologo sott'acqua: Storie dalle acque*, ed. G. Volpe (Florence, 1998), 561–626; S. A. Kingsley, *Shipwreck Archaeology of the Holy Land: Processes and Parameters* (London, 2004).

28 See in this volume M. McCormick, "Ships, Shipwrecks, Trade, and Markets."

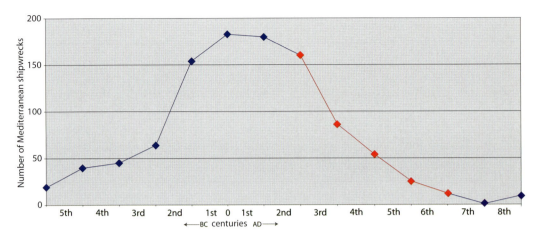

Figure 2.9. Temporal distribution of the 1,072 ancient shipwrecks in the Mediterranean, 6th c. BC–8th c. CE (A. J. Parker, "Cargoes, Containers and Stowage: The Ancient Mediterranean," *International Journal of Nautical Archaeology* 21 [1992]: 89–100, with new data)

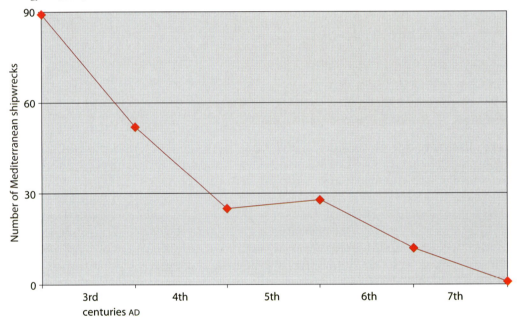

Figure 2.10. Temporal distribution of the 206 Mediterranean shipwrecks in late antiquity, 3rd–8th c. CE; of the 120 wrecked between the 4th and 7th c., only 15 had eastern amphorae in their cargo (Parker, "Cargoes, Containers and Stowage," with new data)

Yet the dangers of the sea during late antiquity were quite real. The precarious status of merchants was compounded by the financial risks posed by the sizable investment involved in chartering a transport vessel. Such concerns surely underlie some of the painted inscriptions (*tituli picti*) that appear on amphorae with increasing frequency between the fifth and seventh centuries—invocations that could have beseeched divine protection for the vessel and its cargo (fig. 2.11). The perils of the sea could destroy a vessel and its cargo, and with them would be lost the considerable funds invested in them. According to an anecdote, John the Almsgiver, at the beginning of the seventh century, entrusted a ship of the Alexandrian church to an unfortunate *naukleros* who had been bankrupted by two successive shipwrecks and was on the verge of killing himself.

To understand this trade, it is worthwhile to examine the background of those who were involved in it. In the West, large-scale trade largely bypassed

Late Roman Amphora 1
with titulus pictus
end of the 5th c. CE
St. Blaise (South of France)

Late Roman Amphora 1B
Antinoopolis, Egypt
(mid-6th c. CE)

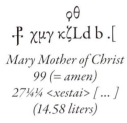

ϙθ
✝ χμγ κζLd b .[

Mary Mother of Christ
99 (= amen)
27¼¼ <xestai> [...]
(14.58 liters)

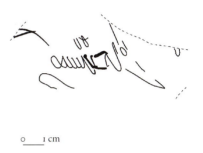

0 ⎯⎯ 1 cm

Figure 2.11. Painted inscriptions on LR 1 amphorae: (a) Late Roman Amphora 1 with titulus pictus, end of the 5th c. AD; Saint Blaise (south of France); (b) Late Roman Amphora 1B, mid-6th c. AD; Antinoopolis, Egypt (Fournet and Pieri, "Les *dipinti* amphoriques d'Antinoopolis," fig. 11a–b)

westerners. Rather, it was controlled by foreigners, specifically foreigners from the East: Greeks, Egyptians, Jews, and especially the *Syrii,* a collective term that designated Syrian, Palestinian, and Phoenician merchants who specialized in large-scale maritime commerce. They plied the Mediterranean and formed communities in the major cities associated with the sea trade (Rome, Ravenna, Naples, Marseille, Arles, and Carthage, among others).[29] Gaul and the Frankish kingdom aptly illustrate their dominance: the familiar examples of Marseille, Arles, Narbonne, Toulouse, Bordeaux, Lyon, Tours, Nantes, and Paris, as well as Trier and Cologne, directly link the discovery of containers of eastern manufacture and the presence of eastern individuals mentioned in the texts. During the late Roman period and the early Middle Ages, the eastern *transmarini negotiatores* were thus essential agents in the distribution of luxury products to the West, products that were likely known and sought after thanks to communities that originated in the East.[30]

Archaeology and papyrology can give us a fairly precise notion of who these merchants were. To the extent that they have been preserved, inscriptions painted on amphorae in fact mention specific names. Thus several examples of contemporaneous (early sixth-century) LR 1, found in two different locations within Egypt—Alexandria and Hermopolis Magna / Antinoopolis—record an individual named Apollinarios (fig. 2.12),[31] inscribed by the

29 C. Dietrich, *Der Handel im westlichen Mittelmeer während des Frühmittelalters*, AbhGött, Philol.-hist.Kl. 144 (Göttingen, 1985), 170–86.

30 A. d'Ors, "Los transmarini negociatores de la legislación visigoda," in *Estudios de Derecho Internacional: Homenaje al Prof. Barcia Trelles* (Santiago de Compostela, 1958), 467–83.

31 J.-L. Fournet and D. Pieri, "Les *dipinti* amphoriques d'Antinoopolis," in *Antinoupolis,* ed. R. Pintaudi, Scavi e materiali 1 (Florence, 2008), 175–216.

χμγ † ϟθ / Θεου χάρις / Ἀπολλιναρ(ίου)
Mary Mother of Christ † Amen / By the Grace of God / Apollinarios

Figure 2.12. Amphorae of Apollinarios, a merchant of the 6th c. AD (Fournet and Pieri, "Les *dipinti* amphoriques d'Antinoopolis," figs. 20–23)

same hand on the neck of each vessel in black ink, much like the label of a bottle. It is tempting to interpret these inscriptions as naming a merchant who, judging from the dating of these amphorae, lived during the first half of the sixth century. He would not have been Egyptian, for the name Apollinarios was no longer in use in Egypt in the sixth century. In this case it can only be the name of one of these famous *transmarini negotiatores* who bound Asia Minor to Egypt.

The Standardization of Amphorae: A Difficult Question

Contrary to received wisdom, standardization is relatively rare in late antique amphora forms, certainly for a large proportion of Mediterranean amphorae, whether of African, Italian, or eastern origin. In fact, a single type of amphora can encompass considerable variation in capacity, sometimes amounting to several liters. One of the most revealing examples is the African *spatheion* of the fourth and fifth centuries: the African cargo of the wreck of the Dramont E found on the southern French coast shows no discernible difference between the amphora type Keay 25.2 and the spatheion, both of which vary in capacity and size.[32] The coexistence of different "standard" units of measure (often fractional units) is seen mainly in eastern amphorae, although it is sometimes difficult to specify the morphological variants that might give rise to errors in classifying amphorae chronologically or typologically.[33] The absence of standardization is particularly characteristic of Cilician amphorae and Cypriot LR 1 vessels. Variations in the capacity of amphora types over the course of time further complicate efforts to associate sizes with specific units of measure. Such is the case with the LR 4, whose capacity increased between the fifth and seventh centuries, a phenomenon that

---

32 M. Bonifay, *Études sur la céramique romaine tardive d'Afrique,* BAR International Series 1301 (Oxford, 2004), 125–29.
33 For example, the differences posited by D. P. S. Peacock and D. F. Williams (*Amphorae and the Roman Economy: An Introductory Guide* [London, 1986], 185–86) among the LR 1 type are not plausible, since the amphorae that illustrated their "Class 44" are in fact two examples of a single form datable to the sixth and seventh centuries. Examples associated with fifth-century forms do not appear in this typology, although these constitute the vast majority of examples of LR 1 in the western Mediterranean.

can be explained only as the market's response to high demand. Ultimately, the proliferation of forms in late period amphorae tells us little about their contents. Their diversity was the result of a long evolution, dictated in part by the demands of maritime transport. Periods of commercialization and technological development of course had an effect, but so did the variations in the contents of amphorae, the sites in which they were manufactured, and local traditions. The same factors account for the diversity of late Roman amphorae, especially those from the East, in which differences are expressed even more markedly. The types and their variants are particularly numerous during this period, a consequence not just of the multiplicity of manufacturing regions and their particular workshops but also of a deliberate intent to promote the vessels' contents in a highly competitive market.

Late eastern amphorae are by definition containers intended for large-scale commerce, manufactured in the thousands (even millions). It would thus be difficult to see no relationship between the product and its packaging, which should (one would think) reflect and promote the product. The notion that commodities might change because of the size of the amphorae or their intended market is implausible. The commonplace manufacture during the late period of smaller-capacity amphorae, replicating standard models, is characteristic of Greek cultural areas since early antiquity. It has a twofold significance in the composition of freight. First, these small units served to fill the empty spaces left by large-diameter units.[34] Second, they were more easily marketable, ready to be sold on the retail market if they were not intended for barter or for specific buyers. It is unlikely that an amphora type from a single point of origin would have served to trade two products as dissimilar as oil and wine, which did not compete with one another and which were subject to distinct metrological systems. Varying contents in a single kind of container is not (or is only rarely) found during the Roman period, when packaging was clearly intended to designate a specific product.[35] The same phenomenon seems to have held true in late antiquity, even if a few exceptional examples attest to multiple uses—for example, the spheroid amphora LR 2, associated in certain specific cases with the shipment of both oil and wine.[36]

The question of the primary content of certain containers is sometimes complicated by the frequent reuse of amphorae; in addition, they might have had multiple uses when they were employed near their place of manufacture, serving to store various products (for example, honey, dried fruit, legumes, dried meats, fish, or cheese).[37] It is thus important to distinguish containers intended for bringing products to market in the context of medium- and long-distance trade from those used locally for a variety of purposes. The main techniques used to sell and promote products were not fundamentally different in antiquity than they are today: a product's commercial success depends not only on its quality and its reputation but also on how it is marketed. Just as important for producers seeking to capture particular markets was their capacity to adapt to competition. In this context, packaging played an important role. Clearly, consumers would have expected to know what an amphora was transporting purely on the basis of its form. The simplest means of promoting the product that amphorae contained was to disseminate them over as wide a territory as possible, and the simplest means of managing and redistributing containers arriving in a port would have been their packaging.

---

34 The phenomenon, now well attested, was exhaustively treated by Claude Santamaria in his study of the shipwreck Dramont E at Saint-Raphaël, which brought to light the fact that African *spatheia* were principally used to fill the empty spaces between the amphorae. C. Santamaria, *L'épave Dramont "E" à Saint-Raphaël (Ve siècle ap. J.-C.),* Archaeonautica 13 (Paris, 1995), 117–18.

35 Such designation was made even clearer with the dissemination, beginning in the second century AD, of series of containers devised to market specific products. Moreover, might not the series of flat-bottomed amphorae, manufactured in Gaul, Africa, and Italy from the second to the fifth century (their common origin suggested by typological details), have been created in order to associate a specific kind of container with wine?

36 Karagiorgou, "LR2"; S. Demesticha, "Some Thoughts on the Production and Presence of the Late Roman Amphora 13 on Cyprus," in *Trade Relations in the Eastern Mediterranean from the Late Hellenistic Period to Late Antiquity: The Ceramic Evidence,* ed. M. B. Briesce and L. E. Vaag (Odense, 2005), 169–78; P. van Alfen, "Newer Light on the Yass1 Ada Shipwreck: The On-going Restudy of the LRA2/13 Amphoras," in *Tradition and Transition,* forthcoming.

37 In the context of local uses, Egyptian LR 7 amphorae contained fish and milk products. See M. Egloff, *Kellia: La poterie copte: Quatre siècles d'artisanat et d'échanges en Basse-Égypte,* Recherches suisses d'archéologie copte (Geneva, 1977), 111; J. A. Riley, "Coarse Pottery," in *Excavations at Sidi Khrebish Benghazi (Berenice),* Libya Antiqua supp. 5 (Tripoli, 1979), 2:225.

Finally, tradition was an important factor. For the manufacturers of containers, in direct partnership with regional agricultural producers, knowledge of changes in how containers would be used must have influenced their form. The long lineages of amphorae are often rooted in regions in which the agricultural traditions were strong.[38]

In trying to determine the nature of the contents, we have less information for late antiquity than we do for earlier periods. The painted or engraved inscriptions that during the Roman period convey a great deal of information no longer indicate the commodity being transported; they are instead limited to measures of capacity or to Christian invocations. Most often, we must content ourselves with examining the inside surfaces of amphorae. In order to transport commodities such as wine or fish sauces, containers had to be made watertight by coating their interiors with resin. The incompatibility of resin and oil has long been recognized.[39]

The relationship between the weight of the container and that of the merchandise was a constant concern among potters in antiquity. Modest technical revolutions in that respect are evident during the late Roman Empire. Progress was made in minimizing the tare (empty) weight of containers without excessively increasing their fragility; late antique eastern Mediterranean amphorae are striking for their lightness and the thinness of their walls. Beyond their decorative effect and the practical utility of making the vessels easier to grasp, the corrugations present almost without exception on the bellies of amphorae were intended to improve the firing of the clay and reduce the areas of limiting contacts between amphorae as well as the risk of breakage during sea transport.

The unusual appearance of amphorae with Greek inscriptions painted in red ochre or black ink on their neck and shoulder also warrants mention. These amphorae have long been known by epigraphers, especially papyrologists, for whom the frequently attested inscriptions are an indispensable resource for studying early Byzantine paleography.

The data in these inscriptions (*tituli picti,* or *dipinti*) most often consist of the weight or volume of the commodities transported, the names of people or institutions, abbreviated theological formulas (incipits and *isopsephia*), and Christian symbols. The inscriptions offer a form of protection, though their purpose is primarily commercial, and they appear in the same location on each amphora.

The metrological system used to mark the capacity of these amphorae is complex and difficult to interpret because of the use of ornate or highly stylized cursive scripts. The unit of measure, the *sextarius* (Greek ξέστης), apparently varied depending on the commodity being transported, the region in which it was produced, and the regions to which it was being shipped, as well as the period. To date, attempts to correlate the capacity of late period amphorae with the known values of the sextarius have not been successful, as the system in use seems to be different from those in effect during the Roman Empire or the medieval period.[40] Peter G. van Alfen, in an essay published in 1996, considered the possible association of the capacities recorded with one or several metrological systems that were in use during the proto-Byzantine period (the sextarius or a multiple of three *litrai*).[41] He determined that the various methods of calculation were apparently not consistently followed, and consequently it is difficult to arrive at a standard unit of capacity for the late Roman period. Contrary to the hypothesis advanced by Michael Decker of a commercial and economic unit of measure to which a standardization of containers might attest,[42] the study recently undertaken on the imported amphorae found at Antinoopolis reveals the use of diverse and regional metrological

---

38 That is the case, for example, with bag-shaped amphorae made in the Near East beginning in the Bronze Age, whose basic form changed little until the medieval period.

39 The discussion is summarized in N. Ben Lazreg, M. Bonifay, and P. Trousset, "Production et commercialisation des *salsamenta* de l'Afrique ancienne," in *Actes du VIe colloque d'Histoire et d'Archéologie de l'Afrique* (Paris, 1995), 103–42.

40 Mabel Lang (*Graffiti and Dipinti*, Athenian Agora 21 [Princeton, N.J., 1976]) sought to demonstrate that the general system used for amphorae found in the Agora at Athens corresponded to the Cypriot *sextarius* (= 0.546 l), but this accords with only a few examples of LR 1. Similarly, the units of measure based on the Byzantine *metron,* and its subunit, the *litra,* are no longer convincing. F. H. van Doorninck, "Giving Good Weight in Eleventh-Century Byzantium: The Metrology of the Glass Wreck Amphoras," *INA Quarterly* 20 (1993): 8–12.

41 P. G. van Alfen, "New Light on the 7th C. Yassı Ada Shipwreck: Capacities and Standard Sizes of LRA 1 Amphoras," *JRA* 9 (1996): 210–13.

42 M. Decker, "Water into Wine: Trade and Technology in Late Antiquity," in *Technology in Transition, A.D. 300–650,* ed. L. Lavan, E. Zanini, and A. Sarantis, Late Antique Archaeology 4 (Leiden, 2007), 65–92.

systems.⁴³ Examining other sites from this perspective may further extend these findings.

The fact that late eastern amphorae, and particularly the LR 1, were somewhat standardized implies a rigorous and well-developed system of controls, but it also points to a certain freedom in the manufacture of containers. Only through the joint study of the inscription and the container can we understand this process, although such study requires complete amphorae with legible inscriptions. The case of Antinoopolis reveals that the measurement of the contents was determined by subtracting the weight of the empty amphora from the weight of the full amphora. Indications of the tare weight, calculated as a multiple of the Roman pound, in fact appear on the necks of amphorae. Once the amphora was filled with wine, the container was weighed again and, after a table of equivalents was consulted, the volume in sextarii was indicated on the shoulder or on the plaster stopper. Steelyards found in shipwrecks such as those at Dor and at Yassı Ada are very likely associated with the weighing of amphorae.⁴⁴ Such a method would imply that on the agricultural estates, at the moment when the containers were filled, individuals were present who were charged with verifying the integrity of the process and defending against fraud; but in the absence of textual sources, these agents remain unknown. The inscriptions of the tare weight and the sextarius were affixed at the same moment, which makes centralized control in the *horrea* or in the redistribution centers appear unlikely. The rigorous topography of the inscriptions on the LR 1 amphorae, as well as the relatively homogeneous style of the scripts, plausibly suggests an itinerant body of professionals specializing in this trade, able to make their way to the various viticultural estates. However, it also seems that the units of weight and the value of the sextarius might have varied according to the region.

The Structures of Production: Complexity of Methods and Premises

The study of the centers in which eastern Mediterranean amphorae were manufactured in late antiquity is perhaps the field in which progress has been slowest and remains, for the moment, least satisfactory.

Whereas the relationships between the manufacture of amphorae and the production of the goods intended to be shipped are understood, at least broadly, knowledge of the precise organization of amphora workshops continues to be elusive. Whether they were public or privately held enterprises remains unknown, as does how the state and the Church affected the process. Nonetheless, it seems likely that we are dealing with fairly loose and heterogeneous productive enterprises, differing somewhat according to region. Papyrological documentation apparently shows that in Egypt, for example, the system was by and large privately held; the manufacture of amphorae was often subcontracted or delegated to a part-time potter through a landowner or an ecclesiastical estate.⁴⁵ Egyptian LR 7 amphorae often contain *tituli picti* on the belly or stamps on the stoppers that suggest either the given names of agricultural landowners or the name of ecclesiastical estates.

The case of LR 1 amphorae is equally revealing, for the names that appear among the painted inscriptions can be plausibly interpreted as Cilician names of private landowners and occasionally of ecclesiastical estates. Several symbols and signs inscribed on the amphora—for instance, crosses that imply a church workshop—also occasionally suggest a closer relation between the Church and their production (fig. 2.13).

The yield of the workshops is similarly unknown to us; it might have been as diverse as suggested by the few potters' establishments found up to the present day, where no single function and organization consistently appear. Knowledge of the sequence of operations, which could shed light on the use of raw materials, related production, the traditions of pottery manufacture, or even technologies, remains sketchy. We likewise know little about the environment of the workshops, for the data only rarely

---

43 Fournet and Pieri, "Les *dipinti* amphoriques d'Antinoopolis."
44 S. Kingsley and K. Raveh, *The Ancient Harbour and Anchorage at Dor, Israel, Results of the Underwater Surveys, 1976–1991*, BAR International Series 626 (Oxford, 1996), 69–72; G. K. Sams, "The Weighing Implements," in *Yassı Ada I, a Seventh-Century Byzantine Shipwreck*, ed. G. F. Bass and F. G. van Doorninck Jr. (College Station, Tex., 1982), 202–30; in this volume, see B. Pitarakis, "Weighing Instruments" in "Daily Life at the Marketplace in Late Antiquity and Byzantium."

45 S. Bacot, "Le commerce du vin dans les monastères d'Égypte à l'époque copte," in *Le commerce en Égypte ancienne*, ed. N. Grimal and B. Menu, Bibliothèque d'étude 121 (Cairo, 1998), 269–88.

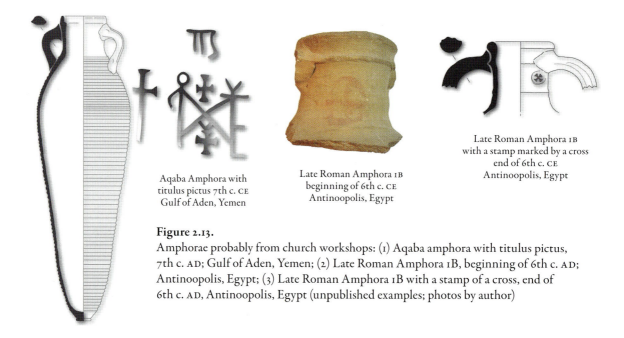

Figure 2.13.
Amphorae probably from church workshops: (1) Aqaba amphora with titulus pictus, 7th c. AD; Gulf of Aden, Yemen; (2) Late Roman Amphora 1B, beginning of 6th c. AD; Antinoopolis, Egypt; (3) Late Roman Amphora 1B with a stamp of a cross, end of 6th c. AD, Antinoopolis, Egypt (unpublished examples; photos by author)

specify the context of these complexes (urban, suburban, or rural) or whether they operated at a regional or provincial level (as independent workshops or as guilds). On this point, the manufacture of LR 1 is again a good example of the complex system of production as it was defined in the East during late antiquity.

At present we know of several sites where LR 1 amphorae were manufactured, since some twenty workshops have been identified, mainly in Cilicia and Isauria.[46] Unfortunately this census, first carried out by Jean-Yves Empereur and Maurice Picon at the end of the 1980s, has only rarely led to excavations.[47] Moreover, even today we know practically nothing about the output of the workshops in which these amphorae were manufactured—what types the workshops made, or how long they functioned. Despite the apparent homogeneity of this type of amphora, whose forms were highly standardized, the workshops themselves were diverse in size, ranging from the modest rural establishment at Rhosos to the large complex at Seleukeia Pieria. Cyprus may be the exception to the general paucity of information about manufacturing, since two workshops were recently excavated on the island, both on the southern coast: one at Paphos and the other at Zygi. They were discovered in the 1990s, and the excavations remain partial: the kilns have been studied, but the complexes as a whole are still unknown.[48] The extent of the area of production, straddling several provinces (Cilicia I and II, Isauria, Syria I, Rhodes, and Cyprus), suggests shared economic interests

---

46   J.-Y. Empereur and M. Picon, "Les régions de production d'amphores impériales en Méditerranée orientale," in *Amphores romaines et histoire économique: Dix ans de recherche* (Rome, 1989), 223–48.

47   M. Ricci, "Elaiussa Sebaste: Context, Production and Commerce," in Böhlendorf-Arslan, Osman Uysal, and Witte-Orr, eds., *Çanak: Late Antique and Medieval Pottery and Tiles*, 169–80; F. Burragato, M. di Nezza, A. F. Ferrazzoli, and M. Ricci, "Late Roman 1 Amphora Types Produced at Elaiussa Sebaste," in Bonifay and Tréglia, eds., *LRCW 2*, 671–88; A. F. Ferrazzoli and M. Ricci, "Un centro di produzione delle anfore LR 1: Elaiussa Sebaste in Cilicia (Turchia): Gli impianti, le anfore," in *LRCW 3: Third International Conference on Late Roman Coarse Wares, Cooking Wares and Amphorae in the Mediterranean: Archaeology and Archaeometry, Comparison between Western and Eastern Mediterranean* (Oxford, 2008).

48   S. Demesticha, "The Paphos Kiln: Manufacturing Techniques of LR1 Amphoras," *Rei Cretariae Romanae Favtorvm Acta* 36 (2000): 549–53; eadem, "Amphora Production on Cyprus during the Late Roman Period," in Bakirtzis, ed., *De Rome à Byzance, de Fostat à Cordoue*, 469–76; eadem, "Some Thoughts on the Production"; S. Demesticha and D. Michaelides, "The Excavation of a Late Roman 1 Amphora Kiln in Paphos," in Villeneuve and Watson, eds., *La céramique byzantine et proto-islamique en Syrie-Jordanie*, 289–96.

that extended far beyond the borders of the *chora*, regional as well as provincial in scope.

The few sites that provide information reveal little about production methods. Several kiln structures that date to the fifth and sixth century have been found at Sinope on the Black Sea,[49] and refuse dumps for LR 7 wasters have been discovered in Egypt. We know of several workshops that made LR 4; they were scattered over a vast region that comprises Gaza, Askalon, and the Negev, which suggests that the territory constituted a substantial manufacturing presence.[50] The workshop situated to the north of Askalon in particular offers a fairly complete example of a factory that was integrated into an extensive rural operation. Finally, of the considerable number of late Byzantine structures that survive, several specializing in the manufacture of spindle-shaped amphorae have been found at Aqaba.[51] The few physicochemical analyses that have been performed have established the origins of amphorae from Beirut with absolute certainty.[52]

Given the scarcity of available data, we have only a patchy view of the methods by which amphorae were manufactured in the East. At the same time, to advance our knowledge of these amphorae, and to go beyond the question of their manufacture, it is essential that we be able to evaluate how amphora manufacturing was integrated into its economic context—urban or rural, regional or provincial. Thus, defining with some precision the places in which amphorae were produced remains the challenge for specialists now studying the organization of agricultural centers in the East.

Imitations and Forgeries

The existence, both recognized and presumed, of regions that produced imitative packaging—and probably, in certain cases, deliberate forgeries—raises a number of questions. The imitation of a specific type of amphora suggests an intent by those with a more or less comparable product to use the commercial success of the original for their own profit. In late antiquity, the output of imitations was limited in both number and chronological scope. Most often, a few containers were copied very faithfully from originals and integrated among ordinary locally manufactured goods. The container most frequently imitated was apparently the LR 1B amphora, intended mainly for the transport of wine. Several workshops are known today that were established far from the traditional regions of production, distributed over geographic areas as diverse as North Africa, Egypt, and the Black Sea. An example of LR 1B preserved in the Bardo Museum in Tunis that seems to be of North African manufacture was the main evidence leading researchers to posit the manufacture of amphorae imitating LR 1 in that region. The subsequent discovery of a manufacturing structure at Henchir Ech Chkaf, near Salakta, has corroborated these suspicions.[53] In fact, this workshop, whose main activity was the manufacture of African containers at the end of the sixth century and during the first half of the seventh, also produced a small quantity of a type of amphora with clear similarities to LR 1.

The case of Egypt is more suggestive; the recent identification of several centers that manufactured LR 1B in the Delta and in the Nile Valley has confirmed the hypothesis of Holeil Ghaly that Egyptian copies of LR 1B were being manufactured in Nile clay at Saqqara.[54] New areas, identified in surveys undertaken by Pascale Ballet, have brought to light imitations in calcite clay (at Uyun Musa in the Sinai) and in alluvial clay (at Kellia and Bawit in the middle Nile Valley).[55] It is noteworthy that there, as in

---

49 D. Kassab-Tezgör and I. Tatlican, "Fouilles des ateliers d'amphores à Demirci près de Sinope en 1996 et 1997," *Anatolia Antiqua* 6 (1998): 423–42.
50 Y. Israel, "Ashqelon," *Excavations and Surveys in Israel* 13 (1993): 100–105; idem, "Survey of Pottery Workshops, Naḥal Lakhish–Naḥal Besor," *Excavations and Surveys in Israel* 13 (1993): 106–7. D. S. Whitcomb, "Ceramic Production at Aqaba in the Early Islamic Period," in Villeneuve and Watson, eds., *La céramique byzantine et proto-islamique en Syrie-Jordanie*, 298.
51 D. S. Whitcomb, "Ceramic Production at Aqaba in the Early Islamic Period," in Villeneuve and Watson, eds., *La céramique byzantine et proto-islamique en Syrie-Jordanie*, 298.
52 M. Roumié, B. Nsouli, C. Atalla, and S. Y. Waksman, "Application of PIXE using Al Funny Filter for Cluster Analysis of Byzantine Amphorae from Beirut," *Nuclear Instruments and Methods in Physics Research, Section B* 227 (2005): 584–90.

53 J. Nacef, "Nouvelles données sur l'atelier de potiers de Henrich ech Chekaf (Pheradi Maius, Tunisie)," in Bonifay and Tréglia, eds., *LRCW 2*, 581–95.
54 H. Ghaly, "Pottery Workshops of Saint-Jeremia (Saqqara)," *Cahiers de la Céramique Égyptienne* 3 (1992): 161–71, figs. 16a, 16b.
55 P. Ballet, "Un atelier aux sources de Moïse (Uyun Musa)," in *Le Sinaï de la conquête arabe à nos jours*, ed. J.-M. Mouton, Cahiers des Annales islamologiques 21 (Cairo, 2001), 37–50, fig. 9;

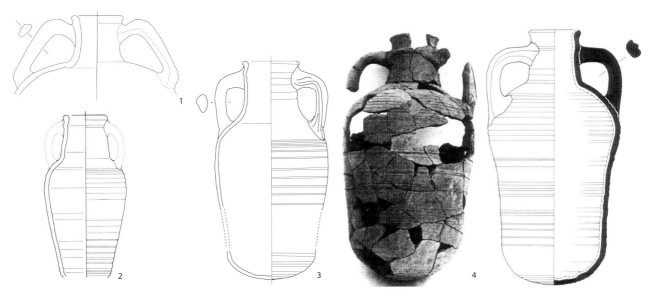

Figure 2.14. Egyptian imitations of LR 1 (approx. scale 1:4): (1) Uyun Musa (Ballet, "Un atelier aux sources de Moïse (Uyun Musa)," fig. 9); (2) Kellia (Ballet, Rassart-Debergh, and Bosson, *La céramique, les inscriptions, les décors*, pl. 23.138); (3) Baouit (Dixneuf, "Les amphores égyptiennes," pl. 181.373); (4) Saqqara (Ghaly, "Pottery Workshops of Saint-Jeremia (Saqqara)," fig. 16a–b)

North Africa, the imitations are of late stage amphorae: they copy only LR 1B models, associated with variants generally dating to the first half of the seventh century (fig. 2.14).

The LR 1 amphorae copied in the Black Sea region are made of a whitish clay characteristic of Sinopean ceramics dating to the sixth and seventh centuries.[56] The Aegean Sea (particularly the island of Kos) might also have been an area in which imitations were manufactured.[57]

P. Ballet and D. Dixneuf, "Ateliers d'amphores de la Chôra égyptienne aux époques romaine et byzantine," in Eiring and Lund, eds., *Transport Amphorae and Trade in the Eastern Mediterranean*, 70–71; P. Ballet, M. Rassart-Debergh, and N. Bosson, *Kellia 2: L'ermitage copte QR 195*, vol. 2, *La céramique, les inscriptions, les décors* (Cairo, 2003), 152–53, pl. 23; D. Dixneuf, "Les amphores égyptiennes du Sinaï à la Moyenne Égypte: Typologie, chronologie, contenu et diffusion: Contribution à l'histoire économique de la période romaine aux premiers temps de l'occupation arabe" (Ph.D. diss., University of Poitiers, 2007).

56 A complete amphora is preserved in the stores of the Sinop Museum. I am grateful to Dominique Kassab-Tezgör for allowing me to consult material from the excavations at the workshops of Demerci.

57 I warmly thank Natalia Poulou-Papadimitriou for providing me with the results of this recent research (presented in Parma in March 2008). N. Poulou-Papadimitriou and S. Didioumi, "Nouvelles données sur la production de l'atelier céramique protobyzantin à Kardamaina (Cos-Grèce)," in *LRCW 3*, forthcoming.

The imitation of LR 1 seems to have been particularly common from the second half of the sixth century onward, at the moment when Cilician manufacture had begun to decline. This synchrony raises the possibility that the emergence of practices associated with counterfeiting reflected a relaxation of controls. At the same time, "officially sanctioned" manufacture and imitations are complex questions, and such speculation is surely premature given the sparse data available at present. Nonetheless, this aspect of manufacture is important for defining the true quantities of commodities exchanged. In the years to come, our current understanding of the manufacture of amphorae in the proto-Byzantine East may well develop in new directions as a result of new discoveries and of new interpretations. Assessing the scope of imitations of amphora types remains a rich line of inquiry. For example, we may well come to discern copies of subtypes of LR 1 in the late calcareous amphorae of Sinope, or imitations of LR 7 in the amphorae of Aqaba.

This brief survey of the manufacture and circulation of amphorae from the eastern Mediterranean suffers from being too schematic. Clearly a more detailed study, by region and by site, would show a more nuanced reality. The main point here has been to show, through a few examples, the areas of inquiry opened by the study of amphorae in the context of a broader understanding of commercial mechanisms. There is no doubt, as surveys and excavations have shown, that the fourth century witnessed a broad recovery in the Mediterranean economy, perhaps to a level comparable to that attained in the first and second centuries of the Common Era. The new element is the emergence of new regions that participated in trade. The founding of Constantinople and the improvement in political, demographic, social, and economic conditions unquestionably favored the eastern Mediterranean. The early Byzantine Empire did not revolve exclusively around Constantinople but was open to other regions and to the Mediterranean as a whole. And by virtue of this openness, it demonstrated a more dynamic character than did the West. What is different from the preceding period is the development of exchanges oriented from East to West.

But the East was not a unitary entity, even if, as we have seen, the production of wine involved the eastern lands in their entirety. Several geographic areas of exchange seem to have divided up the eastern market: the Aegean and the Black Sea, the Near East, and Egypt. And strong differences among these areas emerged between the fourth and the seventh century, reflecting the demands of large centers of consumption, recurring shortages, and the popularity of certain manufactured products that were valued because they were deemed to be of high quality. The importance of eastern trade, demonstrated in large part by the movement of ceramics, lends urgency to the question of what drove the economy. Most frequently cited is the civil and military *annona,* the public service of the state entrusted with distributing basic commodities such as wheat to Constantinople and to the army. The often-accepted explanation is that this institution defined the direction of exchanges and stimulated the economies of neighboring regions. One must nonetheless emphasize, without denying its importance in the provisioning of the capital, that the state guaranteed only a portion of the annona, with the rest depending on private commerce. The same would have held true for the provisioning of other large cities. The leading role of the Church in the provisioning of cities and the armies has often been stressed, but even the Church was only one participant among many in commercial exchanges, and its economic importance varied by region. The role played by the private sector, although difficult to capture, seems to have been important and suggests a fundamentally commercial economy.

Though amphorae may offer a limited contribution to economic history, they nonetheless enable us to follow the stages of development or regression. This commercial economy was able to escape the contraction of the empire's territory and endure political contingencies. But it was not able to survive the extended disruption of production and of the channels of communication that accelerated in the eighth century.[58] The apparent disappearance after the middle of that century of all imported eastern amphorae, with the exception of a few scattered areas (the Aegean basin, the shores of the Sea of Marmara, and the shores of the Black Sea), marks the true end of the economic system inherited from the Roman Empire.

---

58 See, in the present volume, J. F. Haldon, "Commerce and Exchange in the Seventh and Eighth Centuries: Regional Trade and the Movement of Goods," 99–122; P. Armstrong, "Trade in the East Mediterranean in the Eighth Century," in Mango, ed., *Byzantine Trade, 4th–12th Centuries,* 157–78.

• THREE •

Movements and Markets in the First Millennium

Information, Containers, and Shipwrecks

MICHAEL McCORMICK

In memory of Angeliki Laiou, friend and colleague

MARKETS CONCENTRATE WARES, BUYERS, and sellers, a concentration that entails both mental disposition and physical movement. Evidence for mind-sets comes from the finite set of texts that have survived from Byzantium, but it is indirect and so far has attracted little attention. Direct evidence of movement has now reached a critical mass, particularly through study of its physical markers: the containers that packaged wares en route to markets and the ships that helped move them. Archaeologists' wonderful work invites us to think hard about what they have found—or not found—and how we can derive more economic insights from it. Better understanding of how ancient containers were used, new information on the competition of amphorae and barrels, and organizing our knowledge of ancient shipwrecks to foster spatial and temporal analysis suggest new questions and insights. They also turn up limitations to their testimony.

This chapter assesses these different types of evidence from about AD 300 to 1000, and ranges over the Roman and post-Roman world. It starts with ideas and moves to things, beginning with a basic conceptual matter before presenting indirect evidence for the mental disposition toward markets. It then considers ways to deepen the testimony of amphorae for economic history and the implications of late antique barrels for markets and transport systems. Finally, it presents a spatial database of the biggest and most expensive instrument of ancient exchange, ships. All this makes possible some first observations about what shipwrecks do, and do not, tell us about the movements that got goods to markets. Texts, images and material remains, mind-sets, and objects sometimes converge and sometimes conflict. In their discrepancies and convergence lie wisdom and sometimes historical truth. But first, a prior question.

What Is a Market?

"Market" means many things. In literature, ambiguity is rich. In history, it breeds confusion. Are we talking about a place, an institution, an event, a state of mind or type of behavior, or a type of economy, as in "market economy"? All of these we can fruitfully investigate.[1] But we need to be clear in each

1 The research for this study was conducted under the generous conditions of a Distinguished Achievement Award from the Andrew W. Mellon Foundation. Parts of an ancestor of this essay were presented at the symposium "Tradition and Transition" honoring George F. Bass and Frederick van Doorninck at Texas A&M University, and at the Penn Economic History Forum at the University of Pennsylvania. It benefited much from discussions there as well as from conversations at Dumbarton Oaks. Special thanks are due to an anonymous referee who subsequently revealed himself to be Professor van Doorninck. This essay is much the better for his generous and exceedingly well-informed observations, as I have gratefully acknowledged in various places below. Alexander More refined for publication the maps that I designed to illustrate this article, and has my thanks. I was especially gratified that the version of this essay given at Dumbarton Oaks brought pleasure to my friend and close colleague Angeliki Laiou. Neither of us dreamed that this would be the last time that we would work together on the history of the themes so dear to both of us.
See for instance the stimulating debate launched by P. Temin, "A Market Economy in the Early Roman Empire," *JRS* 91 (2001): 169–81, and the pithy comments of A. E. Laiou, "Market," *ODB*

case whether we are thinking of markets as physical places or as economic concepts and, if the latter, *which* economic concept. Are we thinking of markets as "collection[s] of homogeneous transactions" or of "selling opportunities," as "trading zone[s] free [or not] of artificial restrictions on transactions,"[2] or as legal institutions, such as the heavily policed markets in meat, silk, and so on that characterized Constantinople around 900, at least in the eyes of the imperial legislator responsible for the *Book of the Prefect*?[3]

What were markets like in Byzantium? This volume supplies important elements toward an answer for urban or rural, permanent, periodic or occasional markets. Its chapters suggest that we seek to classify Byzantine (and other medieval) markets by size (in terms of volume or value), as wholesale or retail, by spectrum of goods on offer, by place (seaside vs. inland), by position in a system of exchange, by the geographic scale of transactions, or by the degree of regulation or freedom that affected them. Byzantine black markets may have been more important than research to date would indicate. At least one might suspect that. For this society so aspired to regulate transactions that an emperor made a show of riding through markets to check on prices, if the story about the emperor Theophilos (829–42) reflects more than short-term shock at the steep price rise recorded around his time.[4]

Discerning structural patterns should not blind us to change. A complete history of Byzantine markets would clarify how their types and features changed over time, focusing on the markets themselves, their relative importance, their geographic density, and their integration (or lack thereof).[5] At the end of antiquity, the contraction of the capital's population surely connected somehow with the disruption in 618 of the state-subsidized grain shipments of the *annona*—a disruption itself caused mainly by the empire's military loss of Egypt and its merchant fleet.[6] So sweeping a development must have affected the universe of economic transactions at Constantinople, and their role in the Mediterranean economy. We have barely begun to wonder how. For instance, the long period from 400 to 1000 appears to have witnessed at least two major price shifts. What are we to make of the apparent plunge in the price of grain at some point in the seventh century? The price then seems to have jumped in the first half of the ninth, in the caliphate and in Byzantium.[7] How might such secular price change have correlated to the history of markets? Between the seventh and the twelfth century, attestation increases both of Constantinople's permanent market and of different kinds of fairs in the provinces. Even allowing for the growth in surviving evidence, one suspects that real expansion was occurring.[8] Local fairs for instance seem to have proliferated in the late tenth century. The provincial ones grew attractive enough to provoke conflict between merchants and landed aristocrats who wanted to move the markets to their estates.[9]

Insofar as markets were places with built features, archaeology is crucial.[10] Recent discoveries in north-

---

2:1301; eadem, "Exchange and Trade, Seventh–Twelfth Centuries," in *EHB* 2:697–770, esp. 709–10, 730–32, 754–56; and K.-P. Matschke, "Commerce, Trade, Markets, and Money: Thirteenth–Fifteenth Centuries," ibid., 2:771–806, esp. 776–82.

2 G. Bannock, E. Davis, and R. E. Baxter, *The Penguin Dictionary of Economics*, 7th ed. (London, 2003), 242–43.

3 Leo VI, *Book of the Prefect*, ed. J. Koder, *Das Eparchenbuch Leons des Weisen*, CFHB 33 (Vienna, 1991).

4 According to Theophanes Continuatus 3.3, ed. I. Bekker (Bonn, 1838), 87.16–23, according to which the emperor checked prices for food, drink, and clothing in particular. On the increase in grain prices, see note 7 below.

5 Along these lines, L. de Ligt, *Fairs and Markets in the Roman Empire: Economic and Social Aspects of Periodic Trade in a Preindustrial Society*, Dutch Monographs on Ancient History and Archaeology 11 (Amsterdam, 1993), offers a valuable overview of market types and features in the earlier period. For the rich Talmudic evidence on markets in Roman and Byzantine Palestine, see B. T. Rozenfeld and J. Menirav, *Markets and Marketing in Roman Palestine*, Supplements to the Journal for the Study of Judaism 99 (Leiden, 2005).

6 M. McCormick, "Bateaux de vie, bateaux de mort: Maladie, commerce, transports annonaires et le passage économique du Bas-Empire au moyen âge," in *Morfologie sociali e culturali in Europa fra tarda antichità e alto medioevo*, 2 vols., Settimane di studi del Centro italiano di studi sull'alto medioevo 45 (Spoleto, 1998), 1:35–122, at 115; for a recent discussion of the crisis in the grain market at Constantinople and evidence for measures that the government may have taken to address it, see V. Prigent, "Le rôle des provinces d'Occident dans l'approvisionnement de Constantinople (618–717): Témoignages numismatique et sigillographique," *Mélanges de l'École française de Rome: Moyen âge* 118 (2006): 269–99.

7 E. Ashtor, *Histoire des prix et des salaires dans l'Orient médiéval*, Monnaie, prix, conjoncture 8 (Paris, 1969), 453–59; C. Morrisson and J.-C. Cheynet, "Prices and Wages in the Byzantine World," in *EHB* 2:815–78, esp. 830.

8 Laiou, "Exchange and Trade," e.g., 754.

9 Ibid., 731.

10 Two important excavations: J. S. Crawford, *The Byzantine Shops at Sardis*, Archaeological Exploration of Sardis 9 (Cambridge, Mass., 1990), and Y. Tsafrir and G. Foerster, "Urbanism at Scythopolis–Bet Shean in the Fourth to Seventh Centuries,"

western Europe suggest that archaeologists would also do well to watch for the subtle signals of impermanent, occasional, or periodic markets in the Mediterranean.[11] Written evidence proves that ephemeral markets were part of the Mediterranean scene. In 447, a western emperor complained that merchants were abandoning the cities' sanctioned markets and conducting "stealthy business" (*furtiva negotiatio*) in settlements and ports, in informal marketplaces, to the detriment of the imperial treasury.[12] A fifth- or sixth-century African preacher probably reached into his flock's daily experience when he evoked just such an informal market, of all things, in a metaphor expressing the mystery of Christ's resurrection: "O how lovely the beach looks when it's filled with merchandise and it bustles with businessmen! Bundles of different clothing are pulled from the ships, countless people delight at the sailors' cheerful singing, and the rich man dances in the sand!"[13] Beachside markets and the imperial *novella* underscore the diversity of sites that witnessed what we might call "market events." An element of ship's gear, the steelyard scale, also points in the same direction.[14]

Constantinople itself looms as the "supermarket." That is natural but limiting. We tend to think chiefly of the receiving end of Mediterranean transport networks when we think of markets. Yet there must have been "a collection of homogeneous transactions" at those networks' points of departure as well. The farmers whose oil, grain, wine, or animals were carried or driven toward the consumer markets will have been paid for their wares long before the wine was unloaded in Constantinople or Anatolia's pigs reached Pylai (modern Yalova) to be ferried across the Sea of Marmara to the capital.[15] We do not know yet what these markets were like—whether "market" here is shorthand for the transactions of itinerant merchants buying up goods in the country and transporting them down to the sea, or for producers themselves delivering them to the seaside markets, or for something else.

A chance reference in a late antique life of a bishop of the great wine-exporting area of Gaza calls attention to port markets. The implication is that Egyptian merchants congregated on the coast—not further inland—to purchase the region's prized wine. The further implication would be that the transactions that brought the wine from inland to the coast lay in other hands.[16] The coastal traders

---

DOP 51 (1997): 85–146, at 114, 122–23, and, for the Umayyad market, 138–40; see also on the latter and on other contemporary market buildings A. Walmsley, *Early Islamic Syria: An Archaeological Assessment* (London, 2007), 87–97; idem, "Regional Exchange and the Role of the Shop in Byzantine and Early Islamic Syria-Palestine: An Archaeological View"; and L. Lavan, "From *polis* to *emporion*? Retail and Regulation in the Late Antique City" (both in this volume).

11 For instance, dense patterns of coin finds in a particular field, especially cut coins, have been taken to mark impermanent markets: J. Newman, "A Possible Medieval Fair Site at the Albany, Ipswich," *British Numismatic Journal* 64 (1994): 129. For further archaeological traces of a possible Iron Age beachside market in the North Sea, see M. Segschneider, "Trade and Centrality between the Rhine and the Limfjord around 500 AD: The Beachmarket on the Northfrisian Island Amrum and Its Context," in *Central Places in the Migration and Merovingian Periods: Papers from the 52nd Sachsensymposium Lund, August 2001*, Acta Archaeologica Lundensia, series in 8°, 39 (Lund, 2002), 247–56, as well as the studies published in T. Pestell and K. Ulmschneider, eds., *Markets in Early Medieval Europe: Trading and "Productive" Sites, 650–850* (Macclesfield, 2003). The early medieval emporiums of Ribe in Denmark and Kaupang in Norway may have begun as seasonally occupied seaside sites. For instance, at Kaupang, micromorphology showed an ultra-fine stratification of sand layers that seem to have been wind transported, and that separated the first seven charcoal-rich deposits identified as short occupation layers: K. B. Milek and C. A. I. French, "Soils and Sediments in the Settlement and Harbour at Kaupang," in *Kaupang in Skiringssal*, ed. D. Skre ([Oslo], 2007), 321–60, at 328–31.

12 Valentinian III, *Novella* 24 (25 April 447), *CTh* 2, 117–18.

13 Pseudo-Fulgentius of Ruspe, *Sermo 38*, PL 65:901–2; on that text, see E. Dekkers, *Clavis patrum latinorum*, 3rd ed., CCSL (Steenbrugge, 1995), no. 844; cf. M. McCormick, *Origins of the European Economy: Communications and Commerce, A.D. 300–900* (Cambridge, 2001), 84.

14 See below, 87–89, on weighing scales aboard shipwrecks.

15 On pigs at Pylai: Leo of Synada, *Ep.* 54; in *The Correspondence of Leo, Metropolitan of Synada and Syncellus*, ed., trans., and comm. M. P. Vinson, CFHB 23 (Washington, D.C., 1985), 86.26–36; on Pylai as the terminus of a major westward route from Anatolia, C. Foss, *ODB* 3:1760.

16 Mark the Deacon, *Life of Porphyrius of Gaza* (BHG 1570), 58, ed. H. Grégoire and M. A. Kugener, *Marc le diacre: Vie de Porphyre évêque de Gaza* (Paris, 1930), 47.6–7. Although the date and reliability of the text for the saint's biography remain controverted, it is generally thought to have been reworked in the sixth century and, in this detail, surely reflects conditions of that period at the latest: see K. H. Uthemann, "Porphyrius, Bischof von Gaza," *Biographisch-Bibliographisches Kirchenlexikon* (online), www.bautz.de/bbkl/p/porphyrius_b_v_g.shtml, accessed July 2010. The biographer naturally distinguishes clearly between Egyptians and Gazans. In this era, Gaza was in Palestine but on the border of Egypt, as the author himself notes: *Life of Porphyrius* 4, 4.1–2. For one of those other hands, see note 103, below. *Mutatis mutandis*, the ostraca of AD 373 offer a glimpse of how another export ware, African oil, was concentrated at a central warehouse in the port of Carthage before shipment, presumably to Rome, as part of the fiscal supply of the annona: J. T. Peña, "The Mobilization of State

probably did not limit wine exports to their home ports, although well-to-do Egyptians certainly savored Gaza's flowery and pricey white wine.[17] Alexandria's skippers dominated the shipping routes leading to Constantinople, and as antiquity ended they came to be ascendant in all Mediterranean shipping.[18] This dominance makes it likely that the Egyptian merchants who sailed to Gaza to buy wine also exported it far and wide. Although the growth of the Gazan wine industry has been ascribed to increasing local population, the scale of viticulture and of amphora exports across the entire Mediterranean proves that far more than local demand fired the engines of Gazan production.[19] In particular, the Egyptians likely carried this wine to the capital even if the fourth-century archaeological attestation for that trade is still lacking there.[20] Constantinople's stupendous growth parallels that of the Gazan wine industry, and its appetite for wine has left clear tracks in the administrative record—for instance, in the fee schedule of cargo inspectors at Abydos, a key customs station on the way to the capital.[21] But before we look at the containers that traveled and today mark these supply networks and their markets, what new insights can we coax from the well-mined written record?

Modes of Economic Behavior and Markets

Research has identified considerable explicit written evidence on markets.[22] Not much more remains to be found for Byzantine markets before the year 1000. Expanding the net to capture indirect evidence, however, draws in more precious witnesses who, like the

---

Olive Oil in Roman Africa: The Evidence of Late Fourth Century Ostraca from Carthage," in *Carthage Papers*, ed. J. T. Peña, A. I. Wilson, C. Wells, et al., Journal of Roman Archaeology supp. ser. 28 (Portsmouth, R.I., 1998), 116–238.

17 As both surviving amphorae and an eyewitness make clear. For Gaza wine amphorae in Egypt (i.e., "Late Roman Amphora 4"), see D. Pieri, *Le commerce du vin oriental à l'époque byzantine, V^e–VIIe siècles: Le témoignage des amphores en Gaule,* Bibliothèque archéologique et historique 174 (Beirut, 2005), 198–99; in the early seventh century, Patriarch John the Almsgiver decided to save money by shifting from Palestinian to local Egyptian wine, and the fine wine's taste is described: *Life of John the Almsgiver* (BHG 887v), 10, ed. H. Delehaye, "Une vie inédite de saint Jean Aumônier," *AB* 45 (1927): 5–73, here 24.6–14, a text that epitomized no later than the tenth century the precious lost biography by John's associates John Moschus and Sophronius of Jerusalem. For the color, see Corippus, *In laudem Iustini Augusti minoris* 3.98–99, ed. S. Antès, *Corippe (Flavius Cresconius Corippus) Éloge de l'empereur Justin II* (Paris, 1981), 56.

18 See, for instance, the eyewitness report of how Alexandrian shippers of the Egyptian fiscal grain were convoked in the palace by the emperor Justin II (565–578) to debate monophysitism: John of Ephesos, *Historia ecclesiastica,* fragment H, trans. W. J. Van Douwen and J. P. N. Land, "Joannis episcopi Ephesi Syri monophysitae Commentarii de beatis orientalibus et Historiae ecclesiasticae fragmenta," *Verhandelingen der koninklijke Akademie van wetenschappen,* Afdeeling Letterkunde 18 (Amsterdam, 1889), 249.1–27 and the discussion in McCormick, "Bateaux de vie, bateaux de mort," 93–107.

19 P. Mayerson, "The Wine and Vineyards of Gaza in the Byzantine Period," *BASOR* 257 (1985): 75–80, at 75, seems to attribute the expanding Gazan wine industry to local growth, although he is aware of foreign merchants' presence. For Gaza amphorae documented across the entire Mediterranean, see Pieri, *Le commerce du vin oriental,* 197–200.

20 P. Reynolds, "Levantine Amphorae from Cilicia to Gaza: A Typology and Analysis of the Regional Production Trends from the 1st to 7th Centuries," in *LRCW 1: Late Roman Coarse Wares, Cooking Wares and Amphorae in the Mediterranean: Archaeology and Archaeometry,* ed. J. M. Gurt Esparraguera, J. Buxeda i Garrigós, and M. A. Cau Ontiveros, BAR International Series 1340 (Oxford, 2005), 563–611, at 576.

21 It is surely not a coincidence that in this fifth-century inscription, the fees for "all wine freighters (οἰνηγοί) which are carrying wine to the Imperial City" come at the top of the list and are the highest, at "six folles and two pints (*xestai*) [of wine]": J. Durliat and A. Guillou, "Le tarif d'Abydos (vers 492)," *Bulletin de correspondance hellénique* 108 (1984): 581–98, at 583.22–23; cf. G. Dagron and D. Feissel, "Inscriptions inédites du musée d'Antioche," *TM* 9 (1985): 433–55, at 452–55. For the rampant growth of Constantinople, see G. Dagron, *Naissance d'une capitale: Constantinople et ses institutions de 330 à 451,* Bibliothèque byzantine, Études 7 (Paris, 1974), 518–41. Recent archaeology has only strengthened the picture drawn by Dagron: for example, the work of James Crow and his team in surveying the most extraordinary water supply system of the ancient world, which totaled some 400 km in water channels and which kept pace with the demographic growth of the city: see "The Water Supply of Constantinople" at "The Archaeology of Constantinople and Its Hinterland," http://longwalls.ncl.ac.uk/WaterSupply.htm, accessed July 2010.

22 From a rich and growing bibliography see: de Ligt, *Fairs and Markets in the Roman Empire;* É. Patlagean, "Byzance et les marchés du grand commerce vers 830–vers 1030: Entre Pirenne et Polanyi," in *Mercati e mercanti nell'alto medioevo: L'area Euroasiatica e l'area Mediterranea,* Settimane di studi del Centro italiano di studi sull'alto medioevo 40 (Spoleto, 1993), 587–629; N. Oikonomides, "Le marchand byzantin des provinces (IXe–XIe s.)," ibid., 633–60; idem, "The Economic Region of Constantinople: From Directed Economy to Free Economy and the Role of the Italians," in *Europa medievale e mondo bizantino: Contatti effettivi e possibilità di studi comparati,* ed. G. Arnaldi and G. Cavallo, Nuovi studi storici 40 (Rome, 1997), 221–38; A. A. Settia, "*Per foros Italie:* Le aree extraurbane fra Alpi e Appennini," in *Mercati e mercanti nell'alto medioevo,* 187–233; O. Bruand, *Voyageurs et marchandises aux temps carolingiens: Les réseaux de communication entre Loire et Meuse aux VIIIe et IXe siècles* (Brussels, 2002); McCormick, *Origins of the European Economy,* 618–69, as well as the works cited in note 1, above.

African preacher, did not mean to treat the economy as their main subject.[23] Our research strategy needs to reach beyond explicit attestations of markets to encompass implicit allusions to market-conditioned economic behavior, including contemporary interest in information typical of markets, such as price levels. That strategy is important even for the late Roman period, when tax-powered exchange of fiscal grain and goods in kind coexisted with market exchange.

Pretechnological societies had access to much less economic information than we do. Moreover, the cultural blinders through which ancient literary norms filtered reality mean that the relatively well-preserved literary sources shed only intermittent light on markets and economic information relevant to them. Some direct insight does come thanks to the special survival conditions of the Egyptian papyri, which preserve documents actually written by merchants.[24] After antiquity, testimony from the trader's mouth dwindles until we reach the trove of Jewish merchants' letters from the Old Cairo Genizah. Preserved arbitrarily for reasons unrelated to commerce, those letters begin in the eleventh century to illuminate the great "Mediterranean Community" of traders.[25] A wealth of market- and price-related news demonstrates the sensitivity of their writers and readers to the value of economic information and, therefore, underscores the *importance* of the market.

Both the late ancient and later medieval merchants' letters illustrate what Peter Temin has called "modes of economic behavior," which he has categorized into three main types. In the "instrumental" mode of behavior, individuals act to maximize the results of their economic activity, characteristically by means of market exchanges. In the "customary" or traditional mode, people try to do what they have always done, reciprocity characterizes their economic interaction, and change occurs without their realizing it. Finally, the "command mode" is essentially hierarchical. Here actions result from orders given or received, in a dynamic that constitutes the typical form of interaction; change stems from the decisions of identifiable individuals. In a pure form, of course, none of these beasts exists in nature. Any economy consists of varying doses of different behaviors that help shape its overall character and patterns of exchange. Of particular interest here is that recurrent concern with economic information and ascertaining (not fixing) prices points to a behavioral mode which aims to maximize profit and signals that markets will dominate such concerned individuals' economic interaction.

For instance, around 350 an Egyptian businessman wrote from his store and sent cash to a colleague, whom he asked to purchase a series of goods for him, since the local prices, which he listed, were high.[26] In the same Nile Valley, seven centuries later, we are on similar ground. A note from eleventh-century Alexandria signals the impending arrival in Cairo of *Rūm*—either Italian or Byzantine—merchants, hunting for the spices that have vanished from the port city's markets, while other letters report prices spiking under the pressure of northern merchant demand or announce to Indian Ocean correspondents at Aden that sales were slowing in the Mediterranean markets: all appear to be typical cases of the eleventh- and twelfth-century flow of commercial information.[27] When the Roman or Cairo letters report prices, changing supply, and foreign merchants buying up specific goods, they clearly imply an instrumental mode of behavior, and underscore the crucial role of markets in their economies.

Was such economic information valued in the intervening centuries? Faced with a near total absence of merchant testimony, we cannot attach

---

23 A. P. Kazhdan and G. Constable, *People and Power in Byzantium: An Introduction to Modern Byzantine Studies* (Washington, D.C., 1982), 164–78.

24 See note 26, below. On the subtle patterns of preservation of papyrus records, see R. Bagnall, "Models and Evidence in the Study of Religion in Late Roman Egypt," in *From Temple to Church: Destruction and Renewal of Local Cultic Topography in Late Antiquity,* ed. J. Hahn, S. Emmel, and U. Gotter (Leiden, 2008), 23–41, at 34.

25 Beyond S. D. Goitein, *A Mediterranean Society: The Jewish Communities of the Arab World as Portrayed in the Documents of the Cairo Geniza,* 6 vols. (Berkeley, 1967–93), on the Genizah letters' evidence on Byzantine trade and markets connecting to the Muslim world see D. Jacoby, "What Do We Learn about Byzantine Asia Minor from the Documents of the Cairo Genizah?" in *Η βυζαντινή Μικρά Ασία: 6.–12. αι.,* ed. S. Lampakēs (Athens, 1998), 83–95; idem, "Byzantine Trade with Egypt from the Mid-tenth Century to the Fourth Crusade," *Thesaurismata* 30 (2000): 25–77; and K. S. Durak, "Commerce and Networks of Exchange between the Byzantine Empire and the Islamic Near East from the Early Ninth Century to the Arrival of the Crusaders" (Ph.D. diss., Harvard University, 2008).

26 *P. Oxy.* 34:2729, as published and discussed in J.-M. Carrié, "Papyrologica numismatica (1)," *Aegyptus* 64 (1984): 203–27.

27 For these examples, see Goitein, *A Mediterranean Society,* 1:44–45.

much significance to such a silence. But are there signals, direct or indirect, that economic information was valued, and that news about markets did flow but has passed nearly undocumented? Let us start with late Rome as our point of departure. Its sophisticated trading economy supplied the mental categories and conceptual apparatus inherited by Byzantium and the early medieval West. They thus help interpret the later evidence.[28]

Occasionally writings other than letters document the demand for economic information. Around 350, the Greek treatise known from its Latin translation as *Expositio totius mundi* offers what have generally been valuable insights into trade in various regions of the empire, whoever the author might have been, and whatever his objectives.[29] As we have him, it is true that the author rarely discusses price levels directly when describing the wares, women, and worship of different Mediterranean cities. Often the *Expositio* simply mentions that a place abounds in everything ("abundans omnibus," etc.).[30] Frequently it specifies what a town or region exports, and sometimes it notes wares that are particularly abundant. For example, the author touts the textiles of Skythopolis, Laodikeia, Byblos, Tyre, and Beirut; Alexandria's spices; the cheese, lumber, and iron of Dalmatia; and Sicily's wool, wheat, and draft animals.[31] Their very frequency surely indicates that such statements were reckoned economically useful information for the readers. They also reveal price awareness.

Though the surviving text directly addresses prices only once, that passage confirms that in the author's mind, the abundance he so frequently mentions correlates with low prices. Because an emperor was there, Gaul enjoys an abundance of everything. But (*sed*), he adds, everything comes at a high price. The contradiction between abundant supply and high prices implied by the adversative "but" signals unambiguously the author's understanding that abundant supply normally entailed lower prices.[32] We may speculate that prices in Gaul rose to meet the demand fueled by the hefty salaries of the numerous army and palatine officials who attended the emperor, salaries whose traces can still be seen in the piles of surviving coins issued by Gaul's capital.[33] Detritus of the long-distance supply that filled that demand subsists in Trier's Roman garbage, all the way down to the oysters dredged in the Mediterranean and carted north to the delicate palates stationed in the German frontier's hinterland. For the northern capital's market, Ausonius's poem on the comparative delights of exotic oysters was no literary mirage.[34]

---

28 The ideological assumptions of the ruling class are a distinct and important aspect of this question, that is, essentially one of economic mentality. See the complementary analysis of A. E. Laiou, "Economic Thought and Ideology," in *EHB* 3:1123–44.

29 To observe that this imperfectly transmitted work reflects the rhetorical genre of the praise of cities does not deny the author's attempts to describe, in addition to the beauty of the women and the festivals of different ports, what we would call patterns of supply and demand in the late Roman economy. That a commercial milieu might have pretensions to emulate in its own way one of the classic types of contemporary literary practice offers rather a wonderful testimony to the penetration of Hellenistic cultural values across a broad spectrum of the late Roman population. F. Jacques, "Les moulins d'Orcistus: Rhétorique et géographie au IVᵉ s.," in *Institutions, société et vie politique dans l'Empire romain au IVᵉ siècle ap. J.-C.*, ed. M. Christol, Collection de l'École française de Rome 159 (Rome, 1992), 431–46, among others, has suggested that the *Expositio* reflects ancient rhetorical categories of urban praise which lessen but do not entirely invalidate the authority of its economic information. See however the full discussion of K. Ruffing, "Ökonomie als Kategorie in der antiken deskriptiven Geographie: Berichtsweise und Eigenart der expositio totius mundi et gentium," *Münstersche Beiträge zur antiken Handelsgeschichte* 23.1 (2004): 88–130, with further references, as well as the example of Cilician wine exports in note 70, below.

30 E.g., *Expositio totius mundi et gentium* 26, ed. and trans. J. Rougé, SC 124 (Paris, 1966), 160.2, about Caesarea (Maritima); 29, 162.2–3, Askalon and Gaza; 34, 170.2, Alexandria; 51, 186.2, Macedonia, etc. It might be worthwhile to investigate whether any conclusions can be drawn from the absence of this assertion.

31 *Expositio totius mundi* 31, 164.6; 35, 170.5–6: "Omnes autem species aut aromatibus aut aliquibus negotiis barbaricis in ea abundant"; 53, 190.7–9: "Caseum itaque dalmatenum et tigna tectis utilia, similiter et ferrum, tres species cum sint utilia abundans emittit"; 65, 208.4–5, respectively.

32 *Expositio totius mundi* 58, 196.3–4: "Sed propter maioris [i.e., the emperor's] praesentiam, omnia in multitudine abundat, sed plurimi pretii."

33 For the predominance of Trier's mint, see C. H. V. Sutherland, *The Roman Imperial Coinage*, vol. 6, *From Diocletian's Reform (A.D. 294) to the Death of Maximinus (A.D. 313)* (London, 1973), 141–62; J. P. C. Kent, *The Roman Imperial Coinage*, vol. 8, *The Family of Constantine I: A.D. 337–364* (London, 1981), 125–38, etc. Cf. C.-F. Zschucke, *Die römische Münzstätte Trier: Von der Münzreform der Bronzeprägung unter Constans und Constantius II 346/348 n. Chr. bis zu ihrer Schliessung im 5. Jahrhundert*, 3rd ed., Kleine numismatische Reihe der Trierer Münzfreunde 5 ([Trier], 1997), 8–14.

34 For the oysters discovered in a dark earth layer that is dated by coins after 327, see H. G. Attendorn, H. Merten, F. Strauch, et al., "Römische Austernfunde aus den Grabungen in der Pauluskapelle des Domkreuzganges in Trier," *Trierer Zeitschrift* 59 (1996): 89–118; Ausonius, *Opera* 27.3, ed. R. P. H. Green, *The Works of Ausonius* (Oxford, 1991), 194–95.

So the *Expositio* shows us real interest in supply or, as the author and his contemporaries were more inclined to phrase it, in "abundance," as well as in price movements. We need therefore to watch for references to the "abundance" of wares, just as we should be alert to their "dearth," which is how ancient and medieval people tended to think of what we generally call "demand." Criticism that terms such as "supply" and "demand" are anachronistic is a red herring. Just because a term or concept did not exist in antiquity in no way precludes our exploring whether an analogous reality may have existed then. Otherwise, we would have no truck with possible viral or bacteriological infections, as have been proposed for the Antonine and Justinianic pandemics; it would be illegitimate to consider even the questions of ancient demography and medieval rural technology or, indeed, propaganda or power symbolism, none of which corresponds clearly to ancient concepts.

The *Expositio*'s emphasis on "abundance" and "dearth" in different towns suggests that contemporaries expected late antique merchants to be alert to shifting circumstances. A Syrian preacher confirms that around 400, people thought merchants were on the lookout for economic news, and adjusted their behavior accordingly. He drove home a purely spiritual message by comparing the good Christian to a good merchant. The simile implies a sharp eye for economic information: "Like the merchant who conducts his trade and knows how to make a profit in his business not just by one route or in one manner, but who watches carefully all about him, with quick wit (ἐντρεχῶς) and alertly: if he should fail to make a profit, he turns to another deal—for his whole purpose is to make money and grow his business[.]"[35] This is clearly instrumental behavior in Temin's sense, and implies that the audience understood economic behavior in terms of profit, risk (i.e., failing to make a profit), and markets.

That the preacher's listeners spontaneously grasped the value attached to economic information makes sense if markets played an important role in the sophisticated late Roman trading world. A miracle story shows that, from their suburban villas, even families connected to the civil service kept an eye on market prices. It also fills in a few details about wine, a key market ware, and the vintner's perspective on its production and sale. Around 420, Donatus produced a commercial crop of high-quality wine in his villa near Uzalis (modern Tunisia), and stored it in his cellar's (*apotheca*) two hundred containers (*vasa*). He awaited the moment when the price would peak before offering it for sale.[36] When that time came, Donatus went to each container to check the quality of the wine, accompanied by one of his men who was an expert wine taster. To their horror, the wine had turned very dark (*teterrimus color,* a hint that the wine of Uzalis was usually white?) and tasted awful. Each container was the same: the wine was too bad even for vinegar. What was he to do, facing loss worse than if the grapes had been destroyed on the vine (presumably because of the additional costs incurred in harvesting, pressing, and storing them)? Sell it for a song? Or just pour it out? Fortunately, Donatus's investment was saved by the relics of St. Stephen, newly arrived in Africa from Jerusalem. Exposing the wine to the relics restored its color and taste overnight, and the happy Donatus was able to sell an excellent product at a good price.[37] The

---

35 Pseudo-Macarius/Symeon, *Sermo* 29.2.1, in *Sermones 64,* ed. H. Berthold, *Makarios/Symeon Reden und Briefe,* GCS (Berlin, 1973), 262.25–263.6: Ὥσπερ γὰρ ὁ ἔμπορος τὴν ἐμπορίαν αὐτοῦ πραγματευόμενος οὐ διὰ μιᾶς ὁδοῦ οὐδὲ διὰ μιᾶς προφάσεως οἶδε πορίζειν τὸ κέρδος τῆς ἐμπορίας αὐτοῦ, ἀλλ᾽ ἐντρεχῶς καὶ νηφόντως πανταχόθεν περισκοπεῖ, ἐὰν τύχῃ αὐτὸν ἐντεῦθεν ἀποτυγχάνειν τοῦ κέρδους, ἑτέρῳ πράγματι ἐπιβάλλεται—ὅλος γὰρ ὁ σκοπὸς αὐτῷ ἐστι τοῦ κερδῆσαι καὶ πολυπλασιάσαι τὴν ἐμπορίαν αὐτοῦ—, οὕτω καὶ ἡμεῖς τὴν εὐχὴν τῆς προσδοκίας ἡμῶν ... καταρτίσωμεν ...". On Macarius/Symeon, see B. Baldwin and A. M. Talbot, *ODB* 2:1270.

36 The fact that Donatus stored the wine shows that he was producing for the higher-priced market for aged wines: A. Tchernia, *Le vin de l'Italie romaine: Essai d'histoire économique d'après les amphores,* Bibliothèque des Écoles françaises d'Athènes et de Rome 261 (Rome, 1986), 28–32.

37 *Miracula S. Stephani facta Uzali* (*BHL* 7860–61) 2.3, PL 41:849–50: "Hic in fundo suo suburbano cum loco et nomine vocitato probi generis vina quotannis condere et conservare consueverat. Interea, ut possessoribus mos est, commodorum quaestuum causa, quoslibet terrae repositos fructus tunc malle venales emptoribus publicare, cum votis exoptatorum lucrorum avariora concurrunt pretia temporum, visum est memorato domino praedii, cum quodam homine suo, vini scilicet gustatore peritissimo, apothecam suam primitus intrare, ac per singula vasa examinando vina approbare ... " and "inspiciuntur denuo cuncta per ordinem vasa: vinum hauritur, nitor in colore conspicitur, sapor in gustu approbatur, tristitia in gaudium commutatur, et quid quantumque fides in Christo ejusque gloriosissimo Amico valeat reperiri, cunctisque audientibus mirantibusque succeditur: denique illa probatissima vina condigno pretio emptoribus distribuuntur. Ecce qualiter divina providentia utilitatibus hominum deservit ...". The Miracles do not specify that the buyers of the wine are merchants, although this is certainly possible with *emptores.*

story leaves no doubt that this father of an imperial bureaucrat assumed the workings of the market in late Roman Uzalis, for he calculated his sales on the basis of expert information on quality and on changing prices.

The value attached to commercial information recurs on the other side of the economic upheavals that ended antiquity, in the ninth century. In the less developed economy of the early medieval West, the sources run richer than in contemporary Byzantium. An emphasis on places in which particular wares could be had in abundance shows up in a Scandinavian trader's story, written down around 900 at the instruction of King Alfred of Wessex.[38] Another traveler reports the abundance in Estland, along the Baltic coast, of "very much honey and fishing," as well as the tragic fact that the locals had no ale. He also mentions ship ropes, which would have been valuable within Scandinavia.[39] Furs and the honey he describes are well known as long-distance trade goods originating in the north and shipped into and beyond the Mediterranean.[40] And the news of no ale in the north looks like a tip for traders operating within that Northern Arc whose commerce was just then linking with Constantinople and the caliphate, as we can see from Byzantium's treaties with the Rus and the recent archaeology of Sweden's ninth-century trading town of Birka.[41] In any case, the interest of Alfred the Great's court in writing up the geographic and economic information conveyed by the two travelers accords well with the Anglo-Saxons' general interest in trade, which, at least among the literate elite, appears comparatively greater than among their contemporary Frankish peers.[42]

Those who aspired to govern the polyglot Frankish empire found even basic economic information hard to come by, as a command issued by Louis the Pious (814–40) seems to indicate. When the Carolingian emperor tightened royal control over the striking of coins, he specified that certain counts were to seek information, apparently about coinage and counterfeiting, either from other counts or from merchants traveling hither and thither. Louis assumed that merchants possessed special economic information, in this case about monetary conditions in other towns.[43]

Western sources also echo economic information from the Mediterranean. For example, a neurotic French count was famously troubled by Venetian traders' price information about a distant market. Around 880, merchants swarmed around his pilgrim caravan when it camped in a meadow outside of Pavia en route home to Frankland from Rome—another ephemeral "market event." Curious, the count asked the merchants if "I got a good deal" (*utrum bene negotiatus sum*) on the expensive textile he had bought in Rome. The Venetians asked how much he had paid. It was indeed a good deal, they told him: it would have cost more in Constantinople. The future holy man was horrified that he had unwittingly "cheated" the merchant in Rome. He promptly sent the difference in price back to the Roman dealer, a gesture that, clearly, the narrator reckoned pretty much a miracle when he told

---

However, the use of *distribuo* for the sale reinforces the idea that Donatus was selling to multiple parties, and perhaps even at retail.
38 Ohthere reported that the wealth of his fellows in Norway stemmed from tribute paid to them by the far northern tribes of "Finnas" (i.e., Sami), and he specifies the goods that he and others like him acquired in this way: marten, reindeer, and bear pelts; bird feathers; ship ropes from whale; and seal hide. Earlier he had described acquiring valuable walrus tusks ("teeth"): Old English *Orosius*, 46, 45; *Ohthere's Voyages: A Late 9th-Century Account of Voyages along the Coasts of Norway and Denmark and Its Cultural Context*, ed. J. Bately and A. Englert, Maritime Culture of the North 1 (Roskilde, 2007), on which see also the valuable critical analysis of J. Bately, "Ohthere and Wulfstan in the Old English *Orosius*," ibid., 18–39.
39 Old English *Orosius*, 48.
40 McCormick, *Origins of the European Economy*, 730–32; to that evidence must now be added the zooarchaeological evidence for fur-processing that emerged from Björn Ambrosiani's excavation of Birka in the 1990s, in the same small zone as a house with clear eastern connections: see B. Wigh, *Animal Husbandry in the Viking Age Town of Birka and Its Hinterland*, Birka Studies 7 (Stockholm, 2001), 120–23, and note 41, below.
41 McCormick, *Origins of the European Economy*, 967–68, no. 780; 970, no. 811; B. Ambrosiani, "Birka im 10. Jahrhundert unter besonderer Berücksichtigung der Ostverbindungen," in *Europa im 10. Jahrhundert: Archäologie einer Aufbruchszeit*, ed. J. Henning (Mainz, 2002), 227–35.
42 McCormick, *Origins of the European Economy*, 13.
43 This capitulary is very plausibly attributed to Louis the Pious and dated around 820. Unfortunately the sole manuscript (Paris, BnF, lat. 4788, fols. 117–18) is damaged and the details of some of its provisions have been lost. After Louis insisted on limiting the striking of coins to the count's immediate control in certain places and detailed the punishment for counterfeiters, he specified that counts of towns that had no mint were to seek information, apparently about coinage and counterfeiting, either from other counts or from traveling merchants: ed. A. Boretius and V. Krause, MGH Capit 1:300.1–5, no. 147.

the tale around 940.⁴⁴ The story presumes that Venetians trading at Pavia would know the prices of expensive textiles in Constantinople's market and seek price information from Rome. On the basis of the economic "law of one price," it also implies, as we would expect, that Rome and Constantinople at this time were two different markets.

A little-known document shows similar awareness at Aachen of price differences in an even more distant market. Everyone has heard how Hārūn al-Rashīd sent Charlemagne an elephant. Many know about the next embassy, which delivered fabulous gifts from Baghdad to the Frankish court—remarkable spices and drugs, a brass water clock, and a magnificent tent for Charlemagne to use in the field.⁴⁵ But it is virtually unknown that the king leaned on his followers to collect counter-gifts for Baghdad. A letter from the Frankish court to the archbishop of Salzburg specifies that the king would like the archbishop to send him gold or a fine textile (*pallium*). The royal adviser notes that the textile seemed to be very expensive in the caliphal heartland.⁴⁶ Possibly—although not necessarily, for Charlemagne had intense relations with ecclesiastical leaders in the Arab world, and merchants from his empire traded in the Middle East—the information about prices in Baghdad came from the caliph's envoys.⁴⁷ Nevertheless, the courtier's comment about the cost of fine wares in Baghdad shows not only that Charlemagne's entourage sought to maximize diplomatic impact for the lowest cost. It also reveals that economic information about a very distant market was, at least occasionally, valued among the Frankish elite. Charlemagne's advisers, too, were familiar with Temin's instrumental mode of economic behavior.⁴⁸

A last voice from the West takes us back to Byzantium itself. Notwithstanding their philological challenges, the Old Church Slavonic materials generated by the missions of Constantine (Cyril) and Methodius offer wonderful insights. Constantine, Apostle of the Slavs, likely preached his homily on the discovery of the relics of St. Clement in the coastal city of Cherson between 861 and 863. Like few other contemporary religious texts I know, this sermon appeals to merchant interest. Constantine deploys what looks like commercial imagery calculated to catch the attention of an audience that must have included traders assembled in the Black Sea port for a Greek religious service. At one point, Constantine seems to compare the acquisition of the saint's relics to a great business deal, and he certainly reminds his audience how avidly they listen to old merchants' tales of their lives on the road. Although Constantine emphasizes wondrous stories of past trading exploits, he likely expects his listeners to prick up their ears at information about business.⁴⁹ It does not seem to me accidental that the patriarch of Constantinople had compared spiritual preparations for death and eternal life to an easy business deal in a homily delivered

---

44 Odo of Cluny, *Vita Geraldi Aureliacensis* (*BHL* 3411) 1.27, PL 133:658B–C. For critical discussion of this passage, see McCormick, *Origins of the European Economy*, 680 n. 47.

45 McCormick, *Origins of the European Economy*, 893–94, nos. 271 and 277; cf. 890–91, nos. 254–56.

46 The conventional wisdom is that gold was cheaper in the caliphate than in the Carolingian empire, since the legal norm for gold to silver exchange in the caliphate was 1:10 and, about a half century after Charlemagne's death, in western Frankland 1:12: P. Spufford, *Money and Its Use in Medieval Europe* (Cambridge, 1988), 51–52. Nevertheless, the rate fluctuated in the caliphate and it is possible that in 807, the situation looked a little different. Some kind of textile certainly figured among the most important wares exported by the Rhadanite merchants from the Franks to the caliphate around 885: McCormick, *Origins of the European Economy*, 689.

47 On Charlemagne's relations with Arabs, see M. McCormick, *Charlemagne's Survey of the Holy Land: Wealth, Personnel, and Buildings of a Mediterranean Church between Antiquity and the Middle Ages* (Washington, D.C., 2011), and McCormick, *Origins of the European Economy*, 670–95.

48 *Formulae Salzburgenses* 62, ed. K. Zeumer, MGH Form 453–55, with the additional text recovered by B. Bischoff, *Salzburger Formelbücher und Briefe aus Tassilonischer und Karolingischer Zeit*, SBMünch (Munich, 1973), no. 4, Formula 2.2, p. 34 (cf. pp. 13–14), which adds the size of the tent, reveals Charlemagne's efforts to collect countergifts for Harun from his subordinates, and shows that the king's advisers especially wanted gold and *pallium*, the latter being particularly expensive in Iraq: "Aurum, si valetis, aut pallium mittite, quia in suis provinciis valde hoc pretiosum esse videtur." Strictly construed, the *hoc* should refer only to the pallium. The exact nature of the fine textile designated by "pallium" in this and other contemporary sources is not clear to me, and deserves further investigation.

49 Constantine the Philosopher, *Sermon on the Discovery of the Relics of St. Clement*, Old Church Slavonic version, 1, ed. and Latin trans. J. Vašica, "Slovo na prenesenie moštem preslavnago Klimenta neboli legenda chersonská," *Acta academiae velehradensis* 19 (1948): 38–80, here 73–74; trans. 64–65; the text is also available in T. Butler, *Monumenta bulgarica* (Ann Arbor, 1996), 8–9, with a translation that I have not followed. My late colleague Horace Lunt has assured me that Butler's understanding of this difficult passage is not preferable to mine. For further discussion, see McCormick, *Origins of the European Economy*, 188 n. 56.

a couple of years earlier.[50] The metaphor in any event suggests that Photius, too, expected merchants in his audience in the Hagia Sophia.[51]

Writing to a bishop on Crete, another ninth-century Byzantine ecclesiastic disparaged certain prelates' conduct. Theodore Stoudite says they behave like peasants who produce abundant harvests and large herds and then watch carefully, waiting for times of dearth in order to buy and sell with maximum advantage: they act more like merchants than bishops.[52] The implication is that ambitious farmers (γεωργοί) timed their buying and selling to the prices on the food market, which fluctuated according to yields and season. Given that the overwhelming majority of Byzantines were farmers, Theodore's criticism suggests that instrumental behavior was well known among his contemporaries and even practiced by some bishops.[53] The story tells us about no particular farmer or bishop. Nor does it bother to explain the logic of waiting for the right moment to jack up prices and profits. This tells us that contemporary readers understood how the market worked. Unwittingly, Theodore offers excellent indirect evidence on the instrumental mode of behavior, and therefore on the importance of markets in ninth-century Byzantium.

Against a backdrop of nearly no testimony from the merchants themselves, scattered indirect evidence makes it hard to deny that on either side of the economic transformations that separated late antique and early medieval society, some people at least placed a premium on economic information that was useful in markets. Members of the elite instinctively assumed the existence and workings of markets. This indirect evidence suggests that Temin's instrumental mode of economic behavior was important in early medieval and Byzantine society. It reinforces explicit records of market exchange.[54] It may well suggest that the instrumental mode of behavior and the markets it implies were dominant then. Nevertheless, few will question that the command mode played a significant role in the early Byzantine economy, and it probably was not entirely absent later in the first millennium. It would also be hard to imagine a Byzantine countryside or townscape devoid of economic reciprocity. The challenge for future economic historians will be to imagine ways of gauging the relative importance of the three modes of behavior, and to determine how that relative importance may have changed over time and over the differentiated economic space from the capital to the Anatolian plateau or the Balkan valleys. Such a geographically scaled understanding would lead to a more exact knowledge of the Byzantine economy and its markets. Another way of approaching that problem comes from the archaeology of containers.

Amphorae, Barrels, and Economic History

Because of their indestructibility, variety, and ubiquity as transport containers for relatively high-value foodstuffs, ceramic amphorae provide some

---

50 Photius, *Homilia* 2.3, ed. V. Laourdas, Φωτίου ὁμιλίαι, Hellēnika, Paratēma 12 (Thessalonike, 1959), 15.10–25, esp. 13–14: "... ἡ πραγματεία, δι' ἧς ἐμπορεύεσθαι ταῦτα δυνατόν, ἀταλαίπωρος...".

51 The Old Church Slavonic Life of Constantine-Cyril 4.1–2, ed. and Latin trans. F. Grivec and F. Tomšić, *Constantinus et Methodius Thessalonicenses, Fontes* (Zagreb, 1960), 99 and trans., 173; cf. the ed. of T. Lehr-Spławiński, *Konstantyn i Metody* (Warsaw, 1967), 138; Eng. trans.: M. Kantor, R. S. White, and A. Dostál, *The Vita of Constantine and The Vita of Methodius* (Ann Arbor, 1976), 9. The affinity reinforces the explicit assertion of Constantine's biographer that he studied with Photius before the latter assumed the patriarchate. On this score, P. Lemerle, *Le premier humanisme byzantin: Notes et remarques sur enseignement et culture à Byzance des origines au Xᵉ siècle* (Paris, 1971), 161–64, has challenged the literal exactness of the *Life*, and particularly Dvornik's extravagant interpretation, even as he allows the possibility of a link between the two men. I see no reason for a biographer operating under the authority of the Roman popes to invent a connection for his hero that will have seemed damaging in the West. The apparent echo of Photius's unusual simile in Constantine's own composition strengthens the testimony of the exceedingly well-informed anonymous biographer on Constantine's link with Photius.

52 *Ep.* 11 to Anastasius, bishop of "Knosia," ed. G. Fatouros, *Theodori Studitae Epistulae*, 2 vols., CFHB 31 (Berlin, 1991–92), 1:38.116–21: "οἵτινες ὅλην φροντίδα κέκτηνται τάχα ἐπὶ τοῦ σπεῖραι πολλὰ καὶ ἀμήσασθαι καὶ ἐπὶ τοῦ φυτεῦσαι τοσαῦτα καὶ καρπώσασθαι καὶ ἐπὶ τοῦ προσθεῖναι καὶ πληθύναι βουκόλια ἢ ποίμνια, ὥσπερ τινὲς γεωργοὶ καιροσκοποῦντες καὶ καταπραγματευόμενοι τὰς ἐνδείας πρὸς τὸ πωλεῖν καὶ ἀγοράζειν ταῦτα καὶ ἐκεῖνα, πραγματευτικῶς καὶ ἐμπορικῶς οἱονεὶ πολιτευόμενοι, ἀλλ' οὐκ ἐπισκοπικῶς καὶ ἱερατικῶς...". On "Knosia" as Knossos, see, e.g., Fatouros, ibid., 1:153*. A similar thought occurs in John Chrysostom, *In Kalendas* 6, PG 48:962, who nevertheless expresses it quite differently.

53 Exactly the same criticism was leveled at a contemporary Carolingian bishop, underscoring both a deep structural similarity between the two economies and mental commonalities among ecclesiastics. The similarity extends even to an explicit comparison of the bishop with merchants: Notker Stammerer, *Gesta Karoli magni imperatoris* 1.23, ed. H. F. Haefele, MGH ScriptRerGerm, n.s. 12, 2nd ed. (Berlin, 1980), 31.4–10.

54 See notes 8 and 9, above.

of the best data for ancient patterns of production, shipment, and exchange, market or otherwise. We can use recent advances in ceramic knowledge to deepen our understanding of how ancient economies worked. As the Egyptian merchants gathered in the port of Gaza or Donatus's deferred wine sale suggest, we should think hard about the chain of transactions that moved a packet of cloth, a liter of oil, wine, or grain from the site of production through the warehouse and finally on to the market and the consumer. Careful analysis of the ostraca found in Carthage's circular harbor provides exquisite details of how, in the spring and summer of 373, African oil was moved by sea and land to Carthage, and how it was weighed and stored before transshipment.[55] Although the documents appear to reflect the state fiscal apparatus of the annona, they, like the records of earlier Spanish oil shipments, provide precious operational insights into how Romans imagined and organized the movement, inventory, and management of goods en route from production to consumption zones.

Amphora production and distribution have illuminated the changing geography and rhythms of shipments as proxies for the movement of foodstuffs.[56] Containers will contribute more still if we mobilize all the archaeological and textual evidence about them. With new precision, thin sections and the chemistry of amphora fabrics ascribe particular amphorae to specific zones of production marked by the archaeological finds of kilns and wasters.[57] Meticulous scrutiny of amphora features—presence or absence of pitch, cork or ceramic stoppers, types and distribution, modes of opening—has produced a notable advance in our knowledge of the links between specific types of containers and the wares they contained. In the absence of macroscopic vestiges of their contents, gas chromatography and mass spectrometry can identify the types of pitches, and distinguish oil from wine products.[58] Ancient DNA fragments—macroscopically invisible but preserved in the surface of the amphora—have identified the olive oil laced with oregano and, possibly, mastic, that once filled long-submerged Chian amphorae. If the technique is validated and reproduced, it will supply amazing new insights into the wares transported by the thousands of surviving amphorae and millions of amphora fragments that once traveled to Byzantine markets.[59] Such advances will enable us to progress from counting containers to estimating the economic significance of the wares they once contained.

The experimental and ergonomic archaeology of amphora forms can contribute more to grasping the realities of Mediterranean transport. What were the operational advantages of particular designs, and what can they suggest about shippers' priorities, about loading and unloading the cargo? Packing in ship holds was connected with amphora shape; for instance, tapered ends could wedge layers of amphorae in place, and boards braced African cylindrical amphorae.[60] The ergonomics of design hint at how and where amphorae were loaded as cargo, details that in turn could yield insight into the events (markets?) or locales in which their ownership changed hands. Rather like barrels, the large cylindrical amphorae that carried African liquids could have been *rolled* short distances for loading and unloading and probably stowed and transported fairly easily on rafts, flat-bottomed scows, or carts. Is this why their small handles do not protrude beyond the body of the vessel?

What did it take to place into a ship's hold large amphorae such as the highly efficient cylindrical

---

55 Peña, "Mobilization of State Olive Oil."
56 Tchernia, *Le vin de l'Italie romaine,* remains exemplary for the earlier period; for the later period, see Pieri, *Le commerce du vin oriental,* with further references, as well as the valuable reflections of H. Elton, "The Economy of Southern Asia Minor and LR 1 Amphorae," in Gurt Esparraguera, Buxeda i Garrigós, and Cau Ontiveros, eds., *LRCW 1: Late Roman Coarse Wares,* 691–95.
57 Pieri, *Le commerce du vin oriental,* e.g., 80–81, about LRA 1. The valuable website of Simon Keay and David Williams, "Roman Amphorae: A Digital Resource," http://ads.ahds.ac.uk/catalogue/archive/amphora_ahrb_2005/, illustrates thin sections of the fabrics of various amphorae wherever possible.

58 See the important conclusions of M. Bonifay and N. Garnier, "Que transportaient donc les amphores africaines?" in *Supplying Rome and the Empire: The Proceedings of an International Seminar Held at Siena-Certosa di Pontignano on May 2–4, 2004, on Rome, the Provinces, Production and Distribution,* ed. E. Papi, Journal of Roman Archaeology supp. ser. 69 (Portsmouth, R.I., 2007), 9–31.
59 M. C. Hansson and B. P. Foley, "Ancient DNA Fragments inside Classical Greek Amphoras Reveal Cargo of 2400-Year-Old Shipwreck," *Journal of Archaeological Science* 35 (2008): 1169–76.
60 See A. J. Parker, "Cargoes, Containers and Stowage: The Ancient Mediterranean," *International Journal of Nautical Archaeology* 21 (1992): 89–100, and especially the discussion of the boards and packing of the African cylindrical amphorae in the fifth-century wreck Dramont E (or 5): C. Santamaria, *L'épave Dramont "E" à Saint-Raphaël (Ve siècle ap. J.-C.),* Archaeonautica 13 (Paris, 1995), 117–20.

Figure 3.1.
Africana 2D Grande. This type of cylindrical amphora, which runs 109–17 cm long and has an average capacity of 45 to 50 L, was manufactured in the areas of Leptiminus and Hadrumetum in the 3rd and 4th c.; oil and wine seem to have been its main contents (photo courtesy of the Museo Arqueológico Municipal de Cartagena and Archaeological Data Service, Keay and Williams, "Roman Amphorae: A Digital Resource")

Africana 2D Grande, whose production continued into the fourth century (fig. 3.1)? A 68-liter capacity implies that if they carried olive oil, the oil alone would have weighed some 63 kilograms, to which must be added the weight of the amphora itself, another 19.5 kilograms. That surely made the amphora difficult for a single stevedore to handle without some sort of a hoist or crane with hooks—thus no need for big handles—even if the hoist were just a block and tackle hung from the ship's yardarm.[61]

---

61 The specific density of olive oil is 0.9150–0.9180 at 15.5° C. Hence 68 L × 0.92 = 62.56 kg. See the valuable table 1 and dis-

Figure 3.2.
Kapitän 2. The design of this 3rd- and 4th-c. amphora, apparently from the Aegean, lent itself to being handed off between stevedores; about 75 cm high, it held considerably less than, e.g., an Africana 2D Grande (photo courtesy of the Matrica Museum and Archaeological Data Service, Keay and Williams, "Roman Amphorae: A Digital Resource")

On the other hand, what could explain the long, tapered design of smaller amphorae such as the presumably Aegean Kapitän 2 (fig. 3.2) or Dominique

cussion of amphora capacities and weights in D. P. S. Peacock and D. F. Williams, *Amphorae and the Roman Economy: An Introductory Guide* (London, 1986), 51–53 (at 52), who called for more work and reporting of empty amphora weights twenty years ago. Compare for the dimensions and capacity Keay and Williams, "Africana 2D Grande," in "Roman Amphorae," http://ads.ahds.ac.uk/catalogue/archive/amphora_ahrb_2005/character.cfm?id=6&CFID=1795221&CFTOKEN=57363093, accessed July 2010. M. Bonifay, *Études sur la céramique romaine tardive d'Afrique*, BAR International Series 1301 (Oxford, 2004), 474 (cf. 472), suspects that this type of amphora may have been used for a salt fish preparation, in which case the contents probably weighed more. Laboratory analysis did not detect lipids: see Bonifay and Garnier, "Que transportaient donc," 23, fig. 8, where they further suggest the possibility of wine; in this case, the *titulus pictus*, "OLEI," would refer to a secondary usage, unlike the classical merchants' *tituli picti* as clarified by J. T. Peña, "Two Groups of *tituli picti* from Pompeii and Environs: Sicilian Wine, Not Flour and Hand-picked Olives," *Journal of Roman Archaeology* 20 (2007): 233–54.

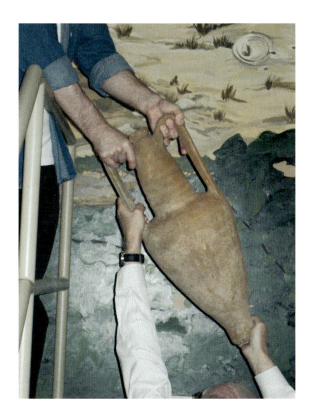

Figure 3.3.
Handing off a Kapitän 2 amphora. Two Harvard stevedores demonstrate the ergonomic advantages of the design of Kapitän 2 amphorae: four fingers of the lower worker's right hand are cupped into the hollow base while his thumb grasps the rilled exterior and his left hand guides the amphora toward the worker aboard a (pretended) ship; the long handles allow both workers to maintain a firm grasp until the amphora is securely handed off (my thanks to Dr. Joseph A. Greene and the Semitic Museum of Harvard University, as well as to Avia Navickas and Michael Actis-Grande for taking the photos)

Pieri's Late Roman 9? At first blush, it is difficult to understand what practical purposes could be served by so odd-looking a shape, with its long and narrow hollow foot and dangerously protruding rabbit-ear handles ill-suited to rolling and prone to breaking. But an experimental and ergonomic approach explains much about the design. The conelike shape is perfect for cradling a full amphora against one's stomach and chest. Personal experience at lifting and carrying a Kapitän 2 shows that this form distributes the weight across one's body, easing the load on the back and arms when, say, one carried it from a loading stack to a ship.[62] Most importantly, the protruding extremities seem designed to minimize the risk of dropping the container and its valuable wine at the most perilous moment in its life, when one laborer passed it to another, especially in wet conditions. The hollow rilled base is perfectly suited to a firm grip with the right hand—four fingers fit easily into the base, while the palm cups against the rim of the amphora foot and its rilled exterior—and the left hand securely grasps the lower part of one long handle. In this way, a stevedore such as the professorial one depicted in figure 3.3 could even stand in the waves and hand the amphora up to a waiting collegial deckhand: the long rabbit-ear handles allow the deckhand to grasp with both hands the upper ends of both handles and pull it up into a smallish ship while the stevedore still holds the amphora securely.[63] The hollow rilled base would help keep a wet amphora from slipping out of one's grasp. The same design facilitated handing the container down through a hatch to packers waiting in the hold.

Such an operational approach should interest more than amphoralogists. If the ergonomic interpretation of the design is correct, amphorae like this one were particularly well tailored to beachside loading or unloading. That could point to the predominance of multiple, small-scale beachside sales or deliveries in the production zone whence these amphorae stemmed. The ways in which these smaller, tapered containers were manipulated must in any case have differed considerably from the handling of the large cylindrical African amphorae. Should we therefore suspect that such African containers entailed fairly elaborate port facilities, while these Aegean amphorae lent themselves to more improvised landings and loadings? This hypothesis

---

62 For Kapitän 2, see Keay and Williams, "Kapitän 2," in "Roman Amphorae," http://ads.ahds.ac.uk/catalogue/archive/amphora_ahrb_2005/details.cfm?id=154&CFID=1795221&CFTOKEN=57363093, accessed July 2010. For LRA 9, see Pieri, *Le commerce du vin oriental*, 137–38.

63 It is a pleasure to thank my colleague Dr. Joseph A. Greene of Harvard's Semitic Museum, who cheerfully helped organize my experiment with one of our intact Kapitän 2 amphorae, accession number 1907.61.3. Today, empty, this amphora weighs 6 kg. Museum summer interns Avia Navickas of Boston College and Michael Actis-Grande of Pennsylvania State University were good sports in carting the amphora around and taking the photos, and have my thanks.

certainly could be reconciled with the sort of archipelago-hopping and beaching that was a familiar feature of navigation in the island- and vineyard-dotted Aegean Sea.[64]

An operational approach clarifies the logic behind the changing size and shape of amphorae. Pieri's recent study of Gaza amphorae (Late Roman Amphora type 4) has shown that fifth-century potters developed a variant form that doubled capacity.[65] But why did the potters choose to expand it in the fashion that they did? Rather than simply ballooning LRA 4's basic oval shape outward and preserving the same proportions, the potters extended vertically the coil of clay that they laid down to form the wall of the amphora, producing an amphora of approximately the same diameter, but twice as long and thus double the capacity. Was this shape a coincidence? Or did some local operational necessity persuade the potters of the Negev desert to change the shape of the LRA 4B to resemble a cigar? We will return to this question below.

Progress in localizing major amphora types invites us to read the texts anew. That schedule of fees for inspecting Constantinople-bound cargoes at Abydos (mentioned above) helps clarify around 500 the critical question of the economic significance of particular amphorae, even as the identification in Cilicia of the production of LRA 1 illuminates the logic of the inscription. Inspectors collected the top fees from "all wine freighters," to the tune of "six folles and two pints (*xestai*) [of wine]."[66] Given what we know from the amphorae, we can legitimately surmise that "all wine freighters" transported north in particular the production of Palestine, whether from Gaza in LRA 4 or in the Palestinian bag-shaped amphorae that were also imitated in Egypt.[67] However, the schedule qualifies the high fee for "all wine freighters" by adding "except only those from Cilicia."

The tariff is generally set according to cargo type: wine, oil, dried vegetables, bacon, and wheat. The sole exception identifies a cargo only by geography and occurs two lines later. It specifies that "Cilician shippers pay to the naval personnel [of this station] three folles." The implication of the double mention of Cilicia seems to be that Cilician shippers were transporting wine, a deduction comforted by the reference to Cilicia's extensive wine exports in the *Expositio totius mundi*.[68] If we may assume that "Cilicia" is fair administrative shorthand for the production area of the amphora known as LRA 1, whose kilns in fact occur overwhelmingly in Cilicia, then we may deduce two things. The first is that LRA 1 (i.e., Cilician amphorae) indeed transported wine, perhaps predominantly around 500.[69] Second, if, as might seem inherently likely, the Abydos fees correlate in some approximate way with values of the cargoes, then Cilicians either enjoyed a special fiscal privilege at this station or Cilician wine was of significantly lower value than Gazan wine, olive oil, dried vegetables, or bacon.[70] Given that Gaza wine is widely attested as a prestige drink, came from further away, and had inherently higher sea transport costs (as well as significant overland expenses for many vineyards, as we will see), the latter seems to make sense.[71] We thus gain a precious insight into the economic significance of specific cargoes. The freight of a ship loaded with LRA 4 or bag-shaped amphorae—that is, Palestinian and perhaps other

---

64 For this pattern of navigation in the Aegean, see the middle Byzantine examples in McCormick, *Origins of the European Economy*, 420–21.

65 Pieri, *Le commerce du vin oriental*, 105–6 for LRA 4B; its 24–26 L compare to the 13–15 L of the earlier LRA 4A (ibid., 104).

66 See note 21, above.

67 For the production zones, see Pieri, *Le commerce du vin oriental*, 109–10, 124–25.

68 Οἱ οἰνηγοὶ πάντες οἱ τὸν οἶνον κομίζοντες εἰς τὴν βασιλίδ<α ταύ>την πόλειν, πλὴν μόνων τῶν Κιλίκων, κλασσικοῖς τῶν στενῶν φόλλις ἓξ καὶ ξέστας δύο, . . . οἱ Κίλικες ναύκληροι κλασσικοῖς τῶν στενῶν φόλλις τρῖς: ed. Durliat and Guillou, "Le tarif d'Abydos," 583.22–25; for the *Expositio*, see below, note 70. On the varied evidence for Cilician wine production, see M. Decker, "The Wine Trade of Cilicia in Late Antiquity," *ARAM* 17 (2005): 51–59.

69 See Pieri, *Le commerce du vin oriental*, 80–85, for the production zone (ten sites in Cilicia, three on Cyprus, and one each on Rhodes and the facing mainland) and for wine as the primary content in LRA 1's original use. Elton, "Economy of Southern Asia Minor," emphasizes that an amphora type produced over such a long period and in so many places inevitably was used for more than just wine, a point borne out by some labels on some amphorae.

70 For wine assessed at 6 folles and 2 xestai (of wine), see above, note 68. Oil, dried vegetable, and bacon cargoes are assessed at 6 folles, against the 3 folles paid for Cilician wine freights, and the 3 folles plus one measure paid for wheat: Durliat and Guillou, "Le tarif d'Abydos," 584.24–29. It therefore looks significant that the *Expositio*, 29, 162.3–4, states that Askalon and Gaza export "the best wine" (*uinum optimum*) whereas it notes (39, 176.1–3) that Cilicia makes "much wine" (*faciens multum uinum*). The cheaper rates for a Cilician product may have created an incentive for more shippers to use the typically Cilician LRA 1.

71 On the prestige of Gaza wine, see the sources collected in Pieri, *Le commerce du vin oriental*, 112–13.

sorts of wine—was worth considerably more than the same ship loaded with LRA 1—that is, Cilician wine—indeed, perhaps twice as much. Should we conclude that Cilician wine catered to a more "mass market" than Gazan?

Future economic archaeology will need to consider the volume of production of different kilns over time. It would be highly desirable to obtain archaeomagnetic dates for the last firing of the amphora kilns, and compare them with the dates assigned to specific amphorae from various find sites around the empire. As we get a better handle on the places of amphora production and distribution, their chronology, the content of amphorae, and even the first glimmer of the relative value of those contents, scholars can correlate this new knowledge with the now invisible markets through which these amphorae passed.[72]

When the grapes were pressed, only higher-value wine made it into export containers. At least in the Mediterranean, low-value wine destined for local consumption seems mainly to have been put in large bladders for overland transport toward its final, local place of disposition.[73] It may be that some better wine was also transported by this method from the press and, after conditioning, transferred into heavy export amphorae or even into archaeologically invisible barrels.[74] Certainly the Carthage ostraca seem to show that bladders played an important role—conveying half to three-quarters of the total, according to J. Theodore Peña's reconstruction—in the initial movement of oil from the sometimes remote countryside to Carthage.[75] At Carthage the olive oil was transferred to amphorae, weighed, and recorded, apparently in preparation for export as part of the annona, the process that generated the ostraca of 373. At the analogous moment in the less-well-documented commercial sector, was the transfer to amphorae or barrels sometimes equivalent to a "market event," a (today) imperceptible commercial transaction in which the producer was paid by a merchant? That might be the implication of the African vintner's story. How many such commercial transactions did a given liter of export oil or wine undergo en route to delivery and how did that chain of transactions change over time? At what point in the chain of distribution and marketing was a particular type of amphora filled or emptied? That is, was an amphora discarded at or before the final transaction purchasing its contents? Differing answers will imply different insights into the microstructure of markets. For instance, around 626, the Yassı Ada ship was carrying as a secondary cargo a surprising array of differently formatted LRA 1 amphorae that were presumably filled with wine or, in some cases, olive oil. Their capacities ranged between 4.5 and 14.8 liters. If this ship was not, as has been hypothesized, on a run exclusively to deliver supplies to Heraclius's army, but (perhaps in addition to a hypothetical fiscal transport) was going to market, its wide variety of amphora sizes could suggest that any merchant aboard her avoided the middlemen—wholesalers?—who acquired and broke larger shipments into smaller lots for sale to consumers.[76] Greater variety in the standard sizes transported

---

72   See on this challenge Elton, "Economy of Southern Asia Minor."

73   Tchernia, *Le vin de l'Italie romaine*, 39.

74   On the conditioning of wine in udders after pressing, and wagon transport of udders to locations where wine was poured into amphorae, see É. Marlière, *L'outre et le tonneau dans l'Occident romain*, Monographies Instrumentum 22 (Montagnac, 2002), 190; cf. Bonifay and Garnier, "Que transportaient donc," 22. Animal membranes are supposed to have been unsuitable for sea transport since the rats which will have infested Roman ships loved to eat them: Marlière, *L'outre et le tonneau*, 189. On rats and Roman ships, see M. McCormick, "Rats, Communications and Plague: Towards an Ecological History," *Journal of Interdisciplinary History* 34 (2003): 1–25, at 9–14. For all aspects of the ancient technology of wine production, especially in the Holy Land, see R. Frankel, *Wine and Oil Production in Antiquity in Israel and Other Mediterranean Countries* (Sheffield, 1999).

75   Peña, "Mobilization of State Olive Oil," 212.

76   P. G. van Alfen, "New Light on the 7th-c. Yassı Ada Shipwreck: Capacities and Standard Size of LRA1 Amphoras," *Journal of Roman Archaeology* 9 (1996): 189–213, at 192–201, 213, on the possibility that the range of sizes was driven by consumer demand in a changing marketplace. On the other hand, F. van Doorninck Jr., "Byzantine Shipwrecks," in *EHB* 2:899–905, at 901, inclines toward identifying this wreck as a fiscal cargo of taxes in kind, for reasons that for now are only sketched in F. van Doorninck, "The Ship of Georgios, Priest and Sea Captain: Yassıada," in *Beneath the Seven Seas: Adventures with the Institute of Nautical Archaeology*, ed. G. F. Bass (London, 2005), 92–97. Although we do not know how much of the structures of the sixth-century annona transport system survived the catastrophic loss in 618 of Egypt and the great home port of Alexandria, imperial legal texts indicate that system had allowed shippers to transport for their own advantage duty-free wares above and beyond their required fiscal cargo; see McCormick, "Bateaux de vie, bateaux de mort," 80–93. If van Doorninck's interpretation of Yassı Ada as a fiscal transport should prove correct, then the rather motley assembly of LRA 1 amphorae could be the first archaeological example of such a shipper's personal, secondary cargo; the new LRA 13 amphorae, the bulk of the cargo, would be the fiscal cargo.

might suggest that the structure of the market had simplified in seventh-century Byzantium.

At the receiving end, how were the wares stored, organized, and moved to the consumer? The archaeology of late antique shops, such as at Sardis and Skythopolis (Beth Shean), can illuminate retail operations and their links with regional and longer-distance trade, as well as the social and economic role of market shops in the changing cityscape of late antiquity.[77] One step further back in the chain of supply are two warehouses from around 500, which have recently been discovered and excavated at an important late Roman town and at a military installation. Because the storehouses in the harbor of Classe (Magazzino no. 17) and at the fort of Dichin, on the Danube, perished catastrophically with their wares still stacked in place, they will shed exceptional light on how late Romans thought about and managed goods that were imported en route to a consumption site, whether it was part of the state supply service or of the private sector. The homogeneity or heterogeneity of the wares in a particular area of the storehouse—such as the six amphorae of three or four types originally stacked in a row at Dichin, or the manifestly grouped sets of amphorae in the warehouse at Classe—quantities, units, and proximity of one type to others all should illuminate what the goods were as well as how they were manipulated, especially when those data are compared to written records generated by such operations, whether they be the Carthage ostraca or countless papyrus receipts of Egypt.[78] As figure 3.4 shows, at Classe's Warehouse 17 the amphorae were stored on the ground floor *by our modern types*: here the excavators have, in addition to one barrel, identified sets of amphorae—Keay 26f–g, 57a–b, 62r, and a set of large amphorae attributed to the same production area as Keay 35b—as well as tableware and lamps. The quantities in this particular warehouse do not seem huge—I count some three dozen of the "syringe" amphorae Keay 26f–g at the stage in the excavation when photo VII.27 (fig. 3.4) was taken—but substantial nonetheless.[79] Recent work identifies the contents of these amphorae variously as fish or olive preserves or wine.[80] Thus, pending full study and publication of the site, we might suppose it to be a warehouse loaded mainly with African food products. However, the fine ware and lamps, apparently present in commercial quantities, were also made in Africa. The warehouse also might have stored sacks of grain, including on a second floor, as the artist's reconstruction suggests (fig. 3.5). Now at this date, Africa was under the Vandals and Ravenna was controlled by either Odoacer or Theoderic, circumstances that doubly rule out identifying these wares as annona shipments: they must have traveled to the head of the Adriatic as commercial wares. The early evidence from the remarkable Warehouse 17 of

---

77 See Walmsley, "Regional Exchange and the Role of the Shop," in this volume, 311–30.

78 For the Classe warehouse excavated in 2004–05, see the preliminary indications and photos in A. Augenti, "Gli scavi 2004–2005 nel porto di Classe—area I," in *Felix Ravenna: La croce, la spada, la vela: L'alto Adriatico fra V e VI secolo,* ed. A. Augenti and C. Bertelli (Milan, 2007), 34–36; E. Cirelli, *Ravenna: Archeologia di una città,* Contributi di archeologia medievale 2 (Borgo San Lorenzo, 2008), 133, figs. 113, 134. It is a pleasure to acknowledge all that I learned from visiting the site of Warehouse 17 with its excavator, Prof. Andrea Augenti, who also alerted me to the parallel find of Dichin and kindly answered my follow-up questions, even as he and his students work on the definitive study and publication of this important discovery. In what we may presume were the different circumstances of a military storeroom ("store building 2") of the fort on the Danube, the row of amphorae consisted of two almost intact LRA 1, presumably containing wine, a badly fragmented imitation LRA 2, a lower Danubian amphora, and two standard LRA 2's whose splintering suggested that they exploded in the fire that destroyed the warehouse, and thus probably contained olive oil. If the LRA 1's contained the usual wine, as the excavator deduces from their nearly intact state, this would have been a row of mixed contents. The same set of storerooms also contained stocks of grain, pulses, lentils, military equipment, and cooking vessels, although it is not possible to discern the logic of their organization from the interim report: V. G. Swan, "Dichin (Bulgaria): Interpreting the Ceramic Evidence in Its Wider Context," in *The Transition to Late Antiquity: On the Danube and Beyond,* ed. A. G. Poulter, Proceedings of the British Academy 141 (Oxford, 2007), 251–80, esp. 252–55; cf. P. Grinter, "Seeds of Destruction: Conflagration in the Grain Stores of Dichin," ibid., 281–88. On LRA 2 as a container associated with the state supply service and on oil as its likely main contents, see O. Karagiorgou, "LR2: A Container for the Military *annona* on the Danubian Border?" in *Economy and Exchange in the East Mediterranean during Late Antiquity: Proceedings of a Conference at Somerville College, Oxford, 29th May, 1999,* ed. S. Kingsley and M. Decker (Oxford, 2001), 129–66, at 146–49.

79 Cirelli, *Ravenna,* 132–33, mentions huge quantities of identical items—e.g., 1,889 Hayes 2a lamps, although this apparently totals not a single deposit but the finds in a zone that contained multiple warehouses.

80 Bonifay and Garnier, "Que transportaient donc," 23–24, fig. 8, identify the contents of Keay 26 (= Spatheion 1) as olive or fish preserves, or wine; Keay 57 shows no sign of lipids, while the oil detected in Keay 62 might be due to reuse; the area that produced Keay 35B had fish-processing installations, and fish residues appear in such amphorae.

Figure 3.4. Classe, Warehouse 17, photo VII.27. Destroyed by fire ca. 500, this two-story structure contained grain, amphorae, quantities of fine ware, and one barrel. The amphorae—stored by type, and perhaps containing mostly fish products—and fine ware were all African; the amphorae were kept upright by holes cut in the floor that held their feet (photo courtesy of Prof. Andrea Augenti, Department of Archaeology, University of Bologna)

Classe thus points to a commercial network whose northern terminal appears to be defined by geography rather than by product type or range. Was this typical of the structures that supplied the markets of late antiquity and Byzantium? Was this one merchant's property? How many shiploads or parts of shiploads are we looking at?

The weight of empty amphorae is critical for estimating transport costs, grasping details of ergonomics and operations, and understanding market networks. Large ones like Dressel 20 containers held some 70 to 75 liters of Spanish olive oil and were heaped by the ton at the giant used amphora dump of Monte Testaccio in Rome. They cannot often have gone directly to individual consumers, who could neither afford the large outlay such a quantity entailed nor manage handily the 100 kilograms or so of a full amphora, which is why a mountain of them piled up in one place.[81] Monte Testaccio gives an idea of what to expect of a dump associated with a very big central distribution center or market. Physically more manageable, Gaza wine amphorae contained 13- or 26-some liters. If such amphorae were as efficient as contemporary LRA 1 or 2 amphorae, the smaller ones will have weighed some 17 to 20 kilograms when filled; the larger, some 34 to 40 kilograms.[82] They could conceivably have been sold

[81] Calculated at 75 liters × 0.92 (the specific density of olive oil) = 68.85 kg. The weight of Dressel 20 amphorae runs about 30 kg, for an amphora efficiency rating (i.e., of liters of contents per kg of vessel weight) of 2.3; on that concept, see van Alfen, "New Light," 208, who also gives the capacity efficiency ratings for LRA 1 and 2. I am grateful to Prof. José Remesal Rodríguez of the University of Barcelona for informing me about the weight of Dressel 20.

[82] The specific density of white wine runs between 0.990 and 1.010. Taking it as 1.0, 13 L would weigh 13 kg; if it were as efficient

Movements and Markets in the First Millennium

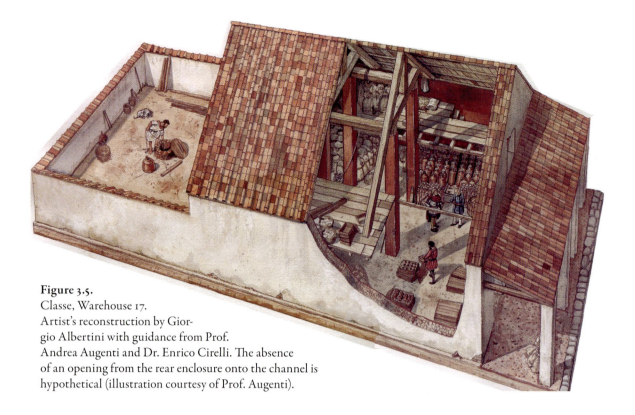

Figure 3.5.
Classe, Warehouse 17. Artist's reconstruction by Giorgio Albertini with guidance from Prof. Andrea Augenti and Dr. Enrico Cirelli. The absence of an opening from the rear enclosure onto the channel is hypothetical (illustration courtesy of Prof. Augenti).

at retail as well as wholesale, though much must have depended on the price.

Knowing which sizes occur on which sites helps clarify whether distance inland and the necessity of overland transport distinguished the distribution of large and small types of the same container. It opens the way to investigating whether market hierarchies—wholesale versus retail markets?—may explain such differentiated distribution patterns.[83]

Recent work even pinpoints links between specific amphora production shops in Africa and particular long-distance markets. Several smallish ships freighting homogeneous cargoes carried in amphorae as well as fine wares fired in Neapolis (modern Nabeul, Tunisia) or Sullecthum (modern Salakta, Tunisia) went down off the coast of Gaul, whose land sites often yield just these wares. Unsurprisingly, the coastal origin of African products recorded at Alexandria broadly resembles the pattern in other great centers around Mediterranean shores. But the absence of those types and the predominance in Egypt's interior—including the oasis of Bahariya in the western desert—of fine ware produced inland in Tunisia suggest a different story. These markets may have been served by caravans traveling overland from inland Tunisia, thus anticipating the medieval caravan trade.[84]

---

as LRA 1 (i.e., 1.9 L per kg of empty amphora), a small LRA 4 amphora would have weighed about 19.8 kg; if it were as efficient as LRA 2 (3.3 L per kg), it will have weighed 16.9 kg when filled. I have calculated the possible weight ranges of the bigger LRA 4 in the same way.

83   One can do this, for example, with the archaeological contexts of France analyzed by Pieri, *Le commerce du vin oriental*, 7–66, with respect to the smaller and larger Gaza wine amphorae LRA 4A and LRA 4B, although the apparently exclusively later date of LRA 4B2 (ca. 550–700) limits this particular comparison to a period when the transport into inner Gaul of both sizes of amphorae was on the decline. Nevertheless, it does show that away from the Mediterranean, the late larger amphorae reached only a few major centers: Bordeaux, Cathedral (cemetery) and Place Camille-Jullian phase 2 (11 amphorae), 50, 105, and 107 (where the smaller form also occurs in phases dated earlier); Lyons, Avenue Adolphe-Max (where both forms occur, although it is not clear that they come from the same phase in occupation levels stretching from the fourth to the sixth century of this site, which awaits

full publication), see 52, cf. 105, 155; Toulouse, Donjon du Capitole (there the LRA 4A comes from an early fifth-century context at the Place Esquirol, so it certainly does not testify to contemporary imports of both sizes to the same northern site), see 48, cf. 105, 155.
84   For the distribution of the production centers of Nabeul, Salakta, and central Tunisia and the possibility of caravan transport, see Bonifay, *Études*, 451–56. For the medieval caravans

Identifying the workshops that produced specific wares uncovers imitations manufactured in places far from their models.[85] The market appeal of locally produced knockoffs of the ubiquitous African dishes and lamps in Gaul, Spain, or Greece seems intuitively clear. But what are the market implications of late Roman packaging that mimics what we can now begin to think of as "branded" amphora types, such as the wine containers of Cilicia or Gaza? If imitation amphorae are indeed a form of geographically misleading late Roman brand recognition, did they target consumers or merchant intermediaries—suggesting that they contained wares similar to the imitated type?[86] Indeed, might doing so sometimes have had some fiscal advantage?[87]

Another factor sheds light on the relative cost of some products and, therefore, the strength of demand. Some large-scale winepresses discovered in the Negev desert lay one or two or more days' travel inland from the sea. Kilns that produced Gaza-type amphorae have been specifically identified at Mefalsim and Naḥal Bohu (about 15 km from the coast) and, apparently, at Beersheba, three times as far inland.[88] A large winepress installation and signs of amphora production have recently been discovered at Beershema (ancient Birsama).[89] The kiln locations indicate that here wine was put into the amphorae—presumably the very ones in which it would be shipped overseas—quite near the inland site of production. That is the same system revealed by Egyptian papyri.[90] The distance inland of the big winepress installations at Elousa (Halutza, ca. 45 km inland, in fig. 3.6), Sobata (Shivta, ca. 60 km inland), and Eboda/Oboda (Avdat, ca. 80 km inland) in a region that featured only overland transport raises the question of how these export wines reached the coast. Starting from the shipping fees recorded in Diocletian's Price Edict, scholars have long recognized that ancient land transport generally was more expensive than water and especially sea transport.[91] More recent scrutiny has stressed the effectiveness of Roman overland transport systems when there was no alternative and when demand could justify the cost.[92] Bottling export wine a few days' journey from the sea testifies both to the organizational infrastructure that delivered the product to Egyptian merchants on the coast and to the great value of the potent wine.[93] But how, in operational terms, did wine bottled in the Negev get to the sea for shipment to overseas markets?

---

between Tunisia and Egypt, see Goitein, *A Mediterranean Society,* 1:276–81.

85   See Bonifay, *Études,* 458–62, who judiciously distinguishes between technological and more general borrowing and true imitation wares.

86   Bonifay and Garnier, "Que transportaient donc," 14. See also N. Kruit and K. Worp, "Geographical Jar Names: Towards a Multi-Disciplinary Approach," *Archiv für Papyrusforschung und verwandte Gebiete* 46 (2000): 65–146, who marshal the papyri's rich array of geographic names that designated different types of amphorae (often associated with wine), and thus can illuminate "brands." I owe this reference to the kindness of Dr. Leslie MacCoull.

87   See note 70, above, on a possible fiscal incentive for the spread of LRA 1.

88   See Y. Israel, "Survey of Pottery Workshops, Naḥal Lakhish–Naḥal Besor," *Excavations and Surveys in Israel* 13 (1993): 106–7, who states that the survey intended to identify kiln workshops producing Gaza amphorae identified ten such. He does not list them, nor can they be identified from his map. Although the wording is confusing, he seems to say (107) that a workshop producing LRA 4 was indeed found at Beersheba. A kiln was also found at Halutza, but the type of ceramic produced there was unclear; see further note 99, below. For a convenient recent list of wine and oil presses in the region, see S. Kingsley, *A Sixth-Century AD Shipwreck off the Carmel Coast, Israel: Dor D and the Holy Land Wine Trade,* BAR International Series 1065 (Oxford, 2002), 126–27, 131, as well as the comprehensive study and catalogue of Frankel, *Wine and Oil Production in Antiquity.* On the economic development of these places and the wine trade, see I. Shatzman, "Economic Conditions, Security Problems and the Deployment of the Army in Later Roman Palestine: Part I: Economy and Population," in *The Late Roman Army in the Near East from Diocletian to the Arab Conquest,* ed. A. Lewin, P. Pellegrini, Z. T. Fiema, et al., BAR International Series 1717 (Oxford, 2007), 153–200, at 167–78.

89   B. J. Dolinka, "Be'er Shem-Birsama of the *Notitia Dignitatum*: A Prolegomenon to the 2006 Excavations," in Lewin et al., eds., *The Late Roman Army in the Near East,* 111–18, esp. 115–17 on wasters from the kiln production of Gaza amphorae.

90   J.-P. Brun, *Archéologie du vin et de l'huile dans l'Empire romain* (Paris, 2004), 145, 148.

91   A. H. M. Jones, *The Later Roman Empire, 284–602: A Social, Economic, and Administrative Survey* (Oxford, 1964), 842.

92   The growing literature on this question is summarized and much new data is adduced by C. E. P. Adams, *Land Transport in Roman Egypt: A Study of Economics and Administration in a Roman Province* (Oxford, 2007).

93   See on these winepresses Mayerson, "Wine and Vineyards of Gaza," and the references above, note 88. Export wines required a longer shelf life and the capacity to withstand the summer heat, and therefore tended to be stronger than most locally consumed wines: Tchernia, *Le vin de l'Italie romaine,* 29–30, hence surely part of their appeal. Gregory of Tours confirms that in Gaul, the wines of Laodikeia and Gaza were reckoned quite robust: *Historiarium libri X* 7.29, ed. B. Krusch and W. Levison, MGH ScriptRerMerov 1.1, 2nd ed. (Hanover, 1951), 348.11–12: "Misitque pueros unum post alium ad requirenda potentiora vina, Laticina videlicet adque Gazitina."

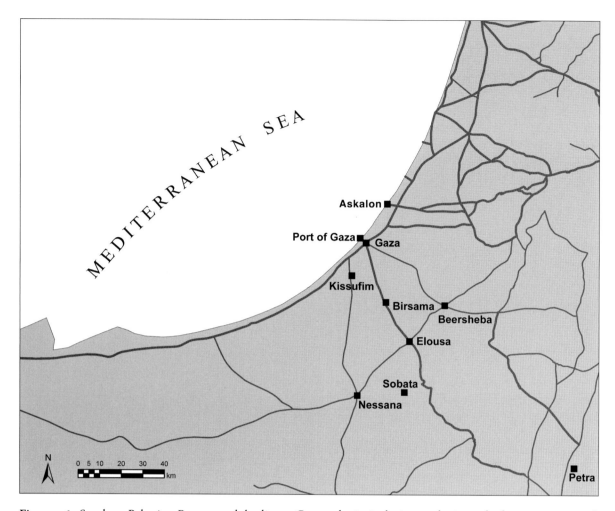

Figure 3.6. Southern Palestine. Roman roads leading to Gaza and principal wine-producing and other sites mentioned in the text (drawn by A. More)

By no coincidence, these inland vineyards lay mostly along the ancient Incense Road linking Petra with Gaza, which the military considerably improved in late antiquity.[94] In this part of the world, we would expect camels to play an important role in overland shipment.[95] In fact, a just-published terra-cotta bottle from the coast at Askalon (fig. 3.7) hints at the infrastructure that moved the wine to the coast.[96] Bottles of analogous design have turned up in Egypt, at Nag Hammadi (fig. 3.8), in Alexandria, and also at Aphrodisias.[97] They take the form of camels carry-

---

94 See, e.g., I. Roll, "Crossing the Negev in Late Roman Times: The Administrative Development of *Palaestina Tertia Salutaris* and of Its Imperial Road Network," in Lewin et al., eds., *The Late Roman Army in the Near East*, 119–30, with references to further bibliography; cf. C. Ben-David, "The Paved Road from Petra to the 'Arabah—Commercial Nabataean or Military Roman?" ibid., 101–10.

95 Discussion of the role camels played in late Roman logistics has taken off since the work of R. Bulliet, *The Camel and the Wheel* (Cambridge, Mass., 1975); see especially R. S. Bagnall, "The Camel, the Wagon and the Donkey in Later Roman Egypt,"

BASP 22 (1985): 1–6, and Adams, *Land Transport in Roman Egypt*, 52–56, 72–73, 79–81, with further references.

96 B. L. Johnson, *Ashkelon 2: Imported Pottery of the Roman and Late Roman Periods* (Winona Lake, [Ind.], 2008), 135, no. 392, where the object is implicitly dated to the Roman period. One is of course sorely tempted to think that these bottles once served wine to late Romans.

97 Oxford, Ashmolean Museum, inv. Dept. of Antiquities 1892.1176, from Nag Hammadi, ascribed to the third century; the different amphorae seem to be depicted on the similar camel bottle in the museum at Alexandria: see Pieri, *Le commerce du vin oriental*, 128, fig. 82. For the Aphrodisias bottle, see S. Applebaum, "Animal Husbandry," in *The Roman World*, ed. J. S. Wacher (London, 1987), 2:504–26, here 524, fig. 19.9. I owe

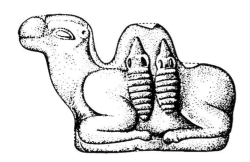
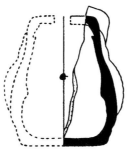

Figure 3.7.
Ceramic bottle in the form of a sitting camel loaded with amphorae. Askalon, A16/87.38.74.L87.FG22,23.(5) (courtesy of Prof. Lawrence E. Stager and the Leon Levy Expedition to Ashkelon)

Figure 3.8. Ceramic figurine of a standing camel loaded with amphorae, assigned to the 3rd century; from Nag Hammadi, Egypt (photo courtesy of Ashmolean Museum, University of Oxford, inv. Dept. of Antiquities 1892.1176)

ing amphorae two to a side, which sounds like the usual camel load of four *keramia* mentioned in the papyri. The Askalon bottle shows long, cylindrical amphorae reminiscent notably of the Gaza amphora LRA 4B, which was certainly manufactured in the Negev wineries.[98] In fact four of the large-format LRA 4B filled with wine—weighing some 25 kilograms, plus the weight of the amphora itself—would fit well the normal camel load specified in Diocletian's Price Edict and documented by the papyri.[99]

---

my knowledge of this last bottle to the kindness of Dr. Günder Varinlioğlu and her thorough follow-up on a conversation we had in the Images Collections at Dumbarton Oaks.
98 Pieri, *Le commerce du vin oriental*, 109–10.
99 Ibid., 105, notes capacities of 13–16 and 24–26 L for LRA 4A and B, respectively. The specific gravity of a sweet white wine

This mode of transport in turn probably answers the question raised earlier, why Negev potters, when they made bigger containers for their wine, did so by elongating the base container. As the bottles suggest, sets of long amphorae lay better against a camel's side than ones that would simply have expanded the original, rounder shape.

Could camel caravans transporting the precious white wine have been a familiar sight along the roads linking the desert vineyards to the sea? The answer comes from a spectacular mosaic pavement discovered in 1977 in the western Negev, at Kissufim, some 15 kilometers south of Gaza. A founder's inscription dates the floor of this basilical church to AD 576–78. Among other images, it shows a camel driver with a stick and a bunch of dates, together with a camel carrying amphorae, apparently four per side (fig. 3.9).[100]

---

should be above 1.002; the weight of the wine is therefore 24 × 1.002 (at least), to which must be added the weight of the container. One wonders immediately whether the inland kilns were producing both large and small versions of LRA 4. Judging from the ruler in the photo, Israel, "Survey of Pottery Workshops," 107, fig. 113, seems to show one of the large format amphorae at a kiln at Naḥal Bohu, i.e., 15 km inland. Even assuming a poor capacity efficiency ratio for LRA 4B of 1 kg per liter of wine carried, each large amphora, when filled, would weigh 50 kg. The hypothetical total maximum burden (4 × 50 kg =200 kg), which surely errs on the heavy side, comes close to the Diocletianic load of 600 Roman pounds (i.e., 194 kg), depending of course on the weight of LRA 4B, which Pieri does not specify. See Adams, *Land Transport in Roman Egypt*, 80.
100 R. Cohen, "The Marvelous Mosaics of Kissufim," *Biblical Archaeology Review* 6.1 (1980): accessed at the Biblical Archaeology Society Online Archive, on 26 November 2008; R. Cohen, "Kissufim," in *The New Encyclopedia of Archaeological Excavations in the Holy Land*, ed. E. Stern, A. Lewinson-Gilboa, and J. Aviram, vol. 4 (Jerusalem, 1993), 876–78; Y. Hirschfeld, "The Monasteries of Gaza: An Archaeological Review," in *Christian Gaza in Late Antiquity*, ed. B. Britton-Ashkelony and A. Kofsky (Leiden, 2004), 61–88, at 80–81. For the inscription, see *SEG* 30 (1983): 482–83, nos. 1688–93. The amphorae depicted on the mosaic were presumably the smaller LRA 4A, which were approximately half the size of the LRA 4B. The latter would appear to be heavy for a dromedary (see note 99, above). It

Figure 3.9. Orbikon the camel driver and his amphora load. From the mosaic pavement, dated AD 576–78, of a church at Kissufim, Israel, which stood 5 km from the Roman road connecting the Negev wineries to Gaza; collection of the Israel Antiquities Authority (photo © The Israel Museum, Jerusalem)

The site is on a wadi—and thus at least seasonally well supplied with water—5 kilometers off the Roman road that connected the wine-exporting centers of Elousa and Birsama to Gaza.[101] Date, site, and subject all point to the conclusion that the mosaic stems from the logistical system that delivered wine to the international port of Gaza. Camel caravans could have delivered their loads of amphorae in, at most, one or two nights of travel at their expected rate of some 60 kilometers a night; thus multiple trips per week were likely.[102] The trade of "Orbikon," as the mosaic names the driver, must have been remarkably profitable if he contributed to financing the magnificent mosaic.[103]

Whether one or more market events intervened between the bottling, transport by caravan, and seaside sale is unclear but worth asking. How in any case did it happen that the inland towns produced amphorae of the same type as Gaza's coastal workshops: Did Gaza entrepreneurs travel up-country to establish the export trade with migrant potters? Did local producers spontaneously imitate the prestigious coastal containers in order to sell their own production in its market niches? Or was respecting the norms of the metropolis expected of even distant potters?[104] Whatever the explanation, Palestine's

---

is a pleasure to thank Dr. Günder Varinlioğlu, who brought this mosaic to my attention. Given the date, one wonders whether the sumptuous decoration reflects a moment of prosperity that arose from the inheritance and concentration of wealth following the demographic changes wrought by the Justinianic plague.

101 The wadi empties into the Mediterranean less than 10 km southwest of Gaza; its modern vegetation is clearly visible on Google Earth.

102 L. Herbison and G. W. Frame, "Camels," in *Encyclopædia Britannica*, Encyclopædia Britannica Online, 2008, www.search.eb.com/eb/article-233465, accessed 26 November 2008.

103 The main donor was a deacon. Cohen, "Mosaics of Kissufim," identifies "OPBIKON" as a Greek personal name. I have not found a clear parallel. A plausible explanation comes to me

from Prof. Michael Sokoloff of the Hebrew University, via the good offices of my friend Prof. Deborah Tor of Notre Dame University. Sokoloff observes a name attested in Syriac documents of approximately this period that seems very close indeed to the camel driver's—"'WRBYQ"—and refers to J. P. Margoliouth, *Supplement to the Thesaurus Syriacus of R. Payne Smith* (Oxford, 1927), 10. Finally, according to Tor, late antique personal names ending in "–on" occur in both Aramaic and Hebrew in the Jerusalem Talmud. Both colleagues have my warm thanks.

104 Shatzman, "Economic Conditions," 176, deserves credit for raising this question. But his answer, that it was local producers attempting to lend a prestigious cachet to their product for the local market, appears to me unlikely if Tchernia's position on what did and did not make it into export amphorae (*Le vin de l'Italie romaine*, 29–30, 39) is well founded. For the apparent role of cities and their territories in defining amphora designs, see Reynolds, "Levantine Amphorae," 575.

sophisticated viticultural society and its feeder crafts required an overland transport industry to move the heavy amphorae to the coast. That industry presumably picked up where, in the third century, the slackening caravan trade of the old Incense Road left off. Barring some kind of special subvention, the further implication is that the profit to be made from southern Palestine's inland vineyards was hefty enough to justify the overland transport of amphorae heavy with wine. Nor was Palestine the sole such case. Land transport was probably also important for the ceramic and agrarian production of contemporary Africa, for example.[105]

Nevertheless, the contrast with other viticultural regions reinforces the impression that some Gaza wineries lay unusually far inland. Connoisseurs still appreciate the wines of the Moselle Valley and of Turkey's Marmara coast, regions that combine favorable soils and climate conditions with immediate access to waterways. Nergis Günsenin's research has shown that at Mount Ganos (modern Gaziköy), the amphora kilns stood close to the vineyards on the western shore of the Sea of Marmara. It may even be that clay was transported 20 kilometers across the sound to the island of Marmara, so that amphorae could be fired in the beachside kilns and filled with the island's wine.[106] Similarly, the many late Roman winepresses discovered in recent years in the Moselle Valley are located smack-dab in what still rank among Germany's choicest vineyards. That soil could have been used for vineyards, so powerful reasons militated for putting the presses right there.

From here, the barrels that dominated the Moselle wine industry could be rolled 20 or 30 meters down the slope to the riverbank. Cheap boat transport then moved them to Trier or the Rhine, the frontier zone, and beyond.[107]

The effort to understand production and transport facilities and their links to markets should encompass deeper synergies that helped shape the cost and conditions of production as well as distribution. The deduction that the big export industry of African Red Slip Ware piggybacked on state-sponsored transport of Africa's oil and—perhaps mainly—grain is by now familiar: stacks of dishes, bowls, and lamps traveled as a secondary cargo aboard subsidized ships whose main task was moving the annona to the capitals.[108] But another synergy is less well known. Massive production of olive oil generated tons of a by-product of extraordinary utility to the ceramic industry in a Mediterranean ecology where wood was at a premium: crushed olive pits and pressing waste, which burned hot and true. Pressing olives for oil produced an essentially free fuel for the kilns that made the masses of African amphorae and dishes exported around the late Roman Empire.[109] Presumably this valuable by-product encouraged ceramic production in other oil-producing areas as well, including in the kilns which fired the amphorae that transported the wine of Gaza.[110]

---

105   See M. Mackensen, *Die spätantiken Sigillata- und Lampentöpfereien von el Mahrine (Nordtunesien): Studien zur nordafrikanischen Feinkeramik des 4. bis 7. Jahrhunderts,* Münchner Beiträge zur Vor- und Frühgeschichte 50 (Munich, 1993), 1:57–59, emphasizing that the ceramic kilns of El Mahrine were favorably situated near major Roman roads leading to Carthage some 45–50 km away, depending on the route, and to other inland markets. The seasonal flow of the nearby lower Medjerda looks unpromising for regular water transport; ibid., 1:57 n. 34. For the deduction that significant quantities of olive oil were transported by land, including in large udders, to the weighing station of Carthage, where it was put in amphorae, see Peña, "Mobilization of State Olive Oil," 185–92, including on the relatively higher cost of udders. A similar situation is imaginable for Byzacena; see Bonifay and Garnier, "Que transportaient donc," 22.

106   N. Günsenin, "Medieval Trade in the Sea of Marmara: The Evidence of Shipwrecks," in *Travel in the Byzantine World,* ed. R. Macrides (Aldershot, 2002), 125–35, at 129–34, argues this from the absence of clay on the island of Marmara for the kilns that were built on its beach there, in order to fill the amphorae on the island where the grapes were grown.

107   For instance, at Piesport (Germany) the Roman wine press is 30 m from the river bank, as anyone can verify on Google Earth. On the press, see K.-J. Gilles in S. Faust, K.-J. Gilles, J. Hupe, et al., *Führer zu archäologischen Denkmälern des Trierer Landes,* Schriftenreihe des Rheinischen Landesmuseums Trier 35 (Trier, 2008), 158, with further references.

108   Bonifay and Garnier, "Que transportaient donc," 22, develop the plausible hypothesis that the fine ware traveled first and foremost with cargoes of grain rather than oil. On ceramics piggybacking on subsidized African annona transports, see, e.g., McCormick, "Bateaux de vie, bateaux de mort," 75–80, with further references.

109   On the highly probable use of waste from olive pressing to fire the kilns at El Mahrine, see Mackensen, *Die spätantiken Sigillata- und Lampentöpfereien,* 1:55–56, although he does not adduce any bioarchaeological evidence for that practice at this site. I am grateful to Prof. Alan Walmsley for discussion of the recent bioarchaeology of Syria and Palestine, including the burning properties of olive pits. See also the experimental data in T. Miranda, A. Esteban, S. Rojas, et al., "Combustion Analysis of Different Olive Residues," *International Journal of Molecular Sciences* 9 (2008): 512–25.

110   On olive production, see, in addition to the works cited in note 88, J. Magness, *The Archaeology of the Early Islamic Settlement in Palestine* (Winona Lake, Ind., 2003), 92–93.

A final packaging problem has often been raised. The extent to which barrels replaced amphorae in late antique holds remains imponderable. Experimental archaeology is needed to work out the exact efficiency advantage of Roman barrels, but they obviously were lighter than amphorae. Judging from modern barrels—bound with metal hoops, which should be heavier than the wooden ones that apparently predominated in antiquity[111]—a recent study of Roman barrels observed that a modern cask holding 225 liters weighs 57 kilograms, for a capacity efficiency of 4, which surpasses even the 3.7 rating attributed to some Africana 2 amphorae.[112] Given a wood barrel's inherent strength, one suspects that their efficiency only increased as barrels became bigger. A second advantage has passed practically unnoticed: the estimated capacity of the biggest Roman barrels commonly surpassed 1,000 liters, and barrels of 500 liters were anything but rare. One even approached 1,500 liters.[113] This size is reminiscent of *dolia,* the huge pottery vessels used for storage rather than transport, and in fact Roman texts mention these wooden vessels in the same breath as dolia.[114] Even if it could have been manufactured in durable fashion with the kind of capacity efficiencies we have seen for LRA 1 and 2, an equivalent transport amphora would have weighed more than half a ton when empty. Although building materials prove that late Romans moved heavy objects, such wine transport containers sound impractical and, in any case, do not appear to be attested in the late Roman period.[115]

According to a recent study, the barrel's efficiency advantage explains its progressive triumph over the amphora.[116] That efficiency advantage was probably clearest for high-volume transports. One would imagine that the skilled labor and the not inexpensive wood required to make them may have made barrels more costly than amphorae of similar capacity. It is conceivable that amphorae of the usual sizes, say some 20 to 100 liters, competed successfully with barrels. Indeed, rivalry with the barrel may in some way have spurred the apparent increase in efficiency of late antique amphorae.[117] However, for high-volume transports, the efficiency advantage of the barrel was probably hard to beat. Thus the historic shifts toward—or away from—barrels may be another token of the aggregate scale of the transportation of liquids and other goods. In fact, this hypothesis seems borne out by the relative proportions of surviving Roman barrels. Of the 88 barrels whose sizes can be estimated, 16 (18 percent) fall in the groups whose capacity runs between 2.5 and 100 liters, that is, common amphora sizes. The remaining 72 (82 percent) run between 120 and 1,440 liters, and the overwhelming majority of them could have held more than 400 liters.[118]

Celts invented barrels and Roman soldiers carried them across the empire. The great majority that survive come from northwestern Europe, a circum-

---

111 Marlière, *L'outre et le tonneau,* 170. However, Charlemagne insisted that on his well-run royal estates, some barrels at least should have iron hoops: "Volumus ut bonos barriclos ferro ligatos, quos in hostem et ad palatium mittere possint, iudices singuli praeparatos semper habeant"; *Capitulare de villis* 68, ed. A. Boretius, MGH Capit 1 (1883), 89.36–37. His statement shows both that the innovation coexisted with wooden hoops by ca. 800 at the latest and that iron hoops were considered superior.

112 Marlière, *L'outre et le tonneau,* 12; more precisely, the capacity efficiency of this modern barrel would be 3.95. For calculations of efficiency, see note 81, above. On the French shopping website Twenga.com I found modern oak wine barrels of approximately the same dimensions (95 × 70 cm) weighing 45 kg, which produces an even better efficiency capacity of 5. Peacock and Williams, *Amphorae and the Roman Economy,* 52, table 1, report Africana 2 Grande efficiencies between 3.27 and 3.59.

113 See Groups 3 and 5 of Marlière, *L'outre et le tonneau,* 164, 166.

114 E.g., in the early third century, Ulpian, *Dig.* 33.6.3, discussing whether the legacy of wine included the containers, seems to consider immobile *cupae* (on which term see below) as a subset of barrels (*cupae* or *cuppulae*), ed. *CIC* 1:509.17–19: "in doliis non puto verum, ut vino legato et dolia debeantur, maxime si depressa in cella vinaria fuerint aut ea sunt, quae per magnitudinem difficile moventur. in cuppis autem sive cuppulis puto admittendum et ea deberi, nisi pari modo immobiles in agro velut instrumentum agri erant." Cf. the African Arnobius the Elder, *Adversus nationes* 2.23, ed. C. Marchesi (Turin, 1953), 93.6–8, whose argument against innate Platonic ideas enumerates banal objects that someone raised with no experience of the outside world would be unable to recognize, including *dolia* and *cupae*: "Quid si adicias quaerere rota quid sit aut tribula, vannus dolium cupa, trapetum vomis aut cribrum, mola buris aut sarculum?"

115 For the earlier dolia ships, see Tchernia, *Le vin de l'Italie romaine,* 138–40.

116 Marlière, *L'outre et le tonneau,* 12.

117 See note 203, below.

118 Marlière, *L'outre et le tonneau,* 157–69; she suspects that the disproportion is an illusion created by the taphonomic circumstance that most barrels are known because they were used to line wells, a purpose that required large barrels. While there is certainly truth in this observation, I am not at all sure that it is the sole explanation of the apparent predominance of large barrels. Prof. van Doorninck rightly insisted in his comments on this essay that it takes a relatively high volume of goods contained for barrels to make economic sense over amphorae.

stance that may reflect their place of origin's preference for them. It certainly reflects conditions favoring preservation—barrels were often recycled there as well-linings and survive below the water table—and Europe's highly developed archaeological traditions. Barrels probably displaced amphorae at important sites in Roman Gaul in the second century.[119] But depictions in Spain and Italy prove that ancient barrels were not confined to northern Europe, and, as we will see below, they were also familiar in the late antique Levant.[120] The question of when and how much they came to figure as Mediterranean transport packaging remains unanswered. Sea evidence of any sort of organic container is scant. But barrels have been detected on board four ancient wrecks so far. In the English Channel, a late third-century wreck on the Isle of Guernsey carried many barrels and smaller kegs.[121] Off the French Riviera, a mid-second-century ship showed traces of barrel hoops and a seventh-century wreck preserved the bottom of a barrel, thanks to a layer of pitch that enclosed it.[122] A ship that went down off Grado around 150 also had a barrel in the bow.[123] Another barrel has turned up in what was probably the warehouse area of the early imperial harbor of Fos-sur-Mer.[124]

On land, written sources expand the picture. Lexically the situation is complicated by the way the word for a "storage tank" for wine (Lat. *cupa*—hence, via Low Germanic, our "cooper") came, between the first and third centuries, to include wooden transport barrels within its semantic field. A wooden tank in the original sense was found in Pompeii.[125] By 238, the wine producers around Aquileia were using lots of barrels for various purposes, including shipping, and the emperor Maximinus improvised a pontoon bridge from their casks; funerary inscriptions of coopers confirm the rise of the barrel in northeast Italy.[126] At Rome's river port, an inscription assigned to the late third century records fees for unloading and storing wine barrels (*cupae*); it implies that the bulk of fiscal wine imported up the Tiber arrived in the wooden containers. The scale of Roman consumption surely contributed to the comparative advantage of using very high-capacity barrels: that they were big explains why the highest fees went to the crane operators whose task was probably to move the casks from the river boat to the shore.[127]

Barrels loomed large in fifth-century Rome's sea imports, if we can judge from Valentinian III's attempt to restore or refurbish the state-organized river transports that brought goods up the Tiber—surely from the city's seaport at Portus Romanus. The emperor fixed the minimum capacity of such vessels as "twenty barrels" (*cupae*). It seems inherently expensive and therefore unlikely that wares would have been transferred at the harbor from amphorae or other containers into barrels for shipment the last 25 kilometers upstream to Rome's river port.[128] Barrels so dominated imports reaching Rome by sea that they furnished the standard measure for riverboat sizes. Valentinian III issued this law at Rome, and it explicitly concerns local transport; it does not necessarily imply that the "barrel" or "ton," as it

---

119 Marlière, *L'outre et le tonneau,* cf. 177.
120 See ibid., 40–43, 117–24, for summaries of the geography of archaeological attestation and iconographic evidence based on her extensive catalogues. For eastern written evidence of barrels in the late antique and medieval periods, see below, 76.
121 St. Peter Port 1, my 794 in the *Digital Atlas of Roman and Medieval Civilization* (see below, 81) (A. J. Parker, *Ancient Shipwrecks of the Mediterranean and the Roman Provinces*, BAR International Series 580 [Oxford, 1992], no. 1007 [hereafter cited as Parker]); Marlière, *L'outre et le tonneau,* 52–55.
122 Port-Vendres 3, my 702 (Parker no. 806); Marlière, *L'outre et le tonneau,* 59–60; and Saint-Gervais 2, my 789 (Parker no. 1001), on which see M. P. Jézégou, "Le mobilier de l'épave Saint-Gervais 2 (VIIᵉ s.) à Fos-sur-Mer (B.-du-Rh.)," in *Fouilles à Marseille: Les mobiliers (Iᵉʳ–VIIᵉ siècles ap. J. C.),* ed. M. Bonifay, M.-B. Carre, and Y. Rigoir, Études massaliètes 5 (Paris, 1998), 343–51, at 345. The Saint-Gervais barrel is not in Marlière.
123 My 350 (Parker no. 464); C. Beltrame and D. Gaddi, "Preliminary Analysis of the Hull of the Roman Ship from Grado, Gorizia, Italy," *International Journal of Nautical Archaeology* 36 (2007): 138–47, at 138; Marlière, *L'outre et le tonneau,* 89.
124 Marlière, *L'outre et le tonneau,* 60–61.

125 See note 114, above, on Ulpian and, in general, the discussion in Tchernia, *Le vin de l'Italie romaine,* 285–87.
126 Herodian, *Regnum post Marcum* 8.4.4, ed. C. M. Lucarini (Munich, 2005), 165.30–166.12, whose Greek periphrase for barrels—"κενὰ οἰνοφόρα σκεύη περιφεροῦς ξύλου"—the *Scriptores historiae augustae, Maximini* 22.4, ed. A. Chastagnol, *Histoire auguste: Les empereurs romains des IIᵉ et IIIᵉ siècles* (Paris, 1994), 672, rendered simply as "Ponte itaque cupis facto," indicating that the term had become unambiguous by the fourth century. On this and on the tombs of coopers, see Tchernia, *Le vin de l'Italie romaine,* 286–88.
127 *CIL* 6:1785, 31391, as analyzed and discussed by J. Rougé, "Ad ciconias nixas," *REA* 59 (1957): 320–28; for Roman cranes, see A. I. Wilson, "Machines in Greek and Roman Technology," in *The Oxford Handbook of Engineering and Technology in the Classical World,* ed. J. P. Oleson (Oxford, 2008), 337–66, at 342–45.
128 Valentinian III, *Novella* 29, *CTh* 2:127–28; that these were river vessels follows from the novel's title *De naviculariis amnicis,* on the manuscript authority of which see ibid., 2:71. On Tiber navigation, see McCormick, *Origins of the European Economy,* 485–86, with 406 n. 64.

were, was becoming a standard unit of ship capacity around the Roman Mediterranean.[129] Nevertheless, this development has consequences for late antique cargoes, as we will see when considering ship sizes.

The scarcity of ceramic dolia for storing wine has seemed puzzling in the rural establishments of Africa Proconsularis.[130] The riddle resolves when we listen to local late Roman texts, for cupae are not uncommon there. Mostly the term means the containers where wine was stored. As a young girl, St. Augustine's mother Monica used to sneak drinks when she was sent with a slave girl to fetch wine from the family storage cask ("de cupa uinum depromere"). In order to clarify a point in Scripture, Augustine mentions the familiar wine casks (*cupae*) arrayed on beams between the columns of wine cellars.[131] Some cupae were in fact transportable, as we learn from judicial proceedings of December 320 investigating the charge that a Donatist bishop and his ecclesiastical associates had stolen *acetum*—vinegar or fermented wine or must that was mixed with water to make *posca*, the refreshing drink of Roman civilization—from the state, or, more specifically, from a temple of Sarapis, along with the barrels (*cupas*) that contained it.[132]

What did such barrels transport? As at Rome and in St. Monica's cellar, wine is clearly the ware most frequently associated with cupae. For instance, a formula ascribed to Hero of Alexandria for calculating the volume of a cupa (κοῦπα) assumed it contained wine.[133] But late Roman barrels held other wares also. Operating on the empire's eastern front, Maurice foresaw that the late sixth-century army should travel with barrels (βουττία) of water, which he clearly distinguishes from ceramic *pithoi*.[134] Salt sounds plausible even if the documented case is exceptional, a trick that Frontinus (d. AD 103/4) claims floated supplies to a besieged northern Italian town in 43 BCE.[135] Beer seems irresistible if unproven.[136] A barrel from a probable dock area has remains of sardines embedded in the pitch that sealed it, and glass for recycling filled another shipboard barrel.[137]

Whether they be barrels or amphorae, containers are not the contained: understanding what they tell us about markets requires recognizing that their evidence about wares is indirect, and that further analysis must be undertaken in light of the wares and markets themselves. Thus, though learning that Palestinian containers around 450 represented an increasing proportion of total amphora imports into Gaul—where African containers had traditionally dominated—truly marks a step forward, it has

---

129 Tchernia, *Le vin de l'Italie romaine*, 291, seems to think otherwise.

130 J.-P. Brun, "Les pressoirs à vin d'Afrique et de Maurétanie à l'époque romaine," *Africa*, n.s., 1 (2003): 7–30, at 12, 14; cf. Bonifay, *Études*, 473.

131 *Confessiones* 9.8 (18), ed. L. Verheijen, CCSL 27 (Turnhout, 1981), 144.34–56; cf. her nursemaid's admonition, ibid., 9.8 (17), 143.24–30. Augustine invokes the image of the *cupa* probably although not unambiguously in the sense of a storage cask: e.g., *De moribus ecclesiae catholicae et Manichaeorum* 2.16.44, ed. J. Bauer, CSEL 90 (Vienna, 1992), 129.6–7: "magis ne inerit illud fel cum in cupa, quam cum in acinis fuerit?"; *Quaestiones in Heptateuchum* 2, *Quaestiones Exodi* 109, ed. J. Fraipont, CCSL 33 (Turnhout, 1958), 1213.1840–44, depicting the casks of wine arrayed on beams between the columns of wine cellars: "quod uulgo uocamus ancones, sicut sunt in columnis cellarum uinariarum, quibus incumbunt ligna quae cupas ferunt"; or ibid., 4, *Quaestiones Numerorum* 32, 254.745–47: "primitiae autem de fructibus quidem, sed iam redactis ab agro, sicut de massa, de lacu, de dolio, de cupa, quae primitus sumebantur." Or consider the happy hope in *De bono uiduitatis*, "that I might always find wine in my barrel (*in cupa mea*)": *Sermo* 11.3, ed. C. Lambot, CCSL 41 (Turnhout, 1961), 163.91–92, a genuine sermon reworked by Caesarius of Arles: see Dekkers, *Clavis patrum latinorum*, no. 111. The 200-some wine containers in which Donatus was aging his wine near Uzalis are identified only as *vasa*, and could have been wooden *cupae* as well: see notes 36 and 37, above.

132 *Gesta apud Zenophilum* (= *Appendix ad Optatum* 1), ed. C. Ziwsa, CSEL 26 (Vienna, 1893), 193.27–94.1; 195.2–24; 196.19–26. The barrels are referred to as belonging to the fisc ("de cupis fisci") and as being "in templo Sarapis" (193.29–30). The implication is probably that the state had taken over and was storing things in a temple building that had gone out of use. I am grateful to Roger Bagnall for discussing this passage with me. For examples of the imperial government using disused temples, see Bagnall, "Models and Evidence in the Study of Religion in Late Roman Egypt," 33. On the Roman drink, see Tchernia, *Le vin de l'Italie romaine*, 13. The East Asian predilection for vinegar-based drinks is helping to make them fashionable again today: see, e.g., T. Cecchini, "Case Study: Dropping Acid," *New York Times Style Magazine*, 9 November 2008, 52.

133 *Stereometrica* 1.51.1–2, ed. J. K. Heiberg, *Heronis Alexandrini opera quae supersunt omnia*, 5 (Stuttgart, 1976): 54.28–56.9; cf. 1.52, 56.10–17, on βούτης, apparently designating another kind of barrel. See in general Marlière, *L'outre et le tonneau*, 173–74, which considers chemical traces of wine inside Roman barrels.

134 Maurice, *Strategicon* 10.4, ed. G. T. Dennis, trans. E. Gamillscheg, *Das Strategikon des Maurikios*, CFHB 17 (Vienna, 1981), 348.41–350.51.

135 Frontinus attributes the stratagem to Aulus Hirtius (who had served with Caesar in Gaul) at the siege of Modena: *Strategemata* 3.14.3, ed. R. I. Ireland (Leipzig, 1990), 86.

136 Marlière, *L'outre et le tonneau*, 173.

137 Ibid., 61; on the Grado wreck, see note 123, above.

rightly been noted that the correct inference to draw about markets and goods is not that one region outpaced another but that new imports of one ware, Palestinian wine, entered the marketplace alongside the long-standing imports of African oil.[138] Since local wine was surely available, the new import indicates the development of specialized demand in late Roman Gaul.

Valuable though it is, such a conclusion is tempered by an elementary but essential observation. To assess the volume of imports—indispensable for considering the value of the imports—one must multiply the estimated number of containers by the volume of the contained. It is plainly misleading to think solely in terms of the ratio of eighteen African to sixty eastern Mediterranean amphorae that have been identified as arriving at Marseille between ca. 425 and 450, when the total contents of the recovered African containers came to around 1,260 liters, versus a total of 1,138 liters for the latter.[139] The obvious next step is to compare the value of the contents. If the African amphorae held oil of the very highest quality, and the eastern ones conveyed wine of similar quality, we could get a first crude estimate of their relative values from Diocletian's Price Edict, according to which the most expensive oil would cost 40 denarii and the highest-quality wine would cost 30 denarii per sextarius. By these hypothetical lights, the value of the oil imported into Marseille would be about 50 percent higher than that of the wine.[140]

Much work remains to be done before the containers that transported wares to markets can shed their full light on the economy of which they were a part. The ships that carried those containers are no less promising. That promise is not without its own complications, however, and it is to the accumulating wealth of shipwreck evidence, including the containers, that we turn next.

Ships and Markets

As the postulated Gaza camel trains suggest, wares, markets, and the merchants who made them happen were by no means confined to the sea. Nor was water transport limited to long-distance voyages. The coastal geography of the Byzantine Empire encouraged shorter-range shipping. Then as now, Constantinople's magnificent setting made very short water trips an essential part of the capital region's transport infrastructure.[141] The smaller vessels just discovered at Yenikapı, the site in Istanbul of the Theodosian harbor, should illustrate this vital component on the spectrum of Byzantine navigation.[142] At a larger scale, the Aegean and the Black Sea are recognizably distinct shipping zones, and some of the ships on them likely specialized in short-distance routes.[143] But a short distance need not always mean small ships. A very big middle Byzantine vessel bearing, if they were filled, an apparent minimum of 200 tons worth of local wine amphorae has been found off the island of Marmara in that wine-producing region of Mount Ganos. Could this have been a barge that specialized in short-distance deliveries? If so, the vessel may have been transporting new amphorae to be filled with fresh wine on the island vineyard or moving just-filled amphorae to some nearby depot, presumably the nearby harbor of Ganos.[144]

---

138 Pieri, *Le commerce du vin oriental*, 168. See further the considerations of Elton, "Economy of Southern Asia Minor."
139 Bonifay, *Études*, 446–47. The comparison is of course hypothetical and approximate. We have arbitrarily assumed that the oil and wine were each of top quality; differing assumptions produce different results, but this at least shows that the exercise is possible. Bonifay compares African Keay 35 with eastern LRA 1, 3, and 4; he does not specify the proportion of Keay 35A vs. 35B, which he identifies (471–73) as likely containing mostly wine and fish sauce or oil, respectively. For wine in LRA 1, see above, note 69; for LRA 3 and 4, Pieri, *Le commerce du vin oriental*, 101, 110–14.
140 Diocletian, *Edictum de maximis* 2.1–7, 3.1–2, ed. S. Lauer, *Diokletians Preisedikt* (Berlin, 1971), 100–103. At 0.547 L, the oil comes to 2303.47 sextarii worth 92,138.9 d. (1260 / .547 = 2303.47 sextarii × 40 d.); the wine to 62,413.16 d. (1138 / .547 =2080.44 sextarii × 30 d.).

141 For examples of very local ninth-century ship movements, see McCormick, *Origins of the European Economy*, R386b, R582.
142 The best publication to date is the exhibition catalog *Gün ışığında: İstanbul'un 8000 yılı; Marmaray, Metro, Sultanahmet kazıları* (Istanbul, 2008), 165–299, a copy of which I owe to the kindness of Alessandra Ricci of the Koç Institute for Anatolian Studies, Istanbul. I am grateful to my colleagues Nergis Günsenin, Sheila Matthews, Cemal Pulak, and Korhan Bircan for arranging for me to visit the extraordinary excavation site in June 2008, and for helpful discussion of the ongoing discoveries.
143 McCormick, *Origins of the European Economy*, 543–44. See also the discussion of potential (as suggested by geography) or actually documented local shipping nodes in the *TIB*, e.g., 1:103–4; 3:96–97, etc., and the comments of A. J. Parker, "Artifact Distributions and Wreck Locations: The Archaeology of Roman Commerce," in *The Maritime World of Ancient Rome*, ed. R. L. Hohlfelder, Memoirs of the American Academy in Rome, supp. vol. 6 (Ann Arbor, 2008), 177–96, at 190–94.
144 Günsenin, "Medieval Trade," 129–31, "Tekmezar I." The possibility of a barge is suggested by the proportions of the amphora spread reported by Günsenin (40 × 20 m), the huge size of the cargo (which she estimates as a minimum of 21,600

The Nile aside, eastern Mediterranean rivers were less favorable than western European ones for extensive fluvial merchant shipping. Yet there must have been short-range river transport on the lower stretches of some Byzantine rivers outside the Danube.[145] Western Europe's river shipping is deeply documented. Current archaeological, environmental, and historical investigations of it can serve as a model for what some day might be possible along the navigable rivers of the middle Byzantine Empire.[146]

Yet ever since Hesiod,[147] Mediterranean minds connected commerce to the sea. Countless ancient and Byzantine writers casually allude to the connection. Preaching not far from the harbor at Hippo, Augustine spontaneously linked shipping, a cosmopolitan outlook, and moneymaking. Four great careers tempted his flock: farming, state service, the law courts, and the sea. Of the last, the African bishop concluded: "'Sailing and trading,' another says, 'that's great!' It's great to know many provinces, make money everywhere, not be beholden in town to some mighty man, to always travel in foreign lands and nourish the mind on a variety of business and nations, and then to come home, rich with the profits!"[148] Around the same time, for Severian of Gabala—whom Photius would repeat ca. 850—all things answered to God's purpose: by God's command, the sun supplies its rays, the earth its fruits, and the sea delivers merchandise.[149] Although he was well aware that some traders traveled overland, Chrysostom also associated merchants and the sea.[150] In the very different world of the eighth-century caliphate, John of Damascus's native city was scarcely coastal and he spent much of his life in the desert monastery of Mar Saba. Yet he too smelled salt water when he thought of merchants. He draws on examples to illustrate the all-pervasive role of faith in life: farmers rely on the soil to survive, and merchants entrust their lives to the wood (of ships).[151] In Constantinople a century later, Photius thought of merchants on long roads burdened by harsh weather and bandits, and by dangerous sea voyages.[152]

John of Damascus echoed an earlier Greek father when he reasoned that absent the sea, merchants would not be able to "import what was in short supply in each place, or export what was surplus." Among late Romans and Byzantines, even men of the cloth grasped the economics of transport, of supply and demand, displaying once again their familiarity with Temin's instrumental mode of economic behavior. These ecclesiastics understood that the sea linked supply and demand: it connected markets.[153] Or

---

amphorae), and the photos of the wreck shown at the Spring Symposium of Byzantine Studies, Birmingham, U.K., April 2000. The harbor is about 20 km distant across the sound.

145 A. Kazhdan, *ODB* 3:1797–98. For Danube traffic in this period, see, e.g., McCormick, *Origins of the European Economy*, 553–57.

146 To cite only a few examples from the French-speaking world: A. Dumont, ed., *Archéologie des lacs et des cours d'eau* (Paris, 2006); É. Rieth, *Des bateaux et des fleuves: Archéologie de la batellerie du néolithique aux teomps modernes en France* (Paris, 1998); and the articles, with further bibliography, in O. Kammerer and O. Redon, eds., *Le fleuve*, Médiévales 36 (Paris, 1999).

147 Hesiod, *Opera et dies* 631–49.

148 Augustine, *Enarrationes in Psalmos*, In Ps. 136:3, ed. E. Dekkers and J. Fraipont, CCSL 40:20–22.

149 Severian of Gabala, *In incarnationem domini*, ed. R. F. Regtuit, "Severian of Gabala: Homily on the Incarnation of Christ (CPG 4204)" (Ph.D. diss., Vrije Universiteit, Amsterdam, 1992), 248.219–221: Πάσης τοίνυν τῆς κτίσεως στασιαζούσης ὁ θεὸς ἐκέλευσε τῇ κτίσει μὴ ἀφηνιᾶν, ἀλλὰ παρέχειν τὸν ἥλιον τὴν ἑαυτοῦ ἀκτίνα, τὴν γῆν τοὺς ἑαυτῆς καρπούς, τὴν θάλασσαν τὰς ἐμπορίας, τοὺς ἀστέρας τὴν ἑαυτῶν φαιδρότητα. Cf. Photius, *Bibliotheca* cod. 277, ed. R. Henry, *Photius, Bibliothèque*, 8 vols. (Paris, 1959–91), 8:134.37–42, who erroneously ascribes the work to Chrysostom, and gives the variants of the "vulgate" version of the text—including the interesting addition of the words ἰχθύας καί before τὰς ἐμπορίας, which drives home the association no less powerfully: the sea conjures up fish and business.

150 Chrysostom often seems to assume that merchants go to sea, for instance when he says that no merchant stops going to sea just because he has suffered a shipwreck and lost his cargo, *Epistola ad Theodorum lapsum* 1, ed. J. Dumortier, *Jean Chrysostome: A Théodore*, SC 117 (Paris, 1966), 48.13–16, or when he compares a merchant's relation with the sea to that of a farmer with the land, *In Iohannem homiliae* 19.3, PG 59:124. Of course he was well aware that some merchants also travel overland. Elsewhere, for instance, he observes that merchants face danger on both land and sea, from robbers as well as pirates: *In Genesim homiliae* 63.5, PG 54:546.

151 John of Damascus, *Expositio fidei* 84, ed. P. B. Kotter, *Die Schriften des Johannes von Damaskos*, 2, Patristische Texte und Studien 12 (Berlin, 1973), 187.13–16: Ἐκτὸς γὰρ πίστεως ἀδύνατον σωθῆναι· πίστει γὰρ πάντα, τά τε ἀνθρώπινα τά τε πνευματικά, συνίστανται. Οὔτε γὰρ γεωργὸς ἐκτὸς πίστεως τέμνει γῆς αὔλακα, οὐκ ἔμπορος μικρῷ ξύλῳ τὴν ἑαυτοῦ ψυχὴν τῷ μαινομένῳ τῆς θαλάσσης πελάγει παραδίδωσιν . . . .

152 Photios, *Homilia* 2.3, ed. Laourdas, 15.10–19.

153 Theodoret of Cyr, *Ep.* 30.8, ed. Y. Azéma, *Théodoret de Cyr: Correspondance*, 1, SC 40 (Paris, 1955), 96.3–14, developing an idea that was wittily apropos in a letter addressed to the bishop of Seleukeia, the port of Antioch: Τέμνειν ἡ θάλαττα τὰς ἠπείρους ἀμφοτέρας νομίζεται, τὸν μέσον τούτων χῶρον κατέχειν διαταχθεῖσα. Ἂν δέ τις τὸ ἀληθὲς ἐρευνῆσαι θελήσῃ, συνάπτει μᾶλλον ἢ τέμνει τὰ πέρατα· ῥᾳδίαν γὰρ τοῖς ἐμπόροις καὶ ταχεῖαν τῶν ἀναγκαίων ποιεῖσθαι τὴν κομιδὴν παρέχουσα, τὴν ἀντίπεραν ἤπειρον τρέχειν ἐνταῦθα παρασκευάζει, καὶ ταύτην πρὸς ἐκείνην ὁρμᾶν, καὶ τὴν ὀθόνην ἐκτείνειν, καὶ κινεῖν τὰ πηδάλια. Εἰ δὲ

rather, they understood that ships connected Mediterranean markets. One of the single most expensive capital goods in the ancient economy, ships constitute a key chapter in economic history even without their cargoes. A. J. Parker's foundational catalogue of Mediterranean shipwrecks marked a new phase in assembling that data for economic history.[154] But the data have not remained static. Intensifying exploration discovers new ships in remarkable numbers. The past fifteen years have brought a dozen to light around the island of Marmara.[155] The spectacular discoveries at Yenikapı have repeatedly been revised upward, reaching some thirty vessels as of June 2008. Seventeen new ships were discovered in Sardinia in 1999–2000.[156] Individual wrecks show up almost monthly.

Scholars have turned to the new data with alacrity. Splendidly detailed excavation and publication of well-preserved wrecks such as Yassı Ada open rare but magnificent windows on *one* specific voyage that, as it turns out, failed to reach its destination. Given their tremendous cost in money and man hours, such publications will remain rare. Moreover, the full interpretive potential of these well-published excavations emerges only when they are set against the large data set of all imperfectly known wrecks. As frustrating as hundreds of poorly published wrecks can be, such large numbers muffle the "noise" of imperfection and error. Historians and archaeologists often struggle to accept this fundamental precept of modern economic investigation, conditioned as we are to exhaustively investigate one small source or site at the expense of the wider view made possible by hundreds of sometimes faulty pieces of data.

The abundant if imperfect new data evince broad patterns to which each shipwreck adds a uniquely revealing stroke. The patterns of ancient communications, their intensity, and their infrastructure offer precious proxy data illuminating the arteries and pulse of the ancient economy. The wrecks do not tell us directly how much cargo was loaded in Alexandria or Askalon, traveled up the Aegean, and was actually unloaded at Constantinople in a given period. But they do testify to the communications that moved on this and other routes, and so indirectly to the shipments that actually arrived. In other words shipwrecks, much like the amphorae, offer another type of indirect information: proxy data, such as modern economists use to assess current economic developments. To maximize the testimony of shipwrecks on the ancient economy, three considerations seem basic. We need to derive new data from independent sources to compare with the wrecks; we should leverage the economic significance of the shipwreck data by viewing it in aggregate in a geodatabase; finally, we must know what we do not know.

Texts tell us more if we mine them beyond the voyages they explicitly document to derive new analytical data from the proxy data they contain. From written sources we can construct databases of communications that lend themselves to different kinds of spatial analysis: the movements of traveler X from Rome to Constantinople or of letter Y from Carthage to Rome.[157] Scholars have yet to draw on the superb prosopographies of the late Roman or middle Byzantine periods to compare the travels they document with shipwrecks. The methodological advantage is clear: travelers' movements recorded in texts survive independently of the shipwrecks. Because of this independence, and because information on travelers' movements is considerably more

---

καὶ ἤπειρος ἦν ἡ θάλασσα, τίς ἂν ἴσχυσε τῶν ἐμπόρων, τοσαύτης ὁδοῦ προκειμένης, ἢ τὸ ἐνδέον ἑκάστῃ χώρᾳ φέρειν, ἢ τὸ περιττὸν ἐκφέρειν; Νῦν δὲ αὕτη τὰ νῶτα τοῖς πλεῖν βουλομένοις παρέχουσα, καὶ τῶν πωλούντων καὶ τῶν ὠνουμένων τὰς χρείας ἀποπληροῖ. John of Damascus echoed this thought, explicitly invoking supply of what is in surplus and demand for what is lacking, in *Sacra parallela*, PG 96:48C: Θάλασσα συνάπτει δι' ἑαυτῆς ἀκώλυτον τοῖς ναυτιλομένοις τὴν ἐπιμιξίαν παρεχομένη, καὶ πλούτου πρόξενος ἐμπόροις γίνεται, καὶ τὰς τοῦ βίου χρείας ἐπανορθοῦται ῥᾳδίως· ἐξαγωγὴν μὲν τῶν περιττῶν τοῖς εὐθηνουμένοις παρεχομένη, ἐπανόρθωσιν δὲ τοῦ λείποντος χαριζομένη τοῖς ἐνδεέσιν.

154 Parker, *Ancient Shipwrecks*. This essay was already completed when I gained access to the thoughtful comments of Parker, "Artifact Distributions and Wreck Locations," with its valuable suggestions on how, e.g., to detect economically significant patterns from cargo distributions.

155 Günsenin, "Medieval Trade," 129–32; cf. her website: www.nautarch.org.

156 R. D'Oriano and E. Riccardi, "Les épaves d'Olbie," in *Barbares en Méditerranée de la Rome tardive au début de l'Islam*, ed. S. Kingsley (London, 2004), 89–95.

157 This is the method that I applied for the eighth and ninth centuries in McCormick, *Origins of the European Economy*, 592–604. More studies are beginning to apply similar methods, for instance the network analysis of affinities among peoples and places in the ninth-century northern seas as they appear in the *Life* of the missionary St. Anskar, mapped against the archaeologically documented movement of material goods in the same period by S. M. Sindbæk, "The Small World of the Vikings: Networks in Early Medieval Communication and Exchange," *Norwegian Archaeological Review* 40 (2007): 59–74.

abundant and precise than that on the wrecks will ever be, they expand and correct the testimony from the sea bottom.

Other series of data call out for similar treatment. As we have seen, archaeologists are making the origins and movement of ceramic vessels ever more clear. But so far the resulting patterns over time and space are rarely laid out *next* to those related to shipwrecks and people. Coins offer more exact chronology and geography. A new study of how Byzantine coins moved around the Mediterranean uncovers directional axes that fit what we know of shipping, of ceramics, and of broad economic trends.[158] A next important step would compile the numismatic data into a geodatabase and, again, compare in detail movements of coins with those of ships, people, and ceramics.

Each type of source opens another window on a different facet of the reality of early shipping and the economic movements it implies. For example, late Roman astrologers drew horoscopes for merchants in northern ports who anxiously awaited ships overdue from the southern Mediterranean. In some ways, the wreck evidence looks different from that offered by fifth-century astrology. The horoscopes show what the freighters loaded for northern markets. In an African port, one had taken on camels, expensive curtains, bed furnishings, and silver-decorated litters; in Alexandria, another had stowed papyrus, pet birds, bronze cooking vessels, and a specially designed cabinet filled with medicine.[159] The warm conditions of the Mediterranean may militate against preserving the bones of pet birds and camels; so far only the medicine cabinet and cookware have archaeological parallels on the seabed.[160] Of course, the missing cargoes of papyrus, curtains, and the like are largely perishable. In other ways, however, the horoscopes fit the wreck evidence—for instance, when they underscore the potential variety of a ship's cargo.[161] Certainly the Genizah letters indicate that diversity was common, even within packaged shipping bundles.[162] Some well-preserved and excavated wrecks do show substantial variety of cargo.[163] But did cargo heterogeneity vary by period and routes?

Meticulous studies of individual shipwrecks show us more when viewed against the broader backdrop of all shipwrecks. Like it or not, economic history requires simplifying and aggregating the data. We must organize the available shipwreck data in geodatabases, the only practical way of analyzing complexes of evidence which number in the hundreds. A geodatabase is a spatial database whose essential data—shipwrecks, geographic coordinates, date, types of cargo, size, and so on—can be interrogated over time and space. Indispensable breadth can be achieved only at the cost of depth. Our geodatabase includes approximate geographic coordinates, and it functions as part of a Geographic Information System (GIS)—in our case, ARCMAP 9.2. To that end,

---

158 C. Morrisson, "La monnaie sur les routes fluviales et maritimes des échanges dans le monde méditerranéen (VIᶜ–IXᶜ siècle)," in *L'acqua nei secoli altomedievali (Spoleto, 12–17 aprile 2007)*, Settimane de studio del centro italiano di studi sull'alto medioevo 55 (Spoleto, 2008), 631–70.

159 *Catalogus codicum astrologorum graecorum*, vol. 1, *Codices florentini*, ed. A. Olivieri (Brussels, 1898), 102–4; cf. ibid., vol. 6, *Codices vindobonenses,* ed. G. Kroll (Brussels, 1903), 14; and esp. G. Dagron and J. Rougé, "Trois horoscopes de voyages en mer," *REB* 40 (1982): 117–33, here 123–25, 129–30.

160 E. Ciabatti, F. Nicosia, E. Riccardi, et al., "La nave delle spezie," *Archeo: Attualità del passato* 58 (1989): 22–31, from a wreck of the second–first century BCE, off Livorno; copper cookware: Grazel 2 (my 358; Parker no. 483). I am grateful to my colleague Noreen Tuross for insights into the effect of salt water on bone. Since part of the point of the astrologer's handbook is to show how marvelous the identifications of the cargoes were, it is not impossible that the author selected particularly unusual cargoes. Nevertheless, with more than 700 ancient shipwrecks from the Roman Empire, one might expect a bit more overlap!

161 See in general Parker, "Cargoes, Containers and Stowage," 89–90, 96.

162 Goitein, *A Mediterranean Society,* 1:332–39.

163 For mixed cargoes from the fifth and eleventh centuries, see, e.g., Santamaria, *L'épave Dramont "E,"* 27–97. Yassı Ada's detectible cargo consisted essentially of two types of amphorae: see G. F. Bass, "The Pottery," in G. F. Bass, F. H. van Doorninck Jr., et al., *Yassı Ada,* vol. 1, *A Seventh-Century Byzantine Shipwreck* (College Station, Tex., 1982), 155–88; van Alfen, "New Light," 202–13, has deduced from their metrology that different subtypes of LRA 1 could have been designed for three different types of liquids. Prof. van Doorninck suggests (personal communication) that these liquids should be interpreted as red (ῥούσιον, i.e., boiled sweet) and white (ἄσπρον, i.e., dry) wine and olive oil, on the basis of the density ratios of the two types of wine recorded in the poorly dated Byzantine metrological treatise that may have been compiled in the eleventh or twelfth centuries and is preserved in the fourteenth-century MS, Vatican, Biblioteca Apostolica, Pal. graec. 367, fols. 88–91, ed. E. Schilbach, *Byzantinische metrologische Quellen* (Düsseldorf, 1970), Text III.1, pp. 126–30, here 127.119–21. He kindly informs me further that after Yassı Ada's hold was loaded as full as possible with globular amphorae, reused LRA 1 amphorae were packed into the small space left between them and the deck beams. The Serçe Limanı wreck carried some perishable cargo, in addition to glass for recycling and wine and olive oil amphorae as well as some small packages of Islamic ceramics; G. F. Bass, ed., *Serçe Limanı: An Eleventh-Century Shipwreck* (College Station, Tex., 2004), 265–71.

some of my students and I worked with Harvard's Center for Geographic Analysis to build a simple geodatabase of shipwrecks from the first 1,500 years of our era.[164] A rough first draft involved a handful of key data about 1,034 shipwrecks at the time that this study was drafted. We aim to put it online as part of the free, Web-based set of geodatabases that form *The Digital Atlas of Roman and Medieval Civilization*.[165] The *Digital Atlas* will facilitate the creation of fine maps in standard cartographic format as well as interfaces with Google Earth or other satellite photos, and the format lends itself to spatial analyses of the sort that follow.

As of May 2008, ongoing research had added 220 (27 percent more) new wrecks, including northern ones, to those that Parker's magnificent repertory had already assembled for our period.[166] We have also updated the data on many older wrecks. Of the new wrecks, 136 are Mediterranean and strikingly few are undated. This increased success in determining their age reflects advancing knowledge of later ceramics, which remain the essential element in dating most wrecks.[167]

Figure 3.10 shows all 309 shipwrecks, old and new, broadly dated to the period between AD 300 and 1500. Right off the bat it refutes the argument that mapping shipwrecks reveals only where people like to scuba dive. Even leaving aside the deepwater wrecks emerging from robotic surveys—some of which the surveyors have generously communicated to us and figure on this map—the distribution of wrecks depicted in figure 3.10 is in no way confined to vacation hot spots. Second, the new wrecks are equally distributed in the western and eastern Mediterranean. Third, the poorly dated wrecks occur mostly along the same shipping routes as the new dated wrecks, perhaps hinting that they went down around the same time.

The new late Roman finds show continuing activity in the western Mediterranean. They also thicken the evidence for shipping in the eastern basin that was notably scarce in the original repertory. In fact, the new Mediterranean wrecks from 300 to about 1000 lie predominantly in the eastern sea; more ships from the High Middle Ages, down to 1500, occur in the western Mediterranean, even as finds continue in the east. Insofar as general navigating conditions allowed, ships on long-distance runs preferred the safer, northern rim of the sea. Although ships certainly sailed along the southern shores, local conditions there may have induced them to stay farther out to sea, and because of the state of modern archaeology as well as seabed conditions in the coastal countries, wreck reports in any case remain exceedingly rare.[168] Nevertheless, the ships from the southern rim are not completely invisible, at least indirectly. The powerful economic impetus emanating from late Roman Africa and Alexandria seems to me to explain the clustering of wrecks in two bottlenecks on the northbound routes. Shipwrecks with African cargoes, likely headed for Rome, cluster off the west coast of Sicily.[169] Similarly, some of

---

164   The main work on this particular database has been done by myself, Dr. J. Kirsten Atagouz, Kelly Lyn Gibson, and Alex Medico More, with unwavering GIS support from Dr. Guoping Huang, Dr. Wendy Guan, and of course Professor Peter Bol and the entire staff of Harvard's new Center for Geographic Analysis. Many colleagues in underwater archaeology have generously supplied additional information.

165   This project, the *Digital Atlas of Roman and Medieval Civilizations,* has been publicly available in a beta version since May 2010 under the aegis of the Center for Geographic Analysis of Harvard University: darmc.harvard.edu.

166   As of July 2010, the total has grown to 1,064.

167   Only seven newly discovered wrecks are dated with no greater specificity than between AD 1 and 1500; so far, just under half of all new wrecks (fifty-four) have been dated to within one century.

168   On this navigational fact, see J. H. Pryor, *Geography, Technology, and War: Studies in the Maritime History of the Mediterranean, 649–1571*, 2nd ed. (Cambridge, 1992), 20–24. As Prof. van Doorninck observes, Synesius makes exactly this nautical point when ca. AD 400 he described his voyage out of sight of the African coast in his *Ep.* 5, in *Synesii Cyrenensis epistolae*, ed. A. Garzya (Rome, 1979), 13.14–15.10. Obvious exceptions are the ships from Dor, Israel: see Kingsley, *A Sixth-Century AD Shipwreck*, 1–5, who notes (4) the fortuitous erosion of the sand deposits that had covered these wrecks, and the report of ship cargoes dating from the fourth century BC to the seventh century AD in the eastern port of Alexandria: www.archeologie-sous-marine.culture.fr/. Signs of suspected shipwrecks were also detected off Askalon, but they are believed to be deeply buried in the sediment piled up by local conditions: S. Wachsmann, "Underwater Survey, 1996–1997," in *Ashkelon*, vol. 1, *Introduction and Overview (1985–2006)*, ed. L. E. Stager, J. David Schloen, and D. M. Master, Final Reports of the Leon Levy Expedition to Ashkelon 1 (Winona Lake, Ind., 2008), 97–99. Note that the maps that I made for this article do not show ships whose dating spans exceed three centuries; there are some poorly dated wrecks in this zone.

169   Late Roman wrecks off Sicily: Imera (my shipwreck no. 383, Parker no. 514, with African amphorae); "Isis" (my no. 387; not in Parker), with presumably a grain cargo, and a few amphorae, mostly African, see A. M. McCann, "The Isis Shipwreck, Skerki Bank," in *Barbarian Seas: Late Rome to Islam,* ed. S. Kingsley (London, 2004), 54–60; Levanzo 1 (my 446, unpublished, knowledge of which I owe to Jeffrey G. Royal) with ceramic tubes and

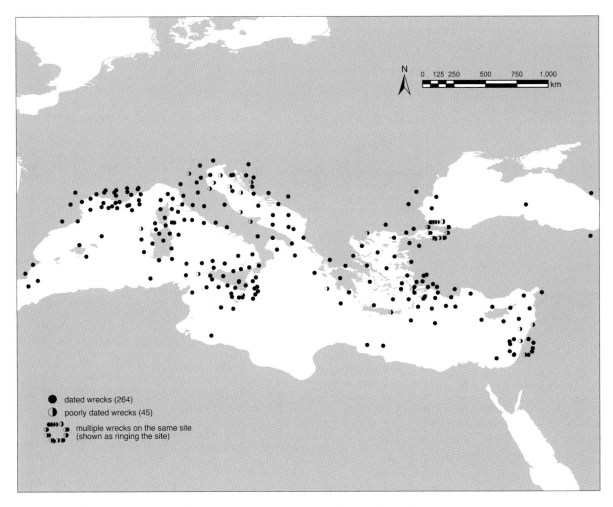

Figure 3.10. Total sites of new and old shipwrecks, AD 300–1500 (drawn by A. More)

the ships that went down off Rhodes, at the eastern entrance to the Aegean, must have been bound from or to Constantinople, possibly from Alexandria as well as other Levantine ports.[170] The chronology also

echoes long-term shipping rhythms. Rhodes-area wrecks date from the entire period between 300 and 1500: the markets of the Aegean and Constantinople never lost their attraction.[171] Off western Sicily,

---

tableware, both of which would fit Africa well (cf. on African "vaulting" tube production Bonifay, *Études*, 441–42); Triscina 3 (my no. 935, Parker no. 1179), "'spatheia' and cylindrical amphoras," which is a good description of a typically African cargo. Capo Granitola 4 (my 170; Parker no. 232) was carrying "Asiatic" marble, and so not obviously on the Africa to Rome route, if the description is reliable. One or another of these particular ships could have been heading farther north, toward Marseille or Arles, but in the grand stream of shipping, until sometime in the fifth century they will have been far fewer than those making for the great capital. For the contraction of the Roman market, see note 206, below.

170 On the rise of Alexandria to late antique shipping supremacy, see McCormick, *Origins of the European Economy*, 104–10; for Egyptian merchants trading in Palestinian wine, see note 16, above. The database shows nine late antique wrecks between the fourth and seventh centuries. Four of the cargoes are unidentified

amphorae, two show LRA 1 (mainly from Cilicia) amphorae, and one has amphorae attributed to the Aegean. Two seem to have cargoes from Palestine, judging from the description or identification of their amphorae: Iskandil Burnu 1 (my 388, Parker no. 518, late sixth century) and Pefkos (my 624; Parker no. 795).

171 In addition to the late antique wrecks enumerated in the preceding note, see Datca 2 (my 250; Parker no. 352), seventh–eighth centuries; Bozborun (my 83; Parker no. 111), late ninth century; Marmaris 1 (my 490; Parker no. 657), eighth–ninth centuries; Mandalya Gulf 3 (my 483, Parker no. 644), tenth century; Serçe Limanı Zone (my 841; Parker no. 1074), tenth–eleventh centuries; Kotu Burun (my 415; Parker no. 557), eleventh century; Çomlek Burun (my 231; not in Parker), eleventh–twelfth centuries; Serçe Limanı 1 (my 840; Parker no. 1070), ca. 1025; Camirus (my 129; Parker no. 167), thirteenth century; Knidos 4 (my 412; Parker no. 551), thirteenth–fourteenth centuries; Bozborun

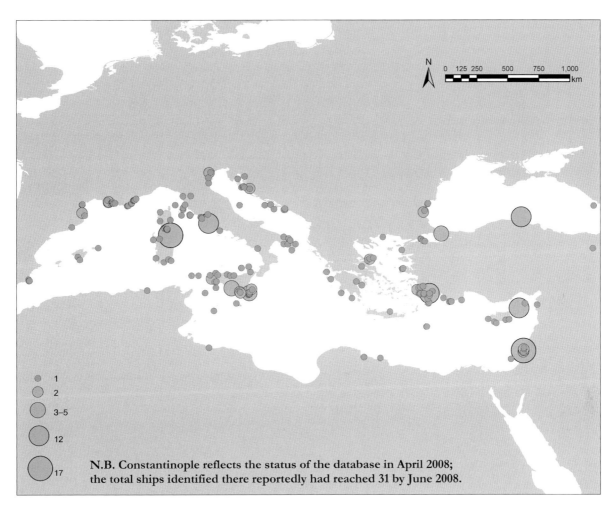

Figure 3.11. Numbers of dated shipwrecks by location, AD 300–1500; totals as of 2008 (drawn by A. More)

on the other hand, there is a considerable gap, beginning in the fifth century or so when the population, and therefore the demand that animated the city market of Rome, experienced catastrophic contraction. So far as we can see today, wrecks off western Sicily linking southern Europe and northern Africa pick up again only after 1000.[172]

Armed Nave and Bozborun Galley (my 84–85; not in Parker), fifteenth–sixteenth centuries.

172 For late antique wrecks, see note 169, above. The first wreck after about 600 is Scoglio della Formica 2 (my 829; Parker no. 1053), ninth–eleventh centuries; Skerki Bank 1 (my 855; not in Parker), eleventh–thirteenth centuries; San Vito Lo Capo (my 810; not in Parker) and Marsala 1 and 2 (my 493, 494; Parker nos. 663–64), all twelfth century; Castellammare del Golfo (my 195; Parker no. 276) and Rocca di San Nicola 1 (my 764, Parker no. 989), both fifteenth century.

Refining the map of datable shipwrecks to distinguish clusters of ships in the same locations throws into stronger relief the coast of southern Palestine, the entrance to the Aegean at Rhodes, and especially eastern Sicily (see fig. 3.11). The big cluster on Sardinia reflects the spectacular discovery in 1999 of seventeen ships. Fourteen apparently date to the hitherto poorly documented fifth century AD and seem to have been destroyed at dock at the same time, around 450, perhaps by a Vandal attack.[173] The value of these ships in shedding light on of the most obscure moments in Roman economic history should be extraordinary when they are suitably published.

Much ink has flowed over the famous charts of shipwrecks that first caught economic historians'

173 See note 176, below.

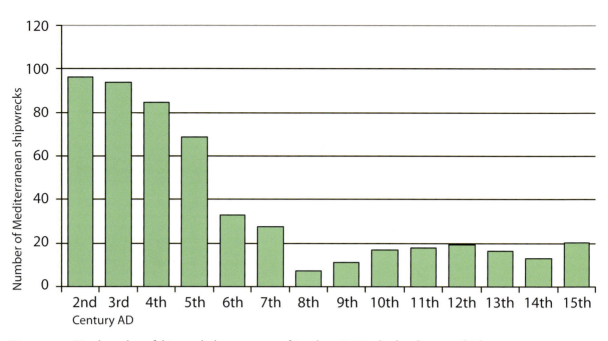

Figure 3.12. Total number of shipwrecks by century as of April 2008. Wrecks dated over multiple centuries are prorated; e.g., a wreck of 400–600 is counted as half a wreck in the 5th c. and half in the 6th (drawn by author).

attention.[174] Figure 3.12 graphs from our database the total numbers of datable shipwrecks, including less precisely dated ones, from the second century to ca. 1500.[175] It is tempting to see in this graph the broad trend of Mediterranean shipping and, through it, a *very* rough indicator of the general level of activity of the economy these vessels once served. Decline there is in late antiquity, but the drop is nowhere near as steep as it appeared in Parker's summary of the data available two decades ago.[176] Slow recovery seems to begin in the ninth century. From the eighth century forward, some believable rhythms are clear within the aggregate numbers of wrecks and lend those numbers general plausibility. Thus ship numbers decline in the fourteenth century, when plague sharply reduced Mediterranean populations and economies and created real difficulties for shipping, which conveyed the contagion. On the other hand, it seems strange that wrecks attributed to the thirteenth century should be fewer than those assigned to the twelfth. Moreover, it seems difficult to compare directly the absolute numbers of shipwrecks presently attributed to the period after 700 or 800 with those in the preceding centuries. The raw numbers of datable wrecks from the ninth to the fifteenth century remain distinctly lower than those of antiquity, yet no one doubts the vitality and great numbers of perhaps considerably bigger ships active

---

174 K. Hopkins, "Taxes and Trade in the Roman Empire (200 B.C.–A.D. 400)," *JRS* 70 (1980): 101–25, here, 106, fig. 1; R. MacMullen, *Corruption and the Decline of Rome* (New Haven, 1988), 8–9, figs. 6–7; Parker, *Ancient Shipwrecks*, 549, fig. 3; etc.

175 The graph accounts differently for the evidence by prorating shipwrecks dated to multiple centuries, rather than locating them at the chronological midpoint of their dating span. This approach may well give a better impression of the situation in our period, at the possible cost of blurring the differences between some centuries. Data for this graph are derived from 724 datable wrecks. Prorating the shares of ships according to the different centuries that fall within their dating span excludes shares that fall outside of the period 100–1500. For example, for a ship dating between 300 BC and AD 500, 1/8 is assigned to each century. Hence only 4/8 of the ship appears in the total of ships graphed between AD 100 and 1500.

176 Some differences between the two series of data indubitably reflect real change in our knowledge due to major discoveries— e.g., the fourteen new fifth-century ships found in a destruction layer at Olbia in Sardinia (see D'Oriano and Riccardi, "Les épaves d'Olbie"), or the spectacular new discoveries of Yenikapı, Istanbul. Others merely echo our different methods of counting: Parker included all ships datable to any span, and classified them according to the arithmetical midpoint of that span (see fig. 2.9). I included only ships that could be dated down to three centuries (a few) or less. See also note 179, below.

in the twelfth, thirteenth, or fifteenth centuries. Is it conceivable that the absolute numbers of ships afloat remained below those of antiquity at a time when one is inclined to think that the global economy was outstripping the balmy days of the early Roman Empire? If we allow that medieval ships were bigger and more efficient, a reduction in numbers seems at least plausible. But it is also likely that medieval ships were better built. From the twelfth century on, it is certain that the spread of charts and the compass improved navigation. These innovations must have lowered the sinking rate of ships afloat.[177] It is also possible that ships from the eighth century onward are less visible on the sea bottom because amphora typologies remain underdeveloped or because barrels progressively replaced amphorae, as western ships and their wooden containers proliferated across the Mediterranean Sea.[178]

The value of a geodatabase for understanding shipping changes over time emerges most clearly when we focus on centuries, decades, and, where possible, even shorter periods. Just because we find many fourth- and sixth-century shipwrecks along the same route does not mean that the route stayed equally active over the fifth century. Figure 3.13 displays 174 more closely dated wrecks that went down between 300 and 700.[179] Our knowledge ranges from bare mentions of unpublished survey discoveries to the sumptuously documented Yassı Ada wreck; mostly the publications are woefully incomplete. Even so, for this period, the evidence is now abundant enough that we can observe in figure 3.13 real structure, and real structural change.

Fourth- and fifth-century ships overwhelmingly predominate in the western Mediterranean; sixth- and seventh-century ships, conversely, dominate the eastern sea. This spatial and chronological distribution appears to reflect the differing fates of the two halves of the Roman Empire. In the fourth and fifth centuries, the late Roman world of markets and ships centered on the western part of the empire. The center of gravity shifted dramatically east over the next two centuries. It may be something like conventional wisdom that both east and west flourished more or less equally in the fourth century and that, in the course of the fifth century, the west declined while the east stayed the same or surged ahead. The map of these 174 wrecks suggests that this picture is too simple. If shipwrecks roughly track economic activity, then the map invites a rather startling question: might the western empire actually have been outperforming the eastern half, at least in the fourth century?[180]

Figure 3.13 further suggests the profound structuring effects of the two mega markets of the later Roman Empire: in the fourth and, to a lesser extent, the fifth century, the market—or exchange center— of Rome dominates visible Mediterranean shipping. In the sixth and seventh centuries, the center of gravity shifts to the routes leading to Constantinople, even if the capital itself remains, for the moment, underrepresented. But other, finer-grained developments also appear: thus, on the coast of Spain near Cartagena, we see mostly fourth- and fifth-century activity. Nevertheless, a rare shipwreck occurs in the sixth century precisely in the corner of Spain that the Byzantines reconquered and held for several generations. Similarly, we might be seeing in the seventh-century ships off the heel of Italy the demand created by the Byzantine forces who then held that strip of land against the Lombard invaders. The exceptional cluster of seven seventh-century wrecks off Syracuse echoes the beleaguered Byzantine government's deepening reliance on Sicily to finance those dark decades' desperate wars against the all-conquering Muslims.[181] Indeed, the

---

177 On the problem of the sinking rate, see below, 94–96. On developments in navigation and ship construction, see F. C. Lane, *Venice, a Maritime Republic* (Baltimore, 1973), 119–34, and Pryor, *Geography, Technology, and War*, 25–86.
178 F. C. Lane, "Progrès technologiques et productivité dans les transports maritimes de la fin du moyen âge au début des temps modernes," *RH* 510 (1974): 277–302, at 278.
179 These ships are all dated to, at most, a three-century span that falls within this period. When a wreck's date spans multiple centuries, it is recorded under the latest century, which may bias the picture somewhat toward the later century in each case. Thus the rather high numbers of fifth- and seventh-century ships could well reflect a fair number of wrecks from the preceding century. See also next note.

180 Of the forty-two wrecks assigned by our method to the fifth century, sixteen have date spans that would allow them to date from the fourth and one from the third century, making the fifth-century total less impressive overall. Fourteen have date spans that end in the first half of the fifth century; none have spans that end between 451 and 499.
181 McCormick, "Bateaux de vie, bateaux de mort," 77–80; C. Morrisson, "La Sicile byzantine: Une lueur dans les siècles obscurs," *Quaderni ticinesi di numismatica e antichità classiche* 27 (1998): 307–34; Prigent, "Le rôle des provinces." C. Zuckerman, "Learning from the Enemy and More: Studies in 'Dark Centuries' Byzantium," *Millennium* 2 (2005): 79–135, essentially accepts this broader point (see, e.g., 105, on the share of the Italian

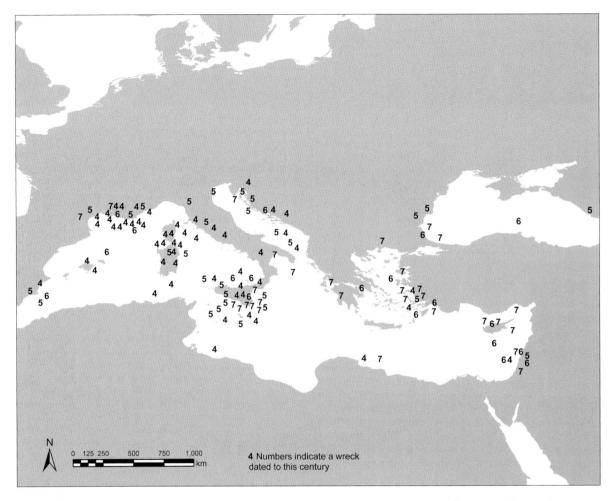

Figure 3.13. Dated shipwreck sites, ca. AD 300–700; these 132 sites contain 174 ships. Each is assigned a number identifying the century to which it is dated (drawn by A. More)

appearance of fifth-century wrecks on the *southeastern* coast of Sicily—ships therefore probably *not* en route to or returning from Rome—likely reflects the growing attractive power, at Rome's expense, of Constantinople and the east for the annona and associated products. That flow of African grain and oil continued after the Vandal conquest, when it can only have been commercial, not fiscal. Land archaeology shows that African fine and coarse wares and petty coins, including those issued by Vandals, moved along just this shipping axis.[182]

Sea routes cannot be isolated from the overall economic networks of which they were an integral part. If we imagine the shipping routes implied by these wrecks as arteries, we quickly see that the economic organism also needed capillaries to move the goods to markets. As Gaza's camel trains suggest, sea shipment often implies land or river transport of goods.[183] By the same token, the numbers

territories in contemporary imperial revenues), while offering a different but plausible interpretation of the unusual term *nauticatio* in the *Liber pontificalis*.

182   J. W. Hayes, *Excavations at Saraçhane in Istanbul*, vol. 2, *The Pottery* (Princeton, N.J., 1992), 5–7, with further references;

Bonifay, *Études,* 479–82; Morrisson, "La monnaie sur les routes," 644–45, 655.

183   This system would probably have included significant redistribution centers such as, e.g., Carthage, Pozzuoli, Narbonne, and Ostia for the high imperial period; these, as Tchernia among others has insisted, must have assembled goods from different regions and reexported them elsewhere, complicating efforts to track ships' courses based on the heterogeneous geographic profiles of some cargoes, notwithstanding valuable stud-

of ships under way must somehow reflect the numbers of people and the strength of demand in particular markets. Consider the best explored example, along the French coast; there, the size and structure of the interior market fed by river and road transport from southern sea routes surely changed a number of times between 300 and 1000.[184] The Tetrarchic reintegration of Gaul into the greater Roman political economy and the rise of the new capital at Trier must have reinvigorated Mediterranean shipping funneling into the Rhone corridor. The *Expositio totius mundi* testifies to just such an influx of goods. The subsequent collapse of the Rhine frontier and the imperial retreat down to Arles will have disrupted the further reaches of the supply network, and amputated demand.[185] The broader Gaulish market to which shipping led undoubtedly shrank in tandem with these changes in demand.

Each change presumably affected the intensity of shipping along the sea routes feeding the inland river and road transport network that, for several generations, conveyed wares north to Trier, the voracious consumer city on the Moselle. This effect appears to be exactly what we see in figure 3.14. In our period, fourth-century shipwrecks predominate on the maritime approaches to Marseille and the Rhone River transport system north to Trier. A little to the east, at Nice, the map reveals an equally clear link between the capillaries of inland transport systems—here the Roman roads—and the artery, the sea route. It also shows how wrecks seem to dwindle away in the fifth century as the area under imperial control shrank and the Gaulish market as a whole contracted violently both in size and, we may suspect, in purchasing power. Yet this corner of our geodatabase also indicates that a few ships continued to serve the demand of Merovingian markets, now starkly reduced—but not stilled—as the papyrus and Gaza wine made famous by Henri Pirenne continued to reach the Rhone until about 700.[186]

The summary reports of ship's gear and cargoes illustrate another aspect of the geodatabase's potential for the history of markets. Invented in the late first century AD, the portable and handy steelyard weighing scale (see fig. 16.5) spread across the entire Roman Empire. It could weigh goods quickly and accurately in quantities running from a few ounces to 400 Roman pounds (ca. 130 kg).[187] An operational approach again suggests interesting questions. How were steelyard balances used aboard ship, and what might that use tell us about changes in the economy? Their spread was likely connected with what appears to be the late Roman tendency to measure by weight rather than by volume the sorts of commodities transported by ship.[188] Considering the mass and time involved, it seems unlikely that steelyards, which typically run up to 50 or 100 pounds, were used in the process of loading ballast or cargo. Instead, experienced captains probably adjusted ballast by eye as they inspected the amount and types of cargoes they would be carrying, particularly since standardized amphora sizes aided them in estimating cargo weights.

In fact, the Byzantines associated scales mainly with buying and selling—that is, with markets.[189]

---

ies such as P. Reynolds, *Trade in the Western Mediterranean, AD 400–700: The Ceramic Evidence,* BAR International Series 604 (Oxford, 1995); see A. Tchernia, "Épaves antiques, routes maritimes directes et routes de redistribution," in *Nourrir les cités de Méditerranée: Antiquité-Temps modernes,* ed. B. Marin and C. Virlouvet (Paris, 2003), 613–21. Carthage, Constantinople, Marseilles, Alexandria, and Antioch presumably played this kind of role to some degree, as yet uncertain, between the fourth and seventh centuries.

184 See the exemplary study of wine shipments along this route in the republican and early imperial period: Tchernia, *Le vin de l'Italie romaine.*

185 E. M. Wightman, *Gallia Belgica* (London, 1985), 267–81, 300–311, remains a good place to start; for more recent developments, see, e.g., H. W. Böhme, "Lahnstein und der Mittelrhein in spätrömischer Zeit," in *Berichte zur Archäologie an Mittelrhein und Mosel,* ed. H.-H. Wegner, vol. 8, Trierer Zeitschrift für Geschichte und Kunst des Trierer Landes und seiner Nachbargebiete; Beiheft 27 (Trier, 2003), 11–19.

186 H. Pirenne, *Mahomet et Charlemagne,* 3rd ed. (Paris, 1937). For recent thinking about these two imports into Gaul, and the complicated question of just what sea route ended when, see McCormick, *Origins of the European Economy,* 35–36, 704–8. For the latest on the Gazan wine trade to Gaul, see Pieri, *Le commerce du vin oriental,* as well as idem, "Regional and Interregional Exchanges in the Eastern Mediterranean during the Early Byzantine Period: The Evidence of Amphorae," in this volume, 27–49.

187 P. Weiss, "Schnellwaage," *Der Neue Pauly* (Brill, 2008; Brill Online), www.brillonline.nl/subscriber/entry?entry=dnp_e1104120, accessed 15 April 2008.

188 See van Alfen, "New Light," 205.

189 This is true in obvious contexts, for example patriarch John the Almsgiver's control of weights and measures in Alexandria: Leontius of Neapolis, *Vita Ioannis Eleemosynarii* (*BHG* 886d), 2, ed. A. J. Festugière, *Léontios de Néapolis, Vie de Syméon le Fou, Vie de Jean de Chypre,* Bibliothèque archéologique et historique 95 (Paris, 1974), 348.2–11: πάντα ἐν ἑνὶ καμπανῷ καὶ ζυγῷ καὶ μοδίῳ καὶ ἀρτάβῃ πωλεῖν καὶ ἀγοράζειν; cf. the frequent mentions in the *Book of the Prefect,* which regulates sealing of weights and measures in Constantinople's markets: *Das Eparchenbuch* 11.9,

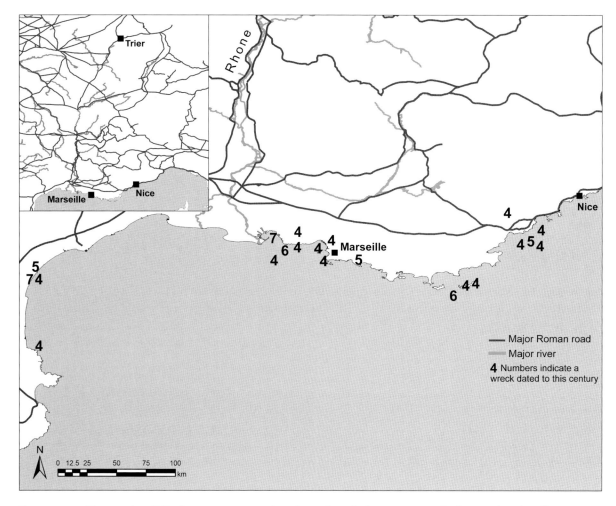

Figure 3.14. Shipwrecks off Gaul, ca. AD 300–700 (numbers identify the century to which a wreck is dated) (drawn by A. More)

One can easily imagine shipboard merchants using steelyard balances to weigh quantities of textiles, oil, or grain they bought or sold. Balances on board might suggest that in many cases their owners were directly buying and selling at shipside—retail—rather than transporting goods for delivery to a wholesale distributor. The chronological distribution of these balances within the geodatabase provides further food for thought. Weighing scales of any sort are not common among wreck finds; only twelve occur among our hundreds of more or less datable Mediterranean wrecks. Nevertheless, they are twice as frequent aboard late Roman and medieval wrecks as the more abundant wrecks from the earlier Roman Empire.[190] This hints that

---

116.524–27, on wax dealers tampering with steelyard balances; also, like Leontius, the regulator distinguishes between (gross) wares sold with steelyards and those weighed more finely with conventional balances, 10.5 (112.489–91) or 13.1 (118.565–66); cf. G. Vikan and A. Cutler, "Balance Scales," *ODB* 1:247; G. Vikan, "Steelyard" and "Weights," *ODB* 3:1947, 2194–95; and B. Pitarakis, "Daily Life at the Marketplace in Late Antiquity and Byzantium," in this volume, 401–5. The pseudepigraphical work of John "of Jerusalem," *De sacris imaginibus contra Constantinum Caballinum* 14, PG 95:331, which seems to have been written between 775 and 787, possibly at Constantinople, inveighs against bishops whose main concern is making money and wondering how they could "sell grain, distribute wine, weigh oil with a steelyard (πῶς καμπανίσωσι τὸ ἔλαιον), deal in wool or raw silk." On this work, see M.-F. Auzépy, "L'*Adversus Constantinum Caballinum* et Jean de Jérusalem," *BSl* 56 (1995): 323–38.

190 Of the approximately 410 datable Mediterranean wrecks in our geodatabase from before ca. AD 300, only 5 (1.2 percent) are recorded as having had weighing devices aboard. Such devices are reported on 7 (2.5 percent) of the 280-some wrecks known after

Figure 3.15. Late Roman mosaic of a beachside market. Wares are being unloaded from the ship drawn up toward the beach, and weighed with a balance scale on the left (photo courtesy of the Institut national d'archéologie et d'art, Musée du Bardo, Tunis)

between 300 and 1500, shippers were more likely to buy and sell goods directly in markets that lacked established weighing procedures or stations, markets perhaps like the beachside one depicted in the late Roman sermon quoted above, or in the African mosaic shown in figure 3.15 (though that has a balance rather than a steelyard scale). The evidence made available by the geodatabase of shipwrecks tallies with Valentinian III's law against covert markets.[191] More ship landings could have represented instant mini-market events: some—many?—shipboard merchants engaged directly in buying and selling at shipside rather than simply transporting goods for delivery to established permanent markets. One suspects that in later centuries such informal, beachside markets dodged the tax mechanisms of the Byzantine state. Ninth-century Italy points in this direction, as do the efforts of its kings to repress such markets,[192] providing evidence of more atomized or unregulated markets alongside permanent ones. Though this may be only a first impression, it hints at how much light the gear observed aboard shipwrecks can shed on market structures when the data are viewed in aggregate.

Seeing Shipwrecks, Cargoes, and Economies: Some Caveats

Along the coast of late Roman Gaul and in the plague conditions of the fourteenth century, the rise and fall of numbers of shipwrecks look to correlate well with broader economic trends. But are we seeing more or less directly the rise and fall of economies? Some important caveats apply. To truly understand what we know, we need to know what we do not yet know, and how those unknowns can affect the economic interpretation of shipwrecks.

The growing number of the nautical equivalent of field-walking surveys is crucial. Those organized by the Institute of Nautical Archaeology of Texas A&M University seem especially promising, particularly insofar as they record in a given area *all* visible wrecks from *all* periods, including that important group, "undated."[193] Knowledge of undated wrecks is imperative if we are to identify the margin of error. When we know all discernible shipwrecks, even those in small (but perhaps well-chosen) zones

---

300. Given that considerably more early Roman wrecks have been more fully excavated, the absence is more striking. Indeed, five out of the seven postclassical ships with weighing scales occur between the fourth and seventh centuries.
191 See note 12, above.
192 McCormick, *Origins of the European Economy*, 781.

193 See, for instance, the invaluable surveys organized and regularly summarized by the Institute of Nautical Archaeology: e.g., J. Leidwanger and D. S. Howitt-Marshall, "Episkopi Bay and Beyond: Recent Collaborative Fieldwork and New Prospects on Cyprus," *Institute of Nautical Archaeology Quarterly* 33.2 (2006): 13–14; J. G. Royal, "Description and Analysis of the Finds from the 2006 Turkish Coastal Survey: Marmaris and Bodrum," *International Journal of Nautical Archaeology* 37 (2008): 88–97.

leading to and from key market centers, we can plot better charts of the rise and fall of wrecks, and maybe also gain a better sense of the rise and fall of traffic. To gauge the changing intensity of traffic, blanks—places or periods without wrecks—on underwater survey maps are no less important than signs marking the presence of wrecks, particularly if we have a clear grasp of the factors that shape their visibility.

Fathoming the ships' economic significance depends on understanding the broader economy that produced the wrecks. Thus, although some might see an apparent drop in shipwrecks in the sixth or the fourteenth centuries as directly indicating economic decline, other considerations complicate such an inference. If, for example, the overall population declined *at the same rate* as shipwrecks dropped—think Justinianic plague or the Black Death—that would suggest no per capita economic decline in shipping. If in fact the wrecks declined at a *slower* rate than the population dropped, the decline could actually indicate an *increase* in per capita economic activity. That is not at all unthinkable: studies of the late medieval Black Death have shown that once they overcame the initial disarray caused by the massive die-off, survivors inherited the wealth of the deceased and, one way or another, some social groups began to do much better than before the plague.[194] The first hints might be coming from archaeology that something similar was afoot in the late Roman economy toward the end of the sixth century.[195] We can adjust for such complications, but we need to remember them.

Ship sizes have attracted attention. Late Roman decline has sometimes been connected with decreasing ship capacities.[196] Nevertheless, there is also a consensus that throughout the premodern period, smaller ships must have been the most common cargo carriers in the Mediterranean. Parker estimated that such smaller ships would have borne under 75 tons of cargo.[197] Now the number of ships for which we can *directly* estimate carrying capacity is very limited, essentially just the well-preserved, fully excavated and published vessels. Another rather rough but useful benchmark is easier to come by: approximate wreck length.[198]

The data are numerous and interesting. Useful approximate lengths are known for 108 Mediterranean vessels.[199] Of the fifty-three more or less well dated late Roman and medieval wrecks in our geodatabase that offer this evidence, the modal length (twelve ships, 22.6 percent) is 20 meters, the size of Yassı Ada. Nine (16.9 percent) are at least 30 meters long. Over half—twenty-nine (54.7 percent)—run between 20 and 50 meters long, and sixteen of those are pre-700 (i.e., the picture is not distorted by the bigger late medieval ships). For the early Roman Empire, we can adduce lengths for fifty-five ships. The largest size class is approximately as well represented in the first three centuries of our era as in the later period: thirty ships (53.5 percent of the total number) run above 20 meters long. The one probable aberrant case—a giant ship (ca. 104 meters)—was likely built for one specific voyage. Otherwise, the longest ancient vessel measures 45 meters; the longest late Roman ship, about 50 meters.[200] Two differences nonetheless reinforce the conventional

---

194   See, for instance, D. Herlihy, *Medieval and Renaissance Pistoia: The Social History of an Italian Town, 1200–1430* (New Haven, 1967), 142–47; C. Dyer, *Making a Living in the Middle Ages: The People of Britain, 850–1520* (New Haven, 2002), 278–86.

195   On archaeological evidence for the economic dynamism of Byzacena ca. 600, see Bonifay, *Études*, 482; for Syria-Palestine after Justinian, see Magness, *Early Islamic Settlement*, 195–214; Walmsley, *Early Islamic Syria*, 34–45. For a possible reflection of this growth in per capita wealth connected with Negev wine transport, see note 100, above.

196   Pryor, *Geography, Technology, and War*, 26–27, with further references.

197   Parker sorts ancient freighters into three different size classes: the smallest, under 75 tons of cargo (always the most numerous group); medium ships, with cargoes ranging from 75 to 200 tons; and the largest, with cargoes over 250 tons: Parker, *Ancient Shipwrecks*, 26; cf. McCormick, *Origins of the European Economy*, 95–96, 415–18.

198   Since the overwhelming majority of preserved shipwrecks are cargo vessels, and therefore "round" ships, there is little danger that the picture will be confused with large numbers of "long" narrow warships. Two caveats about the data: first, in many cases, the length measurement probably or certainly represents the part of the hull that can be seen or is preserved. It is therefore a minimum figure. Second, in other cases, the measurements derive from the cargo deposit, which sometimes can spread on the sea bottom or be disturbed, thereby producing a measure that may more or less exceed the actual hull of the ship.

199   In the state of the database used for this chapter, length could be approximated for 126 vessels, but 17 vessels were under 10 m (10 before the fourth century; 7 from the fourth to the fifteenth century) and excluded from consideration as being very poorly preserved or, most frequently, ships' boats and the like.

200   The giant ship, Fiumicino 12 (my 303; Parker no. 412), is believed to be preserved in the mole of the Claudian harbor, and to have been specially constructed to transport an obelisk from Egypt. It is clearly an exception.

wisdom that ship sizes ran somewhat bigger under the early Roman Empire: at 25 meters, the modal length in the first three centuries—nine ships—exceeds that in the later period by 25 percent. Also, twelve ships (21.4 percent of the total) are 30 meters or longer. In the future it will be important to compare and strengthen these data with other types of evidence developed by imaginative scholars. For instance, anchors often show up on the sea bottom. The patterns of evolution and the distribution of their types and sizes should reflect the size of the ships they once anchored.[201]

So it is fair to say that the evidence today confirms that ships in our period ran somewhat smaller than in the earlier Roman Empire. If we assume that the sinking and visibility rates of the later vessels remained the same as earlier (on which see below), then we might deduce that overall transport volume fell after about 300—and we might be tempted further to argue that this fall is a sign of economic contraction. That latter claim may be true, but several factors complicate it.

Beyond the state of harbor maintenance—whether harbors that silted up from ancient erosion were dredged to maintain depths for bigger ships—I have argued elsewhere that the subsidy system devised by the Roman state to ensure the transport of fiscal grain to the capitals created incentives to build smaller ships.[202] If the subsidized ships were free to pursue their own commercial ambitions after making the required voyage to deliver grain or oil to the capital, it was in the shipowner's interest to have a smaller ship that could be unloaded faster—then as now, delays at unloading were clearly a problem—so that he could quickly return to sea and business. Under these conditions, one could imagine that smaller ships transported cargoes more intensively than bigger ships, increasing the velocity at which goods moved.

A second element, arising from what we have seen about containers, complicates the deductions that we can draw from ship size: how might changes in packaging have affected effective cargoes, that is, cargoes minus the weight and volume of containers? For goods such as grain, transported loose or in sacks, the amount moved at one time by a smaller ship would certainly have decreased. However, it has been claimed that late antique amphorae were more efficient than those of the high Roman Empire: that is, as potters made them thinner, lighter, and stronger, the ratio of the weight of the container to its contents dropped.[203] If that is correct, then the actual total weight of a ship's cargo traded and transported in heavy amphorae will have fallen as later amphorae became lighter. In other words, a smaller ship using the lighter amphorae could transport the same amount of wares as its larger predecessors. This crucial consideration in the economics of transporting amphorae deserves more systematic scrutiny.

What we have seen of late Roman barrels indicates that regardless of changes in the number and size of transport ships, we must allow for a decline in the proportion of cargoes shipped in amphorae between the third and the seventh centuries. I see

---

201 This thoughtful suggestion comes from Prof. van Doorninck.
202 McCormick, "Bateaux de vie, bateaux de mort," 103–5. The case for accelerated erosion in the late Roman period is well made for northwestern Europe by H. Löhr, "Intensivierte Bodenerosion als Folge römischer Landnutzung in der Trierer Talweite und ihrem Umfeld," in *Kelten, Germanen, Römer im Mittelgebirgsraum zwischen Luxemburg und Thüringen,* ed. A. Haffner and S. von Schnurbein, vol. 5, Kolloquien zur Vor- und Frühgeschichte 1 (Bonn, 2000), 175–99. One suspects that some of the widely attested silting up of eastern ports occurred in late antiquity, insofar as similar causes explain similar effects in the eastern empire, although detailed study and verification are necessary. The find circumstances of the ships in the Theodosian harbor of Constantinople, in what is now the dry land site of Yenikapı at what was once the mouth of the river Lykos, indicate that they owe their extraordinary preservation to having been buried as the harbor silted up. See the eloquent image in R. Asal, "İstanbul'un ticareti ve Theodosius Limanı," in *Gün ışığında,* 180–89, at 187, fig. 5. Early reports indicate that the earliest Yenikapı wrecks come from the seventh century, providing a first element toward establishing the chronology of decline of Constantinople's greatest late antique harbor.

203 Pieri, *Le commerce du vin oriental,* 68, states that makers of late Roman eastern amphorae were able to reduce to a minimum the weight of the amphora in relation to its content, but supplies no details. See van Alfen, "New Light," 208, a useful discussion of amphora efficiency, and calculates the efficiency of LRA 1 at 1.9 L per kg of amphora, while that of LRA 2 was strikingly superior at 3.3 L per kg of empty amphora. Because the otherwise precious online catalogue of amphora types of Keay and Williams, "Roman Amphorae: A Digital Resource," ads.ahds.ac.uk/catalogue/archive/amphora_ahrb_2005, accessed multiple times between June and October 2008, normally lists the approximate capacity but not the empty weight of amphorae, it is difficult to verify and develop Pieri's assertion. However, the calculation for the earlier Roman amphora Dressel 20 (see note 81, above), shows that it was slightly more efficient than the LRA 1 but less efficient than the LRA 2. The table of weights and capacity efficiencies in Peacock and Williams, *Amphorae and the Roman Economy,* 52, table 1, does not seem to provide obvious support for the claim that amphora efficiencies generally improved.

no clear way at present to quantify this change and assess how much of the drop in visible cargoes can be attributed to the use of containers that almost never leave remnants on the seabed. The ingenious method for detecting increased use of barrels on Roman sites in Gaul or among imports to Rome nevertheless suggests a way forward. André Tchernia made a persuasive case that the sudden decline in wine amphorae at Ostia in the second century means not that the Romans were drinking less but that much of the wine had begun arriving in barrels, which left no archaeological traces.[204] Similarly, in the Roman north, the proportion of wine to oil amphorae is strikingly lower in military camps than in comparable civilian settlements, suggesting that the soldiers received their wine in kegs.[205] Tchernia at first hesitated to draw the same conclusion from a similar fourth-century decline in wine amphorae at Ostia, attributing it instead to a sharp drop in the population of Rome, an opinion then not contradicted by the apparent absence of evidence for barrels in Roman Africa.

Today most scholars tend to place Rome's urban decline later, in the late fourth or even fifth century.[206] We have seen that wine barrels were in fact familiar in Africa. Moreover, some classes of African amphorae formerly associated with olive oil have now been claimed for wine. Thus African, Italian, and Gaulish transports in barrels as well as amphorae newly identified as wine containers, not changes in demand, probably account for some of the shift in proportions of amphorae associated with particular wares in the fourth-century Roman market.[207] In those regions of the late Roman world that had the wood required for barrels, we can watch between the second and the fifth centuries for the disappearance of export amphora series—or, in the case of wine, of amphorae lined with the resin used to seal their interior. If other wares from the same areas continue to flow to consumers at various sites, and no obvious competing wine supply appears, then we might well hypothesize that such changing patterns in ceramics reflect new packaging rather than a shift in what is being exported and imported. Further clues as to when and where barrels became dominant may lurk in the design of docks. What is the history of ramps at the water's edge? At what time and in what place did they begin to appear at quaysides alongside steps? It is possible that ramps were suited to rolling barrels into vessels, particularly if their design turns out to match changes in naval architecture.[208] The obvious places in the Mediterranean where such a shift could have occurred are Gaul, the head of the Adriatic, perhaps heavily wooded parts of southern Italy, Africa, southern Asia Minor, and the forested Black Sea coast.[209] It may be a coincidence, but it is strik-

204 Tchernia, *Le vin de l'Italie romaine,* 292–99. A recent excavation and ceramic study executed at Ostia with an eye to statistical exploitation came to a similar conclusion, albeit very cautiously phrased; see A. Martin, "Imports at Ostia in the Imperial Period and Late Antiquity: The Amphora Evidence from the DAI-AAR Excavations," in Hohlfelder, ed., *The Maritime World of Ancient Rome,* 105–18, at 112.
205 Marlière, *L'outre et le tonneau,* 193.
206 On Rome's fifth-century decline, see, e.g., R. Meneghini and R. Santangeli Valenzani, "La trasformazione del tessuto urbano tra V e IX secolo," in *Roma dall'antichità al medioevo: Archeologia e storia nel Museo nazionale romano Crypta Balbi,* ed. M. S. Arena, P. Delogu, L. Paroli, et al. (Milan, 2001), 20–33; cf. B. Lançon, *Rome in Late Antiquity: Everyday Life and Urban Change, AD 312–609* (Edinburgh, 2000), 14. N. Purcell, "The Populace of Rome in Late Antiquity: Problems of Classification and Historical Description," in *The Transformations of Urbs Roma in Late Antiquity,* ed. W. V. Harris, Journal of Roman Archaeology, supp. ser. 33 (Portsmouth, R. I., 1999), 135–61, at 137–50, rather elusively develops an interesting argument that the city was shrinking before 410, whereas E. Lo Cascio, "Canon frumentarius, suarius, vinarius: Stato e privati nell'approvvigionamento dell'Vrbs," ibid., 163–82, sees a population of some 600,000–700,000 until that date. For African amphorae newly ascribed to the transport of wine, see Bonifay, *Études,* 463–73, and esp. Bonifay and Garnier, "Que transportaient donc," 20–25, concerning, e.g., some Africana 2 Grande con gradino, many spatheia, Keay 25 and Keay 35A.

207 C. Panella, "Rifornimenti urbani e cultura materiale tra Aureliano e Alarico," in Harris, ed., *The Transformations of Urbs Roma,* 183–215, at 199–205.
208 Inclined ramps leading into the water appear amid conventional docks in late Roman and early medieval river ports. The angle seems suited to the ramplike square bows of flat-bottomed ancient and medieval riverboats of the type found at Zwammerdam, Mainz (Ship 6), and Pommerœl, Belgium. It has been observed that these bows facilitated cargo handling on riverbanks without built-up docks. The combination of bow and ramp wharf design seems to me particularly well adapted to rolling barrels on and off the boats. I have seen such ramp wharves in regions in which barrels were certainly common—for instance, in the Roman river port of Aquileia and the Merovingian port on the Meuse at Namur.
209 That major amphora-producing centers of late antiquity such as Gaza or perhaps some parts of Africa tended not to have abundant wood supplies certainly offers cause for reflection along these lines. However, Cilicia and Cyprus perhaps have a different story, which indicates how complex the situation might have been. The possibility of a shift to carrying mostly barrels may also somewhat complicate the impression of western Mediterranean home ports in decline that I have sketched elsewhere, given that

ing that the shipboard barrels identified to date have come from Gaul and the region of Aquileia, shores that were known to use barrels. In any case, as we have seen, vessels serving late antique Rome indubitably increased their use of barrels to ship wine.

While it is clear that even the late Byzantine Empire continued to manufacture and use amphorae, we do not yet know how extensively and in which specific geographic areas and transportation types barrels may have competed with amphorae before and after the triumph of the Italian shippers. The formula attributed to Hero of Alexandria shows that barrels were familiar in the great Egyptian port as well, or at least in the Greek-speaking world; certainly, as we have already seen, the Byzantine army used water barrels on the eastern front.[210] A late antique martyr's tale of a theater skit in Heliopolis (modern Baalbek, Lebanon) mocking Christian baptism featured a mime in a barrel. Set at the time of the emperor Licinius, the story is no later than the sixth century, since Malalas records it. The Antiochene author felt no need to explain what a barrel (βοῦττις) was.[211] The Farmer's Law also provides a valuable clue to the middle Byzantine spread of barrels to the kind of inland village communities it seems to presuppose. Scholars date the Law variously to sometime between the seventh and the ninth centuries. The original version specifies a penalty for the theft of wine from ceramic vats (ἐκ πίθου) or from the wine tub (ἐκ ληνοῦ) itself. However, manuscripts of the twelfth and thirteenth centuries add the words ἢ ἀπὸ βουττίου (var. βουτζίου), "or from a barrel."[212]

Analysis of the size and operational features of middle Byzantine warships suggests that they too probably used barrels for drinking water. A liquid measure based on barrels also appears in an eleventh-century letter in the Cairo Genizah that could testify to the practice of Byzantine or Italian merchants.[213] Although the archaeological record is silent, barrels are often mentioned—particularly in connection with wine—as Byzantine administrative and archival documents proliferate from the tenth or eleventh century onward.[214] In sum, the evidence today indicates that barrels were (again?) gaining importance in the Byzantine economy by around 1000.

This brings us back to ship size. If the capacity efficiency of ancient barrels was indeed 1:4 or higher, these containers made up no more than 20 percent of the weight of a wine cargo.[215] By contrast, for wine transported in amphorae such as LRA2, the container alone would represent 35 percent of the cargo. Put another way, to carry a certain amount of Cilician wine a ship would require 15 percent less capacity if it used barrels rather than amphorae. Although plenty of cargo still traveled around the Roman Mediterranean in amphorae—particularly, we might imagine, goods from the less wooded eastern Mediterranean—a larger proportion of significantly smaller ships would suffice to transport the same volume of wine or anything else shipped in a barrel.[216] It is thus obviously vital to study patterns of amphora and barrel efficiency systematically, in

---

some of these ports are likely candidates for favoring barrels: cf. McCormick, "Bateaux de vie, bateaux de mort," 93–107.

210 See notes 133, 134, above.

211 John Malalas, *Chronographia* 12, 50, ed. I. Thurn, CFHB 35 (Berlin, 2000), 241.50–242.67; cf. *Chronicon Paschale*, ed. L. Dindorf, CSHB (Bonn, 1832), 513.13–18. Both versions do mention that the barrel was "of a bath," βαλανείου. It sounds big enough for the martyr to have submerged himself. Judging from the sixth-century medical writer Aetius of Amida, who was active in Constantinople and Alexandria, barrels or barrel-like tanks were becoming common for bathing in his time, for he advises that if someone cannot go to the baths to care for a particular illness, he should bathe in "a tub or what they call a barrel (ἐν σκάφῃ ἢ τῇ καλουμένῃ βούττῃ)": *Libri medicinales* 3.134, ed. A. Olivieri, *Aëtii Amideni libri medicinales I–IV*, Corpus medicorum Graecorum 8.1 (Leipzig, 1935), 314.15–16.

212 *Nomos georgikos* 69, ed. I. Medvedev, E. Petrovskaja, and E. Lipšic, *Vizantijskij zemledel'českij zakon* (Leningrad, 1984), 121, with the apparatus. For the dates of the MSS that include the interpolation, see 28–30, 32–33.

213 J. H. Pryor and E. Jeffreys, *The Age of the Dromon: The Byzantine Navy, ca 500–1204*, Medieval Mediterranean 62 (Leiden, 2006), 359–73. I suspect that the words in an eleventh-century Judaeo-Arabic letter (Cambridge University Library TS 12.241), transliterated as "bty' rwmy'" (363 n. 566) and understood as referring to Byzantium, could also be translated as "Italian barrel," given that in these documents the Arabic word *Rūm* refers either to Italians or to Byzantines.

214 E. Trapp, W. Hörandner, J. M. Diethart, et al., eds., *Lexikon zur byzantinischen Gräzität besonders des 9.–12. Jahrhunderts*, vol. 1 (Vienna, 2001), s.vv. βαγενάρης, etc.; βαρίλλιον; βούττη, etc.; and βούτζιον, borrowed, respectively, from Slavic, medieval Latin, and, in the last two cases, Italian.

215 As calculated from modern oak barrels by Marlière, *L'outre et le tonneau*, 12; see also note 112, above, for a more efficient barrel. Lane, "Progrès technologiques et productivité," 278, presents an even higher efficiency for medieval barrels—10 percent of cargo weight—which would represent a capacity efficiency of 1:9. Clearly there is room for experimental archaeology here.

216 If these figures all are sustained by further study, the extraordinary efficiency of 3.7 for Africana 2 reported by Marlière (*L'outre et le tonneau*, 12) perhaps reflects competition with barrels.

order to clarify the extent to which changes in them may have affected ship sizes and transport costs.

The near invisibility in the underwater archaeological record of organic containers such as barrels and the consequent changing visibility of late antique cargoes lead to another essential point.[217] An approximate idea of what data we lack allows better use of the splendid new data that we have. What are we really seeing in the 1,034 wrecks inventoried so far in our geodatabase? To clarify this problem, we must investigate two further issues: cargo visibility and what we might call the *sinking rate*.

Starting with the latter, we need to ask what proportion of all ships afloat went—and stayed—down. Presumably, only a relatively small fraction of ships sank. But was it 1, 5, or 10 percent, or more? To quantify roughly the percentage of ships that were lost, we can use early modern insurance data. Although, as noted earlier, we may suspect that late medieval and early modern navigational technology was superior to that of our period, the later evidence is perhaps as close as we can come to an archival analogue for loss rates in the first millennium. Notarial records of sixteenth-century Venetian insurance claims suggest something like at least 5 percent of ships were lost each year.[218] Rough-and-ready though it is, such a calculation gives an initial sense of how small a fraction we are seeing of ships that were actually afloat in a given year and could potentially have sunk. Given a perhaps optimistic 5 percent sinking rate, the database total of 1,034 ships would imply that in any single year between 300 and 1500, only an average of 17 ships were sailing in the Mediterranean.[219] That is obviously far too low a number. A considerable gap separates the *actual sinking rate* of Mediterranean ships and the number of wrecks that have been discovered so far.

Was the fraction of all ships that sank a random sample of all ships afloat? Some types of vessels or cargoes may have been more likely to be lost than others. Did the proportions change over time, reflecting improvements in construction or navigational technology, or simply altered security conditions, or greater risk aversion among shippers? We must weigh the raw statistics in the light of these considerations.

Further, does not the very fact that it is lying on the bottom of the sea indicate that a wreck is *not* typical of the ships then afloat? One hint will surprise no one who has ever owned a wooden vessel: ancient sources place different values on old and new ships. The Rhodian Sea Law shows that "old" ships were worth 40 percent less than new ships. They were also reckoned less safe.[220] So were more wrecks old rather than new ships? This is not simply a technical question of naval architecture. Answering yes would mean that the sinking rate rose in periods when, for whatever reasons—less capital available for building new ships, soaring lumber prices, or such red-hot demand for ships that anything able to float is put to sea—economic factors drove up the proportion of old ships under way, and therefore the number of

217 All four of the wrecks that yielded barrels were fairly well preserved and also carried amphorae (see the references cited in notes 121–23, above). It is safe to guess that the barrels were not the first thing that archaeologists noticed on them. Given the mixed character of many cargoes in our period, the lesser visibility of barrels complicates but does not render impossible the detection of late antique wrecks. It does suggest, however, that some amphora scatters on the sea bottom presently classified as traces of an act of jettison may in fact represent the nonperishable part of the cargo or gear from a shipwreck.

218 More careful research into the quantitative history of Venetian shipping is needed to make possible a final assessment. But for starters, a rough-and-ready estimate from Venetian insurance records indicates an average of ca. twenty ships per year lost in a fashion that might produce a shipwreck, out of a total of at least several hundred ships. For example, for 1592–93, A. Tenenti, G. A. Catti, and A. Spinelli, *Naufrages, corsaires et assurances maritimes à Venise, 1592–1609* (Paris, 1959), 69–89, tally, in addition to thirteen ships pillaged or captured, sixteen "naufrages," two ships destroyed by fire, and one disappeared. In 1590, Venice had ca. 136 great and light galleys, if I read aright F. C. Lane, *Venetian Ships and Shipbuilders of the Renaissance* (1934; reprint, New York, 1979), 242; round ships of all classes mentioned in various sources in 1499 come to 107 (ibid., 239). Both figures, especially the second, are presumably subsets of the real numbers; adding them together and dividing by the losses yields a loss rate of 7.8 percent for what is presumably a partial subset of the total number of insured ships. Another approach starts with Lane's statement that there were thirty-seven "large round ships in 1558–9" (240). For 1592 I count seven nave or galleons (i.e., round ships) lost; for 1593, twelve. These figures would suggest higher loss rates for this important subgroup of Venetian vessels—i.e., 18.9 percent and 32.4 percent—*if* the number of large round ships had not increased over the previous thirty-three years.

219 If 1,034 is 5 percent of total ships at sea, then there must have been 20,680 ships afloat in the entire Mediterranean between 300 and 1500, or 17.23 ships per year. Obviously that hypothetical number shrinks even further if the equation uses the higher sinking rates discussed in note 218, above.

220 *Lex Rhodia* 2.16, ed. W. Ashburner, *The Rhodian Sea-Law* (Oxford, 1909), 3.7–11. On preference for new ships as safer, see McCormick, *Origins of the European Economy*, 406 with note 69. See also note 224, below, on merchants who put heavy cargoes in old ships.

Table 3.1 Life spans of eleventh-century ships from Skuldelev, Denmark

Ship no.	Launch date	Major repairs (N)	Repair dates	Sinking date	Life span (yrs)
1	ca. 1030	3	1. ca. 1043 or after 1045 2. ca. 1042 or ca. 1059 3. undetermined	ca. 1064	34+
2 (warship)	1042	1+?	1060s	1070s	28+
3	1030s	1	after 1035	ca. 1064	24+
5 (warship)	1030s–40s (from recycled wood)	"many repairs"	last time ca. 1064	ca. 1064	24–34
6	ca. 1030	1 rebuilding/conversion 1 repair	undated	ca. 1070s	40+

SOURCE: O. Crumlin-Pedersen and O. Olsen, eds., *The Skuldelev Ships*, vol. 1, *Topography, Archaeology, History, Conservation and Display*, Ships and Boats of the North 4.1 (Roskilde, 2002), 66–67, 339, 341 (ship 1); 66–68, 340 (ship 2); 67, 340 (ship 3); 67–68, 340–41 (ship 5); 68, 341 (ship 6).

wrecks. Even adjusted for population fluctuations, sinking rate does not mirror economic performance in a linear fashion.

In this respect, the meticulous dendrochronological studies of the Skuldelev vessels in the Baltic—a region that supplied mercenaries to the Byzantine armed forces—offer what is to date the best group portrait of medieval ship aging (see table 3.1). They help address the crucial question of what "old" means in an ancient or medieval ship's life span, even if the distinctive northern tradition of naval architecture and chemistry of the Baltic Sea should make us cautious about simply extrapolating the answer to Mediterranean shipping. These ships were deliberately scuttled in an effort to block the Roskilde fjord against an enemy attack. Old, less valuable ships may well have been selected for destruction. It thus appears that the normal life span for Baltic vessels may have ranged from about twenty-five to forty years, a surmise that furnishes at least a point of comparison for Mediterranean vessels. Of course we cannot forget that the construction techniques and environmental conditions of the two nautical cultures differed considerably.

To date, the best comparable evidence from the Mediterranean comes from the Serçe Limanı wreck. Less than 20 percent of the Serçe Limanı ship's hull survived and none of the timbers proved suitable for dendrodating the ship, whose artifacts point to a sinking date of around 1025. It seems to have undergone a comprehensive refurbishing of the hull, entailing considerable rebuilding "a long time" after it was originally built; the specialist who most carefully studied the structure suspects that the Serçe Limanı ship "was launched a decade or two before" sinking. That estimate looks conservative, in light of the Baltic evidence and the thoroughness of the hull's refurbishing.[221] Nevertheless, the fifteenth-century archival evidence from Venice suggests that maximum life spans for late medieval ships in the Mediterranean were only thirteen or fourteen years; a decade was closer to the norm.[222] Our understanding of the economic history of the Mediterranean would gain much from considering the cost of renewing the vast shipping fleets that crisscrossed the inland sea, and the possibly changing average age of transport ships. Naturally only the most privileged conditions supply this kind of detailed insight

221 J. R. Steffy, "Construction and Analysis of the Vessel," in Bass, ed., *Serçe Limanı*, 153–69, at 165.
222 Lane, *Venetian Ships*, 263.

into individual ship's life histories. In their absence, one wonders about simpler indicators of age. For instance, the number of repairs per square meter of preserved timbers could serve as a kind of crude index of ship age.[223] It could help identify periods when, for example, a red-hot economy kept in service ships that should have been retired and thus drove up the sinking rate.

Other factors besides age might put a ship at risk: were certain types of shipping, ships of certain sizes, ships bearing certain cargoes, or ships on certain routes more likely to be lost and therefore overrepresented in the shipwreck record? By denying indemnities to any merchant foolish enough to freight heavy cargoes in an old ship, the Sea Law tells us something about contemporary perceptions of the link between cargoes and sinking.[224] Cargoes raise the further question of visibility: out of the total ships that went down, what fraction are we able to *see*? Up until very recently, we could see no ships in very deep waters, so scholars thought that ancient shipping was exclusively coastal. Now, as figure 3.10 shows, robotic surveys are discovering surprising numbers of deep-sea wrecks.[225] What features best explain what we see and do not see in a particular environment? Certainly underwater sediment deposit can play a critical role in concealing archaeological deposits on the sea bottom: sand buried the late Roman and early Arab ships at Dor, Israel, until erosion uncovered them in 1991.[226] And, as more than one observer has noted, the nature of a ship's cargo is fundamental.

For most sites in our geodatabase, cargo in the form of amphorae signals the existence of a Mediterranean shipwreck. This brings us to the annona paradox. If the backbone of late Roman shipping consisted of annona transport—and the movement every year around 540 of 8 million units of tax grain from Alexandria to Constantinople indicates to me that fiscal grain transport loomed large—then we should expect a significant share of shipwrecks with cargoes not dominated by amphorae, for grain traveled loose or in sacks.[227] So far, some 136 out of our 1,034 wrecks date from the era of late Roman annona shipments and offer some data about the main cargo, which for 119 (88 percent) was amphorae. Sixteen more ships are probably not grain ships either, since their main cargoes were building materials, ceramics, millstones, and metal. The sole candidate for the sort of voyage that must have dominated the late Roman sea lanes is a seventh-century wreck that has been identified as loaded with a grain cargo: the quite remarkable Saint-Gervais 2, which also offers one of the rare barrels.[228] Of course, since the ship sank off Marseille, it can scarcely have been on an annona run between Africa and Constantinople.

Nevertheless, the situation is not dire insofar as oil and wine traveled in amphorae and at least at times figured in the late Roman annona. Archaeologists increasingly suspect that one type of amphora, LRA 2, is connected with the fiscal supply system, since it tends to show up on sites that most likely benefited from the system—military bases.[229] If this association proves correct, it may become possible to identify ships that were on annona runs, as

---

223 Bass and van Doorninck, eds., *Yassı Ada*, record no repairs to what is left of the hull, although ample attention is devoted to the ship's carpenter's tools. Ships of course were routinely repaired while under way: see for instance the story of the ship's carpenter aboard the merchantman sailing from Constantinople to Gaul ca. 660–68, in McCormick, *Origins of the European Economy*, 855 no. 24. In this case, Prof. van Doorninck informs me that the Yassı Ada ship appeared to be very new, and that "bark was still adhering to one of the half-timber ceiling strakes in the bottom part of the hull." Dor D: Kingsley, *A Sixth-Century AD Shipwreck*, 16–20, mentions no repairs on the handful of strakes and other wooden elements recovered from this wreck.
224 Merchants who shipped heavy or costly cargoes aboard "old" ships had no right to indemnification: *Lex Rhodia* 3.11, 18.1–5.
225 See most recently on this theme, with further references, A. M. McCann, "Cosa and Deep Sea Exploration," in Hohlfelder, ed., *The Maritime World of Ancient Rome*, 37–50.
226 Kingsley, *A Sixth-Century AD Shipwreck*, 5; see also Royal, "2006 Turkish Coastal Survey," 96, on the sand cover that impedes survey detection of cultural deposits in Bodrum Bay.

227 Justinian, Edict 13.8, *CIC* 2:783.8–11, requires Egypt to ship 8 million unspecified units of grain to Constantinople. Over the past decade, disagreement has grown among specialists over which unit is meant here, in part because they have different understandings of the organization and finality of the grain levy and of the size of Constantinople's population. If the units are the standard Egyptian *artabai*, J. Durliat, *De la ville antique à la ville byzantine: Le problème des subsistances,* Collection de l'École française de Rome, 136 (Rome, 1990), 257–58, would convert the total to 160,000 metric tons. B. Sirks, "Some Observations on *Edictum Justiniani* XIII.8," in *Nourrir les cités de Méditerranée: Antiquité, temps modernes,* ed. B. Marin and C. Virlouvet (Paris, 2003), 213–22, calculates instead 245,000 metric tons if the units were *artabai*. If, however, as Sirks believes (214), the units are *modii italici*, he would calculate the total at 54,500 metric tons. Cf. most recently Prigent, "Le rôle des provinces," 270–73.
228 See note 122, above.
229 See Karagiorgou, "LR2: A Container for the Military Annona on the Danubian Border?"

opposed to those carrying private goods; there are some candidates in our database.²³⁰ Yet even if grain ships sometimes also carried amphorae, we are still left with a lot of missing ships. Can this be explained in part by the dynamics of sinking? Ships loaded with heavy amphorae or building materials are the most likely to have reached the bottom and stayed there.²³¹ Depending on how much ballast they carried, wooden ships that were not so heavily loaded need not have sunk to the bottom, unless and until they became waterlogged and lost their natural buoyancy. So long as they still floated, they could wash up on shore or rocks and be broken up. Another critical factor in preserving those ships that did reach the bottom is the nature of the seabed as shaped by the underwater topography, currents, and geology. For instance, rocky exposed shores were obviously a danger zone for ancient vessels, but generally we cannot expect to find much coherent shipwreck evidence there.²³² Cargo type and weight will join with the differing types of seabeds in different areas of the Mediterranean as critical elements in gauging the representativeness of the recorded wrecks. Only by remembering what we probably cannot see will we fully grasp the meaning of what we do observe.

As the evidence about shipwrecks grows and suggests fine details in how shipping patterns changed, we must weigh with care the reams of new data, integrating them into a broader explanatory picture of the changes experienced by ancient and medieval economies. Nevertheless, it is the very success of today's archaeologists in multiplying the data about containers and ships that enables a more critical—and ever more accurate—picture of change, growth, and decline in the movements, markets, and economies of the first millennium.

* * * * * * * *

Mind-sets, markets, containers, shipping, and exchange go together in the late ancient and early medieval Mediterranean, but they often do so in complicated ways. The term "market" is polysemantic; we need consistently to be clear on which meaning we are using. Even in the centuries when we rarely hear directly from the merchants themselves and when the records run thin, indirect indicators of commercial information about prices and market conditions are scattered across the written evidence. The allusions and the attitudes they document reveal an awareness of instrumental behavior, in Temin's economic sense, among the privileged classes who dictated the words preserved in our sources. This means that markets mattered throughout the first millennium.

To clarify with rigor the geographic and chronological trends in the structures of exchange that met in markets, we must seek, align, and compare reliable proxy indicators—that is, independently preserved series of data on communications with an economic component such as shipwrecks and the movements of individuals, coins, and ceramics. Where they converge we will find trade and markets, or at least exchange and distribution, mostly but not exclusively over long and midrange distances. Although this chapter has been more concerned with how we use the accumulating new evidence than what conclusions we may draw from it, the reflections nevertheless suggest some general if preliminary observations about the structure and development of the Mediterranean economies.

Down to the seventh century, the combined indicators of shipwreck patterns and pottery distribution sketch remarkably detailed pictures of links between producers and marketing areas; the complex array of amphorae and barrels, their designs and imitations, and their movements around the Mediterranean drive home the extraordinary sophistication of the economy the late Romans created. In particular, our growing knowledge of amphorae and of the extension of barrels helps untangle the supply chains that delivered goods to the late Roman marketplace, which in itself seems to have been changing. An operational and ergonomic approach to the containers deepens this understanding. As we consider the great question of collapse or transformation, the

---

230 LRA 2 amphorae are found, e.g., in the Cefalù wreck, fifth–sixth century, my 204 (Parker no. 292); Prasso, fifth–seventh century, no. 709 (Parker no. 900); Vendicari, no. 960, late fourth–early seventh century (Parker no. 1211).

231 Oleson and Adams, "Formation, Survey, and Sampling of the Wreck Sites," in *Deep-water Shipwrecks off Skerki Bank: The 1997 Survey*, ed. A. M. McCann and J. P. Oleson, Journal of Roman Archaeology, supp. ser. 58 (Portsmouth, R.I., 2004), 31, and especially the discussion of the "wrecking event" in K. Muckelroy, "The Archaeology of Shipwrecks," in *Maritime Archaeology: A Reader of Substantive and Theoretical Contributions*, ed. L. E. Babits and H. Van Tilburg (New York, 1998), 267–90, at 275.

232 This is of course an oversimplification. For a more sophisticated analysis and discussion of the correlation of topography, geological deposit, slope, sea horizon, and fetch, based on British waters, see Muckelroy, "The Archaeology of Shipwrecks," 270–74.

image of camel trains hauling the precious white wine of the Negev down to the sea at Gaza for shipment to the markets of Marseille or Constantinople emphasizes the logistical sophistication of late Roman market supply systems. It also underscores their fragility. Both texts and ship gear point to merchants' efforts to move away from state-regulated and -taxed markets in cities to more informal marketplaces, in settlements or on waterside landings, perhaps in rhythm to the loosening of the state's grip on society.

The world changed dramatically in the second half of our period, and those changes are reflected in the amphora arrays, shipwrecks, and price patterns of the Mediterranean economy. Constrained though we are by the drying up of written information that accompanied the economic transformations that we still perceive only dimly in much of the seventh- and eighth-century Mediterranean, indirect indications in the written sources reveal that members of the literate elite remained aware of the markets in their midst and of at least some of their workings. They further imply that what a modern economist would recognize as market conditions were present between ca. 350 and 1000, even if we cannot yet gauge more exactly when and where specific proportions of economic exchanges belonged to market as opposed to other types of exchange.

We are living in the golden age of Mediterranean archaeology. The rich new testimony of material culture obliges us to return, critically, to the written record. We must begin to think operationally and even experimentally about the objects that testify to ancient transport and markets, and learn to view the spectacular but rare wrecks that have been fully published against the massive aggregate of all known Mediterranean shipwrecks. Aggregation imposes simplification and quantification and requires a summary geodatabase. Even an early draft of such a geodatabase enables us to see the growth of the data since Parker's achievement of 1992 and to detect some new nuances. But the new data must be understood in the light of the economic conditions that shape ship movements. With them in mind, we can begin to visualize the changing patterns by which ancient and medieval ships tried to bring amphorae, barrels, and sacks of goods to market. Of course, in those cases that we can actually observe underwater, they failed, mortally, to do so. Success at understanding Byzantium's markets will entail getting more comparative data from new approaches to texts, drawing on land and sea finds and organizing the new data into geodatabases. We must think more and harder about what exactly we are seeing on the sea bottom, compared to what once sailed the sea surface.

• FOUR •

Commerce and Exchange in the Seventh and Eighth Centuries
Regional Trade and the Movement of Goods

JOHN F. HALDON

It is generally agreed that between the early seventh and the middle of the ninth century, the commercial networks of the Mediterranean and circum-Mediterranean worlds changed fairly dramatically. Urban social and economic life, along with many other features of late Roman culture, also changed radically across the course of the seventh century. It also seems generally agreed that by the middle of the eighth century the situation had stabilized, politically and economically; that a new social and political elite was evolving in the Byzantine world; that the state could largely conduct its operations by using money once more, though in many instances it had never ceased to be able to do this; and that by the early ninth century the beginnings of a real economic recovery can be detected in both the archaeological and the textual evidence. In the present contribution I will attempt to further break down and periodize the processes of change and the particular elements that together constituted those processes. The focus will be on the evidence for regional exchange across the Byzantine world, as well as across its borders or frontiers. Schematically, we can differentiate between the local, the regional, and the supraregional levels, so I will concentrate largely on the first two. By "local" I mean the areas around settlements that can be reached within a maximum of two or three days on foot, and that thus represent the absolute maximum distances across which productive activities could be carried on.

First of all, some basic premises. Whatever else the archaeological and textual evidence tells us about the fate of towns in the course of the seventh century, it is quite clear that the great majority of formerly urban settlement centers remained occupied. Even if we also know of several that were displaced or deserted—almost all located along the frontier where the warfare of the later seventh and early eighth century was most intense, and abandoned deliberately—most were not. The point is hardly new, but it is worth underlining. They changed in character, of course, as their occupied spaces shrank or were relocated within an originally larger area, but they continued to be settled, to bear their traditional names, and in many cases to support the presence of an ecclesiastical, military, or other establishment—although we rarely have much idea of how many people were actually involved. What has often not been appreciated is the degree to which older, established urban centers lost some of their functions to newer foci of activity: for Anatolia, work and discussion of these issues is in its infancy, although already it is apparent that a highly regionalized and locally varying (and inconsistent) hierarchy of settlement and fortification was evolving during the seventh to ninth centuries (now generally referred to as the transitional period, rather than a dark age).[1] For the

---

I am grateful to Cécile Morrisson, to the participants of the Dumbarton Oaks Spring Symposium 2008, and to the anonymous reviewers for their helpful comments and constructive criticism.

1 Note the discussion in J. Crow, "Byzantine Castles or Fortified Places in Pontus and Paphlagonia," in *Archaeology of the Countryside in Medieval Anatolia,* ed. T. Vorderstrasse and J. Roodenberg (Leiden, 2009), 25–43; P. Niewöhner, "Archäologie und die 'Dunklen Jahrhunderte' im byzantinischen Anatolien,"

southern Balkans it has been shown that—in some areas, at least—many formerly rural and usually upland settlements evolved an entirely new aspect, acquired sometimes quite elaborate defenses, and reflected the diffusion of urban qualities and functions away from settlements of a traditional urban character—a result of shifting government emphases in respect of defense, security, and fiscal administration, to the extent that we may reasonably challenge the distinction traditionally drawn between urban and rural.[2]

But all such communities or groups of communities needed food, services, various goods for ordinary day-to-day purposes, and the people and skills to provide them. Even a highly ruralized former town, where the population was largely involved in agricultural work, would require some such things. We should assume, therefore, that production for exchange and market activity, however limited, must always have continued at any continuously settled site.

The second point is that many such centers were also foci for members of the state or provincial elite. And right through the difficult second half of the seventh and into the eighth century, members of these elites were regularly in receipt of substantial sums in gold from the state in return for their service as military leaders, fiscal officials, and so forth. Elites continued to have demands and perceived needs for things that lesser people could neither afford nor aspire to, and demand of this sort—except in very unusual circumstances and for very limited periods—stimulated both production of the goods in demand and the commercial trade to get them to the point of sale.

In consequence, and whatever the transformations in the urban landscape and the settlement hierarchy of the Byzantine world, it seems reasonable to assume that there was always a reasonably active, even if very highly localized and at times and in places very low-level, market economy connecting rural settlements with their nearer functionally different neighbors (and here we could employ central place theories and landscape modeling as a framework for thinking about routes to markets that are lowest cost or are between centers of production and centers of consumption, resource catchment areas, and so forth).[3] Our problem is to understand how this arrangement worked at times when coin was in scarce supply, or when political conditions made rural life dangerous or untenable; doing so entails grasping the impact of a relatively high degree of militarization of the provincial fiscal system, which was organized around the supply and maintenance of soldiers, whether a local permanent garrison or a transient force of considerable size. We should not forget that even at the height of the commercial economy of the late Roman world in the fifth and sixth centuries, there were always areas that, because of location, or short-term local problems, or whatever reason, were relatively demonetized and devoid of market opportunities, and where the state, in par-

---

in *Post-Roman Towns, Trade and Settlement in Europe and Byzantium,* ed. J. Henning, vol. 2, *Byzantium, Pliska, and the Balkans,* Millennium-Studien zu Kultur und Geschichte des ersten Jahrtausends n. Chr. 5.2 (Berlin, 2007), 119–57; and idem, "Sind die Mauern die Stadt? Vorbericht über die siedlungsgeschichtlichen Ergebnisse neuer Grabungen im spätantiken und byzantinischen Milet," with a geoarchaeological contribution by H. Brückner and M. Müllenhoff, *AA* (2008): 181–201.

2 See A. W. Dunn, "Heraclius' 'Reconstruction of Cities' and Their Sixth-Century Balkan Antecedents," in *Acta XIII Congressus Internationalis Archaeologiae Christianae,* Studi di Antichità Cristiana 14 (Vatican City, 1998), 795–806; idem, "From *polis* to *kastron* in Southern Macedonia: Amphipolis, Khrysoupolis, and the Strymon Delta," in *Archéologie des espaces agraires méditerranéens au Moyen Âge,* ed. A. Bazzana, Castrum 5 (Madrid, 1999), 399–413; and C. Kirilov, "The Reduction of the Fortified City Area in Late Antiquity: Some Reflections on the End of the 'Antique City' in the Lands of the Eastern Roman Empire," in Henning, ed., *Post-Roman Towns, Trade and Settlement,* 2:3–24. For theoretical approaches to the urban/rural dichotomy, see, e.g., L. Leontidou, "Post-modernism and the City: Mediterranean Versions," *Urban Studies* 30 (1993): 949–65, and esp. idem, "Alternatives to Modernism in (Southern) Urban Theory: Exploring in-between Spaces," *International Journal of Urban and Regional Research* 20 (1996): 178–95.

3 For example, J. Koder, "Land-use and Settlement: Theoretical Approaches," in *General Issues in the Study of Medieval Logistics: Sources, Problems and Methodologies,* ed. J. F. Haldon, History of Warfare 36 (Leiden, 2005), 159–83; G. Bellavia, "Extracting 'Natural Pathways' from a Digital Elevation Model: Applications to Landscape Archaeological Studies," in *Archaeological Informatics: Pushing the Envelope,* ed. G. Burenholt, Proceedings of the 2001 Computer Applications and Quantitative Methods in Archaeology Conference, Visby, Sweden, BAR International Series 1016 (Oxford, 2001), 5–12; and the essays in G. Lock, ed., *Beyond the Map: Archaeology and Spatial Technologies* (Amsterdam, 2000). For some general considerations on both historical and archaeological approaches to the period from the sixth to the ninth century, see J. F. Haldon, "Social Transformation in the Sixth–Ninth Century East," in *Social and Political Life in Late Antiquity,* ed. W. Bowden, A. Gutteridge, and C. Machado, Late Antique Archaeology 3.1 (Leiden, 2006), 603–47.

ticular the army and the public post, sometimes provided a temporary market.

Of course, all things are relative. A "flourishing market exchange" in a provincial town of the middle of the eighth century is not necessarily the same as it would have been in the same provincial town in the middle of the sixth century. Furthermore, inland centers, even if located at major nodal points, have far fewer openings for trade beyond the very local than does, say, a coastal settlement with a decent beach or landing place and a productive agrarian hinterland. There are also natural factors to bear in mind—disease, earthquake, bad harvests, and famine. The still hotly debated impact of the appearance of plague in the 540s and its recurrence at intervals until the middle of the eighth century in the whole eastern Mediterranean and Near Eastern zone clearly must have been dramatic—affecting population, the production and availability of resources in labor power and goods, demand, and levels of production. But generalizing in this way throws up a series of difficulties, since in many areas the degree of regional and even of local variation seems to have been substantial.[4] In addition, the written accounts are themselves contradictory, especially in the early Islamic world, where some texts contain graphic accounts of the horrific consequences and high mortality of visitations of the plague while others seem to reflect a relatively flourishing commercial and agrarian economy—a picture borne out to some extent, for some areas, by the archaeological evidence.[5] In considering demand, exchange routes, and production, unfortunately, it is as yet impossible to establish the local constraints imposed by such factors and their effect on markets other than by making a series of sometimes potentially dubious assumptions not necessarily supported by any clear evidence. Thus, though we may be able to draw some conclusions about the degree of demand or the level of exchange (insofar as the material evidence permits a degree of quantification), for much of the area with which we are concerned we can say little at present about the precise causal relationships underlying the patterns that emerge, beyond the very generalizations that we have already noted are so problematic.[6]

In focusing on local and regional exchange, therefore, we might look for evidence of production and commerce at three different levels, each involving progressively greater distances, smaller volumes of higher-value goods, and fewer people. At the first level is the highly localized circuit of agricultural produce or other goods from areas of production and harvest to the nearest market center, and the return of various manufactures to the rural centers. At a slightly higher level, we have the movement of goods and people between such market centers, some of which may be ports. And finally, there is movement between provincial centers of this sort and the nearest larger ports or metropolitan centers. Locating archaeological and textual evidence for the types of goods that were moved between these different levels and within them is, for this period at least, rather more difficult.

Demand

There seems little point in discussing trade and exchange unless we also look at demand—who wanted what, in what quantities, and from which places? The political elite of the empire, both at Constantinople and in the provinces, had demands that could be met only by the import of luxury commodities and by the movement of products such as wine, olive oil, fish, meat on the hoof, and spices across sometimes considerable distances. They continued to receive substantial salaries in gold coin, and as far as we can tell such payments never stopped. While it may signify no more than one individual's tastes,

---

4 See in particular M. McCormick, "Toward a Molecular History of the Justinianic Pandemic," in *Plague and the End of Antiquity: The Pandemic of 541–750*, ed. L. K. Little (Cambridge, 2007), 290–312; L. I. Conrad, "Die Pest und ihr soziales Umfeld im Nahen Osten des frühen Mittelalters," *Der Islam* 73 (1996): 81–192.

5 See the material assembled by M. Morony, "'For whom does the writer write?' The First Bubonic Plague Pandemic According to Syriac Sources," in Little, ed., *Plague and the End of Antiquity*, 59–86, esp. 72–81; and compare it with, for example, A. Walmsley, "Production, Exchange and Regional Trade in the Islamic East Mediterranean: Old Structures, New Systems?" in *The Long Eighth Century: Production, Distribution and Demand*, ed. I. L. Hansen and C. Wickham (Leiden, 2000), 265–343, and idem, "The Village Ascendant in Byzantine and Early Islamic Jordan: Socio-economic Forces and Cultural Responses," in *Les villages dans l'empire byzantin (IVᵉ–XVᵉ siècle)*, ed. J. Lefort, C. Morrisson, and J.-P. Sodini, Réalités Byzantines 11 (Paris, 2005), 511–22.

6 See H. N. Kennedy, "Justinianic Plague in Syria and the Archaeological Evidence," in Little, ed., *Plague and the End of Antiquity*, 87–95; L. I. Conrad, "Epidemic Disease in Central Syria in the Late Sixth Century: Some New Insights from the Verse of Hassan ibn Thabit," *BMGS* 18 (1994): 12–58.

contacts, or interests, the fact that a fragment of a T'ang marbled ware vessel of the later eighth or early ninth century was recovered from the fortress at Methone in the Peloponnese suggests that possibilities were broad.[7] And there is no reason to believe that the middling strata of rural as well as urban society did not also push the market to provide various goods not produced locally, whether these should count as "luxuries" or not. Such demands will have been present especially in those areas where rural production for the market, as opposed to a largely subsistence economy, was itself an important feature of the local and, in consequence, the regional economy.[8] The ecclesiastical establishment, with its bishops and their clergy spread across the empire, generated similar demands; and the presence of soldiers, even in relatively limited numbers, created a market of some sort for leather goods, cloth, metalwork, and livestock, quite apart from foodstuffs. Naturally, such demands might not always be met, and in the most isolated areas they might have been satisfied only rarely, although satisfying them certainly represents one way through which both gold and bronze coins might reach regions distant from the capital or the army. The movement of livestock, in particular sheep, from the grazing lands of central Anatolia to be sold in Constantinople, both to state purchasers and to private households, has been invoked as one likely mechanism by which coin might reach the interior of the region without the involvement of the army or fiscal system, but the amounts are uncertain and were probably always relatively insignificant.[9]

Moreover, it is by no means unlikely that for locally based and regular transactions some arrangements for credit were employed, as had been the case on large estates in the period up to the Persian and then Arab invasions of the seventh century. For supplies for the military, of course, transactions could be written off against taxes due, a system about which we know quite a lot.[10] The continued minting of a fairly stable gold coinage throughout our period certainly made the employment of such instruments entirely practical. In this respect, therefore, the degree of actual monetization of the economy as a whole and regionally—that is, the extent and velocity of circulation of bronze as well as gold—is perhaps less important than the degree to which the gold coinage could be relied on as a sound basis for the calculation and exchange of notional values.[11]

The extent to which estate management and the organization of labor changed between the sixth and eighth or ninth centuries (even if the ratio of estates to nontenant communities and landowners had altered) remains unclear, although continuity and flexibility in such micromanagerial arrangements are highly likely. But shifts in the incidence of emphyteutic leaseholding, for example, along with the breakup of some large estates in the Anatolian regions of the Byzantine state, are probably reflected in changes in local and possibly regional patterns of demand and the distribution of goods, as peasant households in some communities became less dependent on labor contracts to estates, more subject to local military and fiscal demands, or both.[12] By the same token, the reduction in the money supply in the provinces after 658 (see below) will have increased the difficulty of estate management in some cases—those in which estate managers paid their labor force in credit chits exchangeable for petty cash—thereby inducing shifts in patterns of estate administration

---

7 N. D. Kontogiannis, "A Fragment of a Chinese Marbled Ware Bowl from Methoni, Greece," *Byzantinistica* 4 (2002): 39–46.
8 See in particular the discussion in S. A. Kingsley, "Late Antique Trade: Research Methodologies and Field Practices," in *Theory and Practice in Late Antique Archaeology*, ed. L. Lavan and W. Bowden (Leiden, 2003), 113–38.
9 M. F. Hendy, *Studies in the Byzantine Monetary Economy, c. 300–1450* (Cambridge, 1985), 565–66.
10 P. Sarris, "Rehabilitating the Great Estate: Aristocratic Property and Economic Growth in the Late Antique East," in *Recent Research on the Late Antique Countryside*, ed. W. Bowden, L. Lavan, and C. Machado (Leiden, 2004), 55–71, at 65–67; J. F. Haldon, *Warfare, State and Society in the Byzantine World, 565–1204* (London, 1999), 140–47.
11 See N. Oikonomidès, "Σε ποιό βαθμό ήταν εκχρηματισμένη η μεσοβυζαντινή οικονομία;" in *Ροδωνία: Τιμή στον M. I. Μανούσακα*, ed. Ch. Maltezou, Th. Detorakes, and Ch. Charalampakes (Rethymno, 1994), 363–70.
12 So the accounts in the letters from the 820s of Ignatios the deacon might suggest, e.g., *Epp.* 7 and 8, *The Correspondence of Ignatios the Deacon: Text, Translation and Commentary*, ed. C. Mango, with S. Efthymiadis, CFHB 39 (Washington, D.C., 1997), 38–44; for ecclesiastical estates mismanaged by local bishops, see Theodore Stoudite, *Theodori Studitae Epistulae*, ed. A. Fatouros, 2 vols., CFHB 31 (Vienna, 1991–92), no. 11.85–125. See A. Kazhdan, "Ignatios the Deacon's Letters on the Byzantine Economy," *BSl* 53 (1992): 197–201. For shifts in landlord-tenant relations across the period from the sixth to the eighth centuries, see J. F. Haldon, *Byzantium in the Seventh Century: The Transformation of a Culture*, rev. ed. (Cambridge, 1997), 132–41; M. Kaplan, *Les hommes et la terre à Byzance du VIe au XIe siècle* (Paris, 1992), 161–69, 186–218; and for estate management and labor in the sixth century, P. Sarris, *Economy and Society in the Age of Justinian* (Cambridge, 2006), 29–70.

and finance.[13] The degree to which a reduced supply of low-denomination petty coinage affected ordinary day-to-day exchange activities will thus also have varied considerably from region to region, depending not only on distance from markets and sources of ready money but also on estate structure and landlord–tenant relationships. In some areas (major urban centers such as Constantinople and its economic hinterland), market-based exchanges may have continued relatively uninterrupted, in spite of significant disturbances in the broader economy; in others, its cessation or at least disruption had a more visible impact on the fabric of society and economy, as the archaeological evidence presented below will illustrate. In both cases, regional particularities played a key role.

Ceramic Evidence

The evidence of ceramics, both fine and coarse wares, can tell us a great deal about how certain types of goods were moved around as articles of trade and exchange, how far they traveled, and to what sort of context. It can also be very misleading—a few sherds of a particular type of tableware can be used to generate an exaggerated picture of the volume of trade, for example, in the absence of adequate samples and carefully plotted distribution maps tracking how regular and how far such commerce or exchange of goods actually was. But we cannot do without it; and so, bearing in mind some of these caveats, a brief survey of what types of pottery were still being moved around the Byzantine world from the later seventh century onward will provide a basic framework for our discussion. It is now generally agreed that as patterns of long-distance exchange were transformed over the later sixth and seventh centuries, there was an increasing regionalization of commerce, although it is important to note that this does not mean that trade over longer distances ceased. Indeed, quite the contrary was true—ceramics from Egypt and Palestine were still reaching Corinth, for example, in the early eighth century.[14] The ceramic evidence suggests a series of less extended, overlapping inter- and intra-regional networks, which moved goods by stages, rather than single routes traversing really long distances. We can find the occasional exception, but the generalization still holds. As a result, during the second half of the seventh century the distribution of many fine and coarse wares becomes increasingly localized.[15] The evidence for this is now so well established that it hardly needs to be demonstrated.

It is this more regionally nuanced pattern that appears to dominate from around the turn of the seventh to eighth centuries and into the ninth.[16] A major problem is the enormous uncertainty that still remains about typologies and their chronology—we know far more about seventh-century ceramics than those of the eighth and ninth centuries. Indeed, it is now becoming clear that some of the pottery whose production had been assumed to cease by the later seventh century in fact continued to be produced well into the eighth, throwing into doubt some of the conclusions about the dates of occupation levels on sites. At the same time, changes in form may also reflect shifts in both food preparation methods and

---

13 Sarris, *Economy and Society in the Age of Justinian*, 50–68; idem, "The Origins of the Manorial Economy: New Insights from Late Antiquity," *EHR* 119 (2004): 279–311.

14 For a very positive assessment, see, for example, J.-P. Sodini, "Production et échanges dans le monde protobyzantin (IVᵉ–VIIᵉ s.): Le cas de la céramique," in *Byzanz als Raum: Zu Methoden und Inhalten der historischen Geographie des östlichen Mittelmeerraumes*, ed. K. Belke, F. Hild, J. Koder, and P. Soustal, DenkWien 283 (Vienna, 2000), 181–208; and for a variety of regional examples, see J. Boardman, "Pottery," in *Excavation in Chios, 1952–1955: Byzantine Emporio*, ed. M. Balance et al. (Athens, 1989), 88–121, at 92–93, 106; E. Prokopiou, "Ἀμαθούντα, ἀνατολικὴ νεκρόπολη: Τάφο ὀστεοφυλάκιο τοῦ 7ου μ.Χ. αἰ.," in *Reports of the Department of Antiquities of Cyprus* (Nicosia, 1995), 264–67; the annual reports on the excavations at Perissa on Thera by E. Geroussi, "Annual Reports on Excavations at Perissa on Thera," *Ἀρχ.Δελτ.* 45–49 (1990–94); and the summary of Cypriot ceramics of the later seventh century in M. Touma, "Chypre: Céramique et problèmes," in *The Dark Centuries of Byzantium*, ed. E. Kountoura-Galaki (Athens, 2001), 267–91; and see B. L. Johnson, "Late Roman Imports at Corinth from Egypt and Syro-Palestine," *AJA* 89 (1985): 335–36.

15 There is a good summary of material and general trends in Sodini, "Production et échanges"; also J. Vroom, "Late Antique Pottery, Settlement and Trade in the East Mediterranean: A Preliminary Comparison of Ceramics from Limyra (Lycia) and Boeotia," in Bowden, Lavan, and Machado, eds., *Recent Research on the Late Antique Countryside*, 281–331.

16 J. W. Hayes, *Excavations at Saraçhane in Istanbul*, vol. 2, *The Pottery* (Princeton, N.J., 1992), 7. For possible connections between Constantinople and Islamic Bosra, for example, see F. Sogliani, "Le testimonianze ceramiche tardoantiche e medievali a Bosra (Siria): Per un primo contributo alla conoscenza delle tipologie," in *Ravenna, Costantinopoli, Vicino Oriente*, Corso di Cultura sull'Arte Ravennate e Bizantina 41 (Ravenna, 1994), 433–62, at 442–43. For southern Italy, see C. Raimondo, "Aspetti di economia e società nella Calabria bizantina," in *Histoire et culture dans l'Italie byzantine*, ed. A. Jacob, J.-M. Martin, and G. Noyé, Collection de l'École française de Rome 363 (Rome, 2006), 407–43.

diet, and thus a number of important changes can be detected in the culture of food and cooking.[17]

The greater localization of production is illustrated by the appearance at several coastal sites in southern and western Asia Minor of local imitations of late Roman wares, as well as by the production of relatively crude coarse and kitchen wares for purely local use.[18] In the Peloponnese and the Aegean regions, local production of both fine and coarse wares predominates after the end of the seventh century, and this dominance continues to hold well into the ninth century.[19] Coastal sites demonstrate a greater variety of imports, as we might expect, but they come largely from neighboring regions of the Aegean. And networks shifted in emphasis and extent. Even where local wares can be clearly identified, as at Anemourion, for example (although the chronology remains vague), the presence of substantial quantities of Cypriot Red Slip Ware suggests a somewhat wider range of contacts.[20] Some of the finer glazed wares produced at Constantinople reached Crete, the Aegean, mainland centers such as Athens and Corinth, and the Peloponnese, as well as sites in western Asia Minor such as Sardis, Magnesia on the Maeander, and Miletos, Kyaneai, and Limyra in Lycia; they also—but apparently in small amounts—penetrated inland as far as Amorion, and into the Black Sea as far as Cherson. In the lower town at Corinth there is ceramic evidence of contacts with Sparta and the island of Melos, and a single early ʿAbbāsid coin may suggest a further-reaching association. At Corinth, small quantities of Constantinopolitan Glazed White Ware have been located in late eighth- and early ninth-century contexts.[21]

Interregional and indeed international networks thus remained in use, as the evidence from a number of southern and western Anatolian coastal sites suggests, even if in some cases new sources of products were found for former late Roman markets.[22] While pottery from North Africa certainly is reduced to

---

17   See P. Armstrong, "Trade in the Eighth Century in the East Mediterranean," in *Byzantine Trade, 4th–12th Centuries: The Archaeology of Local, Regional and International Exchange*, ed. M. Mundell Mango, Papers of the Thirty-eighth Spring Symposium of Byzantine Studies, St John's College, University of Oxford, March 2004, Society for the Promotion of Byzantine Studies 14 (Aldershot, 2009), 157–78; and on food preparation and ceramic forms, see P. Arthur, "Pots and Boundaries: On Cultural and Economic Areas between Late Antiquity and the Early Middle Ages," in *LRCW 2: Late Roman Coarse Wares, Cooking Wares and Amphorae in the Mediterranean: Archaeology and Archaeometry*, ed. M. Bonifay and J.-C. Tréglia, BAR International Series 1662 (Oxford, 2007), 5–27; J. Vroom, "Medieval Ceramics and the Archaeology of Consumption in Eastern Anatolia," in Vorderstrasse and Roodenberg, eds., *Archaeology of the Countryside in Medieval Anatolia*, 235–58.

18   See Vroom, "Late Antique Pottery, Settlement and Trade," 288–308; eadem, "New Light on 'Dark Age' Pottery: A Note on Finds in South-western Turkey," in *Rei Cretariae Romanae Fautorum Acta* 39 (2005): 249–55. On crude local coarse wares, see W. Bowden, *Epirus Vetus: The Archaeology of a Late Antique Province* (London, 2003), (focusing on Butrint).

19   H. Anagnostakes and N. Poulou-Papadimitriou, "Η πρωτοβυζαντινή Μεσσήνη (5ος–7ος αιώνας) και προβλήματα της χειροποίητης κεραμικής στην Πελοπόννησο," *Σύμμεικτα* 11 (1997): 229–322; N. Poulou-Papadimitriou, "Βυζαντινή κεραμική απο τον ελληνικό νησιωτικό χώρο και απο την Πελοπόννησο," in Kountoura-Galake, ed., *The Dark Centuries of Byzantium*, esp. 240–41. See also F. Curta, *The Making of the Slavs: History and Archaeology of the Lower Danube Region, c. 500–700* (Cambridge, 2001); and see also S. Gutierrez, *Cora de Tudmīr, de la antigüedad tardia al mundo islámico: Poblamiento y cultura material* (Madrid, 1996), esp. 178–86; T. Völling, "The Last Christian Greeks and the First Pagan Slavs in Olympia," in Kountoura-Galaki, ed., *The Dark Centuries of Byzantium*, 303–23. Most recently, see Vroom, "New Light on 'Dark Age' Pottery," 249–55.

20   See the survey in A. Lampropoulou, E. Anagnostakes, V. Konte, and A. Panopoulou, "Συμβολή εις την ερμηνεία των αρχαιολογικών τεκμηρίων της Πελοποννήσου κατα τους σκοτεινούς αιώνες," in Kountoura-Galake, ed., *The Dark Centuries of Byzantium*, 189–229, with conclusions at 221–22; and, e.g., R. Etzeoglou, "Le céramique de Karyoupolis," in *Recherches sur la céramique byzantine: Actes du Colloque organisé par l'École Française d'Athènes et l'Université de Strasbourg II*, ed. V. Déroche and J.-M. Spieser (Athens and Paris, 1989), 151–56, for the production of a range of local ceramic types and the kilns where they were produced. For Anemourion, see the summary report in J. Russell, "Anemurium: The Changing Face of a Roman City," *Archaeology* 33.5 (1980): 31–40; and esp. C. Williams, "A Byzantine Well-deposit from Anemourium (Rough Cilicia)," *AnatSt* 27 (1977): 175–90, with Vroom, "New Light on 'Dark Age' Pottery," 249–55. The ceramic profile here is of the dominance of Phokaian and related wares, with an admixture of Palestinian wares, until the 650s, followed by a period of local production and the appearance of some glazed wares, although not from Constantinople.

21   G. D. R. Sanders, "New Relative and Absolute Chronologies for 9th to 13th Century Glazed Wares at Corinth: Methodology and Social Conclusions," in Belke et al., eds., *Byzanz als Raum*, 153–73, esp. 162–65; a good summary for the Aegean is in J. Vroom, "The Other Dark Ages: Early Medieval Pottery Finds in the Aegean as an Archaeological Challenge," in *Economic Landscape: Modern Methods for Ancient Productions, Trento 29–30 April 2005*, BAR International Series (Oxford, forthcoming).

22   While the evidence is sparse, late Roman glassware disappears from finds in China dated to the sixth to seventh century, to be replaced by vessels from the Islamic world or imitations of them: see H. Kinoshita, "Foreign Glass Excavated in China, from

a trickle after the end of the seventh century, the ceramic record indicates continued regular contacts with the Levant through the eighth and into the ninth century that brought both imported fine ware and amphorae, although it is very difficult to quantify the scale and frequency of such connections.[23] By the same token, there is solid evidence of Red Slip Ware being imported from Egypt to Cyprus at the end of the seventh and in the early eighth century, and indeed the chronology for these Cypriot wares has now been pushed well into the later eighth century; for that reason, sites at which it has been found and which had previously been thought to exhibit no eighth-century ceramic activity can now be looked at anew.[24] Likewise, wares from Palestine and Syria are also found on the island, suggestive of the open communications within this subregion.[25] Another type of fine and semi-fine ware, of good quality and with painted decoration (referred to as "Central Greek Painted Ware"), appears beginning in the early seventh century around the Aegean and southern Balkans at sites such as Argos, Corinth, Athens, Thessalonike, and Constantinople. It also reached Crete, Thasos, Delphi, and Demetrias. In southern Italy the production of a range of local decorated semi-fine and coarse wares thrived, representing an important regional tradition independent of the areas to the north and east. The Red Line-Painted and other Slip Wares found at sites in southern Italy, in and around Naples, for example, as well as at other southern Italian sites (both those within Byzantine territory and in Lombard-controlled regions), were especially prominent. Many of these bear striking similarities to contemporary decorated wares from Egypt and Palestine. That such wares are found at these sites and many others in the eastern Mediterranean basin in levels of the later seventh and eighth centuries suggests contacts, regular if not frequent, between the regions concerned. Ceramics associated with sites at Athens, Corinth, and Aegina are also found at Otranto in southern Italy. Even small and relatively insignificant coastal settlements seem to have maintained contacts with areas at some distance, as at Diaporit near Butrint in Albania, for example, or Aphiona on Kerkyra. At Butrint and neighboring sites in particular, the turn of the eighth to ninth century appears to mark a watershed in the pattern of exchange. From the later eighth century on, the evidence is of an increasing volume of exchange with Italian centers. Importantly, however, the presence of Crimean transport amphorae at both Butrint and northern Italian coastal sites such as Commacchio shows that while local patterns of exchange were altering, certain longer-distance commodities remained continuously in demand.[26]

Inland, particularly in Asia Minor, where it has long been recognized that localized production and distribution predominated throughout the late Roman period, there is little doubt that the pattern of production must have remained more or less the same at the most general level, although considerable dislocation of both centers of production and of ceramic types surely sometimes occurred in the unsettled conditions of the second half of the seventh century, even in the areas nearest to Constantinople—we simply have, at the moment, no real analysis of the regional ceramic types to draw on. This is precisely why sites such as Amorion or Euchaita, or the small rural site at Çadır Höyük near Yozgat (to the south of Euchaita), are potentially of such importance, because in theory at least they should inform

---

the 4th to 12th Centuries," in Mundell Mango, ed., *Byzantine Trade, 4th–12th Centuries*, 253–61.

23 Vroom, "Late Antique Pottery, Settlement and Trade"; eadem, "New Light on 'Dark Age' Pottery"; and eadem, "Limyra in Lycia: Byzantine/Umayyad Pottery Finds from Excavations in the Eastern Part of the City," in *Céramiques antiques en Lycie (VIIᵉ S. a.C.–VIIᵉ S. p.C.): Les produits et les marchés*, ed. S. Lemaître (Bordeaux, 2007), 261–92.

24 See Vroom, "Limyra in Lycia."

25 J. W. Hayes, "Pottery," in A. H. S. Megaw et al., *Kourion: Excavations in the Episcopal Precinct* (Washington, D.C., 2007), 435–75, at 436, 438.

26 Details summarized, with literature, in Poulou-Papadimitriou, "Βυζαντινή κεραμική," 236–37. For the Italian material, see G. Noyé, "Quelques observations sur l'évolution de l'habitat en Calabre du Vᵉ au XIᵉ siècle," *RSBN*, n.s., 25 (1988): 57–138; and P. Arthur and H. Patterson, "Ceramics and Early Medieval Central and Southern Italy: A 'Potted History'," in *La storia dell'alto medioevo Italiano (VI–X secolo) alla luce dell'archeologia*, ed. R. Francovich and G. Noyé (Florence, 1994), 409–41. For a brief overview, see C. J. Wickham, "Early Medieval Archaeology in Italy: The Last Twenty Years," *Archeologia Medievale* 26 (1999): 7–20; Vroom, "The Other Dark Ages"; and most recently S. Gelichi, "Flourishing Places in North-eastern Italy: Towns and *emporia* between Late Antiquity and the Carolingian Age," in *Post-Roman Towns, Trade and Settlement in Europe and Byzantium*, ed. J. Henning, vol. 1, *The Heirs of the Roman West*, Millennium-Studien zu Kultur und Geschichte des ersten Jahrtausends n. Chr. 5.1 (Berlin, 2007), 77–104. For Diaporit and Aphiona, see Bowden, *Epirus Vetus*, 201–11.

us of the extent to which ceramics from far away reached inland, how far local production radiated out from such sites, and how their size and location affected the movement of goods. The red-fabric wares identified at Amorion, which seem to be local versions of the Constantinopolitan GWW I (a type of Glazed White Ware) and are dated to the first half of the ninth century and perhaps earlier, may have traveled—it will be interesting to learn how far.[27] And even if still highly regional in its economy, Amorion seems to have been a good deal better off than Euchaita. The latter, in contrast, was a fortress town, which—although the home of a saint's cult, the center of an ecclesiastical province, and an important military base—appears from our limited evidence to date to have been really very much poorer. A few fragments of both glazed and unglazed Constantinopolitan White Ware have been found from surface collection, but it is at the moment impossible to say whether these represent any sort of substantial commercial activity. By the same token, there appear to be a number of local coarse wares, not yet firmly identified, which may come from the region around Euchaita, and which may be distributed only on a regional and subregional basis.

Sagalassos in Pisidia had been a major center for pottery production from the first century BC, remaining a substantial producer into the very first years of the seventh century AD. In the fourth and fifth centuries its pottery reached much of southern and western Anatolia and its coastal regions, as well as traveling as far as Egypt (and archaeological evidence of the import of Nile fish show that the trade was reciprocal). Yet by the early seventh century, Sagalassos was exporting—still in substantial quantities—almost exclusively to centers around it on the Anatolian plateau, including Amorion, and rarely reaching coastal sites. Conversely, very little African Red Slip material, even from Cilicia and northern Syrian centers such as Antioch, or Phokaian ware appears to have reached either Sagalassos or Amorion, although routes across Anatolia from Constantinople were regularly traveled by both military and nonmilitary personnel. And in the later seventh century, local semi-fine and coarse kitchen wares, found at a number of rural sites around Sagalassos itself (which remained partly occupied), were being produced and distributed in the immediate region. Localization appears to be the standard pattern.[28]

Yet while this conclusion may indeed reflect the still very limited amount of data available, it seems to also reflect a more exaggerated version of probably well-established patterns of inland exchange reaching back to well before any period of crisis. At the small defended rural settlement at Çadır Höyük, a local imitation of late sixth- and seventh-century African Red Slip Ware has been identified, along with other local ware of a slightly later date, and it is difficult to know the origin of this copy of another localized version. At Euchaita, a few sherds of Constantinopolitan Glazed White Ware datable to the seventh–eighth and the ninth–tenth centuries have been recovered, but there is no way of knowing how it reached the area (and substantially greater quantities of unglazed white ware of the same periods have also been found, probably reflecting the existence of an as yet unidentified local or regional production center). At Amorion, only very sparse evidence of the Constantinopolitan glazed white products has so far come to light, suggesting that when the Sagalassos production ceased it must have been forced back on its own resources.[29] At other inland centers, such as Ankara, highly regionalized production predominated after the middle of the seventh century, with very little evidence for any interregional movement. Indeed, throughout the Byzantine world and

---

27 See A. E. Laiou and C. Morrisson, *The Byzantine Economy* (Cambridge, 2007), 75.

28 See A. K. Vionis, J. Poblome, and M. Waelkens, "Ceramic Continuity and Daily Life in Medieval Sagalassos, SW Anatolia (ca. 650–1250 AD)," in Vorderstrasse and Roodenberg, eds., *Archaeology of the Countryside in Medieval Anatolia*, 191–13; H. Vanhaverbeke, A. K. Vionis, J. Poblome, and M. Waelkens, "What Happened After the Seventh Century AD? A Different Perspective on Post-Roman Rural Anatolia," ibid., 177–90.

29 Local conditions were obviously crucial in such cases: at Amorion, there was clearly a specific market, and as the distances involved were not too great (Sagalassos is about 240 km south of Amorion) goods in bulk could be transported. See S. Mitchell, E. Owens, and M. Waelkens, "Ariassos and Sagalassos 1988," *AnatSt* 39 (1989): 63–77, esp. 74–77; and C. S. Lightfoot, "Amorium Excavations 1994: The Seventh Preliminary Report," *AnatSt* 45 (1995): 105–38, at 122 (C. Wagner, "Pottery"). For Sagalassos, see H. Vanhaverbeke, F. Martens, M. Waelkens, and J. Poblome, "Late Antiquity in the Territory of Sagalassos," in Bowden, Lavan, and Machado, eds., *Recent Research on the Late Antique Countryside*, 247–79; and for Çadır Höyük, see the summary in M. Cassis, "Çadır Höyük: A Rural Settlement in Byzantine Anatolia," in Vorderstrasse and Roodenberg, eds., *Archaeology of the Countryside in Medieval Anatolia*, 1–24. For Euchaita, see J. F. Haldon, H. Elton, and J. Newhard, "The Avkat Archaeological Project 2009," *AnatArch* 15 (2009): 17–18.

beyond, the industrial-scale production of ceramics for export seems to have fallen off; they were replaced by locally produced wares, on the one hand, and by household-produced wares, on the other. In Asia Minor, such phenomena could indicate both a shrinkage in demand for professionally produced wares and a decline in urban markets, as well as concomitant effects on well-established inland patterns of commerce and movement of goods. Recent work in the Göksu (Kalykadnos) Valley (in south-central Asia Minor) has identified a locally produced painted coarse ware that seems to reflect both local production centers and local market demands, since it apparently is not found outside the region. There is some slight evidence that this pattern of demand and exchange continues beyond the seventh century.[30]

None of this means that there were no contacts with the wider world: survey work in the Lycian highlands has revealed the presence of Cypriot Red Slip Wares, for example, and at one such site a small amount of Constantinopolitan White Ware has been found. At Limyra, some 6 kilometers inland from Phoinix on the south Lycian coast, there is evidence for contacts with a number of nearby coastal sites as well as with Cyprus, Egypt, and the Near East. In more distant regions that had been tied in with a wider late Roman network, such as Cherson in the Crimea, the ceramic evidence shows a very marked decline in non-locally produced wares after the middle of the seventh century (although Constantinopolitan wares have been identified). At Cherson, the exception to this localization is represented by the amphorae associated with the southern Pontos, where commercial links—which may also have been supported or directed to some extent by state officials—appear to have been continuous throughout. Conversely, however, Crimean amphorae continued to be traded westward into the Aegean and Adriatic throughout the eighth and ninth centuries. Likewise at Bosporos/Kerch, ceramics from the southern Black Sea littoral and from Constantinople dated to the seventh into the ninth century (and later) confirm unbroken commercial connections, even if on a reduced scale compared with trade in the sixth century.[31]

One link for which we might expect to find some archaeological evidence is that between the southern coast of the Black Sea, in particular Paphlagonia, and the capital, since we know that grain was delivered to Constantinople on state-contracted ships in the early ninth century, and probably long before. Yet the nature and volume of this traffic is unclear and there is as yet no identifiable archaeological link, in part because we have no ceramic typology for Paphlagonian sites that can be related to ceramics in Constantinople. Whether such a relationship is reflected in the incidence of the standard globular amphorae and glazed white wares of the seventh and eighth centuries at sites throughout the Aegean, or in the presence of Constantinopolitan wares at sites around the Black Sea coast from contexts dating to the middle or later ninth century onward, is at present difficult to say.[32]

---

30 See M. P. C. Jackson, "Local Painted Pottery Trade in Early Byzantine Isauria," in Mundell Mango, ed., *Byzantine Trade, 4th–12th Centuries*, 137–43, esp. 142–43; also idem, "Medieval Rural Settlement at Kilise Tepe in the Göksu Valley," in Vorderstrasse and Roodenberg, eds., *Archaeology of the Countryside in Medieval Anatolia*, 71–83.

31 See R. M. Harrison, "Amorium Excavations 1991: The Fourth Preliminary Report," *AnatSt* 42 (1992): 207–22, at 216. For the Lycian material, see S. Mitchell, "The Settlement of Pisidia in Late Antiquity and the Byzantine Period: Methodological Problems," in Belke et al., eds., *Byzanz als Raum*, 139–52, at 146; and Vroom, "Limyra in Lycia." For Cherson, see A. I. Romančuk, "Torgovlya Chersonnesa v VII–XII vv.," *Byzantinobulgarica* 7 (1981): 319–31; A. I. Romančuk and O. R. Belova, "K probleme gorodskoi kul'tury rannesrednevokovogo Khersonesa," *ADSV* 54 (1987): 52–68, at 56–59; and esp. A. Sazanov, "Les ensembles clos de Kherson de la fin du 6ᵉ siècle au troisième quart du 7ᵉ s.: Les problèmes de la chronologie de la céramique," in *Les sites archéologiques en Crimée et au Caucase durant l'Antiquité tardive et le haut Moyen Âge*, ed. M. Kazanski and V. Soupault (Leiden, 2000), 253–93. For Kertch, see the relevant chapters in *Materialy po arkheologii, istorii i etnografii Tavrii*, vol. 6 (Simferopol, 1998); and the Amastris region amphorae: J. Crow and S. Hill, "The Byzantine Fortifications of Amastris in Paphlagonia," *AnatSt* 45 (1995): 251–65.

32 See *The Great Palace of the Byzantine Emperors, Being a First Report on the Excavations Carried Out in Istanbul on Behalf of the Walker Trust (The University of St Andrews, 1935–1938)* (London, 1947), 46; Hayes, *Excavations at Saraçhane*, 12, 19; G. D. R. Sanders, "Pottery from Medieval Levels in the Orchestra and Lower Cavea," *BSA* 90 (1995): 451–57; idem, *Byzantine Glazed Pottery at Corinth to c. 1125* (Birmingham, 1995), 232–33, 259–60; F. Waagé, "The Roman and Byzantine Pottery," *Hesp* 2 (1933): 321–22 (for Athens' Agora excavations); Ch. Bakirtzis and D. Papanikola-bakirtzi, "De la céramique byzantine en glaçure à Thessalonique," *Byzantino-Bulgarica* 7 (1981): 421–36, at 422 (various Greek sites); A. L. Jakobson, *Keramika i keramicheskoe proizvodstvo srednevekovoi Tavriki* (Leningrad, 1979), 83–93; and the summary in A. I. Romančuk, "Die byzantinische Provinzstadt vom 7. Jahrhundert bis zur ersten Hälfte des 9. Jahrhunderts (auf Grund von Materialien aus Cherson)," in *Besonderheiten*

In summing up what the ceramic evidence can tell us, I will focus on the routes that were traveled. Since we still lack much of the archaeology that would help, speculating about these remains a slightly risky venture, especially for local exchange relationships—for example, between villages within the same territory—but the survey at Sagalassos is beginning to suggest possible patterns.[33] On a larger scale, in contrast, it is possible to pick out some important connections: (1) Constantinople into the Aegean and Peloponnese and around the coast of Asia Minor across to Cyprus; (2) Cyprus to Egypt and the North African littoral to the west of Egypt, north to the southern and southwestern Asia Minor coast, and a little inland and across to Syria/Palestine; (3) the south Italian and Sicilian network across to the eastern shore of the Adriatic; (4) Cherson and the Crimea via Constantinople and around into the Adriatic, and from Constantinople to Cherson or into Asia Minor along the major routes 1, 2, or 3; (5) Constantinople and along the southern Pontic coast; (6) single routes across from Constantinople to Sicily, central Italy and Rome, and Ravenna and the Adriatic region; (7) a south and central Adriatic zone that connects with the northern Adriatic, especially after the later eighth century; and (8) Constantinople north and west into Thrace. Yet these are not constant—on the contrary, whereas the connection between Cherson, the Adriatic region (Butrint), and northeast Italy (Commacchio) seems to survive across the eighth and into the ninth century (as evidenced by the presence of Crimean transport amphorae), the relationship between the Aegean and the Adriatic in respect of other goods clearly became increasingly tenuous around the year 800 or so, as the western and eastern Adriatic coastal regions developed a closer commercial or exchange-based association. Similar shifts within the broader patterns and apparent continuities may also become visible as the evidence is more thoroughly analyzed. As far as the links between Constantinople and some of the inland centers of Anatolia are concerned, the extent to which these reflect the limited needs of imperial officers and officials of various sorts and reflect any sort of commerce is unclear. Volume must count for something: whereas the 20,000 sherds from the Saraçhane site in Constantinople obviously represent a substantial level of demand over several centuries, the significance of the handfuls of sherds at many sites remains ambiguous, to put it mildly.

Numismatic Evidence

The evidence of coins is notoriously difficult to evaluate, and it is all too easy for historians to make erroneous generalizations because they simply overlook problems familiar to numismatic specialists. I will attempt to summarize what can be said about the import of the coin evidence for the issues I want to talk about here.

Changes in the weight and value of the coin produced by the government, as well as the number of coins struck, reflected both regional monetary tradition and the general economic situation within the empire's remaining territories.[34] The numismatic evidence suggests that issues of the bronze petty coinage were deliberately curtailed beginning about 658 or soon thereafter, a curtailment that has been associated with the probable internal restructuring of the mechanisms of tax collection (and by definition, therefore, with the ways in which the army was paid and supplied).[35] This contrasts with the relatively constant gold content of the precious metal coinage from the middle of the seventh to the ninth century and beyond. The purity of the gold *nomisma* was in fact slightly reduced during the second half of the seventh century, and only slowly restored by the early ninth century; but this fluctuation was trivial compared with the changes that affected the bronze coinage. Through a careful analysis of dies, however, it has now been demonstrated that there was a real reduction in the issue of gold coinage during the later seventh and into the early ninth century, a reduction that parallels the much more dramatic

---

der byzantinischen *Feudalentwicklung,* ed. H. Köpstein, BBA 50 (Berlin, 1983), 57–68, at 65–66.

33 See the important discussion in Vanhaverbeke et al., "What Happened After the Seventh Century AD?"

34 See the survey of the role of coin in the Byzantine economy in C. Morrisson, "Byzantine Money: Its Production and Circulation," in *EHB* 3:909–66.

35 See Haldon, *Byzantium in the Seventh Century,* 226–27, 232–44, with earlier literature; Hendy, *Studies,* 641; and M. Phillips and A. Goodwin, "A Seventh-Century Syrian Hoard of Byzantine and Imitative Copper Coins," *NC* 157 (1997): 61–87, esp. 75–78. For state policies and intervention at this point, see W. Brandes, *Finanzverwaltung in Krisenzeiten: Untersuchungen zur byzantinischen Administration im 6.–9. Jahrhundert* (Frankfurt am Main, 2002), 281–368, 418–26.

cutback in the amount of bronze issued across the same period and a massive increase in gold issues from the reign of Theophilos onward. Thus, while the government clearly continued to produce gold in quantity during the extended period of crisis and economic adjustment which stretched from the middle of the seventh to the later eighth century, this evidence shows that the amount was greatly reduced. The consequences have yet to be fully analyzed, but the picture derived from this analysis must affect our understanding of the nature of exchange relations and commerce throughout the empire's remaining lands.[36] The dramatic fall in the numbers of bronze issues recovered from archaeological sites across Asia Minor for the period ca. 660 until the early ninth century or later, corroborated by the relatively small number of such issues in collections, illustrates the change in the economic circumstances under which exchange and the appropriation of surplus through tax took place. The pattern is borne out even in Constantinopolitan contexts such as Kalenderhane, where, although bronze issues were undoubtedly available throughout the period, issues for the emperors from Constantine IV through to Theophilos are sparse and follow the same contours.[37]

The curtailment of production of the petty coinage after this time means not that no small-scale exchange activity took place but merely that it must have been substantially reduced, or at least constrained by other mechanisms. Nor should we conclude that a reduction in the number of coins minted is the only way to explain why such coinage is absent. A similar disappearance of casual finds of bronze and a sharp reduction in the number of hoards of both bronze and gold from archaeological contexts in Greece after the 580s, and more particularly after the first decade of the reign of Heraclius, have been associated with the withdrawal of Roman forces, for example, rather than with a reduction in either minting or in exchange activity as such; a dramatic reduction of coins from archaeological contexts in the northern Peloponnese from the 630s onward can also be connected with Heraclius's closure in 629–30 of the mint at Thessalonike, which in the context of a strongly regional distribution of coins clearly affected the areas previously supplied from that mint.[38] And finally, the continued production of bronze to service the state's requirements for its military and fiscal apparatus may be demonstrated by the dispatch of specific consignments of bronze to particular locations associated with certain political or military events, as well as the reforms of the bronze coinage undertaken by Constantine IV.[39]

---

36 See the detailed survey of the evidence in C. Morrisson, "La monnaie d'or byzantine à Constantinople: Purification et modes d'altérations (491–1354)," in C. Brenot, J.-N. Barrandon, J.-P. Callu, J. Poirier, R. Halleux, and C. Morrisson, *L'or monnayé*, vol. 1, *Purification et altérations de Rome à Byzance*, Cahiers Ernest Babelon 2 (Paris, 1985), 113–87, esp. 123–27; Morrisson, "Byzantine Money," 920–29; and now, with the new analysis of emissions and levels of circulation, F. Füeg, *Corpus of the Nomismata from Anastasius II to John I in Constantinople, 717–976: Structure of the Issues, Corpus of Coin Finds, Contribution to the Iconographic and Monetary History* (Lancaster, Pa., 2007), esp. 166–71.
37 M. F. Hendy, "Roman, Byzantine and Latin Coins," in *Kalenderhane in Istanbul: The Excavations,* ed. C. L. Striker and Y. D. Kuban (Mainz, 2007), 175–276, at 179–82 with fig. 79; D. M. Metcalf, "Monetary Recession in the Middle Byzantine Period: The Numismatic Evidence," *NC* 161 (2001): 111–55.

38 B. Callegher, "La circulation monétaire à Patras et dans les sites ruraux environnants (VIᵉ–VIIᵉ siècles)," in Lefort, Morrisson, and Sodini, eds., *Les villages dans l'empire byzantin*, 225–35, esp. 232–33.
39 See the survey by C. Morrisson, "Byzance au VIIᵉ siècle: Le témoignage de la numismatique," in Βυζάντιος: Αφιέρωμα στον Ανδρέα Στράτον (Athens, 1986), 1:149–63, at 156–59. See P. Grierson, "Coinage and Money in the Byzantine Empire, 498–c. 1090," in *Moneta e scambi nell'alto Medioevo*, Settimane di studio del centro italiano di studi sull'alto medioevo 8 (Spoleto, 1960), 411–53, at 436 with table 2; and Hendy, *Studies*, 496–99, 640–41; see also W. Brandes, *Die Städte Kleinasiens im 7. und 8. Jahrhundert*, BBA 56 (Berlin, 1989), 226–27. For recent excavation results that demonstrate the same pattern, see M. Galani-Krikou, "Θήβα 6ος–15ος αιώνας: Η νομισματική μαρτυρία απο το πολιτιστικό κέντρο," Σύμμεικτα 12 (1998): 141–70, esp. 152–55; Bowden, *Epirus Vetus*, 67, for Albania. It should be noted that while many of the sites in which this pattern emerges have been the subject of excavations limited to very restricted areas, the same pattern emerges even from those sites—for example, in Greece and the Peloponnese—where much more extensive soundings or excavations have taken place. Thus, its universal application can hardly be doubted, although, as noted, the chronology and the causes may vary according to local and regional political variations and fluctuations—see below, and for the south Balkans, Curta, *The Making of the Slavs*, 169–81; idem, *Southeastern Europe in the Middle Ages, 500–1250* (Cambridge, 2006), 74–75. But the basic pattern from the later 660s onward seems to be confirmed throughout the empire's remaining territories. See the comments in C. Morrisson, "Survivance de l'économie monétaire à Byzance (VIIᵉ–IXᵉ s.)," in Kountoura-Galaki, ed., *The Dark Centuries of Byzantium*, 377–97, esp. 383; and for some of the material, Lampropoulou et al., "Συμβολή εις την ερμηνεία," esp. 221–24. C. S. Lightfoot, "Byzantine Anatolia: Reassessing the Numismatic Evidence," *RN* 158 (2002): 229–39, notes that bronze coins at Amorion and in its hinterland might argue for a countertrend. Yet the role of the city as a garrison across this period, and its political importance, would suggest that the pattern here is hardly different from that at other such sites, even if regionally

Differences between the Balkan pattern of coin finds and that of Asia Minor underline these points. In the Balkans in particular, researchers have noted an association from the middle of the seventh century between finds of bronze, coastal regions and sites, and military or naval activity. Substantial amounts of bronze from Athens (especially issues of Constans II, Philippikos, and Leo III) and Corinth (especially of Phocas, Heraclius, Constans II, and Constantine IV) have reasonably been connected with military activity and the presence of soldiers, a point borne out by the actual distribution patterns within the excavated areas. Bronze coin of seventh-century emperors from sites in the Dobrudja and the coast of Bulgaria—notably Mesembria, where there was a substantial imperial naval and military presence—contrasts with the absence of such material from inland regions; this disparity again suggests the movement of coin via ships, whether military or commercial, and a qualitative difference in the sort of exchange activity possible in coastal and metropolitan as opposed to inland regions. In addition, an association has been drawn between precious metal coins—silver in particular, but also gold—from hoards in territories associated with so-called barbarian rulers and the deliberate dispatch of such coinage to foreign rulers in return for their support, whether military or diplomatic. Finds of specially minted gold (lightweight solidi) issued by the Constantinople mint, usually discovered on the south Ukrainian steppe, contrast with gold found in the northwest Balkans, Hungary, and western Romania; the latter, originating from the mints at Constantinople as well as on Sicily, suggest specifically targeted payments for both diplomatic and military support. A similar interpretation has been offered for finds in particular of silver hexagrams or *miliaresia* of Heraclius, Constans II, and Constantine IV, both from the Caucasus and from the northern Balkans.[40]

But the Anatolian pattern does not contrast so sharply with the Balkans in its essentials, particularly when casual finds from areas around or associated with fortresses, or from military or administrative sites, are taken into account. Finds from Sardis, Ankara, and Ephesos may in fact present a similar pattern, which has a similar explanation. Scattered finds around sites such as Amorion may point in the same direction.[41] On the other hand, the pattern in both the Balkans and Asia Minor, and within distinct zones of both areas, contrasts very sharply with the continued widespread and concentrated use of copper coins throughout former imperial territories now under Islamic control, where the archaeological as well as numismatic material shows virtually no disruption to the patterns of economic activity that had been established before the 630s, even if it demonstrates a shift in the patterns and networks of distribution from the early eighth century onward.[42] I would suggest that this difference is a result not simply of the Islamic conquests or of the economic dislocation caused by warfare in either Asia Minor or the Balkans, but rather of longer-term regional variations already evident in the preceding period. There were other important regional variations: the numismatic, ceramic, and textual evidence for Sicily, for example, shows that the island did not suffer to the same extent as the Balkans and Asia Minor from a dearth of coinage in the later seventh and eighth centuries, that its commerce seems to have been quite

---

nuanced. For the consigning of bronze, see the evidence summarized by Hendy, *Studies*, 641–42, 659–62.

40 The evidence, with earlier literature, is presented in detail by F. Curta, "Byzantium in Dark-Age Greece (the Numismatic Evidence in Its Balkan Context)," *BMGS* 29 (2005): 113–46. See also C. Morrisson, V. Popović, and V. Ivanišević, with P. Culerrier et al., *Les trésors monétaires byzantins des Balkans et d'Asie Mineure (491–713)* (Paris, 2006), esp. 41–73; V. Ivanišević, "Les trésors balkaniques, témoins des invasions et de leurs routes," ibid., 75–93; I. Touratsoglou, "La mer Égée au VIIe siècle: Le témoignage des trésors," ibid., 95–104; and P. Culerrier, "Les trésors d'Asie Mineure," ibid., pp. 105–10.

41 Hendy, *Studies*, 640–42.
42 See P.-L. Gatier, "Les Villages du Proche-Orient protobyzantin: Nouvelles perspectives (1994–2004)," in Lefort, Morrisson, and Sodini, eds., *Les villages dans l'Empire byzantin*, 101–19; H. MacAdam, "Settlements and Settlement Patterns in Northern and Central Transjordania, ca. 550–ca. 750," in *The Byzantine and Early Islamic Near East*, vol. 2, *Land Use and Settlement Patterns*, ed. G. R. D. King and A. Cameron, Studies in Late Antiquity and Early Islam 1 (Princeton, N.J., 1994), 49–93; and Y. Tsafrir and G. Foerster, "From Scythopolis to Baysân—Changing Concepts of Urbanism," ibid., 95–115, for generalized continuity in central and northern Syria, Palestine, and western Jordan. For the coinage, see Walmsley, "Production, Exchange and Regional Trade," 332–39; L. Domascewica and M. Bates, "Copper Coinage of Egypt in the Seventh Century," in *Fustat Finds: Beads, Coins, Medical Instruments, Textiles, and Other Artifacts from the Awad Collection*, ed. J. Bachrach (Cairo, 2002), 88–111; C. Foss, "The Coinage of Syria in the Seventh Century: The Evidence of Excavations," *Israel Numismatic Journal* 13 (1994–99): 119–32; idem, *Arab-Byzantine Coins: An Introduction, with a Catalogue of the Dumbarton Oaks Collection*, Dumbarton Oaks Byzantine Collection Publications 12 (Washington, D.C., 2008), 18–55, 112–18; and Phillips and Goodwin, "A Seventh-Century Syrian Hoard."

robust, and that it continued to serve as an important stepping-off point for travelers eastward.[43] And even Cyprus, which was thought to have suffered disaster at the hands of the Arabs in the middle of the seventh century, can now be shown to have remained a major producer and exporter of table- and kitchenwares to the Levant and southern Anatolia well into the eighth century.[44]

In this respect the provenance of coins is interesting, for it shows a marked localization of coin distribution—if we exclude, that is, finds related to subsidies and tribute or payments to neighboring peoples.[45] Thus, whereas for the period 491–641 only 80 percent of the coins from the Saraçhane site in Constantinople were minted in the capital, the remainder deriving from other mints across the empire, in the following period, 641–867, 100 percent of coins excavated were from the local mint. Similar statistics prevail at other sites: of the coins excavated from the Athenian Agora for the first period, 50 percent are Constantinopolitan, whereas in the later period this proportion rises to 95 percent; at Bari in the first period some 15 percent of coins came from Constantinople and more than 70 percent from Italy and the mint in Sicily, whereas in the later period all the coins were from the Sicilian mint; and so on. In Italy in general after the sixth century there is a marked regionalization of coinage use and distribution.[46] In Cyprus at the Kourion site several mints are represented up to the year 630, after which Constantinople dominates completely. Of course, this domination almost certainly reflects the closure of a number of mints under Heraclius at that time.[47] But the diffusion of Byzantine coins to regions outside the empire, both in the East and in the West, is much more restricted after the middle of the seventh century, a further indicator of the localization of networks of exchange at this time (although in part, as noted above, reflecting the dispatch of coin in various forms, especially silver and gold, as subsidies or payments to neighbors). Again, however, these signs of restriction do not demonstrate that no longer-distance exchange survived: a small number of coins of the late seventh and of the late eighth centuries minted in Sicily have been excavated from the lower town at Corinth, suggestive of continued contacts along the route from Sicily to Constantinople via the northern Peloponnese, a picture repeated at other coastal sites.[48]

In general terms, the evidence seems to show pretty clearly that money-based exchange was never entirely interrupted, though there is good reason to believe that in the absence of particular conditions, the intensity and degree of such activity could be quite patchy and limited for some one hundred years after the middle of the seventh century. The evidence from hoards for both the Balkans and Asia Minor during the seventh century is indicative, as in their number and size as well as in their composition the hoards emphasize the degree of disruption and insecurity. Yet in the Balkans in particular, small-denomination currency continued to be employed in centers of imperial administration and military activity, chiefly found in coastal regions rather than inland. The evidence for Asia Minor is beginning to

---

43 The evidence is collected and discussed in C. Morrisson, "La Sicile byzantine: Une lueur dans les siècles obscurs," *Quaderni ticinesi di numismatica e antichità classiche* 27 (1998): 307–34. See also eadem, "Survivance de l'économie monétaire," and E. Kislinger, "Byzantinische Kupfermünzen aus Sizilien (7.–9. Jh.) im historischen Kontext," *JÖB* 45 (1995): 25–36, with further literature, and the discussion above.

44 Armstrong, "Trade in the East Mediterranean in the Eighth Century."

45 F. Curta, "Byzantium in Dark-Age Greece," 117–22; J. Smedley, "Seventh-Century Byzantine Coins in Southern Russia and the Problem of Light Weight Solidi," in *Studies in Early Byzantine Gold Coinage,* ed. W. Hahn and W. E. Metcalf (New York, 1988), 111–30.

46 E. A. Arslan, "La circolazione monetaria in Italia (secoli VI–VIII): Città e campagna," in Jacob, Martin, and Noyé, eds., *Histoire et culture dans l'Italie byzantine,* 365–85. All of the Byzantine coins found in Mallorca except one (a half follis of Constantine IV), for example, were minted in Sicily or Naples. The half follis from the Constantinople mint may perhaps indicate imperial military activity of some sort. See L. Ilisch, M. Matzke, and W. Seibt, *Die mittelalterlichen Fundmünzen, Siegel und Gewichte von Santueri, Mallorca* (Tübingen, 2005), 22–25. A similar picture is already found in the Peloponnese before the early seventh century; see Callegher, "La circulation monétaire à Patras," 232. For the Constantinopolitan material, see Füeg, *Corpus of the Nomismata,* and its review by C. Morrisson, in *RN* 164 (2008): 513–15.

47 M. F. Hendy, "Late Roman and Early Byzantine Coins," in Megaw et al., *Kourion,* 400–421, at 403.

48 See Morrisson, "Survivance de l'économie monétaire," esp. 383–87; eadem, "La diffusion de la monnaie de Constantinople: Routes commerciales ou routes politiques?" in *Constantinople and Its Hinterland,* ed. C. Mango and G. Dagron (Aldershot, 1995), 77–90, esp. 78–81; A. Avramea, *Le Péloponnèse du IVe au VIIIe siècle: Changements et persistances,* Byzantina Sorbonensia 15 (Paris, 1997), 72–81. For diffusion outside the empire, see Morrisson, "La diffusion de la monnaie de Constantinople," 83–89; eadem, "Byzantine Money," 962–64.

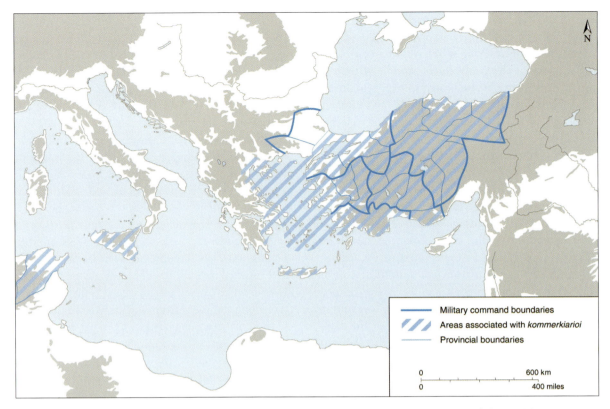

Figure 4.1. Provinces associated on lead seals with *kommerkiarioi* and *apothēkai*, ca. 660–732 (after Haldon, *The Palgrave Atlas of Byzantine History*, map 6.5)

suggest that the same was true there.[49] Older coins also continued in use, and not only where local demand was not being met by the supply of contemporary issues—this certainly seems to be the case at Byzantine Corinth, to choose one example among many, where for certain strata over half of all coins were more than fifty years old when they were deposited. Inelasticity of supplies of gold and silver at different periods had a direct impact on this practice.[50] As I have said, an absence of coins need not signify an absence of exchange. Systems of reciprocity, relying on both bartered goods and the use of instruments of credit, may have enabled the maintenance of most economic relationships at a local level through any changes. And it is perfectly possible, albeit awkward, to conduct day-to-day transactions using a high-value coinage, provided the conditions for such transactions and the required degrees of credit and reciprocity can be met.[51]

Sigillography

An apparently important indicator of the relevance of trade and commerce across the imperial frontiers is the evidence of lead seals of the officials called *kommerkiarioi*. From the 660s until the year 731, the

---

49 See, for example, the evidence for the Cyclades and the Peloponnese, assembled in V. Penna, "Νομισματικές νύξεις για την ζωή στις Κυκλάδες κατα τους 8ο και 9ο αιώνες," in Kountoura-Galake, ed., *The Dark Centuries of Byzantium*, 399–410, and eadem, "Η ζωή στις Βυζαντινές πόλεις της Πελοποννήσου: η νομισματική μαρτυρία (8ος–12ος αι. Μ.Χ.)," in *Μνήμη Martin J. Price*, Βιβλιοθήκη της Ελληνικής Νομισματικής Εταιρείας 5 (Athens, 1996), 195–264; the summary of other scattered material in Morrisson, "Survivance de l'économie monétaire," esp. 389–91; and, for the evidence from hoards, Touratsoglou, "La mer Égée au VIIᵉ siècle," and Culerrier, "Les trésors d'Asie Mineure."
50 An issue discussed in C. Morrisson, "The Re-use of Obsolete Coins: The Case of Roman Imperial Bronzes Revived in the Late Fifth Century," in *Studies in Numismatic Method Presented to Philip Grierson*, ed. C. N. L. Brooke et al. (Cambridge, 1983), 95–111, and eadem, "Byzantine Money," 942–44; see also, for the later Roman period, J. Banaji, *Agrarian Change in Late Antiquity—Gold, Labour and Aristocratic Dominance* (Oxford, 2001), 70–77. For Corinth, see Sanders, "New Relative and Absolute Chronologies," 155–56.
51 See Sarris, "Rehabilitating the Great Estate."

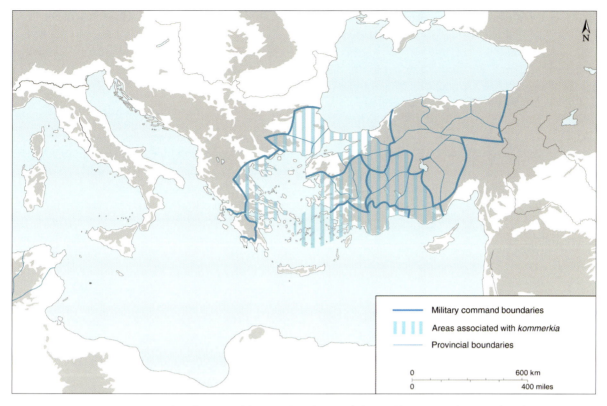

Figure 4.2. Provinces associated with imperial *kommerkia* after 732 (after Haldon, *The Palgrave Atlas of Byzantine History,* map 6.6)

activities of the *genikoi kommerkiarioi* and the associated provincial *apothēkai* (state warehouses or granaries) have a strong internal accent, and they have been connected with a range of duties related to fiscal administration and supplying Constantinople and the imperial armies. This is not the place to go into that particular issue, but it is interesting that from the 730s onward, seals of *genikoi kommerkiarioi* of *apothēkai* no longer occur.[52] Instead, seals of *kommerkiarioi* and of an institution referred to as the *basilika kommerkia* appear increasingly to be associated with specific locations at which the import or export of goods could be supervised—Mesembria, Thessalonike, Kerasous, and so forth (see figs. 4.1 and 4.2).[53]

There are also seals for specific provinces within military commands (such as Asia, for example, which appears on a seal of the basilika kommerkia in the second half of the eighth century).[54] The seals for kommerkiarioi associated with ports along the Black Sea coast—Herakleia, Amastris, Ionopolis, Kerasous, Trebizond, Sinope, and others; with riverine emporiums such as Charax on the Parthenius River, some 10 kilometers south of Amastris; or with Abydos, Nikomedeia, and Thessalonike highlight points of exit or entry for commerce.[55] From the later

---

52   There are isolated cases of officials from the later period that have the title or function of *genikos kommerkiarios,* although they are not associated with an *apothēkē* and their authority was presumably more general or supervisory. See, e.g., *DOSeals* 4:89, no. 32.17, a ninth-century seal of Eugenios, *genikos kommerkiarios* of Chaldia.

53   See the list in Brandes, *Finanzverwaltung in Krisenzeiten,* app. 7; app. 1, nos. 206–81; and in A.-K. Wassiliou and W. Seibt,

Die byzantinischen Bleisiegel in Österreich, vol. 2, *Zentral- und Provinzverwaltung,* Veröffentlichungen der Kommission für Byzantinistik 2.2 (Vienna, 2004), see selected seals in the series nos. 142–67.

54   N. P. Lihačev, "Datirovannye vizantiyskie pečati," *Izvestiya Rossiyskoy Akademii Istorii Material'noy Kul'tury* 3 (1924): 153–224, at 203, dated to either 755/56 or 770/71: see Brandes, *Finanzverwaltung in Krisenzeiten,* 559 (no. 252), and p. 386.

55   N. Oikonomidès, "Silk Trade and Production in Byzantium from the Sixth to the Ninth Century: The Seals of Kommerkiarioi," *DOP* 40 (1986): 33–53, at 48–49; see, for example, the seals of kommerkiarioi of a variety of ports or frontier regions through which merchants and traders passed: *DOSeals,* vol. 4,

eighth century, there is sound evidence for the levying of a duty on trade, referred to as the *kommerkion*, and kommerkiarioi were undoubtedly associated with its collection.⁵⁶ We should consider in this light the Byzantine-Bulgarian treaty of 715–18 (renewed again, a century later, after the accession of Leo V). Trade was permitted by each side on condition that certain political arrangements were respected (such as the return of deserters and traitors on the demand of their own government or ruler); licenses were issued to merchants permitted to cross the border; and maxima in the value of exportable goods were also stipulated. The trade itself seems to have been sufficiently significant for both sides to take it very seriously, and for the Bulgars to wish to regulate it on their own side.⁵⁷

Textual Evidence

How extensive, therefore, was commerce between the regions and provinces of the empire? On the basis of the evidence reviewed so far, we may conclude that commercial enterprise within the empire continued unbroken throughout the period from the later seventh century into the ninth century (in many cases in a more localized, short-hop fashion), and that there was a trough in the later seventh to later eighth centuries. Grain ships still traveled from the southern Black Sea coast to Cherson in the middle years of the seventh century, and hint at the ways in which the imperial capital was supplied after the loss of Egypt.⁵⁸ Because the Black Sea littoral never suffered from the sort of devastation that affected parts of southern and eastern Asia Minor or even on occasion the southern and central Aegean region, we might reasonably assume an uninterrupted, if differently nuanced, pattern of shipping and commerce.⁵⁹ Throughout the eighth and well into the ninth century, it is quite clear that Amastris was an important focus of Black Sea trade, especially to Cherson.

no. 23.1 (Amaseia); nos. 32.15–24 for Chaldia (which included Trebizond). Seals of kommerkiarioi attached to Cherson in the period ca. 830–70, for example, bear no titles at all: see I. V. Sokolova, "Les sceaux byzantins de Cherson," in *Studies in Byzantine Sigillography*, ed. N. Oikonomidès, vol. 3 (Washington, D.C., 1993), 99–111, nos. 17–18 and further references. For other seals for specific ports or entrepôts for the period from the later eighth or ninth century onward (Abydos, Debeltos, Dekapolis, Nikomedeia, Thessalonike, Nicaea, Christoupolis, etc.) see the indexes in *DOSeals*; Wassiliou and Seibt, *Die byzantinischen Bleisiegel*; or indeed any of the other major catalogues; Brandes, *Finanzverwaltung in Krisenzeiten*, 366 with n. 732; and F. Curta, "L'administration byzantine dans les Balkans pendant la 'grande brèche': Le témoignage des sceaux," *Byzantinistica* 6 (2004): 155–89, dealing with the Balkan evidence from the later seventh to ninth centuries. For Charax, see note 64, below, and G. Zacos and A. Veglery, *Byzantine Lead Seals*, vol. 1, parts 1–3 (Basel, 1972), no. 1559 (hereafter cited as ZV), a ninth-century seal of Nikephoros, kommerkiarios of Partheniou, presumably the area around the river and the commercial center at Charax itself.

56 See *Theophanis Chronographia*, ed. C. de Boor, 2 vols. (Leipzig, 1883–85), 469–70 (Constantine VI reduced the *kommerkion* of 100 lbs in gold levied on the fair at Ephesos), 475 (Eirene reduces the *kommerkia* levied at Abydos and Hieron), 487 (Nikephoros I offers high-interest loans to the Constantinopolitan shipowners while still levying the "customary *kōmerkia*"). See H. Antoniadis-Bibicou, *Recherches sur les douanes à Byzance: L' "octava," le "kommerkion" et les commerciaires* (Paris, 1963), 182–84, 232–34; Oikonomidès, "Silk Trade and Production in Byzantium," 48–49; idem, "Le kommerkion d'Abydos, Thessalonique et le commerce bulgare au IXᵉ siècle," in *Hommes et richesses dans l'Empire byzantin*, vol. 2, *VIIIᵉ–XVᵉ siècle*, ed. V. Kravari, J. Lefort, and C. Morrisson (Paris, 1991), 241–48; Sokolova, "Les sceaux byzantins de Cherson"; and A. W. Dunn, "The *Kommerkiarios*, the *Apotheke*, the *Dromos*, the *Vardarios*, and *The West*," *BMGS* 17 (1993): 3–24, esp. 11–12. For simple kommerkiarioi, see, e.g., ZV, nos. 968, 1811 (of Petros and of Konstantinos, both *hypatos, genikos kommerkiarios*), 1862 (Eirenaios, *diakon, archōn tou blattiou, kommerkiarios* of Abydos), 1599 (Sergios, *kommerkiarios* of Nikomedeia), 2182 (of ?Michael, *genikos kommerkiarios*), 2264 (of Niketas, *basilikos silentiarios, archōn tou blattiou*, and *genikos kommerkiarios*), and 2635A (anon., with the same titles as 2264), all from the eighth century. Further discussion in Brandes, *Finanzverwaltung in Krisenzeiten*, 424–26, summarizing the detailed prior analysis.

57 See, with older literature and sources, N. Oikonomidès, "Tribute or Trade? The Byzantine-Bulgarian Treaty of 716," in *Studies on the Slavo-Byzantine and West-European Middle Ages: In memoriam Ivan Dujcev*, Studia Slavico-Byzantina et Mediaevalia Europensia 1 (Sofia, 1988), 29–31; P. Philippou, "Η βυζαντινή-Βουλγαρική συνθήκη ειρήνης του 716," Βυζαντιακά 13 (1993): 171–84. See also M. McCormick, *Origins of the European Economy: Communications and Commerce, A.D. 300–900* (Cambridge, 2001), 604–6.

58 For grain ships delivering to Cherson, see *Vita S. Martini Papae* 261 (P. Peeters, "Une vie grecque du pape Saint Martin I," *AB* 51 [1933]: 225–62 [*BHG* 2259]). For a sample of the seals: ZV 1, nos. 180 (Paphlagonia and Ionopolis, AD 692/93); 164 (Lazica and Kerasous, AD 689/90); 178 (Lazica, Kerasous, Trebizond, AD 691/93); 179 (Lazica, Kerasous, Trebizond, AD 692/93); 250 (Kerasous, AD 735/36); 2765 (seal of the general *kommerkiarios* of the coast of Pontos, AD 727/28); 2894 (Sinope and the Pontos, AD 832/33 or 847/48); see also Lihačev, "Datirovannye vizantiyskie pečati," 198–99, no. 9 (Herakleia, AD 734/35); 199, no. 10 (Kerasous, AD 738/39); 165–66, no. 3 (seal of the general *kommerkiarios* of the *apothēkē* of Honorias, Paphlagonia, the coast of Pontos and Trebizond, AD 721/22[?]). For a summary of some of the material from Cherson, see A. I. Romančuk, *Studien zur Geschichte und Archäologie des byzantinischen Cherson*, ed. H. Heinen (Leiden, 2005), esp. 205–10, 235–37, on the ceramic evidence.

59 See below, 117–18 with notes 73–77.

Good evidence is provided by amphorae associated with Amastris and found in quantities along the northern Pontic coast, although the commodity they carried is not certain—perhaps oil from nuts, which seems to have been a major product of the hinterland of Amastris; the Rus's later attack on that port, with its twin harbors and well-defended *kastron*, suggests its importance as a relatively wealthy center of commerce.[60] The evidence of a lead seal from the later seventh or early eighth century of an imperial kommerkiarios of the apothēkē of "Honorias, Paphlagonia, and the Pontic coast," found in Sudak (Sougdaia, modern Surož in the Crimea), illustrates the relationship, while Amastris had its own apothēkē.[61] Port-to-port trade on a small scale and longer-distance commerce around the Black Sea and the Aegean islands and coastal zones, as well as to Constantinople from these regions, should probably be assumed to have continued with only minimal disruption, although the dominance of Constantinople as a gross importer should be borne in mind.[62]

The literary evidence suggests that coastal cities such as Attaleia, Smyrna, Ephesos, Amastris, and Trebizond continued to serve as local market centers and entrepôts for commerce, however much their physical shape was changed. The sigillographic evidence likewise suggests that towns or ports such as those listed above, as well as Kerasous and Sinope, were the foci of local and longer-distance commercial activities of some sort. The ceramic and other archaeological evidence, where it is available, offers support for this picture.[63] At Amastris, for example, as well as at Sinope and Ionopolis, substantial structures identified with (commercial) warehouses, converted from original uses that remain unknown, have been dated, very approximately, to the middle Byzantine period—after the sixth century; these may suggest the importance of both grain storage and other related exchange activities, whether state-sponsored or not. Not far from Amastris, according to a ninth-century account of travels around the Pontic coast and its hinterland, there was also an important commercial center on the Parthenius River at a place referred to (from its location) simply as Charax, undefended though well-protected by the rivers between which it was situated.[64] There was certainly a regular annual grain traffic to Constantinople in the first half of the ninth century, conducted by contracted *naukléroi*, from particular regions such as the Aegean and Paphlagonia to Constantinople, and managed through the general *logothesion*. The emperor Nikephoros I introduced a series of measures intended to indemnify or insure the government with regard to the activities of such shipowners or naukléroi. Naukléroi from the island of Androte, located off the northern Anatolian coast in Paphlagonia, who had defrauded the government of some of the grain they were to transport are mentioned in a letter of the deacon Ignatios, written in the 820s.[65] The Acts of the council of 787 in Nicaea

---

60 Crow and Hill, "The Byzantine Fortifications of Amastris," 251, 261; K. Belke, *Paphlagonien und Honorias, TIB* 9, DenkWien 249 (Vienna, 1996), 142. The date of the attack remains in dispute: see ibid., 78–89 (AD 941); A. Markopoulos, "La vie de saint Georges d'Amastris et Photius," *JÖB* 28 (1979): 75–82 (AD 860, with some authorities preferring the authorship of Ignatios the deacon and thus a *terminus ante quem* of 843).
61 For the seal, see V. Šandrovskaja, "Das Siegel eines χαλκοπράτης aus Sudak," in *Studies in Byzantine Sigillography*, ed. N. Oikonomidès, vol. 6 (Washington, D.C., 1999), 43–46, at 46; Brandes, *Finanzverwaltung in Krisenzeiten*, 565; and *TIB* 9:162 and n. 28. For other seals of either kommerkiarioi of the apothēkai or the imperial kommerkia, of Paphlagonia or the Pontic coast, Lazica, Honorias, Kerasous, Sinope, and Trebizond, see the catalogue in Brandes, *Finanzverwaltung in Krisenzeiten*, 601, 603, 605–6, 608–10.
62 And see J. Shepard, "'Mists and Portals': The Black Sea's North Coast," in Mundell Mango, ed., *Byzantine Trade, 4th–12th Centuries*, 421–41, esp. 424–27.
63 See Brandes, *Die Städte Kleinasiens*, 124–31 ("Städte mit relativer Kontinuität"); and the catalogue of seals of kommerkiarioi and apothēkai, as well as basilika kommerkia, in Brandes, *Finanzverwaltung in Krisenzeiten*, apps. 7, 10.
64 See Crow and Hill, "The Byzantine Fortifications of Amastris," 252; A. A. M. Bryer and D. Winfield, *The Byzantine Monuments and Topography of the Pontos*, 2 vols. (Washington, D.C., 1985), 1:81–82; *TIB* 9:220. The location and identity of the emporium at Charax were discussed in detail in C. Mango, "A Journey Round the Coast of the Black Sea in the Ninth Century," *Palaeoslavica* 10 (2002): 255–64, at 259–60; the text in question is in an expanded version of *Vita S. Andreae*, composed by Nicetas David Paphlagon (see ed. S. A. Paschalides [Thessalonike, 1999], 157–59).
65 Nikephoros I's measures: Theoph., 487. Ignatios's letter is written on behalf of the ship captains to Democharis, the general logothete, to beg for leniency, and refers to the annual shipment for the public treasury (*demosios logos*), clearly implying that they were subject to the authority of the general *logothesion*: *Ep.* 21, *The Correspondence of Ignatios the Deacon*, 67–68; comm. 178–81; with discussion in Brandes, *Finanzverwaltung in Krisenzeiten*, 494–98, though he argues that the state-contracted ships were for the supply of the military (*tagmata* and others) of Constantinople. While this is entirely possible, it seems to me just as likely that they supplied a range of other government needs also. See also *Prosopography of the Byzantine Empire, 641–886*, ed. J. R. Martindale, CD-ROM (Aldershot, 2001), Anonymi 34; R.-J. Lilie, C. Ludwig, T. Pratsch, and I. Rochow et al., *Prosopographie der mittelbyzantinischen Zeit, Erste Abteilung (641–867)*, 6 vols. (Berlin,

refer to a commercial voyage from Cyprus to the Syrian coast undertaken ca. 785, and the presence of the painted wares referred to above across the Aegean and Syrian/Palestinian coastal regions may suggest a more regular and frequent contact, regardless of the political and military situation. Since it seems clear that Venetian merchants were trading with Constantinople, Alexandria, the Black Sea, and the Levant by the end of the eighth century, it is a priori likely that Byzantine traders could also be similarly linked with other regions, even if the extent and volume of such traffic cannot be known.[66]

Apart from coastal cities possessing port facilities and markets, an important opportunity for trade was offered by the numerous yearly fairs, or *panēgyreis*, held on particular saints' days in many towns. Trebizond, Ephesos, Sinope, Euchaita, Chonai, Myra, Thessalonike, Nikomedeia—all held a yearly market. Since this tradition goes well back into the late Roman period, it is highly likely that where conditions allowed these fairs continued through the seventh and eighth and into the ninth centuries; indeed, many continue to be celebrated today (or, in Turkey, continued until 1921). There are a number of literary references to such fairs, and to the fact that they took place once a year, suggesting the limited nature of the commercial activity carried on outside of highly localized trade. A particularly clear example comes from a ninth- or tenth-century hagiography, admittedly some time after the period under discussion but probably not atypical for the rural hinterland, in which a peasant farmer in Paphlagonia travels to the yearly market of his district with his cart laden with products that he wishes to exchange—"some by sale and some by barter."[67]

The text implies that this was a regular and yearly event, and a merchant who bought and sold using substantial amounts of gold coin is also mentioned. The much-discussed example of the annual fair at Ephesos—at which, according to Theophanes, a tax of 100 pounds of gold, representing 10 percent of the total transactions, was raised—at least suggests the local importance of such events, and the role of the government in extracting its share of their profits, even if the figure given in the text is suspicious. That the old city continued to function as an attraction for pilgrims and thus hosted some commercial activity is also suggested by the visits of westerners there during the eighth century, as well as by the presence of ships and merchants in the early 830s.[68] Just as important, the distribution of military pay may have been coordinated with such events, both in order to enable soldiers to purchase their requirements more easily and to allow the coin in which their salaries were issued to percolate into a wider network of exchange relationships. In Euchaita in the year 811, the annual pay of the troops coincided with the festival of St. Theodore Tiro in February, but it is unclear to what extent the issue of annual pay to the troops generally followed the calendar of saints' *panēgyreis* and to what extent fairs at towns where soldiers were based were predicated on this event.[69]

Merchants and traders appear fairly consistently in literary sources from the later seventh through the eighth century and beyond. In 715, for example,

---

1999–2002), no. 10602 (hereafter cited as *PmbZ*), with further literature; and the comment of A. E. Laiou, "Exchange and Trade, Seventh–Twelfth Centuries," in *EHB* 2:697–770, at 711.

66   See *Sacrorum Conciliorum nova et amplissima Collectio*, ed. J. D. Mansi (Florence, 1759–98), 13:77–80; and see also *PmbZ*, no. 3846 (Konstantinos of Konstantia). For Venice, see now D. Jacoby, "Venetian Commercial Expansion in the Eastern Mediterranean, 8th–11th Centuries," in Mundell Mango, ed., *Byzantine Trade, 4th–12th Centuries*, 371–91, esp. 371–73.

67   For late Roman antecedents: A. H. M. Jones, *The Later Roman Empire, 284–602: A Social and Administrative Survey* (Oxford, 1964), 855–56; Byzantine fairs: S. Vryonis, "The Panēgyris of the Byzantine Saint: A Study in the Nature of a Medieval Institution, Its Origins and Fate," in *The Byzantine Saint*, ed. S. Hackel (London, 1981), 196–228; idem, *The Decline of Medieval Hellenism in Asia Minor and the Process of Islamization from the Eleventh through the Fifteenth Century* (Berkeley, 1971), 39–41; and esp. A. E. Laiou, "Händler und Kaufleute auf dem Jahrmarkt," in *Fest und Alltag in Byzanz*, ed. G. Prinzing and D. Simon (Munich, 1990), 53–70 (repr. in eadem, *Gender, Society and Economic Life in Byzantium* [Aldershot, 1992], art. XI). For the peasant: *Synaxarium Constantinopolitanum*, ed. H. Delehaye, Propylaeum ad AS Novembris (Brussels, 1902), 721.24–25 ("De Metrio agricola . . ."), and Laiou, "Händler und Kaufleute," 68–70.

68   See Theoph., 469–70; and discussion in M. Gerolymatou, "Ἐμπορικὴ δραστηριότητα κατα τους σκοτεινούς αιώνας," in Kountoura-Galaki, ed., *The Dark Centuries of Byzantium*, 347–64, at 361–62, with previous literature; for westerners: McCormick, *Origins of the European Economy*, 171–72; and for Ephesos in the 830s, see G. Makris, ed., *Ignatios Diakonos und die Vita des Hl. Gregorios Dekapolites*, ByzArch 17 (Stuttgart, 1997), 9, 53.10–12 (*BHG* 711).

69   See Theoph., 489; Vryonis, "The Panēgyris of the Byzantine Saint"; on Euchaita, see F. Trombley, "The Decline of the Seventh-Century Town: The Exception of Euchaita," in *Byzantine Studies in Honor of Milton V. Anastos*, ed. S. Vryonis Jr. (Malibu, 1985), 65–90, at 72, 85 and n. 51. For the date of the *miracula S. Theodori*, see T. Artun, "The Miracles of St. Theodore Tērōn: An Eighth-Century Source?" *JÖB* 5 (2008): 1–11.

a mutinous army on the northwestern coast of Asia Minor attempted to use merchant vessels to transport itself to Constantinople, but was unable to seize enough ships to accommodate the whole force (probably a few thousand soldiers at the most).[70] Most merchants would have operated along the coastal routes and by sea, as we have now seen. At Ravenna the ceramic evidence at the end of the seventh century shows quite clearly that wine continued to be imported from as far afield as the Aegean region (in amphorae associated in particular with Chios and Sardis), Palestine, and Calabria, while sherds from amphorae of Egyptian provenance indicate commerce with that region as well. It is unlikely that much, if any, of this trade was directly managed by the exarchate.[71] By the later tenth and early eleventh century, explicit textual evidence shows that long-standing regular annual markets were an entirely normal aspect of provincial life. They were frequented by both local and foreign merchants and farmers, they took place at established and "traditional" locations, local landlords might be in competition to attract the market, and the merchants themselves might be organized in partnerships to maximize their capital resources. On the basis of the eighth- and ninth-century sources referred to already, it would seem reasonable to argue that many of these markets existed (with or without major interruptions, according to the conditions of the times) across the period dealt with here.[72]

Although of course it is from the preceding period, the *Life* of Theodore of Sykeon, whose mother ran an inn on a major east–west thoroughfare in the region of Ankyra in the 580s and after, may offer some indication of inland conditions in general in Asia Minor, for here merchants appear hardly at all—the customers of the inn and others who passed through the village were chiefly imperial officials and soldiers.[73] But that traders did operate inland is evident from occasional references in texts: for example, in 716 the general Leo (shortly to become the emperor Leo III) seems to have had no difficulty in organizing a traveling market for the district around Amorion, which could supply under truce the Arab armies encamped at that fortress.[74] In 782 an Arab raiding force bottled up by Byzantine troops in Bithynia was able to negotiate itself out of difficulties (aided by the seizure of the two Byzantine emissaries sent by the empress Eirene)—and interestingly, the deal included access to markets where the Arab soldiers could buy provisions.[75] But probably a sense of the general situation is conveyed by the fact that although Byzantine troops mustered for the yearly campaigning season in Anatolia had to bring several days' provisions with them, they were thereafter supplied by the provincial authorities through compulsory purchase and extraordinary levies. Provisions were deposited at key locations—in granaries or storehouses, according to a ninth-century Arabic report—from which they were collected by the army and loaded onto pack animals, carts, and the soldiers themselves as they passed through. The same Arab source notes (in marked contrast to the situation in the Islamic world) that "there is no market in the Roman camp. Each soldier is obliged to bring from his own resources the biscuit, oil, wine, and cheese that he will need," a point confirmed by numerous references in Byzantine sources.[76]

---

70 Theoph., 385–86.

71 See S. Cosentino, "L'approvvigionamento annonario di Ravenna dal V all' VIII secolo: L'organizzazione e i riflessi socio-economici," in *Ravenna: Da capitale imperiale a capitale esarcale*, Atti del XVII Congresso internazionale di studio sull'alto medioevo, Ravenna, 6–12 giugno 2004 (Spoleto, 2005), 405–34, at 428, with further literature.

72 See in particular Laiou, "Händler und Kaufleute."

73 For the expense and problems of land transport, see Jones, *Later Roman Empire*, 841–44; J. F. Haldon and H. Kennedy, "The Arab-Byzantine Frontier in the Eighth and Ninth Centuries: Military Organisation and Society in the Borderlands," *ZRVI* 19 (1980): 79–116, at 87–88; W. Harris, "Between Archaic and Modern: Some Current Problems in the History of the Roman Economy," in *The Inscribed Economy: Production and Distribution in the Roman Empire in the Light of the "Instrumentum Domesticum,"* Journal of Roman Archaeology, supp. ser. 6 (Ann Arbor, 1993), 11–29, at 27–28. See also *Vie de Théodore de Sykéon*, ed. and trans. A. J. Festugière, 2 vols., SubsHag 48 (Brussels, 1970), §6, for Theodore's mother's inn on the main route through the village.

74 C. S. Lightfoot, "The Survival of Cities in Byzantine Anatolia: The Case of Amorium," *Byzantion* 68 (1998): 56–71; E. W. Brooks, "Byzantines and Arabs in the Time of the Early Abbasids," *EHR* 15 (1900): 728–47, at 738.

75 For the Arab expedition of 782, see Brooks, "Byzantines and Arabs in the Time of the Early Abbasids," 737–39; A. D. Beihammer, *Nachrichten zum byzantinischen Urkundenwesen in arabischen Quellen (565–811)*, Poikila Byzantina 17 (Bonn, 2000), 419–23 (nos. 345–47).

76 See Abū l-Kāsim ʿUbayd Allāh b. ʿAbd Allāh b. Khurradādhbih, *Kitāb al-Masālik waʾl-Mamālik*, in *Bibliotheca Geographorum Araborum*, ed. M.-J. De Goeje (1899; repr., Leiden, 1967), 6:76–85, at 83, 85; and for supplying armies in general, Haldon, *Warfare, State and Society*, 143–76, where sources and further literature are given.

By the same token, some areas did suffer a quite dramatic collapse in both urban and rural life. Recent work in Cappadocia, in the area south of Nazianzos and along the major route north from Tyana, which combines the results of historical and archaeological investigation with paleo-environmental work, has yielded some startling results. Using precisely datable half-yearly laminations (thin compressed layers) reaching back to the third century AD, researchers can show that agricultural production must have ceased almost entirely at exactly the time when Arab invading forces are reported by both Byzantine and Arab sources to have ravaged and occupied the area on an almost annual basis—between the years 664 and 678. They can also show that agrarian and pastoral activity resumed some 250 years later, when, according to the written sources, Byzantine aristocratic landlords began to recolonize the area—a vivid example of the effects of this sort of human activity on the settlement and economy of the region. The extent of the areas involved remains unclear, however, since the pollen evidence reflects winds and a range of local factors that influence our interpretation. And it is also clear that a neighboring region may have been much less affected if it managed to avoid such intense hostile activity. Consequently, crude generalizations should be avoided, since there might be substantial variation within even a fairly small region.[77]

A final category of evidence may point to other types of movement across and within imperial territory. The finds and distribution patterns of Byzantine belt buckles, specifically those of the so-called Corinth type and its variants, may well indicate the movement of imperial officials—more particularly, soldiers or military officers as well as nonmilitary personnel. Soldiers and those associated with them served both as a conduit for the movement of goods and as a focus of exchange activity with local populations; and concentrations of such belt buckles in Istria, Sardinia, the Peloponnese, Epiros, and the Crimea, and of other types in Bithynia and parts of Anatolia (for example, an eighth-century "Avar"-style belt buckle tongue has been excavated from the Byzantine settlement at Boğazköy in central Anatolia, and a number of buckle parts have been recovered from the "dark age" strata at Amorion), hint at the nature of some of these movements, whether of the soldiers themselves or of the accoutrements they wore.[78]

Roads and Transport

The extent to which the condition of roads affected the overland movement of goods associated either with the state or with private commerce is very difficult to determine. The fifth- and sixth-century evidence points to the very poor condition of many roads.[79] Yet as often as not, alternative routes were brought (or brought back) into use, and they were protected—and possibly maintained—by garrisons of soldiers located in strategically placed forts, to which the soldiers were accompanied by their families. There is plenty of evidence for the continued and frequent use of a network of official routes across both the southern Balkans and Asia Minor throughout the period (see figs. 4.3 and 4.4), maintained in part at the expense of the state (through a system of

---

77 See J. F. Haldon, "'Cappadocia will be given over to ruin and become a desert': Environmental Evidence for Historically-Attested Events in the 7th–10th Centuries," in *Byzantina Mediterranea: Festschrift für Johannes Koder zum 65. Geburtstag,* ed. K. Belke, E. Kislinger, A. Külzer, and M. Stassinopoulou (Vienna, 2007), 215–30; and A. England, W. J. Eastwood, C. N. Roberts, R. Turner, and J. F. Haldon, "Historical Landscape Change in Cappadocia (Central Turkey): A Paleoecological Investigation of Annually-Laminated Sediments from Nar Lake," *The Holocene* 18 (2008): 1229–45.

78 In general, see the survey in M. Schulze-Dörrlamm, *Byzantinische Gürtelschnallen und Gürtelbeschläge im Römisch-Germanischen Zentralmuseum,* vol. 1, *Die Schnallen ohne Beschlag, mit Laschenbeschlag und mit festem Beschlag des 5. bis 7. Jahrhunderts* (Mainz and Bonn, 2002); and in particular, E. Nallbani, "Précisions sur un type de ceinture byzantine: La plaque-boucle du type Corinthe au haut Moyen Âge," *TM* 15 (2005): 655–71. For the Amorion material, see M. Lightfoot, "Belt Buckles from Amorium and in the Afyon Archaeological Museum," in *Amorium Reports,* vol. 2, *Research Papers and Technical Reports,* ed. C. S. Lightfoot, BAR International Series 1170 (Oxford, 2003), 81–103; and the Boğazköy belt-tongue: A. Schachner, "Die Ausgrabungen in Boğazköy-Hattuša 2007," *AA* (2008): 113–61, at 131 and fig. 24.

79 On the state of roads in the later fourth and fifth centuries, see *Theodosiani libri XVI cum constitutionibus Sirmondianis,* ed. T. Mommsen, P. Meyer, et al. (Berlin, 1905), 15.3.4 (AD 412), remarking upon "the immense ruin of the highways" throughout the prefecture of Oriens. The western sections of the Via Egnatia, the major route from Constantinople to the Adriatic coast, were, according to one report, barely passable in the middle of the fifth century: see Malchus of Philadelphia, *Fragments* §18, in *FGH* 4:127 [= *Excerpta historica iussu imp. Constantini Porphyrogeniti confecta,* vol. 1, *Excerpta de Legationibus,* 2 parts, ed. C. de Boor (Berlin, 1903), 1:158]. According to Procopius, parts of the Via Egnatia were almost impassable in wet weather; see *Buildings* 4.8.5.

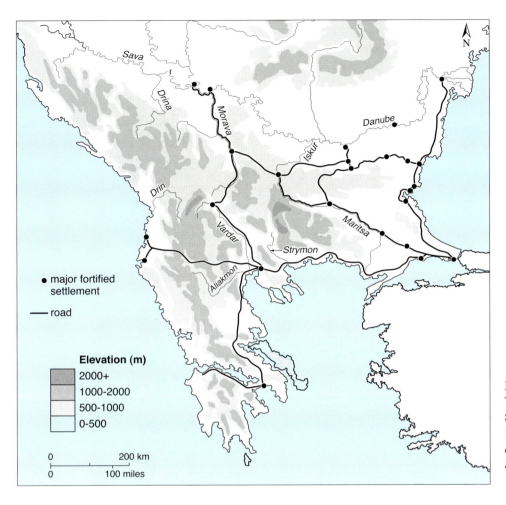

Figure 4.3. The Balkans, ca. 800 (after Haldon, *The Palgrave Atlas of Byzantine History,* map 6.8)

impositions on local communities), carrying a traffic not just of military and administrative officials but also of private persons. Such traffic seems to have passed along the Albanian stretches of the Via Egnatia and the parallel routes employed after its central sections had fallen into disrepair. Here a number of small cemeteries characterized by a type of stone-lined grave apparently used for members of the same family or kinship group included weapons and other items of personal dress associated with what seem to be military emplacements—forts and garrisons. These goods belong to the so-called Komani-Kruja culture, named for the sites where they were first identified; similar goods have been found across northern Albania and into Macedonia and southern Thrace as well as on Kerkyra and in the northern Peloponnese. Except in the case of the Kerkyra graves, which contained no weapons, they have been tentatively linked either with the route of the Via Egnatia or with areas in which a Byzantine military presence continued largely uninterrupted through the seventh, eighth, and ninth centuries; often, they are closely related to reoccupied fortified hilltop sites. In the coastal regions of Istria and likewise along its northern border region, cemeteries accompanied by particular types of grave goods can be associated with military emplacements, and they almost certainly reflect the presence of soldiers permanently stationed with their families and drawn from local or "imported" populations—in this case, a connection with "Avars" from the regions to the north of the Danube basin has been made on the basis of the grave goods, in particular belt buckles and weapons.[80] Banditry or warfare in both the Balkans and in Anatolia influenced the pattern of movement.

80 For the Komani-Kruja materials, see W. Bowden, "The Construction of Identities in Post-Roman Albania," in Lavan and Bowden, eds., *Theory and Practice in Late Antique Archaeology,* 56–78, esp. 59–62, and idem, *Epirus Vetus,* 204–11; E. Nallbani,

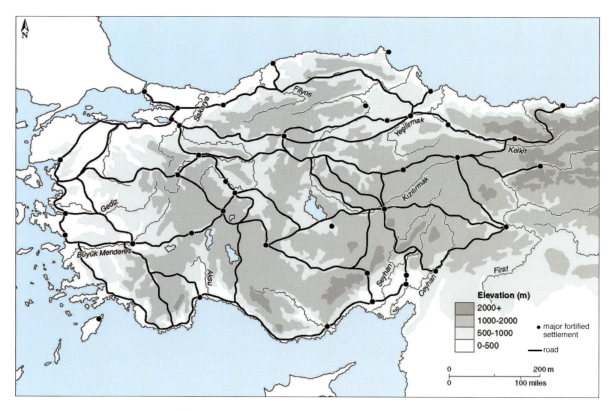

Figure 4.4. Asia Minor, ca. 800 (after Haldon, *The Palgrave Atlas of Byzantine History,* map 6.9)

Such disruption varied by both season and region, however. While it must have contributed to the interruption of the movement of goods across the areas affected, and thus to the further localization of economic subsystems, in the longer term the movement of goods and resources around and across the networks and circuits I noted previously was compromised only marginally.[81] There also appears to have been an increasing reliance on beasts of burden for the movement of goods and people, rather than on wheeled vehicles drawn by draft animals, and this shift may in turn have affected the ways in which goods, whether in bulk or not, were transported. Large, heavy amphorae, easily stacked and carried on ships or carts, were less easily managed on mules or donkeys, a factor that may have contributed to the increased regionalization of exchange in inland regions (although some transport amphorae were certainly made for use with animals).[82] For example, ninth- and tenth-century evidence shows that wine or oil could be carried, in considerable quantities, in large leathern skins of 50-liter capacity slung on mules; other goods—grain and dried fruits, for instance—were transported in panniers slung in pairs, two pairs per animal. It is entirely possible that the disappearance of imported amphorae from

"Transformations et continuité dans l'ouest des Balkans: Le cas de la civilisation de Komani (IVᵉ–IXᵉ siècles)," in *L'Illyrie méridionale et l'Epire dans l'Antiquité,* ed. P. Cabanes and J.-L. Lamboley (Paris, 2004), 481–90; and, for the military association, Curta, *Southeastern Europe in the Middle Ages,* 103–7. For the Istria material, see M. Torcellan, *Le tre necropoli di Pinguente* (Florence, 1986).

81 For a brief survey of the road systems and the economic hinterlands they connected, see Hendy, *Studies,* 69–138; Haldon, *Warfare, State and Society,* 51–60; M. Kaplan, "Quelques remarques sur les routes à grande circulation dans l'empire byzantin du VIᵉ au XIᵉ siècle," in *Voyages et voyageurs à Byzance et en Occident du VIᵉ au XIᵉ siècle,* ed. A. Dierkens and J.-M. Sansterre (Liège, 2000), 83–100; A. Avramea, "Land and Sea Communications, Fourth–Fifteenth Centuries," in *EHB* 1:57–90; K. Belke, "Communications: Roads and Bridges," in *The Oxford Handbook of Byzantine Studies,* ed. E. Jeffreys, J. Haldon, and R. Cormack (Oxford, 2008), 295–308.

82 R. W. Bulliet, *The Camel and the Wheel* (Cambridge, Mass., 1975); and see, in this volume, M. McCormick, "Movements and Markets in the First Millennium: Information, Containers, and Shipwrecks," 70–71.

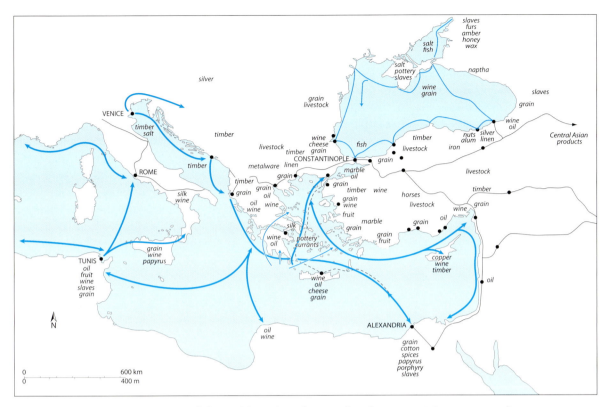

Figure 4.5 Sources of goods, ca. 850 (after Haldon, *The Palgrave Atlas of Byzantine History,* map 6.12)

certain parts of the Roman world reflects not just changes in patterns of exchange and export/import of goods but also changes in the mode of their transportation. The picture thus becomes even more complicated than it might appear at first sight.[83]

Implications

What does all this evidence mean? The first conclusion that can safely be drawn is that we must factor into our understanding a very high degree of quite localized differentiation, particularly across the period 650–800 or so (see fig. 4.5). One area can be devastated and suffer an absolute collapse of social and economic life; an area not too far away, either separated by obvious natural features or merely out of range of frequent and regular hostile action, can remain relatively flourishing and display a considerable degree of continuity. Relatively small coastal settlements with good access to commercial routes can flourish, while similar settlements inland can be quite poor. Larger settlements inland can thrive if they are centers of communications, of the army, and of administration; lesser settlements can be quite impoverished, despite the presence of church and state. Another conclusion is that some types of settlement thrive on an entirely seasonal basis, remaining for much of the year relative backwaters but flourishing during a few weeks of an annual fair—Euchaita and Ephesos are just two examples. This differentiation by zone reflects a combination of the effects of economic disruption and dislocation caused by hostile action and the established regional variations dependent on site location and context. Consider the differences between the Taurus and Anti-Taurus frontier region, the relatively protected Pontic-Marmara region, and the southern and western Asia Minor coastal zone, as well as the approximate demarcation between the fairly well protected strategic hinterland of Constantinople and the less

---

83 See *Constantine Porphyrogenitus: Three Treatises on Imperial Military Expeditions,* ed., English trans., and comm. J. F. Haldon, CFHB 28 (Vienna, 1990), [C] 142–44; and for the capacities involved, E. Schilbach, *Byzantinische Metrologie, HAW* 12.4, Byzantinisches Handbuch 4 (Munich, 1970), 248–63.

well protected zone behind the frontier regions: in three out of these four cases, the differences also reflect geographical divisions. The ceramics and the numismatic material are only just beginning to reveal these inflections and nuances.

At the same time, it is clear that patterns can alter over relatively short cycles—a good example is the changing pattern evidenced in the Butrint material, as a shift from an eastern to an Adriatic emphasis takes place in the later eighth and early ninth centuries, even as goods from the Crimea continue to move into the area. So in many respects, we are still very dependent on textual evidence. Finally, subsistence or marginal economies tend to maintain themselves at key tipping points—relatively poor and marginal zones can flourish when the capacity of the economy as a whole is such as to draw them into a wider network of economic relationships. When the overall balance is disturbed to the degree that that capacity disappears, as happened in the later seventh and early eighth centuries across much of the Byzantine world, then areas with adequate local resources may be able to maintain a substantial degree of continuity, but those without such reserves will quickly be thrown back on a highly localized and semi-autarkic set of relationships. Location, geography, and human activity all play a complex and interlocking role, and we can understand the great variety of local economic histories within the broader picture, and avoid misleading generalizations, only if we take this into account.

The Middle and Late Byzantine Periods

• FIVE •

Regional Networks in the Balkans in the Middle and Late Byzantine Periods

ANGELIKI E. LAIOU[†]

LET ME SAY AT THE OUTSET HOW PLEASANT and comforting it is to me to see the revived interest in Byzantine trade that has developed over the past few years—maybe a couple of decades. It signals considerable progress in the study of Byzantine economic history. A number of factors have contributed to this development, and I will signal only two, which in my view are the most significant. One is, undoubtedly, the advances in archaeology, which is now carried out with sophistication and with a view toward uncovering and studying not only elite products but also more humble ones. The other is the liberation of Byzantine economic history from the primitivist models, the outcropping of the Finley-Jones views, as Sean Kingsley and Michael Decker have called them,[1] a liberation that, while not yet complete, is very much in evidence, as a number of the papers in this Symposium show. Such views had for some considerable time informed the study not only of the late antique and early Byzantine period but of subsequent periods as well.[2]

The study of international exchange had suffered less than that of regional and interregional exchange, and for good reason.[3] The export (or import) of luxury items, thought to constitute the objects of international trade, can easily fit the model of an economy based on status and embedded in politics, in which exchange is controlled in one way or the other, and where one or two large centers of demand and production are sufficient. Regional and interregional trade engage different productive forces and different modes of distribution.

What does one mean by regional trade? The definitions depend partly on distance and partly on

---

This draft was communicated to Peter Temin in advance of the Symposium, in April 2008. It has been edited minimally here by Cécile Morrisson, completing the references indicated by the author with the help of Demetra Papanikola-Bakirtzi, Johannes Koder, and Rowan Dorin. When there was some doubt as to which publication Laiou had in mind, the reference has been inserted between square brackets. The few sentences where the style was adapted to the oral presentation have been left unchanged.

1 S. Kingsley and M. Decker, introduction to *Economy and Exchange in the East Mediterranean during Late Antiquity: Proceedings of a Conference at Somerville College, Oxford, 29th May, 1999*, ed. S. Kingsley and M. Decker (Oxford, 2001), 3.

2 E.g., M. F. Hendy, [*Studies in the Byzantine Monetary Economy, 300–1450* (Cambridge, 1985)]; J. Haldon, ["Production, Distribution and Demand in the Byzantine World, c. 660–840," in *The Long Eighth Century: Production, Distribution and Demand,* ed. I. L. Hansen and C. Wickham (Leiden, 2000), 225–64]; C. Wickham, ["Overview: Production, Distribution and Demand," ibid., 345–77]; M. Angold, [*Byzantine Government in Exile: Government and Society under the Laskarids of Nicaea, 1204–1261* (London, 1975)].

3 E.g., É. Patlagean, "Byzance et les marchés du grand commerce vers 830–vers 1030: Entre Pirenne et Polanyi," in *Mercati e mercanti nell'alto medioevo: L'area Euroasiatica e l'area Mediterranea*, Settimane di studi del Centro italiano di studi sull'alto medioevo 40 (Spoleto, 1993), 587–632. Some scholars, however, have stressed the role of non-economic international circulation of goods and money: P. Grierson, "Commerce in the Dark Ages: A Critique of the Evidence," *Transactions of the Royal Historical Society*, 5th ser., 9 (1959): 123–40 (repr. in idem, *Dark Age Numismatics* [London, 1979], art. II).

function. One concept based on distance calls long-distance trade, as opposed to regional trade, that which extends over 100 kilometers by land, or covers the distance from Egypt to Africa by sea.[4] The borderline between local and regional trade would be 50 kilometers by land or one day's sailing.[5] Distance, of course, is not the only factor, and perhaps not the primary one, since its role can vary, depending on more functional aspects, such as the purpose of the transactions and the pull of major centers of consumption. For regional trade, I use the definition that locates it within a radius of 50 to 300 kilometers. In terms of function, it would implicate transactions that were more large-scale than those of local trade, and goods that were produced and consumed within the region; and the merchants would be professionals, not the producers who would frequent local markets. The types of product exchanged are usually thought to be more expensive and lighter than those of local trade, but not luxury items, which are thought to form the commodities of interregional and international trade, but I do not think that this is a good distinguishing factor.[6]

It is necessary to introduce nuances and amplifications into this definition. Some distinctions do not hold: regional trade is not necessarily domestic, as it can also take place across frontiers—John Haldon has already noted this in connection with Cyprus, the southern coast of Asia Minor, and Syria-Palestine, and the recently completed dissertation of my student, Koray Durak,[7] makes the same point for a period that extends to the late eleventh century. Trade between the Byzantine Empire and Bulgaria is both regional and international in the sense that it implicates two different political entities. Trade between Crete and Egypt, which in the tenth century and after included herbs and cheeses from Crete and spices from Egypt to Crete, implicates commodities that are semiluxury on one leg and luxury on the other. Indeed, in terms of commodities, the same commodity can be the object of regional transactions as well as long-distance, international ones, as will be argued in the case of eleventh- to twelfth-century ceramics. A real difference exists in the conditions in which international trade takes place: it is subject to strictures, limitations, and bilateral arrangements, such as, for example, affected the Bulgarian trade. The treaty of 716 had permitted the export to Bulgaria of "garments and red leather of a price up to 30 pounds of gold," and it has plausibly been suggested that this exchange would have taken place in Mesembria, which would then have functioned as a port of trade.[8] In the early tenth century, the *Book of the Prefect* set down specific terms regarding the exchange of silks for the linen and honey brought by the Bulgarians.[9] In other words, there is an institutional component to international trade that is absent from regional and interregional trade within the Byzantine Empire. The distinction between the products exchanged in regional and in interregional/long-distance trade is also not a stable one, but changes with time and economic conditions: thus, in the thirteenth century and after, exchange between the Black Sea area and the northern Aegean, on the one hand, and Venice and Genoa, on the other, was not limited to the luxuries that in the first instance one associates with long-distance trade, but very much involved bulk products, primarily wheat and alum. Thus the various categories of trade are not clear-cut; they become blurred at the boundaries, as the same commodities (grain, for instance) at times circulate between contiguous areas and at other times travel over long distances. I use the term "regional trade" here to refer to exchanges within a limited geographic range (the geographic component) that involve commodities which are produced within that area. When the exchange involves the resale of

---

4   J. Durliat, *De la ville antique à la ville byzantine: Le problème des subsistances,* Collection de l'École française de Rome 136 (Rome, 1990), 513–14; A. E. Laiou, "Exchange and Trade, Seventh–Twelfth Century," in *EHB,* 2:705.

5   A. E. Laiou and C. Morrisson, *The Byzantine Economy* (Cambridge, 2007), 81; J. H. Pryor, *Geography, Technology and War: Studies in the Maritime History of the Mediterranean, 649–1571* (Cambridge, 1988), 139–52.

6   The above is an adaptation of de Ligt's definitions for fairs: L. de Ligt, *Fairs and Markets in the Roman Empire: Economic and Social Aspects of Periodic Trade in a Pre-industrial Society,* Dutch Monographs on Ancient History and Archaeology 11 (Amsterdam, 1993), 15, 82–83, 88–89.

7   K. Durak, "Commerce and Networks of Exchange between the Byzantine Empire and the Islamic Near East from the Early Ninth Century to the Arrival of the Crusaders" (Ph.D. diss., Harvard University, 2008).

8   See Theophanes the Confessor, *Theophanis Chronographia,* ed. C. de Boor, 2 vols. (Leipzig, 1883–85), 1:497–99; N. Oikonomides, "Tribute or Trade? The Byzantine-Bulgarian Treaty of 716," in *Studies on the Slavo-Byzantine and West-European Middle Ages: In memoriam Ivan Dujčev,* Studia Slavico-byzantina et Medievalia Europensia 1 (Sofia, 1988), 29–31.

9   *Eparchenbuch* 9.6.

commodities from or to greater distances, this will be noted.

If the existence of local trade may be assumed except in the most extreme of circumstances, that of regional networks is not self-evident. It is their development that we are concerned with here, and for that there are certain preconditions. There has to be a level of effective demand that cannot be adequately met by local exchange either because it is too large or because it involves specialty products. Large, concentrated demand for alimentary products, typically associated with the existence of large cities (but which could also be the result of the presence of an army in a particular location), cannot be met by the production of the immediate hinterland: it has been estimated that in medieval societies an urban population of ten to twenty thousand could not be provisioned from the immediate hinterland, which necessarily means regional or interregional trade in foodstuffs.[10] In the Balkans, Constantinople is the obvious case in point, but it is, of course, far from a unique case: Thessalonike and, after the tenth century, certainly in the eleventh–twelfth, Corinth, Monemvasia, and other cities[11] were large enough to depend on regional and perhaps interregional trade. The second point, specialty products, is exemplified by the sale of Bulgarian honey in Thessalonike or the dispersion of pottery from Thessalonike and Serres in the Palaiologan period. Channels of distribution are important and require good communications, which are not simply a given: effective demand helps develop good communications, and is reinforced by them.

Let us look at the development of regional trade networks in Thrace and Macedonia. These are privileged areas, since Thrace has the strong magnet of the great consumption center that was Constantinople, and Macedonia has the equally important magnet of Thessalonike, not only a major consumption and production center but also a port. At times, both areas were very insecure: Thrace in the seventh and eighth centuries, and from time to time afterward, and Macedonia whenever there were troubles with the Bulgarians. These areas also had, since Roman times and throughout much of the Byzantine period,

a good network of roads, doubtless built for military reasons but also able to serve peaceful ones: the two major such roads were the Via Egnatia and the so-called Military or Imperial Road (Via Militaris or Regia, *basilikē hodos*), traversing the Balkans diagonally, from Belgrade to Braničevo and Niš, then to Philippopolis, Adrianople, and Constantinople.[12] The Via Egnatia, difficult of access in the late seventh century, began to be reopened toward the end of that century, and seems to be functioning partly in the 830s and fully by the late ninth century, at least in times of peace. Alternatively, communications along the southern shore of Thrace were carried out by sea, also a dangerous but, it seems, not unusual enterprise.[13] By the end of the ninth century, people could travel along the entire length of the Via Egnatia.[14] The way inland would have followed the rivers or the river valleys of Axios, Strymon, and Nestos.[15] The lower part of the Via Regia, as far north as Philippopolis, seems to have been recently reopened in the late eighth century, when the empress Eirene

10 J. Landers, *The Field and the Forge: Population, Production and Power in the Pre-industrial West* (Oxford, 2003), 114.

11 W. Treadgold, *A History of the Byzantine State and Society* (Stanford, 1997), 702.

12 K. Belke, "Roads and Travel in Macedonia and Thrace in the Middle and Late Byzantine Period," in *Travel in the Byzantine World,* ed. R. Macrides (Aldershot, 2002), 73–90.

13 Despite grave dangers posed by Slavs such as those "Slavic robbers" who, in the 830s, robbed ships that tried to cross the Strymon River: G. Makris, ed., *Ignatios Diakonos und die vita des Hl. Gregorios Dekapolites,* ByzArch 17 (Stuttgart, 1997), 86; or those of a "sklavinia" in the hinterland of Thessalonike who rebelled against imperial authority or, at the very least, launched a destructive expedition in the surrounding area (ibid., 110). On his first trip, St. Gregory went to Thessalonike from Constantinople by sea from Ainos to Christopolis (Kavalla), and then to Thessalonike land, having persuaded the Slavic "robbers" to let him cross the Strymon. Interestingly, he was then able to go, in the service of a monk, from Thessalonike to Corinth overland, and then on board ship, braving the Arab pirates, to Rhegion and then to Rome (86–88). Travel between Thessalonike and Constantinople took place both by land (though Anastasios and George the *protokangelarios* took a ship at Maroneia) and by sea (112–16).

14 As did Anastasius Bibliothecarius in 870: Belke, "Roads and Travel," 78–79. [N. Oikonomides, "The Medieval Via Egnatia," in *The Via Egnatia under Ottoman Rule (1380–1699): Halcyon Days in Crete II,* ed. E. Zachariadou (Rethymnon, 1996), 9–16 (repr. in idem, *Social and Economic Life in Byzantium* [Aldershot, 2004], art. XXIII)]; A. E. Laiou, "Η Θεσσαλονίκη, η ενδοχώρα της και ο οικονομικός της χώρος στην εποχή των Παλαιολόγων" (Thessalonike, its hinterland and its economic space), in Διεθνές Συμπόσιο Βυζαντινή Μακεδονία 324–1430 μ. Χ., Θεσσαλονίκη, 29–31 Οκτωβρίου 1992, Πρακτικά Μακεδονική Βιβλιοθήκη 82 (Thessalonike, 1995), 183–94, at 184.

15 N. Oikonomidès, "Le kommerkion d'Abydos: Thessalonique et le commerce bulgare au IXe siècle," in *Hommes et richesses dans l'Empire byzantin,* vol. 2, *VIIIe–XVe siècle,* ed. V. Kravari, J. Lefort, and C. Morrisson (Paris, 1991), 241–48, at 245–47.

visited the city and rebuilt Veroe (Stara Zagora) and Anchialos, in 784.[16] If Theophanes' account of the travels is accurate, Eirene went first to Veroe, then to Anchialos, and finally to Philippopolis, from where she returned to Constantinople. Whatever the reason for this somewhat crisscross journey, it is clear that not only was the southern part of the main route open at this time but there were roads connecting Veroe to Anchialos, a fairish long way away, and Veroe to Philippopolis. At the same time, communications by sea between Constantinople and the Black Sea coast must have been open at least since the Byzantine-Bulgarian treaty of 716; in any case, the Black Sea was controlled by Byzantine ships.

For the commercial networks of Thrace in the period down to the eleventh century, the available information is primarily Constantinopolitan or connected to Constantinople. It has been established, on the basis primarily of Arab sources of the eighth and ninth centuries, that Constantinople was provisioned in agricultural products from the Thracian hinterland, first the area adjacent to the city and then further inland. By the tenth century, Raidestos, to the south of Constantinople, had become a major center of agricultural production and diffusion, and so it remained throughout the Byzantine era. Mesembria, Anchialos, and in the ninth century Develtos (which replaced Mesembria) also functioned as export centers for the trade of the Bulgarian hinterland, that is, agricultural products.[17] It has also been argued, on the basis of texts and the seals of *kommerkiarioi,* that in the late ninth century the products of the Bulgarian hinterland reached Constantinople by land as well, along the Via Regia, which led from Sofia to Constantinople.[18] Independent evidence supports the idea that commerce with parts of the Bulgarian hinterland increased over time. The Bulgarian merchants in the *Book of the Prefect* sold linen and honey and they bought Byzantine and Syrian silks. In 969, the Russian Prince Svetoslav described Presthlavitza as a commercial center where, along with products from Hungary, Bohemia, and the Rus, one could find gold, silks, fruit, and wine "from Greece."[19] Indeed, archaeological finds include fine White Ware ceramics and objects in high-quality glass.[20] While the jewelry of the Preslav treasure might be there as a gift from Byzantium, the other objects, especially those mentioned by Svetoslav, seem to belong best to the context of commercial exchange. The Byzantine products sold here would be luxury products (silks), but also semiluxury commodities (fruit and wine).

The expansion of regional trade inland, intensifying in the eleventh and twelfth centuries, is a natural function of the rise in demand, which one may plausibly suggest developed with the revival of cities and city functions, as it seems to have occurred since the early ninth century; it continued, as an overall pattern, through the twelfth century at least. The demand of the capital for agricultural goods and raw materials, as well as for Bulgarian linen, would have been a particular stimulus for exchange involving the northern part of the region.

This, then, was the situation in the ninth to tenth centuries with regard to Thrace. The southern and easternmost part of Thrace had connections with centers of trade—mostly with Constantinople is what we hear about, but perhaps with other centers of consumption as well. For the products to reach the distribution centers, there must have been smaller networks, whose composition we cannot know. The question that arises naturally, and especially given the debate about the nature of the Byzantine economy, is the degree to which the commodities involved were exchanged through commercial channels or were inscribed in a system of non-economic exchange, primarily that of (tribute or) tax. Secondarily, there is the question of the medium through which these transactions were conducted.

Starting from the geographic north, to the extent that exchanges involved Bulgarian-ruled territories and given that these territories were independent until 1018, there is no question of a fiscally driven

---

16 Theophanes, ad 6276, *The Chronicle of Theophanes Confessor: Byzantine and Near Eastern History, AD 284–813,* trans. C. Mango and R. Scott (Oxford, 1997), 142–43.
17 Oikonomidès, "Le kommerkion d'Abydos," 247–48.
18 Ibid., 247. By this time, the *kommerkiarioi* were imperial officials who controlled imports and exports and collected the customs duties: N. Oikonomides, "Silk Trade and Production in Byzantium from the Sixth to the Ninth Century: The Seals of Kommerkiarioi," *DOP* 40 (1986): 50 (repr. in idem, *Social and Economic Life in Byzantium,* art. VIII). In the seventh and eighth centuries, according to this scholar, the kommerkiarioi had been important merchants dealing primarily in silk, who received from the emperor official rights in their province (33–53).

19 Reported in the *Russian Primary Chronicle*: N. Oikonomides, "Presthlavitza, the Little Preslav," *Südost-Forschungen* 42 (1983): 1–19.
20 I. Jordanov, "Preslav," in *EHB,* 2:669.

exchange. Nor did the Bulgarians pay tribute to the Byzantines. From early on, the exchange seems to have involved merchants: the treaty of 716 mentions the *emporeuomenoi* of both states, who were required to have their merchandise stamped with an official stamp.[21] In 893, two Byzantine merchants with friends in high places tried to divert the trade of the Bulgarian hinterland from Constantinople to Thessalonike—these were commercial exchanges, involving merchants, on whom our two Byzantines also imposed higher customs duties, which they collected. The complaints of the Bulgarian merchants provoked the attacks of Tsar Symeon.[22] The Bulgarian merchants in the *Book of the Prefect* are just that.

Further south, within Byzantine Thrace, fiscal grain must have ceased being significant in the second half of the eighth century: since 769, when Constantine V forced the collection of taxes in cash rather than in kind, there was a fiscally driven commercialization of production, with all that means for monetization. What does raise a question is the fact that the area had a number of large estates, especially well documented in the eleventh and twelfth centuries; so one would have to address the question of whether the products of the region—primarily, of course, agricultural ones—were sold to merchants who then resold them to centers of concentrated demand, including Constantinople, or whether important landlords collected their rents (in kind, in such a scenario) and transferred them to their urban dwellings, thus taking a considerable proportion of urban demand (Constantinopolitan in the case of Thrace, Thessalonian in the case of Macedonia and perhaps western Thrace) out of the commercial circuit. In the tenth and eleventh centuries, the seals of the *horreiarioi* mark the presence of warehouses that stored grain from imperial estates, perhaps for consumption in Constantinople. In Thrace, these were in Herakleia and Philippopolis, so that some of the production of the area probably moved outside the regional commercial network.[23] In the *Book of the Prefect* there is no hint that any of the commodities entering Constantinople did so in any conditions other than market ones; the question still remains, however, as to the proportion of the goods that did so.

Finally, we must consider the issue of the medium of payment. For Byzantine Thrace, especially its southern regions, there is no reason to believe that transactions were carried out in any medium other than cash in the ninth to tenth centuries. On the other hand, the first Bulgarian empire (680–971) issued no coinage of its own, and it is assumed that it was mostly a barter economy. Certainly, the Bulgarian merchants in Constantinople in the early tenth century bartered their products, whether because they found Byzantine silks more serviceable than money or because the Byzantines themselves preferred to barter with them rather than export their own coinage (but commission fees between the Byzantines themselves were paid in cash).[24] Coin finds from the area of Preslav show that some Byzantine money circulated, and also that the quantity of Byzantine coins increased very considerably, almost doubling, during the period of Byzantine rule (971–1185).[25] The decision of the emperor Michael IV (1034–41) to demand the Bulgarian taxes in cash must have played a role in the monetization of exchange.[26]

---

21 Theophanes, ed. De Boor, 1:497; Laiou, "Exchange and Trade," 704.
22 Theophanes Continuatus, ed. I. Bekker (Bonn, 1838), 357–58: (ἀνδράσιν ἐμπορικοῖς καὶ φιλοκερδέσι καὶ φιλοχρύσοις); *Ioannis Scylitzae synopsis historiarum,* ed. I. Thurn (Berlin, 1973), 175–76: ἀνδράσιν ἐμπορικοῖς καὶ φιλοκερδέσι; Oikonomidès, "Le kommerkion d'Abydos," 246ff.; Laiou, "Exchange and Trade," 726. Skylitzes' phrasing suggests that Constantinople would no longer import the Bulgarian trade directly. So the enterprise would also involve a further exchange, from Thessalonike to Constantinople.
23 J.-C. Cheynet, "Un aspect du ravitaillement de Constantinople aux Xe–XIe siècles d'après quelques sceaux d'*hôrreiarioi*," in *Studies in Byzantine Sigillography,* ed. N. Oikonomidès, vol. 6 (Washington, D.C., 1999), 1–26 [repr. in idem, *La société byzantine: L'apport des sceaux* (Paris, 2008), 209–36].
24 [*Eparchenbuch* 1.13, 1.14, 1.19 (*synetheiai* due to the *primmikerios* or the *grapheus* by the new *didaskalos* or the new *taboullarios*); 4.5 (6 *nomismata* due to the guild by the new *vestioprates*); 6.4 (*kankelarion*); 6.11, 22.1 (*arrabona*); 6.9, 6.13 (fine to pay to the guild); 7.2, 8.1 (price of silk textiles); 1.4, 1.5, 1.9ff., 2.8, 11.5, 11.7, 12.1, etc. (fines); 21.2 (profit of the *bothroi*); 21.9 (fees due to the *prostates* of the *bothroi*); 1.6ff., 1.25, 22.3 (various *misthoi*).]
25 Jordanov, "Preslav," 670.
26 One hopes that the hoarding of coins in Matak near Nim (1 *solidus* and 7 *histamena*), which has been connected with this policy, is an isolated instance: I. Touratsoglou, "Ἀπό τα νομισματικά πράγματα στα Βαλκάνια των Μακεδόνων: Με αφορμή το 'θησαυρό' Ἰσταμένων Θεσσαλονίκη 2000," in *Βυζαντιό Κράτος καὶ Κοινωνία, μνήμη Ν. Οἰκονομίδη,* ed. A. Avramea, A. E. Laiou, and E. Chrysos (Athens, 2003), 523–41, at 526. [Laiou's "hopes" are confirmed by the context of this find: it belongs with a series of Dalmatian hoards formerly connected by D. M. Metcalf to the wreck of a ship loaded with 10 *kentēnaria* of gold recovered by Stephen of Dioclea (*Coinage in the Balkans* [Thessalonike, 1975],

In the eleventh and twelfth centuries, a period in which the Byzantine economy was in a virtuous cycle, regional exchange networks are visible throughout the empire. Cities thrived, commercial exchanges intensified, and manufactured products, not only luxury ones but pottery, glass, and perhaps others, circulated. In Thrace, given the relative peace in the region and the demand generated from increased urban populations, the hinterland seems to have been integrated more fully into the commercial networks. The well-known example of Raidestos, a very important center of grain collection and export to Constantinople, shows the impeccable workings of a market that functioned on market principles, where prices were formed freely on the ground.[27] This fact is so well known that there is no reason to dwell on it here. Philippopolis and its hinterland must have become a major producer of agricultural products in the eleventh century, as also the hinterland of Mosynopolis, in the south (see below); Veroe and the Hebros Delta were also important in the twelfth century.[28] All of these towns or, increasingly, cities were, in terms of distance, situated within a radius of less than 300 kilometers from Constantinople, the only exception being Philippopolis (372 km).[29] All were situated along major land or sea routes (see fig. 5.1). The products of their hinterland would, presumably, have arrived at the centers of distribution, if I may call them that, on the large number of smaller roads about which we have information from a much later period, and which seem to have been ubiquitous.[30]

Trade networks in the interior of the Balkans are not easy to determine with great precision. Here, we have a valuable source of information, the foundation charter of the monastery of the Theotokos, in Petritzos, south of the city of Philippopolis, dated 1083 (see fig. 5.2). Its founder was a Georgian noble, Gregory Pakourianos, a great soldier in the service of the Byzantine Empire and a man who, only two years earlier, had been an emperor maker.[31] He endowed his monastery with very considerable properties that had been given him by imperial decrees as reward for his services, as well as with those that had been given to his late brother, Apasios. The properties were in three solid blocks: the one that included the properties of his brother was in the eastern part of the theme of Thessalonike/western part of Strymon, at the Strymon Delta. It consisted of the city of Kaisaropolis and the village communities of Prilongion and Sravikion. The second was centered on Philippopolis, and the third was in and around Mosynopolis in the south on the Via Egnatia, Peritheorion, and Xanthe. They consisted of villages and towns, such as Stenimachos in the north and Peritheorion in the south, houses and other real estate in the city of Mosynopolis, and a great deal of arable land, vineyards, trees, mills (both water mills and those that were operated by animal power), mountain land, pasture land, lakes, and so on. Together with those of his brother, they were in the themes of Thessalonike, Voleron, Serres, Philippopolis, and Xanthe, and in the region of Komotene. They were,

---

48–49). I. Mirnik ("The Coinage of Romanos III Argyros in the Archaeological Museum of Split," *Vjesnik za Arheologiju i historiju Dalmatinsku* 87–89 [1998–99]: 305–60) connects them to the increasing Ragusan trade at that time. See in this volume R. W. Dorin, "Adriatic Trade Networks in the Twelfth and Early Thirteenth Centuries," 235–79 C.M.]

27 See G. Bratianu, "Une expérience d'économie dirigée: Le monopole du blé à Byzance au XIᵉ siècle," *Byz* 9 (1934): 643–62 [repr. in idem, *Études byzantines d'histoire économique et sociale* (Paris, 1938), 129–81]; A. Harvey, *Economic Expansion in the Byzantine Empire, 900–1200* (Cambridge, 1989), 236–38; M. Kaplan, *Les hommes et la terre à Byzance du VIᵉ au XIᵉ siècle: Propriété et exploitation du sol* (Paris, 1992), 468–70; P. Magdalino, "The Grain Supply of Constantinople, Ninth–Twelfth Centuries," in *Constantinople and Its Hinterland,* ed. C. Mango and G. Dagron (Aldershot, 1995), 40–43.

28 C. Asdracha, *La région des Rhodopes aux XIIIᵉ et XIVᵉ siècles: Étude de géographie historique* (Athens, 1976), 180–219 (production), 219–31 (trade and monetary circulation); J. L. Teall, "The Grain Supply of the Byzantine Empire, 330–1025," *DOP* 13 (1959): 87–190; A. E. Laiou, "Introversion and Extroversion, Autarky and Trade: Urban and Rural Economy in Thrace During the Byzantine Period," in *4th International Symposium on Thracian Studies Byzantine Thrace: Evidence and Remains (Komotini, 18–22 April 2007),* forthcoming. At the time of the Third Crusade, a large part of Frederick Barbarossa's army was sent to take and plunder the *civitas opulentissima* of Veroe (= Stara Zagora): Ansbert, "Historia de Expeditione Friderici Imperatoris," in *Quellen zur Geschichte des Kreuzzuges Kaiser Friedrichs I.,* ed. A. Chroust (Berlin, 1928), 44, 45. The city can have become "very rich" only through trade, and that regional trade.

29 Varna lies at a distance of 260 km. The distance of Great Preslav to Constantinople would be about the same.

30 Bclkc, "Roads and Travel," 86ff.

31 See P. Lemerle, *Cinq études sur le XIᵉ siècle byzantin* (Paris, 1977); A. E. Laiou, "L'étranger de passage et l'étranger privilégié à Byzance, XIème–XIIème siècles," in *Identité et droit de l'Autre,* ed. L. Mayali (Berkeley, 1994), 69–88; and eadem, "Introversion and Extroversion"; I have used the Petit edition of the *typikon* (L. Petit, "Typikon de Grégoire Pacourianos pour le monastère de Petritzos (Bačkovo) en Bulgarie, texte original," *VizVrem* 9, supp. 1 [St. Petersburg, 1904]), hereafter cited as Petit.

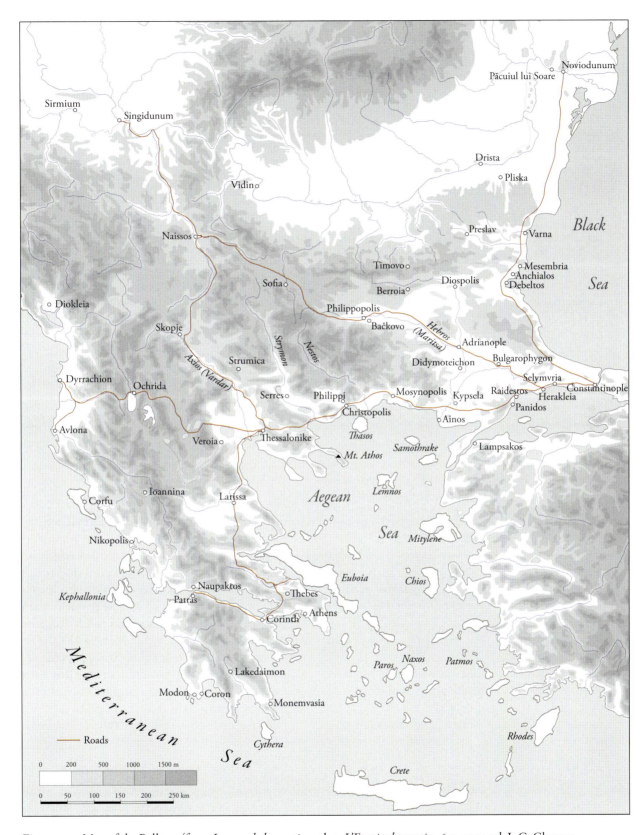

Figure 5.1. Map of the Balkans (from *Le monde byzantin*, vol. 2, *L'Empire byzantin, 641–1204*, ed. J.-C. Cheynet, Nouvelle Clio [Paris, 2006], courtesy CNRS, UMR 8167)

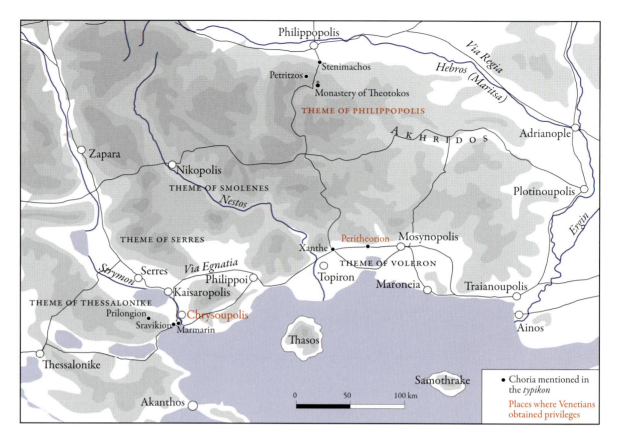

Figure 5.2. Venetian privileges in and around Pakourianos's estates (after C. Asdracha, in Lemerle, *Cinq études,* facing 176)

he tells us, functioning and income-producing.³² The properties he gave to his monastery were going concerns and in the past had yielded very considerable revenues, according to Pakourianos.³³ In his *praktikon* (foundation charter), Pakourianos provides rather generously for subsidies for the *hēgoumenos* and the monks, as well as for commemorative services. Just these two expenses, paid in good coin (*histamenon trachy*), add up to about 14 pounds of gold a year. It has been estimated that the total outlay in cash would be about 20 pounds of gold a year, and the value of expenses in kind about 79 pounds of gold. Ten pounds of gold were to be kept as a reserve at all times, and the rest of the money would be invested in land.³⁴ He also expected that revenues would increase in time, as he and his successors effected land improvements, and perhaps as he constructed towers, doubtless for defensive purposes. He obtained privileges from the emperor to ensure that in such a case these increased revenues would also be free of taxes.³⁵ A hundred years later, according to an elegant study by Michael Hendy, the abbot buried the sum of 10 pounds of gold in order to protect it from the marauding crusaders of Frederick Barbarossa. Of the 786 coins, 239 date from the reign of Alexios I (1081–1118); they had been in the monastic reserves almost from the beginning.³⁶

The ubiquity of coins on the estates of Pakourianos, even before these were turned over to the mon-

---

32 On the domains, see Petit, paras. 2, 14; Lemerle, *Cinq études,* 180, 190–91.
33 Lemerle, *Cinq études,* 166–68. Cf. Petit, para. 14.
34 C. Morrisson, "Byzantine Money: Its Production and Circulation," in *EHB* 3:949.
35 Petit, para. 55.
36 M. F. Hendy, "The Gornoslav Hoard, the Emperor Frederick I, and the Monastery of Bachkovo," in *Studies in Numismatic Method Presented to Philip Grierson,* ed. C. N. L. Brooke, J. G. Pollard, B. H. I. H Stewart, and T. R. Volk (Cambridge, 1983), 179–91 (repr. in idem, *The Economy, Fiscal Administration and Coinage of Byzantium* [Northampton, 1989], art. XI).

astery, presupposes the sale of a considerable part of the production of the monastery.[37] One has to remember, of course, that there was a Byzantine army stationed in Philippopolis, so it is possible that some of the production of the monastery was sold to the state, and was thus taken out of regional trade. But there was also an imperial grain storehouse, with state grain from imperial estates, which might have been used for the army.[38] In any case, the position of the three hostels built by Pakourianos, as well as the content of the Venetian commercial privileges (on which more below), makes it very likely that his production, or considerable parts of it, was commercialized. If the cash mentioned in the *typikon* came from the rents of the peasantry, then we are looking at local trade, which, I suspect, would have been unlikely to satisfy the demands of the two important cities and other smaller ones, unless we posit the existence of merchants who bought the crops from the peasants and then sold them both to the cities of the immediate area and elsewhere along a regional network. If the peasants paid their rent in kind, on the other hand, then the monastery itself was involved in the cash-producing trade. The monastery also had an unusually large domanial reserve, which would have meant concentrated production that could, again, be channeled to regional trade. Through his own holdings and those of his brother, Gregory Pakourianos had access to important markets: Philippopolis, for one, and also Mosynopolis on the Via Egnatia in the south, not far from Xanthe, and Peritheorion by the sea.[39] Pakourianos built three hostels on his property, apart from the preexisting ones: one was at a crossroads near the large village of Stenimachos, southeast of Philippopolis, where an (annual?) fair also took place. Of the other two hostels, one (Marmarin, Sravikion) was located at the Strymon Delta, near a bridge, and the other in Prilongion, to the west of Marmarin near the sea (see fig. 5.2). Marmarin is mentioned by al-Idrīsī as a river flowing outside the walls of Chrysoupolis (the editor says that al-Idrīsī is mistaken and the river is the Maritsa),[40] a city renowned for "the beauty of its markets and the importance of its commerce."[41] All three were for the use of travelers, which very much suggests that they were built and maintained for merchants or people moving commodities. The two coastal places are accessible from Philippopolis by road and they are, of course, very much accessible from Mosynopolis. Philippopolis had access to the sea through four networks of roads. A circuitous route could lead, south of the Via Regia, to the valley of the Nestos, down to Xanthe and Peritheorion. A second, eastern route would follow the Hebros Valley (and so the Via Regia) to Adrianople and eventually to the Via Egnatia. More interesting for us are the vertical routes: the route Philippopolis-Stenimachos-Achridos-Mosynopolis and the route from Philippopolis-Stenimachos, crossing the Arda, to Xanthe and Peritheorion. This last route is

---

37 Michael Hendy thinks that there was a dearth of coin in the interior, even in the twelfth century. He believes that the coin mentioned in the typikon came from revenues gained in the monastery's properties in the themes of Voleron and Thessalonike and transferred to Petritzos, thus from the coast to the interior: M. F. Hendy, in *DOC* 4:277. Paul Lemerle, on the other hand, believes that the cash was collected from the dues of the *paroikoi*. I have no problem with Hendy's interpretation, as long as it means that the production of Petritzos was marketed in these coastal cities and towns, and not that the cash revenues came from the production of the southern estates.

38 Asdracha, *La région des Rhodopes*, 154–62; Cheynet, "Quelques sceaux d'*hôrreiarioi*," 12, cites Leon, horreiarios of Philippopolis in the tenth century.

39 On Mosynopolis, Xanthe, and Peritheorion, see Asdracha, *La région des Rhodopes*, 104–9, 93–96, and 98–104, respectively. Asdracha says that Mosynopolis was destroyed in 1206 and never recovered (106); she thinks it is the Messene mentioned by Kantakouzenos.

40 In fact, al-Idrīsī is quite correct as to the location of Marmarin at the Strymon Delta. He is wrong in thinking it a river, and clearly confuses it with the Strymon; see *La Géographie d'Édrisi: Traduite de l'arabe d'après deux manuscrits de la Bibliothèque Nationale*, by P.-A. Jaubert, 2 vols. (1836–40; repr. Amsterdam, 1975), 2:297 (hereafter cited as al-Idrīsī): "Cette dernière ville ['Akhrisoboli la Maritime'] est agréable et remarquable par la beauté de ses marchés et par l'importance de son commerce. Auprès de ses murs coule une rivière connue sous le nom de Marmari." On Marmari(o)n (bandon of Zabalta, theme of Serres), see Asdracha, *La région des Rhodopes*, 184, 200. See also P. Gautier, "Le typikon du sébaste Grégoire Pakourianos," *REB* 42 (1984): 112–13.

41 Al-Idrīsī, 2:297. Chrysoupolis is near the ancient Amphipolis on the Strymon Delta: see A. Dunn, "The Rise and Fall of Towns, Loci of Maritime Traffic, and Silk Production: The Problem of Thisvi-Kastorion," in *Byzantine Style, Religion, and Civilization: In Honour of Sir Steven Runciman*, ed. Elizabeth Jeffreys (Cambridge, 2006), 38–71; idem, "Loci of Maritime Traffic in the Strymon Delta (IV–XVIII cc.): Commercial, Fiscal, and Manorial," in Οι Σέρρες και η περιοχή τους από την αρχαία στην μεταβυζαντινή κοινωνία: Σέρρες, 29 Σεπτ.–3 Οκτ. 1993, Πρακτικά, 2 vols. (Thessalonike, 1998), 2:343, 345–46; idem, "From *polis* to *kastron* in Southern Macedonia: Amphipolis, Khrysoupolis, and the Strymon Delta," in *Archéologie des espaces agraires méditerranéens au Moyen Âge*, ed. A. Bazzana, Castrum 5 (Madrid, 1999), 408, 411f.

thought to be the one mentioned in the typikon of Pakourianos.[42]

The chronicles of the first three crusades attest that the production of agricultural goods was very high in the areas along the Via Regia from Serdica (Sofia) southward, and suggest the existence of regional trade and the underlying monetization of the area. It should be remembered that the forces of the crusaders were very large, and they certainly must have taxed the resources of the areas through which they passed, especially Thrace.[43] Most destructive was the army of Frederick Barbarossa, which spent eight and a half to nine months on Byzantine soil, most of the time in Thrace.[44] The fact that the participants of the First Crusade were expected to buy their provisions along the way, and that money changers seem to have been present, indicates that such was the case in Thrace already in the eleventh century. Better information from the twelfth century (Second Crusade: 1147–49; Third Crusade: 1187–92) allows us to be more specific. In Sofia, the French members of the Second Crusade were able to get provisions from the governor. In Philippopolis, there was a Latin settlement outside the walls of the city, "who sold a great many supplies to travellers."[45] The existence of a settlement of western merchants in Philippopolis in the middle of the twelfth century is proof positive that at this time, and doubtless for some time before, the city was a center of concentration and, it follows, of dissemination of agricultural products. The list of cities where the crusaders were permitted to buy and sell in 1100–1101 is enlightening. It includes Philippopolis, Adrianople, and Didymoteichon, all three on the Via Regia, as well as Panidos (= Panion, near Raidestos), Raidestos, and Selymbria, in the vicinity of Constantinople.[46] Panidos and Raidestos were very active in the grain trade, we have seen that Philippopolis was also, and so must the others have been; al-Idrīsī mentions Chrysoupolis, Christopolis, Panidos, Raidestos, Herakleia, and Selymbria as rich commercial cities.[47] Part of Frederick Barbarossa's army stayed in Philippopolis for about five months, while he traveled south and stayed in Adrianople for three and a half months.[48] The resources of both areas as well as the distribution system collapsed during this time; it is a wonder that they did not do so during the earlier crusades, which suggests a well-functioning regional network in the area (see fig. 5.1).

The chrysobulls with commercial privileges issued to the Venetians are a good source for the expansion of trade networks in inland Thrace in the eleventh to twelfth centuries. I do quite recognize that since 1082, Venetian merchants possessed the right and privilege to trade everywhere in the empire, and thus the fact that a place is not specifically mentioned in the grant does not indicate that it was not important as a commercial center. On the other hand, I assume that when places or cities *are* specifically mentioned, this suggests that the Venetians had specifically asked that they be, presumably because they thought them particularly important.

In Thrace, the Venetians had requested and received, in 1082, the right to trade along the shore from Thessalonike to Constantinople (including Chrysoupolis and Peritheorion, where the Pakourianoi had properties), and Adrianople on the Maritsa River.[49] We have already seen that at the time of the Second Crusade there was an active "Italian" colony of merchants just outside the walls of Constantinople. By the end of the twelfth century, the Venetians requested privileges in the entire "provinces" (themes) of Strymon, Voleron, and Thessalonike, and in a host of areas in the interior: the provinces of Thrace and Macedonia, Adrianople and Didymoteichon, as well as the provinces of Philippopolis, Veroe, Morra and Achridos—that is, exactly where

---

42 Asdracha, *La région des Rhodopes*, 34–39.

43 The First Crusade, including that of 1100–1101, must have numbered in toto 150,000–200,000 people; the Second Crusade may well have numbered 100,000, while for the Third Crusade we have the figure of 100,000 men.

44 A. E. Laiou, "Byzantine Trade with Christians and Muslims and the Crusade," in *The Crusades from the Perspective of Byzantium and the Muslim World*, ed. A. E. Laiou and R. P. Mottahedeh (Washington, D.C., 2001), 157–96, at 161–62. The First Crusade spent two to two and a half months on Byzantine soil in the Balkans, the Second Crusade two and a half to three months.

45 Odo of Deuil, *De Profectione Ludovici VII in Orientem: The Journey of Louis VII to the East*, ed. V. G. Berry (New York, 1948), 45, 43. On the issue of the provisioning of the crusaders, see Laiou, "Byzantine Trade," 163ff. For Philippopolis in the Third Crusade, see *Nicetae Choniatae Historia*, ed. J. L. van Dieten, CFHB 11.1 (Berlin, 1975), 403.

46 Albert of Aix, *Historia Hierosolymitana*, RHC HOcc 4 (Paris, 1879), 559; Laiou, "Byzantine Trade," 165. Hendy, "Gornoslav Hoard," 180, thinks "Rusa" is Rus Koy (= Kosan), not Xanthe or Komotene, and he is doubtless correct.

47 Al-Idrīsī, 2:120–21, 297–98.

48 Hendy, "Gornoslav Hoard," 180.

49 M. Pozza and G. Ravegnani, eds., *I trattati con Bisanzio, 992–1198* (Venice, 1993), 40.

one concentrated part of the estates of the monastery lay—and the "episkepseis" (large estates, perhaps imperial) of Tzouroulos, Theodoroupolis, Arkadiopolis (Lule-Burgas), Messene (between Arkadiopolis and Tzouroulos), and Boulgarophygon. This attests to the expansion of Venetian interest and activities in the Byzantine Empire, but also confirms what we know from other sources: that these inland areas had grown rich, one assumes through the sale of their products in regional exchange. And it also reminds us that there are points where regional and interregional/international networks meet, when commercial activity intensifies, and the market is greatly enlarged. Of course, this change cannot necessarily be credited to the Venetians, who may well have replaced Byzantine merchants in internal trade.

The composition of the estates of Pakourianos and the routes linking them suggest, among other things, that Philippopolis and its production can be thought as belonging to both trade regions: the eastern, Thracian one, with Constantinople as one of the major centers, and the western, Macedonian one. The products of the hinterland that arrived at the Strymon Delta might then travel east or west.

The border between the economic regions of Thrace and Macedonia lies along the Strymon or the Nestos River, a fact that is supported by the evidence of monetary circulation. If we look at the areas of circulation of bronze coins in the fifth to the midseventh century, we find two neatly differentiated zones: coinage from the mint of Constantinople circulated in Moesia Secunda, Thracia, Haemimons, and Rhodope (= the diocese of Thrace), while coins from the mint of Thessalonike circulated in (today's Greek province of) Macedonia and the two Dacias; that would make the Nestos River the frontier.[50] Between the late eleventh and the thirteenth centuries, another numismatic division delineates two broad zones. The Balkan regions north of the Rhodope mountains and to the east used as petty coin the billon trachy (the *stamenon* of western sources); this is the eastern zone. In the western zone, in Greece and the Peloponnese, the lower-value copper *tetarteron* predominated. Thessalonike primarily used the tetarteron, but it served both zones of numismatic circulation: in the twelfth century, its mint issued both billon trachea and tetartera.[51]

The regional trade of Macedonia is connected with the great city of Thessalonike, which serves as a magnet, given its large market and the variety of products that it could send to the interior. I will not discuss this network in any detail; in any case, I have already indicated how I think regional trade networks developed and functioned. Here I will simply make a few supplementary points that emerge from the study of Macedonian trade. The first point is the obvious one that regional networks can change direction. Thus, in the late seventh century, the city of Thessalonike sought its grain, when it did not come by sea from the east, in southern parts: in Thessaly and particularly in the region of Demetrias and Phthiotid Thebes.[52] Its hinterland to the west, its natural hinterland, was, apparently, too unruly for much exchange to take place there. The situation to the east was also difficult for some time. When St. Gregory the Decapolite tried to reach Thessalonike from Constantinople (before 841), he went by sea up to Christopolis and then, when he tried to cross the Strymon, he was attacked by Slav robbers who apparently made a habit of attacking travelers. Since he was a saint, he managed to leave and continue his journey by foot. On the other hand, he seems to have been able to travel by land from Thessalonike to the south, as far as Corinth, without mishap, at least not of the kind he met earlier.[53] A while later, another monk, along with a Byzantine official who was in disgrace, managed to reach Constantinople by land; the saint himself preferred the sea route.[54] The commercial network of Thessalonike that included Thessaly, particularly Demetrias, continued in the later ninth century.

By the second half of the ninth century, trade became active between Thessalonike and lands to the west, at least as far as the city of Veroia (63 km

---

50 C. Morrisson, "La diffusion de la monnaie de Constantinople: Routes commerciales ou routes politiques?" in *Constantinople and Its Hinterland*, ed. C. Mango and G. Dagron (Aldershot, 1995), 79; C. Morrisson, V. Popović, and V. Ivanišević, with P. Culerrier et al., *Les trésors monétaires byzantins des Balkans et d'Asie Mineure (491–717)* (Paris, 2006), 62–63.

51 Hendy, *Studies*, 434–47, 601–2; *DOC* 4:1, 129–30; Morrisson, "Byzantine Money," 935–36, 960.

52 P. Lemerle, *Les plus anciens recueils des miracles de Saint Démétrius et la pénétration des Slaves dans les Balkans*, 2 vols. (Paris, 1978–80), 1:211, 218, miracle 2.4, §§254, 268; on this affair, see Durliat, *De la ville antique*, 401ff. Demetrias was an important center in the late ninth century (Laiou, "Exchange and Trade," 727).

53 Makris, ed., *Ignatios Diakonos*, 86, 88.

54 Ibid., 114–16.

away). Furthermore, the Axios, a navigable river, became an avenue of exchange with the interior; it is explicitly stated that in the late ninth and early tenth century, ships sailed up the river, carrying merchandise and increasing the wealth of the city.⁵⁵ The source that describes all this new activity claims that it was due to the fact that the Bulgarians had converted to Christianity (in 865), and that therefore peaceful relations were possible, and goods circulated by land and sea.⁵⁶ Thus there was a regional network, extending to the west and north of Thessalonike, that also involved areas of the state of Bulgaria; we see again that regional trade need not be confined within national boundaries. In the tenth century, Thessalonike was apparently a gateway to the interior as far as Belgrade, a distance of 507 kilometers, which Constantine VII pronounced to be a leisurely eight-day journey.⁵⁷ However, there is no indication of significant commercial activity anywhere near this far north at this time.

It is the part of this network that included "Bulgaria" that two merchants from Greece (who were also imperial officials?) tried to expand in the 890s. The "Bulgaria" in question is not the Black Sea coast but the hinterland—around Philippopolis, for instance. The effort to divert the Bulgarian trade from Constantinople to Thessalonike (with a considerable increase of the duties paid by the Bulgarians) has been interpreted as an effort to decentralize trade and help the economy of Thessalonike.⁵⁸ It is a plausible assumption that the two merchants might have had commercial interests in the network that linked Thessalonike to parts south, and were trying to establish an interregional network from the Bulgarian interior to some parts of Greece.⁵⁹

The regional network of Thessalonike, insofar as it included Bulgaria, still at a low level of monetization and with no coins of its own, was probably in part an exchange of commodities, although precious metals in some form may have been used, as well as Byzantine coins. The city produced pottery; glass; metal objects made of copper, iron, tin, and lead; and perhaps silk.⁶⁰ Presumably, this is what was sold to the interior, in exchange for foodstuffs, and possibly linen. The text mentions in Thessalonike a profusion of linen cloth, very thin and of excellent quality, and some of this may have come from Bulgaria, as it did in Constantinople. In this period, there is no identifiable pottery from Thessalonike with dispersion anywhere else. On the other hand, Constantinopolitan Polychrome Ware and Glazed White Ware dating from the late tenth to the late eleventh century

---

55 Kameniates, *De expugnatione Thessalonicae* 6.8. For a discussion of this, see A. E. Laiou, "The Byzantine City: Parasitic or Productive?" in *Byzantium: The Economic Turn,* ed. M. Whittow (Oxford, forthcoming). The most recent study of Thessalonike in this period is by Ch. Bakirtzis: "Imports, Exports and Autarky in Byzantine Thessalonike from the Seventh to the Tenth Century," in *Post-Roman Towns, Trade and Settlement in Europe and Byzantium,* ed. J. Henning, vol. 2, *Byzantium, Pliska, and the Balkans,* Millennium-Studien zu Kultur und Geschichte des ersten Jahrtausends n. Chr. 5.2 (Berlin, 2007), 89–118.

56 Kameniates, *De expugnatione Thessalonicae* 9.2–4, ed. G. Böhlig, CFHB 4 (Berlin, 1973): ἐξ ὅτου γὰρ ἡ κολυμβήθρα τοῦ θείου βαπτίσματος τὸ τῶν Σκυθῶν ἔθνος τῷ χριστωνύμῳ λαῷ συνεμόρφωσε καὶ τὸ τῆς εὐσεβείας γάλα κοινῶς ἀμφοτέροις διείλετο, πέπαυτο μὲν ἡ τῶν πολέμων στάσις, . . . ἔνθεν αἱ τῆς γεωργίας ἀφθονίαι, ἐκεῖθεν αἱ τῆς ἐμπορίας χορηγίαι. (4.) γῆ γὰρ καὶ θάλασσα λειτουργεῖν ἡμῖν ἐξ ἀρχῆς ταχθεῖσαι πλουσίαν καὶ ἀδάπανον τὴν περὶ ἕκαστον ἐδωροφόρουν. "The Bulgarian trade with Thessalonike coming down the Nestos-Strymon-Axios rivers seems to have increased ever since the peace with the Bulgarians in 815; indications from the seals of *kommerkiarioi,* of the second half of the ninth century, attest to this importance. The new customs officials in Thessalonike had jurisdiction over Thessaly, Kephallonia, the theme of Thessalonike and the West of Greece" (Laiou, "Exchange and Trade," 726; citing Oikonomidès, "Le kommerkion d'Abydos," 241–48).

57 Constantine Porphyrogennetos, *De administrando imperio,* ed. G. Moravcsik, trans. R. J. H. Jenkins (Washington, D.C., 1967), chap. 42.

58 Oikonomidès, "Le kommerkion d'Abydos," 246–48.

59 Interestingly, although this endeavor failed in the tenth century, one of the permanent markets of the city was called the "Sthlavomese," the "market of the Slavs," presumably referring to those west of Thessalonike: N. Oikonomidès, ed., *Actes de Docheiariou,* 2 vols. (Paris, 1984), no. 4, l. 27.

60 Kameniates 9.8–9 (ed. Böhlig, 499–501): ἐντεῦθεν χρυσίου καὶ ἀργυρίου καὶ λίθων τιμίων παμπληθεῖς θησαυροὶ τοῖς πολλοῖς ἐγίνοντο, καὶ τὰ ἐκ Σηρῶν ὑφάσματα ὡς τὰ ἐξ ἐρίων τοῖς ἄλλοις ἐπινενόητο. περὶ γὰρ τῶν ἄλλων ὑλῶν, χαλκοῦ καὶ σιδήρου κασσιτέρου τε καὶ μολύβδου καὶ ὑέλου, οἷς αἱ διὰ πυρὸς τέχναι τὸν βίον συνέχουσι, καὶ μνησθῆναι μόνον παρέλκον ἡγοῦμαι, τοσούτων ὄντων ὡς ἄλλην τινὰ δύνασθαι πόλιν δι' αὐτῶν δομεῖσθαί τε καὶ ἀπαρτίζεσθαι. 58.7–8 (568–69): ἐτελεῖτο δὲ ταῦτα ἐφ' ὅλοις νυχθημέροις δέκα, τῆς πληθύος ἀεὶ τῶν χρημάτων εὐφορουμένης ἀπὸ τῆς πόλεως, τῆς τε λοιπῆς ἀναγκαίας ὕλης, ὅση διὰ σηρικῆς ἐσθῆτος εὐπρεπὴς ἦν καὶ ὅση διὰ λίνου τοῖς ἀραχνείοις ἤριζεν ὑφάσμασιν, ὡς ὄρη καὶ βουνοὺς ἐκτελεῖσθαι τὰς τούτων σωρείας, ἄλλων ἐπ' ἄλλοις ἐπιτιθεμένων καὶ τὸν ὑποκείμενον τόπον πληρούντων. χαλκῶν γὰρ καὶ σιδηρέων σκευῶν ἢ τῶν ἐξ ἐρίων ἐσθημάτων οὐμενοῦν οὐδ' ὅλως ἐφρόντισαν, περιττὴν ἡγούμενοι τὴν κτῆσιν αὐτῶν. For the archaeological information regarding such activities (except for silk, very difficult to attest archaeologically), see Bakirtzis, "Imports, Exports," 108, on pottery; 111, on glass; 99–100, on metalwork, but referring to an earlier period.

have been found in Thessalonike, confirming the links between these two cities.⁶¹

The commercial activity of Thessalonike by land and by sea appears to have been substantial in the tenth century. Monetary finds do not, however, seem to confirm this. Of the 285 bronze coins found recently, only 15 belong to the period between the seventh and the tenth century.⁶² The dissonance between monetary finds and other sources is, unfortunately, not rare.

In the eleventh and twelfth centuries the relative peace in the western Balkans, following the victories of Basil II over the Bulgarians, doubtless played a role in the evident flourishing of Thessalonike. The greatly expanded hinterland to the northwest—that is, Serbia—begins to enter the commercial networks. The regional trade network is partly deduced from the Venetian privileges of 1198. The provinces of Kastoria, Servia, Veroia, Skopje, Strumica, Prilep, Pelagonia, and Moglena are an enlarged regional market trading with Thessalonike. In the documentation, the themes of Strymon and Voleron are mentioned in geographic proximity to Thessalonike rather than to the east.⁶³ Thessalonike produced, among other things, silk, as attested by Benjamin of Tudela; and it produced pottery that was disseminated widely, in places that included northern Greece, Serbia, and Bulgaria.⁶⁴ The presence in Prilep, Skopje, and Niš of pottery that may have originated in Thessalonike and Constantinople clearly indicates that there were, indeed, trade relations with the northwestern Balkans in the twelfth and early thirteenth centuries. In the early thirteenth century, local imitative production begins.⁶⁵ Pottery may easily have been one of the items exchanged for the agricultural products of Macedonia. Pottery production is also attested in the city of Veroia and the town of Kitros, to the south of Veroia.⁶⁶ I take this conjunction of production for diffusion into a large area along with the existence of more centers of production in smaller cities as an indication of hierarchization of both production and trade, regional and interregional.

Some information may be gleaned about the regional and interregional trade that found its way to Thessalonike in the twelfth century from the description of the great fair that took place on the feast of St. Demetrios. Apart from the Italian, Spanish, French, Egyptian, and Syrian merchants—all, it seems, bringing cloth—there are the Byzantine merchants. They come "from everywhere," says the source, but it mentions specifically those from the south, Boeotia and the Peloponnese, who trade in textiles (doubtless silks). There is no mention of specific products from western Macedonia or the western Balkans: the fair seems to have specialized in textiles and cattle, and we do not know of commercialized production of textiles in areas west of Thessalonike. On the other hand, merchandise does come to the fair from Bulgaria and the Black Sea: it comes by way of Constantinople, and by land, carried on the backs of "numerous" horses and mules, although we do not know what it was.⁶⁷

Thessalonike had a mint that produced both gold and copper coins in the eleventh century. The "dramatic" increase of issues in 1081–85 has been attributed by Michael Hendy to the presence of Alexios I and his army, on campaign against the Normans. The mint continued to produce gold, electrum, and copper coins after the monetary reform of Alexios I. The bulk of the issues was in copper tetartera. A recent discovery brought to light a hoard of fourteen gold *histamena* of the period 976–1055. They were found in the port, and Ioannis Touratsoglou suggests that they may have belonged to a sea captain/merchant.⁶⁸

Let us look at our third region, Greece and the Peloponnese. A differentiating characteristic of these areas is that there are no cities of the size and concentration of Constantinople or Thessalonike to act as magnets for regional and interregional trade.

---

61 I. Kanonides, "Μεσοβυζαντινή εφυαλωμένη κεραμική με λευκό πηλό από ανασκαφές οικοπέδων στη Θεσσαλονίκη," in *VIIe Congrès international sur la Céramique Médiévale en Méditerranée, Thessaloniki, 11–16 octobre 1999: Actes,* ed. Ch. Bakirtzis (Thessalonike, 2003), 71–76.
62 Bakirtzis, "Imports, Exports," 112.
63 Pozza and Ravegnani, eds., *Trattati,* 130.
64 Benjamin of Tudela, *The Itinerary of Benjamin of Tudela: Travels in the Middle Ages,* trans. M. N. Adler (Malibu, 1983), 10; J. Vroom, *Byzantine to Modern Pottery in the Aegean: 7th to 20th Century; An Introduction and Field Guide* (Utrecht, 2005), 87 (Painted Fine Sgraffito Ware).
65 M. Bajalović-Hadzi-Pesić, "Ornamentation of Medieval Serbian Tableware—Byzantine Heritage," in Bakirtzis, ed., *VIIe Congrès international sur la céramique médiévale en Méditerranée,* 90.

66 Laiou and Morrisson, *The Byzantine Economy,* 118, with references and map, 120. Al-Idrīsī (2:296) describes Kitros as "a considerable city, strong, commercial, and well populated."
67 Pseudo-Lucian, *Timarione,* ed. R. Romano (Naples, 1974), 53–55.
68 *DOC* 4:129–30; Touratsoglou, "Από τα νομισματικά πράγματα," 527–28.

This statement needs to be nuanced. Thessaly, specifically Demetrias, had traded with Thessalonike since at least the seventh century, and seems to have done so in the early ninth century,[69] exporting agricultural products. And Corinth developed into a major center of regional and interregional trade. Its industrial production as well as its size (15,000–20,000 people in the late eleventh and twelfth centuries)[70] of necessity posit regional trade, as does the existence of other important cities in the region (Halmyros, Larissa, Patras, Sparta, Athens, Thebes); these formed as many foci of trade of one kind or another, unless one were to argue that urban effective demand was kept down by the local large landlords feeding their urban households on the products of their estates. But even that extremely conservative and choleric landlord Kekaumenos, a great advocate of living off one's land, could not escape the fact that there were merchants around and that his autarkic ideal was far from realistic.[71]

One important difference with the earlier period should be noted. The city of Halmyros replaced Demetrias as a center of collection and export of the agricultural production of Thessaly, as is well known. But this trade seems to have been reoriented in the twelfth century. Thessalonike no longer looks like an important trade partner. The connections of Halmyros are with its hinterland to the west, from where came agricultural products. According to the Venetian documents, Halmyros is linked with commercial links to Corinth, and also to Constantinople by sea; in fact, this second route appears to be well established ("taxegio de Armiro"). There even seem to be people trading from Almyros to Syria, Palestine, and Egypt, but not to Thessalonike.[72] This shift in regional trade patterns should be further investigated.

It has long been recognized, and so I will not insist upon it, that rising demand led to increased productivity or at least production, and to the sale of agricultural commodities locally, regionally, and interregionally.[73] Almyros, as we have just seen, was a center where the products of the hinterland were concentrated and then exported. The area around Thebes had rich agricultural production and animal husbandry in the eleventh and twelfth centuries, and some of the wealth of the city certainly came from the commercialization of this production. Sparta and its area grew rich on the sale of olive oil.[74] When the study of unglazed ceramics is further advanced, it will doubtless provide precious information about the specificities of the movement of agricultural goods and of the ceramic containers themselves. In the area under discussion, for example, specifically in Boeotia, unglazed ware, especially amphorae of the Günsenin 3/Saraçhane 61 type, proliferated in this period, with finds concentrated in rural sites.[75] The amphorae, which can be used for the transport of liquids—wine, oil, and honey, all produced in Boeotia—bespeak trade in agricultural products but also in unglazed pottery: all of which in turn means considerable product specialization. Günsenin 3 amphorae have also been found in Sparta, a famous exporter of olive oil.[76] As places of production of this pottery, northeastern Turkey and central Greece, Boeotia, and Athens have been variously suggested.[77] The detailed study of regional and interregional trade in unglazed ceramics of the middle Byzantine period would have a lot to teach us. It is, in any case, clear that centers of consumption and distribution of agricultural products also both produced ceram-

---

69 *AASS* 4:666, vita of Blasios of Amorion.

70 G. D. R. Sanders, "Corinth," in *EHB* 2:653–54.

71 Kekaumenos: G. G. Litavrin, *Sovety i rasskazy Kekavmena* (Moscow, 1972), 188–90; see also A. E. Laiou, "Economic Thought and Ideology," in *EHB* 3:1127.

72 *DCV*, nos. 35 (1112), 108 (1142), 151 (1161), 152 (1191), 202 (1168), 212 (1169), 236 (1170), 238 (1171); *NDCV*, nos. 21 (1168), 190 (1169).

73 On central Greece, see A. Harvey, "Economic Expansion in Central Greece in the Eleventh Century," *BMGS* 8 (1982–83): 21–29.

74 Harvey, *Economic Expansion*, 145, 147; A. Dunn, "Historical and Archaeological Indications of Economic Change in Middle Byzantine Boeotia and Their Problems," in *B' Diethnes Synedrio Voiotikon Meleton* (Athens, 1955), 755–74. See the elegant churches of twelfth-century Mani.

75 J. Vroom, *After Antiquity: Ceramics and Society in the Aegean from the 7th to the 20th Century A.C.: A Case Study from Boeotia, Central Greece* (Leiden, 2003), 153–55.

76 G. D. R. Sanders, "Excavations at Sparta: The Roman Stoa, 1988–91," *BSA* 88 (1993): 283.

77 J. W. Hayes, *Excavations at Saraçhane in Istanbul*, vol. 2, *The Pottery* (Princeton, N.J., 1992), 76 (Boeotia or Athens); J. F. Cherry, J. L. Davis, and E. Mantzourani, with J. W. Hayes, "Introduction to the Archaeology of Post-Roman Keos," in J. F. Cherry, J. L. Davis, and E. Mantzourani, *Landscape Archaeology as Long-term History: Northern Keos in the Cycladic Islands*, Monumenta Archaeologica 16 (Los Angeles, 2001), 351–64, at 354–55; Vroom, *Byzantine to Modern Greek Pottery in the Aegean*, 97–99.

ics and traded them within the region, as is the case in Sparta and Larissa, for example.⁷⁸

The Peloponnese seems to have encompassed a set of regional markets, as well as having trade relations with Thebes and doubtless Athens.⁷⁹ As we will see, there is a very active subsystem around the Corinthian Gulf that encompasses Athens, Thebes, Corinth, and perhaps Euripos (Nigroponte). In 1082, the Venetians specifically requested access to Nauplion and Corinth, but we know that Venetian merchants were in Sparta already in the tenth century; they maintained an active trade in Sparta throughout the twelfth century. In 1198, they also got access to the regions of Patras and Argos as well as Modon.⁸⁰ al-Idrīsī speaks of about fifty "cities" in the Peloponnese, sixteen of which are important and renowned. Among them is, of course, Corinth, but also Sparta ("an important and flourishing city"), Patras, Argos, and others.⁸¹ A number of Venetian commercial contracts have Corinth as their destination or as the starting point for trade to Constantinople, Almyros, southern Greece, and the rest of the Peloponnese.⁸² This, of course, is both regional and interregional trade. What is more interesting is a look at some of the commodities that we know were exported from Corinth: I will speak first of the products of the Peloponnese and then of the manufactured products of the city itself. Corinth exported olive oil, presumably from the region around it; for the Venetians to pick it up in Corinth, merchants—originally certainly Byzantines, then probably Venetians as well—had to bring it there. From Corinth, good-quality cotton was exported (4,000 light lbs., valued at 64 "old" *hyperpyra*—the place of production is not known, although it could be the area around Lake Kopais, that is, the Theban hinterland; this cotton was exported to Constantinople).⁸³ There is some indication that Corinth also served as a point of collection and export of olive oil from Sparta.⁸⁴ Together with the contracts that mention Corinth as a point of departure for trade in southern Greece and the Peloponnese, it is clear that Corinth was one of the important centers of regional trade (and interregional and international, of course).

Let us now turn to the trade in manufactured products and raw materials. In the twelfth century, Athens and Thebes were linked through the silk industry. Thebes had become one of the great centers of silk production, as we know from narrative sources, both Byzantine and other.⁸⁵ Its great workshops produced purple silk cloth, one supposes together with silk textiles of lower quality.⁸⁶ Great silk manufacturing operations and the demand for their products do not develop from one day to the next, and so the fact that our information starts around the mid-twelfth century (with Niketas Choniates' description of the raid of Roger II of Sicily in 1147) does not mean that this is when the silk industry began. Besides, Venetians are attested there since 1071,⁸⁷ and the Venetian privilege of 1082 already mentions Thebes as a place where the Venetians wished to trade; the only commodity specifically associated with Thebes in the Venetian documentation is silk, which does not mean that nothing else was exported, but nevertheless points up the importance of the city's silk industry.⁸⁸ The

---

78 For Sparta, see notes 74 and 76, above, and A. Bakourou, E. Katsara, and P. Kalamara, "Argos and Sparta: Pottery of the 12th and 13th Centuries," in Bakirtzis, ed., *VIIᵉ Congrès International sur la Céramique Médiévale en Méditerranée*, 233–36; J. Dimopoulos, "Byzantine Graffito Wares Excavated in Sparta (12th–13th Centuries)," in *Çanak: Late Antique and Medieval Pottery and Tiles in Mediterranean Archaeological Contexts*, ed. B. Böhlendorf-Arslan, A. Osman Uysal, and J. Witte-Orr, Byzas 7 (Istanbul, 2007), 336–41. For Larissa as a possible center of the production of glazed ceramics in the late twelfth to early thirteenth century, see D. Papanikola-Bakirtzi, "Ἐργαστήρια εφυαλωμένης κεραμικής στο Βυζαντινό κόσμο," in Bakirtzis, ed., *VIIᵉ Congrès International sur la Céramique Médiévale en Méditerranée*, 53.
79 The distance from Thebes to Corinth is 54 km as the crow flies. The vita of St. Loukas Stereiotes shows how easy and common communications were between Boeotia and Corinth: D. Sofianos, Ὅσιος Λουκᾶς: Ὁ βίος τοῦ Ὁσίου Λουκᾶ τοῦ Στειριώτη: Προλεγόμενα – μετάφραση – κριτική ἔκδοση τοῦ κειμένου (Athens, 1989), paras. 41, 42.
80 Pozza and Ravegnani, eds., *Trattati*, 40, 130.
81 Al-Idrīsī, 2:124–26.
82 *DCV*, nos. 35 (1112), 65 (1135), 67 (1135), 68 (1136), 69 (1136), 80 (1142), 97 (1150), 145–47 (1161), 185 (1167), 192 (1168), 202 (1168), 314 (1179), 336 (1183), 451 (1200).

83 Ibid., no. 192 (1168) [concerning a shipment of cotton from Corinth to Constantinople].
84 Ibid., no. 65 (1135). Of course, the Venetians also collected oil from Sparta itself.
85 *Nicetae Choniatae Historia*, 74; Benjamin of Tudela, *The Itinerary*, 10.
86 Benjamin of Tudela, *The Itinerary*, 10; *DCV*, no. 243 (1171) ("pro samito uno ulati").
87 D. Jacoby, "Silk in Western Byzantium before the Fourth Crusade," *BZ* 84–85 (1991–92): 494 (repr. in idem, *Trade, Commodities and Shipping in the Medieval Mediterranean* [Aldershot, 1997], art. VII).
88 Pozza and Ravegnani, eds., *Trattati*, 40.

remnants of dye workshops have been found in the city, but otherwise the archaeological record is thin and, as has been pointed out, the evidence for the silk industry is primarily documentary or narrative.[89] Despite the valuable archaeological work undertaken in the area, the archaeological record does not, at the moment, provide many answers.[90] We do all remember, of course, that medieval textile industries do not easily leave an archaeological record, and that Thebes, like Corinth and other cities with continuous habitation, has not been and cannot be properly excavated.

Athens was a great producer of murex shells, from which the dye came that gave the best and most expensive purple color. That production, or part of it, was sold, we assume, to the silk works of Thebes, as was the soap that was needed to clean the silk.[91] Possibly, Thebes also got murex from Kastorion/Thisbe, on the Corinthian Gulf; heaps of murex shells have been found here and are clearly related to the production of purple dye, but, unfortunately, they have not been dated and Archibald Dunn uses them as evidence for both the early and the middle Byzantine period.[92] It also received murex from its closest port, Chalkis (Euripos = Nigroponte).[93] Thus both the area close to Thebes and Athens sent this important and expensive item to the city. In the case of Athens, this may be considered regional trade, of a somewhat different kind from what we have seen until now, since the product that we know was sent to Thebes from Athens was an expensive one. What Athens got from Thebes we do not know—possibly silks or simply money. It is no wonder that both Athens and Thebes prospered during the eleventh and twelfth centuries, when Athens enjoyed a building boom as seen in a number of churches built at the time.[94] The catchment area for Athenian trade seems to extend to the north as well; its metropolitan, Michael Choniates, was informed of the excellence of the makers of agricultural implements of the town of Gardiki in Thessaly, and requested that cart makers be sent there from Athens.[95]

The end product of the Theban silk industry was sold in Constantinople or reached it through non-commercial means, that is, in the form of tax, if Benjamin of Tudela is to be believed on this point.[96] It is also probable that some of it, and of varying qualities, was the object of regional trade, in an economy that was flourishing, with cities increasing in size and demand becoming differentiated and moving down the socioeconomic scale.[97] A Venetian document dated August 1159 and redacted in Thebes is a quittance for a *colleganza* (total: 150 hyperpyra "paleokenurgos"—new, but of "old" weight)[98] whereby the merchants would travel by land to all of "Catodica" (southern Greece or the theme of Hellas) and the Peloponnese, back to Thebes, "and from Thebes up to Thessalonike." The journey lasted for three to four months, beginning in May 1159.[99] A number of other documents show that Thebes was the starting point for commercial trips to southern Greece and the Peloponnese.[100] For the trip to

---

89 Ch. Koilakou, "Βυζαντινά εργαστήρια (βαφής) στη Θήβα," *Technologia* 3 (1989): 23–24; Dunn, "The Problem of Thisvi-Kastorion," 38–71.
90 There are two archaeological projects, the Boeotian Archaeological-Geological Expedition (directed by A. Snodgrass and J. Bintliff), and the Thisbe Basin Survey, directed by T. Gregory.
91 M. Kazanaki-Lappa, "Medieval Athens," in *EHB* 2:644–45.
92 Dunn, "The Problem of Thisvi-Kastorion," 46, 53–58. Al-Idrīsī, 2:125, calls the gulf between Naupaktos and Corinth the "port of the dyers," "Sabbughun" or "Mers' al-Sabbughun," and says that it was navigable by small ships only. All others had to circumnavigate the Peloponnese.
93 J. Koder, F. Hild, and P. Soustal, *Hellas und Thessalia, TIB* 1 (1993), 164.
94 Kazanaki-Lappa, "Medieval Athens," 642.

95 *Michaelis Choniatae Epistulae*, ed. F. Kolovou, CFHB 41 (Berlin, 2001), no. 43. For the location, see A. Avramea, *Η Βυζαντινή Θεσσαλία μέχρι του 1204: συμβολή εις την ιστορικήν γεωγραφία* (Athens, 1974), 162–63. Unfortunately, the destination of the soap, olive oil, and ecclesiastical vestments cut and dyed and sewn in Athens and carried on Monemvasiot ships (Kolovou, no. 84) cannot be determined. The statement of Michael Choniates that Athens did not produce silk as other places did (no. 60) should be taken as a comparative claim: Athens did not produce as much silk as Thebes.
96 Benjamin of Tudela, *The Itinerary*, 15; Jacoby, "Silk in Western Byzantium," 489–90.
97 The fact that there was social stratification in the period and that demand was boosted even by rich peasants has been recognized by M. F. Hendy, "'Byzantium, 1081–1204': The Economy Revisited, Twenty Years On," in *The Economy*, art. III, 9.
98 *DOC* 4:1, 56 and n. 85 with references.
99 *DCV*, no. 137 (1159).
100 Ibid., nos. 235 (1170), 239 (1171), 426 (1195). A document dated 1185 shows a contract redacted in Thebes for the merchant (Pietro Morosini) to go to Durazzo by land, then to Venice; from Venice he was to go to Corinth by sea and then, by land, to reach the investor (Vitale Voltani) in Thebes, and clear the accounts (the contract was for 250 "old-new" hyperpyra); or, depending on political conditions, Morosini was to go from Venice to Constantinople, either directly (by sea) or indirectly (docking at Durazzo and traveling by land to Constantinople). In either case, the accounts would be cleared in Constantinople: no. 353 (1185).

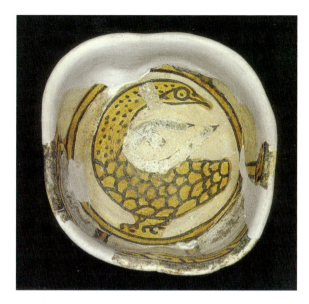

Figure 5.3. Polychrome Ware vessel with a bird, Benaki Museum

the southern parts of Greece, the Peloponnese, and Thessalonike and back to Thebes to have taken only three to four months indicates that there were well-established routes, with inns and other necessary infrastructure, and with either commercial agents with whom the merchants dealt or other good information about markets. I find it hard to believe that the Venetians developed these inland markets and suggest therefore that they represent preexisting networks of regional trade.

The entire Corinthian Gulf and places inland formed an industrial triangle with very active trade between Thebes, Athens, Corinth, and Euripos. Pottery was implicated in this trade, as it was with regional trade within the Peloponnese. As is well known, pottery is something of a guide for the movement of other goods as well, whereas it has also been pointed out that the movement of other consumer goods can point to the direction in which pottery moved.[101]

Glazed White Ware, found more or less everywhere, and Polychrome Ware (see fig. 5.3) are elite pottery from Constantinople. In the tenth to eleventh centuries, they are found in Thebes and the Boeotian countryside, but in small quantities. They are also found in Sparta, Lakonia, Milos, Xanthos, Crete, and elsewhere.[102] This is of no interest to us except as an indicator for other things, and that is the size of provincial demand. It has been pointed out that in Corinth the importation of Constantinopolitan White Ware and Polychrome Ware increased greatly through the eleventh century; indeed, the overall peak of demand for this luxury pottery is thought to be the third quarter of the eleventh century.[103] Regional trade it is not, but indication of constantly and significantly rising demand it is.

Corinth and Sparta produced good glazed pottery in this period; Argos is a smaller center of production in the Peloponnese in the twelfth century and subsequently. Both cities also imported glazed ceramics, both from Byzantine centers of production and, in the thirteenth century, from Italy.[104] For Boeotia, we have good information resulting from the intensive surveys conducted in the framework of the Boeotia Project. The data come from various sites, including Thebes itself, although the fact that Thebes has had continuous habitation and is still an important city means that the archaeological

---

101 Vroom, *After Antiquity,* 241.
102 P. Armstrong, "From Constantinople to Lakedaimon: Impressed White Wares," in *Mosaic: Festschrift for A. H. S. Megaw,* ed. J. Herrin, M. Mullett, and C. Otten-Froux (Athens, 2001), 57–58; G. D. R. Sanders, "Byzantine Polychrome Pottery," ibid., 89–103.
103 Hayes, *Excavations at Saraçhane,* 2:35–37, G. D. R. Sanders, "An Overview of the New Chronology for 9th- to 13th-Century Pottery at Corinth," in Bakirtzis, ed., *VIIe Congrès International sur la Céramique Médiévale en Méditerranée,* 37 (he thinks Polychrome Ware is an exclusively eleventh-century production); G. D. R. Sanders, "New Relative and Absolute Chronologies for the 9th- to 13th-Century Glazed Wares at Corinth: Methodology and Social Conclusions," in *Byzanz als Raum: Zu Methoden und Inhalten der historischen Geographie des östlichen Mittelmeerraumes im Mittelalter,* ed. K. Belke, F. Hild, J. Koder, and P. Soustal (Vienna, 2000), 164.
104 Bakourou, Katsara, and Kalamara, "Argos and Sparta," 233–36.

information is quite sporadic and incidental to rescue excavations. It shows the existence of plain glazed ware in Boeotia since the late ninth century.[105] In the same period, petty coins reappear, as they do elsewhere in the Byzantine Empire, pointing to a livelier trade.[106] Between the tenth and early thirteenth centuries, glazed ware of types common in central Greece increase in number, to the extent that Joanita Vroom speaks of a boom in the number of ceramics, especially in the different types of decorated ware, and especially in rural sites; in Thebes itself, the number of sherds recovered is doubtless limited by the obstacles to archaeological work that I have already mentioned. The ceramics in question include Slip-Painted Ware (eleventh–twelfth century), Green and Brown Painted Ware (late eleventh–twelfth century [Morgan] or mid-twelfth to early thirteenth century [Sanders]), Fine Sgraffito Ware (twelfth century; see fig. 5.4), Painted Fine Sgraffito Ware (mid-twelfth century; see fig. 5.5), and Incised Sgraffito Ware (second half of the twelfth century to early thirteenth century).[107] The place of production of a number of these wares appears to be somewhere in central Greece: Corinth and Thebes itself have been proposed as possibilities, although no kilns have been found in Thebes;[108] I have a theory that Athens (where kilns have been found) is a good candidate for large production of ceramics, but any proof or disproof of this must await the forthcoming study of Charalambos Bouras on medieval Athens.[109]

The proliferation of pottery types and the quantity of pottery in Thebes and its hinterland in the middle Byzantine period are sure signs of the increase in demand, not only here but more gener-

Figure 5.4. Fine Sgraffito bowl found in Corinth, Museum of Ancient Corinth, from Papanikola-Bakirtzi, ed., *Art of Sgraffito*, 171, no. 198)

Figure 5.5. Painted Fine Sgraffito bowl, Benaki Museum

ally in central Greece and the Peloponnese. They are also signs that production responded to demand, with differentiated wares. The increase of demand in the countryside, exemplified by the glazed ceramics from an undetermined Greek center in eastern Phokis,[110] is underwritten by the prosperity of the

105   Vroom, *After Antiquity*, 121.
106   For this, and for the high degree of monetization in the twelfth century, see Hendy, *Studies*, 310–12, 424–28, 435–37; Dunn, "Economic Change in Middle Byzantine Boeotia," 765–66; M. Galani-Krikou, "Thebes: 6th–15th c," in Επετηρίς Εταιρείας Βοιωτικών Μελετών IIIA, ed. V. Aravantinos (Athens, 2000), 901.
107   Vroom, *After Antiquity*, 150–53, 163–64, 285–86; also Aegean Ware and Zeuxippus Ware (late twelfth–thirteenth century), and Zeuxippus derivatives, probably of local production, middle–third quarter of the thirteenth century: P. Armstrong, "Byzantine Thebes: Excavations on the Kadmeia, 1980," *BSA* 88 (1993): 295–335, here 306–13, 328.
108   Wasters of unglazed pottery and of uncertain date have been found in the Kadmeia: Armstrong, "Byzantine Thebes," 335.
109   Ch. Bouras, Βυζαντινή Αθήνα, 10ος, 11ος, 12ος αι. (Athens, 2010), 112, 113, nn. 919–41; Laiou and Morrisson, *The Byzantine Economy*, 118; Vroom, in *After Antiquity*, 363, mentions workshops of the early Turkish period in Athens.

110   P. Armstrong, "Some Byzantine and Later Settlements in Eastern Phokis," *BSA* 84 (1989): 1–47. These are rural sites near Atalanti and Orchomenos. The (unsystematically collected) finds

peasantry, itself resulting from a rise in population, rise in urban population, and increase in production. And the fact that very similar types of glazed pottery—Fine Sgraffito Ware, Green and Brown Painted Ware, Slip-Painted Ware, Incised Sgraffito Ware—circulated widely in central Greece, the Peloponnese, Thessalonike, and elsewhere, combined with the existence of many centers of production (Corinth, Athens, Sparta, Argos, and in all probability Thebes), shows very active trade at the regional level. Let me explain. Corinth, of course, is the best known of the production centers of pottery (and also of glass, but glass is not very useful for our purposes because its study is still in its infancy), thanks to the exemplary excavations of the American School of Classical Studies at Athens. The first, and still the major, publication by Charles H. Morgan II established the typology and the chronology of the ceramics.[111] The chronology has since been disputed, primarily by G. D. R. Sanders, who has pushed it forward by a hundred years or so, carrying with it the chronology of much of the other ceramics production, which has frequently been established on the basis of comparison with the Corinthian one.[112] The numerous publications on the ceramics production of the Peloponnese can help us with the question of regional trade. I repeat first of all the fact that we find both concentrated production in Corinth and production in other centers. Second, and importantly, a particular type of pottery, commonly known as Measles Ware (see fig. 5.6), was produced only in the Peloponnese, namely, in Corinth and Sparta. Morgan has established that some of the Measles Ware of Sparta were imported from

Figure 5.6. Measles Ware bowl from Sparta excavations showing feline with mane moving right, Mystras Museum (from Papanikola-Bakirtzi, ed., *Art of Sgraffito*, 26, no. 2)

Corinth, while others were made locally, imitating Corinthian wares.[113] Measles Ware is found only in a few sites other than Sparta and Corinth, but also in Albania and Italy, including Padua and Venice.[114] We have already seen a commercial connection between Corinth and Sparta, involving olive oil. The presence of Corinthian pottery in Sparta and also its local imitation strengthen the idea that there was regional trade involving these two cities and the Lakonian hinterland. Further, the export of both Corinthian and Spartan ware to Italy[115] ties in very well with the relations of these two cities with Venice. Among the other finds in Sparta are champlevé pottery (a type of Aegean Ware or Incised Ware, late twelfth century) and locally made Sgraffito Ware.[116]

include Green and Brown Painted Ware, Slip-Painted Ware, Sgraffito, Aegean Ware, and Zeuxippus derivatives. The author thinks that Fine Sgraffito Ware from these sites is close both in decoration and in form to Corinth examples and those found on the Pelagonessos shipwreck, though in terms of fabric they show similarities to those of Pelagonessos, Constantinople, and Athens but not to those of Corinth (43). There is also some evidence of production of glazed pottery in a village (46).

111 C. H. Morgan, *The Byzantine Pottery*, Corinth 11 (Cambridge, Mass., 1942).
112 See, for example, Sanders, "An Overview of the New Chronology," 35–44; idem, "Corinth Workshop Production," in *Byzantine Glazed Ceramics: The Art of Sgraffito*, ed. D. Papanikola-Bakirtzi (Athens, 1999), 159–64; idem, "New Relative and Absolute Chronologies," 153–73; and idem, "Recent Developments in the Chronology of Byzantine Corinth," in *Corinth: The Centenary, 1896–1996*, ed. C. K. Williams and N. Bookidis, Corinth 20 ([Princeton, N.J.], 2003), 385–99.

113 Morgan, *The Byzantine Pottery*, 95ff.
114 Sanders, "Excavations at Sparta," 267; Vroom, *Byzantine to Modern Pottery in the Aegean*, 89.
115 S. Gelichi, "La ceramica bizantina in Italia e la ceramica italiana nel Mediterraneo orientale tra XII e XIII secolo: Stato degli studi e proposte di ricerca," in *La ceramica nel mondo bizantino tra XI e XV secolo e i suoi rapporti con l'Italia: Atti del Seminario, Certosa di Pontignano (Siena), 11–13 marzo 1991*, ed. idem (Florence, 1993), 9–46; V. François, "Sur la circulation des céramiques byzantines en Méditerranée orientale et occidentale," in *La céramique médiévale en Méditerranée: Actes du VIe Congrès de l'AIECM2, Aix-en-Provence, 13–18 Novembre 1995* (Aix-en-Provence, 1997), 231–33; Laiou and Morrisson, *The Byzantine Economy*, 118.
116 Sanders, "Excavations at Sparta," 260, 264.

Champlevé pottery may in fact have originated in Corinth and Sparta (or the eastern Mediterranean), but has wide dissemination, as does Sgraffito Ware.[117] Indeed, one of the best known of champlevé ceramics is the so-called Digenes and the Girl, from Corinth (see fig. 5.7). Sparta (along with Corinth) has also been proposed as the origin of Green and Brown Painted Ware, which is found mostly in the Peloponnese, but also elsewhere in the eastern Mediterranean, Cherson, the Balkans, and Venice.[118] The connection between regional trade, production, and interregional trade becomes obvious.

A phantom "leading undetermined site"[119] of large and organized production in the late twelfth century and early thirteenth century floats over ceramics and trade in ceramics. It produced excellent-quality Incised Sgraffito Ware (Aegean Ware), the pottery found in the Kastellorizo shipwreck[120] (see fig. 5.8) and the Skopelos shipwreck (in the Northern Sporades Islands).[121] In the middle of the twelfth century, a ship that foundered off Pelagonisi (also in the Northern Sporades) carried beautifully made Fine Sgraffito Ware that seems to ceramicists to be close to the production of Corinth (see fig. 5.9); 1,500 pieces have been recovered, but neither the place of production of the pottery nor the destination of the ship has been fully determined.[122] Demetra Bakirtzi has, however, pointed out that the pottery on these shipwrecks as well as that securely attributable to Constantinople and Corinth was manufactured

Figure 5.7. Champlevé plate, Digenes and the Girl, Museum of Ancient Corinth (from Papanikola-Bakirtzi, ed., *Art of Sgraffito*, 184, no. 211)

Figure 5.8. Incised Sgraffito bowl from Kastellorizo shipwreck showing stylized fishes with long tails, Benaki Museum (from Papanikola-Bakirtzi, ed., *Art of Sgraffito*, 148, no. 170)

117 See Vroom, *Byzantine to Modern Pottery in the Aegean*, 84–93.
118 Vroom, *After Antiquity*, 151–52, with reference to Vroom, *Byzantine to Modern Pottery*, 83.
119 Morgan, *The Byzantine Pottery*, 127.
120 G. Filotheou and M. Michailidou, "Βυζαντινά πινάκια από το φορτίον ναυαγισμένου πλοίου κοντά στο Καστελλόριζο," *Αρχ. Δελτ.* 41 (1986): 271–330.
121 P. Armstrong, "A Group of Byzantine Bowls from Skopelos," *Oxford Journal of Archaeology* 10.3 (1991): 335–45. The author thinks that a group of glazed bowls from the Ashmolean Museum similar to those of the Kastellorizo shipwreck come from a shipwreck off the island of Skopelos.
122 Ch. Kritzas, "Το βυζαντινόν ναυάγιον Πελαγοννήσου Αλοννήσου," *Αρχαιολογικά Ανάλεκτα εξ Αθηνών* 4.2 (1971): 176–82; E. Ioannidaki-Dostoglu, "Les vases de l'épave byzantine de Pélagonnèse-Halonnèse," in *Recherches sur la céramique byzantine*, ed. V. Déroche and J.-M. Spieser, BCH supp. 18 (Athens, 1989), 157–71. A. H. S. Megaw and R. E. Jones have found similarities in the clay of Red Sgraffito Ware found in Constantinople and the Pelagonisi ceramics: "Byzantine and Allied Pottery: A Contribution by Chemical Analysis to Problems of Origin and Distribution," *BSA* 78 (1983): 235–65, at 237.

in large and well-organized workshops, with division of labor.[123] Clearly, the ships carried objects of interregional and international trade, which must also have been highly organized, although we do not

123 Papanikola-Bakirtzi, "Εργαστήρια εφυαλωμένης κεραμικής," 63–64.

Figure 5.9. Fine Sgraffito Ware from the Pelagonisi shipwreck with stylized tree in central medallion; Nea Anchialos, archaeological site storage (from Papanikola-Bakirtzi, ed., *Art of Sgraffito*, 134, no. 147)

know any of the details.[124] What I have tried to do here is show the earlier step: regional trade, which we should think of as both riding on the coattails of interregional trade and feeding it.

The evidence from coins is helpful to our inquiry up to a point. Coin finds in Corinth increase abruptly beginning with the reign of Basil I (867–86), rising dramatically after 970 or so.[125] The problem is that the vast majority of the twelfth-century coins are tetartera or half-tetartera, the copper coin of small-scale transactions. Only a few gold and electrum coins, and a smaller number of silver *miliaresia*, have been found. During the reign of Alexios I (1081–1118) and again from 1143 to 1195 a "Balkan" mint, other than those of Thessalonike and Constantinople, is attested; Michael Hendy considers it very likely that it was established in either Corinth or Thebes, for the administrative reason that Thebes was the capital of the themes of Hellas and Peloponnesos, while Corinth had earlier been the capital of the theme of Peloponnesos.[126] This mint, wherever it was based, produced tetartera and half-tetartera. The coins are perfectly adequate for small, everyday transactions, but they do not reflect either regional trade or the interregional/international trade of both Thebes and Corinth; notably, the Venetian documents register their transactions in gold coins, which are not money of account since specific types of coin are mentioned. Actually, the dearth of precious metal coins in the archaeological record is a generalized phenomenon in central and southern Greece. I know of no persuasive explanation for this disjunction between the numismatic evidence and the rest of the archaeological, documentary, and historical evidence. In any case, the increase in copper coins is rightly interpreted as an indicator of the high level of monetization in the area.

Conclusion

It is evident that regional trade during the long period we have been examining took different forms. In Thrace and Macedonia, it was considerably affected by the needs of the two great centers of consumption. At first, the centers of exchange were along the coasts of the northern Aegean and the Black Sea. The extension of trade networks into the hinterland went hand in hand with the establishment of more or less normal military and political conditions, and with the upward demographic curve that began some time in the second half of the eighth century. It must have been hindered by the low monetization of the interior, which, however, I do not think was acute starting after the middle of the eleventh century. The multiplication of smaller cities, both along the coast and inland, is a witness to the well-functioning trade activities of the twelfth century. The agricultural production of that part of the Balkans was doubtless exchanged not only for money but also for some of the manufactured products of the cities: this is clear for the tenth century, and clear in the twelfth century, with the dissemination of Thessalonian pottery in the interior. Until the end of the period, the hinterland's part in regional exchange remained heavily dependent on agricultural products.

Central and southern Greece and the Peloponnese exhibit a different pattern. The general demographic trend and the effects of a virtuous cycle are not much different from in the rest of the empire. But when documentation of various kinds becomes more abundant, in the ninth century, and especially

---

124 François, "Circulation des céramiques byzantines," 235.
125 Morrisson, "Byzantine Money," graph 6.9; Sanders, "Corinth," 649; V. Penna, "Numismatic Circulation in Corinth from 976 to 1204," in *EHB* 2:655–58.
126 *DOC* 4:9, 131.

in the eleventh and twelfth centuries, an important difference from the northern areas is evident: there is much more trading activity *within* the region, involving both agricultural products and manufactured items. One explanation of this phenomenon may lie in the fact that the regional products were specialized: olive oil comes in different qualities, as does wine; silk cloth and pottery also were manufactured in different qualities, and these industries need raw materials, available in the region. We can therefore see quite clearly the differentiated production, which doubtless reflects differentiated demand, as well as the greater wealth of virtually all segments of the population that made it possible.

The increase in effective demand in these southern areas may well have been influenced by interregional trade, in the sense that imports from other areas had an impact on people's decision to invest in the kind of goods to which they had been exposed as consumers. Constantinopolitan silks were known to the upper class and the church. Pottery from the Arab world may have influenced some designs of Peloponnesian pottery. The White Ware and Polychrome Ware of Constantinople were relatively abundant in the eleventh and twelfth centuries, but had been imported in smaller quantities earlier. Significantly, the form of mid-tenth-century Corinthian chafing dishes imitate the form of Constantinopolitan ones.[127] I understand the impact of interregional trade to be the following: people are exposed to imported items used by the upper class; as the population becomes wealthier, its taste for some type of similar product becomes demand; local production responds, producing items that are similar to the imported ones, but cheaper and more affordable; because tastes differ, pottery, for example, is produced in many centers, and is also diffused within the region through trade. The pattern is reproduced on a regional scale, as when the production of pottery in Sparta imitates "imported" Corinthian wares. And it is reproduced for a time in the northern areas, when Serbian potters start making imitative ware, in the thirteenth century.

This brings me to my final point. Trade networks develop and function in complex and interrelated ways. While local, regional, and interregional trade have distinguishing characteristics, and broadly speaking respond to different kinds and levels of demand, nevertheless they meet at several points, and the existence of one exerts varying, multidimensional, and multidirectional influences on the other. In this context, I think that regional trade occupies a nodal place in a society's economic development. It is the point where both demand and production become differentiated and specialization sets in; where the productive forces of a large segment of the population become active; where demography, urbanization, and monetization meet and reinforce each other; it is the point at which products become commodities. This is how the market expands, and the economy with it. I do not want to be misunderstood. Long-distance trade, whether domestic or foreign, is very important to an economy. I hope I have demonstrated the effects of the pull of demand from outside the region on regional economies. And I have long argued that it was the virtual monopolization of Mediterranean trade by Italian merchants of foreign markets that played a seminal role in altering the structure of demand for Byzantine products, in the eventual demise of Byzantine industries, and in profound changes in regional patterns of trade. But international trade has always received scholarly attention; the story of *regional* trade in the Byzantine Empire, its structures and its conjunction with foreign trade, has yet to be told.

---

127 See, for example, Sanders, "New Relative and Absolute Chronologies," 165.

• SIX •

Regional Networks in Asia Minor during the Middle Byzantine Period, Seventh–Eleventh Centuries

An Approach

JOHANNES KODER

THE DECLINE OF MONETIZATION AND OF markets characterizes the beginning (and the end) of the middle Byzantine period.[1] Discussions of commercial networks of any size (and consequently also regional networks) imply that there is a demand for goods or services not adequately available everywhere. On a local and regional level, an incentive to produce a surplus and offer this surplus to the inhabitants of cities or citylike settlements is achieved only when population density is sufficient in a given central locality within reachable distance. Without these requirements, production often remains at the level of self-sufficiency.[2] The borders defining local, regional, and superregional trade are indeed fluid, and they depend on many factors (for instance, on expected earnings). In principle, however, they can roughly be defined by the average transit time to a particular marketplace. I consider the term "local" to be applicable to a distance of one or in some instances perhaps up to two days of travel, and the term "regional" to encompass generally a distance of more than one day but at most ten days of travel.[3]

The transit of goods can take place regularly or as the result of special occasional needs. The nature of these occasions can be either civilian, such as trade fairs, which were normally associated with ecclesiastical festivals, or military, such as wars or maneuvers. Concrete incentives for the *regular* trade of goods—especially with the intention of everyday selling at periodic markets,[4] which is the aspect that will be addressed here—include commodity or labor shortages that occur to a certain degree within areas of concentrated settlement. Such shortages are characteristic not just of everyday foodstuffs but also of goods in the nonfood sector. There was certainly a lasting demand for wood of every quality (probably

---

I am grateful to Klaus Belke and Friedrich Hild, both of Vienna; to the anonymous readers; and to Alice-Mary Talbot, of Dumbarton Oaks, for many valuable suggestions, additions, and improvements.

1 C. Morrisson, "Survivance de l'économie monétaire à Byzance (VIIᵉ–IXᵉ s.)," in *The Dark Centuries of Byzantium*, ed. E. Kountoura-Galaki (Athens, 2001), 377–97; A. E. Laiou and C. Morrisson, *The Byzantine Economy* (Cambridge, 2007), 38–42.

2 Among the factors influencing and advancing an economy's development are general conditions beyond conscious human control. These include subconscious influences, the relationship between individual effort and conditions created by the efforts of earlier generations for their own benefit, and factors determined by nature. See, in general, T. Shanin, ed., *Peasants and Peasant Societies* (Harmondsworth, 1971); for Byzantium, see A. Harvey, *Economic Expansion in the Byzantine Empire, 900–1200* (Cambridge, 1989), 1–13, 198–243 (chap. 6, "Interaction between Town and Country"). For the example of development in Austria, see also F. Mathis, *Unter den Reichsten der Welt—Verdienst oder Zufall? Österreichs Wirtschaft vom Mittelalter bis heute* (Innsbruck, 2007). But Gilbert Dagron, relying on Karl Polanyi and his school, has rightly confirmed that in premodern civilizations

"the economy is closely embedded in social relations and has not yet acquired its proper rationality or autonomy": G. Dagron, "The Urban Economy, Seventh–Twelfth Centuries," in *EHB* 2:396.

3 Expressed as physical distance, "local" may be measured as within 30 km (and only occasionally more), and "regional" as up to ca. 300 km; but I prefer to express these differentiations in time and not by length, as the experience of distance may vary depending on seasonal, topographical, and other factors. See also Laiou and Morrisson, *The Byzantine Economy*, 81–82.

4 For merchants, markets, and fairs, see A. Laiou, "Exchange and Trade, Seventh–Twelfth Centuries," in *EHB* 2:728–32.

including a significant portion used for firewood, depending on the region),[5] for charcoal,[6] and for hemp, flax, and leather as well as for pottery and small quantities of iron or iron ore.[7]

Although not a direct focus of this chapter, the question of how much importance we should attach to self-sufficiency and the issue of profit maximization needs to be addressed at least briefly. Angeliki Laiou has rightly stressed the strong presence of the central government in Byzantium in comparison with contemporary states in western and central Europe.[8] The early Byzantine system of taxation probably forced landowners to produce a surplus over the long term; Jacques Lefort has also discussed this equilibrium between self-sufficiency and an interest in profit maximization,[9] which was partially forced by "the state" (a term not used in its modern sense).

Charles Brand discussed examples that suggest the existence of elements of a free market in the eleventh and twelfth centuries.[10] The well-known position of Kekaumenos, who distanced himself from emperor and state and who indirectly advocated self-sufficiency, may have polarized the landowners in remote provinces and the upper classes in Constantinople.[11] But perhaps his position simply reflects the prevalent attitude among those of his contemporaries who lived in regions that had (at times) a low, irregular demand for production and trade as the result of a small number of urban and quasi-urban settlements and a weak state.

At this time, it is not possible to give a detailed picture of networks in Asia Minor during the middle Byzantine period.[12] I therefore propose to present some general thoughts on the topic and to relate these to several exemplary territories and places. I will concentrate geographically on the interior of western and central Asia Minor, though I will not neglect coastal regions entirely (see fig. 6.1). Although I accept Marlia Mundell Mango's view that there is no general "de facto divorce within the Eastern Empire of Late Antiquity from medieval Byzantium,"[13] I will begin chronologically with the period after the fall of the Sasanid Empire and the first phase of expansion of the Arabs, who were motivated by Islam to create new political realities.[14]

---

5   A. Dunn, "The Exploitation and Control of Woodland and Scrubland in the Byzantine World," *BMGS* 16 (1992): 235–98. Depending on their availability, the primary sources of domestic fuel were low-quality wood and dried dung (Greek *zarzakon*, Turkish *tezek*); see also Harvey, *Economic Expansion*, 128 and n. 43. If a town is *adendros* and *axylos*, then it is a *chora aoiketos*, as John Mauropous calls Euchaita in the mid-eleventh century; see *The Letters of Ioannes Mauropus, Metropolitan of Euchaita: Greek Text, Translation and Commentary*, ed. A. Karpozilos (Thessalonike, 1990), letter 64. But *chortoi, phrygana,* and *papyrou hylē* were also used as fuel in ovens and cooking stoves, as attested for the ninth/tenth centuries in the *Book of the Prefect, Eparchenbuch* 18.3.
6   Charcoal was needed especially in all areas of metal production and processing. Although the amounts required were low, there was also a regular demand for charcoal for incense burners in the ecclesiastic/liturgical sector.
7   However, we know practically nothing about mining in the middle Byzantine period. See K.-P. Matschke, "Mining," in *EHB* 1:115–20, esp. 118–19, and also the detailed overview by B. Pitarakis, "Mines anatoliennes exploitées par les Byzantins: Recherches récentes," *RN* 153 (1998): 141–85.
8   A. E. Laiou, "Economic and Noneconomic Exchange," in *EHB* 2:689–90. See also Harvey, *Economic Expansion*, 163–97 ("The Patterns of Demand").
9   J. Lefort, "The Rural Economy, Seventh–Twelfth Centuries," in *EHB* 1:300ff., adduced the well-known examples of Baris near Miletos and of Radolibos in Macedonia. Also helpful is Nicolas Oikonomides' observation that under the emperors of the Isaurian dynasty, the private *kommerkiarioi* disappeared and were replaced by civil servants of the *basilika kommerkia*. See N. Oikonomides, "The Role of the Byzantine State in the Economy," in *EHB* 3:987–88. Thus, we can assume that from the mid-eighth century onward, the settlements with an *apothēkē kommerkion* were commercial centers. But as the seals of *kommerkiarioi* include only regions, not toponyms, they are not helpful for the purposes of this chapter. A seal dated to 741/42 mentions *basilika kommerkia* in Kato Hexapolis, but this region is identified only until the sixth century with the regions of Melitene, 'Arqa, and Arabissos. See F. Hild and M. Restle, *Kappadokien*, *TIB* 2 (1981), 191.

10 C. M. Brand, "Did Byzantium Have a Free Market?" *ByzF* 26 (2000): 63–72.
11 Kekaumenos, *Strategicon*, ed. B. Wassiliewsky and V. Jernstedt (1896; repr., Amsterdam, 1965), esp. chap. 52, 218–19; for discussions of land use and distribution of agricultural products, see A. E. Laiou, "Economic Thought and Ideology," in *EHB* 3:1125–26, and A. Dunn, "Rural Producers and Markets: Aspects of the Archaeological and Historiographic Problem," in *Material Culture and Well-Being in Byzantium (400–1453)*, ed. M. Grünbart et al. (Vienna, 2007), 101–9. Though this chapter deals mainly with Macedonia, the general issues are relevant to other parts of the Byzantine Empire.
12 See, generally, A. Avramea, "Land and Sea Communications, Fourth–Fifteenth Centuries," in *EHB* 1:74–77; more detailed information is found in the chapters on "Verkehrsverbindungen/Straßen" in the introductions to volumes 2, 4, 5, 7, 8, and 9 of the *TIB*, and in F. Hild, *Das byzantinische Straßensystem in Kappadokien*, Veröffentlichungen der Kommission für die Tabula Imperii Byzantini 2 (Vienna, 1977).
13 M. Mundell Mango, "Action in the Trenches: A Call for a More Dynamic Archaeology of Early Byzantium," in *Proceedings of the 21st International Congress of Byzantine Studies*, ed. E. Jeffreys (London, 2006), 83–98, esp. 85.
14 These events resulted in the region's separation from the Roman Empire and the new political structuring of populations along the southern rim of the eastern Mediterranean and

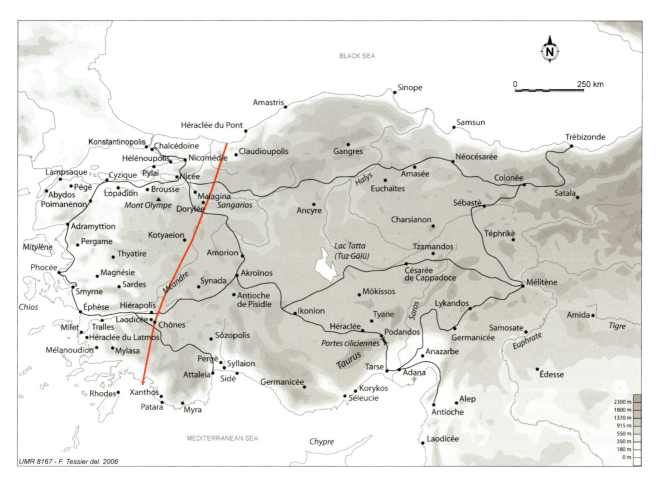

Figure 6.1. Asia Minor: places under discussion and eastern border of fertile areas, according to Byzantine land survey manuals (after map courtesy of the Institut d'études byzantines, CNRS, Paris)

The logical end for the period under discussion is the decade after the Battle of Mantzikert, when society, economy, trade, and politics were again lastingly altered because of the conquest of significant parts of Asia Minor by the Seljuks and because of the Crusades that followed.[15]

The Size and Chronology of Settlements

A chronologically differentiated knowledge of settlement density and population size is a necessary starting point for a discussion of the regional transport of goods. In all urban and military settlements, including the *aplēkta* (military camps),[16] the participation of inhabitants in agricultural production was to a certain degree the norm;[17] at the same time, a significant portion of the (civilian and military) population not engaged in production had to be

---

in the hinterlands. The consequent dissolution of the Mediterranean community had long-lasting economic and social repercussions. For these developments in the sixth century and earlier, see H. G. Saradi, *The Byzantine City in the Sixth Century: Literary Images and Historical Reality* (Athens, 2006).

15 This period is partially covered by Alan Harvey's discussion (in Harvey, *Economic Expansion*) of developments after the "dark centuries."

16 On the *aplēkta* at Malagina, Dorylaion, Kaborkin, Koloneia, Kaisareia, Dazimon, and Bathys Rhyax, see J. Haldon, ed., trans., and comm., *Constantine Porphyrogenitus: Three Treatises on Imperial Military Expeditions,* CFHB 28 (Vienna, 1990), 80–81, 155–57. The financial burden imposed on the affected population by the *aplēkta* and *mitata* must have been great. See Michael Attaleiates, *Diataxis,* ed. and trans. P. Gautier (Paris, 1981), 4.1425–51 and esp. 5.1652–52, 1675–76: Ἐξκουσσευθήσονται δὲ καὶ ἀπὸ μιτάτου ἀρχόντων ταγματικῶν ἢ θεματικῶν, ἔτι τε . . . φοσσάτων διατροφῆς καὶ ἀπλήκτων ἐπὶ πόλεμον ἀπιόντων ἢ ὑποστρεφόντων.

17 See Theophanes the Confessor, *Theophanis Chronographia,* ed. C. de Boor, 2 vols. (1883–85; repr., Hildesheim, 1980), 1:394: ἐξέρχονται ἐκ τοῦ κάστρου εἰς τὸν κάματον.

sustained not only from the surrounding countryside but also from more distant producers.[18]

Written sources rarely comment on the terminology of settlement types and on such aspects of settlements as their size, organization and centrality, buildings, population, social stratification, or economy. Seals of *kommerkiarioi* and coins offer only limited information. The archaeological and monumental record is a richer source of information, as long as the surviving remains (monuments, ruins, or other traces) have been documented sufficiently. Problems of chronology arise. For the period under discussion, the main problems of chronology do not concern dating when a monument was constructed or modified (though some degree of uncertainty often remains); of greater importance, particularly after the sixth century, is the question of continuity or discontinuity of settlement activity during the period of transition from the early Byzantine era to the Middle Ages.[19] Archaeological information on the development process of late antique cities in Asia Minor is often seen, almost stereotypically, as fitting into the following three phases:

1. Increased building activity (particularly of churches and other ecclesiastical buildings) in the late fourth and fifth centuries

2. The renewal of structures and fortifications in the "age of Justinian"[20]

3. Modifications and renovations that are "post-Justinianic" (i.e., dated from the last third of the sixth century onward), often with the statement—correct as far as it goes—that no evidence for major building activities can be found after the beginning of the seventh century, a qualifier that has opened the road to misunderstandings and misleading generalizations about the history of settlement development[21]

An example for this uncertainty of the end of settlement activity is Mokisos in Cappadocia (most probably Viranşehir near Helvadere). The city was founded under the emperor Anastasius and expanded by Justinian I[22] (see fig. 6.2). With more than twenty churches, it covered an area of approximately 45 hectares in a high valley (above 1,400 m) extending north to Hasan Dağ (3,270 m).[23] The area could support a maximum population of approximately 13,500.[24]

18 In this context, the population density of the area as a whole is of less importance and can lie far below 20 inhabitants per km². See J. Koder, Τὸ Βυζάντιο ὡς χώρος (Thessalonike, 2004), 202–8; for corresponding estimates for Austria (ca. 84,000 km²) that show 1.5 million inhabitants for the period around 1300, see R. Sandgruber, *Ökonomie und Politik* (Vienna, 1995), 16; a maximum of 900,000 inhabitants (ca. 12/km²) is estimated by F. Bruckmüller, *Sozialgeschichte Österreichs,* 2nd rev. ed. (Vienna, 2001), 65–66. For 1520/30, an estimate of 1.2–1.5 million inhabitants (ca. 14–18/km²) is proposed by Sandgruber, *Ökonomie und Politik,* 51.
19 W. Brandes, *Die Städte Kleinasiens im 7. und 8. Jahrhundert,* BBA 56 (Berlin, 1989), 80–131, defines four urban development patterns: reduction, relocation, decline, and relative continuity. See also the summary of T. Loungis, "Ἡ ἐξέλιξη τῆς βυζαντινῆς πόλης ἀπό τον τέταρτο στο δωδέκατο αἰώνα," *Byzantiaka* 16 (1996): 33–67, esp. 49–50. Many valuable observations on the fundamental change of urban structures can be found in J.-M. Spieser, "L'évolution de la ville byzantine de l'époque paléochrétienne à l'Iconoclasme," in *Hommes et richesses dans l'Empire byzantin,* vol. 1, *IVᵉ–VIIᵉ siècle* (Paris, 1989), 97–106. B. Ward-Perkins's answer to the question raised in his essay's title, "Can the Survival of an Ancient Town-Plan Be Used as Evidence of Dark-Age Urban Life?" in *Splendida civitas nostra (Festschrift A. Frova),* ed. G. Cavalieri Manasse (Rome, 1995), 223–29, is negative.

20 See H. Leppin, "(K)ein Zeitalter Justinians—Bemerkungen aus althistorischer Sicht zu Justinian in der jüngeren Forschung," *HZ* 287 (2007): 659–86, who emphasizes the formulaic quality of the term "age of Justinian." See also idem, "Justinian I. und die Wiederherstellung des Römischen Reiches: Das Trugbild der Erneuerung," in *Sie schufen Europa,* ed. M. Meier (Munich, 2007), 176–94. Justinianic building activity is "confirmed" by Procopius of Caesarea, though he often attributes to Justinian buildings erected by the emperor Anastasius.
21 Many examples for the evidence of monuments can be found in the topographical catalogues of the volumes of the *Tabula Imperii Byzantini* dedicated to Asia Minor (with bibliography); see the helpful considerations of J.-P. Sodini, "Marble and Stoneworking in Byzantium, Seventh–Fifteenth Centuries," in *EHB* 1:135–43, and C. Morrisson and J.-P. Sodini, "The Sixth-Century Economy," ibid., 184–87 (with bibliography). For analogous examples in the Peloponnese, see A. Avraméa, "Pénétration et installation des Slaves: Sources et archéologie," chap. 4 in *Le Péloponnèse du IVᵉ au VIIIᵉ siècle: Changements et persistances,* Byzantina Sorbonensia 15 (Paris, 1997), 67–104, esp. 80–86.
22 *Procopii Caesariensis Opera Omnia,* ed. J. Haury, rev. G. Wirth, 3 vols. (Leipzig, 1962–64), 2:5.4.15–18. See also A. Berger, "Viranşehir (Mokisos), eine byzantinische Stadt in Kappadokien," *IstMitt* 48 (1998): 349–429, and for historical data 415–19; Hild and Restle, *Kappadokien,* 238–39.
23 The area of built settlement extends through the valley, encompassing a length of ca. 900 m and a width between 400 m and 700 m. The acropolis, situated in the northwest corner, covered ca. 1.5 hectares. See Berger, "Viranşehir," 421.
24 For calculating probable upper limits for urban population numbers, see Appendix I. A total of 13,500 inhabitants required

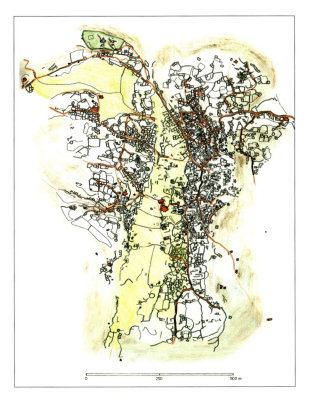

Figure 6.2. Mokisos, town plan (after A. Berger, "Mokisos," *Antike Welt* 31.1 [2000]: fig. 4)

The monumental evidence for settlement activity within the city is secure into the early seventh century, which means that the settlement outlasted the Justinianic plague and the change in climate that occurred around the same time. The city was located in a protected site, but not far from the road leading from Koloneia to Tyana, whose importance was rising in the Byzantine period; it was close to an important transit route for merchants and soldiers (see fig. 6.3).[25] There is no monumental or other evidence for the date of the end of settlement activity, since water scarcity at the site (a result of geological shifts) became a problem only in the late eighteenth or early nineteenth century.[26]

No evidence for when settlement activity actually ended or significantly declined over a longer period is available from Mokisos or from other ruined sites where enough building material (spolia) or undatable quarry stone or ashlar from the late antique period was available for use in new periods of building activity. Reliance on degradable materials, such as wood, clay and straw, or unfired brick, also often rendered later additions not identifiable. Such constructions could decay without leaving evidence of their period or cause of destruction;[27] in many cases, datable evidence was left behind only after destruction by fire. Moreover, well into the twentieth century, these strata (being of minor interest to classical archaeologists) were commonly removed without being adequately documented or sampled. Thus in dating the end of activity for settlements in Asia Minor, archaeology often relies on the general historical information that this area was subjected to Arab invasions in the seventh century; yet historians often base their chronologies on dates obtained from archaeological publications. For such cases, then, we are dealing with circular reasoning. Thus, the conventional "dating" of the end of activity at a given settlement often provides only a terminus post quem. For the early Byzantine period, the possibility should be acknowledged that many (of course not all)[28] urban and quasi-urban settlements showed significant levels of habitation long after the last preserved datable evidence for building activity.

---

about 13,905 tons of grain cultivated on 432–567 km² arable land; see Appendix II.

25 Berger, "Viranşehir," 419–20.
26 Ibid., 366–67; but see also Brandes, *Die Städte Kleinasiens*, 108, 118–19.

27 See also the introductory remarks of P. Niewöhner, "Frühbyzantinische Steinmetzarbeiten in Kütahya: Zu Topographie, Steinmetzwesen und Siedlungsgeschichte einer zentralanatolischen Region," *IstMitt* 56 (2006): 407–73, at 407: "Das liegt in erster Linie an der Lehmbauweise, die in jener zentralanatolischen Region üblich war und zur Folge hat, dass dort kaum ein frühbyzantinisches Monument mehr aufrecht steht."
28 An example of well-documented decline in the seventh century is Sagalassos. See M. Waelkens et al., "Sagalassos und sein Territorium: Eine interdisziplinäre Methodologie zur historischen Geographie einer kleinasiatischen Metropole," in *Byzanz als Raum: Zu Methoden und Inhalten der historischen Geographie des östlichen Mittelmeerraumes*, ed. K. Belke, F. Hild, J. Koder, and P. Soustal (Vienna, 2000), 261–88, with bibliographical references. Although Sagalassos was in the same general historical situation, its urban development took a different course. See *Sagalassos*, vol. 5, *Report on the Survey and Excavation Campaigns of 1996 and 1997*, ed. M. Waelkens and L. Lootseds (Louvain, 2000). This would seem to confirm Philipp Niewöhner's theory that the de-urbanization of settlements does not proceed in a linear fashion as the number of inhabitants drops; see P. Niewöhner, *Aizanoi, Dokimion und Anatolien: Stadt und Land, Siedlungs- und Steinmetzwesen vom späteren 4. bis ins 6. Jahrhundert n. Chr.*, Archäologische Forschungen 23, Aizanoi 1 (Wiesbaden, 2007).

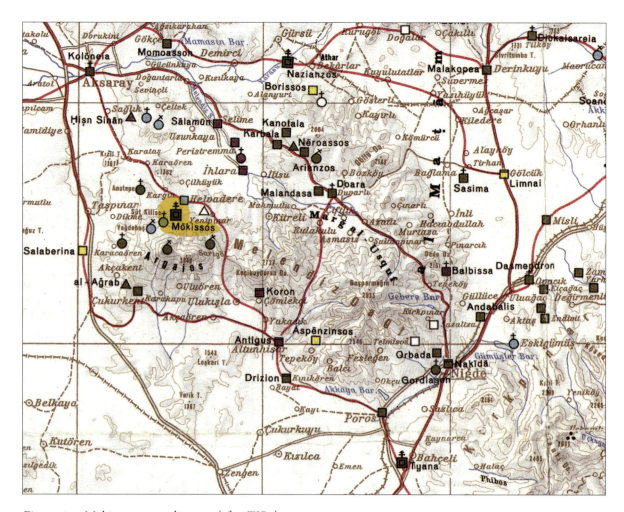

Figure 6.3. Mokisos, surrounding area (after *TIB* 2)

Roads (Road Networks)

Generally, the courses of routes and streets in the preindustrial period are largely determined by topographical conditions and the landscape contours. To be sure, in late antiquity and continuing into the early Byzantine period, in Asia Minor emphasis was mainly placed on the Aegean coastal cities, especially on Ephesos as the traditional connector to Rome, while Constantinople remained a destination of minor significance. But in principle, changes in local, regional, and transregional route systems, even in the first half of the twentieth century, came about only in response to changes in the natural landscape, such as erosion, earthquakes, or other earth movements, as well as changes in the network of waterways. As Ian Booth's study on trade routes in northwest Asia Minor has shown (see fig. 6.4), this general principle is not altered by the temporary abandonment of some transit routes due to political events associated with the desertion of settlements.[29] During the Roman period, the construction of roads[30] was normally intended to improve the speed, quality, and safety of travel by vehicle (especially for

---

29 I. Booth, "Ghazis, Roads and Trade in North-west Anatolia 1179–1291," *BMGS* 31.2 (2007): 127–45.

30 D. H. French, "The Roman Road-System of Asia Minor," in *Aufstieg und Niedergang der römischen Welt,* part 2, vol. 7.2, *Politische Geschichte (Provinzen und Randvölker: Griechischer Balkanraum; Kleinasien),* ed. H. Temporini and W. Haase (Berlin, 1980), 698–729; idem, "A Road Problem: Roman or Byzantine?" *IstMitt* 43 (1993): 445–54; and idem, *Roman Roads and Milestones of Asia Minor,* vol. 1, *The Pilgrim's Road,* BAR International Series 105 (Oxford, 1981); G. Radke, "Viae publicae Romanae," in *RE* supp. 13 (1973): 1415–1686.

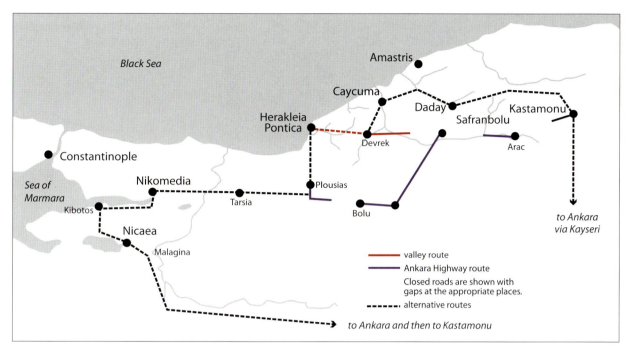

Figure 6.4. Trade routes in northwest Asia Minor (after Booth, "Ghazis, Roads and Trade," fig. 2)

military and postal transport).³¹ But as a rule, the Roman road system did not deviate from the pre-Roman system except when the requirements of construction demanded—for example, if the building of a bridge in place of a ford made it necessary to relocate a river crossing.³²

Nor did the decline of Roman roads usually result in road relocation.³³ Regional and transregional routes generally remained constant during the Byzantine period.³⁴ But the importance of certain roads may have changed, for at the beginning of the period under investigation the focus of importance for Asia Minor's superregional network of roads was definitively transferred from Ephesos to Constantinople.³⁵ The dating of the *end* of the use of roads is at least as uncertain as it is for settlements: the abandonment of a particular route can only rarely be determined on the basis of direct archaeological

---

31 See, e.g., Basilika 56.17.22 = *CI* 12.50.22: Καὶ ἔστιν ἀγγαρεία μὲν ἡ πάροδος ἡ διὰ τῆς δημοσίας ὁδοῦ τῆς καὶ δρόμον ἐχούσης, ὡς τυχὸν ἐντεῦθεν ἐπὶ Τύρον· παραγγαρεία δὲ ἡ διὰ τῆς πλαγίας ὁδοῦ. Καὶ ὅτι τὸ παλαιὸν ἦν ὁ πλατὺς δρόμος ὁ λεγόμενος διὰ ὀχημάτων· τοῦτον τοίνυν ἀναιρεῖ ἡ διάταξις λέγουσα εἶναι, ἡνίκα δεήσει παρερχομένων στρατιωτῶν ἤτοι πρεσβευτῶν ἤτοι ὅπλων. Τοῖς δὲ δεσπόταις τῶν ζώων παρεχέσθωσαν τὰ μισθώματα. One goal was the establishment of standard minimum widths for fortified and paved roads. The width postulated by Procopius, *Wars,* ed. G. Haury, rev. G. Wirth, vol. 1 (Leipzig, 1962), 5.14.7—εὖρος δέ ἐστι τῆς ὁδοῦ ταύτης ὅσον ἁμάξας δύο ἀντίας ἰέναι ἀλλήλαις (for which see also Radke, "Viae," 1438)—is probably valid for arterial roads (see, e.g., French, *Roman Roads and Milestones,* 1:21: ca. 3.0–3.5 m); it cannot be confirmed by measurements of road remains in Asia Minor, which were all less than 3 m wide. Imposition of a standard made possible wagon transport and the construction of bridges, supporting walls, protective buildings, and road stations. (In Asia Minor there were no road tunnels such as that found at Furlo, Italy.)

32 It seems also likely to me that where topographically possible, dirt trails continued to be used in parallel with paved or fortified roads. Such trails could be useful for (wagonless) caravans or for driving livestock.

33 The onset of a decline in the interior of Asia Minor is usually connected with the Persian wars of the sixth century.

34 The routes were not affected by the (partial) change from vehicles to animals after the sixth century—see R. W. Bulliet, *The Camel and the Wheel* (1975; repr., New York, 1990)—as becomes clear in the chapters on "Verkehrsverbindungen/Straßen" in the introduction to volumes 2, 4, 5, 7, 8, and 9 of the *Tabula Imperii Byzantini* and in Hild, *Das byzantinische Straßensystem in Kappadokien.*

35 Avramea, "Land and Sea Communications," 74–77. See also F. Hild, "Verkehrswege zu Lande: Die Wege der Kreuzfahrer," in *Handelsgüter und Verkehrswege: Aspekte der Warenversorgung im östlichen Mittelmeerraum (4. bis 15. Jahrhundert),* Veröffentlichungen zur Byzanzforschung 18 (Vienna, 2010), 105–25.

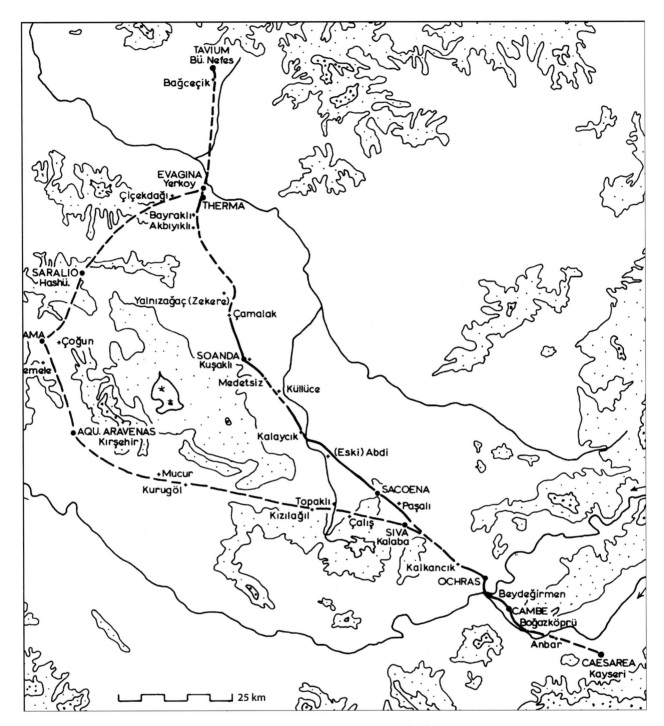

Figure 6.5. Roman road near Topaklı (after French, "Roman Roads," fig. 1)

Figure 6.6. Roman road near Topaklı at Kalaycik, traces of premodern paving directly under the dirt road (photo by author)

evidence.[36] For the most part, the (approximate) determination of such dates is based on indirect archaeological information (such as the destruction of bridges, road stations, etc.), combined with historical information. Indeed, the use of traditional routes often extended beyond the Ottoman period.[37] The example of the Roman road from Tavium to Kaisareia is characteristic of this continuity: this road crosses the modern road heading north from Topaklı about 10 kilometers outside of the town (see fig. 6.5);[38] it can be followed there, as well as at several neighboring villages,[39] for long stretches over the countryside, though it has been partially built over and destroyed by modern regional roads (see fig. 6.6). As in other places,[40] even in the twenty-first century the local inhabitants refer to the road as the "old Baghdat's road" ("eski Bağdat yolu"), as it was still in use into the twentieth century, though archaeological documentation ends with the late Roman period.

It also should be mentioned that the use of roads changed between the sixth and ninth centuries. Fewer vehicles were employed, and the transportation of goods and persons by beasts of burden (camels, horses, mules, and donkeys) increased, though the use of oxcarts is documented, especially for short distances by those in agriculture, the building trade, and the military.[41]

Agrarian Productivity in Asia Minor

Climate, water resources, and the conditions of the natural environment are the primary determinants of agrarian productivity;[42] transformations in these factors—which often cannot be verified today—affect farming and animal husbandry. In Asia Minor, the basic physico-geographical structures of the middle Byzantine period generally correspond to a high degree to those found today. The fertile rolling country, river valleys, and delta plains of the west and southwest contrast with the landscapes to the east; between the two areas, a transitional zone extends from the Black Sea coast east of the lower Sangarios River,[43] east of Dorylaion, Kotyaeion, and Laodikeia, to the Aegean coast east of the Knidos Peninsula (see fig. 6.1). To the east of this transitional zone, the landscape rises in central Anatolia continually to a level of approximately 1,000 meters, whereas in eastern Anatolia the level clearly surpasses 1,500 meters. The *Book of the Prefect* indirectly confirms

---

36 See the examples in French, "A Road Problem."

37 See generally F. Taeschner, *Das anatolische Wegenetz nach osmanischen Quellen*, 2 vols., Türkische Bibliothek 22–23 (Leipzig, 1924–26).

38 35° 05' 58" N, 34° 49' 25" E; on the road from Topaklı to Kozaklı, see D. French, "A Study of Roman Roads in Anatolia: Principles and Methods," *AnatSt* 24 (1974): 143–49, esp. 145, with fig. 1.

39 The villages of Gerce (39° 06' 45" N, 34° 48' 24" E), Kalaycik, and Abpi.

40 See, e.g., French, *Roman Roads and Milestones*, 1:16–18.

41 For the changes, see K. Belke, "Von der Pflasterstraße zum Maultierpfad? Zum kleinasiatischen Wegenetz in mittelbyzantinischer Zeit," in *Byzantine Mikra Asia (6os–12os ai.)*, ed. S. Lampakes (Athens, 1998), 267–84. Theodoros Stoudites, for example, rode from the Kathara monastery through Lopadion, Perperina, Parion, and Horkos to Lampsakos on his trip into exile, ἐποχηθέντες ἐφ' οἷς ἔτυχε ζῴοις, *Theodori Studitae Epistulae*, ed. G. Fatouros, 2 vols., CFHB 31 (Berlin, 1991–92), 1:3.59. See also K. Belke, "Verkehrsmittel und Reise- bzw. Transportgeschwindigkeit zu Lande im Byzantinischen Reich," in *Handelsgüter und Verkehrswege*, 45–58.

42 See generally W.-D. Hütteroth and V. Höhfeld, *Wissenschaftliche Länderkunden—Türkei* (Darmstadt, 2002); M. F. Hendy, *Studies in the Byzantine Monetary Economy, c. 300–1450* (Cambridge, 1985), 44–54; and especially the recent article by J. Haldon, "'Cappadocia will be given over to ruin and become a desert': Environmental Evidence for Historically-Attested Events in the 7th–10th Centuries," in *Byzantina Mediterranea: Festschrift für Johannes Koder zum 65. Geburtstag*, ed. K. Belke, E. Kislinger, A. Külzer, and M. Stassinopoulou (Vienna, 2007), 215–30, an excellent example of a successful combination of written sources and palynological evidence.

43 For the significance of the Sangarios region, see C. Foss, "Byzantine Malagina and the Lower Sangarius," *AnatSt* 40 (1990): 161–83 = idem, *Cities, Fortresses, and Villages of Byzantine Asia Minor*, Variorum Collected Studies 538 (Aldershot, 1996), art. VII; for the late period, see I. Booth, "The Sangarios Frontier: The History and Strategic Role of Paphlagonia in Byzantine Defence in the 13th Century," *ByzF* 28 (2004): 45–86.

the frontiers of these landscapes in Asia Minor when it prohibits the butchers of Constantinople from purchasing herds of sheep in Nikomedeia or even in Constantinople itself; instead, in order to ensure a lower price, they are told to buy them beyond the Sangarios River.[44] Thus, the region west of the Sangarios in western Asia Minor (like parts of the European hinterland of the imperial city, in Thrace)[45] was probably dominated by farming, whereas animal husbandry was restricted—it sufficed to supply the farmers but not Constantinople.

Land survey manuals from the middle Byzantine period take into account these qualitative differences in the terrain, since they distinguish between three regions: those of superior, of high, and of lesser quality, as differentiated by measuring ropes, whose lengths vary between 10 and 12 *orgyiai* (21.1–25.3 m).[46] Included in the first group were large parts of Optimaton and of the themes (provinces) of Opsikion, Boukellarion, Thrakesion, and Kibyrraioton in western Asia Minor; to the second, the European parts of the empire (Dysis, "the West"); and to the third, low-quality group, the remaining areas of Asia Minor (Anatole, "the East")[47] (see fig. 6.7). Similarly, other texts generally recognize three types of terrain quality (*poiotēs*). The first (superior) category comprises meadow land (*chortokopoumenon libadion*), irrigated land (*hypardos topos*), properties located near the sea (*parathalassion <chōraphion?>*), and land within settlements (*esothyron <chōraphion?>*). The second category comprises all cultivated (*speiromenē <gē?>*) land in arid (*anydros <gē?>*) regions outside of settlements (*exōthyros <gē?>*). The third comprises pasture land (*nomadiaia <gē?>*) and steppe (*chersaia <gē?>*).[48]

Because the agrarian productivity of individual landscapes varies, so does the supply radius of the hinterlands of urban settlements (local trade); thus the quality of the terrain is also a significant factor in the regional traffic of goods. Productivity, together with population, influences both the distance that goods are transported and their volume. Two—extreme—examples of terrain variation may be cited here:

ONE The land around the Lake of Nicaea in western Asia Minor is highly fertile.[49] Therefore it may have been easy to promote agricultural production in the Nicaean territories in the years after 1204, when the population there suddenly increased (with an influx of refugees from Constantinople). Stretching from Nicaea to the southeast, this rolling country remains nearly as fertile for another 50 kilometers, to about Bilecik, an area that encompasses the entire Sangarios region. It is only east and south of this river, toward Dorylaion/Eskişehir and Kotyaeion/Kütahya, that the fertility gradually declines: the amount of land around Dorylaion or Kotyaeion

---

44 Οἱ μακελάριοι μὴ συναντάτωσαν τοῖς ἀπὸ τῶν ἔξωθεν ἐρχομένοις προβαταρίοις τοῖς τὰς ἀγέλας ἐμπορευομένοις καὶ εἰσάγουσιν ἢ ἐν Νικομηδείᾳ ἢ ἐν τῇ πόλει, ἀλλ' ἐν τῷ πέρα τοῦ Σαγάρου, ὡς ἂν εὐωνοτέρα ἡ πρᾶσις τοῦ κρέατος ᾖ, δηλονότι τοῦ ὀφειλομένου κέρδους τοῖς σφάττουσιν ἐγγινομένου, ἀλλὰ μὴ τοῖς ἐμπόροις; *Eparchenbuch* 15.3.

45 For Thrace, see A. Külzer, *Ostthrakien (Europa)*, TIB 12 (2008), 212–20.

46 Based on E. Schilbach, *Byzantinische Metrologie*, HAW 12.4, Byzantinisches Handbuch 4 (Munich, 1970), 22–24. The longer the rope, the larger the surface (and the lesser the quality of the land) for the same amount of tax.

47 Ἐν παντὶ τόπῳ τῆς ἀνατολῆς τὸ σχοινίον ὀργυιῶν γίνεται ιβ', ἐν δὲ Θρᾳκησίῳ καὶ τῷ Κιβυρραιώτῳ ὀργυιῶν ι' διὰ τὸ τοῦ τόπου εὔχρηστον. Τὸ αὐτὸ γίνεται καὶ ἐν τῇ δύσει, ἤγουν μετὰ ι' ὀργυιῶν μετροῦσι, πλὴν ποιοῦσιν ὑπεξαίρεσιν κατὰ δέκα σχοινία σχοινίον α'; *Géométries du fisc byzantin*, ed. J. Lefort et al. (Paris, 1991), 62–63 (§51 = Paris. Suppl. gr. 676), similarly 184 (§286 = vv. 14–17 of a didactic poem, which is ascribed to Michael Psellos); for the circumstances see also Lefort, "The Rural Economy," 299–300. Further, almost all treatises state that the bases for measurement differed by *themata*.

48 Λέγεται δὲ πρώτη μὲν ποιότης τὸ χορτοκοπούμενον λιβάδιον, ὁ ὕπαρδος τόπος, τὸ παραθαλάσσιον καὶ τὸ ἐσώθυρον, δευτέρα δὲ ἡ σπειρωμένη μὲν ἄνυδρος δὲ καὶ ἐξώθυρος, τρίτη ἡ νομαδιαία καὶ χερσαία; Lefort et al., eds., *Géométries*, 62–63 (§53 = Paris Suppl. gr. 676, 12th/13th c.). The text should be dated earlier than an eleventh-century tax reform, perhaps to the reign of Leo VI (see ibid., 34–35). The three categories are described essentially in the same fashion, albeit more poetically, by another text, which calls the first category "honey and milk" (μελίγαλος γῆ) and describes rich black and red earth soils with a deep layer of humus, near riverbanks; the second is coarse, mixed with sand, or even very sandy, and requires irrigation; the third is stony scrubland, not arable but usable as grazing land. See *Géométries*, 40 (§4 = Vind. jur. gr. 10, 2nd half of the 13th c.); the text should be dated after the tax reform already mentioned. Representative prices are given for all three soil grades: for the first category, 1 *nomisma* for 1 *modios*; for the second category, the same price for 2 *modioi*; and for the third category, for 3 *modioi*.

49 In that region today, vegetables (various types of legumes, zucchini, onions, etc.) are systematically planted around olive trees in olive groves; on vegetables, arboriculture, and olives, see Harvey, *Economic Expansion*, 141–46. The contribution of B. Geyer, Y. Koç, J. Lefort, and C. Châtaigner, "Les villages et l'occupation du sol au début de l'époque moderne," in *La Bithynie au Moyen Âge*, ed. B. Geyer and J. Lefort, Réalités byzantines 9 (Paris, 2003), 411–30, esp. 424–25, offers concrete information about the productivity of this region, based on an early Ottoman register.

Figure 6.7. Dysis and Anatole: Provinces of Optimaton, Opsikion, Boukellarion, Thrakesion, and Kibyrraioton (after G. Ostrogorsky, *Geschichte des Byzantinischen Staates,* 3rd ed. [Munich, 1963], 248 and courtesy of the Institut d'études byzantines, CNRS, Paris)

dedicated to supplying those settlements must necessarily have been greater per inhabitant than for the region around the Lake of Nicaea.

TWO The opposite case is found in central Anatolia, for the steppelike terrain of Lake Tatta/Tuz gölü (see fig. 6.8). No agrarian production is possible within the approximately 16,000 square kilometer (11,000 sq. mi.) area around this great salt lake—independent of the frequent rise and fall in the lake's water level. Even pasture farming is possible on only a limited basis. Thus, the larger settlements in this area (such as the city of Koloneia/Aksaray directly to the east) could not have been provisioned with local goods.

Exemplary Regions and Places

By discussing several examples, I will now substantiate and elucidate the foregoing thoughts on settlements and the networks between them. (For the period under investigation, we can accept that the focus of importance for Asia Minor's superregional network of roads had long before definitively transferred from Ephesos to Constantinople.) The choice of these examples does not reflect the written sources[50] or an economic-geographic system; rather, those sites were selected whose spatial expansion

50 For example, the twenty *poleis* in the *Thrakesion thema* listed by Constantine VII Porphyrogennetos, *De thematibus,* ed. A. Pertusi (Vatican City, 1952), 68. See C. Foss, "Archaeology and the 'Twenty Cities' of Byzantine Asia," *AJA* 81 (1977): 469–86 = idem, in *History and Archaeology of Byzantine Asia Minor,* art. II.

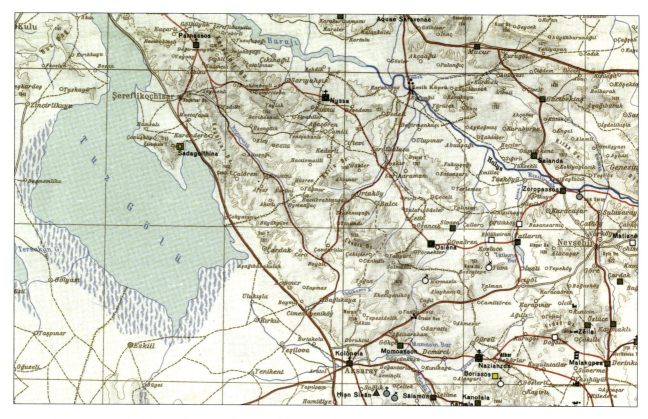

Figure 6.8. Lake Tatta and surrounding area (after *TIB* 2)

and types and dates of monumental structures suggest that an urban or quasi-urban settlement or fortification persisted after the mid-seventh century.[51] Another criterion is that, judging from the climatic and geographic conditions of the time, their water supply was sufficient.[52]

Landscapes in Western Asia Minor

The first group of examples comes from outermost northwestern Asia Minor, an area of high agricultural productivity (i.e., the most valuable type of area, according to Byzantine land survey manuals). After the middle of the ninth century, most of this area—perhaps even the area in its entirety—was fully settled, albeit less densely than it was in the late antique period (before the so-called Justinianic plague), as described by Hierokles.[53] The surpluses achieved here may be seen as only partly related to the need to fulfill demand from the relatively large "urban" populations in this region, some of whom were not involved in agrarian production. This production capacity made possible a high volume of exports. Until the decade after 1071, these exports went above all to Constantinople; but central and eastern Anatolia as well depended on this region, at least for the provisions of military troops located there (in the *aplēkta* of Malagina, Dorylaion, and Kaborkin).[54] The result was frequent regional over-

---

51 Settlements of a purely military character are not discussed here.

52 Attempts in the following discussion to calculate the maximum possible number of inhabitants are based on considerations explained in Appendix I.

53 Hierokles, *Synekdemos,* ed. E. Honigmann (Brussels, 1939); see J. Koder, "The Urban Character of the Early Byzantine Empire: Some Reflections on a Settlement Geographical Approach to the Topic," in *The 17th International Byzantine Congress: Major Papers, Dumbarton Oaks/Georgetown University, Washington, D.C., August 3–8, 1986* (New Rochelle, N.Y., 1986), 155–87.

54 For the thirteenth century, the productivity of the region is confirmed by the well-known exports of the "Empire of Nicaea" to areas ruled by the Seljuks. See A. E. Laiou, "The Agrarian Economy, Thirteenth–Fifteenth Centuries," in *EHB* 1:320–21 (with bibliography), and E. Mitsiou, "Versorgungsmodelle im

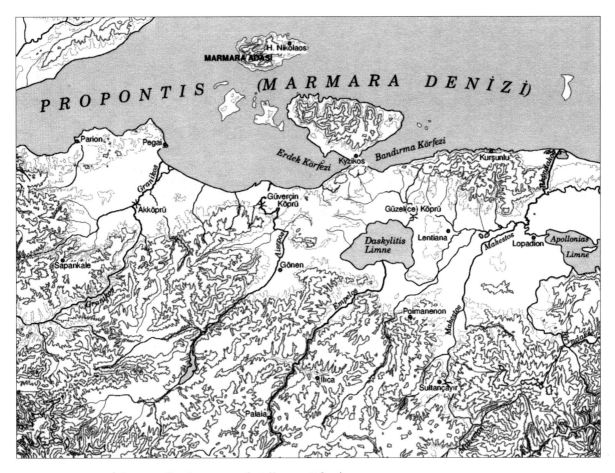

Figure 6.9. Mysia (after K. Belke, "Mysien und Hellespont," fig. 1)

land transport, both to the ports of the Propontis and to the east.

MYSIA Mysia, located between the Troas to the west and Bithynia and Phrygia to the east, is central to this region (see fig. 6.9). Mysia is subdivided by many streams that drain northward into the Propontis,[55] several of which form lakes in the flatlands after passing out of mountainous terrain. Its dense network of roads corresponded to the density of settlement. One main road that ran along the Propontis at a varying distance from the coast linked the port bays of Lampsakos[56] with those of Parion, Pegai,

Kyzikos, and other harbors as far as Apameia.[57] The coastal road was met or crossed by roads to the port towns from the south. Thanks to the many streams, regional road courses can often be identified through the remains of bridges. Thus, there are two bridges over the Granikos: though one, the Akköprü, has long been known,[58] the other was discovered only recently by William Aylward.[59] Both are found near the point where the coastal road is crossed by a road leading north to the port of Pegai, approximately 10 kilometers distant.

Unlike the sites of Parion and Kyzikos, the Pegai Peninsula is abandoned today; thus it provides conclusive evidence of the extent of the settlement (see

---

Nikäischen Kaiserreich," in *Handelsgüter und Verkehrswege*, 223–40.

55 The most important rivers are Granikos, Aisepos, Makestos, and Rhyndakos.

56 For the importance of Lampsakos, see Dagron, "Urban Economy," 2:394, with reference to G. G. Litavrin, "Provintsialnyi viz. gorod na rubeže XII–XIII vv.," *VizVrem* 37 (1976): 17–29.

57 See the lemmata in K. Belke, *Bithynien und Hellespont*, TIB 13 (forthcoming), s.v.

58 Akköprü is on the road from Biga to Karabiga, directly south of Güleç (between the village and the modern highway).

59 W. Aylward, personal communication, June 2007.

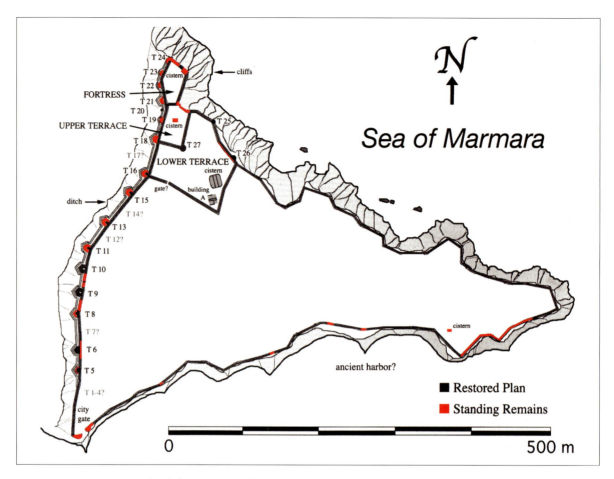

Figure 6.10. Pegai, town plan (after W. Aylward, "The Byzantine Fortifications at Pegae," pt. 1, 181)

fig. 6.10). The ruins of the city cover a triangular peninsula that is tapered to the north; to the west it ends at a city wall ca. 500 meters long. A small acropolis is found at the highest point in the northwest corner.[60] The habitable area comprised almost 11 hectares—of a sufficient size to accommodate a maximum of about 3,300 inhabitants, who might have been supplied without difficulty from the surrounding areas.[61] The (ancient) port was located on the southern side of the settlement (the coastline to the north is characterized by steep cliffs), but, after ca. 2 kilometers, the road extending south from Pegai leads to a bay in the western part of Erdek körfezi.[62] Today a fishing port, this bay bore in the medieval period the name of κόρφος τῆς Πήγας[63] and it likely served as the city's port.

Many other bridges mark the course of the coastal road: the Güvercin bridge[64] crossed the Aisepos about 5 kilometers south of the mouth of the stream; to the east, the Güzelce bridge,[65] near Dogruca bridge,[66] crossed (north–south) the

---

60 40° 24′ 53″ N, 27° 19′ 31″ E; it has a large cistern; to the south-southwest are an upper and a lower terrace, each protected by a forewall. See W. Aylward, "The Byzantine Fortifications at Pegae (Priapus) on the Sea of Marmara," pts. 1 and 2, *Studia Troica* 16 (2006): 179–203; 17 (2007): 90–105; also K. Belke, "Mysien und Hellespont," *RBK* 6 (2002): 863–65, with further bibliography.

61 The maximum demand for grain was 2,344–3,399 tons per annum, produced on an area of cultivation measuring 105.6–138.6 km² (see Appendix II).

62 See A. Horn and W. Hoop, *Durch die Nordägäis nach Istanbul: Izmir—Marmarameer—Istanbul: Nautischer Reiseführer* (Hamburg, 1989), 60–61.

63 See A. Delatte, *Les Portulans grecs,* 2 vols. (Paris, 1947–58), 229.21 (Port. II), 242.2–7, 337.3 (Port. II and VI, v.l. Σπίγα) and other portolans.

64 See Belke, *Bithynien und Hellespont,* s.v.

65 Ibid., s.v. Tolype.

66 40° 15′ 41.9″ N, 28° 03′ 09.4″ E, about 3 km south-southeast of Dogruca (formerly Debleke), several hundred meters south of the modern highway from Bandirma to Canakkale.

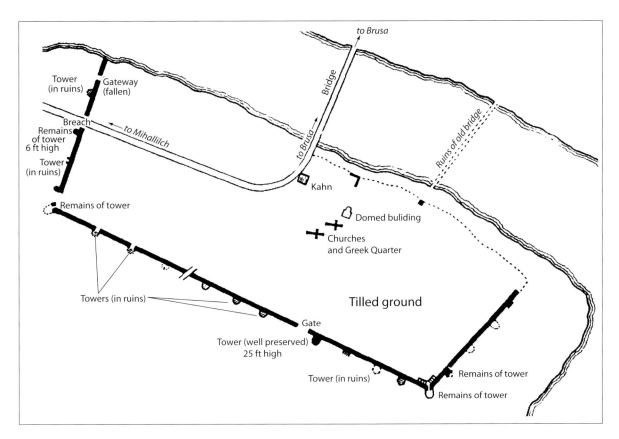

Figure 6.11. Lopadion, town plan (after K. Belke, "Mysien und Hellespont," fig. 6)

Empelos, a tributary of the Gönen Cayı. The piers of another bridge over the Rhyndakos[67] near Lake Apollonias (to the north) are still extant. This bridge connected Lopadion[68]/Uluabat (see fig. 6.11), a city of ca. 7 hectares,[69] with the main road running parallel to the coast toward the port of Daskyleion, a settlement protected by a fortress.[70]

THE HINTERLAND OF THE PROPONTIS (POI-MANENON) In the hilly, sometimes almost mountainous country south of the coastal areas of the Propontis, urban settlements were rarer. The functions of central markets probably were often transferred to fortresses that, because of their size, may have served as refuges for the local population in times of war.[71] A characteristic example is Poimanenon,[72] above the village of Eski Manyas. It is surrounded by fertile hills and lies above a strong spring, the source of a small stream flowing north.

---

67 The south-southwestern end of the bridge: 40° 12′ 13.7″ N, 28° 26′ 28.6″ E.
68 See Belke, *Bithynien und Hellespont*, s.v.
69 Walls preserved throughout the terrain seem to indicate that Lopadion had an urban character. The site, found in a fertile plain near Lake Apollonias/Uluabat and the outlet of the Rhyndakos, was only fortified as a garrison (not as a civilian settlement) by John II Komnenos. The northeast flank of the site, which is nearly square in plan (approx. 475 × 150 m), abuts the Rhyndakos. Within its walls Lopadion covers an area a little larger than 7 hectares, but the settlement seems to have extended outside the fortifications to the southwest, and along the river to the west. See C. Foss, "The Defenses of Asia Minor against the Turks," *GOTR* 27 (1982): 159–61 = idem, in *Cities, Fortresses, and Villages of Byzantine Asia Minor*, art. V; Belke, "Mysien und Hellespont," 860–62. For a possible maximum of 2,100 inhabitants, a demand for grain of 2,163 tons per annum (area under cultivation, 67.2–88.2 km²) can be assumed (see Appendix II).

70 J. Lefort, "Les grandes routes médiévales," in Geyer and Lefort, eds., *La Bithynie au Moyen Âge*, 467–68; Belke, *Bithynien und Hellespont*, s.v.
71 For example, the anonymous text *De obsidione toleranda* (10th c.) stipulates the "next" *kastron* as a place of refuge for farmers, their supplies, and their animals; see *Anonymus De obsidione toleranda*, ed. H. van den Berg (Leiden, 1947), §71s., pp. 57–58.
72 See Belke, *Bithynien und Hellespont*, s.v.

The location of the site and the building remains suggest it was a fort with market functions rather than an urban settlement;[73] the broad outer wall indicates its use as a refuge by the inhabitants of the surrounding villages (including Eski Manyas). In any case, because of its central location, Poimanenon very likely served as a market for these villages, especially since it lay near a main road.[74] This road led from Kyzikos in the north over the Güzelce bridge, ca. 20 kilometers away, through Melitoupolis[75] and Eski Manyas to Poimanenon.[76] Several meters of paved road directly south of the fortified hill are preserved (see fig. 6.12).[77] After Poimanenon, the road continued southwest to the Makestos River near the Sultançayır bridge[78] and on to Smyrna.

Another example is Palaia. About 3 kilometers south of Kadıköy and 10 kilometers from modern Balya, a prominence is found near the confluence of two streams. The area is fertile, with abundant water, and the prominence is covered with small trees and shrubs. The remains of a fortification wall can be seen on the north and east sides of the prominence,

Figure 6.12. Road remnants near Poimanenon (photo by author)

indicating by its dimensions a quasi-urban settlement whose character was mainly as a fortification.[79]

The examples above correspond to those areas of western Asia Minor with above-average population densities and high-quality agrarian production. The trade in foods and other daily goods played a major role not only in regional urban centers and their (immediate) vicinities but also in superregional trade relations with Constantinople and with areas of Asia Minor to the east.

BITHYNIA, ASIA, AND CARIA Significant trade in everyday necessities also occurred in large portions of the provinces of Bithynia,[80] Asia, and Caria. But many urban settlements along the west coast of Asia Minor between the Gulf of Edremit and the Gulf of Iasos have left almost no trace, and the few remains that have survived are not sufficient to give an idea of the size of communities such as Myrina, Phokaia, or Smyrna. Useful examples of urban settlements from the Byzantine period are Pergamon and Miletos.[81]

---

73 However, Anna Komnene, *Alexias,* book 14.5.5 (*Annae Comnenae Alexias,* ed. D. R. Reinsch and A. Kambylis, 2 vols., CFHB 40 [Berlin, 2001], 1:445), mentions Poimanenon as a πολίχνιον ἐρυμνότατον (see also Stephanos Byzantinos 530: πόλις ἤτοι φρούριον), the same phrase used for Koloneia (*Alexias,* 12.7.3; p. 377) and for Kedros (*Alexias,* 15.4.1; p. 470), which were indeed market towns. Similarily Kourikon is called a πόλις ἐρυμνοτάτη (*Alexias,* 11.10.9; p. 353).

74 Poimanenon's hinterland was densely populated; directly east of the fortress on another and somewhat lower hill, 40° 00' 05" N, 28° 03' 20" E, the remains of a second fortress can be seen. Judging from the masonry, the preserved portions can be dated as contemporaneous with the Laskarid phase of Poimanenon, though it can be assumed that a previous complex existed here; directly north of these fortress remains an early Muslim building (a tekke?) can be identified. Spolia were used in the construction of both buildings, and numerous ceramic and brick sherds are found dispersed over both hills. See F.-M. Kaufmann and J. Stauber, "Poimanenon bei Eski Manyas: Zeugnisse und Lokalisierung einer kaum bekannten Stadt," *Studien zum antiken Kleinasien* 2 / *Asia Minor Studies* 8 (1992): 43–85.

75 See Belke, *Bithynien und Hellespont,* s.v. Miletupolis.

76 It probably led east around the fortress hill and at its highest point met the entrance to the fortress.

77 40° 00' 093" N, 28° 03' 07.8" E. At the south entrance to the village (i.e., the upper entrance, located at the fortress), remains of paving are also preserved (40° 00' 31.3" N, 28° 02' 57.4" E).

78 The bridge runs west–east; in 2007 it lay in an area of large-scale street construction and was thus not directly accessible (west bridgehead at 39° 41' 59" N, 28° 09' 51" E); see Belke, *Bithynien und Hellespont,* s.v.

79 See Belke, "Mysien und Hellespont," 859–60. Today, Balya is found on the same stream as and ca. 7 km above Palaia; there, a tree-covered rise might also be identified as a fortress hill, although no building remains can be discerned.

80 Geyer and Lefort, eds., *La Bithynie au Moyen Âge,* esp. Lefort, "Les grandes routes médiévales," 461–72.

81 For Ephesos no recent studies of the "Byzantine" city walls are available; in general, see C. Foss, *Ephesus after Antiquity: A Late Antique, Byzantine and Turkish City* (Cambridge, 1979), and idem, "Archaeology and the 'Twenty Cities'," 472–75. But Sabine Ladstätter has informed me (in a letter of 1 February 2008) that it seems certain that the wall was not erected before the reign of Justin II, since the workshops above Hanghaus II can be dated to

Pergamon was located near the road that, coming from the east, connected the city with the port bay of Myrina and with the road along the Aegean coast. Its *chora* contained portions of the fertile Kaikos Valley.[82] With direct access to at least 300 square kilometers of farmland, it was largely self-sustaining. In 716, Pergamon was briefly captured by Maslama;[83] this event was interpreted as the end of the life of the city, even though the Patriarch Nikephoros (d. 815) explicitly calls it a *polis*.[84] Klaus Rheidt has identified evidence of building construction ("eine christliche Kultstätte"), beginning in the area of the *kastron,* that he has dated to the tenth century and has connected with the restoration of the town (see fig. 6.13).[85] This would indicate a break in the eighth and ninth centuries, but the discussion should be reopened, since Philipp Niewöhner has recently made the case for continuity of settlement over the "dark" centuries, including Pergamon.[86] The first restoration phase included the theater terrace. According to Rheidt, it was only as the result of a population boom that occurred after 1071 and certainly by the twelfth century that the residential city expanded to ca. 19 hectares—a size that, he argues, might have accommodated up to 4,200 inhabitants.[87] The houses were relatively small, each built for an individual family.

The second example, Miletos/Palatia in Caria (see fig. 6.14), was located a two days' journey south of Ephesos on the Aegean coastal road in a partially fertile *chora* that encompassed an area of approximately 120 square kilometers between Lake Bafa (Bathys) and the rather marshy estuary plain of the Maeander River. Quite possibly this area saw a steep decline in population after the Arab incursion of 650.[88] Thus, during the Byzantine period the inhabited area was considerably smaller than the area inside the so-called Wall of the Goths (built on top of a wall of the Hellenistic period). But the inhabited area beyond the theater, the fort, and the Byzantine wall may still have covered up to 10 hectares (though it must be noted that housing density may have varied greatly). The theater, which was accessible from the fortress above, was densely covered by small housing units constructed of quarrystone, brick rubble, and lime mortar; the inhabited area continued directly into the fort above. The remaining areas of the city probably showed less dense building distribution.[89] It can be postulated that in the periphery beyond the city walls were agricultural settlements that were

---

his reign. The combination of residential buildings, theater, and adjoining fortress is noteworthy in that analogous arrangements are found in Miletos and Pergamon (as noted below). Also, a settlement in former Olympieion can be identified based on geophysical measurements. Workshops and graves near the church of St. Mary date from the eleventh century.

82 Located a short day's journey from the (also Byzantine) spa town of Allianoi. See H. Müller, "Allianoi: Zur Identifizierung eines antiken Kurbades im Hinterland von Pergamon," *IstMitt* 54 (2004): 215–25.

83 *Theophanis Chronographia* 390, in the year 6208.

84 Patriarch (806–15) Nikephoros names a total of twelve cities in Asia Minor. See *Nicephori archiepiscopi Constantinopolitani opuscula historica,* ed. C. de Boor (Leipzig, 1880; repr., New York, 1975), 52–53; I. Čičurov, *Mesto "Chronografii" Feofana v rannevizantijskoj istoriografičeskoj traditsij (IV–načalo IX v.)* (Moscow, 1981), 145. Pergamon as *polis* of the theme of Thrakesion: Constantine VII Porphyrogennetos, *De thematibus,* Asia 17.17; see also Foss, "Archaeology and the 'Twenty Cities'," 479–81.

85 K. Rheidt, "Byzantinische Wohnhäuser des 11. bis 14. Jahrhunderts in Pergamon," *DOP* 44 (1990): 195–204, at 203; idem, *Die Stadtgrabung,* part 2, *Die byzantinische Wohnstadt,* Altertümer von Pergamon 15.2 (Berlin, 1991), 197–98; see also idem, "The Urban Economy of Pergamon," in *EHB* 2:623–29.

86 P. Niewöhner, "Archäologie und die 'dunklen Jahrhunderte' im byzantinischen Anatolien," in *Post-Roman Towns, Trade and Settlement in Europe and Byzantium,* ed. J. Henning, vol. 2, *Byzantium, Pliska, and the Balkans,* Millennium-Studien zu Kultur und Geschichte des ersten Jahrtausends n. Chr. 5.2 (Berlin, 2007), 119–57, esp. 129–30.

87 Rheidt, "Byzantinische Wohnhäuser," 203. According to my estimate, a *maximum* of ca. 5,700 inhabitants can be calculated for this area, and thus also a demand of approx. 5,871 tons of grain (that can be produced on an area of 182–240 km²); see Appendix II.

88 A similar population drop was experienced by the region of Limyra after the battle near its harbor Phoinix (Finike) in the year 655; see S. Cosentino, "Constans II and the Byzantine Navy," *BZ* 100 (2007): 577–603.

89 See W. Müller-Wiener, "Milet," *RBK* 6 (1999): 362–77; P. Niewöhner, "Byzantinische Steinmetzarbeiten aus dem Umland von Milet," *Anadolu ve Çevresinde Ortaçağ* 1 (2007): 1–28; idem, "Sind die Mauern die Stadt? Vorbericht über die siedlungsgeschichtlichen Ergebnisse neuer Grabungen im spätantiken und byzantinischen Milet," with a geoarchaeological contribution by H. Brückner and M. Müllenhoff, *AA* (2008): 181–201. For Miletos's residential buildings, the respective coastlines should be taken into consideration; it must be noted not only that the mouth of the Maeander migrates but also that the Anatolian Plate sinks in the area of Miletos and the sea level generally rises. I kindly thank Volkmar von Graeve, for valuable information given in Miletos on 24 May 2007, and Philipp Niewöhner, for discussing problems of the Byzantine wall and giving me information on the size of the Byzantine city on 28 and 31 August 2008.

Figure 6.13. Pergamon, town plan (after K. Rheidt, "The Urban Economy of Pergamon," in *EHB* 2, fig. 2)

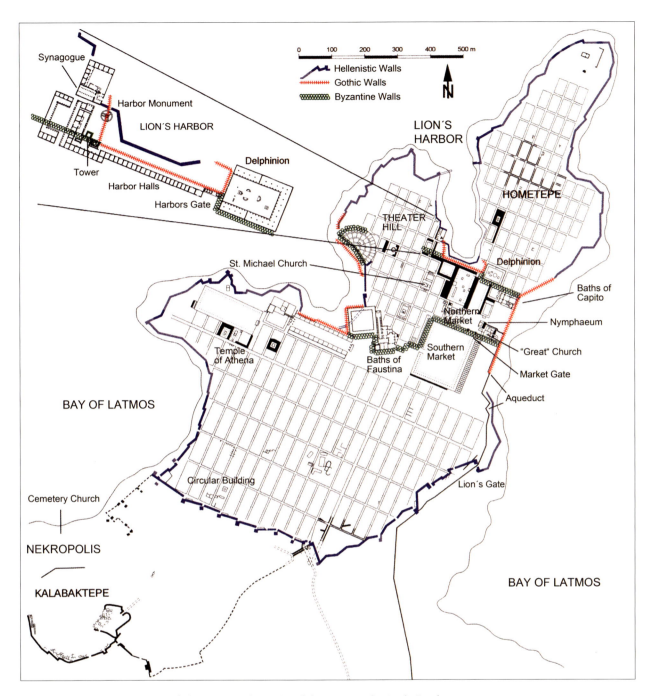

Figure 6.14. Miletos, town plan (after P. Niewöhner, "Sind die Mauern die Stadt?" 183)

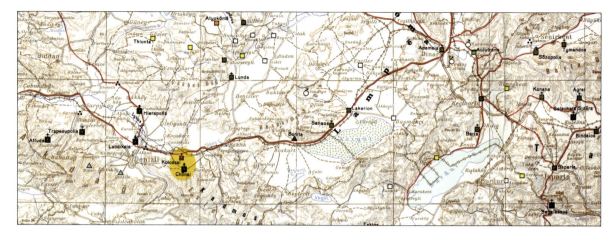

Figure 6.15. Chonai, surrounding area (after *TIB* 7)

connected economically to Miletos. Thus, the size of population may have reached that of Pergamon.

Central and Eastern Asia Minor

Compared to the west, settlement density was considerably lower in central Asia Minor, including the southern coast, for here the fertile landscapes (mostly running along the rivers) are often contained and separated from one another by mountain ranges,[90] many of which are covered with partially degraded forests (macchia) or by steppe-like high plateaus with little or even no agrarian production. Between some agrarian settlements and castles (which functioned as "central places," as described by Central Place Theory), many plateaus in central Asia Minor probably served only as grazing land even before 1071.[91] In addition to the region of Mokisos discussed above, three more examples will be mentioned here.

CHONAI AND THE LYKOS VALLEY The first example is Chonai, the famous pilgrimage site and successor settlement to Kolossai, located ca. 4 kilometers to the south of ancient Kolossai. At Kolossai[92] and just to the south in the valley of the Lykos River, an area characterized by hills and small streams, settlement evidence extends until the ninth century; at the edge of the mountain range, corresponding evidence exists for the medieval mountain fortification near Chonai, dating it from the eighth century onward. In light of the small expansion of the area of the fort, it is possible to place Chonai, Niketas Choniates' "prosperous and big city,"[93] directly below the fort, at present-day Honaz. The size of the Byzantine

---

90 This is true also for the inland parts of Caria—a useful example might be the ancient and late antique fortress town of Alinda, which is situated along two mountain ridges above the modern village of Karpuzlu, ca. 50 km to the south of Aydın. It controls a fertile plain that is surrounded by mountains at all sides and watered by a southern tributary of the Maeander River, accessible from roads leading from Tralleis/Aydın to Mylasa/Milas and to the Knidos Peninsula. The settlement was—probably after the sixth century—reduced to the upper town, where the remains of a densely built housing area, and perhaps also a church, are to be found inside the ancient fortification wall. This restoration phase still cannot be dated, though the probability of a dating to the seventh or eighth century is high (P. Ruggendorfer, personal communication on 3 June 2009). As Constantine Porphyrogennetos, *De thematibus,* Asia 3, mentions it as a (fortified?) town in Thrakesion, its existence is probably documented at least until the tenth century. See also P. Ruggendorfer, "Survey-Projekt Alinda: Die Kampagne 2007," *ArSonTop* 26 (2009): 37–44, esp. 40–41; B. Öhlinger and P. Ruggendorfer, "Development and Transformation of a North-Karian Settlement," in *Mylasa, Labraunda, Milas Çomakdağ,* ed. F. Kuzucu and M. Ural (Istanbul, 2010), 139–51, esp. 146–48; information on the Alinda Survey: http://homepage.univie.ac.at/elisabeth.trinkl/forum/forum0908/48alinda.htm, accessed July 2010.

91 The military treatise *De velitatione* reflects the settlement reality of central and eastern Asia Minor in the late ninth and tenth century: see G. Dagron and H. Mihaescu, *Le traité sur la guérilla (De velitatione) de l'empereur Nicéphore Phocas (963–969)* (Paris, 1986), esp. the commentary "Places fortes et villages," 225–31.

92 K. Belke and N. Mersich, *Phrygien und Pisidien,* TIB 7 (1990), 309–11. See also Foss, "Archaeology and the 'Twenty Cities,'" 484–85.

93 πόλις εὐδαίμων καὶ μεγάλη; *Nicetae Choniatae Historiae,* ed. J. L. van Dieten, CFHB 11.1 (Berlin, 1975), 178.15; see Belke and Mersich, *Phrygien und Pisidien,* 222–25.

Figure 6.16. Cistern near Camurlu (photo by author)

Figure 6.18. Road near Kilistra (photo by author)

settlements such as Laodikeia[94] (18 km to the northwest) and Hierapolis[95] (11 km to the north)—both of which were located, like Chonai, close to the Lykos Valley—or to Trapezoupolis (35 km to the west) and Attuda (another 10 km to the west)[96] (see fig. 6.15).

All of these sites were located close to the great west–east route connecting Ephesos and Smyrna via Laodikeia with Apameia and further with Pisidian Antioch,[97] from which it continued to Ikonion. This last part of the route probably corresponded to the Roman Via Sebaste.[98] Remains of the road can be seen 15–30 kilometers southwest of Konya, above Lystra, in Gökyurt, partly dug from the living rock, partly as roadbed ashlar. Further remains are found between Camurlu and Erinkaya and at several points south of Kizilören, site of a Han (caravanserai), near Camurlu, where an accessible cistern is

Figure 6.17. Cistern near Camurlu (photo by author)

settlement cannot be determined, because the area today is inhabited and built over. The Lykos Valley is fertile; the area of arable farm land directly accessible to Chonai comprised about 150 square kilometers, with a potential of producing 3,700–4,800 tons of grain. Thus, Chonai probably was self-sufficient and could export foodstuffs to neighboring urban

---

94 Laodikeia's medieval site cannot be determined with precision. It was either near Denizli or 13 km to the west, near Hisar. *Nicetae Choniatae Historiae*, 638.28: αἱ Χῶναι καὶ ἡ ἀγχιτέρμων ταύτῃ Φρυγικὴ Λαοδίκεια." See Belke and Mersich, *Phrygien und Pisidien*, 323–26, 273–74.
95 Belke and Mersich, *Phrygien und Pisidien*, 268–72.
96 Ibid., 407–8, 195–96.
97 Ibid., 188–89, 185–87. Antioch was a traffic junction: Kotyaeion (ibid., 312–16) could be reached (to the north) via Akroinon (177–78), and the south coast could be reached primarily via the Via Sebaste—on which see F. Hild, "Die Via Sebaste in Kleinasien," in *Hypermachos: Festschrift für Werner Seibt zum 65. Geburtstag*, ed. C. Stavrakos, A.-K. Wassiliou, and M. K. Krikorian (Wiesbaden, 2008), 59–71; and French, "A Road Problem," 447–48. Other routes went via Akroterion (Belke and Mersich, *Phrygien und Pisidien*, 179–80) to Perge (H. Hellenkemper and F. Hild, *Lykien und Pamphylien*, TIB 8.1 [2004], 360–72) and Attaleia (ibid., 297–41), and via Sagalassos (Aglasun near Isparta; Belke and Mersich, *Phrygien und Pisidien*, 368–69).
98 K. Belke (with contributions by M. Restle), *Galatien und Lykaonien*, TIB 4 (1984), 176–78; see Hild, "Via Sebaste."

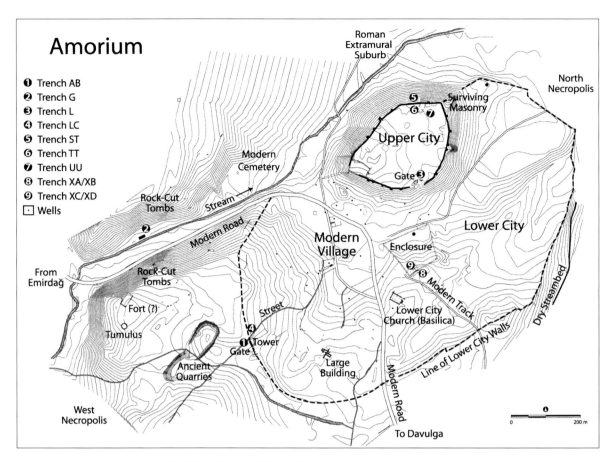

Figure 6.19. Amorion, town plan (after C. S. and M. Lightfoot, *Amorium*)

preserved (see figs. 6.16 and 6.17),[99] and also in Kilistra (see fig. 6.18).

In short, much of the area described here consists of valleys and basins that were arable as long as adequate freshwater resources (and not saltwater, such as Lake Tatta or Acıgöl) were available. The areas of fertile land were separated from one another by large mountain ranges. Given the overall low number of (fortified) urban settlements and large fortress towns, the possible amount of agrarian production (and pasture farming) should have been sufficient for this region; furthermore, although some surplus would have been available for troops moving through the region, this surplus production would hardly have been high enough to support a *regular* export worth noting.

AMORION The second example is Amorion, which during this period was the capital and headquarters of the Anatolikon theme (see fig. 6.19).[100] It lies 12.5 kilometers to the east of the modern city Emirdağ, between two streambeds. The site was surrounded by a fortification wall, long stretches of which still

---

99 The cistern, about 8.2 km from Kizilören (37° 49′ 22″ N, 32° 07′ 52″ E), still carries several m³ of water; it has a circular retrieval opening with a stone cap, as well as an entrance (closed with ashlar spolia) accessible by seventeen steps.

100 See research reports from R. M. Harrison in *AnatSt* 38–46 (1988–96) and from C. S. Lightfoot et al. in *DOP* 51–53, 55, 57–59 (1997–1999, 2001, 2003–05); see also C. S. Lightfoot and E. A. Ivison, introduction to *Amorium Reports*, vol. 1, BAR International Series 1070 (Oxford, 2002), 1–31; C. S. Lightfoot, ed., *Amorium Reports*, vol. 2, *Research Papers and Technical Studies*, BAR International Series 1170 (Oxford, 2003); and idem, "The Survival of Cities in Byzantine Anatolia: The Case of Amorium," *Byzantion* 68 (1998): 56–71. Very useful is the survey in C. S. and M. Lightfoot, *Amorium: A Byzantine City in Anatolia: An Archaeological Guide* (Istanbul, 2007); see also Belke, *Galatien und Lykaonien*, 122–25.

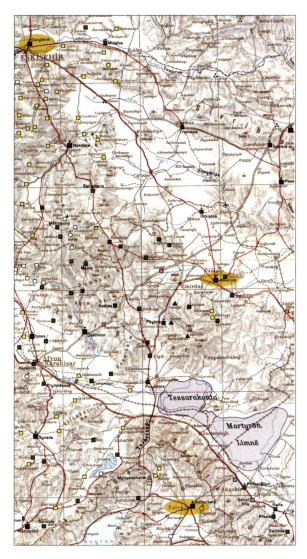

Figure 6.20. The region of Dorylaion, Amorion, and Antiocheia (after *TIB* 4)

stand, encompassing some 70 hectares; more than 50 hectares of the enclosed area are habitable, and are only partially occupied by a modern village. Approximately 4.5–5.0 hectares of the urban area belong to the "Upper City," which had its own fortifications during the Byzantine period, although it has to be said that its physical position—only some 20 meters higher than the "Lower City"—was not very good for defensive purposes. The perseverance of the Byzantine administration in holding and reoccupying the site in the face of all attacks during the middle Byzantine period, despite its less than ideal topography, demonstrates the importance of this junction of main Byzantine/Arab roads coming from Dorylaion, Ankyra, Ikonion, and Pisidian Antioch

(see fig. 6.20). For example, the stronghold was evidently rebuilt sometime after its sack by the army of al-Muʿtasim (838), since it was attacked again by the emir of Tarsos in 931.[101]

With an area of 50 hectares, the garrison and civilian population of Amorion could have reached a *maximum* figure of 15,000,[102] though Byzantine sources claim that 30,000 persons were captured or killed during the Arab sack in the summer of 838.[103] The landscape in the territories around Amorion, near the headwaters of the Sangarios River, is mostly fertile, able to provide not only sufficient crops to feed the inhabitants and pay their taxes but also a surplus to be exported and to supply passing armies.

Anazarbos The third example, Anazarbos (or Anabarzos), lies close to a northern tributary of the Pyramos River, 100 kilometers east of Tarsos. Since the time of Theodosius II it served as the capital of Cilicia secunda. The urban area borders a fertile plain[104] of about 160 square kilometers (see fig. 6.21; for the surrounding area, see fig. 6.22); accordingly, the *Geoponica* praises the production of olive oil in this region.[105] Anazarbos extends about 1.5 kilometers to the north, and is bordered to the east by a mountain 220 meters high, topped by a large fortress. The town was destroyed in the sixth century by two earthquakes (in 525 and 561), and its population was decimated by the Justinianic plague. The reduced city walls, probably to be dated to the early

---

101 Ad-Dahabi, as quoted by A. A. Vasiliev, *Byzance et les Arabes,* vol. 2, *Les relations politiques de Byzance et des Arabes à l'époque de la dynastie macédonienne,* part 2, *Extraits des sources arabes, traduits par M. Canard* (Brussels, 1950), 238; Ibn al-Athir 1.332; 3.86, 337; 7.17, quoted by E. W. Brooks, "The Arabs in Asia Minor (641–750), from Arabic Sources," *JHS* 18 (1898): 183; Vasiliev, *Byzance* 2:2, 152; Georgios Monachos, *Chronicon Breve* (PG 110:1024).
102 The figure corresponds to a *maximum* demand of ca. 15,000 tons of grain. This quantity needs a *maximum* production area of 480–630 km² (assuming that none of the inhabitants were engaged in agriculture, which is unlikely); see Appendix II.
103 *Theophanes Continuatus,* ed. I. Bekker, CSHB [33] (Bonn, 1838), 125–32.
104 κατὰ τὴν Ἀνάβαρζαν καὶ τὸν Ποδανδὸν καὶ τὰς λοιπὰς παροδεύων χώρας, καὶ βλέπων τὰ ἐν ποσί, κτήσεις τε ὀρῶν πολυτελεῖς καὶ χωρία εὐφυῆ τε καὶ πάμφορα; *Ioannis Scylitzae synopsis historiarum,* ed. I. Thurn (Berlin, 1973), 311.95–96; see *Ioannis Zonarae epitomae historiarum libri xviii,* ed. T. Büttner-Wobst, vol. 3, CSHB 46 (Bonn, 1897), 537.
105 φασὶ δὲ ἐν Ἀναζάρβῳ τῆς Κιλικίας παῖδας ἁγνοὺς γεωργεῖν τὴν ἐλαίαν, καὶ διὰ τοῦτο εὐφορωτάτην εἶναι τὴν παρ' αὐτοῖς ἐλαίαν; *Geoponica sive Cassiani Bassi scholastici De re rustica eclogae* 9.2.6, ed. H. Beckh (Leipzig, 1895).

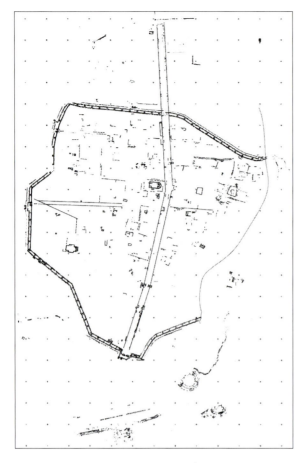

Figure 6.21. Anazarbos, town plan (courtesy of H. Birk and R. Posamentir, Project Anazarbos, German Archaeological Institut Istanbul and Istanbul Üniversitesi)

sixth century, enclose an area of ca. 65 hectares and include the mountain fortress; the walls consisted of a moat, forewall, and main wall and are in evidence for their entire course. Correspondingly, area-wide pottery finds date only to the sixth century. At least one later phase of construction can be identified; this upper phase is identified as Arabic, with pottery in the masonry of the wall dated to the eighth and tenth centuries;[106] and still in the twelfth century

---

106 See F. Hild and H. Hellenkemper, *Kilikien und Isaurien*, *TIB* 5 (1990), 178–85, with bibliography; M. H. Sayar, *Die Inschriften von Anazarbos und Umgebung,* part 1, *Inschriften aus dem Stadtgebiet und der nächsten Umgebung der Stadt,* Inschriften griechischer Städte aus Kleinasien 56.1 (Bonn, 2000), for a historical overview and the written sources; R. Posamentir and M. H. Sayar, "Anazarbos—Ein Zwischenbericht aus der Metropole des ebenen Kilikien," *IstMitt* 56 (2006): 317–57, esp. 354–55, with further comments by Richard Posamentir in a lecture (Vienna, 27 November 2007); further, R. Posamentir, "Kulturkontakt als Impuls architektonischer Innovation: Austausch

Figure 6.22. Anazarbos, surrounding area (after *TIB* 5)

the city was considered to have a large population (*polyanthropos*) and as being easy to defend, since the walls of the city and fortress were intact.[107] After its destruction by the Mamluks in 1375, the territory of the settlement remained uninhabited and therefore all of it is accessible for investigation. A distinctive and particularly remarkable feature is that more than a third of the area enclosed by the walls shows no evidence of settlement after late antiquity. One possible explanation might be that—as in the case of Nicaea—not only was it easier for later possessors and inhabitants to restore the still-existing (remains of) earlier walls than to build entirely new fortifications but also the topographical situation offered

---

und Inspiration in Anazarbos, einer vergessenen Grenzstadt zwischen Ost und West," in *Austausch und Inspiration: Kulturkontakt als Impuls architektonischer Innovation: Kolloquium anlässlich des 65. Geburtstages von Adolf Hoffmann,* ed. F. Pirson and U. Wulf-Rheidt, Diskussionen zur archäologischen Bauforschung 9 (Mainz, 2008), 89–106. A general volume on Anazarbos in the series Istanbuler Forschungen is planned.

107 ἡ γὰρ πόλις αὕτη, κουροτρόφος οὖσα καὶ πολυάνθρωπος, ἐρυμνοῖς διείληπται τείχεσι καὶ πετρῶν ἀποτόμων ὕπερθεν ἵδρυται, τότε δὲ μᾶλλον ἀσφαλεστέρα γεγένηται παρὰ τῶν εἰς αὐτὴν ὡς εἰς κρησφύγετον συνελθόντων, ἁπάντων ὄντων φρακτῶν καὶ κρατίστων, ἐπιτειχίσματα προσειληφυῖα καὶ μηχαναῖς παντοίαις διαληφθεῖσα; *Nicetae Choniatae Historiae* 25.16–17.

more security. Another is that Anazarbos might have served as a military gathering point, whether for Byzantine armies on their way to Syria or for Arabic armies marching to central Asia Minor.[108] That the town remained partially inhabited until the fourteenth century may be explained by its location, as it was situated near a highway running north to Kaisareia and Hierapolis and extending 30 kilometers to the south of Anabarzos, to a coastal road leading from Tarsos to the east.[109]

Unlike western Asia Minor, large inland portions of central and eastern Asia Minor were characterized by isolated agricultural zones of variable (in some cases, quite low) quality. These zones were separated by mountains and steppes, and in many places even nomadic stock farming was possible on only a limited basis.[110] For this reason, and as the east and southeast were threatened by enemy raids,[111] the primary market for agrarian production in the seventh to eleventh centuries was local, although occasional surpluses might have been used to supply armies. Surpluses normally found their way to the free (regional) market only secondarily.

Combining Concrete Information with General Patterns

After reviewing the problems in reconstructing networks in Asia Minor during the middle Byzantine period as briefly illustrated in the examples above, one might, as a next step, attempt to connect these and other settlements in Asia Minor's two distinct landscape categories (recognized as such by Byzantine land surveyors) with theoretical models of land use and development. Two such models that might be applied together are Johann Heinrich von Thuenen's Location Theory (Theorie der isolierten Orte) and Walter Christaller's Central Place Theory (Zentralörtliche Theorie), as I have pointed out elsewhere.[112] In an earlier study on this subject, I considered the regions of Honorias, Paphlagonia, Galatia, Lykaonia, and Isauria (see fig. 6.23), all of which were landscapes of lesser productive capabilities.[113] That study produced the following results: after the middle of the sixth century, archaeologically datable settlement density fell in all of the regions examined. Although coastal areas in the north and south of Asia Minor were less affected, the population of the inland areas of Isauria and in Paphlagonia declined sharply (see fig. 6.24). I therefore concluded that for a prolonged period, no economic or trade networks existed in the interior of central Asia Minor; it seemed instead that isolated settlements were connected only locally with their immediate hinterland.

But these conclusions were not supported by specific examples. The study did not reflect critically on archaeological information relevant to the end of settlements, and it did not take into account the agriculturally productive regions of western Asia Minor. This chapter suggests that for future studies, those conclusions should be revised in two ways.

First, the significance of structural constants should receive more attention. The differences between western Asia Minor and the interior regions of central and eastern Asia Minor—specifically, their agricultural possibilities and their histories of settlement—should be taken into consideration. And further, the persistent demand for goods in medium- and long-distance trade, which also contributed to the revival of regional trade after catastrophes, should be considered when continuities are analyzed.

Second, the standard account should be more rigorously tested against empirical evidence. Although the examples presented above are not sufficient to support a detailed, area-wide assessment, they do add nuance to a one-sided general view by calling into question both the uniform and early dating of settlement decline to around the first half

---

108 Perhaps also the sometimes noxious climate may have been a partial explanation.
109 The so-called Amanikai Pylai of the road are still preserved northeast of Aigai (36° 55' 16" N, 35° 57' 57" E), in a garbage dump near the lading port of the oil pipeline near Ceyhan.
110 For an excellent description of this type of landscape in Asia Minor, see X. de Planhol, *De la plaine pamphylienne aux lacs pisidiens, nomadisme et vie paysanne* (Paris, 1958), 23–64.
111 For the typology of military campaigns along the eastern frontier, see also I. Stouraitis, *Krieg und Frieden in der politischen und ideologischen Wahrnehmung in Byzanz (7.–11. Jahrhundert)*, Byzantinische Geschichtsschreiber, supp. 5 (Vienna, 2009).

112 See J. Koder, "Land Use and Settlement: Theoretical Approaches," in *General Issues in the Study of Medieval Logistics: Sources, Problems and Methodologies*, ed. J. F. Haldon, History of Warfare 36 (Leiden, 2006), 159–83.
113 J. Koder, "Παρατηρήσεις στην οικιστική διάρθρωση της κεντρικής Μικράς Ασίας μετά τον 6ο αιώνα: Μια προσέγγιση από την οπτική γωνιά της 'θεωρίας των κεντρικών τόπων'" ("Observations on the settlement structure of central Asia Minor after the sixth century: An approach using 'Central Place Theory'"), in *Byzantine Asia Minor (6th–12th cent.)*, ed. S. Lampakēs (Athens, 1998), 245–65, esp. 256–57 with figs. 1, 6.

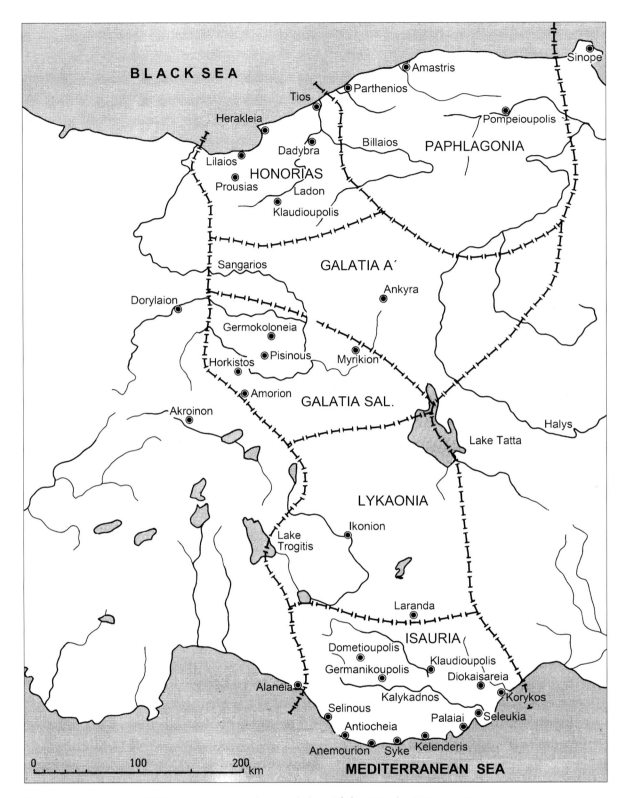

Figure 6.23. Central Asia Minor, provinces and "central places" (after J. Koder, "Παρατηρήσεις στην οικιστική διάρθρωση")

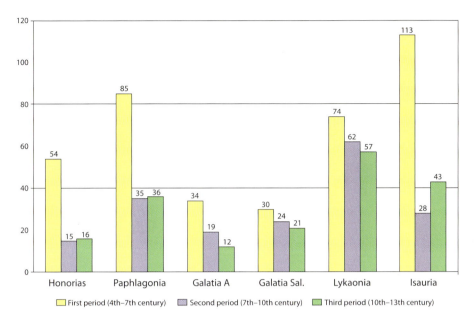

Figure 6.24. Central Asia Minor, changes in city population according to the number of archaeologically datable settlements (after J. Koder, "Παρατηρήσεις στην οικιστική διάρθρωση")

of the seventh century and the standard assumption that the demise of these settlements lasted to the beginning of the ninth century. Thus, more new case studies supported by survey evidence are needed.[114] Additional evidence, such as data on the economic function of bishoprics and on the innovative role in reviving regional trade played by large-scale property ownership (with military nobility as well as monasteries being the landowners), should be included.

Therefore, for the period between 650 and 750, it might become apparent that *urban* settlement density—important on a regional level—indeed declined, but that general population density, which had already fallen after the 540s, declined far less, as population density may have increased in rural settlements. These conditions also facilitated a regeneration of urban and quasi-urban settlement structures. Likewise, in this scenario regional trade weakened after the sixth century but certainly did not totally end. If we connect this recommended approach with the observations made recently by Philipp Niewöhner concerning development and changes in Asia Minor's settlement typology,[115] we will find roughly two centuries of continual "darkness" to be no more probable than a millennium of "decline and fall."

---

114 Such case studies should rest on surveys like that in Paphlagonia or in the region of Ikonion. See, e.g., R. Matthews, "Project Paphlagonia 2001," *AnatArch* 7 (2001): 20–21, and D. Baird, "Konya Plain Survey," *AnatArch* 7 (2001): 16.

115 Niewöhner, "Archäologie und die 'Dunklen Jahrhunderte'"; also idem, *Aizanoi, Dokimion und Anatolien,* and idem, "Frühbyzantinische Steinmetzarbeiten in Kütahya." But see also the preliminary results coming from the Konya Plain Survey Project: D. Baird, "Settlement Expansion on the Konya Plain, Anatolia, 5th–7th Centuries A.D.," in *Recent Research on the Late Antique Countryside,* ed. W. Bowden, L. Lavan, and C. Machado (Leiden, 2004), 219–46; and the results of a survey of agrarian settlements in central Lycia: A. Sanlı-Erler, *Bauern in der Polis: Ländliche Siedlungen und agrarische Wirtschaftsformen im zentrallykischen Yavu-Bergland,* Tübinger althistorische Studien 1 (Bonn, 2006).

Appendixes

APPENDIX I

Population Figures for Densely Built-up Settlements

A difficult and at the same time intriguing problem is presented by the population figures for settlements that were densely built-up. James Russell accepted the number of "300 a hectare" though he regarded it as "a very high index."[116] I attempted to verify the figure for post–late antique cities, relying on some fortified examples,[117] by taking as a basic unit the single-family house with a ground floor used as a professional and dwelling area and in some cases one upper story used for dwelling only, and then tallying a possible maximum number of units (and inhabitants) for settlements with an area defined by an enclosing wall, a sufficient number of ruined houses to calculate a hypothetical number of inhabitants, or both.[118] The result seems to me to confirm Russell's figure of 300 inhabitants as a realistic possible maximum population density per hectare.

City	City Area (ha)	Housing Area (ha)	Households	Inhabitants	Inhabitants per ha
Thessalonike	290	230	15,800	79,000	273
Nikaia	130	100	7,500	37,500	288
Mistra	21	16	1,200	6,000	286
Ioannina	17	14	1,050	5,300	303
Pergamon	12	9	800	4,000	333

116 J. C. Russell, "Late Ancient and Medieval Population," *TAPS* 48.3 (1958): 93 (he discusses "290 and 261 persons to the hectare" for the cities of the Muslim caliphate of Córdoba, 92; see also his significantly lower estimations for Selcuk cities in Asia Minor, 99–100). See also the figures in Laiou and Morrisson, *The Byzantine Economy*, 130–31, and Loungis, "Η εξέλιξη της βυζαντινής πόλης," 66, relying on Litavrin, "Provintsialnyi," 17–29, esp. 24, 27, for Lampsakos (173 households and ca. 900 inhabitants).

117 The following calculation presupposes that the houses on average correspond to one household (equal to a mean value of 5 persons). Also taken into consideration was a tentative pertinent share of 20–25 percent of the surrounding streets, places, and common buildings (such as churches):

118 Pergamon is one example; see M. Klinkott, *Die Stadtmauer*, part 1, *Die byzantinische Befestigungsanlage von Pergamon mit ihrer Wehr- und Baugeschichte*, Diskussionen zur archäologischen Bauforschung, Altertümer von Pergamon 16.1 (Berlin, 2001), town plan at the end of the volume; Rheidt, "Byzantinische Wohnhäuser"; see also idem, "Urban Economy of Pergamon."

APPENDIX II

Annual Supply of Grain

The minimum amount of grain required to supply 100 persons annually is between 20 and 29 tons. If those 100 persons are not themselves engaged in agricultural production, then to determine the total grain needed one must add the same amount again to meet the producer's needs, as well as a portion set aside for seed grain and at least 25 percent for losses in transit between producer and consumer. In the end up to ca. 100 tons of grain are required per annum for 100 nonproducers;[119] for that annual output, between 3.2 and 4.2 square kilometers are required for agrarian production, assuming a two-crop rotation.

119 For details of these calculations, see J. Koder, *Gemüse in Byzanz: Die Frischgemüseversorgung Konstantinopels im Licht der Geoponika*, Byzantinische Geschichtsschreiber, supp. 3 (Vienna, 1993), 100–103. For other calculations, see (with bibliography) M. Kaplan, *Les hommes et la terre à Byzance du VIᵉ au XIᵉ siècle: Propriété et exploitation du sol* (Paris, 1992), 80–85; Lefort, "The Rural Economy," 259–61; and Laiou and Morrisson, *The Byzantine Economy*, 64–66.

APPENDIX III

Byzantine and Modern Names of Sites Mentioned

Adramyttion / Edremit (Karataş)
Aisepos / Gönen Çay (river)
Akroinon / Afyon
Akroterion / Eğridir
Alinda / Karpuzlu
Amorion / Hisar(köy)
Anazarbos (Anabarzos) / Anavarza
Ankyra / Ankara
Antiocheia Pisidias / Yalvaç
Apameia / Dinar
Apameia / Mudanya
Apollonias / Uluabat (lake)
Artake / Erdek
Attuda / Asar
Bathys limen / Bafa gölü (lake)
Bonita / Çardak
Chonai / Honaz
Daskyleion / Ergili
Dorylaion / Eskişehir
Empelos / Sığırcı çayı / Koca çayı (river)
Ephesos / Ayasuluk / Selçuk
Eski Manyas / Soğuksu
Granikos / Biga (river)
Hierapolis / Komana
Hierapolis / Pamukkale
Iasos / Kiyikişlacık
Ikonion / Konya
Kaikos / Bakır çayı (river)
Kaisareia / Kayseri
Kilistra / Gökyurt
Knidos peninsula / Reşadiye Yarimadasi
Koloneia / Aksaray
Kolossai → Chonai
Kotyaeion / Kütahya

Kyzikos / Balkız
Lampsakos / Lapseki
Laodikeia / Denizli
Lopadion / Uluabat
Lykos / Aksu (river)
Lystra / Gökyurt
Maeander / Büyük Menderes (river)
Makestos / Simav çayı (river)
Malagina / Karaçahisar
Mantzikiert (Manzikert) / Malazgird
Melitoupolis (Miletoupolis) / Melde
Miletos / Palatia / Balat
Mokisos / Viranşehir near Helvadere
Mylasa / Milas
Myrina / Karadut
Nicaea / İznik
Nicomedia / İzmit / Koçaeli
Palaia / Kadıköy, Balya
Parion / Kemer
Pegai / Karabiga
Pergamon / Bergama
Phoinix / Finike
Phokaia / Foça
Poimanenon / Eski Manyas
Pyramos / Ceyhan (river)
Rhyndakos / Koca su (river)
Sagalassos / Ağlasun
Sangarios / Sakarya (river)
Smyrna / İzmir
Tarsos / Tarsus
Tatta Limne / Tuz gölü
Tralleis / Aydın
Trapezoupolis / Seyne
Tyana / Kemerhisar

• SEVEN •

Business as Usual?

Archaeological Evidence for Byzantine Commercial Enterprise at Amorium in the Seventh to Eleventh Centuries

CHRISTOPHER LIGHTFOOT

CITIES, TOWNS, AND LARGE SETTLEMENTS form the basis for any effective commercial activity, since it is only in such places that markets can thrive and workforces can be concentrated. De-urbanization in the seventh century has long been seen as compounding the problems caused by a severe contraction in both the production of and the demand for goods throughout the Byzantine Empire. Combined, these factors are taken to signify the impoverishment of the state and a sharp decline in the standard of living for the majority of its population. Yet an increasing amount of archaeological evidence suggests that the infrastructure of communities and communications in Byzantine Anatolia may have been more robust and sustainable than had previously been recognized. In this chapter new discoveries, principally from Amorium (Amorion), will be discussed, and the argument will be made that there existed a vigorous environment of regional supply and demand in central Anatolia that was relatively unaffected by the decline in long-distance trade and was only partially reliant on state support.

It has often been stated, almost as a given fact, that the Byzantine Empire was "always centered on the Mediterranean and on the Black Sea."[1] It is, of course, irrefutable that maritime warfare, trade, and travel played an important part in the history of Byzantium, just as first the Aegean, then the eastern Mediterranean, and finally the whole of the Mediterranean basin contributed significantly to the rise and development of ancient Greece. Yet it is worth observing that not all civilizations were dependent on maritime power and trade for their success or survival, and one might contend that the Byzantine Empire was no more based on the sea than were two other great "Anatolian" empires—those of the Hittites and the Ottomans. In the period under discussion in this chapter (the dark age and the middle Byzantine periods between the mid-seventh and the late eleventh centuries) it is certainly possible to argue that a somewhat distorted view of reality is provided by this focus on the Mediterranean littoral. The only major provincial cities that are usually regarded as having survived the end of antiquity are placed along the coasts where they had access to harbors.[2] Inland sites, on the other hand, are often excluded from the list of Byzantine settlements that could claim to be "towns" or "cities," despite the fact

---

[1] A. E. Laiou and C. Morrisson, *The Byzantine Economy* (Cambridge, 2007), 8; see also C. Wickham, "The Mediterranean around 800: On the Brink of the Second Trade Cycle," *DOP* 58 (2004): 168 ("the Aegean heartland of the Byzantine Empire"); T. E. Gregory, *A History of Byzantium* (Oxford, 2005), 10. By contrast, fifty years ago George Ostrogorsky regarded Asia Minor as "the basis and foundation of medieval Byzantium": G. Ostrogor-

sky, "The Byzantine Empire in the World of the Seventh Century," *DOP* 13 (1959): 3.

[2] W. Brandes, "Byzantine Cities in the Seventh and Eighth Centuries—Different Sources, Different Histories," in *The Idea and the Ideal of the Town between Late Antiquity and the Early Middle Ages,* ed. G. P. Brogiolo and B. Ward-Perkins (Leiden, 1999), 25; see also J. H. W. G. Liebeschuetz, *The Decline and Fall of the Roman City* (Oxford, 2001), 292; C. Wickham, *Framing the Early Middle Ages: Europe and the Mediterranean, 400–800* (Oxford, 2005), 626; M. Rautman, *Daily Life in the Byzantine Empire* (Westport, Conn., 2006), 119.

Figure 7.1. Sketch map of Byzantine Anatolia (courtesy of Pamlyn Smith Designs)

that contemporary Arab sources emphasized the size and importance of places such as Amorium, the capital of the Anatolic theme in central Anatolia (see fig. 7.1).[3] A few scholars, however, have detected an increase in the importance (if not in the physical size) of some inland cities, tracing their rise to the late antique period. Ankyra (modern Ankara) is a case in point.[4] At Amorium, too, there is good archaeological evidence to show that during the late fifth and sixth centuries considerable improvements were made to the appearance and amenities of the city— for example, with the construction of the all-new fortifications, the aisled basilica (Church A), and the bathhouse, all in the Lower City.[5] While evidence is still lacking that might shed light on Amorium's possible decline, partial abandonment, or even ruin during the first half of the seventh century, excavations at various points across the site attest to continued, substantial occupation in the subsequent centuries. Indeed, encroachment on open areas around Church A and the bathhouse after ca. 650 suggests a marked increase in the density of settlement (see fig. 7.2).[6] Such dark-age construction work finds few parallels elsewhere in Byzantine Anatolia.[7] It is not to

---

3   C. S. Lightfoot, "Trade and Industry in Byzantine Anatolia—The Evidence from Amorium," *DOP* 61 (2007): 270–71. For references in Ibn Khurradādhbih, see M. Whittow, *The Making of Byzantium, 600–1025* (Berkeley, 1996), 153, 184.

4   C. Foss, "Late Antique and Byzantine Ankara," *DOP* 31 (1977): 42–68; S. Mitchell, *Anatolia: Land, Men, and Gods in Asia Minor*, vol. 2, *The Rise of the Church* (Oxford, 1993), 84–90; Wickham, *Framing the Early Middle Ages*, 406–7.

5   E. A. Ivison, "Amorium in the Byzantine Dark Ages (Seventh to Ninth Centuries)," in *Post-Roman Towns, Trade and Settlement in Europe and Byzantium,* ed. J. Henning, vol. 2, *Byzantium, Pliska, and the Balkans,* Millennium-Studien zu Kultur und Geschichte des ersten Jahrtausends n. Chr. 5.2 (Berlin, 2007), 35.

6   Ivison, "Amorium in the Byzantine Dark Ages," 46–48; for a brief account of recent discoveries around Church A, see C. Lightfoot and E. Ivison, "Amorium 2008," *AnatArch* 14 (2008): 25–27.

7   Wickham, *Framing the Early Middle Ages,* 629. Only in Arab-occupied Syria does prosperity and activity continue,

Figure 7.2. Dark age buildings immediately to the west of the Lower City bathhouse (photo by author)

be confused with a phenomenon common elsewhere that saw abandoned public buildings and spaces taken over for private dwellings and workshops during the sixth century.[8] Rather, the new construction at Amorium should probably be associated with the arrival of the Army of the Anatolics and the elevation of the city to the status of capital of the new theme of Anatolikon in the second half of the seventh century.

Likewise, it has been stated that "after Ancyra and Amorium were sacked by the Arabs in 838, Amorium never fully recovered, though Ancyra regained much of its importance as a trading center after some rebuilding by Michael III."[9] Again, archaeology has been able to prove otherwise. From the late ninth century there began a period of massive reconstruction at Amorium, involving the building not only of new fortification walls around the Upper City and the Enclosure but also of dwellings and workshops across the entire site. It follows that Byzantine Amorium must have had a sizable population, which was engaged in a number of different trades and professions. In addition, Church A was completely rebuilt in the tenth and eleventh centuries.[10] Much use was

---

although here, too, the evidence is uneven and intermittent; see C. Foss, "Syria in Transition, A.D. 550–750: An Archaeological Approach," *DOP* 51 (1997): 264–67.

8 H. G. Saradi, *The Byzantine City in the Sixth Century: Literary Images and Historical Reality* (Athens, 2006), 307–8. Likewise, the process of "deurbanization" at seventh-century Apameia in Syria is quite different; Foss, "Syria in Transition," 265.

9 W. Treadgold, *A History of the Byzantine State and Society* (Stanford, 1997), 573. For the building inscription, see D. French, *Roman, Late Roman and Byzantine Inscriptions of Ankara: A Selection* (Ankara, 2003), 196–97, no. 80.

10 E. A. Ivison, "Middle Byzantine Sculptors at Work: Evidence from the Lower City Church at Amorium," in *La sculpture byzantine, VIIe–XIIe siècles: Actes du colloque international organisé par la 2e Éphorie des antiquités byzantines et l'École française d'Athènes (6–8 septembre 2000)*, ed. C. Pennas and C. Vanderheyde, BCH supp. 49 (Paris, 2008), 489–91. There are instances of churches in Lycia that were constructed or rebuilt on a similar

Figure 7.3. Tomb 65 at Church A, constructed from reused Phrygian doorstones of the Roman period (2nd–early 3rd c.), located outside the wall of the south aisle (photo by E. Schoolman)

made in all this work of earlier Byzantine spolia, indicating that the physical appearance of the city was now radically altered. There is also ample evidence from the wealth of pottery, glass, and small finds to show that Amorium must have served as a flourishing market for both agricultural produce and manufactured goods. Several wealthy families must have resided there, too, for they not only lavished money on the refurbishment of Church A but were then also honored with prestigious tombs within its precincts (see fig. 7.3).[11] The city declined (and, indeed, may have been expeditiously evacuated) only after the Battle of Manzikert in 1071, when the unforeseen arrival of the Seljuk Turks imposed a new geopolitical reality on the Anatolian plateau.

The coin finds at Amorium reflect this picture of sustained economic activity in both the dark ages and the middle Byzantine period (see table 7.1).[12] There is no discernible break in the sequence of issues from the mid-sixth through the mid-ninth century, although there are marked peaks in the reigns of Constans II and Theophilos (see fig. 7.4). After the destruction of the city in 838, there comes a slight hiatus; but finds pick up again in the reign of Nikephoros II and continue until the 1080s.[13] To date only one postreform issue of Alexios I has been

---

lavish scale in the ninth century; C. Foss, "The Lycian Coast in the Byzantine Age," *DOP* 48 (1994): 36–37, 50.

11 C. S. Lightfoot, Y. Arbel, E. A. Ivison, J. A. Roberts, and E. Ioannidou, "The Amorium Project: Excavation and Research in 2002," *DOP* 59 (2005): 249–52.

12 For some preliminary, general remarks, see C. Lightfoot, "Byzantine Anatolia: Reassessing the Numismatic Evidence," *RN* 158 (2002): 229–39. Of a total of some 856 coin finds, including unidentified specimens, recovered from the site up to and including the 2009 season, 130 have been securely identified as belonging to the period between the reigns of Constans II (641–68) and Theophilos (829–42). Here a list of all the Byzantine coins by reign has been extracted from the annual finds reports; see table 7.1. A full catalogue and discussion of the coins found at Amorium between 1987 and 2006 will appear shortly; C. Katsari and C. S. Lightfoot, with a contribution by A. Özme, *Amorium Reports*, vol. 4, *The Amorium Mint and the Coin Finds* (forthcoming).

13 A silver *miliaresion* of Michael III (SF8346) was found at Church A during excavations in 2008: C. Lightfoot, E. Ivison, O. Koçyiğit, and M. Şen, "Amorium Kazıları 2008," *KazSonTop* 31 (2010): 136, 143, pl. 6. This was the first and, so far, only coin of

Table 7.1 Byzantine Copper Alloy Coins found at Amroium (1997–2009)

Anastasius I (491–518) 3	Basil I (867–86) 4
Justin I (518–27) 1	Leo VI (886–912) 10
Justinian I (527–65) 6	Constantine VII (913–59) 16
Justin II (565–78) 5	Romanos I Lekapenos (920–44) 17
Tiberius II (578–82) 8	Nikephoros II, Phokas (963–69) 19
Maurice Tiberius (582–602) 7	
Phocas (602–10) 6	Anonymous folles
Heraclius (610–41) 16	
Constans II (641–68) 30	Class A1 (970–76?) 8
Constantine IV (668–85) 7	Class A2 (976?–ca. 1030/35) 71
Justinian II, first reign (685–95) 7	Class B (ca. 1030/35–1042?) 12
Leontios (695–98) 1	Class C (1042?–ca. 1050) 29
Tiberios III (698–705) 6	Class D (ca. 1050–60) 9
Justinian II, second reign (705–11) 1	Class G (ca. 1065–70) 31*
Anastasios II (713–15) 1	Class I (ca. 1075–80) 17
Leo III (717–41) 4	Class I var. (ca. 1080?) 2
Constantine V (741–75) 2	Class I or J 1
Leo IV (775–80) 5	
Constantine VI and Eirene (790–97) . . . 2	Signed folles
Nikephoros I (802–11) 7	
Leo V (813–20) 7	Constantine X and Eudocia (1059–67) . 34
Michael II (820–29) 13	Romanos IV (1068–71) 5
Theophilos (829–42) 37	Michael VII (1071–78) 6
	Alexios I (1081–1118) 1

* Includes a hoard of 22 folles.
This list excludes several other coins that are clearly Byzantine but have not been securely identified.

Figure 7.4. Copper alloy follis of Theophilos with his son Constantine (photo by E. Schoolman)

recovered; they represent the last Byzantine coins from Amorium. There is a plethora of middle Byzantine anonymous folles, numerous examples of which turn up every year, but it is the relatively small yet significant number of dark-age issues that is remarkable, especially in Anatolia. The pattern of coin finds at Amorium is thus seriously at odds with the numismatic evidence from almost every other Byzantine site, with the exception of Constantinople itself.[14] The only valid explanation is that the excavations at Amorium have indeed revealed the unprecedented remains of a thriving city.[15]

The evidence from Amorium may be exceptional, but it should also be pointed out that this is in part only because little archaeological work has been done elsewhere in central Anatolia to document the prosperity and vitality of the region in the Byzantine period.[16] There are clues, however, to a different reality, one in which the Anatolian hinterland played a vital role in the survival of the empire. Little can yet be said about the density of population in this region in Byzantine times, but it could be argued that it remained, as previously in Roman times, an important source of manpower. Most of the thematic troops were stationed in Anatolia, and it is likely that many of the soldiers were recruited locally.[17] Efforts were certainly made by successive emperors to augment the pool of reserves by transplanting peoples to the region.[18] Similarly, the Byzantine soldier's rations consisted principally of wheat, wine, and meat—all staple products of the Anatolian plateau. In addition, fresh fish and salt, seen as "two essential elements," could be found in the lakes and rivers of central Anatolia.[19] There is also evidence to show that some fish, presumably dried or otherwise preserved, and marine mollusks were at times imported from the coast.[20]

Nevertheless, it has been stated that "the [Byzantine] economy became focussed on the coastal fringes of Asia Minor, the Greek islands, Cyprus, and the North African littoral."[21] As a result the economic value of the Anatolian plateau has been played down and large tracts of land have been relegated to the status of poor-quality, arid pasturage—in Byzantine times fit only for stock rearing.[22] It is certainly true that animal husbandry played an important role; large quantities of domesticated animal bones recovered during the excavations at Amorium make this obvious, and in numerous instances butchering marks have been noted.[23] Similar evidence has been found elsewhere, notably at Pessinus.[24] Sheep, goats, and to a lesser extent cattle and pigs must have been a

---

Michael III recorded at Amorium, but it suggests some reoccupation of the site as early as the mid-ninth century.

14 M. F. Hendy, "The Coins," in *Excavations at Saraçhane in Istanbul*, vol. 1, R. M. Harrison et al., *The Excavations, Structures, Architectural Decoration, Small Finds, Coins, Bones, and Molluscs* (Princeton, N.J., 1986), 279; see also C. Morrisson, "Byzantine Money: Its Production and Circulation," in *EHB* 3:912–13, fig. 6.6.

15 For the traditional view of dark-age coinage in Anatolia, see W. Treadgold, *Byzantium and Its Army, 284–1081* (Stanford, 1995), 169; L. Brubaker and J. Haldon, *Byzantium in the Iconoclast Era (ca. 680–850): The Sources* (Aldershot, 2001), 149. Only Byzantine Sicily has been regarded as an area where, in the eighth century, there was a "more active circulation of coinage"; Wickham, *Framing the Early Middle Ages*, 125–26 (with references in n. 174 to C. Morrisson, "La Sicile byzantine: Une lueur dans les siècles obscurs," *Quaderni ticinesi di numismatica e antichità classiche* 27 [1998]: 307–34; quotation, 125), 127.

16 For general remarks on the paucity of data on the countryside of Anatolia, especially in the early medieval period, see G. Varinlioğlu, "Living in a Marginal Environment: Rural Habitat and Landscape in Southeastern Isauria," *DOP* 61 (2007): 288. The problem is exacerbated by the lack of a secure chronology for local coarse ware ceramics of the Byzantine period.

17 Although Anatolia has been described as "poor land with poor communications," it is nevertheless accepted that in the eighth century the thematic armies based there "came to be supplied locally, and indeed recruited locally": Wickham, *Framing the Early Middle Ages*, 127.

18 For references to refugees and deportations, see Laiou and Morrisson, *The Byzantine Economy*, 45.

19 Laiou and Morrisson, *The Byzantine Economy*, 15; see also 21–22. For salt working in Bithynia, see M. Gérolymatou, "Le commerce, VIIᵉ–XVᵉ siècle," in *La Bithynie au Moyen Âge*, ed. B. Geyer and J. Lefort, Réalités byzantines 9 (Paris, 2003), 488–89. For the provisioning of Byzantine armies, see J. F. Haldon, *Warfare, State and Society in the Byzantine World, 565–1204* (London, 1999), 143–76.

20 Lightfoot, "Trade and Industry," 275.

21 R. Hodges and D. Whitehouse, *Mohammed, Charlemagne and the Origins of Europe* (London, 1983), 75; see also Wickham, *Framing the Early Middle Ages*, 125.

22 Whittow, *The Making of Byzantium*, 29–30; Laiou and Morrisson, *The Byzantine Economy*, 24, 43; see also J.-C. Cheynet and T. Drew-Bear, "Une inscription d'Akroïnos datant de Constantin Porphyrogénète," *REB* 62 (2004): 217; Rautman, *Daily Life*, xiii. For a more balanced view that envisages mixed farming, see M. Decker, "Frontier Settlement and Economy in the Byzantine East," *DOP* 61 (2007): 256–62.

23 E. Ioannidou, "Animal Husbandry," in *Amorium Reports*, vol. 3, *The Lower City Enclosure: Finds Reports and Technical Studies*, ed. C. S. Lightfoot and E. A. Ivison (Istanbul, 2012).

24 A. Ervynck, W. Van Neer, and B. De Cupere, "Animal Remains from the Byzantine Castle," in *Excavations in Pessinus: The So-called Acropolis: From Hellenistic and Roman Cemetery to Byzantine Castle*, ed. J. Devreker, H. Thoen, F. Vermeulen, et al. (Ghent, 2003), 375–82.

common sight in Byzantine Anatolia. In addition, it is clear from literary and artistic references as well as archaeological finds that the Byzantines enjoyed the hunt and that game such as deer and wild boar was exploited to supplement the food supply.[25] Indeed, these and other wild animals were common in the Anatolian countryside until fairly recent times. Other domesticated animals, essentially the beasts of burden (which included oxen and camels as well as horses), required stabling and provisioning through the harsh winter months.[26] The supply of animals to the army alone must have ensured a vigorous trade in livestock, fodder, and equipment.[27] There is no suggestion that the Byzantine army became ineffective during the dark ages, and so it must be assumed that a number of basic services and supplies continued to be furnished, at least in the vicinity of thematic garrison posts. The need to supply provisions, equipment, and services necessitated the existence of a developed economy, attracting craftsmen, traders, and, presumably, people in less visible professions. So, with the soldiers' presence there undoubtedly came a certain degree of affluence, since their spending power and consumption demands would have stimulated the local economy.

The contraction of the Byzantine state in the seventh century is apparent in geographical, demographic, and economic terms. Numerous cities that had formerly flourished as centers of wealth and population became severely impoverished and were no longer able to sustain a complex social organization. Many different factors contributed to their demise, including both natural and man-made disasters. It was probably the combination and frequent repetition of these events that wreaked havoc on urban populations, thereby preventing any chance at recovery.[28] Available evidence suggests that coastal cities in particular were severely affected, although it has to be admitted that much less is known about inland cities.[29] Survey work in the territory around Sagalassos in Pisidia has shown that even in the sixth century the city itself was contracting, but at the same time rural communities were growing in size and number.[30] It is possible that social and political factors contributed to this apparent pattern of migration from the city, since smallholders may have found conditions in the countryside more attractive under the protection of local magnates or rural monasteries.[31] In these circumstances it is not surprising that an increase in village trades and crafts has been noted. Likewise, the countryside may have offered greater security or, at least, lessened the effects of plague, earthquake, and invasion. Some of these rural communities developed so rapidly that they quickly took on the appearance of "new" cities. There are numerous examples of Byzantine settlements in central Anatolia—at Binbirkilise, for example, and other sites near Konya (Iconium) and Niğde, as well as those in Phrygia.[32]

---

25 For Byzantine hunting, see A. Karpozilos, J. W. Nesbitt, and A. Cutler, "Hunting," in *ODB* 2:958. For wild animals in Roman Asia Minor, see J. Nollé, "Boars, Bears, and Bugs: Farming in Asia Minor and the Protection of Men, Animals, and Crops," in *Patterns in the Economy of Asia Minor,* ed. S. Mitchell and C. Katsari (Swansea, 2005), 62–66.

26 One may note the funerary stele of a camel driver or, more properly, the owner of a camel caravan, dated to the sixth century, in Ankara; French, *Inscriptions of Ankara,* 203–4, no. 84.

27 *Chartoularioi* of the Anatolic theme have been associated with horse-breeding ranches in central Anatolia; see *DOSeals* 3:144, 147, no. 86.9.

28 For the effects of the Justinianic plague, see P. Sarris, "Bubonic Plague in Byzantium: The Evidence of the Non-Literary Sources,"
in *Plague and the End of Antiquity: The Pandemic of 541–750,* ed. L. K. Little (Cambridge, 2007), 119–32, esp. 131.

29 See Foss, "The Lycian Coast," 1–52, esp. 48–49.

30 Dr. Hannalore Vanhaverbeke, personal communication; see also H. Vanhaverbeke et al., "What Happened after the 7th Century AD? A Different Perspective on Post-Roman Anatolia," in *Archaeology of the Countryside in Medieval Anatolia,* ed. T. Vorderstrasse and J. Roodeberg (Leiden, 2009), 177–78. Earlier reports had suggested that in the early Byzantine period (ca. 450/75–ca. 640/50) there was a reduction in the number of sites "resulting in a near abandonment of the city's territory by the mid-7th century": H. Vanhaverbeke and M. Waelkens, *The Chora of Sagalassos: The Evolution of the Settlement Pattern from Prehistoric until Recent Times,* Studies in Eastern Mediterranean Archaeology 5 (Turnhout, 2003), 286–87.

31 Laiou and Morrisson, *The Byzantine Economy,* 32.

32 W. M. Ramsay and G. L. Bell, *The Thousand and One Churches* (London, 1909); A. Berger, "Viranşehir (Mokisos), eine byzantinische Stadt in Kappadokien," *IstMitt* 48 (1998): 349–429, pls. 45–62; K. Belke (with contributions by M. Restle), *Galatien und Lykaonien, TIB* 4 (1984), 155 (Dağören mevkii, near Karapınar). See also R. Ousterhout, "The 1994 Survey at Akhisar-Çanlı Kilise," *ArSonTop* 13.2 (1996): 165–80; N. Asutay, "Zwei byzantinische Denkmäler aus Phrygischen Hochlands: Kirche G und H im Dorf Ayazin," *IstMitt* 48 (1998): 437–42, pl. 65; N. Karakaya, "2005 Yılı, Kayseri'nin Yeşilhisar İlçesi, Erdemli Vadisi'ndeki Kaya Yerleşimi Yüzey Araştırması," *ArSonTop* 24.2 (2007): 501–10; B. Y. Olcay Uçkan, "Frigya (Phrygia) Bölgesindeki Kaya Kiliseleri," *ArSonTop* 24.2 (2007): 101–12; Decker, "Frontier Settlement," 238–45. New, ongoing excavations at Han, only some 40 km WNW of Amorium, have revealed extensive Byzantine remains, suggesting that it was an important supply and provisioning station on the main highway from Dorylaeum

There is no apparent equivalent around the west and south coasts of Anatolia to these developments on the central plateau.[33] In Bithynia, however, where a regional survey of the Byzantine remains has been conducted more rigorously than elsewhere, evidence has been found to suggest that the larger and more important cities survived the calamitous seventh century and that a number of large villages developed in the eighth through tenth centuries.[34] While the region's proximity to the capital is cited as the principal reason for this relative prosperity, it should be noted that its military, ecclesiastical, and strategic importance must also have played a role. It may well be that it served not only as a source of supply for Constantinople but also as an important conduit in the movement of troops, merchants, and pilgrims, and in the exchange of goods to and from the central plateau. Additionally, the major cities of Nicaea, Nikomedeia, and, probably, Prusa remained vital military, administrative, and economic centers throughout the Byzantine period.[35] In the dark ages Cotyaeum (modern Kütahya) also gained prominence as "one of the centers of the Opsician theme" and a strategic fortress on the main highways across Anatolia.[36]

The end of Roman and Byzantine thalassocracy in the Mediterranean in the mid-seventh century must be linked directly with the sudden collapse in maritime trade, although it is impossible to say exactly what is cause and what is effect in the concurrent decline in activities such as shipbuilding, tree felling, amphora production, and other related ceramic industries.[37] Nevertheless, in cities such as Amorium, which lay many days' journey from the nearest seaport, it should be apparent that the effects of this disruption to commerce and productivity would have been felt much less severely and then only indirectly. The economic viability of Amorium, in other words, rested on other sectors of production, notably agriculture and stock rearing. Recent excavations there have provided tangible evidence for the scale of production in one sector, viticulture and wine making. To date, eight installations used for pressing grapes to make wine have been identified within the area known as the Enclosure at the center of the Lower City (see fig. 7.5). All can be confidently dated to the eighth and early ninth century from the stratigraphical and other archaeological evidence.[38] It has been claimed, however, that viticulture did and does not exist on the Anatolian plateau "on account of its altitude and harsh continental climate."[39] This misconception appears to be based partly on a famous passage in one of the *Letters* of Leo of Synada, in which the bishop complains of the lack of olive oil and wine in his see, and partly on a misunderstanding of the habitats of wild and cultivated vines.[40] The wild olive, too, is found only

---

to Amorium; A. O. Alp and M. D. Çağlar, "Eskişehir-Han İlçesi ve Başara Köyü Kazıları," *KazSonTop* 30.1 (2009): 192–93.

33 The rural settlements of southeastern Isauria, some of which were large enough to have been given the status of a *komopolis*, are imprecisely dated but appear to have reached the peak of their prosperity in the sixth century: Varinlioğlu, "Living in a Marginal Environment," 308–12. The villages and farms of Byzantine Anatolia were probably similar, at least in the sixth century, to those in Palestine in their size, layout, and function: Y. Hirschfeld, "Farms and Villages in Byzantine Palestine," *DOP* 51 (1997): 70–71.

34 R. Bondoux, "Les villes," in *La Bithynie au Moyen Âge*, ed. Geyer and Lefort, 408.

35 For the importance of Nicaea, capital of the theme of Opsikion, see M. Angold, "The City Nicaea ca. 1000–ca. 1400," in *İznik throughout History*, ed. I. Akbaygil, H. İnalcık, and O. Aslanapa (Istanbul, 2003), 27–28, and C. Foss, "The Walls of Iznik," ibid., 252–54. For Nikomedeia, see C. Foss, *Survey of Medieval Castles of Anatolia*, vol. 2, *Nicomedia* (London, 1996), 16–18.

36 C. Foss, *Survey of Medieval Castles of Anatolia*, vol. 1, *Kütahya* (Oxford, 1985), 3. Little trace of the Byzantine city below the castle has been found or recorded.

37 For a survey of Byzantine shipwrecks, confirming the absence of any examples that can be "confidently assigned" to the latter part of the seventh and the eighth century, see F. van Doorninck Jr., "Byzantine Shipwrecks," in *EHB* 2:902.

38 Lightfoot, "Trade and Industry," 273–74, figs. 2–3; C. Lightfoot, O. Koçyiğit, and H. Yaman, "Amorium Kazısı 2005," *KazSonTop* 28.1 (2007): 275–76, 281, pls. 4–5, 7; C. Lightfoot, O. Koçyiğit, and H. Yaman, "Amorium Kazısı 2006," *KazSonTop* 29.1 (2008): 450, pl. 9; C. S. Lightfoot, "Excavations at Amorium: Results from the Last Ten Years (1998–2008)," in Vorderstrasse and Roodeberg, eds., *Archaeology of the Countryside*, 141–42, figs. 6–7, 10. For full discussion of the archaeological contexts, see E. A. Ivison, "Excavations at the Lower City Enclosure, 1996–2008," in Lightfoot and Ivison, eds., *Amorium Reports* 3, esp. 29–60.

39 J. Lefort, "The Rural Economy, Seventh–Twelfth Centuries," in *EHB* 2:249. For rock-cut installations identified as wine presses of indeterminate date in western Phrygia, see T. T. Sivas, "Survey of Phrygian Settlements and Rock-cut Monuments in Western Phrygia," in *The Mysterious Civilization of the Phrygians*, ed. H. and T. T. Sivas (Istanbul, 2007), 77–92, esp. 88–89.

40 *Ep.* 43, in *The Correspondence of Leo, Metropolitan of Synada and Syncellus*, ed., trans., and comm. M. P. Vinson, CFHB 23 (Washington, D.C., 1985), 68–70; see also Cheynet and Drew-Bear, "Une inscription d'Akroïnos," 217 n. 6; Lightfoot, "Excavations at Amorium," 139. Maps showing the distribution range of the wild grapevine do indeed indicate that it is not found on the Anatolian plateau, although the cultivated vine thrives there; see D. Zohary, "The Domestication of the Grapevine *Vitis vinifera* L.

Figure 7.5. Installation C, comprising a pressing tank, screw press weight, and dismantled stone spout used for the collecting vat, located southeast of the bathhouse and west of the Byzantine street (photo by author)

in western and southern Anatolia and, although the domesticated variety grows inland, it is not as common on the plateau as the vine.[41] Today there are vineyards but no olive groves in the countryside around Amorium.[42] Furthermore, there is no doubt

from the configuration of the various installations that they were used for treading and pressing grapes (see fig. 7.6) and not for processing olives.

The precise extent and capacity of the installations does not concern us here, except insofar as their existence implies large-scale production for commercial purposes. Their creation in the mid-seventh century and use during the eighth century presupposes not only a flourishing countryside but also the existence of several subsidiary industries, including that of local haulers, needed to bring the vintage into the city. In addition, various components were necessary and these required different skills, ranging from the digging of nearby wells to the supply of stone troughs, lever supports, and press weights. The latter are to be found scattered throughout the Anatolian countryside and, although some may belong to the Roman period, it is clear that many are of Byzantine date,

---

in the Near East," in *The Origins and Ancient History of Wine*, ed. P. E. McGovern, S. J. Fleming, and S. H. Katz (Amsterdam, 1996), 24, map 2.1; P. E. McGovern, *Ancient Wine: The Search for the Origins of Viniculture* (Princeton, N.J., 2003), 2, map 2.

41 J.-P. Brun, *Le vin et l'huile dans la Méditerranée antique: Viticulture, oléiculture et procédés de transformation* (Paris, 2003), 123–26; S. Mitchell, "Olive Cultivation in the Economy of Roman Asia Minor," in Mitchell and Katsari, eds., *Patterns in the Economy of Asia Minor*, 83–93; Laiou and Morrisson, *The Byzantine Economy*, 109; 10, map 2. For olive cultivation around Sagalassos, see Vanhaverbeke and Waelkens, *Chora of Sagalassos*, 53–55.

42 The same is true at Çadır Höyük in the modern province of Yozgat, where Byzantine levels have also been excavated: A. Smith, "Plant Use at Çadır Höyük, Central Anatolia," *Anatolica* 33 (2007): 170–71, table 2. See also S. M. Paley, "The Excavations at Çadır Höyük, 2004," *KazSonTop* 27.1 (2006): 355–57, figs. 12–14; idem, "The Excavations at Çadır Höyük," *KazSonTop* 28.1 (2007): 520–24, figs. 3–6. New survey work at Euchaita (Avkat) has also provided evidence for cereal and wine produc-

tion, whereas the olive does not grow in the region; J. Haldon, H. Elton, and J. Newhard, "The Avkat Archaeological Project," *AnatArch* 14 (2008): 20.

Figure 7.6. Installations E and F, grape-treading floors, located east of the Byzantine street (photo by E. Schoolman)

since these examples bear decorative crosses or have been carved out of reused Roman funerary stelae (fig. 7.7).[43] Large terra-cotta storage jars or *pithoi* are also associated with the wine-making installations at Amorium, which may be taken to indicate that pottery production continued at the site in the dark ages. On the other hand, there is very little evidence for the use of amphorae at Amorium, a fact that has caused some surprise among scholars who are used to studying amphorae as indicators of trade and industry.[44] Yet, here again one is trapped by what might be called the "maritime mind-set." Transport amphorae are regarded as ubiquitous, having been found on innumerable coastal sites and shipwrecks, but in fact they are less than ideal containers for transporting liquids such as wine over long distances by land.[45] Carts with wooden barrels would undoubtedly have made more sense in central Anatolia, but there is little trace in the archaeological record of such items

---

43 C. S. Lightfoot, "Stone Screw Press Weights," in *Amorium Reports,* vol. 2, *Research Papers and Technical Reports,* ed. idem, BAR International Series 1170 (Oxford, 2003), 73–77, esp. pls. V/7–8, 10–12. A screw press weight from Çaykoz near Pessinus is made out of a marble statue base of the second half of the second century: I. Claerhout and J. Devreker, *Pessinous, Sacred City of the Anatolian Mother Goddess: An Archaeological Guide* (Istanbul, 2008), 138–39. For an honorific inscription to Constantine I, dated 324–27, that was later reused as a press weight, see French, *Inscriptions of Ankara,* 88, no. 4 (where the recarving is regarded as "recent"). The same stone is elsewhere stated to have been recut in late antiquity but is seen as a type "exclusively used for producing olive oil": Mitchell, *Olive Cultivation,* 92. In Bithynia similar stone press weights are attributed to the Roman and "proto-Byzantine" periods: A. Pralong, "Matériel archéologique errant," in *La Bithynie au Moyen Âge,* ed. Geyer and Lefort, 246–47, nos. 71, 78.

44 B. Böhlendorf-Arslan, "Stratified Byzantine Pottery from the City Wall in the Southwestern Sector of Amorium," in *Çanak: Late Antique and Medieval Pottery and Tiles in Mediterranean Archaeological Contexts,* ed. eadem, A. O. Uysal, and J. Witte-Orr, Proceedings of the First International Symposium on Late Antique, Byzantine, Seljuk, and Ottoman Pottery and Tiles in Archaeological Contexts (Çanakkale, 1–3 June 2005), Byzas 7 (Istanbul, 2007), 291.

45 The same conclusion has also been drawn with regard to the transportation of olive oil overland: Mitchell, *Olive Cultivation,* 98.

Figure 7.7. Press weight at Pessinus (photo by author, courtesy of the Pessinus Excavations)

as wine casks and wineskins.[46] This, indeed, may be taken as a cautionary tale, for whereas the Roman and late antique worlds were filled with mass-produced material goods of a basically indestructible nature (fine ware pottery and mold-made lamps, for example), during the less affluent dark ages it is possible that more goods were made from organic materials that are not so well preserved in archaeological contexts.

Silk is one such material that is well known, both from the literary sources and remaining examples. The centers of production and the international trade that linked Byzantium with both the West and the Islamic world have been much discussed.[47] Dress clearly played an important role in Byzantine society as a signifier of rank and wealth, and expensive items of silk clothing were readily available, at least in the markets of the more important urban centers. Yet relatively little silk has been recovered from Byzantine contexts. Indeed, one recent study states that "no high-status Byzantine sarcophagi have been discovered with surviving remains" and so doubts "the Byzantine use of silk to encase relics or important corpses."[48] At Amorium the remains of embroidered silk shrouds and garments, some decorated with gold thread, have been found in two of the graves excavated in the narthex of Church A.[49] Both tombs can be dated to the middle Byzantine period between the late ninth and the mid-eleventh century. They attest not only to the wealth and high social status of those buried in them but also to the availability of fine silks to wear, even in death, at places that might be regarded as remote from the sophistication of Constantinople. Texts tell of ceremonies in the capital on major religious holidays at which silk garments are both worn by and handed out as gifts to members of the imperial court.[50] The Amorium finds indicate nothing so grand, although they clearly demonstrate on a lower level the importance of the wearing and display of such garments in a distinctly urban context.

---

46 The *Life* of Lazaros of Galesion mentions the transportation of wine in containers made of animal hide; see K. Smyrlis, *La fortune des grands monastères byzantins: Fin du Xe–milieu du XIVe siècle*, Monographies du Centre de Recherche d'Histoire et Civilisation de Byzance 21 (Paris, 2006), 222. I am very grateful to Professor Kostis Smyrlis for bringing this reference to my attention.

47 See, for example, N. Oikonomidès, "Silk Trade and Production in Byzantium from the Sixth to the Ninth Century: The Seals of *Kommerkiarioi*," *DOP* 40 (1986): 33–53; G. C. Maniatis, "Organization, Market Structure, and Modus Operandi of the Private Silk Industry in Tenth-Century Byzantium," *DOP* 53 (1999): 263–332; D. Jacoby, "Silk Economics and Cross-Cultural Artistic Interaction: Byzantium, the Muslim World, and the Christian West," *DOP* 58 (2004): 197–240.

48 L. Brubaker, "The Elephant and the Ark: Cultural and Material Interchange across the Mediterranean in the Eight and Ninth Centuries," *DOP* 58 (2004): 194.

49 Lightfoot, "Trade and Industry," 276–77; P. Linscheid, "Middle Byzantine Textiles from Amorium, Anatolia," *Archaeological Textiles Newsletter* 38 (2004): 25–27; P. Linscheid, "Middle Byzantine Textiles from Excavations at Amorium, Turkey," in *Methods of Dating Ancient Textiles of the 1st Millennium AD from Egypt and Neighbouring Countries: Proceedings of the 4th Meeting of the Study Group "Textiles from the Nile Valley," Antwerp, 16–17 April 2005*, ed. A. de Moor and C. Fluck (Tielt, 2007), 88–96. More textiles, yet to be studied and analyzed, were recovered from tombs on the south side of Church A in the 2008 and 2009 seasons; see C. Lightfoot, "Amorium 2009," *AnatArch* 15 (2009): 24.

50 Philotheus, *Listes de préséance*, ed. and trans. N. Oikonomidès (Paris, 1972), 203; *Liutprandi Cremonensis Antapodosis, homelia paschalis, historia Ottonis, relatio de legatione Constantinopolitana*, ed. P. Chiese (Turnhout, 1998), 6.10. I wish to thank Dr. Cécile Morrisson for bringing these references to my attention.

Other organic goods are also attested. There is, for example, archaeological evidence for the production of luxury leather goods, perhaps even astrakhan, at a workshop also dated to the middle Byzantine period and located just to the north of Church A.[51] How much commercial activity these finds represent is hard to judge, but, as in other periods, long-distance trade in such luxury goods must have been a relatively minor part of the local economy. Other pieces of evidence, however, suggest that a wide variety of goods found their way to Amorium in Byzantine times. Arab medical texts, for example, mention that among the various plants and drugs that were obtained from the Byzantines, sweet flag (*Acorus calamus* L.) came specifically from Amorium.[52] It is uncertain whether the plant was grown and processed there, although there is as yet no evidence for its presence among the archaeobotanical residues that have been studied at the site; but in more general terms, it does show that Anatolia played an important and otherwise unsuspected role in Byzantine commercial activity.

Books, too, may have had a part in such international trade, and they apparently formed part of the booty taken from Amorium in 838.[53] Although no remains of parchment have been found, the excavations have produced a number of bronze bookbinding pins (SF2935, SF3615, SF3666, and SF5514) and, in 2008, a bronze book ring (SF8271) (fig. 7.8), used to secure the cover with straps.[54] Sadly, such small items

Figure 7.8. Bronze book ring, found during excavations in the Church A complex (photo by E. Schoolman)

are often overlooked or misinterpreted, but it would not be altogether surprising to find more examples in the collections of local Turkish museums.[55] There can be no doubt that although the level of literacy may have declined, Byzantine Anatolia was not completely illiterate. Inscriptions of the standard (Roman) types—honorific, dedicatory, and funerary—become extremely rare, but there is enough evidence to suggest that the written word continued to impart its meaning to at least some of the population that lived on the central plateau. The clergy, tax collectors, and imperial administrators were always literate; stone carvers and fresco painters also continued to add names, dates, and other information to their work.[56] Graffiti and inscribed stamps found on Byzantine coarse ware pottery from Amorium shed

---

51 Lightfoot, "Trade and Industry," 275–76, fig. 6.

52 This information derives from a paper presented at the Thirty-second Byzantine Studies Conference; see K. Durak, "Arabic Pharmacological Literature: An Alternative Source of Evidence for Byzantine-Arab Commerce in the Early Middle Ages," in *Thirty-Second Byzantine Studies Conference, November 10–12, 2006, The University of Missouri–St. Louis, Abstracts*, 24.

53 The latter information comes from Prof. Irfan Shahîd; compare Brubaker, "The Elephant and the Ark," 182, attributing such booty to the capture of Ankara and Amorium by Hārūn al-Rashīd in the 790s. For philosophical, medical, and scientific books sought in Byzantium by the Arabs, see H. Kennedy, *When Baghdad Ruled the Muslim World: The Rise and Fall of Islam's Greatest Dynasty* (Cambridge, Mass., 2005), 255–56.

54 Bookbinding pins found elsewhere include examples from the acropolis at Xanthos and, seemingly, the Church of St. Nicholas at Demre: J. des Courtils and D. Laroche, "Xanthos—Le Letoon: Rapport sur la campagne de 1998," *Anatolia Antiqua* 7 (1999): 376, fig. 4; S. Y. Ötüken, "2004 Yılı Aziz Nikolaos Kilisesi Kazısı ve Duvar Resimlerini Belgeleme, Koruma-Onarım Çalışmaları," *KazSonTop* 27.1 (2006): 299, pl. 3. Compare *DOCat* 2:96–97, no. 142, pl. 66 (said to have been found in Constantinople). Book pins have also been found at sites in Italy, including

Byzantine Otranto; see L. Allason-Jones, "The Small Finds," in *Excavations at the Molia di Monte Gelato: A Roman and Medieval Settlement in South Etruria*, ed. T. W. Potter, A. C. King, et al., British School at Rome Archaeological Monograph Series 11 (London, 1997), 244, no. 22, fig. 171; A. J. Hicks and M. J. Hicks, "The Small Objects," in *Excavations at Otranto*, vol. 2, *The Finds*, ed. F. D'Andria and D. Whitehouse (Lecce, 1992), 291, no. 38, fig. 10:5. Another book pin was found during the Iznik kiln excavations at Nicaea in 2008: Dr. V. Belgin Demirsar Arlı, personal communication.

55 For a pin and ring from Pliska, see J. Henning and L. Dontcheva-Petkova, *Parvoprestolna Pliska: 100 Godini archeologitcheski Proutchvanija* (Frankfurt am Main, 1999), 42–43, nos. 67–68, pl. 6. For finds from the Crimean Chersonesus, see J. A. Szirmai, *The Archaeology of Medieval Bookbinding* (Aldershot, 1999), fig. 6.15. Three book rings, initially misidentified as belt buckles, have been recorded in the Afyonkarahisar Museum: M. Lightfoot, "Belt Buckles from Amorium and in the Afyon Archaeological Museum," in *Amorium Reports* 2:87, nos. 21–23, pls. VI/27–29.

56 For inscribed fresco fragments from Church A, see Johanna Witte-Orr's report in C. S. Lightfoot, Y. Mergen, B. Y. Olcay, and

further light on this aspect of daily life. Indeed, literacy is an important factor in any attempt to assess the commercial viability of a community, although in most cases all that now remains of the account books, inventory lists, sales of contract, and so on are the lead seals of the *kommerkiarioi*.[57]

The excavations at Amorium provide a rare glance into other aspects of activity. At one level the almost constant refurbishment of Church A in the tenth and eleventh centuries called on the skills of architects, stone masons, mosaicists, and fresco painters. It is impossible to tell if these professionals and craftsmen were drawn from a local labor pool or brought in from elsewhere, but some of their materials as well as their technical skills and artistic influences can be traced to the wider world. So, for example, analyses of the pigments used to color the middle Byzantine carved stones and frescoes found in the church revealed that in addition to common, presumably local, ingredients such as red ocher and charcoal, the craftsmen were able to use more unusual and exotic pigments such as gamboge and ultramarine.[58] Both of these would appear to have been obtained through trade from the Far East. At the other end of the scale, the evidence provided by the numerous examples of middle Byzantine glass bracelets and wheel-made terra-cotta lamps found at Amorium shows that the local population shared many of the small items of material culture with other communities across Anatolia.[59]

Any surpluses produced from the land in central Anatolia during the Byzantine period would obviously have been converted by means of trade and exchange into wealth, and this in turn would have stimulated the local economy as well as being filtered back to the capital and the imperial treasury. Such gains may not have been great, especially in the dark ages, but those to whom any surplus wealth accrued should not necessarily be regarded as behaving in the same way as the local elites of earlier times. Lavish self-promotion by means of public building projects, honorific statues, and inscriptions was no longer the norm, so it is not surprising that we cannot trace such evidence after the sixth century.[60] Stone working and construction work did not cease, however, as the numerous carved stone church furnishings that litter the Anatolian countryside attest.[61] It has been suggested that no stone was quarried during the dark ages, but this surely cannot be the whole truth, even if builders could often draw on large quantities of spolia from ruined or abandoned Roman and early Byzantine buildings.[62] At Amorium, in fact, apart from the frequent reuse of Roman tombstones (especially in the first-phase fortification wall around the Upper City mound), there is relatively little evidence for spolia from the Roman imperial period. Most is recycled Byzantine material.[63] Similarly, it is certain that the use of tiled roofs remained prevalent in the dark ages for buildings of all types at Amorium, and it therefore may be assumed that the production of bricks and tiles persisted throughout the Byzantine period.[64] The larger, public buildings were still constructed of masonry and brick, but the fact that the small workshops and domestic quarters had

---

J. Witte-Orr, "The Amorium Project: Research and Excavation in 2000," *DOP* 57 (2003): 284–85, figs. 9–10.

57 No lead seals of kommerkiarioi have been found as yet at Amorium. For seals naming Amorium, see *DOSeals* 3:166–67, nos. 88.1–4. For kommerkiarioi of the Anatolikoi, see *Studies in Byzantine Sigillography*, ed. N. Oikonomides, vol. 3 (Washington, D.C., 1999), 172 (see no. 8), 179–80 (see no. 1766). I thank Dr. Olga Karagiorgou for her help and advice on this subject.

58 E. A. Hendrix, "Painted Polychromy on Carved Stones from the Lower City Church," in *Amorium Reports* 2:132; J. Witte-Orr, "Technical Study of Frescoes and Mosaics from the Lower City Church," ibid., 147; M. Wypyski, "Analysis of the Pigments Used in the Lower City Church Frescoes," ibid., 157–58.

59 For the glass bracelets, see C. S. Lightfoot, "Glass Finds at Amorium," *DOP* 59 (2005): 179–80; for the lamps, see my comments in M. A. V. Gill, "Middle Byzantine Terracotta Lamps," in *Amorium Reports* 2:67.

60 As, for example, is noted for Bithynia; see Pralong, "Matériel archéologique errant," 225–26.

61 For examples found in Phrygia, see E. Parman, *Ortaçağda Bizans Döneminde Frigya (Phrygia) ve Bölge Müzelerindeki Bizans Taş Eserleri* (Eskişehir, 2002); P. Niewöhner, "Frühbyzantinische Steinmetzarbeiten in Kütahya: Zu Topographie, Steinmetzwesen und Siedlungsgeschichte einer zentralanatolische Region," *IstMitt* 56 (2006): 407–73. For epigraphic evidence, see Cheynet and Drew-Bear, "Une inscription d'Akroïnos"; Ivison, "Amorium in the Byzantine Dark Ages," 30.

62 Laiou and Morrisson, *The Byzantine Economy*, 64.

63 For example, Lightfoot, Mergen, et al., "Amorium Project, 2000," 289, fig. 14; Lightfoot, Arbel, et al., "Amorium Project, 2002," 245–46, 257–58, figs. 14–15, 22–3; C. S. Lightfoot, O. Karagiorgou, O. Koçyiğit, H. Yaman, P. Linscheid, and J. Foley, "The Amorium Project: Excavation and Research in 2003," *DOP* 61 (2007): 374–76, fig. 27.

64 Lightfoot, "Trade and Industry," 279–80, fig. 10; J. Witte-Orr, "Bricks and Tiles from the Triangular Tower at Amorium," in Böhlendorf-Arslan, Uysal, and eadem, eds., *Çanak: Late Antique and Medieval Pottery and Tiles*, 295–308. It has, however, been argued that "in the countryside . . . tiles disappeared in favour of wooden planks or thatch for roofing": Laiou and Morrisson, *The Byzantine Economy*, 40.

dry-stone or mud-brick walls on stone foundations does not necessarily signal "impoverishment." These were the age-old materials and techniques used for such construction on the Anatolian plateau, and there is unfortunately little evidence to say if Roman housing in Phrygia was any different.

Other major aspects of commercial enterprise include the production of pottery and metalwork. Ken Dark's *Byzantine Pottery* rightly draws attention to the ubiquitous nature of pottery both in Byzantine daily life and in the archaeological record.[65] At Amorium the finds of pottery sherds are more numerous than any other category of material, and although some clearly belong to other periods, the vast majority of these sherds can be securely placed in the Byzantine period. The finds of coarse wares vastly outnumber those of fine wares, and of the latter only a small proportion can be identified as imports. The first sherd of Constantinopolitan Petal Ware to be recorded at Amorium (fig. 7.9) was found only during the 2008 season.[66] However, the fact that much of the Byzantine pottery found at Amorium was probably produced locally proves not that inland patterns of trade and distribution had changed markedly since Roman and early Byzantine times but only that they were much reduced in scale after the mid-seventh century. Indeed, the "mysterious" jars with multiple handles found in a ninth-century destruction layer behind the Lower City walls are not unique to Amorium; two examples are also known from Kastamonu in Paphlagonia.[67] I would argue, therefore, that the focus on coastal sites and maritime trade has distorted our perspective and led to a misunderstanding of the way in which inland markets operated on a more regional and local basis. I am not aware, for example, that in the early Byzan-

Figure 7.9. Small fragment of glazed Petal Ware, found during excavations in the Church A complex (photo by E. Schoolman)

tine period African Red Slip Ware reached sites on the Anatolian plateau in any great quantity.

International trade in Byzantine metalwork has attracted much more attention than the mechanisms that allowed this industry to survive and flourish in the domestic market.[68] But continued traditions of metalworking may suggest a relatively greater use of copper vessels and utensils during the dark ages, since tablewares of imported pottery and glass were no longer readily available.[69] Bronze or copper alloy vessels and objects of the Byzantine period are well represented in Turkey, both at sites and in museums.[70] Nor should these objects be seen in isolation; rather, they formed part of a much larger category of metalwork that included prestige items such as jew-

---

65 K. Dark, *Byzantine Pottery* (Stroud, 2001), 8, 23. For a comprehensive survey of Byzantine glazed pottery from sites in Turkey, including material from Amorium, see B. Böhlendorf-Arslan, *Die glasierte byzantinische Keramik aus der Türkei,* 3 vols. (Istanbul, 2004), 220–25, 424–35, nos. 391–446, pls. 104–10.

66 Lightfoot, Ivison, et al., "Amorium Kazıları 2008," 136. For Petal Ware, see Dark, *Byzantine Pottery,* 122–23.

67 Böhlendorf-Arslan, "Stratified Byzantine Pottery," 288–90, nos. 67–70, fig. 12. One of the Kastamonu jars is now in the Istanbul Archaeological Museum, but the other, which remains unpublished, is still in the local museum: *İstanbul Arkeoloji Müzeleri Yıllığı* 3 (1949): 32, fig. 17 (recorded as coming from the *ilçe* of Araç). My thanks go to Dr. Marlia Mundell Mango for bringing this example to my attention.

68 M. Mundell Mango, "Beyond the Amphora: Non-Ceramic Evidence for Late Antique Industry and Trade," in *Economy and Exchange in the East Mediterranean during Late Antiquity: Proceedings of a Conference at Somerville College, Oxford, 29th May, 1999,* ed. S. Kingsley and M. Decker (Oxford, 2001), 87–106.

69 For finds at Amorium, see Lightfoot, Karagiorgou, et al., "Amorium Project, 2003," 358, 360, figs. 10–12.

70 For example, at Beycesultan: G. H. R. Wright, "Some Byzantine Bronze Objects from Beycesultan," *AnatSt* 50 (2000): 165–70; idem, "Beyce Sultan—A Fortified Settlement in Byzantine Phrygia," *Anatolica* 33 (2007): 146, figs. 18–19. For additional comments, see Lightfoot, "Trade and Industry," 282 (esp. n. 44).

Figure 7.10. Pair of gold basket earrings found in Tomb 18 in the atrium of Church A (photo by E. Schoolman)

elry and other personal and devotional ornaments.[71] The find of a pair of gold basket-type earrings (fig. 7.10) in an eleventh-century tomb at Amorium raises interesting questions about continuity of styles and cross-cultural awareness in the Byzantine world. The type has its antecedents in the sixth century as well as parallels in the Islamic world; the earrings from Amorium are directly comparable to a pair in the Tiberias Hoard, for which coins provide a *terminus ante quem* of 1036.[72] Likewise, a number of small pendant bronze crosses have been found in tombs both at Church A and in the extensive cemetery outside the city.[73] Even if these were made locally or by itinerant craftsmen, they belong firmly to a tradition that spanned the empire both chronologically and geographically. The front cover of a reliquary cross or encolpion, found in an extramural tomb at Amorium in 2006, belongs to a well-known and common type.[74] No list of find spots of encolpia in Anatolia can ever be exhaustive, since new examples are constantly turning up, frequently as a result of illicit excavations in the countryside.[75] In addition, no firm conclusions can yet be made about the center(s) of production for the raw metals, the molds, or the crosses themselves, but it should be noted that central Anatolia has not been ruled out as one area in which Byzantine metalworking thrived.[76]

It is, therefore, necessary to reassess the role played by Anatolia in the survival of the Byzantine Empire. The wealth of archaeological evidence that is now slowly coming to light suggests that despite the frequent Arab incursions in the second half of the seventh and throughout the eighth century, some urban centers remained and the countryside continued to provide the basic resources not just for subsistence but also for surplus wealth. Other areas of the empire during the dark ages were less fortunate. For example, although recent studies suggest that Corinth and the rural sites in the Isthmian countryside were able to weather the various storms of plague, earthquake, and invasion during the period from the third through the early seventh century, thereafter "the lights of the Corinthian crossroads dim and go out."[77] The same does not hold true for the Anatolian crossroads.

---

71 The finds of metalwork at Amorium are numerous and varied, including hanging lamp ornaments and censers; they are to be published in a separate report. For similar material found elsewhere, see G. Köroğlu, "Bizans Dönemi Buhurdanları ve Halûk Perk Müzesi'ndeki Örnekler," in *Tuliya*, vol. 1 (Istanbul, 2005), 261–308; S. Atasoy, *Bronze Lamps in the Istanbul Archaeological Museum*, BAR International Series 1436 (Oxford, 2005), 87–91, nos. 146–54; idem, "İstanbul Arkeoloji Müzesi'ndeki el şeklinde bronz kandil/mum taşıyıcılar," in *Muhibbe Darga Armağanı*, ed. T. Tarhan, A. Tibet, and E. Konya (Istanbul, 2008), 109–14; M. Feugère, "An Early Byzantine Chained Ornament from Sulumağara (Islahiye)," in ΠΑΤΡΙΣ ΠΑΝΤΡΟΦΟΣ ΚΟΜΜΑΓΗΝΗ: *Neue Funde und Forschungen zwischen Taurus und Euphrat*, ed. E. Winter, Asia Minor Studies 60 (Bonn, 2008), 283–86.

72 See A. Kirin, ed., *Sacred Art, Secular Context: Objects of Art from the Byzantine Collection of Dumbarton Oaks, Washington, D.C., Accompanied by American Paintings from the Collection of Mildred and Robert Woods Bliss* (Athens, Ga., 2005), 84, no. 31 (with references).

73 C. Lightfoot and E. Ivison, "Amorium 2006," *AnatArch* 12 (2006): 31; Lightfoot, Koçyiğit, and Yaman, "Amorium Kazısı 2005," 273, fig. 2. For examples from Hierapolis, see P. Arthur, *Byzantine and Turkish Hierapolis (Pamukkale): An Archaeological Guide* (Istanbul, 2006), 92, fig. 35.

74 Lightfoot, Koçyiğit, and Yaman, "Amorium Kazısı 2005," 273, pl. 3; see also C. and M. Lightfoot, *Amorium: A Byzantine City in Anatolia: An Archaeological Guide* (Istanbul, 2007), 161. For the same type, see B. Pitarakis, *Les croix-reliquaires pectorales byzantines en bronze*, Bibliothèque des Cahiers archéologiques 16 (Paris, 2006), 195–99, nos. 19–35.

75 Pitarakis, *Croix-reliquaires*, 126–30, fig. 78.

76 Ibid., 175.

77 D. K. Pettegrew, "The Busy Countryside of Late Roman Corinth: Interpreting Ceramic Data Produced by Regional Archaeological Surveys," *Hesp* 76 (2007): 778–79.

• EIGHT •

Byzantine Glazed Ceramics on the Market

An Approach

DEMETRA PAPANIKOLA-BAKIRTZI

THE PROGRESS MADE IN RECENT YEARS IN the study of Byzantine ceramics is evident. The increasing number of books that, even if they do not have Byzantine ceramics as their subject, have been given a cover depicting ceramic vessels of this period is sufficient to demonstrate at a glance the broader interest that the ceramics of the Byzantine world have lately attracted.[1] This interest has been shown not only by historians of art, curators of museums, and those studying everyday life but also by other historians, particularly those specializing in the economic history of Byzantium.

The aim of the present chapter is to draw information from the recent progress in the study of Byzantine glazed pottery in order to contribute to the consideration of the subject under discussion—trade and markets in Byzantium—by using glazed ceramics to instantiate economic patterns. This is not the first time that evidence for trade relations, routes, and commercial transactions has been provided by the location of ceramic products a long way from their point of production.[2] But beyond the presentation of new archaeological data that might enrich the map of the movement of ceramic glazed wares, this chapter principally attempts to investigate the

This essay is dedicated to the memory of Angeliki Laiou, an enthusiastic friend of Byzantine ceramics who introduced me to the exciting world of Byzantine economic history and encouraged my participation in the Dumbarton Oaks Spring Symposium.

Both my presentation and essay benefited by the generous help and support of the symposiarch, Cécile Morrisson. I am also indebted to Alice-Mary Talbot for her valuable comments. Many thanks go to Sylvie-Yona Waksman for her kind assistance on archaeometric issues, as well as to Lena Demetriadou, Aspasia Dina, Anastasia Drandaki, Maria Hatzicosti, Dimitris Nalpantis, Christina Pavlidou, Guy Sanders, Larisa Sendikova, Ioulia Tzonou, and Nikos Zekos for their help in illustrating this article. Finally, my appreciation goes to Irini Papanicolas, Xenophon Moniaros, and Matthew Milliner for their very useful comments and care in editing my text.

1 C. Jouanno, *Digénis Akritas, le héros des frontières: Une épopée byzantine* (Turnhout, 1998); K. Charalambidis, *Δοχίμιν* (Athens, 2000); Niketas Eugenianos, *A Byzantine Novel: Drosilla and Charikles,* ed. and trans. J. B. Burton (Wauconda, Ill., 2004); L. Garland, ed., *Byzantine Women: Varieties of Experience, A.D. 800–1200* (Aldershot, 2006); E. D. Maguire and H. Maguire, *Other Icons: Art and Power in Byzantine Secular Culture* (Princeton, N.J., 2006); A. E. Laiou and C. Morrisson, *The Byzantine Economy* (Cambridge, 2007).

2 D. Pringle, "Pottery as Evidence for Trade in the Crusader States," in *I comuni italiani nel regno crociato latino di Gerusalemme: Atti del Colloquio "The Italian Communes in the Crusading Kingdom of Jerusalem,"* ed. G. Airaldi and B. Z. Kedar (Genoa, 1986), 449–75; P. Armstrong, "From Constantinople to Lakedaimon: Impressed White Wares," in *Mosaic: Festschrift for A. H. S. Megaw,* ed. J. Herrin, M. Mullett, and C. Otten-Froux (London, 2001), 57–67; V. François, "Sur la circulation des céramiques byzantines en Méditerranée orientale et occidentale," in *La céramique médiévale en Méditerranée: Actes du VIe Congrès de l'AIECM2, Aix-en-Provence, 13–18 Novembre 1995* (Aix-en-Provence, 1997), 231–36; eadem, "Réalités des échanges en Méditerranée orientale du XIIe au XIXe s.: L'apport de la céramique," *DOP* 58 (2004): 241–49; V. François and J.-M. Spieser, "Pottery and Glass in Byzantium," in *EHB* 2:585–601; Laiou and Morrisson, *The Byzantine Economy,* 115–21, 184–88; I. Dimopoulos, "Trade of Byzantine Red Wares, End of the 11th–13th Centuries," in *Byzantine Trade, 4th–12th Centuries: The Archaeology of Local, Regional and International Exchange,* ed. M. Mundell Mango, Papers of the Thirty-eighth Spring Symposium of Byzantine Studies, St John's College, University of Oxford, March 2004, Society for the Promotion of Byzantine Studies 14 (Aldershot, 2009), 179–90.

trade and *market* characteristics of Byzantine glazed pottery by studying the products themselves.

The focus here is on tablewares, which constitute the majority of glazed ceramics and were valuable and salable intrinsically and not only for their contents, as was usually the case with amphorae. I will examine their form, size, and decoration and will discuss their "quality" in an effort to determine their trade and market characteristics, affording a deeper understanding of the reasons for and mechanisms of their demand, diffusion, and distribution.

Tablewares for the New Elite (tenth century to first half of the thirteenth century)

From the seventh century onward the lead-glazing technique gradually began to spread, becoming established by the end of the ninth century.[3] This practice allowed new possibilities for ceramics and determined their future course of development. Furthermore, the glazing of ceramic vessels, especially of tableware, influenced their appearance and shaped their trade and market characteristics. For the period from the tenth to the first half of the thirteenth century, the ceramic production from two locations is here examined: the glazed ceramic wares attributed to the workshops of the Byzantine capital itself and the glazed ceramic products of Corinth, a large administrative and commercial center. The ceramic finds from two shipwrecks—one at Pelagonnesos-Alonnesos in the Sporades in the northwest Aegean, the other at Kastellorizo, near the island of Rhodes—are also discussed.

Tablewares from the Capital

A large category of glazed ceramics with characteristic "white" clay has been attributed to Constantinopolitan workshops.[4] Recent excavations related to structures for the Istanbul Metro have brought to light evidence of glazed pottery production near what is now the Sirkeci Railway Station. Archaeologists uncovered what appear to be the remains of a kiln as well as many ceramic wasters, such as uncompleted and deformed vessels.[5] Deformed white fabric vessels, very possibly wasters, point to the existence of related manufacturing activity, at least in the neighboring area. However, the archaeometric analyses of the excavated white fabric ceramic material did not support their attribution to the workshop found at Sirkeci.[6]

David Talbot Rice's pioneering work on Byzantine glazed pottery, Robert Stevenson's publication on the ceramic wares found in the Great Palace, Urs Peschlow's article on the pottery from Hagia Eirene, and more recently John W. Hayes's publication on the pottery found in the excavations of Hagios Polyeuktos (Saraçhane) have provided the classification and typology of Glazed White Ware and a framework for dating it.[7] These glazed ceramics make their appearance as early as the seventh century and have a continuous presence until the middle of the thirteenth century. Over their long history, they present a variety of forms, which mainly correspond to vessels that could have served as table containers for food and drink (fig. 8.1).

The drinking vessels are in the shape of cups or mugs with one or two handles, and thus closely resemble the shape of a skyphos or kantharos. These vessels may also take the form of a small bowl with a low or stemmed foot. Generally, the food vessels are large and shallow dishes. There are also plates with an almost flat body and tall legs, known as "fruit stands," and hemispherical bowls that, because of

---

[3] For problems related to the emergence of glazing technique in Byzantium, see J. W. Hayes, *Excavations at Saraçhane in Istanbul*, vol. 2, *The Pottery* (Princeton, N.J., 1992), 13, 15; S. Y. Waksman, A. Bouquillon, N. Cantin, and I. Katona, "Approche archéométrique des premières 'Byzantine Glazed White Ware' et de productions glaçurées romaines et romaines tardives," *Rei Cretariae Romanae Acta* 40 (2007): 1–6; eidem, "The First Byzantine 'Glazed White Wares' in the Early Medieval Technological Context," in *Archaeometric and Archaeological Approaches to Ceramics*, ed. S. Y. Waksman, BAR International Series 1691 (Oxford, 2007), 129–35.

[4] Hayes, *Excavations at Saraçhane*, 2:12–37.

[5] Ç. Girgin, "Sirkeci'de sürdürülen kazı çalışmalarından elde edilen sonuçlar," in *Gün Işığında: İstanbul'un 8000 yılı: Marmaray, Metro, Sultanahmet kazıları* (Istanbul, 2007), 97–105.

[6] S. Y. Waksman and Ç. Girgin, "Les vestiges de production de céramiques des fouilles de Sirkeci (Istanbul): Premiers éléments de caractérisation," *Anatolia Antiqua* 16 (2008): 458, 467–68, figs. 25b, d, e, f.

[7] D. T. Rice, *Byzantine Glazed Pottery* (Oxford, 1930); R. B. K. Stevenson, "The Pottery, 1936–1937," in *The Great Palace of the Byzantine Emperors, Being a First Report on the Excavations Carried out in Istanbul on Behalf of the Walker Trust (The University of St Andrews, 1935–1938)* (Oxford, 1947), 1:38–50, pls. 16, 17, 22; U. Peschlow, "Byzantinische Keramik aus Istanbul: Ein Fundkomplex bei der Irenenkirche," *IstMitt* 27–28 (1977–78): 363–414; Hayes, *Excavations at Saraçhane*, 2:12–37.

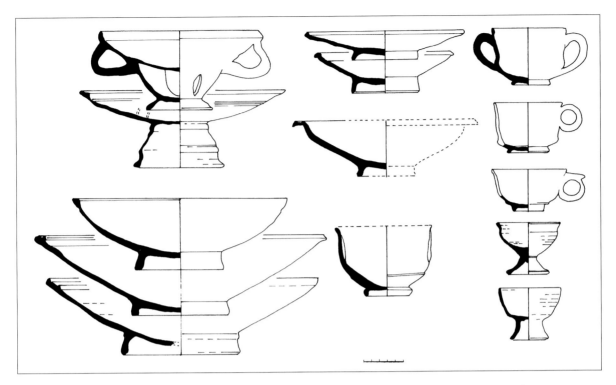

Figure 8.1. Forms of Glazed White Wares (line drawing by C. Malia after Hayes, *Excavations at Saraçhane;* Morgan, *The Byzantine Pottery;* and Papanikola-Bakirtzi, Mavrikiou, and Bakirtzis, *Byzantine Glazed Pottery in the Benaki Museum*)

their shape and size, must have been used as vessels for the serving of communal food rather than as individual crockery. Apart from the ordinary dishes and bowls, there are some other forms of vessels, such as the *saltzaria* or *gararia* (chafing dishes),[8] that were also communal and served a particular purpose. As is well known, these were self-heating vessels, used to keep sauces hot at the table. The sauces were made from animal fats and included the famous garum, made mainly of fish blood.[9]

The variety of the forms (fig. 8.1), on the one hand, and the presence of a number of specialized vessels on the other indicate a way of life and of eating that might be called demanding, refined, and "urbane." Within this context one can recognize the existence of an elite dining culture, which used a variety of vessels as well as cutlery (sets of forks and knives).[10] Study of the decoration of these vessels attributed to the capital's workshops makes another aspect of their character apparent. The most dominant type of decoration clearly imitates the ornamentation on metal utensils, both in their decorative effects and in their iconography. The effort is obvious and the result is quite successful. For example, it is evident that the relief decoration of the largest group of the white clay Constantinopolitan tablewares (Glazed White Ware II), which was achieved

8 Ch. Bakirtzis, Βυζαντινά Τσουκαλολάγηνα, 2nd ed. (Athens, 2003), 55–65; for a discussion on chafing dishes from Corinth, see G. D. R. Sanders, "New Relative and Absolute Chronologies for 9th- to 13th-Century Glazed Wares at Corinth: Methodology and Social Conclusions," in *Byzanz als Raum: Zu Methoden und Inhalten der historischen Geographie des östlichen Mittelmeerraumes im Mittelalter*, ed. K. Belke, F. Hild, J. Koder, and P. Soustal (Vienna, 2000), 165.

9 *Geoponica sive Cassiani Bassi scholastici De re rustica eclogae* 20.40, ed. H. Beckh (Leipzig, 1895); for the trade of fish sauce in amphorae during late antiquity and earlier, see A. Opaiţ, "A Weighty Matter: Pontic Fish Amphorae," in *Transport Amphorae and Trade in the Eastern Mediterranean*, ed. J. Eiring and J. Lund (Aarhus, 2004), 101–21.

10 I. Anagnostakis and T. Papamastorakis, "'. . . and Radishes for Appetizers': On Banquets, Radishes, and Wine," in Βυζαντινών διατροφή και μαγειρίαι: Πρακτικά ημερίδας "Περί της διατροφής στο Βυζάντιο," ed. D. Papanikola-Bakirtzi (Athens, 2005), 147–48.

with a stamp or a mold,[11] follows a model of relief decoration on *anaglypha asēmia* (silver vessels),[12] imitating the result attained by repoussage in metal objects of this kind. Geometric motifs, themes from the plant and animal kingdoms, and, more rarely, human figures appear in relief, usually on the bottom of the clay vessels, below the yellow or, more rarely, green glaze. For example, we can observe a close resemblance between the relief decoration of the twelfth-century silver bowl from Beryozovo,[13] now in the State Hermitage Museum, and the relief decoration of glazed white ceramic vessels depicting animals (fig. 8.2).[14] The quality of the relief motifs on clay vessels is frequently poor, and in some cases the patterns are hardly recognizable. As a result, their decorative role is often minimized, and emphasis is placed instead on their apotropaic function and meaning.[15] However, the two purposes are not mutually exclusive: nothing prevents a decorative pattern from serving an apotropaic role even in ceramic vessels with hardly readable designs.[16] In my opinion, the low quality of these motifs can be explained by the abrasion and the wear of the stamps or molds used in the decorative process. Furthermore, the lack of clarity in the decorative motifs could be attributed

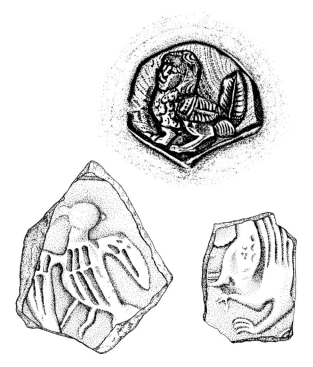

Figure 8.2. Relief decoration on metal and ceramic vessels (drawing by T. Zontanos after photos in Maguire, "The Feasting Cycle," fig. 5, and Papanikola-Bakirtzi, Mavrikiou, and Bakirtzis, *Byzantine Glazed Pottery in the Benaki Museum,* cat. nos. 51 and 59)

11   Hayes, *Excavations at Saraçhane,* 2:18–29; Armstrong, "From Constantinople to Lakedaimon," 63–64; D. Papanikola-Bakirtzi, P. Mavrikiou, and C. Bakirtzis, *Byzantine Glazed Pottery in the Benaki Museum* (Athens, 1999), 37.
12   M. Mundell Mango, "From 'Glittering Sideboard' to Table: Silver in the Well-appointed *triclinium*," in *Eat, Drink, and Be Merry (Luke 12:19)—Food and Wine in Byzantium: Papers of the 37th Annual Spring Symposium of Byzantine Studies in Honour of Professor A. A. M. Bryer,* ed. L. Brubaker and K. Linardou, Society for the Promotion of Byzantine Studies 13 (Birmingham, 2003), 137.
13   V. P. Darkevich, *Svetskoe iskusstvo Vizantii* (Moscow, 1975), 193–94, fig. 299; *Sinai, Byzantium, Russia: Orthodox Art from the Sixth to the Twentieth Century,* ed. Y. Piatnisky et al. (St. Petersburg, 2000), 91, no. B68.
14   For the interpretation of this depiction, see H. Maguire, "The Feasting Cycle and the Meanings of Hybrids in Byzantine Ceramics," in *VIIe Congrès International sur la Céramique Médiévale en Méditerranée, Thessaloniki, 11–16 Octobre 1999: Actes,* ed. Ch. Bakirtzis (Athens, 2003), 205–10; Maguire and Maguire, *Other Icons,* 47–55.
15   V. François, "Ὕπαγε Σατανα: Des fonctions apotropaïque et prophylactique de la vaisselle de table à Byzance," *CahArch* 51 (2003–04): 58. Their function as control devices to identify products of individual potters or workshops was suggested by John Hayes; see Hayes, *Excavations at Saraçhane,* 2:21.
16   H. Maguire, "The Feasting Cycle," 205–10; Maguire and Maguire, *Other Icons,* 74–82.

to a short delay in stamping the soft clay. The existence of relief motifs inside closed forms, such as in the interior of chafing dishes lids, can be explained by the simple observation that these vessels were not always closed.

If we look at examples of the famous Polychrome Ware (fig. 8.3),[17] a subgroup of Glazed White Wares, we will see that to a large extent they are reminiscent of metal utensils decorated with polychrome enamel (fig. 8.4). Similarities of metalwork with Polychrome Ware have already been pointed out in earlier scholarship.[18] Polychrome Ware also imitates vessels made of gold or silver with precious stones around their

17   D. T. Rice, "The Byzantine Pottery," in *Second Report upon the Excavations Carried Out in and near the Hippodrome of Constantinople on Behalf of the British Academy in 1928,* ed. S. Casson, D. T. Rice, and D. F. Hudson (London, 1929), 29–35; idem, *Byzantine Glazed Pottery,* 10–19, pls. 3–9; Hayes, *Excavations at Saraçhane,* 2:35–37; G. D. R. Sanders, "Byzantine Polychrome Pottery," in J. Herrin, M. Mullett, and C. Otten-Froux, eds., *Mosaic,* 89–103.
18   J. C. Anderson, "Tiles, Books, and the 'Church Like a Bride Adorned with Pearls and Gold'," in *A Lost Art Rediscovered: The Architectural Ceramics of Byzantium,* ed. S. E. J. Gerstel and

Figure 8.3. Polychrome Ware; fragment of bowl found in Corinth (photo courtesy of the American School of Classical Studies at Athens)

Figure 8.4. Clothing pendant decorated with enamel (photo courtesy of the Dumbarton Oaks Byzantine Collection, Washington, DC)

rim. For example, the rendering of the rims of two fragmentary dishes of the Benaki Museum[19] makes it obvious that they are imitating the gem-studded rim of precious vessels such as the paten with the Last Supper in the Louvre and the paten with Christ Blessing in the Procuratoria of San Marco in Venice.[20] Polychrome Ware was found in many places, including—albeit in small quantities—even remote sites, such as Synaxis near Maroneia in Thrace.[21] It has been suggested that an elite demand was behind the diffusion as well as the creation of Polychrome Ware.[22]

The presence of the Constantinopolitan White Wares has been widely recorded. Records illustrate their great diffusion throughout the Byzantine world and beyond,[23] during a period stretching from the eighth to the first half of the thirteenth century. The characteristic milky or chalky color of their clay makes them readily recognizable and is the main reason that they have been easily identified among archaeological finds everywhere. The excavations of the American School of Classical Studies in Corinth, which has carefully recorded and analyzed its finds,[24]

J. A. Lauffenburger (Baltimore and University Park, Pa., 2001), 126–29.

19 Papanikola-Bakirtzi, Mavrikiou, and Bakirtzis, *Byzantine Glazed Pottery in the Benaki Museum,* cat. nos. 15 (inv. no. 13603), 16 (inv. no. 17546).

20 *The Glory of Byzantium: Art and Culture of the Middle Byzantine Era, A.D. 843–1261,* ed. H. C. Evans and W. D. Wixom (New York, 1997), inv. nos. 28, 29.

21 Ch. Bakirtzis and G. Hatzimichalis, Σύναξη Μαρωνείας (Athens, 1991), 124; *Late Byzantine Glazed Pottery from Thrace: Reading the Archaeological Finds,* ed. D. Papanikola-Bakirtzi and N. Zekos (Thessalonike, 2010), 38.

22 Laiou and Morrisson, *The Byzantine Economy,* 76.

23 Hayes, *Excavations at Saraçhane,* 2:12; Armstrong, "From Constantinople to Lakedaimon," 57–58, fig. 6.1, with a list of findspots of White Wares and earlier references; E. D'Amico, "Glazed White Ware in the Italian Peninsula: Proposals for a Study," in *Çanak: Late Antique and Medieval Pottery and Tiles in Mediterranean Archaeological Contexts,* ed. B. Böhlendorf-Arslan, A. Osman Uysal, and J. Witte-Orr, Proceedings of the First International Symposium on Late Antique, Byzantine, Seljuk, and Ottoman Pottery and Tiles in Archaeological Contexts (Çanakkale, 1–3 June 2005), Byzas 7 (Istanbul, 2007), 215–38.

24 The Byzantine ceramics from Corinth have received the fullest study. Glazed ceramic wares in particular attracted early attention and were assigned a volume of their own in the Corinth series by C. H. Morgan, *The Byzantine Pottery,* Corinth 11 (Cambridge, Mass., 1942). Although this publication continues to be a point of reference, its conclusions have been updated and modified by more recent studies; see Sanders, "New Relative and Absolute Chronologies," 153–73; idem, "Recent Developments in the Chronology of Byzantine Corinth," in *Corinth: The Centenary,*

reveal the presence of Constantinopolitan ceramics in an important administrative and commercial center during the period in question. The presence of Constantinopolitan ceramics in Corinth can now be sketched in as follows: they appear sparingly in the latter part of the eighth century but by the early ninth century disappear, perhaps because of Arab raids. In the second half of the tenth century, Glazed White Wares make their reappearance. Constantinopolitan wares were most common in the third quarter of the eleventh century (1050–75), gradually falling off in the final decades of the century. After 1100, imported Constantinopolitan ceramics were essentially sidelined by locally produced wares that flooded the Corinthian market.[25]

The frequency and density of finds of Constantinopolitan White Wares in the capital itself[26] as well as in various other locations like Corinth, where in the third quarter of the eleventh century they constituted almost 80 percent of glazed pottery,[27] indicate a considerable production. A systematic, mainly maritime trade supplied crockery to the markets of the empire's great administrative and commercial centers and, through them, to smaller markets in their periphery.[28] Whether White Wares were the main or the supplementary cargo is difficult to ascertain. It would be wrong to be too dogmatic, since both scenarios are plausible.

Thus, glazed tablewares from the capital—shaped to serve foodstuffs prepared for a discriminating taste, and decorated to imitate precious metal utensils—were widely diffused through systematic trade to meet consumerist demands of a public that had begun to seek a refined way of life and that, it appears, enjoyed a degree of culture and high aesthetic principles. The profile of this public, whose requirements the market met by offering glazed ceramic vessels from the capital, matches the profile of a rising socioeconomic section of the population that had begun to be "urbanized" and to acquire the consciousness of an elite.[29]

Tablewares from the Big City

Returning to Corinth, we can see how and through what mechanisms the production of a "big city"[30] was able to displace the imported tablewares from the capital. Production of glazed ceramic wares in Corinth seems to have begun at the end of the ninth century. Their presence was limited and, as mentioned above, was overshadowed by the glazed wares imported from Constantinople. This picture changed at the end of the eleventh century with the new practice of investing the bare clay with a milky slip coating underneath the glaze,[31] which enabled the local tableware utensils to compete against the great advantage of ceramics made from white clay—their light-colored surface. Such surfaces were always desirable, both because as they are more suitable for decoration and because of their refined appearance. Exploitation of these advantages provided scope for daring decorative proposals with fine results and for the production of articles that competed with the imported wares, reduced their number, and forced them out of the local market. For example, Dark-on-Light Slip-Painted Ware (fig. 8.5) obviously imitates and competes with the Polychrome Ware of the Constantinopolitan workshops (see fig. 8.3). The local workshops were bold enough to develop sgraffito decoration (fig. 8.6) that also successfully imitated metal utensils and thus were able to displace the imported wares in the market. For example, the

---

1896–1996, ed. C. K. Williams II and N. Bookidis, Corinth 20 ([Princeton, N.J.], 2003), 385–99. For the later Byzantine ceramics, see T. Mackay, "More Byzantine and Frankish Pottery from Corinth," *Hesp* 36 (1967): 249–320; G. D. R. Sanders, "An Assemblage of Frankish Pottery at Corinth," *Hesp* 56 (1987): 159–95; C. K. Williams and O. H. Zervos, "Frankish Corinth: 1991," *Hesp* 61 (1992): 133–91; C. K. Williams, "Italian Imports from a Church Complex in Ancient Corinth," in *La ceramica nel mondo bizantino tra XI–XV secolo e i suoi rapporti con l'Italia*, ed. S. Gelichi (Florence, 1993), 263–82.

25 Sanders, "New Relative and Absolute Chronologies," 163–66; idem, "Recent Developments," 390–97.
26 In the excavations of Hagios Polyeuktos the Glazed White Wares occur in massive quantities—more than 20,000-odd sherds; see Hayes, *Excavations at Saraçhane*, 2:12.
27 Sanders, "New Relative and Absolute Chronologies," 164, fig. 5.
28 A. E. Laiou, "Exchange and Trade, Seventh–Twelfth Centuries," in *EHB* 2:746–48; Laiou and Morrisson, *The Byzantine Economy*, 82; for maritime routes, see A. Avramea, "Land and Sea Communications, Fourth–Fifteenth Centuries," in *EHB* 1:77–88.

29 For a definition of the city and of the urban economy during the eleventh and twelfth centuries, see G. Dagron, "The Urban Economy, Seventh–Twelfth Centuries," in *EHB* 2:393–396, 401–5; Laiou and Morrisson, *The Byzantine Economy*, 130–33.
30 For the expansion of the cities from the late eighth to twelfth centuries, see A. E. Laiou, "The Byzantine Economy: An Overview," in *EHB* 3:1147–56.
31 Sanders, "New Relative and Absolute Chronologies," 166; idem, "Recent Developments," 394.

Figure 8.5. Bowl with dark-on-light slip-painted decoration, Corinth (photo courtesy of the American School of Classical Studies at Athens)

Figure 8.6. Unfinished bowl with fine-sgraffito decoration, Corinth (photo courtesy of the American School of Classical Studies at Athens)

Figure 8.7. Bowl with fine-sgraffito decoration of a mounted hunter, Corinth (photo courtesy of the American School of Classical Studies at Athens)

Figure 8.8. Mounted figure on a silver plate of the Alanos treasure (line drawing by C. Malia after Ballian and Drandaki, "Silver Treasure," fig. 3)

sgraffito representation of a mounted falconer on a ceramic bowl from Corinth[32] (fig. 8.7) seems to imitate mounted figures on metal vessels like those on the silver plates of the Konstantinos Alanos treasure (fig. 8.8).[33] Through their quality and decoration, such ceramic wares won over the consumers who, amid other motivations, were seeking refined ware to enhance their social status.

32 E. D. Maguire, "Ceramic Arts of Everyday Life," in *The Glory of Byzantium*, cat. no. 183; P. Armstrong, "Iconographic Observations of Figural Representation on Zeuxippus Ware," in *Ritual and Art: Byzantine Essays for Christopher Walter*, ed. P. Armstrong (London, 2006), 80–81.

33 A. Ballian and A. Drandaki, "A Middle Byzantine Silver Treasure," Μουσείο Μπενάκη 3 (2003): 47–80; Mundell Mango, "From 'Glittering Sideboard' to Table," 139–41.

It is likely that the development in the ceramic market occurring in Corinth was also taking place in most of the other administrative and commercial centers of the empire during the twelfth century. Such development is apparent from the case of Sparta, where there is evidence of local production by the middle of this century.[34] The demand for glazed tableware was initially served by White Wares from Constantinople;[35] local production later replaced these, meeting the needs of a discriminating public that knew how to recognize quality and innovation. The products of both these Peloponnesian workshops, as far as we can observe, not only displaced the Constantinopolitan imports from their own local markets but also began to be exported regionally and interregionally in the Peloponnese and central Greece[36] as well as internationally to other markets abroad, such as those of Italy.[37]

Tablewares from the Big Workshops

THE PELAGONNESOS-ALONNESOS SHIPWRECK
As mentioned above, further information on the character of glazed ceramic wares for the middle Byzantine period has been gleaned from the study of two shipwrecks: one at Pelagonnesos-Alonnesos and the other at Kastellorizo. The 1960 excavation of a ship that sank between Pelagonnesos and Alonnesos in the Northern Sporades around the middle of the twelfth century revealed that its main cargo was glazed ceramic tableware with impressive fine-sgraffito decoration (figs. 8.9 and 8.10).[38] The obvious homogeneity of these ceramics was confirmed by the analysis of their fine-grained, red-orange clay, which was used for all the glazed ceramics from the wreck.[39] The vessels were also homogeneous in form and shape: for the most part, they were relatively large shallow crockery of the plate and dish type with vertical walls, and there were also a few smaller, deep hemispherical bowls. Their fine-sgraffito decoration was of a similar kind, too. On a small number of vessels, the fine-sgraffito decoration was accompanied by painted decoration and belonged to the Painted Fine Sgraffito Ware. It follows, then, that the glazed ceramic wares of Pelagonnesos-Alonnesos that sank in the waters of the northern Aegean were a collection of ceramics from one workshop, or at least from workshops in the same area that used soil from the same geological region.

The key features of the Pelagonnesos-Alonnesos vessels were their high quality and their imitation of metal utensils. The vessels of the shipwreck have meticulous, smooth surfaces; flat floors; and well-formed walls. A great number of them have overall white slip coatings and are glazed inside and out, features that in most Byzantine ceramics were restricted to the interior surface. In its execution, the decoration is characterized by delicate, meticulous, and steady craftsmanship that shows persistent attention to detail. Traces of the use of a compass,[40] which testifies to hand finishing, indicate the special care that was taken over the decoration—possibly in a separate section of a well-organized workshop.[41] Moreover, the quality of the glazing is astonishingly high: the glaze on some of the vessels, even after centuries of immersion in salt seawater, has retained its glossy sheen.

The shapes of the ceramics from the Pelagonnesos-Alonnesos wreck clearly imitate those of metal vessels (see fig. 8.11). A comparison with the limited

---

34 A. Bakourou, E. Katsara, and P. Kalamara, "Argos and Sparta: Pottery of the 12th and 13th Centuries," in Bakirtzis, ed., *VIIe Congrès International sur la Céramique Médiévale en Méditerranée*, 233–34; *Byzantine Glazed Ceramics: The Art of Sgraffito*, ed. D. Papanikola-Bakirtzi (Athens, 1999), 187; J. Dimopoulos, "Byzantine Graffito Wares Excavated in Sparta (12th–13th Centuries)," in Böhlendorf-Arslan, Osman Uysal, and Witte-Orr, eds., *Çanak: Late Antique and Medieval Pottery and Tiles*, 336–42.
35 Armstrong, "From Constantinople to Lakedaimon," 56–67.
36 J. Vroom, *After Antiquity: Ceramics and Society in the Aegean from the 7th to the 20th Century A.C.: A Case Study from Boeotia, Central Greece* (Leiden, 2003), 192.
37 For example, on the diffusion of Peloponnesian Measles Ware, see H. Patterson, "Contatti commerciali e culturali ad Otranto dal IX al XV secolo: L'evidenza della ceramica," in *La ceramica nel mondo bizantino tra XI–XV secolo e i suoi rapporti con l'Italia*, ed. Gelichi, 108, fig. 4; François, "Circulation des céramiques byzantines," 233, map 1.
38 Ch. Kritzas, "Τὸ Βυζαντινὸν ναυάγιον Πελαγοννήσου Ἀλοννήσου," Ἀρχαιολογικὰ Ἀνάλεκτα ἐξ Ἀθηνῶν 4.2 (1971): 176–82; E. Ioannidaki-Dostoglou, "Les vases de l'épave byzantine de Pélagonnèse-Halonnèse," in *Recherches sur la céramique byzantine*, ed. V. Déroche and J.-M. Spieser, BCH supp. 18 (Athens, 1989), 157–71; Papanikola-Bakirtzi, ed., *Art of Sgraffito*, 122–42.
39 A. H. S. Megaw and R. E. Jones, "Byzantine and Allied Pottery: A Contribution by Chemical Analysis to Problems of Origins and Distribution," *BSA* 78 (1983): 237, 251–52.
40 C. Vogt, "Technologie des céramiques byzantines à glaçure d'époque Comnène, Les décors incisés: Les outils et leurs traces," *CahArch* 41 (1993): 99–110.
41 D. Papanikola-Bakirtzi, "Ἐργαστήρια εφυαλωμένης κεραμικής στο βυζαντινό κόσμο," in Bakirtzis, ed., *VIIe Congrès International sur la Céramique Médiévale en Méditerranée*, 64.

Figure 8.9. Fine-sgraffito dish with a cheetah taking a gazelle, Pelagonnesos-Alonnesos shipwreck (photo courtesy of the Hellenic Ministry of Culture)

Figure 8.10. Fine-sgraffito dish, Pelagonnesos-Alonnesos shipwreck (photo courtesy of the Hellenic Ministry of Culture)

number of metal utensils that have survived reveals not only exactly similar forms but also details peculiar to metal, including the almost flat bottom, with a very low, almost rudimentary foot or a band-shaped foot, and the tooth-shaped tip of the lip. The imitation of metal vessels is not limited to shape and form, however, but also obviously extended to the decoration. Some have suggested that engraved metalwork is the prototype for Sgraffito Ware.[42] The silver plates of the Konstantinos Alanos treasure confirmed the relationship of metalwork with sgraffito decoration and pointed to the immediate model of Byzantine fine-sgraffito.[43] Beyond close parallels in figural decoration, like those on the Corinthian plate with the falconer, similarities can be observed in more simple motifs such as spirals and palmettes. It is difficult to ignore that both metal and ceramic vessels follow identical arrangements in medallions and bands. Of great importance also are some details in the execution of the decoration, such as the dots and the scale pattern in the background of the scenes (fig. 8.12). These details show that ceramic workshops were attempting to come close to metal prototypes and to give ceramic products the appearance of metal ones. In other words, these similarities illustrate the perceived hierarchy and value of materials, expressed in the tendency of the cheaper to imitate the more expensive.[44] The vessels' high quality implies that the wares were created in professional workshops with talented artists who had access to the metal models.[45] Their apparent intention to transfer elements from the expensive metal vessels onto those of clay also suggests that the cheaper glazed ceramics were in demand by consumers and had a market; such a market was most likely the destination of the unfortunate ship.

THE KASTELLORIZO SHIPWRECK   In 1970, the wreckage of a ship was found in the open sea off

---

42 A. Lane, "The Early Sgraffito Ware of the Near East," *Transactions of the Oriental Ceramic Society* 15 (1937–38): 41; E. D. Maguire and H. Maguire, "Byzantine Pottery in the History of Art," in D. Papanikonla-Bakirtzi, E. D. Maguire, and H. Maguire, *Ceramic Art from Byzantine Serres* (Urbana, Ill., 1992), 14–16.

43 P. Armstrong, "Byzantine Glazed Ceramic Tableware in the Collection of the Detroit Institute of Arts," *Bulletin of the Detroit Institute of Arts* 71 (1997): 8–9; eadem, "Figural Representation," 82.

44 Maguire and Maguire, "Byzantine Pottery," 14–15; Ballian and Drandaki, "Silver Treasure," 57.

45 Armstrong, "Byzantine Glazed Ceramic Tableware," 8–9; eadem, "Figural Representation," 92.

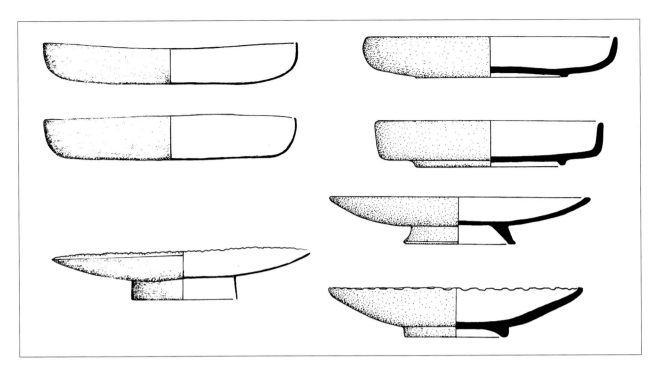

Figure 8.11. Forms of metal (left) and ceramic (right) vessels (drawing by C. Malia)

Figure 8.12. Line drawing of decorative patterns on metal (left) and ceramic (right) vessels (drawing by C. Malia)

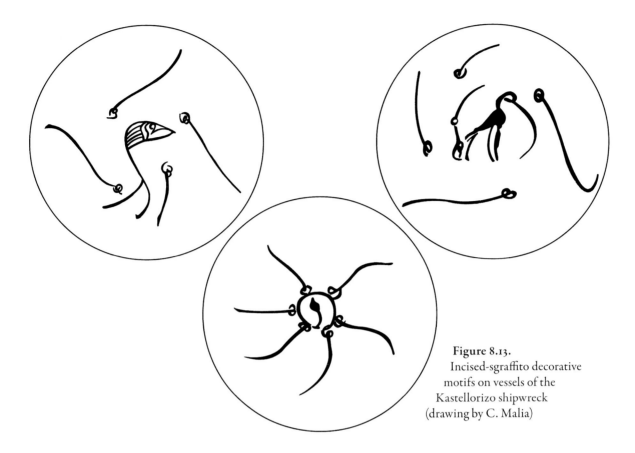

Figure 8.13.
Incised-sgraffito decorative motifs on vessels of the Kastellorizo shipwreck (drawing by C. Malia)

the island of Kastellorizo, east of Rhodes. A large part of its cargo consisted of glazed tableware.[46] The ceramics are homogeneous in their clay, which is coarse-grained with inclusions and reddish, often with a kind of orange tint, in color.[47] There is also clear homogeneity and standardization in the forms, which are large-sized bowls with ring-shaped bases. A small number are marginally different, having a widely flaring foot.

Although the ceramics belonged to different groups with regard to their type of decoration, there was homogeneity within the decorative groups. Most of the ceramics had incised-sgraffito decoration, displaying birds and fishes among fronds (fig. 8.13). A small number belonged to fine-sgraffito, mostly depicting birds. A limited number were decorated with groups of animals rendered in champlevé; these also differed from the rest in form, having the widely flaring foot noted above. Vessels with brown and green painted decoration were also recorded. Another group of ceramics belonged to the slip-painted type, in which whorls and twisted motifs create a lattice of white lace on the red clay. The homogeneity in the clay, forms, and even decoration within the groups leads to the conclusion that the ceramic wares on the wrecked ship were from one workshop or from a group of workshops within a particular area.[48] Because its distinct decorative motifs make the incised-sgraffito group easily recognizable, ceramics that belong to it can be straightforwardly identified

46   G. Philotheou and M. Michaelidou, "Βυζαντινά πινάκια από το φορτίο ναυαγισμένου πλοίου κοντά στο Καστελλόριζο," Ἀρχ. Δελτ. 41 (1986): 271–329; Papanikola-Bakirtzi, ed., *Art of Sgraffito,* 143–56.
47   See descriptions of the clay in Philotheou and Michaelidou, "Βυζαντινά πινάκια."

48   A combined archaeological and archaeometric study by Waksman and Wartburg indicates that wares such as those carried by the ship sunk off Kastellorizo have homogeneous clay; see S. Y. Waksman and M.-L. von Wartburg, "'Fine-Sgraffito Ware,' 'Aegean Ware,' and Other Wares: New Evidence for a Major Production of Byzantine Ceramics," *Report of the Department of Antiquities of Cyprus* (2006): 369–85. See also M. J. Blackman and S. Redford, "Neutron Activation Analysis of Medieval Ceramics from Kinet, Turkey, especially Port Saint Symeon Ware," *Ancient Near Eastern Studies* 42 (2005): 87, 96–98, 100, table 3.

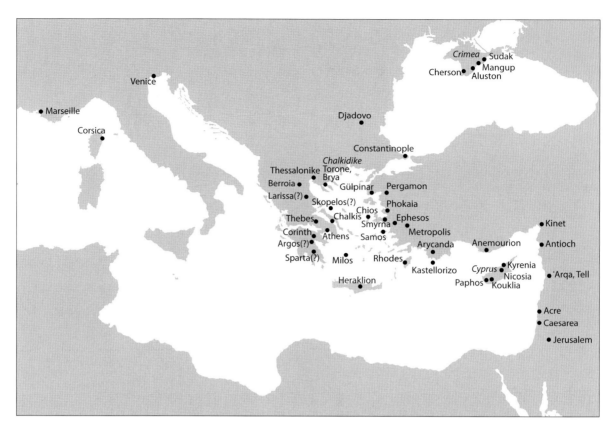

Figure 8.14. The distribution of Incised Sgraffito Wares similar to those of the Kastellorizo shipwreck (drawn by author)

among excavation material in numerous sites.[49] Vessels such as those from Kastellorizo have been uncovered in significant numbers in various sites in Asia Minor.[50] They have also been found in large numbers in Syro-Palestinian sites[51] and in Cyprus,[52] as well as in Constantinople,[53] in Crimea,[54] and in Greece.[55] Their presence has even been recorded in Italy[56] and southern France.[57] This geographical den-

---

49 Not every incised-sgraffito decoration is related to Kastellorizo wares; moreover, not every example of Incised Sgraffito Ware is Aegean Ware, as it was defined by Megaw.

50 L. Doğer, *Izmir Arkeoloji Müzesi Örnekleriye: Kazıma Dekorlu Ege-Bizans Seramikleri* (Izmir, 2000); B. Böhlendorf-Arslan, *Die glasierte byzantinische Keramik aus der Türkei*, 3 vols. (Istanbul, 2004), map 4.

51 Pringle, "Pottery as Evidence for Trade," 451–75; E. J. Stern and S. Y. Waksman, "Pottery from Crusader Acre: A Typological and Analytical Study," in Bakirtzis, ed., *VIIe Congrès International sur la Céramique Médiévale en Méditerranée*, 167–80; M. Avissar and E. J. Stern, *Pottery of the Crusader, Ayyubid, and Mamluk Periods in Israel*, Israel Antiquities Authority Reports 26 (Jerusalem, 2005).

52 A. H. S. Megaw, "An Early Thirteenth-Century Aegean Glazed Ware," in *Studies in Memory of David Talbot Rice*, ed. G. Robertson and G. Henderson (Edinburgh, 1975), 34–45; M.-L. von Wartburg, "Cypriot Contacts with East and West as Reflected in Medieval Glazed Pottery from the Paphos Region," in Bakirtzis, ed., *VIIe Congrès International sur la Céramique Médiévale en Méditerranée*, 158–59.

53 Hayes, *Excavations at Saraçhane*, 2:48; François, "Circulation des céramiques byzantines," 234, map 4; Böhlendorf-Arslan, *Die glasierte byzantinische Keramik*, 175–76, map 5.

54 A. L. Yakobson, *Keramika i keramicheskoe proizvodstvo srednevekovoj Tavriki* (Leningrad, 1979), 128, fig. 81.

55 It has been suggested that a group of Byzantine bowls in the Ashmolean Museum, similar to those from the Kastellorizo shipwreck, came from another shipwreck located off the island of Skopelos in the Sporades in the northwest Aegean; see P. Armstrong, "A Group of Byzantine Bowls from Skopelos," *Oxford Journal of Archaeology* 10.3 (1991): 335–47; François, "Circulation des céramiques byzantines," 234, map 4.

56 S. Gelichi, "La ceramica bizantina in Italia e la ceramica italiana nel Mediterraneo orientale tra XII e XIII secolo: Stato degli studi e proposte di ricerca," in *La ceramica nel mondo bizantino tra XI–XV secolo e i suoi rapporti con l'Italia*, ed. idem (Florence, 1993), 18–19; François, "Circulation des céramiques byzantines," 234, map 4.

57 L. Vallauri and G. Démians d'Archimbaud, with F. Parent and C. Richarté, "La circulation des céramiques byzantines,

sity indicates a systematic diffusion mainly within an area stretching from the Black Sea to Cyprus and along the length of the Asia Minor coastline down to the Syro-Palestinian coast (fig. 8.14).

The ceramics from the wreck off Kastellorizo are all large hemispherical bowls that display no great attention to the finishing of their surfaces. For example, a good number of them were warped during the production process and no effort was made to remove the marks of the tool used to shape the outside cheek of the vessel. The decoration was executed with a swift, sure line; the incised-sgraffito decoration in particular is rendered freely and confidently. There is no evidence suggesting that it imitates metal models. The subject is chased onto the coating with a steady, free hand. Fishes and birds rendered in a few lines among fronds and tendrils show freedom of execution, imagination in concept, and artistic creativity. Thus, at the beginning of the thirteenth century, glazed ceramic tableware had become established and had created its own market niche. There was no longer any need to imitate metal vessels, because ceramics had evolved their own way of expression, which would be completed in the following period.

Tablewares for All
(thirteenth–fourteenth centuries)

Examination of the ceramics from the Kastellorizo wreck has already brought us to the thirteenth century, the first half of which was a period of significant change in the character of glazed ceramic vessels. Certain features of the Kastellorizo ceramics have already been noted, such as their hasty finish and their departure from metallic models. This last observation is particularly true of a type of vessel closely related to those of Kastellorizo, which A. H. S. Megaw has analyzed under the name "Low-ring Base Ware" in his "An Early Thirteenth-Century Aegean Glazed Ware."[58] On these vessels, familiar motifs, such as the well-known birds of Kastellorizo vessels and incised multiple concentric circles, are enriched with green coloring. The presence of the color splashes dispels any impression that the ceramic vessels might have served as imitations of metal ones.

But the ceramics that appear to signal a real new departure are the much-discussed Zeuxippus Ware. When Megaw so termed a type of ceramics with thin sides, elegant shapes, and fine design (figs. 8.15 and 8.16),[59] nobody could have foreseen that he would begin a discussion that has continued to capture the interest of scholars for half a century. Megaw verified that during the life span of this type of ceramics, in the first half of the thirteenth century, changes occurred that would determine the development of Byzantine ceramics throughout the late Byzantine period. These changes concern the methods of producing Zeuxippus Ware—more specifically, the firing technique and the decoration process.

One change in production was the adoption of a new firing technique using tripod stilts, which made possible a more efficient use of space inside the kilns.[60] This technical innovation strongly influenced the development of the glazed ceramics market in the Byzantine Empire and boosted production in late Byzantine workshops. Another change was that on most class II vessels sgraffito was applied while the ceramics were on the wheel, so that the rotating motion could be used to draw concentric circles without the aid of a compass.[61] Furthermore, the practice emerges of enriching the sgraffito decoration with color, in this case brownish-yellow brushstrokes.[62]

In a recent archaeological and archaeometric study on Zeuxippus Ware, Sylvie-Yona Waksman and Véronique François have extensively examined this intriguing ware, with very interesting results.[63] Among other conclusions, this important study

---

chypriotes et du Levant chrétien en Provence, Languedoc et Corse du Xᵉ au XIVᵉ siècle," in Bakirtzis, ed., *VIIᵉ Congrès International sur la Céramique Médiévale en Méditerranée*, 144–47.
58   Megaw, "Aegean Glazed Ware," 39, 42.

59   A. H. S. Megaw, "Zeuxippus Ware," *BSA* 63 (1968): 67–88.
60   D. Papanikola-Bakirtzi, "Τριποδίσκοι ψησίματος των βυζαντινών και μεταβυζαντινών αγγείων," in *Αμητός: Τιμητικός τόμος για τον καθηγητή Μ. Ανδρόνικο* (Thessalonike, 1986), 641–48; eadem, ed., *Art of Sgraffito*, 21; Laiou and Morrisson, *The Byzantine Economy*, 184.
61   Megaw, "Zeuxippus Ware," 77–81.
62   This is the same period when the incised designs of the Low-ring Base Ware were embellished with green color. See Megaw, "Aegean Glazed Ware," 39–40.
63   S. Y. Waksman and V. François, "Vers une redéfinition typologique et analytique des céramiques byzantines du type Zeuxippus Ware," *BCH* 128–29 (2004–05): 629–724. See also an earlier study focused on similar questions, A. H. S. Megaw, P. Armstrong, and H. Hatcher, "Zeuxippus Ware: An Analytical Approach to the Question of Provenance," in Bakirtzis, ed., *VIIᵉ Congrès International sur la Céramique Médiévale en Méditerranée*, 91–100.

Figure 8.15. Zeuxippus Ware vessel with a lion attacking a gazelle, Cherson (courtesy of the National Preserve of Tauric Chersonesos, photo by C. Williams)

Figure 8.16. Zeuxippus Ware vessel with a lion attacking a serpent, Cherson (courtesy of the National Preserve of Tauric Chersonesos, photo by C. Williams)

demonstrates that the clay composition of Zeuxippus class I B with the brownish-orange glaze does not correspond to that of Zeuxippus Ware sensu stricto as described by the authors. It continues to be difficult to follow the diffusion of Zeuxippus Ware, since it remains unclear which features are "sensu stricto" "genuine," "derivative," or "imitative." Even class II, which seemed to be relatively uniform, presents several differentiations. However, its examples can be more easily identified because of their characteristic yellow-brown sgraffito decoration with refined features and motifs. In this context, it is important to note that both "genuine" and "derivative" examples of class II can usually be found at the same sites.

The vessels of Zeuxippus Ware II were widely spread or diffused.[64] They have been found in significant numbers in Constantinople,[65] Thrace,[66] on the coast of Asia Minor,[67] and at crusader sites in Syro-Palestine,[68] Cyprus,[69] Egypt,[70] and Italy.[71] They have even been recorded in southern France and Corsica.[72] The presence not only of class II but of Zeuxippus Ware in general is limited in Greece (except Thrace).[73] In this context one may note the frequency of Zeuxippus Ware class II among the finds in Crimea mainly at the port of Cherson, and particularly the number of vessels that feature impressive pictorial decoration with mounted figures and fantastic animals (see figs. 8.15 and 8.16).[74] The central role of the maritime cities of Italy, especially of Venice and Genoa, is evident since the aforementioned locations constituted markets for their com-

---

64 Megaw, "Zeuxippus Ware," 87, 88; François, "Circulation des céramiques byzantines," 234, map 3.
65 Böhlendorf-Arslan, *Die glasierte byzantinische Keramik,* 172–75.
66 Papanikola-Bakirtzi and Zekos, *Late Byzantine Glazed Pottery from Thrace.*
67 Böhlendorf-Arslan, *Die glasierte byzantinische Keramik,* 178–307.
68 Avissar and Stern, *Pottery in Israel,* 48–50.
69 Megaw, "Zeuxippus Ware," 84–86.
70 V. François, *Céramiques médiévales à Alexandrie* (Cairo, 1999), 110–12, fig. 25.
71 G. Berti and S. Gelichi, "'Zeuxippus Ware' in Italy," in *Materials Analysis of Byzantine Pottery,* ed. H. Maguire (Washington, D.C., 1997), 85–104.
72 Vallauri, Démians d'Archimbaud, et al., "La circulation des céramiques byzantines," 147–48, fig. 9.
73 Dimopoulos, "Trade of Byzantine Red Wares," 189.
74 Yakobson, *Keramika,* 120–26, figs. 75–77; A. Romančuk, "Befunde der glasierten Keramik der spätbyzantinischen Zeit in Chersonesos: Örtliche Herstellung und Import," in Bakirtzis, ed., *VIIe Congrès International sur la Céramique Médiévale en Méditerranée,* 101–14, fig. 1–3; eadem, *Glazurovannaja posuda pozdnevizantijskogo Chersona* (Ekaterinburg, 2003), 141–76.

mercial activities. It is difficult to interpret the trade in "genuine" Zeuxippus Ware class II more precisely, since its place of origin remains unknown.[75] The diffusion of Zeuxippus Ware class II, along the coastline of Asia Minor down to Cyprus and the Levant,[76] exhibits similarities to that of the wares found in the Kastellorizo shipwreck (see fig. 8.14), suggesting common distribution patterns. It also indicates that the old trade paths continued to be in use at least until the middle of the thirteenth century.

Archaeological research has demonstrated that the amount of glazed ceramics found from the thirteenth century onward significantly increased over earlier periods. Moreover, it has shown that glazed pottery workshops proliferated, operating not only in urban centers but also in small rural towns and even in villages. Confirmation of such growth is provided by the increased number of textual references to ceramic production in rural areas during this period.[77] However, it is difficult to determine whether these references are to glazed pottery workshops. The glazed ceramics that can be dated from the thirteenth century onward are both smaller and deeper than those of the previous period. Their form and size indicate that these vessels were for individual use and for the consumption of liquid foods such as soups and broths. The change in diet and eating vessels has been discussed elsewhere at length and need not concern us here.[78] However, investigating the ceramic tablewares of a number of glazed pottery production centers active in the period of the thirteenth to the fourteenth centuries can help pinpoint their trade and market characteristics.

Tablewares from Constantinople

For many years, the question of whether Constantinople was a center for the production of glazed ceramic wares in the late Byzantine period remained open, but an answer has been supplied by the recent excavations near the Sirkeci railway station.[79] This site uncovered tripod stilts, as well as red fabric sherds from vessels that did not complete the production process; in particular, they are missing the final coat of glaze. By studying the rubble from the workshop and comparing the wasters with ceramics found at various times during excavations in Constantinople, such as those in the Mangana area,[80] we can gain a relatively good picture of Constantinopolitan late Byzantine ceramics. Most of the ceramics are hemispherical bowls demonstrating a refined decoration with various types of sgraffito side by side. There is a rich variety of subject material, including plain geometric circles, knots and lattices, monograms, and animal figures. To an overwhelming degree, the quality of these ceramic wares is high, and they demonstrate confident execution of the decoration and knowledge of the secrets of how to apply coatings and glazes so that they adhere well to the body of the vessel. Recent clay analysis indicates differences between the red fabric of the ceramics from Sirkeci and vessels of Fine Sgraffito Ware and Aegean Ware, as well as Zeuxippus Ware classes Ia and II.[81] The features of the group that, thanks to the wasters at Sirkeci, we can ascribe to the production of Constantinople during the late Byzantine period[82] are reminiscent of a group of vessels from the thirteenth century known as Elaborate Incised Ware (fig. 8.17).[83] Véronique François has suggested that very possibly they were produced in

---

75 Waksman and François, "Zeuxippus Ware," 629–724; S. Y. Waksman, with A. I. Romanchuk, "Byzantine Chersonesos, an Investigation of the Local Production of Ceramics by Chemical Analysis," in Böhlendorf-Arslan, Osman Uysal, and Witte-Orr, eds., Çanak: Late Antique and Medieval Pottery and Tiles, 394.
76 François, "Circulation des céramiques byzantines," 233, map 3–4.
77 J. Lefort, "Anthroponymie et société villageoise (Xᵉ–XIVᵉ siècle)," in Hommes et richesses dans l'Empire byzantin, 2 vols. (Paris, 1989–91), 2:236–37.
78 Papanikola-Bakirtzi, ed., Art of Sgraffito, 21; eadem, "Εργαστήρια," 45; J. Vroom, "Byzantine Garlic and Turkish Delight," Archaeological Dialogues 7.2 (2000): 204; eadem, After Antiquity, 238; and eadem, "The Changing Dining Habits at Christ's Table," in Brubaker and Linardou, eds., Eat, Drink, and Be Merry (Luke 12:19), 191–222; for everyday food in Byzantium, see J. Koder, "Η καθημερινή διατροφή στο Βυζάντιο με βάση τις πηγές," in Papanikola-Bakirtzi, ed., Βυζαντινών διατροφή και μαγειρίαι, 17–30.

79 Girgin, "Sirkeci," 97–105.
80 R. Demangel and E. Mamboury, Le Quartier des Manganes (Paris, 1939), 136–48.
81 Waksman and Girgin, "Les vestiges de production de céramiques des fouilles de Sirkeci (Istanbul): Premiers éléments de caractérisation," 467.
82 S. Y. Waksman, N. Erhan, and S. Eskafen, "Les ateliers de céramiques de Sirkeci (Istanbul): Resultats de la campagne 2008," Anatolia Antiqua 17 (2009): 457–67.
83 Ibid., 458, 466 fig. 3.5. As it was introduced by David Talbot Rice (see Byzantine Glazed Pottery, 34–40), the term Elaborate Incised Ware was an effort to group ceramics according to style and did not designate the production of a specific center; V. François, "Elaborate Incised Ware: Un témoin du rayonnement de la culture byzantine à l'époque paléologue," Byzantinoslavica 61 (2003): 151–68.

Figure 8.17. Elaborate Incised Ware; the decoration of a bowl found in Thessalonike (drawing by C. Malia)

Figure 8.18. Thessalonike Ware; bowl with sgraffito decoration (photo courtesy of the Hellenic Ministry of Culture)

the Byzantine capital itself. Future clay analysis may confirm similarities between the red fabric ceramics of Sirkeci and Elaborate Incised Ware. The record of the diffusion of this ware would then offer an initial picture of the movement of the products of the workshops of Constantinople during the first part of the late Byzantine period, indicating that these wares were dispersed over an appreciable area, particularly in locations in Bulgaria and on the Black Sea.[84]

Tablewares from Thessalonike

Archaeological work has make possible a comprehensive understanding of glazed ceramic production in late Byzantine Thessalonike (second half of the thirteenth–fourteenth centuries).[85] The examples of this production are of good quality and reflect the technical skills of Thessalonian potters. At the same time they bear the evidence of swift completion and mass production, with decorative subjects vividly rendered and characterized by naive freshness and ingenuity (fig. 8.18).

It is likely that the glazed ceramics of late Byzantine Thessalonike were sold in local workshops and outlets, some of which may have been in the center of the city, particularly at the site of the ancient Agora.[86] They must also have been available for purchase in the regular, weekly street markets that were held in the city, as well as at the Demetria, the great annual commercial fair in Thessalonike, which, according to written sources, was held in October outside the western walls of the city.[87] Apart from Thessalonike, they have also been found in Chalkidike and the Strymon Valley. According to present archaeological data, they are absent from Thrace, although they have been found in Venice (fig. 8.19). The diffusion of the ceramic products of Thessalonike's late Byzantine workshops supports the observation that after the thirteenth century, Constantinople and Thessalonike belonged to two dif-

---

84 François, "Elaborate Incised Ware," 153 (map).

85 D. Papanikola-Bakirtzi, "Εργαστήριο εφυαλωμένης κεραμεικής στη Θεσσαλονίκη: Πρώτες παρατηρήσεις," in *Αφιέρωμα στη μνήμη Στυλιανού Πελεκανίδη* (Thessalonike, 1983), 377–87; eadem, "The Palaeologan Glazed Pottery of Thessaloniki," in *L'art de Thessalonique et des pays balkaniques et les courants spirituels au XIVᵉ siècle, Recueil des rapports du IVᵉ Colloque serbo-grec* (Belgrade, 1987), 193–204; eadem, ed., *Art of Sgraffito*; eadem, "'Πολύτιμα' εργαστηριακά απορρίμματα εφυαλωμένης κεραμικής από τη Θεσσαλονίκη," in *Κερμάτια Φιλίας Τιμητικός Τόμος για τον Ιωάννη Τουράτσογλου* (Athens, 2009), 451–67.

86 Papanikola-Bakirtzi, "Εργαστήριο," 379 n. 2.

87 K.-P. Matschke, "Commerce, Trade, Markets, and Money: Thirteenth–Fifteenth Centuries," in *EHB* 3:779–82.

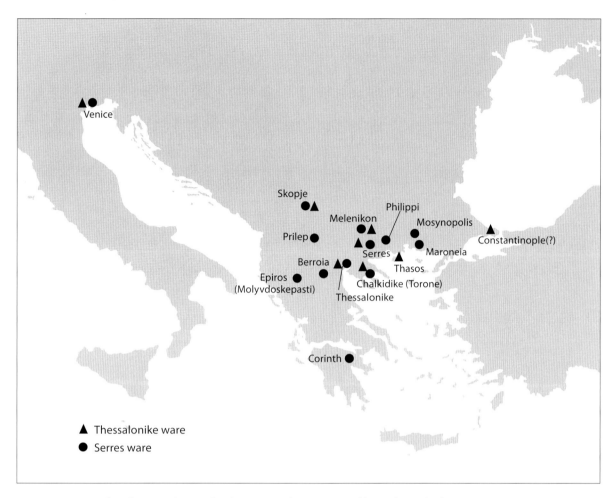

Figure 8.19. The distribution of Thessalonike Ware and Serres Ware (drawn by author)

ferent commercial subsystems.[88] The first, which included Constantinople, operated in Thrace, Bulgaria, and, in particular, the Black Sea coast. The second, which included Thessalonike, operated in Greece and the western Balkans, particularly Serbia, with links to Venice. References to the discovery of products from the workshops of Thessalonike in Constantinople[89] should be reexamined carefully in the light of the new finds at Sirkeci, which show significant similarities to the products from Thessalonike, such as related decorative motifs and persistent use of the champlevé technique in the rendering of decorative motifs. Even a version of the so-called bird of Thessalonike seems to have been produced in Constantinople.[90]

Tablewares from Serres

The town of Serres—the administrative, agricultural, and economic center of the Strymon Valley[91]—

---

88 K. Dieterich, "Zur Kulturgeographie und Kulturgeschichte des byzantinischen Balkanhandels," *BZ* 31 (1931): 37–57; A. Laiou, "Η Θεσσαλονίκη, η ενδοχώρα της και ο οικονομικός της χώρος στην εποχή των Παλαιολόγων," in *Διεθνές Συμπόσιο Βυζαντινή Μακεδονία 324–1430 μ.Χ., Θεσσαλονίκη, 29–31 Οκτωβρίου 1992*, Πρακτικά Μακεδονική Βιβλιοθήκη 82 (Thessalonike, 1995), 186–87.
89 C. Bakirtzis and D. Papanikola-Bakirtzi, "De la céramique byzantine en glaçure à Thessalonique," *Byzantinobulgarica* 7 (1981): 436.
90 Waksman, Erhan, and Eskafen, "Les ateliers de céramiques de Sirkeci," 465–66, fig. 3b.
91 A. E. Laiou, "Κοινωνικές δυνάμεις στις Σέρρες στο 14° αιώνα," in *Οι Σέρρες και η περιοχή τους από την αρχαία στην μεταβυζαντινή κοινωνία: Σέρρες, 29 Σεπτ.–3 Οκτ. 1993*, Πρακτικά, 2 vols. (Thessalonike, 1998), 2:203–19, esp. 211–12.

has been linked to the production in the second half of the thirteenth and the fourteenth centuries of vessels with a sgraffito type of decoration enriched with bright green and yellow colors (fig. 8.20).⁹² The discovery of wasters, whose numbers are constantly rising, leaves no room for doubt that these ceramics were produced in Serres.⁹³ Existing archaeological data suggest that the diffusion of these vessels was abundant in Melenikon and Thessalonike; significant in the Strymon Valley; more sparse in Chalkidike and at more remote sites in eastern Macedonia, such as Philippi; and sporadic in Thrace. Isolated examples of Serres ceramics have been recorded even in Epiros, Corinth, and Venice (see fig. 8.19).⁹⁴

When considering the mode of interregional transport, we should focus on small-scale trade, following the route along the Strymon Valley to Chalkidike,⁹⁵ as well the Via Egnatia to Thessalonike and to Prilapos and Skopje to the north, to Philippi and, occasionally, Thrace to the east. The isolated examples found in Epiros, Corinth, and Italy were quite possibly transported there in the baggage of travelers. The insertion of a vessel into a wall of the monastery of Molyvdoskepasti in Epiros, which suggests that some pious traveler donated the vessel in question as a memento of a trip, reinforces this view.

The case of Melenikon is of particular interest for the Serres ceramics. In this well-known Byzantine town, the mass of finds with similarities to the ceramics from Serres⁹⁶ is so great that it suggests that very possibly Melenikon was also a center for the production of a related type of vessel. Though Serres and Melenikon are today in different countries, the distance between them is small and permits such an assumption.

Figure 8.20. Serres Ware; dish with brown-yellow and green sgraffito decoration (photo courtesy of the Hellenic Ministry of Culture)

The main feature of Serres Ware vessels is the use of bright colors, which in conjunction with their sgraffito decoration gives a vivid polychrome impression. In my opinion this feature was in effect their marketing trademark. In the market of, say, Thessalonike their bright colors would have attracted buyers as they competed against the mostly monochrome yellow Thessalonian vessels. The suggested existence of Serres Ware imitations⁹⁷ in Thessalonike indicates, I believe, the attention that Serres vessels received in the market of Thessalonike. The same colorful characteristic would have won them attention also in the Chalkidike markets. They even reached Thrace after capturing the interest of buyers. The colorful Serres Ware may well have brought something very unusual and exotic to the market: it is worth remembering that the method of firing ceramics in kilns with rods that was used in the workshops of Serres has its roots in the Islamic world.

92 Papanikonla-Bakirtzi, Maguire, and Maguire, *Byzantine Serres*; H. Maguire, "Feathers Signify Power: The Iconography of Byzantine Ceramics from Serres," in *Οι Σέρρες και η περιοχή τους*, 2:383–98.
93 Papanikola-Bakirtzi, ed., *Art of Sgraffito*, 222, 223, and cat. nos. 259, 260, 266, 276, 271, 273, 274, 277.
94 D. Papanikonla-Bakirtzi, "Serres: A Glazed-Pottery Production Center during the Late Byzantine Period," in Papanikonla-Bakirtzi, Maguire, and Maguire, *Byzantine Serres*, 32–33; Papanikola-Bakirtzi and Zekos, *Late Byzantine Glazed Pottery from Thrace*, 14, cat. nos. 18, 32, 33, 81.
95 A. Dunn, "Loci of Maritime Traffic in the Strymon Delta (IV–XVIII cc.): Commercial, Fiscal, and Manorial," in *Οι Σέρρες και η περιοχή τους*, 2:339–60.
96 B. Cvetkov, *Khudožestvena keramika ot Melnik* (Sofia, 1979).

97 D. Papanikonla-Bakirtzi, "Serres Ware," in Maguire, ed., *Materials Analysis of Byzantine Pottery*, 143; S. Wiseman, E. De Sena, S. Landsberger, R. Ylangan, S. Altaner, and D. Moore, "Compositional Analyses of Ceramics from Serres and Thessaloniki," ibid., 160.

Tablewares from Mikro Pisto, Gratianou, and Mosynopolis in Thrace

The rubble from the ceramics workshop in Mikro Pisto (fig. 8.21), on the foothills of the Rhodope range in Thrace, has provided information about a site for the production of glazed ceramics during the thirteenth century—not in some administrative or commercial center of the region but at a location on the Via Egnatia.[98] This evidence supports the hypothesis of pottery production in agricultural areas and on road arteries, and therefore implies overland transportation. The discovery of the remains of similar workshop rubble in Byzantine Gratianou (fig. 8.22), which lies a short distance from Mikro Pisto, forces us to assume that related workshops with similar production were operating in the same general area.[99] Moreover, recent excavations in Maximianoupolis (the Byzantine Mosynopolis) provide strong evidence for the local production of glazed tablewares in the thirteenth century (fig. 8.23).[100]

By and large, most of the pottery from Thrace belongs to, resembles, or has some kind of connection with Zeuxippus Ware. The material connected directly or indirectly with Zeuxippus Ware, mainly brownish-yellow-colored class II though with a number of variations, could be divided into three not always distinct categories. The first, matching strict criteria and Megaw's specifications, could be classed among the "genuine" Zeuxippus Wares; the second, similar to the first, may have been manufactured by a workshop closely related to that producing "genuine" wares; a third category could comprise the pottery ascribed to the local Thracian workshops.[101] These observations imply that the cradle of Zeuxippus Ware should be sought within coordinates somewhere between Thrace and the Black Sea coast, as far as the Crimean Peninsula.[102]

The record of the thirteenth-century products from Mikro Pisto, Gratianou, and Mosynopolis indicates that their diffusion was local and perhaps

Figure 8.21. Deformed and broken bowl (waster) from Mikro Pisto (photo courtesy of the Hellenic Ministry of Culture)

regional, but limited to Thrace. By examining the characteristics of the ceramic products of a region not far from Constantinople, such as Thrace, we can recognize their quality, which demonstrates good knowledge of firing and glazing as well as of the trends of decoration. The ceramic products aimed to please local and regional consumers by providing a fashionable daily crockery, a goal that they appear to have met, given the limited number of imported ceramics found by archaeological excavations in the thirteenth-century context.

Tablewares from Pergamon

The ceramics of Pergamon are representative of the ceramics of late Byzantine workshops from Asia Minor more generally. The systematic excavations undertaken at Pergamon and especially the careful study of the finds there have made possible detailed description of the local production of glazed ceramics wares during the late Byzantine period (thirteenth century).[103] The local glazed production of

---

98 N. Zekos, "A Glazed Pottery Workshop in Thrace," in Bakirtzis, ed., *VIIe Congrès International sur la Céramique Médiévale en Méditerranée*, 455–66.
99 Papanikola-Bakirtzi and Zekos, *Late Byzantine Glazed Pottery from Thrace*, 99–104.
100 Ibid., 53–54.
101 Ibid., 13.
102 Ibid., 52–53.

103 J.-M. Spieser, *Byzantinische Keramik aus der Stadtgrabung von Pergamon*, Pergamenische Forschungen 9 (Berlin, 1996), 45–48; S. Y. Waksman and J.-M. Spieser, "Byzantine Ceramics Excavated in Pergamon: Archaeological Classification and Characterization of the Local and Imported Production by PIXE and INAA Elemental Analysis, Mineralogy, and Petrography," in

Figure 8.22. Bowl with sgraffito decoration enhanced with brownish yellow splashes, Gratianou (photo courtesy of the Hellenic Ministry of Culture)

Figure 8.23. Bowl with sgraffito decoration enhanced with brownish yellow splashes, Mosynopolis (photo courtesy of the Hellenic Ministry of Culture)

this period includes Slip-Painted Wares, Plain-Glazed ceramics with yellow-brown, yellow mustard, or green glaze as well as Plain-Sgraffito Wares with concentric circles and other geometric motifs, again under a yellow-brown, yellow mustard, or green glaze. Another group attributed to local workshops has sgraffito decoration enriched with yellow-brown splashes similar to those found on Zeuxippus Ware II. Sherds of this group have been identified as "derivatives" of Zeuxippus. A local slip-painted group is also recorded. The ceramics whose production can be assigned to Pergamon had limited diffusion, which can be described as regional and perhaps interregional.[104]

Tablewares for a Multicultural Market (twelfth–fifteenth centuries)

Let us now turn to Cyprus and examine the market, trade image, and character of ceramic tablewares produced on an island with a strong Byzantine tradition under Latin rule. Because of its history and its geographical position in the southeastern corner of the Mediterranean, Cyprus constitutes a special case; beginning in the eleventh century it was caught in the maelstrom of the crusaders' expeditions, and from 1191 on it was part of the crusading world of the East, under the French Lusignans. For these reasons the study of the glazed ceramic wares from Cyprus is of particular interest, as we examine the character of the ceramic tablewares of a place that was transformed from a Byzantine eparchy at the end of the twelfth century to an independent feudal kingdom.

Examination of the glazed ceramic wares found during various excavations has revealed the presence of well-known versions of different types of Byzantine glazed ceramic wares from the second half of the twelfth and the early thirteenth century. The presence of wares such as Green and Brown Painted Ware, Slip-Painted Ware, and also various types of Sgraffito Wares (Fine Sgraffito, Incised Sgraffito, and Champlevé) has been recorded.[105] Recent clay analyses of these red fabric wares have revealed their

---

Maguire, ed., *Materials Analysis of Byzantine Pottery*, 105–34; Waksman and François, "Zeuxippus Ware," 670.

104 Finds from Troy and Kyme are probably products of Pergamene workshops; see Waksman and François, "Zeuxippus Ware," 685.

105 D. Papanikola-Bakirtzi, "Glazed Pottery in Byzantine Medieval Cyprus (12th–15th Centuries)," in *Byzantine Medieval Cyprus*, ed. D. Papanikola-Bakirtzi and M. Iacovou (Nicosia, 1998), 129–31, cat. nos. 60–64; Wartburg, "Cypriot Contacts," 153–66.

Figure 8.24. Paphos Ware; brown and green incised-sgraffito bowl with a dancer (photo courtesy of the Benaki Museum, Athens)

similarity, and for this reason Sylvie-Yona Waksman and Marie-Louise von Wartburg have argued that they came from the same place of production.[106] Among ceramic finds, mainly from excavations in the Paphos area, a significant representation of Zeuxippus vessels (class Ia and class II) is also recorded.[107] Similar types of Byzantine glazed pottery have been recorded in a number of sites of the crusader Levant, first by Denys Pringle and more recently by Edna Stern, M. James Blackman, and Scott Redford.[108] These finds indicate that products of Byzantine workshops not only continued to appeal to a public belonging to Byzantine culture, as did the Cypriots, but also was attractive to the crusader population. The conclusions drawn from the diffusion of these Byzantine wares are that a small-scale interregional and "international" trade supplied glazed ceramics to the markets of Cyprus and also to the crusader towns on the Anatolian and the Levantine coasts during the late twelfth and early thirteenth century.

Local production of glazed pottery in Cyprus first appears at the beginning of the thirteenth century, in the Paphos region,[109] following the decentralization of glazed pottery production in the Byzantine world. Thus, although Cyprus was no longer part of the Byzantine Empire, the same production trends can be observed there as in the rest of the Byzantine world. The Cypriot glazed vessels of the thirteenth century seem to have all the related characteristics: rather small and deep forms, traces of the use of tripod stilts for their firing, and incised-sgraffito decoration, which after the middle of the century is enhanced with splashes of green and yellowish-brown color (fig. 8.24). Products from the Cypriot workshops of Paphos have been found in significant numbers in the southern Asia Minor,[110] Syria, and Palestine.[111] They have also been recorded in Egypt.[112] The frequency and density of finds of Cypriot wares in these lands may justify the hypothesis of short-distance trade between Cyprus and the coasts opposite it.[113] However, it is also possible that a good number of these wares would have been transported in the baggage of travelers, pilgrims, merchants, sailors, and soldiers, the motley crowd that then made up the population of the Levant. Products from Paphos apparently ceased to be conveyed to the continental lands opposite once the crusader statelets there were abolished and the Mamluks became dominant (1291).[114] Isolated and sporadic finds in

106 Waksman and Wartburg, "'Fine-Sgraffito Ware,' 'Aegean Ware,'" 369–85.
107 Megaw, "Zeuxippus Ware," 84–86; Waksman and François, "Zeuxippus Ware," 665–66; Wartburg, "Cypriot Contacts," 156–60.
108 Pringle, "Pottery as Evidence for Trade"; Avissar and Stern, *Pottery in Israel*, 40–52; Blackman and Redford, "Medieval Ceramics from Kinet," 84–87.

109 D. Papanikola-Bakirtzi, *Μεσαιωνική εφυαλωμένη κεραμική της Κύπρου: Τα εργαστήρια Πάφου και Λαπήθου* (Thessalonike, 1994).
110 S. Bilici, "Bazi Örnekleriye Alanya Kalesi Kazılarında Bulunan Ithal Kibris Sirli Seramikleri," *Adalya* 11 (2008): 384, 385, 393, 396. I am most grateful to Scott Redford for bringing this article to my attention.
111 Avissar and Stern, *Pottery in Israel*, 57–62, with earlier bibliography.
112 François, *Céramiques médiévales à Alexandrie*, 112–13, figs. 27–29.
113 Such trade was very likely based in the port of Limassol; see N. Coureas, "Commercial Activity in the Town of Limassol during the Fourteenth and Fifteenth Centuries," *Επετηρίδα Κέντρου Επιστημονικών Ερευνών* 27 (2002): 21–41.
114 For the marginal importance of Cyprus in the shipping networks in the eastern Mediterranean before and after 1291, see D. Jacoby, "Greeks in the Maritime Trade of Cyprus around the Mid-Fourteenth Century," in *Κύπρος—Βενετία: Κοινές ιστορικές τύχες*, ed. Ch. Maltezou (Venice, 2002), 59–83.

Italy,[115] and even in southern France,[116] seem not to be products of systematic trade. Instead they likely supplemented occasional trade,[117] or can be accounted for as ceramics that accompanied travelers,[118] or were mementos from a trip to the exotic East.

Toward the fourteenth century, Cypriot glazed ceramics started to develop their own characteristics; though they continued to display the decorative techniques of Byzantine pottery, their iconography became receptive to influences from the crusader world that surrounded the island. Richly attired ladies and ironclad knights armed with shields and spears appear frequently on Cypriot glazed vessels, as do scenes of falconry and courtly life (fig. 8.25).[119] They obviously were influenced by pictorial elements linked with a visual vocabulary that dominated the eastern Mediterranean through this period. Cypriot glazed tablewares from this period closely resemble Port Saint Symeon Wares, which were produced in a number of sites in the Levant during the thirteenth century.[120] This group of ceramics features figural depictions as well as other decorative motifs, such as coats of arms, that are very similar to those of Cypriot wares.

Meeting the Market Demands

Having dealt at length with various aspects of the trade and market characteristics of Byzantine glazed ceramics, we can now better understand the ways in which their production from the tenth to fifteenth centuries met market demands.

Figure 8.25. Brown and green sgraffito dish with a knight and his bride, Cyprus (photo courtesy of the Department of Antiquities, Cyprus)

During the tenth and eleventh centuries the workshops of Constantinople seem to have been almost exclusively responsible for the production of glazed table wares. The workshops of the capital supplied these ceramics to the markets of the entire empire and beyond. This great diffusion of Constantinopolitan ceramics presupposes considerable production and distribution, as well as commercial activity associated with the merchandise that must have been interregional, and internationally carried mainly on ships.

From the end of the eleventh to the early thirteenth century, production of glazed ceramic wares was undertaken by workshops that were active in the big cities and in the administrative and commercial centers, such as Corinth. The adoption of an innovative white coating on ceramics made from red clay was a limiting factor in the spread of Constantinopolitan wares to the markets. According to archaeological data, the production of workshops such as those of Corinth, as well as those that supplied the ceramic cargo found in the shipwrecks of Pelagonnesos-Alonnesos and Kastellorizo, was considerable, standardized, specialized, and of high quality. The size and quality of production are sufficient to conclude that the workshops of the middle Byzantine centuries had a professional structure and organization. I would venture that they had par-

---

115 F. Saccardo, L. Lazzarini, and M. Munarini, "Ceramiche importate a Venezia e nel Veneto tra XI e XIV secolo," in Bakirtzis, ed., *VIIe Congrès International sur la Céramique Médiévale en Méditerranée,* 408, fig. 12.
116 Vallauri, Démians d'Archimbaud, et al., "La circulation des céramiques byzantines," 148–49.
117 N. Coureas, "Provençal Trade with Cyprus in the Thirteenth and Fourteenth Centuries," Επετηρίδα του Κέντρου Επιστημονικών Ερευνών 22 (1996): 69–92.
118 François and Spieser, "Pottery and Glass," 606–7; François, "Réalités des échanges," 244.
119 D. Papanikola-Bakirtzi, *Colours of Medieval Cyprus: Through the Ceramic Collection of the Leventis Municipal Museum of Nicosia* (Nicosia, 2004), 44–45.
120 A. Lane, "Medieval Finds at Al-Mina in North Syria," *Archaeologia* 87 (1937): 19–78; S. Redford, S. Ikram, E. M. Parr, and T. Beach, "Excavations at Medieval Kinet, Turkey: A Preliminary Report," *Ancient Near East Studies* 38 (2001): 58–138; Blackman and Redford, "Medieval Ceramics from Kinet," 101–5.

allels with the well-known majolica workshops in fifteenth-century Italy, about which ample information is provided by an illustrated treatise written by Cipriano Piccolpasso around 1557.[121]

The quality of the products from the middle Byzantine workshops, both in the capital and in other centers of the empire, as well as the clear tendency of glazed clay wares to imitate metalwares permit their placement in the category of semiluxury goods. These tablewares were most likely intended for an upwardly mobile section of the population, whose economic position and aesthetic sensibilities led it to desire and purchase goods that resembled those enjoyed by the upper classes.[122] The data provided by archaeological research—in particular information gathered from the dispersal of specific wares, as well as the examination of shipwrecks—indicate that transport of the wares was regional, certainly interregional, occasionally international, and mainly maritime.

The image and character of late Byzantine glazed ceramics were shaped in the first half of the thirteenth century, when extensive changes occurred in the technology, location, and structure of workshops. Archaeological finds leave no room for doubt that the production of glazed ceramics was decentralized in the late Byzantine era. Decentralization is consistent with the emergence of regional economies that followed the political fragmentation and disarticulation in Byzantium after 1204. Functioning workshops existed not only in the administrative centers, such as Thessalonike, or centers in the hinterland, such as Serres and Pergamon, but also on road arteries, such as in Mikro Pisto in Rhodope, on the Via Egnatia.

The quality of the wares, after the middle of the thirteenth century, varied from average to good; and clear signs of "mass" production are evident, such as the lack of concern for detail and of particular attention during the different stages of production. The finishing of the decoration was achieved quickly, on the wheel. Concentric circles were made not, as before, with a compass but with the rotation of the wheel and are therefore really whorls. The very good quality of Elaborate Incised Ware is an exception, and further investigation into its origin is needed. Production in these late Byzantine decentralized workshops was promoted by the use of tripod stilts for firing the vessels in columns, the one inside the other. Thus, the use of tripod stilts and the practice of decorating the vessels on the wheel led to distinctive differences in the manufacturing process of the tableware of this period as well as in its character.

The features of the ceramics dated after the middle of the thirteenth century lead to the view that these workshops, in contrast to the middle Byzantine ones above termed "professional," had a family workshop structure, very similar to that found until quite recently in traditional glazed pottery workshops in the Aegean and the eastern Mediterranean regions.[123] Production was mainly carried out by family members, with occasional help from hired hands. It is likely that the distribution of the workshop products would have been handled largely by the workshops themselves, which also functioned as sales outlets. In addition, the potters would have displayed their wares at the regular markets and fairs in their areas.[124] This does not, of course, preclude the regional distribution of the ceramics by retailers, within the limited scale of land or seacoast trade.[125]

In contrast to the glazed tablewares of the eleventh to twelfth centuries, which were viewed as semiluxury items and objects of social prestige, the glazed vessels produced after the middle of the thirteenth century had the features of vessels widely used by broad strata of the population.[126] Indeed, all vessels of the late Byzantine phase could literally be called "everyday utensils": the difference between the poor and the rich, we believe, was not in the quality but in the number that they could afford. In this connection, it should be noted that the glazed ceramics of the tenth to twelfth centuries include a comparatively large number of wares with holes for metal

---

121 Cipriano Piccolpasso, *I tre libri dell'arte del vasaio*, ed. A. Caiger-Smith and R. Lightbown, 2 vols. (London, 1980).
122 Laiou, "The Byzantine Economy: An Overview," 1150–52; Laiou and Morrisson, *The Byzantine Economy*, 121, 232.
123 B. Psaropoulou, *Τελευταίοι τσουκαλάδες του ανατολικού Αιγαίου* (Athens, n.d.). It might be noted that not all pottery workshops were producing glazed wares.
124 Laiou, "Exchange and Trade," 709–10; Matschke, "Commerce, Trade, Markets, and Money," 779–82; J. Lefort, *Villages de Macédoine*, vol. 1, *La Chalcidique occidentale* (Paris, 1982); A. I. Lampropoulou, "Οἱ πανηγύρεις στὴν Πελοπόννησο κατὰ τὴν μεσαιωνικὴ ἐποχή," in *Η καθημερινή ζωή στὸ Βυζάντιο* (Athens, 1989), 291–310; C. Asdracha, "Les foires en Épire médiévale: La fonction justificative de la mémoire historique," *JÖB* 32 (1982): 437–46.
125 Laiou, "The Byzantine Economy: An Overview," 1159.
126 Laiou and Morrisson, *The Byzantine Economy*, 187.

clamps that were used to hold broken parts together. The need to prolong the lifespan of a ceramic vessel, albeit with its use restricted to solid, dry foodstuffs, shows that it was not easy to acquire these utensils and that they were not inexpensive. This practice of mending broken vessels seems to languish after the middle of the thirteenth century.

Finally, examination of the case of Cyprus showed that in the late twelfth to early thirteenth centuries the same patterns of international trade continued to supply the markets of the crusader Levant with tablewares made in Byzantine workshops. The appearance of local glazed wares in Cyprus in the first half of the thirteenth century coincides with the decentralization of the production of glazed ceramics throughout the Byzantine world and the gradual replacement of imported wares with domestically produced wares in the Cypriot market. At this time Cypriot glazed wares even reached neighboring sites, principally to meet the needs of the crusader population that had settled there.

Cypriot ceramics, toward the fourteenth century, were influenced by the world of the crusaders. Cypriot glazed wares of this time, like Port Saint Symeon Ware, depict knights, ladies, and coats of arms, all part of a visual artistic language understood and accepted by all the people, Christians and Muslims, locals and foreigners, then living in the area of the eastern Mediterranean.[127] The ceramic evidence demonstrates extensive interregional as well as international communication. The study of glazed clay ceramics, goods for everyday use that evolved and circulated beyond the reach of religious and other restrictions, demonstrates that the relationships that developed in the Levant during the thirteenth and fourteenth centuries were complex and multilateral. The market and the consuming public were concerned with culture, and the exchanges were not just regional, interregional, and international but also intercultural.

The growing focus of archaeological and archaeometric research on Byzantine glazed ceramics will result in the attribution of more ceramic groups to specific workshops and centers of production. In addition, the increasing care and attention given by excavators of Byzantine sites to pottery finds will contribute to the documentation of their diffusion, attention that can shed a unique light on previously concealed Byzantine trade patterns.

127 Blackman and Redford, "Medieval Ceramics from Kinet," 84–87. See also M. Georgopoulou, "Orientalism and Crusader Art: Constructing a New Canon," in *Medieval Encounters: Jewish, Christian and Muslim Culture in Confluence and Dialogue*, ed. C. Robinson (Leiden, 1995), 289–321.

West and East: Local Exchanges in Neighboring Worlds

• NINE •

Local and Interregional Exchanges in the Lower Po Valley, Eighth–Ninth Centuries

SAURO GELICHI

Beyond Pirenne

Looking at the Mediterranean, but also focusing much more locally on the north of Italy and particularly on the Po Valley plain, historians and archaeologists seem to agree that the population was largely self-sufficient in its production and distribution of commodities in the years between the seventh and the tenth centuries.

Whether one follows the view put forward by the great Belgian historian Henri Pirenne,[1] or advocates the theory that signs of a crisis can be seen well before the advent of the Arabs,[2] there is no doubt that even the most recent historiography tends to treat the eighth century as a period of stagnation,[3] with low vitality and little creation or use of medium- or long-range trading networks.[4] This is not to suggest that trade relations completely ended, since valuable merchandise would in any case have continued to circulate for a restricted elite.[5] However, the crisis would have been felt in terms of what may be called the intermediary systems, and trade relations would have been reduced to a very local and regional scale. More recently even Michael McCormick, who sees the flourishing of Venice at the end of the eighth century as the turning point of the European and Mediterranean economy,[6] pays no attention to the features and the nature of earlier trade relations, even in those areas that contributed to the origins of the future Serenissima.

The analysis of those areas and of their economies, therefore, may be useful not only to establish more firmly the origin and fate of a unique city like Venice but also to evaluate whether the eighth century should be seen as a sort of long, stagnant waiting period or as revealing, at least in certain situations and specific places, more dynamic features.

The purpose of this chapter therefore is to discuss the scale of the northern Italian economy between the late Longobard age and the early Carolingian age, drawing on archaeological sources. Its objective is to demonstrate how the eighth century may be seen as a time of considerable vitality with regard to medium- and long-range trade, how this vitality must have been connected to an inadvertent

---

[1] As is well known, Henri Pirenne defined his theory at the beginning of the last century and published a synthesis in his famous volume *Mahomet and Charlemagne* (H. Pirenne, *Mahomet et Charlemagne* [Paris, 1922]). His theory has been broadly discussed; for a recent article, see P. Delogu, "Reading Pirenne Again," in *The Sixth Century: Production, Distribution and Demand*, ed. R. Hodges and W. Bowden (Leiden, 1998), 15–40.

[2] Pirenne's theory has been discussed, from an archaeological viewpoint, particularly by R. Hodges and D. Whitehouse, *Mohammed, Charlemagne and the Origins of Europe* (London, 1983), rev. in trans., *Mahomet, Charlemagne et les origins de l'Europe* (Paris, 1996).

[3] See I. L. Hansen and C. Wickham, eds., *The Long Eighth Century: Production, Distribution and Demand* (Leiden, 2000).

[4] See also C. Wickham, *Framing the Early Middle Ages: Europe and the Mediterranean, 400–800* (Oxford, 2005), and idem, "Overview: Production, Distribution and Demand, II," in Hansen and Wickham, eds., *The Long Eighth Century*, 345, 358–60.

[5] Wickham, *Framing the Early Middle Ages*. A similar position has been developed by B. Ward-Perkins, *The Fall of Rome and the End of Civilization* (Oxford, 2005).

[6] M. McCormick, *Origins of the European Economy: Communications and Commerce, A.D. 300–900* (Cambridge, 2001), 523–31.

system created by the Longobard rulers following the establishment of peace with the Byzantines in 680, and, lastly, how the flourishing of Venice may be rooted in these events.

The Economy of Northern Italy during the Eighth Century: A Historical and Archaeological Assessment

More than ten years ago, Ross Balzaretti published a highly interpretive article that discussed in particular northern Italy's economy between the eighth and the ninth centuries;[7] it essentially uses written sources, particularly a treaty between the Longobards and the inhabitants of Comacchio (a town that developed in the early Middle Ages at the mouth of the River Po; fig. 9.1) about trade on the River Po and its effluents.[8] As the people from Comacchio were obliged to pay duties on trade, the record of these taxes (paid in cash but also in kind) makes it possible to get an idea of the goods they exchanged along those rivers.

The Liutprand Capitulary, one of the few written sources of the eighth to ninth centuries, explicitly refers to the types of goods circulated,[9] but there is a danger of misjudging its importance. When consulting this source, scholars tend to focus on salt,[10] not only because of its role in early medieval nutrition but also because the tax on salt was actually mentioned as the principal duty that had to be paid in the port stations. This suggests that salt was the most sought-after commodity and that the people from Comacchio provided large quantities of it, but says nothing about the role and the importance of the other traded goods.

Indeed, the archaeological evidence considered by Balzaretti, recovered from the urban excavations and from the monasteries, suggests an alternative scenario. The archaeology of the principal cities that for different reasons are mentioned in the capitulary (Cremona, Mantua, Pavia) seems to indicate a lack of long-distance trade and exchange: the traditional long-distance traders are totally absent and, further, the quality of their material structures does not offer signs of the settlements' vitality. At the same time, even the monasteries' archaeology points toward a sort of impasse, though data on important urban or rural coenobia have not yet been published, with the exception of San Salvatore a Brescia.[11]

Essentially, the scarcity of both material and written sources seems to fit the theory of economic decline. The signs of dynamism displayed by the Liutprand Capitulary refer to the inner Po Valley. This could be described as a sort of constrained vitality;[12] and the goods attested in the capitulary,

---

7 R. Balzaretti, "Cities, Emporia and Monasteries: Local Economies in the Po Valley, c. AD 700–875," in *Towns in Transition: Urban Evolution in Late Antiquity and the Early Middle Ages,* ed. N. Christie and S. T. Loseby (Aldershot, 1996), 213–34.

8 This source, known as the Liutprand Capitulary, has been dated to 715 or 730. The *habitatores* of Comacchio were in fact the pact's contracting party (represented at this time by a *presbyter,* a *magister militum,* and two *comites*) and, generically, the Longobards. The text is known thanks to a thirteenth-century copy, which is kept in the Archivio Vescovile di Cremona; it was first published by L. M. Hartmann in 1904 (*Zur Wirtschaftsgeschichte Italiens: Analekten* [Gotha, 1904], 74–90). G. C. Mor has also examined the capitulary, with a different interpretation; see "Un'ipotesi sulla data del 'Pactum' c. d. Liutprandino coi 'milites' di Comacchio relativo alla navigazione sul Po," *AStIt* 135 (1977): 493–502. Its text has also been discussed particularly with regard to relations with the Padano River ports by G. Fasoli, "Navigazione fluviale: Porti e navi sul Po," in *La navigazione mediterranea nell'Alto Medioevo,* Settimane di studio 25 (Spoleto, 1978), 565–607.

9 See, for example, the tribute in pepper and cinnamon paid by the Comaclenses to the monastery of Bobbio in the ninth century: A. Castagnetti, M. Luzzati, G. Pasquali, and A. Vasina, eds., *Inventari altomedievali di terre, uomini e redditi* (Rome, 1979), 138.

10 On salt cultivation, and on the roles of Comacchio and Venice within the salt trade system, see the standard studies by Hartmann, *Zur Wirtschaftsgeschichte Italiens;* M. Merores, "Die venezianischen Salinen der älteren Zeit in ihrer wirtschaftlichen und sozialen Bedeutung," *Vierteljahrschrift für Sozial- und Wirtschaftsgeschichte* 13 (1916): 71–107; and G. Volpe, *Medio Evo italiano* (Florence, 1923), 256; as well as J.-C. Hocquet, *Le sel et la fortune de Venise,* vol. 2, *Voiliers et commerce en Méditerranée* (Villeneuve-d'Ascq, 1979). On salt production in Comacchio, see L. Bellini, *Le saline dell'antico delta* (Ferrara, 1962). Further, regarding the role of salt in relation to the Liutprand Capitulary, see M. Montanari, "Il Capitolare di Liutprando: Note di storia dell'economia e dell'alimentazione," in *La civiltà Comacchiese e Pomposiana dalle origini preistoriche al tardo medioevo* (Bologna, 1986), 461–75.

11 This monastery was founded by King Desiderio and his wife Ansa, ca. 750. The archaeological sequence of the excavations was already known by the end of the 1980s (G. P. Brogiolo, "Trasformazioni urbanistiche nella Brescia longobarda: Dalle capanne in legno al monastero regio di San Salvatore," in *Italia Longobarda,* ed. G. C. Menis [Venice, 1991], 101–19), but a more recent series of monographs have pushed their date back by a few years: see G. P. Brogiolo, ed., *S. Giulia di Brescia, gli scavi dal 1980 al 1992: Reperti preromani, romani e altomedievali* (Florence, 1999); G. P. Brogiolo, F. Morandini, and F. Rossi, eds., *Dalle "domus" alla corte regia: S. Giulia di Brescia: Gli scavi dal 1980 al 1992* (Florence, 2005).

12 S. Gelichi, "Tra Comacchio e Venezia: Economia, società e insediamenti nell'arco nord adriatico durante l'Alto Medioevo,"

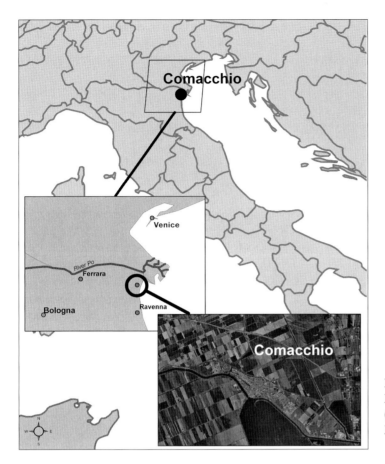

Figure 9.1.
Location of Comacchio (Ferrara)
(drawn by Laboratorio di Archeologia
Medievale—Venezia)

which were certainly exotic (for instance, the spices and maybe the garum), have been interpreted as luxuries directed at an elite client base.

Thus we see, on the one hand, a drastic reduction in Mediterranean trade—the collapse of the bulk utilitarian commodities system,[13] which was characteristic of the late antique economy—and, on the other hand, a very high level of circulation of luxury goods. The latter phenomenon has always existed, and therefore it does not help our understanding of the qualitative and quantitative level of Mediterranean trade.

It is important to underline that there is a remarkable lack of evidence in the archaeology of northern Italy for the new settlements (towns or emporiums) that appear in the written sources from the seventh to eighth centuries (fig. 9.2). Among these settlements are a number of centers from the Venetian lagoon plexus (or at the borders of the lagoon), such as Torcello,[14] Olivolo,[15] Cittanova,[16] Costanziaco,[17]

---

in *Genti nel Delta da Spina a Comacchio: Uomini, territorio e culto dall'antichità all'alto medioevo*, ed. F. Berti, M. Bollini, S. Gelichi, and J. Ortalli (Ferrara, 2007), 380–82.

13 Wickham, *Framing the Early Middle Ages;* Ward-Perkins, *The Fall of Rome.*

14 On Torcello, see E. Crouzet-Pavan, *La mort lente de Torcello: Histoire d'une cité disparue* (Paris, 1995). On its archaeology, see L. Leciejwicz, E. Tabaczyńska, and S. Tabaczyński, *Torcello: Scavi 1961–62* (Rome, 1977). For the most recent excavations, see L. Leciejwicz, ed., *Torcello: Nuove ricerche archeologiche* (Rome, 2000).

15 On the excavations carried out at the nearby church of S. Pietro di Castello (the antique Olivolo), which have provided fifth- to seventh-century contexts, see S. Tuzzato, "Le strutture lignee altomedievali a Olivolo (S. Pietro di Castello–Venezia)," in *Studi di archeologia della X Regio in ricordo di Michele Tombolani* (Rome, 1994), 479–85; S. Tuzzato, V. Favero, and M. Josè Vinals, "San Pietro di Castello a Venezia: Nota preliminare dopo la campagna 1992," *Quaderni di Archeologia* 9 (1993): 72–80.

16 On Cittanova, see D. Calaon, "Cittanova (VE): Analisi GIS," in *IV Congresso Nazionale di Archeologia Medievale,* ed. R. Francovich and M. Valenti (Florence, 2006), 216–24 (with the earlier bibliography).

17 The area of Costanziaco, in the northern lagoon, has been partially investigated. In particular, excavations have been carried out on San Lorenzo di Ammiana island; see E. Canal, L. Fersuoch,

and Malamocco.[18] In the northern part of the lagoon area, the episcopal *castrum* of Grado (Udine) emerged, while in the south are Chioggia (Venice), the site of Gavello, nearby Adria (Rovigo),[19] and Comacchio, on the delta of the Po. The archaeology of these areas looks very different, but its analysis has rarely concentrated on their origins.

In the Venice lagoon, for instance, the archaeology has developed quite atypically, in that the most important element has been the discovery of its classical origins (or "Romanity"); the researchers did not focus their excavations on understanding the original phases of the settlement.[20] In general, the archaeology carried out has not taken account of the postclassical phases, even though the historical evidence suggests that they are worthy of study.

To use a maritime metaphor (pertinent to these places and topics): if in antiquity taking refuge meant landing in a safe place, then attempting new ways could have suggested adventure in unknown far-off seas (and often in stormy weather)—as I am trying to do with my research. Take, for example, Comacchio, which is known from the written sources only from the beginning of the eighth century, but presumably has a much earlier history, both in the episcopal sequence and in the date of its foundation.[21] A strategy of effective investigation therefore requires more active consideration of the material sources.

A Small Lagoon and a Small Settlement? Comacchio during the Early Middle Ages

Today Comacchio is a small town lying near the delta of the River Po, renowned for its fish and its charming historical center. Not inhabited during Roman times, it emerged only toward the beginning of the eighth century with the appearance of the extraordinary capitulary mentioned above.[22] At present, there is no reason and no archaeological evidence to ascribe a more ancient origin to it. As the site is termed *castrum* in some early medieval written sources, its defensive function seems clear, given the fortification of the exarchate borders undertaken by the Byzantine authorities toward the beginning of the seventh century.[23]

This interpretation, which should not necessarily be rejected out of hand, gives these places a history whose processes replicate those suggested for another lagoon area which emerged in that very same period, that of Venice. The inhabitants may have been encouraged to move from the mainland to the lagoon islands not so much by long-term economic trends as by events connected to the barbarian inva-

---

S. Spector, and G. Zambon, "Indagini archeologiche a S. Lorenzo di Ammiana (Venezia)," *Archeologia Veneta* 12 (1989): 71–96; E. Canal, *Testimonianze archeologiche nella Laguna di Venezia: L'età antica* (Venice, 1998), 33–44. See also E. Canal, "Le Venezie sommerse: Quarant'anni di archeologia lagunare," in *La laguna di Venezia,* ed. G. Caniato, E. Turri, and M. Zanetti (Verona, 1995), 206–21.

18 The location of the ancient Metamacum/Metamauco does not seem to coincide with the present village of Malamocco.

19 On Gavello, and in general on Adria and its territory in the early Middle Ages, see L. Casazza, *Il territorio di Adria tra VI e X secolo* (Padua, 2001).

20 It is not possible to detail all the scientific knowledge of this period developed by Italian archaeologists, but see W. Dorigo, *Venezia origini: Fondamenti, ipotesi, metodi* (Milan, 1983). For a critical analysis of this type of archaeology, see S. Gelichi, "Venezia tra archeologia e storia: La costruzione di una identità urbana," in *Le città italiane tra la tarda antichità e l'alto Medioevo,* ed. A. Augenti (Florence, 2006), 151–83; idem, "Tra Comacchio e Venezia," 368–73.

21 The first definite bishop is dated to the second half of the eighth century; on the episcopal sequence, see L. Bellini, *I vescovi di Comacchio* (Ferrara, 1967), and the observations of A. Samaritani, *Medievalia e altri studi* (Ferrara, 1961). For a synthesis of the problems, see E. Grandi, "La cristianizzazione del territorio," in Berti et al., eds., *Genti nel Delta,* 420–26. Concerning the archaeology of Comacchio, see a synthesis in S. Gelichi and D. Cal-

aon, "Comacchio: La storia di un emporio sul delta del Po," ibid., 387–416.

22 Although the bibliography on Comacchio is abundant, there is still a need for up-to-date publications containing historical synthesis. Concerning the early Middle Ages, see, on the territory of Comacchio in the Roman era, J. Ortalli, "I Romani nel Delta: Una prospettiva archeologica," in Berti et al., eds., *Genti nel Delta,* 233–55; for the phase of transition between antiquity and the Middle Ages, see again Gelichi and Calaon, "Comacchio: La storia," 387–416.

23 Comacchio is sometimes called *castrum* and its inhabitants labeled *milites,* but no ancient (or humanistic) written source associates its foundation with the establishment of a fortification to defend the borders of the exarchate during the Byzantine age, despite the suggestions of some scholars: for instance, see C. Diehl, *Études sur l'administration byzantine dans l'exarchat de Ravenne (568–571)* (Paris, 1888), 57; A. Guillou, *Régionalisme et indépendance dans l'Empire byzantin au VIIe siècle: L'exemple de l'Exarchat et de la Pentapole d'Italie* (Rome, 1969), 58; A. Vasina, "Il territorio ferrarese nell'alto medioevo," in *Insediamenti nel Ferrarese: Dall'età romana alla fondazione della cattedrale* (Florence, 1976), 81; S. Patitucci Uggeri, "Il *castrum* Ferrariae," ibid., 153–58. About this issue and the significance for these territories of some of these terms (including κάστρον) in the written sources, see Gelichi, "Tra Comacchio e Venezia," 380–81.

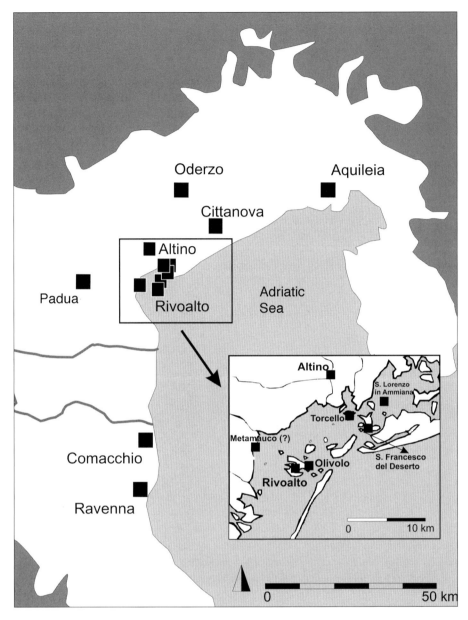

Figure 9.2. The northern Adriatic arc and some of the places mentioned in the text (drawn by Laboratorio di Archeologia Medievale—Venezia)

sions and the subsequent Byzantine responses: in other words, for reasons connected to safety rather than trade.[24]

24 For a different interpretation of this phenomenon than the traditional one, see C. La Rocca, "Città scomparse in area veneta nell'alto medioevo: Dati archeologici, fonti scritte e memoria storiografica," in *L'Adriatico dalla tarda antichità all'eta carolingia* (Florence, 2005), 287–99; S. Gelichi, "La nascita di Venezia," in *Roma e i Barbari,* ed. J.-J. Aillagon (Milan, 2008), 584–87.

Leaving aside for the moment the question of the origins of Comacchio, which are still difficult to determine in the absence of targeted research, it is surprising that archaeology has not yet highlighted or analyzed its features during the period about which written sources inform us. In short, if Comacchio really was an important nodal point for the economy of the Lombard Kingdom in the first half of the eighth century, it is amazing that

Figure 9.3. Comacchio: posts recovered in the 1920s in the northwest area of the settlement (photo by Soprintendenza per i Beni Archeologici per l'Emilia-Romagna—Bologna)

no trace of this central role has emerged from material sources. It is for this reason, and with the aim of verifying the archaeological record of this central role, that some years ago my colleagues and I began a research project in these areas. The main aim was to gain a better understanding of settlement and socioeconomic processes in the northern Adriatic between the seventh and ninth century—a period that is obviously crucial for understanding the origins of Venice.

The archaeological evidence from Comacchio is, today, very unequal in quality. It includes finds recovered at the beginning of the twentieth century when areas in the northwest of the present settlement were drained (where formerly a sugar refinery was located)[25] (fig. 9.3); tombs and wall remains recovered during the 1970s in the northeast area of the settlement (the area of the monastery of Sant'Agostino) and in the historical center (via Mazzini);[26] and some stratigraphical excavations from the late 1990s, in front of the monastery of Santa Maria in Aula Regia and again in the northwest area, in conjunction with a building being divided into lots.[27]

We can add to these investigations the excavation carried out between 2007 and 2008 in the area around the cathedral, as well as the more recent stratigraphical excavations in the village of San Francesco. Further, we should not forget the gen-

25 On the excavations of that period (with bibliography), see Gelichi and Calaon, "Comacchio: La storia," 387–94. A number of these findings have already been discussed by S. Patitucci Uggeri, "Problemi storico-topografici di Comacchio tra tardo-antico e altomedioevo: Gli scavi di Valle Ponti," in *Actes du XIe Congrès International d'Archéologie Chrétienne* (Rome, 1989),

2301–15; eadem, "Il Delta Padano nell'età dei goti," in *XXXVI Corso di Cultura sull'Arte Ravennate e Bizantina* (Ravenna, 1989), 269–322.

26 S. Patitucci Uggeri, "Il *castrum Cumiacli*: Evidenze archeologiche e problemi storico-topografici," in *La civiltà Comacchiese,* 273.

27 D. Calaon, "Lo scavo di Villaggio San Francesco 1996 (COM 96): Le strutture portuali di Comacchio?" in Berti et al., eds., *Genti nel Delta,* 505–30; G. Bucci, "COM 03, Villaggio San Francesco," in ibid., 553–56; eadem, "COM 01, via Mazzini," ibid., 557–63.

Figure 9.4. Comacchio, San Francesco village, excavations, 2008: waterfront on the canal (8th c.) (photo by Laboratorio di Archeologia Medievale—Venezia)

eral archaeological researches in the territory of Comacchio, which have brought to light several early medieval contexts, such as the church and the cemetery of Motta della Girata.[28] In all, this evidence is very significant and needs to be considered carefully, but here it would be better to discuss two specific contexts that help us understand the topography and the socioeconomic character of the settlement in the centuries under consideration: the area of the San Francesco village/former sugar refinery and the area around the cathedral.

The evidence from the first site indicates very clearly that we are dealing with an area constructed for use as a port. For instance, the numerous remains of posts, bank structures, and wooden platforms are suggestive of port structures. The ceramic material recovered (89 percent unglazed ware, 55 percent of which are amphorae dated to the eighth to ninth centuries) confirms the nature of the context and the chronology. New archaeological investigations should make possible a new reconstruction of this area, as recently excavated trenches have started to demonstrate. At this point, however, the mercantile character of the place continues to be prominent. Of the three trenches opened in the autumn of 2008, one has brought to light a waterfront, on the canal: this is perfectly preserved and filled with fragments of early medieval amphorae (fig. 9.4). A second trench underlines the presence here of docks. The most recent excavations confirm that the northwest area of Comacchio was occupied by port structures in an area of ca. 75,000 square meters.

Analysis of the surrounding environment enables us to see how the port area was naturally protected by the lagoon and was effectively linked to the external seashore areas by a tidal canal that ensured a constant flow of salt water from outside (fig. 9.5). Via this canal, goods from Mediterranean and

---

28 See the recent article by C. Corti, "Santa Maria in Padovetere: La chiesa, la necropoli e l'insediamento circostante," in Berti et al., eds., *Genti nel Delta,* 531–52; eadem, "La frequentazione nell'area di Santa Maria in Padovetere: Materiali dalla chiesa e dall'insediamento circostante," ibid., 569–89.

Figure 9.5. Comacchio in the early Middle Ages in relation to the water canals (drawn by Laboratorio di Archeologia Medievale—Venezia)

Adriatic sea routes could reach the port. Wharves and wooden jetties formed quays and areas for warehouses, while local flat-bottomed boats, suitable for traveling along the shallow waters of the rivers in the Po Valley plain, would have guaranteed distribution of the goods inland.

A second area of recent archaeological investigation is located near the cathedral (fig. 9.6).[29] Excavations have been under way for about two years and the sequence that has been recovered, though of extraordinary interest for many reasons, cannot be discussed until published in full.

The most significant preliminary data are linked to the first occupations of the area. The most ancient traces of occupation of the site, dated to before the seventh century at the latest, are represented by a series of wooden households (fig. 9.7). These buildings seem to be associated with manufacturing (probably glassworks), perhaps connected with the cult building (probably the episcopal church) that was constructed in that area.

From this moment onward (eighth to ninth centuries) the sequence seems to change: the production facilities and the households are covered by a necropolis, which was in use until at least the tenth to eleventh century, when important new renovations appear to have taken place in the church (and presumably also nearby). From the recovered material of this period we are able to gain a better understanding of the nature of the early medieval church, which was most probably located under the area occupied by the cathedral (rebuilt in the seventeenth century): this church seems to be characterized by a mosaic pavement, with walls made of marble slabs and a possible chancel screen (or iconostasis), constructed in the ninth century, of which

---

29 S. Gelichi, ed., *L'isola del vescovo: Gli scavi archeologici intorno alla Cattedrale di Comacchio = The Archaeological Excavations near the Comacchio Cathedral* (Florence, 2009).

Figure 9.6. Comacchio, cathedral area, excavations, 2007–08: a general view (photo by Laboratorio di Archeologia Medievale—Venezia)

Figure 9.7. Comacchio, cathedral area, excavations, 2007–08: the earliest phases of the area (7th c.) (photo by Laboratorio di Archeologia Medievale—Venezia)

we have a few precious fragments (fig. 9.8). What is interesting here is not only the presence of a cult building of apparently high quality but also significant contemporary materials not commonly found in what we understand to be the characteristic material culture of the eighth to ninth centuries in the northern Italy region.

Single-firing glazed ware,[30] unglazed ware (fig. 9.9),[31] coins (fig. 9.10),[32] and above all amphorae (see below) are important, especially because of the quantities found, and they are predominant among the residual material from the layers dated to the medieval and modern period. These finds certainly associate the cathedral area with privilege and high rank, but importantly they also reflect quite closely the economy and trading activities of the emporium.

The combination of this old and new data immediately raises questions about the role of Comacchio in the framework of early medieval settlement of the

30 This pottery presents analogies with the so-called Forum Ware of Roman-Laziale production—see L. Paroli, "La ceramica invetriata tardo-antica e medievale nell'Italia centro meridionale," in *La ceramica invetriata tardoantica e altomedievale in Italia,* ed. L. Paroli (Florence, 1992), 33–61; M. Sannazaro, "La ceramica invetriata tra età romana e medioevo," in *"Ad mensam": Manufatti d'uso da contesti archeologici fra Tarda Antichità e Medioevo,* ed. S. Lusuardi Siena (Udine, 1994), 242–50—but mineral-petrographic analyses have ascertained that it was not produced in that area. To date, pottery of this type has been recovered in Romagna (S. Gelichi and M. G. Maioli, "Emilia-Romagna," in *La ceramica invetriata tardoantica e altomedievale in Italia,* ed. Paroli, 216–17 n. 1 [from Rimini], 265 nn. 10, 11 [from Imola]), in Comacchio itself (ibid., 272–73 nn. 4, 5; S. Gelichi, C. Negrelli, G. Bucci, V. Coppola, and C. Capelli, "I materiali da Comacchio," in Berti et al., eds., *Genti nel Delta,* 632–38; Gelichi, ed., *L'isola del vescovo,* 39), and, above all, in the Venice lagoon (L. Paroli, I. de Luca, F. Sbarra, M. Bortoletto, and C. Capelli, "La ceramica invetriata altomedievale in Italia: Un aggiornamento," in *VIIe Congrès International sur la Céramique Médiévale en Méditerranée, Thessaloniki, 11–16 Octobre 1999, Actes,* ed. Ch. Bakirtzis [Athens, 2003], 485–86). It is possible that it was manufactured in the Delta area of the Po River (perhaps in Comacchio itself).

31 This pottery, made with a fine fabric, is represented by only a single form: a sort of jug, almost always with double handles and with a flat base (Gelichi, ed., *L'isola del vescovo,* 38–39). And though this pottery shows parallels with Roman products recorded in eighth-century deposits (e.g., the Crypta Balbi in Rome), the mineral-petrographic analyses of the fabrics seem to indicate, at least for the vessels recovered in Comacchio, that its production was probably local.

32 For example, Mauricius Tiberius (582–602) *decanummius,* Ravenna; Constans II (643–ca. 650) *follis,* Ravenna; Louis the Pious (819–22) *denarius,* Venice; Hugh of Provence (926–57) *denarius,* probably Venice (courtesy Alessia Rovelli).

Figure 9.8. Comacchio, cathedral area, excavations, 2007: fragment of the chancel screen (9th c.) (photo by Laboratorio di Archeologia Medievale—Venezia)

Figure 9.9. Comacchio, cathedral area, excavations, 2007–08: early medieval unglazed ware (photo by Laboratorio di Archeologia Medievale—Venezia)

Po Valley area. What is the relationship between this place and the economy of the Po Valley? Who were the participants (active or passive) in these trading operations? Did these activities really center mainly or only on salt?

Figure 9.10. Comacchio, cathedral area, excavations, 2007–08: denarius of Louis the Pious (819–22), Venice (courtesy of Alessia Rovelli; photo by Laboratorio di Archeologia Medievale—Venezia)

Mediterranean Exchanges?

In considering the amphorae, which clearly represent an archaeological marker of high significance, it is important to stress that the archaeological evidence about the eighth-century chronology has been recorded only recently (fig. 9.11). In fact, until only a few years ago it was believed that the circulation of amphorae, at least via the Mediterranean, ended in the seventh century, apparently coinciding with the end of long- and medium-distance trade. However, detailed archaeological investigations, paying particular attention to eighth- and ninth-century levels in different areas of the Italian peninsula, have clearly shown that amphorae continue to be present in these two centuries.[33] Even in northern Italy, eighth- and ninth-century amphorae have been found in, for example, Rimini, Verona, and the Venetian lagoon (fig. 9.12).[34]

[33] The early medieval globular amphorae have large bodies with wide curved shoulders, flat or convex bases, conical necks, straight or slightly enlarged lips, sometimes with internal grooves, and either ribbon handles (sometimes with a central large rib) or a loop handle. The dimensions can differ, but generally are attested as high as 50–60 cm (the dimensions of the materials from Comacchio, though conjectural, are fully compatible with those of entire vessels from other places), with lips 7–8 cm in diameter. They derive from the similar Aegean forms LR2 and they have a clear link with the Yassı Ada 2 type (typologically speaking, a variant of the large category LR 2), which is still widespread in the Aegean and the Mediterranean Sea in the seventh century. For a good synopsis, see C. Negrelli, "Produzione, circolazione e consumo tra VI e IX secolo dal territorio del Padovetere a Comacchio," in Berti et al., eds., *Genti nel Delta*, 454–62.

[34] For early medieval amphorae from Verona, see B. Bruno, "Ceramiche da alcuni contesti tardoantichi e altomedievali di Verona," in *La circolazione delle ceramiche nell'Adriatico tra Tarda Antichità ed Altomedioevo: III Incontro di Studio Cer.*

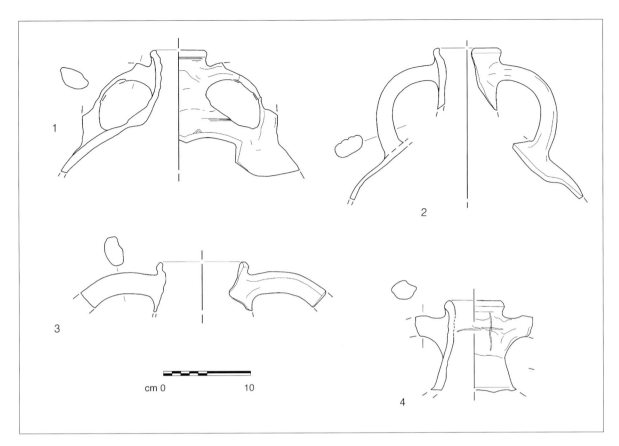

Figure 9.11. Comacchio, settlement area, excavations: early medieval amphorae (drawn by C. Negrelli)

To return to the amphorae recovered in Comacchio, archaeological and archaeometric investigations are still in progress, so it is too early to present a detailed typology. But we can already start to sketch the important questions that this evidence may be able to answer (and begin to guess at what those answers might be): Where do these amphorae come from? What were they carrying? And who were the consumers of these commodities?

First, possible sources of such containers, of extremely uniform shape (but with very different ceramic fabrics), are southern Italy, the eastern Mediterranean, and particularly Syria-Palestine and the Aegean (although possible imports from Pontus cannot be excluded).[35] Their uniformity suggests that the containers may have been sent directly from a single center—presumably the capital of the Byzantine Empire, if we base our judgment on comparisons with the site of Saraçhane in Istanbul studied by J. W. Hayes.[36] The contents of the amphorae are more difficult to determine: reasonable guesses are oil, garum, and wine, but only future scientific

---

am.Is, ed. S. Gelichi and C. Negrelli (Mantua, 2007), 157–82. For the amphorae from the Venice lagoon, see I. Modrzewska, "Bizanyjskie amfory (wydobyte) z laguny weneckiej," in *Studia Zdziejów Cywilizacji (Studia ofiarowane Profesorowi Jerzemu Gąssowkiemu)* (Warsaw, 1998), 267–71; A. Toniolo, "Le anfore," in *Ca' Vendramin Calergi: Archeologia urbana lungo il Canal Grande di Venezia,* ed. L. Fozzati (Venice, 2005), 90–94. For the amphorae recovered in Rimini, see C. Negrelli, *Rimini capitale: Strutture insediative, sociali ed economiche tra V e VIII secolo* (Florence, 2008), 77–80, 94–95.

35 On these transport vessels, the publication by Negrelli, "Produzione, circolazione e consumo," 437–71, is outstanding, particularly about the amphorae, 454–68.

36 J. W. Hayes, *Excavations at Saraçhane in Istanbul,* vol. 2, *The Pottery* (Princeton, N.J., 1992).

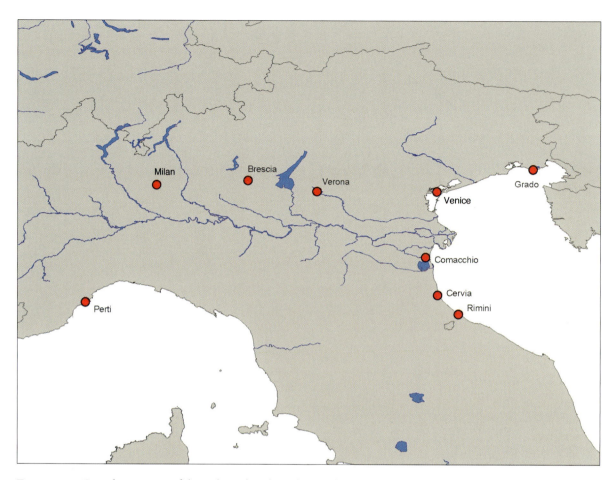

Figure 9.12. Distribution map of the early medieval amphorae of northern Italy (drawn by C. Negrelli)

analysis of their residues, which is certainly feasible, will determine which is correct. These amphorae are important not only for their contents but also simply for their presence, which helps us understand the movement of vessels made of wood or vegetable and animal fiber, which have not been preserved in the archaeological record.

Finally, let us try to answer the last question, which focused on the consumers of these amphorae. Does the amphora evidence correspond with the hypothesis that luxury goods were traded for a limited elite? The lengthy excursus on Comacchio and the character of the emporium trade during the eighth century is very helpful here. Contrary to expectation, the quantity of archaeological evidence found (which suggests only indirectly the real volume of traffic) is of a magnitude that would have seemed unimaginable until recently (see fig. 9.13). It reveals that there were still, during the eighth century, active trading relations with the Byzantines that apparently were neither sporadic nor accidental. Indeed, the economic picture had changed drastically, starting in the last quarter of the seventh and continuing into the first half of the eighth century, with the creation and development of these emporia, for which I believe these finds provide very precise material testimony. The number of round amphorae of Mediterranean origin, but above all the very existence of sites like Comacchio, with complex and extensive infrastructures, is by no means explained by the circulation of a few luxury goods to a limited elite. In addition, other archaeological and historical evidence points to the presence of a relatively high social class during the Longobard reign in the late seventh and eighth century, the *negotiantes*.[37] This

---

37 The figures of the *negotiantes* appear in the legal documents of the Longobard period (from Aistulf's *leges*: C. Azzara and S. Gasparri, eds., *Le leggi dei Longobardi: Storia, memoria e diritto di un popolo germanico* [Milan, 1992], 250–51). Regarding their

Figure 9.13. Reconstruction of early medieval Comacchio (courtesy of Comune di Comacchio; drawn by R. Merlo and Laboratorio di Archeologia Medievale—Venezia)

more detailed analysis of Longobard society in the eighth century, together with the level of its wealth, has been more clearly explored in recent research and seems to agree with the data emerging from the archaeological record.[38]

The history of Comacchio and its excavations would under any circumstances be of continuing archaeological interest, even if of only local significance; but the context in which this site has developed touches on broader topics and problems. In fact, from the eighth century onward the trade networks include Comacchio, placing it in a web of connections that reach across the Mediterranean.

Two themes in particular are apparent: the quantity of trade, archaeologically witnessed by the presence of amphorae, and the transregional nature of this traffic, suggested by the Liutprand Capitulary and other written sources. However, since the archaeological framework is still partly incomplete, it is important to reaffirm that some centers, such as Ravenna, were in decline during this period.[39] On the other hand, the archaeology of other antique coastal cities, such as Rimini, seems to follow a different trajectory.[40] The best evidence, judging from the published material, comes from the Venice lagoon. A recent excavation located in the historical center of Venice, Ca' Vendramin Calergi, has brought to light an archaeological sequence dated from the seventh century, which is paralleled in Comacchio.[41]

---

presence in the Longobard society and their function, see the discussion in S. Gasparri, "Mercanti o possessori? Profilo di un ceto dominante in un'età di transizione," in *Carte di famiglia: Strategie, rappresentazione e memoria del gruppo familiare di Totone di Campione (721–877)*, ed. idem and C. La Rocca (Rome, 2005), 161–62.

38 The observations of Gasparri on the family of the Totoni, as well as his general information on Longobard society, are worth noting (Gasparri, "Mercanti o possessori?" 157–77). On these issues, see also S. Gelichi, "Una discussione con Chris Wickham," *Storica* 34 (2006): 134–47.

39 For Ravenna in this period, the most up-to-date analysis is E. Cirelli, *Ravenna: Archeologia di una città*, Contributi di archeologia medievale 2 (Florence, 2008).

40 See the results of the excavations in the area of Piazza Ferrari, recently published (Negrelli, *Rimini capitale*); the particular attention to excavating the postclassic phases has made possible precise descriptions of the changes of a rich Roman *domus* and its later functional elements. These transformations (from mosaic pavements to beaten pavements) do not influence the characteristics of the contexts, which during the seventh and eighth centuries still include evidence of imported amphorae, fine tablewares, and Islamic coins.

41 The excavation—one of the few sites of the lagoon definitively published—is particularly significant for several reasons. First, it indicates, in this central area of the future Venice, the presence of a settlement dated earlier than the seventh century. Further, it shows the presence of a household that very closely resembles wooden buildings in the north of Italy dated to the same period. Finally, it is remarkable because the associations of materials in the eighth- to ninth-century deposits (amphorae, unglazed pottery, Monochrome Glazed Ware with appliqué decorations) are the same as in the contemporary deposits of Comacchio. On the excavation, see V. Gobbo, "Lo scavo d'emergenza nel cortile occidentale di Ca' Vendramin Calergi,"

Figure 9.14. Nonantola (Modeno), excavations of the monastery: pottery from the 8th c. (on left) and 9th–10th c. (on right) (photo by Laboratorio di Archeologia Medievale—Venezia)

How should we characterize these "new emergent centers"? The contemporary (or slightly later) sources seem to find it difficult to label them.[42] The term "emporium" would probably be most appropriate, not only because it links this area with northern Europe, where a similar phenomenon was occurring,[43] but also because this word more specifically identifies centers with economic characteristics.

The situation of Comacchio is therefore not unique in the eighth century in the northern Adriatic arc. The birth and development of this place, which appears to be linked to the economic policies of the Longobard reign, is also a part of the strong dynamic system in the northern Adriatic arc.[44] Within this system, different locations appear to compete with one another, on two different scales: one is within the Venetian lagoon, signaled by the alternations among different centers of power until the birth of Venice; the other is much wider, and includes the whole northern Adriatic arc, within which Comacchio seems to be a major player. This competition also appears in the written sources, though they are strongly colored by the view of the winners, who are the *Venetici* people.[45] It eventually ended with the consolidation of the settlement

---

in Fozzati, ed., *Ca' Vendramin Calergi*, 41–57; on the material, idem, "Le ceramiche della prima fase medievale," in ibid., 95–102.

42 S. Gelichi, "Flourishing Places in North-eastern Italy: Towns and *emporia* between Late Antiquity and the Carolingian Age," in *Post-Roman Towns, Trade and Settlement in Europe and Byzantium*, ed. J. Henning, vol. 1, *The Heirs of the Roman West*, Millennium-Studien zu Kultur und Geschichte des ersten Jahrtausends n. Chr. 5.1 (Berlin, 2007), 83–84.

43 The bibliography on northern European emporiums is very rich. Among the most important works are R. Hodges, *Dark Age Economics: The Origins of Towns and Trade, A.D. 600–1000* (New York, 1982), and, more recently, T. Pestell and K. Ulmschneider, eds., *Markets in Early Medieval Europe: Trading and "Productive" Sites, 650–850* (Macclesfield, 2003).

44 I have discussed these issues in "The Eels of Venice: The Long Eighth Century of the Emporia of the Northern Region along the Adriatic Coast," in *774: Ipotesi su una transizione,* ed. S. Gasparri (Turnhout, 2008), 81–117.

45 See the *Istoria Veneticorum* by John the Deacon, the first chronicle that tells about the initial phases of Venetian history (Comacchio appears in 3.44 and 3.12).

around Rivoalto, the heart of the future Venice, to which the Frankish kings were politically close.[46]

I believe that this research has cast new light on the economic characteristics (especially the question of local versus international factors) that seem to define northern Italy between the late Longobard age and the early Carolingian age, demonstrating that Mediterranean trade did not completely cease, but instead developed in many different ways (and to varying extents). Fragmentation, which remains the real paradigm of early medieval Europe and the Mediterranean (as Chris Wickham has argued), took a different form in these regions. Paradoxically, it seems that the Carolingian renaissance actually reduced the international economic role of the Po Valley area—as at least the archaeological evidence from the important monastery of Nonantola, on the far fringes of this economic system, suggests (fig. 9.14).[47]

---

[46] The Carolingians attempted several times to conquer Venice and to come to agreements with the Venetians: R. Hodges, *Towns and Trade in the Age of Charlemagne* (London, 2000), 62. For several reasons, and in particular the nature of the location, the area of the Venice lagoon must have appeared to the Franks more interesting than the southern coastal centers.

[47] This is demonstrated by two contexts, of the eighth and ninth–tenth centuries respectively, recovered during the recent excavations within the monastic complex. See S. Gelichi and M. Librenti, "Nascita e fortuna di un grande monastero altomedievale: Nonantola e il suo territorio dalla fondazione al XIV secolo," in *Monasteri in Europa occidentale (secoli VIII–XI): Topografia e strutture,* ed. F. De Rubeis and F. Marazzi (Rome, 2007), 239–57; S. Gelichi, M. Librenti, and A. Cianciosi, *Nonantola e l'abbazia di San Silvestro alla luce dell'archeologia: Ricerche, 2002–2006* (Carpi, 2006).

• TEN •

Adriatic Trade Networks in the Twelfth and Early Thirteenth Centuries

ROWAN W. DORIN

It appears that regional trade has finally found its scholarly footing. For medieval economic historians, long-distance maritime trade was for many decades the center of attention, the absence of far-reaching trade networks (whether real or supposed) often being seen—*à la* Pirenne—as an indication of economic dormancy. In the post–World War II era, interest in the history of local trade began to move out of the shadows, though it was all too frequently sidestepped with a token nod to its ubiquity and resilience. Meanwhile, regional trade was sandwiched awkwardly between these two analytic categories, with evidence of such trade often squeezed into local or long-distance models rather than interpreted discretely. Recent scholarship, however, has begun to highlight both the economic importance of regional trade systems and their structural differentiation from both long-distance and local trade. This is especially true for the early Middle Ages. Richard Hodges's work on the North Sea and that of Michael McCormick, Chris Wickham, and many others on the Mediterranean have brought to light considerable and persuasive evidence for the vitality of regional maritime trade systems prior to the tenth century.[1] Their economic importance was fundamental; McCormick has described the eighth and ninth centuries as "an age of predominantly regional shipping zones," while Wickham has similarly maintained that "most exchange, and the most important bulk exchange, took place inside rather than between regions."[2] Building on this work, Wickham has also argued that the subsequent expansion of long-distance trade was driven by the increasing internal complexity and dynamism of these early regional systems—a challenging hypothesis, at the very least.[3] However, the excitement generated by a new appreciation of the scope and activity of these early medieval trade networks has not inspired comparable work on later centuries, even though regional trade continued to play a crucial role in the economic life of Europe and the Mediterranean.[4] Indeed, such networks not

The topic of this chapter was first suggested to me by Angeliki Laiou, beloved teacher and mentor, who guided its development and sharpened its arguments. I am grateful to the editor for including it in this volume dedicated to her memory, and I would also like to thank the editor for her own helpful criticisms. I owe further thanks to David Abulafia, Sauro Gelichi, Michael McCormick, and Gherardo Ortalli for their suggestions, and to Dumbarton Oaks for granting me a short-term predoctoral residency to facilitate completion of the essay.

1 R. Hodges, *Dark Age Economics: The Origins of Towns and Trade, A.D. 600–1000* (New York, 1982); idem, *Towns and Trade in the Age of Charlemagne* (London, 2000); M. McCormick, *Origins of the European Economy: Communications and Commerce, A.D. 300–900* (Cambridge, 2001); C. Wickham, *Framing the Early Middle Ages: Europe and the Mediterranean, 400–800* (Oxford, 2005), esp. 693–824. A cautious synthesis of the scholarship on the Mediterranean is offered in S. T. Loseby, "The Mediterranean Economy," in *New Cambridge Medieval History*, vol. 1, *c. 500–c. 700*, ed. P. Fouracre (Cambridge, 2005), 605–38.
2 McCormick, *Origins of the European Economy*, 547; Wickham, *Framing the Early Middle Ages*, 707.
3 Wickham, *Framing the Early Middle Ages*, 707.
4 In the 1970s, David Abulafia, Michel Balard, and others conducted pioneering research into regional trade networks in the central and late Middle Ages, but subsequent work has not advanced much beyond their early insights. See D. Abulafia, *The*

only persisted into the central Middle Ages; in many cases, they flourished and transformed themselves into ever more sophisticated and interconnected systems. The foundations of regional trade may have been laid down in the eighth and ninth centuries, but much of the edifice was built in the twelfth and thirteenth.

The Adriatic Sea offers perhaps the most striking example of such growth; it is certainly the best documented. Between the early twelfth and the mid-thirteenth centuries, the region underwent profound political and economic transformations. The Venetian sphere of influence expanded so dramatically that by the late thirteenth century Venice could justifiably see itself as the "Queen of the Adriatic"; it was largely during this period that Venice established the economic dominance over the Adriatic sea-lanes that so marked the subsequent history of the region. Ancona rapidly rose to international commercial prominence, and equally rapidly reverted to purely regional importance. The Byzantine grip on the eastern Adriatic coast was loosened, and then eliminated altogether after 1204—a development that heralded major reconfigurations in the political economy of the sea and its coasts. The regional trade network both influenced and responded to these developments as commercial interconnections within the Adriatic became increasingly intense, diverse, and formalized.

The wealth of surviving written evidence also allows us to examine the dynamics of a regional trade system in considerable detail. We can follow a wide variety of bulk commodities as they move along the coasts and across the sea. We can determine ways in which the long-distance trade that had arisen from earlier intraregional networks now coexisted and connected with them. We can even glean specific knowledge about some of the people who wove these trade networks as they sailed the sea, although far more remain unknown and unknowable. The Adriatic offers insights into larger problems concerning regional trade: how did micro-ecological variations shape the development of trade networks, and what factors countered or amplified their effects? How did local, regional, and long-distance trade interact? How did dominant commercial powers engage with—or seek to control—regional trade systems, and how did neighboring communities respond? Who carried out the commerce by which such systems were created, and how did institutional factors influence their movements? What follows is an effort to answer some of these questions, via the specific historical experience of the medieval Adriatic.

Coasts, Currents, and Connectivity

Both the opportunities for commercial exchange and the mechanics of trade were intimately connected to the rhythms of the sea and the landscapes along its shores and hinterlands; they can be fully understood only within this physical context. From a geographic perspective, the Adriatic is virtually a closed sea (see fig. 10.1).[5] Only the narrow Strait of Otranto, a 72-kilometer-wide channel between Apulia and Albania, permits access to the rest of the Mediterranean. The northern coast of the sea is generally flat and smooth, with extensive lagoons surrounding Venice and the rest of the Po Delta. The western or "Italian" coast is sandy, low-lying, and smooth, with shallow waters along most of its length. With the exception of certain areas of Molise and the Gargano Peninsula, most of the immediate hinterland is well-suited to the growing of the staple Mediterranean crops: grain, olives, and grapes. The eastern coast, by contrast, is mostly rocky and infertile, and is separated from its Balkan hinterland by the Dinaric Alps. The region has always faced a severe dearth of arable land, although the innumerable islands and inlets along the shore have provided it with a surfeit of natural harbors.[6] As a result, its inhabitants have always been linked closely with the sea, and fish (relatively abundant here as compared with the western coast) has formed a staple of the local diet. Only at the southern edge of the eastern shore, in modern Albania, are there sizable tracts

---

Two Italies: Economic Relations between the Norman Kingdom of Sicily and the Northern Communes (Cambridge, 1977), and M. Balard, *La Romanie Génoise*, 2 vols. (Rome, 1978). The work of Angeliki Laiou is an important exception insofar as the eastern Mediterranean is concerned; see in particular her "Exchange and Trade, Seventh–Twelfth Centuries," in *EHB* 2:697–770.

5 For a detailed description of the natural geography of the Adriatic, see P. Cabanes et al., *Histoire de l'Adriatique* (Paris, 2001), 13–21.

6 Even in places where the soil is highly fertile, such as the region immediately surrounding Ragusa (modern Dubrovnik), the terrain is often too steep to be readily cultivable.

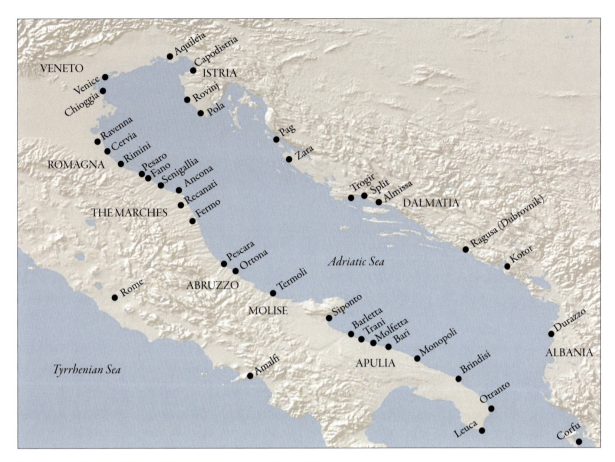

Figure 10.1. The twelfth- and thirteenth-century Adriatic (drawn by author)

of arable land. However, they are small in comparison with the vast plains extending inland from the Italian shore, and malarial infestations have long limited their productivity.

Both the tide and the currents in the Adriatic are fairly weak, and they were thus largely unimportant for medieval navigation.[7] It was instead the winds that were crucial. The three principal winds in the Adriatic are the bora, a northeast wind that is particularly frequent in the upper Adriatic; the maestral, which also blows from the northeast; and the sirocco, a moist southerly wind over most of the sea, although along the upper reaches of the western coast it is often an easterly.[8] All three winds are particularly dangerous during winter, and it is therefore not surprising that medieval mariners generally sought to avoid undertaking lengthy voyages within the Adriatic between November and February. Moreover, the direction and strength of the winds during January and February rendered travel up the Adriatic extremely difficult. If the Venetian government frequently sought to limit the maritime ventures of its citizens during the winter months (as will be discussed below), it was because the dangers of such voyages were well-known—and very real. At no point, however, was the Adriatic truly "closed" to navigation during the winter. While mariners

---

7 The following discussion of Adriatic currents and wind patterns is drawn from A. Simović, ed., *Navigational Guide to the Adriatic: Croatian Coast,* 2nd ed. (Zagreb, 2000), 26–30; *Weather in the Mediterranean,* vol. 1, *General Meteorology,* 2nd ed. (London, 1962), 75–86; and J. Ferluga, "Les îles dalmates dans l'empire byzantin," in *Byzantium on the Balkans: Studies on the Byzantine Administration and the Southern Slavs from the VIIth to the XIIth Centuries* (Amsterdam, 1976), 97–130, at 124–27.

8 These three are not the only winds in the Adriatic—for example, the *lebić* (also known as *garbin*) blows from the southeast, and the northerly *tramontana* is frequent in the southern Adriatic—but they are the most important for navigation.

understandably preferred to avoid winter sailing, commercial opportunities or political exigencies often trumped navigational concerns.[9]

The winds, currents, and topography of the Adriatic therefore rendered the eastern coast more conducive to medieval navigation than the Italian shore. Given the limitations of medieval ship riggings, the prevalence of easterly winds in the Adriatic considerably hampered navigation up the western shore. Moreover, the western shore was smooth and low-lying, whereas the eastern coastline (particularly Dalmatia) was rife with islands and inlets that provided refuge during storms or from pirate attacks. Furthermore, the Dinaric Alps that run along the eastern coast served as visual markers to facilitate navigation—an important concern in an era without compasses. But while the many advantages of the eastern side of the Adriatic made it the preferred route for medieval mariners, the sea-lanes along the western coast were hardly inactive. As the commercial success of Ancona and the Apulian ports attests, the Italian shore was certainly not unnavigable. Nevertheless, in the absence of pressing geographical, political, or commercial considerations, most Adriatic shipping opted for the eastern route, then as now.

In an era when coastal tramping was the norm, the importance of coasts and coastlines cannot be overstated. Mediterranean shipping has almost always been conducted close to the shore, which offers smoother sailing and higher navigability than the open seas, and can also provide refuge during storms.[10] However, the Adriatic offered greater ease of crossing than most of the other open spaces in the Mediterranean. The maestral winds could drive ships from west to east, and the sirocco (at least when it blew as a southerly) enabled them to sail in the reverse direction. Voyages from one coast to another could therefore be conducted with comparative ease for most of the year. This was especially true in the central Adriatic; as one moves southward, trans-Adriatic crossings become steadily more difficult. But even the Strait of Otranto could be crossed by ancient and medieval seafarers, assuming favorable winds.[11]

We know very little about the boats that sailed the sea-lanes of the Adriatic prior to the late Middle Ages. However, depictions of ships in mosaics and illuminated manuscripts from the period indicate that they were lateen rigged (that is, they used triangular rather than square sails) and generally had one or two masts. While the lateen rigging allowed the ships more maneuverability than their square-rigged counterparts (since they could sail more closely to the wind), the wide and shallow configurations of the hulls and keels of medieval Adriatic ships would have considerably reduced their ability to hold a course into the wind.[12] The seasonal patterns of prevailing winds in the Adriatic were therefore crucially important to the rhythms and directions of seaborne commerce.

The vast majority of intra-Adriatic trade was carried out on various types of relatively small boats with rounded prows and sterns, whose names were used so interchangeably that no meaningful distinction can be made between them. Large-scale trade in the Adriatic was carried out by *naves,* the typical roundships of the twelfth-century Mediterranean, most of which had a carrying capacity of at least 90 tons. Venice occasionally relied on the *tarida,* which was lower, longer, and narrower than a roundship and had only a single deck. While the tarida had a smaller carrying capacity than the roundship, it was popular as a military supply vessel due to its greater maneuverability.[13] Although galleys were vitally important for the contemporary Levant

---

9   See McCormick, *Origins of the European Economy,* 458–67.
10 For a striking visual presentation of the importance of the coasts to Adriatic shipping, see the maps of late sixteenth- and early seventeenth-century pirate attacks and shipwrecks in A. Tenenti, *Naufrages, corsaires et assurances maritimes à Venise, 1592–1609* (Paris, 1959), plates 2, 5. However, new archaeological research is providing evidence for a higher frequency of blue-water sailing than has previously been thought; see A. M. McCann, "Cosa and Deep Sea Exploration," in *The Maritime World of Ancient Rome,* ed. R. L. Hohlfelder, Memoirs of the American Academy in Rome, supp. vol. 6 (Ann Arbor, Mich., 2008), 37–50.
11 Ships generally opted to sail from the Italian coast to the island of Corfu (just south of the strait) or vice versa, rather than directly across the strait itself. According to the twelfth-century Muslim geographer al-Idrīsī, the voyage from Corfu to Otranto took one day. See *Géographie d'Édrisi: Traduite de l'arabe d'après deux manuscrits de la Bibliothèque Nationale,* trans. P. A. Jaubert, 2 vols. (Paris, 1836–40), 2:121. See also McCormick, *Origins of the European Economy,* 463–64.
12 See J. Pryor, *Geography, Technology, and War: Studies in the Maritime History of the Mediterranean, 649–1571* (Cambridge, 1988), 31–38.
13 U. Tucci, "L'impresa marittima: Uomini e mezzi," in *Storia di Venezia,* vol. 2, *L'età del comune,* ed. G. Cracco and G. Ortalli (Rome, 1995), 627–59, at 639–40; F. C. Lane, *Venice, a Maritime Republic* (Baltimore, 1973), 46; M. A. Bragadin, "Le navi, loro strutture e attrezzature nell'alto medioevo," in *La naviga-*

trade, they were rarely used for Adriatic trade during this period. Because of the cost of the oar crews and their reduced carrying capacity, galleys were too expensive to be used for the transportation of bulk commodities (which made up almost the entirety of intra-Adriatic shipping). By contrast, the square-rigged cog was specifically designed for the transport of bulk commodities, and was thus among the most important ship types in the later medieval Mediterranean. However, it was a Baltic innovation and is not attested in Venetian documents until 1315.[14]

The limitations of medieval ships and the restrictions posed by the Adriatic wind patterns should not be overemphasized, for contemporary mariners understood and adapted to these conditions. Moreover, the dimensions of the Adriatic itself facilitated movement. A ship traveling at 4 knots (which seems to have been standard for a medium-sized vessel) could cross from Venice to Istria in under twenty-four hours. Ragusa (Dubrovnik) could be reached in a further four or five days of sailing, and under good sailing conditions a fast ship could travel from Venice to Corfu in less than nine days.[15] A round-trip within the Adriatic could therefore be completed in under a month, assuming favorable winds. In an era when merchants and mariners regularly spent months sailing on the open Mediterranean, a timescale of weeks was rapid indeed. The difficulties and dangers faced by medieval Adriatic mariners were not negligible, but they were far from insuperable. In comparative terms, the medieval Adriatic was a highly navigable sea—and this navigability was an essential feature of its trade networks.

Another essential feature of these networks was the pattern of micro-ecological variation along the shores, a theme emphasized in the recent work of Peregrine Horden and Nicholas Purcell.[16] Micro-ecologies, as Horden and Purcell construe them, are not purely ecological, geological, or climatic constructions, but are "derived from the set of available productive opportunities and the particular interplay of human responses to them found in a given period."[17] The mutual complementarity of micro-ecologies, coupled with their access to distributive networks, is responsible for the extraordinary "connectivity" of the Mediterranean, which Horden and Purcell see as a defining characteristic of the sea since antiquity.

There is much that is useful in this approach. As they rightly argue, micro-ecological variations and the complementarity that they generated were important engines of exchange. *Ceteris paribus,* two communities that both produced salt as a principal export commodity were less likely to trade with each other than two communities of which only one produced salt. When a given micro-ecology could not satisfy local demand, opportunities for exchange arose. Such micro-ecological complementarity was particularly pronounced in the Adriatic, for nowhere else in the Mediterranean are two coasts with such differing micro-ecologies so accessible to one another by sea. With a few notable exceptions (particularly salt and timber), the commodities produced on the western side of the Adriatic were not widely produced on the eastern, and vice versa. Thus, the patterns of micro-ecological diversity along both the coasts and their hinterlands were a crucial factor in the movement of goods within the sea. However, they did not single-handedly define the possibilities for exchange. The opportunities created by micro-ecological complementarity were worthless without willing suppliers or a corresponding demand for the commodities that could be produced. In the sixth century, for example, Ravenna imported wine and oil from Istria; seven hundred years later, the movement of staple agricultural commodities was almost exclusively in the opposite direction, from west to east.[18] This shift is a reminder of the importance of urban spaces as demand centers, a phenomenon on which Horden and Purcell place too little emphasis.[19] In the case of sixth-century Ravenna, as for

---

zione mediterranea nell'alto medioevo: 14–20 aprile 1977 (Spoleto, 1978), 389–407, at 405.

14 U. Tucci, "La navigazione veneziana nel Duecento e nel primo Trecento e la sua evoluzione tecnica," in *Venezia e il Levante fino al secolo XV,* ed. A. Pertusi (Florence, 1973), 821–41, at 839.

15 Lane, *Venice,* 48. The question of place-names is invariably tricky, and I have aimed for clarity over consistency. Cities and regions are thus cited in their most familiar form, with modern or medieval equivalents given as appropriate following the first mention.

16 See, in particular, P. Horden and N. Purcell, *The Corrupting Sea: A Study of Mediterranean History* (Oxford, 2000). For a clarification and defense of their method, see idem, "Four Years of Corruption: A Response to Critics," in *Rethinking the Mediterranean,* ed. W. V. Harris (Oxford, 2005), 348–75.

17 Horden and Purcell, *Corrupting Sea,* 80.

18 See Cassiodorus, *Variarum Libri XII* 12.24.

19 Horden and Purcell, *Corrupting Sea,* 89–122; idem, "Four Years of Corruption," 369–71.

medieval Venice and other Adriatic cities, commodity exchange was often driven by the demands of an expanding population. These demands often outstripped the productive capabilities of the surrounding region, and thus required food to be imported from further away. Moreover, urban areas offered economic institutions (markets, currency exchange, controlled weights and measures, regulated dispute adjudication, and so forth) unavailable in less-settled localities, as well as a wider variety of commercial offerings. Large cities like Ancona or Ragusa offered manufactured goods that would have been unavailable in more remote communities; similarly, those cities that enjoyed commercial ties with communities outside the Adriatic were often sources of commodities that bore no relation to the micro-ecologies of the cities themselves—spices and silks being only two of the most obvious examples. The presence of such exogenous commodities in the markets of certain Adriatic cities certainly helped foster trade within the sea. Thus, while micro-ecological complementarity was a very significant factor in the patterns of Adriatic exchange, it was neither a sufficient condition for exchange nor the sole economic stimulant within the sea.

Horden and Purcell's principal goal is to demonstrate the continuing connectivity of the Mediterranean throughout recorded human history, and in this effort they succeed admirably. From the perspective of economic history, however, their methodology is not only inappropriate but dangerously misleading. It makes little provision for diachronic evolution, and is even less helpful in attempting to explain it.[20] Equally problematic is the highly binary nature of their model of connectivity. Connection between two localities either occurs or does not occur; at times, the frequency and intensity of the connection seem virtually irrelevant. A onetime exchange of a given commodity between two coastal hamlets can appear as important for overall connectivity as the frequent exchanges between Ancona and Zara (Zadar). This approach risks making a single voyage appear to be of equal economic importance with centuries of commercial activity. It might (and indeed does) produce a conceptual map of the Mediterranean that is rife with linkages, but from the perspective of economic history, such a map is not especially useful. Though we cannot always securely establish the relative economic importance of individual connections between communities, we must at least acknowledge that differences existed—and that such differences had genuine economic consequences. The following analysis therefore makes use of micro-ecologies, but as a conceptual tool rather than as an overriding framework, and it seeks to be sensitive to changes over time, wherever the concentration of evidence permits.

The evidence for Adriatic trade during the period is almost entirely textual; the exchange of locally produced ceramics within the Adriatic is largely a phenomenon of the late thirteenth century and afterward, though ceramic imports from elsewhere in the Mediterranean can occasionally be used to corroborate the written record where long-distance trade is concerned. While the survival rate of twelfth- and early thirteenth-century documentary evidence is significantly lower than for subsequent centuries, a considerable amount has been preserved. The notarial documents in the Venetian archives are a particularly rich source of information. Among the hundreds of surviving commercial contracts from the period, roughly sixty refer specifically to Adriatic trade; altogether they concern more than fifty separate ventures between 1098 and 1259.[21] Nearly all of them are standard *colleganza* contracts, or quittances thereof. In such contracts, an investor typically entrusted capital to a particular merchant for use in an overseas venture, the profits to be shared according to prior agreement.[22] Both commodities and destinations often go unspecified, as such matters were regularly left to the discretion of the merchant undertaking the voyage. It is probable

---

20 For a penetrating critique along these lines, see W. V. Harris, "The Mediterranean and Ancient History," in idem, ed., *Rethinking the Mediterranean*, 1–42, at 34–38.

21 The use of approximations here is intentional, since the notarial documents are frequently ambiguous. Almost all of the relevant contracts are printed in R. Morozzo della Rocca and A. Lombardo, eds., *Documenti del commercio veneziano nei secoli XI–XIII*, 2 vols. (Rome, 1940), and A. Lombardo and R. Morozzo della Rocca, eds., *Nuovi documenti del commercio veneto dei secoli XI–XIII*, Monumenti storici, n.s., 7 (Venice, 1953).

22 *Colleganza* was a Venetian name for the more common *commenda*. In certain cases, the recipient also invested his own funds in the venture; such a contract is usually referred to as a "bilateral *colleganza*." For an illuminating study of the commercial possibilities and limitations embedded in the structure of such contracts, see J. H. Pryor, "Mediterranean Commerce in the Middle Ages: A Voyage under the Contract of *commenda*," *Viator* 14 (1983): 132–94.

that many of the extant medieval Venetian contracts that omit references to a final destination actually concerned intra-Adriatic ventures, but there is usually no means by which these can be identified.

These contracts, though often revealing, must be used with caution. To begin with, they are all concerned with the commercial activities of Venetian merchants, rarely mentioning merchants from other Adriatic communities. They are therefore highly skewed toward the experience of the lagoon city. Moreover, the selective transmission of such documents—generally due to their inclusion in testamentary bequests to churches or monasteries—limits their potential to support any meaningful quantitative analysis. Finally, they generally represent the commercial experience of the kinds of Venetian citizens who would have been making major testamentary bequests in the first place: namely, the wealthy ones. The trends in the documentation therefore cannot always be extrapolated for Venice as a whole, let alone the entire Adriatic. Fortunately, the evidence from these contracts can be corroborated and supplemented by the extant diplomatic records from throughout the Adriatic, as well as medieval chronicles, geographic surveys, travelogues, and other contemporary sources.

The Adriatic as Venetian *Contado*

It is appropriate, if hardly novel, to begin with Venice, for the most striking feature of the twelfth- and thirteenth-century Adriatic trade system was the rapid expansion of Venetian control. Venice had established itself as the principal city of the Adriatic well before 1100, but its early dominance was mainly political, even if the underlying impetus was economic: the security of the Adriatic as a corridor for Venetian long-distance maritime trade. Over time, however, control over commodity movement within the Adriatic became increasingly important to Venice, as the city came to depend on the resources of the sea's coasts and hinterlands for its very existence. Just as the medieval Italian communes sought to establish a monopoly over the economic life of their surrounding countryside (*contado*), so too did Venice increasingly attempt—with considerable if not absolute success—to control intra-Adriatic shipping. Of course, while the city may have risen from the waves, it was hardly independent from the nearby mainland. Much of its food supply originated in the lands bordering the Venetian lagoon, and, as surnames such as Trevisano ("from Treviso") attest, so too did much of the city's population. Moreover, just as many noble families in Genoa, Pisa, and elsewhere owned considerable landholdings in their city's contado, many Venetian patrician clans possessed estates on the mainland. As early as 829, a Venetian doge is recorded as having possessed extensive lands near the shores of the lagoon and around Treviso. This pattern certainly continued into the period under question and became de rigueur for the Venetian upper classes in subsequent centuries.[23] In many respects, therefore, the mainland surrounding the Venetian lagoon played the role of a typical contado.

Yet the Adriatic came to replicate many aspects of a contado as well. Although it would be incorrect to suggest that the Adriatic *was* the Venetian contado (for, if nothing else, this equation marginalizes the role of the surrounding terra ferma and ignores many of the politico-juridical elements of a typical contado), medieval Venice gradually came to rely on the Adriatic to fulfill many of the conventional functions of an agricultural hinterland.[24] As discussed above, exchange in the medieval Adriatic was generally prompted either by demand that could be satisfied by a complementary micro-ecology within the region or by an urban center's inability to supply itself adequately from its immediate surroundings. In the twelfth and early thirteenth centuries, the city of Venice epitomized both conditions. Only with respect to fish and salt was it fully self-sufficient, and much of its salt was imported from Chioggia on the southeastern edge of the lagoon. Furthermore, by the twelfth century the productive capabilities of the nearby terra ferma were decidedly

---

23 See G. Luzzatto, "Les activités économiques du patriciat vénitien," *Annales d'histoire économique et sociale* 9 (1937): 25–57; and M. Pozza, "I proprietari fondiari in terraferma," in *Storia di Venezia,* vol. 2, Cracco and Ortalli, eds., *L'età del comune,* 661–80.

24 The nature of the medieval contado has been much disputed in Italian historiography; a balanced overview may be found in G. Chittolini, "The Italian City State and Its Territory," in *City States in Classical Antiquity and Medieval Italy,* ed. A. Molho, K. Raaflaub, and J. Emlen (Ann Arbor, Mich., 1991), 589–602. The classic account of the economic role of the contado (with an emphasis on the Tuscan communes) is E. Fiumi, "Sui rapporti economici tra città e contado nell'età comunale," *Archivio Storico Italiano* 114 (1956): 18–68; for more recent approaches, see the essays collected in T. Dean and C. Wickham, eds., *City and Countryside in Late Medieval and Renaissance Italy: Essays Presented to Philip Jones* (London, 1990).

insufficient to meet the growing Venetian demand for a wide range of commodities, and Venice therefore turned to the Adriatic to make up the shortfall. The phrase "intra culfum," which occurs repeatedly in contemporary Venetian documents, was more than a navigational criterion used by the Venetian government: it was a linguistic reflection of a perception of the Adriatic as a discrete geographical and economic unit, and one that Venice would seek increasingly to dominate.

One of the principal economic functions of a contado was to provide the metropole with a steady flow of immigrants. The Adriatic likewise proved a continual source of population inflow for Venice and of manpower for its industries, with Ragusans and Apulians captaining Venetian ships, and Dalmatian sailors regularly serving aboard the city's galleys (particularly from the early fourteenth century onward).[25] In the later Middle Ages, and likely in earlier centuries as well, many residents of Venice hailed from the eastern coast of the Adriatic.[26] However, the most critical economic role of a contado was not the supplying of men but the production of staple commodities—primarily grain, oil, and salt, as well as wine, wood, and other foodstuffs. For much of Venice's early history, the city's immediate surroundings were presumably able to adequately satisfy its demand for basic staple goods. Venice was particularly well supplied with salt; the shallow waters of the lagoon were distinctly suited to the establishment of saltworks, and by the eleventh century nearby Chioggia was already the site of a thriving salt industry. Timber was available nearby, for the heavy forests of the upper Adriatic (particularly in Istria) had not yet been depleted by centuries of overexploitation. Venice was also blessed with an abundance of fish, for the surrounding lagoons were among the most productive fishing zones anywhere in the Mediterranean.[27] Thus, even in times of crop failures, Venetians could at least fall back on fish to sustain themselves. Yet fish was never the mainstay of the local diet. For medieval Venice, as for the Mediterranean world in general, the staple diet was based on grain—whether wheat, barley, or other crops.[28] As the city's population expanded in the twelfth century, reaching an estimated 80,000 inhabitants by the year 1200,[29] Venice began to seek foodstuffs from coastal communities throughout the Adriatic (see fig. 10.2). For the next four centuries, grain imported from within the Adriatic would be a crucial element of the Venetian diet, and in the later Middle Ages such imports made up the majority of the city's grain supply.[30] Only toward the end of the sixteenth century did grain production in the Veneto expand sufficiently that it was possible for local sources to outstrip maritime imports.[31]

In general, it was cities on the Italian coast that came to serve as the principal supply centers for the staple food commodities that Venice lacked. The inhospitable micro-ecologies of the eastern Adriatic shore, with its rocky coastline and mountainous hinterland, could barely provide enough food for its own inhabitants, let alone an exportable surplus. The lone exception was Albania, which provided Venice with grain from the early thirteenth century onward, and possibly earlier.[32] But Albanian grain was considered to be of inferior quality (at least by later writers), and the surviving documentation suggests accordingly that Albanian grain was sought primarily during times of widespread scarcity, rather than as usual practice.[33] It is possi-

25 See Lane, *Venice*, 20, 168.
26 See, for example, B. Krekić, "Venetians in Dubrovnik (Ragusa) and Ragusans in Venice as Real Estate Owners in the Fourteenth Century," in *Dubrovnik: A Mediterranean Urban Society 1300–1600* (Aldershot, 1997), art. XI, 1–48.
27 The lagoons were particularly productive in comparison to Mediterranean fishing overall, although the scarcity of fish in the Mediterranean has been exaggerated by Braudel and subsequent historians. For a more balanced interpretation of fish yields in the Mediterranean, see Horden and Purcell, *Corrupting Sea*, 190–92.

28 Ibid., 201.
29 Lane, *Venice*, 18.
30 Venetian merchants also purchased grain from the Black Sea and other parts of the Byzantine Empire, although such imports seem to have remained fairly limited prior to the late thirteenth century. See A. E. Laiou, "Monopoly and Privileged Free Trade in the Eastern Mediterranean (8th–14th century)," in *Chemins d'outre-mer: Études d'histoire sur la Méditerranée médiévale offertes à Michel Balard*, ed. D. Coulon et al. (Paris, 2004), 511–26, at 521–25.
31 See M. Aymard, *Venise, Raguse, et le commerce du blé pendant la seconde moitié du XVIe siècle* (Paris, 1966).
32 In 1210, Michael Doukas granted the Venetians the freedom to export grain from the Despotate of Epiros; see G. L. T. Tafel and G. M. Thomas, eds., *Urkunden zur älteren Handels- und Staatsgeschichte der Republik Venedig*, 3 vols. (Vienna, 1856–57), no. 224.
33 Fernand Braudel, *The Mediterranean and the Mediterranean World in the Age of Philip II*, trans. Sîan Reynolds (New York, 1972), 595.

Figure 10.2. Documented grain movements in the Adriatic Sea, 1100–1260 (drawn by author)
NOTE: This map is intended to be illustrative rather than exhaustive. Many highly probable grain movements have been left unmarked, for lack of extant contemporary evidence, while a few documented exchanges have been omitted in the interests of cartographic clarity. The varying thickness of the lines is meant to convey the intensity of traffic, but should be taken as suggestive.

ble that Albania was also a source of wine and oil, since the area around Durazzo (Durrës) is known to have had vineyards and olive orchards during the period, but unfortunately the surviving commercial documents concerning voyages to Durazzo make no reference to the ships' cargoes.[34] The establishment of the Venetian-controlled Duchy of Durazzo following the Fourth Crusade played a major role in securing the city's access to Albanian foodstuffs; of the seven surviving contracts that specifically mention Durazzo as a final destination (as opposed to merely a port of transit), all but one date from the years of the duchy.[35] Evidence of Venetian trade with Albania largely drops off after 1213 (when Venice lost control of Durazzo), although trade may have continued intermittently over the succeeding decades. Venice still seems to have turned its attention toward the southeastern Adriatic when alternative sources of grain proved insufficient; a report of an attack by Istrian pirates on a ship returning from Durazzo in 1227 (in the midst of a severe famine in Venice) suggests that the Albanian grain market remained open to Venetian traders.[36]

Throughout the late twelfth and thirteenth centuries, the predominant sources of staple commodities

---

34 A. Ducellier, *La façade maritime de l'Albanie au Moyen Âge: Durazzo et Valona du XIe au XVe siècle* (Thessalonike, 1981), 62.
35 *DCV,* nos. 501, 507; *NDCV,* nos. 60, 61, 69, 71; and L. Frizziero, ed., *San Maffio di Mazzorbo e Santa Margherita di Tor-*

cello (Florence, 1965), no. 25. The lone exception is *NDCV,* no. 60, which immediately antedates the official establishment of the duchy.
36 *Consilia et Ordinamenti,* no. 70 (September 1227), in *Deliberazioni del Maggior Consiglio di Venezia,* ed. R. Cessi, 3 vols. (Bologna, 1931–50), 1:189 (hereafter cited as *DMCV*).

for Venice lay on the western shores of the Adriatic.[37] Much of the grain, oil, and wine that was transported to the city originated near the communities along the central and southern Italian coast, for the microecologies of their surrounding regions were generally conducive to the cultivation of wheat, olives, and grapes. Commercial relations between Venice and these regions dated back centuries, but starting in the mid-twelfth century these relations became increasingly regular. They also became increasingly regulated, especially after a severe famine from 1224 to 1227 prompted Venice to focus diplomatic efforts on securing its access to staple foodstuffs from within the Adriatic.

Unfortunately, there are no surviving private commercial documents concerning Venetian trade with central Italy prior to the very end of the twelfth century, so specific features of this commerce must be inferred largely from the diplomatic record. The earliest relevant treaty is from 1141: in it Fano, a small maritime community in the Marches, offered its submission to the doge and Commune of Venice in return for promises of military support against its nearby rivals.[38] Venice promised that citizens of Fano—and merchants in particular—would be safe, secure, and treated as Venetians within Venetian territory. The reciprocal promises from Fano to Venice did not single out merchants, but gave corresponding assurances of security and parity between citizens of the two cities, as well as additional legal privileges to Venetians involved in disputes with Fanese citizens. The revenue from weights and measures used by foreign merchants was to be given to Venice. Fano also promised to pay an annual tribute of one *miliarium* of oil to the church of San Marco and an additional *centenarium* of oil per year to the ducal *camera*.[39] Unlike all subsequent treaties between Venice and the coastal cities of central Italy, the 1141 treaty with Fano is primarily a political and military agreement, in which commercial factors are mentioned only summarily. However, the apparent dominance of noncommercial elements is misleading. The submission of Fano was not part of a larger pattern of Venetian territorial acquisitions in central Italy, nor was Fano a significant port, or even a valuable strategic site.[40] What, then, did Venice stand to gain by involving itself in the regional squabbles of the Marches? Gino Luzzatto has suggested that Venice sought to establish its tutelage over some cities in order to counter the independent power of Ancona in the central Adriatic, but this hypothesis is undermined by the absence of sustained Venetian efforts to establish a presence in the region beyond this isolated instance.[41]

Yet it is possible that Venice's interest in Fano was predominantly commercial. Even if the bulk of the treaty's text deals with politico-military affairs, all of the clauses concerning these affairs come after those that concern trade. Moreover, the specific concessions offered to the Venetians in Fano would have been attractive primarily to merchants. For-

---

37 See G. Rösch, *Venedig und das Reich: Handels- und verkehrspolitische Beziehungen in der deutschen Kaiserzeit* (Tübingen, 1982), 135–79. The best overall survey of Venetian diplomatic and commercial relations with the cities of the Marches in the period concerned remains G. Luzzatto, "I più antichi trattati tra Venezia e le città marchigiane (1141–1345)," *Nuovo Archivio Veneto* 11 (1906): 5–91, cited hereafter as *VCM*; Luzzatto's overall interpretation is updated in Silvano Borsari's short article "Le relazioni tra Venezia e le Marche nei secoli XII e XIII," *Studi Maceratesi* 6 (1970): 21–26. Venetian-Apulian commercial relations have also been well studied; the best synthesis remains F. Carabellese and A. Zambler, *Le relazioni commerciali fra la Puglia e la Repubblica di Venezia dal secolo X al XV: Ricerche e documenti*, 2 vols. (Trani, 1897–98), hereafter cited as *PRV*. J.-M. Martin's *La Pouille du VIᵉ au XIIᵉ siècle* (Rome, 1993), an otherwise exhaustive survey of early medieval Apulia, unfortunately focuses little on external commerce. Little has been written on twelfth- and thirteenth-century commercial relations between Venice and the other regions along the Italo-Adriatic coast (principally because of the extreme paucity of surviving sources); P. D. Pasolini, "Delle antiche relazioni fra Venezia e Ravenna," *AStIt*, ser. 3, 13 (1871): 72–92, 222–47, is primarily diplomatic and rife with errors.
38 A. B. Langeli, ed., *Il patto con Fano, 1141* (Venice, 1993).
39 The miliarium, as a measurement for oil, had a capacity of 630 liters; the centenarium, naturally, had one-tenth of that capacity. Modern equivalents for weights and measures are adapted from A. Schaube, *Handelsgeschichte der romanischen Völker des Mittelmeergebiets bis zum Ende der Kreuzzüge* (Munich, 1906), 415–16; F. C. Lane, *Venetian Ships and Shipbuilders of the Renaissance* (Baltimore, 1934), 245–46; J.-C. Hocquet, "Métrologie du sel et l'histoire comparée en Méditerranée," *AnnalesESC* 29 (1974): 393–424; and Rösch, *Venedig und das Reich*, 203.
40 Admittedly, Venice's 1141 treaty with Fano was followed by a series of treaties with Istrian cities (see Langeli, *Fano*, 15). However, while control of the Istrian peninsula was clearly necessary to Venetian security, control over Fano was not (nor, at any rate, did possession of a minor beachhead in the Marches offer any real security).
41 Luzzatto, "I più antichi trattati," 5. Attilio Langeli, the most recent editor of the treaty, adopts a more bluntly imperialist interpretation. Although he rightly notes that Venice "conquistò una piazza, non un territorio" (Langeli, *Fano*, 13), he does suggest that the submission of Fano gave Venice control over a maritime city that was important for control of the Adriatic. This considerably overstates the strategic importance of Fano.

eign weights and measures were penalized in favor of Venetian ones, which both facilitated Venetian trade and improved the terms of trade for Venetian merchants. More importantly, Venetians involved in legal disputes with the Fanese were to be tried by a Venetian judge (*in curia illius vestri missi*), rather than in a local Fanese court. This requirement offered clear advantages for merchants, especially since they were most likely to be interacting closely with the Fanese in circumstances that might lend themselves to legal disputes. Furthermore, the selection of oil for the city's tribute indicates that Fano's position as a source of staple commodities was not overlooked in the drafting of the treaty.[42] Control over Fano did not offer Venice access to a major harbor, or the ability to dominate Adriatic shipping lines—but it did provide Venice a secure source for the agricultural products of the Marches. The trade with Fano was evidently important enough to merit the city's active protection; in 1141 (the same year as the treaty was signed), Venice warned Ancona not to restrict Venetian trade with either Fano or nearby Pesaro, which suggests that Venice's commercial interests in Fano were already well established and a major concern at the time the treaty was concluded.[43] It therefore seems likely that the treaty was prompted by stronger commercial interests (at least on the Venetian side) than has been previously suggested.

Venice's 1141 warning to Ancona highlights two additional features of its commercial relations with central Italy. The first is that a substantial proportion of Venice's trade with the region was conducted via relatively small coastal communities, such as Pesaro and Fano. These cities were not insignificant; indeed, they were evidently important enough that highborn Venetians were willing to serve as *podestà* in their local governments.[44] But they were hardly comparable in size or economic importance to Ancona or the major Apulian ports. The surviving commercial documents bear witness to this pattern of Venetian involvement. In the eight contracts that mention a specific destination along the central Italian coast, three mention Ancona, while Pesaro, Fano, Ortona, Ravenna, Pescara, and Rimini are each mentioned once.[45] The individual amounts invested in these ventures are lower than usual for intra-Adriatic commerce;[46] half of the contracts are for amounts below £50, and none are for more than £100.[47] Given that the journey from Venice to central Italy was fairly short, and that the cargo holds were generally filled with bulk commodities, this phenomenon is not surprising. Voyages to nearby cities were less costly than voyages to distant ones, and Venice was not importing shiploads of high-value luxury commodities from the cities along the central Italian coast.

The warning to Ancona is also indicative of Venice's stormy relationship with its Adriatic neighbor. Ancona was the only other Adriatic city to enjoy a significant international commercial presence, which enabled it to exercise considerable control over the surrounding region. Having ruthlessly crushed all prior Adriatic competitors (such as Comacchio, which was razed to the ground in 946), Venice was hardly about to tolerate Anconitan ambitions. As a result, Venice and Ancona spent much of the twelfth and thirteenth centuries alternating between open (and usually inconclusive) warfare and tenuous peace. Despite the intermittent hostilities, commercial ties remained strong. In 1152, Venice even granted Anconitans full commercial rights in Venice and Venetian territories—although these were rescinded upon the outbreak of war two decades later.[48] Yet even without a formal agreement, trade between the two cities continued to flourish; as mentioned above, Ancona appears as a destination in the surviving Venetian contracts more often than any other central Italian coastal city. No specific commodity information survives prior to the mid-thirteenth

---

42 Fano was also a source of wine; a contract from July 1200 (*DCV*, no. 449) concerns a shipment of wine to be brought from Fano to Venice.

43 Archivio di Stato, Venice, Codex diplomaticus Lanfranchi, 1100–1199, anno 1141, p. 1; and Liber Pactorum i, fols. 187v–188r; both cited in D. Abulafia, "Ancona, Byzantium and the Adriatic, 1155–1173," *Papers of the British School at Rome* 52 (1984): 195–216, at 204 n. 48.

44 For example, Doge Rainier Zeno (r. 1252–68) was serving as podestà in Fermo when he was elected doge in 1252, as noted by Martino da Canale (*Les estoires de Venise: Cronaca veneziana in lingua francese dalle origini al 1275* [Florence, 1972], 126).

45 *DCV*, nos. 438, 449, 450, 543, 660, 709, 711, 831; the earliest of these dates from June 1198; the latest, from September 1255. All of these cities are located in Romagna, the Marches, or the Abruzzi.

46 See figure 10.4 (p. 275).

47 All monetary references are expressed in Venetian currency, except where otherwise noted; the Venetian pound (*libra denariorum venetialium*) is indicated by £ and the solidus by *s*.

48 See *VCM*, 7–8. Unfortunately, only a brief summary of the treaty text has survived.

century (aside from a single reference to the export of wine), but here, as elsewhere, the commerce was almost certainly dominated by the principal agricultural products of the micro-ecologies along the Italian coast: grain, oil, and wine.

The other major source of Venetian foodstuffs lay further south, in Apulia. The region was rich in agricultural products, with venerable olive orchards around Bari, vineyards near Trani, and grain predominating in the areas below the Gargano Peninsula.[49] Venetians already had active settlements in Apulia during the early twelfth century, and these settlements grew in importance during the period;[50] by 1257, Venice had consuls in Trani and Barletta (as permitted by a privilege from Manfred of Sicily).[51] The earliest formalization of economic relations between Venice and Apulia occurred in 1139, when Roger II of Sicily signed a commercial treaty (now lost) with the Venetians.[52] In 1154, another treaty was signed between Venice and Roger's successor; unfortunately, this too is lost.[53] By 1166, Venetian trade with southern Italy had evidently grown significant enough that Doge Vitale II Michiel refused to provide the Byzantines with Venice's usual assistance against the Normans for fear of risking good relations with Apulia.[54] The first treaty for which the text has survived dates to 1175, when William II of Sicily reduced by one-half the tolls levied on Venetian ships entering Apulian ports and promised royal protection to all Venetian ships (except corsairs and those in the service of the Byzantine emperor).[55] Then, in 1199, the civic authorities of Brindisi signed a friendship agreement with two representatives of the Venetian fleet, promising to exclude Pisan and Genoese corsairs from the city's port.[56] Private documents also indicate that Venetian trade with Apulia was flourishing during the period in question. There are nine surviving Venetian contracts concerning voyages to Apulia between the mid-twelfth and early thirteenth century, more than for any other destination within the Adriatic.[57] One contract, from November 1190, concerns an investment of £374, the largest recorded for an intra-Adriatic voyage prior to the late 1220s;[58] all save the earliest (from 1159) are for amounts between £50 and £200 (that is, within the normal range). As was true of loads originating on the central Italo-Adriatic coast, no details on the cargoes of the ships traveling from Apulia to Venice are available prior to the 1220s, but once again they almost certainly comprised the same staple agricultural goods (grain, oil, and wine) that were the region's principal export commodities.

Although Venice's trading relations with the central and southern Italo-Adriatic coast had been somewhat formalized by the diplomatic agreements discussed above, the treaty provisions were fairly broad and the treaties themselves few in number. Thus these relations remained very flexible and largely unregulated during the twelfth and early thirteenth centuries. There were no specific restrictions on the import or export of commodities, nor

49 Martin, *La Pouille*, 400.
50 *DCV*, no. 41; and see Abulafia, *The Two Italies*, 78.
51 *PRV* 2:110–22, and no. 6. Venice certainly had consuls in the Kingdom of Sicily by 1239, but it is unclear whether they were located in Apulia or elsewhere. The increasing importance of commercial ties between Venice and Apulia is suggested by the fragments of Apulian proto-majolica found in Venice from the first half of the thirteenth century onward; see F. Saccardo, "Venezia: Le importazione ceramiche tra XII e XIII secolo," in *Ceramiche, città e commerci nell'Italia tardo-medievale: Ravello, 3–4 maggio 1993*, ed. S. Gelichi (Mantua, 1998), 49–73, at 50–51; and F. Saccardo, L. Lazzarini, and M. Munarini, "Ceramiche importate a Venezia e nel Veneto tra XI e XIV secolo," in *VIIe Congrès International sur la Céramique Médiévale en Méditerranée, Thessaloniki, 11–16 Octobre 1999: Actes*, ed. Ch. Bakirtzis (Athens, 2003), 395–420, at 410–14.
52 *PRV* 1:7. An earlier treaty between Venice and Bari, dating to 1122, does not include any specifically commercial clauses beyond the standard reciprocal promises to protect the other city's citizens.
53 *PRV* 1:7. This treaty is mentioned in Andrea Dandolo, *Chronica per extensum descripta*, in *Rerum Italicarum Scriptores*, vol. 12, pt. 1, fasc. 3, ed. E. Pastorello (Bologna, 1939), 245–46.
54 Dandolo, *Chronica*, 249. As there are no other surviving references to this event, the reliability of Dandolo's account has been disputed; see F. Chalandon, *Jean II Comnène (1118–1143) et Manuel I Comnène (1143–1180)*, 2 vols. (Paris, 1912), 2:586.

55 *PRV*, no. 3. The reciprocal treaty, offering privileges to Apulians (and all Sicilian subjects) in Venetian territories, has not survived.
56 E. Winkelmann, ed., *Acta imperii inedita seculi XIII [et XIV]...*, 2 vols. (Innsbruck, 1880–85), vol. 1, no. 583.
57 These documents are *DCV*, nos. 136, 391, 397, 410, 441, 569; and *NDCV*, nos. 48, 49, 61. The 1159 contract involves an investment of £20 *veronensium*, which would have been worth roughly £40 *venetialium*. During most of the twelfth century, Veronese currency (which was coined by the official imperial mint at Verona) was the standard coinage in Venice; only after 1183 did Venetian coinage become prevalent. See F. C. Lane and R. C. Mueller, *Money and Banking in Medieval and Renaissance Venice*, vol. 1, *Coins and Moneys of Account* (Baltimore, 1985), 107–8. Several surviving contracts were also drawn up by Venetians in Apulia, but do not necessarily concern intra-Adriatic trade; one such contract is mentioned in *DCV*, nos. 282, 283.
58 *DCV*, no. 391.

did either signatory seek to establish a monopoly position within the other's markets. But the limitations of this system became strikingly apparent between 1224 and 1227, when Venice (along with much of northern Italy) was faced with a severe famine.[59] The Venetian government immediately took steps to secure the city's food supply. In July 1224, it began offering subsidies to private merchants for grain imported from the upper and mid-Adriatic; these subsidies were frequently renewed in the following years.[60] Such measures were evidently insufficient, particularly since (as the documentary record attests) the upper and mid-Adriatic had little surplus to offer—not a single surviving contract from the famine years mentions a city in Dalmatia or on the central Italian coast as a destination for Venetian merchants.[61] An isolated reference to a 1227 commercial voyage from Durazzo suggests that Albanian grain may have provided some relief during the famine, but it was on southern Italy that Venice focused most of its hopes, sending galleys to Apulia to collect every available scrap of foodstuffs.[62] In 1226, Frederick II of Sicily intervened in Venice's favor, greatly reducing the restrictions on the export of grain and other foodstuffs from Apulian ports.[63] Not surprisingly, the effects of Frederick's action were striking. Venetian merchants and government representatives rushed to southern Italy to purchase grain in massive quantities. Four contracts for voyages from Venice to Apulia survive from 1226 alone, as well as repeated references in the contemporary proceedings of the Venetian government preserved in the *Liber Comunis*.[64] Giovanni Stagnario, a private merchant, was commissioned by the Venetian government in March 1227 to travel to southern Italy and gather food; he returned with 2000 *modii* of grain from Siponto and other Apulian ports.[65] The enormous profit that Stagnario received from this expedition is also an important reminder of the frequent possibilities for commercial gain offered by the exchange of bulk commodities; Levantine trade was not the only source of commercial riches during the Middle Ages.

A key aspect of Venice's response to the famine was its attempted monopolization of commodity movement within the Adriatic. As the Venetian government realized, the purchasing of grain by a Venetian merchant in Brindisi was of little use to the mother city if the merchant sold all of it in Ancona before returning to Venice. As a result, beginning in December 1225, Venetians sailing anywhere in the Adriatic—specifically, north of Leuca (Leukas) or Modon (Methoni)—were forbidden to unload wares at any port except Venice.[66] It is unlikely that the ban ever succeeded entirely, although there are no recorded instances of attempted evasion. Still, the benefits of this policy were clear, and it must have proved effective enough to be considered a feasible policy for the future. The experience of the famine had revealed the weaknesses of the existing supply structures all too clearly. The succeeding decades would find Venice not only strengthening its ties with the communities that offered access to staple commodities but also increasing its grip on the movement of these commodities within the Adriatic.[67] In June 1228, Venice established an alliance with a confederation of four cities in the Marches (Recanati, Castelfidardo, Osimo, and Umana), receiving

---

59 The years 1225 and 1226 saw widespread famines throughout much of western Europe; see F. Curschmann, *Hungersnöte im Mittelalter: Ein Beitrag zur deutschen Wirschaftsgeschichte des 8. bis 13. Jahrhunderts* (Leipzig, 1900), 85, 170–72.

60 *Precepta, Iuramenta, Interdicta*, nos. 73, 124, 133, 161, in *DMCV* 1:67, 80, 82, 94; and *Consilia et Ordinamenta*, no. 31, in *DMCV* 1:172.

61 Evidence from the *Liber Comunis* indicates that trading activity between Venice and the cities of the central Italo-Adriatic coast did not cease entirely. However, the evidence for active exchange is sparse, and commerce with these regions certainly seems to have decreased considerably from earlier periods. See, for example, *Plegii et Pagatores*, no. 118, in *DMCV* 1:31; *Precepta, Iuramenta, Interdicta*, no. 32, in *DMCV* 1:55; and *Precepta, Iuramenta, Interdicta*, no. 108, in *DMCV* 1:74, all of which attest to Venetian-Anconitan trading relations during the period.

62 See *Consilia et Ordinamenti*, no. 70, in *DMCV* 1:74; and *Precepta, Iuramenta, Interdicta*, no. 109, in *DMCV* 1:189.

63 *PRV* 1:11. In gratitude for Frederick's assistance, Venice honored him with a major celebration of thanksgiving during his visit to the city in March 1232.

64 *DCV*, nos. 627, 629, 633, 638; *Precepta, Iuramenta, Interdicta*, no. 188 (June 2, 1226), in *DMCV* 1:103, in which Giovanni Scandallaro traveled to Apulia after swearing to act in the best interests of Venice; *Plegii et Pagatores*, no. 152, in *DMCV* 1:39; and *Precepta, Iuramenta, Interdicta*, no. 202, in *DMCV* 1:109.

65 *Consilia et Ordinamenta*, nos. 36, 46, 49, 50, in *DMCV* 1:178–83. For a detailed account of Stagnario's voyage, see *PRV* 1:11–12. The Venetian modius was composed of four *staria*, each of which was equivalent to roughly 83 liters.

66 *Precepta, Iuramenta, Interdicta*, no. 161, in *DMCV* 1:94.

67 The political consequences of the famine can also be seen in the commitment to supplementing the city's grain supply in the *promissio* of the new doge, Jacopo Tiepolo, in 1229; see G. Graziato, *Le promissioni del doge di Venezia: Dalle origini alla fine del Duecento* (Venice, 1986), 18–19.

full commercial access in the allied territories and exemptions from tolls.[68] Then, in July 1228, Venice allied itself with Cingoli, another Marchigian city slightly further inland.[69] Meanwhile, the doge had declared that all Venetians could trade goods anywhere on the western coast of the Adriatic above the Gargano Peninsula except for Ancona and its territory, and that Anconitan goods could not be transported anywhere but to Venice unless they had been produced in the Gargano, in which case they could also be taken to Acre.[70] Although the latter restrictions were immediately denounced by the papacy (which was then in league with Ancona) and went largely unenforced, they were nevertheless a foreshadowing of future Venetian dominance over Ancona's commercial liberties.

In general, most of the Venetian treaties with the coastal Italian cities were focused on securing Venice's free access to the cities' grain and staple commodity supplies. In a 1234 commercial treaty with Ravenna, Venice agreed to pay tax on the export of wine and grain from Ravenna in return for the latter's commitment not to sell any surplus grain, wine, meat, oil, cheese, or figs to any city other than Venice. Ravenna could, however, continue to import these commodities from the Marches and Apulia to satisfy local needs.[71] According to Venice's 1239 treaty with Recanati, for example, Venice gained the right to export grain and all other commodities in unlimited quantities, as well as full liberty to enter within the city walls after the payment of the appropriate duties (which were limited to a maximum of eight *denarii* per *soma* of any merchandise).[72] In 1260, Venice signed a treaty with Fermo after a short period of hostilities between the two cities. Venice could export unlimited quantities of wine and grain, although Fermo reserved the right to ban the export of the latter if prices rose above 30 solidi per *starium* (a high price indeed).[73] The common theme among all of the treaties signed with coastal cities in Romagna and the Marches is Venice's free access to the agricultural produce of the co-signatories. Venice's inability to feed itself had become painfully self-evident, and the city's government was determined to minimize the possibility of future shortfalls by strengthening relations with the producers of basic foodstuffs—and, where possible, establishing limitations on their movement within the upper Adriatic.

Ancona was the only sizable community on the central Italian coast that continually managed to rebuff Venetian efforts to either control its trade or restrict its commercial freedoms during the first half of the thirteenth century. Venice frequently responded by banning its merchants from traveling to Ancona at all; at the height of the famine, the city's government declared that any Venetian who went to Ancona without a special ducal permit would have to forfeit his entire cargo and pay a fine of £30 12s.[74] Even in a 1264 treaty between the two cities, in which Ancona was forced to considerably curtail its international commerce following a crushing Venetian victory, Venice was unable to compel Ancona to fall in line with its increasing monopolization of intra-Adriatic staple commodity movement. Ancona was allowed to import foodstuffs and other goods from throughout the Adriatic and trade these same goods freely within the sea, although it could not sell salt or cotton in the northern Adriatic. The city was also allowed to import 2,000 amphorae of wine and 100 miliaria of oil from northern Italy each year (including Ferrara, Bologna, and Lombardy).[75] Venice, on top of eliminating its only contemporary Adriatic rival for long-distance maritime trade, received full commercial rights in Ancona—except, tellingly, it could neither export grain from its rival nor import wine or salt to it.[76] Viewed from the perspective of Venetian control over long-distance trade, the treaty was a decisive triumph—at least on paper.[77] In light of Venice's ongoing efforts to establish a complete monopoly over the Adriatic trade of staple commodities, however, it was a marked setback.[78]

---

68 *VCM*, no. 7.
69 Ibid., no. 9.
70 *Consilia et Ordinamenta*, no. 97, in *DMCV* 1:197–98. The reference to the Gargano suggests that wood may have been an important element in Anconitan trade with Acre.
71 Pasolini, "Venezia e Ravenna," 226.
72 *VCM*, no. 10. The capacity of the soma depended on the specific merchandise.
73 Ibid., no. 11. Venetian commercial relations with Fermo were already well established in the first half of the thirteenth century; see *DCV*, nos. 694, 707, 745.

74 *Consilia et Ordinamenta*, no. 4, in *DMCV* 1:166.
75 The Venetian amphora had a capacity of 600 liters.
76 *VCM*, no. 12; R. Cessi, *La repubblica di Venezia e il problema adriatico* (Naples, 1953), 69–72.
77 Ancona openly flouted the treaty restrictions on international commerce, prompting a resumption of open warfare a decade later. See *VCM*, 16–18.
78 This setback is even more pronounced if one accepts David Abulafia's interpretation of the Venetian-Anconitan rivalry,

If Venice was not powerful enough to completely control Ancona's intra-Adriatic commerce, it was certainly not powerful enough to impose its economic program on the Kingdom of Sicily. Therefore, the commercial side of Venice's diplomatic efforts in southern Italy was directed principally toward securing the city's access to Apulian grain, and only minimally toward regulating the flow of staple goods in the Adriatic. A 1232 treaty between Venice and Frederick II of Sicily opened the ports of the kingdom to Venetian traders but did not exempt them from duties. Frederick's subjects were allowed to bring goods to Venice, but only if they were produced within the kingdom itself.[79] A 1257 treaty between Venice and Frederick's son Manfred renewed most of the conditions of the 1232 agreement, while also establishing that the duties paid by the Venetians on grain would be lower than those paid by Manfred's own subjects. Again, merchants from southern Italy were welcome to bring domestically produced commodities to Venice, but nothing else.[80] However, they were banned from carrying salt north of Zara or Ancona; they could not bring salt even to Venice. This prohibition stemmed from the Venetian desire to maintain control of the salt commerce in the upper Adriatic. Venice sought to keep all channels open insofar as the grain supply was concerned, but it was well supplied with salt from non-Apulian sources, and therefore could safely afford to shut out southern Italian merchants in the interests of preserving its monopoly. Thus, while the treaties that Venice signed with the Kingdom of Sicily are markedly less stringent than those with the cities of central Italy, they are still distinguished by Venice's overall concern with both securing its access to staple foodstuffs and regulating their movement where feasible.

The demand for grain also prompted Venice to establish a *muda* system for Puglia in the thirteenth century. The muda was a particularly Venetian commercial institution, in which the government proclaimed a specific period for the loading or unloading of goods in either Venice or a foreign territory. A fleet of ships, often (though not always) outfitted privately, then traveled in convoy to its destination.[81] The most famous was the semiannual Levantine muda, in which Venetian ships sailed to Constantinople, Alexandria, or Acre in spring or autumn, then returned together in time for a specific unloading period. The advantages to this system lay not only in the security of convoy travel but also in the price stability that it created, since the purchasing and selling of certain kinds of bulk merchandise were confined to specific—and well-publicized—periods of time. This latter feature made the muda system highly attractive for the grain trade, in which major price fluctuations could either lead to significant social disruption or force the city's government to provide expensive subsidies. Moreover, convoys offered vital protection to the grain-laden ships during periods of widespread famine. Unlike the Levantine muda, the Apulian muda occurred only when grain supplies seemed dangerously low. However, Venetians residing in Apulia were allowed to send shipments of grain to the mother city whenever they wished, even when the muda was imposed.[82] Although little information survives concerning the thirteenth-century Apulian muda, it was yet another means by which Venice sought to control the movement of staple commodities within the Adriatic.

Foodstuffs were not the only commodities that Venetian merchants sought in the Apulian ports; cotton and wool were also important exports for southern Italy. Although Venice imported its highest-quality textile materials from elsewhere in the Mediterranean, the Apulian ports were certainly exporting wool by the late twelfth century and the intra-Adriatic cotton trade was active by

---

namely that it stemmed neither from any direct concurrence on the Levantine trade routes nor from a desire to control the central Adriatic, but rather from the obstacle that a commercially independent Ancona posed to Venice's intra-Adriatic monopoly on the exchange of staple commodities (see Abulafia, "Ancona, Byzantium and the Adriatic," 207). This interpretation certainly seems plausible from the mid-thirteenth century onward. But in light of the absence of earlier Venetian efforts to restrict commodity movements within the Adriatic (except within the upper reaches of the sea), it does not fully explain the twelfth-century hostility between the two cities—unless Venice was genuinely afraid that Ancona might cut off its access to Apulian grain.

79 *PRV*, no. 4.
80 Ibid., no. 6.

81 For a lucid discussion of the Venetian *muda*, see F. C. Lane, "Fleets and Fairs: The Functions of the Venetian *muda*," in *Venice and History* (Baltimore, 1966), 128–41; see also G. Luzzatto, "Navigazione di linea e navigazione libera," in *Studi di storia economica veneziana* (Padua, 1954), 53–57.
82 G. Luzzatto, *Storia economica di Venezia dal'XI al XVI secolo* (Venice, 1995), 36–37.

the late twelfth or early thirteenth century.[83] By the mid-thirteenth century, Venice was actively regulating the cotton trade in the upper Adriatic; in the 1257 Venetian treaty with Manfred of Sicily, the latter's subjects were banned from transporting cotton north of Zara or Ancona (the same restriction that applied to salt).[84] Similarly, Venice's 1264 treaty with Ancona banned the latter from reexporting cotton from southern Italy to anywhere else in the Adriatic.[85] While none of the surviving Venetian commercial contracts specifically mention Apulian wool or cotton, the treaty provisions suggest that intra-Adriatic exchange of these commodities was sufficiently active to warrant Venice's imposition of restrictions on their movement.

Despite the existence of numerous treaty provisions limiting the freedom of non-Venetian participants in the grain, salt, and cotton trade, Venice was not yet powerful enough to fully impose its restrictive economic program on the entire Adriatic. However, it could quite easily establish and enforce restrictions on the activities of its own citizens. A series of official Venetian proceedings that survive for the mid-1220s reveal that navigation restrictions were frequently imposed during the winter months, since, as mentioned earlier, the sailing conditions in the Adriatic in winter were unpredictable and often dangerous. In November 1224, for example, the doge declared that Venetians could not sail south of Siponto on the western coast of the Adriatic, or south of Ragusa on the eastern coast, without ducal permission; this order was renewed in October 1226 and March 1228.[86] In February 1227, the doge banned Venetians from sailing south of Ravenna or Zara; one year later, a similar order was issued with the boundaries shifted to Senigallia (in the Marches) and Istria.[87] In later decades, foodstuffs were subjected to special restrictions at any time of year. In May 1251, Venetians were banned henceforth from carrying food to any Adriatic port except Venice (as had been the case during the 1224–27 famine).[88] In May 1253, a similar order was issued, but this time the limits applied only to the upper Adriatic (north of Romagna), and exceptions were made for cities with special ducal privileges.[89] These decrees ensured that Venetian ships carrying staple foodstuffs could not be diverted to other destinations by the promise of higher prices, a change that might have endangered the city's food supply. For obvious reasons, Venice was also concerned about food being exported outside the Adriatic; such activity was accordingly banned in June 1256.[90]

In the mid-thirteenth century, the intra-Adriatic trade in salt also became an issue of concern for Venice. Until that point, Venice had been well supplied by the flourishing saltworks in neighboring Chioggia, though some restrictions had been established in order to protect its supply. Beginning in 1184, for example, a ducal seal was required to export Chioggian salt outside the lagoon, and in 1228 Venetians were banned from transporting salt south of Ravenna or Quarnar (just south of Istria).[91] But in general, control of the salt trade was of minimal immediate concern to Venice during the twelfth and early thirteenth century. However, beginning around 1232 the rapid collapse of the Chioggian salt industry (due in part to debilitating Venetian tax policies, which effectively privileged Cervian salt over local Chioggian production) forced Venice to seek other sources from which to supply itself.

Fortunately, the Adriatic Sea was comparatively rich in salt. Within the upper Adriatic, the other major source was Cervia, which had been under the control of Ravenna throughout the preceding centuries. Venice aggressively sought to control first the commerce of Cervian salt within the upper Adriatic, sending galleys into the port of Badareno (through which Ravenna accessed the Adriatic) in 1234 to prevent Ravenna from shipping Cervian salt northward. As Chioggian production declined, Venice fought for control of Cervia itself. From 1243

---

83 G. De Gennaro, "Le lane di Puglia nel basso Medioevo," in *La lana come materia prima, i fenomeni della sua produzione e circolazione nei secoli XIII–XVII*, ed. M. Spallanzani (Florence, 1974), 149–67, at 152–54, 167.

84 *PRV*, no. 6.

85 *VCM*, no. 12; Cessi, *Il problema adriatico*, 69–72.

86 *Plegii et Ordinamenta*, no. 8, in *DMCV* 1:132; and *Consilia et Ordinamenta*, nos. 8, 83, in *DMCV* 1:167, 193. In the latter two cases, the southern boundary along the Italian coast was fixed at Leuca and Tronto (in the Abruzzo), respectively.

87 *Consilia et Ordinamenta*, nos. 29, 80, in *DMCV* 1:172, 192.

88 *Liber Comunis*, 14 May 1252: "De illis qui carrigant victualia infra culfum," in *DMCV* 2:45.

89 *Liber Comunis*, 5 March 1253: "De non portandis victualibus et mercibus, nisi Venecias, et cetera," in *DMCV* 2:46.

90 *Liber Comunis*, 14 May 1251: "De illis qui carrigant victualia infra culfum," in *DMCV* 2:49.

91 J.-C. Hocquet, *Le sel et la fortune de Venise*, 2 vols. (Villeneuve-d'Ascq, 1978–79), 2:170–71; *Consilia et Ordinamenta*, no. 104, in *DMCV* 1:200.

to 1248, and then again from 1252 to 1254, Venice actually wrested it from Ravenna. In 1261, the feuding cities signed a treaty by which Ravenna ceded an annual volume of Cervian salt to Venice.[92] The coast between Ravenna and the Gargano Peninsula had almost no domestic salt industry in the Middle Ages, but south of the Gargano, the sandy littorals of Apulia lent themselves to the production of this staple good. However, their output was largely reserved for consumption within the Kingdom of Sicily—and there was enough salt elsewhere in the Adriatic that Venice saw little point in seeking access to Apulia's production. As mentioned above, Venice did include a provision in the treaty of 1257 banning Manfred's subjects from transporting salt north of Zara or Ancona.[93] The provision suggests that Venice was willing to forgo access to the product itself, rather than renounce its right to control the movement of salt within the upper Adriatic. The eastern shores of the Adriatic rarely figured into Venice's system of provisioning itself, given the region's general paucity of arable land. But the numerous archipelagoes along the coast harbored countless saltworks, and there were major ones as well on the island of Pag and around Zara. The latter sites were already producing abundant salt in the eleventh and twelfth centuries, and were probably a source of salt for Venice starting in the mid-thirteenth.[94] Strict Venetian control over the Adriatic salt trade did not begin until the late thirteenth century; as of 1272, Venetians entering into the Adriatic with salt from the Mediterranean (particularly Ibiza, Sardinia, and Cyprus) could unload it only in Venice, and in 1281 the Great Council required all Venetian merchants to import salt on the return trip of each voyage.[95] However, the developments in the first half of the century—namely, the decline of nearby saltworks and Venice's increasing concern with commodity movement in the Adriatic—laid the groundwork for what was to become one of the Venetian state's most absolute monopolies.

The importance of the Adriatic region as a source of Venetian manpower has already been noted. Much of the population inflow was the product of voluntary immigration, but part of it stemmed from the urban demand for domestic slaves.[96] Though domestic slavery may not have been a widespread phenomenon in twelfth- and thirteenth-century Venice itself, Venetian participation in the slave trade was considerable.[97] In the early Middle Ages, the bulk of the slaves passing through Venice were supplied from Carolingian conquests and raids; in later centuries, by contrast, they were drawn from the Balkans, which emerged as one of the principal sources of slaves in the high and late medieval Mediterranean world.[98] In each of the attested cases of urban Venetian domestic servitude from the period, the slave concerned was of Balkan descent. In 1125, for example, the heirs of Pietro Stagnario noted the manumission of Dobramiro, their father's former slave, who was of Croatian origin.[99] In 1199, Bratemiro, a slave *ex genere Sclavorum,* was sold to a certain Domenico of Chioggia. In 1211, Giacomo della Scala made provisions in his will for the freeing of Draga, a female slave whose name implies a Balkan origin.[100] The regular (if infrequent) appearance of Balkan slaves in the surviving Venetian commercial contracts suggests that while the slave trade was perhaps not yet as vigorous as it would become at the very end of the thirteenth century, nor as fundamental as it had been during the early Middle Ages, it was nevertheless an important component of Venetian economic exchange with the eastern Adriatic coast during the period in question.[101]

To what extent was the movement of slaves and other commodities to and from Venice carried out by the Venetians themselves? The surviving documentation suggests that it was generally Venetian

---

92 Hocquet, *Le sel et la fortune de Venise,* 1:172–75.
93 *PRV,* no. 6.
94 Hocquet, *Le sel et la fortune de Venise,* 1:169.
95 Ibid., 1:315; 2:253–54.
96 Given the difficulty of establishing a clear dividing line between slavery and servitude in the High Middle Ages, I use the terms "slaves" and "slavery" throughout.
97 Venetian involvement in the slave trade was nothing new; Michael McCormick has recently argued that the slave trade in fact formed the basis of early Venetian prosperity (McCormick, *Origins of the European Economy,* 763–77).
98 In the early Middle Ages, the Balkans were also a major source of slaves for the Byzantine Empire and its slave trade; see Y. Rotman, *Les esclaves et l'esclavage de la Méditerranée antique à la Méditerranée médiévale, VIe–XIe siècles* (Paris, 2004), 97.
99 *DCV,* no. 49.
100 *DCV,* nos. 442, 535.
101 For the later Middle Ages, see C. Verlinden, "Le relazioni economiche fra le due sponde adriatiche nel basso Medio Evo alla luce della tratta degli schiavi," in *Momenti e problemi della storia delle due sponde adriatiche: Atti del 1° Congresso internazionale sulle relazioni fra le due sponde adriatiche (Brindisi-Lecce-Taranto, 15–18 ottobre 1971),* ed. P. F. Palumbo (Rome, 1973), 105–39.

merchants and sailors who carried them from Adriatic communities to Venice itself, rather than waiting for the commodities to be brought to the Rialto by others. This is not surprising; in the twelfth and thirteenth centuries, the Venetian merchant marine dwarfed that of the Adriatic cities, and Venice was the commercial city par excellence. But while Venetians undoubtedly dominated their city's intra-Adriatic trade routes (and, indeed, its trade routes in general), non-Venetians also played an active role. Admittedly, the extent of non-Venetian participation in Venice's overall intra-Adriatic trade is difficult to gauge: little relevant documentation survives that might illuminate its scale. Consequently, we have no way of knowing how much of the southern Italian grain was carried to the lagoon city on Apulian ships rather than Venetian ones, or how often Ragusan slave traders brought their wares to Venice rather than waiting for Venetian merchants to come to the Dalmatian markets, and so on.

Although we do not know what proportion of Venice's intra-Adriatic trade was accounted for by non-Venetian participants, it was far from negligible. All of Venice's treaties with the cities along the central Italian coast allowed the co-signatories permission to trade freely (or very nearly so) in Venice. Both the 1232 and 1257 treaties between Venice and the Kingdom of Sicily specifically allowed southern Italian merchants to bring domestically produced goods to Venice (although the latter treaty excluded salt and cotton).[102] Even Venice's 1264 treaty with Ancona, which greatly restricted the latter's commercial freedoms, still allowed Ancona to bring goods produced within the Adriatic to Venice (again excepting salt and cotton).[103] Essentially, the Venetian need for staple foodstuffs outweighed the city's desire to completely control the movement of those commodities within the Adriatic. The availability of grain on the Rialto was more important than the allegiance of the ships on which it was transported. Dalmatian merchants came to Venice, too, and they settled in the city in large numbers. In Ragusa's 1205 treaty with Venice, its merchants were exempted from taxes on Balkan commodities that they brought to Venice, though the treaty severely limited their ability to import goods to Venice from beyond the Adriatic and banned them from engaging in commerce with foreign traders during their visit to Venice.[104]

From the mid-twelfth century onward, Venice massively expanded its control over the economic life of the Adriatic. Commercial ties were formalized, navigation restrictions were imposed, and commodity movements were monopolized. The city's efforts were not motivated by Venetian interests in the Levant, nor by a virulent strain of civic imperialism—though these factors undoubtedly colored the developments. Rather, they were a direct and rational response to well-founded concerns about Venice's ability to sustain itself. Other parts of the Adriatic could provide what the city's immediate surroundings could not, and an intensification of intra-Adriatic commercial exchange was the natural result. But while Venice was dependent on the Adriatic for its survival, the communities engaged in the supplying of Venice also depended on the city for their economic livelihoods.[105] The relationship between a city and its contado was never unidirectional, and the Venetian experience was no exception. If the coastal cities of the Adriatic gradually accepted Venetian restrictions over their commercial freedom in return for a guaranteed market for their wares, it was not always a case of weaker powers being subjugated by a dominant power; rather, it was often an acknowledgment that the expansion of trade could bring mutual rewards.

Commercial Exchange within the Adriatic

The influence of Venice was felt throughout the Adriatic, but not all sea routes led inexorably toward the lagoon city. Because the sea was navigable, intra-Adriatic trade was conducted both laterally (that is, along a given coast) and transversally (between opposing coasts). Of course, some voyages involved both lateral and transverse trade: a Dalmatian ship might cross the Adriatic to southern Italy and stop at several Apulian ports to buy grain before return-

---

102 *PRV*, nos. 4, 6.
103 *VCM*, no. 12.

104 The text is now lost, although its provisions have been recreated from later treaties; see S. M. Stuard, "Ragusa and the Silver Trade: Ragusan Trade with the Balkan Interior, 1205–1358" (Ph.D. diss., Yale University, 1971), 26–27.
105 In some cases, like the 1141 treaty with Fano, Venice also offered its protection to the co-signatory—but during the period such cases were rare outside the upper Adriatic.

ing to the eastern coast.¹⁰⁶ However, such a voyage served the same redistributive function—namely, moving grain from the west coast to the east coast—regardless of how many Apulian ports the Dalmatian ship visited during its trip. From the regional perspective of commodity exchange, the movement of grain from Apulia to Dalmatia is the crucial factor; it is unimportant whether such grain was purchased in one port or many. From the perspective of the grain merchants in medieval Brindisi or Otranto, in contrast, such port-hopping was vitally important. Attention to such movements would be equally crucial for a close examination of short-distance maritime trade routes or of the individual activity of Adriatic ports. But in order to avoid burying the large patterns of intra-Adriatic commodity exchange beneath a bewildering array of detail, the analysis below will focus primarily on broad movements of commodities within the Adriatic—either along the same shore or across to the opposing one—rather than the specific itineraries by which individual vessels orchestrated this movement.

Much of the lateral commercial traffic along the western coast was occasioned by the simple inability of major urban centers to supply themselves with sufficient basic foodstuffs from their immediate surroundings.¹⁰⁷ Venice was not the only Adriatic city that expanded beyond the productive capabilities of its hinterland; Ravenna, for example, faced a similar problem. In its 1234 treaty with Venice, it insisted on maintaining its freedom to import food from Apulia and the Marches—a stipulation which clearly implies that Ravenna was unable to consistently supply its food needs from the surrounding countryside.¹⁰⁸ Ancona was an even larger urban center, and the city's demand for foodstuffs was a particularly important engine of lateral exchange on the western coast. Free access to Adriatic grain was so vital that the papacy (which had declared the city to be a papal protectorate) regularly intervened in Adriatic affairs in order to secure the Anconitan food supply. In 1245, Pope Innocent IV declared that the citizens of Ancona were free to trade throughout Apulia and the Kingdom of Sicily, though since both regions were under imperial rather than papal control, his proclamation had no practical effect.¹⁰⁹ Even under the crushing terms of the city's 1264 treaty with Venice, Ancona managed to preserve its right to import agricultural goods from anywhere on the Italo-Adriatic coast.¹¹⁰ Given Venice's increasing monopolization of intra-Adriatic staple commodity movement, Ancona's preservation of this commercial freedom was no mean feat, and the clause is a testament to the critical importance of the western Adriatic coast to the Anconitan food supply.

There were also communities along both coasts with specific needs that could often be satisfied only by nearby urban centers, which enjoyed a density of skilled labor (for manufactured goods) or a concentration of capital (for long-distance trade). For example, the monks of S. Maria di Tremiti, a Benedictine monastery on the small island of San Nicola off the Gargano Peninsula, turned to Anconitan markets to provide commodities that were unavailable in their tiny archipelago. A surviving *pagina recordationis* from 1128 indicates that cheese was produced on the Tremiti islands, but gives no hint as to the Anconitan goods that induced the monks to sail from their monastery to the great port city in the first place.¹¹¹ Perhaps they sought more varied foodstuffs than the ecology of the archipelago could sustain, or perhaps they came for more specialized merchandise—wax for their candles, incense for their services, tools for their workers—all of which would have been available in the markets of Ancona. Similar circumstances probably animated the harbors of countless other Adriatic port cities on both the eastern and western coasts, although the surviving documentary evidence for such activity is unfortunately scarce.

---

106 Such a route is attested in an early medieval vita of St. Leucius, in which the saint travels aboard a Dalmatian ship in order to travel from Otranto to Brindisi. It is probable that this segment formed part of a larger trading voyage from Dalmatia to Apulia and back again. See *Vita S. Leucii, AASS* Jan. I, XI, 672.

107 Contemporaries were well aware of the consequences of local shortfalls, particularly where port cities were concerned. As one Anconitan chronicler noted ca. 1200, "civitates que sunt in portibus constitute vix possunt de labore proprio frumentum et anonam habere ad sufficientam, cum plures constet esse in illis nautas et mercatores"; Boncompagno da Signa, *Liber de obsidione Ancone*, in *RIS* 6, pt. 3, ed. G. C. Zimolo (Bologna, 1939), 17.

108 Pasolini, "Venezia e Ravenna," 226. F. C. Lane (*Venice,* 58) incorrectly dates this treaty to 1238 rather than 1234.

109 A. Theiner, ed., *Codex diplomaticus dominii temporalis S. Sedis,* 3 vols. (Rome, 1861–62), no. 210. A year later, the pope insisted on Anconitan commercial privileges in Durazzo—but the city's Epirote rulers seem to have ignored this as well (ibid., no. 227).

110 *VCM,* no. 12.

111 A. Petrucci, ed., *Codice Diplomatico del Monastero Benedettino di S. Maria di Tremiti (1005–1237)* (Rome, 1960), no. 96.

In other cases, the patterns of exchange along the western Adriatic coast were less firmly established, with the dynamics of supply and demand varying from month to month and year to year. Such is the case with the commercial relationship between Fermo and Termoli during the early thirteenth century. The terms of a 1225 treaty between the two cities indicate that trading links had been active for some time; indeed, the treaty was an attempt to rectify the ill will that had arisen after the cities had imposed sanctions on each other's merchants.[112] The commodities specifically named in the treaty include wool, linen, iron, wax, pepper, salt, oil, vegetables, meat, cheese, animals, and eels, but the treaty itself is unconcerned with the directional flow of the goods. Fermo, of course, lay in a fertile agricultural region, with sufficient supplies of grain, oil, and wine that its output would be actively sequestered by Venice in the mid-thirteenth century, as mentioned earlier.[113] It was also an active fishing port; even today, fish and eels are mainstays of the local diet. Termoli, by contrast, was backed by a mountainous hinterland for which it was the principal port. Subsistence farming and sheepherding seem to have been the surrounding region's principal economic activities, though there was some grain production in the area.[114] It is probable that Termoli often offered wool in exchange for the agricultural produce of Fermo, but the trade dynamics of salt, linen, wax, iron, and pepper are unclear (though the latter two were presumably imported from elsewhere).[115] Given that most other contemporary treaties are considerably more explicit about the directionality of commodity movement, the ambiguity in the Fermo-Termoli treaty seems quite deliberate—a reminder that even if the broad movements of goods within the Adriatic often adhered to enduring and predictable patterns, smaller-scale exchanges between neighboring cities and regions were much more mutable.[116]

On the eastern side of the Adriatic, the relative unity of the micro-ecologies along the Dalmatian coast limited the opportunities for large-scale lateral exchange. Moreover, because the Dalmatian terrain was hardly conducive to agricultural production, urban-based demand could not prompt lateral exchange in the same way that it did on the western shore. Only further south, in Albania, did significant opportunities present themselves for commerce between communities along the eastern shore. While Venice apparently dominated the export market for Albanian grain, there was nevertheless a sizable Ragusan presence in Durazzo during the twelfth and thirteenth centuries.[117] The Ragusans became particularly active in the Albanian port after the Venetian-controlled Duchy of Durazzo collapsed in 1213, since they faced no local hostility (unlike their Venetian competitors) and their presence was actively encouraged by Durazzo's new overlords, the despots of Epiros.[118] The Ragusans had already been granted commercial privileges in the despotate in 1206, in return for a promise to import horses and armaments. According to these privileges, Ragusan merchants were exempted from the *kommerkion* (the traditional Byzantine commercial duty of 3 percent *ad valorem*), the despot renounced the right of the fisc, and Ragusans could not be collectively penalized for grievances committed by an individual Ragusan merchant.[119] Once Durazzo fell to the Despotate of Epiros in 1213, Ragusans would

---

112 W. Hagemann, "Un trattato del 1225 tra Fermo e Termoli finora sconosciuto," in *Studi in onore di Riccardo Filangieri* (Naples, 1959), 175–88, at 184–87. The treaty also notes that the trade could be carried out either by land or by sea, although the mountainous terrain of the region around Termoli probably rendered the maritime route more attractive to medieval merchants.

113 Although wine was the principal export commodity of Fermo in the later thirteenth century, it is not mentioned in the treaty, perhaps because the civic government wished to maintain stricter controls on its trade.

114 See M. Fondi, *Abruzzo e Molise*, Regioni d'Italia 12 (Turin, 1977), 15–149; and G. Brancaccio, *Il Molise medievale e moderno: Storia di uno spazio regionale* (Naples, 2005), 15–62.

115 No medieval saltworks are attested in the vicinity of either city; see Hocquet, *Le sel et la fortune de Venise*, 1:94–96.

116 For general twelfth- and thirteenth-century commercial developments in Molise and the Abruzzo, see D. Aquilano, "Insediamenti, popolamento e commercio nel contesto costiero abruzzese e molisano (sec. XI–XIV): Il caso di Pennaluce," *Mélanges de l'École française de Rome: Moyen Âge* 109.1 (1997): 59–130.

117 See A. Ducellier, "La côte albanaise au Moyen Âge: Exutoires locaux ou ports de transit?" *Études balkaniques* 8 (1985): 200–204, reprinted in idem, *L'Albanie entre Byzance et Venise, X^e–XVe siècles* (London, 1987), art. XIX.

118 Ducellier, *Façade maritime*, 186. The Duchy of Durazzo was established by Venice in 1205 following the Fourth Crusade, and was directly administered by the Venetian government for the next decade.

119 F. Miklosich and J. Müller, eds., *Acta et diplomata graeca medii aevi sacra et profana*, vol. 3 (Vienna, 1865), no. 12. For the *kommerkion*, see H. Antoniadis-Bibicou, *Recherches sur les dou-*

have enjoyed these privileges in Durazzo as well. Later treaties in 1234 and 1237 extended these privileges even further, assuring Ragusan merchants of protection from pirate attacks and of the protection of their property should they die within the despotate.[120]

The Ragusans came to Durazzo seeking salt, and evidently in great quantities.[121] The many lagoons along the Albanian coast (particularly north of Durazzo) rendered the region ideal for the production of the staple, and with Venice able to provision itself from saltworks in the upper Adriatic, Ragusa evidently faced little competition. The Dalmatian city's interest in the Albanian saltworks is striking: every surviving Ragusan contract for trade in Durazzo in the thirteenth century concerns the purchase of salt. The quantities involved were substantial—Ragusans seem to have bought more than one hundred tons of salt from Durazzo in 1243, and almost six hundred tons in 1248.[122] The intensity of this commerce is somewhat surprising, since the Dalmatian coastline was itself highly conducive to salt production. However, the level of Ragusan interest in Albanian salt clearly suggests that either local production was inadequate or that the commercial privileges that the city enjoyed in the despotate were generous enough to compensate for the longer transport distance. Moreover, Ragusa was supplying not merely its own needs but also those of its Balkan hinterland. Although Balkan demand was somewhat sated by the salt mines in Bosnia and Hungary, Ragusa nevertheless served an important intermediary function for the transit of Albanian salt.[123]

Salt was one of the very few commodities produced throughout the Adriatic. As it was produced on both the western and eastern coasts, it was usually traded laterally (since coastal tramping was generally preferred to trans-Adriatic crossings whenever possible). Only in the upper Adriatic, where most of the salt came from the major production centers of the northwestern coast, was there an active transverse trade. The movement of the salt was largely controlled by Venice; in 1182, for example, a treaty between Venice and Capodistria required all salt entering Istria to pass through Capodistria, and it also had to carry the seal of the Venetian doge unless it was being used for personal consumption.[124] Consequently, Venice was able to exercise a large degree of regulatory control over the regional commerce of salt. In the twelfth century, the Chioggian saltworks were the main suppliers for the upper Adriatic, just as for Venice itself. Thereafter, however, Cervian salt became more and more common in Istria. It seems to have circulated fairly freely until the mid-thirteenth century, when Venice was finally able to establish controls on its movement.[125] The eastern coast also had abundant saltworks during the period, particularly in the region around Pag, an island in the Dalmatian archipelago near Zara. Pag was already producing abundant salt in the eleventh century, and it continued to be a major source of Adriatic salt for centuries thereafter. Much of its production was purchased by Zaratine merchants, who then redirected it into the Balkan hinterland. Indeed, the profits from the salt trade with Pag were so crucial to Zara's economic livelihood that by cutting off Zara's access to the saltworks of Pag, Venice was able to hasten the end of Zaratine resistance to Venetian rule in the late twelfth century.[126]

The central and southern Italo-Adriatic coast also witnessed a lively lateral salt trade during the period. The Apulian coast had considerable saltworks, especially in the area around Siponto (immediately south of the Gargano Peninsula), and Cervia supplied the coast and interior of Romagna. But the regions in between—namely, the Marches and Abruzzo—had no domestic salt industry, and thus relied on imports.[127] Given that salt was generally too bulky to be carried overland in high volumes

---

anes à Byzance: L' "octava," le "kommerkion" et les commerciaires (Paris, 1963), 107–55.
120 *Acta et diplomata graeca*, nos. 14, 15.
121 The Ragusans may have purchased wheat as well, since the 1234 treaty between Ragusa and Epiros allowed Ragusa to export grain freely from the despotate except in times of dearth. However, it is unclear whether Ragusan merchants purchased this grain in Albania or elsewhere in the despotate, which by this point included Thessaly, a major grain-producing region.
122 Ducellier, *Façade maritime*, 188–90.
123 Hocquet, *Le sel et la fortune de Venise*, 2:612–14.

124 M. Pozza, ed., *Gli atti originali della cancelleria veneziana*, vol. 1, *1090–1198* (Venice, 1994), 97–98.
125 Hocquet, *Le sel et la fortune de Venise*, 1:168–69.
126 Ibid., 1:179.
127 Pescara, in Abruzzo, may have had a domestic salt industry by the late thirteenth century—but no local saltworks are attested before 1316. See Hocquet, *Le sel et la fortune de Venise*, 1:94–96.

for any significant distance, maritime transportation was the preferred mechanism of redistribution (with inland waterways playing an additional, and integral, distributive role). Unfortunately, no commercial contracts survive that might illuminate the details of this trade, though its existence is confirmed by the recurring references to the importation of salt in contemporary treaties from the cities in the region.[128]

Until the late thirteenth century, the salt commerce in the Adriatic was conducted almost entirely laterally, from Apulia to Ancona, or from Durazzo to Dalmatia, and so forth. Only in the upper parts of the sea, between Chioggia and Istria, was there an active transverse salt trade (and there the crossing might almost be considered lateral). While salt may have been transported from one coast to another in other parts of the Adriatic, no such exchanges are attested before the second half of the thirteenth century. In June 1262 the procurator of the Venetian count of Ragusa purchased 12,000 *modii ragusini* of salt from three Apulian ports, and there is no reason to believe that the transaction was unusual.[129] Twenty-five years later, in a 1288 treaty between Ancona and Zara, the exchange of salt between the two coasts was discussed extensively; the Zaratine saltworks were evidently poised to supply much of the demand in Ancona and its surrounding region.[130] But in general this was a late thirteenth-century phenomenon, and in the twelfth and early thirteenth centuries, salt was rarely traded between the eastern and western shores.

The lateral nature of the salt trade was largely paralleled by the contemporary timber trade. Like salt, wood was not confined to any one region or coast in the Adriatic. A major axis ran from Durazzo to Ragusa, which grew in importance as Ragusan shipbuilding developed in the later Middle Ages.[131] The northern Adriatic was largely self-sufficient; the Istrian forests had ample supplies to furnish both Venetian needs and the demands of other communities in the upper Adriatic. Further south on the Italian shore, the Gargano Peninsula was a vital source of sturdy timber for communities along both the central and southern Italian coast. Like the salt trade, the timber trade seems to have been almost entirely confined to individual coasts during the twelfth and early thirteenth centuries. Only in the later Middle Ages, as local forests began to be exhausted and local shipbuilding industries grew (particularly in Ragusa), did the timber trade expand to connect the opposing shores.[132]

While salt and timber were largely traded along a particular coast, a considerable proportion of intra-Adriatic trade was conducted transversally, that is, between the eastern and western coasts. Such commerce was facilitated by the favorable navigation conditions for trans-Adriatic trade, particularly in the central Adriatic. Though it is impossible to determine from the surviving records whether trans-Adriatic trade outweighed lateral trade in either the value or the quantity of the goods exchanged, there is no question that it involved the greater variety of commodities. Most lateral trade was prompted by the inability of local regions to fully satisfy the ever-increasing demands of urban centers, rather than by micro-ecological complementarity. Ancona imported foodstuffs from Apulia not because the Marches were not suitable for the cultivation of grain, but because the Marches could not produce grain in sufficient quantities. The cargoes of the ships sailing on the trans-Adriatic trade routes, by contrast, were dominated by commodities that could be produced solely (or almost solely) on the opposite coast.

The importance of such trans-Adriatic trade is suggested by the contemporary Ragusan diplomatic record (see fig. 10.3). Notwithstanding Ragusa's spectacular commercial success during the later Middle Ages, in earlier centuries its economic circumstances were similar to those of the other Dalmatian coastal cities. Its rich archives therefore offer a means of indirectly examining the commercial experience of the neighboring urban centers in general, as well as understanding the trade networks of Ragusa itself. By 1260, Ragusa had established commercial treaties with a dozen communities on the western Adriatic coast (excluding Venice). By comparison, there are only two Ragusan commercial treaties in which

---

128 See, for example, the Fermo-Termoli treaty mentioned above (Hagemann, "Fermo e Termoli," 184–87); see also the 1264 treaty between Ancona and Venice (*VCM*, no. 12), in which the former retained the right to control its own salt imports.
129 T. Smičiklas, ed., *Codex Diplomaticus Regni Croatiae, Dalmatiae et Slavoniae* (Zagreb, 1904–), vol. 5, nos. 731, 754 (hereafter cited as *CDS*). The Ragusan modius had approximately one-tenth the capacity of the Venetian modius.
130 *CDS*, vol. 6, no. 526.
131 Ducellier, "Côte albanaise," 201.

132 Braudel, *Mediterranean*, 141–42.

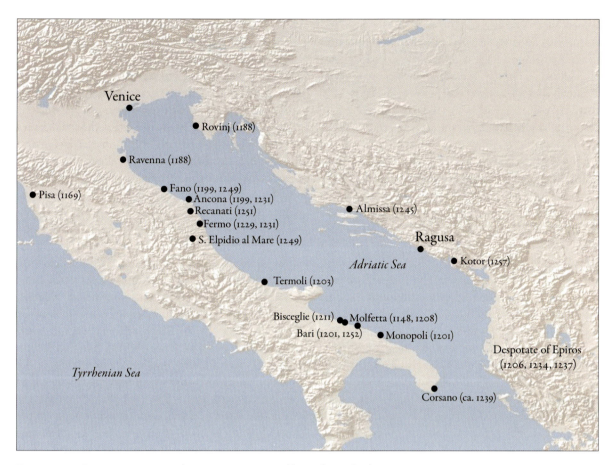

Figure 10.3. Ragusan commercial treaties, 1100–1260 (drawn by author)

the co-signatory is another Dalmatian city (both date from the mid-thirteenth century), plus a treaty with Rovinj, on the Istrian Peninsula.[133] Admittedly, Ragusa also received commercial privileges in Albania in the thirteenth century, as mentioned earlier. But even if the market of Durazzo was a popular destination for Ragusan merchants, the enormous effort that Ragusa invested in its relations with the cities on the opposite shore underscores the crucial importance of the Italian coast to its trade network. The city's political allegiance to Venice ensured that economic relations between them were close, but the treaties spanned the entire Italian coast, from Ravenna to Corsano (at the mouth of the Adriatic), and the co-signatories ranged in size from great ports like Ancona and Bari to tiny communities like S. Elpidio a Mare, near Fermo. Almost all of the surviving treaties offer assurances of personal security for merchants and sailors, as well as broad promises of reciprocal freedom of maritime trade. Some, such as Ragusa's 1203 treaty with Termoli, expressly exempted Ragusan merchants from duties in the port of the co-signatory.[134] Others, like Ragusa's 1148 treaty with Molfetta and its 1211 treaty with Bisceglie, provided for reciprocal exemptions.[135] In every instance, however, the treaty was signed not in Ragusa but in the territory of the co-signatory. The uniformity of this trend indicates that Ragusan proactivity was the driving force behind these

---

133   Most of the treaty texts are reproduced in *CDS,* vols. 1–5; and in J. Radonić, ed., *Acta et diplomata Ragusina,* vol. 1 (Belgrade, 1935), hereafter cited as *ADR.* The original text of Ragusa's treaty with Molfetta was lost in the late twelfth century; its provisions are known from the document concerning the treaty's renewal in 1208. For Ragusa's 1188 treaty with Rovinj, see S. Ljubić, ed., *Listine o odnosajih izmedju Jurnoga Slavenstva i Mletačke Republike od godine 960 do 1469* (Zagreb, 1868–91), 1:14. The two commercial treaties with other Dalmatian cities are with Almissa (in 1245) and Kotor (in 1257); see *ADR,* nos. 26, 33.

134   *ADR,* no. 14.
135   Ibid., nos. 15, 16.

agreements, for it was Ragusa that sent its ambassadors up and down the Italo-Adriatic coast in search of commercial privileges.[136] Moreover, the existence of treaties in which Ragusa was exempted from duties in the other city's port, but not vice versa, suggests that the exchange was largely conducted by Ragusan vessels sailing to the western coast, rather than Italian ships sailing to Dalmatia.[137]

The earliest known Ragusan treaty with another Adriatic city dates from 1148, and concerns reciprocal trading privileges with the Apulian port of Molfetta. Only two other commercial agreements survive from before the very end of the twelfth century; in 1188 Ragusa signed treaties with both Rovinj (Rovigno) and Ravenna.[138] The turn of the twelfth century saw a marked increase in Ragusa's formal trading ties with other Adriatic communities, with six treaties signed between 1199 and 1210, and a further twelve signed between 1211 and 1252. But while it is tempting to thus see the early thirteenth century as a period of explosive growth for Ragusa's commerce in the Adriatic, the individual treaties were usually responses to existing trading relationships, not vehicles for initial contact. The text of Ragusa's 1201 treaty with Monopoli, for example, includes a warm greeting that implies existing ties between the two cities.[139] Consequently, it is likely that commercial relations with Monopoli had been established earlier, and that the treaty merely marked a new step in the evolution of the trading relationship. It is thus probable that the expansion of Ragusa's intra-Adriatic activity was a phenomenon of the late twelfth century, or possibly even earlier.

Though the chronology of Ragusa's commercial expansion in the Adriatic is impossible to pinpoint precisely, the intensity of its interest in the Italian coast is indisputable. At first glance, however, the general absence of Ragusan commercial relations with other Dalmatian cities—especially Zara and Split—is striking. In the twelfth century, at least, Byzantine suzerainty over most of the eastern coast may have obviated the need for formal treaties between the communities that lay along it. But no such political unity existed in the thirteenth century—and yet there are only two surviving commercial treaties between Ragusa and other Dalmatian cities, and none before 1245. It is thus unlikely that the apparent Ragusan disinterest in eastern Adriatic communities is the result of a skewed documentary record. Rather, it reflects the simple consequences of the similar micro-ecologies along the Dalmatian coast—and the complementary micro-ecology of the opposite shore. It is therefore not surprising that the trading patterns of other communities that shared Ragusa's micro-ecology demonstrated a similar east–west, rather than lateral, dynamic. Ragusa may be the best documented of the medieval Dalmatian cities, but it was by no means the only one that was actively engaged in commerce with the opposite shore. Split was certainly trading with the Apulian towns by the mid-twelfth century; in 1160, a merchant from Split was selling merchandise in Terlizzi, near Bari.[140] In the late twelfth century, Kotor (Cattaro) is known to have had particularly close relations with Bari. By 1195, Kotor had officially subjected itself to the ecclesiastical authority of the metropolitan of Bari; that same year its merchants were exempted from duties in Bari by a privilege from the Empress Constance, which spurred further activity in Bari and the surrounding region over the succeeding decades.[141] While there are no surviving commercial agreements between the Apulian ports and either Zara, Trogir (Traù), or Split, it is highly probable that all three also maintained active economic ties with southern Italy, especially in light of ceramic evidence from the thirteenth century.[142]

---

136 D. Abulafia, "Dalmatian Ragusa and the Norman Kingdom of Sicily," *SEER* 54 (1976): 412–28, at 416.

137 Italian ships did, however, visit Dalmatia, as evidenced by Ragusa's efforts ca. 1190 to protect Apulian shipping from the attacks of the Cazichi pirates. See *ADR*, no. 8.

138 For Rovinj, see Ljubić, *Listine o odnosajih izmedju*, 1:14; for Ravenna, see *CDS*, vol. 2, no. 14.

139 *ADR*, no. 12; and see Abulafia, "Dalmatian Ragusa," 416.

140 F. Carabellese, ed., *Codice diplomatico barese*, vol. 3, *Le pergamene della cattedrale di Terlizzi (971–1300)* (Bari, 1899), no. 87; and Martin, *La Pouille*, 438.

141 G. B. Nitto di Rossi and F. Nitti di Vito, eds., *Codice diplomatico barese*, vol. 1, *Le pergamene del Duomo di Bari (952–1264)* (Bari, 1897), no. 65. Slavko Mijušković overemphasizes the importance of the ecclesiastical ties at the expense of the much more important imperial privilege in his article "Bari, Cattaro ed i dinasti serbi dei secoli XII–XIV," in *Navigazioni mediterranee e connessioni continentali (secoli XI–XVI)*, ed. R. Ragosta (Naples, 1982), 111–14.

142 See D. Whitehouse, "Apulia," in *La ceramica medievale nel Mediterraneo occidentale: Siena, 8–12 ottobre 1984; Faenza, 13 ottobre 1984* (Florence, 1986), 573–86, at 579. However, large-scale ceramic imports from southern Italy to Split (and elsewhere in Dalmatia) are largely a product of the late thirteenth century, when Apulian ceramic production itself became more developed; see J. Buerger, "The Medieval Glazed Pottery," in *Diocletian's*

In some cases, formal agreements may simply have been lost during the upheavals of succeeding centuries; it is also possible that no treaties ever existed, and that trade was conducted without formal concessions. And in some cases, privileges in the Italian cities were acquired indirectly—thereby eliminating the need for separate agreements. In 1257, for example, a treaty between Venice and Manfred of Sicily included Zaratines among the beneficiaries of the concessions that were being extended; when the treaty was reconfirmed two years later, the privileges were extended to Ragusan merchants as well.[143] The cities of the Marches were also popular destinations for the merchants of the major Dalmatian communities. Commercial ties between Fermo and Split almost certainly antedated the thirteenth century, since in a document from 1200, Fermo reminded Split of the preexisting treaty of friendship between them.[144] In 1236, Ancona and Trogir also signed a treaty; while it did not include specifically commercial provisions, the general assurances of protection of each other's citizens were presumably aimed at facilitating trade.[145]

For Dalmatia, as for Venice, the great appeal of the western Adriatic coast stemmed from its agricultural surpluses. Most of the eastern coast between Istria and Albania is too mountainous or infertile to sustain much cultivation of wheat or olives, and north of Split the relatively harsh climate contributes to the absence of widespread agriculture.[146] Consequently, the Dalmatian cities relied heavily on imports of wheat and oil, particularly as their populations increased beyond the productive capabilities of their hinterlands. In 1572, when a visitor to Ragusa remarked that in the city "Il ne se mange ung seul grain de bled qu'il ne faille aller cercher à cinq cens mil d'icy," he was simply noting a perennial feature of Dalmatian urban life.[147] It is no coincidence that Ragusa's earliest surviving intra-Adriatic commercial treaty is with Molfetta, the center of Apulian oil production.[148] The crucial importance of the trade in foodstuffs from Italy to the eastern coast is revealed by the surviving commercial contracts from late thirteenth-century Dalmatia, many of which specifically refer to imports of Apulian grain.[149] Much of the grain and oil was probably consumed in the Dalmatian cities themselves, although some of it was transported overland to Serbia.[150]

The western coast offered other commodities as well, even if these were never as important as the staple foodstuffs in the overall patterns of exchange. Wine was the principal export commodity of Fermo, and since Fermo had commercial ties with both Split and Ragusa in the twelfth and early thirteenth centuries, it seems probable that wine filled at least part of the cargo holds of the ships setting forth toward the eastern coast.[151] Furthermore, in light of Ragusa's continual efforts to acquire Albanian salt in the early thirteenth century, it is possible that its merchants also looked for salt in Ravennan and Apulian markets, both of which offered the mineral in abundance. But the presence of saltworks both elsewhere in the Dalmatian archipelago and along the western Adriatic coast makes it unlikely that salt represented a major component of the east–west Adriatic trade during the period. A 1292 treaty between Ragusa and Ancona also discusses the export of silk and rope cordage from the latter city.[152] Although the agreement dates from the very end of the thirteenth century, it is highly probable that luxury and manufactured goods played a role in the exports from the Italian ports in earlier decades, too, especially given the limited international trade network of the Dalmatian cities and their relatively small size (at least compared to major urban centers like Ancona).

Palace: American-Yugoslav Joint Excavations, vol. 3 (Split, 1979), 5–123, at 75–76.
143 *PRV,* no. 7.
144 *Monumenta spectantia historiam Dalmatarum,* Archivio Storico per la Dalmazia 1, vol. 1, fasc. 3 (Rome, 1926), 11.
145 Ibid., fasc. 2, 4.
146 Cabanes et al., *Histoire de l'Adriatique,* 19.
147 E. Charrière, *Négociations de la France dans le Levant,* 4 vols. (Paris, 1848–60), 3:245; cited in Braudel, *Mediterranean,* 578.
148 Martin, *La Pouille,* 438.
149 See, among others, *CDS,* vol. 6, nos. 125, 260, 284, 309, 339 (the contracts range from 1275 to 1279); see also T. Raukar, "Il porto di Spalato e le relazioni commerciali nell'Adriatico del tardo Medio Evo," *Rivista storica del Mezzogiorno* 15–16 (1980–81): 117–28, at 127; and V. Foretić, "Curzola e la penisola italiana tra Medio Evo e Rinascimento," *Rivista storica del Mezzogiorno* 14 (1979): 91–108, at 95.
150 Mijušković, "Bari, Cattaro," 143–44; and C. Lozzi, "Relazioni tra la Repubblica Marinara di Ancona e la Repubblica di Ragusa e gli Slavi dell'Adriatico," in *Convegno di studi storici: "Federico Barbarossa, Ancona, e le Marche," Ancona, 19–20 aprile 1969* (Castello, 1972), 41–46, at 43.
151 *VCM,* 15.
152 *ADR,* nos. 44, 45.

The eastern coast probably imported textiles, too, particularly from southern Italy. The intra-Adriatic textiles trade, which would prove so lucrative and important in later centuries, begins to appear regularly in the documentary record around the mid-thirteenth century.[153] A limited textile industry existed in Dalmatia and its Balkan hinterland, but domestic production of both the primary materials and the finished products evidently proved insufficient to meet rising local demand.[154] It therefore turned to the western coast to make up the shortfall. Although no surviving commercial contracts refer to the movement of textiles between the western and eastern shores, provisions for the regulation of the cotton trade in surviving Venetian treaties indicate some experience in the import and export of textiles. In 1257, as mentioned above, Venice banned the subjects of Manfred of Sicily from exporting cotton north of Ancona or Zara.[155] Yet they remained free to sell their cotton in Albania, much of Dalmatia, and the southern half of the Italo-Adriatic coast—and they surely exploited this freedom. A few years later, in 1264, Venice banned Ancona from reexporting cotton from southern Italy to Dalmatia or any Italian coastal city north of Rimini.[156] From these provisions, it can be deduced that the cotton trade was already active in the Adriatic in the mid-thirteenth century (and probably earlier), although in the second half of the century the movement of cotton in the northern Adriatic was evidently heavily controlled by Venice.

What did the eastern coast offer in return for these imports? Unlike the Italian coast, which produced an abundance of agricultural products that could be traded, the Dalmatian coast had few commercial resources. Dalmatia was well forested, but again there is no evidence that timber was transported across the Adriatic during this period. Salt was also widely produced, but in the twelfth and thirteenth centuries, the production of Dalmatian saltworks was often insufficient to satisfy even local demand, let alone be sold to the opposite shore, and the shortfall only increased in later periods. The region did produce wine, which was certainly exported westward during the late thirteenth century and possibly earlier as well, but there is no evidence to suggest that this trade was particularly active or lucrative at this time.[157] Given the Dalmatian coast's limited production of exportable commodities, most of the exports of the Dalmatian ports originated in the Balkan hinterland, and Dalmatian traders served as middlemen. Animal products—principally leather, hides, and fur pelts—seem to have been particularly common; they were specifically mentioned in the 1292 Ragusa-Ancona treaty and reappear frequently in later documentation.[158] Wax was also an important export commodity in the late thirteenth century, and probably earlier as well.[159] As Ragusa was an exporter of horses and armaments to Albania, it is possible that these commodities were a component of its trade with the Italian coastal cities. The Dalmatian shipbuilding industry may also have served as a source of export commodities, since in 1160 a certain Sabbato of Split sold a small boat to an Apulian for 9½ *perperi*.[160] Unfortunately, the document does not indicate whether the ship was originally made in Dalmatia or was acquired elsewhere by Sabbato.[161]

The bulk of Dalmatian imports, however, were paid for through the export of Balkan slaves, whose importance has already been mentioned. In Apulia, references to slaves *ex genere Sclavorum* begin in the mid-eleventh century, and continue through to the later Middle Ages.[162] In 1121, a certain Pietro of Bari purchased a female slave and her child, both

---

153   For the medieval textile trade, see M. F. Mazzaoui, *The Italian Cotton Industry in the Later Middle Ages, 1100–1600* (Cambridge, 1981); and for the later Middle Ages, J.-K. Nam, *Le commerce du coton en Méditerranée à la fin du Moyen-Age* (Leiden, 2007).
154   See D. Kovačević-Kojić, "La laine dans l'exportation des matières premières de la Bosnie médiévale," in *La lana come materia prima*, ed. Spallanzani, 289–90; and J. Tadić, "Jugoslavia e paesi balcanici: Produzione e esportazione della lana," ibid., 291–97.
155   *PRV*, no. 6.
156   *VCM*, no. 12.
157   In the 1292 treaty between Ancona and Ragusa, the Anconitans are permitted to both import and export wine to and from Ragusa, suggesting that Dalmatian wine production was of interest to Italian traders. See *ADR*, no. 44.
158   *ADR*, no. 44.
159   In 1297, for example, 301 pounds of wax were sold at Ragusa to Venetian traders (Dubrovnik Archives, *Diversa Cancellaria*, III, fol. 75b; cited in Stuard, "Ragusa and the Silver Trade," 175).
160   *Codice diplomatico barese*, vol. 3, no. 87.
161   The Dalmatian shipbuilding industry was certainly active during the period. Indeed, despite the general brevity of al-Idrīsī's remarks on the Dalmatian coastal cities, in half of the entries he comments on the high number of ships possessed by the city concerned. See al-Idrīsī, *Géographie d'Édrisi*, 2:263–67.
162   Martin, *La Pouille*, 437.

ex genere sclavorum, for 56 *miliareni de ramesinis,* and in 1183 a female slave in Barletta is described in the same way.[163] These references, together with considerable other evidence for Balkan slaves in Apulia, suggest the presence of an active slave trade between the eastern and western Adriatic coasts.[164] In Ragusa, for example, 236 slaves (mostly domestic) are recorded as having been exchanged between November 1280 and January 1284; since the total urban population of the city was under 4,000, the slave population was evidently a very significant component—even granting that some of the slaves may have been sold to non-Ragusans.[165] Given that Ragusa was the principal Adriatic outlet for Balkan slaves, it is not surprising that the city drew wrathful condemnations from the rulers of the afflicted populations. In 1253, Prince Crnomir of Bosnia addressed a complaint to Ragusa in which he expressed his deep concern for the safety of his rural subjects, who lacked protection from the foreign traders who regularly captured and enslaved them.[166] But despite such protests, the slave trade was too profitable for it to be readily abandoned by Dalmatian merchants. Ragusan documents from the 1280s suggest that a female slave cost on average 10 *hyperpera*—more than the residence of a skilled artisan.[167] The medieval slave trade was lucrative indeed. There is also evidence for a lateral slave trade along the Dalmatian coast, not simply from east to west across the Adriatic. A 1279 treaty between Ragusa and Kotor provided for matching duties on slaves exchanged between the two ports, which suggests that in the later thirteenth century, at least, an intra-Dalmatian market for slaves had developed.[168] However, it is unlikely that the slave trade along the eastern coast ever approached the level of the trans-Adriatic slave trade, given that the merchants in most of the Dalmatian ports had fairly easy access into the Balkan hinterland and could thus avoid the use of intermediaries if they so chose.

In both antiquity and the later Middle Ages, the most important of the Dalmatian export commodities were derived from the rich Balkan ore deposits.[169] From the late thirteenth century onward, silver, lead, copper, and other precious metals were extracted in enormous quantities from the great Serbian and Bosnian mines and transported overland to the Dalmatian coast to be exported to the Adriatic and the Levant. The economic importance of these commodities became even more critical as the Bosnian slave trade declined in the fourteenth century.[170] But metal and mineral exports probably played a minimal role in the Dalmatian economy of the twelfth and early thirteenth centuries. There are no textual references to Balkan mining activity prior to 1254 (when the mines at Brskovo in northern Montenegro are first attested) and there are no references to Bosnian mines before the mid-fourteenth century.[171] Since the documentary references rarely pinpoint the start of mining activity at a given site, the textual evidence almost always postdates the initial activity—especially since many of the mines seem to be fairly active by the time they are first mentioned. But it is impossible to determine the extent to which mining was already under way during this period. Admittedly, the rise in documentation of Balkan mining closely parallels the rise in medieval Balkan documentation in general. Prior to the late thirteenth century, local sources are extremely rare; thereafter both the archival materials and the references to mining become plentiful. It thus might seem reasonable to assume that mining

163 *Codice diplomatico barese,* vol. 5, *Le pergamene di S. Nicola di Bari II, periodo normanno (1075–1194),* ed. F. Nitti di Vito (Bari, 1902), no. 66; *Codice diplomatico barese,* vol. 8, *Le pergamene di Barletta, Archivio Capitolare (897–1285),* ed. F. Nitti di Vito (Bari, 1912), no. 141.
164 See J.-M. Martin, "L'esclavage en Pouille (fin du Xᵉ siècle–milieu du XIIIᵉ siècle)," in *I rapporti demografici e popolativi,* Congressi sulle relazioni tra le due sponde adriatiche 2 (Rome, 1981), 55–74.
165 S. M. Stuard, "To Town to Serve: Urban Domestic Slavery in Medieval Ragusa," in *Women and Work in Preindustrial Europe,* ed. B. Hanawalt (Bloomington, Ind., 1986), 39–55, esp. 42.
166 L. Stojanović, ed., *Stare srpske povelje i pisma,* 1 vol. in 2 (Belgrade, 1929–34), 1:25.
167 Stuard, "To Town to Serve," 47.
168 *ADR,* no. 41.

169 The most comprehensive treatment of the topic is M. J. Dinić, *Za istoriju rudarstva u srednovekovnoj Srbij i Bosni,* 2 vols. (Belgrade, 1955–62); K. Jireček, *Die Handelsstrassen und Bergwerke von Serbien und Bosnien während des Mittelalters* (Prague, 1879), remains fundamental. Desanka Kovačević offers an excellent survey in "Les mines d'or et d'argent dans la Serbie et la Bosnie médiévales," *AnnalesESC* 15 (1960): 248–58.
170 This decline was due to competition from Genoese slave traders in the Black Sea, a decrease in the persecution of the Bosnian Bogomils (who had been a major source of the slaves), and the efforts of Bosnian rulers, who became steadily more capable of protecting their subjects from slave raiders (Stuard, "Ragusa and the Silver Trade," 191–94).
171 Kovačević, "Mines d'or," 249.

activity in the Balkans was already under way in the twelfth or early thirteenth century (if not earlier) and that documentary references simply have not survived, a position adopted by many scholars of Balkan mining.[172] Nevertheless, the absence of any mention of metals in the surviving treaties pertaining to Dalmatian communities is troubling. Admittedly, exports of silver and gold may have been in effect hidden in the coinage used for commercial transactions, but specific provisions relating to the exchange of gold and silver were often included in other contemporary treaties, such as the 1232 treaty between Venice and the Kingdom of Sicily.[173] Nor is lead or copper mentioned in the extant diplomatic record, although significant exports of both commodities are well attested in later documentation. Moreover, when the Ragusan notarial charters first become plentiful (around 1278) the slave trade is clearly thriving, while mining activity seems to be of lesser importance (though rapidly expanding).[174] Consequently, though some Balkan mining activity was presumably under way in the early to mid-thirteenth century, and possibly even in the twelfth century as well, it was almost certainly on a small scale. Thus the precious metal ores that would prove so critical to intra-Adriatic trade in later centuries were probably not a major component of the Dalmatian export commodities during this period.[175]

While Dalmatia enjoyed vibrant commercial links with the Italian coast, the trans-Adriatic commercial activity of Albania is almost impossible to determine with any certainty due to the lack of sources. However, it is unlikely that east–west exchange in the southern Adriatic was particularly active during the twelfth and thirteenth centuries. Unlike the Dalmatian city-states, whose microecologies were highly complementary with those along the western coast, Albania had ample domestic supplies of agricultural staples. It had no need to import salt, for the saltworks around Durazzo provided surpluses for export to other Adriatic markets. In addition, it had access to the Balkan hinterland, with its supplies of animal products and slaves. In times of scarcity, Albania no doubt imported foodstuffs from southern Italy, and it may have also turned to other coastal cities in the Adriatic for manufactured or luxury commodities. But what trade did occur was probably sporadic, for the structural features that inspired the vibrant east–west exchange elsewhere in the Adriatic were largely absent in Albania. Moreover, navigation across the lower Adriatic was considerably more difficult than in the central and upper parts of the sea, as a result of both the strong currents in the Strait of Otranto and the unfavorable wind patterns; this would have further discouraged east–west commerce.

Thus far, the discussion of intra-Adriatic exchange has focused on the redistribution that arose from commercial operations. But there was another important and regular mechanism by which commodities were moved throughout the Adriatic: piracy. Though medieval pirates operated outside formalized structures of commerce, they nevertheless served a redistributive function that was in many ways analogous to conventional trade. However, one cannot discuss pirates as a discrete class of individuals, for many of those who engaged in acts of piracy did not treat it as a trade. Rather, it was simply one of the various means by which commodities could be acquired. In periods of famine, for example, ships carrying foodstuffs regularly had their cargoes seized by desperate communities. The merchants aboard sometimes received compensation for their losses—but not always. Piracy should be usually understood—at least from an economic perspective—as one among several mechanisms of exchange and redistribution in the medieval Adriatic, practiced by a variety of different individuals depending on the circumstances.[176]

Some individuals and groups did engage in piracy as a regular means of sustenance, however, and might be appropriately labeled "pirates" in the conventional sense of the term. Almost all of them were based in the islands along the eastern coast of

---

172 See Jireček, *Handelsstrassen,* 42; S. Vryonis Jr., "The Question of the Byzantine Mines," *Speculum* 37 (1962): 1–17, at 17; but cf. Kovačević, "Mines d'or," 249–50.
173 *PRV,* no. 4.
174 Stuard, "Ragusa and the Silver Trade," 191–93.
175 I therefore disagree with David Abulafia, who argues that silver was the most important Dalmatian export commodity during the late twelfth and early thirteenth centuries. See Abulafia, "Dalmatian Ragusa," 417; and idem, "East and West: Comments on the Commerce of the City of Ancona in the Middle Ages," *Atti e memorie della Società dalmata di storia patria* 26 (1997): 49–66, at 52.

176 Adriatic piracy of a slightly later period is discussed in I. B. Katele, "Captains and Corsairs: Venice and Piracy, 1261–1381" (Ph.D. diss., University of Illinois at Urbana-Champaign, 1986).

the Adriatic, which provided a multitude of concealed harbors and defensible positions along the main shipping routes. In the year 1000, Doge Pietro II Orseolo of Venice famously waged yet another major offensive against the Narentani pirates, who were based in the Dalmatian archipelago and had been obstructing Adriatic shipping.[177] Over the course of the campaign, Orseolo not only crushed the pirates but also elicited widespread acceptance of Venetian suzerainty in the region. Yet it was not long before the pirates returned to prey on Adriatic shipping, and pirate attacks are a recurring theme in contemporary annals. In April 1224, Leonardo Simeticulo, a Venetian merchant, was attacked by Dalmatian pirates while traveling from Ancona to Pescara, and all his merchandise (including cloth, iron, and copper) was stolen.[178] A few years later, in September 1227, Vitale Caraciacanape and several other merchants from Venice and Chioggia lost an estimated £1,233 worth of merchandise after they were beset by Istrian pirates while returning to Venice from Durazzo.[179] And of course, Venetian vessels were not the only ones that were attacked. In 1224, the coast around Ancona was repeatedly ravaged by pirates from Almissa and Split (perhaps the same who attacked Leonardo Simeticulo), and Ancona responded by confiscating the property of all the citizens of Split within its territory.[180] Two years earlier, Pope Honorius II had gone so far as to send a papal delegate to Dalmatia to preach a crusade against the Almissan pirates, but his efforts failed entirely.[181]

Given the very real threat of piracy, various efforts were undertaken in order to provide protection for commercial shipping. In the thirteenth century, Venice regularly dispatched fleets to police the Adriatic, a practice that later developed into a permanent institution.[182] During the 1224–27 famine, Venice sent its grain fleets in convoys with military escorts so that the desperately needed foodstuffs would not be intercepted.[183] Since pirates were often supported by local governments (whether overtly or not), some cities turned to diplomacy to protect their maritime commerce. In 1201, for example, Bari promised to keep the local Apulian pirates from attacking Ragusan vessels; this may have been a response to Ragusan efforts a decade earlier that forced the Cazichi pirates (based in Dalmatia) to cease their attacks on Apulian ships traveling to the eastern shore.[184] In 1240, Frederick II ordered one of his admirals to outfit several ships to protect Apulian waters from Dalmatian pirates.[185] In 1245, Ragusa reached an agreement with the Almissan pirates to halt attacks on the city's shipping, presumably in return for a large payment.[186] And of course, Venice regularly launched military strikes against major pirate strongholds, though even its most concerted efforts were unable to eradicate the threat altogether. But if pirates posed a continual threat to Adriatic shipping, it was because there was shipping for them to prey on. And the shipping was not only Venetian—it was Apulian, Ragusan, Anconitan, Zaratine, and more. The east–west regional relationships that had been established in the twelfth century multiplied and diversified with increasing rapidity from the early thirteenth century onward, and lateral ties proliferated as well. The complementarity of micro-ecologies enabled this exchange to occur; the increasing demand driven by the expanding urban centers necessitated it.

The Adriatic as Conduit and Corridor

It is important not to make too firm a division between regional and long-distance trade, for the two were vitally interwoven. While the great galleys and roundships that sailed through the Strait of Otranto toward eastern Mediterranean markets were vastly outnumbered by the countless smaller vessels that sailed up and down the Adriatic coasts, the commodities and profits from the long-distance trade networks were fed into the regional trade system, and vice versa. Venice's grain purchases in Apulia were funded by the profits of its luxury trade

---

177 For references to earlier Venetian anti-piracy campaigns, see McCormick, *Origins of the European Economy*, 528.
178 *Precepta, Iuramenta, Interdicta,* no. 52, in *DMCV* 1:60.
179 *Consilia et Ordinamenti,* no. 70, in *DMCV* 1:189.
180 Lozzi, "Repubblica marinara," 45.
181 G. Fejér, ed., *Codex diplomaticus Hungariae ecclesiasticus ac civilis,* 11 vols. (Buda, 1829–44), 3.1:307–8.
182 See Cessi, *Il problema adriatico,* 64–65; and L. B. Robbert, "A Venetian Naval Expedition of 1224," in *Economy, Society, and Government in Medieval Italy: Essays in Memory of Robert L. Reynolds,* ed. D. Herlihy et al. (Kent, Ohio, 1969), 141–51, at 147.

183 Luzzatto, *Storia economica di Venezia,* 36–37; and see *Precepta, Iuramenta, Interdicta,* no. 109, in *DMCV* 1:189.
184 *ADR,* no. 8.
185 J.-L.-A. Huillard-Bréholles, ed., *Friderici secundi . . . Historia diplomatica,* 6 vols. (Paris, 1852–61), 5:687.
186 *CDS,* vol. 4, no. 233.

with the Levant, and the same was true for Ragusan hides or Cervian salt. The commodities purchased in the markets outside the Adriatic often served to drive exchange within it, just as the coinage used by Venetian merchants to purchase southern Italian wheat would have been used by Apulian merchants to pay for their own acquisitions in the markets of the East.

It was not only the extra-Adriatic commodities themselves that spurred intra-Adriatic exchange. The simple mechanics of medieval navigation were equally important. Because ships had to stop regularly to stock up on food and fresh water, the merchants aboard could engage in small-scale trade in each port they visited. Whether this involved selling pepper in Bari en route to Ancona or purchasing furs in Ragusa en route to Venice, the merchants who engaged in long-distance trade were not so narrowly focused as to ignore commercial opportunities available on the Adriatic leg of their journey. Many of the surviving Venetian colleganza contracts specify that the merchant is to stop in Apulia or Durazzo on his way to a Levantine destination. More often, this would have been simply left to the discretion of the merchant, for the standard terms of such contracts gave the merchants considerable freedom of action within the overall framework of a specified voyage. This intra-Adriatic port-hopping may also have served as an additional generator of local exchange, since increased activity along the shores of the Adriatic would have lowered transportation costs for nonluxury and bulk commodities. We lack information on contemporary shipping rates, but the structure of medieval shipping itself suggests that such a reduction would be a plausible consequence of increased maritime commercial activity. This trend would have been reinforced by the need for ballast in larger ships; given that most returned from the Levant carrying high-value, low-weight commodities, the addition of bulky staple commodities (like grain or salt) would have weighed down, and thereby stabilized, the ship. The Venetian galley convoys were something of an exception to this interaction of long-distance and regional trade systems in the Adriatic, for they rarely stopped in Adriatic ports for commercial reasons.[187] However, as the surviving contracts for Venetian trade attest, a significant proportion of Venice's long-distance maritime commerce occurred outside of such galley convoys.

Since an understanding of this commerce is crucial to an understanding of the Adriatic trade system in general, it is to Venice—the dominant commercial center of first the Adriatic and then the eastern Mediterranean—that we now turn our attention. From the earliest days of its existence, Venice had been economically linked to Constantinople, and trade with the city on the Bosporus remained the foundation of Venice's commercial preeminence during the twelfth and thirteenth centuries. The generous provisions of the chrysobull issued by Alexios I in 1082 gradually enabled Venice to dominate much of the Constantinopolitan commerce, and the massive Venetian quarter in the Byzantine capital was a striking indication of the onetime colony's rise to prominence.[188] And the frequency and value of the commercial interactions between the two cities seem to have increased steadily during the twelfth century, with the exception of a few instances of open hostility—particularly in the years immediately following 1171, when Manuel I suddenly expelled the Venetians from the empire and confiscated their goods. The Fourth Crusade in 1204 led to a partial collapse of the Byzantine economy, but the powerful Venetian presence in Constantinople itself, as well as the establishment of Venetian bases throughout the Aegean, ensured that the sea-lanes connecting the two cities remained active commercial passageways.[189] Of course, the Venetian ships sailing through the Strait of Otranto were not headed only for Constantinople; they could also be found at commercial emporia throughout the eastern and western Mediterranean. Occasionally they sailed in search of bulk commodities—Thessaly and Sicily both sold

---

187 On the basis of this observation, Jorjo Tadić suggests that the major long-distance trade routes along the western coast of the Balkans in the Middle Ages had almost no influence on the economic life of the region—but this conclusion ignores not only the role of broad commodity movements but also the fact that not all of Venice's long-distance shipping took place in regulated galley convoys during the period. See his "La côte occidentale des Balkans et ses liaisons maritimes et continentales (XIe–XVIe siècles)," in *Navigazioni mediterranee e connessioni continentali (secoli XI–XVI)*, ed. R. Ragosta (Naples, 1982), 103–4.

188 See Laiou, "Exchange and Trade," 751–52.

189 See D. Jacoby, "The Economy of Latin Constantinople, 1204–1261," in *Urbs Capta: The Fourth Crusade and Its Consequences/La IVe Croisade et ses conséquences*, ed. A. E. Laiou (Paris, 2005), 195–214, esp. 196–99.

grain to Venice during the twelfth century[190]—but the great galley convoys that set forth from the port of S. Nicolò di Lido in Venice were generally in pursuit of luxury goods: spices, silks, gems, high-quality manufactured goods, and the like.

As noted above, the geographic and navigational conditions of the Adriatic were such that the eastern shores were preferred for voyages whose final destination lay outside the Adriatic. Even when the ships were to stop in Apulia before continuing their journeys, it is likely that they sailed down the eastern coast and then crossed westward to Apulia, rather than sailing down the western coast for the entire journey.[191] Given the importance of the Dalmatian and Albanian coasts to Venice's commercial interests, the city's ongoing efforts to control key points along the eastern Adriatic shore are easily understood. So long as the entire coastline was in Byzantine hands, and Veneto-Byzantine relations remained friendly, Venice was assured of safe passage along the eastern littoral (aside from the constant—and significant—threat from piracy). But as effective Byzantine control over the region weakened during the twelfth century, Venice began to intervene more and more frequently in local politics in order to guarantee that the coastal harbors and shipping lanes remained open to its vessels. The existence of hostile cities, like Zara, not only irked Venice by flouting the commercial system that it sought to impose in the Adriatic but also posed a very real threat to the unimpeded movement of Venetian ships along Venice's principal axis of long-distance maritime commerce. Venice was unwilling to tolerate such a threat. The conquest of Zara by the armies of the Fourth Crusade is the most notorious of Venice's responses to Dalmatian defiance in the twelfth and thirteenth centuries, but the incident was by no means isolated.

Control over the eastern coast—or at least freedom of navigation along its length—would have been largely meaningless were the Strait of Otranto not also open to Venetian vessels. Until the eleventh century, this had not been a serious concern, for Byzantium controlled both sides of the strait. But the Norman expansion in southern Italy during the late eleventh century transformed the political dynamics of the narrow sea passage. Venice accordingly helped the Byzantines resist the Norman efforts to acquire a foothold in Albania in 1081. In 1155, Venice assisted with the fleeting Byzantine reconquest of several Apulian coastal cities (which were promptly retaken by the Normans). For a few years following the Fourth Crusade in 1204, Venice itself controlled much of the eastern side of the strait, and in later centuries the city assiduously strove to secure its freedom of movement.[192] But in general, the Strait of Otranto lay outside direct Venetian domination during the period concerned—an acceptable state of affairs, so long as its two sides were not both dominated by a hostile power. Indeed, Venetian diplomatic efforts during the twelfth and thirteenth centuries were strikingly successful at maintaining open relations with the powers that controlled the strait, even when those same powers were warring with each other.[193] Given the importance to Venetian prosperity of free passage in and out of the Adriatic, failure to maintain these relations would have been catastrophic.

Venice was not the only Adriatic city that had long been active along the major trade routes of the medieval Mediterranean. In Apulia, the city of Brindisi had played host to foreign merchants for more than a thousand years before settlers first established themselves on the islands of the Venetian lagoon. Along with Bari, Otranto, Trani, and other Apulian ports, Brindisi continued to be involved in Mediterranean commerce in the Middle Ages. The participation of these cities was a product both of their hinterland's agricultural wealth and of their privileged geographic position on the protruding heel

---

190 For Thessaly, see al-Idrīsī, *Géographie d'Édrisi,* 2:291, 296; and Benjamin of Tudela, *The World of Benjamin of Tudela: A Medieval Mediterranean Travelogue,* ed. S. Benjamin (Madison, N.J., 1995), 123–25. For Sicily, see D. Abulafia, "Pisan Commercial Colonies and Consulates in Twelfth-Century Sicily," *English Historical Review* 93 (1978): 68–81, at 69–71. However, the Venetians did not import salt from outside the Adriatic until the last quarter of the thirteenth century; see Hocquet, *Le sel et la fortune de Venise,* 1:98.

191 See *DCV,* nos. 31, 437, 847.

192 In 1495 and 1528, Venice occupied the major Apulian ports, and considered another invasion in 1580. But as Braudel rightly noted, it was neither the Apulian ports nor even the Balkan coast that dominated the entrance to the Adriatic, but the island of Corfu just south of the Strait of Otranto—which Venice conquered in 1386 and held until the end of the Venetian Republic in 1797 (see Braudel, *Mediterranean,* 126–27). Modon and Coron (Koroni), the "Eyes of the Republic" on the western coast of the Peloponnese, were also crucial to the security of Venetian shipping routes to the Levant.

193 See Cessi, *Il problema adriatico,* 39–83.

of the Italian peninsula. Yet while the eleventh century was a period of great expansion for the Apulian ports, their involvement in twelfth- and thirteenth-century long-distance trade networks was mainly passive—they welcomed the ships of many, but sent forth few of their own.[194] Greeks, Sicilians, and others sailed up through the Strait of Otranto toward the nearly continuous line of ports along the southeastern Italian coast. Amalfitans, for example, were present in Bari in sufficient numbers during the twelfth century to merit special mention in an 1132 treaty between Roger II of Sicily and the city.[195] These visitors were drawn by the fertile offerings of the Apulian plateau, which provided the ports with abundant supplies of grain, oil, and wine; in return, they often brought manufactured goods and Levantine luxuries. These exchanges kept the region's ports busy during the period. Al-Idrīsī, a Muslim geographer writing in the mid-twelfth century, described the port of Otranto as having "flourishing markets where much commerce is done" and Trani as having "a very well-known market."[196] Long-distance maritime trade was never a central pillar of the Apulian economy; the region's economy was overwhelmingly agrarian, and it does not appear to have been highly commercialized during this period.[197] But surpluses were evidently common enough to attract foreign merchants to the Apulian ports, and the ensuing exchange played an important, if not fundamental, role in the region's economic system.

Apulian ships and sailors were not entirely absent from the sea-lanes of the Mediterranean. They were certainly active in Alexandria in the mid-twelfth century, since Apulian merchants are mentioned in the contemporary account of Benjamin of Tudela, a rabbi who traveled extensively throughout the eastern Mediterranean. He noted, in addition, that Trani was "an important commercial center, rich from its trade with the East," and that Otranto was "a port flourishing from the trade with the East and especially with Palestine."[198] The sailors of Bari, who had gained international fame after stealing the body of St. Nicholas from Myra in 1087, seem to have been the most active of their Apulian neighbors during the early twelfth century. Bari's maritime preeminence was shattered, however, after the city resisted the accession of William I to the throne of Sicily and in 1156 was razed to the ground in retribution. By the thirteenth century, Brindisi had returned to its ancient prominence as the most commercially active port in Apulia, with especially close trade connections with Sicily. In a letter sent from Frederick II to one of his admirals in 1240, the city was referred to as "caput terrarum maritimarum Apulie."[199] Brindisi certainly had trading relations with Egypt during the early thirteenth century, since in 1227, a citizen of Trani who was then residing in Brindisi invested money and merchandise in a ship bound for Alexandria.[200] Perhaps the city's merchants were active in the Syrian trade as well; it seems likely that other Apulian ports were involved in the Levant trade too, though probably to a lesser extent. In May 1197, for example, Henry VI Hohenstaufen granted the Teutonic Knights of St. Mary in Jerusalem the right to establish a hospital in Barletta, thereby strengthening the city's ties to the eastern Mediterranean.[201] Staple foodstuffs were undoubtedly the principal export commodities, as was always the case for Apulia, but the near-absence of commercial evidence leaves the rest of the cargoes, as well as their destinations, to the realm of sheer speculation.

Ragusa also seems to have been involved in long-distance Mediterranean commerce during the

---

194 See in particular G. Cassandro, "I porti pugliesi nel Medioevo," *Nuova Antologia* 507 (September 1969): 3–34, esp. 11–13, 19–22; and H. Patterson, "Contatti commerciali e culturali ad Otranto dal IX al XV secolo: L'evidenza della ceramica," in *La ceramica nel mondo bizantino tra XI e XV secolo e i suoi rapporti con l'Italia: Atti del Seminario, Certosa di Pontignano (Siena), 11–13 marzo 1991*, ed. S. Gelichi (Florence, 1993), 101–23.
195 C. Brühl, ed., *Rogerii II. regis diplomata Latina*, Codex diplomaticus regni Siciliae, series prima, Diplomata regum et principum e gente Normannorum, vol. 2.1 (Cologne, 1987), no. 20.
196 Al-Idrīsī, *Géographie d'Édrisi*, 2:120, 264. Not all of the port activity was commercial—the Sicilian navy used the Apulian ports (especially the southernmost ones), as did many of the western European pilgrims traveling to and from the Holy Land in the twelfth century. But this activity served to supplement, not supplant, the commercial functions of the ports.
197 J.-M. Martin's characterization of Apulia as having "une agriculture de subsistance" (*La Pouille*, 442–43) seems overly restrictive, however, given the export activity of the Apulian ports.

198 Benjamin of Tudela, *Travelogue*, 101, 112, 272.
199 *Friderici secundi . . . Historia diplomatica*, 5:686.
200 F. Davanzati, *Dissertazione sulla seconda moglie di Manfredi e su' loro figliuoli* (Naples, 1791), no. 80; cited in W. Heyd, *Histoire du commerce du Levant au moyen-âge*, 2 vols. (Leipzig, 1885–86), 1:419.
201 R. Filangieri di Candida, ed., *Codice diplomatico barese*, vol. 10, *Pergamene di Barletta del R. Archivio di Napoli (1075–1309)* (Bari, 1927), no. 37.

period, although here again solid evidence is lacking.[202] The city's archives provide ample evidence of Ragusan activity in the Levant beginning in the late thirteenth century, but the paucity of earlier documentation obscures its origins. Despite sporadic Venetian efforts to hinder Ragusa's mercantile ambitions, the Dalmatian city seems to have maintained a Mediterranean presence from the twelfth century onward. The city's merchants were certainly active in the Ionian Sea in the early thirteenth century; both Epiros and Corfu offered Ragusa commercial privileges, and Ragusan merchants are recorded in Modon in 1242.[203] Ragusan ships may have also been present in the Aegean, since in the early thirteenth century the despot of Epiros repeatedly offered his protection to Ragusan merchants and exempted them from the kommerkion in his territory (which extended from Albania to the Aegean).[204] Unfortunately, no evidence survives to indicate whether Ragusan merchants subsequently traveled to the eastern parts of the despotate either by sea or via the overland route through the Balkans.

The chronicle of Benjamin of Tudela also hints at Ragusan involvement in the contemporary Levant trade. In listing the geographic origins of the merchants operating in Alexandria during his visit there, he cites "Rakuvia," which may refer to Ragusa.[205] A treaty of 1169 between Pisa and Ragusa promised Pisan protection for Ragusans in Constantinople, which suggests that their presence in the Byzantine capital was already established in the 1160s.[206] Three commercial agreements between Venice and Ragusa from the early and mid-thirteenth century give additional evidence for Ragusan involvement in long-distance commerce at this time. These agreements specified the duties to be imposed on merchandise brought from Romania, Egypt, Tunis, and the Barbary Coast and carried to Venice aboard Ragusan vessels.[207] The very precise wording of these treaties suggests that the Dalmatian city's commercial presence beyond the Strait of Otranto, if not already well established, was certainly being felt. Unfortunately, we have no concrete evidence as to the specific cargoes of the Ragusan ships—nor do we know whether the ships of other Mediterranean powers sailed to the city.[208] In later periods, Ragusan cargo holds frequently carried silver, lead, copper, timber, and hides and other animal products to the Levant. They probably did so in the twelfth and thirteenth centuries as well, but at present this cannot be affirmed with any degree of certainty. Despite the scarce documentation, however, the wide array of circumstantial evidence strongly suggests that Ragusan merchants were indeed involved in long-distance maritime trade during this period.[209]

The most active of all Venice's Adriatic competitors on the long-distance maritime trade routes was the "ancient and celebrated" city of Ancona.[210] The twelfth and thirteenth centuries witnessed the city's first rise to international commercial prominence, which began to fade only after Venice finally succeeded in imposing a humiliating treaty on its competitor in 1264. So famous was its port, which had first been expanded under Trajan, that it became the subject of a medieval mariner's expression: "Unus Petrus in Roma, una turris in Cremona, unus portus in Ancona."[211] In the late twelfth century, Ancona enjoyed a particularly close commercial relationship with Constantinople. This was a relatively new phenomenon—the Anconitans do not seem have had regular economic ties with the Byzantine capital prior to

---

202 See B. Krekić, *Dubrovnik (Raguse) et le Levant au Moyen Age* (Paris, 1961).
203 *Acta et diplomata graeca*, vol. 3, nos. 12, 14, 15; Krekić, *Dubrovnik*, nos. 4, 5, 6, 7.
204 *Acta et diplomata graeca*, vol. 3, no. 12.
205 Benjamin of Tudela, *Travelogue*, 272.
206 *ADR*, no. 8; and see Lozzi, "Repubblica marinara," 42–23.
207 *ADR*, no. 18. In addition, Venice twice banned Ragusa from trading in Egypt because of the papal embargo—this may not be clear evidence that Ragusa was engaged in trade with Egypt, but at the very least such trade was feasible enough that Venice saw the need to specifically outlaw it. See Ljubić, *Listine o odnosajih izmedju*, 1:33, 3:394.
208 Ceramic evidence from Split clearly demonstrates close Dalmatian commercial ties with the wider Mediterranean, but whether the ceramics were brought there by Dalmatian merchants, or arrived as cargoes on the ships of Venetians or others, cannot be determined. See H. Zglav-Martinac, *Ulomak do ulomka: Prilog proučavanju keramike XIII.–XVIII. stoljeća iz Dioklecijanove palače u Splitu* (Split, 2004), esp. 113–23.
209 This differs markedly from the position taken by Jorjo Tadić, who argued that in the twelfth and thirteenth centuries, Ragusan ships navigated almost exclusively in the Adriatic and Ionian seas, and that no evidence survives to indicate that the cities along the eastern Adriatic coast had any maritime commercial relations with territories beyond these seas (Tadić, "Côte occidentale," 102). In my opinion, this argument discounts too easily the evidence from the Venetian-Ragusan treaties.
210 Al-Idrīsī, *Géographie d'Édrisi*, 2:266.
211 M. Natalucci, "Ancona, Repubblica marinara," in *Federico Barbarossa, Ancona, e le Marche*, 18–40, at 28; the origin of the expression is unattributed.

1150—but it developed rapidly.[212] Moreover, Anconitan activity not only served to counterpoint deteriorating Byzantine-Venetian relations but may well have been inspired by the rising hostilities between Venice and its former overlord. In 1157, according to the Byzantine court historian John Kinnamos, Manuel I Komnenos "recognized the Venetians' nation as malicious and stubborn, and thought it very important to lay claim to Ancona. Thereby he might to a large extent humble the Venetians' pride and from there very easily wage wars in Italy."[213] Accordingly, Manuel sent money to Ancona to promote his (ultimately unsuccessful) efforts to reconquer the lost Byzantine territories in Italy. Two decades later, he sent more money to the city to help it in its struggle against Frederick Barbarossa, and he seems to have extended trading privileges to the Anconitans as well.[214] The effect of Manuel's political intervention was striking: supposedly the Anconitans spontaneously accepted Byzantine overlordship and received "the same civic rights enjoyed by Roman [i.e., Byzantine] citizens."[215] These developments all helped strengthen the economic ties between Ancona and Byzantium, and by the late twelfth century, Anconitans seem to have had their own church, colony, and consul in Constantinople.[216]

Given that al-Idrīsī in the mid-twelfth century described Ancona as "one of the greatest cities of the Christian world," it seems likely that the city already maintained a certain commercial presence in the Mediterranean before it adopted Byzantine suzerainty.[217] However, the profits from the ensuing trade with Constantinople no doubt increased the capital available for other long-distance ventures, and it is certain that during the succeeding century Ancona's Mediterranean activity increased markedly. Anconitan ships sailed not only to the Bosporus but also to other Levantine destinations.[218] According to the Anconitan chronicler Boncompagno da Signa (writing ca. 1200), many of Ancona's citizens were away conducting business in Alexandria, Constantinople, and the Byzantine Empire during the German siege of the city in 1173–74.[219] In 1231, some of the city's merchants were thrown into jail in Alexandria, and the pope had to intervene with the sultan to seek their release.[220] In 1257, the city founded a colony at Acre.[221] Even if there are no surviving Anconitan notarial sources from before the fourteenth century, the presence of the city's merchants in the great trading cities of the Levant clearly indicates Ancona's involvement in the spice and luxury trade. Moreover, not only was Ancona's port the finest on the central Italo-Adriatic coast, but it also lay at the end of the road leading across the Apennines to northwestern Italy. The city was therefore able to sell the luxuries of the East to the inhabitants of the prosperous Tuscan city-states. Just as Venice's Mediterranean commerce relied on access to transalpine and northern Italian markets, so too did Ancona's long-distance maritime trade depend on its access to markets across the Apennines.

Ancona's commercial interests in the Balkans, together with the city's economic ties to the Tuscan city-states, also serve as a reminder that the long-distance trade routes in the Adriatic ran not only north–south through the sea but also east–west. The trade routes between Ancona and northwestern Italy were mirrored on the other side of the Adriatic by

---

212   S. Borsari, "Ancona e Bisanzio nei secoli XII–XIII," ibid., 67–76, at 71.
213   John Kinnamos, *Epitomē*, ed. A. Meineke, CSHB 25–26 (Bonn, 1836), 170; trans. as *The Deeds of John and Manuel Comnenus by John Kinnamos*, trans. C. M. Brand (New York, 1976), 130. See also *Nicetae Choniatae Historia*, ed. J. L. Van Dieten, CFHB 11.1 (Berlin, 1975), 97–98.
214   Abulafia, "Ancona, Byzantium and the Adriatic," 195–216.
215   Choniates, *Historia*, 202.
216   *VCM*, 35–36. Niketas Choniates states that Manuel Komnenos gave the Anconitans their own quarter in Constantinople (Choniates, *Historia*, 199). See also A. Pertusi, "The Anconitan Colony in Constantinople and the Report of Its Consul, Benevento, on the Fall of the City," in *Charanis Studies: Essays in Honor of Peter Charanis*, ed. A. E. Laiou-Thomadakis (New Brunswick, N.J., 1980), 199–218, at 199–200.
217   Al-Idrīsī, *Géographie d'Édrisi*, 2:253. Al-Idrīsī's description counters the argument of Zimolo, the editor of Boncompagno da Signa's chronicle in the *Rerum Italicarum Scriptores*, who saw Manuel's privileges as providing the initial impetus for Anconitan merchants to trade abroad. While they no doubt facilitated the growth of Anconitan maritime trade, al-Idrīsī's remark suggests that Ancona was already a city of more than purely regional importance by the mid-twelfth century. See Boncompagno da Signa, *Liber de obsidione Ancone,* 12 n. 2; and Abulafia, "Ancona, Byzantium and the Adriatic," 205.
218   See D. Abulafia, "The Anconitan Privileges in the Kingdom of Jerusalem and the Levant Trade of Ancona," in *I comuni italiani nel regno crociato di Gerusalemme,* ed. G. Airaldi and B. Z. Kedar (Genoa, 1986), 525–70, esp. 557–58.
219   Boncompagno da Signa, *Liber de obsidione Ancone,* 17.
220   C. Baronius (Baronio), ed., *Annales ecclesiastici ab anno 1198 . . .,* 15 vols. (Lucca, 1747–56), vol. 2, a. 1231, no. 56.
221   S. Paoli, ed., *Codice diplomatico del Sacro militare ordine gerosolimitano oggi di Malta . . .,* 2 vols. (Lucca, 1733–37), vol. 1, no. 132.

the routes running from the Dalmatian city-states into the central Balkans or down the eastern coast and thence overland to northern Greece and Constantinople. Consequently, a vigorous trade flourished between the shores of the central Adriatic. As discussed earlier, slaves were probably the major export of the Balkan heartland, and the trade in timber may have been significant as well.[222] Ancona managed to control much of the transport traffic across the Adriatic, a traffic so lucrative that, according to David Abulafia, it may have even been the foundation of the city's economic prosperity in the late twelfth century,[223] though firm evidence of this is lacking. Regardless of its importance in relation to the city's long-distance maritime commerce, in absolute terms it brought considerable wealth to the city's coffers.

Pisa was a particularly active participant in this trans-Adriatic trade network.[224] As mentioned above, the Tuscan commune signed a treaty with Ragusa in 1169;[225] while no evidence of commerce survives to prove that Pisans visited Ragusa with any regularity, Pisan activity elsewhere in the region suggests that the treaty with Ragusa was part of a larger Dalmatian program. In 1188, Pisa signed a treaty with Zara that exempted its citizens from all duties if they arrived by land. If they arrived by sea, the Pisans had to pay four *romanati,* unless they were trading wine or salt, in which case the duty was reduced to two romanati.[226] The inclusion of this provision suggests that both wine and salt were important commodities along the trade route.

From the perspective of long-distance trade, however, the principal appeal of the Dalmatian ports was their relatively easy access to the overland route to Constantinople, which ran roughly along the ancient Via Egnatia from Durazzo to Thessalonike and then on to Constantinople. It is not surprising, therefore, that we find Ragusans present in Durazzo from at least from the mid-twelfth century onward.[227] The overland route was well-known in the period, and al-Idrīsī's *Geography* described it at length.[228] On the western endpoint, the city of Durazzo, whose position as a mercantile crossroads once drew the praise of Catullus,[229] was a thriving commercial center in the twelfth century. Al-Idrīsī described Durazzo as "a flourishing city, abundant in resources, home to numerous markets and in a prosperous position."[230] Despite al-Idrīsī's remark, the city's wealth came not from any abundance in natural resources—the surviving documentation makes almost no reference to the exchange of local products—but rather from its participation in the transit trade.

It is in this context that we should understand the provision in the Pisan-Ragusan treaty of 1169 offering protection for Ragusan merchants in Constantinople, and the importance of the overland route can be seen in the effects of 1204 on Italian activity in Dalmatia.[231] The breakup of the Byzantine Empire naturally led to the political fragmentation of the territories along the Via Egnatia, and without the security offered by unbroken Byzantine control, the trade route temporarily fell into disuse. The Pisan presence in Dalmatia disappeared entirely in the decades following 1204, and resumed only gradually later in the thirteenth century.[232] By the 1230s the trade route's revival may have begun, since the protection afforded to Ragusans in the Despotate of Epiros in 1234 was possibly intended

---

222 Abulafia, "East and West," 52. If mining activity was in fact under way in the twelfth- and early thirteenth-century Balkans, then silver and other metals were no doubt an important component of this trade; however, as discussed above (261–62), this is unlikely to have been the case.
223 Abulafia, "Ancona, Byzantium and the Adriatic," 206.
224 Florence was evidently not directly involved in this trade, however: there is no evidence of Florentines in Zara before 1299, or in Split before 1357. Florentine-Ragusan relations were probably established in the early fourteenth century, though the earliest evidence of them is much later. See A. Fradelli, "Pisani e fiorentini in Dalmazia," *Atti e memorie della Società Dalmata di Storia Patria* 31 (2002): 161–209.
225 *ADR,* no. 8.
226 *CDS,* vol. 2, no. 209. For the use of *romanati* as a unit of account in the eleventh- and twelfth-century Adriatic, see *DOC* 3.1:58–59.

227 Ducellier, *Façade maritime,* 75.
228 Al-Idrīsī, *Géographie d'Édrisi,* 2:286–98. The route used in the twelfth century differed slightly from the classical Via Egnatia; see N. Oikonomides, "The Medieval Via Egnatia," in *The Via Egnatia under Ottoman Rule (1380–1699): Halcyon Days in Crete II,* ed. E. Zachariadou (Rethymnon, 1996), 9–16, esp. 12–14.
229 Catullus, *Carmina* 36.15.
230 Al-Idrīsī, *Géographie d'Édrisi,* 2:120.
231 *ADR,* no. 8. David Abulafia argues that "the Pisan treaty must be seen in the context of Pisan attempts to inherit in the Greek Empire rights enjoyed until lately by the Venetians" ("Dalmatian Ragusa," 415). Although this may have been part of the Pisan strategy, this interpretation overlooks subsequent Pisan activity in Zara, and also places too little emphasis on the commercial potential of the overland route to Constantinople through the Balkans.
232 Fradelli, "Pisani e fiorentini," 179–84.

to aid overland as well as maritime traffic.[233] Similarly, Anconitan treaties with Trogir in 1236 and Zara in 1258 may have been prompted by a resurgent interest in the economic potential of the dormant route.[234] However, the instability brought on by the post-1204 political disunity prevented the route from ever again reaching its twelfth-century peak.

Not surprisingly, it was the Venetians, not the Dalmatians, who dominated the overland route to and from Constantinople during much of the period. According to Anna Komnena, Durazzo already had a substantial Italian (primarily Venetian) community in the late eleventh century.[235] The Venetians' presence in Durazzo was largely a consequence of Alexios I's chrysobull in 1082, which gave them a church and allowed them to own property in the city.[236] As mentioned above, Venetian ships regularly stopped at Durazzo en route to the Levant, but many Venetians also traveled to Durazzo overland from Greece or Constantinople. In March 1161, Filippo di Albiola received 200 *perperi auri* for a journey that he was to make overland from Constantinople to Durazzo, and then by sea to Venice. The same itinerary (in reverse) was specified in an 1183 contract concerning a voyage by Pietro da Molin. Two years later Pietro Morosini traveled from Thebes overland to Durazzo and then sailed up to Venice.[237] Since Morosini's starting point was Thebes, a major center of silk production, it seems quite probable that he was carrying silk, a hypothesis supported by the fact that he was specifically instructed to travel overland (and therefore could not have been transporting bulk merchandise).[238] Indeed, the appeal of the overland route to Durazzo lay precisely in the security it afforded the transport of high-value, low-weight goods like silk.

But all this changed following the Fourth Crusade. Venice's establishment in 1205 of the Duchy of Durazzo, a colony directly administered by the Venetian government, temporarily increased the importance of the city as a stopping point for Venetian vessels traveling to and from the Levant. Following the collapse of the Venetian duchy in 1213, Ragusan merchants became a significant presence in Durazzo. But no evidence survives to suggest that the overland route to Thessaly and Constantinople continued to be much used in the following decades. Henceforth, the axis of Durazzo's trade ran north–south rather than east–west.

The transformations wrought by extra-Adriatic developments on the intra-Adriatic trade networks of Albania and Dalmatia serve as an important reminder of the interconnections between regional and long-distance commerce. Just as Venetian victories in the Bosporus reconfigured the commercial function of Albania, so Venetian victories in the Adriatic largely eliminated the Anconitan presence in the Levant. The medieval Adriatic was tightly linked to the rest of the Mediterranean world, and developments in the one had consequences for the other. But whereas regional trade generally followed a course toward increasing intensity and complexity during this period, the long-distance activities of the Adriatic cities show a less uniform trend. Some, like Venice, continued along a path of expansion on which they had already embarked in the preceding centuries. The Apulian ports, by contrast, seem to have stalled after their eleventh-century flourishing. Ragusa and Ancona both emerged on the international markets—but while the thirteenth century marked the first glimmerings of greatness for one, it marked a temporary end to Mediterranean commercial prominence for the other.

The Human Adriatic: Patterns of Social Participation

Who were the people who created and sustained these trade networks? In general, we do not know, our ignorance the lamentable consequence of a historical record that privileges large-scale commerce and the elites who were usually responsible for it. The world of small-scale mariners is hidden behind the heavy veil of the intervening centuries, although its effects are visible in the very existence of cities like Venice and Ragusa, which relied so heavily on the maritime imports brought to their harbors by these *caboteurs,* whose presence can be detected indirectly.

---

233 Krekić, *Dubrovnik,* no. 3.
234 *CDS,* vol. 4, no. 10; and *Monumenta spectantia historiam Dalmatarum,* vol. 2, fasc. 8, p. 30.
235 Anna Komnena, *Alexiadis libri XV,* 6.5.
236 See M. Pozza and G. Ravegnani, eds., *I trattati con Bisanzio, 992–1198* (Venice, 1993), 35–45.
237 *DCV,* nos. 150, 349, 353.
238 For the Theban silk industry, see D. Jacoby, "Silk in Western Byzantium before the Fourth Crusade," *BZ* 84–85 (1991–92): 452–500.

For example, thousands of twelfth- and thirteenth-century contracts concerning the saltworks of the Venetian lagoon do survive, and while these deal overwhelmingly with questions of ownership and management, the salt that was actually produced was almost certainly transported and sold throughout the upper Adriatic not by the great merchants of the Rialto (for it goes virtually unmentioned in their extant documents) but by small-scale traders.[239] For many such traders, commerce formed only part of their activities. In the medieval Mediterranean, as in modern times, individuals regularly took on multiple roles. Those who carried out the cabotage along the shores of the Adriatic were not necessarily professional merchants, earning their living solely by acting as middlemen between other parties. Some, especially in Dalmatia, would have also been fishermen; elsewhere, some might have been farmers; others still might have themselves gathered the salt that was to fill their cargo holds. Some, evidently, were even monks; the aforementioned *pagina recordationis* from 1128 indicates that the monks of S. Maria di Tremiti were able to travel to Ancona with their *famuli* for trading purposes without being subject to the usual taxes, so long as they gave one meal and two wheels of cheese to the Anconitan authorities.[240] Unfortunately, this fleeting reference tells us nothing about what commodities they bought or sold (other than perhaps cheese), nor how often they made the journey. However, it does serve as a testament to the polyactivity of some of the individuals who engaged in small-scale Adriatic commerce. They were traders, certainly, but much else besides.

Not until three centuries later do we have a record that offers fuller insights into the identities of these shadowy caboteurs, together with their routes and cargoes. Preserved by chance in an administrative register concerning farms around Fano is the log of journeys made by a small boat (*burchio*) belonging to the local Malatesta clan.[241] Between July 1409 and February 1410, the burchio made forty trips to the ports around Fano—primarily to Senigallia, but to Ancona and to smaller ports such as Casebruciate and Cesano as well. Though the burchio was most often used to bring firewood from Senigallia to Fano, it also carried grain, salt, wine, and horses to other destinations. From the register, we can also determine the origins of many of the men involved in these journeys. Of the twenty-seven voyages for which the *patronus* (who served as both captain and trader) is named, twenty-four were captained by men from the Marches (most of whom served multiple times over the ten-month period); of the remaining three, one was captained by Nicolo da Lacroma of Ragusa and two by Tommaso de Drogasse of Zara. Among the fourteen named sailors, however, only two were from the Italian peninsula—the other twelve were all Dalmatians (a striking testament to the region's maritime expertise).[242] While these voyages were carried out much later than the period in question, they are broadly representative of the cabotage that animated the Adriatic shores throughout the medieval period: local traders carrying relatively small quantities of staple commodities and making regular journeys to nearby communities.

Whereas the absence of documentary evidence conceals the identities of the medieval Adriatic caboteurs, the Venetian archives offer an altogether happier outlook for an investigation into the identities of the large-scale merchant-mariners (at least those based in Venice), their investors, and the *naucleri* who captained the ships used for this trade.[243] These occupational divisions are necessarily arbitrary, since the boundaries between them were often blurred. The same men might serve as investors for one venture and traders for another, and many

---

239 See S. Perini, ed., *Chioggia medioevale: Documenti dal secolo XI al XV*, 3 vols. (Venice, 2006). Interesting light is shed by *Consilia et Ordinamenta*, no. 104, in *DMCV* 1:200, which threatens salt traders who contravene Venetian shipping restrictions with the loss of their "platem seu barcam"—that is, small flat-bottomed boats with limited carrying capacity.
240 Petrucci, *S. Maria di Tremiti*, no. 96.
241 S. Anselmi, "Per la storia economica del piccolo cabotaggio: L'attività di un burchio adriatico (1409–1410)," *Nuova rivista storica* 62 (1978): 521–48. The register was compiled by Antonio de Andriuccio da Saxoferato on behalf of the Malatesta (who owned both the farms and the burchio concerned). Although Antonio compiled at least thirteen volumes, only the volume from 1409–10 has survived.
242 All, except those from Ragusa, are identified as *schiavo*.
243 The term *nauclerus* is usually, though inadequately, translated as "shipmaster." This term is used particularly by F. C. Lane, although he employed others as well; compare his "Venetian Seamen in the Nautical Revolution of the Middle Ages," in *Venezia e il Levante fino al secolo XV*, ed. A. Pertusi (Florence, 1973), 403–29, at 408—where *nauclerus* is translated as "sailing master"—with his *Venice, a Maritime Republic* (Baltimore, 1973), 50—where he uses the more standard "shipmaster."

mariners engaged in trade themselves. The documentation provides less insight into the many intermediaries whose active involvement was so crucial to the development of sophisticated trade networks: the sailors who sailed the ware-laden ships, the dockworkers who loaded and unloaded the boats, the innkeepers who so often brokered the exchanges, and a host of others.[244] But though the analysis that follows here focuses primarily on the men—and they were mostly men—who were most directly involved in the trade, it is with due awareness of the less visible human infrastructure that underpinned their activities.

We turn first to the great Venetian merchants, the individuals who both invested in and carried out the large-scale intra-Adriatic trade described in the extant commercial contracts. Their identities emerge most clearly because it was they who gathered together before the Rialto notaries to set down the terms of their ventures, and whose bequests to Venetian churches and monasteries enabled their personal documents to survive through the centuries. One important observation is that the individuals who were active in the Adriatic—whether making or accepting investments—were generally the same individuals who were active in the waters beyond the Strait of Otranto. Of the thirty merchants named in the intra-Adriatic contracts for whom at least two records of separate voyages (to any destination) survive, twenty-three were engaged in the Levant trade as well. From a purely economic standpoint, this is not surprising. The navigation conditions of the Mediterranean and technical limitations of medieval ships prevented Venetian merchants from making two return voyages to the Levant in a single year, but under favorable conditions they could travel to the Levant and back, and subsequently make a second round-trip within the Adriatic.[245] This strategy was adopted by a certain Marco Tiepolo in 1190: in March he set sail to Messina (only a short journey from the mouth of the Adriatic), then returned to Venice, then set sail again in August for Constantinople, presumably returning the following spring.[246] There were, of course, some merchants who apparently confined most of their efforts within the Adriatic. Between 1235 and 1253, for example, Gabriele Marignoni invested in nine recorded commercial ventures. Of the six contracts for which the destination is specified, five are limited to locations within the Adriatic (Ancona, Zara, and Fermo), while the sixth—for a voyage by land or sea to Hungary (Ungaria)—may also have been carried out within the sea.[247]

The contracts also suggest that involvement in intra-Adriatic trade was not limited to a single social class; members of prominent ducal families appear alongside men of more modest means. Roughly one-fifth of the individuals mentioned in the intra-Adriatic contracts bear surnames of great Venetian clans: Badoer, Contarini, Falier, Michiel, Morosini, and the like. There is no discernible relationship between the size of the investment and the social status of the investor, and patrician investors do not seem to have consistently invested either more or less in individual contracts than did their nonpatrician counterparts. Nor did the patricians limit themselves merely to financing these voyages and leaving the active trading to others; around 1190, Domenico Corner journeyed to Apulia, and three decades later Domenico Gradenigo twice did the same.[248] Individuals often played both roles—financing some voyages, and accepting investments for others—just they did in the general Mediterranean trade. In August 1198, for example, Domenico Aldoino invested £50 in another Venetian merchant's voyage to Apulia; two years later, he accepted £50 for a voyage to Ancona and Dalmatia.[249] The absence of a hierarchy of trading destinations in twelfth- and thirteenth-century Venice—at least as expressed by the social status of the merchants involved—is mirrored by the contemporary Genoese

---

244 Their importance has recently been highlighted by K. L. Reyerson, *The Art of the Deal: Intermediaries of Trade in Medieval Montpellier* (Leiden, 2002), esp. chap. 3. See also C. M. de la Roncière, *Firenze e le sue campagne nel Trecento: Mercanti, produzione, traffici* (Florence, 2005).
245 Tucci, "Navigazione veneziana," 829.
246 *DCV*, nos. 377, 388.
247 *DCV*, nos. 694, 707, 711, 709, 715, 745. For Marignoni's other ventures, see *DCV*, nos. 701, 809, 820. This specialization seems to have accelerated markedly in the thirteenth century, likely as a result of increasing commercial opportunities within the Adriatic; see my remarks in "Les activités économiques des familles vénitiennes dans l'Adriatique, 12ᵉ–13ᵉ siècles," in *Réseaux familiaux à la fin de l'Antiquité et au Moyen Age*, ed. B. Caseau (Paris, forthcoming).
248 *DCV*, nos. 391, 397, 569, 633.
249 See *DCV*, no. 450; and *San Maffio di Mazzorbo*, no. 48.

experience. There, too, the same merchants who conducted regional trade within the western Mediterranean basin were also active in Genoa's Levant trade. Guglielmo Burono, the son of a distinguished member of the twelfth-century consular aristocracy, regularly invested in voyages to Syria, Sicily, and Sardinia alike. His cousin, Ingo de Flexo, did the same for Syria and Sicily—suggesting that no stigma or particular specialization was attached to regional rather than long-distance trade.[250]

The career of Tommaso Viadro, a Venetian merchant active in the Adriatic in the late twelfth and early thirteenth centuries, offers a particularly illuminating case study.[251] He lived in the parish of San Maurizio, almost midway between the Piazza San Marco and the Rialto bridge, and his family seems to have been quite wealthy—his younger sister married into the prominent Gradenigo family, and his older sister's dowry was worth at least £800, a substantial sum.[252] The origins of his family's wealth are unknown, but his father Pietro was evidently prosperous and prominent enough to win the hand of Giacomina Ziani, either the daughter or the niece of the spectacularly rich Sebastiano Ziani.[253] The Viadro and Ziani families maintained close relations during Tommaso's lifetime. In several cases, members of the Viadro family served as witnesses for the Ziani's commercial contracts, and the Ziani made several investments in Tommaso Viadro's commercial activities: Pietro Ziani (later doge) invested £152 in one of his voyages to Syria, and in 1209 the Dogaressa Maria Ziani gave £120 to Viadro in a maritime loan.[254] Such familial involvement was the norm in Venice; on at least two occasions Viadro was involved in commercial transactions with his brothers, and he was also given his sister's dowry to invest by her husband.[255] Despite his distinguished lineage, Viadro seems to have preferred maritime commerce to politics—a choice also made by his nephew Domenico Gradenigo. It was his older brother Stefano who took on whatever familial political obligations may have been expected. Stefano served as podestà first of Chioggia and then of Pola in the early 1220s—another indication of the family's prominence in early thirteenth-century Venice, and possibly another reflection of their close ties to the Ziani, since Pietro had by then been elected doge.[256]

Tommaso Viadro's surviving commercial contracts concern at least sixteen separate voyages, of which at least seven were conducted exclusively within the Adriatic. Like most Venetians who traded within the Adriatic, Viadro was also active in the Levant; indeed, his name first appears in a June 1197 contract in which it is noted that he received £100 from Filippo Marcello the previous August

---

250 E. Bach, *La cité de Gênes au XIIe siècle* (Copenhagen, 1955), 109–13.

251 More than thirty commercial contracts concerning Tommaso Viadro have survived, making him one of the best-documented merchants of the period. Most of these have been published in *NDCV*; there are summaries of all but one in *San Maffio di Mazzorbo*. A single unpublished contract survives from June 1197 (ASV, San Maffio di Mazzorbo pergamene, busta 1, Fonti Viadro, June 1197). But despite the comparative wealth of these sources, Viadro has received far less attention than have some other contemporary Venetian merchants. His commercial activities are briefly discussed in Luzzatto, *Storia economica di Venezia*, 24, 77–78; a fuller discussion of the Viadro family in general can be found in K. Takada, "Aspetti della vita parentale della nobiltà veneziana nel Duecento: L'esempio della famiglia Viaro del ramo di San Maurizio," *Archivio Veneto* 145 (1995): 5–29. I would like to thank Marco Pozza for directing my attention to the Fonti Viadro.

252 *San Maffio di Mazzorbo*, no. 22.

253 This relationship between Giacomina and Sebastiano Ziani is a matter of some contention. In 1197, Giacomina Viadro and Pietro Ziani (Sebastiano's eldest son) signed an agreement concerning their adjacent properties in the parish of San Giovanni di Rialto in which Giacomina refers to Pietro as her *consanguineus*. This term appears in only one other contemporary Venetian source, where it means "sibling," and hence Irmgard Fees has argued that Giacomina was Pietro's sister. However, Giacomina's name is never mentioned in any of the chronicles that refer to either Pietro or Sebastiano; and since *consanguineus* can also denote a more general familial relationship, it is possible that Giacomina and Pietro were merely cousins. Regardless, the Viadro and Ziani families enjoyed close ties. See I. Fees, *Reichtum und Macht in mittelalterlichen Venedig: Die Familie Ziani* (Tübingen, 1988), 41–42.

254 *NDCV*, nos. 54, 73. See also Fees, *Reichtum und Macht*, 42 n. 191. The involvement of Venetian doges in trade was widely accepted until the 1270s; thereafter, they faced steadily increasing restrictions on their commercial activities. See L. Buenger Robbert, "Domenico Gradenigo: A Thirteenth-Century Venetian Merchant," in *Medieval and Renaissance Venice*, ed. T. Madden and E. Kittell (Chicago, 1999), 27–48, at 33.

255 *San Maffio di Mazzorbo*, no. 22; and Fonti Viadro, February 1256. In the first instance (July 1207), Viadro and his two brothers (Giacomo and Stefano) received in collegantia his sister's dowry from Viadro's sister and her husband Rainiero Vitturo. In the second, Viadro received £135 and 35 *perperi auri* from his brother Stefano in October 1218, while they were both in Candia.

256 *Chioggia medioevale*, nos. 418, 419; *NDCV*, no. 82.

to be invested in copper and sold in Alexandria.²⁵⁷ Over the next two decades, Viadro returned to Alexandria at least twice and was also active in Syria and Crete. His first recorded intra-Adriatic voyage was likely in the autumn of 1199;²⁵⁸ between April and August of that year he engaged in three recorded colleganza contracts totaling £250 for commerce in Apulia and Dalmatia.²⁵⁹ In early 1203, Viadro set out again to trade within the Adriatic with at least £400 gathered from four investors.²⁶⁰ The following year, he went to Durazzo in the spring on a galley commanded by Giacomo Zaccaria and received £200 from Domenico Aldoino in November for trade in Brindisi and Durazzo.²⁶¹ The establishment of the Venetian duchy in Durazzo in 1205 was a strong incentive for Viadro (and other Venetians) to expand their commercial activity there; Viadro not only accepted money in the summer and winter of 1207 for the purposes of trading in Durazzo but also sold merchandise destined for the Albanian market to a certain Giuliano Derardo of Bologna in June 1207.²⁶² In 1211 Viadro received a land grant in Crete, where he seems to have remained moderately active in trade for the remainder of his life (he died sometime before 1224).²⁶³ His only attested son, Pietro, seems to have been less interested in maritime trade than was his father; most of his surviving documents concern the acquisition and maintenance of territorial possessions near Treviso.²⁶⁴

The Viadro documents provide strong evidence of patrician involvement in intra-Adriatic trade—his investors included members of the Badoer, Corner, and da Molin families—and of course Viadro himself possessed a distinguished lineage. Moreover, the investments made in his journeys also align closely with the general pattern in the Venetian documentation. The average investment per contract in Viadro's Adriatic ventures is £93, close to the general intra-Adriatic average of £102.²⁶⁵ Similarly, most of Viadro's contracts (eleven out of fourteen) fall between £50 and £150, though the general evidence points to a higher frequency of small investments (see figs. 10.4 and 10.5). Not surprisingly, the average investment in Viadro's Adriatic ventures is lower than the average investment in his Levantine ones (£133);²⁶⁶ in both duration and expense, voyages to the Levant were considerably more demanding than those within the Adriatic. But here again, there is no significant difference between the amounts invested by members of high-ranking Venetian families and those from less exalted backgrounds. The largest recorded investment in his Adriatic ventures (£200) is from Domenico Aldoino, a member of an established but not particularly prominent Venetian family; the lowest (£38) is from Pietro da Molin, scion of a powerful patrician clan.²⁶⁷ Given the low survival rate of contemporary documentation, there is no way to prove conclusively that Viadro was "typical" of Venetian merchants trading in the Adriatic. However, his own commercial activities (activity in both the Levant and the Adriatic), the socioeconomic dynamic of the investors that he attracted (both patrician and nonpatrician), and the size of the investments that he received (generally £50 to £200) do make Viadro's career appear broadly representative of Venetian upper-class mercantile involvement in the Adriatic.

The surviving contracts frequently specify the identity of the *nauclerus* for the voyage; he essentially served as the captain of the ship during this period, though authority was partially shared with the merchants on board (particularly so far as changes of des-

257 *Fonti Viadro*, June 1197.
258 Although the dates of the contracts suggest that the voyage was to be carried out in the autumn of 1199, the contracts themselves do not specify a particular date.
259 *NDCV*, nos. 48, 49, 50. The previous year (1198) Viadro had received £150 from Pietro Zorzi for a voyage to Arta, on the Ionian coast just beyond the mouth of the Adriatic (*NDCV*, no. 47).
260 *NDCV*, nos. 56, 57, 58, 59.
261 *NDCV*, nos. 60, 61.
262 *NDCV*, nos. 69, 71; *San Maffio di Mazzorbo*, no. 25. Given that the merchandise was sold in exchange for 100 *perperi auri veteres pesantes ad pondum Durachii* (to be paid upon Derardo's return to Venice), Alain Ducellier has suggested that Viadro's main purpose was to acquire Byzantine currency (Ducellier, *Façade maritime*, 132).
263 For the land grant, see Tafel and Thomas, *Urkunden*, no. 229; for Viadro's continuing commercial activity, see *NDCV*, nos. 78, 82. *San Maffio di Mazzorbo*, no. 52 (June 1224), refers to "Petrus Viadro filius quondam Tomaso Viadro."
264 *Fonti Viadro*, varia. A certain Tommaso Viadro is recorded as a *iudex examinator* in a 1260 dispute over a saltwork near Chioggia, but his precise relationship to his namesake is unclear (see *Chioggia medioevale*, no. 654).

265 The latter excludes investments made in non-Venetian currencies, which account for roughly one-fifth of the surviving contracts.
266 These calculations do not include those investments for which no destination is specified, such as the substantial investment of £800 (a marked outlier) from his sister's dowry.
267 *NDCV*, nos. 61, 71.

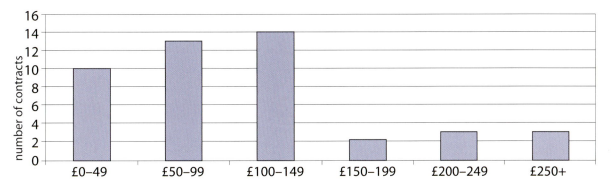

Figure 10.4.
Amounts invested per contract in Adriatic ventures (general), 1100–1260 (from *DCV*; *NDCV*; *San Maffio di Mazzorbo*)

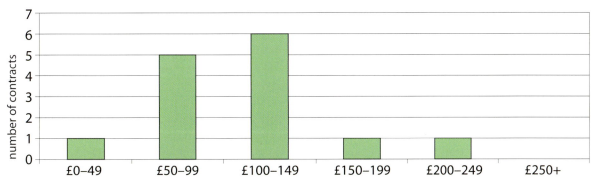

Figure 10.5.
Amounts invested per contract in Adriatic ventures (Viadro) (from *DCV*; *NDCV*; *San Maffio di Mazzorbo*)

tination were concerned). Unlike the *capitani* and *comiti* of the Levantine galleys, the intra-Adriatic *naucleri* do not appear to have hailed from patrician families. Moreover, many of the *naucleri* mentioned in the surviving Venetian contracts bear distinctly non-Venetian surnames, and in some cases their non-Venetian origins (for example, Ragusa) are explicitly stated, suggesting that the *naucleri* on Venetian ships hailed from throughout the Adriatic.[268] Like the merchants whom they transported (along with their wares), some of the *naucleri* active in the Adriatic also ventured beyond the Strait of Otranto. In 1226, for instance, Deodatus Blanco was the *nauclerus* for a voyage to Trani and Brindisi; some two decades earlier he had served in the same capacity on Tommaso Viadro's trip to Syria.[269]

The evidence also suggests that the *naucleri* themselves regularly engaged in trade. In 1159, a certain Manolesso Lipefina lent £20 *veronensium* to Giovanni Russo for a journey to Apulia on which Russo himself was the *nauclerus*.[270] Another *nauclerus*, Bartolomeo Fazio, made four recorded trading voyages to ports in the upper Adriatic between 1198 and 1201, receiving small investments for each trip.[271] This coupling of the roles of merchant and *nauclerus* was certainly not unique to the Adriatic; in one seventh-century Byzantine hagiographic text, the terms *naukleroi* and *emporoi* are even used interchangeably.[272] As the eleventh-century documents from the Cairo Genizah contain frequent references

---

268 In *DCV*, no. 409, the *nauclerus*, Samarico Lombardo, is from Apulia. In *DCV*, no. 629, the *nauclerus*, Blasio di Bistino, is from Ragusa.
269 *DCV*, nos. 461, 626.
270 *DCV*, no. 136. For the use of Veronese currency in twelfth-century Venice, see above, note 57.
271 *DCV*, nos. 438, 449, 453, 543.
272 Laiou, "Exchange and Trade," 706; the text concerned is the *Miracles of St. Demetrios*. The ancient Roman use of *nauclerus* is just as problematic as the medieval usage and offers few insights; see the extended discussion in J. Rougé, *Recherches*

to captains carrying goods for their own trading purposes, it appears that naucleri-traders were a regular feature of Islamic shipping along the southern Mediterranean shore.²⁷³ In the late thirteenth century, the Cretan merchants of Greek origin who engaged in maritime trade generally served as both trader and sailor, and the same seems to have been true of Greek merchants active in the Black Sea grain trade in the late fourteenth century.²⁷⁴ Most tellingly, both the Rhodian Sea Law and the Venetian maritime code promulgated by Doge Rainier Zeno in 1255 specifically discuss the quantities of merchandise that mariners could bring aboard their ships for trading purposes.²⁷⁵ It is not surprising, therefore, that we find the naucleri of the medieval Adriatic also engaging in small-scale trade.²⁷⁶

It is unclear whether the naucleri owned the boats that they themselves captained; comparative evidence from elsewhere in the Mediterranean shows a variety of practices. Most of the Greek merchants mentioned in the extant fourteenth-century notarial records from the Black Sea were also sailors or owners of small boats, and many seem to have been joint sailor-owners.²⁷⁷ However, evidence from the Cairo Genizah suggests that this vertical integration of commerce and shipping was not universal in the Mediterranean. In the eleventh century, at least, the men who owned the ships used for commercial ventures along the southern shores of the Mediterranean were usually distinct from those who sailed them. For example, one boat was named after its captain, Ibn al-Iskandar, but owned by two other men.²⁷⁸ In general, the ships were owned by government officials (ranging from the sultan himself to Muslim judges) and, above all, by merchants (particularly those belonging to large business houses).²⁷⁹ In contemporary Genoa, ship ownership and management were concentrated in a single individual insofar as small ships were concerned.²⁸⁰ Starting in the mid-twelfth century, however, the trend toward fractional ownership of vessels meant that large ships rarely belonged to any single individual, let alone the nauclerus. Even in recorded cases of single ownership, the owner and nauclerus appear to have been distinct, as in an 1198 voyage from Genoa to Catalonia aboard a ship belonging to the Genoese merchant Ugolino da Levanto in which the nauclerus was a certain Salvo of Savona.²⁸¹

Into which paradigm, therefore, did the naucleri of the medieval Adriatic fall? Three pieces of evidence suggest that while some Adriatic naucleri may indeed have owned their ships, those cases cannot be generalized. First, the early fifteenth-century burchio mentioned above was owned by the Malatesta clan, who chartered it out to various captains.²⁸² Thus, the naucleri of the later medieval Adriatic were not necessarily the owners of the ships on which they sailed. Second, according to the Venetian maritime code promulgated by Doge Rainier Zeno in 1255, the nauclerus was to fulfill entirely separate functions from

---

sur l'organisation du commerce maritime en Méditerranée sous l'empire romain (Paris, 1966), 229–58.

273 S. D. Goitein, *A Mediterranean Society: The Jewish Communities of the Arab World as Portrayed in the Documents of the Cairo Geniza*, 6 vols. (Berkeley, 1967–93), 1:311.

274 A. E. Laiou-Thomadakis, "The Byzantine Economy in the Mediterranean Trade System: Thirteenth–Fifteenth Centuries," *DOP* 34–35 (1980–81): 177–222, at 196–97; and eadem, "The Greek Merchant of the Palaeologan Period: A Collective Portrait," Πρακτικά τῆς Ἀκαδημίας Ἀθηνῶν 57 (1982): 96–132, at 107, 118.

275 Rhodian Sea Law, 3.22 (referring specifically to *naukleroi*), in Νόμος Ῥοδίων Ναυτικός—*The Rhodian Sea Law*, ed. W. Ashburner (Oxford, 1909), 102–3; 1255 Zeno Code, Article 50, in R. Predelli and A. Sacerdoti, eds., *Gli statuti marittimi veneziani fino al 1255* (Venice, 1903), 122–23. Although the Zeno Code refers to "merchatores et marinarii" and not specifically to "naucleri," the broad phrasing of the statute suggests that naucleri were encompassed within its provisions.

276 The occupational pattern of sailor-trader may not have been the rule in the medieval Mediterranean. According to E. H. Byrne, twelfth- and thirteenth-century Genoese naucleri apparently did not engage actively in trade, drawing their profits instead from the sailing and management of their ships; see *Genoese Shipping in the Twelfth and Thirteenth Centuries* (Cambridge, Mass., 1930), 12. However, given the frequency with which naucleri seem to have engaged in trade elsewhere in the medieval Mediterranean, I have some reservations about the categorical certainty of Byrne's conclusion. To be sure, the Venetians might have simply adopted the Byzantine custom of dual occupations, but it seems more likely that the commercial activities of Genoese naucleri are simply underrepresented in the surviving records.

277 Laiou-Thomadakis, "Byzantine Economy," 196–97; and eadem, "Greek Merchant," 107.

278 Goitein, *Mediterranean Society*, 1:309.

279 Ibid., 310–11. Goitein suggests that some of the shipowners may have been skippers (i.e., naucleri) by calling, but no instances are recorded among the 148 boats that he examined. See also A. L. Udovitch, "Time, the Sea and Society: Duration of Commercial Voyages on the Southern Shores of the Mediterranean during the High Middle Ages," in *La navigazione mediterranea nell'alto medioevo* (Spoleto, 1978), 503–63, at 519–20.

280 Byrne, *Genoese Shipping*, 12.

281 J. E. Eierman et al., eds., *Bonvillano (1198)*, Notai liguri dei secoli XII e XIII 3 (Genoa, 1939), no. 35.

282 See Anselmi, "Piccolo cabotaggio," 521–48.

the patronus (who both owned the ship and oversaw the shipping expedition); indeed, the nauclerus was to report on certain contraventions of the code perpetrated by the patronus.[283] This clearly suggests a division between the naucleri and the shipowners, at least in the mid-thirteenth century. However, the provisions in the code that concern naucleri generally refer only to ships with a carrying capacity of more than 200 *migliaia*, which would have exempted most of the ships active in the Adriatic. Moreover, though naucleri appear in almost every one of the surviving intra-Adriatic contracts, they are mentioned only rarely within the code overall, which assigned to them a considerably more limited role than their frequency in the extant documentation would suggest. The provisions of the code therefore seem to bear little relationship to the reality of intra-Adriatic shipping. Yet if separate ownership and captaining of the ships was de rigueur in Venice's long-distance trade, it seems probable that such a division was at least not unusual within the confines of the Adriatic. Finally, we know that in Venice from the eleventh century onward, ownership of a ship was often divided among multiple investors, as in Genoa and elsewhere in the Mediterranean, and some naucleri did indeed own shares.[284] Overall, it seems safe to assume that some of the Adriatic naucleri owned their own ships (especially when the ships were small), as was the case in contemporary Genoa, while many others either owned them only in part or else were hired by shipowners to manage the ships on their behalf.[285]

The patterns of Venetian social involvement in the Adriatic trade reveal many parallels with the city's general trade in the Mediterranean: there was considerable overlap in the merchants involved, the amounts invested fell generally within the same range, and some of the naucleri active in the Adriatic also captained ships bound for the Levant. But in one respect, Venice's pattern of intra-Adriatic mercantile involvement differed strikingly from its involvement in the wider Mediterranean: the participation of women. In only two of the roughly sixty surviving Venetian contracts concerning intra-Adriatic trade between 1100 and 1260 is a woman an active participant.[286] By contrast, more than one-eighth of all Venetian commercial contracts from the same period involve women in some capacity.[287] Active female involvement in the Mediterranean trade in general was certainly not an exclusively Venetian phenomenon; of the 4,500 extant Genoese colleganza contracts recorded between 1155 and 1216, nearly one-quarter of them involve women acting either for themselves or on behalf of a family member.[288] How then can the comparative underrepresentation of women in intra-Adriatic trade be explained? The two surviving contracts offer little guidance: one consists of a sea loan of £40 (one of the smallest recorded amounts); the other, a quittance for a colleganza for £400 (one of the largest). The woman in the former case bears an uncommon surname and loaned money to a nauclerus-trader. In the latter case, the woman was the widow of a member of an established (if not especially prominent) Venetian family; she was acting on behalf of her late husband in concluding an earlier transaction with a patrician merchant. Is it possible that most female investors were attracted by the greater state control over the Levant trade, with its systems of mude and convoys? Did the higher potential returns from the commerce of luxury goods appeal to them, despite the higher risk? Unfortunately, unless new sources are discovered that add to the paucity of existing material, these questions must remain unanswered.

A Connected Sea

The portrait of the Adriatic sketched in the preceding pages shows a region moving toward ever-greater commercial integration, though against a background of considerable international upheaval and steadily increasing Venetian control of commodity movement within the sea. The commodity exchange that animated its shores had multiple

---

283   1255 Zeno Code, Article 33, in *Statuti marittimi veneziani*, 102. See also G. Bonolis, *Diritto marittimo medievale dell'Adriatico* (Pisa, 1921), 169–70, for a discussion of the functions of *padroni* and *naucleri* delineated in the code.

284   See, for example, *DCV*, no. 519, in which Leonardo Urso owns part of a ship in which he also serves as the nauclerus. For fractional ownership in Venice, see Lane, *Venetian Ships and Shipbuilders of the Renaissance*, 116.

285   This corresponds with the view of F. C. Lane, who noted that "on a twelfth-century merchant vessel, the *nauclerus* was not necessarily the owner" (*Venice*, 50).

286   *DCV*, nos. 543, 638.

287   This figure is based on an analysis of the documents in the *DCV* and *NDCV*.

288   See M. Angelos, "Women in Genoese *Commenda* Contracts, 1155–1216," *JMedHist* 20 (1994): 299–312, at 300.

interdependent causes; in the Adriatic, as in the medieval Mediterranean more generally, no one factor was sufficient to drive exchange. Concentrated (and growing) urban demand for staple commodities had to be matched by surplus production elsewhere within the sea. Regions with complementary micro-ecologies had to be accessible by navigable sea-lanes. Hinterlands had to be connected to the seaports by secure overland routes. The medieval Adriatic was an exemplar of this model. The grain and oil production of the western Adriatic coast and Albania fed the citizens of Venice, Ancona, Ragusa, and other large coastal centers. Salt from Durazzo could be easily transported along the coast to Ragusa; grain from the Marches could be easily carried across the central Adriatic to Dalmatia. Slaves and hides could be carried from the Balkan interior to Zara through passes in the Dinaric Alps, to be exchanged for staple foodstuffs and manufactured goods that would then be carried back across the mountain passes.

Intra-Adriatic trade was predominantly *bulk* trade, and in the twelfth and thirteenth centuries the movement of bulk goods within the sea generally adhered to broad patterns. While salt and timber moved in many directions within the sea (though usually laterally), the chief agricultural commodities—especially grain and oil—moved from south to north and from west to east. Perhaps this is not surprising—the Apulian plateau and Po plain were more conducive to the cultivation of wheat and olives than were the Veneto marshes or the mountainous Dalmatian coast. But neither can the direction of movement be taken for granted. As the sixth-century letter of Cassiodorus to the *tribuni maritimorum* indicates, there was a time when communities along the western shore sought staple foodstuffs—wine, oil, and wheat—from the eastern coast.[289] Local production possibilities were vitally important, but other factors also stimulated the exchange of commodities and influenced the directions of this exchange: demand patterns, navigational trends, and political factors all helped shape the trade networks within the sea. Furthermore, bulk commodities were not the only cargoes traveling along the Adriatic sea-lanes, for luxury goods from the Levant were frequently carried through the Strait of Otranto—and prior to 1204, overland through the southern Balkans to the eastern Adriatic coast as well. The influx of these commodities into the Adriatic region, together with structural features of medieval long-distance shipping, ensured that extra-Adriatic commerce was not an isolated phenomenon but rather was closely intertwined with local and regional trade networks.

Long-distance trade not only influenced the workings of the regional trade networks but also profoundly shaped their growth. It was above all the expansion of Venetian control over commodity movements within the Adriatic, particularly from the second quarter of the thirteenth century onward, that transformed an accumulation of individual commercial linkages into a truly integrated system. The expansion of this control came after Venice had already established its supremacy in the long-distance trade of the eastern Mediterranean. The prosperity and growth engendered by Venetian success outside the Adriatic greatly amplified the lagoon city's function as a demand center for commodities within the sea, and Venice's need to ensure secure access to these commodities drove the monopolistic program that so defined the Adriatic trade system by the mid-thirteenth century. Yet though Venetian dominance of regional trade within the Adriatic was supported by its dominance of long-distance trade in the eastern Mediterranean, the two were nevertheless separate achievements. Regional preeminence was hardly an automatic by-product of Levantine hegemony; it had to be negotiated, fought for, and defended in its own right. Indeed, while the city's nodal position between the eastern Mediterranean and northwestern Europe may have facilitated its success in long-distance trade, its position at the head of the lagoon rendered it less able to supervise Adriatic trade than could cities further south, such as Ancona or Split. Although the thirteenth century saw the limits of Venetian control inching ever further southward, the comparative weakness of this control in the southern portions of the sea is underscored by the vigorous non-Venetian activity there; it is no coincidence that Dalmatian diplomatic and commercial activity was more intense in Apulia than along more northern stretches of the western Adriatic coast.

Other aspects of the Adriatic trade system remain to be explored. The role played by coastal hinterlands is still insufficiently understood, though the importance of the Serbian mountains or the grain fields on the Apulian plateau is clear. Simi-

---

289 Cassiodorus, *Variarum Libri XII* 12.24.

larly, fluvial and terrestrial connections in the Adriatic region have made only brief appearances in the preceding pages, even though goods were not always transported by sea; overland and river routes were also important conduits of exchange along the shores of the medieval Adriatic, and they require much more research.[290] And, as often mentioned, we know little about the caboteurs, or the sailors who rigged and sailed the roundships and taride, or even the merchants who hailed from Ragusa, Brindisi, or anywhere except Venice. Only echoes of their activities are left behind, in the historical traces of the commercial linkages that they helped forge. None of these medieval merchants and mariners, none of these captains and caboteurs, none of the countless men—and, occasionally, women—who traveled the sea-lanes of the Adriatic thought in terms of "microecologies" or "connectivity." But in responding to economic opportunities and braving the unpredictable seas, they collectively created vibrant trade networks that continued to flourish long after they had vanished from memory.

In the succeeding decades and centuries, Venice expanded its control over commodity movement to the very mouth of the Adriatic and beyond. The textile trade expanded enormously, with Tuscan cloth being carried to Ancona for export to Dalmatia and the Levant. Balkan metals replaced Balkan slaves as the chief export of the Dalmatian coast. Venice began to seek out staple foodstuffs from beyond the Strait of Otranto: grain from Thessaly and the Black Sea; salt from Ibiza, Sardinia, and Cyprus. Overland trade routes through the western Balkans were revived, leading to an enormous expansion of regional commercial activity. The Apulian ports declined further, while Ragusa underwent a dramatic rise to Mediterranean prominence. But the economic integration of the Adriatic, the fundamental achievement of the trade networks that had developed in the twelfth and thirteenth centuries, continued unabated. The linkages that had been established among regions and between coasts proved too strong to be permanently severed by political upheavals, religious turmoil, or linguistic barriers. More than eight hundred years have passed since Tommaso Viadro set out for Brindisi and Durazzo, and since the monks of the Tremiti islands brought their wheels of cheese to Ancona. But the commercial ties that these voyages forged and the connectivity they exemplified have remained defining features of the Adriatic ever since.

---

290 Their importance in the northern Adriatic is ably discussed in Rösch, *Venedig und das Reich,* 31–46.

• ELEVEN •

Annual Fairs, Regional Networks, and Trade Routes in Syria, Sixth–Tenth Centuries

ANDRÉ BINGGELI

Muslim tradition holds that before the advent of Islam the city of Mecca regulated trade between Syria and Yemen by controlling an organized regional network of more than a dozen annual intertribal fairs in the Arabian Peninsula, the famous *aswāq al-ʿArab*.¹ According to the tradition, this annual cycle started with the fair of Dūmat al-Jandal in the north of the peninsula, at the crossroads of trade routes in the desert frontier region between the Byzantine and Persian empires, and culminated during the great fair of ʿUkāẓ, well known for its contests of poetry, which was organized on neutral ground at another junction of roads between Mecca and Ṭāʾif.² The precise role of these fairs in pre-Islamic Arabia and their relationship to early Islamic traditions is the subject of ongoing scholarly debate, and it is now commonly admitted that the annual cycle was partly reconstructed in later historiography to coincide with the Meccan *ḥajj*.³ After the advent of Islam, these fairs disappeared quite rapidly, but what was the fate of the institution in other parts of the caliphate? Away from the Arabian Peninsula, their existence and economic role in the Islamic Empire have scarcely been studied, while their counterparts in the West and to a lesser extent in Byzantium have been given much attention over the past decades.⁴ The aim of this chapter is to present literary

---

1 On the *aswāq al-ʿArab*, see H. Kindermann, "al-Sūq," in *Encyclopédie de l'Islam, Supplément* (Leiden, 1938), 228–29 (French edition); S. al-Afghānī, *Aswāq al-ʿArab* (Damascus, 1960); G. W. Heck, "The Precious Metals of West Arabia and Their Role in Forging the Economic Dynamic of the Early Islamic State" (Ph.D. diss., King Faisal Center for Research and Islamic Studies Riyadh, 2003), appendix K.
2 See, for example, the account by al-Yaʿqūbī, *Taʾrīkh*, ed. M. T. Houtsma, 2 vols. (Leiden, 1883), 1:313–14, trans. and comm. in R. G. Hoyland, *Arabia and the Arabs: From the Bronze Age to the Coming of Islam* (London, 2001), 109–10. Other accounts are given by Ibn Ḥabīb, *Kitāb al-Muḥabbar,* ed. I. Lichtenstädter (Hyderabad, 1361/1942), 263–68; see also note 11, below.
3 The issue of the economic importance of fairs is part of the larger debate on the commercial history of Arabian trade in the sixth–seventh centuries, especially the role of Mecca in transArabian trade, revived with the controversial volume by P. Crone, *Meccan Trade and the Rise of Islam* (Princeton, N.J., 1987). On the role played by Islamic historiography in the reconstruction of this cycle, see J. Wellhausen, *Reste arabischen Heidentums,* 2nd ed. (Leipzig, 1927), 84–101, esp. 88; U. Rubin, "Meccan Trade and Qurʾānic Exegesis (Qurʾān 2:198)," *BSOAS* 53 (1990): 421–28.
4 See R. Brunschvig, "Coup d'œil sur l'histoire des foires à travers l'islam," in *La Foire,* Recueils de la Société Jean Bodin 5 (Brussels, 1953), 43–74, for a comprehensive overview. A list of fairs in the eastern provinces of the caliphate is given by A. Miquel, *La géographie humaine du monde musulman jusqu'au milieu du 11ᵉ siècle,* 4 vols. (Paris, 1967–88), 4:151–54. At the same time, archaeological discoveries in Jordan over the past decades have focused considerable attention on the institution of permanent markets, also known by their Arabic name *sūq/aswāq*, and their impact on urban changes; see R. Foote, "Commerce, Industrial Expansion, and Orthogonal Planning: Mutually Compatible Terms in Settlements of Bilâd al-Shâm during the Umayyad Period," *Mediterranean Archaeology* 13 (2000): 25–38; and A. Walmsley, "Production, Exchange and Regional Trade in the Islamic East Mediterranean: Old Structures, New Systems?" in *The Long Eighth Century: Production, Distribution and Demand,* ed. I. L. Hansen and C. Wickham (Leiden, 2000), 265–343, at 274–83. On fairs in Byzantium, see P. Koukoules, Βυζαντινῶν βίος καὶ πολιτισμός, 6 vols. (Athens, 1948–57), 3:270–283; S. Vryonis, "The *Panēgyris* of the Byzantine Saint: A Study on the Nature of a Medieval Institution, Its Origins and Fate," in *The Byzantine Saint,* ed. S. Hackel (London, 1981), 196–227; and A. E. Laiou, "Händler und Kaufleute auf dem Jahrmarkt," in *Fest und Alltag*

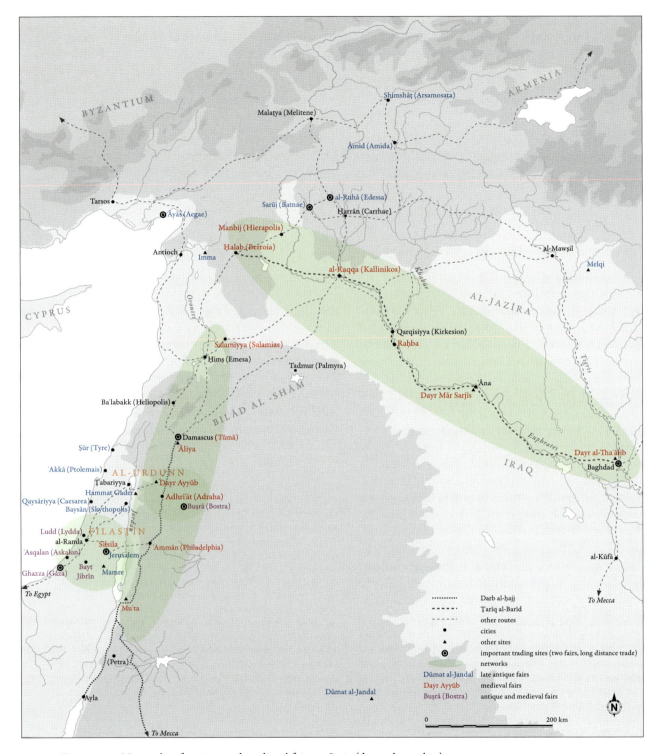

Figure 11.1 Networks of antique and medieval fairs in Syria (drawn by author)

282   ANDRÉ BINGGELI

evidence that has gone unnoticed concerning a network of annual fairs throughout Bilād al-Shām and the Jazīra that bears some similarity to the traditional cycle of pre-Islamic Arabia, and thereby provides new insight into this institution in the early Islamic period (see fig. 11.1). These fairs, taking place from Upper Mesopotamia to the Mediterranean and from northern Syria to Palestine, are listed in a series of Arabic astronomical and chronological treatises, calendars, and almanacs from the ninth to the thirteenth centuries.[5]

Almanacs as Literary Evidence for Fairs during the Islamic Period

The earliest extant treatise that preserves such entries is the *Kitāb al-Azmina*, the "Book of Times" of Ibn Māsawayh (d. 857), a Christian physician at the court of the ʿAbbāsid caliphs in Baghdad in the first half of the ninth century.[6] The book comes in the form of a calendar or an almanac, from October to September, with entries for each month and for special days of the year. The author collected and reorganized a wide range of material concerning the motion of stars, meteorological phenomena, seasonal agricultural activities, observations on the habits of animals and plants, advice for a balanced diet and good hygiene, and finally information on Christian feasts and fairs—seven altogether, all situated in southern Bilād al-Shām. He mostly derived his information from earlier written material collected in the eighth century by Arab traditionists from Iraq in their books of the *anwāʾ*, which record astronomical and meteorological lore concerning the motion of stars and seasonal changes with references to the old poetic tradition of the Arabs. The mention of fairs is a novelty, however, and it is our contention that here Ibn Māsawayh may have been using an original Syrian source from the eighth century.[7]

Three other works from the second half of the tenth and the early eleventh centuries—the *Kitāb al-Dalāʾil*, the "Book of Signs" of Ibn Bahlūl (d. 968), a notable of the Church of the East in Baghdad;[8] the *Kitāb al-Azmina wa-l-Amkina*, the "Book of Times and Places" of al-Marzūqī (d. 1030), a philologist at the court of the Buyids in Ispahan;[9] and *al-Āthār*

---

in Byzanz, ed. G. Prinzing and D. Simon (Munich, 1990), 53–70, reprinted in eadem, *Gender, Society and Economic Life in Byzantium* (Aldershot, 1992), art. XI. For the Roman period, see in particular L. de Ligt, *Fairs and Markets in the Roman Empire: Economic and Social Aspects of Periodic Trade in a Pre-industrial Society,* Dutch Monographs on Ancient History and Archaeology 11 (Amsterdam, 1993); Z. Safrai, *The Economy of Roman Palestine* (London, 1994); and B. T. Rozenfeld and J. Menirav, *Markets and Marketing in Roman Palestine,* Supplements to the Journal for the Study of Judaism 99 (Leiden, 2005), esp. 58–69.

5   For other parts of the Islamic world, the importance of almanacs and calendars for the writing of economic history has already been emphasized; see C. Cahen, "Un traité financier inédit d'époque fatimide-ayyubide," *Journal of the Economic and Social History of the Orient* 5 (1962): 139–59, reprinted in idem, *Makhzūmiyyāt: Études sur l'histoire économique et financière de l'Égypte médiévale* (Leiden, 1977), 1–21. Such calendars existed in all parts of the medieval Islamic world: on al-Andalūs and the famous tenth-century *Calendar of Cordoba,* see R. Dozy and C. Pellat, *Le Calendrier de Cordoue* (Leiden, 1961), and M. Forcada, "Books of *Anwāʾ* in al-Andalus," in *The Formation of al-Andalus,* part 2, *Language, Religion, Culture and the Sciences,* ed. M. Fierro and J. Samsó, Formation of the Classical Islamic World 47 (Aldershot, 1998), 305–28; on the Egyptian tradition, see the works of C. Pellat, especially *Cinq calendriers égyptiens,* Institut français d'archéologie orientale, Textes arabes et études islamiques 26 (Cairo, 1986); on the Yemenite tradition, see D. M. Varisco, *Medieval Agriculture and Islamic Science: The Almanac of a Yemeni Sultan* (Washington, 1994), and idem, *Medieval Folk Astronomy in Arabia and the Yemen* (Aldershot, 1997). It is notable, however, that fairs are mentioned only in calendars produced in Syria and Iraq.

6   Ibn Māsawayh, *Kitāb al-Azmina,* ed. P. Sbath as "Kitāb al-Azmina: Le *Livre des temps* d'Ibn Massawaïh, médecin chrétien célèbre décédé en 857," *Bulletin de l'Institut d'Égypte* 15 (1932/33): 235–57 (hereafter cited as Ibn Māsawayh), reprinted in *Beiträge zur Geschichte der arabisch-islamischen Medizin: Aufsätze,* ed. F. Sezgin, vol. 7, *Aus den Jahren 1931–1935* (Frankfurt, 1991), 183–205; trans. and comm. in G. Troupeau, "Le *Livre des temps* de Jean Ibn Māsawayh," *Arabica* 15 (1968): 113–42. On Ibn Māsawayh, see M. Ullmann, *Die Medizin im Islam,* Handbuch der Orientalistik, ser. 1, Erg. 6, 1 (Leiden, 1970), 112–15; and F. Sezgin, *Geschichte des Arabischen Schrifttums,* vol. 3, *Medizin-Pharmazie-Zoologie-Tierheilkunde* (Leiden, 1970), 231–36.

7   The sources used by Ibn Māsawayh and the seven fairs mentioned by him are examined in A. Binggeli, "Foires et pèlerinages sur la route du hajj: À propos de quelques sanctuaires chrétiens et musulmans dans le sud du Bilād al-Shām d'après le *Kitāb al-azmina* d'Ibn Māsawayh (9ᵉ s.)," *Aram* 18–19 (2006–07): 559–82.

8   Ibn Bahlūl, *Kitāb al-Dalāʾil,* ed. Y. Habbi (Kuwait, 1408/1987), hereafter cited as Ibn Bahlūl; for a facsimile edition of the manuscript, see *The Book of Indications: Kitāb al-Dalāʾil by Al-Ḥasan Ibn al-Bahlūl (Tenth Century A.D.),* Publications of the Institute for the History of Arabic-Islamic Science, Facsimile Editions 10 (Frankfurt-am-Main, 1985). On Ibn Bahlūl and his work, see J. Habbi, "Le livre des signes de Al-Ḥasan b. Bahlūl," *OrChr* 68 (1984): 210–12; idem, "Les sources du Livre des signes de al-Ḥasan Ibn Bahlūl," in *Deuxième congrès international d'études arabes chrétiennes,* Orientalia Christiana Analecta 226 (Rome, 1986), 193–203.

9   Al-Marzūqī, *Kitāb al-Azmina wa-l-Amkina* (Hyderabad, 1332/1914); reprint, ed. F. Sezgin, 2 vols., Publications of the Institute for the History of Arabic-Islamic Science, Natural Sciences

al-Bāqiyya ʿan al-Qurūn al-Khāliyya, the "Chronology of Ancient Nations," completed around 1000 by the famous scientist from Khwarizm, al-Bīrūnī (d. 1048)[10]—preserve similar lists. All of these works are more developed chronological treatises, with comparative studies of calendars in the traditions and civilizations of the Greeks, Arabs, Persians, Jews, Sabaeans, and different Christian churches. Like Ibn Māsawayh's almanac, though on a much larger scale, they interlace mathematical, astronomical, meteorological, and historical information with observations concerning the customs and creeds of different people. The lists of fairs that were held in Bilād al-Shām and the Jazīra are generally found in sections relating to the calendar of the Greeks. The pre-Islamic fairs of the Arabian Peninsula are also listed, but in special sections on the festivals of the Arabs during the *Jāhiliyya* period or in chapters dedicated to the calendar of the Arabs.[11] Fairs in more remote regions of the Islamic Empire are sometimes to be found in other chapters; a group of fairs in Central Asia is thus mentioned by al-Bīrūnī in his chapter on the Sogdians, who were renowned as traders and merchants.[12]

The authors of these works drew on a large number of sources and show an encyclopedic ambition, although on occasion they also record some original information. Al-Bīrūnī, for example, is very scrupulous about giving his source, whether written or just popular lore, for each entry in his chapters on the calendar of the Greeks.[13] Nine fairs are listed, all in Bilād al-Shām and all known from earlier sources, with one exception: for 24 September, al-Bīrūnī first indicates "nothing mentioned" (i.e., he found nothing in his written sources), then goes on to cite the fair of Thaʿālib (in Iraq) and a meteorological phenomenon noted by "practical observers."[14] This information appears as the author's own addition to the sources he was compiling.

Ibn Bahlūl and al-Marzūqī have the most extensive lists, but analysis of them is difficult because several fairs are mentioned in only one or the other work, often with scribal errors. In his section on the months of the Greeks, Ibn Bahlūl names eighteen fairs spread across the whole territory of Bilād al-Shām, including Palestine, southern Syria and Jordan, northern Syria and the Jazīra (Upper Mesopotamia), and even Alexandria.[15] In another section, he mentions a fair near Baghdad in the monastery of Harqil.[16] That this last fair appears in a section dedicated to the liturgical calendar of the Church of the East (the Nestorians) suggests that the information here derives from a different type of source—possibly from the author's personal knowledge as a clergyman of the Church of Baghdad. Al-Marzūqī similarly has a comprehensive list of thirteen fairs, but many names are garbled and therefore difficult to identify. Moreover, a couple of these were held in more eastern provinces of Iran (Khuzistān and Khurassān).[17] Since al-Marzūqī is the only author to mention these Iranian fairs, this information must also have been transmitted on an independent circuit.

Finally, a much later source—the *Kitāb ʿAjāʾib al-Makhlūqāt,* the "Cosmography" of al-Qazwīnī (d. 1283)—also gives a short list of eight fairs.[18] All of these fairs are known from previous sources and it is uncertain whether they were still held in al-Qazwīnī's time. The literary genre itself appears to be very conservative, with many mishaps in the pro-

---

in Islam 53–54 (Frankfurt-am-Main, 2001), hereafter cited as al-Marzūqī.

10 Al-Bīrūnī, *Al-Āthār al-Bāqiyya ʿan al-Qurūn al-Khāliyya,* ed. C. E. Sachau as *Chronologie orientalischer Völker von Albêrûni* (Leipzig, 1923), hereafter cited as al-Bīrūnī; trans. C. E. Sachau as *The Chronology of Ancient Nations: An English Version of the Arabic Text of the Athâr-ul-Bâkiya of al-Bîrûnî, or "Vestiges of the Past"* (London, 1879).

11 Ibn Bahlūl, 194–212; al-Marzūqī, 2:169–170; al-Bīrūnī, 328.

12 Al-Bīrūnī, 233–35; on Sogdian merchants and trade, see E. de la Vaissière, *Histoire des marchands sogdiens,* Bibliothèque de l'Institut des Hautes Études Chinoises 32, 2nd rev. ed. (Paris, 2004) ; English trans. by J. Ward, *Sogdian Traders: A History,* Handbuch der Orientalistik, ser. 8, 10 (Leiden, 2005).

13 At the end of his chapter on the days of the Greek calendar, the author concludes: "This is the calendar used by the Greeks, to which we have added all that Sinān [ibn Thābit] has mentioned in his *Kitāb al-Anwāʾ*" (al-Bīrūnī, 275).

14 Al-Bīrūnī, 274; on the fair of Thaʿālib, see note 60, below.

15 Only one fair in October, named the festival of *Mawtāt* [?] (Ibn Bahlūl, 89), was not identified. Since all the fairs referred to in this section, except the fair of Alexandria, were held inside Bilād al-Shām, this fair probably also took place there; it is not to be mistaken for the fair of Muʾta, already mentioned as occurring in November (Ibn Bahlūl, 98).

16 Ibn Bahlūl, 228; on the fair of Harqil, see note 59, below.

17 Four fairs mentioned by al-Marzūqī were not identified: one fair in October, named al-Qādisān, that was held at Sūq al-aswāq and lasted a week (2:283, line 7–8), and three fairs in September—in the Jund Nīshābūr (2:291, line 4), in al-Sūs (2:291, line 10), and a last incomprehensible name for a fair that also lasted a week (2:291, line 10). In many places the edition appears to be faulty; some corrections are proposed in the following pages.

18 Al-Qazwīnī, *Kitāb ʿAjāʾib al-Makhlūqāt,* ed. F. Wüstenfeld, 2 vols. (Göttingen, 1848–49); hereafter cited as al-Qazwīnī.

cess of copying and transmission; new information is scarce, and what is written about fairs often may be relevant not to the date of the composition but to an earlier situation. Therefore, we must be very careful when using these sources, especially in dating the historical data they convey. Later sources frequently have value only insofar as they confirm earlier lists.

Moreover, none of these texts gives much information about the organization of the fairs named. At most, they specify the date and the place when the fair was held, as well as its length. Unlike narrative or juridical sources that tell us about fairs in other parts of the late antique and medieval world, our documents do not describe how these actually operated: Where were they held? How were they organized? Who took part in them? What was exchanged? Such questions may be answered only indirectly by comparison with other regions or periods, or when these fairs happen to be mentioned in other sources. The main interest of these documents lies in the consistency, not to say regularity, of the image they convey of this area during the first centuries of the Islamic Empire. Indeed, one is immediately struck by the relatively equal geographical distribution of fairs across Bilād al-Shām and the Jazīra, with the exception of the desert regions in its middle. The list of fairs is certainly not exhaustive, but the network is sufficiently dense to allow speculation on the ways in which these fairs relate to one another, on a regional scale, both geographically and chronologically. For the other regions of the Islamic Empire, fairs receive only scattered mention and, it appears, mostly as later additions to the earlier group, so their inclusion in this inquiry would be too hazardous. This chapter therefore seeks to use the aforementioned literary evidence to advance a tentative reconstruction of a regional trade network in Bilād al-Shām and the Jazīra, by analyzing how these fairs interact with each other, by examining how they develop in relation to trade routes, and by highlighting more general trends. In the process, it connects the appearance and disappearance of fairs over time with the economic necessities and political changes that took place more generally in Syria during the period spanning the sixth to the tenth centuries.

List of Fairs in Bilād al-Shām

Including the *aswāq al-ʿArab* of the Arabian Peninsula, close to fifty different fairs in total are mentioned in the five works. Of these, eighteen were held within the boundaries of the provinces of Bilād al-Shām and the Jazīra, and can be identified with a great degree of certainty. They are listed here in the order of the calendars from October to September.

Adhriʿāt, ancient Adra[h]a or modern Derʿa, in southern Syria: the fair was held on 13 October, according to Ibn Māsawayh and al-Qazwīnī; al-Bīrūnī puts it in August.[19]

Ḥalab or Aleppo, ancient Berroia, in northern Syria: the fair was held on 16 October, according to Ibn Bahlūl and al-Marzūqī.[20]

(Dayr) Mār Sarjīs, the "monastery of Saint Sergius" at ʿĀna on the Middle Euphrates, at the frontier between the provinces of the Jazīra and Iraq: the fair was held in October, according to al-Marzūqī, who is the only author to mention it.[21]

Al-Raqqa, ancient Kallinikos, in northern Syria on the Euphrates: the fair was held in November, on the occasion of the "festival day" of the church of al-Raqqa; al-Marzūqī is the only author to mention it.[22]

Muʿta, a village, today between Kerak and Petra in southern Jordan: the fair was held in November, according to Ibn Māsawayh and Ibn Bahlūl.[23]

Tūmā in Damascus: the fair was held near the eastern gate of the city, Bāb Tūmā. It is mentioned in all the calendars and was held on 1 December.[24]

Filasṭīn: the exact location is not specified; according to the different calendars, the fair of Filasṭīn started within a day or two of 23 April.[25]

---

19 Ibn Māsawayh, 242; al-Qazwīnī, 1:55; Al-Bīrūnī, 272; see Binggeli, "Foires et pèlerinages," 573. On the fairs of Adhriʿāt, Buṣrā, and Dayr Ayyūb, see I. Shahīd, *Byzantium and the Arabs in the Sixth Century*, vol. 2.2 (Washington, D.C., 2009), 33–40.
20 Ibn Bahlūl, 89; al-Marzūqī, 2:283.
21 Al-Marzūqī, 2:283 (sūq Māsarjisān). On Dayr Mār Sarjīs (Māsarjīs or Māsarjisānā), see al-Shābushtī, *Kitāb al-Diyārāt*, ed. K. Awwād, 2nd ed. (Baghdad, 1966), 228–29; Ibn Faḍlallāh al-ʿUmarī, *Masālik al-Abṣār fī Mamālik al-Amṣār*, vol. 1, ed. A. Zakkī Bāshā (Cairo, 1924), 271–72; Yāqūt, *Muʿjam al-Buldān*, ed. F. Wüstenfeld as *Jacut's geographisches Wörterbuch*, 6 vols. (Leipzig, 1866–70), 2:693.
22 Al-Marzūqī, 2:283 (read *sūq ʿīd* [instead of *ʿnd*] *kanīsat al-Raqqa*).
23 Ibn Māsawayh, 243; Ibn Bahlūl, 98; see Binggeli, "Foires et pèlerinages," 569–71.
24 Ibn Māsawayh, 245 (on 25 December); Ibn Bahlūl, 105; al-Marzūqī, 2:288; al-Bīrūnī, 248; al-Qazwīnī, 1:55; see Binggeli, "Foires et pèlerinages," 576–77.
25 Ibn Māsawayh, 250; al-Marzūqī, 2:288 (*sūq Krw* [?] *bi-Filasṭīn*); al-Qazwīnī, 1:57. Ibn Bahlūl (98) has the entry concerning the fair of Filasṭīn in November.

This was the feast day of Saint George, one of the most celebrated saints in Syria and Palestine. His main sanctuary was found in the town of Lydda, a renowned pilgrimage site from the late fifth century until the crusader period.[26] Since evidence exists for a large pilgrimage fair in Lydda on Saint George's day, we can assume that Lydda/Ludd was the location of the fair of Filasṭīn in late antiquity. The foundation of al-Ramla by Sulaymān b. ʿAbd al-Malik, the governor of the Jund (military district of) Filasṭīn at the beginning of the eighth century, certainly caused the economic decline of neighboring Ludd.[27] Perhaps the fair was then moved to the new administrative capital.[28] But it is more likely that it remained in Ludd, ensuring limited trading activity for the declining city during the festival of Saint George, which, according to medieval sources, was still celebrated well into the tenth century.[29]

Dayr Ayyūb, the "monastery of Job," in the modern village of Shaykh Saʿd near Derʿa in southern Syria: the fair was held at the end of April or the beginning of May and is recorded in all the lists except Ibn Māsawayh's.[30]

Buṣrā, ancient Bostra in southern Syria: the fair, which is mentioned by all the authors except al-Marzūqī, was held in mid-July; Ibn Bahlūl and al-Bīrūnī even refer to it twice.[31]

Salamiyya, ancient Salamias, between Damascus and Aleppo; the fair was also held in mid-July.[32]

ʿĀliya, a village on the southern outskirts of Damascus; Ibn Bahlūl and Ibn Māsawayh disagree about when it was held, claiming July and September, respectively.[33]

ʿAmmān, ancient Philadelphia, in Jordan: the fair, at the beginning of August, the 5th or the 10th, is mentioned in all lists except al-Marzūqī's. Al-Bīrūnī does not say explicitly that a fair was held in ʿAmmān; he refers only to fairs "in al-Urdunn and in the districts of Filasṭīn" on 5 August.[34] Since ʿAmmān belonged in the Jund Filasṭīn from the end of the ninth century onward, al-Bīrūnī may have been referring here to the fair of ʿAmmān.[35]

Bayt Jibrīn or Bayt Jibrīl, ancient Eleutheropolis or Beth Guvrin, in Palestine; the fair is mentioned at different dates in August by Ibn Bahlūl and al-Marzūqī.[36] Since Bayt Jibrīn also was found in the Jund Filasṭīn, al-Bīrūnī's aforementioned entry concerning fairs "in the districts of Filasṭīn" could also be referring to the fair of Bayt Jibrīn. A fair was already being held at Eleutheropolis as early as the fourth century, according to the *Life of Epiphanios*; its season is not specified, however.[37]

Al-Urdunn: this fair is the most problematic. Al-Bīrūnī puts it in August and al-Qazwīnī in December. Ibn Bahlūl mentions a fair in August in the district of al-Urdunn, "near" (ʿind) Bayt Ḥarīr, or more likely "on the festival day" (ʿīd) of Bayt Ḥarīr.[38] This otherwise unknown toponym could be interpreted as a scribal error for Bayt Jibrīn, and thus a duplication of the former entry, but doing so would contradict the ascription of the district. So it must be assumed that a fair was also held in August somewhere in the Jund al-Urdunn, in Galilee, on the banks of the Jordan River or around Lake Tiberias.[39]

---

26 See P. Maraval, *Lieux saints et pèlerinages d'Orient: Histoire et géographie des origines à la conquête arabe* (Paris, 1985), 298–99; D. Pringle, "Churches in the Crusader Kingdom of Jerusalem," in *Ancient Churches Revealed,* ed. Y. Tsafrir (Jerusalem, 1993), 28–39, at 32–33.
27 Walmsley, "Production, Exchange and Regional Trade," 283.
28 That is the opinion of M. Gil, *A History of Palestine, 634–1099* (Cambridge, 1992), 241.
29 Al-Muqqadasī, *Aḥsan al-Taqāsīm fī Maʿrifat al-Aqālīm,* ed. M. J. De Goeje, Bibliotheca Geographorum Arabicorum 3 (Leiden, 1877), 183, mentions the festival of Ludd. For other references prior to the tenth century, see Binggeli, "Foires et pèlerinages," 565–66.
30 Ibn Bahlūl, 142 (read *Dayr Ayyūb* [instead of *Abūn*]); al-Bīrūnī, 260–61; al-Qazwīnī, 1:57; see Binggeli, "Foires et pèlerinages," 573–76. In a garbled citation, Al-Marzūqī, 2:287 (*sūq al-Dayr bi-arḍ S.w.ā.r.t* [?] *min Sūq al-Ahwāz*), may be referring to the same fair, although he locates it in Khuzistān. For the precise location of Dayr Ayyūb, see R. Dussaud, *Topographie historique de la Syrie antique et médiévale* (Paris, 1927), 329.
31 Ibn Māsawayh, 253; Ibn Bahlūl, 168, 172; al-Bīrūnī, 267, 272; al-Qazwīnī, 1:57; see Binggeli, "Foires et pèlerinages," 571–73.
32 Ibn Bahlūl, 168; al-Marzūqī, 2:289 (read *Salamiyya* [instead of *Salima*]); al-Bīrūnī, 272.

33 Ibn Māsawayh, 256; Ibn Bahlūl, 194; see Binggeli, "Foires et pèlerinages," 577–78.
34 Ibn Māsawayh, 255; Ibn Bahlūl, 196; al-Qazwīnī, 1:59; al-Bīrūnī, 272; see Binggeli, "Foires et pèlerinages," 566–69.
35 On the administrative division of the Jund Filasṭīn during the Islamic caliphate, see D. Sourdel, "Filasṭīn," in *EI²* 2:932–35 (French edition).
36 Ibn Bahlūl, 183 (read *ʿīd* [instead of *ʿnd*] *Bayt Jibrīl bi-Filasṭīn wa-yaqūmu sūquhā*); al-Marzūqī, 2:290.
37 *Vita Epiphanii* 1–2 (PG 41:25 BC).
38 Ibn Bahlūl, 177 (*wa-fīhi taqūmu ayḍan sūq bi-nāḥiyat al-Urdunn ʿnd* [or *ʿīd?*] *Bayt Ḥarīr*); al-Bīrūnī, 272; al-Qazwīnī, 1:55.
39 The frontiers of the Jund Filasṭīn (capital al-Ramla) and Jund al-Urdunn (capital Ṭabariyya) varied through time, but the two districts correspond roughly to the Byzantine provinces of Palaestina Prima and Palaestina Secunda; see P. M. Cobb, "Al-Urdunn," in *EI²* 10:952–53 (French edition).

In late antiquity a fair was held in Hammat Gader (al-Hamma), the thermal springs of Gadara on the eastern shore of Lake Tiberias, at the beginning of summer.⁴⁰ The two festivals could be related.

'Asqalān, ancient Askalon on the southern coastline of Palestine: the fair is cited on 15 August by Ibn Bahlūl; though al-Marzūqī does not explicitly mention it, he refers to the festival of Askalon on the same day.⁴¹

Silsila in Jerusalem: this fair is mentioned only by Ibn Bahlūl on 25 August, where it appears in a jumbled citation with two scribal errors.⁴² There is little doubt that the fair was held in Jerusalem, which the author generally calls Īliyāʾ, the ancient Aelia Capitolina.⁴³ As for the name of the fair, we propose reading it as *silsila* (chain), instead of *sīsla*; it could be referring to Qubbat al-Silsila, the Dome of the Chain, one of the minor construction works on the Ḥaram al-Sharīf, built under ʿAbd al-Malik.⁴⁴ Bāb al-Silsila, the Gate of the Chain, might appear more plausible, as fairs were often held at the periphery of cities, but that gate was built at the end of the twelfth century and the name does not appear in sources before the fourteenth century.⁴⁵ A big fair in Jerusalem with "countless people of various nations" coming to trade is also described by the pilgrim Arculf two decades after the Arab conquests. It lasted for several days around 12 September, probably on the occasion of the Feast of the Cross (14 September).⁴⁶ The two fairs could be related in some way.

Manbij, ancient Mabbug or Hierapolis, in northern Syria: the fair is mentioned on 1 September in all the lists except Ibn Māsawayh's.⁴⁷

Raḥba in the Jazīra, a foundation of early ʿAbbāsid times, in northeastern Syria on the Euphrates: the fair is mentioned by al-Marzūqī on 21 September and possibly by Ibn Bahlūl on 20 July, with a scribal error in the manuscript.⁴⁸

A Pre-Islamic Legacy

Although they are mentioned in texts of the Islamic period, many of these fairs, like the sūq Filasṭīn that was seen to be connected to the festival of Saint George, originated in late antiquity or early Byzantium and first developed around a Christian sanctuary on the feast day of the local saint—the so-called *panēgyris* mentioned in Greek sources and still observed today.⁴⁹ Some of these fairs could even have been rooted ultimately in pagan festivals that were eventually Christianized or Islamized in the course of time.⁵⁰

Muslim authors seem generally unaware of the Christian background of most of these fairs. In contrast, Ibn Bahlūl, as a clergyman of the Church of the East, often makes the link between a fair and the Christian festival that occasioned the commercial event. In his *Kitāb al-Dalāʾil*, fairs are mentioned either in the main body of the chapter dedicated to each month, as in other chronological treatises, or at the end of the chapter, in a special section where feast days of Christian saints are listed.⁵¹ The festival and fair of Bayt Jibrīn was held on 15 August; the

---

40 Epiphanios of Salamis, *Panarion* 30.7, ed. K. Holl as *Ancoratus, Panarion (Haereses 1–33)*, GCS 25 (Leipzig, 1915), 342 (PG 41:416–17). See M. Tardieu, *Les paysages reliques: Routes et haltes syriennes d'Isidore à Simplicius* (Louvain, 1990), 13–14; Safrai, *Economy of Roman Palestine*, 252, 257. Although no other source refers explicitly to a fair in early Islamic times, there is evidence of a persistent interest regarding the site of Hammat Gader under the Umayyads; see Muʿāwiya's famous Greek inscription, in Y. Hirschfeld, *The Roman Baths of Hammat Gader* (Jerusalem, 1997), 239.

41 Ibn Bahlūl, 177; Al-Marzūqī, 2:290.

42 Ibn Bahlūl, 178 (read *wa-yawm* [or *wa-yaqūmuʾ*] *sūq Silsila bi-Īliyāʾ* [instead of *Āliyāʾ*] *wa-ʿīduhā*).

43 See, for example, Ibn Bahlūl, 193 (*ʿīd kanīsat al-Qiyāma allātī bi-Īliyāʾ*), referring to the festival of the Church of the Anastasis in Jerusalem. On the use of this name in Arabic sources, see P. M. Cobb, "A Note on ʿUmar's Visit to Ayla in 17/638," *Der Islam* 71 (1994): 283–88, at 284–85.

44 See G. Le Strange, *Palestine under the Moslems: A Description of Syria and the Holy Land from A.D. 650 to 1500* (1890; repr., Beirut, 1965), 151–53; A. Elad, *Medieval Jerusalem and Islamic Worship: Holy Places, Ceremonies, Pilgrimage*, Islamic History and Civilization 8 (Leiden, 1999), 47–48.

45 M. H. Burgoyne, "The Gates of the Ḥaram al-Sharīf," in *Bayt al-Maqdis, ʿAbd al-Malik's Jerusalem, Part One,* ed. J. Raby and J. Johns, Oxford Studies in Islamic Art 9 (Oxford, 1992), 105–24, at 118–19.

46 Adamnan, *De locis sanctis* 1.1.8–10. On a possible reference to the same fair in an eleventh-century document of the Genizah, see Gil, *A History of Palestine,* 242.

47 Ibn Bahlūl, 187; al-Marzūqī, 2:291 (read *Manbij* [instead of *m.n.ī.j*]); al-Bīrūnī, 273; al-Qazwīnī, 1:59.

48 Al-Marzūqī, 2:291; Ibn Bahlūl, 169 (read *Raḥba* [instead of *r.ʿ.n.h*]).

49 See Vryonis, "The *Panēgyris* of the Byzantine Saint"; de Ligt, *Fairs and Markets in the Roman Empire,* 35–39.

50 A famous example is the intercommunity trade fair of the Terebinth at Mamre near Hebron, attended by Christians, pagans, and Jews, that was Christianized under Constantine; see Sozomen, *Historia ecclesiastica* 2.4.

51 These two approaches to categorizing fairs probably caused the duplication of the information in the case of Buṣrā and perhaps Bayt Jibrīn; see above, with notes 31, 38.

author notes that according to the Melkites, the date coincides with the Dormition of the Virgin.[52] The same connection is made in the case of the fair of ʿAsqalān. Al-Marzūqī specifies that 15 August was the feast day of the "death of Mary, daughter of ʿImrān according to the People of the Book," and that a great festival for all Christians was held on this occasion in ʿAsqalān.[53] Bayt Jibrīn is not known to have possessed a pilgrimage shrine dedicated to the Mother of God in antiquity, but ʿAsqalān did have a big church dedicated to "the Virgin called the Green" (Maryam al-Khaḍrāʾ), which was burned down by the Muslims around 940. It was not rebuilt later, as the bishop did not receive permission to undertake new work.[54] In both cities, it is most likely that the mid-August fairs arose locally in connection to the festival of the Dormition of the Virgin.

In most cases, however, the festival that was the occasion for the fair is not clearly stated and must be deduced with the help of liturgical and hagiographical sources. The fair of Aleppo, for example, took place on 16 October, the day following the feast day of two local Aleppine saints, Mār Asyā and Mār Ishʿayāʾ, according to liturgical calendars of the Syrian Orthodox (Jacobite) Church.[55] The Christian festival and the trade fair that were organized in the same city on the same day were doubtless connected. Similarly, the fair of ʿAmmān was held on 10 August and thus coincided with the feast day of the deposition of the relics of the local martyr Aelianos in his martyrium, as given in the *Passion of Aelianos* and liturgical calendars used in Palestine.[56] Again, the fair must have been related in some way to the consecration feast of the shrine of Aelianos.

Evidently, all these fairs did not have equal importance throughout late antiquity and early Islam. In the case of Aleppo and ʿAmmān, a simple panēgyris on the saint's festival day must originally have been held around the shrine of the saint or the martyr. These saints had only a local reputation, and certainly the associated commercial activities were initially insignificant. At some point later, the panēgyris developed from a local event into a more important gathering, and in the subsequent Islamic period, the religious aspect of the Christian festival may well have been forgotten, as the fair became a purely commercial event. The fact is that these gatherings generally enjoy strong continuity, even through political changes, precisely because in most cases their religious and social dimension cannot be dissociated from their commercial purpose.

The shrine at the center of the event guaranteed a fair's success, and it is sometimes mentioned in the calendars. Several fairs are said to have been organized near monasteries or churches on the day of the local festival. As its name indicates, the fair of Dayr Ayyūb took place around the monastery dedicated to the patriarch Job, a famous pilgrimage site for Christians and later for Muslims, from the late fourth century to the present day.[57] At its origin the fair probably coincided with the festival of the patriarch Job, on 6 May. The fair of al-Raqqa was held during the festival of the church of al-Raqqa, but we have no other sources to identify this church or its patron saint.[58] Ibn Bahlūl mentions a fair that was held for five days (between Palm Sunday and Good

---

52 Ibn Bahlūl, 183.
53 Al-Marzūqī, 2:290; Ibn Bahlūl, 177.
54 Yaḥya Ibn Saʿīd, *Taʾrīkh,* ed. J. Kratchovsky and A. Vasiliev as "Histoire de Yahya-Ibn-Saʿïd d'Antioche, continuateur de Saʿïd-ibn-Bitriq," *PO* 18 (1957): 719. The church of the Mother of God is also mentioned in the seventh-century miracles of Anastasios the Persian, ed. B. Flusin as *Saint Anastase le Perse et l'histoire de la Palestine au début du VIIᵉ siècle,* 2 vols. (Paris, 1992), 1:150–51.
55 P. Peeters, "Le martyrologe de Rabban Sliba," *AB* 27 (1908): 129–200, at 140; F. Nau, "Un Martyrologe et douze ménologes syriaques," *PO* 10 (1915): 53, 64, 93, 97, 108, 128; S. Brock, "A Calendar Attributed to Jacob of Edessa," *Parole de l'Orient* 1 (1970): 415–29, at 421. The feast day is also mentioned by Ibn Māsawayh, 242. On these two Aleppine saints, see V. Sauma, *Sur les pas des saints au Liban* (Beirut, 1994), 101, 184–87; and J.-M. Fiey, *Saints syriaques,* Studies in Late Antiquity and Early Islam 6 (Princeton, N.J., 2004), 99–100.
56 G. Garitte, "La Passion de S. Élien de Philadelphie (ʿAmman)," *AB* 79 (1961): 413–46, at 424, 445–46; idem, *Le calendrier palestino-géorgien du Sinaiticus 34 (Xᵉ siècle),* SubsHag 30 (Brussels, 1958), 298–99. See also a tenth-century Syriac Melkite calendar among the Sinai new finds (MS Sinai Syr. M52N): Philothea of Sinai, *Nouveaux manuscrits syriaques du Sinaï* (Athens, 2008), 515.
57 Egeria, *Itinerarium* 16.4–6; John Chrysostom, *Homilia ad populum Antiochenum* 5.1 (PG 49:69); al-Harawī, *Kitāb al-Ishārāt ilā Maʿrifat al-Ziyārāt,* ed. J. Sourdel-Thomine (Damascus, 1953), 16.
58 The only churches known to Syriac sources are the cathedral church of al-Raqqa and the monasteries of the Column and of Mār Zakkai on the outskirts of the city. They are mentioned in particular in the account of the election of Dionysios of Tel-Maḥre to the patriarchate in 818; see Michael the Syrian, *Chronicle* 12.10, ed. J.-B. Chabot as *La Chronique de Michel le Syrien, patriarche jacobite d'Antioche (1166–1199),* 4 vols. (Paris, 1899–1910), 3:43. Syriac sources provide evidence for the existence of a Syrian Orthodox community in al-Raqqa up until the early thirteenth century; see C. F. Robinson, "Ar-Raqqa in the Syriac

Friday) during the festival of the monastery of Harqil, also known as Dayr Ḥazqiāl, near al-Nuʿmāniyya on the Tigris south of al-Madāʾin.⁵⁹ Although al-Bīrūnī does not make the link, the fair of Thaʿālib on 24 September most probably took place at Dayr al-Thaʿālib, a monastery on the outskirts of Baghdad. In a chapter on the "feasts of the Nestorians," he mentions that the monastery's festival was held precisely at that time of the year, on the last Saturday of September.⁶⁰ The fair at Dayr Mār Sarjīs in October was certainly connected to the festival of the patron saint of the monastery, the martyr Sergius, on 7 October. The poet Abū Nuwās (d. 813) evokes the pleasures of pilgrimage to a Sergius shrine (Māsarjusāna), most probably in ʿĀna, and he even compares it to the great Meccan ḥajj.⁶¹

By investigating the religious and devotional circumstances of a fair's origin, we can in some cases locate more precisely the whereabouts of the event. With the exception of Dayr Ayyūb and Muʾta, both connected to shrines in rural areas, all the fairs that are mentioned in the calendars take place in an urban setting. In many cases, when the shrine can be identified from archaeological remains or literary descriptions, they appear to have been situated outside the city walls. In Damascus, one fair was held near Bāb Tūmā, the northeastern gate of the city, and the other in the village of ʿĀliya, now in the southern suburbs of the modern city, where a shrine devoted to the prophet Moses was located.⁶² The martyrium of Aelianos in ʿAmmān was built to the east of the city, next to the cave where, according to the *Passion of Aelianos*, his body had first been deposited.⁶³ The shrines of Ishʿayāʾ or Asyā are not mentioned in Greek, Syriac, or Arabic sources that give lists of the churches of Aleppo. Nonetheless, the tomb of Mār Ishʿayāʾ the Aleppine is still revered today by the Syrian Orthodox Church, and there is an annual procession to it on 15 October. The tomb is found in a Muslim neighborhood outside Bāb al-Naṣr, the northern gate of the medieval city; in this local tradition some recollection of an antique shrine dedicated to the saint may linger. If indeed the fairs of ʿAmmān and Aleppo are to be connected to the shrines of these two saints, it is notable that both took place outside the antique and medieval city walls. In Askalon, according to Talmudic sources, a permanent market that at some point became a fair existed in antiquity. Its relation to the fair of the Dormition of the Virgin on 15 August is not altogether clear, but here again the event originally took place around a pagan shrine "outside the established urban confines of the city."⁶⁴ The organization of fairs on the outskirts of the city is commonly observed in other periods and regions as well. Such placement offers the space needed for so important a commercial event. It also makes unnecessary the entrance of large numbers of foreigners into the city, as it provides a neutral ground for exchange between rural and urban, sedentary and nomadic populations. The location of many fairs on the verge of semi-arid regions seems to point to the latter function.

Trade Networks and Regional and Interregional Exchange

We will now examine the range and scope of these fairs, using the theoretical apparatus elaborated by Luuk de Ligt for the Roman Empire.⁶⁵ On the basis of four criteria— "duration," "distance," "volume," and "type of transaction"—he distinguished three categories of fairs in preindustrial societies, corresponding to different types of exchange: (1) local fairs, of limited duration (one or two days), with a small catchment area (up to 50 kilometers in radius), and direct exchange between producers and consumers; (2) regional fairs that last for one or

---

Historical Tradition," in *Raqqa*, vol. 2, *Die Islamische Stadt*, ed. S. Heidemann and A. Becker (Mainz-am-Rhein, 2003), 81–85.

59 Ibn Bahlūl, 228; see J.-M. Fiey, "Sur le calendrier syriaque oriental arabe de Bar Bahlūl (942/968 A.D.)," *AB* 106 (1988): 259–71, at 264.

60 Al-Bīrūnī, 274, 310. On the location of Dayr al-Thaʿālib, see al-Shābushtī, *al-Diyārāt*, 24–26; Ibn Faḍlallāh al-ʿUmarī, *Masālik al-Abṣār*, 278; Yāqūt, *Muʿjam al-Buldān*, 2:651.

61 See E. Wagner, *Abū Nuwās: Eine Studie zur arabischen Literatur der frühen ʿAbbāsidenzeit* (Wiesbaden, 1965), 111. Other pilgrimage shrines dedicated to Sergios (and his companion Bakchos) were known in late antiquity, especially the famous shrine in Ruṣāfa; see E. K. Fowden, *The Barbarian Plain: Saint Sergius between Rome and Iran* (Berkeley, 1999), and J.-M. Fiey, "Les Saints Serge de l'Iraq," *AB* 79 (1981): 102–14.

62 On Bāb Tūmā, see N. Elisséeff, *La description de Damas d'Ibn ʿAsākir* (Damascus, 1956), 298. On ʿĀliya, see J. Sourdel-Thomine, "Les anciens lieux de pèlerinage damascains d'après les sources arabes," *BEODam* 14 (1952–54): 65–85, at 73.

63 Garitte, "La Passion," 445–46. For a tentative connection of this martyrium with archaeological remains, see 423.

64 Safrai, *Economy of Roman Palestine*, 257.

65 De Ligt, *Fairs and Markets in the Roman Empire*, 78–91.

two weeks and involve an area with a radius of up to 300 kilometers, with large-scale transactions; and (3) interregional fairs, that can last for up to two months, with merchants coming from more than 300 kilometers away; the commodities exchanged in these grand fairs can include luxury goods, and the merchandise may eventually be transported elsewhere; in any case, such trade requires warehouses and storage facilities.

Before considering how long fairs lasted, it is worth noting that they were concentrated in two times of year: spring, during the months of April and May, when two fairs were held (Filasṭīn and Dayr Ayyūb), and the long summer and autumn period from July to early December (especially mid-July to mid-October), when all the other fairs were organized. These two periods correspond to important stages in the annual agricultural cycle, sowing (early spring) and harvest (summer and early autumn). They were generally viewed as sacred times in many Semitic religions of antiquity, and religious festivals and fairs were usually held during these periods of truce.[66] Rivalries were put aside, commercial taxes were abolished, and ancient authors often observe how trade seemed to benefit from some kind of supernatural power that was active during these sacred periods.[67] That these were still the two main trading seasons in the medieval period to some extent recalls the pre-Islamic and even pre-Christian heritage of many of these fairs with roots in Semitic religions; but primarily, it underscores that these fairs met an economic necessity in following the seasonal calendar of agriculture. It is very likely that originally the timing of these fairs coincided with the marketing of agricultural and pastoral produce, although it is difficult to judge the extent to which they still served this function in the medieval period. These were also the seasons when trading routes were passable, and the lack of a single fair during the winter months, from late December to mid-April, could imply that these fairs depended partly on long-distance trade, whether by sea or by land routes.

The duration of fairs in Bilād al-Shām, when specified in the calendars, varied between one and six weeks. The spring fairs of Filasṭīn and Dayr Ayyūb lasted a week;[68] Salamiyya and Adhriʿāt, two weeks;[69] and Buṣrā, a month or more.[70] The length could also vary over time as a particular fair's importance changed. For example, al-Bīrūnī observes that the fair of Buṣrā had declined between the Umayyad and ʿAbbāsid periods: "On this day [i.e., 10 Tammūz], they begin to hold the fair of Buṣrā during twenty-five days; in the time of the Banū Umayya this fair used to last thirty to forty days."[71]

The catchment area of these fairs is more difficult to assess, and, like their duration, it certainly changed over time. The first element to be considered in an attempt to define it more precisely is the distance between fairs. Except in Ḥawrān and Filasṭīn, two regions discussed below, the distance between two fairs ranged from 80 to 250 kilometers. To the south of Damascus, the fairs of Buṣrā, ʿAmmān, and Muʾta are set out along a line at regular intervals of 100 kilometers. To the north of Damascus the distances between Salamiyya, Aleppo, and al-Raqqa are closer to 200 kilometers; these greater distances are probably explained in part by the geography of northern Syria, which results in cities being further apart. When two fairs, such as those of Aleppo and Adhriʿāt in mid-October or Buṣrā and Salamiyya in mid-July, were held at the same time, the distances between them are doubled, to 500 and 350 kilometers, respectively. The concurrent fairs on

---

66 Among other references, see J. Henninger, *Les fêtes de printemps chez les sémites et la Pâque israélite* (Paris, 1975); D. Sourdel, *Les cultes du Hauran à l'époque romaine*, Bibliothèque archéologique et historique 53 (Paris, 1952), 109–11; and T. Kaizer, *The Religious Life of Palmyra: A Study of the Social Patterns of Worship in the Roman Period* (Stuttgart, 2002), 203–11; for Arabia, see Wellhausen, *Reste arabischen Heidentums*, 96–101.

67 On the abolition of taxes during fairs in late antiquity, see de Ligt, *Fairs and Markets in the Roman Empire*, 256–58. In pre-Islamic Arabia, in contrast, taxes were levied at all fairs except ʿUkāẓ by the tribes under whose protection the fairs were organized; see M. Lecker, "Were Customs Dues Levied at the Time of the Prophet Muḥammad?" *Al-Qanṭara* 22 (2001): 19 43, at 24–29. Buṣrā appears to have been under the protection of the Jafnids, who collected taxes there, although it is not certain that the same was true of the pre-Islamic fair; see M. Lecker, "The Levying of Taxes for the Sassanians in Pre-Islamic Medina," *Jerusalem Studies in Arabic and Islam* 27 (2002): 109–26, at 115–20. Concerning supernatural events, Adamnan, *De locis sanctis* 1.1.10, tells how rain miraculously washed away all the refuse the day following the end of the fair of Jerusalem; see also the description of the fair of Edessa by Gregory of Tours, *De gloria martyrum* 32.

68 Ibn Bahlūl, 98; al-Marzūqī, 2:287, 288; al-Bīrūnī, 260. One week is the most common duration of fairs in other regions: see al-Bīrūnī, 234 (sūq al-Ṭawāwīs), 235 (sūq al-Sharj); and al-Marzūqī 2:283 (sūq al-Qādisān).

69 Al-Marzūqī, 2:289; al-Bīrūnī, 272; according to Ibn Bahlūl (168), the fair of Salamiyya lasted only eight days.

70 Ibn Bahlūl, 172; al-Bīrūnī, 271.

71 Al-Bīrūnī, 267; trans. Sachau, *Chronology*, 259.

either side of the Jordan Valley in August and those of Dayr Ayyūb and Filasṭīn in April were separated by some 150 kilometers. All these figures suggest that a distance of 80 to 250 kilometers could be a first rough estimate of the catchment area of these fairs.

Other evidence, however, seems to indicate that the fairs of Bilād al-Shām could also draw visitors from farther afield. The fair of Jerusalem in the seventh century was said to attract "countless people of various nations."[72] In his description of the fair of Dayr Ayyūb, Master Thietmar, a thirteenth-century pilgrim from Germany, lists "Arabs, Parthians, Idumians, Syrians, and Turks" among those gathered for the annual event.[73] Although the reference applies to a later period, it makes clear that the event had acquired an interregional importance after the Crusades. The commercial activities of the Meccan tribe of Quraysh in the cities of Buṣrā, Adhri'āt, and Gaza at the time of the rise of Islam are frequently referred to in Arabic sources.[74] In one biographical tradition, Muḥammad himself is said to have encountered at the fair of Buṣrā the monk Baḥīra who recognized him as a future prophet.[75] The importance of the fair of Buṣrā in the Umayyad period confirms that it certainly had not lost its drawing power beyond its own region. The same apparently held true in other parts of the Islamic Empire. In his chapter on the Sogdians, al-Bīrūnī notes that in al-Ṭawāwīs "the merchants of all countries gather and hold a fair of seven days duration."[76]

The region of Ḥawrān is a densely populated area where three fairs were held within 30 to 40 kilometers of one another: Dayr Ayyūb in April, Buṣrā in July, and Adhri'āt in October. Al-Bīrūnī's remark on the first of these annual events provides some insight into how these fairs were connected:

Nisān 23. People hold a fair at Dayr Ayyūb. Abū Yaḥyā b. Kunāsa says that the Pleiades disappear under the rays of the sun during forty days, and this fair is held when the Pleiades appear. So the Syrians make them rise fifteen days earlier than in reality they rise, because they are in a hurry to settle their affairs. This fair lasts seven days. Then they count seventy days until the fair of Buṣrā. Through these fairs, that are held alternately in certain places, the commerce of these countries has been promoted and their wealth been increased. They have proved profitable to the people, to both buyers and sellers.[77]

Trying to explain the commercial appeal of the event, the astronomer calculates the date of the fair according to the position of stars, without taking into account that the fair originally coincided with the Christian festival of the patriarch Job on 6 May, the precise time when the Pleiades appear in the sky. It is likely that the festival had lost its importance or even ceased to be celebrated. The shrine dedicated to Job at the center of the fair, now Islamized and transformed into a mosque, was the only vestige of the event's religious and social origin.[78] The date of the fair had itself been moved forward, apparently for purely commercial purposes (probably influenced by the nearby and concurrent fair of Buṣrā), and al-Bīrūnī clearly underlines the fact that the fairs of Dayr Ayyūb and Buṣrā were interdependent and part of a set annual cycle that fulfilled a regional economic function. From the sixth to the eighth centuries, Buṣrā was by far the most important fair in the region. By the very end of the tenth century, when al-Bīrūnī was writing, it had lost some of its former fame and it had been shortened, though it still lasted longer and was more significant than its two counterparts.[79] Conversely, the fair of Dayr Ayyūb, which may originally have served only as a local market, was acquiring new status and its date had been changed to give it more visibility. The

---

72   See note 46, above.
73   *Magister Thietmari Peregrinatio* 3, ed. J. C. M. Laurent (Hamburg, 1857); trans. C. Deluz, in *Croisades et pèlerinages: Récits, chroniques et voyages en Terre Sainte XIIe–XVIe siècle*, ed. D. Régnier-Bohler (Paris, 1997), 928–58, at 934.
74   See Crone, *Meccan Trade*, 115–18, who cites the sources on the commercial activities of the Quraysh tribe from Mecca in Syria, particularly in Buṣrā, Adhri'āt, and Gaza.
75   Ibn Hishām, *Sīrat al-Nabawiyya*, ed. F. Wüstenfeld as *Das Leben Muhammed's nach Muhammed Ibn Iskâk bearbeitet von Abd-el-Malik Ibn Hishâm*, 2 vols. (Göttingen, 1858–60), 1:119; see Crone, *Meccan Trade*, 219–20. On the trading activities of the Quraysh in Jordan and Palestine, see also A.-L. de Prémare, *Les fondations de l'Islam: Entre écriture et histoire* (Paris, 2002), 33–81.
76   Al-Bīrūnī, 234; trans. Sachau, *Chronology*, 221.

77   Al-Bīrūnī, 260–61; trans. Sachau, *Chronology*, 251.
78   J.-F. Legrain, "Variations musulmanes sur le thème de Job," *BEODam* 37–38 (1985–86): 51–114.
79   The most northern portion of the highway between Damascus and Mecca deviated from its original course in the 'Abbāsid period and went directly from Damascus through Adhri'āt to 'Ammān, bypassing Buṣrā. This shift may account for the waning importance of the fair of Buṣrā after the Umayyad period.

process is confirmed by Thietmar's report, some two or more centuries later, that it was an event of international scope. Moreover, the three annual fairs of Dayr Ayyūb, Buṣrā, and Adhriʿāt, within a circle of some 40 kilometers in diameter and held alternately every two or three months from spring to autumn, formed a trading network that ensured the prosperity of the region of Ḥawrān by providing a regional commercial outlet.[80]

Filasṭīn offers a slightly different picture, as its three fairs—in Bayt Jibrīn, ʿAsqalān, and Jerusalem, only 30 kilometers from one another—were held at approximately the same time, during the second half of August. Summer was the high season, and the competition between neighboring fairs could have enhanced trade. But it is also possible that one could overshadow the other, if two events were held simultaneously at insufficient physical distance. Assuming that these were not just local fairs, they likely either followed each other directly, enabling merchants to go from one to the other, or offered specialized goods, catering to different buyers and sellers. For now, we lack the evidence to do more than speculate.

Of de Ligt's four criteria, the volume and type of commodities exchanged at these fairs are the most difficult to determine. Sometimes Arab geographers give a glimpse of the locally and regionally produced agricultural and manufactured goods that could be traded in these fairs. The tenth-century geographer al-Muqaddasī praises ʿAsqalān for the quality of its silkworms and manufactured textiles.[81] From al-Raqqa came fine soap and olives.[82] ʿAmmān was renowned for grain, sheep, and honey; Aleppo, for cotton and clothing; al-Ramla and Filasṭīn, for figs and olive oil; and Damascus for precious fabric, copperware, olive oil, figs, raisins, and nuts.[83] Indeed, al-Bīrūnī specifies that the December fair of Damascus (sūq Tūmā) was called "the fair of the cutting of the ben-nut."[84] Buṣrā was famous since antiquity for its wine and its grain.[85]

Many of the cities in which the fairs were held are also described by Arab geographers as important trading centers. Ibn Ḥawqal, a contemporary of al-Muqqadasī, reports that al-Raqqa was a thriving city before the time of Sayf al-Dawla, the emir of Aleppo and northern Syria between 945 and 967. It was then the most important city in the district of Diyār Muḍar, and its prosperity was due to its low prices and beautiful markets.[86] A recent archaeological survey has also revealed an important commercial and industrial area for the production of glass and ceramics, just outside the city. Its main period of activity spans the late eighth century, when the city of al-Raqqa was chosen as the caliphal residence by Hārūn al-Rashīd, until it declined and fell into ruin at the end of the ninth or the beginning of the tenth century.[87] Ibn Ḥawqal (citing al-Iṣṭakhrī) reports that before the Byzantine reconquest by Nikephoros in 961, Aleppo "was very populous, and the people were possessed of much wealth, and commerce throve, for the city lies on the high road between Iraq and the fortresses (al-Thuġūr), and the rest of Syria"; he also mentions its beautiful markets.[88] Many of the cities in which fairs were held combine a location on a main commercial route and all the facilities needed for long-distance trade: well-supplied markets, industrial quarters, accommodations, and warehouses. Although fairs are never explicitly mentioned in these texts, the existence of such infrastructure suggests that they functioned as redistribution centers in an interregional trading network.

---

80 This regional trading network functioned much like those known in other regions, such as late Byzantine Peloponnesos and Epiros; see C. Asdracha, "Les foires en Épire médiévale: La fonction justificative de la mémoire historique," *JÖB* 32 (1982): 437–46; D. A. Zakythinos, *Le Despotat grec de Morée*, 2nd ed., 2 vols. (London, 1975), 2:253–54.

81 Al-Muqaddasī, *Aḥsan*, 174; see Gil, *A History of Palestine*, 240.

82 Al-Muqaddasī, *Aḥsan*, 141, 145; see S. Heidemann, "The History of the Industrial and Commercial Area of ʿAbbāsid Al-Raqqa, called Al-Raqqa Al-Muḥtariqa," *BSOAS* 69 (2006): 33–52, at 41.

83 Al-Muqaddasī, *Aḥsan*, 180–81. For the production of cotton in Aleppo and northern Syria, see A.-M. Eddé, *La principauté ayyoubide d'Alep (579/1183–658/1260)*, Freiburger Islamstudien 21 (Stuttgart, 1999), 496, 514–15. Olive oil has been an important Palestinian export since antiquity; see Gil, *A History of Palestine*, 236–37.

84 Al-Bīrūnī, 248; trans. Sachau, *Chronology*, 237.

85 Al-Muqqadasī, *Aḥsan*, 152; al-Ṭabarī, *Taʾrīkh al-Rusul wa-l-Mulūk*, ed. M. J. De Goeje, 3 vols. (Leiden, 1879–1901), 1:1089; see M. Sartre, *Bostra: Des origines à l'islam*, Bibliothèque archéologique et historique 117 (Paris, 1985), 129–30.

86 Ibn Ḥawqal, *Kitāb Ṣūrat al-Arḍ*, ed. J. H. Kramers as *Opus geographicum auctore Ibn Haukal*, Bibliotheca Geographorum Arabicorum 2 (Leiden, 1873), 225; see also al-Muqaddasī, *Aḥsan*, 141.

87 Heidemann, "Al-Raqqa Al-Muḥtariqa."

88 Al-Iṣṭakhrī, *Kitāb al-Masālik wa-l-Mamālik*, ed. M. J. De Goeje as *Viae Regnorum: Descriptio ditionis Moslemicae*, Bibliotheca Geographorum Arabicorum 1 (Leiden, 1870), 61; Ibn Ḥawqal, *Kitāb Aḥsan al-Aḥsan*, 177; trans. Le Strange, *Palestine*, 360.

Warehouses might also serve in redistribution, on a smaller, more regional scale. Before its decline in al-Muqaddasī's time, Bayt Jibrīn is said to have catered to the provincial capital of al-Ramla, acting as the district's granary in the middle of a land of riches and plenty.[89] Already in the fourth century, the *Life of Epiphanios* describes the attempt of the saint, who was a native of Eleutheropolis, to sell his widowed mother's sole possession, an ox yoke, at his city's fair.[90] This story suggests that it served mainly as a market for local and regional exchange rather than long-distance trade.

All in all, assessing the fairs listed in these calendars according to the four criteria of duration, distance, volume, and type of transaction leads to the conclusion that they appear to have catered to regional and interregional exchange. Each and every fair had its own characteristics that changed over time. For example, the fair of Buṣrā, which lasted forty days in the Umayyad period and attracted merchants from the Ḥijāz, doubtless had an interregional dimension in late antiquity and early Islam. In contrast, the fair of Bayt Jibrīn, which served as a cattle and stocking market for its district, probably had only regional importance inside the Jund Filasṭīn. But they had in common a function beyond the local scale. The texts that have preserved lists of fairs inside Bilād al-Shām were all produced in the regions of Iraq and Iran and for these lists relied mainly on earlier written sources. Were Syrian fairs only of local importance, it is unlikely that their fame would have spread to such remote eastern regions.

Routes, Ports, and Foreign Trade

While the regions of Ḥawrān and Filasṭīn constituted two small networks on a regional scale, most fairs were part of larger networks that must be examined in relation to trade routes and foreign trade in a broader historical perspective. As their development in the Islamic period is part of long-term economic trends, it is best to begin by considering them in comparison with what is known of fairs in late antiquity. Three main groups of fairs that coincide partially with existing late antique networks can thus be distinguished inside Bilād al-Shām.

A first group of fairs south of Damascus covers southern Syria and Jordan. Most of these fairs (Damascus, Buṣrā, ʿAmmān, Muʾta) are set out roughly along a north-to-south axis that follows the Via Nova built by Trajan; it coincides with the caravan route between the Ḥijāz and Syria, and later the *Darb al-ḥajj*, the pilgrimage route from Damascus to Mecca.[91] The fairs are usually located at important crossroads along the highway. ʿAmmān is at the crossroads with the westbound road across the Jordan River to Jerusalem and Filasṭīn, while Buṣrā and Adhriʿāt are on another road from the Ḥawrān to Ṭabariyya and al-Urdunn. That fairs are found on major routes—and, more important, at crossroads—does not come as a surprise, and the same pattern can be observed in other regions. Although the volume of traffic and the particular type of trade along this highway between the Ḥijāz and Syria have been the subject of much scholarly debate, the existence of commercial relations in the sixth and seventh centuries is beyond question.[92] The Islamic traditions are unanimous in describing the trading activities of the Meccan tribe of Quraysh in Adhriʿāt and Buṣrā, the latter probably serving as one of the main emporiums for ingoing and outgoing caravans.[93] There is no reason to deny the existence of the fairs of Buṣrā and Adhriʿāt before the advent of Islam. The development of these fairs and others along this highway is evidently related to the considerable prosperity and economic growth of the Balqāʾ and Ḥawrān regions during the sixth to eighth century, as attested by extensive archaeological excavations in Jordan over the past decades.[94] If we can credit our sources, the

---

89 Al-Muqaddasī, *Aḥsan*, 174.
90 *Vita Epiphanii* 1–2 (PG 41:25 BC).
91 On the portion of the Damascus–Mecca highway in southern Bilād al-Shām and northern Ḥijāz that was separated into three concurrent branches, see G. R. D. King, "The Distribution of Sites and Routes in the Jordanian and Syrian Deserts in the Early Islamic Period," *Proceedings of the Seminar for Arabian Studies* 17 (1987): 91–105; Y. Frenkel, "Roads and Stations in Southern Bilād al-Shām in the 7th–8th Centuries," *Aram* 8 (1996): 177–88.
92 For a recent reassessment of the issues at stake in the debate on Meccan trade, see G. W. Heck, "Arabia without Spices: An Alternate Hypothesis," *JAOS* 123 (2003): 547–76; and P. Crone, "Quraysh and the Roman Army: Making Sense of the Leather Trade," *BSOAS* 70 (2007): 63–88.
93 See note 74, above.
94 See R. Paret, "Les villes de Syrie du Sud et les routes commerciales d'Arabie à la fin du VIᵉ siècle," in *Akten des XI. internationalen Byzantinistenkongresses, München, 1958*, ed. F. Dölger and H.-G. Beck (Munich, 1960), 438–44. On the economic development of Ḥawrān during the sixth to eighth centuries,

peak of activity of this regional network was reached under the Umayyads, as al-Bīrūnī's remark on the length of the fair of Buṣrā during that period suggests. With two annual fairs, Damascus appears to have had special status in the network as the highway's northern terminus. Moreover, in the Umayyad period the city was the capital of the Islamic Empire, generating a growing demand for all kinds of commodities. Ibn Māsawayh, author of the earliest extant calendar, mentions exclusively these fairs in southern Bilād al-Shām. In later sources, this network is often listed only in part, as if its importance was already on the wane, while networks in other regions were in expansion.

The second group of fairs makes up a network in Palestine. It comprises Jerusalem, ʿAsqalān, Bayt Jibrīn, the fair of Filasṭīn in Ludd or al-Ramla, and possibly the fair of al-Urdunn near Ṭabariyya (Tiberias). Although no comparable source systematically documents fairs in antiquity, no fewer than ten fairs in Palestine are recorded in various Christian and Jewish Talmudic sources of the fourth to seventh centuries: Jerusalem, Skythopolis (Baysān), Eleutheropolis, Butna (Mamre) near Hebron, Hammat Gader on the eastern shore of Lake Tiberias, and the coastal cities of Gaza (Ghazza), Askalon, Ptolemais (ʿAkkā), Maritime Caesarea (Qaysāriyya), and Tyre (Ṣūr).[95] In some places, such as Jerusalem, Eleutheropolis, or Askalon, the continuity between antiquity and the Islamic period is obvious. We have also seen that other fairs attested in our medieval sources have their roots in the earlier period. Conversely, it is likely that some of the antique fairs continued to exist into Islamic times. Nonetheless, it is striking that apparently none of the numerous antique fairs on the Mediterranean coastline, except for Askalon, continued into the Islamic period.

Located at the south of the coastline of Palestine, Gaza was the terminus of one of the branches of the route from Arabia in the sixth to seventh centuries, but also more generally of incoming trade from the Red Sea, and the fairs that were held in that seaport probably benefited from its status as an international market.[96] Farther north, beyond the limits of Palestine, in the fifth to sixth centuries Aegae (Āyās) in Cilicia was the site of a tax-free maritime fair lasting forty days.[97] In one of his letters, Theodoret of Cyrrhus reports that it was visited by large numbers of merchants from the western provinces of the empire.[98] This annual fair probably served as a commercial outlet for the Far Eastern trade of spices and silk. The continuous string of maritime fairs along the eastern Mediterranean coastline thus played a role in antiquity as trading centers and contributed to the prosperous trans-Mediterranean trade in the Roman Empire. Yet during the first centuries of the caliphate, our sources appear to completely ignore the Mediterranean coastline. Even ʿAsqalān, though a prosperous city in the medieval period, had acquired a bad reputation as a harbor, probably because of silting, and al-Muqaddasī describes its "unsafe harbor" and "brackish waters."[99] The fair that was held there was apparently not oriented toward the sea. Although it has been shown that maritime trade in the Mediterranean was not altogether extinct after the Islamic conquests, its decline both in volume and scope was significant in the eighth to ninth centuries in comparison with the former.[100] There was no

---

see M. Sartre, "Le Hawran byzantin à la veille de la conquête musulmane," in *Proceedings of the Second Symposium on the History of Bilad al-Sham during the Early Islamic Period up to 40 A.H./640 A.H.: The Fourth International Conference on the History of Bilad al-Sham,* vol. 1 (Amman, 1987), 155–67. The archaeological evidence brought to light over the past decades for the prosperity of the Balqāʾ during the same period is impressive; see H. I. MacAdam, "Settlements and Settlement Patterns in Northern and Central Transjordan, ca. 550–ca. 750," in *The Byzantine and Early Islamic Near East,* vol. 2, *Land Use and Settlement Patterns,* ed. G. R. D. King and A. Cameron, Studies in Late Antiquity and Early Islam 1 (Princeton, N.J., 1994), 49–93; A. Walmsley, *Early Islamic Syria: An Archaeological Assessment* (London, 2007).

95 See de Ligt, *Fairs and Markets in the Roman Empire,* 255–56, with references; Safrai, *Economy of Roman Palestine,* 239–62.

96 On the antique fairs in Gaza, see F. K. Litsas, "Choricius of Gaza and His Descriptions of Festivals at Gaza," *JÖB* 32 (1982): 427–36.

97 Theodosius, *De Situ Terrae Sanctae* 32.

98 Theodoret of Cyrrhus, *Epistulae* 70 (PG 83:1240 A–C).

99 Al-Muqaddasī, *Aḥsan,* 174; trans. Le Strange, *Palestine,* 40. Among the earlier sources that provide evidence for important maritime activities in Askalon, see in particular the numerous references in the sixth-century *Vita Nicolai Sionitae,* ed. G. Anrich as *Hagios Nikolaos: Der heilige Nikolaos in der griechischen Kirche,* 2 vols. (Berlin, 1913–17), 1:3–35; see H. Magoulias, "The Lives of Saints as Sources of Data for the History of Commerce in the Byzantine Empire in the VIth and VIIth Cent.," Κληρονομία 3 (1971): 303–30, esp. 314.

100 Pirenne's thesis (*Mahomet et Charlemagne* [Brussels, 1937]) of a complete interruption of trans-Mediterranean trade after the Islamic conquests that would account for the so-called dark ages in western Europe has been strongly disputed; see a reassessment in C. Picard's preface to the most recent edition (Paris, 2005) with

major disruption in the occupation of the coastal cities after the Islamic conquests. On the contrary, the Umayyads implemented a clear policy of fortifying the coastline against Byzantine attacks.[101] However, the real expansion of commercial activity in harbors and the recovery of maritime trade in the Mediterranean took place only in the later ninth and tenth centuries under the Ṭūlūnids and the Fāṭimids.[102] These factors might explain why our sources do not mention fairs along the coastline.

The third group of fairs, those north of Damascus, cover northern Bilād al-Shām and the Jazīra. Most of these fairs are situated in a crescent that follows the Euphrates axis from Aleppo to Baghdad, which was also a portion of one of the main highways of the caliphate: the Ṭarīq al-Barīd, the post road.[103] Here again, fairs are located at important crossroads. Aleppo was the terminus for the roads toward the north and the east. Manbij, al-Raqqa, Raḥba, and ʿĀna (Dayr Mār Sarjīs) are all situated at strategic points with crossings on the river. Salamiyya is at the crossroad of the north-to-south route between Aleppo and Damascus and the eastbound route across the desert that meets the Euphrates Valley at Raḥba. Comparing this network to the geographic distribution of fairs in northern Syria and Mesopotamia during late antiquity again brings to light major changes between the two periods.[104]

Our knowledge of their geographic distribution is naturally very uneven, dependent on available material; yet it is striking that the main annual fairs of late antiquity that are known—Arsamosata (Shimshāṭ), Amida (Āmid), Edessa (al-Ruhā), and Batnae (Sarūj)—are all set along a northern route across Armenia that was a branch of the trade route to Central Asia in the Roman and early Byzantine period.[105] The one-month fair in Edessa during the annual festival of the apostle Thomas was certainly one of the major attractions for merchants, as its fame stretched to the western parts of the empire. It functioned as an emporium for spices and perfumes.[106] The fair of Batnae at the beginning of September had an equally high reputation as an exchange market for goods from India and China, probably including silk.[107] The western terminus of this route for spices and silk trade was either Antioch or the seaport of Aegae, where, as already mentioned, every year an international maritime fair was held for forty days. During the medieval period, the fairs were set along the Euphrates axis much further to the south. Thus in northern Syria there appears to be no real continuity between the Byzantine and the Islamic periods, probably because the frontier lines moved with the Islamic conquests, radically changing the routes of long-distance trade on which the network of the Byzantine period depended.[108] Indeed, the Euphrates route did not exist as such in the sixth century, since it lay on the frontier between the Byzantine and the Persian empires. Conversely, in the ninth and tenth centuries, the northern route through Edessa passed through regions disputed between the Arabs and the Byzantines that were continually changing hands.

---

the main references, in particular R. Hodges and D. Whitehouse, *Mohammed, Charlemagne and the Origins of Europe* (London, 1983), and M. McCormick, *Origins of the European Economy: Communications and Commerce, A.D. 300–900* (Cambridge, 2001). More specifically on maritime trade inside the caliphate, see E. Ashtor, *A Social and Economic History of the Near East in the Middle Ages* (Glasgow, 1976), 100–109.

101 See A. Borrut, "Architecture des espaces portuaires et réseaux défensifs du littoral syro-palestinien dans les sources arabes (7e–11e siècles)," *Archéologie islamique* 11 (2001): 21–46.

102 See Walmsley, "Production, Exchange and Regional Trade," 291–99.

103 On the Ṭarīq al-Barīd in the Umayyad and ʿAbbāsid periods, see A. J. Silverstein, *Postal Systems in the Pre-Modern Islamic World* (Cambridge, 2007), 60–66, 92–99.

104 See de Ligt, *Fairs and Markets in the Roman Empire*, 255–56, with references. A fair at Imma on the highway between Aleppo and Antioch in the fifth century is mentioned in Theodoret of Cyrrhus, *Historia Religiosa* 7.2–3. Another fair more to the east in Melqi near Arbela is mentioned in the early seventh-century *History of Mar Qardagh*; see J. Walker, "The Legacy of Mesopotamia in Late Antique Iraq: The Christian Martyr Shrine at Melqi (Neo-Assyrian Milqia)," *Aram* 18–19 (2006–07): 483–508, at 498.

105 The Far Eastern trade route parted in two branches in Seleucia-Ctesiphon, one going north to Antioch, the other south to Petra via the Persian Gulf; see J. I. Miller, *The Spice Trade of the Roman Empire: 29 B.C. to A.D. 641* (Oxford, 1969), chap. 7.

106 Gregory of Tours, *De gloria martyrum* 32; John of Ephesos, *Lives of Eastern Saints* 21, *PO* 17 (1923): 293; and *Vita Symeonis Stylitae Iunoris* 1; see Magoulias, "The Lives of Saints," 306.

107 Ammianus Marcellinus, *Res gestae* 14.3.3; on the fair of Batnae, see U. Monneret de Villard, "La Fiera di Batnae e la traslazione di S. Tomaso a Edessa," *AttiLinc, Rendiconti, Classe di Scienze Morali, Storiche e Filologiche*, ser. 8, 6 (1951): 77–104.

108 It is worth noting, however, that the fair of Batnae in antiquity and the fair of Manbij in the medieval period were both held at the beginning of September. It is unlikely that two important fairs took place so close to one another in time and space (the two cities are less than 100 km apart). It may be that the fair of Batnae was at some point transferred to Manbij.

The development of the network of fairs in northern Bilād al-Shām documented in our sources is certainly related to the development of the Euphrates axis to Baghdad, which accompanied the shift of political and economic power from Bilād al-Shām to Iraq under the ʿAbbāsids. Without question, the Euphrates became an important commercial route for inland transportation in the late eighth and ninth centuries.[109] After it became the caliphal residence for a little more than a decade under Hārūn al-Rashīd (786–809), al-Raqqa is known to have been one of the region's main river ports.[110] Raḥba, a city newly founded, according to the legend, in the early ninth century by Mālik b. Ṭawq under the caliphate of al-Maʾmūn (813–33), was also known as a port for inland transportation. Its position on the Ṭarīq al-Furāt, the Euphrates road between al-Raqqa and Baghdad, was highly strategic, at the point where the caravan routes from Damascus, Salamiyya, Ḥimṣ, and Ḥamā reach the Euphrates Valley; it was also the starting point of the routes toward al-Mawṣil to the east and the Diyār Muḍar to the north along the Khābūr Valley.[111] The clear caliphal policy to develop the Jazīra, already in place under the last Umayyads; the economic growth of the region in the eighth and ninth centuries; and its subsequent decline in the second half of the tenth century under Ḥamdanid rule thus delineate the historical framework within which the network of fairs in northern Bilād al-Shām developed and reached its heyday.[112]

* * * * * * * *

Our sources on annual fairs in Bilād al-Shām provide only scarce evidence to analyze the realia and the particularities of these trading events inside the Islamic Empire as opposed to other regions of the antique and medieval world. Nonetheless, they attest without any doubt to the continuity and vitality of this institution from late antique into Islamic times, albeit with important regional disruptions caused by the changing patterns of international trade brought by the establishment of the caliphate inside regions that had been previously controlled by the Byzantines. The networks for regional and interregional trade, first in Filasṭīn and along the Damascus–Mecca highway, both inherited from late antiquity, then in the northeast along the Euphrates axis, developed in accordance with the economic expansion and decline of the regions in which they were established, following the shift of power inside the Islamic Empire from Damascus to Baghdad, and more generally from Bilād al-Shām to the more eastern provinces of Iraq and Iran.

---

109 See the famous description of Baghdad as the center of the universe, with merchandise coming from all parts of the world down the Euphrates and the Tigris, in al-Yaʿqūbī, *Kitāb al-Buldān,* ed. M. J. De Goeje, Bibliotheca Geographorum Arabicorum 7 (Leiden, 1892), 237. In an often-cited passage of Ibn Khurradādhbih, one of the trade routes of the Jewish Rādhānite merchants from the West is said to have been across the sea to Antioch, then along the Euphrates to Baghdad and the Far East: *Kitāb al-Masālik wa-l-Mamālik,* ed. M. J. De Goeje, Bibliotheca Geographorum Arabicorum 6 (Leiden, 1889), 154.

110 For the development of shipping activities at the port of al-Raqqa, see the extensive references in S. Heidemann, "Die Geschichte von ar-Raqqa/Ar-Rāfiqa: Ein Überblick," in Heidemann and Becker, eds., *Die Islamische Stadt,* 9–56, at 29 and nn. 221–22. To these can be added an early mention of trade along the Euphrates in an alternative version of the martyrdom of Anthony (d. 799), ed. B. Pirone as "Un altro manoscritto sulla vita e sul martirio del nobile qurayshita Rawḥ," in *Biblica et Semitica: Studi in memoria di Francesco Vattioni,* ed. L. Cagni, Dipartimento di Studi Asiatici, Series Minor 59 (Naples, 1999), 479–509, at 505.

111 See E. Honigmann and T. Bianquis, "Raḥba," in *EI*² 8:407–10 (French edition); T. Bianquis, "Raḥba et les tribus arabes avant les Croisades," *BEODam* 41–42 (1989–90 [1993]): 23–51; M.-O. Rousset, "La ville de Raḥba Mayādīn et sa région IXᵉ–XIVᵉ siècle," *BEODam* 52 (2000): 243–61.

112 On the development of the Jazīra already into a prosperous province under the last Umayyads, see C. Robinson, *Empire and Elites after the Muslim Conquest: The Transformation of Northern Mesopotamia,* Cambridge Studies in Islamic Civilization (Cambridge, 2000), 33–62; A. Borrut, *Entre mémoire et pouvoir: L'espace syrien sous les derniers Omeyyades et les premiers Abbasides (v. 72–193/692–809),* Islamic History and Civilization 81 (Leiden, 2010), 383–466.

• TWELVE •

Trade and Economy in Antioch and Cilicia in the Twelfth and Thirteenth Centuries

SCOTT REDFORD

In this chapter I consider the coincidence, or lack thereof, of states and markets. In its first section, I propose that the founding of the Principality of Antioch on the model of the Byzantine Duchy of Antioch led to a geographical, administrative, and economic imbalance. Geography linked the city of Antioch and its hinterland more closely with the Cilician plain/Çukurova to the north, but the principality's major port, Laodikeia/al-Lādhaqiyya/Lattakia/Lazkiye, and all of the principality's territory south of it along the northern Syrian coast lay apart. This disjunction between geography and polity had important implications for the economy of the region and the nature of the principality itself, as the chapter's second section—an examination of specific questions raised by medieval period excavations in the region—makes clear.

Askew: Polity and Historical Precedent

In the late eleventh and early twelfth century, the Norman Principality of Antioch constituted itself largely along the lines of the Byzantine Duchy of Antioch, and Byzantine territories in northern Syria were geographically askew. Antioch lies on the Orontes/ʿĀṣī/Asi River some 30 kilometers distant from the Mediterranean (figs. 13.1 and 13.2). The port town called Port Saint Symeon/al-Suwaydiya/Samandağ near the mouth of the Orontes had replaced the nearby silted-up Hellenistic and Roman port of Seleukeia Pieria/Çevlik sometime after the sixth century. Medieval societies preferred ports that were viable without dredging, and therefore far from the mouths of rivers. Medieval Muslims called the Orontes Nahr al-ʿĀṣī, "the Rebellious River," for its frequent and often violent flooding, but the city of Antioch had no immediate alternative to its mouth as the location for a port.[1]

[1] Every student of this region needs to acknowledge a debt to two very different books, Claude Cahen's *La Syrie du nord à l'époque des croisades et la principauté franque d'Antioche* (Paris, 1940) and Friedrich Hild and Hansgerd Hellenkemper's *Kilikien und Isaurien*, TIB 5 (1990). These two books give far more copious and various information than what is found in this chapter. Rather than being comprehensive, I have here presented textual, numismatic, survey, and excavation data pertaining to a reexamination of well-known issues based on recent archaeological fieldwork in the region. Acknowledgments are due to the following scholars: Timothy Beach, Kinet excavation director Marie-Henriette Gates, Fokke Gerritsen, symposiarch Cécile Morrisson, Pagona Papadopoulou, and Alice-Mary Talbot.

For Port Saint Symeon, see T. Vorderstrasse, *Al-Mina: A Port of Antioch from Late Antiquity to the End of the Ottomans* (Leiden, 2005), 13–17, with bibliography. British excavations here in the 1930s found remains dating back to the ninth century BCE, but there were gaps in the occupation sequence: the site presumably resumed its role as riverine port for the Antioch region after the silting up of the harbor of Seleukeia Pieria. Moreover, the British excavations touched only on the harbor: the town lay several kilometers to the north, presumably somewhere under the modern town of Samandağ.

For the provincial organization of the region after the Byzantine reconquest of Antioch in 969, see J.-C. Cheynet, "The Duchy of Antioch during the Second Period of Byzantine Rule," in *East and West in the Medieval Eastern Mediterranean*, ed. K. Ciggaar and M. Metcalf, vol. 1, *Antioch from the Byzantine Reconquest until the End of the Crusader Principality*, Orientalia Lovaniensia Analecta 147 (Louvain, 2006), 1–16. The thirteenth-century geographer Yāqūt, in *Muʿjam al-Buldān*, ed. F. Wüstenfeld as *Jacut's geographisches Wörterbuch*, 6 vols. (1866–70; reprint, Frankfurt, 1994), 1:385, wrote that the journey from Antioch to the coast was

Figure 12.1. The eastern Mediterranean (drawn by J. Cookson)

Instead of the less-than-ideal site of Port Saint Symeon, the Norman principality's major port—and its second city, as it had been under Byzantine rule—was Laodikeia (after the Normans finally wrested that city from the Byzantines for good in 1108). Laodikeia is located southwest of Antioch, separated from it by the mountain range behind Jabal Aqrā'/Mount Cassius/Kel Dağ. These mountains are heavily forested, difficult to negotiate, and, at the coast, plunge directly into the sea. Major commercial contact between Antioch and Laodikeia was therefore much more likely to take place either by sea, via Port Saint Symeon, or by a circuitous land route following the Orontes upstream as it turned inland and ran parallel to the coast in the Ghāb Valley. From there, the route likely followed the modern road from Jisr al-Shughūr across the coastal mountains to the sea.[2]

Circuitous as it was, this land route would have presented few difficulties in the first half of the twelfth century, when the dominion of the principality extended through much of the Ghāb Valley, through which the Orontes flows. That changed after the fall of Edessa/al-Ruhā/Urfa in 1144, the failure of the Second Crusade in 1149, and the consequent consolidation of Zangid rule. And with the final fall of the fortress town of Ḥārim/Harenc to the armies of Nūr al-Dīn in 1164, the hinterland of Antioch shrank to the ʿAmuq/ʿAmq/Amik/Amık plain. Ḥārim lies at the edge of this plain, just 40

---

two parasangs, and that at a harbor named al-Suwaydiya goods from Frankish ships were loaded on to pack animals and taken to Antioch. Writing in the middle of the twelfth century, al-Idrīsī called al-Suwaydiya a *furḍa*, or small port (*Nuzhat al-Mushtāq fī Ikhtirāq al-Āfāq*, ed. U. Scerrato et al., as *Opus geographicum, sive "Liber ad eorum delectationem qui terras peragrare studeant,"* 9 vols. [Naples, 1970–78], 6:645).

2 See H. Kennedy, *Crusader Castles* (Cambridge, 1994), 79–84, for the castle of Bourzey/Rochefort and passing mention of Shughūr, both of which guarded the approaches to this route.

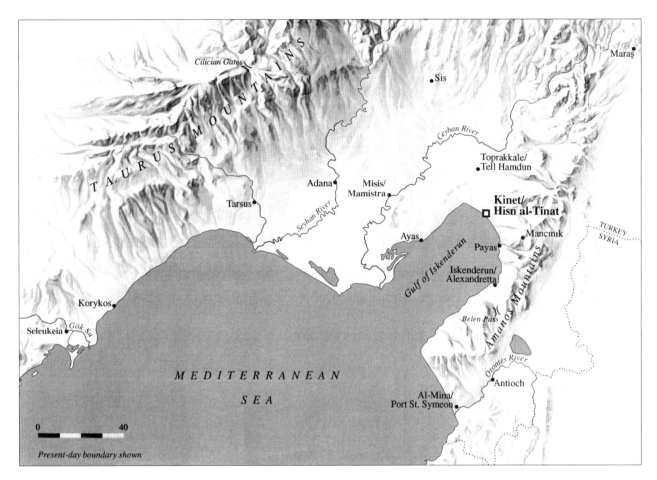

Figure 12.2. The northeastern corner of the Mediterranean, showing the regions of the plain of Cilicia and Antioch (drawn by J. Cookson)

kilometers east of Antioch. The ʿAmuq plain itself measures about 30 by 40 kilometers.[3]

Laodikeia served as the principal port for northern Syria in general. It was the largest town of the southern coastal domains of the Principality of Antioch, which abutted those of the County of Tripoli and were, again, largely coterminous with the territories of the earlier Byzantine duchy. After the crusader conquest of the region in 1098, the tenacious efforts of the Byzantine emperor Alexios I Komnenos to hold on to Laodikeia (with no such insistence on Port Saint Symeon) underscores its importance as a port. The fall of Laodikeia to the armies of Saladin in 1188 has been viewed as ushering in a new era, pushing Antioch into the embrace of Armenian Cilicia and away from contact with Tripoli and Acre to the south because the land link was severed between Antioch and Frankish coastal possessions to the south. By including Cilicia with Antioch in this chapter, I tip my hand. Whatever the status of Laodikeia, given the impediments of Zangid and later Ayyūbid Aleppo to the east, and the mountainous terrain to the south, the geography of the region links the city of Antioch to the north (Cilicia) more tightly than it does to the south.[4]

---

[3] For preliminary results of recently concluded Italian excavations at this site, see S. Gelichi, "Il castello di Harim: Un sito fortificato tra musulmani e crociati nella Siria del nord," *Archeologia Medievale* 30 (2003): 431–52. J. Casana, "The Archaeological Landscape of Late Roman Antioch," in *Culture and Society in Later Roman Antioch,* ed. I. Sandwell and J. Huskinson (Oxford, 2004), 104, provides the estimate of the size of the ʿAmuq.

[4] H. E. Mayer, *The Crusades* (Oxford, 1988), 255, attributes the decline of Antioch in the thirteenth century to its separation from other Frankish states to the south after the loss of Laodikeia. See A. Lane, "Medieval Finds at Al Mina in North Syria," *Archaeologia* 87 (1938): 23: "Saladin had threatened it [Antioch], and captured in 1188 its second port of Latakia; thereafter the harbour

Geography, Natural Resources, Agriculture, and Industry

What is this geography? The major link between Antioch and Cilicia runs through the Belen/Baylān pass in the Amanos Mountains some 50 kilometers northwest of Antioch.[5] This pass joins the ʿAmuq plain to the Mediterranean. The mighty fortress of Baghrās/Gaston/Bakras was located near its landward end and guarded the northern approach to the city. On the stretch of the Mediterranean directly west and north of this pass lay such ports as Alexandretta/al-Iskandarūna/İskenderun, Baia/Bayās/Payas, Portella/Sarı Seki, and Canamella/Ḥiṣn al-Ṭīnāt/Kinet. These ports were small, but on the whole must have been easier to maintain than the strategic but unstable Port Saint Symeon, given its proximity to the mouth of the Orontes. As one moves northward, this coastal zone offers direct access to the broad expanse of the Cilician plain lying to the north and west.

The core territory of the Principality of Antioch was thus relatively small: a very fertile, well-watered, and heavily cultivated plain, the ʿAmuq, open to trade and invasion from the east, and open to the west to the sea via the Orontes Valley, wedged between two mountain ranges: Jabal Mūsā/Musa Dağı and the Amanos to the north and Jabal Aqrāʾ to the south.

However much Byzantine precedent affected the shape of the early Norman Principality, like most of the eastern Mediterranean coastal regions, the economy of this region, like that of Smooth Cilicia, was strongly linked to Egypt, the economic heavyweight in the region. In Islamic, Byzantine, and crusader times alike, its timber, pitch, and iron (scrap, ingots, and artifacts) supplied Egypt, which was deficient in iron and wood, especially wood for shipbuilding.

The presence of these resources constituted another reason for Norman Antioch to engage with its northern neighbors in Armenian Cilicia. The Amanos Mountains, like the Taurus to the north of Cilicia, are rich in iron, which was either quarried from open pit mines or extracted from hematite boulders in streambeds and alluvial fans. Compared with the Mediterranean basin in general, which is dry in the summer and wet in the winter, the Amanos Mountains have more precipitation in the summer and in total, leading to a dense forest cover similar to that along the Black Sea. This atypical climate, combined with a relatively narrow coastal plain cut by seasonal and perennial torrents, was conducive to the traditional lumbering methods of Mediterranean and Pontic Anatolia (as well as of the Mediterranean basin in general): trees were harvested high in the coastal mountains and then, in the late winter or early spring, with the increase in volume of snowmelt torrents, their trunks were floated downstream for collection by boats with the beginning of the sailing season. Arabic sources from the tenth to fourteenth and Latin sources from the twelfth to fourteenth centuries mention the large-scale export of pine and oak from this region; the high pitch content of Cilician pine made it especially valuable for ship construction. Lumbering and metallurgy were complementary industries, as branches and smaller tree limbs were turned into charcoal at these seaside camps. Charcoal was used for fuel-hungry metallurgy. In turn, the iron smithy was a vital part of an economy that produced, consumed, and exported—and therefore shod—large numbers of equids.[6]

---

at the mouth of the Orontes became more important than ever." When I call Islamic Aleppo an impediment, I mean this in a military sense. This essay does not address commercial and economic links between Antioch and that part of Syria under Islamic rule except in passing.

5 The Amanos were called the equivalent of "the Black Mountain" in many languages, and Jabal Lukkām in Arabic. Their Ottoman Turkish name, Gavur Dağı (Infidel Mountain), may come precisely from their strong association with Christians through earlier monastic settlement, though little of it survived the Mamluk conquest.

6 See M. Lombard, *Espaces et réseaux du haut Moyen Âge* (Paris, 1972), 113–16, 114, for the Cilician pine (*Abies cilicica*) with its high pitch content; J. McNeill, *The Mountains of the Mediterranean World* (Cambridge, 1992), for the relationship between fuel and mining (238), for the floating of tree trunks down mountain rivers (242), for the relationship of the Taurus timber trade to Egypt in later centuries (246ff.), for the forest cover of the Taurus (289); D. Jacoby, "The Supply of War Materials to Egypt in the Crusader Period," *Jerusalem Studies in Arabic and Islam* 25 (2001): 119–25, for the export of timber and iron from Cilicia to Egypt in the twelfth and thirteenth centuries. To my knowledge, the passage from a contemporaneous source that best ties together mountains, sea, logging, rivers, and the use of timber from those mountains for shipbuilding is Ibn Saʿīd's account of this trade in and around the Black Sea port of Sinope in the mid-thirteenth century; see his *Kitāb al-Jughrāfiyā*, ed. I. al-ʿArabī (Beirut, 1970), 195. All of the ingredients itemized here for the Sinope region were also found at the time in Cilicia and Antioch

During its early years, in the first decade of the twelfth century, the Principality of Antioch expanded its borders north through the Baylān pass, up the coast, and far into the eastern Cilician plain, conquering and refortifying cities like Anazarbos/'Ayn Zarba/Anavarza. Despite the subsequent Armenian riposte, a different kind of Frankish presence continued in the region: in the mid- and late twelfth and thirteenth centuries, the northern coastal plain between the Amanos and the sea and the Amanos Mountains themselves were dotted with castles, forts, and ports belonging to the Knights Templar (who were active in the area beginning in the 1130s, and granted castles here from the 1150s on). They were joined by the Teutonic Knights in the thirteenth century. Guarding against Armenian-Antiochene conflict and Muslim invasion did not preclude these military orders from becoming engaged in the harvesting of the resources mentioned above, which they sold to Genoese and Venetian merchant ships, for export largely to Ayyūbid, and later Mamluk, Egypt.[7]

As the German armies of the Third Crusade found out in June and July of 1190, the Cilician plain was no place to be in the summer. It harbored malarial coastal swamps undrained since Roman times, and the intense, humid summer heat caused the populace annually to forsake the coast and lowlands for the surrounding mountains, leaving the plains empty. Swamps, torrents, sandbars, and dunes rendered large stretches of the Cilician coast uninhabitable summer *and* winter, and thus inhospitable for maritime trade. The two main ports of Cilicia, Āyās/Lajazzo/Yumurtalık and Korykos/Kız Kalesi, lay distant from the mouths of rivers.[8] Despite these disadvantages, the presence of a long growing season, fertile soil, and plentiful pastures, both upland and lowland, made the Cilician plain and piedmont of the Amanos and Taurus mountains into a major center for agriculture and animal husbandry. A population of agriculturalists that leaves the lowlands for the mountains for the summer can easily bring with it flocks of sheep and goats, and less easily larger quadrupeds, to graze in upland summer pastureland. The seasonal transhumance of farming communities must have been disrupted by the influx of nomadic tribes of Türkmen in the twelfth and Mongols in the later thirteenth century. Be this as it may, Armenian Cilicia continued to be known for the export of

---

save the arsenal itself. Iron ore is currently mined in the region of Payas and Kırıkhan; see, e.g., Ş. Koç and M. A. Değer, "Genesis of Bauxite Bearing Iron Ore Deposits from Payas (Hatay) District," *Mineral Research Exploration Bulletin* 113 (1991): 73–86. Excavations at Kinet uncovered part of a twelfth-century iron workshop. Elsewhere at the site, burned and cracked river boulders of hematite were recovered. Given the small (but constant) scale of iron production at Kinet, it makes sense that alluvial hematite was collected, either complementing or replacing pit mining; see S. Redford, "A 12th Century Iron Workshop at Kinet, Turkey," *Byzas* 11 (2012) (forthcoming). On booty taken by Mamluk armies in the form of quadrupeds, see Ibn al-Dawādārī, *Kanz al-Durar wa Jam'i al-Ghurar*, ed. U. Haarman (Freiburg, 1971), 8:177, for a raid in AH 673/AD 1274–75 that netted cattle, riding animals (horses, mules, donkeys), slave girls, and mamluks; Ibn Shaddād, *Tārīkh al-Malik al-Ẓāhir*, ed. A. Hutait (Wiesbaden, 1983), 107 (sheep/goats, cattle, and slaves); and Mufaḍḍal, *Ägypten und Syrien zwischen 1317 und 1341 in der Chronik des Mufaḍḍal b. Abī l-Faḍā'il*, ed. and trans. S. Kortantamer (Freiburg, 1973), 11 (cattle and water buffalo). See also C. Favre and B. Mandrot, "Voyage en Cilicie," *Bulletin de la Société de Géographie*, n.s. 6, 8 (1878): 21: "dans la plaine on se sert de chariots grossiers attelés de deux buffles et qui, lorsque le sol n'est pas marécageux, avancent sans trop de difficulté. Le mode de transport le plus usité, même dans les passages de montagne, est le chameau."

7 On the arrival of the Templars in this region, see J. Burgtorf, "The Military Orders in the Crusader Principality of Antioch," in Ciggaar and Metcalf, eds., *East and West in the Medieval Eastern Mediterranean*, 233. The standard work on the subject is still J. Riley-Smith, "The Templars and the Teutonic Knights in Cilician Armenia," in *The Cilician Kingdom of Armenia*, ed. T. S. R. Boase (Edinburgh, 1978), 92–117. Robert Edwards has argued that the massive donjon separating the south bailey from the central bailey at Anazarbos is a crusader work, and therefore dates to the period of Frankish control of eastern Cilicia, which ended around 1110; see his *The Fortifications of Armenian Cilicia* (Washington, D.C., 1987), 68–69.

8 The importance of Āyās as a port is well known and documented, especially in the Genoese archives. The *maître* of these archives, Michel Balard, makes the following generalization in *Les Latins en Orient* (Paris, 2006), 245, concerning the direction of trade: from Āyās camlet and cotton cloths were sent west, or to Cyprus, while wood and iron were sent to Egypt and Syria. For more detailed information of the structure of the Italian trading community, see C. Otten-Froux, "L'Aias dans le dernier tiers du XIIIᵉ siècle d'après les notaires génois," *Asian and African Studies* 22 (1988): 147–71; and P. Racine, "L'Aias dans la seconde moitié du XIIIᵉ siècle," *Rivista di Bizantinistica* 3 (1992): 173–206. Korykos has never been excavated, but a hint of the richness of thirteenth-century trade at the other, western end of Smooth Cilicia is provided by excavations at Yumuktepe, a coastal site near Mersin west of Korykos: see G. Köroğlu, "Yumuktepe in the Middle Ages," in *Mersin-Yumuktepe: A Reappraisal*, ed. I. Caneva and V. Sevin (Galatina, 2004): 103–32, and eadem, "Yumuktepe Höyüğü Ortaçağ Kazısından Küçük Buluntular," *VI Ortaçağ ve Türk Dönemi Kazı Sonuçları ve Sanat Tarihi Sempozyumu*, ed. M. Denktaş et al. (Kayseri, 2002), 515–35.

camlet, a cloth made of goat or camel hair, well into the fourteenth century.⁹

Arabic and Latin sources from the thirteenth and fourteenth centuries repeatedly mention a wealth of quadrupeds: sheep and goats, horses, mules, donkeys, and water buffalo, often taken as booty. Mamluk sultans demanded mules, horses, and donkeys as tribute from the kings of Armenian Cilicia. The large role played by animal husbandry here also led to associated industries: tanning, weaving, and the export of wool, cloth (especially camlet), and hides. Water buffalo and cotton (the latter mentioned in Italian documents) lead us to posit the irrigated cultivation of low-lying areas despite the difficulties mentioned above. Even though the region possessed plentiful water and a hot climate, sugarcane never seems to have been grown in either the Antioch region or the Cilician plain. Perhaps its absence is explained by the heavy investment needed for sugarcane plantations, or the lack of political stability. Certainly it was not for lack of the slaves needed for the labor-intensive work of its cultivation. In the early thirteenth century, slaves were either captured during nearby wars or traded long distance, from the Black Sea steppes through Sivas and Cilicia to Egypt; the Sivas route gained in importance when that town became the regional center for Mongol governance in the second half of the thirteenth century.

The resources of the ʿAmuq plain, the fertile hinterland of the Principality of Antioch proper, were much the same as those of Cilicia to the north. In the Hellenistic and Roman periods, expansion of olive and vine cultivation into the foothills of the Jabal Aqraʿ, and to a lesser extent the Amanos, had led to massive deforestation around Antioch. As the population declined in the late fifth to sixth centuries, settlement retreated to the ʿAmuq plain, where increased alluviation caused by deforestation had earlier encouraged the development of a large new lake in the middle of the ʿAmuq. This deforestation also resulted in the landslides and floods that have led some to misperceive Antioch as a "lost city" buried under the alluvium.¹⁰

The extensive canal system in the ʿAmuq plain that had contributed so much to the wealth of Roman Antioch declined in the early Byzantine era, although some canals seem to have been in use through the early Islamic period. But the lush riverine environments of the medieval ʿAmuq contributed to a thriving pisciculture. Several freshwater bodies of water were used to farm eels—indeed, the export of dried eels from Antioch under the principality was so profitable that their sale was given as a gift to monasteries. Despite, or perhaps because of, this aquatic environment, the ʿAmuq plain attracted nomadic pastoralists: Bedouins in earlier times, and Türkmen by at least the thirteenth century.¹¹

Settlement in the ʿAmuq plain in the Frankish period seems to follow general patterns found throughout the medieval Near East. Thus, many of the settlement mounds (*tell/höyük*) that form such

---

9 The continuator of the history of William of Tyre said of summer in the Cilician plain: "Car les pleins d'Ermenie en esté sont chaus et enfermés. La montaigne est fresche et saine. Dont les habitans de la terre ont lor maneirs en la montaigne, et demorent illueques por la chalor dou tens, des l'entree de juing jusques a la metié de septembre, et d'illueques en avant descendent au plain por ce que la terre est tempree et meins enfermé": *La continuation de Guillaume de Tyr (1184–1197)*, ed. M. R. Morgan (Paris, 1982), 99. For a study of a Roman port on the shores of the Gulf of Iskenderun abandoned to coastal sand dunes (and only partially reinhabited thereafter in the thirteenth century), see J. Tobin, *Black Cilicia: A Study of the Plain of Issus during the Roman and Late Roman Periods* (Oxford, 2004). For information about fourteenth-century trade in Āyās, see *Merchant Culture in Fourteenth-Century Venice: The Zibaldone da Canal,* ed. and trans. J. Dotson (Binghamton, 1994), 110–12; and Francesco Balducci Pegolotti, *La pratica della mercatura,* ed. A. Evans (Cambridge, Mass., 1936), 59–63. See also W. Heyd, *Histoire du commerce du Levant au Moyen-Âge,* 2 vols. (Leipzig, 1885–86), 1:365–72, 2:73–92 for Armenian Cilicia; he notes the establishment of Venetian factories for the weaving of camlet (2:82). For another excellent overview of the trade of Armenian Cilicia, also mainly based on western European archival documents, see P. Bedoukian, *Coinage of Cilician Armenia* (New York, 1962), 25–87. Since camlet was the major cloth produced in Armenian Cilicia, it is important to know what it was made of. Most authors follow Heyd's argument (2:703–5) in tracing its origins not to camel but goat hair, but Bedoukian (38) translates documents referring to the Venetian purchase, manufacture, and transport of camel wool/hair.

10 Casana, "Archaeological Landscape," 110–12. F. Gerritsen et al., "Settlement and Landscape Transformations in the Amuq Valley, Hatay: A Long-Term Perspective," *Anatolica* 34 (2008): 265–66, note that the heaviest exploitation of the uplands of the Jabal Aqraʿ occurred in the fifth and sixth centuries AD along with a consolidation of settlements in the plain as large estates expanded there.

11 See Cahen, *La Syrie du Nord,* 474, and Burgtorf, "The Military Orders," 228, for the lucrative trade in eels and other fish. Riley-Smith, "The Templars," 110, citing Ibn al-Athīr, points to Templar attacks on Türkmen tribes in the ʿAmuq in the early thirteenth century. In the fourteenth century, the Moroccan traveler Ibn Baṭṭūṭa noted that the ʿAmuq "is occupied by Türkmens with their animals on account of its fertile pasture and extent": *The Travels of Ibn Baṭṭūṭa,* trans. H. A. R. Gibb, 5 vols. (Cambridge, 1958–2000), 1:105.

a prominent feature of the landscape in the ʿAmuq were reinhabited and refortified in the twelfth and thirteenth centuries. This change in settlement pattern, shared with other regions of Anatolia, Syria, and northern Mesopotamia, can be linked to various and contradictory factors: war, nomadification, prosperity, and demographic expansion. Publications based on the recent University of Chicago ʿAmuq survey note the trend, but do not try to explain it, aside from noting that these fortified hilltop settlements did not constitute a frontier. Some mound-top settlements must have been islands, whose inhabitants engaged in the fishing industry mentioned above. Here, as in many other examples to the north and south of Antioch, the hand of the state or another central authority is evident in their regular layout.[12]

As late as the late tenth century, the Antioch native and doctor Ibn Buṭlān described the landscape between Antioch and Aleppo as well-populated and consisting of plentiful pastureland, water, and villages, with grain and barley grown under olive trees—a sight familiar to travelers to the region today. Silk and wine were also produced and exported, so mulberry groves and vineyards must also have figured prominently in the landscape.[13] As was the case in Cilicia, the nearby mountains, which held the summer residences of the nobility and monasteries (and Cursat/Quṣayr, the castle of the patriarch of Antioch), must have also supported the summer pasture of flocks of sheep and goats that wintered on the plain. Certainly, even a principality restricted to the ʿAmuq plain, Jabal Aqrāʾ, and Amanos would have possessed more than adequate agricultural resources to support a medium-size city like Antioch. Especially after the loss of direct contact with its southern territories in 1188, the Principality of Antioch became a city-state, coveted by the Armenian Kingdom to the north. It was this covetousness that led to various alliances, including one between Antioch and the Seljuks of Rūm that was itself counterbalanced by close relations between Lusignan Cyprus and Armenian Cilicia.

The geographical work of al-Idrīsī, completed in 1154 at the Palermitan court of the Norman king Roger II, contains information about Antioch not found in other sources. Given the importance of Antioch and Antiochenes to the Normans, it is not surprising that a great deal of information was available to a geographer far away in Norman Sicily, who could also rely on earlier works like that of the tenth-century geographer Ibn Ḥawqal. Al-Idrīsī's account draws, as it were, the water of the environs of the city into the cityscape. In it, water "penetrates" the streets of the city, great and small; its markets; and even its mansions (quṣūr). Likewise, the rural landscape replicates itself within the circuit of the Justinianic walls, which contained mills, legume gardens, and orchards. The word for mills (arḥāʾ, sing. raḥan) must here refer to waterwheels, the famous noria/nāʿūra still found on the Orontes in Syria, that lifted water from the river into the city, as well as water mills turned by streams flowing from Mount Silpius. As for the markets of the city, al-Idrīsī mentions that they were thriving, and produced marketable goods

---

12 Gerritsen et al., "Settlement and Landscape," 278–79. These settlements combined with major fortified settlements in the uplands. See J. Casana and T. Wilkinson, "Settlement and Landscapes in the Amuq Region," in *The Amuq Valley Regional Projects,* ed. K. A. Yener, vol. 1 (Chicago, 2005), 45: "Many of the Early and Middle Islamic settlements in the central Amuq Valley must have been located within or on the edge of the extensive marsh that had inundated much of the area. . . . In some cases, it is clear that Islamic settlements were located on top of older Bronze and Iron Age tell sites such as Karatepe, which would have formed islands in the marsh[.]" (The authors use the solecism "Middle Islamic" to refer to the period of Byzantine reoccupation and Frankish rule.) This type of resettlement must have been tied at least in part to the thriving pisciculture discussed above. See T. Vorderstrasse, "Archaeology of the Antiochene Region in the Crusader Period," in Ciggaar and Metcalf, eds., *East and West in the Medieval Eastern Mediterranean,* 323–24, for the fortified and planned mound-top medieval settlement of Çatal Höyük in the ʿAmuq plain, which she calls a "village site . . . which might date partially to the crusader period." I have linked the medieval settlement of mound tops by Byzantines, Armenians, crusaders, Artuqids, and Ayyūbids in the Euphrates Valley in southeastern Turkey to the use of the river as a frontier and trade route; see S. Redford, *The Archaeology of the Frontier in the Medieval Near East: Excavations at Gritille, Turkey* (Philadelphia, 1998), 68–75. For fortified settlements in the territories of the Kingdom of Jerusalem in the twelfth century, see R. Ellenblum, *Crusader Castles and Modern Histories* (Cambridge, 2007), 84–102, where he critiques the unthinking use of the term "castle," proposes a tripartite hierarchy for walled settlements, and argues strongly against modern ideas of the frontier in the medieval period. He states: "The most important conclusion is that the defensibility of a certain site is not the only—or even major—criterion for its function" (101).

13 Part of Ibn Buṭlān's narrative is preserved in Yāqūt, *Muʿjam,* 1:382–85; in describing the landscape between Antioch and Aleppo, he calls it capable of being traversed in a day and a night (383). Large waterwheels were present in the Antiochene hinterland until the twentieth century; see J. Weulersse, "Antioche: Essai de géographie," *BEODam* 4 (1934): 44, 49 n. 1.

of excellent quality. Specifically, he mentions the local manufacture of plain (or monochrome) cloth, watered silk, and two other kinds of cloth whose exact nature is hard to ascertain. Other manufacturing in the city included the making of iron swords or knives. Glassmaking was in the hands of the Jewish community. The 1930s excavations attested to the manufacture in the medieval period of several varieties of glazed ceramics in at least two areas of the city.[14]

With the tenth-century Byzantine reconquest of the region, as we learn from historical sources, the mountains and hills of the Amanos and Jabal Aqrā' came to again be covered with monasteries (even if published archaeological evidence gives little if any indication of monastic resettlement before the late twelfth to thirteenth century). Although little is known of the early history of monastic settlement in the area around Antioch, certainly reincorporation of this region into a Christian state beginning in the late eleventh century contributed to an increase in pilgrimages—especially, although not exclusively, from Georgia and Armenia. Monasteries were expanded and rebuilt, and reoccupied the hilly and mountainous surroundings of Antioch and further north in the Amanos. This development must have helped spur olive as well as wine production, though the major surviving index of the wealth of at least some of the monasteries of Jabal Aqrā' and the Amanos does not come from monastic typica or detailed archaeological field study but consists simply of the high quality and luxury of manuscripts they produced.[15]

Pilgrimage may not have been as big a business here as further south in the Levant, but it still must have contributed to the financial well-being of the principality. It can be seen not only in the revival of interest in urban Antiochene shrines, and in monasteries such as those of St. Simeon the Younger and St. Barlaam, but also in the transit trade of larger pilgrimage circuits. As we know, the Ayyūbids permitted, and profited from, western Christian pilgrimage to holy sites deep in their territory. The late thirteenth-century treasure of ecclesiastical silver found in Ruṣāfa/Sergiopolis well east of Aleppo may constitute evidence of a pilgrimage itinerary linking that town to Antioch via Aleppo.[16]

Genoese, Pisan, and Venetian merchants all conducted business in the principality and in the baronial and royal Cilician Armenia (the Genoese received a trade concession at Port Saint Symeon in 1101, and the Venetians were granted trade concessions by Antioch in 1143). Port Saint Symeon was operational during the period of the crusader siege of Antioch in the winter of 1098–99, but, as noted above, it is likely that Laodikeia was the principal-

---

14 Al-Idrīsī, *Nuzhat*, 6:645. These locally manufactured cloths included *al-Isbahānī*, named after the Persian city of Isfahan, and *al-tasatturī*. In his account of Antioch after the crusader conquest during the First Crusade, William of Tyre twice mentions quantities of silk being found in the city; see *A History of Deeds Done beyond the Sea*, trans. E. A. Babcock and A. C. Krey, 2 vols. (New York, 1943), 1:260, 297. On forging blades, see Cahen, *La Syrie du Nord*, 476. Benjamin of Tudela reports that "10 Jews dwell here, engaged in glass-making," by which he must have meant 10 Jewish families. He also reports different information on the water supply of the city: "The city lies by a lofty mountain. . . . At the top of the mountain is a wall, from which a man appointed for that purpose directs the water by means of 20 subterranean passages to the houses of the great men of the city": *The Itinerary of Benjamin of Tudela*, trans. M. Adler (London, 1907), 16. By contrast, he notes the presence of 100 Jews in Laodikea.

Excavations in the 1930s uncovered evidence for medieval glazed pottery production of Monochrome and Sgraffito Wares in two areas of the city. First, a kiln was found in the north of the city. Second, two dozen tripods used in kilns were found to the southeast of the city; see F. O. Waagé, "The Glazed Pottery," in *Antioch-on-the-Orontes*, vol. 4.1, *Ceramics and Islamic Coins*, ed. idem (Princeton, N.J., 1948), 101–2 and fig. 95. Casana, "Archaeological Landscape," 116, has identified water mills in valleys leading down to the 'Amuq; as noted above, if these existed in Antioch proper, they must have been placed on the streams coming into the city from Mount Silpius. For a brief discussion of archaeological evidence for water mills near the 'Amuq, and Antioch's streams and water adduction systems, see Casana and Wilkinson, "Settlement and Landscapes," 43.

15 Al-Idrīsī, *Nuzhat*, 6:645, mentions a large monastery in the Amanos Mountains north of Suwaydiya. See also A. Saminsky, "Georgian and Greek Illuminated Manuscripts from Antioch," in Ciggaar and Metcalf, eds., *East and West in the Medieval Eastern Mediterranean*, 17–78; and J. Weitenberg, "The Armenian Monasteries in the Black Mountain," ibid., 79–93. W. Djobadze, *Materials for the Study of Georgian Monasteries in the Western Environs of Antioch on the Orontes* (Louvain, 1976), 108, estimates that there were thirteen or fourteen Georgian monasteries near Antioch. The same author, in his *Archeological Investigations in the Region West of Antioch on-the-Orontes* (Stuttgart, 1986), 188ff., notes that the only datable pottery from three monasteries investigated archaeologically was the thirteenth-century tricolored sgraffito known as Port Saint Symeon Ware. Excavations at Kinet have extended the chronological range of production of these ceramics from the late twelfth through the early fourteenth centuries and decoupled them from the Mamluk conquest of Antioch in 1268, a date on which Djobadze insists for the abandonment of monastic life.

16 T. Ulbert et al., *Resafa*, vol. 3, *Der Kreuzfahrerzeitliche Silberschatz aus Resafa-Sergiupolis* (Mainz, 1984).

ity's main port. Whether permanent—as opposed to seasonal—Italian settlement began in Antioch in the period just before the battle of Ḥaṭṭīn in 1187 (as Jonathan Riley-Smith has posited for the southern Outremer cities), we do not know.[17] Even if this was the case, the presence of large, thriving, and diverse local Christian communities of merchants and artisans in Antioch (and likely fewer Muslims and Jews than elsewhere) must have made its urban population markedly different from that of other Frankish Levantine cities, and the city's distance from the sea must at least have reduced the number of Italians. The circumstances of the fall of the city to the armies of the First Crusade, without the kind of extensive and extended naval blockade that marked later crusader-Italian sieges, also militated against the quick and easy establishment of separate Italian trading emporiums, and later colonies, within the fabric of the city.

The thirteenth-century commercial boom that swept the eastern Mediterranean also engulfed Antioch and Armenian Cilicia. This boom can be attributed to many factors, including the long truces between Franks and Ayyūbids, the conquest of Cyprus in 1191 and the founding of the Lusignan kingdom there, the spread of Italian trading colonies on Cyprus and on other islands of the northern Mediterranean, and the rise of unitary Anatolian states such as the Seljuk Sultanate of Rūm and the Kingdom of Armenian Cilicia.

With the establishment and stability of these states came a proliferation of currencies. Although the argument thus far might lead one to expect a currency community between the billon and copper of Antioch and silver and copper of Cilician Armenia, in the thirteenth century the weight and purity of Armenian silver trams aligned them more closely with the silver dirhams of the Rūm Seljuks to the north than with the coinage of Syrian Ayyūbids to the east and south. Given the vast number of Antiochene helmet deniers minted, it seems logical to suggest, with Michael Metcalf, that they were a principal method of payment for the Templars guarding the northern borders of the principality. This hypothesis has been supported by the recovery of a hoard of Antiochene deniers from the site of Kinet, which, under the name of al-Ṭīnāt/Canamella, was a Templar fort and port in the Mediterranean marchland between Franco-Norman Antioch and Armenian Cilicia. Settlement at Kinet lasted from the mid- to late twelfth through the early fourteenth centuries. Helmet deniers were used throughout the occupation sequence, alongside first copper coins from Antioch and then Armenian *kardez*. Only one Armenian silver tram was recovered from the site. On the basis of hoard findspots, Metcalf has argued that Antiochene billon deniers did not circulate further than Antioch and its vicinity and the Templar marches.[18]

Asymmetry: States, Markets, and Economic Actors

The first half of this chapter has painted a broad canvas, largely describing the historical geography and natural resources of Cilicia and Antioch and its environs. It has relied principally on written sources and numismatic evidence, but has also drawn on publications of the ʿAmuq survey undertaken recently by the University of Chicago. I will now employ more specific archaeological data—especially but not exclusively ceramics, from two sites, Port Saint Symeon and Kinet—to deepen and broaden issues raised earlier. Tasha Vorderstrasse has recently reevaluated the 1930s excavations at Port Saint Symeon, while a Bilkent University project at Kinet, under the direction of Marie-Henriette Gates, has recently concluded a program of excavation and survey that began in 1992.[19] I am currently working on the final publication of excavations in the medieval levels at Kinet.

---

17 J. Riley-Smith, *The Crusades: A History*, 2nd ed. (New Haven, 2005), 224–26, argues that the change in the flow of luxury trade from Egypt to Syria in the 1180s precipitated a change in the nature of Italian trading colonies in the Outremer, as permanent representatives were appointed and some Italians became year-round residents.

18 D. M. Metcalf, *Coinage of the Crusades and the Latin East*, 2nd ed. (London, 1995), 138, phrases his point as a question: "Did the Templars receive financial support for their work in guarding the northern marches of the Latin East?" The noncongruence of currencies between Antioch and its neighbors might be explained by the limited circulation of Antiochene coinage: "The Antiochene deniers seem to have been very much a city coinage, of which the use was concentrated in Antioch itself and on the coast" (139). Metcalf will be publishing the hoard of deniers from Kinet.

19 Vorderstrasse, *Al-Mina*; S. Redford, S. Ikram, E. M. Parr, and T. Beach, "Excavations at Medieval Kinet, Turkey: A Preliminary Report," *Ancient Near Eastern Studies* 38 (2001): 58–138.

Here, I will use some of the data from these two sites to examine three specific questions that may help us better understand the place of this region in the eastern Mediterranean economy of the twelfth and thirteenth centuries. I hope that what follows can be considered synecdochically, with the reader also keeping in mind the production and trading of more perishable goods *not* surviving in the archaeological record (cloth, leather, wood, etc). These questions are

1. What is the overlap of sovereign states, characterized by legal, fiscal, and military regimes, with markets—places of production and consumption?

2. What is the intersection between the monopolistic practices of these states and those of the Italian mercantile republics?

3. How can demand be stimulated by the creation of taste?

There is very little evidence for material products of a unitary state in Antioch, where, as we have seen, even the billon currency was restricted in circulation and was used in the Templar marches, an area that Jonathan Riley-Smith has called "a semi-independent territory in which the Templars went their own way, with little reference to their nominal lords in Cilicia."[20] In contrast, the military fortifications of Armenian Cilicia display commonality of workmanship and design consistent with a degree of centralized patronage and organization.[21] The lack of a distinctive material culture is a problem in the study of the crusader states of the Outremer in general. In the realm of ceramics, Acre produces distinctive unglazed bowls, and Cyprus and the Levantine coast shared the medieval production of a unique type of glazed frying pans that may reflect a culinary tradition distinct from that of Byzantium, Islamic Syria, or Anatolia.[22] The issue of gold and silver coins by Outremer states that imitated the coinage of their Islamic neighbors—first Egypt, then Syria—is well known. Without delving into this topic here, I would like to point to it simply as an example of the overlap of sovereign states with economic zones.

Port Saint Symeon ceramics have been considered another example of crusader material culture. The 1930s excavations by Sir Leonard Woolley at Port Saint Symeon uncovered evidence of production there of a distinct tricolor glazed, incised ware. The scholar who published medieval finds from Port Saint Symeon, Arthur Lane, called this ware Port Saint Symeon ceramics, and linked its production to the city's alleged rise in importance after the fall of Laodikeia in 1188. Lane also neatly tied the end of the production of these ceramics to 1268, when Antioch fell to the armies of the Mamluk sultan Baybars,[23] even though there was no archaeological evidence that the site was burned, destroyed, or abandoned at that time.

In a seminal 1985 article, Denys Pringle called Port Saint Symeon Ware "Crusader ceramics *par excellence*" due to two factors: the localization of its production at the main port of Antioch in the thirteenth century and its widespread distribution. As had Lane, Pringle observed the importance of Italian maritime trading networks in spreading Port Saint Symeon Ware as far west as Genoa and Marseille, to the Crimea, and all around the eastern and central Mediterranean. He also noted its distribution at inland sites in Syria, Anatolia, and northern Mesopotamia. This wide export stimulated imitation in

---

20 Riley-Smith, "The Templars," 110. This area, of course, would have answered to the Templar commandership in Antioch itself.
21 On commonalities of Armenian defensive masonry, see Edwards, *Fortifications of Armenian Cilicia*, 18–24. Edwards (37) argues against the association—made here—between standardized, increased building and the foundation and subsequent prosperity of the Armenian Kingdom in the thirteenth century. It is true that Armenians by that time had already lived and ruled under Byzantine suzerainty for a century, but I believe that much of the rise in castle building must be tied both to commerce and governance in the thirteenth century and to the concurrent neglect of cities. Edwards characterizes a typical settlement of the Cilician plain under Armenian rule as "a large garrison fort with a number of scattered villages in the immediate area. The villages were agricultural settlements" (45). But surely it took time—precisely the twelfth century, which Edwards equates with the thirteenth as a period of castle building with standardized planometric and masonry types—for the cities of the plain to become depopulated, and for their defensive walls to fall into ruin.
22 For the latest publications on these two ceramic types, see S. Y. Waksman et al., "Elemental and Petrographic Analyses of Local and Imported Ceramics from Crusader Acre," *Atiqot* 59 (2008): 157, and V. François et al., "Premiers éléments pour une caractérisation des productions de Beyrouth entre domination franque et mamelouke," in *VIIe Congrès International sur la Céramique Médiévale en Méditerranée, Thessaloniki, 11–16 Octobre 1999: Actes,* ed. Ch. Bakirtzis (Athens, 2003), 325–40.
23 Lane, "Medieval Finds," 45–46.

the cities around the Tyrrhenian Sea, the Crimea, inland Syria and Mesopotamia, and Cyprus. (Interestingly enough, the potters of the Aegean, where the production of glazed ceramics was well established and varied, did not succumb to the desire to imitate Port Saint Symeon ceramics.)[24]

Recent archaeological fieldwork has rendered problematic the one-to-one identification of the production of Port Saint Symeon ceramics with territories of the Franco-Norman Principality of Antioch. The evidence assembled demonstrates that Port Saint Symeon Ware was produced in this region *before* the principality was established, and *outside* its boundaries. In addition to Port Saint Symeon itself, evidence of production has been uncovered at the coastal sites of Kinet, Epiphaneia/Kanīsat al-Sawdāʾ, and Mamistra/Mopsuestia/al-Maṣṣīṣa/Misis. Its ubiquity at medieval sites in the Cilician plain suggests that it was likely produced in Tarsus, Adana, Āyās, and other port sites in Armenian Cilicia as well. There is *no* evidence, however, for its production to the south of Jabal Aqrāʾ, in Laodikeia or elsewhere. This most widely traded of all medieval Mediterranean glazed ceramics was produced in the Kingdom of Armenian Cilicia and in part of the Principality of Antioch, a geographical zone of production spanning two sovereign states.

The widespread production of Port Saint Symeon ceramics in this northeastern corner of the Mediterranean helps explain the breadth of their export: there were many production centers, all located near or on the sea. This is a pattern seemingly copied from the Aegean, where the production of glazed ceramics in the twelfth century was decentralized and mostly near the sea. However, it is incorrect to identify these ceramics exclusively with one polity or another: the key identification seems instead to be with maritime commerce. In this part of the Mediterranean, the promotion and internationalization of Port Saint Symeon ceramics, a preexistent local ware, seem to have coincided with the commercial boom of the early thirteenth century. Therefore, the key actors apparently were the Italian maritime republics engaged in the trade in commodities (chiefly grain and timber) in the region—especially Genoa, given the close relation of early Ligurian sgraffito ceramics to Port Saint Symeon ceramics.[25]

The trend of decentralization does not appear to have applied only to ceramics: the recovery of much slag, an iron ingot, a crushed hematite boulder, hundreds of iron nails, sickles, horseshoes, and arrow points, as well as the discovery of a small furnace from twelfth-century levels at Kinet, attests to ongoing small-scale iron smelting there. Indeed, it is hard to imagine the state supplying the kind of organization needed to produce *centrally all* of the large number of horseshoes and nails demanded by the Egyptians from the Armenian Kingdom as annual tribute (along with horses and other equids) in the late thirteenth and early fourteenth centuries. More generally, decentralization and multiplication of production centers must have been fostered in order to promote the carrying trade: at the very least, the standardization of size, glaze, type, and decoration of Port Saint Symeon ceramics over multiple production areas argues for direct intervention and management by merchants of the Italian maritime republics beginning in the early thirteenth century.

Of course, port revenues were an important—probably the major—source of income for the rulers of the Frankish states of the Outremer, who undoubtedly were cognizant of that fact. Nonetheless, like those elsewhere in the eastern Mediterranean, nonstate actors imbedded in or clinging to the littoral belonging to those states, and yet not entirely subject to their laws, actively participated in this trade and, through preferential treaties, deprived the

---

24 D. Pringle, "Pottery as Evidence for Trade in the Crusader States," in *I comuni italiani nel regno crociato di Gerusalemme: Atti del Colloquio "The Italian Communes in the Crusading Kingdom of Jerusalem,"* ed. G. Airaldi and B. Kedar (Genoa, 1986), 451–75; see G. Berti and S. Gelichi, "Considerazioni sulla cosiddetta 'ceramica crociata'," in *L'ambiente culturale a Ravello nel medioevo,* ed. P. Peduto and F. Widemann (Bari, 2000), 249ff., for the relationship between Port Saint Symeon Ware and the *graffita arcaica tirrenica* produced in Liguria. For an analysis of Port Saint Symeon ceramics found in Genoa and Marseilles, see C. Capelli et al., "Caratterizzazione archeometrica di ceramiche graffite medievali (*Port Saint Symeon Ware*) rinvenute a Beirut, Genova e Marsiglia," in *XXXVIII Convegno Internazionale della Ceramica* (Albisola, 2006), 81–86.

25 Racine, "L'Aias," 192, 198, notes the residence in Āyās in the late thirteenth century of Genoese and Ligurian craftsmen, including weavers, carpenters, and tanners. Once we know this stratum of Latin society to have been even temporarily resident in Āyās and other cities along the coast—along with better-known merchants and officials—the mechanism for cultural contact and transferal of both techniques and artistic motifs and styles becomes easier to understand.

state of revenue. Italian merchants are the most obvious nonstate actors, but in this region the Templars, too, profited at the expense of the kingdom and principality whose borders they were guarding.

Port Saint Symeon ceramics define a zone of economic activity that unites Antioch and Armenian Cilicia: a new idea, but perhaps not a revolutionary one. What is equally if not more interesting is recently uncovered archaeological evidence that Port Saint Symeon ceramics were produced *after* the Mamluk conquest of Antioch, or Port Saint Symeon, and of the coastal zone to the north of the Baylān pass. This finding underscores that a cultural and economic product often associated with a political entity may in fact be noncongruent with it, both temporally and spatially. The implications of such noncongruence in this case remain to be explored.

Kinet appears to have been a port controlled by the Templars, an organization that directly answered neither to Antioch nor Sis, the Armenian Cilician capital. And yet it participated in a regional network of decentralized but highly standardized production of iron ingots, nails, and other simple objects, as well as glazed ceramics whose shape and decoration varied little from that made in other regional centers. This port also sold timber to the Genoese. Although for much of its medieval existence Kinet lay within the boundaries of the Kingdom of Armenian Cilicia, all but minor transactions were made with the currency of the Principality of Antioch. It may be argued that this was a border region, which is true, but currency use argues for more integration with Antioch. If so, one is hard-pressed to find evidence of the famous state monopolies on salt, sugar, honey, soap, and even ship timber known from such other medieval Mediterranean states as Norman Sicily and Lusignan Cyprus.

David Jacoby has argued for a change in shipping patterns in the thirteenth century, contending that the seasonal milk run around the eastern Mediterranean was replaced by direct point-to-point shipping, with cabotage to secondary ports proceeding from major ports like Acre. In essence, this is an argument for a two-tiered system of trading cities. According to this model, ships would travel from Venice or Genoa directly to, say, Famagusta, with their produce then distributed to the largest port in Cilicia, Āyās, or to Port Saint Symeon, and from there to a minor port like Kinet. Major cities would similarly follow this pattern in gathering goods for consumption or export.[26]

Data from neutron activation analysis of glazed Aegean pottery found at Kinet contradict this model. In a decade-long research project, M. James Blackman of the Smithsonian Institution and I sampled and analyzed dozens of sherds imported to Kinet from the Aegean from all levels of the site's century-and-a-half medieval occupation. We found that the majority of the sherds of Aegean wares found at Kinet, a site thousands of kilometers distant from the Aegean, were made from the same clay, and therefore were probably all made in or near the same place, even though they were produced over 150 years, and with a variety of techniques. It is hard to think of a small port like Kinet receiving pottery from only one production center in the Aegean over such a long time had it received its imports, as it should have by virtue of its size, as the result of redistribution from a "central place." Given the close identification of Kinet with the Templars in both Frankish and Islamic sources, it is likely that multiple networks were in operation simultaneously, and that a port in the Aegean associated with the Templars may have furnished these ceramics. Similar special arrangements in production and distribution networks for other products and groups must be envisaged as operating alongside the prevalent cabotage model.[27]

In the same study, we also analyzed sherds of Port Saint Symeon Ware found at Kinet, as well as pottery from 1930s British excavations at Port Saint Symeon itself. In addition, we sampled unpro-

---

26 E.g., in "Everyday Life in Frankish Acre," *Crusades* 4 (2005): 118–19, D. Jacoby argues for direct trade with single ports like Acre, with cabotage up and down the coast. He maintains, "Local ships practising cabotage along the Levantine coast provided Acre with victuals, raw materials, half-finished and finished products. Wine came from Antioch and Laodicea, silk stuff and ceramics from Antioch, spices, salt fish and flax from Egypt, planks, scrap iron and iron ingots, nails and horseshoes from Ayas in Cilician Armenia" (92).

27 M. J. Blackman and S. Redford, "Neutron Activation Analysis of Medieval Ceramics from Kinet, Turkey, Especially Port Saint Symeon Ware," *Ancient Near Eastern Studies* 42 (2005): 83–186. In excavations at Corinth, the consistent recovery of Seljuk *fulūs* minted in Antioch before the First Crusade points to another possible special relationship between the two ports; see D. M. Metcalf, "Six Unresolved Problems in the Monetary History of Antioch, 969–1268," in Ciggaar and Metcalf, eds., *East and West in the Medieval Eastern Mediterranean*, 293–96.

venienced pieces of Port Saint Symeon Ware in museum collections. Chemical signatures for the clays from the production centers of these two ports were identified. Gratifyingly, we found the chemical data to be congruent with stylistic and iconographic difference in the ceramics' decoration. As a result, we can introduce to this context the idea of "workshop production" familiar to archaeologists, art historians, and economists alike. Ceramics made at the smaller port of Kinet were consistently simpler in decoration and subject matter. Ceramics chemically identified as having been made in Port Saint Symeon consistently were better drawn, and featured subject matter that was iconographically more complex. The best-known example of pottery so identified was the famous Dumbarton Oaks amphora (cover image), whose clay fabric is the same as that of vessels found in excavations at Port Saint Symeon itself.[28]

Aside from assuring art historians that visual analysis can be meaningful, and economists that workshops actually existed, how does this discovery affect our thinking about the economy of maritime trade in the thirteenth-century Mediterranean? If stylistic and iconographic complexity can be associated with a larger production center, and simpler production with a smaller provincial center, we can persuasively argue for a sliding scale of prices based on skill and length of time of production (and not on material). Market destination, in these two cases, might also affect price. Port Saint Symeon was closer both to the larger, more sophisticated (and wealthier) Antiochene market and to the long-distance, point-to-point transport ships taking products around the Mediterranean basin. Kinet can be seen as producing ceramics more cheaply, and quickly, for a more local market.

Whether these conclusions are correct or not, the consistent use of avian, floral, astrological, and debased royal imagery on Port Saint Symeon ceramics made them equally acceptable in the Caucasus, Mesopotamia, Cairo, the Crimea, and France, to name some of the more far-flung points where these ceramics have been recovered. I would argue that the Italian merchant republics worked to create taste—using standardized nonreligious imagery to appeal to a wide variety of markets around the Mediterranean. As is well known, in the early thirteenth century, ceramics changed from an incidental to a principal maritime cargo. But we can apply the lessons learned from the analysis of Port Saint Symeon ceramics to other manufactured products—like the camlets and leather goods mentioned above—that have now disappeared or await identification in museum basements and church treasuries. As trade networks became more efficient, and peace reigned, it was in the interest of Italian merchants to produce, or stimulate the production of, goods that were salable in a wide variety of destinations, and these goods must have been produced at a variety of prices for different markets: different in being rural or urban, rich or poor, coastal or inland, but not different in being Christian and Muslim.[29]

---

28 Blackman and Redford, "Medieval Ceramics from Kinet," 101–3. See also Helen Evans, ed., *Byzantium: Faith and Power (1261–1557)*, 398–99 for a brief discussion of the imagery on this amphora.

29 S. Redford, "On *Sāqīs* and Ceramics: Systems of Representation in the Northeast Mediterranean," in *France and the Holy Land: Frankish Culture at the End of the Crusades,* ed. D. Weiss and L. Mahoney (Baltimore, 2004), 282–312. A consideration of cultural borrowing between Antioch and Aleppo may begin with the examination of ceramics and other finds from the recent Aleppo citadel excavations. That part closest to Port Saint Symeon Ware can be found in V. Daiber, "Sgraffiato-Keramik von der Aleppiner Zitadelle," in *Qal'at Halab* 1.4, ed. K. Kohlmeyer and W. Khayyata (forthcoming). I am grateful to Julia Gonnella for this reference.

• THIRTEEN •

Regional Exchange and the Role of the Shop in Byzantine and Early Islamic Syria-Palestine

An Archaeological View

ALAN WALMSLEY

Much traditional medieval economic history has stressed long-distance commerce: partly because documentary sources overstress luxuries ... and partly because of what one might call the mercantilist romanticism of Venetian galleys ploughing the seas, and of wharves loaded with bales of cloth. In reality, however, most exchange, and the most important bulk exchange, took place inside rather than between regions.[1]

Chris Wickham, in his impressive and compelling 990-page book on the medieval economy of Europe and the Mediterranean, respectfully reminds us, in a chapter titled "Systems of Exchange" ("the core of the book"),[2] that Western scholarship has traditionally emphasized those aspects of economic exchange relevant to its own recent past: transregional trade systems, a belief in codependency between commerce and empire, the pivotal role of a merchant class (the Venetians, for instance), and a deeply symbiotic relationship between economic complexity and successful elites. From a postcolonial perspective—today increasingly dominant in many disciplines, including archaeology[3]—most of these assumptions require difficult, probing questioning or, at the very least, a rephrasing of issues and a detailed reanalysis of data from new perspectives. The 2008 Byzantine Spring Symposium at Dumbarton Oaks, which was the genesis of this volume, represented a most positive move in that direction, given its expressed emphasis on regional exchange, markets, and the marketplace.[4]

Defining and understanding local trade networks and the major function played by regional markets in such systems lie at the core of this chapter, which centers on Byzantine and early Islamic Syria-Palestine (roughly the sixth to eighth centuries AD). At least that is my intention, just partially achieved in this offering, as hitherto only sporadic research has taken place into commercial exchange at the medial level in the eastern Mediterranean during these centuries. Instead, most studies have consistently dealt with the character and extent of interregional trade—that is, those networks that spanned the Mediterranean and in some cases reached quite far inland—focusing in particular on the movement of luxury goods and prestige items, or at least on those types of objects easily recoverable from archaeological contexts and amenable to historical-cultural analysis. An interest in interregional networks during late antiquity grew, in part, out of a tradition of research into Roman imperial systems made possible by surviving written sources and, for archaeologists, the high visibility of trade networks in the material culture record. Overwhelmingly, archaeological research has emphasized the extensive ceramic

1 C. Wickham, *Framing the Early Middle Ages: Europe and the Mediterranean, 400–800* (Oxford, 2005), 707.
2 Ibid., 693.
3 See, for an informative introduction, C. Gosden, *Archaeology and Colonialism: Cultural Contact from 5000 B.C. to the Present*, Topics in Contemporary Archaeology (Cambridge, 2004).

4 Special thanks are due to Dumbarton Oaks, especially Cécile Morrisson and Alice-Mary Talbot, for issuing the invitation to speak at the Symposium and for organizing such a stimulating and informative meeting.

record produced by a century or more of excavation: fine wares (notably late Roman slip wares),[5] lamps, different amphora groups,[6] and increasingly the much-neglected coarse wares.[7] There is no denying that important work was done—from basic studies on matters of chronology, production, and technology to more complicated considerations of premodern political systems and contact exchange—yet this emphasis on interregional trade ignored or obscured a huge sector of the economy: namely, exchange systems at the regional and even subregional level.

By understanding the range, purpose, and health of regional trade networks, researchers may be able to provide detailed insights into developments in social and political structures at the subelite level, and especially into the ability of individual communities to identify and withstand, through adaptive strategies, potentially deadly challenges to their survival. Written sources rarely consider these groups, even though they constitute the financial and cultural basis of a society. As scholarship has increasingly questioned the worth of a hierarchical approach to history and sought to contextualize the actions of a ruling class, archaeology has stepped in with much new information along with the theoretical, methodological, and empirical techniques to deal with it—though we must ask different questions of data sourced from archaeology if we are to gain fresh insights.

Cognizant of the issues just outlined (on which much more really needs to be done), I will attempt in this chapter to identify and analyze the activity of local trade networks in Byzantine and early Islamic Syria-Palestine from two different, but closely related, perspectives. The first section presents two different categories of material culture, specifically ceramics and low-value (copper alloy) coinage, in an effort to map out the geographical reach and level of activity in regional trade networks.[8] Work to date reveals that local networks were especially vibrant in the sixth to eighth centuries (and almost certainly beyond, but verifiable evidence is currently lacking), and contributed significantly to the uninterrupted prosperity of Syria-Palestine over this period. These networks facilitated not only local exchange but also, on a wider scale, the transportation of commodities from outside the immediate region, as these two systems were very likely interdependent. The second section looks at the economic and social role of the shop at the local level. Archaeological evidence for a shop-based market system has expanded greatly in recent years, providing a detailed understanding of the system of exchange within an urban context and demonstrating the crucial role of the shop in everyday commercial exchange. However, its social function as an urban institution has been relatively neglected. This chapter concludes by reflecting on the shops, their keepers, the suppliers, and the patrons as an operating system of both economic exchange and cultural interaction in postclassical Syria-Palestine. By focusing attention on how the physical centrality of the shop was matched by its defining social role on a daily basis, the study of the shop and its contents also promises to offer fascinating and revealing insights into changing social outlooks in towns.

---

5   The classic and still current study is in J. W. Hayes, *Late Roman Pottery: A Catalogue of Roman Fine Wares* (London, 1972); idem, *A Supplement to Late Roman Pottery* (London, 1980). Subsequent archaeological work has made some limited, but significant, improvements to Hayes's conclusions, most notably in extending the period of use (by changing the terminal dates) for some of the later forms.

6   For recent studies, see J. Eiring and J. Lund, eds., *Transport Amphorae and Trade in the Eastern Mediterranean: Acts of the International Colloquium at the Danish Institute at Athens, September 26–29, 2002,* Monographs of the Danish Institute at Athens 5 (Aarhus, 2004); D. Pieri, *Le commerce du vin oriental à l'époque byzantine, V^e–VIIe siècles: Le témoignage des amphores en Gaule,* Bibliothèque archéologique et historique 174 (Beirut, 2005); P. Reynolds, "Levantine Amphorae from Cilicia to Gaza: A Typology and Analysis of Regional Production Trends from the 1st to 7th Centuries," in *LRCW 1: Late Roman Coarse Wares, Cooking Wares and Amphorae in the Mediterranean: Archaeology and Archaeometry,* ed. J. M. Gurt Esparraguera, J. Buxeda i Garrigós, and M. A. Cau Ontiveros, BAR International Series 1340 (Oxford, 2005), 563–611.

7   See the assessment of coarse ware studies in L. Joyner, "Searching for the Holy Grail: Late Roman Ceramic Analysis in the Levant," in Gurt Esparraguera, Buxeda i Garrigós, and Cau Ontiveros, eds., *LRCW 1: Late Roman Coarse Wares,* 547–62, as well as other essays in that groundbreaking volume dedicated to understanding common wares in the late antique Mediterranean.

8   Ceramics and coins were chosen because these material groups are relatively abundant and a substantial number of reasonably thorough studies have already been undertaken, but other classes of finds—notably, glass, lamps, and worked stone—show great promise; see, for instance, the wide-ranging essays on glass in M.-D. Nenna, ed., *La route du verre: Ateliers primaires et secondaires du second millénaire av. J.-C. au Moyen Âge,* Travaux de la Maison de l'Orient méditerranéen 33 (Lyon, 2000).

Regional Networks
Pottery

Previous studies of locally produced ceramics dating to late antique and early Islamic Syria-Palestine (fig. 13.1) have shown that the spatial distribution of pottery from a production nucleus rarely extended beyond 100 kilometers; although examples did occasionally cross this limit, they did so rarely and only exceptionally were found at a radius greater than 150 kilometers. The most likely reasons for the 100-kilometer limit were economic and social.[9] The primary economic disincentive was distribution costs, which by land were always expensive (compared to water) and could vary according to available transport routes and the nature of the terrain to be crossed. Once distribution costs exceeded revenues from sales, a commodity would no longer be traded—a basic rule of central place theory; but since most of the population lived in rural areas, profits were optimized by organizing a distribution network that reached into the countryside,[10] a point we will return to later.

Transport expenses would have comprised duties levied at provincial borders,[11] market fees at the point of sale, and either ownership overhead or the hire and sustenance of drovers and their pack animals.[12] Mules, donkeys, and camels were the main means of transport in late antiquity and early Islamic times;[13]

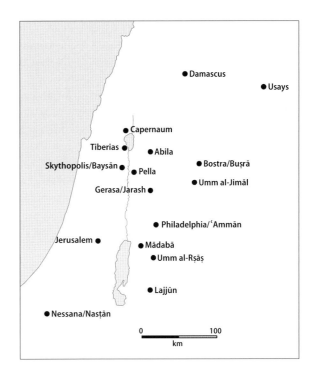

Figure 13.1. The southern half of Syria-Palestine in late antiquity and the early Islamic period (major sites discussed) (drawn by author)

as the seventh-century Christian pilgrim Arculf commented, wagons and carts were rarely seen in Palestine.[14] With pack animals, a three-day journey could have averaged a hundred kilometers (62.5 miles), perhaps a little more.[15] Some indication of probable distances achieved by trading caravans can be seen in voyages undertaken in the region before the construction of modern roads. In the nineteenth century, C. M. Doughty was able to cover 140 kilometers in three long days on a largely flat and well-traveled route between 'Ammān and al-Ḥisā' as part of the annual pilgrimage to the Ḥijāz.[16] A more mountainous terrain would have slowed progress, but not necessarily as much as we might expect. Early in the twentieth century, Gertrude Bell was able to travel on horseback the road between Jerusalem and al-Ṣalṭ, crossing the depression of the Jordan

---

9   For an insightful general study of factors encouraging regionalization in Jordan, see P. Bienkowski, "The North-South Divide in Jordan: Ceramics, Regionalism and Routes," in *Culture through Objects: Ancient Near Eastern Studies in Honour of P. R. S. Moorey,* ed. T. F. Potts, M. Roaf, and D. L. Stein (Oxford, 2003), 93–107.

10 R. L. Morrill, *The Spatial Organization of Society,* 2nd ed. (North Scituate, Mass., 1974), 61–65. Costs exceed profits until a threshold volume of sales is reached (i.e., local consumers offer only a limited market base), after which profits increase before being eroded by expenses (transport, taxes); as expenses rise, profits ultimately are reduced to zero.

11 Probably a head tax for each animal, assessed depending on the goods being carried; more expensive commodities drew a higher rate, as in the Palmyrene Tariff of AD 139. Boundary taxes would have hindered exchange between provinces, as will be seen below.

12 The government obtained pack animals by requisition; see C. J. Kraemer, *Excavations at Nessana,* vol. 3, *Non-Literary Papyri* (Princeton, N.J., 1958), 209–11, document 74 (dated to the late seventh century): a demand for two camels and two drovers with pack saddles and straps to work the Caesarea–Skythopolis route.

13 A. Walmsley, "Roads, Travel, and Time 'across Jordan' in Byzantine and Early Islamic Times," in *Studies in the History and Archaeology of Jordan,* vol. 10 (Amman, 2009), 459–66.

14 J. Wilkinson, *Jerusalem Pilgrims before the Crusades* (Warminster, 1977), 106.

15 See ibid., 16–28, who settles on 12 to 19 miles a day on trails, depending on conditions.

16 C. M. Doughty, *Travels in Arabia Deserta,* 2nd ed., 2 vols (London, 1921), 1:58–66; the third day, traveling the flat and monotonous road from Qaṭranah to al-Ḥisā', took 12 hours.

Rift Valley, in two short days—a total distance of a little over 80 kilometers.[17] With loaded pack animals such a trip would have taken longer, and by foot it would have been even slower.

In addition to economic imperatives, social factors may have also played a significant role in limiting distances traveled. Jews preferred to complete a journey within six days—three days out and three days back—so that the traveler would be home for the holy day and related social activities at the week's end. While the same requirement did not hold for Christians and Muslims, they probably also preferred to complete a journey within a week.

Three case studies of distinctive ceramic types reveal that the 100–150 kilometer range for regional trade networks applied equally between the sixth and ninth centuries. In all three examples, the pottery was of superior manufacture (one reason why it is commonly described in archaeological reports), being well prepared and finished; in two cases the external surface was also embellished with bold painted designs.

In the sixth to seventh centuries, an appealing category of table ware usually referred to as "Jerash Bowls," named after their known production site in north Jordan, radiated out in an area defined by the Jordan Rift Valley on the west, the Wādī Yarmūk to the north, and the Wādī Mūjib on the south (fig. 13.2).[18] Most discoveries fit within a radius of 50 kilometers from Jarash, with only two locations known outside the 100-kilometer radius. This suggests that the maximum range of sales was 50 kilometers (requiring a round trip of four days) with maximum economic benefits being attained at around 20 to 30 kilometers out, depending on conditions, or a two-day journey there and back. The specimens found at sites in a radius of 50 to 100 kilometers from Jarash were probably sourced through a secondary market, such as Skythopolis/Baysān for the north Jordan Valley,[19] and Philadelphia/ʿAmmān or Mādabā

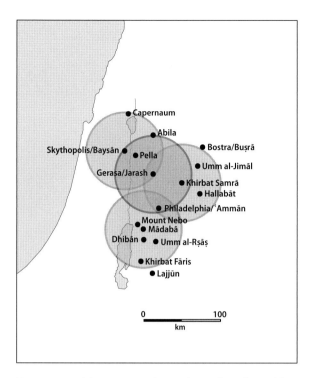

Figure 13.2. Major sites with Jerash Bowls and possible distribution networks (drawn by author)

for the middle Jordan plateau.[20] As the distribution map shows, Jerash Bowls were predominantly a product of Arabia, both manufactured and marketed there, but also with lines of distribution northwestward to the former Dekapolis towns in eastern Palaestina Secunda, a politico-cultural grouping to which Jarash also formally belonged.[21] The Jerash

17 G. L. Bell, *The Desert and the Sown* (London, 1907), 4–18.
18 See A. Walmsley, "Economic Developments and the Nature of Settlement in the Towns and Countryside of the Levant, ca. 565–800 CE," *DOP* 61 (2007): 319–52, at 331, with references.
19 Skythopolis was endowed with extensive markets in late antique and early Islamic times, including a new complex dated to the reign of the caliph Hishām (724–43); see E. Khamis, "Two Wall Mosaic Inscriptions from the Umayyad Market Place in Bet Shean/Baysan," *BSOAS* 64 (2001): 159–76; Y. Tsafrir and G. Foerster, "Urbanism at Scythopolis–Bet Shean in the Fourth to Seventh Centuries," *DOP* 51 (1997): 85–146.

20 For ʿAmmān, see A. Binggeli, "Foire et pèlerinages sur la route du Hajj: À propos de quelques sanctuaires chrétiens et musulmans dans le sud du Bilad al-Šam d'après le *Kitab al-azmina* d'Ibn Masawayh (9e s.)," *Aram* 18–19 (2006–07): 559–82, at 566–69, where the fair of ʿAmmān is described based on a ninth-century source; also the likely marketplace next to the cathedral in the lower town (site of a later khan) in A. Northedge, *Studies on Roman and Islamic ʿAmman: The Excavations of Mrs C.-M. Bennett and Other Investigations,* vol. 1, *History, Site and Architecture,* British Academy Monographs in Archaeology 3 (Oxford, 1992), 59–61. For Mādabā, see D. C. Foran, T. P. Harrison, et al., "The Tall Mādabā Archaeological Project, Preliminary Report of the 2002 Field Season," *ADAJ* 48 (2004): 79–96, at 91 and fig. 10.13–14, for two likely Jerash Bowls; below, the possible commercial role of Mādabā/Mount Nebo is discussed further.
21 A perceptive analysis of the Decapolis can be found in D. F. Graf, "Hellenisation and the Decapolis," *Aram* 4 (1992): 1–48. Jarash, it is worth noting, does not appear among the towns of Arabia and Palestine depicted in an eighth-century church mosaic at Umm al-Raṣāṣ (Kastron Mefaʿa) in Jordan (the northernmost town shown is Philadelphia/ʿAmmān); see M. Piccirillo and E. Alliata, *Umm al-Rasas—Mayfaʿah I: Gli scavi del com-*

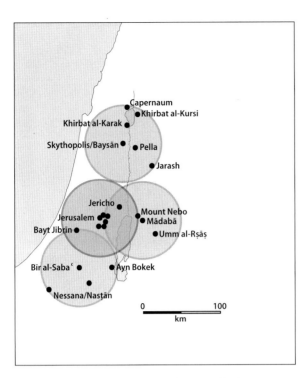

Figure 13.3. Sites with and distribution of Palestinian Fine Ware of the 7th to 9th c. AD (drawn by author)

ash Bowls and church mosaics display a shared iconographic and representational tradition, made easy by the use of frames in mosaic compositions,[23] and reveal a smooth crossover between religious and secular contexts not challenged until the iconoclastic explosion experienced by Christians and Muslims alike in eighth-century Syria-Palestine.[24]

The second example, called Palestinian Fine Ware, was a popular pottery type in southern Syria-Palestine during the seventh to ninth centuries; it was likely a product of the Jerusalem area and inspired by precious metal prototypes current in Jerusalem.[25] A distribution map of this ware shows a cluster of sites within a 30- to 50-kilometer radius of Jerusalem (fig. 13.3), with three further groupings in the north Jordan Valley, on the central Jordanian plateau, and in the Naqab/Negev area. The most distant sites, at around 150 kilometers, were Capernaum on Lake Tiberias in the north and Nessana (Nasṭān) in the south. Again, the spread of Palestinian Fine Ware indicates the use of subsidiary distribution centers such as Skythopolis for the north Jordan Valley and Mādabā for Jordan,[26] with material moving the greatest distances across more favorable terrain such as the conduit of the Jordan Rift Valley and the

Bowls constituted part of a highly visual culture that dominated late antique and early Islamic Jordan. Using a corpus of imagery drawn from a Hellenistic and indigenous past and depicted in many church mosaics, communities centered on Jarash and Mādabā were to simultaneously claim a warmly embraced social memory as their own, broadcast a new self-defining identity, and confirm a confident presence at the culmination of the political, cultural, religious, and financial success of Christians in their society.[22] In this celebratory environment, the Jer-

---

plesso di Santo Stefano, Studium Biblicum Franciscanum Collectio Maior 28 (Jerusalem, 1994), 121–230, a possible indication of Jarash's weaker link with the towns to its south.

22 Significant contributions to comprehending the meaning behind the rich material imagery of these mosaics can be found in C. Bertelli, "Visual Images of the Town in Late Antiquity and the Early Middle Ages," in *The Idea and Ideal of the Town between Late Antiquity and the Early Middle Ages,* ed. G. P. Brogiolo and B. Ward-Perkins, Transformation of the Roman World (Leiden, 1999), 127–46; G. W. Bowersock, *Mosaics as History: The Near East from Late Antiquity to Islam,* Revealing Antiquity 16 (Cambridge, Mass., 2006); L.-A. Hunt, "The Byzantine Mosaics of Jordan in Context: Remarks on Imagery, Donors and Mosaicists," *PEQ* 126 (1994): 106–26; M. Piccirillo, "The Activity of the Mosaicists of the Diocese of Madaba at the Time of Bishop Sergius in the Second Half of the Sixth Century AD," in *Studies in the History and Archaeology of Jordan,* vol. 5, *Art and Technology*

Throughout the Ages, ed. K. 'Amr, F. Zayadine, and M. Zaghloul (Amman, 1995), 391–98; and also G. Fowden, "Late-Antique Art in Syria and Its Umayyad Evolutions," *JRA* 17 (2004): 282–304, although with some distracting language. Below, a stylistic link between mosaic designs and ceramic decoration is discussed further.

23 P. M. Watson, "Pictorial Painting on Pottery and Its Demise in the Mid-7th Century A.D.: The Case of the Jerash Bowls," *Aram* 6 (1994): 311–32.

24 From the local perspective, see S. Ognibene, "The Iconophobic Dossier," in *Mount Nebo: New Archaeological Excavations, 1967–1997,* ed. M. Piccirillo and E. Alliata, Collectio Maior 27 (Jerusalem, 1998), 373–89; eadem, *Umm al-Rasas: La chiesa di Santo Stefano ed il problema iconofobico* (Rome, 2002); R. Schick, *The Christian Communities of Palestine from Byzantine to Islamic Rule,* Studies in Late Antiquity and Early Islam 2 (Princeton, N.J., 1995), 180–219.

25 J. Magness, *Jerusalem Ceramic Chronology, circa 200–800 CE,* JSOT/ASOR Monograph Series 9 (Sheffield, 1993), 166–71; earlier (but with major errors in dating), M. Gichon, "Fine Byzantine Wares from the South of Israel," *PEQ* 106 (1974): 119–39; also Walmsley, "Economic Developments and Settlement," 330–31.

26 Mount Nebo, too, may have functioned as a subsidiary market center because, as a pilgrimage site associated with Moses, it was well connected to Jerusalem by road. In addition to Piccirillo and Alliata, eds., *Mount Nebo,* see the useful summary of discoveries in M. Piccirillo, "Mount Nebo," in *New Encyclopaedia of Archaeological Excavations in the Holy Land,* ed. E. Stern (Jerusalem, 1993), 1106–18.

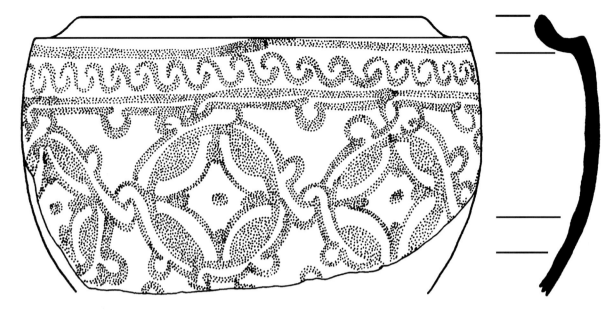

Figure 13.4. Mosaic-style decoration on a deep bowl in "Palace Ware" from Pella, Jordan, 9th or 10th c. AD (courtesy of Pella Archaeological Project, University of Sydney)

desert routes of the Naqab, often used for travel to Saint Catherine's monastery near Mount Sinai.[27]

The highly regional nature of ceramic production and distribution so far seen in the late antique and early Islamic periods persisted in the later eighth and ninth centuries, when a new ware type—characterized by the extensive and, at times, sophisticated use of red paint—appeared. This third example considered here, Red Painted Ware, occurs in four main varieties differentiated by fineness, shape, and paint. The earliest, based on the Pella finds, are the jars found embedded in the AD 749 earthquake debris.[28] These were wheel-made of a well-prepared clay, expertly fired to a light buff to pale orange color and decorated in red with bold abstract designs of swirls, stars, palm fronds, and wavy to zigzag lines: practical, appealing, but devoid of images. The second variety consists of high-walled cups decorated on the outside and sometimes inside with drooping loops and wavy lines, manufactured at Jarash as found in Kiln 4 of the so-called Umayyad House on the south *decumanus*.[29] The Jarash cups were very similar in shape (though not fineness) and function to the contemporary thin, elevated wall cups in Palestinian Fine Ware, and perhaps were a response to the popularity of the Jerusalem products. The third variety consisted of plates, reminiscent in function of the Jerash Bowls but seemingly not made at Jarash, again exuberantly but abstractly decorated with circles and wavy lines, but no images. The last variety was the so-called Palace Ware, a skillfully constructed ceramic product—technologically skillful, morphologically

---

27 Note the requisition preserved in the Nessana papyri for a guide to take pilgrims to the Sinai: Kraemer, *Nessana*, 3:205–7.

28 A. Walmsley, "The Umayyad Pottery and Its Antecedents," in *Pella in Jordan 1: An Interim Report on the Joint University of Sydney and The College of Wooster Excavations at Pella, 1979–1981*, ed. A. McNicoll, R. H. Smith, and B. Hennessy, 2 vols. (Canberra, 1982), 1:143–57; idem, "Tradition, Innovation, and Imitation in the Material Culture of Islamic Jordan: The First Four Centuries," in 'Amr, Zayadine, and Zaghloul, eds., *Studies in the History and Archaeology of Jordan*, 5:657–68; also idem, "Economic Developments and Settlement," 341–42.

29 M. Gawlikowski, "Céramiques byzantines et omayyades de Jerash," in *Hellenistic and Roman Pottery in the Eastern Mediterranean—Advances in Scientific Studies: Acts of the II Nieborów Pottery Workshop*, ed. H. Meyza and J. Mlynarczyk (Nieborów, 1995), 83–86; idem, "A Residential Area by the South Decumanus," in *Jerash Archaeological Project*, vol. 1, *1981–1983*, ed. F. Zayadine (Amman, 1986), 107–36, although perhaps the Umayyad House was actually a commercial structure that was a constituent part of the mosque-market complex in this area of Jarash; see H. Barnes, L. Blanke, et al., "From 'Guard House' to Congregational Mosque: Recent Discoveries on the Urban History of Islamic Jarash," *ADAJ* 50 (2006): 285–314; L. Blanke, K. Damgaard, et al., "From Bathhouse to Congregational Mosque: Further Discoveries on the Urban History of Islamic Jarash," *ADAJ* 51 (2007): 177–97.

Figure 13.5. Sites with and distribution of Red Painted Ware, dating to the 7th to 9th or 10th c. AD (drawn by author)

elegant, and stylistically decorated—whose elaborate interlacing designs are directly linked to the mosaic traditions of the time (fig. 13.4). Apart from the cups, the production center for Red Painted Ware has not been located, and the chemical dissimilarity between the jars and Jerash Bowls suggests that there was at least one other point of manufacture.[30] Nevertheless, the findspots of the other Red Painted Ware varieties point to a location not too distant from Jarash, probably near 'Ammān. The distribution of Red Painted Ware, though it took place a century or more later, is structurally very close to that of the Jarash Bowls, with two secondary distribution centers for the north Jordan Valley and east of the Dead Sea—probably Tiberias and Mādabā, respectively. Red Painted Ware was a popular item around Mādabā, and an extensive corpus has been recovered at Mount Nebo and Umm al-Raṣāṣ in particular (fig. 13.5).[31]

30   P. Duerden and P. Watson, "PIXE/PIGME Analysis of a Series of Byzantine Painted Bowls from Northern Jordan," *Mediterranean Archaeology* 1 (1988): 96–111, at 108–10.
31   See Piccirillo and Alliata, eds., *Mount Nebo*; C. Sanmorì and C. Pappalardo, "Ceramica dal monastero della Theotokos nel Wadi 'Ayn al-Kanisah—Monte Nebo," *Lib.ann* 50 (2000): 411–30 and pls. 39–42; Piccirillo and Alliata, *Umm al-Rasas—Mayfa'ah I*.

These three classes of pottery repay study at this stage because their distinctive characteristics enable them to be easily identified by excavators (even if sometimes misdated), and thus they are often published. We can therefore make indicative distribution studies. Though their quality and aesthetic appeal undoubtedly raised their production costs, that expense would have been offset by a higher production to distribution cost ratio and increased demand. Together, these factors would have favored a wider dispersal of these ceramic classes than of coarser common wares, such as cooking vessels (which are notoriously difficult to classify without chemical analysis of the fabric). The distribution maps show that the optimum range for these better-quality decorated wares was 30 to 50 kilometers; money could still be made by onselling the ceramics to a secondary market point on the periphery, from which the goods could be redistributed for another 30 to sometimes 50 kilometers. Only rare examples were distributed outside this 100-kilometer range, and they were nearly always found at sites that were on easily traversed routes (such as the north Jordan Valley) or were privileged places (such as the royal establishments at remote Usays and al-Rīsha, where specimens of Red Painted Ware were found).

Coins

An equally prolific source of useful evidence for economic structures in late antique and early Islamic Syria-Palestine is provided by the numismatic history of sites, until recently troublesome for these periods but now much improved following the latest advances in the identification and dating of the transitional coinages.[32] The coin evidence produced

32   See now a constantly growing and impressive list of publications, such as recently S. Album and T. Goodwin, *Sylloge of Islamic Coins in the Ashmolean*, vol. 1, *The Pre-reform Coinage of the Early Islamic Period* (Oxford, 2002); H. J. Bone, "The Administration of Umayyad Syria: The Evidence of the Copper Coins" (Ph.D. diss., Princeton University, 2000); C. Foss, *Arab-Byzantine Coins: An Introduction with a Catalogue of the Dumbarton Oaks Collection*, Dumbarton Oaks Byzantine Collection Publications 12 (Washington, D.C., 2008); idem, "The Coinage of Syria in the Seventh Century: The Evidence of Excavations," *Israel Numismatic Journal* 13 (1994–99): 119–32; T. Goodwin, *Arab-Byzantine Coinage*, Studies in the Khalili Collection 4 (London, 2005); idem, "The Arab-Byzantine Coinage of Jund Filastin: A Potential Historical Source," *BMGS* 28 (2004): 1–12; N. G. Goussous, *Nummiyat nuhasiyah Umawiyah jadidah min majmu'ah khassah: musahamah fi i'adat nazar fi nummiyat bilad al-Sham*

by excavations, increasingly being taken seriously by project directors, largely corroborates the conclusions drawn from the ceramic data about the strength of regional economies in the sixth to ninth centuries, but with some interesting caveats. Site-retrieved isolated coin finds and hoards, both characterized by an enhanced reliability because of their archaeological contexts,[33] together present a consistent and similar picture of the monetary economy in each century.

Analysis of site finds of base coinage dating to the sixth and early seventh century, during which time coinage was sourced from outside the region, reveal considerable regionalism in the distribution and circulation of low-value coinage. In a pioneering 1964 study of Byzantine and Arab-Byzantine coins, Michael Metcalf observed that sites and hoards in Palestine and Arabia exhibited localized consignment patterns and that, more surprisingly, these were subsequently preserved in a discernible pattern of a "preponderance" of particular mints and authorities at one place. On this he commented: "it is quite remarkable that the outlines of the original pattern of consignment should not have become more blurred through the process of ordinary monetary circulation."[34] The evidence from the adjacent sites of Gerasa/Jarash, Pella, and Skythopolis, spread in this period over two provinces (Gerasa was in Arabia, while Pella and Skythopolis—the capital city—were in Palaestina Secunda), shows ample proof of regionality in coin distribution and subsequent circulation, and much of that proof is in the detail. All three sites reveal that a high proportion of the base metal coins from the reigns of Justin I, Justinian, and Justin II were sourced from the mints of Constantinople and Nikomedeia, not the regionally significant center of Antioch (fig. 13.6). Official consignments probably explain this phenomenon, now a recognized characteristic of this region and expressed, in the seventh century, by the widespread replication of the Justin II and Sophia type from Nikomedeia to meet the continuing needs of the marketplace—and to satisfy an unshakable preference for this coin type about a century after its extensive introduction.[35] In this instance the trait was regional and transprovincial, but largely limited to the Jarash–Skythopolis axis. Yet within the regional pattern, local variations can be discerned. For example, Pella had a much higher incidence of coins from Nikomedeia, which indicates that this mint was commissioned to supply coins to Palaestina Secunda during the reigns of Justinian and Justin II, whereas Gerasa received a higher number of coins minted in Thessalonike as well as Antioch. Unusually, Gerasa also had some Alexandrian 12-nummi issues, elsewhere before the end of the century found only in coastal Palaestina Prima.[36] That these very specific supply patterns survived for so long—well into the following century—demonstrates emphatically the very limited economic horizons of towns in sixth-century Palestine and Arabia,

---

[Rare and inedited Umayyad copper coins] (Amman, 2004); A. Oddy, "Whither Arab-Byzantine Numismatics? A Review of Fifty Years' Research," *BMGS* 28 (2004): 121–52; H. Pottier and C. Foss, *Le monnayage de la Syrie sous l'occupation perse (610–630) = Coinage in Syria under Persian Rule (610–630)*, Cahiers Ernest-Babelon 5 (Paris, 2004); H. Pottier, I. Schulze, and W. Schulze, "Pseudo-Byzantine Coinage in Syria under Arab Rule (638–670): Classification and Dating," *RBN* 154 (2008): 87–161; also a comprehensive review of the topic in L. Ilisch, "Islamic Numismatics," in *A Survey of Numismatic Research, 1996–2001*, ed. C. Alfaro and A. Burnett (Madrid, 2003), 637–61, at 638–40.

33 The emphasis on site retrieval necessarily excludes hoards or coins obtained through the market, of which the "only sure provenance is the international transit lounge at Zurich airport": M. Phillips, "Currency in Seventh-Century Syria as a Historical Source," *BMGS* 28 (2004): 13–31, at 17.

34 D. M. Metcalf, "Some Byzantine and Arab-Byzantine Coins from Palaestina Prima," *Israel Numismatic Journal* 2 (1964): 84–98, at 87.

35 Album and Goodwin, *Islamic Coins*, 1:89; N. Amitai-Preiss, A. Berman, and S. Qedar, "The Coinage of Scythopolis-Baysan and Gerasa-Jerash," *Israel Numismatic Journal* 13 (1994–99): 133–51, at 135–39; Metcalf, "Coins from Palaestina Prima," 86; C. Morrisson, "La monnaie en Syrie byzantine," in *Archéologie et histoire de la Syrie*, ed. J.-M. Dentzer and W. Orthmann (Saarbrücken, 1989), 191–204, at 194; A. Oddy, "The Early Umayyad Coinage of Baisân and Jerash," *Aram* 6 (1994): 405–18; see also A. Walmsley, "Coin Frequencies in Sixth and Seventh Century Palestine and Arabia: Social and Economic Implications," *Journal of the Economic and Social History of the Orient* 42 (1999): 324–50, for a (now dated) comparative study of Byzantine coins retrieved from the excavations at Jarash and Pella.

36 See E. J. Prawdzic-Golemberski and D. M. Metcalf, "The Circulation of Byzantine Coins on the South-eastern Frontiers of the Empire," *NC* 123 (1963): 83–92, at 86–87, G. Bijovsky, "Review: Bruno Callegher. *Cafarnao* IX. *Monete dall'area urbana di Cafarnao (1968–2003)*. Jerusalem 2007; Cécile Morrisson, Vladislav Popović† and Vujadin Ivanišević, *Les trésors monétaires byzantines des Balkans et d'Asie Mineure (491–713)*. Paris 2006," *Israel Numismatic Research* 3 (2008): 192–99, at 196 n. 8; and Metcalf, "Coins from Palaestina Prima," 85, although Metcalf's suggestion that the occurrence of Alexandrian coins resulted from a reopening of eastern land routes between Egypt and Mesopotamia through Jarash is not easily supported by other archaeological evidence (in particular the ceramics mentioned earlier).

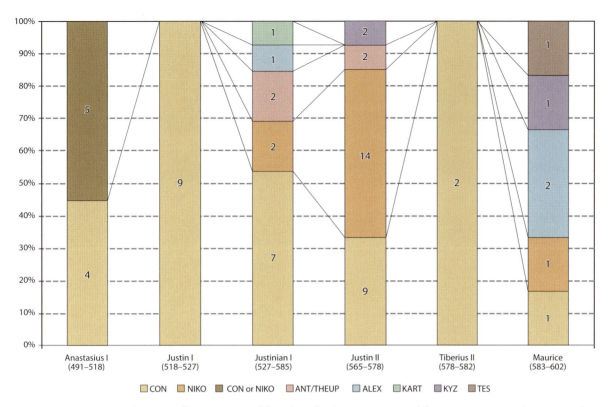

Figure 13.6. The origin by mint of base coinage of the 6th and 7th c. AD, recovered from excavations at Gerasa/Jarash

a pattern repeated in the other regions of Syria-Palestine such as at Bayrūt and in the north of Syria.[37]

The intense localization of coin circulation in the sixth century is matched by that in the seventh century,[38] during which local issues increasingly came to supply market needs. As Byzantine coinage—traded by whatever mechanism—became scarce and then ceased by ca. 660, substitute coinage was locally produced to take its place. The initial production of a replica coinage was instituted under Sasanid rule and probably centered on Emesa/Ḥimṣ;[39] it was followed by a more extensive minting in regional centers in the 650s to 670s, thus shortly after the Islamic expansion into Syria-Palestine.[40] Produced as a substitute coinage, the early Islamic replica currency intermingled freely with introduced Byzantine coinage in the north of Syria-Palestine and seems to have been generally accepted—indeed, more readily at Apameia and Dayhis than the next coin type, the so-called Umayyad Imperial Image series of 660–80.[41] In the south, the substitute coinage had a mixed reception, but it took on a significant role in the monetary economy of Filasṭīn

---

37 For Bayrūt, which had a distinct bias for the small-module coins of Anastasios, see K. Butcher, "Coinage in Sixth-Century Beirut: Preliminary Observations," *Berytus* 43 (1997–1998): 173–80; for a detailed study for sites around Antioch, dominated by issues from Antioch and Constantinople, see T. Vorderstrasse, "Coin Circulation in Some Syrian Villages (5th–11th centuries)," in *Les villages dans l'Empire byzantin (IVe–XVe siècle)*, ed. J. Lefort, C. Morrisson, and J.-P. Sodini (Paris, 2005), 495–510.

38 This period, whose numismatics was previously much neglected, has now been retrieved. See note 32, above.

39 A meticulous, detailed, and convincing study can be found in Pottier and Foss, *Monnayage de la Syrie*.

40 Well covered in Album and Goodwin, *Islamic Coins*, 1:77–81, which should be read in tandem with C. Foss's review, "The Coinage of the First Century of Islam (review of Stephen Album and Tony Goodwin, *Sylloge of Islamic Coins in the Ashmolean Museum*, volume 1: *The Pre-Reform Coinage of the Early Islamic Period* [Ashmolean Museum, Oxford 2002])," *JRA* 17, fasc. 2 (2004): 748–60.

41 A. Nègre, "Monnaies orientales des maisons d'Apamée: Étude comparative," in *Apamée de Syrie: Bilan des recherches archéologiques, 1973–1979: Aspects de l'architecture domestique d'Apamée: Actes du colloque tenu à Bruxelles les 29, 30 et 31 mai 1980*, ed. J. Balty, Fouilles d'Apamée de Syrie, Miscellanea 13 (Brussels, 1984), 249–59; C. Morrisson, "Déhès: Campagnes I–III (1976–1978), Recherches sur l'habitat rural: Les monnaies," *Syria* 57 (1980): 267–87; see also Foss, "Coinage of Syria," 125–29.

Figure 13.7. An unusual double Standing Caliph copper alloy coin (27 mm diam.; 8.1 g [cleaned]) recovered from recent excavations at Jarash, reflecting the region's continuing preference for a large-module, dual-figure monetary unit; enlarged (courtesy Islamic Jarash Project)

as much less Byzantine coinage reached there, perhaps owing to the distance from Byzantium. At Jarash, Pella, and Skythopolis, however, this coinage found little acceptance, with few examples found during excavation, probably because there was a local preference for the sixth-century types and their later transitional replacements.[42] Even with the attempted adoption over all Syria-Palestine of a standardized and centralized coinage in the 690s, the so-called Standing Caliph series, provincial differences in iconography and metrology persisted. In the towns of the Jund al-Urdunn this type gained no acceptance at all, except for the production of an issue depicting two standing figures (fig. 13.7).[43] Overall, then, the differing regional preferences in the coinage of the seventh century show a strong persistence of localized economies.

Compared to the often-unbridled regionalism of the seventh-century coinage of Syria-Palestine, only partially constrained by the more centralized Standing Caliph series of the 690s, the eighth-century reformed coinage displays much greater unity, a unity that extended outside of Syria-Palestine. Yet even here elements of regional expression emerged, both in the variability of fabric and in the use of distinctive symbols in addition to the standard *shahadah* (declaration of faith). Thus there was a continuing preference, at first, for large-flan coins struck at the mints of Skythopolis/Baysān and Jarash (ca. 700–730s), which preserved a memory of the heavy coins of Justin II and Sophia; but these were eventually superseded in the late 730s by the small-module fish *fals* type of Baysān.[44] With this change at Baysān, as elsewhere in Syria-Palestine at about the same time, a numismatic memory traceable back over 160 years was largely discarded within little more than a generation after 'Abd al-Malik's reform of the coinage, and by the 730s the small-module *fulūs* had become the monetary standard.[45]

Paralleling the relatively analogous stylistic regime of the eighth-century coinage is an extension to the distance from their mint that copper coins circulated, revealing a growing transregional acceptance of monetary units. While most eighth-century site finds show that coins continued to be products of mints in the local province, the proportions of coins from more distant places increased over those seen in the seventh century, although only precious coinage moved considerable distances—sometimes, as bullion, beyond the borders of the Islamic world. At Ṭabariyya, capital of the Jund al-Urdunn, exca-

42 Album and Goodwin, *Islamic Coins*, 82, 1:89; Amitai-Preiss, Berman, and Qedar, "Coinage."

43 This curious coin type, which appears reasonably often in the seventh-century coin repertoire at Jarash but not outside its immediate area, displays a clear relationship to the Standing Caliph type—especially in the inclusion of the title and name of 'Abd al-Malik, as seen on the specimen published here.

44 L. Ilisch, *Palästina IVa Bilâd aš-Šâm I*, Sylloge Nummorum Arabicorum Tübingen (Tübingen, 1993), 28; N. Schindel, "A Hoard of Umayyad Copper Coins from Baysan," *NC* 166 (2006): 385–92.

45 Ilisch, *Palästina*, 10, nos. 23–31 (Iliyā/Jerusalem); 14, nos. 64–77 (al-Ramla, but some medium-sized modules, as would be expected of a provincial capital); 32–34, nos. 345–76 (Ṭabariyya, late 730s and 740s, some displaying palm, tendriled urn, and lion symbols); also H. Gitler, "The Coins," in Piccirillo and Alliata, eds., *Mount Nebo*, 563, for a hoard of small-module *fulūs* from Mount Nebo in Jordan; and A. Walmsley, "The Early Islamic Coin Hoard," in *Excavations at Tall Jawa*, vol. 4, *The Early Islamic House*, ed. M. Daviau, Culture and History of the Ancient Near East 11.4 (Leiden, 2009), 391–412, for an excavated hoard of anonymous small-module fulūs found near Mādabā.

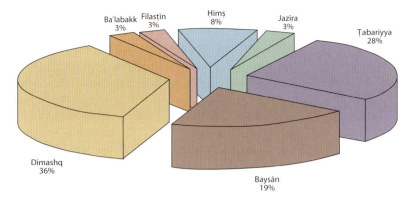

Figure 13.8. Origins of the coins recovered from excavations within the town of Ṭabariyya, the early Islamic capital of the Jund al-Urdunn (from Berman, "The Coins")

vations within the town produced the following numbers of identifiable coins (fig. 13.8). From the Ṭabariyya mint: 10; Baysān: 7 (total from al-Urdunn: 17); Dimashq, a very active mint: 13, plus one from Ba'labakk (total 14); Filasṭīn: 1; Ḥimṣ: 3; and the Jazīra: 1, showing the dominance of local mints.[46] Given that the mint in Damascus was more active, the strong showing of the al-Urdunn mints is even more significant. A corpus from Ruṣāfa, an atypical site because of its status as the Umayyad dynastic capital under Hishām (724–43), is nonetheless still dominated by nearby provincial mints: Qinnasrīn, its own province: 23 fulūs; Ḥimṣ, a prolific mint: 12; the Jazīra: 5; Dimashq: 44, here indicative of fiscal ties with the administrative capital; al-Urdunn: 2; Filasṭīn: 3; and Egypt: 1.[47] Generally, the coins originating in a more distant province probably reached their destination in stages through trade, not consignment, though the numerous Damascus coins at Ruṣāfa were likely an exception.

Ceramics, Coins, and Regional Trade

From the sixth to early ninth centuries, regional economies were demonstrably strong in Syria-Palestine. Ceramics reveal energetic commercial networks usually active within a radius of 30 to 50 kilometers from a central site, with distribution of higher-grade commodities that have higher cost:profit ratios up to 100 kilometers (or through one subsidiary point). More costly goods, for instance steatite stone vessels from the north coast of the Ḥijāz,[48] probably traveled through a system of overlapping market networks; the greater demand for, and hence value of, these items ensured that buyers would absorb the greater costs added not just by the land transportation but also by the market and border taxes. Base coinage reflects a similar arrangement, but we have a more detailed knowledge of its working. The circulation of copper alloy coins in the sixth and seventh centuries was very limited, but in the eighth the system began to expand. Longer lines of communication were formed, and even everyday coinage intended for small change could travel great distances. Simultaneously, new ceramic fashions were beginning their sweep of the Islamic world in styles characterized by shimmering glazes and thin, metal-inspired cream vessels that hinted at riches but avoided the danger of being made from prohibited metals. This, then, was the precursor of a system of long-distance trade and Islamic world awareness that expanded out of the Muslim realm, reaching from Scandinavia to China on a scale that surpassed that of the Roman Empire.

The Shop, Markets, and Shoppers
Shops and Markets

Pottery and coins reveal the overarching structure of distribution networks in Byzantine and early

---

46 A. Berman, "The Coins," in *Excavations at Tiberias, 1973–1974: The Early Islamic Periods*, ed. D. Stacey, IAA Reports 21 (Jerusalem, 2004), 221–45, at 222–23. The pattern is repeated with the anonymous issues, of which 26 can be ascribed to al-Urdunn and Filasṭīn and 17 to Dimashq and Ḥimṣ (two of the most prolific coin-producing provinces), which makes the al-Urdunn/Filasṭīn figure even more significant.

47 L. Ilisch, "Die islamischen Fundmünzen," in *Resafa*, vol. 4, *Die Große Moschee von Resafa—Ruṣafat Hišam*, ed. D. Sack (Mainz, 1996), 111–32. Only the coins attributable to a specific mint are used in these calculations.

48 A. Kisnawi, P. de Jesus, and B. Rihani, "Preliminary Report on the Mining Survey, Northwest Hijaz, 1982," *Atlal* 7 (1983): 76–83.

Islamic Syria-Palestine (even if these reconstructions continue to be unsophisticated given the current state of knowledge), but they do not answer the question of how this system operated on the ground. This section investigates the role of the shop from an economic and social perspective: specifically, it examines exchange systems within towns and villages and especially the pivotal role of the shop. The shop was crucial not only in local commerce but also in society more generally. The markets, the shopkeepers, the suppliers, and the patrons operated within a complex system of economic exchange and cultural interaction, in which the physical centrality of the shop was matched by its influential role in daily community life.

From an archaeological angle, there is little doubt that shop-based market complexes served a pivotal function in the economic life of towns and villages in Byzantine and early Islamic Syria-Palestine. While the archaeological evidence for such activity in major centers—for instance, Damascus and Jerusalem—is obscured by later developments, data from other, second-level urban sites are compelling.[49] Examples include Ruṣāfa (Hishām's capital in north Syria), with an enclosed market shared between the famous pilgrim church of St. Sergius and a large congregational mosque;[50] Palmyra/Tadmūr, where a market street with more than 100 shops has been revealed;[51] Pella, with a shop-lined street and an central ecclesiastical complex with a sizable commercial annex;[52] a new street-based market at Baysān, founded in the time of Hishām as recorded in a mounted mosaic inscription;[53] likewise a new market street at Arsūf on the Mediterranean coast;[54] and (lastly for our purposes) Jarash, where existing market units around the south *tetrakionia* plaza were enlarged to meet expanding commercial needs and developed further with the construction of a congregational mosque. In all cases—and most of the above examples were founded in the first Islamic century or two—the expansion was an ordered, sympathetic addition to towns unaccompanied by the urban chaos imagined by earlier writers on the development of the so-called Oriental city.

In understanding market development in the sixth to eighth centuries, it is also significant that extensive market areas were included in the new foundation of ʿAnjar in the Biqāʿ valley of Lebanon. This often discussed but usually misrepresented site,[55] established during the caliphate of al-Walīd I (705–15), was equipped with streets lined with nearly one hundred shops (many more were planned); these numerous street shops were supplemented with an enclosed court lined with twenty more shops located opposite the mosque and next to a major public building, seemingly a reserved area intended to serve a different function. While ʿAnjar's intended purpose (or, more likely, purposes) is disputed, a commercial function is difficult to exclude—but who were the intended customers, and where were they living? ʿAnjar is hardly a large urban site, which suggests that much of the target market lived not within the walled settlement but in the fertile and productive agricultural hinterland of al-Walīd's model town.

When considering economic life in Byzantine and early Islamic Syria-Palestine, however, few writers have paid sufficient attention to matters of commodity production and exchange systems in

---

49 Detailed in R. Foote, "Commerce, Industrial Expansion, and Orthogonal Planning: Mutually Compatible Terms in Settlements of Bilad al-Sham during the Umayyad Period," *Mediterranean Archaeology* 13 (2000): 25–38; eadem, "Umayyad Markets and Manufacturing: Evidence for a Commercialized and Industrializing Economy in Early Islamic Bilad al-Sham" (Ph.D. diss., Harvard University, 1999); also Walmsley, "Economic Developments and Settlement," 344–47.

50 T. Ulbert, "Beobachtungen im Westhofbereich der Großen Basilika von Resafa," *Damaszener Mitteilungen* 6 (1997): 403–16 and pls. 72–76.

51 Kh. al-Asʿad and F. M. Stepniowski, "The Umayyad Suq in Palmyra," *Damaszener Mitteilungen* 4 (1989): 205–23.

52 On the shops, see P. Watson in A. W. McNicoll, P. C. Edwards, et al., "Preliminary Report on the University of Sydney's Seventh Season of Excavations at Pella (Ṭabaqat Faḥl) 1985," *ADAJ* 30 (1986): 155–98, at 177–81; on the church annex, see R. H. Smith and L. P. Day, *Pella of the Decapolis*, vol. 2, *Final Report on the College of Wooster Excavations in Area IX, the Civic Complex, 1979–1985* (Wooster, Ohio, 1989), reinterpreted in A. Walmsley, "The Social and Economic Regime at Fihl (Pella) and Neighbouring Centres, between the 7th and 9th Centuries," in *La Syrie de Byzance à l'Islam VIIᵉ–VIIIᵉ siècles: Actes du colloque international*, ed. P. Canivet and J.-P. Rey-Coquais (Damascus, 1992), 249–61.

53 Khamis, "Two Wall Mosaic Inscriptions"; Tsafrir and Foerster, "Urbanism at Scythopolis."

54 I. Roll and E. Ayalon, "The Market Street at Apollonia-Arsuf," *BASOR* 267 (1987): 61–76. This street, repeatedly renovated, had a long history from the seventh to eleventh centuries.

55 See, however, the excellent reassessment in R. Hillenbrand, "ʿAnjar and Early Islamic Urbanism," in *The Idea and Ideal of the Town between Late Antiquity and the Early Middle Ages*, ed. G. P. Brogiolo and B. Ward-Perkins, Transformation of the Roman World 4 (Leiden, 1999), 59–98.

rural communities, let alone to how these systems operated. In part the omission has reflected a lack of information, but the lacuna is beginning to be filled. One excellent and overlooked example is the site of Umm al-Raṣāṣ (Kastron Mefaʿa), a large village comprising a walled zone originally of Diocletianic date and an extramural suburb in which was located the extensive ecclesiastical complex, featuring the church of St. Stephen. This site, despite its goodly size and many churches, was not the seat of a bishop but belonged to the See of Mādabā; it was, potentially, a *kōmē*, or bourgade.[56] Or almost, for it is unlikely that Umm al-Raṣāṣ supported a population of 1,000 souls, although it would have held almost that many.[57] An understandable passion for the mosaic-rich church of St. Stephen has distracted scholarship, to some extent, from paying sufficient attention to the walled zone, occupied well into the ninth century, yet its layout is very revealing (see figs. 13.9 and 13.10). Following a localized grid, a street led southward for 110 meters from the north gate, apparently a later addition to the original Diocletianic plan intended to facilitate access to the extramural suburb located immediately to the north, as depicted on two mosaics at Umm al-Raṣāṣ.[58] This street, which probably once led to the blocked south gate, was lined with rows of shops one room deep along the northern section, and hence could serve both the walled zone and the extramural suburb. In the center, at the point where an axial east–west street once crossed the north–south one, more shops lined the still-open western part of the cross street; these were generally larger, with some two-room units on the north side and, on the south side, four shops were fronted by a common courtyard, a complex that could be secured at night. Another unit, possibly commercial, marked the terminus of the street running east–west, perhaps consisting of specialty shops fronted by a securable court. In all, the walled zone had more than thirty shops lining these two streets, including units within securable compounds. Here is preserved evidence for a local, village-based market, intended to serve not only Kastron Mefaʿa but also the rural hinterland. A second feature of Umm al-Raṣāṣ is a self-contained ecclesiastical complex with an attached market built around the closed eastern (main) gate. Reached by a closable lane from the north–south street, the complex comprised a double church group on the south, a bath of Umayyad date (fronted by shops?) on the east, shops on the west, and a large, perhaps ceremonial, room to the north (fig. 13.10).[59] Other units, commercial and residential, flanked the ecclesiastical core on the west and south sides. Umm al-Raṣāṣ offers a clear case of a village market infrastructure, consisting of units serving various commercial functions. The markets would have served both the local community and those living in the surrounding countryside, which at Umm al-Raṣāṣ—given its location in the *bādiyah* (steppe lands east of the mountain ranges of Syria and Jordan)—would have included a large nomadic component.

Similar in disposition and function was Subaytah/Shivta in the Negev, planned around radiating streets from two pools at the village core to facilitate water collection; it had three churches and several markets, occasionally running straight along

---

56   A. E. Laiou, "The Byzantine Village (5th–14th Century)," in *Les villages dans l'Empire byzantin (IVe–XVe siècle)*, ed. J. Lefort, C. Morrisson, and J.-P. Sodini, Réalités Byzantines 11 (Paris, 2005), 31–54, at 38, with references; also P.-L. Gatier, "Les villages du Proche-Orient protobyzantin: Nouvelles perspectives (1994–2004)," ibid., 101–19.

57   Population figures are notoriously difficult to calculate. While most previous studies seem generous in their estimates for Roman and Byzantine times, they tend to be pessimistic for the early Islamic period; see recently A. Lewin and P. Pellegrini, *Settlements and Demography in the Near East in Late Antiquity: Proceedings of the Colloquium, Matera, 27–29 October 2005*, Biblioteca di Mediterraneo antico 2 (Pisa, 2006). The figure for Umm al-Raṣāṣ, based on the assumption of seven people for each domestic unit, suggests a population in the mid-500s; a similar calculation for the large village of Umm al-Jimāl in north Jordan resulted in a figure of about 750 inhabitants.

58   J. Bujard and M. Jogin, "La fortification de Kastron Mayfaʿa/Umm al-Rasas," in ʿAmr, Zayadine, and Zaghloul, eds., *Studies in the History and Archaeology of Jordan*, 5:241–49, at 243–45; mosaic in Piccirillo and Alliata, *Umm al-Rasas—Mayfaʿah I*, 209–10. The two depictions of Kastron Mefaʿa are in St. Stephen's church and the so-called Church of the Lions. That in the Church of the Lions appears more faithful to the actual layout of the site (see next note).

59   Bujard and Jogin, "Fortification de Kastron Mayfaʿa," 241–43. The mosaic of Kastron Mefaʿa in the Church of the Lions clearly depicts the double church as well as the streets, including the later blocked eastern leg of the street running east–west. The complex is reminiscent of the church-market arrangement at Pella (see above and Smith and Day, *Pella of the Decapolis*, vol. 2; Walmsley, "Social and Economic Regime"); both appear to be market inns (*funduq*), on which see O. R. Constable, *Housing the Stranger in the Mediterranean World: Lodging, Trade, and Travel in Late Antiquity and the Middle Ages* (Cambridge, 2003), especially chap. 2. The building opposite (north of) the mosque at ʿAnjar is probably a funduq as well.

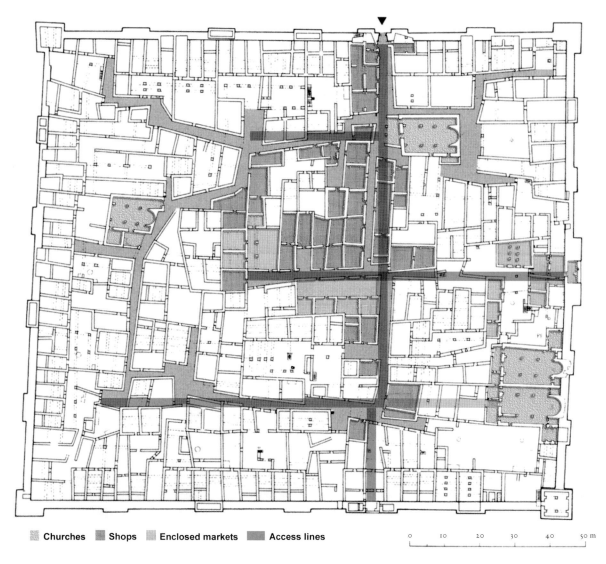

Churches ■ Shops ■ Enclosed markets ■ Access lines   0 10 20 30 40 50 m

Figure 13.9. Plan of Umm al-Raṣāṣ (Kastron Mefaʻa) in Jordan, showing shop-lined streets and more specialist commercial units (modified from E. Wirth, *Die orientalische Stadt im islamischen Vorderasien und Nordafrika* [Mainz, 2002], 36)

sections of the streets but especially of the enclosed type, in one case next to a church (the North church).[60] At Khirbat Susiyah, shops likewise faced out onto a street at the entrance to the village, with their construction forming part of a domestic unit.[61] Thus, as these other examples suggest, the commercial arrangements evident in the village plan of Umm al-Raṣāṣ should not be considered in any way "exceptional" but rather normal for the times.

Nevertheless, other villages in Syria-Palestine do not exhibit the presence of market structures as clearly as at Umm al-Raṣāṣ and Subaytah. For instance, Sergilla (north Syria), Shāʻra (Ḥawrān), and Umm al-Jimāl (north Jordan) are large,

60 Y. Hirschfeld, "Social Aspects of the Late-Antique Village of Shivta," *JRA* 16 (2003): 392–408. We should dismiss obfuscating pronouncements on these village settlements, such as "They were not laid out in the Roman grid pattern, nor were their streets wide or straight, but followed the usual haphazard eastern system with many blind alleys": H. D. Colt, ed., *Excavations at Nessana (Auja Hafir, Palestine)*, vol. 1 (London, 1962), 7.

61 Y. Hirschfeld, "Farms and Villages in Byzantine Palestine," *DOP* 51 (1997): 33–71, at 64.

Figure 13.10. View of the northern area of the enclosed church market at Umm al-Raṣāṣ (Kastron Mefaʿa) (photo by author)

sprawling sites composed of agglomerated courtyard units,[62] some of which may have taken on the role of *funduq,* or market inns. Umm al-Jimāl has two church complexes that are reminiscent of the double church complex at Umm al-Raṣāṣ, and may well likewise have been funduq.[63] Unfortunately, ascribing function to buildings can often be extremely difficult, especially when such deductions are based only on survey plans, for buildings often had multiple uses, and their functions often changed over time.

Shops and Shoppers

Evidence on how shops operated at the micro level in Byzantine and early Islamic Syria-Palestine is not common, but it is not entirely lacking. A particularly informative example was unearthed at Skythopolis, where a line of shops on the "Street of Monuments" located at the back of a colonnade opposite the Nymphaeum was destroyed in an intense fire during the sixth century.[64] While the shops gave up a large number of finds—mostly pottery, lamps, and glass—these items were neither precious nor, unfortunately, very revealing about the possible activities that were undertaken in the shops, unless they were the commodities for sale.[65] The only glimpse of function

62   Gatier, "Villages du Proche-Orient"; Hirschfeld, "Social Aspects of the Late-Antique Village."
63   On this site, see the detailed report in B. de Vries, *Umm el-Jimal: A Frontier Town and Its Landscape in Northern Jordan,* vol. 1, *Fieldwork 1972–1981,* Journal of Roman Archaeology supp. ser. 26 (Portsmouth, R.I., 1998), esp. 236–39.

64   S. Agady et al., "Byzantine Shops in the Street of the Monuments at Bet Shean (Scythopolis)," in *What Athens Has to Do with Jerusalem: Essays on Classical, Jewish, and Early Christian Art and Archaeology in Honor of Gideon Foerster,* ed. L. V. Rutgers, Interdisciplinary Studies in Ancient Culture and Religion 1 (Louvain, 2002), 423–506. The destruction is dated to sometime in the first half of the sixth century, on the basis of coin finds, but the ceramics and lamps suggest a date later in that century, or even in the seventh.
65   The problem with that suggestion is the wide chronological range given to the objects, especially the lamps. However, it is possible that the suggestion is correct and the dating is in error.

came from shop 1, which turned up *eulogia* tokens and ampullae, perhaps intended for devotees on their way to the central church on the mound overlooking the lower town. Shop 4 holds some interest, as it produced three glass weights, one almost complete and marked with Γ·H (8 ounces). Almost a century later another row of shops was destroyed, this time by an earthquake that entombed their contents. The shops were built during the reign of the caliph Hishām on the authority of a local governor,[66] and their excavation produced pottery, metalwork, jewelry (damaged, so perhaps being stored as bullion?), and coins, in addition to a victim.[67] Among the coins from these shops as well as from other shops destroyed in the earthquake were eight hoards, most of which were identified as shopkeepers' tender. One shop produced two hoards, one of fourteen dirhams with some jewelry and the other of thirty-one dinars (a lot of money); another shop contained a hoard of thirty-six dirhams and twenty-eight fulūs, mostly of the Baysānī fish type mentioned earlier. Other hoards also consisted of a mixture of precious and base coins, indicating the ongoing monetary basis of the market economy. Also found during the excavation of the 749 destruction level at Skythopolis were two instruments of measure, one a balance in copper alloy with markings in Greek and Arabic and the other a copper-lead alloy weight inscribed only in Arabic, which indicate the continuing reliance on a weight standard in the marketplace.[68]

Discoveries at nearby Pella, a town that never matched the importance of Skythopolis, have nonetheless revealed the diverse activities undertaken in shops in daily commerce. The excavation of a shop on the main mound, destroyed in 659/60, produced eight complete Gaza wine amphorae, apparently once stored on an upper level. A diverse group of iron objects, dating to the 749 earthquake, were found in a blacksmith's workshop in the commercial annex to the central church.[69] One dinar, fourteen dirhams, and fourteen fulūs were recovered from rooms in the commercial annex, in addition to the skeletons of two human and many animal victims, the latter including seven camels.[70]

As these examples suggest,[71] and rather unsurprisingly, the business conducted in shop-based markets largely dealt with ordinary daily transactions involving the exchange of commodities based on a controlled system of weights within a monetary economy. A further detailed insight comes from the recent excavations at Jarash, directed by me.[72] In the 2006 and 2007 seasons, a row of five shops was excavated on the west side of the *cardo,* built to harmonize the irregular space created between the old Roman-period north–south street and the different orientation required for the mosque (fig. 13.11). The northernmost of these shops, located adjacent to the semicircular staircase that gave entrance into the mosque compound, was found to have been subdivided into ten storage bins accessed by way of an axial walkway (shop 5, fig. 13.12). In one bin, deep inside the shop, a small group of intact ceramic vessels was found, composed of four casseroles and a juglet of local manufacture. Their date, firmly established by other work at Jarash and Pella,[73] is in the eighth and ninth centuries. In the adjacent bin at the rear of the shop no commodities were found, but instead a reused fine stone tablet measuring 18.0 by 17.5 centimeters was discovered, leaning almost upright against a support stone. Preserved on it, written with a charcoal stylus, are eleven lines of clear writing in a cursive Arabic script that, after an initial invocation (the *bismillah*), list the shopkeeper's accounts (fig. 13.13)—for example, "payable from Abū al-Ṣaqar, one dirham"; "from Zayd, three-quarters of a dirham"; "from Ḥārith, dirhamayn

---

66 Khamis, "Two Wall Mosaic Inscriptions."
67 Briefly mentioned in Y. Tsafrir and G. Foerster, "Bet Shean Excavation Project—1988/1989," *Excavations and Surveys in Israel 1989/1990,* vol. 9 (1991): 120–28, at 126–27.
68 N. Amitai-Preiss, "Umayyad Coin Hoards from the Beth Shean Excavations of the Hebrew University," *Israel Numismatic Journal* 14 (2000–2): 224–38 and pl. 27.
69 McNicoll, Edwards, et al., "Seventh Season," 177–81; Smith and Day, *Pella of the Decapolis,* 2:70.

70 Smith and Day, *Pella of the Decapolis,* 2:67–71; discussed in Walmsley, "Social and Economic Regime," 260–61.
71 See, in addition, Foote, "Umayyad Markets and Manufacturing."
72 Preliminary reports of the Islamic Jarash Project, a partnership between the Department of Antiquities of Jordan and the University of Copenhagen, will be found in Barnes, Blanke, et al., "'Guard House' to Congregational Mosque"; Blanke, Damgaard, et al., "From Bathhouse to Congregational Mosque"; A. Walmsley, "The Friday Mosque of Early Islamic Jarash in Jordan: The 2002 Field Season of the Danish-Jordanian Islamic Jarash Project," *Journal of the C. L. David Collection* 1 (2003): 110–31. The Department of Antiquities' active encouragement of the work at Jarash is greatly appreciated by the Copenhagen team.
73 Walmsley, "Tradition, Innovation, and Imitation."

Figure 13.11. Aerial photograph of the eighth-century mosque and adjoining shops at the south tetrakionia of Jarash; view to southwest, taken in 2008 (APAAME_20081029_RHB_187; courtesy of Bob Bewley and David Kennedy)

[two dirhams]"; and "from Umm ʿUbād [a woman], three *darāhim*."[74]

Although the totals are small, a number of significant deductions can be drawn from this important find. First, the text shows that the silver-based dirham had become the accepted standard unit of currency, in real terms and in calculating credit, after centuries in Syria-Palestine of an essentially bimetallic monetary system, based on gold and copper. The major role of silver in the marketplace is reinforced by the widespread recovery from major eighth-century archaeological contexts of dirhams from shops and markets, as already seen above.[75] This reorientation not only occurred rapidly, within two generations, but also permanently affected how commerce was transacted. Second, the tablet text reveals that a particular type of store credit, widely known in the later Islamic world,[76] was a well-established method of commercial exchange by the later eighth to ninth century. As in later times, the booked amounts may have represented not the full commodity price but a residual debt after an initial cash payment, or installments owed, although we would not expect the utilitarian

---

[74] The tablet is being studied by Fanny Bessard, a doctoral student at the Sorbonne and a team member of the Islamic Jarash Project. She has provided a translation and report on the tablet, on which this discussion is based. See Bessard in A. Walmsley, L. Blanke, et al., "A Mosque, Shops and Bath in Central Jarash: The 2007 Season of the Islamic Jarash Project," *ADAJ* 52 (2008): 109–38.

[75] Shops at Jarash have also produced at least two dirham hoards, one a large mid-eighth-century earthquake hoard (unpublished) and the second a smaller group of eight coins, found in a ceramic juglet, for which see A. Naghaway, "Umayyad Dirhams from Jarash (Arabic)," *ADAJ* 46 (2002): 127–33.

[76] S. D. Goitein, *A Mediterranean Society: The Jewish Communities of the Arab World as Portrayed in the Documents of the Cairo Geniza,* vol. 1, *Economic Foundations* (Berkeley, 1967), 197–202 and index.

Figure 13.12. View to west of shop 5 located between the street and mosque at Jarash, adjacent to a major entrance into the mosque from the street (IJP_D3253, photo by author)

vessels found in the shop to come with a high price tag. Next, while the text begins with the bismillah, there are no obviously Muslim names recorded on the tablet; therefore, the clients may have been predominantly, if not all, Christians, even though the shop was located next to the mosque.[77] However, the keeping of shop accounts in a smoothly applied and confident freehand Arabic, in which only occasional diacritical marks were applied,[78] demonstrates the acquiescence of Jarash society to the everyday use of Arabic in the marketplace during the eighth to ninth century, as also indicated by the weights and measures recovered at Skythopolis. Finally, it should be noted that this tablet is not the only one known from Jarash. A second was excavated in an adjacent shop in 2007, although the text is very faint, and a third was unearthed as part of the Yale mission of 1928–34 but never published in full.[79] That they were

---

77 A continuing Christian presence at Jarash has been known since the work of the Yale joint mission; the excavations revealed that many of the churches continued in use well into Islamic times, but how far is not always clear from the reports found in C. H. Kraeling, ed., *Gerasa, City of the Decapolis* (New Haven, 1938). Nevertheless, my own recent observations (with special thanks to Abdul Majid Mejali of the Department of Antiquities) at the Mortuary Church and the Bishop Genesius Church reveal considerable architectural embellishments, notably added benches along the sidewalls of the nave aisles, as well as major repairs that would seem to date to early Islamic times, as suggested by recently discovered Arabic inscriptions in these churches.

78 On the sporadic but not random application of diacritical marks in early Islamic times, see A. Kaplony, "What Are Those Few Dots For? Thoughts on the Orthography of the Qurra Papyri (709–710), the Khurasan Parchments (755–777) and the Inscription of the Jerusalem Dome of the Rock (692)," *Arabica* 55 (2008): 91–112. The occasional use of marks is not a failing but reveals the writing abilities of the scribe: that is, the skill to produce a text quickly in which just enough detail was provided for the reader to recall the meaning.

79 The tablet is on display in the Jordanian Archaeological Museum in Amman, and is currently being studied by Bessard along with the two recent finds. Tablets with Arabic texts were found at Qaṣr al-Ḥayr al-Gharbī in Syria and are displayed in the National Museum, Damascus; for one published example, see D. Schlumberger, *Qaṣr el-Heir el Gharbi,* Bibliothèque archéologique et historique 120 (Paris, 1986), 28.

Figure 13.13. The inscribed marble tablet from shop 5 with the accounts of a shopkeeper written in charcoal; they reveal the dominant role of silver coinage in the marketplace and the common use of store credit, perhaps representing the balance owing on a transaction (IJP_D3500, photo by A. Simpson)

apparently in use at Jarash shows that account keeping in Arabic had become common practice, indeed the norm, sometime after the middle of the eighth century, and that the residents of Jarash, the greater number of whom would have been Christians, habitually communicated in Arabic. This was only one part, but perhaps a significantly reinforcing part, of the profoundly momentous process by which eastern Christianity was to adopt Arabic as its own language and, along with it, build a new identity that was both Arab and Christian.[80]

* * * * * * * *

The mechanisms of intraregional exchange in Byzantine and early Islamic Syria-Palestine are being increasingly understood through modern archaeological research. Ceramics and coins, while offering slightly differing perspectives, reveal a local economic network that was founded on a distribution system with an optimal reach of 30 to 50 kilometers.

---

80 S. H. Griffith, "The Church of Jerusalem and the 'Melkites': The Making of an 'Arab Orthodox' Christian Identity in the World of Islam (750–1050 CE)," in *Christians and Christianity in the Holy Land: From the Origins to the Latin Kingdoms*, ed. O. Limor and G. A. G. Stroumsa, Cultural Encounters in Late Antiquity and the Middle Ages (Turnhout, 2006), 175–204; idem, *The Church in the Shadow of the Mosque: Christians and Muslims in the World of Islam*, Jews, Christians, and Muslims from the Ancient to the Modern World (Princeton, N.J., 2008); A. M. H. Shboul and A. G. Walmsley, "Identity and Self-image in Syria-Palestine in the Transition from Byzantine to Early Islamic Rule: Arab Christians and Muslims," in *Identities in the Eastern Mediterranean in Antiquity*, ed. G. Clarke (Sydney, 1998), 255–87. Note also the total dominance of reformed Arabic-language coinage in the marketplace by the mid-eighth century: Walmsley, "Early Islamic Coin Hoard."

Beyond that distance, the exchange of commodities could occur up to 100 kilometers away from a production point, an outcome probably achieved through secondary market points. Coins of the sixth and seventh centuries show the considerable extent to which these distribution systems remained self-reliant, but in the eighth century the evidence suggests a widening of horizons. Archaeological evidence also brings new insights into how exchange functioned at the local level. Towns, villages, and the countryside were served by new and long-established shop complexes and markets, in which commodities drawn from local and distant places could be found and services offered. In the eighth century a system of credit was customary, even the norm, in commerce, and Arabic had become firmly established as the everyday language of trade. Thus in areas as diverse as financial systems, weights and measures, and language, a tangible change can be observed as Byzantium gave way to Islam in the towns of seventh- and eighth-century Syria-Palestine. Accordingly, the study of trade is not only a matter of economic history but also a key to comprehending social transformations at the end of antiquity.

Markets and the Marketplace

• FOURTEEN •

From *polis* to *emporion*?
Retail and Regulation in the Late Antique City

LUKE LAVAN

Commercial Pressure and the End of the Classical City

THE END OF CLASSICAL MONUMENTAL STREETS has attracted much scholarly attention, since the publication of Jean Sauvaget's study of Laodikeia in 1934.[1] In this work, Sauvaget proposed a model of urban evolution in which the ancient street was gradually obliterated by the encroachment of stalls, followed by masonry shops, with the remaining empty space turned to the advantage of their owners. Sauvaget believed that this process happened during the early Islamic period. In 1985, Hugh Kennedy developed these ideas further, arguing that the commercially vibrant *madina* emerged at the expense of the politico-aesthetic classical *polis*. He suggested, on the basis of three archaeological sites with evidence of encroachment, that this development had its origins in the late antique period, and was driven by the needs of commerce.[2] Others, such as Évelyne Patlagean and Charlotte Roueché, lent weight to these ideas by pointing to the increasing number of cellular shops found in city centers during late antiquity.[3] Later, Bryan Ward-Perkins challenged Kennedy's chronology, pointing to the continued building of well-ordered colonnaded avenues of shops even within the Umayyad period. Marlia Mundell Mango also suggested, on the basis of the *Book of the Prefect*, that such facilities survived until the ninth century at Constantinople.[4] Yet despite these arguments, Isabella Baldini Lippolis and Helen Saradi have recently described late antiquity as a period in which street porticoes and other public spaces were being lost, without blaming commerce.[5] With such

---

I wish to dedicate this essay to my mother-in-law Van Bui-Duc, who helped look after my newborn son Aidan during its writing. Without her assistance I would not have been able to have finished it. I would also like to thank Toon Putzeys, Catherine Saliou, and Cécile Morrisson for their comments. Putzeys's research on the function of shops, which he has kindly shared with me, has been invaluable. Harriet Gemmel's dissertation on the architectural design of the Sardis shops, which I supervised in 2009, has also been inspiring. In addition, I thank my father for proofreading the text, and Michael Mulryan for library work. Several scholars provided clarifications by e-mail on specific points, especially Axel Gering, Elias Khamis, and Feriştah Alanyalı, who kindly sent me her excellent excavation report on the Patara shops. All errors are my own.

1 J. Sauvaget, "Le plan de Laodicée-sur-mer," *BEODam* 4 (1934): 81–114.

2 H. Kennedy, "From *polis* to *madina*: Urban Change in Late Antique and Early Islamic Syria," *Past and Present* 106 (1985): 3–27; on street encroachment beginning in late antiquity, see 11–13.

3 More shops in city centers: É. Patlagean, *Pauvreté économique et pauvreté sociale à Byzance, 4ᵉ–7ᵉ siècles* (Paris, 1977), 59–61, 233ff.; D. Claude, *Die Byzantinische Stadt im 6. Jahrhundert* (Munich, 1969), 52ff.; *ALA*, no. 230.

4 B. Ward-Perkins, "Urban Survival and Urban Transformation in the Eastern Mediterranean," in *Early Medieval Towns in the Western Mediterranean*, ed. G. P. Brogiolo, Documenti di Archeologia 10 (Padua, 1995), 143–53; M. Mundell Mango, "The Commercial Map of Constantinople," *DOP* 54 (2000): 203–4.

5 Street porticoes and public spaces lost: I. Baldini Lippolis, "Private Space in Late Antique Cities: Laws and Building Procedures," in *Housing in Late Antiquity: From Palaces to Shops*, ed. L. Lavan, L. Özgenel, and A. Sarantis, Late Antique Archaeology 3.2 (Leiden, 2007), 197–237; H. G. Saradi, *The Byzantine City in the Sixth Century: Literary Images and Historical Reality* (Athens, 2006), 271–94, esp. 203, 205.

divergent views, there is clearly a need to reconsider how sources for this question are being used. Were urban avenues being lost, and was this the result of commercial pressure?

Narratives of the encroachment of streets in late antiquity principally depend on book 15 of the Theodosian Code.[6] These texts are often seen as confirming both the reality of street encroachment and the source of this pressure: lax regulation of private interests, especially those of a commercial nature.[7] Scholarly discussions of these laws, which mainly concern late fourth- to early fifth-century Constantinople, are usually illustrated with a few (often undated) archaeological examples from distant provinces.[8] These cases are presented as supporting a bleak view of the deterioration of classical monumentality, disappearing beneath the emerging cabins and hovels of the middle ages. Such a situation can be confirmed for the fifth century in the West. However, the match is poor for the fourth century in the West and especially poor for the fourth- to sixth-century East.[9] Examples of street encroachment can be found even here, but these are normally on side streets, or within minor cities that were losing urban status. In provincial capitals and medium-sized cities, the overwhelming impression is of the continuity of the main colonnaded avenues to the late sixth or early seventh century.[10] New avenues, lined with cellular shops, were still being erected in the East: they can be seen at Aizanoi, Side, Skythopolis, and Jerusalem in the fourth to sixth century, and at Umayyad ʿAnjar and at Gerasa in the early eighth century. If the legal texts on encroachment had been lost, such a model would probably never have been suggested for the East. It cannot be derived from eastern archaeology alone, unless one is indifferent to the dating of late antique and early medieval structures covering urban sites.[11]

It seems that there are a number of different processes taking place within the late antique city, which scholars have conflated into a single narrative of urban decay. Arguably, this has been done in order to fit the archaeology to the mental images evoked by a straightforward reading of the codes. Certainly there is evidence for the privatization of duplicate or redundant civic public buildings. Furthermore, in some cities, minor roads came to be blocked off and neglected. However, in these same cities, this development was counterbalanced by work on the main avenues, which were increasingly monumentalized, a process which can be seen at Ostia or at Sagalassos.[12] There is little evidence that commerce contributed to either of these developments. Rather, archaeology reveals examples of ordered markets of wooden stalls with *topos* inscriptions, even for the sixth century; of ordered subdivisions of porticoes into shops; and of planned rows of new shops built as unified, even

---

6   E.g., *CTh* 15.1.39: "We order that the buildings commonly called *parapetasia*, or others which are attached to the walls of cities, or to public buildings, and on account of whose condition the neighborhood is threatened with fire or some other danger, or which occupy the space of public squares, or interfere with the porticos of public edifices, shall be demolished and destroyed" (given at Constantinople, AD 398). Unless otherwise specified, all translations are my own.

7   E.g., T. W. Potter, *Towns in Late Antiquity: Iol Caesarea and Its Context* (Oxford, 1995), 85–90, 102.

8   Archaeological examples used to illustrate encroachment: Kennedy, "From *polis* to *madina*," 11–13 (three examples); Saradi, *The Byzantine City*, 280–87, esp. 285–87 (four examples on main avenues, including one from Vandal Carthage and one that was cleared away in antiquity). Baldini Lippolis, "Private Space," 206–12, gives two examples on fora and six examples on streets, while the rest deal with the privatization or subdivision of public buildings; of her street examples, some are post-antique, and several encroach to allow the building of a large monumental structure, as they did in earlier centuries; Baldini Lippolis's two convincing examples come from Vandal Africa, not the East.

9   Encroachment in the fifth-century West, on major avenues, occurred in Wroxeter, York, Emerita, Barcelona, Valencia, and Carthage; in the fourth century, on major streets of minor centers, in Roselle and Luni. This will be detailed in my forthcoming study on streets.

10   Encroachment in the fourth- to sixth-century East on minor roads in major/medium centers: Messene, Gortyn, Pella, Sagalassos. In minor centers: Ariassos, Delos. Alleged encroachments of major avenues tend to be a continuation of earlier arrangements (as at Perge and Side), or coincide with general (post-antique) urban decline, as at Apameia and Skythopolis. This will be detailed in my forthcoming study on streets. For colonnaded streets at Constantinople into the medieval period, see M. Mundell Mango, "The Porticoed Street at Constantinople," in *Byzantine Constantinople: Monuments, Topography and Everyday Life*, ed. N. Necipoğlu (Leiden, 2001), 47–50.

11   See L. Lavan, "Street Space in Late Antiquity," in *Proceedings of the 21st International Congress of Byzantine Studies, London, 21–26 August, 2006*, vol. 2, *Abstracts of Panel Papers*, ed. E. Jeffreys with J. Gilliland (Aldershot, 2006), 68–69.

12   On Ostia, see A. Gering, "Plätze und Straßensperren an Promenaden: Zum Funktionswandel Ostias in der Spätantike," *Römische Mitteilungen* 111 (2004): 299–382. On Sagalassos, see L. Lavan, "The Streets of Sagalassos in Late Antiquity: An Interpretative Study," in *La rue dans l'Antiquité: Définition, aménagement et devenir de l'Orient méditerranéen à la Gaule: Actes du colloque de Poitiers 7–9 Septembre 2006*, ed. C. Saliou et al. (Rennes, 2008), 201–14.

aesthetically pleasing parades. Finally, there are several examples of market buildings still repaired and kept in use. In most cities of the East, there is evidence for a high degree of spatial order in the main public areas of the city. Public property was generally respected, private land boundaries continued unchanged, and the overall classical aesthetic of middle to large eastern cities was generally maintained, with great avenues, fountains, and public plazas, as long as prosperity remained.[13]

Regrettably, very little attention has been given to excavations which confirm that streets were still cleaned and maintained until the sixth or seventh century AD.[14] Rather, encroachment walls covering a main avenue always gain more attention, whether dated or not, even though they are much rarer.[15] New impressions of urban order are starting to emerge from a fresh study of the legal evidence: Catherine Saliou has argued in a recent article that our understandings of late Roman laws on "encroachment" are too simplistic, and that a more ordered attempt to commercialize porticoes and to regulate their commercial potential can be detected within late antiquity. She sees not individual initiative but rather collective activity, regulated and encouraged by imperial and civic government.[16] Further, it seems reasonable to ask to what extent we can read late antique laws against encroachment as representing evidence of a change from earlier periods, given our lack of any comparable collection of laws surviving from those times. Perhaps the laws of book 15 of the Theodosian Code could be seen rather as a testimony to the survival of an active tendency to regulate and to protect public space. This tendency had always existed in Greco-Roman cities. The fact that these laws were carried into book 8 of the Justinianic Code, and were added to by new laws of Justinian, suggests that such interests endured.[17] Indeed, the nature of the sixth-century rule book of Julian of Askalon, or the late fifth-century collection of laws in the *Liber Syro-Romanus,* suggests that such concerns were very much alive, even if they were now applied only to main avenues and not to the back streets.[18]

Before Saliou's intervention, Saradi had herself (in 1998) highlighted the activity of patrons in developing porticoes of colonnaded streets. Yet in 2006 she still believed that this represented a "chaotic situation," "the dissolution of civic public space."[19] She identified that there was little dated archaeological evidence for portico encroachment before the later sixth century, but preferred to privilege the legal evidence, stating that "the dissolution of civic urban space... began in the 4th century" (p. 291), and that "archaeological excavations illustrate the phenomenon mentioned in the literary sources. The space between the columns of the porticoes was gradually walled up; walls projecting from the back divided the porticoes into separate compartments, while other structures encroached on the street" (p. 272).[20] In this chapter I will take a different approach, focusing not on the legal texts but on archaeological, epigraphic, and literary evidence for organized retail activity in central and eastern Mediterranean cities. This tells its own independent story of the organization of retail in late antique cities. It seems that impressions gained from the Theodosian Code can

---

13   See Lavan, "Street Space"; idem, "Streets of Sagalassos"; and idem, "Social Space in Late Antiquity," in *Objects in Context, Objects in Use: Material Spatiality in Late Antiquity,* ed. L. Lavan, E. Swift, and T. Putzeys, Late Antique Archaeology 5 (Leiden, 2007), 134–35.
14   Streets kept open to the sixth century include Narbonne, Utica, Castel San Pietro, Ravenna, Tomis, Ephesos, Aphrodisias, Sagalassos, Apameia, Bostra, Caesarea Palaestinae, and Skythopolis, as will be described in my wider study on streets, to be published in the near future.
15   For undated encroachment walls covering a main avenue, see the Thamugadi oil press, now an iconic image of encroachment, in Potter, *Towns in Late Antiquity,* 67–68, and post-antique phases of Sagalassos in Lavan, "Streets of Sagalassos," 206.
16   New perspectives: C. Saliou, "Identité culturelle et paysage urbain: Remarques sur les processus de transformation des rues à portiques dans l'Antiquité Tardive," *Syria* 82 (2005): 207–24.
17   New laws of Justinian: *CI* 1.4.26.8–9, 10.30.4.11–14 (7–8).
18   C. Saliou, trans., *Le traité d'urbanisme de Julien d'Ascalon: Droit et architecture en Palestine au VIe siècle,* Travaux et mémoires du Centre de recherche d'histoire et civilisation de Byzance, Monographies 8 (Paris, 1996); W. Selb and H. Kaufhold, eds., *Das syrisch-römische Rechtsbuch,* 3 vols. (Vienna, 2002).
19   Patrons and porticoes: H. Saradi, "Privatisation and Subdivision of Urban Properties in the Early Byzantine Centuries: Social and Cultural Implications," *BASP* 35 (1998): 17–43. Chaos and dissolution: eadem, *The Byzantine City,* 285, 291.
20   Saradi, *The Byzantine City,* 272, implies that the lack of excavated evidence is a result of poor technique. There is some basis for this claim in the case of early excavated sites such as Apameia and Gerasa, which were crudely "cleared." However, this is to underestimate the visibility of late antique subdivision walls, which were normally built in mortared stone rather than, as later, in unmortared rubble. The former have been detected by Mediterranean archaeology since the 1960s at the latest. On well-dug sites such as Aizanoi, Xanthos, Caesarea Maritima, Sepphoris, and Skythopolis, late antique encroachment on the main monumental avenues is generally absent until the last years of the sixth or beginning of the seventh century.

be substantially modified, and perhaps be contradicted, by considering other sources for the period, on their own terms.

It is worth stressing at the outset that what is being questioned is the interpretation of legal evidence, not its inherent value. Admittedly, legal texts provide some specific instances of emperors or governors clearing away unauthorized constructions, and these should be taken seriously. At Constantinople in 398 private buildings were removed from around the *horrea publica,* and in 409 they were removed from the Great Palace.[21] But are these measures really indicative of chaotic encroachment and dissolution of the central areas of eastern cities? If they are, can they be taken as representative? It is worth remembering that Cato the Elder was praised for demolishing houses that encroached on public ground/against public buildings in the early second century BC and that Domitian sought to restrict the display of goods by shop owners within porticoes.[22] Such initiatives do not indicate dissolution of urban space but rather reflect attempts to regulate: in the sixth century as much as in the late Republic or early Empire. Thus, until someone excavates traces of stalls or shops blocking a major commercial artery in a prosperous Eastern city that are dated to late antiquity (and those at Palmyra are not),[23] there seems to be no basis for asserting that unregulated commerce was responsible for the decline of the classical street in the late antique East.

Regulated Stalls
Structural Evidence

Tim Potter's discovery of market stalls on the forum of Iol Caesarea sparked considerable interest. These structures were small (3–4 m by 2–3 m), irregular rectangles, marked by slits cut into the paving in front of a portico. Large numbers of small fourth-century bronze coins from retail transactions were found in the paving cracks beneath, providing a likely use date in the fourth to fifth century.[24] Potter was able to suggest parallels at two other sites (Paestum and Philippi), though neither had features as clear as the indentations discovered at his own site. Nevertheless, he was quick to point out that market stalls (tables) had been depicted on a fresco of a forum from Pompeii.[25] Probably, such stalls had been common throughout antiquity, but only now were actually permitted to break the surface of the paving with holes and channels. The stalls at Iol Caesarea were small-scale market structures comparable to those of earlier periods, though they were semipermanent huts rather than tables. However, these stalls were confined to the portico, and permanent stone squats were not allowed to develop on the forum, even in the fourth and fifth centuries, as they were in later periods.

A similar, though more regular, set of late market stalls comes from Sagalassos in southwest Turkey, and deserves to be considered in detail.[26] Here, excavations led by Marc Waelkens have uncovered substantial areas of public space, including a colonnaded street and two public squares, which show ample evidence of organized urban retail in late antiquity. This was not immediately apparent to the excavators, who on uncovering the Upper Agora in the early 1990s concentrated on the built architecture and honorific monuments of the plaza. The site was then covered in sand and turned into a stone depot and conservation area. However, during a postdoctoral fellowship at the Katholieke Universiteit Leuven, I was able to reexamine the area, using detailed drawings taken by the site supervisor, Peter Cosyns. I identified a number of postholes and topos inscriptions that had not been considered important at the time, and had been accidentally eliminated from later "neat" drawings (fig. 14.1). Recleaning and survey in 2006 confirmed the postholes and made it possible to record three of the stalls, with their topos inscriptions (fig. 14.2).

---

21 Clearing encroachment at Constantinople: *CTh* 15.1.38; *CTh* 15.1.47 = *CI* 8.11.17. In AD 406, a general law for all public buildings in the city was issued (*CTh* 15.1.46; *CI* 8.10.9).
22 Cato the Elder and encroachment: Livy, *Epit.* 39.44; Plut. *Vit. Cat. Mai.* 19. Domitian: Mart. *Epigrams* 7.61.
23 Palmyra: the shops built over the street are dated to the Umayyad period, based on Umayyad pottery and coins found beneath the floors of the shops: Kh. al-As'ad and F. M. Stepniowski, "The Umayyad Suq in Palmyra," *Damaszener Mitteilungen* 4 (1989): 210–11, 220.

24 Stalls at Iol Caesarea: Potter, *Towns in Late Antiquity,* 36–39.
25 Stalls at Paestum: E. Greco and D. Theodorescu, *Poseidonia-Paestum,* vol. 1, *La "curia,"* Collection de l'École Française de Rome 42 (Rome, 1980), 10–12 (not seen); Philippi: observed by Potter, *Towns in Late Antiquity,* 75, 77; Pompeii, Insula of Julia Felix: R. Ling, *Roman Painting* (Cambridge, 1991), 163–64.
26 For a fuller description, see L. Lavan, "The Agorai of Sagalassos in Late Antiquity: An Interpretative Study," *Anatolian Studies* (forthcoming).

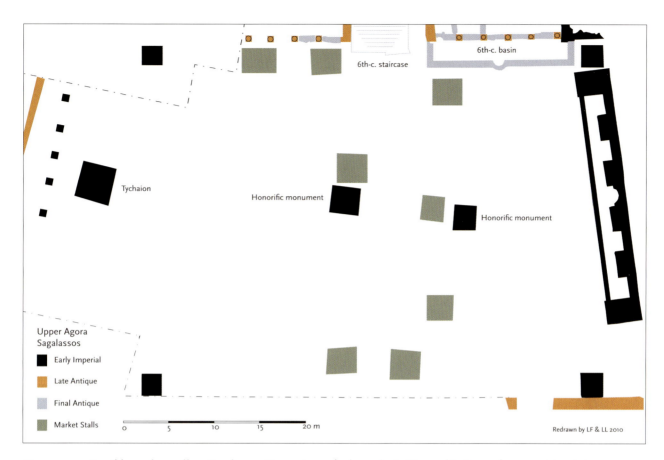

Figure 14.1. Possible market stalls at Sagalassos, Upper Agora (redrawn by L. Figg and L. Lavan from provisional site drawings, 2010)

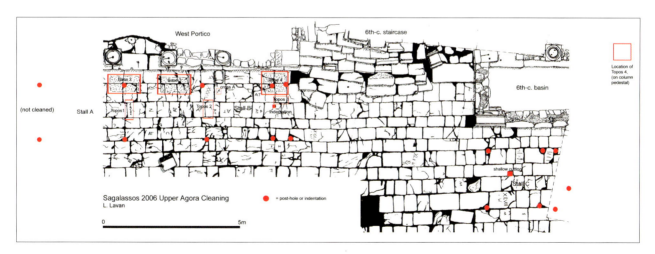

Figure 14.2. Possible market stalls at Sagalassos, detail; Sagalassos Upper Agora cleaning, 2006 (after P. Cosyns)

The postholes were cut right through the paving of the agora. These holes, measuring between 15 and 30 centimeters across, belonged to square structures, measuring approximately 3 × 3 meters. They were generally four-posters, although two stalls had six posts, while still being square. The absence of any trace of stone remains strongly suggests that the stalls were entirely wooden. If no stone survives today, there probably never was any then, given that the structures appear to have belonged to the last phase and the Upper Agora has seen very little robbing of stone since antiquity. However, the holes are substantial: not post pipes but postholes, designed to support deep-set timbers, with the putative aid of stone and earth packing. Thus, this was no ephemeral effort: either the wooden stalls were allowed to stand semipermanently, or they were slotted into permanent casings within the paving on market day.

The postholes are likely to represent wooden market stalls in a regulated market, rather than postantique huts, as the structures appear to have been almost identical: regular in alignment, design, and size. Given their coherence, they probably reflect a single regulatory regime across the marketplace, and thus are probably of the same date. They are likely to date from late antiquity, most probably the sixth century: in several places they cut through the foundations of a number of honorific monuments, which had been removed from the plaza, probably at the time of the construction of North-East Building's northern wall (late fifth to early sixth century), which includes several honorific monuments.[27] Further, the line of three stalls revealed by the 2006 cleaning also seems to leave a space for access to the sixth-century staircase, which led down into the agora from the Bouleuterion Church on the west; additionally, one of the stalls seems to respect the position of a basin of sixth-century date (and so must postdate it). The letter forms of one of the two topos inscriptions accompanying these stalls are of the fourth to seventh century (a round cursive μ, whose use is normally dated to the fourth century and especially after). This all suggests that the stalls are late antique in date, most probably fourth–seventh century.

Topos Inscriptions

At least four topos inscriptions can be seen on the Upper Agora of Sagalassos. Two are chiseled to be read at a right angle to the western portico, both set within the same line of slabs and apparently underscored with a nonepigraphic diagonal "signature line." They are closely associated with two of the wooden stalls. The inscriptions seem to be personal names—perhaps the tradesmen who were allowed to work here.[28] Judging from the letter forms (the cursive μ), the first dates to the fourth to seventh century. The second is much more difficult to date, but its signature line, alignment, and setting, on the same row of slabs, suggests that it belongs with the previous inscription.[29] Two further topos inscriptions were set on a different alignment, aligned with the portico. The third inscription is chiseled into the paving and may relate to the trade of shops in the adjacent portico rather than to the stalls on the plaza. It reads τοπος χαλκο|τυπων (the place of the bronzesmiths). The fourth inscription, scratched onto a column pedestal in the adjacent portico, is preceded by a cross and reads +τοπος ΔΑΠΗ[vac. | -- ΜΩΝ. This is too fragmentary to read, although an upholsterer (*δαπηδιμα) is among the options which have been tentatively suggested. This should date to the fifth to sixth century based on the cross, and should predate the late basin of the sixth century which covered the paving in this area.[30]

The significance of the stalls and topos inscriptions is that they appear to reveal a regulated market of the sixth century AD. The topos inscriptions, which are aligned *perpendicularly* to the portico, are clearly associated with stalls, though they bear only personal names. The topos inscriptions aligned *parallel* to the portico do not appear to belong to a particular stall, and they specify (artisanal) trades. Probably we are dealing here with a division between what was sold on the plaza and goods set out on the paving outside of artisanal workshops. Apparently there were two systems of organization, only one of

---

27 Sagalassos, North-East Building's northern wall (late fifth to early sixth century): see Lavan, "Streets of Sagalassos," 205–6.

28 The first reads μακεδυρα or perhaps μακεδυια / μακεαυρα / μακεδυια and the second Ζα....ες.

29 A further possible topos inscription that includes a round cursive μ—ΔΙΟμ (*Diomedes*?), aligned with the portico—occurs on the paving next to one of the stalls toward the north center of the plaza.

30 I am grateful to Catherine Saliou and Denis Feissel for offering readings of these difficult inscriptions.

which relates to the stalls on the plaza. In this case, there seems to be something of a match between the last function of the shops in the portico behind each topos inscription, as recorded by archaeology: a metal workshop and a possible *fullonica,* with a basin fed by tubing, from the late sixth/early seventh century.[31] Yet the evidence is not quite so simple: as noted above, this topos inscription and basin appear to belong to two different phases, so one should be wary of seeing this as a definite match. Rather, it is safer just to note active regulation of stalls within the Upper Agora during late antiquity, some if not all of which dates from the late sixth or early seventh century.

Elsewhere in Turkey, a handful of sites provide us with comparable topos inscriptions, though without stalls and place inscriptions in association. Such texts can be interpreted as place markers without any commercial function for people of different status, as in theaters (at Bostra, for example).[32] Yet in streets and squares, and especially when set directly in front of shops, they do seem to have a commercial function. At Aphrodisias, the finest set occurs on columns outside shops which were set within the Hall of the Theater Baths, to serve the fourth-century "Tetrastoon" square: here we see well-cut inscriptions defining the "place of Alexander, barber," as well as two other individuals. In the adjacent Tetrastoon, there are no cellular shops at all, but nonetheless two topos inscriptions on columns—for the "men of Hierapolis."[33] Nothing can confirm that they are place inscriptions specifically for commerce, but the context seems persuasive: in an alcove within the same square, evidence for a stall comes from a price list of foodstuffs that was scratched into the plaster: this was one spot at least where agricultural goods were on sale within the covered porticoes of the square. From the south agora of the same city comes another inscription which might represent a stall rather than reserved seating: that of Zoticos the Peddler.[34]

At Perge, a τοπος θερμοπουλου (place of the restaurant) midway down the main street is highly visible, being carved on a monumental arch.[35] Here a commercial identification is unquestionable, because no individual is described, only a trade. Whether it referred to a stall or a full-scale restaurant cannot be determined: probably both existed here, comparable to the stall which St. Symeon the Fool operated at Emesa for a couple who ran a thermopolion. Another topos inscription on a colonnaded street comes from Sagalassos: τοπος ..λιανου (place of (?Ju)lian) but with no further details to elucidate its meaning.[36] On the adjacent Lower Agora there is an inscription in the paving in late cursive letters: νικα η τυχα δε|τερασεβδο|μαδης+ (the fortune of the people of the second week triumphs+).[37] Could this reflect the possibility of a regular cyclical market giving time-limited spatial rights to stall holders? Augustine alludes to such an arrangement in early fifth-century Africa: he mentions stalls that were temporary, which people complained were not currently set up.[38]

One thing seems certain: known topos inscriptions represent only a fraction of those which once existed: probably only those which were the most deeply inscribed have survived. Do they represent the assertions of individuals? Perhaps. But, as Roueché notes, *I. Iasos* 256 reveals that a topos inscription could be authorized by a civic official, and this process seems to have carried on in late antiquity.[39] Two late antique topos inscriptions from around the northwest city gate at Sagalassos are cut by the same hand, and the two inscriptions directly associated with stalls on the Upper Agora also bear a common signature line. This suggests a degree of regulation. Increasingly, the context of topos inscriptions is revealing a degree of structure, whether in agorai, on public seats, or in theaters, which suggests the involvement of public authorities. This kind of regulation would have suited Julian of Askalon. It would also have fit with the urban rules of Constantinople, which can be seen in imperial laws

---

31 A metal workshop and a possible fullonica were found in this area. A basin and tubing were set in this area in the final phase, late sixth/early seventh century: for all this see Lavan, "Agorai of Sagalassos."
32 Bostra theater topos inscriptions: *IGLSyr* 13.1, nos. 9156–63.
33 Aphrodisias, topos inscriptions from hall of the Theater Baths: *ALA,* nos. 191–93. "Men of Hierapolis": *ALA,* nos. 196–97.
34 Zoticos the Peddler: *ALA,* no. 206.

35 Perge, "τοπος θερμοπουλου": LL site visit 2005.
36 Topos inscriptions on Sagalassos streets: Lavan, "Streets of Sagalassos," 201–14.
37 Inscription in Lower Agora: Lavan, "Agorai of Sagalassos."
38 Booths in the street: August. *Psalm* 81.2.
39 For topos inscriptions in general, see *ALA,* nos. 187–211 with commentary; Roueché specifically cites *Die Inschriften von Iasos,* ed. W. Blümel (Bonn, 1985), no. 256.

governing behavior in its public squares, and which Saliou reads in laws that regulated the commercial occupation of its porticoes.[40]

Literary and Pictorial Evidence

On one occasion we do have a description of the late antique clearance of stalls from a major street. At Edessa in 496–98, as part of a cleaning and whitewashing operation, a governor removed wooden booths built by artisans.[41] Yet there is no indication that anything had been built in masonry: probably they were still only light wooden booths like those mentioned by Libanius in orations of 356 and 384, set between columns in the porticoes of Antioch.[42] The stalls he describes are wooden, small-scale, and were vulnerable unless occupied. In the latter oration he notes that they need to be well maintained: they must be kept in use to stop the wooden building materials being robbed, or age making them unsightly. Libanius states that levies on such stalls provide a source of civic income. In *Or.* 11 he sees them as testifying to the commercial vibrancy of the city: he first discusses them in the context of an encomium on his hometown. He wrote this as an individual who was especially keen to praise the monumentality of Antioch. If the stalls irredeemably damaged the fabric of the great street, or obscured its beauty, why did he include them?

A century later, the Yakto mosaics depicting the colonnaded avenues of the city provide the clearest answer to this question: here we see elegant porticoes which are unencroached, with only temporary stalls.[43] The stalls are not kiosks but rather tables: the same type as appear in the Rossano Gospels' sixth-century depiction of Christ cleansing the temple of traders, recalling the slightly simpler tables seen in the Pompeii forum fresco centuries earlier.[44] In sixth-century Emesa, we again hear of tables, which could be easily tipped over, being used to sell foodstuffs, while, in sixth-century Gaza, Choricius described a festival market that had stalls covered in fabrics and laurels, with no mention of stone structures.[45] Thus, the roofed wooden structures described by Libanius on the great street of Antioch were probably exceptional, as were the stalls made out of planks and other materials in the porticoes of the main avenue at Constantinople, which Zeno ordered to be replanned and clad in marble.[46] Similarly, the semi-permanent stalls of Sagalassos have so far been found only on the main square, not on the streets and lesser plazas. There, tables were more likely used.

Functions

Aside from establishing that regulated stalls did exist, we are able to describe in some detail the types of goods sold on them. Sometimes we are able to create a general impression of what was being sold but not to tie it definitely to stalls. Chrysostom mentions meat and bread sold in the marketplace, and seems to imply wine, while also mentioning vegetables and shoes. During the reign of Julian, Christians, worried about pagan holy water sprinkled on foodstuffs, saw meat, fruit, vegetables, and bread on sale in Near Eastern agorai.[47] At least this last reference seems to imply open displays: surely the trick was to make fruit and vegetables shine in the sun, a practice known to stallholders everywhere. However, in some cases we can explicitly connect goods to a stall. The price list from an alcove of the Tetrastoon of Aphrodisias includes honey, wine, oil,

---

40 For regulation of behavior in the "basilica" courtyard at Constantinople, see *CI* 8.12.21 (AD 440). On regulation at Constantinople more generally, see Saliou, "Identité culturelle," 214–18, highlighting particularly *CI* 8.10.12 (Zeno, last quarter of fifth century), on which she further comments in eadem, *Les lois des bâtiments* (Beirut, 1994), 283–84.

41 Stalls at Edessa: Josh. Styl. 29 (AD 496–97), 32 (AD 497–98).

42 Stalls at Antioch: Lib. *Or.* 11.254 (AD 356), *Or.* 26.21 (AD 384). Only in the first oration does Libanius definitely locate the colonnades thus occupied as on a street, though this placement is likely in the second oration also: I owe these insights to the seminal article of Saliou, "Identité culturelle," 212–14.

43 Yakto mosaic: J. Lassus, "La mosaïque de Yakto," in *Antioch-on-the Orontes*, vol. 1, *The Excavations of 1932*, ed. G. W. Elderkin (Princeton, N.J., 1934), 114–56, at 134–35. See also in this volume B. Pitarakis, "Daily Life at the Marketplace in Late Antiquity and Byzantium," 398.

44 Yakto mosaic stall: Lassus, "Mosaïque de Yakto," 134–35. See the Rossano Gospels, fol. 2r; the connection is made by Mundell Mango, "The Porticoed Street," fig. 3. For the Pompeii fresco, see note 25, above.

45 For Emesa (stalls of the pastry chefs and bean seller), see *Vita S. Symeonis Sali*, part 4, p. 151; ed. L. Rydén in A.-J. Festugière, ed., *Léontios de Néapolis: Vie de Syméon le Fou et Vie de Jean de Chypre* (Paris, 1974) 55–104 (hereafter cited as *v. Sym.*). On Gaza, see Choricius, *Or.* 1.93, 2.59–65 (not seen).

46 Porticoes of the Mese at Constantinople: *CI* 8.10.12.6 (Zeno); Saliou, "Identité culturelle," 214–18.

47 For meat and wine, see Joh. Chrys. *Ad Theodorum lapsum (Treatise)* 19.7–10; vegetables: *Hom. in Ac.* 9.5 (PG 60.84); bread and meat and fruit and vegetables: Theod. *Hist. eccl.* 3.15.2.

bread, and, less certainly, vegetables, pulses, and storax, a fragrant gum.[48] At Gaza, under Julian, we learn that hot dishes were kept on the boil in the marketplace.[49] At Emesa, pastry chefs were selling on tables outside a church, while Symeon sold beans, lentil soup, and fruit in the same city, from what sounds like a self-contained stall, which depended on a thermopolium.[50]

The impression conveyed by these snippets of evidence is that the stalls in a city were mainly given over to foodstuffs, sometimes unprocessed.[51] All of these things could have been brought in from the countryside on a daily basis. They might come on donkeys, such as those which Libanius described carrying corn and hay into Antioch each day, and which went back home before midday. Alternatively, people might bring them in unaided: like St. Hilarion of Gaza, who himself carried wood, collected in the countryside, into cities of Sicily for sale.[52] There were at least some stalls given over to the sale of manufactured goods. Libanius envisages a tailor working in one of the semipermanent stalls in between the colonnades of the porticoes at Antioch. Other stalls selling artisanal goods may have been connected to shops within porticoes, which, as mentioned earlier, sold manufactured goods, cooked meals, and services. This seems to be the case for at least some of the stalls at Sagalassos. As we will see, shop owners had certain rights to use the portico space in front of their premises.[53] However, it is possible that some finished goods were sold on market tables by visiting tradesmen, such as the shoes being offered for sale on tables in the Pompeii forum fresco.

Market Buildings

Thus far we have considered stalls set within public squares and streets, sometimes set inside porticoes. In addition, stalls could be set within designated market buildings. These might include civil basilicas: the covered markets of antiquity, which Vitruvius saw as providing winter cover for the gatherings of traders.[54] It seems that these continued to be used for commercial activities in the fourth- and early fifth-century West. At Rome, it appears that money changers were among the occupants of the Basilica Aemilia in the early fifth century.[55] Unfortunately, such precision is not possible elsewhere. Repairs in the fourth and early fifth century to civil basilicas outside of provincial capitals are likely to have been in part commercially oriented, rather than used for law courts, as civic judicial magistrates were now rare, and the jurisdiction of governors was now mainly concentrated in *metropoleis*.[56] A small fourth-century apsed hall at Cuicul is particularly interesting: an inscription names it as the *basilica vestiaria*. It coexisted with a civil basilica, both built on the same square during the period 364–67.[57] Andrew Wilson has highlighted an almost identical structure at Thamugadi, to which has been connected an inscription dedicated under the same governor who built a *forum vestiarium adiutricianum*.[58] We also have mentions of a basilica of the skin dressers (βασιλικῆς τῶν Γουναρίων) in sixth-century Constantinople, but it is worth remembering that in the East at this date, *basilica* could also mean a portico (such as fronted

---

48 List of commodities: *ALA*, no. 213, painted as a rough graffito on the wall of a recess in the theater wall facing onto the Tetrastoon, listed as "?4th c." by Roueché, because it was on plaster that seems to date from the time of the building of the Tetrastoon (later fourth century), though the inscription could of course have been added a little later.
49 Gaza boiling pots: Sozom. *Hist. eccl.* 5.9.4.
50 Emesa: *v. Sym.* part 4, p. 151. Symeon seems to have been given control over the distribution and sale of the foodstuffs, with only occasional oversight from the thermopolium.
51 Antioch had food stalls on a main colonnaded street: Lib. *Or.* 11.251–52.
52 Antioch, donkeys bringing produce: Lib. *Or.* 50.25; Hilarion carrying wood: Sozom. *Hist. eccl.* 5.10.
53 Shoes: Joh. Chrys. *Hom. in Ac.* 9.5 (PG 60.84); tailor at Antioch: Lib. *Or.* 11.254.

54 Civil basilicas providing winter cover for traders: Vitr. *De arch.* 4.1.4.
55 Basilica Aemilia: money changers' coins in destruction layer on basilica floor, the latest of which is AD 409; see R. Reece, "A Collection of Coins from the Centre of Rome," *PBSR* 50 (1982): 117, 127, 131–33.
56 Repairs to civil basilicas: T. Putzeys and L. Lavan, "Commercial Space in Late Antiquity," in *Objects in Context, Objects in Use: Material Spatiality in Late Antiquity,* ed. L. Lavan, E. Swift, and T. Putzeys, Late Antique Archaeology 5 (Leiden 2007), 108.
57 Cuicul, *basilica vestiaria*: *CIL* 8. 20156 = *ILS* 5536 (AD 364–67); civil basilica: *AE* (1946): 107 = *CRAI* (1943): 381–83 (AD 364–67); C. Lepelley, *Les Cités de l'Afrique romaine au bas-empire,* vol. 2, *Notices d'histoire municipale* (Paris, 1981), 404; P. A. Février, *Djemila* (Alger, 1971), 56.
58 Thamugadi: S. Gsell, "Notes d'archéologie algérienne," *BAC* (1901): 308–23, no. 10; *AE* (1909): 4; A. Ballu, *Les Ruines de Timgad: Sept années de découvertes 1903–1910* (Paris, 1912), 144–45 (AD 364–76); A. I. Wilson, "Urban Production in the Roman World: The View from North Africa," *PBSR* 70 (2002): 241.

shops on colonnaded streets).[59] Certainly there is no evidence that civil basilicas served commercial functions beyond the early fifth century, by which time they had fallen into general disuse in the West and only a few survived in the East (mainly in provincial capitals, where they could still house the law courts).[60]

Somewhat better attested is the use of specialized market buildings (see figs. 14.3 and 14.4). These continued to be occupied, built, and repaired from the late third to the early fifth century in the West, and to the sixth century in the East. They took a variety of forms, as Hellenistic market buildings, tetragonal agorai, or macella. New macella were built at Madauros in 379–83, at Antioch (likely under Valens).[61] At Constantinople, the *Notitia Urbis* of 425 lists four macella, at least two of which must have been built after 337, as they were located in a new quarter of the city.[62] Repairs to macella are known from archaeology at Wroxeter, Verulamium, Sagalassos, and Apameia, and from epigraphy at Isernia, Lepcis Magna, and Ostia.[63] These repairs, where we have details, seem to have been conservative, maintaining the existing fabric of the buildings, with few modifications to their functional layout: macella were still in some cases courtyard buildings with a portico and a central roundel, designed to host stalls rather than cellular shops. At Sagalassos, the traditional roundel of the macellum survived until the end of antiquity despite the building of rows of shops within its interior in the sixth century. Further, at Bulla Regia and Thamugadi the erection of statues during the fourth to fifth century took place within early imperial macella which were not modified structurally at all.[64] Yet examples of an alternative type of macellum (a square block of cellular rooms surrounding a small courtyard) were constructed at Geneva in the late third or fourth century (confirmed by a bone dump), and possibly at Athens at the beginning of the fifth century. In both cases they were built on or adjacent to the forum/agora of their city, making their identification as organized market buildings likely.[65] However, they had no central pavilion.

Textual evidence from the fourth to sixth century also seems to support the continued use of macella, at least for meat, while evidence of their use for selling fish, important in the early imperial period, is currently lacking.[66] A law of 367 provides regulations governing trade in pigs to be set up on bronze tablets in the swine market (*in foro suario*) at Rome, which sounds like a macellum.[67] In sixth-century Antioch, the macellum was still the place where pig's flesh was cut up.[68] This testimony, of Malalas, is the latest evidence we have for macella as public buildings with such a clear purpose: for specialized meat selling, thus keeping nasty smells of meat waste out of the main public plaza. However, the story of macella in late antiquity is not entirely one of continuity and new building. There is evidence of the abandonment of these structures at Naples (by the mid-sixth century), Philippi (sometime before 550), and Gerasa (after late fifth but before later sixth century).[69] The disuse of the structure at Naples is not unexpected, as most secular public buildings in Italy were being abandoned around this time. It is more surprising at Philippi and Gerasa, as here it occurred within the last monumental phase of the city, when churches coexisted with public plazas and other secular public buildings. But these two examples do not negate

---

59 Constantinople, basilica of the skin dressers: *Chron. Pasch.* Olympiad 327, AD 531 (*Chronicon Paschale,* ed. L. Dindorf, CSHB [Bonn, 1832]); R. Janin, *Constantinople byzantine: Développement urbain et répertoire topographique,* 2nd ed. (Paris, 1964), 160–61. On the term *basilica,* see G. Downey, "The Architectural Significance of the Use of the Words *Stoa* and *Basilike* in Classical Literature," *AJA* 41 (1937): 194–211. *Chronicon Paschale* does use *embolos* to describe a portico in the passage just cited, possibly to make a distinction—perhaps *embolos* designated a single portico and *basilica* a row.

60 Civil basilicas disused: see appendix, §6.

61 New macella/market buildings: see appendix, §2.

62 Constantinople, macella: *Not. Const.* 6.27 (*regio* 5), 9.17 (*regio* 8, post-Constantinian *regio*), in *Notitia Dignitatum Accedunt Notitia Urbis Constantinopolitanae et Laterculae Provinciarum,* ed. O. Seeck (1876; reprint, Frankfurt, 1962); Socrates *Hist. eccl.* 1.38.9. At least two macella still existed at Rome in the early fourth century: *Not. Rom.* 2, 5; *Notitia Regionum Urbis XIV* in A. Nordh, *Libellus de regionibus urbis Romae,* Acta Instituti Romani regni Sueciae 3 (Lund, 1949), 75, 80. At Antioch, Lib. *Or.* 11.256 appears to describe one (a place for the regulated display and sale of meat).

63 Repairs to macella: see appendix, §2.

64 Continuity of occupation: see appendix, §3.

65 New macella: see appendix, 1 also with Complutum.

66 Fish and late macella: C. de Ruyt, *Macellum: Marché alimentaire des Romains,* Publications d'histoire de l'art et d'archéologie de l'Université catholique de Louvain 35 (Louvain-la-Neuve, 1983), 271–73.

67 Rome, pig market regulations: *CTh* 14.4.4.4 (AD 367).

68 Antioch, place where pork meat was cut up: Malalas 9.5, 12.7. Analyzed by G. Downey, *A History of Antioch in Syria from Seleucus to the Arab Conquest* (Princeton, 1961), 632–67, and chapter 14 n. 3.

69 Disuse of macella: see appendix, §4.

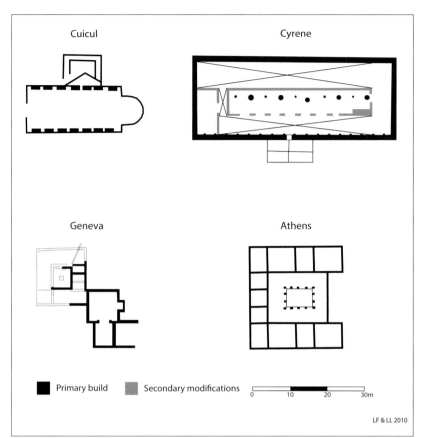

Figure 14.3. Comparative plans of some new-built late antique market buildings: the *basilica vestiaria* at Cuicul, the replanned Hellenistic market building at Cyrene, a macellum identified by bone dumps at Geneva, and a possible macellum from Athens (drawn by L. Figg and L. Lavan, 2010)

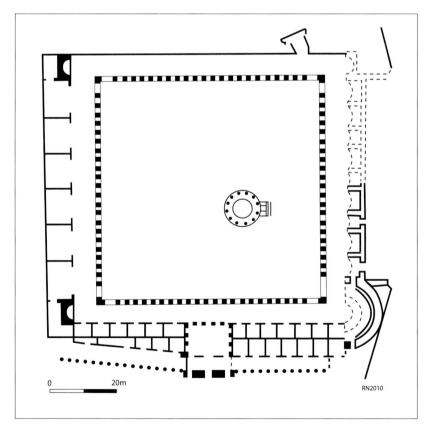

Figure 14.4. Tetragonal agora of Side: partially rebuilt in late antiquity

From polis *to* emporion? *Retail and Regulation in the Late Antique City*   343

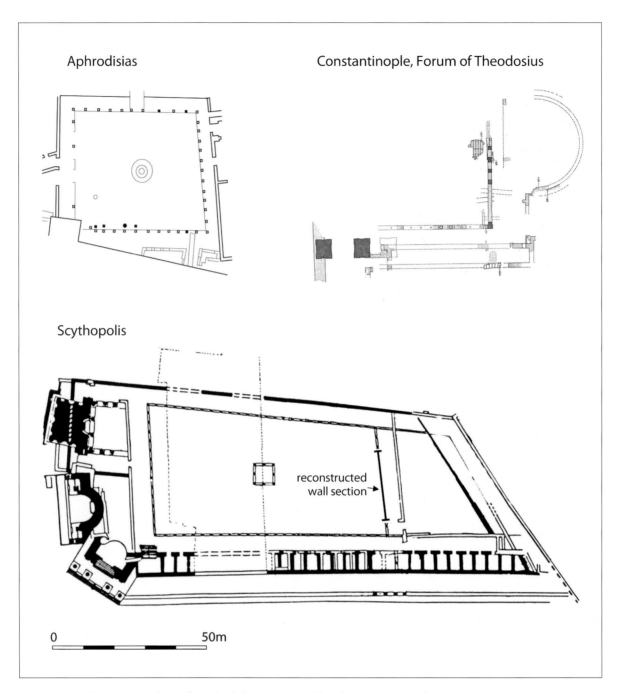

Figure 14.5. Comparative plans of new-built late antique public plazas, at same scale

the general picture, which suggests that wherever classical urbanism survived intact, in the fourth to sixth century, macella were preserved, repaired, and built anew.

Traditional Hellenistic market buildings show less continuity than Roman macella. A small new market building is known from Cyrene, dating from the final period of monumental building on the agora (probably late fourth/early fifth century). This was an open hall, 38.45 by 7.65 meters, built within the earlier structure. Elsewhere, they were at best not spoliated (Pednelissos, Melli), or were demolished (Selge). Tetragonal agorai consisted of four rows of porticoed shops surrounding a central courtyard (for

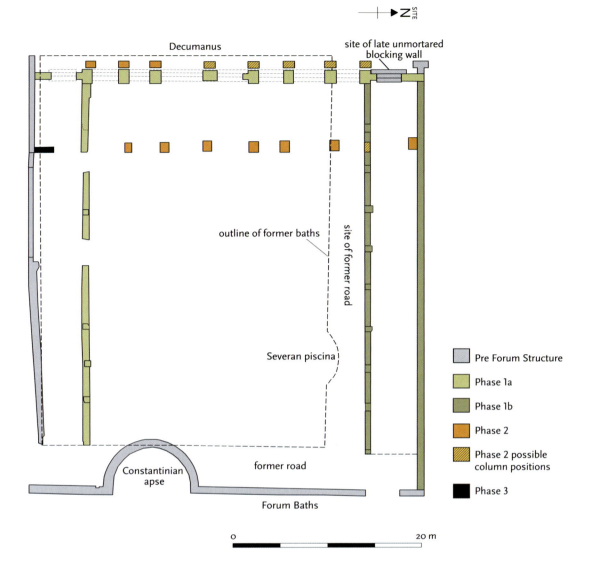

Figure 14.6. New 4th-c. plaza at Ostia (*Foro della Statua Eroica*), apparently a *macellum* in an early 5th-c. inscription, currently under excavation by the universities of Kent and Berlin (Humboldt) (drawn by A. Bates, L. Bosworth, and L. Figg, 2010)

stalls?). These show signs of late repair at Perge and Side, while at Ephesos the agora was totally rebuilt in the fourth century and further repaired in the later sixth.[70] However, the markets at Phaselis and Elaiussa Sebaste were converted into churches.[71]

Such secondary plazas might have had specialized commercial functions, such as the *forum olitorium*

---

70 See L. Lavan, "Fora and Agorai in Mediterranean Cities: Fourth and Fifth Centuries A.D.," in *Social and Political Life in Late Antiquity,* ed. W. Bowden, C. Machado, and A. Gutteridge, Late Antique Archaeology 3.1 (Leiden, 2006), 245–46.

71 In Phaselis, the church is thought to have been built in the fifth to no later than the middle of the sixth century, because of the style of its polygonal apse: J. Schafter, ed., *Phaselis: Beiträge zur Topographie und Geschichte der Stadt und ihrer Hafen,* Istanbuler Mitteilungen 24 (Tübingen, 1981), 96–97. In Elaiussa Sebaste, mosaics from the church have been dated from the fifth to sixth century AD on stylistic grounds, while the lettering on a funerary inscription found inside the building has been dated to the sixth century: E. Equini Schneider, ed., *Elaiussa Sebaste I: Campagne di scavo, 1995–1997,* Bibliotheca archaeologica 24 (Rome, 1999); eadem, ed., *Elaiussa Sebaste II: Un porto tra Oriente e Occidente,* 2 vols., Bibliotheca archaeologica 37 (Rome, 2003), 2:248–50, 538–50.

(vegetable market) built *a fundamentis* at Thignica in 326–33, known only from an inscription.[72] Notably, new fora/agorai of the period (see figs. 14.5 and 14.6) seem to have a decidedly commercial appearance: the late fourth-century Tetrastoon at Aphrodisias was simply a four-porticoed square without public buildings, as was the final phase of the forum of Coimbriga, the fourth-century *foro* at Ostia, the fourth-century agora of Skythopolis, and the forum of Theodosius at Constantinople, as identified by Berger.[73] A simple square with three porticoes from the last monumental phase of St. Bertrand de Comminges seems to belong to this same group, although it has not been dated.[74] The squares at Coimbriga and Skythopolis did have shops, but not those at Aphrodisias, St. Bertrand, or Ostia: they could only have held stalls. It could be argued that the plaza at Aphrodisias had a mainly representational function, as it is adjacent to the theater and has produced not only imperial statues but also painted acclamations for governors.[75] For the plaza at Ostia this seems less likely, as it is actually set back from the main road behind a porticoed façade and is adjacent to the main forum, to which one might expect political activities to be drawn.

The new plaza at Ostia (now known as the *Foro della Statua Eroica*) is currently under excavation by the universities of Kent and Berlin, directed by Axel Gering and myself. This paved rectangle, built over a former baths complex, has only three porticoes on its four sides and no monumental buildings within it, though it is ca. 42 × 46 meters, equivalent in size to the Tetrastoon at Aphrodisias. Its main construction phase dates shortly after the reign of Constantine, but there are also signs of a secondary restoration program. The plaza's paving, of reused stone slabs, was relaid a second time, following a destruction, and the architectural façade along the street frontage also seems to be secondary, reusing parts of the roadside steps of the first phase. The site had already been excavated in the early to mid-twentieth century, notably by the unskilled workmen of Mussolini. However, excavation diaries, studied by Axel Gering, have revealed one highly significant fact: that the Ostia "macellum" inscription seems to have come from an architrave found in this area. The inscription seems to fit the sequence of the plaza recovered by current work: it records a restoration of a macellum by Aurelius Symmachus, prefect of the city of Rome in 418–19.[76] Thus, at least in its final phase, this large late Roman square, equivalent in size to other new fora of the period, seems to have functioned as a macellum, removing foul-smelling residues from the adjacent main square of the city.

The Ostia forum/macellum seems to provide an alternative form for macella in this period, of a porticoed courtyard without shops or roundel. Thus it also seems wise to consider other types of untraditional structure that might also have represented collectively organized shopping areas. The most obvious examples are the new "sigma" shopping plazas of the fourth- to sixth-century Mediterranean (see fig. 14.7). These semicircular exedras of shops were more than simply shopping crescents which enlarged the street shopping area. At Corinth, Skythopolis (in two cases), and Ostia they were actually set behind a street portico/façade, so that they were not integrated within the wider street space of the avenues in which they were set, but were secluded from it.[77] Such architecture failed to maximize the aesthetic potential of the crescent but clearly provided amenity to shoppers, by producing self-contained market areas, perhaps with a central space for stalls. It seems equally possible that some hall-like public buildings, which were converted into cellular shops (see fig. 14.8), might have served as unified macella. Thus, the Hall of the Theater Baths and the Sebasteion at Aphrodisias provided an environment not unlike a mod-

---

72 Thugnica, *forum olitorium*: *CIL* 8.1408.
73 Newly built fora/agorai: Lavan, "Fora and Agorai," 196–202.
74 St. Bertrand de Comminges, "portique en pi": porticoed square dated tentatively to the fourth century, as it is the last monumental phase of the complex, and foundation levels related to it have produced second- and third-century material: G. Fabre and J.-L. Paillet, *Saint-Bertrand-de-Comminges,* vol. 4, *Le macellum* (Pessac, 2009), 115.
75 Statues of Tetrastoon at Aphrodisias: *ALA*, nos. 20, 21 (AD 360–64); R. R. R. Smith, "Late Antique Portraits in a Public Context: Honorific Statuary at Aphrodisias in Caria, A.D. 300–600," *JRS* 99 (1999): 168–71; idem, "A Portrait Monument for Julian and Theodosius at Aphrodisias," in *Griechenland in der Kaiserzeit: Kolloquium zum sechzigsten Geburtstag von Prof. Dietrich Willers,* ed. C. Reusser (Bern, 2001), 125–36. On the painted acclamations, see *ALA*, no. 75, with C. Roueché, "Looking for Late Antique Ceremonial: Ephesos and Aphrodisias," in *100 Jahre Österreichische Forschungen in Ephesos: Akten des Symposions Wien 1995,* ed. H. Friesinger and F. Krinzinger, Archäologische Forschungen 1, DenkWien 260 (Vienna, 1999), 161–68.

76 Ostia macellum repair inscription: *CIL* 14 s.1 4719 (AD 418–19).
77 Sigma plazas: see appendix, §7.

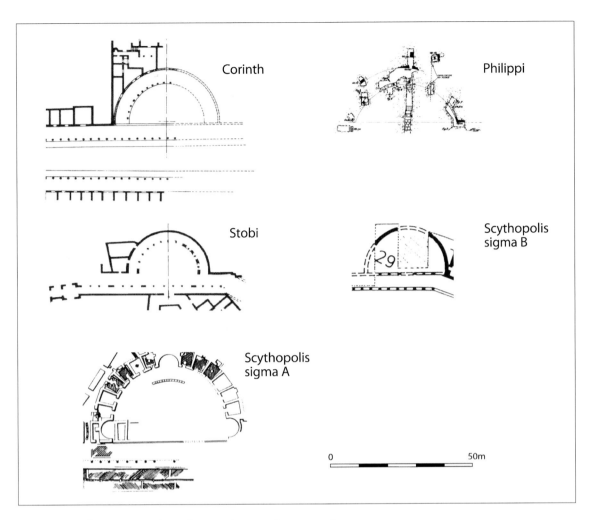

Figure 14.7. Comparative plans of sigma plazas, at the same scale

ern shopping mall, with two aisles of shops lining a central (covered) space; so did the gymnasium and basilica of Herdonia, which were subdivided into cellular units in the fourth century, and the baths' basilica (now museum) of Side, which was reorganized in the same way, likely sometime in late antiquity.[78]

Shops
Definition and Identification

The terms *taberna* and *ergastērion* are in the Roman Empire closely associated with shops. *Taberna* can, however, also mean a hut, shelter, booth, or stall, whereas *ergastērion* can mean a place where work is done with no retail element necessary.[79] However, this should not obscure the fact that in an urban context these terms are widely used to designate buildings housing permanent retail establishments, including rows of purpose-built cellular rooms. It is the latter definition which will be explored in this chapter. Such units, set in prime locations, along main avenues and fora/agorai, spread around the Mediterranean from the fourth century BC onward.[80]

---

78 It is noteworthy that the cellular units in the Hall of the Theater Baths at Aphrodisias could not be locked, except by closing the whole hall.

79 P. W. Glare et al., *Oxford Latin Dictionary*, 8 vols. in 2 (Oxford, 1968–82), s.vv. "ergasterium," "taberna"; G. W. H. Lampe, *A Patristic Greek Lexicon* (Oxford, 1961), s.v. ἐργαστήριον.
80 Cellular tabernae began in Italy in the fourth century BC, and spread with the establishment of Roman cities in the West: see A. MacMahon, *The Taberna Structures of Roman Britain*, BAR British Series 356 (Oxford, 2003), 4–5. No equivalent study

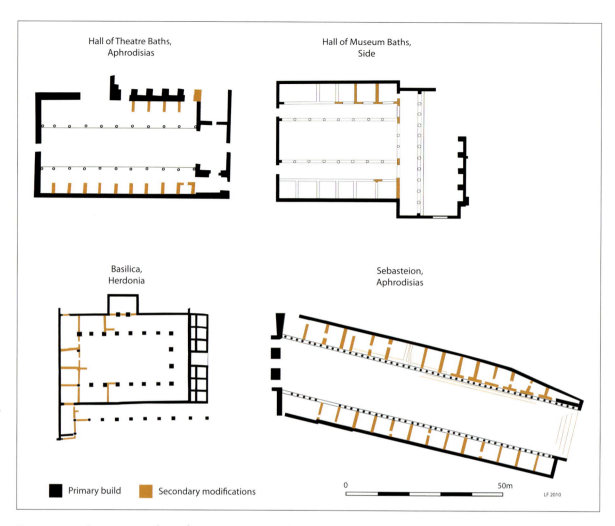

Figure 14.8. Comparative plans of structures converted into halls of cellular rooms in late antiquity (the date of the shops in the Baths at Side is not yet confirmed), at the same scale (drawn by L. Figg, 2010)

The function of these ergastēria/tabernae is easy to distinguish from the stalls found in plazas, streets, or self-contained market buildings. In late antiquity, tabernae do not seem to have carried out the sale of raw food stuff and other agricultural products, but rather the integrated production and sale of artisanal manufactures, from cooked meals and bread to silver ornaments. The production undertaken was very definitely secondary production: not the primary processing of raw materials or other dangerous artisanal activity (such as making pottery), but rather glassblowing, the manufacture of small iron objects, and so on, with facilities designed for display and sale as much as for production. Thus, as will be discussed later, there is evidence of hammer scale from metalworking at Sagalassos, and small glass furnaces for blowing at Aphrodisias. Yet no large-scale productive installations have been located within cellular shops. It seems likely that these arrangements were supposed to allow objects to be manufactured to order by urban patrons, as Cassiodorus (*Var.* 8.31) suggests. A final distinguishing characteristic of tabernae/ergastēria was perhaps their status as permanent points of sale. Libanius describes how agorai could be deserted in winter in Syria because of the rains, which caused the citizens of Antioch to keep to the porticoes. Presumably such seasonal down-

---

has been made for the East, where they form an integral part of Roman colonnaded streets in early imperial phases, though cellular units were present in late Hellenistic market buildings and tetragonal agorai, as at Ephesos and Miletos.

pours seriously disadvantaged stallholders, even if they could find a space under a basilica or portico roof, as Vitruvius envisaged.[81] In contrast, shop owners were able to keep open all of the year, as permanent points of sale.

As I have noted, when found in literary sources the terms *tabernae* and *ergastēria* are commonly identified with the rows of cellular shops found in Mediterranean cities, especially those lining their principal avenues. However, recently there has been some dissent about the automatic attribution of such textual labels to these architectural structures. Penelope Allison has criticized many of the simple assumptions behind the attribution of linguistic labels to architectural spaces: not all shops need have been set in rows of cellular rooms, and not all cellular rooms need have been shops.[82] Taking this line of thinking further, Anthea Harris has suggested that the finds from such units do not necessarily designate commerce.[83] These analyses have some benefit: certainly not all shops were located in purpose-built structures, as Jennifer Baird has demonstrated for Dura-Europos.[84] Conversely, not all cellular shops served as retail spaces in their final phase, from which artefacts found on site relate: they might have been just houses, rather than shops in which artisans also lived. For mixed domestic and commercial use we have some literary evidence: a widow sleeping above a shop at Antioch and owners sleeping in two thermopolia at Emesa.[85] However, there is much architectural and artifactual evidence which seems to confirm the traditional identification of rows of cellular rooms on streets and squares as shops.

Above all, the architectural evidence seems clear: these structures were commonly built as rows of cellular units of one or two stories, frequently fronted by a portico, opening onto the street, sometimes through an entrance which extended across the full width of the façade. Such a structure is perfect for commerce, and it is no surprise that we find these cells within macella and tetragonal agorai, and labeled *ergastēria* on the Yakto mosaic.[86] It is true that within forts, cellular units are interpreted as barrack blocks: but within an urban setting, rows of such units along major avenues of cities would be the most desirable commercial properties. Furthermore, fixtures found within such units frequently indicate commercial activities (such as the multiple basins at Thamugadi, or the counters of Ostia), while the finds at sites such as Sagalassos, Tralleis, and Skythopolis seem to confirm both production and retail, at least in the final period. The topos inscriptions of Aphrodisias and Sagalassos set outside "shops" also suggest that these units had a specialized commercial function. Finds of production materials (e.g., dyestuffs) and especially waste, such as hammer scale, take the case further. Thus, in this chapter I will be treating the rows of cellular units found along main urban streets as having been constructed as shops. Further, because such units continued to be built in ever greater numbers within city centers in the East, I will also assume that most of them continued to be used as shops until the end of the period, an assumption supported by finds from Sagalassos, Skythopolis, Beirut, and elsewhere.

Perhaps the most important arguments for the identification of rows of cellular rooms on main streets as shops are textual. At Constantinople, we know that the buildings lining the main avenue (confirmed as cellular units in a small excavation) were key retail establishments, certainly at the time of the early tenth-century *Book of the Prefect* and probably earlier, as silversmiths were based here in the early seventh century.[87] Further, we hear of collective ownership arrangements for *ergastēria*,

---

81 Agorai deserted in winter in Syria: Lib. *Or.* 11.215–17; basilica providing shelter to traders in winter: Vitr. *De arch.* 4.1.4.
82 P. M. Allison, "Using the Material and Written Sources: Turn of the Millennium Approaches to Roman Domestic Space," *AJA* 105 (2001): 181–208.
83 A. Harris, "Shops, Retailing and the Local Economy in the Early Byzantine World: The Example of Sardis," in *Secular Buildings and the Archaeology of Everyday Life in the Byzantine Empire*, ed. K. Dark (Oxford, 2004), 82–122.
84 J. A. Baird, "Shopping, Eating and Drinking at Dura Europos: Reconstructing Contexts," in Lavan, Swift, and Putzeys, eds., *Objects in Context, Objects in Use*, 413–47.
85 Antioch, widow above shop: Lib. *Or.* 33.6; Emesa, owners sleeping in bean seller's shop and tavern: see v. *Sym.* part 4, pp. 151, 153.

86 Cellular units are found within macella at Sagalassos in a late rebuild and at Geneva and Athens, and in tetragonal agorai at Ephesos, Perge, and Side in a late rebuild and earlier. For full references, see appendix, §2, and Lavan, "Fora and Agorai," 244–45. Cellular units were also occupied in the fourth to fifth century within a macellum of Thasos: J.-Y. Marc, personal communication. On the Yakto mosaic, see Lassus, "Mosaïque de Yakto," 134–35.
87 Constantinople units along the Mese: R. Naumann, "Vorbericht über die Ausgrabungen zwischen Mese und Antiochus-Palast," *IstMitt* 15 (1965): 145–46; *Chron. Pasch.* Olympiad 327, AD 531 (a basilica—i.e., portico—of silversmiths).

which is unsurprising, given that rows of cellular shops are usually built as one phase, as an architectural unit. Thus, for Antioch, we see on the Yakto mosaic a group labeled *ergastēria* (plural) belonging to a martyrion.[88] At Constantinople a friend of Chrysostom owned a group on the Augusteion square, on the south side of Hagia Sophia, while a law of Constantius endowed the same church with income from ergastēria in the city, suggesting state ownership. At Skythopolis, the architectural unity that is the sigma plaza and its shops was built as a single operation by the governor, Theosebius, in 506/7.[89] Furthermore, in a sermon given at Antioch in 387, Chrysostom implies that several artisans of different trades inhabiting the same shop paid rent collectively: given the small size of most shops (ca. 3 ×3 m or 4 × 4 m), this could well refer to traders within a single row.[90] The existence of a sequence of single letters (A, B, Γ, etc.) in front of a row of shops, on successive portico pavements at Beirut, and the uniform use of all units in some rows (such as Tralleis's weaving establishments) suggest the same.[91]

Functions

The trades represented in late antique tabernae/ ergastēria were many, and have been explored in a recent article.[92] Unfortunately, not every trade attested can be explored in equal detail, as the nature of the sources we have is very uneven, reflecting in part the different levels of mess which different artisans produced or how well that residue has survived. Thus, although we hear of ergastēria being used as schools and as painters', barbers', moneychangers', candlemakers', and perfumers' shops, excavations tend to find mainly restaurants, metal workshops, dye shops, and glassblowing establishments. This is a rather poorer material trace than for the early imperial period, when butchers', fishmongers', and potters' shops are known.[93] Such a wider variety of establishments may have continued to exist, but we cannot confirm their presence archaeologically. In the West, where occupation levels and fixtures have been entirely removed by later damage, few identifications are possible. In the East, sudden destructions, as at Skythopolis and Sardis, provide an evidential window which would otherwise be closed. Yet, even on such exceptional sites, some professions are invisible. The evidence is undoubtedly richest for shops in Asia Minor and the Levant. From these sites, supplemented by the occasional text, we can gain at least something of an impression of the nature of artisanal boutiques found in late antique cities.

From both literary sources and archaeological evidence, it seems likely that the most common type of shop was the restaurant. In contrast, metal workshops, glassblowers, and fullonicae, which have equally distinctive architectural fixtures, are mentioned far less often in the texts. The same is true of bakeries. Of other types of late antique shop, we usually have usually only single examples from archaeology (e.g., a mosaicist, perfumer, or goldsmith), or epigraphy (a barber), or perhaps just one literary description (of a painter). In texts, schools are the type of "shop" best represented, at Rome, Antioch, and Athens, though silversmiths are mentioned at both Carthage and Constantinople. This points toward the unremarkable conclusion that restaurants/taverns and schools really were very frequent, while other establishments were less common. Quite how many glassblowers existed in relation to barbers cannot be known. Yet some of the "rare" artisans were probably a little more common than our fragmentary information suggests: Chrysostom and Augustine use metaphors drawing on painters' or perfumers' shops as if they were universally understood, as will be explored shortly.

It is important to note the existence of some trades not represented as occupying shops during late antiquity, in either texts, epigraphy, or archaeology. There were apparently no (or very few) permanent shops for the sale of fruit and vegetables, meat, fodder, clothes, shoes, pottery, ordinary building

---

88   Yakto mosaic: Lassus, "Mosaïque de Yakto," 134–35.
89   Constantinople, shops south of Hagia Sophia, see *Vita Olympiadis* 6; for endowed shops, see Just. *Nov.* 59.5, perhaps referring to *CI* 3.1.2 (AD 357). On Skythopolis, see appendix, §7.
90   Common rent: Joh. Chrys. *Hom. ad pop. Ant.* 16.6 (PG 49.172): "And in the same manner as persons inhabiting the same shop carry on a separate traffic, yet put all afterward into the common fund, so also let us act."
91   Beirut pavement numbers: American University of Beirut, "Module 3: The Byzantine Portico and Shops," *Windows on the Souk,* http://ddc.aub.edu.lb/projects/archaeology/soukex/deliverables/module03.html (accessed July 2010). On the uniformity of shops at Tralleis, see appendix, §13.
92   Survey of shop functions: Putzeys and Lavan, "Commercial Space."

93   MacMahon, *Taberna Structures,* 62–64, 66–68.

materials, or slaves. In some cases, we may assume a gap in our evidence (likely in the case of cobblers and high-class tailors), but in other cases these were goods which we know or may presume were sold on the stalls in specialized buildings or on stalls in the marketplace. This was either because regulations demanded it, or because their value was too low/seasonal for the volume sold to support a shop, which was likely the case for most raw foodstuffs.[94] Perhaps some commodities had to be bought from out-of-town production sites, or direct from the private houses of artisans in the suburbs, who could not afford a street-front studio. There seems little basis to assert that professional service providers, such as lawyers, and notaries commonly held tabernae as offices in this period, rather than their own homes.[95] Rather, one can note a number of small civic and imperial offices on streets and public squares, as at Rome, Cyrene, Caesarea and Emesa, which might have occupied tabernae. Yet, where we have specific details, it is clear that more monumental settings were used, and one would expect city council chambers, basilicas, and praetoria to be the normal settings for such activities.[96]

Urban Setting

According to the rule book of Julian of Askalon, which seems to reflect practice in sixth-century Palestine, the location of different types of artisanal activity was regulated. Some enterprises were entirely excluded from cities, to guard against fire and nuisance.[97] Quite what reality this had is another matter, at least in terms of the urban landscapes revealed by archaeology, which picks up traces of production well. As far as the exclusion of dirty primary production goes, these rules seem to have been respected, up to a point, though occasional breaches are known.[98] In the fourth- to sixth-century East, we rarely find pottery/lime kilns and blast furnaces in city center locations. Admittedly, in reconquest Africa a number of production sites were established in fora and large public buildings. They also appear in other regions under Roman control within the late sixth and seventh century, and then in the Levant under the Umayyads and early ʿAbbāsids.[99] However, for prosperous cities in the fourth-century West and fourth- to sixth-century East we still find production sites on the edge or outside of the city, as at Delphi, Sagalassos, and Dor.[100] What do very definitely occur, in even the most monumental city centers, in contradiction of Julian of Askalon, are small units for secondary production, with retail incorporated: glassblowing shops and metal workshops.[101]

The testimony of archaeology and everyday textual sources reveals a mixed landscape of retail, with

---

94 On unprocessed foodstuffs in the market, see note 47, above.

95 In Cyrene, a government office was definitely in a monumental building on the agora; see Lavan, "Fora and Agorai," 248. In Emesa, a *tabellio* (public notary) had his seat in the agora (here probably not a law court, as this is not a provincial capital); see Procop. *Anecdota* 28.6. Other examples are given in note 96, below.

96 In Antioch, a tax office was established in a former temple: Lib. *Or.* 30.42. The "tax office" at Caesarea was part of a wider *praetorium* complex, and was not a simple taberna; S. P. Ellis sees it as comparable to medium-sized "middle class" houses in the region in "Middle Class Houses in Late Antiquity," in Bowden, Machado, and Gutteridge, eds., *Social and Political Life in Late Antiquity,* 424. There is no solid evidence for the hypothesis that the *secretarium senatus* at Rome was inside a taberna of the Forum of Caesar; see A. Fraschetti, *La conversione da Roma pagana a Roma cristiana* (Rome, 1999), 230–36, with further references. It seems far more likely that a building inscription would record repairs to a monumental structure than to a taberna. On praetoria, see L. Lavan, "The Praetoria of Civil Governors in Late Antiquity," in *Recent Research in Late-Antique Urbanism,* ed. idem, Journal of Roman Archaeology, supp. ser. 42 (Portsmouth, R.I., 2001), 39–56.

97 Julian of Askalon 5.1 (pottery production considered only in villages); 4.3 (bread ovens restricted to the outskirts of cities); 11.1 (glassmakers and ironmongers and foundries must practice on outskirts); 14 (garum makers excluded).

98 Industrial encroachment: in Silchester, the forum was given over to industry in the second half of the third century, and pottery kilns, thought to be fifth century, have been found in one of Thessalonike's abandoned fora; see appendix, §19.

99 Industrial encroachment, sixth–seventh century: see appendix, §§20, 21.

100 Industrial quarters on edge/outside of city—Delphi, peripheral in terms of late city: P. Petridis, "Les ateliers de potiers à Delphes à l'époque paléochrétienne," *Topoi* 8 (1998): 703–10; Sagalassos: J. Poblome, P. Bounegru, P. Degryse, W. Viane, M. Waelkens, and S. Erdemgil, "The Sigillata Manufactories of Pergamon and Sagalassos," *Journal of Roman Archaeology* 14 (2001): 143–66; Dor, by north harbor: A. Raban, "Dor-Yam: Maritime and Coastal Installations at Dor in their Geomorphological and Stratigraphic Context," in *Excavations at Dor, Final Report,* vol. 1A, *Areas A and C: Introduction and Stratigraphy,* ed. E. Stern, Qedem Reports 1 (Jerusalem, 1995), 285–354.

101 Glassblowing occurred in shops within the walls of Delphi, Ephesos, Aphrodisias, and Beirut, and metalworking in Segobriga, Carthage, Sardis, Sagalassos, and Skythopolis (eighth century): see Putzeys and Lavan, "Commercial Space," 85–93.

rows of shops containing different trades, with occasional nodes of concentration. For mixed commerce, we have the finds from shops at Sardis, Aphrodisias (Theater Baths), Sagalassos (Upper Agora), and Beirut, as well as a description of a mixed row from seventh-century Constantinople.[102] For zones of concentrated commerce, we hear of metalworkers in groupings together: thus, according to the *Patria,* Jewish coppersmiths clustered together at Constantinople in the Chalkoprateia until the time of Theodosius II, while a Street of the Silversmiths is known from Carthage and likewise existed on part of the Mese at Constantinople.[103] Carthage also had a Street of Fig Sellers,[104] though those sellers could have been organized in stalls. At Antioch, inns clustered just outside the gates of the city.[105] For metal workers, one might suspect that their relatively valuable products encouraged safety in numbers. Yet, groupings of shops of weavers and dye workers suggest something more complex was going on—perhaps the presence of guilds, who came together by choice or compulsion. A passage of Augustine seems to suggest that, in some cases at least, groups of artisans might assemble together in order to make complex manufacture easier, with a division of labor resembling Fordist mass production:

> like workmen in the street of the silversmiths, where one vessel, in order that it may go out perfect, passes through the hands of many, when it might have been finished by one perfect workman. But the only reason why the combined skill of many workmen was thought necessary was that it is better that each part of an art should be learned by a special workman, which can be done speedily and easily, than that they should all be compelled to be perfect in one art throughout all its parts, which they could only attain slowly and with difficulty. (August. *de civ. D.* 7.4)[106]

In a few cases, the clustering of trades is likely to have had a commercial motive. The book copiers and sellers trading in the "Basilica" courtyard at Constantinople clearly wanted to be close to the city library and the law courts, which concentrated customers for their wares.[107] Thus among shops, it is unsurprising to find restaurants clustered around agorai, which were still important centers of social life. The placing of schools around fora/agorai can perhaps be explained by the desire of teachers to catch the eye of parents visiting the agora for other reasons, or to imitate the style of those "civic" teachers who were lucky enough to enjoy a classroom in the town hall.[108] Perhaps variations in rent influenced where some types of commerce were located: the street of the silversmiths was adjacent to the forum of Carthage in the late fourth century, and similarly occupied the main avenue of Constantinople in the early seventh century, probably because these traders were able to pay higher rents than blacksmiths and their ilk.[109] In some cities, such as Thamugadi, the incidence of fullonicae seems too great to relate to any real retail logic: it has been suggested that intensive commercial cloth finishing for export was their aim, rather than cloth cleaning, as elsewhere.[110] Yet if export was their goal, it seems odd to fill city center shops with such establishments, rather than placing them outside the city. Perhaps the motivation in setting fullonicae within shops, rather than in the suburbs, was to obtain direct access to urban water supply and drains, to provide improved security, or to bestow a mark of status, rather than being there only to sell.

---

102 Of mixed commerce: Thasos, Sardis, Sagalassos (Upper Agora west side), and Beirut, see appendix (§§13, 10, and 14, respectively) for references. For Constantinople, see *Miracles of St. Artemius,* chaps. 18, 21, 26, 29, 36; Mundell Mango, "Commercial Map of Constantinople," 197.
103 Constantinople copper market: *Patria* 3.32; Constantinople, silversmiths on the Mese: *Chron. Pasch.* Olympiad 328, AD 532; Malalas 18.71; Carthage: August. *Conf.* 6.9 (14).
104 Carthage, Street of the Fig Sellers: August. *De moribus Manichaeorum* 19.72.
105 Antioch, inns just outside city gates: Lib. *Or.* 11.231.
106 *Augustinus: De Civitate Dei,* ed. E. Hoffmann, CSEL 40.1, 40.2 (Vienna, 1899–1900).
107 Book copiers and sellers in the "Basilica" courtyard at Constantinople: Agath. 2.29.2.
108 Clustering around agorai, of restaurants (Sagalassos, Antioch, Cyrene) and schools (Rome, Milan, Carthage, Constantinople, Athens, Antioch): see the references collected in Lavan, "Fora and Agorai," 228, 248, 230 n. 94. The article also discusses the continuing social function of agorai.
109 On the location of silversmiths, see note 103, above.
110 High incidence of fullonicae at Thamugadi: Wilson, "Urban Production in the Roman World," 237–41.

Architecture

Although the architecture of cellular shops is relatively simple, its detail reveals much about their nature, as well as much information of value for its own sake. The most important observation that can be made on the design of cellular shops is their striking homogeneity and continuity in basic design, from the Hellenistic period to the early seventh century AD. Many late antique traders operated out of shops dating from earlier periods, to which they felt no need to make major adaptations. Furthermore, the design of shops constructed anew saw no change on earlier designs. Most shops were still built as square, or almost square, one-room units, opening onto the street, although a few (and only a few) eventually expanded by subdividing their portico or knocking through into an adjacent unit. Some shops not arranged in rows surely do escape archaeological identification. But there are so many units arranged in cellular rows, along main streets and plazas, that we have plenty to describe. Within rows, the units were usually regular in size. Their dimensions varied from ca. 10 by 7 meters at Constantinople on the Mese to ca. 2 by 1.75 meters at Sagalassos, with smaller sizes more common.[111] Where elevations survive, most shops seem to have been single-story. In some examples, we may suspect a wooden mezzanine within the vault space or roof rafters, as at Sardis and Sagalassos, where lines of beam holes have been detected.[112] Sometimes shops were two-story, which was definitely the case for some shops at Sardis and at Perge, and for some at Constantinople. Upper levels were reached by staircases, as preserved at Sardis, Aphrodisias (Sebasteion), Iasos, and Side, or, rarely, from a second-level portico, comparable to those of the shops on the Mese at Constantinople.[113] The domestic use of upper stories is suggested by Libanius, but on the Mese an upper gallery of shops is likely.[114]

The shops of the silversmiths at Carthage had a lead roof, or at least lead guttering. Most are likely to have had tile roofs, as depicted on the Yakto mosaic, and confirmed at Sardis and at Justiniana Prima.[115] Other roofs were barrel-vaulted, like those built on the Lower Agora of Ephesos in the fourth century, Sagalassos in the fifth century, at Patara in or after the sixth century, and also at Tralleis (see fig. 14.9). Shops seem to have been vaulted when they were built against another larger structure or hillside.[116] Single-phase conjoined vaults imply collective construction of rows as units. As in earlier centuries, shop fronts in the East usually had formal doorways, of a single leaf (as at the Sebastaion at Aphrodisias and at Sardis) or double-leaf (as at Perge's tetragonal agora and at Sardis). Otherwise, they might be open to the street, with no threshold at all, such as those built at Jerusalem and within the Theater Baths at Aphrodisias. In the West, shops with an open front were more common, and were sometimes closed by a distinctive type of door whose conjoining planks were fitted into special slots in the threshold, one after the other, and closed with a padlock.[117] These slotted threshold blocks continued to be employed for shop doorways at Ostia throughout late antiquity, despite several rises in street levels during the period: being reset higher and higher.[118] The accessibility of the shops to the

---

111 Shop size, Constantinople: see note 87, above. Sagalassos: T. Putzeys, "Contextual Analysis at Sagalassos: Developing a Methodology for Classical Archaeology" (Ph.D. diss., Katholieke Universiteit Leuven, 2007), 213–18 (available at http://users.telenet.be/diplodocus/Phd_CD/index.html; last accessed November 2010).

112 Sardis, possible mezzanine: J. S. Crawford, *The Byzantine Shops at Sardis,* Archaeological Exploration of Sardis 9 (Cambridge, Mass., 1990), 8; Sagalassos, Lower Agora west side shops: LL site observations, 2005.

113 Staircases: LL site observations, 2005; second-level portico: e.g., *CTh* 15.1.45 (AD 406).

114 Libanius mentions a widow above a shop in Antioch, *Or.* 33.6 (above, note 85).

115 Lead roofs: August. *Conf.* 6.9 (14). Tile roofs, Yakto mosaic: Lassus, "Mosaïque de Yakto," 134–35; Sardis, tile: Crawford, *Byzantine Shops at Sardis,* 6. Justiniana Prima, tile with some lead plaques: V. Kondić and V. Popović, *Caričin Grad: Utvrdeno naselje u vizantijskom Iliriku* (Belgrade, 1977), 323. Such tools would have functioned best with collective drain gutters.

116 Vaulted roofs at Ephesos's Lower Agora and Tralleis: see references in the appendix; at Sagalassos (west side of Upper Agora) and Patara: Putzeys, "Contextual Analysis at Sagalassos," 291–95; LL site visits, 2005.

117 Slotted thresholds and other blocks: MacMahon, *Taberna Structures,* 91–99.

118 Ostia, threshold blocks raised: e.g., on the Via di Diana, see Gering, "Plätze und Straßensperren an Promenaden," 346–49 with fig. 27 n. 114, dated around 300 (thanks to coins). South of Case a Giardino: idem, "Die Case a Giardino als unerfüllter Architektentraum: Planung und gewandelte Nutzung einer Luxuswohnanlage im antiken Ostia," *Römische Mitteilungen* 109 (2002): 129–36 with figs. 12, 14, 18, 19 (repaired at the end of third century; a coin of Aurelian gives a terminus post quem).

Figure 14.9. Shops with collective barrel vaults: Ephesos (above), Lower Agora (4th c.), and Patara (below) (6th c.) (photos by author)

major streets, where the main drains ran, could create difficulties with flooding; when storm drains overflowed, this might lead to panicked bailing of water "using tubs and pitchers and sponges" as shopkeepers tried to avoid goods being spoiled, or worse, the foundations of the buildings being undermined, as Chrysostom describes.[119]

Many, though not all, rows of cellular shops were fronted by a portico, especially those built within the fourth to sixth century, in both East and West. They have been detected in nine cases of new shop construction, and were absent in ten cases. It should be noted that the former were generally built on great long avenues, while the latter were generally part of short "parades" of cellular units fitting into preexisting spaces.[120] Porticoes were of varied width, between 2 and 6 meters, corresponding to the varied height of the colonnade. Shops that were built within a preexisting stoa, as secondary subdivisions, obviously could not offer this, although at Sagalassos a light wooden porch, perhaps supporting a brushwood or cloth superstructure, was added to the front of a subdivided portico:[121] an arrangement that was perhaps followed elsewhere. The walkway within porticoes was normally on a raised pavement, above the road, at varying heights, of usually no more than two or three steps. Most of these details are unsurprising: they confirm that the shops built in the sixth and early seventh century were largely the same design as those of the second century AD, or indeed second century BC, and that they persisted in being structures that were well-suited to commerce and amenable to shoppers, being often the result of collective design rather than piecemeal development.

Decoration

It is important to consider the decoration of shops, as these too reveal traces of collective organization and individual initiative in construction or occupation. Within Eastern shops, surviving wall decoration is rare, probably indicating that most shops had only plaster to decorate them, and are in any case very rarely published. At Sardis, individual shops show a variety of window types, doorsills, and floor materials, despite being set within a row with a common front and portico. Alternatively, at some sites rows of rooms seem to be almost identically fitted, as in the Skythopolis sigma.[122] Of other decorations to shops, only a few well-preserved sites can provide details, supplemented by texts. Shop façades occasionally show evidence of collective decoration: frescoes, as at Ephesos and Apameia, where it included garlands, imitation marble panels, and a possible representation of a *noria;* or marble veneer, as on the shops of the Skythopolis sigma.[123] Such decoration might have been a component part in a planned construction of a row of shops, as at Skythopolis. Alternatively, it might possibly reflect a civic requirement for private owners to decorate their façades in a comparable manner, as existed for stalls in the porticoes of the Mese at Constantinople.[124]

---

119 Low entrances and flooding of street: Joh. Chrys. *Hom. in 1 Tim.* 13.3 (PG 62.568).
120 Porticoes graced newly built shops at Ostia, Justiniana Prima, Aizanoi, Ephesos (Arcadiane), Sagalassos (Upper Agora), Sardis, Skythopolis, and Jerusalem. They were absent from Herdonia, Iasos, Metropolis, Ephesos (shops by the Temple of Domitian), Aphrodisias (shops by the Basilica), Sagalassos (Lower Agora, south and west side; Upper Agora, last divisions on the west side), Ariassos (units in stoa—perhaps not shops), Arykanda (Upper Agora and shops below the Main Baths). For references, see appendix, §§10–13.
121 Sagalassos, possible late portico in wood: Lavan, "Agorai of Sagalassos."
122 Sardis decoration: Crawford, *Byzantine Shops at Sardis,* 8–9. Skythopolis: LL site observation, 1998, and E. Khamis, "The Shops of Scythopolis in Context," in Lavan, Swift, and Putzeys, eds., *Objects in Context, Objects in Use,* 448, on mosaic floor in both shops and portico, citing G. Mazor and R. Bar-Nathan, "Scythopolis, Capital of Palestina Secunda," *Qadmoniot* 107–8 (1994): 130–32 (in Hebrew); G. Mazor and R. Bar-Nathan, "The Bet She'an Excavation Project—1992–1994: The IAA Expedition," *Hadashot Arkheologiyot—Excavations and Surveys in Israel* 105 (1996): 1–34 (in Hebrew). The Sepphoris shops have mosaic floors, but few details are published yet: see Z. Weiss, "'Nancy and James Grosfeld 2000 Zippori Expedition': Zippori (Sepphoris)—Archaeological Summer Course, June 25–July 28, 2000," at http://archaeology.huji.ac.il/zippori/2000/zippori-2000-reoprt. html [sic] (accessed July 2010).
123 Shop façades, Ephesos, with frescoes: C. Foss, *Ephesus after Antiquity: A Late Roman, Byzantine and Turkish City* (Cambridge, 1979), 69, for which I have not been able to locate further references; Apameia, painted façade: J. C. Balty, *Guide d'Apamée* (Brussels, 1981), 78; and (on the Skythopolis sigma) R. Bar-Nathan and G. Mazor, "City Centre (South) and Tel Iztabba Area: Excavations of the Antiquities Authority Expedition," *Excavations and Surveys in Israel* 11 (1992): 43–44.
124 Constantinople, stalls on the Mese: CI 8.10.12.6 (Zeno). Such a requirement might of course have been commuted to a compulsory payment for works carried out by the city.

Portico decoration strongly reveals collective arrangements. Tile and stone paving were most frequent. Nevertheless, mosaics in porticoes are quite common, with late antique examples found at sites such as Ephesos, Side, Perge, Beirut, Sepphoris, Skythopolis, and Gerasa.[125] Complex geometric and figured mosaics are known from the porticoes of Ephesos, Skythopolis, and especially Apameia (where a fifth-century pictorial *tessellatum* was followed by a sixth-century *opus sectile*). These are truly spectacular and represent a clear desire to show off, exceeding the decoration of shopping areas in earlier periods.[126] Collective decoration shows that either porticoes were considered private space under a single owner or—as the legislation suggests—public space. This was clearly the case when portico mosaics were dedicated by a *pater civitatis* at Side and at Perge, by a governor at Skythopolis, and by a bishop at Sepphoris.[127]

In the substance of decoration there are some signs of ornament for commercial purposes. At Apameia, the façade was painted with a tariff list for young and old wines: goods for sale either on stalls, or within the shops.[128] Chrysostom mentions shop signs that were gilded, though none has so far been recovered: only a well-cut set of topos inscriptions from columns inside the bath halls of Aphrodisias, which seem to label the shops behind.[129] Yet other signs were religious in nature: we hear from Theodoret of images of St. Symeon Stylites, who became so well-known that small portraits of him were "set up on a column at the entrances of every shop" at Rome. This is a practice which echoes the treatment of paintings of Marcus Aurelius centuries earlier.[130] Inscribed symbols of religious identity have survived on columns in front of late antique shops: single crosses were carved at Sagalassos and Aphrodisias, and menorahs at Aphrodisias, presumably to distinguish owners of different confessions.[131] This is unsurprising when we consider the strength of the Jewish artisan class seen in the Copper Market at Constantinople, in shops at seventh-century Sardis, or in the Emesan tales of St. Symeon the Fool.[132]

Internal Organization

While the design and decoration of shops reveal signs of collective planning and enduring confidence in their design, their internal spatial organization reveals more about their commercial function. It is difficult to reconstruct the interiors of most shop types, as unfortunately we have only a few depictions of the insides of shops and only a small number of descriptions; indeed, for many types of shop we have neither. However, from a combination of these sources with architectural and stratigraphic evidence, we can envisage a number of spatial zones found in most workshops that were strongly related to their commercial function. These zones would be zones of product display and sale, product storage, product manufacture, and, where relevant (as in the case of restaurants), product consumption, and often domestic occupation.

---

125 Portico mosaics: see appendix, §8.
126 Elaborate portico mosaics, Ephesos: see "Alytarch stoa," appendix, §8; Skythopolis, "Byzantine agora": the portico mosaic in the late agora must postdate the fifth century, given the coins and ceramics beneath it, and must predate AD 535, as the building inscription *in situ* fails to title the governor as consular (a title gained in AD 535): Y. Tsafrir and G. Foerster, "Urbanism at Scythopolis–Bet Shean in the Fourth to Seventh Centuries," *DOP* 51 (1997): 122–23; G. Foerster and Y. Tsafrir, "Hebrew University Expedition, Bet Shean Project—1988," *Excavations and Surveys in Israel* 7–8 (1988–89): 31; Bar-Nathan and Mazor, "City Centre (South)," 45 (inscription). Skythopolis sigma, *opus sectile*: see above, note 123. On Apameia's pictorial *tessellatum* with mosaic inscription of AD 469, see Balty, *Guide d'Apamée,* 81; it was followed by an *opus sectile,* which in one section has a mosaic inscription (*IGLSyr* 1318) of the beginning of the sixth century (Balty, 62–63).
127 Legislation on public ownership of porticoes: Saliou, "Identité culturelle," 212–18 (transgressions and alienation of portico space); dedications of mosaics: see note 126, above.
128 Apameia, wine price list: Balty, *Guide d'Apamée,* 78.
129 Shop signs: Joh. Chrys. *Hom. in Heb.* 28.6 (PG 63.200): ταῖς προθήκαις ταῖς ἐπὶ τῶν ἐργαστηρίων. Late antique equivalents of the ceramic shop signs known from Ostia have not so far been identified: see J.-P. Descoeudres, ed., *Ostia, port et porte de la Rome antique* (Geneva, 2001), 415–17, with the most recent literature on this topic.
130 Images of St. Symeon Stylites at Rome: Theod. *Hist. Rel.* 26 (*Théodoret de Cyr, Histoire des moines de Syrie,* ed. and trans. P. Canivet and A. Leroy-Molinghen, SC 234, 257 [Paris, 1977–79]). Imperial paintings: M. Aur. *Correspondence with Fronto* 14, in *The Correspondence of Marcus Cornelius Fronto,* ed. and trans. C. R. Haines, 2 vols. (London, 1919–20).
131 Crosses carved outside shops at Sagalassos: Lavan, "Agorai of Sagalassos." Crosses and menorahs at Aphrodisias: LL site observation, 2005.
132 Jewish artisan class seen in shops—Constantinople: *Patria* 3.32; Sardis: Crawford, *Byzantine Shops at Sardis,* 17–18; Emesa: *v. Sym.* part 4, pp. 154, 163, written about sixth-century Emesa but perhaps better reflecting its seventh-century composition on Cyprus.

Evidence for product display is nowhere as vivid as it is for the early empire, where tomb reliefs provide a great amount of information. We are more reliant on archaeology for late antiquity. Shelving is one way to handle restricted space (attested by wall sockets, nails in walls, and the presence of metal suspension devices). Archaeological remains of shelves found at Sagalassos and Skythopolis testify to the popularity of this method.[133] Niches set into walls, as at Sardis, Sagalassos, and Side, may have held shelves, ideal for product display: they were used in this way in a second-century catacomb fresco from Hadrumetum depicting a glass sale shop.[134] Shelving was perhaps more widespread than we imagine, as with many shops little survives of their elevations. Certain product types could probably just be displayed standing on the ground, like the statues found in the sculptor's workshop at Aphrodisias. Julian of Askalon and imperial legislation anticipated that shops would have use of the portico space in front of their premises, perhaps on payment of a fee.[135] Yet urban authorities seem to have been sensitive about goods left on the street, as revealed by laws against this included in the *Digest*. The only exceptions were for fullers who were permitted to dry cloth outside their premises and cartwrights to keep their work on the street.[136] But it seems likely that at least some pavement stalls were connected to adjacent shops: the topos inscriptions at Sagalassos suggest this, as discussed above.

Restaurants represent a special case, in which display was wound up together with consumption. Many such shops were found along urban avenues and on squares, probably out of dependence on a high volume of customers. Counters facing onto the street, surviving in this period, are known archaeologically only in Italy (at Ostia and Lucus Feroniae), with cavities within, perhaps for charcoals to cook food or keep it hot. In other regions, such installations are rare, though Symeon the Fool warmed himself next to the fire of his thermopolion at Emesa, while sitting outside. From his seat he was able to reach in and take a coal, suggesting a similar open counter.[137] Presumably, the closed frontages of eastern shops encouraged restaurants to bring food out onto tables on the streets, like the pastry chefs in Symeon's story. Restaurants also required some furniture for product consumption: for this, we can rely only on two scenes in the Yakto mosaic; these show couches for eating, as distinct from chairs and a table which is being used for gaming, though a relief from Ostia of the second half of the third century shows a tavern with drinkers sitting at a table.[138] Low benches are sometimes found by excavation, as at Sardis, Skythopolis, and Aphrodisias (Sebasteion), which have been used, in conjunction with other evidence, to suggest restaurants.[139]

The fixtures and fittings associated with product manufacture did of course vary according to trade, with kilns, ovens, stoves, and basins. A glass furnace in a late shop at Aphrodisias was located at the back of the room. At Emesa, the furnace seen by Symeon the Fool was visible from the road, and beggars were able to warm themselves there.[140] Basins and tanks are usually taken as evidence of fullonicae,

133   Archaeological remains of shelves, Sagalassos (Lower Agora east portico): Putzeys, "Contextual Analysis at Sagalassos," 248; Skythopolis (sigma shops): Khamis, "The Shops of Scythopolis in Context," 449; Bar-Nathan and Mazor, "City Centre (South)," 30–46.
134   Niches set into walls, as at Sardis (several), Sagalassos (in two shops: one is an arched recess, not a small niche). In Side, late Roman shops on the street of the episcopeion may have been set with shelves: LL site observation, 2004.
135   Use of portico space by shop owners: Julian of Askalon 36. Saliou, "Identité culturelle," 214–21, sees an echo of such use in late imperial legislation and later Islamic law.
136   Fullers and cartwrights: *Dig.* 43.10.1.4.

137   Counters at Ostia: Gering, "Plätze und Straßensperren an Promenaden," figs. 49 (red), 53, and nn. 48, 58, 60, 73, 129, 154; and J. T. Bakker, *Living and Working with the Gods: Studies of Evidence for Private Religion and Its Material Environment in the City of Ostia, 100–500 AD* (Amsterdam, 1994), catalogue of bars and brothels. Lucus Feroniae: M. Torelli, *Etruria,* 2nd ed., Guide archeologiche Laterza 3 (Rome, 1982), 34. Symeon the Fool describes an oven open to the street and visible from within: *v. Sym.* part 4, p. 151.
138   Tavern scene from Ostia, Isola Sacra: Ostia Antiquarium inv. 135.
139   Benches at Sardis (e.g., W3, W8, E1, E3, E4): Crawford, *Byzantine Shops at Sardis,* figs. 60, 110, 160, 198, 207; Skythopolis: S. Agady et al., "Byzantine Shops in the Street of the Monuments at Bet Shean (Scythopolis)," in *What Athens Has to Do with Jerusalem: Essays on Classical, Jewish, and Early Christian Art and Archaeology in Honor of Gideon Foerster,* ed. L. V. Rutgers, Interdisciplinary Studies in Ancient Culture and Religion 1 (Louvain, 2002), 432 (possible bench); Aphrodisias: R. R. R. Smith and C. Ratté, "Archaeological Research at Aphrodisias in Caria, 1996," *AJA* 102 (1998): 238.
140   Glass furnace, Aphrodisias: Smith and Ratté, "Archaeological Research at Aphrodisias," 238; Emesa: *v. Sym.* part 4, p. 163. A furnace was also against a wall in Alexandria, in a shop not much wider than it: M. Rodziewicz, *Les habitations romaines tardives d'Alexandrie à la lumière des fouilles polonaises à Kôm el-Dikka,* Alexandrie 3 (Warsaw, 1984), 250–51.

as most recently in the shops of Beirut.[141] This might not always be the case: at Side a basin with adjacent cistern was raised to counter height and gave onto a street, suggesting it might have been used as a dispensing point for liquids. However, elsewhere, such tanks are situated at the back of shops, as at Sagalassos in a shop on the north–south colonnaded street, at Sardis, and at Arykanda.[142] These sites seem unlikely to represent fullonicae as identified at Thamugadi, Ostia, or elsewhere, which have a far greater number of basins. Nevertheless, the number of adjacent shops at Sardis with basins suggests some kind of industrial process.[143] Platforms, perhaps for preparing hot food (cooked in charcoal), have been found, without the support of finds, in shops lining the main street at Side, and at Arykanda, and Antioch in Pisidia.[144] At Xanthos, a cooking platform survives at the back of a shop, complete with traces of a ceramic grill, set within a niche.[145] Bakeries could contain both mills and ovens, as in fourth-century Ostia; here these were mainly organized as large-scale units, quasi-factories rather than shops, or in rows of one-oven tabernae, as at Cirencester. Yet a small single-taberna unit with only one oven is known at Ostia, and at Sabratha.[146]

The amount of space given over to storage will have depended on the trade concerned, and on how quickly bulky products were sold; otherwise, the shelves and tables themselves may have sufficed. However, a second story or mezzanine would have also been useful, especially if it could be kept rat-free. Archaeological evidence for food storage comes from *dolia*, often found in the floors of shops—examples come from shops at Ostia, Side, Beirut, and Gerasa.[147] Large numbers of dolia—such as those in the "wine factory" at Barcelona—may indicate a specialized warehouse (for aging wine) rather than just storage for sale.[148] Other small underground cavities are known in shops: one of the late shops by the theater square at Ephesos had an underground space with a round manhole, while at Xanthos the thermopolion by the theater had cavities cut into the rock floor which probably served to refrigerate food.[149] Sometimes storage did not require specialized facilities: a back room at the "hardware store" at Sardis was used for this purpose.[150] Raw materi-

---

141 Basins for fullonicae identification: A. Uscatescu, *Fullonicae y tinctoriae en el mundo romano* (Barcelona, 1994); C. De Ruyt, "Les foulons, artisans des textiles et blanchisseurs," in *Ostia: Port et porte de la Rome antique*, ed. J.-P. Descoeudres (Geneva, 2001), 186–91; A. Barbet et al., *Pompéi, nature, sciences et techniques* (Milan, 2001), 140. Specifically on Beirut tanks: American University of Beirut, "Module 3: The Byzantine Portico and Shops."
142 For Sagalassos and Arykanda: LL site observations, 2005. Sardis: Crawford, *Byzantine Shops at Sardis*, 23–33, commented on by Harris, "Shops, Retailing and the Local Economy," 94–97; Uscatescu, *Fullonicae y tinctoriae*, 128–32.
143 Fullonicae at Thamugadi: no dating evidence is currently available, but they are thought to be late antique from the general urban context: Wilson, "Urban Production in the Roman World," 237–41. More generally, see Uscatescu, *Fullonicae y tinctoriae*.
144 Platforms at Side, Aphrodisias, Arykanda, and Antioch in Pisidia: LL site observation, 2005.
145 Xanthos: A.-M. Manière-Lévêque, "An Unusual Structure on the Lycian Acropolis at Xanthos," in Lavan, Swift, and Putzeys, eds., *Objects in Context, Objects in Use*, 473–94.
146 Two bakeries survive at Ostia into the fourth century: Regio I – Insula XIII – Molino (I/XIII/4) and Regio II – Insula VI – Caseggiato delle Fornaci (II/VI/7): see J. T. Bakker, *The Mills-Bakeries of Ostia: Description and Interpretation* (Amsterdam, 1999), 74–75, 87, who apparently bases his dating on masonry technique typical of this period (coarse modifications in *opus latericium* and *vittatum*). For Cirencester, see J. S. Wacher, "Excavations at Cirencester 1961," *AntJ* 42 (1962): 1–14, at 11, where the excavator believed they were too small for bread ovens, though there was no metal residue. At Ostia, a small bakery survived the late third- or fourth-century installation of the sigma exedra on the *decumanus*: Gering, "Plätze und Straßensperren," 326–42, and see appendix. In Sabratha, the bakery must postdate the dismantling of the apse of the Forum East Temple in Regio 2: A. Wilson, "Commerce and Industry in Roman Sabratha," *Libyan Studies* 30 (1999): 48.
147 Dolia—Ostia, thermopolium: G. Hermansen, *Ostia: Aspects of Roman City Life* (Edmonton, 1981), 131–32; see also A. Gering, *Aphrodisias, Ephesos und das spätantike Ostia: Porträt einer vergessenen Weltstadt* (Berlin, forthcoming), 270–87. Side, along main street: LL site observation, 2004. Beirut: D. Perring, "The Archaeology of Beirut: A Report on Work in the Insula of the House of the Fountains," *AntJ* 83 (2003): 217, notes mid-fifth- to early sixth-century alterations involving the insertion of dolia in the shops, without giving further details. Gerasa, pithos in floor of taberna 20 outside macellum: A. Uscatescu and M. Martín-Bueno, "The Macellum of Gerasa (Jerash, Jordan): From a Market Place to an Industrial Area," *BASOR* 307 (1997): 81.
148 Wine storage, Barcelona, with dolia: J. Beltràn de Heredia Bercero, ed., *From Barcino to Barcinona (1st to 7th Centuries): The Archaeological Remains of Plaça del Rei in Barcelona* (Barcelona, 2002), 70 n. 7, dated by two amphorae used as containers set in the floor of the wine cellar of Dressel 23/Keay XIII type, the other a small Dressel 20. This suggests that the winery was in use in the second half of the third century or early fourth century and may date from around this time.
149 Underground cavities—Ephesos, theater square: LL site observation, 2005; Xanthos, thermopolion: Manière Lévêque, "An Unusual Structure on the Lycian Acropolis."
150 Sardis backroom recycling: Crawford, *Byzantine Shops at Sardis*, 74.

als might alternatively be stocked within the shop itself: as with dumps of bronze for recycling at Skythopolis, and of raw glass, for blowing into vessels, at Alexandria.[151]

Objects

The objects present within shops could reflect both production and retail. Very occasionally, distinctive professional tools have been located by excavations in shops, such as those from the fourth-century sculptor's workshop at Aphrodisias, from sixth-century metalworking establishments at Justiniana Prima, or from restaurants at Sagalassos, Pisidian Antioch, Cyrene, Sardis, and Skythopolis. These latter sites have produced platters, kitchen implements, and serving vessels for hot wine.[152] Such objects evoke the tavern where Symeon the Fool worked, carrying hot water, probably for diluting wine, which was stored in jars at the back of the premises.[153] Occupation deposits producing tools are exceptional, often being the result of sudden abandonment or destruction. In any case, they produce distinctive traces for only a very few trades. For other professions, we are dependent on depictions to know anything at all about different tool groups. From late antique depictions we can see into taverns (at Ostia and Antioch), a carpenter's workshop (Alexandrian ivory), a blacksmith's shop (on textile), a painter's studio, and a school (Vienna Dioscurides).[154] These simple images may represent an inherited iconographic type rather than late antique life. However, overall similarities in architecture and material culture found within shops makes it likely that early imperial depictions from tombs represent a world very close to that of late antiquity.[155] The similarities between them and details of commerce shown in the Yakto mosaic (tables for cutting meat, containers for holding bread) further support this view.[156]

Of other artifacts linked to production, it is wise to consider the presence of small quantities of raw materials, such as the dye found in suspected tinctoria at Sardis, or waste, whether the droplets of glass found at Ephesos, Beirut, and Delphi, the hammer scale from Sagalassos, or the sculptor's stone fragments from Aphrodisias.[157] Even though such traces might make up a small part of the assemblage from a shop, their value as evidential markers is high. The stratigraphic invisibility of most professions should always be kept in mind: the presence of domestic artifacts, from the families of those artisans who slept in the shops, should not negate the significance of distinctive professional items. Thus Harris goes too far in suggesting that the presence of domestic items and just a few professional items (rather than coherent retail assemblages) indicates the house of an artisan rather than his workplace. She is perhaps too optimistic about the readability of the material record, given the number of professions which escape material detection entirely.[158] Yet, it is unsurprising to find domestic assemblages in a shop context: as noted earlier, we have several examples of owners sleeping in their shops. However, Libanius would not have dreamed of sleeping in the shop

---

151 Recycling dumps, Sardis: ibid.; Skythopolis: Khamis, "The Shops of Scythopolis in Context," 456; G. Foerster and Y. Tsafrir, "The Bet Shean Project (1989–1991): City Center (North)—The Hebrew University Expedition," *Hadashot Arkheologiyot—Excavations and Surveys in Israel* 98 (1992): 3–29, at 20 (in Hebrew); Alexandria: Rodziewicz, *Les habitations romaines tardives*.

152 Professional tools, sculptor of Aphrodisias: P. Rockwell, "Unfinished Statuary Associated with a Sculptor's Studio," in *Aphrodisias Papers, 2: The Theatre, a Sculptor's Workshop, Philosophers, and Coin-types*, ed. R. R. R. Smith and K. T. Erim, Journal of Roman Archaeology, supp. ser. 2 (Ann Arbor, Mich., 1991), 127–43; metalworking at Justiniana Prima: C. Popović, "Les activités professionnelles à Caričin Grad vers la fin de V^e et le début du VIIe siècle d'après les outils de fer," in *Caričin Grad 2: Le quartier sud-ouest de la ville haute*, ed. B. Bavant, V. Kondić, and J.-M. Spieser, Collection de l'École française de Rome 75 (Rome and Belgrade, 1990), 269–98. Restaurants of Sagalassos, Antioch in Pisidia, Cyrene, Sardis, and Skythopolis: see Putzeys and Lavan, "Commercial Space," 97–100.

153 Tavern of Emesa: *v. Sym.* part 4, pp. 152, 157.

154 Depictions of taverns, Ostia, late third century AD: Museo delle Navi inv. 1340; at Antioch: Yakto mosaic. Metal workshop: Coptic textile, sixth century: London, Victoria and Albert Museum inv. 2140-1900. Carpenter's workshop in Alexandrian ivory (third or fourth century): Princeton inv. y1956-105. Painter and a medical school: Vienna Dioscurides (fols. 5v, 3v), early sixth century. The school represented is that of Galen, while the metal workshop is a representation of Hephaistos.

155 Early imperial depictions: e.g., G. Zimmer, *Römische Berufsdarstellungen*, Archäologische Forschungen 12 (Berlin, 1982).

156 Similarities between Yakto details and earlier images: T. Putzeys, "Commercial Display," paper summarized in Jeffreys with Gilliland, eds., *Proceedings of the 21st International Congress of Byzantine Studies, London*, 2:244–45; see also idem, "Contextual Analysis at Sagalassos," 213–18.

157 Waste: Putzeys and Lavan, "Commercial Space," 85–93.

158 Domestic artifacts, Sardis: Crawford, *Byzantine Shops at Sardis*, 12–106, 135–50 with figures, reexamined by Harris, "Shops, Retailing and the Local Economy," 92–120. See also Putzeys, "Contextual Analysis at Sagalassos," 332 and 325 (rooms 2 and 4 of western portico), 377 (room 5 of northeast building).

where he held his first school at Antioch, and neither would a silversmith.[159]

Objects associated with selling have been found more widely than those associated with production. Steelyards and balances found in late shops at Thasos, Sardis, Sagalassos, and Skythopolis would have permitted precise quantities to be sold, when used with the weights described by Brigitte Pitarakis in her chapter in this volume.[160] As she notes, civic stone tables for measuring quantities seem to have disappeared. Even so, a building for weighing objects was repaired at Antioch in Pisidia, probably in the fourth century.[161] Within shops and stalls, an essential fitting in the sale area was a cashbox. At Emesa, Symeon used one when selling food from his stall—revealing that even a fast-food restaurant was engaging in monetized commerce, though, when working in a tavern in the same city, Symeon was paid in food rather than cash.[162] Finds of very small denomination bronze coins are very frequent in shops when compared with other types of structure. They were also found concentrated around the market stalls of Iol Caesarea, suggesting that this association is due to commerce.[163]

Overall Assessment

The above description will probably serve to polarize opinions about the identification of cellular units as shops. Proponents of a positive identification will see here conclusive evidence of their commercial character. Revisionists, who see shops as houses, may be less convinced: they will note many cellular rooms empty of fixtures and fittings, without distinctive artifactual traces of retail. My summary will perhaps seem to them like an artful presentation of the facts to support one side of the argument. However, if we admit that our evidence is both fragmentary and complex, and that a conclusion cannot be achieved from simply adding it all up, then it is possible to make a judgment on the balance of the evidence. For me, this should be that rows of cellular units constructed along main avenues and public squares in late antiquity were built as specialized commercial structures. They were sometimes constructed in a single coordinated build with unified decoration (as at Skythopolis). Alternatively, they might be built without unified decoration, but within a single architectural conception (as at Sardis). The continuity of homogeneity of design, perfectly adapted to retail, suggests great confidence in cellular shops, and probably a cultural consensus (if not a hard rule) among civic authorities about how they should be laid out.

These units could have been occupied as houses, but cellular rows were not a preferred house design away from the main avenues. In eighteenth- and nineteenth-century Britain, cellular houses could be found away from the main roads, in back courts as well as side streets: this is not true of cellular units in fourth- to sixth-century cities, which are concentrated in very public areas. Furthermore, the types of fittings, though perhaps occasionally found in houses (e.g., the odd basin or cooking platform), occur with a frequency that suggests something different. The same can be said of the material culture found within, which, while often dominated by domestic finds, contains distinctive traces of raw materials, tools, and production waste not normally found in houses. Finally, the textual, epigraphic, and pictorial evidence (from the Yakto mosaic) seems to clinch the argument. Nothing would have stopped someone from living in a shop without exercising a trade, but, as will be described below, the fact that they continued to be built into the early seventh century, and maintained to the same design, suggests that demand for cellular units as shops remained high in eastern city centers.

---

159 Sleeping in shops: see note 85, above; Antioch, school in shop: Lib. Or. 1.101–4. On the social status of silversmiths, see J.-P. Sodini, "L'artisanat urbain à l'époque paléochrétienne (IVe–VIIe s.)," Ktèma 4 (1979): 94–97. Wealthier shop owners may have left a slave to guard their goods overnight.

160 Balances and weights in shops along the road by the agora at Thasos: J.-Y. Marc, personal communication. Steelyards, at Sardis (E5, E7, E13, E14, E16): Crawford, *Byzantine Shops at Sardis*, 58 and figs. 235–37, 64 and fig. 306, 84 and fig. 412, 88 and fig. 468, 94 and fig. 476; at Skythopolis: Khamis, "The Shops of Scythopolis in Context," 458–59; at Sagalassos, in shops Lower Agora, east portico shops: Putzeys, "Contextual Analysis at Sagalassos," 272.

161 Antioch, *zygostasion* (weighing building): inscription dated after third century (on the basis of the letter form of omicron and the fact that a local man was acting as *logistēs*), perhaps to the fourth century; see, with references, S. Mitchell and M. Waelkens, *Pisidian Antioch: The Site and Its Monuments* (London, 1998), 226, no. 9.

162 Cashbox at Emesa: *v. Sym.* part 4, pp. 151; food payment: p. 152.

163 Frequency of coins in shops: C. Morrisson, personal communication. Iol Caesarea: Potter, *Towns in Late Antiquity*, 36–39.

The Building and Repair of Shops in Late Antiquity

Thus far, my analysis of shops seems to lead to a rather dull conclusion: overwhelming continuity with the Roman past. This seems confirmed by the record of building repair: older shops were being repaired or rebuilt, as at Exeter, Carthago Nova, Ostia, Thessalonike (shops on a street south of the agora), Thasos, Delphi, Herdonia (shops along a street), Ephesos (along Arcadiane), Side (tetragonal agora), Perge (tetragonal agora), Samaria, and Skythopolis.[164] In some cases, the total rebuild of a complex unit of shops (such as the tetragonal agora at Ephesos, or the main colonnaded streets of Antioch in Syria) shows a retention of the same architectural concept, with few changes in plan.[165] However, an analysis of brand-new constructions of shops in this period reveals something rather different: that there was an expansion in the number of shops in city centers. This came in part with the establishment of great new colonnaded streets, but was in part due to the filling of previously empty spaces, and also due to the redevelopment of political buildings, temples, and stoas. That the total number of shops within a city increased seems unlikely, but the shops were certainly given greater prominence in relation to other urban public buildings in core monumental areas.

Rows of cellular shops were built as integral parts of new colonnaded streets at Gorsium, Justiniana Prima, Diocletianopolis, Constantinople, Ephesos, and Skythopolis, still being present on the main streets of early eighth-century ʿAnjar. New shops were built on existing streets at Carthago Nova, Thessalonike (on the street by the forum), Athens, Sardis, Aphrodisias (alongside the basilica and by "Gaudin's gymnasium"), Patara (alongside the baths), Side, Gortyn, and Pella. The Sigma plazas with crescents of new shops added further to this number. Further, a large number of shops were built within agorai, where space permitted, giving them a more commercial character. This happened at Cirencester (just south of the forum), Segobriga (a cryptoporticus divided into shops), Antioch in Pisidia (Tiberia Plataea), Ephesos (theater square), Iasos, Sagalassos (Upper Agora), Arykanda (Upper Agora), Perge (in a square by the Hellenistic south gate), Skythopolis, Sabratha, and Cyrene.

The shops mentioned so far were often squeezed into previously unbuilt corners of streets and squares. However, others replaced, or were set within, former public buildings on these same plazas and thoroughfares. The pressure on space is evident at Constantinople with "very many houses with their shops" being built in the porticoes of the Zeuxippos Baths in 424 (*CTh* 15.1.53), but is also visible in the provinces. At both Gortyn and Sabratha, shops were set across the façade of a temple. At Ephesos, they were placed in the substructures of the Temple of Domitian, lining a major street. At Sagalassos, cellular rooms were built in the stoa by the northwest gate, and in the west and south stoas of the Lower Agora, as they were in a stoa at Metropolis. At Seleukeia-Lyrbe, they filled the bouleuterion, a type of structure destroyed by a "sigma" of shops at Skythopolis in 506/7. At Side, a row was built over a demolished temple, while at Aphrodisias the Sebasteion (a monumental approach to a temple) was converted into a double row, as were the bath halls here and at Side, as well as both the basilica and gymnasium at Herdonia.

Do these developments provide us with archaeological confirmation of the erosion of monumental space by chaotic commercial developments, as described in the Theodosian Code? Well, hardly. Without the legal texts, one would not describe the building of these cellular shops as chaotic. In almost every instance, their construction was undertaken without seriously detracting from the monumental development of the streets and squares in which they were found, at most closing a stoa and almost never blocking actual street space. In the case of Aphrodisias and Sagalassos, the new boutiques coexisted with the continued maintenance and decoration of the agorai in which they were set, with reerected statue monuments and repaired fountains.[166] Furthermore, in many cases, the rows of shops were

---

164 Repairs: see appendix, §§11, 14.

165 Antioch street plan retained: J. Lassus, *Antioch-on-the-Orontes*, vol. 5, *Les Portiques d'Antioche* (Princeton, N.J., 1972), 19–40, esp. 29.

166 Continued decoration of agorai despite new shops—at Sagalassos: Lavan, "The Agorai of Sagalassos"; at Aphrodisias: Smith, "Late Antique Portraits in a Public Context," 155–89; C. Ratté, "The Urban Development of Aphrodisias in Late Antiquity," in *Urbanism in Western Asia Minor: New Studies on Aphrodisias, Ephesos, Hierapolis, Perge and Xanthos*, ed. D. Parrish (Portsmouth, R.I., 2001), 127–30, 135.

clearly planned unified actions (same building materials throughout, same common walls, roof, same sizes and openings) involving a considerable degree of capital outlay: thus the building of the west portico shops on the Upper Agora at Sagalassos involved a great monumental staircase and collective barrel vault, a feature which also appeared in shops built alongside the baths at Patara. These shops, and others with a unified design, must have been the result of large-scale building operations paid for by the city or by an urban patron.

Yet the cellular subdivision of porticoes in front of already-existing shops, at Ostia, Sagalassos, Ariassos, and Petra, was undoubtedly messier, as was the building of a single room out onto the street portico in front of a shop at Sardis: this looks much more like individual initiative: "usurpation." But such developments were comparatively rare within the fourth to sixth century. Furthermore, the main streets of cities in this period were almost always respected, as long as monumental urban occupation continued, in the fourth- to sixth-century East and in the fourth-century West. When urban collapse arrived in the early seventh century, most cities of Asia Minor still had wide main streets lined with shops, as they did in the first two centuries AD. In the Levant, the replacement of main streets by narrowed alley-ways, with shops built on the road paving, seems to be an Umayyad phenomenon, as shown at Apollonia in Palestine and at Palmyra, though it often seems to come even later.[167] The encroachment of main streets in the later fifth- to sixth-century West under the Vandals and Visigoths was not done with shops in mind, and the breakdown of monumental streets in the Levant, from the late eighth century onward, does not seem to be accompanied by any evidence of commercial expansion. Rather, the Umayyad shops lining the streets of Resafa, Gerasa, and 'Anjar suggest that up to this eighth-century turning point, despite some change, ancient cellular shops that respected street space persisted in the Near East.[168]

Retail in a Wider Context
Social Life and Shopping

Retail activities in the late antique city naturally occurred within a wider cultural matrix. While different professions have been well studied as social groups, the place of traders in the city, in relation to urban patrons and others, has been little explored.[169] The open tables in marketplaces would likely have been used by farmers from the rural territory of a city. However, the places reserved for the "men of Hierapolis" in the Tetrastoon at Aphrodisias suggest that some stallholders might have been peddlers on a circuit, selling more specialized goods. About the customers of stalls we hear less, but whatever anecdotes we do have suggest individual shoppers, buying at most for households.[170] Markets adapted to large-scale sales of single products do not seem to have been found within late antique cities, except perhaps at Constantinople, where such a market existed for live animals in the middle Byzantine period.[171] Wholesale markets could perhaps rather be found in the countryside. A single possible example from the provinces comes from Carthage, where the "Street of Fig Sellers" might have involved wholesale retail from stalls.

The shops themselves were occupied by more comfortable traders, who resided permanently in the city. The shops that these people ran generally represented high-value commerce, and in some cases can be reasonably described as boutiques. Although restaurants represent low-value sales, it is worth noting that both the bean shop and the tavern at Emesa were able to permanently employ one person from outside the family.[172] These people were the "middle

167 Apollonia: I. Roll and E. Ayalon, "The Market Street at Apollonia-Arsuf," *BASOR* 267 (1987): 61–76; Palmyra: see note 23, above.
168 For discussion of Resafa, Gerasa, and 'Anjar with recently established plans of streets in the Umayyad period, see A. Walmsley, *Early Islamic Syria: An Archaeological Assessment* (London, 2007), 81–88.

169 Artisanal class, key references: Sodini, "L'artisanat urbain," 71–119; Patlagean, *Pauvreté économique*; E. Zanini, "Artisans and Traders in Late Antiquity: Exploring the Limits of Archaeological Evidence," in Bowden, Machado, and Gutteridge, eds., *Social and Political Life in Late Antiquity*, 373–411; see also Ellis, "Middle Class Houses in Late Antiquity," 413–37. On relationships between artisans and patrons, see J. H. W. G. Liebeschuetz, *Antioch: City and Imperial Administration in the Later Roman Empire* (Oxford, 1972), 197–98.
170 Anecdotes of shoppers: Lavan, "Fora and Agorai," 228–30.
171 Wholesale markets at Constantinople: Mundell Mango, "Commercial Map of Constantinople," 199.
172 Emesa bean seller's shop: *v. Sym.* part 4, pp. 151–52; tavern: pp. 152–53.

classes" of the period, if you were looking for one.¹⁷³ Libanius understood this in describing the rising prestige of Roman law in his time: law was something that once only youngsters from the ergastēria wanted to pursue to improve themselves, but now it was being chosen by the sons of the local gentry.¹⁷⁴ To religious leaders, shopkeepers might seem a critical group to win over, perhaps because their independent resources made them more difficult to lead than the urban poor. Chrysostom addressed many of his sermons to this group, sometimes treating them as the default listeners: he suggests that the rich man should become an artisan of charitable works, while he disapproves of upper-class snobbery about mercantile origins. In pastoral messages specifically aimed at merchants, Chrysostom criticized the closure of shops when the theater is playing, the use of oaths during commercial transactions, and the treatment of apprentices.¹⁷⁵ The *Life of Symeon the Fool* has something of a similar preoccupation with the artisanal class: the conversions of a Jewish glassblower and of a heretical bean seller are key priorities for the saint. The prominence of Jewish artisans in city life must have worried some Church leaders. Here was one group that was used to keeping workshop secrets, and could perhaps keep those of faith. It also had its own secure income and thus perhaps needed bishops a little less than did other groups.

Nevertheless, artisans did have patronage relationships with wealthy families within cities: either as general clients, like the bakers of Libanius, or as artisans working on specific commissions for rich customers. Cassiodorus stressed this relationship in his evocation of the ideal daily round for a Roman nobleman: "to stroll through the forum, to look in at some skillful craftsman at his work, to push one's own cause through the law courts, to play counters, to go to the baths with one's acquaintances, to have a banquet."¹⁷⁶ Here it seems likely that the items being made by the artisan were in fact items being paid for by the elite visitor, who might have wished to discuss fine details during production. Artisans might have participated in the cultural strategies of patrons quite intimately: both Libanius and Chrysostom saw the association of rich men with silversmiths as representing one of the key aspects of their wealth, along with estates, a house, slaves, and money.¹⁷⁷ However, Libanius's own alliance with shopkeepers certainly extended beyond what he could buy: he enjoyed hearing their compliments each day as he passed their shops: in return, he protected them, as he did the guild of bakers against the floggings of the *comes Orientis,* Philagrius.¹⁷⁸ This was a straightforward relationship of patronage, which might have existed with any other social group for political or commercial reasons.

Shops were also places for the meetings of equals. Libanius frequently mentions ergastēria as important places for socializing, while Ammianus describes how the poorest people in Rome spent nights in tabernae, where they liked to gamble and discuss chariot racing.¹⁷⁹ When Chrysostom pleaded for decorum in church (no greetings, chatting, or laughter), he implored his congregation to remember that "the church is no barber's or perfumer's nor any other merchant's shop (ἐργαστήριον) in the marketplace" and reminded them that talk of buying and selling belonged in the shops rather than in church.¹⁸⁰ It is important to keep in mind that perhaps not all "shoppers" were customers, even potentially. The *Life of Symeon the Fool* describes beggars sitting watching a glassblower, just for the fun of it, and for the heat of his fire.¹⁸¹ The urban malls must have contained a fair number of

---

173 Middle classes: see above, note 169.
174 Youngsters from ergastēria study law: Lib. *Or.* 61.21.
175 Positive image for artisanal class: Joh. Chrys. *Hom. in Mt.* 14.2 (PG 57.219: praising artisans for hard work), 49.3 (PG 58.50: the rich man is like an artisan), 58.3 (PG 58.570: the elite are descended from artisans). *Hom. in Rom* 30, 15.25–27. Theaters: *Hom. in Mt.* 6.7 (PG 57.71). Oaths: *Hom. in Ac.* 9.5–6 (PG 60.81–82). Employment of apprentices: *Hom. ad pop. Ant.* 14.1 (PG 49.145).

176 Daily round of nobleman: Cassiod. *Var.* 8.31; *Magni Aurelii Cassiodori Variarum libri XII,* ed. Å. J. Fridh, Magni Aurelii Cassiodori Senatoris Opera 1, CCSL 96 (Turnhout, 1973).
177 Wealth display in land, money, silversmiths, slaves, and house: Lib. *Or.* 31.11–12; wealth display in silversmiths' shops: Joh. Chrys. *Hom. in 1 Cor.* 11.4 (PG 61.93).
178 Shopkeepers greeting Libanius: Lib. *Or.* 2.6; Libanius protecting bakers from flogging: Lib. *Or.* 34.4, 1.206ff., 29.6.
179 Antioch, ergastēria as centers of social gossip: Lib. *Or.* 48.13, 8.4, 31.25; Rome, poorest spend the night in tabernae: Amm. Marc. 14.6.25.
180 Church is no shop: Joh. Chrys. *Hom. in 1 Cor.* 36.5 (PG 61.313).
181 Glassblower: *v. Sym.* part 4, p. 163.

window-shoppers, time wasters, and petty thieves, as they do in any age, drawn as much by the spectacle as by any commercial or social relationships.

Shopping as a Cultural Experience

Here we enter into an understanding of shopping as a cultural experience. It is clear from the layout of colonnaded shopping avenues that amenity as well as function was always at the center of their design. Shopping areas were constructed as public spaces as much, or even more than, as commercial spaces. Colonnaded streets were invested with monumental art, such as the reused mythological statues found at Constantinople and Aizanoi, as well as sundials and professionally cut gameboards. Both were sponsored by urban patrons.[182] Thus, visiting commercial spaces, such as the porticoes of Antioch or Skythopolis, was meant to be enjoyable from the beginning: shops were part of this pleasure, all the more because they were well-ordered, cellular experiences.

Libanius and Choricius sought to delight their readers by describing what they saw: fresh high-quality produce on display.[183] Smell certainly helped to display goods on offer, producing an enticing odor of the kind that seems to have driven Ammianus to distraction. In a rare survival, the frescoes of a restaurant at Ostia were painted with some of the refreshments on offer: olives, turnips, and eggs/peaches.[184] Another attraction of taverns was the serving girls. In Justinian's *Digest,* taverns were places where prostitution might take place, though in an informal manner, evading the law. Tavern girls, like prostitutes, were *infames*: in late Roman laws, illegitimate children fathered by prominent citizens in taverns could not inherit any property, and such citizens could not marry tavern mistresses or their daughters; further, a law of 396 even forbade tavern workers, alongside actors and actresses, from using public seats.[185] High-pitched cries might advertise food (fish at Antioch, cooked food at Rome). Ammianus was not alone in regarding this behavior as vulgar. Choricius of Gaza suggested that merchants at Gaza did not need to shout to advertise, at a festival market in his city, because their wares were of such high quality;[186] merchants of high-value goods everywhere may well have felt the same.

Enthusiasm for the spectacle of urban retail can be seen not only in continued depictions of them in this period, but also in anecdotes and metaphors from late antique literature. Augustine, Chrysostom, and Leontius of Neapolis all found delight or interest in visiting artisans, as the following extracts reveal.

Blacksmith: Augustine, *Enarrationes in Psalmos* 48(2).9, ed. E. Dekkers and J. Fraipont, CCSL 38–40 (Turnhout, 1956)

If you were to enter the workshop of a smith, you would not dare to find fault with his bellows, his anvils, his hammers. But take an ignorant man, who does not know the purpose of each thing, and who finds fault with everything. Yet if he does not have the skill of the workman, and has only the reasoning power of a man, what is he saying to himself? Not without reason are the bellows placed here: the workman knows why, though I do not. In the shop he [the ignorant man] dares not to find fault with the smith, yet in the universe he dares to find fault with God. Therefore, just as "fire, hail, snow, ice, wind of storms, which do His word," and all things in nature, which seem to foolish persons to be made at random,

---

182 Reused statues at Constantinople in *plateia*: Malalas 16.13 (brought by Constantine from all over Greece); the depictions of statues in a colonnaded street on a column of Arcadius, just west of the Forum of Constantine, suggest they were largely mythological: E. H. Freshfield, "Notes on a Vellum Album Containing Some Original Sketches of Public Buildings and Monuments, Drawn by a German Artist Who Visited Constantinople in 1574," *Archeologia* 72 (1922): 87–104 with pls. 15–22. Aizanoi: K. Rheidt, "Aizanoi: Bericht über die Ausgrabungen und Untersuchungen 1992 und 1993," *AA* (1995): 706–7. Sundials and gameboards: see Lavan, "Streets of Sagalassos," 205, 207, 209.
183 Fresh produce display: Lib. *Or.* 11.251–52; Choricius *Or.* 2.59–65, 1.93.
184 Smells: Amm. Marc. 28.3.4; paintings at Ostia: Hermansen, *Ostia,* 131–32, with Gering, *Aphrodisias,* for a discussion.

185 Sex in taverns: e.g., *Joh. Moschus* 188. Legal status of tavern women: *Dig.* 3.2.4.2, 23.2.43.praef., 23.2.43.9). Illegitimate children: *CTh* 4.6.3 (AD 336). Marriage forbidden: *NMarc* 4.1.1 (AD 454), in *Theodosiani Libri XVI cum Constitutionibus Sirmondianis,* ed. T. Mommsen and P. Meyer, vol. 2, *Leges Novellae ad Theodosianum Pertinentes* (Berlin, 1905). Public seats forbidden: *CTh* 15.13.1 (AD 396). "The Fool" working in a tavern at Emesa was also an attraction for customers, who came there specifically to be amused by him: *v. Sym.* part 4, p. 152.
186 Cries: Lib. *Or.* 11.258 (Antioch); Amm. Marc. 28.3.4 (Rome); Choricius: *Or.* 2.59–65, 1.93 (Gaza).

simply "do His word," because they are not made except by His command.

Perfume shop: John Chrysostom, *Homiliae in Johannem* 53.3 (PG 59.205)

For if a man who passes an ointment maker's shop, or sits in one, is impregnated with perfume even against his will, much more is this the case with one who comes to church.

Painter: John Chrysostom, *Homiliae in Acta apostolorum* 30.4 (PG 60.228)

Go into a painter's study, and you will observe how silent all is there. Then so ought it to be here: for here too we are employed in painting portraits, royal portraits (every one of them), none of any private man, by means of the colors of virtue. . . . This is a reform not easy, but (only) by reason of long habit, to be effected. The pencil moreover is the tongue, and the Artist the Holy Spirit.

Dye workshop: *The Arabic Gospel of the Infancy of the Savior* 37 (thought to be a fifth- to sixth-century addition to an earlier text, the Infancy Gospel of Thomas); trans. A. Walker, rev. and ed. K. Knight, in *The Ante-Nicene Fathers* (Buffalo, 1885–96), 8:412.

On a certain day the Lord Jesus, running about and playing with the boys, passed the shop of a dyer, whose name was Salem; and he had in his shop many pieces of cloth which he was to dye. The Lord Jesus then, going into his shop, took up all the pieces of cloth, and threw them into a tub full of indigo. And when Salem came and saw his cloths destroyed, he began to cry out with a loud voice, and to reproach Jesus, saying: Why have you done this to me, O son of Mary? You have disgraced me before all my townsmen: for, seeing that everyone wished the colour that suited himself, you have come and destroyed them all.

Glassblower: *v. Sym.* part 4, p. 165; trans. D. Krueger, *Symeon the Holy Fool: Leontius's Life and the Late Antique City* (Berkeley, 1996), 165–66

Another time he (Symeon) was sitting with his brothers (in poverty) and warming himself near a glassblower's furnace. The glassblower was Jewish. And Symeon said to the beggars joking, "Do you want me to make you laugh? Behold, I will make the sign of the cross over the drinking glass which the craftsman is making, and it will break." When he had broken about seven, one after the other, the beggars began to laugh, and they told the glassblower about the matter, and he chased Symeon away, branding him. As he left, Symeon screamed at the glassblower, saying "Truly, bastard, until you make the sign of the cross on your forehead, all your glasses will be shattered." And again after the (glassblower) broke thirteen others, one after the other, he was shattered and made the sign of the cross on his forehead. And nothing ever broke again. And because of this, he went out and became a Christian.

Having heard all this, one might think that the shopping malls of late antiquity were places reserved for sensuality and sale. But for a few people at least, visits to the shops had a more serious purpose: Augustine's metaphor suggests that when inside a workshop it is wise for a man to yield to the knowledge of the artisan, as only an ignorant man would try to better the wisdom of experience, which has ordered production. Lactantius (*Divine Institutes* 2.9) goes further and suggests that without visits to artisans, one is not able to understand the nature of manufactured goods, and suggests that this is something very necessary for the wellborn to undertake. Thus it seems that a morning at the shops could be very rewarding in late antiquity, even on an intellectual level.

Conclusion

In conclusion, it seems fair to assert the survival of most forms of Roman regulated retail into late antiquity, to the early fifth century in the West and into the sixth in the East, at least in provincial capitals and middle-ranking cities. Structured markets of regulated stalls still existed, as did macella for meat sales. Cellular units on main avenues were still being built and repaired as shops (not houses), as they had been earlier. There is no evidence that these well-defined cellular structures were less important as shops than earlier, or that market buildings and regulated stalls were being abandoned in favor of anarchic commercial developments resulting from individual initiative. Rather, we see the increasing prominence of cellular shops in city centers: they were being built to fit into spaces from which they had previously been excluded, though there were probably not more shops in cities in total than there had been earlier. This "commercialization" of city centers did not cause urban decay or a loss of monumentality. Significantly, the process belongs to the fifth to sixth centuries AD, not the early Islamic period.

For the East, late antiquity can be described as the peak period for commercial amenities in the classical city: they had more colonnaded shops than earlier, and there was more glitzy decoration. This expansion was probably due to the sympathetic attitude of urban notables, who were happy to sacrifice superfluous political buildings and disused temples. They were redefining their cities as urban centers dominated by shops, baths, and churches, but as structures still set within monumental avenues and squares, decorated in a classical manner. In these cities, shopping was still an enjoyable experience, but not one in which the interests of traders were allowed to overwhelm the aesthetic character of civic centers. Market stalls were still regulated as to their location and building materials, specialized market buildings were built to house unpleasant smells, and an attempt was made to ensure that private individuals could not disrupt the amenity of porticoes. Quite who actually carried out spot checks, and ordered demolitions, is not documented. Civic slaves are likely candidates, under the control of the *pateres civitatis*, who were notably active in restoring shop porticoes. But the widespread "order" seen in eastern archaeological evidence for commercial structures does at least provide an urban context in which the prescriptions of Julian of Askalon seem credible.

Appendix

1. Market Buildings, New (all types)

Complutum: In phase 2 of the forum, which is given a terminus post quem (TPQ) by pottery of the very end of the third century, there is a courtyard structure built on the edge of the forum, which has been proposed as a macellum: S. Rascón Marqués, "La ciudad de Complutum en la tardoantigüedad: Restauración y renovación," in *Complutum y las ciudades Hispanas en la antigüedad tardía*, ed. L. García Moreno and S. Rascón Marqués, Acta antiqua complutensia 1 (Alcalá de Henares, 1999), 53–57. **Geneva**: Part of a courtyard building, with some cellular units within it, was discovered above a destruction layer of the second half of the third century AD and featured a column base tentatively dated to the third or fourth century AD: C. de Ruyt, *Macellum: Marché alimentaire des Romains,* Publications d'histoire de l'art et d'archéologie de l'Université catholique de Louvain 35 (Louvain-la-Neuve, 1983), 73–75; L. Blondel, "De la citadelle gauloise au forum romain," *Genava* 19 (1941): 98–118. **Madauros**: Restoration of temple of fortune, transformed into a market: H. G. Pflaum et al., *Inscriptions latines de l'Algérie* (Paris, 1922–[2003]), 1.2103 (AD 379–83). **Constantinople**: Several macella listed in the early fifth-century *notitia* are in new quarters of the city, and so must be late antique developments: e.g., *Not. Const.* 6.27 (Regio 5), 9.17 (Regio 8). See Socrates, *Hist. eccl.* 1.38.9; M. Mundell Mango, "The Commercial Map of Constantinople," *DOP* 54 (2000): 189–207, esp. 193–94. **Athenian Agora**: The "square building" is a courtyard of cellular rooms, of a form suitable for a macellum. It is dated to the beginning of the fifth century because of the similarity of its construction technique to the nearby Palace of the Giants, dated (by coins in construction layers) to this time: see the most recent discussion with reference to earlier literature in I. Baldini Lippolis, "Sistema palaziale ed edifici amministrativi in età protobizantina: Il settore settentrionale dell'Agorà di Atene," *Ocnus* 11 (2003): 13–16. **Antioch**: Temple of Ares on Forum of Valens converted into macellum, probably under Valens, who redeveloped this area: Malalas 9.5, 12.7, analyzed by G. Downey, *A History of Antioch in Syria from Seleucus to the Arab Conquest* (Princeton, N.J., 1961), 632–67, and chapter 14 n. 3. **Cyrene**: New smaller market building (with one phase of repair) 38.5 by 7.65 m. The dating is based on general site "phasing"—after an earthquake of AD 365, from Amm. Marc. 22.16.4, but before the next building phase, which is thought to be the result of successful intercession of Syn. *Ep.* 104, 113, 124, to the imperial court at the turn of the century: S. Stucchi, *L'Agorà di Cirene,* vol. 1.1, *I lati nord ed est della platea inferiore* (Rome, 1965), 307–12. Of archaeological dating there appears none, but it is probably fair to date this last weak monumental phase to approximately the same time as the conversion of the adjacent temple into an audience hall, which mostly likely occurred in the later fourth or fifth century AD. This late market complex was given a new façade in the next phase on the agora, thought to date around 400, on the basis of supposed Austurian destruction: Stucchi, *L'Agorà di Cirene,* 1.1:324.

2. Market Buildings, Repaired (all types)

Wroxeter: The macellum, which was adjacent to the forum, seems to have been repaired in the third century, according to the suggested phasing of the report (trying to make sense of complex earlier excavations), which observes that a herringbone floor seen here is found also in the basilical hall, latrine, and room 11A, possibly associated with a new praefernium, which was added in the early third century. A new courtyard wall is also similar to that of the portico stylobate wall, which is of similar date: P. Ellis, ed., *The Roman Baths and Macellum at Wroxeter: Excavations by Graham Webster, 1985–55,* English Heritage Archaeological Report 9 (London, 2000), 75, and elsewhere. **Ostia**: C. de Ruyt, *Macellum: Marché alimentaire des Romains,* Publications d'histoire de l'art et d'archéologie de l'Université catholique de Louvain 35 (Louvain-la-Neuve, 1983), 124, with *CIL* 14 s.1 4719 (AD 418–19), and see commentary in main text above for new excavations. **Verulamium**: Macellum at Verulamium rebuilt with a new monumental street portico in early fourth century AD: K. M. Richardson, "Report on Excavations at Verulamium: Insula XVII 1938," *Archaeologia* 90 (1944): 81–126, at 88, based on Rhenish and Castor Ware found in the foundation trench (thought late third to early fourth century) and a subsequent repair yielding a coin of Constantius II. **Isernia**: Macellum restored 350–64, with columns and tiles provided by the state: *CIL* 9.2638 = *ILS* 5588 (*PLRE,* Iustinianus 3). **Lepcis Magna:** Portico of macellum restored in 324–26: *IRT* 468; C. Lepelley, *Les Cités de l'Afrique romaine au bas empire,* vol. 2, *Notices d'histoire municipale* (Paris, 1981), 337. **Sagalassos**: *Internal Report* (2006). **Apameia**: Apameia excavation team, personal communication. **Cyrene**: Repair phase of new façade ca. AD 400, see §1, above.

3. Market Buildings, Continuity of Use

Bulla Regia: Statue of Hermes in macellum: A. Beschaouch, R. Hanoune, and Y. Thébert, *Les Ruines de Bulla Regia* (Rome, 1977), 89. **Thamugadi**: Dedication of fourth-century imperial statues on a monument in the market of Sertius, where a tetrarchic statue sacellum with dedications to Jupiter, Hercules, and Victory was reused for monuments of the Valentinianic dynasty: *BCTH* (1896) 284; *AE* (1895) 108 = *BCTH* (1891) 361; C. Lepelley, *Les Cités de l'Afrique romaine au bas-empire,* vol. 2, *Notices d'histoire municipale* (Paris, 1981), 448–51. **Thasos**: Cellular units occupied in the fourth to fifth century within macellum: J.-Y. Marc, personal communication. **Melli and Pednelissos**: L. Vandeput, personal communication. For details of our present knowledge of market buildings,

see V. Köse, "The Origin and Development of Market-buildings in Hellenistic and Roman Asia Minor," in *Patterns in the Economy of Roman Asia Minor,* ed. S. Mitchell and C. Katsari (Swansea, 2005), 139–66. Selge, spoliated, in a church which is stylistically dated based on alleged Syrian influences in architecture to the fourth–fifth century AD: A. Machatschek and M. Schwartz, *Bauforschungen in Selge,* DenkWien 152, Ergänzungsbände zu den Tituli Asiae Minoris 9 (Vienna, 1981), 107–8.

4. Market Buildings: Disuse (all types)

Naples: Out of use by the mid-sixth century, when the church of St. Lorenzo was built over the northern half. It is thought to be built in the early years of John II's episcopate (AD 533–55). See A. Venditti, *L'architettura dell'alto medioevo,* vol. 2, no. 2 of *Storia di Napoli* (Naples, 1969), 812; P. Arthur, *Naples, from Roman Town to City-State: An Archaeological Perspective,* Archaeological Monographs of the British School at Rome 12 (London, 2002), 44. **Philippi**: Macellum demolished and replaced by church Basilica B "c. 550," apparently based on its close resemblance to the church of Hagia Sophia and parallel bands of brickwork and stone (*opus mixtum*), characteristic of Justinian's reign (AD 527–65): C. Koukouli-Chrysanthaki and C. Bakirtzis, *Philippi* (Athens, 1995), 43; see also P. Lemerle, *Philippes et la Macédoine orientale à l'époque chrétienne et byzantine: Recherches d'histoire et d'archéologie,* 2 vols. (Paris, 1945), 1:497ff. **Gerasa**: A. Uscatescu and M. Martín-Bueno, "The Macellum of Gerasa (Jerash, Jordan): From a Market Place to an Industrial Area," *BASOR* 307 (1997): 67–88. Entrances to the macellum were blocked by rebuilt cellular shops, which closed access, sometime in the late fifth to mid-sixth century. See details of dating in §14.

5. Civil Basilicas: Repairs

See L. Lavan and T. Putzeys, "Commercial Space in Late Antiquity," in *Objects in Context, Objects in Use: Material Spatiality in Late Antiquity,* ed. L. Lavan, E. Swift, and T. Putzeys, Late Antique Archaeology 5 (Leiden, 2007), 108.

6. Civil Basilicas: Disuse/Demolition

Rome: Basilica Aemilia on Forum Romanum, demolished in the early fifth century after Alaric's sack, dated by the coins of money changers—the latest of which is AD 409—in the destruction layer on the basilica floor: R. Reece, "A Collection of Coins from the Centre of Rome," *PBSR* 50 (1982): 116–45. **Tarraco**: A fire destroyed the basilica and it was never rebuilt: S. Keay, "Tarraco in Late Antiquity," in *Towns in Transition,* ed. N. Christie and S. T. Loseby (Aldershot, 1996), 30; the destruction is given a TPQ by coins of AD 333–61, found under a fallen column drum: R. Mar and J. Ruiz de Arbulo, "La basílica de la colonia de Tarraco: Una nueva interpretación de llamado foro bajo de Tarragona," in *Los foros romanos de las provincias occidentales* (Madrid, 1988), 33; J. Serra Vilaro, "Excavaciones en

Tarraco," in *Memorias de la Junta Superior de Excavaciones y Antigüedades* 116.5 (1930): 59. The use of the building as a quarry for stonework, some used nearby in the early Christian cemetery (*Die Römischen Inschriften von Tarraco,* ed. G. Alföldy [Berlin, 1975], 91), provides a rough terminus ante quem (TAQ) of late antiquity for this disuse: I. Rodà, "Sarcofagi della bottega di Cartagine a Tarraco," in *L'Africa romana: Atti del VII Convegno di Studio, Sassari 15–17 dicembre 1989,* ed. A. Mastino (Sassari, 1990), 728 n. 4. **Paestum**: Basilica thought to have been converted into a curia in the third century (largely on the basis of building techniques: it has a TPQ of late first to second century AD from ceramics)—but excavators seem unnerved by a third- to fourth-century inscription restoring a basilica mentioned above: E. Greco and D. Theodorescu, *Poseidonia-Paestum,* vol. 1, *La "curia,"* Collection de l'École Française de Rome 42 (Rome, 1980), 16–23, esp. 16, 23; M. Mello and G. Voza, *Le iscrizioni latine di Paestum,* 2 vols. (Naples, 1968–69), 1:242–43, no. 168. **Herdonia**: Basilica converted into hall of cellular "shops": masonry type of *opus mixtum / vittatum / listatum* thought to be "late Roman." In the context of the development of the site, a third- to fourth-century date seems reasonable. The later fourth or fifth century sees a decline of monumentality on the site: J. Mertens, "Dal tardo antico all'altomedieovo," in *Herdonia: Scoperta di una città,* ed. idem (Bari, 1995), 339–41. **Brescia**: Basilica not spoliated in late antiquity: G. P. Brogiolo, "Considerazioni sulle sequenze altomedievali nella zona monumentale della città romana," in *Carta archeologica della Lombardia,* vol. 5, F. Rossi, *Brescia: La città* (Modena, 1996), 261–63. **Carthage**: The collapse of one of the central substructures of the eastern side of the basilica is dated to the mid-fifth century because the distinctive immediate destruction layer contains only pottery of the second half of the fifth century (Hayes 61 and 91) and a coin of Valentianian III (AD 425–55): P. Gros, *Byrsa,* vol. 3, *Rapport sur les campagnes de fouilles de 1977 à 1980: La basilique orientale et ses abords* (Rome, 1985), 33–34, 42–43. **Ephesos**: The whole civil basilica was destroyed sometime after its Christianization, of perhaps the late fourth century, and the construction the Church of St. John on the Aya Suluk under Justinian in the mid-sixth century. The building was partially covered with the peristyle of a house which included the colossal Christianized statues of Augustus and Livia, as well as other spoils from the basilica. A piece of the basilica's dedicatory inscription was found at the Church of St. John, providing a TAQ for the destruction of the reign of Justinian, whose monograms adorn this church: W. Alzinger, "Das Regierungsviertel," *ÖJhBeibl* 50 (1972–75): 266, 299. **Cremna**: Conversion into church, though no details are given, apart from basic observations on the church plan: S. Mitchell et al., *Cremna in Pisidia: An Ancient City in Peace and in War* (Swansea, 1995), 221–22. **Magnesia on the Meander**: Conversion into church described in O. Bingöl, *Magnesia ad Meandrum: Magnesia am Mäander* (Ankara, 1998), who believes this to belong to the central medieval period, without giving structural reasons, although a priori it is more likely to be late antique. **Samaria**: Conversion into church: two apses were added at the north end, a smaller one inside the other; they are, however, not dated more precisely than to late antiquity, from the spolia included in their build: J. W. Crowfoot, K. M. Kenyon, and E. L. Sukenik, *The Buildings at Samaria,* Samaria-Sebaste 1 (London, 1942), 37. **Tiberias**: Excavations by A. Druks in 1964–68 (which seem to be unpublished) are described in Y. Hirschfeld, "Tiberias," in *The New Encyclopedia of Archaeological Excavations in the Holy Land,* ed. E. Stern, vol. 4 (Jerusalem and New York, 1993), 1467: these excavations apparently found mosaics dating to the fifth and sixth century and a rebuilding of the apse that was more suited to a church than to a basilica.

7. Sigma Plazas (semicircular exedras with ranges of cellular rooms, unless stated otherwise)

In general: W. Müller-Wiener, "Das 'Sigma', eine spätantike Bauform," in *Armağan—Festschrift E. Akurgal* (= *Anadolu* 21, 1979/80) (Ankara, 1987), 127. Constantinople sigma plazas (not confirmed as commercial hemicycles): A. Berger, "Tauros e Sigma: Due piazze di Constantinopoli," in *Bisanzio e l'Occidente: Arte, archeologia, storia: Studi in onore di F. De Maffei* (Rome, 1996), 17–31; M. Mundell Mango, "The Porticoed Street at Constantinople," in *Byzantine Constantinople: Monuments, Topography and Everyday Life,* ed. N. Necipoğlu (Leiden, 2001), 37. See the recent discussion of sigma plazas by A. Gering, *Aphrodisias, Ephesos und das spätantike Ostia: Porträt einer vergessenen Weltstadt* (Berlin, forthcoming), 357–65. **Carthago Nova**: Theater cavea leveled and cellular units built around its edge in the fifth century, with a foundation level thought to be of the first half of the fifth century, based on the presence of amphorae LRA 1 and LRA 4, local cooking wares, and African Red Slip (ARS) Ware of the late fourth to early fifth century, esp. Hayes 61 and 91: S. F. Ramallo Asensio, "Carthago Spartaria, un núcleo bizantino en Hispania," in *Sedes Regiae (ann. 400–800),* ed. G. Ripoll and J. M. Gurt (Barcelona, 2000), 579–611; S. F. Ramallo Asensio, E. Ruiz Valderas, and M. C. Berrocal Caporrós, "Contextos cerámicos de los siglos V–VII en Cartagena," *Archivo Español de Arqueología* 69 (1996): 135–90, esp. 140–42; S. F. Ramallo Asensio and E. Ruiz Valderas, "Bizantinos en Cartagena: Una revisión a la luz de los nuevos hallazgos," *Annals de l'Institut d'Estudis Gironins* 38 (1996–97): 1203–19; S. F. Ramallo Asensio and E. Ruiz Valderas, "Cartagena en la arqueología bizantina en Hispania: Estado de la cuestión," in *V Reunió d'arqueologia cristiana hispànica: Cartagena* (Barcelona, 2000), 305–22. **Ostia**: This structure was established with reused material above a bakery (cutting the structure and employing some parts of the bakery—e.g., millstones). The bakery was set within a bath building destroyed in or shortly after the time of Probus (ad 276–82), as suggested by a TPQ of coins from destruction levels in this area. Gering associates the exedra with a generalized fourth-century rebuilding level in this area, though this theory is more suggestive: A. Gering, "Plätze und Straßensperren an Promenaden: Zum Funktionswandel Ostias in der Spätantike," *Römische Mitteilungen* 111 (2004): 326–82, esp. 332–34 (reuse of bakery material) and 335 (coins from destruction levels). **Stobi**: The exedra was built incorporating reused blocks from the adjacent theater: E. Kitzinger, "A Survey of the Early Christian Town of Stobi," *DOP* 3 (1946): 102 n. 73, 116, quoting *Starinar* (1935/36): 156, figs. 16–19, and 152–53, on the date of the abandonment of the theater; see also J. Wiseman, "The City in Macedonia Secunda," in *Villes et peuplement dans l'Illyricum protobyzantin: Actes du colloque organisé par l'École française de Rome 12–14 mai 1982* (Rome, 1984), 289–314, esp. 313 (not seen). **Philippi**: Exedra similar in style to other plazas, reusing earlier architectural blocks: J. Coupry, "Sondage a l'ouest du forum de Philippes," *BCH* 62 (1938): 42–50; S. Provost and M. Boyd, "Application de la prospection géophysique à la topographie urbaine II: Philippes, les quartiers Ouest," *BCH* 126 (2002): 478–79. **Corinth**: R. L. Scranton, *Mediaeval Architecture in the Central Area of Corinth,* Corinth 16 (Princeton, N.J., 1957), 12–14. The hemicycle was made of spolia (14–16). There was apparently no further dating evidence available. **Skythopolis 1**: The north side of the Palladius Street contained a marble paved semicircular plaza with an exedra of rooms that cut into an earlier odeon/bouleuterion. This new development involved the almost complete demolition of a row of shops, and their replacement by a semicircular exedra of new tabernae. The exedra cuts into a fifth-century street portico and is dated by an inscription of ad 506/7: R. Bar-Nathan and G. Mazor, "City Centre (South) and Tel Iztabba Area: Excavations of the Antiquities Authority Expedition," *Excavations and Surveys in Israel* 11 (1992): 43–44; Y. Tsafrir and G. Foerster, "Urbanism at Scythopolis–Bet Shean in the Fourth to Seventh Centuries," *DOP* 51 (1997): 121–22, 130, figs. 28–29. See §8, below, for detail of mosaic. **Skythopolis 2**: A second sigma plaza on Valley Street is shown on Tsafrir and Foerster, "Urbanism at Scythopolis," 121–22, fig. C, but no further details have yet been published. It is not clear if the plaza has rooms arranged around it. **Gadara**: This discovery has not yet been published: W. Thiel, personal communication. **Bostra**: The building of a sigma plaza is mentioned in an inscription, *IGLSyr* 13.9122 (ad 488). It might not have a commercial function, as we cannot know if it had cellular rooms. **Damascus**: Possible sigma plaza with cellular rooms shown in mosaic discussed by Gering, *Aphrodisias, Ephesos und Ostia.*

8. Portico Mosaics Fronting Cellular Shops

Ephesos, Arcadiane: Mosaic paving in its late antique state: R. Heberdey, *ÖJh* 3 (1900): 90; 5 (1902): 53; for overall context, see P. Schneider, "Bauphasen der Arkadiane," in *100 Jahre österreichische Forschungen in Ephesos: Akten des Symposions Wien 1995,* ed. H. Friesinger and F. Krinzinger, DenkWien 260, Archäologische Forschungen 1 (Vienna, 1999), 467–80. **Ephesos, Embolos**: "Alytarch stoa" mosaic is the same phase as portico built in reused material, which must be earlier than ad 440, when a decree was inscribed on one of its reused columns. Stylistic dates for the mosaic have been offered in the late fifth/early sixth century, but are obviously weaker than this structural information: H. Thür, "Die spätantike Bauphase der Kuretenstraße," in *Efeso paleocristiana e bizantina—Frühchristliches und byzantinisches Ephesos,* ed. R. Pillinger, O. Kresten, F. Krinzinger, and E. Ruso (Vienna, 1999), 111–12. **Side**: Must be late antique, as it fronts some late shops by the theater which cover a ruined temple, at the same level: see §10, below, plus site observations by author (hereafter LL), 2004. **Perge**: Mosaic in colonnaded street dated by a mosaic inscription dedicated by a *patēr*, so placing it after the 460s: C. Foss, "The Cities of Pamphylia in the Byzantine Age," in idem, *Cities, Fortresses and Villages of Byzantine Asia Minor* (Aldershot, 1996), art. IV, 37, note 67 with C. M. Roueché, "A New Inscription from Aphrodisias and the Title πατὴρ τῆς πόλεως," *GRBS* 20 (1979): 173–85, esp. 182. **Sepphoris**: Mosaic dated by mosaic inscriptions as the work of the bishop Eutropius: E. Netzer and Z. Weiss, "New Evidence for Late-Roman and Byzantine Sepphoris," in *The Roman and Byzantine Near East: Some Recent Archaeological Research,* ed. J. H. Humphrey, Journal of Roman Archaeology, supp. ser. 14 (Portsmouth, R.I., 1995), 162–76. **Beirut**: American University of Beirut, "Module 3: The Byzantine Portico and Shops," *Windows on the Souk,* http://ddc.aub.edu.lb/projects/archaeology/soukex/deliverables/module03.html (accessed July 2010); D. Perring, "The Archaeology of Beirut: A Report on Work in the Insula of the House of the Fountains," *AntJ* 83 (2003): 217, dates the portico mosaic to the period ad 525–51, based on "stylistic parallels and the construction horizons." **Skythopolis**: Mosaic in sigma square and in portico of Palladius Street dated by mosaic inscriptions to the early fifth century or after, based on the title of the governor, which is praesidal, not consular, and so must be of Palestina II, created in the early fifth century: G. Mazor, "Department of Antiquities Expedition," in "Beth Shean Project 1988," *Excavations and Surveys in Israel* 7–8 (1988–89): 27, with Y. Tsafrir and G. Foerster, "Urbanism at Scythopolis–Bet Shean in the Fourth to Seventh Centuries," *DOP* 51 (1997): 114 n. 126. **Gerasa**: The east portico mosaic was laid out as part of the same program of works as the late fifth- to sixth-century shop rebuild: see the references below, §14, plus E. Olavarri, "Excavaciones en el edificio publico romano junto al Cardo Maximus, Gerasa 1983," in *Jerash Archaeological Project,* vol. 1, *1981–1983,* ed. F. Zayadine (Amman, 1986), 474. Collective portico mosaics with a unified design are not universal: see **Sardis** in §13, below.

9. Shops on Fora/Agorai: The West

Cirencester: Shops were built to close the street to the south of the forum and basilica. Rooms on the north side were turned around, creating a possible new plaza, in the last phase of building on site, reasonably assumed to be fourth century: J. S. Wacher, "Excavations at Cirencester," *AntJ* 42 (1962): 1–14. **Exeter**: Basilica and curia extended and new possible "shops" erected: P. T. Bidwell, *The Legionary Bath-house and Basilica and Forum at Exeter* (Exeter, 1979), 104–9, in period 3A after ca. 340/50, according to coins and pottery. **Complutum**: In phase 2 of the forum, which is given a TPQ by pottery of the very end of the third century, the forum tabernae were refurbished with new pavement: S. Rascón Marqués, "La ciudad de Complutum en la tardoantigüedad: Restauración y renovación," in *Complutum y las ciudades Hispanas en la antigüedad tardía*, ed. L. García Moreno and S. Rascón Marqués, Acta antiqua complutensia 1 (Alcalá de Henares, 1999), 53–57. **Segobriga**: Cryptoporticus on the north side of the forum is subdivided into shops, dated by excavators to third century, on the basis of finds of ceramics which seem to be like ARS Hayes 50, though details of context are not given: J. M. Abscal, M. Almagro-Gorbea, and R. Cebrián, "Segobriga 1989–2000: Topografía de la ciudad y trabajos en el foro," *Madrider Mitteilungen* 43 (2002): 140–41. **Herdonia**: For the shops installed inside the basilica, see §6, above. Another set of cellular rooms was established in the gymnasium, also on the agora, which are thought to date to the same "late Roman" period on the basis here too of *opus mixtum*. A secondary phase of alterations features deposits containing fourth- to fifth-century pottery. However, the gymnasium rooms have doors between rooms rather than out onto the front, and so these might not be shops: J. Mertens, "Dal tardo antico all'altomedievo," in *Herdonia: Scoperta di una città*, ed. idem (Bari, 1995), 339–43. **Rome**: Roman forum, Cassiod. *Var.* 4.30, AD 507/11. **Sabratha**: An attempt to install shops in the precinct of the East Forum Temple. These shops were never completed. They are given a TPQ of the second quarter of the third century or after by the presence of pottery dating from ca. 230/40 to ca. 360, Hayes 50A and 45 (or similar). Excavators think that the wall separating the temenos from the forum was also eliminated as part of the same project, as the present wall looked rough and "late": P. M. Kenrick, *Excavations at Sabratha, 1948–1951*, JRS Monographs 2 (London, 1986), 29–31. I am tempted to see this as an attempt to use a secularized temple temenos as an extension of the forum during the fourth century, though shops in temple temenoi are not unknown earlier.

Shops on Fora/Agorai: The East
10. Shops Built Anew

Delphi: "Roman Agora." The present state of shops is the result of rebuilding; much reused material was used in the façades of the shops: J.-F. Bommelaer, *Guide de Delphes: Le site*, École française d'Athènes, sites et monuments 7 (Athens and Paris, 1991), 89–92. Excavations, not yet fully published, have concluded that the agora saw substantial changes dating to the fourth century AD, which probably included the refurbishment of these shops: P. Petridis, "Delphes dans l'antiquité tardive: Première approche topographique et céramologique," *BCH* 121 (1997): 685, with references to preliminary reports. **Sagalassos, Upper Agora, west side**: Cellular rooms built with a portico and a monumental staircase as part of the fifth-century redevelopment of the west side of the square; the west portico contained in its foundation levels phase 8 ceramics (AD 450/75–550/75): see *Internal Report* (2002): 12. Inspection of walls suggests that shops were planned with the staircase, not before it: LL site observations, 2006. Fill under the stairs contained a coin of Arcadius (AD 395–401): *Internal Report* (1999): 19. Cellular rooms were also built in a secondary phase subdividing the north part of the portico, sometime in the sixth century, when they were covered by a fill containing phase 8 ceramics (AD 450/75–550/75), while room C contained ceramics of the phase from "after the earthquake of A.D. 518" (currently considered to be AD 500): *Internal Report* (2000): 10–16, 33–42. **Sagalassos Lower Agora, west side**: Cellular rooms subdivide this portico, which was rebuilt after destruction of the early sixth century AD ("earthquake of A.D. 500"). The floor levels in the shops contain "LR/EB" fine wares and possible fifth- to seventh-century coarse wares: *Internal Report* (1999): 136, fine and coarse ware from the late sixth to mid-seventh century along with two coins confirming an "Early Byzantine" date for the floor installation: *Internal Report* (2000): 139–45. Occupation material in the shops includes coins (up to Phokas) and pottery up to the first half of the seventh century AD, with a predominance of sixth- to seventh-century material (coarse wares): M. Waelkens et al., "The 1996 and 1997 Excavations Seasons at Sagalassos," in *Sagalassos,* vol. 5, *Report on the Survey and Excavation Campaigns of 1996 and 1997,* ed. M. Waelkens and L. Loots, Acta Archaeologica Lovaniensia Monographiae 11/B (Louvain, 2000), 368; *Internal Report* (1999): 135–36; *Internal Report* (2000): 139–45. **Sagalassos Lower Agora, south side**: Fronted by late cellular units, which have been only partially excavated and are omitted from current site plans. They are visible in a drawing in Notebook LA (92) 16 and other early drawings of the site. When connected to a wall of identical construction built over the Agora Gate, they can be shown to postdate the early sixth-century destruction of this structure: M. Waelkens et al., "The 1994 and 1995 Excavation Seasons at Sagalassos," in *Sagalassos,* vol. 4, *Report on the Survey and Excavation Campaigns of 1994 and 1995,* ed. M. Waelkens and J. Poblome, Acta Archaeologica Lovaniensia Monographiae 9 (Louvain, 1997), 208–10. **Cyrene**: One or two shops installed on the agora of Cyrene in the last monumental phase, ca. AD 400, after a supposed Austurian destruction, one of them thought to be a "*thermopolion*": S. Stucchi, *L'Agorà di Cirene,* vol. 1.1, *I lati nord ed est della platea inferiore* (Rome, 1965), 325–26. The absolute chronology here is not solid, but the assumed broad phasing of the agora, though not easy to challenge from the reports, seems correct and thus gives a date after the disuse of the temples, in the later fourth century or later. **Antioch in Pisidia**: Cellular rooms made out of spolia, including apparently altars, at the east end of Tiberia Platea, on the north side by the propylon: LL site observation, 2003; S. Mitchell and M. Waelkens, *Pisidian Antioch: The Site and Its Monuments* (London, 1998), 147–49. **Aphrodisias, bath hall on the Tetrastoon**: In this hall shops can be seen, which in places do include some reused material. They are at least in part clearly secondary to the original structure (LL field observation, July 2004—walls abut casually against two columns), though no proper study of the hall has ever been undertaken. The south end of the hall has been pierced to create a new entrance from the south, which Kenan Erim thought was a fourth-century development—presumably because it links it to the Tetrastoon, which was built at this time. Although the square may have had a predecessor, it seems reasonable to envisage a late antique date for the transformation of the adjacent bath hall into a colonnaded shopping mall, which was opened up to join this square: K. Erim, *Aphrodisias: City of Venus Aphrodite* (London, 1986), 94–95. **Aphrodisias, Sebasteion, just off agora**: The insertion of two rows of cellular shops into this structure is undated, but should date to the mid-fourth century or probably later; this is an appropriate guess for the end of its pagan use, when sculptures here were edited to remove religious content. A floor deposit from inside one of the shops produced coins of fourth- to sixth-century date, testifying to sixth-century occupation. The earlier coins, too, could well have been lost at this time, and do not prove fourth-century occupancy: R. R. R. Smith and C. Ratté, "Archaeological Research at Aphrodisias in Caria, 1996," *AJA* 102 (1998): 238–39. Sebasteion reliefs editing: C. Ratté, "The Urban Development of Aphrodisias in Late Antiquity," in *Urbanism in Western Asia Minor: New Studies on Aphrodisias, Ephesos, Hierapolis, Perge and Xanthos,* ed. D. Parrish (Portsmouth, R.I., 2001), 133; R. R. R. Smith, "The Imperial Reliefs from the Sebasteion at Aphrodisias," *JRS* 77 (1987): 97–98. **Ephesos, theater square**: Shops on the north side of the square examined by Clive Foss, who thought they were late antique, showing several stages of "rather mediocre rebuilding": C. Foss, *Ephesus after Antiquity: A Late Antique, Byzantine and Turkish City* (Cambridge, 1979), 56. **Iasos**: No published account of these shops was accessible to me. They consist of two cellular units in the southwest corner of the agora, built secondarily against a base of the original colonnade and against a spolia wall partially blocking an agora entrance (LL site observation, 2003). The spolia wall is a fortification wall thought by excavators to be third century

AD, and is certainly posterior to the bouleuterion but anterior to the construction of the shops: R. Parapetti, "Il Bouleuterion: Aspetti archittetonici e decorativi," in *Studi su Iasos di Caria: Venticinque anni di scavi della missione archeologica italiana,* ed. L. de Lachenal, Bollettino d'Arte supp. to nos. 31–32 (Rome, 1986), 107, fig. 4, and 177. One published report does describes a coin hoard, of 280 coin types stopping with those of Gallienus (AD 253–68), recovered from under the floor level of one of these shops. This find might be thought to suggest that the shops were built by the late third century, though it is not at all clear from the report if the hoard was deposited before or after the shops were built: D. Levi, "Iasos: Le campagne di scavo 1969–70," *ASAtene* 47–48, n.s. 31–32 (1969–70): 497–502. **Side, square by nymphaeum, west of the Theater**: Shops were built over a temple, and so are likely to be late fourth to sixth century AD: A. M. Mansel, *Die Ruinen von Side* (Berlin, 1963), 90–94; C. Foss, "The Cities of Pamphylia in the Byzantine Age," in idem, *Cities, Fortresses and Villages of Byzantine Asia Minor* (Aldershot, 1996), art. IV, 37. **Seleukeia-Lyrbe**: The secondary subdivision of the bouleuterion may possibly be into shops like other rooms on this side of agora, at least in the case of the southernmost room. The divisions of the bouleuterion are secondary, but only one wall, which may be of a still later phase, clearly incorporates recycled material. The interior elevation of the façade shows a floor (beam holes) inserted at a height that would suit a shop, below the original lintel line of the building entrance, so making it secondary (LL site observations, 2003). For the plan, see J. Inan, *Toroslar'da bir antik kent: Lyrbe? Seleukia?* (Istanbul, 1998), 112.

11. Shops on Agorai Repaired

Sagalassos, Lower Agora, eastern portico: Shops replanned in late antiquity; provisional date suggested as being late fourth or early fifth century, as coins found in interstices between pavement, probably relating to the use of the shops in this phase, date from AD 391 to 491, especially the later fourth and fifth century: M. Waelkens, D. Pauwels, and J. Van den Bergh, "The 1993 Excavations on the Upper and Lower Agora," in *Sagalassos,* vol. 3, *Report on the Fourth Excavation Campaign of 1993,* ed. M. Waelkens and J. Poblome, Acta Archaeologica Lovaniensia Monographiae 7 (Louvain, 1995), 23–46, at 29. **Arykanda, Upper Agora**: These shops contain much reused building material, suggesting that they at least were repaired, and perhaps were built, in late antiquity (LL site observations, 2003). P. Knoblauch and C. Witschel state they were still in use in late antiquity, but provide no further details: "Arykanda in Lykien: Eine topographische Aufname," *AA* (1993): 254. **Ariassos**: The cellular shops in the stoa in the Hellenistic city center were extended to fill the portico. These walls are clearly secondary and seem in one place to incorporate reused material (LL site observation, 2003). Stephen Mitchell, the surveyor, thought these alterations to be late

Roman. He does not record them on his plan: S. Mitchell, "Ariassos 1990," *AnatSt* 41 (1991): 160, 161, fig. 2. **Perge**: Square in front of Hellenistic south gate contains shops with much reused material. C. Foss, "The Cities of Pamphylia in the Byzantine Age," in idem, *Cities, Fortresses and Villages of Byzantine Asia Minor* (Aldershot, 1996), art. IV, 16, thought they had been extensively rebuilt, though they may be entirely late antique. See A. M. Mansel, "Bericht über Ausgrabungen und Untersuchungen in Pamphylien 1957–1972," *AA* (1975): 60–63.

12. New Shops Built as Part of New Streets

Gorsium: "Tabernae" on the main street behind the colonnade are thought to be fourth century because they are at the same level as the fourth-century street. No precise justification is given for this. However, the excavators entertain a general theory that the whole site was rebuilt after the Roxolani invasions of AD 260. Though it is likely that buildings on this last monumental level are late third or fourth century (with the renaming of the site as Herculia), the generalization of this date across the site can only be tentative. It appears that a TPQ in the case of the nearby Villa Amasia for this later phase is provided only by second-century finds (no later than 160s–70s). Coins of the fourth century in layers above the villa foundation (pits, etc.) do not provide a firm TAQ: J. Fitz, "The Excavations at Gorsium," *ActaArchHung* 24 (1972): 3–52, esp. 11. The tabernae may be barracks, given the frontier location of this site, though they do not appear as distinct as the cellular barracks at Diocletianopolis, which have a clear functional relationship to the fortification wall behind them: K. Madkarov, *Diocletianopol*, vol. 1 (Sofia, 1993), 164–66, 207. **Diocletianopolis**: A further row of rooms (no illustration available) with a portico has been located within the city, along one of its major streets. This seems more likely to represent shops, as they are away from the wall, and have none of the unusual characteristics of the barracks mentioned above. They are dated to the "second half of the 4th c." on the basis of the techniques of construction and the use of spolia (apparently a judgment on the overall evolution of the city): Madkarov, *Diocletianopol*, 1:211. A safer date would probably be anytime after the third century. **Justiniana Prima**: Cellular units (two rooms in depth) were found on the short colonnaded street east of the round plaza. In the first phase, which is assumed like the rest of the site to be sixth century AD, these units are two-story stone and fired brick constructions opening onto a portico: V. Kondić and V. Popović, *Caričin Grad: Utvrđeno naselje u vizantijskom Iliriku* (Belgrade, 1977), 325–26. There are also cellular units that share the same chronological assumptions, on the colonnaded street south of the round plaza, where it has been excavated adjacent to the so-called praetorium. These were made of brick with mortar floors: B. Bavant, "Identification et fonction des bâtiments," in *Caričin Grad*, vol. 2, *Le quartier sud-ouest de la ville haute*, ed. B. Bavant, V. Kondíc, and J. M. Spieser, Collection de l'École Française de Rome 75 (Belgrade and Rome, 1990), 157–60. **Constantinople, Mese**: *Chron. Pasch.* Olympiad 327, AD 531; Theophanes, *Chron.* AD 561/62, recording their destruction by fire; R. Janin, *Constantinople byzantine: Développement urbain et répertoire topographique*, 2nd ed. (Paris, 1964), 157, 180; R. Naumann, "Vorbericht über die Ausgrabungen zwischen Mese und Antiochus-Palast 1964 in Istanbul," *IstMitt* 15 (1965): 145–46, fig. 5, recording three excavated examples. **Ephesos (along the Arcadiane)**: The shops along the Arcadiane include much spolia and, as far as they have been excavated (mainly the façades only), seem to indicate a complete rebuilding. Although the street has recently been suggested to be Severan, on the basis of the typology of its capitals, it was largely rebuilt in late antiquity using spolia. It probably dates from the time of Arcadius, after whom the street was renamed, according to the following inscription: *Die Inschriften von Ephesos*, ed. AAVV (Bonn, 1979–84), 2.557; P. Schneider, "Bauphasen der Arkadiane," in *100 Jahre österreichischen Forschungen in Ephesos: Akten des Symposions Wien 1995*, ed. H. Friesinger and F. Krinzinger, DenkWien 260, Archäologische Forschungen 1 (Vienna, 1999), 467–80, with LL site visit, 2005. **Jerusalem**: The shops on the cardo are part of the late construction, but I was not able to obtain the reports relating to this phase. **Skythopolis, Palladius Street**: Fill from sondages beneath the pavement contains material of the second to third century AD that could be early fourth century at the latest. At the north end of the street, excavations beneath the shops have revealed fragmentary floors with distinctive Roman material dating to the second and third century AD: G. Foerster and Y. Tsafrir, "Center of Ancient Bet Shean—North," in "The Bet Shean Project," *Excavations and Surveys in Israel* 6 (1987–88): 25. This evidence, plus the fact that this street cuts across the alignments of early Roman buildings, has led the excavators to suggest a fourth-century date for the street and its shops. Later development of Palladius Street: the pavement of the portico has been sectioned, revealing an earlier mosaic that is white with geometric designs. It bears the mosaic inscription "In the time of Palladius Porphyrius, the most magnificent governor, the work of the stoa with the mosaic was done": "Department of Antiquities Expedition," in "Bet Shean Project—1988," *Excavations and Surveys in Israel* 7–8 (1988–89): 27. See Y. Tsafrir and G. Foerster, "Urbanism at Scythopolis–Bet Shean in the Fourth to Seventh Centuries," *DOP* 51 (1997): 104: "It is generally agreed that the street in its present state was built in the late fourth century, repaired several times, and remodeled in the early sixth century." There seems no published reason to accept that it was built in the second century as asserted in E. Khamis, "The Shops of Scythopolis in Context," in *Objects in Context, Objects in Use*, ed. L. Lavan, T. Putzeys, and E. Swift, Late Antique Archaeology 5 (Brill, 2007), 443. **Skythopolis, "Byzantine Bazaar" by the northeast

gate: Khamis ("Shops of Scythopolis in Context," 453–54) notes "20 shops in 4 rows two lanes across . . . built inside the city walls at the entrance to the north-east gate. . . . The bazaar was built at the beginning of the 6th c.," drawing on the following sources, which I have not been able to check: G. Mazor and R. Bar-Nathan, "Scythopolis, Capital of Palestina Secunda," *Qadmoniot* 107–8 (1994): 133–34 (in Hebrew), along with G. Mazor and R. Bar-Nathan, "The Bet She'an Excavation Project—1992–1994: The IAA Expedition," *Hadashot Arkheologiyot—Excavations and Surveys in Israel* 105 (1996): 26–27, ills. 31–33 (in Hebrew). Khamis assures me (personal communication) that the dating is based on the occupation finds within the shops, though technically these could be later than the construction. Based on coins, part or all of the bazaar seems to have ceased to function after the time of the Persian invasion of AD 614. **Skythopolis, Valley Street**: Shops expanded by cutting rooms into rock at back, thought to date to the end of the fourth century and beginning of the fifth century, though no reason is given for this by the excavators: G. Foerster and Y. Tsafrir, "The Bet Shean Project (1989–1991): City Center (North)—The Hebrew University Expedition," *Hadashot Arkheologiyot—Excavations and Surveys in Israel* 98 (1992): 22 (in Hebrew). ʿAnjar: Whole site dates to early eighth century, and includes colonnaded cellular units along its main streets: R. Hillenbrand, "ʿAnjar and Early Islamic Urbanism," in *The Idea and Ideal of the Town between Late Antiquity and the Early Middle Ages,* ed. G. P. Brogiolo and B. Ward-Perkins, Transformation of the Roman World 4 (Leiden, 1999), 59–98. **Gerasa**: Shops were built on the main colonnaded street, leaning against the wall of the Umayyad mosque, so as to integrate this unusually aligned structure within the classical urban landscape: A. Walmsley, *New Discoveries at Islamic Jerash,* 24 September 2004, at www.staff.hum.ku.dk/walmsley/IJP/IJP_Prelim2_files/IJP2004report.pdf (accessed July 2010).

13. New Shops on Preexisting Streets

Carthago Nova: "Roman street" museum: square cellular unit aligned with street, made out of reused material (probably part of row) seen in a small trench by LL, 2004. **Carthago Nova**: Row of shops made out of spolia, suggested as fourth century, as they follow an abandonment of the end of the second century, while their own abandonment layer of ashes contains fourth- to fifth-century material: M. D. Làiz Reverte and E. Ruiz Valderas, "Area de tabernae tardorromanas en Cartagena," in *Arte y poblamiento en el SE peninsular durante los últimos siglos de civilización romana,* Antigüedad y cristianismo 5 (Murcia, 1988), 432. **Ostia, on decumanus**: V. Scrinari and M. A. Ricciardi, *La civiltà dell'acqua in Ostia Antica* (Rome, 1996), 2:235, no. 28. **Athens**: New shop at Poikillis in the center of Athens contains much spolia, and was part of a complex for which a date of ca. 420 has been established based on the pottery (presumably from fill levels), and coins of Theodosius and Arcadius from 383–95 and 383 respectively (one very worn), which provide a TPQ: LL site visit, 2003; A. Frantz, *Late Antiquity: AD 276–700,* Athenian Agora 24 (Princeton, N.J., 1988), 67 (and see p. 84 for two further possible examples). **Sardis**: The chronology of these shops is not presented explicitly by J. S. Crawford, *The Byzantine Shops at Sardis,* Archaeological Exploration of Sardis 9 (Cambridge, Mass., 1990), and has been reexamined by A. Harris, "Shops, Retailing and the Local Economy in the Early Byzantine World: The Example of Sardis," in *Secular Buildings and the Archaeology of Everyday Life in the Byzantine Empire,* ed. K. Dark (Oxford, 2004), 82–122, and H. Gemmel, "Late Antique Shops: Aspects of Architectural Design" (B.A. diss., University of Kent, 2009). Harris, "Shops, Retailing and the Local Economy," 86, notes coins from a layer beneath rooms E14–16 of the reign of Zeno (AD 474–91); Crawford, *Byzantine Shops at Sardis,* 104–5. Harris is unwilling to expand this observation into a TPQ for the whole of the row, noting inconsistencies of wall thickness and joints. However, she notes the common use throughout of spolia, fieldstones, and mortar in construction, with varying quantities of brick, as well as similar drains, internal doorways between some units, and the presence of a group with similar double doorways at the center of the row: Harris, "Shops, Retailing and the Local Economy," 85–92; Crawford, *Byzantine Shops at Sardis,* 10; Gemmel, "Architectural Design," 12–13. One could also note the general (but not perfect) common frontage of the shops, which is quite different from the irregular rows of shops of the main street of Side or of many in the West. It is also significant that the row contains only cellular rooms, rather than a mix of types. The shops also seem from all indications (beam holes, two levels of finds from the two floors) to have been two-story throughout: Crawford, *Byzantine Shops at Sardis,* 20–21. This design would have well suited the colonnade roof, whose burnt beams seem to match the 10 cm diameter of joist holes in the north (interior) wall of the shop, suggesting that similar timber was used to cover both the shop interiors and the portico: Gemmel, "Architectural Design," 10, 18, drawing on Crawford, *Byzantine Shops at Sardis,* 6, 8. The colonnade along the whole length of the structure does not have to be contemporary, though it very likely is, and the mosaic in the portico has different patterns in each sector in which it has been found: Gemmel, "Architectural Design," 23, drawing on Crawford, *Byzantine Shops at Sardis,* 5–6. Overall, the shops give the impression of being built by a number of different builders, working not to the same design but within the same regulatory scheme, perhaps set by the city, which likely provided the colonnade. **Aphrodisias, along side of basilica**: Cellular rooms thought perhaps contemporary with the third- to fourth-century restoration of adjacent basilica, or paving in reused slabs of adjacent road. There is no reason given for this, except a theory of a general reorganization of the area: R. R. R. Smith and

C. Ratté, "Archaeological Research at Aphrodisias in Caria 1994," *AJA* 100 (1996): 16–19. **Aphrodisias, by "Gaudin's gymnasium"**: "late tabernae" recorded, with no further details: R. R. R. Smith, "Archaeological Research at Aphrodisias 1989–1992," in *Aphrodisias Papers*, vol. 3, *The Setting and Quarries, Mythological and Other Sculptural Decoration, Architectural Development, Portico of Tiberius, and Tetrapylon*, ed. C. Roueché and R. R. R. Smith, Journal of Roman Archaeology, supp. ser. 20 (Ann Arbor, Mich., 1996), 27. **Ephesos**: Shops expanded from substructures of the Temple of Domitian, narrowing the street: H. Vetters, "Domitianterasse und Domitiangasse," *ÖJh* 50 (1972–75): 311–30, claimed dating as post-Justinianic, but the only dating material mentioned is coins of Galerius in an earlier level. **Patara, alongside the baths**: Shops built after third-century repairs to apse of adjacent baths. Trenches in foundation levels have produced sixth-century ceramics, covering a deeper level with fifth-century material: see F. Alanyalı, "Patara Hurmalık Hamamı 2005–2008 yili arkeoloji ve belegeleme çalişmalarina genel bir bakiş," in *Kültür Varlikarinin Belegelenmesi*, ed. A. Çabuk and F. Alanyalı (Eskişehir, 2009), 117–43, esp. 137, fig. 34, which is a sondage through the floor of one of the shops. **Side**: The two main colonnaded streets are lined with shops, full of spolia, that are recently excavated and not yet published: LL site visit, 2005. **Gortyn**: Shops in front of the podium of the temple by the praetorium are dated to first half of fifth century: see G. Rocco, "Primi risultati di uno studio architettonico del tempio al Pretorio di Gortina," in *Congresso internazionale su Creta romana e protobizantina*, Scuola Archeologica Italiana di Atene 2000, Preatti (Athens, 2000), 60–61 (not seen). **Bostra**: Construction or comprehensive reconstruction of shops on west side of north–south street, between the entrance to central baths "Khan ed-Dibs" and the crossroads, which clearly make secondary use of the door frames, and so are thought to be late antique. This development is placed by the excavators after the fifth century, in their relative phasing of the site, though no reasons are given for that dating in their summary report: J.-M. Dentzer, P.-M. Blanc, and T. Fournet, "Le développement urbain de Bosra de l'époque nabatéenne à l'époque byzantine: Bilan des recherches françaises 1981–2002," *Syria* 79 (2002): 115–16. **Sepphoris**: Excavations have revealed a main street ("the *decumanus*") on which shops, constructed in part from spolia, were built on one side behind a portico. It has been suggested that these are of third- or fourth-century date though no reason is given. The portico was apparently encroached in the "Late Byzantine" or early Islamic period: Z. Weiss, "2007 Sepphoris Expedition Sponsored by the Hebrew University and DOAR Litigation Consulting in Loving Memory of Noam Shudofsky: June 24 – July 20, 2007," 6, 10, at http://archaeology.huji.ac.il/zippori/Zippori_Report07.pdf (accessed July 2010). **Tralleis, by Gymnasium**: Stated as being "fourth century," with no further details given: R. Dinç, "Late Roman–Early Byzantine Shops," in *Tralleis Rehberi/Guide* (Istanbul, 2003), 40–41.

14. Shops on Streets Repaired

Ostia: Late repairs to shops, involving reused material, occur throughout the city: for general surveys, see C. Pavolini, "L'édilizia commerciale e l'édilizia abitativa nel contesto di Ostia tardo-antica," in *Società romana e impero tardoantico*, ed. A. Giardina, vol. 2, *Roma: Politica, economia, paesaggio urbano* (Rome, 1986), 239ff., and A. Gering, *Aphrodisias, Ephesos und das spätantike Ostia: Porträt einer vergessenen Weltstadt* (Berlin, forthcoming), chapters II.1.a–II.5.e. **Thessalonike**: In the shops opening onto the street on the south side of the agora, pottery of the second half of the fourth century was found in deposits directly beneath the floors. In the shops, and pits inside them, fourth-century pottery was found. The excavators believe these finds date the floors only, not the original construction, to the late fourth or early fifth century AD, when the shops were apparently repaired. Pottery in the fill above the floors has been dated to the fifth to sixth century, a time when this agora (one of at least two in the city) ceased to be a public square: A. Boli and Y. Skiadaressis, "The Stratification of the South Wing," in *Αρχαία αγορά Θεσσαλονίκης*, vol. 1, *Πρακτικά*, ed. P. Adam Veleni (Thessalonike, 2001), 87–104, summary 328–29. **Thasos, shops adjacent to agora**: Spolia in floors, seen during LL site visit, 2003, confirmed by J.-Y. Marc, who notes in a personal communication that the floors of these shops, dug in the 1950s, were lowered in the late period. **Herdonia**: Shops along Via Traiana and in forum had walls restored and new floors, at a date thought to be late third or fourth century, no more details given: idem, "Dal tardo antico all'altomedieovo," in *Herdonia: Scoperta di una città*, ed. J. Mertens (Bari, 1995) 342. **Ephesos, Embolos**: Shops behind Stoa of the Alytarch don't seem to have reused material, but their façades do, so repair is likely: LL site observation, 2005. I was unable to find a publication on this. For general context, see H. Thür, "Die spätantike Bauphase der Kuretenstraße," in *Efeso paleocristiana e bizantina—Frühchristliches und byzantinisches Ephesos*, ed. R. Pillinger, O. Kresten, F. Krinzinger, and E. Ruso, DenkWien 282 (Vienna, 1999), 104–20; J. Fildhuth, "Die Entwicklung der ephesischen Kuretenstraße in der Spätantike," in *Die antike Stadt im Umbruch: Colloquium Darmstadt 19.05.2006–20.05.2006*, ed. F. Daubner (Darmstadt, forthcoming). **Beirut**: D. Perring, "The Archaeology of Beirut: A Report on Work in the Insula of the House of the Fountains," *AntJ* 83 (2003): 217, describes a phase of rebuilding of the portico shops ca. 350, with alterations in the mid-fourth to early sixth century, involving inserting dolia, ovens, and mortar floors. **Samaria**: The colonnaded street with its shops at Samaria has been claimed to be as late as those at Jerusalem by J. W.

Crowfoot. He observed Corinthian capitals in Samaria, but he probably did not know an accurate date for the streets at Jerusalem. Crowfoot made no decisive observations that would have dated the street, except to notice a reused second-century block in the back wall, which I think might represent a late repair: J. W. Crowfoot, K. M. Kenyon, and E. L. Sukenik, *The Buildings at Samaria,* Samaria-Sebaste 1 (London, 1942), 50–52. More recent excavations recorded "ugly houses or shops" built in the colonnades with a floor deposit containing coins mainly of Constantius Gallus (AD 351–54): F. Zayadine, "Samaria-Sebaste: Clearance and Excavations (October 1965–June 1967)," *Annual of the Department of Antiquities of Jordan* 12 (1966): 79–80. **Skythopolis**: Shop on Monuments Street: the beaten earth floor in shop 1, renewed several times in late antiquity, produced finds of mid-fourth- to early sixth-century coins and pottery: S. Agady et al., "Byzantine Shops in the Street of the Monuments at Bet Shean (Scythopolis)," in *What Athens Has to Do with Jerusalem: Essays on Classical, Jewish, and Early Christian Art and Archaeology in Honor of Gideon Foerster,* ed. L. V. Rutgers (Louvain, 2002), 432. **Pella**: Shops built on street against (thus after) atrium wall of "Civic Complex Church" in civic complex area, thought by excavators to be late fifth or sixth century, a judgment based on the date of the church, which has many phases and which they describe as having no Constantinian features and mosaic floors of the fifth or sixth century. More securely, below the shops, were found "Late Roman levels": A. McNicholl, R. H. Smith, and B. Hennessey, *Pella in Jordan 1: An Interim Report on the Joint University of Sydney and the College of Wooster Excavations at Pella, 1979–1981* (Canberra, 1982), 106. **Gerasa**: A. Uscatescu and M. Martín-Bueno, "The Macellum of Gerasa (Jerash, Jordan): From a Market Place to an Industrial Area," *BASOR* 307 (1997): 67–88, esp. 75–81. The entrance to the macellum was blocked by cellular shops, sometime in the late fifth to sixth century. These were part of rows lining two streets flanking the macellum on its eastern and southern side. Both the rows were refaced in this period (according to the plan on 69), and in the southern row new cellular shops were inserted in what seems to be a former entrance. Dating evidence for this phase has been retrieved from sondages beneath the floor and the foundations of two shops, respectively. The former included pottery of mid-fourth- to fifth-century date (Hayes 50A), with a local krater rim of the fourth to fifth centuries, and coins ending with Basiliscus (AD 475–76). The latter context included fourth- to fifth-century imported pottery, including ARS Hayes 91, 50A, 50B, and stamped sherd Hayes D (AD 440–500). The latest coins are of Theodosius II (minted AD 402–08). The presence of a Jerash Bowl is taken as excluding a date after the mid-sixth century, though really this material gives only a TPQ, which overall should be taken as of the late fifth century. Occupation evidence from inside the shops is sixth century (pottery in taberna 12), with material in the destruction deposit of the site being of the first decades of the seventh century.

15. Shops Built over or within Existing Structures

Segobriga: Cryptoporticus divided into shops: see §9, above. **Herdonia**: Basilica and gymnasium: see §§6, 9, above. **Gortyn**: In front of temple: see §13, above. **Ephesos**: In the substructures of the Temple of Domitian: see §13, above. **Aphrodisias**: Sebasteion converted into a double row of shops: see §10, above. **Aphrodisias**: Hall of Theater Baths: see §10, above. **Sagalassos, stoa by northwest gate**: This was divided into cellular units as part of, or shortly after, a raising of the level of the structure in the late fourth or early fifth century, which postdates fills containing fourth-century pottery and is associated with a raised road with makeup layers containing pottery of the second half of the fourth century. In my view, the cellular units may slightly postdate this—as their rough walls jar with the careful use of spolia in the raised central dividing wall. A coin of Honorius (AD 393–95) came from the fill under the floor of room 3, while the fill supporting the division wall between rooms 1 and 2 contained a coin of AD 364–75. This raising of the level might be associated with the large-scale works associated with the nearby city wall of AD 400. In their final sixth- to seventh-century phase, finds suggest, these units were occupied as shops or workshops: M. Waelkens et al., "The 1994 and 1995 Excavation Seasons at Sagalassos," in *Sagalassos,* vol. 4, *Report on the Survey and Excavation Campaigns of 1994 and 1995,* ed. M. Waelkens and J. Poblome, Acta Archaeologica Lovaniensia Monographiae 9 (Louvain, 1997), 162–73. **Sagalassos, Upper Agora**: West portico: see §10, above. **Sagalassos, Lower Agora**: West and south stoas: see §10, above. **Metropolis**: Stoa: LL site visit, 2003. **Seleukeia-Lyrbe**: Bouleuterion: see §10, above. **Skythopolis**: Bouleuterion: see §7, above. **Side**: Row built over a demolished temple: see §10, above. **Side**: Bath hall: C. Foss, "The Cities of Pamphylia in the Byzantine Age," in idem, *Cities, Fortresses and Villages of Byzantine Asia Minor* (Aldershot, 1996), art. IV, 35. **Gerasa**: Shops in eastern façade of the Temple of Zeus: J. Seigne, "Recherches sur le sanctuaire de Zeus à Jerash. Rapport préliminaire," in *Jerash Archaeological Project,* vol. 1, *1981–1983,* ed. F. Zayadine (Amman, 1986), 59 (not seen).

16. Shops in Pseudo-Market Buildings

The cellular rooms built inside the Hall of the Theater Baths at Aphrodisias and at Side, along with those in the basilica gymnasium at Herdonia, could be interpreted as organized macella. This seems justified in the case of the Hall of the Theater Baths at Aphrodisias, as there is no visible closing mechanism for the shop fronts, which thus required the whole hall to be closed to secure them, if they were secured at all.

17. Shops Built in Earlier Periods with Occupation Evidence for Late Antiquity

Skythopolis: Shop on monuments street: see §14, above. **Segobriga**: Metal workshop of fourth-century date on forum: one of the tabernae on the south side of the forum has been identified as having housed a metal workshop during the fourth century, presumably on the basis of finds: poster *Foro Romano de Segobriga,* purchased on site November 2004. I could not find details of this in the site report: J. M. Abscal, M. Almagro-Gorbea, and R. Cebrián, "Segobriga 1989–2000: Topografía de la ciudad y trabajos en el foro," *Madrider Mitteilungen* 43 (2002): 123–61. **Complutum**: Production waste of a mosaicist of the fourth century in cellular rooms on forum: Sebastián Rascón Marqués, personal communication. **Delphi**: Blobs of glass identified in occupation layer with second- to third-century pottery sealed by a fill of fourth-century date; only preliminary reports so far: V. Déroche and P. Pétridis, *BCH* 117 (1993): 643.

18. Shops Demolished

Zadar, Dalmatia: The first church was built into a row of three shops. Its second phase is thought to date to the first half or middle of the fifth century, based on mosaics. The tabernae are supposed to have been abandoned in the late fourth or early fifth century but I have been unable to find any dating evidence: P. Vežić in *Actes du XIII CIAC* (Split-Porec, 1994); P. Chevalier, *Ecclesiae Dalmatiae: L'architecture paléochrétienne de la province romaine de Dalmatie (en dehors de la capitale, Salona),* vol. 1, *Catalogue,* and vol. 2, *Illustrations et conclusions* (Split and Rome, 1995), 1:100–107, 2: pl. 28–29. **Corinth**: Southern shops destroyed at end of the fourth century and steps and fountains built over them. Destruction deposits in the shops made into fountains contained coins of the first half of the fourth century: R. L. Scranton, *Monuments in the Lower Agora and North of the Archaic Temple,* Corinth 1.3 (Princeton, N.J., 1951), 117, 131–32; idem, *Mediaeval Architecture in the Central Area of Corinth,* Corinth 16 (Princeton, N.J., 1957), 12–14. **Constantinople**: Shops of the Augusteion square removed, late fourth or early fifth century: *Vita Olympiadis* 6.

19. Industrial Encroachment in City Centers: Fourth and Fifth Century

Silchester: Forum given over to industry in second half of the third century, according to coins of this date and also of the fourth century, found respectively in association with the earliest pits and in the fills of later pits: M. Fulford and J. Timby et al., *Late Iron Age and Roman Silchester: Excavations on the Site of the Forum Basilica 1977, 1980–86,* Britannia Monograph Series 15 (London, 2000), 68–75. **Thessalonike**: Pottery kilns in one of the abandoned fora of the city, thought to be fifth century, though further details not given: A. Valavanidou, "Workshops on the Site of the Ancient Agora of Thessalonica," in *Αρχαία αγορά Θεσσαλονίκης,* vol. 1, *Πρακτικά,* ed. P. Adam Veleni (Thessalonike, 2001), summary 121–30, English summary 329–30.

20. Industrial Encroachment in City Centers: Reconquest Africa

Kilns are found in the forum at Iol Caesarea and in a bath at Leptiminus. **Iol Caesarea**: T. W. Potter, *Towns in Late Antiquity: Iol Caesarea and Its Context* (Oxford, 1995), 48–49, 52–56: these postdate the destruction of the "church," in the silts above which was found a sherd of ARS of ca. 570–600, which Potter thinks might be associated with the occupation of this kiln and an adjacent rectangular post-built structure. **Leptiminus**: L. Stirling, with assistance from D. J. Mattingly and N. Ben Lazreg, "The East Baths and Their Industrial Re-use in Late Antiquity: 1992 Excavations," in *Leptiminus (Lamta): Report no. 2: The East Baths, Venus Mosaic, Cemeteries and Other Studies,* ed. L. Stirling, D. J. Mattingly, and N. Ben Lazreg, Journal of Roman Archaeology, supp. ser. 40 (Portsmouth, R.I., 2001), 53–55, 67: metalworking took place, as indicated by slags coming from a new floor in which Justinianic coins were found; in an adjacent court, debris was uncovered from kilns producing amphorae of Keay types 61–21 (fifth–seventh century) and 8A (probably seventh century only). Such encroachment by production does begin earlier, as it was a feature of the Vandal period. But this earlier encroachment is not by industry but by olive presses, as in the forum of Uchi Maius. The continued spread of these presses was a feature of the reconquest period: A. Leone, "Topographies of Production in North African Cities during the Vandal and Byzantine Periods," in *Theory and Practice in Late Antique Archaeology,* ed. L. Lavan and W. Bowden, Late Antique Archaeology 1 (Leiden, 2003), 257–87.

21. Industrial Encroachment in City Centers: Late Sixth-Century East

Justiniana Prima: Blacksmiths in retail areas within the city (in last antique phase of what is a mid-sixth-century city): V. Kondić and V. Popović, *Caričin Grad: Utvrdeno naselje u vizantijskom Iliriku* (Belgrade, 1977), 327. **Gortyn**: Residential quarter with artisanal activity of seventh-century date: A. Di Vita, "Gortina bizantina," *Studi Tardoantichi* 4 (1987): 341–51; E. Zanini, "Lo scavo nel 'quartiere bizantino' di Gortina: Il contesto metodologico dell'avvio di una ricerca," in *Bisanzio, la Grecia e l'Italia,* ed. A. Iacobini (Rome, 2004), 145–59; E. Zanini and E. Giorgi, "Indagini archeologiche nell'area del 'quartiere bizantino' di Gortina: Prima relazione preliminare (campagna 2002)," *ASAtene* 80 (2002): 898–918; eidem, "Indagini archeologiche nell'area del 'quartiere bizantino' di Gortina: Seconda relazione preliminare (campagna 2003)," *ASAtene* 81 (2003): 913–45, esp. 924–26, with details of seventh-century coins used to provide TPQ for development of this artisanal area. **Ephesos**: Behind Octagon on Embolos, late sixth to seventh century, on the basis of unspecified unpublished finds: H. Thür, "Die spätantike Bauphase der Kuretenstraße," in *Efeso paleocristiana e bizantina—Frühchristliches und byzantinisches Ephesos,* ed. R. Pillinger, O. Kresten, F. Krinzinger, and E. Ruso (Vienna, 1999), 118. **Anemourion**: Large baths, out of use by late fourth century, occupied by pottery kilns and a grain mill by the end of the sixth century: J. Russell, "The Archaeological Context of Magic in the Early Byzantine Period," in *Byzantine Magic,* ed. H. Maguire (Washington, D.C., 1995), 35–50. Dating is probably based on coins, as coins from many of the late structures are late sixth and seventh century.

22. Industrial Encroachment in City Centers: Early Islamic Near East

Skythopolis: Y. Tsafrir and G. Foerster, "Urbanism at Scythopolis–Bet Shean in the Fourth to Seventh Centuries," *DOP* 51 (1997): 135–46, esp. 138. **Gerasa**: J. Schaefer and R. K. Falkner, "An Umayyad Potter's Complex in the North Theatre, Jerash," in *Jerash Archaeological Project 1981–1983,* ed. F. Zayadine (Amman, 1986), 411–60.

• FIFTEEN •

Weighing, Measuring, Paying

Exchanges in the Market and the Marketplace

CÉCILE MORRISSON

in memory of Angeliki, χάρις

If money is undoubtedly "the great wheel of circulation, the great instrument of commerce," as Adam Smith claimed,[1] that is because, as we all know since Aristotle, it is "a measure of all things" on the basis of which exchange can take place.[2] It is only natural that in the fourth century, the bishop of Constantinople, St. John Chrysostom, who was born in the great merchant metropolis of Antioch, heralded "the use of coins [which] welds together our whole life and is the basis of all our transactions,"[3] while a roughly contemporary epigram of Palladas in the *Anthologia Palatina* praised the "fertilizing follis."[4] But money is only one among many other measures, as traditional images of a Byzantine and a western merchant illustrate: the former carries a jar on his shoulder and holds the scales in his left hand (fig. 15.1),[5] while the latter holds the scales in his right hand and the measuring rod in his left, his conspicuous purse hanging from his belt (fig. 15.2). In the words of Peter Spufford, "To be a merchant is to weigh and measure."[6] Money, weights, and measures, plus taxes and various excises, always formed the core of the merchant's culture—as Francesco Balducci Pegolotti put it in the fourteenth century, they are the *cose bisognevoli di sapere a mercatanti di diverse parti del mondo* (topics that the merchants from various parts of the world need to know).[7]

No treatise on the art of commerce comparable to Pegolotti's survives from Byzantium, but much information can be gained from several sources: first, the many laws that governed commerce and ensured security and uniformity in weighing and paying in "markets," be they permanent, weekly, or annual, or local, regional, or international; second, other textual sources giving evidence of daily practice; and, last but not least, the archaeological documentation on instruments of weighing, measuring, and paying. This latter perspective is considered in greater detail in this volume in the chapter by Brigitte Pitarakis, but it cannot be entirely ignored in what follows, which will outline the regulation and enforcement

---

1   I am indebted to the late Angeliki Laiou for having insisted at an early stage of this research on the importance of studying the evolution of measuring practices in the late Byzantine period. This chapter would not have been the same without her advice but unfortunately lacks what she would have added to it later. I am grateful to Christophe Giros for valuable information. Alice-Mary Talbot's accurate reading saved me from several mistakes and improved my English.
 A. Smith, *The Wealth of Nations* (London, 1964), 256.
2   Aristotle, *Politics* 1.3.17: "For money is the first element and limit of commerce" (τὸ γὰρ νόμισμα στοιχεῖον καὶ πέρας τῆς ἀλλαγῆς); trans. H. Rackham, Loeb ed. (Cambridge, Mass., 1972), 45. See O. Picard, "Considérations historiques, éthiques (chrématistique), économiques, juridiques sur la *monnaie* chez Aristote," *Ktèma* 5 (1980): 267–76.
3   PG 51:100.
4   *Anth. Pal.* 9.528: Χριστιανοὶ γεγαῶτες Ὀλύμπια δώματ' ἔχοντες ἐνθάδε ναιετάουσιν ἀπήμονες· οὐδὲ γὰρ αὐτοὺς χώνη φόλλιν ἄγουσα φερέσβιον ἐν πυρὶ θήσει. Cited by C. Mango, "L'attitude byzantine à l'égard des antiquités préromaines," in *Byzance et les images*, ed. A. Guillou and J. Durand (Paris, 1994), 95–120, at 99.

5   See K. Weitzmann, *The Miniatures of the Sacra Parallela, Parisinus Graecus 923,* Studies in Manuscript Illumination 8 (Princeton, N.J., 1979), 58 and fig. 67.
6   P. Spufford, *Power and Profit* (London, 2002), 7.
7   Francesco Balducci Pegolotti, *La pratica della mercatura,* ed. A. Evans (Cambridge, Mass., 1936), 4 (and pl. 1).

Figure 15.1. Byzantine merchant (after *Sacra Parallela*, BnF, Paris. gr. 923, fol. 201v)

Figure 15.2. Western merchant, 14th c. (German manuscript, after Iacopus de Cessolis, *Liber de scacchis;* frontispiece of Spufford, *Power and Profit*)

of weighing, measuring, and paying in Byzantine markets from the fourth through the fifteenth century. In this *longue durée,* the power of tradition and material constraints contributed to a certain degree of continuity. Yet political and economic changes and their consequences require a chronological assessment, which here takes the form of a classic three-period division, paralleling the distribution of our sources: late antique or early Byzantine, middle Byzantine, and late Byzantine.

The Early Byzantine Period (Fourth–Sixth Centuries)

A fourth-century text by Pacatus describes the usurper Maximus (409–11) as staying "at the scales (*lances*) . . . watching the movement of the weights (*momenta ponderum*) and the oscillations of the balances (*nutus trutinarum*) on which are **weighed** the spoils of the provinces. . . . here, **gold** taken from the hands of the women; there, *bullae* torn from the necks of children. . . . Everywhere, **coins** (*pecuniae*) were **counted up**, chests (*fisci*) were filled up, [bronze] **moneys** (*aera*) were heaped up and vessels (*vasa*) were cut up."[8] In a less dramatic way, the same distinction between weighing and counting was made in the marketplace, where it was customary to pay by weight for precious metal, by tally for small change. This long tradition is summed up in the eleventh century in the versified *Synopsis tōn nomōn*, where Psellos answers the question about which commodities were sold "by weight, by measure, or by number" with the following examples: "by weight, such things as gold, silver, and lead; by number, small change (*noummoi leptoi*); and by measure, wine."[9] Market transactions relied on accurate and honest scales or balances, weights, and measures of capacity or length applied to both the various commodities exchanged and the coins used in their payment.

---

8 *Panegyricus Theodosio Augusto dictus* 12.2; *Panégyriques latins,* ed. E. Galletier, vol. 3 (Paris, 1955), 93—cited and translated by M. F. Hendy, *Studies in the Byzantine Monetary Economy, c. 300–1450* (Cambridge, 1985), 189.

9 L. G. Westerink, *Michaelis Pselli poemata* (Stuttgart, 1992), poem 8; ll. 896–99: ὅπερ ἐστὶ τὰ πόνδερε νούμερε μένσουρέ τε, / ὅσα σταθμοῦ καὶ μέτρου τε καὶ ἀριθμοῦ τυγχάνει, / πόνδερε μὲν οἷον χρυσὸς ἄργυρος μόλιβδός τε, / νούμμοι λεπτοὶ τὰ νούμερε, οἶνος τὰ μένσουρέ τε.

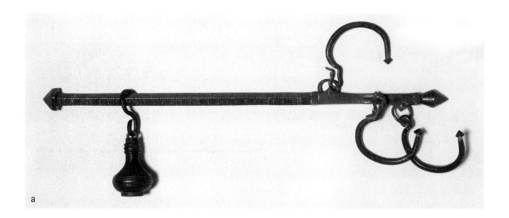

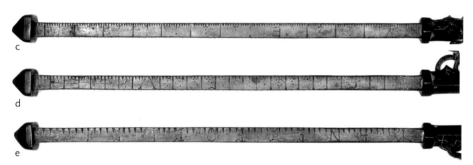

Figure 15.3. Bronze steelyard and weight (48 cm long; 7.5 cm high, weighing 510.3 g; *DOCat*, 1:63, no. 73; BZ 1940.11, from the Bliss collection)

Let us recall briefly the different types of scales and weights, in order to understand better the nomenclature followed in regulation and practice. Heavier commodities were weighed either on a steelyard (Latin *statera*, Greek κάμπανος) or on an equal-arm balance (ζυγός). Many specimens of steelyards, complete or fragmentary, have been found in excavations in western Europe and the Byzantine world (e.g., at Pliska, Sardis, Amorion, and Skythopolis, among many sites) or in shipwrecks such as Yassı Ada or Gruissan.[10] One of the three preserved in Dumbarton Oaks (fig. 15.3a–e) has a four-sided rod, 48 centimeters long, divided into longer (32 cm) and shorter (16 cm) sections.[11] Three of the four sides of the longer section are engraved with varying scales. A counterpoise (7.5 cm high), weighing 510 grams, slid along the longer section and gave the weight when it balanced. On the shorter section, the punched inscription +ΗΔЄCΙΟΥ+ probably gives the name of the owner (fig. 15.3b). This section has three hooks, each attached to a different side of the rod. One hung the steelyard from the hook corresponding to the scale one wanted to read. The hook farthest from the collar served for the lightest amounts, the closest for the heaviest ones. The three marked sides of the longer section are engraved with dotted graduations in *librae* (Roman pounds),[12] referring to weights from ½ pound (1.63 kg) and 1 pound (fig. 15.3a; 3.26 kg) to 12½ pounds (4.07 kg) (fig. 15.3c), from 12 (IB; 3.91 kg) to 38 pounds

10 For more on steelyards see B. Pitarakis, "Daily Life at the Marketplace in Late Antiquity and Byzantium," in this volume, pp. 399–426.
11 *DOCat*, 1: no. 73.

12 Throughout, the "pound" cited is the Roman one (estimated to be ca. 327 g), not any modern weight of that name.

(12.38 kg) (fig. 15.3d), and finally from 40 (M; 13.04 kg) to 95 pounds (30.97 kg) (fig. 15.3e). Another steelyard in the Prähistorische Staatssammlung Munich has a longer arm (73.5 cm), also engraved with three scales, which allowed for the measurement of loads from ¼ pound (81.5 kg) to 32 pounds (10.43 kg) on the first one, from 20 to 71 pounds (6.52 kg to 23.15 kg, in pounds and half pounds) on the second one, and from 42 to 135 pounds (13.69 kg to 44 kg) on the third one (in pounds only). A comparable steelyard in the Museum für Vor- und Frühgeschichte Frankfurt, with a total length of 100.6 centimeters, allows for measuring weights from 75 to 245 pounds (24.45 kg to 79.87 kg).[13] Finally, a larger scale offered for sale in Munich with an arm of 1.25 meters can weigh loads up to 229 pounds (74.65 kg). Taking into account the total weight of such an instrument, with its hooks, chains, and pan (in Latin, *lanx*), its installation must have required great care for any loads above 25 kilos.[14] The signboard of a Roman butcher preserved in Dresden shows how a steelyard, obviously used for smaller loads, was suspended from the shop's beam by two ropes or chains with its arm provisionally lying to the side in a slot in the pole of the stall or the shop (fig. 15.4).[15]

Of much smaller dimensions (ca. 10 cm) and scope were *staterae*, which could be held between two fingers; the counterpoise slid inside one arm incised for the purpose, and the coin or light object was laid on a little pan at the other end.[16] A less sophisticated device consisted of a small scale with unequal arms (7.8 cm long); lacking a counterpoise, it was designed to balance only when a *hyperpyron* was put in the pan.[17] In contrast, big steelyards had sizable counterpoises; those preserved range from 1.4

Figure 15.4. Sign of a Roman butcher with scale suspended from the shop's beam (Dresden Museum; after Garbsch, "Wagen oder Waagen?" pl. 32)

to 2.6 kilos. Their mass could be adjusted by filling the inner part with lead or by adding some lead at its base; tampering and fraud was thus easy, as will be considered below.

Balance scales with equal arms had suspended pans and sometimes could be used even for heavy loads measured with stone weights of some 12 kilos or more; the balance arm would be hung from a strong beam lying on two trestles. But most equal-arm balance scales were used for smaller commodities, such as spices, metal, and of course (and most often) coins. Some of them had a collapsible beam with a joint in each arm, permitting them to be folded and carried in a small container in the pocket.[18] Balances of Byzantine money changers have been recovered also from shipwrecks, such as the late sixth-century ship sunk near the island of Port-Cros (Var, France;

---

13 D. Stutzinger, "Zwei spätantike Schnellwaagen," in *Tesserae: Festschrift für Josef Engemann*, Jahrbuch für Antike und Christentum, Ergänzungsband 18 (Münster, 1991), 304–28 (with references).

14 J. Garbsch, "Wagen oder Waagen?" *Bayerische Vorgeschichtsblätter* 53 (1988): 191–222, at 201–5 and the auction catalogue, with details on both scales. For the first one (Munich Museum Inv. No. 1987, 996) see also *Rom und Byzanz: Archäologische Kostbarkeiten aus Bayern* (Munich, 1998), 171, no. 224. The Yassı Ada steelyard maximal load was 400 pounds (ca. 130 kg).

15 Ibid., pl. 32.

16 B. Kisch, *Scales and Weights: A Historical Outline* (New Haven, 1965), 62 (fig. 26), 65. See Pitarakis, "Daily Life," 407–11.

17 See the specimens discovered in excavations at Pǎcuiul lui Soare (Romania) and Shumen (Bulgaria); see P. Diaconu, "Cîntare pentru verificat greutatea perperilor de Vicina," *Studii și Cercetări di Numismătica* 6 (1975): 243–45.

18 Kisch, *Scales and Weights*, 38–39; see also Pitarakis, "Daily Life," 422–23.

see fig. 15.5).[19] The best preserved are the well-known specimens from the Flinders Petrie collection found in Upper Egypt, but many others have been brought to light in Turkey by Brigitte Pitarakis's survey.[20]

We are concerned here not with the problem of the development of Roman and Byzantine measures[21] but with their use and control. Since Augustus, the emperors had aimed at normalizing and unifying measures in their domain,[22] and Roman standards had gradually become the unique measures of the empire, though they long coexisted with local or unofficial measures.[23] Public control was exercised over the original standard measures (étalons or *Urmaße*) against which all other weights and measures could be checked or copied. In old Rome they were kept in the temples of Juno Moneta or Jupiter Capitolinus; in Egypt, in the Serapeion,[24] before Constantine I transferred them to the cathedral church of Alexandria. In Constantinople they were probably kept in a similar location and from there distributed all over the empire.

These official standard measures, previously controlled by members of the curia, were in the late antique period directly overseen by state officials. These were mainly the *zygostatai,* who were first appointed in each city, according to an edict of Julian in 363,[25] and then elected by the bishop, the inhabitants, and the landlords of the city following a prefectoral edict of 495.[26] In fact they are documented by inscriptions from such places as Bostra,[27] Korykos, Gadara, and Corinth and by many papyri from Egypt.[28] A late antique inscription from Antioch in Pisidia even mentions a *zygostasion*—that is, a building where weighing was carried out and probably the standards were kept.[29]

One of the most enlightening of such inscriptions is that from Andriake, the well-known Lycian port of Myra, where Hadrian had built public granaries that were still in use in the fourth and fifth

---

19 L. Long and G. Volpe, "Origini e declino del commercio nel Mediterraneo occidentale tra età arcaica e tarda antichità: I relitti de La Palud (Isola di Port-Cros, Francia)," in *L'Africa romana: Atti dell'XI convegno di studio Cartagine, 15–18 dicembre 1994,* ed. M. Khanoussi, P. Ruggeri, and C. Vismara (Sassari, 1994), 3:1235–84. Thanks are due to Luc Long for providing the original illustration.
20 T. Sheppard and J. F. Musham, *Money Scales and Weights* (London, 1923), 2–4. See Pitarakis, "Weighing Instruments," in "Daily Life," 419–20.
21 See E. Schilbach, *Byzantinische Metrologie,* HAW 12.4, Byzantinisches Handbuch 4 (Munich, 1970).
22 Cassius Dio 30.9 (cited by E. Schilbach, "'Rechtes Maß von Gott gesetzt': Zur Legitimierung von Maßen in Antike und frühem Mittelalter," in *Acta Metrologiae Historicae V: 7. Internationaler Kongreß des Internationalen Komitees für Historische Metrologie,* ed. H. Witthöft, Sachaüberlieferung und Geschichte 28 [St. Katharinen, 1999], 17–31 at 19 n. 12).
23 On what follows, see the rarely cited but important article by Schilbach, "'Rechtes Maß von Gott gesetzt': Zur Legitimierung von Maßen in Antike und frühem Mittelalter," (above, n. 22).
24 See Sozomen 5.3.3 (*Historia Ecclesiastica = Kirchengeschichte,* ed. and trans. G. C. Hansen, Fontes Christiani 73.2 [Turnhout, 2004], 2:574), on the restitution by Julian to the Serapeion of the Nile *cubitus* and other standards (τὸν πῆχυν τοῦ Νείλου καὶ τὰ σύμβολα) that had been transferred to the cathedral church by Constantine I. Christophe Giros suggests (personal communication) that *symbolon,* which is frequently used by Sozomen to designate a religious insignum, may apply here to insignia of the cult of Serapis.

25 *CTh* 12.7.2 (slightly shortened in *CI* 10.73.2; emphasis mine): "Imp. Iulianus a. ad Mamertinum praefectum praetorio. emptio venditioque solidorum, si qui eos excidunt aut deminuunt aut, ut proprio verbo utar cupiditatis, adrodunt, tamquam leves eos vel debiles nonnullis repudiantibus impediatur. *ideoque placet quem sermo graecus appellat per singulas civitates constitui zygostaten,* qui pro sua fide atque industria neque fallat neque fallatur, ut ad eius arbitrium atque ad eius fidem, *si qua inter vendentem emptoremque in solidis exorta fuerit contentio, dirimatur.* dat. viiii kal. mai. salonae iuliano a. iiii et sallustio conss. (363 apr. 23)." For a *zygostatēs tēs poleos* in Corinth, see L. Robert, *Hellenica,* vols. 11–12 (Paris, 1960), 51. For a mention of Jewish *zygostatai* in Side in the early Byzantine period, see L. Robert, "Inscriptions grecques de Sidè," *Revue de philologie* 32 (1958): 15–51, at 36–37. Denis Feissel (personal communication) knows also of inscriptions mentioning zygostatai in Seleukeia in Isauria, Korykos, Gadara (Μαξιμῖνος ὁ Κ(αι)σαρίας), and Bostra. The zygostatai in Alexandria were controlled by the *augustalis* (Justinian Edict XI, *CIC* 3:777).
26 *Ed. Praef.* 7. See A. Laniado, *Recherches sur les notables municipaux dans l'empire protobyzantin* (Paris, 2002), 173. Several seventh-century seals of a Cypriot zygostatēs called Epiphanios, with the figure of the homonymous saint on the obverse, are published by D. M. Metcalf and A. Pitsillides, *Byzantine Lead Seals from Cyprus* (Nicosia, 2004), no. 299.
27 S. Sari, "A Church at Khirbat Sa'ad: A New Discovery," *Lib. ann* 45 (1995): 526–29, pl. 84, fig. 5; cited by D. Feissel, *Chroniques d'épigraphie byzantine: 1987–2004* (Paris, 2006), no. 863.
28 P.Oxy. LXIII 4395, ca. AD 499–500, in which a zygostatēs certifies the quality of 10 solidi in a loan; cited by C. Zuckerman, *Du village à l'Empire: Autour du registre fiscal d'Aphroditô (525/526),* Centre de recherche d'histoire et civilisation de Byzance, Monographies 16 (Paris, 2004), 103. For other references, see R. Delmaire, *Largesses sacrées et res privata: L'aerarium impérial et son administration du IVᵉ au VIᵉ siècle,* Collection de l'École française de Rome 121 (Rome, 1989), 257 n. 37.
29 S. Mitchell and M. Waelkens, *Pisidian Antioch: The Site and Its Monuments* (London, 1998), 226, no. 9, dated to the third century or later with references to the otherwise rare antique inscriptions where this term occurs: Pergamon, Apollonia on the Rhyndacos, Acmonia (in the *macellum*), and Selge.

Figure 15.5. (a) Balance in its box from the 6th-c. shipwreck of La Palud (Var, France), with (b) close-up of the weight preserved in the box (courtesy L. Long, Département des recherches archéologiques subaquatiques et sous-marines, DRASSM, Marseille)

centuries. The inscription is dated by its mention of Fl. Eutolmios, prefect of the East between 388 and 392, and is located to the right of one of the central doors to the granaries.

Ἐπὶ τοῦ κυρίου μου καὶ τὰ πάντα θαυμασιωτάτου
τοῦ λαμ(προτάτου) καὶ μεγαλοπρεπεστάτου
Φλ(αβίου) [Εὐτολμίου][ἐπάρχου] τῶν ἱερῶν
πραιτωρίων κατεσκευάσθη κατὰ τὰ
ἀποσταλέντα φραγέλλια σιδαρᾶ β΄ καὶ ξέσται
χάλκεοι β΄ ἔχοντες τρία αὐγούστια καὶ μόδιοι
τρῖς κατὰ τὴν ποιότητα τῶν ἀποσταλένων παρὰ
τῆς μεγίστης ἐξουσίας, ἀφ᾽ ὧν ἓν μὲν φραγέλλιον
δέδοτε τῇ Μυρέων μητροπόλι, τὸ δὲ ἕτερον τῇ
Ἀρναιατῶν, ὁμοίως δὲ καὶ ξέστης εἰς Μυρέων
καὶ ὁ ἕ[τερο]ς τῇ Ἀρναιατῶν, καὶ τῶν μοδίων
δύο μὲν Μυρεῦσιν καὶ ἡμιμόδια δύο, ἓν δὲ
Ἀρναιάτες, καὶ ἡμιμόδιον ἕν, ἐπὶ τῷ φροντίδι
τῶν κατὰ καιρὸν πρεποσίτων φυλάττεσθαι
τά τε μέτρα καὶ τὰ σταθμὰ ἀνεπιβούλευτα
τοῖς ὁρρίοις[30]

Under my lord, admirable in all, *lamprotatos* and *megaloprepestatos* Flavios Eutolmios, prefect of the Sacred Praetoria, were prepared according to what had been sent, two iron sticks (*phragellia/flagellia*) and two bronze *xestai* having the three *augoustia* and three *modioi* according to the quantity of the (standards) sent by the supreme authority. Out of these one *phragellion* was given to the metropolis of Myra, the other to that of the Arnaiatai, and similarly one *xestēs* to Myra and the other to the Arnaiatai, and to Myra on the one hand two modioi with two half-modioi, and on the other hand to the Arnaiatai one (*modios*) with one half-modios, while the measures and weights will be kept untampered for the granaries under the *praepositus* of the moment.

Several expressions in the text are problematic. First is the word *phragellion*, which, in his recent com-

---

30 G. Manganaro, "Due note tardoantiche," *ZPapEpig* 94 (1992): 283–94, with updated comment and edition and references to previous publications by H. Grégoire, *Recueil des inscriptions grecques chrétiennnes d'Asie Mineure*, vol. 1 (Paris, 1922), no. 290; M. Wörrle, *Myra: Eine lykische Metropole* (Berlin, 1975), 67–68. I am grateful to Denis Feissel for bringing this text to my attention and for discussing it with me and Brigitte Pitarakis. The

importance of the imperial granaries at Andriake is discussed by K. Belke, "Prokops De Aedificiis book V und Klein Asien," *AnTard* 8 (2001): 116–17. He cites Manganaro's interpretation of the *phragellion* and seems to accept it; but in n. 19, he gives later parallel examples of a linear measure called *bergion* (rod), which support the alternative interpretation offered here.

mentary, Giacomo Manganaro takes in the most obvious meaning of *flagellum* (whip), used to punish defrauders on grain measures in Rome in the fifth century.[31] In an earlier comment, the Austrian scholar and numismatist Wilhelm Kubitschek, who fully recognized the great metrological interest of the inscription, assumed that *flagellum* could be a linear measure. He drew attention to the fact that many "feet measures" (*Fußmaße*) in wood, bone, bronze, or iron were preserved and that "*flagrum* or *flagellum* as instruments of punishment included the representations not only of whips but also of sticks (*Geißel, Gerte, Stecken*) and other things." He added that it was not fortuitous that Hesychios equated φραγέλλια with σκυτάλαι βακτηρίαι.[32] To a modern mind, it indeed makes more sense to distribute standard linear measures together with standard weights rather than a standard instrument of punishment. But the question must be left open.

The phrase *tria augoustia* remained unexplained by Kubitschek, while Manganaro interpreted it as designating standard weights—which are missing from the list, though mentioned at line 11 together with standard measures. He had in mind counterpoises with an imperial bust (*[augoustia] aequipondia*).[33] In order to explain the phrase "*xestai having* the tria augoustia," he even went as far as to suggest that there were "three poises of various weights attached between them and *contained* inside each of the two xestai, which, before being proper *sextarii*, units of measurement for liquids and dry staples, functioned as containers."[34] But the text does not allow the *tria augoustia* to be considered as a separate measure. In the enumeration of the consignment sent by the prefect, the second and third objects mentioned after the *sphragellia* are both introduced by a *kai*: *sphragellia sidara duo* kai *xestai khalkeoi duo* . . . kai *modioi tris*—the *xestai khalkeoi duo* "having" or "bearing" (not "containing") "the *tria augoustia*." Although no other occurrence of *augoustia* or *augousteia* can be retrieved from the Thesaurus Linguae Graecae, in my opinion the phrase can only be understood only as an allusion to *augoustia [laurata]*. The xestai bore the images of the three emperors, engraved or punched as a mark of validity, as found later on silver plate. In the late fourth century and early fifth century, examples of ingots or weights featuring the busts of various combinations of the three ruling emperors of the time (Gratian, Valentinian I, and Valens, 367–78; Arcadius, Honorius, and Theodosius II, 402–8) abound (see fig. 15.6). Although no such marked xestai survive (to be sure, their corpus is rather limited), the hypothesis cannot be ruled out and provides the easiest practical explanation of the text now available.

In general the inscription of Andriake is a vivid example of how the edict of 386—which provided that all official measures, including "*modii* of bronze or stone, *sextarii* (liquid measures), and *pondera* (weights)[,] were to be placed in each station (*mansio*) and city"—was enacted.[35] In 545, Justinian I renewed the regulation in greater detail, explaining that the measures and weights of commodities were to be provided to the cities by the prefects—as evidenced in the Andriake inscription—and the weights of gold, silver, and other metals by the Count of Sacred Largesses. The measures and weights were "to be preserved in the most holy church of each city."[36] The role of the church as depository and guarantor of the weights was not only related to the increasing scope of bishops' functions as leaders of the city;[37] it also derived from the trust that could be placed in the "justice" of the Church. The long association of divine justice with good weights and scales (cf. Leviticus 19:35–36),[38] as well as the insistence in Church teaching on practicing honest weighing and

---

31   Manganaro, "Due note," 285–86, with reference.
32   W. Kubitschek, "Eine Inschrift des Speichers von Andriake," *NZ* 51 (1918): 63–72; Hesychios, *Lexikon* 3.1190, ed. K. Latte (Copenhagen, 2005), 318.
33   Manganaro, "Due note," 284–85. For the interpretation of the busts on these counterpoises, see Pitarakis, "Daily Life," 417–22. The Thesaurus Linguae Graecae search for "augoustia" yields only two instances, both referring to the Spanish city.
34   "Tre di questi αὐγούστ(ε)ια—contrappesi, che in italiano sono anche denominati 'romani', certamente di tre diversi valori ponderali, raccordati tra loro—erano contenuti in ognuno dei due *xestai*, indicati a lin. 4 con una sigla e poi per esteso a lin. 8. . . . ξέστης εἰς . . . καὶ ὁ ἕτερος: a mio avviso, prima che di veri *sextari*, unità di misura per liquidi e aridi, essi avevano funzione di contenitori per I tre pesi-campione."

35   *CTh* 12.6.21 (AD 386). *CTh* 12.6.19 (AD 383) already provided that *mensurae et pondera* must be placed publicly in each mansion. For actual specimens of such measures, see Pitarakis, "Dry and Liquid Measuring Instruments," in "Daily Life," 410–16.
36   *CI, Novella* 218.15; trans. Hendy, *Studies,* 332.
37   J. Durliat, "Les attributions civiles des évêques byzantins: L'exemple du diocèse d'Afrique," in *XVI. Internationaler Byzantinistenkongress, Wien, 4.–9. 1981: Akten,* vol. 2.2, *JÖB* 32.2 (Vienna, 1982), 73–84.
38   "Do not use dishonest standards when measuring length, weight, or quantity. Use honest scales and honest weights."

Figure 15.6. *Exagium solidi* with the three imperial busts of Arcadius, Honorius, and Theodosius II (402–8); on the reverse, a standing female figure (Moneta or Aequitas) holding scales (a. P. J. Sabatier, *Description générale des monnaies byzantines* [Paris, 1862], pl. III, 9 = Bendall, 18, no. 10, from the Cabinet de France or the British Museum [4.78g]; b. Dumbarton Oaks, BZC 60.88.5608 [Bertelè collection], publ. in A. Kirin, ed., *Sacred Art, Secular Context: Objects of Art from the Byzantine Collection of Dumbarton Oaks, Washington, D.C., Accompanied by American Painting from the Collection of Mildred and Robert Woods Bliss* (Athens, Ga., 2005), [3.78g], "slightly broken," 20mm)

assaying, pointed to that reliance. It is well exemplified in the edict proclaimed in Alexandria by John the Almsgiver on his accession to the patriarchate in the early seventh century:

> He insisted that it should not be lawful to use at will different measures (μέτρον) or scales (στάθμιον), whether great or small, throughout the city, but that everything should be bought and sold according to a single standard and weight, whether the "modius" or "artaba" (ἀλλὰ πάντα ἐν ἑνὶ καμπάνῳ καὶ ζυγῷ καὶ μοδίῳ καὶ ἀρτάβῃ πωλεῖν καὶ ἀγοράζειν). . . . He sent out an edict signed by his own hand throughout the whole neighbourhood worded as follows: ". . . I exhort you, beloved, since God hates 'a large and a small balance,' as the holy Scripture says [Deut. 25:13], never to allow such a transgression of law to be seen anywhere amongst you. But if, after the promulgation of this our edict, subscribed by us, anyone shall be proved to have rendered himself open to such a charge, he shall hand over all his possessions to the needy, whether he will or no, and receive no compensation."[39]

Except for the law providing that the *zygostatēs* was to settle disputes that arose between a seller and a buyer of *solidi,* all the other regulation dealing with weighing and measuring was directed at protecting both the state and the taxpayer from possible tampering in fiscal transactions, whether payments in cash or in kind. But they give details on procedures that could also occur in the marketplace. The proper method of weighing to avoid fraud is neatly described in the Theodosian Code 12.7.1, a law of 325 which states that

> when gold is paid, it shall be received with level pans (*aequa lance*) and equal weights (*libramentis paribus*) in such a fashion, naturally, that the end of the cord (*summitas*

---

[39] Leontios of Neapolis, *Leben des heiligen Iohannes der Barmherziger, Erzbischofs von Alexandreien,* ed. H. Gelzer (Freiburg, 1893), 9–10; trans. E. Dawes and N. H. Baynes, *Three Byzantine Saints: Contemporary Biographies* (Oxford, 1948), 211.

lini) is held with two fingers, the remaining three being free and extended towards the tax-receiver (*susceptor*) so as not to depress the weights (*pondera*) by restraining either of the pans suspended from the tongue (*examen*) of the balance, but so as to permit the level and equal movement of the balance (*stater*)."[40]

The correct finger position appears on specimens of an *exagium solidi* (the weight standard for the gold unit) (see fig. 15.6a). In rare cases, cheating could be viewed in a positive light: on his accession, when Justin II reimbursed the debts of Justinian I, the officials who were weighing and paying solidi are described by Corippus as having given "good weight" to the state's creditors: "they pour out solidi and weigh them, and press down the scales with their thumbs."[41]

But in most cases cheating was detrimental to taxpayers or buyers, and allusions to *iniusta* or *iniqua pondera* are frequent.[42] Kekaumenos cites such (morally?) dangerous but highly profitable activities as "making false coins or clipping them, falsifying documents, reengraving seals, and so forth."[43] The life of St. Markianos, the fourth-century *oikonomos* in Constantinople, tells the story of a *trapezitēs* to whom the holy man, then *protector*—that is, a headquarters officer—went regularly at midnight, with his face hidden so as not to be recognized, to "change gold into a lot of small bronze change for his alms to those in need." The banker or money changer used the suspicious night visits as a pretext to weigh the gold coins on an unfairly adjusted (*adikoi*) balance. Puzzled by the recurring visits, the money changer sent a young servant to spy on the saint. He saw a miracle accomplished by Markianos, who had resurrected a poor man whom he had found dead and had washed for his burial. When the servant reported the event to his master, naturally the dishonest *trapezitēs* repented—and on the next visit of the saint, he confessed and reimbursed all that he had unjustly taken.[44] We know of George Koutales, the son of a couple of money changers and pawnbrokers (ἔχων γονεῖς διὰ τοῦ χρυσοκαταλλακτικοῦ καὶ σημαδαρικοῦ πόρου), whose parents were training him to master this business of the precise use of scales and weights (τῶν τε ζυγίων καὶ ἐξαγίων τὴν ἀκρίβειαν). But in spite of his youth he knew their "vain and disreputable profiteering and the weighting of scales and their greedy and usurious rate of interest and the unadulterated exorbitance of interest on pawned objects" (τὴν ματαίαν αὐτῶν αἰσχροκέρδειαν καὶ τὴν τῶν ζυγίων βαρυσταθμίαν καὶ τὴν τῶν τόκων ἀπληστίαν καὶ τὴν τῶν ἐνεχύρων ἀδιάκριτον πολυτοκίαν).[45] The *Parastaseis*, in its eighth-century version, includes the colorful story of a certain Karkinelos, an *argyrokopos* with "balances

---

40 *CTh* 12.7.1 = *CI* 10.73.1 (trans. and comm. by Hendy, *Studies*, 329; emphasis mine): "Imp. constantinus a. ad eufrasium rationalem trium provinciarum. si qui solidos appendere voluerit, auri cocti septem solidos quaternorum scripulorum nostris vultibus figuratos adpendat pro singulis unciis, xiiii vero pro duabus, iuxta hanc formam omnem summam debiti illaturus. eadem ratione servanda, et *si materiam quis inferat, ut solidos dedisse videatur. aurum vero quod infertur aequa lance et libramentis paribus suscipiatur, scilicet ut duobus digitis summitas lini retineatur, tres reliqui liberi ad susceptorem emineant nec pondera deprimant nullo examinis libramento servato, nec aequis ac paribus suspenso statere momentis.* et cetera. proposita xiiii kal. aug. paulino et iuliano conss. (325 iul. 19)."

41 Corippus, *In Laudem Iustini Augusti minoris* 2.395–96, trans. Av. Cameron (London, 1976), 101. The French translation by S. Antès, *Corippe (Flavius Cresconius Corippus): Éloge de l'empereur Justin II* (Paris, 1981), 50 ("on divise en poids égaux les sous d'or épars et d'un coup de pouce on donne une impulsion au plateau de la balance"), is partly incorrect. In the sentence *pondere fusos exaequant solidos et lancem pollice pulsant, exaequare* means to "balance" (horizontally align) the scale. Jean-Pierre Callu agrees (personal communication) with my interpretation and with understanding *fusi* as alluding to the fineness of the gold coins.

42 See Hendy, *Studies*, 332 (citing Cassiodorus and Gregory the Great). The main biblical statements are Proverbs 11.1, "A false balance is an abomination to the Lord, but a just weight is his delight," and Psalm 61.10: "But vain are the sons of men, the sons of men are liars in the balances: that by vanity they may together deceive." This last is commented on by Neophytos Enkleistos, "Ἁγίου Νεοφύτου τοῦ Ἐγκλείστου, Ἑρμηνεία τοῦ Ψαλτῆρος καὶ τῶν Ὠιδῶν," ed. Th. Detorakes, in *Ἁγίου Νεοφύτου τοῦ Ἐγκλείστου Συγγράμματα*, ed. D. Karavidopoulos et al., vol. 4, Ἔκδοση Ἱερᾶς Βασιλικῆς καὶ Σταυροπηγιακῆς Μονῆς Ἁγίου Νεοφύτου (Paphos, 2001), 229–559, at 356–57 (Ps. 61). For other biblical citations about false weights and scales, see D. Hendin, *Ancient Scale Weights and Pre-coinage Currency of the Near East* (New York, 2007).

43 Kekaumenos, *Stratēgikon*, chap. 122; *Cecaumeni Strategicon*, ed. B. Wassiliewsky and V. Jernstedt (St. Petersburg, 1896), p. 51, lines 20–23: τέχνην πολυκερδῆ προξενοῦσάν σοι ἀχρειωσύνην εἴτε κίνδυνον μὴ μετέλθῃς, εἰ καὶ σφόδρα εἶ ἔμπειρος αὐτῆς, οἷον παραχαράσσειν καὶ ψαλίζειν τὰ νομίσματα καὶ φαρσογραφεῖν καὶ βούλλας ἐπισφραγίζειν καὶ τὰ τούτοις ὅμοια.

44 *Βυζαντινὸν Ἑορτολόγιον*, ed. E. Gedeon (Constantinople, 1899), chap. 13, 276–77; cited and commented on by Zuckerman, *Du village à l'Empire*, 79.

45 *Varia Graeca Sacra*, ed. A. Papadopoulos-Kerameus (St. Petersburg, 1909), 62; trans. V. C. Crisafulli and J. W. Nesbitt, *The Miracles of St. Artemios: A Collection of Miracle Stories by an Anonymous Author of Seventh-Century Byzantium*, Medieval Mediterranean 13 (Leiden, 1998), miracle 38, 197–99.

truquées" (false scales, ἐν πλαστοῖς ζυγοῖς) who lived near the place an enormous elephant used for circus games. As the elephant was ruining his house and he could not get the mahout to settle the matter, he finally murdered the mahout and gave his corpse to the elephant to eat. But as the elephant was wild he killed Karkinelos too. Later a golden statue of the elephant was erected on this spot, which became that of the Basilica.[46]

How could such wrongdoings in weighing and measuring be checked and deterred? Valentinian's law of 386, which ordered that standards be placed in each station and city, helps us imagine the procedures: "Each tax-payer, with the established measures of all articles beneath his eyes, shall know what he ought to give the tax-receiver. As a result, if any tax-receiver should suppose that he may exceed the norm of established measures, liquid measures, or weights, he shall know himself liable to a suitable punishment."[47] Those engaged in transactions taking place in public spaces could resort to checking on "established measures" (*constituti modii*) or could appeal to the zygostatēs. As in today's markets, word of mouth and reputation probably directed customers to the trustworthy merchants or money changers, whose honest behavior was proposed as an ideal model and transposed into spiritual life by many preachers.[48] Now the specialized market controllers were not the *agoranomoi,* as previously, but *curiales,* who were responsible for the market and who must have settled disputes arising about transactions.[49] Weights referring to *curiales* (*ephoroi*) show that municipal authorities could issue measures of reference alongside the two official main groups of weights: commercial or commodity weights, which were the responsibility of the praetorian prefect and the prefect of the city, and coin weights, initially controlled by the Count of Sacred Largesses and later by the prefect of Constantinople.[50] They are well known and classified, and we need not take time to review them here.[51]

Most of our information about fraud and its punishment, not surprisingly, concerns money. Counterfeiting gold coinage was considered treason and punished by some manner of execution, including "burning in flames."[52] Clipping and putting into circulation counterfeit solidi were regarded as equally grievous crimes.[53] Casting bronze coins was punishable only by confiscation or minor penalties. But nothing is known about incidents of false measurement, although the insistence of legislation and ecclesiastical texts is abundant proof of that the

---

46 *Patria* §37, *Scriptores Originum Constantinopolitarum,* ed. T. Preger, vol. 1 (Leipzig, 1901), 40; commented on by G. Dagron, *Constantinople imaginaire: Études sur le recueil des Patria* (Paris, 1984), 42–43. Note that in the later tenth-century version of the *Patria* (K III, p. 89; comm. Dagron, 166), the story is modified into an example of an "elephant's memory": the trapezitēs who had once given a slight stroke with a pike to the animal on the Milion as it was on its way to the Hippodrome is struck to death by the animal, who recognized him ten years after the incident. Note that the money changer here is no longer a cheating one. Is law more easily enforced under Leo VI, in a smaller metropolis, than in the early Byzantine capital?

47 *CTh* 12.6.21 (trans. Hendy, *Studies,* 331; emphasis mine): "Imppp. valentinianus, theodosius et arcadius aaa. cynegio praefecto praetorio. modios aeneos seu lapideos cum sextariis atque ponderibus per mansiones singulasque civitates iussimus collocari, ut *unusquisque tributarius sub oculis constitutis rerum omnium modiis sciat, quid debeat susceptoribus dare*; ita ut, si quis susceptorum conditorum modiorum sextariorumque vel ponderum normam putaverit excedendam, poenam se sciat competentem esse subiturum. (386 nov. 28)."

48 St. John Chrysostom, *In principa actorum,* PG 51, col. 100.

49 Laniado, *Recherches sur les notables,* 93 n. 41.

50 D. Feissel, "Le préfet de Constantinople, les poids-étalons et l'estampillage de l'argenterie au VIᵉ et au VIIᵉ siècle," *RN,* ser. 6, 28 (1986): 119–42.

51 See C. Entwistle, "Byzantine Weights," in *EHB,* 2:611–14, with references.

52 P. Grierson, "The Roman Law of Counterfeiting," in *Essays in Roman Coinage Presented to H. Mattingly,* ed. R. A. G. Carson and C. H. Sutherland (Oxford, 1956), 240–61 (reprinted in *Scritti storici e numismatici,* ed. E. A. Arslan and L. Travaini [Spoleto, 2001], 107–28); Hendy, *Studies,* 317–27, with references.

53 *CTh* 9.22.1 (21 July 317; emphasis mine): "omnes solidi, in quibus nostri vultus ac veneratio una est, uno pretio aestimandi sunt atque vendendi, quamquam diversa formae mensura sit. nec enim qui maiore habitu faciei extenditur, maioris est pretii, aut qui angustiore expressione concluditur, minoris valere credendus est, quum pondus idem exsistat. quod si quis aliter fecerit, aut *capite puniri debet, aut flammis tradi, vel alia poena mortifera.* quod ille etiam patietur, *qui mensuram circuli exterioris arroserit, ut ponderis minuat quantitatem, vel figuratum solidum adultera imitatione in vendendo subiecerit*. dat. vii. kal. aug. gallicano et basso coss." Trans. Hendy, *Studies,* 364 (brackets his): "All solidi on which Our face and venerability is to be found are to be valued and sold at one price, however diverse the extent of the image. For that which is spread out with a larger representation of Our face is not worth more, and that which is contracted with a smaller portrait is not to be thought worth less, when the same weight is present. And if anyone should suppose otherwise he is to be capitally punished either by being handed over to the flames or by some other death-carrying punishment. [And indeed he that should nibble away the extent of the outside edge of a solidus, so as to diminish the total of its weight or should nibble away the extent of the outside edge, or should replace a stamped solidus with a false imitation in a sale, is to suffer in the same fashion.]"

practice was common. However, the long tradition of trade, the force of legal and moral penalties, and the disgrace of the *parazygiasitēs* may have led to a certain amount of self-discipline and self-regulation in the marketplace.

The Middle Byzantine Period (Leo VI to the Twelfth Century)

It is impossible to trace the evolution of the previous regulations and practice in the seventh and eighth centuries, although the Basilics took over almost unchanged the Justinianic prescriptions: most likely, however, the shrinkage of cities and the decline of the earlier municipal institutions led to the disappearance or transformation of many elements. The zygostatēs, for instance, was now a member of the *sakellion,* the central financial administration—initially a high-ranked one, as several seventh-century seals of ὕπατος and ζυγοστάτης demonstrate.[54] Some seals call him *basilikos.* In the ninth and tenth centuries he is mentioned in the three official lists of titles and offices (*taktika*) of 842–43 (Uspenskij), 899 (Philotheos), and 971–75 (Escurial). Philotheos gives him the higher dignity of *spatharios* and puts him in the third position in the *sekreton.*[55] After him the same list mentions *metrētai,* who also appear on seals and in the Basilics.[56] A certain Nicholas, "*metrētēs* of the Phylax"—an imperial private treasury, close to the *eidikon*—possessed a lead seal in the eleventh century. To modern editors, he "seems to have been a professional weigher who performed services for the crown."[57] This is not entirely convincing, since we know that the mint department of the *chrysocheion* (gold foundry) was part of the eidikon and that there were also metrētai in the sakellion.[58] Metrētai must have also been imperial officials like the Nicholas, "metrētēs of the Phylax," cited above. The functions of these middle Byzantine officials are unclear, but probably had to do with the measurement of all items coming into and out of the treasuries or kept therein: coins, metal, silk, and other commodities. The standard weights and measures must have also been under their control.[59]

Fortunately the *Book of the Prefect* brings us closer to ordinary dealings in the market, at least that of the capital. As in the late sixth century, the prefect still controls weights, measures, and scales and μέτρα (measures), which are marked by his seal.[60] False weighing (παρακαμπανίζειν) is of course still severely punished by flogging and tonsuring (see fig. 15.7).[61] Moreover, the silk merchants (μεταξωπράται) must use steelyards (ζύγια) and *bolia* (βόλια)[62] sealed with his stamp.[63] Since no surviving Byzantine scales or steelyards bear any imperial stamp or inscription, but only names of individuals, as Brigitte Pitarakis notes in her chapter, we must imagine that they were provided at some point with a lead or wax seal like the official labels or seals appended to

---

54 W. Brandes, *Finanzverwaltung in Krisenzeiten: Untersuchungen zur byzantinischen Administration im 6.–9. Jahrhundert* (Frankfurt am Main, 2002), 642, with references.

55 Hendy, *Studies,* 317–18, with references.

56 Basilics 60.9.1–5; *Synopsis Basilicorum* 10; Zepos, *Jus,* 5:418–19. N. Oikonomides, *Les listes de préséance byzantines des IXᵉ et Xᵉ siècles* (Paris, 1972), 315 n. 162, doubts that they are the same officials as assumed by H. Antoniadis-Bibicou, *Recherches sur les douanes à Byzance: L'"octava," le "kommerkion" et les commerciaires* (Paris, 1963), 138 n. 2.

57 *DOSeals,* 5:68–69, no. 27.1.

58 Cf. the seal of *Petros, metrētēs tou sakellariou* (eleventh century), in V. Laurent, *Le corpus des sceaux de l'Empire byzantin,* vol. 2, *L'administration centrale* (Paris, 1981), 428, no. 818.

59 Note that in Constantine VII Porphyrogennetos, *De thematibus* 15, ed. A. Pertusi (Vatican City, 1952), 61–62, the ἀργυρὰ μινσούρια τὰ ἀνάγλυφα (silver *minsouria* with low relief sculpture) kept in the imperial *vestiarion* in the tenth century were not measures "of the earlier period" as assumed by Hendy (*Studies,* 333), but an early Byzantine *missorium* (silver plate) "inscribed with the name of Jordanes, *stratelatēs* of Anatolia and other peoples of Asia Minor"—i.e., Jordanes, *magister militum* of Leo I in 466–67.

60 *Eparchenbuch* 13.2.

61 Ibid., 16.6. Fol. 43v of the Skylitzes Matritensis (fig. 15.7, below) illustrates the description of Theophilos's weekly visit to the market by Skylitzes. The text does not mention flogging but notes only the interest taken by the emperor in the price of goods, especially food and drink, cloth, and heating materials, and the fear his punishment inspired in the *adikoi* (*Ioannis Scylitzae Synopsis historiarum,* ed. I. Thurn [Berlin, 1973], 50–51). The fact that the Skylitzes Matritensis painter chose the flogging scene as exemplary implies that the punishment was known and practiced in the twelfth century. Zonaras, who describes the same visits, recalls that the emperor, after finding that his brother-in-law Petronas had behaved contrary to the law, had him stripped of his clothes and publicly whipped on his back and on his chest in the marketplace (Zonaras, *Ioannis Zonarae Annales,* vol. 3, *Epitomae Historiarum libri XVIII,* ed. M. Pinder and T. Büttner-Wobst [Bonn, 1897], 356–57).

62 Koder here understands βόλια as *Seidengewichte* (silk weights). But assuming some symmetry in the sentence, one could take it as a name for an equal-arm balance used for silk. That Schilbach (*Byzantinische Metrologie*) does not deal with this word suggests that he did not consider it a weight measure. For a different interpretation of *bolia,* see below, note 69.

63 *Eparchenbuch* 6.4.

Figure 15.7. A flagellation scene in the market of Constantinople, a miniature illustrating Skylitzes' description of Theophilos's weekly visit to the market (photo courtesy of the Biblioteca nacional, Madrid, Skylitzes Matritensis, fol. 43v)

weighing instruments in our open-air markets or shops today.[64] Similar control was exercised over innkeepers (κάπηλοι): their measures were inspected each time they received deliveries of wine. The prefect's assessor (σύμπονος) was to come and force them to "prepare the weights and the vessels in which they sell wine corresponding to those in which they had bought it."[65] Their vessels (ἀγγεῖα) had to be of the proper weight (the *metron* should weigh 30 pounds, or ca. 10 kg, and the *mina* 3 pounds) and bear the usual seal. The innkeepers whose vessels were found not to have the proper weight or not to bear the usual seal were to be "flogged, tonsured, and expelled from the guild."[66] The soap traders were also obliged to have a steelyard (*kampanos*) with such a seal.[67] The silk merchants were subject to a tax called *kankelarion*, not otherwise attested.[68] It was charged "only on hundreds (*kentenaria*),"

---

64 For example, the U.S. Constitution gives Congress the power to "fix the Standard of Weights and Measures" (art. 1, sec. 8). Individual states take slightly different approaches to controlling weights and measures. In New Jersey, for instance, "Each county or municipal superintendent shall cause an inspection of the weights and measures used in trade within his jurisdiction to be made at least once in each year" (*New Jersey Statutes Annotated*, title 51:1-65). "The state superintendent [now the Superintendent of the Division of Weights and Measures] shall provide for himself and for the use of the county and municipal superintendents, seals or certificates of proper form and wording to be attached to duly approved standards of weights and measures" (*NJSA*, title 51:1-58) (information kindly supplied by Joseph Romano, Acting Chief Supervisor, New Jersey State Office of Weights and Measures, on 1 September 2010). In France, according to a decree of 26 May 2004, all instruments used for selling to the public goods up to 30 kg must be verified every two years and impressed with an official stamp.

65 *Eparchenbuch* 19.1: Οἱ τῶν καπήλων προεστῶτες ὀφείλουσιν ἀναγγέλειν τῷ ἐπάρχῳ ὁπηνίκα οἶνος εἰσέλθῃ, ὡς ἂν παρ' αὐτοῦ ἡ οἰκονομία γένηται, ὅπως ὀφείλει πιπράσκεσθαι, προστασσομένου καὶ τοῦ συμπόνου καταναγκάζειν τοὺς καπήλους ἀναλόγως τῇ ἐξωνήσει καὶ τὰ ἀγγεῖα ποιεῖν, ἐν οἷς τὸν οἶνον πιπράσκουσι. The insistence on using similar measures in buying and selling was intended not only to prevent tampering but also to control the profit margins of merchants—an effort for which we have several examples (A. E. Laiou, "Exchange and Trade, Seventh–Twelfth Centuries," in *EHB*, 2:719; J. Koder, "Ἐπαγγέλματα σχετικά με τον επισιτισμό στο Επαρχικό Βιβλίο," in *Πρακτικά του Α' Διεθνούς Συμποσίου "Η καθημερινή ζωή στο Βυζάντιο"* [Athens, 1989], 363–71, at 369–71). This is confirmed by *Eparchenbuch* 13.5, which allows the grocers a profit of 2 *miliaresia* per nomisma (2/12) but punishes them if they are shown, through a check of their *exagia* (nomismata weight), to have earned a greater profit.

66 *Eparchenbuch* 19.4. The proper weight of the *metron* is cited in 19.1.

67 Ibid., 12.9.

68 J. Koder, "'Problemwörter' im Eparchikon Biblion," in *Lexicographica Byzantina*, ed. W. Hörandner and E. Trapp, Byz-Vindo 20 (Vienna, 1991), 185–97, refers (189–90) to the employees (*Untergebene*) of the prefect of that name (καγκελλάριοι) mentioned in a novel of Constantine VII and proposes that the tax took its name from them.

which Johannes Koder assumes to be hundreds of "cords or *bolia*"—presumably bales of silk cloth tied together with cords and sealed.[69] As Koder recently recalled, the sealing of various wares (βουλλεύειν; see *Eparchenbuch* 4.4) was entrusted to the *boullotai* (*Eparchenbuch* 8.3), dependents of the prefect. Two such boullotai are mentioned as very wealthy in the twelfth century: John Tzetzes reports that they owned precious *kodikes* that he could borrow from them.[70]

The regulations were to prevent fraud not only on measures but also on coins: the trapezitai must not accept any clipped miliaresion, nor must they themselves practice filing (*xeein*), clipping (*temnein*), or forging (*parakharattein*). Forgery required specialized skills that the bankers possessed, but filing and clipping were certainly widespread and punished especially among perfumers and grocers.[71] Penalties for forgery were less harsh than in the Roman period or in contemporary western Europe, where counterfeiters were boiled in a cauldron: in Leo VI's time, the culprit was whipped and his property confiscated.

The *Book of the Prefect* is also one of the few sources mentioning the factual context of coin exchange: it commands the *trapezitai* to remain in their shops on the fixed market days with their "assistant" (στήτωρ, *stētōr*)[72] and have the stock of coins present in the front of their stall (ἀββάκιον) in miliaresia (or "with nomismata and miliaresia set out before them").[73] Each banker must have two employees in charge of the heaping up (ἐπισώρευσις, *episōreusis*) of small coins (*noumia*).[74] The presence of the money changer is essential to the functioning of the market, since he provides small change to buyers who have only gold or silver coins.

The famous affair of the *foundax* (depot) of Rodosto (ca. 1075) is one of the rare recorded events that throw some light on the functioning of provincial markets.[75] Before the creation of the foundax by Nikephoritzes, logothete of Michael VII, and the enforcement on its monopoly on wheat trade, "Many carts used to bring the grain to the *kastron* of Raidestos and sell it retail to the hostels (*xenodocheia*) and depots (*katatopia*) of the monasteries, of the Great Church itself, and of many inhabitants, and they would carry out their sale freely without hindrance to whoever wished. . . . Anyone who wanted to buy grain contacted a seller, and if he was not satisfied in a depot (κατατοπίῳ) went to another, eventually to another one, and the sale took place directly from the carts[.]" But afterward the "inhabitants of the region and those of Raidestos" were "forbidden to sell the produce of their lands on their own premises, and their measures (*medimnoi*) were confiscated and the foundax alone became master of the measures (*medimnoi*)."[76] It is clear that the landlords had measures of their own, and transactions taking place on private premises apparently could avoid being taxed (probably on the pretext of their loca-

---

69 *Eparchenbuch* 6.4. Bolia designates either dice (as in Leontius's *Life of Symeon Salos*, ed. L. Rydén, *Das Leben des heiligen Narren Symeon von Leontios von Neapolis* [Uppsala, 1963]; repr. in A.-J. Festugière, *Vie de Syméon le Fou, Vie de Jean de Chypre* [Paris, 1974], 99 [Greek text], 155 [French trans.]) or seals. In Constantine VII Porphyrogennetos, *Le Livre des Cérémonies*, ed. A. Vogt (Paris, 1967), 1:79; 2:144.5, 145.26, *bolia* or *boulla* is applied to the seals of the prefect that are affixed to the urn used for drawing (*tirer au sort*) the starting places of the Hippodrome races; see G. Dagron, "L'organisation et le déroulement des courses d'après le Livre des Cérémonies," *TM* 13 (2000): 151–52. Here obviously it must have applied to a category or package of pieces of silk that were sealed. Cf. *Eparchenbuch* 8.9, which mentions "mantles found wrapped in rolls which did not bear the *boulla* of the prefect." The term has survived in modern Greek to describe a long silk scarf. Therefore Koder ("Problemwörter," 190) understands that the "kankelarion was to be paid by the silk merchants to the exarchs for each hundred of bolia or cords."
70 John Tzetzes, *Epistula* 58 (δύο δέ εἰσι βουλλωταί, πατὴρ Θεόδωρος τὴν κλῆσιν καὶ υἱὸς Κωνσταντῖνος διάκονος); cited by J. Koder in "The Eparch's Authority in the Marketplaces of Constantinople," a paper delivered at the conference "Authority in Byzantium," King's College, London, 15–18 January 2009.
71 *Eparchenbuch* 3.1 (trapezitai), 10.4 (perfumers), 13.2 (grocers).
72 Ibid., 2.3; for a discussion of this term and the unacceptable correction of *statēr* proposed by Sjuzjumov, see Koder, "Problem-

wörter," 186–87, and C. Morrisson, "Manier l'argent à Byzance au Xᵉ siècle," in *Eupsychia: Mélanges Hélène Ahrweiler*, Byzantina Sorbonensia 16, 2 vols. (Paris, 1998), 2:557–65, at 560.
73 The translation of Hendy (*Studies,* 252) is more readily understandable and logical in concrete terms than Koder's "das Geld in Form von Miliaresia" (*Eparchenbuch* 2.3, p. 85).
74 See Morrisson, "Manier l'argent," 561.
75 It also throws light on price formation; see Laiou, "Exchange and Trade," 742–43, and A. E. Laiou and C. Morrisson, *The Byzantine Economy* (Cambridge, 2007), 135.
76 Attaleiates, *Historia*, ed. W. Brunet de Presle and I. Bekker, CFHB (Bonn, 1853), 201–4 = *Historia*, ed. I. Pérez Martin (Madrid, 2002), 148–50. Cf. the analysis and interpretation of P. Magdalino, "The Grain-Supply of Constantinople, Ninth–Twelfth Centuries," in *Constantinople and Its Hinterland*, ed. C. Mango and G. Dagron (Aldershot, 1995), 40–43. My and Christophe Giros's translation follows his except that he has "dispers[e it] to the hostels" instead of "sell it retail to the hostels" and "of local churches" rather than "of many inhabitants" (πολλῶν ἐγχωρίων). See also M. Gerolymatou, *Ἀγορές, ἔμποροι καὶ ἐμπόριο στὸ Βυζάντιο (9ος–12ος αι.)* (Athens, 2008), 198–200.

tion). Attaleiates alludes to the "heavy market tolls" (βαρείας ἀπαιτήσεις ὑπὲρ τῶν τοπιατικῶν) that were required in the new organization and to the *kommerkion* that was charged "from that point not only on the grain, but also on the other commodities that were transported along with the grain."[77] Since we know incidentally of the market tax (τελώνησις) that was collected by some masters of a fair,[78] and since there is no reason why the kommerkion attested in the eighth and ninth centuries should have ceased to be collected in the eleventh century,[79] we may assume that the tax-free transactions in Rodosto in the golden age before the foundax were more the exception than the rule.[80] Most probably the various taxes that appear in the later period, to which we turn now, in fact were established earlier and escape our notice simply because of the bias and gaps of our documentation. Only a few twelfth-century documents point to the existence of some of them. For example, in the chrysobull of Alexios I (1104), Lavra's ships are exempted from the landing tax (*emblētikion*) as well as from the *pratikion* that was levied in exchange for the authorization to sell.[81]

The Late Byzantine Period: Encroachments on the Unified System of Weighing, Measuring, and Paying

In the late Byzantine period, the availability of a large number of archival sources, whether Italian or Byzantine, greatly enlarges the amount of our documentation. But because it is less systematically arranged than before, we have to glean information from numerous texts. Parallel economic growth in Byzantium and in the West added substantially to the complexity of weighing and measuring, as markets in both areas opened with the grant of privileges to merchants of Venice, Pisa, Genoa, and elsewhere. The opening of the markets entailed the use of a much greater variety of measures than before.

"In Gostantinopoli e in Pera si à di più maniere pesi e misure come diviserà qui appresso in questa altra faccia che segue," begins Pegolotti, and the explanation goes on eight more pages, reflecting the diversity of trade in Constantinople.[82] Apparently an implicit rule was that the various commodities were measured according to the standards of their country of origin: for cloth, for instance, "si conviene che'l venditore faccia al comperatore ciascuna pezza tanti picchi secondo la terra ove il panno è fatto, come dirà ordinatamente in questo libro."[83] Gone was the former unity of Byzantine official measures, though their long-established position ensured that they retained an important role. Thus, the account book of Badoer (1436–39) reveals that he kept his accounts in *perperi* and often used Byzantine measures, starting from the carat and the *saggio/exagium* to its larger multiples, the pound or *rotolo* (72 *saggi*) and the *cantar/centenarium* (100 *rotoli*). But equally often he used Italian or other foreign units and carefully noted in his ledger which standard of *pexo* was being employed.[84] When the item was destined for

---

77 Attaleiates, *Historia,* CFHB, 203, lines 1–2.
78 For these merchants and the founders of fairs, see A. E. Laiou, "Händler und Kaufleute auf dem Jahrmarkt," in *Fest und Alltag in Byzanz,* ed. G. Prinzing and D. Simon (Munich, 1990), 53–70, 189–94, and eadem, "Exchange and Trade," 731. For a market tax on the local fair at Kouperion, in Thrace, see ibid., 755. *Nicetae Choniatae Historia*, ed. J. L. van Dieten, CFHB 11.1 (Berlin, 1975), 501, describes the Cuman attack on the city at the time of the feast of Saint George and the fair and blames the "scoundrel from the monastery of Antigonos who had come to tax the festival" and "was fearful lest a copper coin escape him should the people disperse" (trans. H. J. Magoulias, *O City of Byzantium: Annals of Niketas Choniatēs* [Detroit, 1984], 275).
79 See in this volume J. Haldon, "Commerce and Exchange in the Seventh and Eighth Centuries: Regional Trade and the Movement of Goods," 114 n. 58.
80 In the view of A. E. Laiou, the earlier direct sales "seem to have escaped the payment of the *kommerkion,* because they were small-scale and involved large numbers of people" ("Exchange and Trade," 742). A more plausible reason may lie in the sales' private location, since Raidestos, a market renowned for the quality of its wheat (later praised by Pegolotti; see *La pratica della mercatura*), did not have only small-scale exchanges. N. Oikonomides, "The Role of the Byzantine State in the Economy," in *EHB,* 3:999, underlines the existence "of 'satellite' markets around the Constantinople area for those who did not wish to bring their goods into the markets of the capital" since "the *kommerkion* does not seem to have been charged on unofficial sales and purchases."
81 *Actes de Lavra,* ed. P. Lemerle et al., 4 vols. (Paris, 1970–82), 1:286, no. 55, line 62. The *pratikion* is probably the tax *a causa onerandi* from which the Venetian merchants are exempted by the treaty of 1198 between Isaac II and the Venetians: M. Pozza and G. Ravegnani, eds., *I trattati con Bizanzio (992–1198)* (Venice, 1993), 129, §15.
82 Pegolotti, *La pratica della mercatura,* 32–40.
83 Ibid., 37.
84 C. Morrisson, "Coin Usage and Exchange Rates in Badoer's *Libro dei Conti*," *DOP* 55 (2001): 217–44; for weights, see J.-C. Hocquet, "Weights and Measures of Trading in Byzantium in the Later Middle Ages: Comments on Giacomo Badoer's Account Book," in *Kaufmannsbücher und Handelspraktiken vom Spätmittelalter biz zum beginnenden 20. Jahrhundert/Merchant's Books and Mercantile* Pratiche *from the Late Middle Ages to the Beginning of the 20th Century,* ed. M. A. Denzel, J.-C. Hocquet,

resale in Constantinople, he would convert its entry into the Byzantine standard.⁸⁵

For some two centuries Italian merchants, starting with the Venetians in 1265, had been authorized to use their own weights.⁸⁶ In 1304 Andronikos II granted the Genoese "omnimodam livertatem et franchisiam ad ponderandum mercaciones eorum,"⁸⁷ and before 1346 even the merchants from Narbonne enjoyed the same privilege.⁸⁸ The importance to the different communities of weighing and measuring is underlined in several earlier sources going back to the twelfth century, when control of balances, weights, and measures (*staterae, metrae, pesae et mensurae*)⁸⁹ was granted to various institutions. But at that time, their authority did not include the franchise of using foreign weights; it pertained only to Byzantine weights and the profit derived from the right to control them.

The profit from weighing is demonstrated by the story of the church of St. Akindynos in Constantinople: in 1107 the doge donated it to the patriarch of Grado together with its balances (*staterae*), weights (*pesae*), and liquid and capacity measures (*metrae* and *mensurae*), which no other Venetian could possess.⁹⁰ In 1169 the patriarch of Grado leased the revenue of the church, including this monopoly of weighing and measuring, for 500 pounds of Veronese deniers a year (approximately 240 *hyperpyra*, a substantial amount).⁹¹ Note that the Latin names do not imply that the measures were Venetian but instead reflect the origin of the document: *pesae* covers the exagion and its multiples up to the pound, the kentenarion, and the πῆσα itself (= 4 kentenaria, some 128 kg), while *metrae* refers to the current Byzantine unit for wine (μέτρον) and the *misurae* to the μουζούρια, the other name of the modios.⁹²

Other similar Italian documents give details of the fees demanded for weighing on the balances and standards of other colonies: in 1147, in Rodosto, where the weights were deposited in the church of St. George—which was a branch of San Giorgio Maggiore in Venice and enjoyed the same monopoly—for each *miliarion* (*migliaio*?) of wares traded, presumably mostly wheat, two *stamines* (silvered bronze coins worth 1/48 hyperpyron) were demanded from Venetian merchants and four from Byzantines.⁹³

---

and H. Witthöft, Vierteljahrschrift für Sozial- und Wirtschaftsgeschichte 163 (Stuttgart, 2002), 89–116 (translated with slight modifications from idem, "Pesi e misure del commercio veneziano a Bisanzio: Dal libro dei conti di Giacomo Badoer," in his *Denaro, navi e mercanti a Venezia: 1200–1600* [Rome, 1999], 265–93). See now T. Bertelè, "Misure di peso a Bisanzio," with postscript by B. Callegher, in *Bolletino del Museo civicodi Padova* 96 (2007): 189–229.

85 *Il libro dei Conti di Giacomo Badoer (Costantinopoli, 1436–1440)*, ed. U. Dorini and T. Bertelè, Il nuovo ramusio 3 (Rome, 1956), carta 191, p. 384: "charatelo j e sacho j de zera, pexa in Chafa neta cchant. 5 r. 93, la qual zera pexò in Costantinopoli chant 6 r. 28, neta de tara."

86 Zepos, *Jus*, 1:498; G. L. F. Tafel and G. M. Thomas, eds., *Urkunden zur älteren Handels- und Staatsgeschichte der Republik Venedig*, vol. 3, *1256–99* (Vienna, 1857), 73: ἵνα ἔχωσι στατῆρας ἰδίους, μοδίους μέτρα, λίτρας, πήχεις εἰς τοὺς οἰκείους τόπους. The Latin version has *suas staterias, modia, miliaria, libras, pichos* (ibid., 84). The Venetian Commune in Constantinople had two *ponderatores* to whose office all Venetians residing in the empire or the Black Sea region had to register (C. Maltezou, Ὁ θεσμὸς τοῦ ἐν Κωνσταντινουπόλει βενετοῦ βαΐλου (1268–1453) [Athens, 1970], 79, 137–43, documents dating to 1327, 1361, and 1368). D. Jacoby, "Mediterranean Food and Wine in Constantinople: The Long-Distance Trade, Eleventh to Mid-Fifteenth Century," in *Handelsgüter und Verkehrswege: Aspekte der Warenversorgung im östlichen Mittelmeerraum (4. bis 15. Jahrhundert)*, ed. E. Kislinger, J. Koder, and A. Külzer, DenkWien 388 (Vienna, 2010), 127–47, at 146, draws attention to this "Venetian scale" (τὸ ζυγ(ὶ)ν τὸ βενέτικ(ον)) mentioned in the "Pontic" (rightly Constantinopolitan) account (P. Schreiner, *Texte zur spätbyzantinischen Finanz- und Wirtschaftsgeschichte in Handschriften der Biblioteca Vaticana* [Rome, 1991], no. 62, line 111).

87 L. T. Belgrano, "Prima serie di documenti riguardanti la colonia di Pera," in *Atti della Società Ligure di Storia Patria*, vol. 13 (Genoa, 1877–84), 106; see also Zepos, *Jus*, 1:529. For a confirmation of this right in 1317, see Belgrano, 119; cited by M. Balard, *La Romanie génoise: XIIᵉ–début du XVᵉ siècle*, 2 vols. (Rome, 1978), 2:649.

88 Zepos, *Jus*, 1:610.

89 This control was always maintained by Latin churches, and it supplied part of their revenues. See, e.g., the various documents pertaining to the Pisan church of Sts. Peter and Nicholas in Constantinople, whose *introitum* consisted of weighing *statera*, at the rate of 1 staminum per centinarium, or ½ for Pisans, and measuring with *rubo et modio et metro* at the same rate; see J. Müller, *Documenti sulle relazioni delle Città Toscane coll'Oriente cristiano e coi Turchi fino all'anno 1531* (Florence, 1879), nos. VIII (1162), XVI (1180), and XLIII (1197). Schilbach (*Byzantinische Metrologie*, 207), s.v. *rubo*, cites not our Pisan or Venetian documents but only Pegolotti, *La pratica della mercatura* (102, 29), who mentions a *rubo* of 4 *ruotoli* used for weighing wax.

90 Tafel and Thomas, *Urkunden*, 1:103–5, 107–9.

91 *DCV*, vol. 1, no. 225.

92 Ibid., nos. 245, 238–39. The concession applies "to the whole of our maritime section (*ripa*), its houses and taverns, and balances (*stateris*), measures [?] (*rubis*), weights (*ponderibus*) as well as measures used for wine and oil and honey (*mensuris ad vinum et oleum et mel mensurandis*)."

93 If the Venetian *migliaio* (477 kg, approximately 37 1/3 modioi) is implied here, and assuming that we are dealing with wheat (the main object of trade in Rodosto) costing 1/3 hyperpyron in the late twelfth century, we get 2 stamena (1/24 hyperpyron)

"If it were really necessary, the Venetian will have a half *metro* and *rubo* with him and will sell up to 50 pounds and if he wishes to sell above these 50 pounds, he will take the *metro* from the aforesaid church, and for each *metro* he will pay to the church one *tetarteron* and if he weighs on retail (*per minutum*) (?) more than 50 pounds, he must take the *rubo* from the church and give, according to what will appear from the account (*sicut per racionem advenerit*), two *stamines* per *miliare* without any contest."[94]

The importance of a thriving mint, just weights, and commercial regulation for the market and a prosperous economy is highlighted in Gregoras's report of Agathangelos's visit to Cyprus in the 1340s. In his comprehensive general narrative, he pointed to

ὁπόσα τῇ νήσῳ περίεστιν ἄξια θέας, τά τε ἄλλα καὶ ὅσα ἐν θεάτροις, ἐν ἀγοραῖς, ἐν δικαστηρίοις, τὸ ἐν νομίσμασι καὶ χαράγμασι τὸν ἅπαντα χρόνον ὡσαύτως ἔχον καὶ μηδαμῇ μηδ' ὁπωσοῦν τρεπόμενον, καὶ ὅπως ἐν σταθμοῖς καὶ μέτροις πλάστιγξιν εἴη διδόμενά τε καὶ λαμβανόμενα εἴδη καθάπαξ ὠνίων ἅπαντα, οὐχ ὡς τῶν πιπρασκόντων ἕκαστος βούλοιτ' ἄν, ἀλλ' ὡς τὰ τῆς πολιτείας ἀρχαῖα κελεύουσι δόγματα, οὐδ' ὡς τῆς τῶν εὐτυχεστέρων πλεονεξίας τὸ λίχνον παρακερδαίνειν ἐθέλει, ἀλλ' ὡς οἱ σωτῆρες τῆς ἄνωθεν εὐταξίας προστάττουσι νόμοι τὸν ἅπαντα χρόνον[.][95]

what is especially worth seeing on the island, both overall and what is in the theaters, the marketplaces, and the courts—the stability in coins and issues over time that change neither in any way nor in the slightest degree, and how every sort of salable goods in each instance would be sold and bought according to weights and scales [used for] measuring,[96] not as each of the sellers might choose, but as the long-standing principles of the state dictate, not as the appetite for gain of the wealthy wishes to profit unjustly, but as the salvific laws of heavenly order ordain for all time.

An important Byzantine document, the *prostagma* of Andronikos III for the Monemvasiots of Pegai (1328),[97] throws light on the various taxes that could be levied on sea traders and their market transactions.

In no way during the practice of their business will they be hindered by anyone or made liable to requests for *kampanistikon, mesitikon, metritikon, opsonion, skaliatikon, dekateia, tetramoiria, orikē, kastroktisia, mageireia, antinaulon, kormiatikon* or to any other chapter (*kephalaion*) of all these taxes, but they will remain absolutely untouched and undisturbed. Similarly nothing will be demanded for *kommerkion* from those who sell to them [the Monemvasiots] or who buy from them, either beasts or natural commodities or something else, whether in God-honored Constantinople or in other places of my Empire, because of the *dephendeusis* of these Monemvasiots[.][98]

The prostagma had stated in detail the places of their trade and the commodities affected by the reduced rate of kommerkion (2 percent) granted to them:

my Majesty grants . . . the present prostagma according to which is stated that the aforesaid Monemvasiots in whatever affairs they will undertake either in God-honored Constantinople, in Herakleia, in Selymbria,

---

on a total price of 12 2/5 hyperpyra, so the tax amounted to ca. 0.32 percent.
94 Tafel and Thomas, *Urkunden*, 1:103–4, no. XLVII (1145), and 107–8, no. XLIX (1147). The church will possess in perpetuity *suas proprias rubos et metras atque modia sua propria* and hence may gain from any of the above-mentioned measures (*quaecunque his prefatis mensuris lucrari poterit*).
95 Nikephoros Gregoras, *Romaïke Historia* 25.12, ed. B. G. Niebuhr (Bonn, 1855), 3:34. I am grateful to Elizabeth Fisher and Denis Sullivan for their help with the translation.
96 Because there is no connective between μέτροις and πλάστιγξιν, Fisher and Sullivan suggested this translation.
97 Ed., trans., and comm. P. Schreiner, "Ein Prostagma Andronikos' III. für die Monembasioten in Pegai (1328) und das gefälschte Chrysobull Andronikos' II. für die Monembasioten im Byzantinischen Reich," *JÖB* 27 (1978): 203–28. The reader should keep in mind that the data of the forged chrysobull of Andronikos II (1316) are considered as authentic in older studies (F. J. Dölger, "Zum Gebührenwesen der Byzantiner," *Études dédiées à la mémoire d'André Andréadès* [Athens, 1939], 35–59, though Dölger later drew attention to its status as a forgery without dismissing all its contents; idem, *Regesten der Kaiserurkunden des oströmischen Reiches von 565–1453* [Munich, 1977], no. 2383) as well as in recent reference works.
98 Schreiner, "Prostagma," 208–9.

in Raidestos, in Gallipoli and other coastal sites of Macedonia [i.e., Thrace], either in Ainos or other ports of call nearby, be it with grain on the Prosphorion [marketplace in the harbor in Constantinople of that name] or anywhere of their choice, be it with wine, or with *prosphagia pasta* [salted fish or meat], or *xylakhyros* [wood and straw], or *tzokharikē* [woolen cloth][99] or four-footed animals or other wares of their choice, will give as *kommerkion* according to quantity two hyperpyra on a hundred hyperpyra.[100]

I will not dwell on the kommerkion, since this tax—also called *dekaton* (tenth) or *pratikion*, amounting to 10 percent of the value of the merchandise and levied on movements or sale of goods—has been extensively studied,[101] mainly with respect to the exemptions conceded to Italian merchants and their consequences on Byzantine trade and finances.[102] Instead, I will focus on the other charges on the circulation of commodities, their means of transportation, and sales, which have attracted little attention[103] and whose economic significance was relatively restricted, according to Nicolas Oikonomides.[104] In the list in the prostagma we find several charges for the official measuring or weighing of merchandise that were intended to protect from cheating not just the public but also the state, since other taxes—mainly the kommerkion—were based on the value of traded commodities, which in turn was calculated on their weight or other measurement. These charges for measurement were

the *kampanistikon* (weighing tax: from *kampanos*, "balance")[105]
the *metritikon* (measuring tax for liquids)[106]
the *modiatikon* (measuring tax for grain)

The other charges directly related to commercial transactions are

the *mesitikon* (brokerage)[107]
the *skaliatikon* (landing tax)[108]

---

99   Ibid., 207 n., for references on these technical names.
100 Ibid., 206–7.
101 See, principally, Antoniadis-Bibicou, *Douanes*; Oikonomides, "Role of the Byzantine State," 978–80, 1042–43.
102 R.-J. Lilie, *Handel und Politik zwischen dem byzantinischen Reich und den italienischen Kommunen Venedig, Pisa und Genua in der Epoche der Komnenen und der Angeloi, 1084–1204* (Amsterdam, 1984); N. Oikonomidès, *Hommes d'affaires grecs et latins à Constantinople: XIIIe–XVe siècles*, Conférence Albert-le-Grand 1977 (Montreal, 1979), 41ff.; Laiou, "Exchange and Trade," 750–51; and eadem, "The Byzantine Economy: An Overview," in *EHB*, 3:1156–60.
103 Exceptions are Antoniadis-Bibicou, *Douanes*, and, more recently, A. Kontogiannopoulou, *Η εσωτερική πολιτική του Ανδρονίκου Β' Παλαιολόγου (1282–1328): Διοίκηση, οικονομία*, Byzantina keimena kai meletai 36 (Thessalonike, 2004), 247–50, and now eadem, "La fiscalité à Byzance sous les Paléologues (13e–15e siècle): Les impôts directs et indirects," *REB* 67 (2009): 5–57. I am grateful to Anastasia Kontogiannopoulou for letting me consult her article before publication.
104 Oikonomides, "Role of the Byzantine State," 1000.

105 The only comparable evidence of such a tax is found in a chrysobull of Andronikos II for the monastery of the Theotokos in Stèlaria (on the Çesme Peninsula opposite Chios; see V. Kravari, "Nouveaux documents du monastère de Philothéou," *TM* 10 [1987]: 261–356, at 270): among the properties of the monastery were σιδηροκαυσεῖα δύο καὶ ἐσωεργαστήριον ὅμοιον ἕν, μετὰ τῶν δικαιωμάτων αὐτῶν ἤτοι καμπάνου μηνιατικοῦ καὶ καταθέσεως, "two [outer] forges and a similar inner workshop with their rights consisting in weighing, mina measurement, and deposit"; *Actes de Philothée*, ed. W. Regel, E. Kurtz, and B. Korablev, Actes de l'Athos 6 (St. Petersburg, 1913), app. I, 11 (no. 3). I am grateful to Christophe Giros for discussing this text with me; in his view, "Les ateliers dont il est question sont situés à proximité du monastère. Je comprends que le monastère détient deux forges à l'extérieur du monastère (*exôergastèria kai sidèrokauseia duo*) et un atelier semblable (c'est-à-dire un atelier de forge) à l'intérieur du monastère, probablement dans une cour annexe à la cour principale abritant l'église et le réfectoire. Les droits associés à ces forges me paraissent être au nombre de trois. On sait que la livraison de vin pouvait entrer dans la rétribution des ouvriers, ce qui expliquerait la mention de cette redevance dans le texte. La *katathésis* m'est inconnue. Le terme renvoie à un dépôt, mais de quoi: matière première, ou approvisionnement des forgerons?" Anastasia Kontogiannopoulou, whom I also consulted, agreed with this interpretation. See her "La fiscalité," 38–39.
106 It is also mentioned in the imperial document (February 1214) exempting the ships (πλατύδια) of the monastery of Patmos from σκαλιατικόν, κομμέρκιον, . . . πρατίκιον, μετρητίκιον; *Acta and Diplomata Graeca Medii Aevi Sacra et Profana*, ed. F. Miklosich and J. Müller, 6 vols. (Vienna, 1860–90), vol. 6, no. LII, 165–66 = Βυζαντινὰ ἔγγραφα τῆς Μονῆς Πάτμου, vol. 1, Αὐτοκρατορικά, ed. H. L. Vranousē (Athens, 1980), no. 23. The same charges are mentioned in the confirmation of previous exemptions by Theodora Palaeologina, wife of Michael VIII, in July 1269 (XCIII, 225–26 = Vranousē, Πάτμος, vol. 1, no. 36).
107 See Antoniadis-Bibicou, *Douanes*, 136. Her alternate interpretation of *mesatikon* as a measuring tax, derived from *messa* = barrel—attested only in Brabant by Pegolotti, *La pratica della mercatura*, 252 n. 8—is not compelling, since there is no Italian or Greek measure with this signification.
108 *Scalatico* is already mentioned in a twelfth-century document stating that Pisan ships could remain in the Pisan *scala* two months without paying it; Müller, *Documenti*, no. VIII, 10. It also

perhaps the *dekateia* (tenth), if we consider it to be the *dekateia* or *dekatosis* of the *oinara* or *oinaria* charged on the transportation and sale of wine[109]

the *zygastikon* cited in the false chrysobull of 1316; attested in Latin sources,[110] it might refer to weighing with a ζυγός (steelyard) as opposed to with the κάμπανος[111]

I leave aside the other charges in the list: *opsonion* (tax on provisioning, "Verproviantierungs-abgabe"), *tetramoiria* (a tax—4 percent[?]—on a fisherman's catch, according to Christophe Giros, rather than on ships), *orikē* (tax on the exploitation of forests, or on pasture in mountainous areas), *kastroktisia* (repair of forts), *mageireia* (support for feeding the poor, "Leistung für den Unterhalt der Armen"[?]), *antinaulon* (payment in lieu of the obligation to transport certain people or commodities), and *kormiatikon* (a hapax, difficult to interpret).[112] They all apparently concerned the Monemvasiots insofar they were liable to requisitions in kind or in service (*aggareiai*, "corvées"), which these payments could forestall.

Comparable weighing, measuring, and brokerage taxes are clearly described in Pegolotti:

"Pesaggio di mercatantia in Gostantinopoli e in Pera": the seller as well as the buyer must pay 3 carats per cantar on all commodities sold by the cantar (indigo, wax, skins, tallow, raisins, soap, almonds, honey, cotton, rice, gall nuts, figs, orpiment, safflower, henna, cumin, pistachios, sulfur, senna, pitch, litharge, salted meat, cheese, flax, wool, chestnuts).[113]

"Senseraggio di mercatantie in Gostantinopoli e in Pera": the seller as well as the buyer must pay 4 percent "di perperi" for brokerage on all commodities whether they are weighed or not. The tax is usually assessed on value, at 6 percent on grain, or for retail sale (*a minuto*) on pieces (*pezza* of cloth) or on the cask (*botte* of olive oil or wine) at the rate of 3 carats per *pezza* and 2 carats per *botte*, respectively.[114]

Garbellatura is a control tax charged on spices in the same places. Pepper, incense, ginger, mastic, cinnamon, zedoary, and other *spezierie grosse* are taxed at 1 carat per hundredweight; cloves "because their control is tedious" at 1 carat per 10; cubebs, mace, nutmeg, rhubarb, galingale, cardamom, spike lavender, and other *spezierie sottile* at 3 carats per hundred pounds.[115] Comparable control is extended over skins (*cuioa*) by the *cernitori* of the Comune, or over wine that is tasted by the *cernitori* at the rate of 6 carats per 100 *botti* and seen at between 6 and 12 per 100 *botti*.[116]

A special measurement tax (*per farlo picoare cioè misurare*) is charged on woolen cloth (*panni lani*) at ½ carat per *pezza*, or for olive oil (*misuraggio*) at 2 carats per *botte*.[117]

Without examining the other fees exacted for discharging, storing, transporting, binding, or packing,[118] we have a picture of the Constantinople and Pera markets showing that they were efficiently controlled to ensure the security of transactions. Estimating the cost of these fees remains to be attempted. Accepting Oikonomides' low rating of their importance, we may assume that their revenue accrued partly to the public authority (the emperor in Constantinople, the Comune in Pera) and partly to the various inspectors (*pesatori, cernitori*, etc.), as did the *synētheiai* (gratuities) of the early Byzantine period.

The numerous Byzantine documents of the period preserved in monastic archives also give patchy information about taxes exacted on inland fairs, many of which were controlled by churches or monasteries. When in the 1270s Michael VIII confirmed and increased donations to St. Sophia in a

---

figures in Michael VIII's treaty with the Venetians in 1265 (see note 86, above) and in several documents of the Mount Athos archive of the late thirteenth to early fourteenth century; see Kontogiannopoulou, Εσωτερική πολιτική, 249 n. 1102.

109 Oikonomides, "Role of the Byzantine State," 1043.
110 See references in D. A. Zakythinos, *Le chrysobulle d'Alexis III Comnène, empereur de Trébizonde en faveur des Vénitiens* (Paris, 1932), 65, to the treaties drawn respectively between Pisa and the king of Tunis (1353) and between Venice and Tripoli (1356).
111 Antoniadis-Bibicou, *Douanes*, 137.
112 See references and discussion by Schreiner, "Prostagma," 208–9 n.; see also Oikonomides, "Role of the Byzantine State," for *orikē* (1026) and *naulon* (1044); C. Giros, oral communication.
113 Pegolotti, *La pratica della mercatura*, 33–35 (items listed).
114 Ibid., 44–45.
115 Ibid., 44.
116 Ibid., 47.
117 Ibid., 46. *Picoare* derives from *picco*, the Byzantine πῆχυς (some 57 cm; see Schilbach, *Byzantinische Metrologie*, 43). But "when oil is sold in jars, you don't have anything to pay, because they are not measured" (*e quando veni l'olio in giarre non ai a pagare niente, perchè non si misurano*).
118 For a detailed study of such expenses in Badoer, see J. Lefort, "Le coût des transports à Constantinople, portefaix et bateliers au XVe siècle," in *Eupsychia*, 2:413–25.

chrysobull, he mentioned the two villages of Thermon and Loulon,[119] together with the *poron* (a toll exacted on the crossing of fords), the *kommerkion*, the *ennomion* (a tax on common pasture), and the *topiatikon*. This last tax was charged to each vendor, as is still done today in open-air markets, for the right to set up a table or simply display merchandise on the spot.[120] It is probably identical to the *pratikion* and the *plateaticum* attested in Puglia in the Lombard and Norman periods and known in an eleventh-century document as πλάτζα.[121] Among the fairs controlled by Lavra we learn from a 1317 praktikon that the one held twice a year (on St. Nicholas's feast and at Christmas) in the village of Doxompous, southeast of Lake Achinos on the lower Strymon, yielded 10 hyperpyra, and 50 hyperpyra for *gomariatikon* (a commercial tax on each load of merchandise),[122] *kommerkion, opsōnion,* and *katagōgion*.[123] The large praktikon of Pergamēnos and Pharisaios (1321) reports a revenue of 6 nomismata from the fair of St. Constantine in the land of Pinssōn (Pissōn) and 3 nomismata from another fair of St. Elias, whose location is not stated.[124]

Some of these charges and the officials responsible for their collection, or similar ones with different names, still existed in the fifteenth century, as can be observed in the ledger of Badoer, where we encounter

> *sanseria, sanssaria, senseria* (brokerage tax) at a 0.5 percent rate on sales and acquisitions, at 0.25 percent on barter transactions[125]
> *mexura*[126]
> payments to the *pexador*[127]
> the practice of *picar,* measuring in *picchi* in Constantinople and in Pera
> *tarizadori*[128]
> *stimadori*[129]
> *boleta de Griexi*[130] for the seal (*bola*) applied to merchandise, especially textiles (reminding one of the *bolia* in the *Book of the Prefect*)

* * * * * * * *

Markets in Byzantium long benefited from a unified system of control of paying and weighing.[131] In the later period the influence of this long-established

---

119   I. Sakkelion, "Μιχαὴλ Παλαιολόγου ἀνέκδοτον χρυσόβουλλον περὶ τῶν παρ' αὐτοῦ τῇ Μ. Ἐκκλησίᾳ δωρηθέντων κτημάτων," Πανδώρα 15 (1864): 25–32, at 29. The text is reprinted in Zepos, *Jus*, 1:658–67. The chrysobull is analyzed and its date discussed in V. Kravari, "Évocations médiévales," in *La Bithynie au Moyen Âge*, ed. B. Geyer and J. Lefort, Réalités byzantines 9 (Paris, 2003), 88 n. 141.

120   For a vivid representation of a traditional fair in the preindustrial world, see Jacques Callot's seventeenth-century engraving of the Fair of Impruneta (Musée historique lorrain, Nancy). See D. Ternois, "La foire d'Impruneta," in *Jacques Callot 1592–1635, Musée historique lorrain, Nancy 13 juin–14 septembre 1992,* exhibition catalogue (Paris, 1992), 241–56, and J. Lieure, *Jacques Callot: Deuxième partie, Catalogue de l'œuvre gravé* (Paris, 1927), 2:14–16, nos. 361, 478 (image on http://www.impruneta.com/fr/fairs–and–festivals.htm).

121   *Sigillion* of the *katepano* Constantine Opos for the monastery of Montaratro in Capitanate, Trinchera 28, cited by J.-M. Martin, *La Pouille du VIe au XIIe siècle* (Rome, 1993), 429.

122   K.-P. Matschke, "Commerce, Trade, Markets, and Money: Thirteenth–Fifteenth Centuries," in *EHB*, 2:802, understands *gomariatikon* as "a ship freight or cargo bale tax" and refers to Schreiner, "Prostagma," 170.

123   ὑπὲρ τῆς τελουμ(έν)ης πανηγύρε(ως) τοῦ ἁγ(ίου) Νικολ(άου) κ(αὶ) τῆς Χ(ριστο)ῦ γεννήσ(εως) ὑ(πέρ)π(υ)ρ(α) δέκα· ὑπὲρ τοῦ γομαριατικοῦ, τοῦ κομμερκίου μετὰ κ(αὶ) τοῦ ὀψωνίου κ(αὶ) τοῦ καταγωγίου, ὑ(πέρ)π(υ)ρ(α) πεντήκοντα; Lemerle et al., eds., *Actes de Lavra*, 2:170. As in the case of the Monemvasiots discussed above, the *opsonion* and *katagōgion* are requisitions in kind or in service and do not bear on commercial transactions.

124   Ibid., 2:275, no. 89, line 131. See J. Lefort, *Villages de Macédoine*, vol. 1, *La Chalcidique occidentale* (Paris, 1982), 123–25. Fair of St. Elias: see Lemerle et al., eds., *Actes de Lavra*, 2:282, no. 111, line 131; probably located in the region of Hērmeleia in eastern Chalkidike.

125   See references s.vv. in U. Dorini and G. Bertelè, ed., *Il libro dei conti di Giacomo Badoer (Costantinopoli 1436–1440): Complemento e indici* (Padua, 2002). A similar tax in Coron, Venice, or Trebizond was called *mesetaria,* a term more akin to the Greek *mesitikon*.

126   Dorini and Bertelè, eds., *Badoer*, carta 107, p. 217, line 4: "peza 1 de pano chupo, fo quelà che fo chonprada a denar chontadi a perp. 98 la peza zenza mendo e zenza mexura" (one piece of dark cloth, the one which was acquired in cash for 98 hyperpyra, the piece without defect and without measure).

127   Ibid., chap. 43, p. 86, line 15: "per pexador e scrivan al pexo di Griexi" (for the weigher and the secretary at the weight office of the Greeks). Many other examples could be given.

128   E.g., ibid., chap. 11, p. 22, line 8: "e per pichar e tarizar, chontadi ai tarizadori e al pichador a car. 3 per peza" of Flemish cloth (*pani loesti* of Alost).

129   E.g., ibid., chap. 189, p. 380, line 5: "per stimadori e tarizadori, a car. 4½ per bota" of olive oil from Puglia.

130   E.g., ibid., chap. 9, p. 18, lines 29–30: "per boleta al prete del chapetanio e barche de galia e boleta de Griexi e cortexia a quei da la porta, in tuto car. 1 per cholo" ("di stagni fasi": i.e., cargoes of tin in "loads," an equivalent of the Greek γομάριον). On the wards of city gates (*da la porta*), see K.-P. Matschke, "Tore, Torwächter und Torzöllner von Konstantinopel in spätbyzantinischer Zeit," *Jahrbuch für Regionalgeschichte* 96.2 (1989): 42–57.

131   In his first message to Congress on 8 January 1790, President George Washington declared: "Uniformity in the currency, weights and measures of the United States is an object of great

and elaborate tradition was still felt, even though part of the empire's regulatory power devolved to privileged western communities. Charges and regulations of transactions can now be better apprehended than before; they were not higher or tighter in Constantinople than in other trading places of the Mediterranean. They aimed at, and certainly contributed to, the smooth and correct functioning of very active markets, which Brigitte Pitarakis will describe in the following chapter, using archaeological and iconographical evidence.

importance, and will, I am persuaded, be duly attended to" (http://teachingamericanhistory.org/library/index.asp?document =324).

• SIXTEEN •

Daily Life at the Marketplace in Late Antiquity and Byzantium

BRIGITTE PITARAKIS

EXCAVATIONS CARRIED OUT IN THE URBAN centers of late antique cities across the Mediterranean have given us rich insights into the organization of the crafts industry and commercial space in this period. The interior layout of shops and workshops, their facilities, and their contents have received increased attention from scholars in the past few years.[1] Archaeological work in the eastern Mediterranean in such cities as Apameia,[2] Palmyra,[3] Beirut,[4] Jarash,[5] Pella,[6] and Bet Shean[7] has allowed

I would like to express many thanks to Dr. Zeynep Kızıltan, director at the Istanbul Archaeological Museums; to Şehrazat Karagöz, curator, and Turhan Birgili, photographer at the Istanbul Archaeological Museums; to Edine F. Süleymanoğlu, curator at the Pera Museum; to M. Özalp Birol, General Manager, Suna and Inan Kıraç Foundation Culture and Arts Enterprises; to Chris Entwistle, curator, Late Roman and Byzantine Collections, Department of Prehistory and Europe, British Museum; and to Halûk Perk, Istanbul, for providing the required publication rights and photographs of objects from their collections. I am also indebted to Nicolas Beaudry, Pascale Chevalier, F. van Doorninck, Michael Featherstone, Denis Feissel, Jean-Luc Fournet, Sharon Gerstel, Georges Kiourtzian, Garo Kürkman, Christos Merantzas, Cécile Morrisson, Jean-Pierre Sodini, Gülrû Tanman, and Marianna Yerasimos for their generous help.

1 The best case study is provided by the Byzantine shops in Sardis; see J. S. Crawford, *The Byzantine Shops at Sardis*, Archaeological Exploration of Sardis 9 (Cambridge, Mass., 1990). A recent reassessment of the function of the Sardis shops is by A. Harris, "Shops, Retailing and the Local Economy in the Early Byzantine World: The Example of Sardis," in *Secular Buildings and the Archaeology of Everyday Life in the Byzantine Empire*, ed. K. Dark (Oxford, 2004), 82–122. For recent synthetic surveys on the commercial areas of late antique cities, see L. Lavan, "Fora and Agorai in Mediterranean Cities: Fourth and Fifth Centuries A.D.," in *Social and Political Life in Late Antiquity*, ed. W. Bowden, A. Gutteridge, and C. Machado, Late Antique Archaeology 3.1 (Leiden, 2006), 195–249; E. Zanini, "Artisans and Traders in the Early Byzantine City: Exploring the Limits of Archaeological Evidence," ibid., 373–411; T. Putzeys and L. Lavan, "Commercial Space in Late Antiquity," in *Objects in Context, Objects in Use: Material Spatiality in Late Antiquity*, ed. L. Lavan, E. Swift, and T. Putzeys, Late Antique Archaeology 5 (Leiden, 2007), 81–109; L. Lavan, "The Monumental Streets of Sagalassos in Late Antiq-

uity: An Interpretative Study," in *La rue dans l'Antiquité: Définition, aménagement, devenir: Actes du colloque de Poitiers, 7–9 Septembre 2006*, ed. P. Ballet, N. Dieudonné-Glad, and C. Saliou (Rennes, 2008), 201–14. In this volume, see A. Walmsley, "Regional Exchange and the Role of the Shop in Byzantine and Early Islamic Syria-Palestine: An Archaeological View," and L. Lavan, "From *polis* to *emporion*? Retail and Regulation in the Late Antique City."

2 Apameia, Syria, offers a clear illustration of the process of passage from classical urbanism to the medieval city. The whole area around the eastern cathedral of the episcopal quarter, after its abandonment as a religious center, was covered with shops arranged around the courtyards of earlier structures. See J.-C. Balty, "Le groupe épiscopal d'Apamée, dit 'cathédrale de l'Est': premières recherches," in *Apamée de Syrie: Bilan de recherches archéologiques 1969–1971, Actes du colloque tenu à Bruxelles les 15, 17 et 18 avril 1972*, ed. J. and J.-C. Balty (Brussels, 1972), 193–94; C. Jourdain, "Sondages dans l'insula 'au triclinos,' 1970 et 1971," ibid., 113–42.

3 Kh. al-As'Ad and F. M. Stepniowski, "The Umayyad Suq in Palmyra," *Damaszener Mitteilungen* 4 (1989): 205–23.

4 D. Perring, "Excavations in the Souks of Beirut: An Introduction to the Work of the British-Lebanese Team and Summary Report," *Berytus* 43 (1997–98): 9–43; D. Perring, H. Seeden, P. Sheehan, and T. Williams, "BEY 006, 1994–1995, The Souks Area," *Bulletin d'archéologie et d'architecture libanaises* 1 (1996): 176–206.

5 M. Gawlikowski, "A Residential Area by the South Decumanus," in *Jerash Archaeological Project*, vol. 1, *1981–1983*, ed. F. Zayadine (Amman, 1986), 107–36.

6 A. McNicoll, R. H. Smith, and B. Hennessy, *Pella in Jordan 1: An Interim Report on the Joint University of Sydney and the College of Wooster Excavation at Pella, 1979–1981* (Canberra, 1982); A. W. McNicoll, P. C. Edwards, J. Hanbury-Edison, B. Hennessy, T. F. Potts, R. H. Smith, A. Walmsley, and P. Watson, *Pella in Jordan 2: The Second Interim Report on the Joint University of Sydney and College of Wooster Excavation at Pella, 1982–1985* (Sydney, 1992).

7 E. Khamis, "The Shops of Scythopolis in Context," in Lavan, Swift, and Putzeys, eds., *Objects in Context, Objects in*

the study of a broader time span, illustrating the transition from the Byzantine agora to the Islamic *sūq*.[8] By contrast with earlier periods, our knowledge of the development of commercial areas in medieval cities in Anatolia, Greece, and the Balkans is unfortunately much more limited.[9] However, despite the restricted archaeological possibilities in the commercial center of Constantinople, the *Book of the Prefect*, a legal text from the year 912, provides us with important data on industrial and commercial activities in the capital.[10]

Even when possible, archaeological excavation of commercial spaces does not always convey a satisfactory understanding of the activities that were carried out there.[11] Studies to date of artifacts used in commercial transactions preserved in museums and private collections clearly demonstrate that the archaeology of the late antique and Byzantine marketplace provides only a fragmentary view of reality. My purpose in this chapter is to provide a fuller view of the marketplace through a combined study of objects, iconographical and written sources, and archaeology. I will attempt to reveal the movable structures and buoyant dynamics of the marketplace by exploring traces of commercial activity outside the shop walls. Pack animals carrying goods in the colonnaded streets, merchants plying their trade in a wooden stall, encounters between merchants and customers, people eating, drinking, and entertaining themselves—all will illuminate for us the blind spots in archaeology in a wide chronological span from late antiquity to the Byzantine age.

First, the examination of available visual sources supplemented by written accounts will help illustrate the context of daily exchanges with an emphasis on vendors of food and drink and on money changers, ubiquitous figures in the marketplace throughout the history of Byzantium. Second, I will examine the various categories of instruments for weighing and measuring, which offer material evidence for the exercise of trade. To elucidate the context of the use of these instruments and discuss their dating, I will focus on examples found in archaeological excavations. But since the full variety of measuring tools for dry and liquid goods is not represented in the archaeological record, I will also refer to written and visual sources or, when possible, to examples kept in museums. In the latter case, the original context of use is often revealed by inscriptions on the objects. Finally, I will consider the whole range of these instruments taken together in order to stress the motive forces that conditioned their decoration and inscriptions. I will attempt to illustrate the role of the numerous apotropaic and religious devices in the fight against fraud, a central concern affecting everyday life in the marketplace in all periods.

Use, 439–72; S. Agady et al., "Byzantine Shops in the Street of the Monuments at Bet Shean (Scythopolis)," in *What Athens Has to Do with Jerusalem: Essays on Classical, Jewish, and Early Christian Art and Archaeology in Honor of Gideon Foerster,* ed. L. V. Rutgers, Interdisciplinary Studies in Ancient Culture and Religion 1 (Louvain, 2002), 423–506.

8   See also discussion in M. Mundell Mango, "The Commercial Map of Constantinople," *DOP* 54 (2000): 203. Mention should also be made of the pioneering works by J. Sauvaget, "Le plan de Laodicée-sur-mer," *BEODam* 4 (1935): 81–114; idem, *Alep: Essai sur le développement d'une grande ville syrienne des origines au milieu du XIXᵉ siècle* (Paris, 1941).

9   On Amorion in Phrygia, an extremely important site for illustrating the continuity of commercial and industrial activities well into the dark ages, see Chris Lightfoot's chapter in this volume, "Business as Usual? Archaeological Evidence for Byzantine Commercial Enterprise at Amorium in the Seventh to Eleventh Centuries." For Corinth, see R. L. Scranton, *Mediaeval Architecture in the Central Area of Corinth,* Corinth 16 (Princeton, N.J., 1957), 37, 48–49, 58–60, 67–68, 77–78; for Thessalonike, see C. Bouras, "Imports, Exports and Autarky in Byzantine Thessalonike from the Seventh to the Tenth Century," in *Post-Roman Towns, Trade and Settlement in Europe and Byzantium,* ed. J. Henning, vol. 2, *Byzantium, Pliska, and the Balkans,* Millennium-Studien zu Kultur und Geschichte des ersten Jahrtausends n. Chr. 5.2 (Berlin, 2007), 89–118. Archaeological testimonies about industrial installations in Greece in the period from the fifth to the fifteenth century are presented in Ἀρχαιολογικά τεκμήρια βιοτεχνικών εγκαταστάσεων κατά τη Βυζαντινή εποχή 5ος–15ος αιώνας: Ειδικό θέμα του 22ου συμποσίου Βυζαντινής και Μεταβυζαντινής αρχαιολογίας και τέχνης, Ἀθήνα, 17–19 Μαΐου 2002 (Athens, 2004). For a thorough survey on production and trade throughout the boundaries and the history of the Byzantine Empire, see A. E. Laiou and C. Morrisson, *The Byzantine Economy* (Cambridge, 2007).

10 *Eparchenbuch;* see Mundell Mango, "Commercial Map of Constantinople," 189–207; eadem, "The Porticoed Street at Constantinople," in *Byzantine Constantinople: Monuments, Topography and Everyday Life,* ed. N. Necipoğlu (Leiden, 2001), 29–51; M. Kaplan, "Les artisans dans la société de Constantinople aux VIIᵉ–XIᵉ siècles," ibid., 245–60; T. Thomov and A. Ilieva, "The Shape of the Market: Mapping the Book of the Eparch," *BMGS* 22 (1998): 105–16.

11 "[I]n the overwhelming majority of cases the contents of a commercial space have not been conserved in the archaeological deposits that we can recover, not only because the commercial material itself may well have been perishable, but also because once any commercial property has been abandoned, its stock is rarely left lying idle in the empty shops": Zanini, "Artisans and Traders," 386.

The Context of Daily Exchanges and the Marketplace

The Transport of the Goods to the Marketplace

The caravan of laden camels depicted on a mosaic pavement from the Great Colonnade at the Agora of Apameia in the Museum of Damascus, dated 469 by an inscription, or the camel driver Mouchasos on the border of a mosaic pavement from the church of St. George in Deir el-'Adas, Syria, dated 722, illustrates the role of pack animals in daily exchanges in Byzantium.[12] More common pack animals throughout the Mediterranean were the mule and the donkey.[13] Despite the scarcity of visual sources for the medieval period, an eloquent testimony is the representation of a young monk accompanying a donkey laden with two pottery jars in the painted cycle of St. Gerasimos at the church of St. Nikolaos Orphanos, Thessalonike, dated to the fourteenth century. The monk holds a pitcher into which he is about to pour water from one of the jars with the aid of a funnel.[14]

Wine, on the other hand, was usually transported in skins. In the seventh-century *Life of St. Symeon the Fool,* there is a story about a muleteer who was on his way to buy some wine for his home. We learn that the man transported the wine in skins (ἀσκήδια).[15] Pack animals loaded with liquids were also part of military expeditions. A military treatise by Constantine Porphyrogennetos mentions the use of paired flasks (ζυγοφλάσκια) for imperial wine, while the wine for the *magistroi* and *patrikioi* is transported in wineskins (ἀσκία). The text also mentions leathern flasks (σκορτζίδια) for the imperial oil.[16] According to the context of use, different sizes of wineskins were available. The altar table in the representation of the Communion of the Apostles on the sixth-century Riha paten in Dumbarton Oaks, for example, shows two wineskins framed by liturgical vessels of similar size.[17]

In relation to the nature of the load, the estimated capacity of each pack animal was fixed officially. In a fifth- or sixth-century customs tariff from Anazarbos in Cilicia, the unit of measure in use is the γόμος, abbreviated by the letters γο.[18] In the military treatises of Constantine Porphyrogennetos we learn that the maximum load that could be borne by pack animals on military expeditions was eight *modioi,* in order to prevent them from being overburdened and consequently unable to complete the journey.[19] Bulkier goods exceeding the capacity of a pack animal had to be carried in carts.[20]

---

12 C. Dulière, *Mosaïques des portiques de la grande colonnade,* Fouilles d'Apamée de Syrie, Miscellanea 3 (Brussels, 1974), 25, pl. 21; J. Balty, *Mosaïques de Syrie* (Brussels, 1977), 110–11, no. 50; P. Donceel-Voûte, *Les pavements des églises byzantines de Syrie et du Liban: Décor, archéologie et liturgie,* 2 vols., Publications d'histoire de l'art et d'archéologie de l'Université catholique de Louvain 69 (Louvain-la-Neuve, 1988), 45–49, figs. 20–21, 23; K. M. Dunbabin, *Mosaics of the Greek and Roman World* (Cambridge, 1999), 185, fig. 199. Many other examples are to be found in late antique mosaic pavements. A man leading a camel laden with baskets and amphorae appears on the mosaic floor of a basilica found in the fields of the kibbutz Kissufim in the Negev. A dedicatory inscription provides the date 576; see R. Cohen, "A Byzantine Church and Its Mosaic Floors at Kissufim," in *Ancient Churches Revealed,* ed. Y. Tsafrir (Jerusalem, 1993), 277, pl. 22c. The laden camel is also a recurring motif in the decoration of fifth-century clay lamps from North Africa. See A. Ennabli, *Lampes chrétiennes de Tunisie (Musées du Bardo et de Carthage)* (Paris, 1976), 107, no. 422, pl. 22; L. Wamser and G. Zahlhaas, eds., *Rom und Byzanz: Archäologische Kostbarkeiten aus Bayern,* exhibition catalogue (Munich, 1998), 136, no. 155. For a bronze lamp in the Louvre taking the shape of a dromedary laden with four baskets, see M.-H. Rutschowscaya and D. Bénazeth, eds., *L'Art copte en Égypte: 2000 ans de christianisme,* exhibition catalogue (Paris, 2000), 196, no. 219.

13 See, for example, the representation of a laden donkey on a mosaic pavement in the nave of the church of Choeifat in Khaldé, Lebanon, dated to the sixth to seventh century: Donceel-Voûte, *Les pavements des églises byzantines,* 360, fig. 344.

14 A. Tsitouridou, *Ὁ ζωγραφικὸς διάκοσμος τοῦ Ἁγίου Νικολάου Ὀρφανοῦ στὴ Θεσσαλονίκη: Συμβολὴ στὴ μελέτη τῆς Παλαιολόγειας ζωγραφικῆς κατὰ τὸν πρώιμο 14ο αἰώνα,* Βυζαντινὰ μνημεῖα 6 (Thessalonike, 1986), 177–78, pl. 71. Color illustrations in *Ayios Nikolaos Orphanos: The Wall Paintings,* ed. Ch. Bakirtzis (Thessalonike, 2003), 78–79. See also M. Parani, *Reconstructing the Reality of Images: Byzantine Material Culture and Religious Iconography (11th–15th Centuries),* Medieval Mediterranean 41 (Leiden, 2003), 226, fig. 236.

15 *Life of Symeon the Fool* 165.1; Léontios de Néapolis, *Vie de Syméon le Fou et Vie de Jean de Chypre,* ed. A.-J. Festugière and L. Rydén (Paris, 1974), 99.

16 *Constantine Porphyrogenitus: Three Treatises on Imperial Military Expeditions,* ed., English trans., and commentary J. F. Haldon, CFHB 28 (Vienna, 1990), 102–3.

17 *DOCat,* 1:12–15, no. 10, pl. 11.

18 G. Dagron and D. Feissel, *Inscriptions de Cilicie,* Travaux et mémoires du Centre de recherche d'histoire et civilisation de Byzance, Monographies 4 (Paris, 1987), 170–73, no. 108, pl. 45.

19 Haldon, ed., *Constantine Porphyrogenitus: Three Treatises,* 120–21, 240.

20 Illustrations of laden carts are part of the iconographic repertory of mosaic pavements from late antiquity. See the oxcart laden with wineskins in the depiction of the scene of Dionysos giving the gift of wine to Ikarios on a late second- or early third-century AD pavement from the House of Dionysos in Nea Paphos, Cyprus: Dunbabin, *Mosaics of the Greek and Roman World,* 227–28, fig. 240.

Depictions of the Marketplace

Depictions of street scenes and markets are not common in the repertory of late antique and Byzantine art. The topographic border illustrating Antioch in the famous mosaic of the Megalopsychia Hunt from the village of Yakto near Daphne, now in the Hatay Archaeological Museum in Antakya and dated to the third quarter of the fifth century, is therefore of exceptional importance (fig. 16.1).[21] The composition, capturing a day in the life of Antioch, offers a visual complement to Libanius's laudatory description of the commercial activities of this city.[22] Boys carrying baskets of provisions, porters of both sexes carrying bundles, a man carrying what appears to be a rolled carpet, women in conversation, parents of both sexes holding their children by the hand, men riding saddled horses—all pass along a section of the colonnaded street, which appears to be reserved for food sellers. One of these latter, who stands between a building called τὸ Δημόσι(ο)ν, a public bath, and another labeled ὁ περίπατος, or meeting place, is selling what would appear to be bread rolls or doughnuts, displayed on a table. The image brings to mind the ταβλία τῶν πλακουνταρίων, or tables of the pastry sellers, mentioned in the *Life of St. Symeon the Fool*.[23] The other activities are more difficult to identify and various interpretations are possible. There is a man standing behind a bench carrying elongated objects that, according to Doro Levi, may be fishes. Antioch indeed had an abundant supply of sea and lake fish.[24] Another merchant stands behind a high counter broadening upward. Here Levi favors the identification of a butcher's chopping block. The next composition is more obscure. Two men are shown swinging a pair of utensils with long handles in a cylindrical vessel set on a tripod with long legs. Levi proposes a brazier, while the red mass under the instruments, which he identifies as shovels, would suggest that these are meat sellers mincing their meat.[25] A more recent study of the scene identifies the figures as men cooking meat on skewers.[26] However, the absence of fire and the long legs of the tripod, as well as the relatively shallow dimensions of the vessel, would imply that the contents are not hot. Judging from the list of goods sold by grocers (σαλδαμάριοι) in the tenth-century *Book of the Prefect*, such spatulas as those here might have served for selling cheese, butter, or honey.[27]

The above scenes are placed in an area adorned with statues, perhaps a city square or forum, which was equally a meeting place for people who entertained themselves with games or ate and drank in nearby taverns.[28] At two different points in this topographic border we find dice players seated on folding chairs, facing each other across a gaming table. As counterparts, there are two instances of a servant pouring out drinks to a reclining customer. Taverns were clearly still an indispensable feature of the marketplace. Excavations carried out in the agorai of late antique cities in the Mediterranean frequently reveal the remains of restaurants or taverns.[29] To round out our view, let us turn to Con-

---

21 J. Lassus, "La mosaïque de Yakto," in *Antioch-on-the-Orontes*, vol. 1, *The Excavations of 1932*, ed. G. W. Elderkin (Princeton, N.J., 1934), 128–50; D. Levi, *Antioch Mosaic Pavements*, vol. 1 (Princeton, N.J., 1947), 330–31, pl. 79–80; *IGLSyr* 3.2:544–48, no. 998; C. Kondoleon, ed., *Antioch: The Lost Ancient City*, exhibition catalogue (Princeton, N.J., 2000), 115.
22 Libanius, *Oration XI: The Antiochikos*, chaps. 254–58, 266–67; *Antioch as a Centre of Hellenic Culture as Observed by Libanius*, trans. with an intro. by A. F. Norman, Translated Texts for Historians 34 (Liverpool, 2000), 59–63.
23 *Life of Symeon the Fool* 146.2–3, ed. Festugière and Rydén, 80; S. A. Ivanov, *Holy Fools in Byzantium and Beyond* (Oxford, 2006), 133. Bread sellers standing behind similar tables are depicted on a late sixteenth- to early seventeenth-century icon in Corfou. See J.-C. Cheynet, "La valeur marchande des produits alimentaires dans l'Empire byzantin," in Βυζαντινῶν διατροφή καὶ μαγειρίαι: Πρακτικά ἡμερίδας "Περί τῆς διατροφῆς στὸ Βυζάντιο," ed. D. Papanikola-Bakirtzi (Athens, 2005), 34, fig. 2.
24 Libanius, *Oration XI: The Antiochikos*, chaps. 254–58, 266–67; see Norman, trans., *Antioch as a Centre of Hellenic Culture*, 60–61: "Everything is at hand. All you need do is to lend an ear to the fish-sellers crying their wares" (chap. 258).
25 Levi, *Antioch Mosaic Pavements*, 331.
26 Kondoleon, *Antioch*, 115.
27 *Eparchenbuch* 13.1. Given the table habits of the Byzantines, an alternative use for the spatulas might have been to crush and blend a foodstuff into a sauce.
28 On the forum/agora as a place for social encounters, see Lavan, "Fora and Agorai," 215–24.
29 The great amount of animal bones (sheep, goat, horse, pig, and also shellfish), pottery fragments, and glassware in the form of goblets and flasks together with knives and masonry benches in some of the seventh-century shops in Sardis, for instance, made possible the identification of restaurants and a wine shop next to a number of dye shops. See Crawford, *Byzantine Shops at Sardis*, E1–E3 and W1–W3 (restaurants); E4 (wine shop), 18, 34, 38, 43–45, 52, and fig. 35 (restitution of the interior of E1). See also the discussion in Harris, "Shops, Retailing and the Local Economy," 92–94, 97, 116. For a discussion on the taverns and restaurants in late antique cities, see Putzeys and Lavan, "Commercial Space," 97–100; Lavan, "Fora and Agorai," 228–29; see also J. A. Baird, "Shopping, Eating and Drinking at Dura-Europos: Reconstruct-

Figure 16.1. Topographic border of Antioch from the Megalopsychia Hunt Mosaic; Yakto village, near Daphne, 5th c., Hatay Archaeological Museum, Antakya, inv. no. 1016 (after Levi, *Antioch Mosaic Pavements*, pl. 79)

stantinople and the *Life of St. Andrew the Fool*. When hungry, the holy man often goes to the Artopoleia, where the sellers of beans, bread, cheese, and fruit give him some of the goods they sell.[30] In the same neighborhood, the holy man frequents a tavern, called a καθαροπότιον.[31] Taverns specializing in wine flavored with myrrh (ἐσμυρνισμένον οἶνον) are mentioned in other commercial areas, such as the

---

ing Contexts," in Lavan, Swift, and Putzeys, eds., *Objects in Context, Objects in Use,* 423–32; J. Vroom, "The Archaeology of Late Antique Dining Habits in the Eastern Mediterranean: A Preliminary Study of the Evidence," ibid., 313–61.

30 *The Life of St. Andrew the Fool,* ed. L. Rydén (Uppsala, 1995), 94–95, ll. 1232–35. Rydén dates the *Life* to the tenth century, while Cyril Mango suggested that the text was produced between the years 680 and 695: C. Mango, "The Life of St. Andrew the Fool Reconsidered," *RSBS* 2 (1982): 297–313, esp. 309–10, reprinted in idem, *Byzantium and Its Image: History and Culture of the Byzantine Empire and Its Heritage,* Variorum Reprints (London, 1984), art. VIII.

31 *Life of St. Andrew the Fool,* 38–39, l. 389–90. See also ll. 408, 1397; Appendix l. 172.

Antiphoros, a food market adjoining the Forum of Constantine.³² Elsewhere we find a φουσκάριον, a place in which φούσκα, a cheap and much-diluted acidulous or sour wine, was sold.³³

Further insights into the Byzantine marketplace are provided by the late thirteenth-century painted composition of the weekly procession of the Hodegetria icon in Constantinople in the narthex of the Blachernitissa in Arta, Epiros.³⁴ According to the Spanish traveler Pero Tafur, who visited the capital in 1437–38, a market was held in the square in front of the church of the Hodegetria every Tuesday, when the procession took place.³⁵ The market scenes unfold below the central panel depicting the religious procession on the western wall of the narthex (fig. 16.2). In the background are rows of women watching the event from the windows and balconies of two-story houses above the porticoed street. The emphasis on female attendance in this composition, similarly attested in the market scenes below, may be connected with the conversion of the Blachernitissa from a male monastery into a nunnery sometime before 1230.³⁶ The first merchant on the left, who stands behind his counter, is serving drinks in small pots (φωκάδια) to a group of men swinging jugs in their hands.³⁷ The next inscription identifies a woman selling vegetables (ἡ λαχανοπώλισσα) that look like turnips or radishes.³⁸ As demonstrated by their recurrent use in scenes of the Last Supper in the Palaiologan era, these were common products on the table of the Byzantines. Further to the right, fruits identified as ὀπωρικά, probably apples and pears, are being sold in baskets. The market scenes continue on the southwestern pilaster (fig. 16.3). At the top, there is an old woman with a row of small globular buckets hanging from a large chain around her neck. Two men standing in front of her drink from the vessels that she hands them. In all likelihood she is selling water or perhaps a kind of juice, as was the practice on feast days.³⁹ From travelers' accounts and other texts about this procession we also learn that officials of the church and attendants

32   *Life of St. Andrew the Fool*, 36–37, ll. 351–52 and 309 n. 1. About the Antiphoros, see C. Mango, "Le terme *antiforos* et la *Vie* de saint Marcien économe de la Grande Église," *Mélanges Jean-Pierre Sodini, TM* 15 (2005): 317–28.

33   *Life of St. Andrew the Fool*, 28–29, ll. 235–36. For a discussion on the meaning of the word φούσκα, see also L. Rydén, "Gaza, Emesa and Constantinople: Late Antique Cities in the Light of Hagiography," in *Aspects of Late Antiquity and Early Byzantium*, ed. L. Rydén and J. O. Rosenqvist (Uppsala, 1993), 139; idem, "Style and Historical Fiction in the Life of Andreas Salos," *XVI. Internationaler Byzantinistenkongress, Wien, 4.–9. Oktober 1981: Akten*, vol. 2.3, *JÖB* 32/3 (Vienna, 1982), 178–79; E. Kislinger, "Φοῦσκα und Γληχῶν," *JÖB* 34 (1984): 49–53. In the *Life of Symeon the Fool*, the word stands for a kind of soup, sold together with lentil soup, beans, and different kinds of fruit; see 146.6; 153.5, 18; 165.8.

34   M. Acheimastou-Potamianou, *Η Βλαχέρνα της Άρτας: Τοιχογραφίες*, Βιβλιοθήκη της εν Αθήναις αρχαιολογικής εταιρείας 264 (Athens, 2009), 89–92, 133–35, figs. 44, 52–55. The scene develops on the shallow arch on the southern wall of the narthex and on the southwestern pilaster, which supports the arch. It is identified by the inscription Ἡ χαρὰ τῆς ὑπεραγίας Θεοτόκου τῆς Ὁδηγήτριας τῆς ἐν τῇ Κωνσταντινουπόλει (Feast of the All-Holy Theotokos Hodegetria in Constantinople). See also M. Acheimastou-Potamianou, "The Byzantine Wall-Paintings of Vlachernae Monastery (Area of Arta)," in *Actes du XVe Congrès international d'études byzantines, Athènes, 1976*, vol. 2, *Art et archéologie: Communications* (Athens, 1981), 12–14; eadem, "The Basilissa Anna Palaiologina of Arta and the Monastery of Vlacherna," in *Les femmes et le monachisme byzantin: Actes du symposium d'Athènes, 28–29 mars 1988 = Women and Byzantine Monasticism: Proceedings of the Athens Symposium, 28–29 March 1988*, ed. J. Y. Perreault, Publications of the Canadian Archaeological Institute at Athens 1 (Athens, 1991), 43–49; eadem, "Η ζωγραφική της Άρτας στο 13ο αιώνα και η μονή της Βλαχέρνας," in *Πρακτικά Διεθνούς Συμποσίου για το Δεσποτάτο της Ηπείρου (Άρτα, 27–31 Μαΐου 1990)*, ed. E. Chrysos (Athens, 1992), 185–86; B. N. Papadopoulou, *Η Βυζαντινή Άρτα και τα μνημεία της* (Athens, 2002), 82–83. The composition is also discussed in Mundell Mango, "Commercial Map of Constantinople," 205.

35   Pero Tafur, *Travels and Adventures, 1435–1439*, trans. and ed. M. Letts (New York, 1926), 141–42.

36   See A.-M. Talbot, "Affirmative Action in the 13th Century: An Act of John Apokaukos concerning the Blachernitissa Monastery in Arta," in *ΦΙΛΕΛΛΗΝ: Studies in Honour of Robert Browning*, ed. C. N. Constantinides et al. (Venice, 1997), 399–409; S. E. J. Gerstel, "Painted Sources for Female Piety in Medieval Byzantium," *DOP* 52 (1998): 91. On the presence of women in the marketplace of Constantinople, see A. E. Laiou, "Women in the Marketplace of Constantinople (10th–14th Centuries)," in Necipoğlu, ed., *Byzantine Constantinople*, 261–73.

37   Acheimastou-Potamianou, "Byzantine Wall-Paintings," 13. One may wonder whether the drink served here is not the φούσκα, or a kind of sour wine, discussed above: *Life of St. Andrew the Fool*, 28–29, ll. 235–36.

38   In early Byzantium a common word used for the seller of vegetables is *krambitas*. See the tombstone of a *krambitas*, dated to the fifth to sixth century from Lerna, in the Argolid, at the Archaeological Museum of Corinth; J. Koder, "Η καθημερινή διατροφή στο Βυζάντιο με βάση τις πηγές," in Papanikola-Bakirtzi, ed., *Βυζαντινών διατροφή και μαγειρίαι*, 23, fig. 6. Radishes are believed to offer an antidote to drunkenness. See E. Anagnostakis and T. Papamastorakis, "'. . . and Radishes for Appetizers': On Banquets, Radishes and Wine," ibid., 162–66.

39   See, for example, the mention of juices to be distributed at the feast of the Savior and the feast of the Holy Anargyroi in the typikon of the Pantokrator monastery: P. Gautier, "Le typikon du Christ Sauveur Pantocrator," *REB* 32 (1974): 94–95; *BMFD*, 2:761.

Figure 16.2. Procession of the Hodegetria in Constantinople and market scenes, narthex of the church of the Blachernitissa, Arta, western wall, late 13th c. (photo courtesy of D. Christos Merantzas, Pythagore Database, University of Ioannina)

Figure 16.3. Old woman with buckets around her neck (top) and Khazar selling caviar on an equal-arm balance scale (bottom), narthex of the church of the Blachernitissa, Arta, southwestern pilaster, late 13th c. (photo courtesy of D. Christos Merantzas, Pythagore Database, University of Ioannina)

of the icon distributed holy water to the sick and holy oil to the faithful.⁴⁰ It is therefore also possible that the old woman is distributing holy water. Further down, another merchant is identified as a "Khazar selling caviar" (ὁ χάζαρης πουλῶν τὸ χαβιάρι). Standing behind a wooden table, he weighs the caviar on a balance scale, observed by his customer, who holds a white money-bag in his left hand. This composition is an interesting indication of the consumption of caviar, which, in Byzantine times, was not a luxury product as it is today.⁴¹ The term "caviar" was applied to the processed, salted roe of several fish species, whose quality and prices differed widely. High-grade caviar may have been reserved for the imperial court and aristocracy, but several other brands were affordable to people of more modest means. In retail shops caviar was sold stuffed in the tail of the fish's skin, called φούσκα, while individual portions ready to be served were sold in wicker baskets.⁴² As Nicolas Oikonomides observed, the merchants plying their trade in the market of the Hodegetria might be identified with the παζαριῶται whom the Venetian

---

40 C. Angelidi, "Un texte patriographique et édifiant: Le 'discours narratif' sur les Hodègoi," *REB* 52 (1994): 141, ll. 115–21; 149, ll. 253–57. See also C. Angelidi and T. Papamastorakis, "The Veneration of the Virgin Hodegetria and the Hodegon Monastery," in *Mother of God: Representations of the Virgin in Byzantine Art,* ed. M. Vassilaki, exhibition catalogue (Athens, 2000), 379.
41 E.g., Ptochoprodromos eats caviar and people make fun of him as χαβιαροκαταλύτης: *Ptochoprodromos,* ed. H. Eideneier,

Neograeca Medii Aevi 5 (Cologne, 1991), 144, poem 4, line 104.
42 On the consumption and trade of Black Sea caviar in Byzantium, see D. Jacoby, "Caviar Trading in Byzantium," in *Mare et litora: Essays Presented to Sergei Karpov for His 60th Birthday,* ed. R. Shukurov (Moscow, 2009), 349–63; see also Cheynet, "La valeur marchande des produits alimentaires," 40 n. 47; P. Schreiner, *Texte zur spätbyzantinischen Finanz- und Wirtschaftsgeschichte in Handschriften der Biblioteca Vaticana* (Vatican City, 1991), 50.

Figure 16.4. Expulsion of the Merchants from the Temple, Protaton church, Mount Athos, early 14th c. (after Gouma-Peterson, "Christ as Ministrant," fig. 11)

merchant Giacomo Badoer, living in Constantinople from 1436 to 1440, distinguished from respectable traders keeping shops (*botegier*).[43]

The Expulsion of the Merchants from the Temple is another scene that provides a glimpse into the marketplace in Byzantium. The central figure here, as in the well-known sixth-century miniature from the Rossano Gospels, is the money changer, who has picked up his table in such a hurry that he drops his coins.[44] The iconographic type of this scene was more or less firmly fixed by the ninth century.[45] The scene gained greater popularity in the decorative program of Palaiologan churches in Greece and the Balkans. In the early fourteenth-century painted panel in the Protaton church on Mount Athos, the money changer carries a big money-bag and the box of his balance scale, which has fallen onto the ground together with numerous coins (fig. 16.4).[46] The balance scale is drawn with precision. One can even distinguish the bracket with a hinged pointer, indicating perfect horizontality.[47] The money changer stands amid a crowd of bird sellers, goats, and sheep. In the same scene at the contemporary church of St. Nikita in Čučer, near Skopje in Macedonia, one merchant has a birdcage and others have heavy bags

---

43 N. Oikonomidès, *Hommes d'affaires grecs et latins à Constantinople (XIIIᵉ–XVᵉ siècles)*, Conférence Albert-le-Grand 1977 (Montreal, 1979), 107. See *Il libro dei conti di Giacomo Badoer: Costantinopoli, 1436–1440*, ed. U. Dorini and T. Bertelè, Il Nuovo Ramusio 3 (Rome, 1956).

44 G. Cavallo, *Codex Purpureus Rossanensis* (Rome, 1992), 80, fol. 2r, fig. 3.

45 T. Gouma-Peterson, "Christ as Ministrant and the Priest as Ministrant of Christ in a Palaeologan Program of 1303," *DOP* 32 (1978): 197–216.

46 Ibid., 204, fig. 11.

47 A similar bracket with pointer in copper alloy that once belonged to a balance scale was found in Byzantine levels in Corinth; see G. R. Davidson, *The Minor Objects*, Corinth 12 (1952; reprint, Meriden, Conn., 1987), 216–17, no. 1674, pl. 98.

around their necks, while yet another man carries a large jug on his shoulder. Here, the money changer's box is left open on the ground, revealing the compartments in the various shapes of the weights, pans, and balance arm of the scale.[48]

The above images provide visual evidence for the use of wooden stalls by street sellers and money changers in late antiquity and Byzantium. In late antiquity, the colonnaded streets were equipped with holes at regular intervals into which were fitted the shafts of the wooden stalls, aligned in continuous rows, while the numerous topos inscriptions found on the columns or paving stones of late antique agorai bear the name of the traders who owned stalls at specified places.[49] These stalls can also be identified by lists of commodities for sale scratched or painted on various spots. For example, text in very irregular cursive, scratched on the plaster lining of a recess on the outer, east-facing wall of the Theater building in Aphrodisias, dated to the fourth century, gives a list of common foodstuffs (honey, wine, bread, pulses) and what appears to be storax, or a fragrant gum. The quantities of the commodities are not given, but against each entry is a figure expressed in myriads that seems to correspond to the prices.[50]

Complementary information on the stalls may be gleaned from written sources. From a passage of Niketas Choniates we learn, for example, that the Selçuk sultan Kılıç Arslan was unable to cross the forum without being mocked by the money changers, who rattled the iron parts of their tables at him during his visit to Manuel I in 1162.[51] The most widespread word for stalls or counters in Byzantine texts is ταβλία. In the *Book of the Prefect*, the word ἀββάκιον is used for the tables of the goldsmiths, linen merchants, and perfumers.[52] Another common word for stalls was προβολή.[53] Depending on their nature, the goods displayed on the wooden stalls were contained in sacks, baskets, or other special containers. In the fruit-gathering season it appears that greengrocers displayed their best wares in glass vessels (ὑελίνων σκευῶν), as in the case of the choice figs for sale in a shop in the *Life of St. Andrew the Fool*.[54] And in the chapter of the *Book of the Prefect* on the perfumers, we read that the latter displayed their fragrances in small vessels, κάβια, set out on counters.[55]

Material Culture of Exchange: Instruments for Weighing and Measuring
Weighing Instruments

The weighing instruments used in the marketplace fall into two major categories: the steelyard (κάμπανος) used for gross weights and the symmetrical balance scale (ζυγός) used for smaller commodities.[56] The steelyard is a sort of lever divided by an

---

48 Gouma-Peterson, "Christ as Ministrant," 204, fig. 13; G. Millet and A. Frolow, *La peinture du Moyen Âge en Yougoslavie (Serbie, Macédoine et Monténégro)*, vol. 3 (Paris, 1962), pl. 41.1–2. A similar box is set on the table of Julian the tax collector in his representation in the twelfth-century Sinai manuscript of the liturgical homilies of Gregory of Nazianzus, Sinai Cod. 339, fol. 73v: K. Weitzmann and G. Galavaris, *The Monastery of Saint Catherine at Mount Sinai: The Illuminated Greek Manuscripts*, vol. 1, *From the Ninth to the Twelfth Century* (Princeton, N.J., 1990), 144, fig. 478. See also G. Galavaris, *The Illustrations of the Liturgical Homilies of Gregory Nazianzenus*, Studies in Manuscript Illumination 6 (Princeton, N.J., 1969), fig. 9.

49 See the discussion in L. Lavan, "The Agorai of Sagalassos in Late Antiquity: An Interpretative Study," *Anatolian Studies* (forthcoming), and idem, "From *polis* to *emporion*?" above, 333–76; T. W. Potter, *Towns in Late Antiquity: Iol Caesarea and Its Context* (Oxford, 1995), 36–38, 52; Zanini, "Artisans and Traders," 391–94. On place inscriptions from the Agora of Aphrodisias, see *ALA*, nos. 198–206. See also J.-P. Rey-Coquais, *Inscriptions grecques et latines de Tyr*, Bulletin d'Archéologie et d'Architecture Libanaises 3 (Beirut, 2006), 90–92; Lavan, "Monumental Streets of Sagalassos," 206–7.

50 *ALA*, no. 213. In the late antique period, large sums were often expressed in myriads. A myriad was calculated on different currency bases, depending on the time and place. Lists of goods for sale painted on the façades at some two-story shops in Apameia built in the second century are thought to be of later date. See L. Reckmans, "Fresques des portiques de la grande colonnade," in *Apamée de Syrie: Bilan des recherches archéologiques,*

1965–1968, ed. J. Balty (Brussels, 1969), 118, 121; J.-C. Balty, *Guide d'Apamée* (Brussels, 1981), figs. 81–82; Mundell Mango, "Commercial Map of Constantinople," fig. 17.

51 *Nicetae Choniatae Historia*, ed. J. A. van Dieten, CFHB 11.1 (Berlin, 1975), 120, ll. 82–85; the passage is mentioned in M. F. Hendy, *Studies in the Byzantine Monetary Economy, c. 300–1450* (Cambridge, 1985), 248.

52 *Eparchenbuch* 2.3, 9.7, 10.1.

53 Ibid., 13.2. For other occurrences of the word προβολή, see N. Oikonomides, "Quelques boutiques de Constantinople au Xe s.: Prix, loyers, imposition (Cod. Patmiacus 171)," *DOP* 26 (1972): 347–48; Ph. Koukoules, Βυζαντινῶν βίος καὶ πολιτισμός, 6 vols. (Athens, 1948–57), 2.1:236.

54 *Life of St. Andrew the Fool*, 102, ll. 1347–49.

55 *Eparchenbuch* 10.1.

56 For the complementary use of steelyards and balance scales, see the prescriptions in the *Book of the Prefect*: *Eparchenbuch* 10.5, 13.1. See also G. Vikan and J. Nesbitt, *Security in Byzantium: Locking, Sealing and Weighing*, Dumbarton Oaks Byzantine Collection Publications 2 (Washington, D.C., 1980), 29–34; J. Nesbitt, "Steelyards and Weights," in *Sacred Art, Secular Context: Objects of Art from the Byzantine Collection of Dumbarton*

axis, usually called a *fulcrum,* into two unequal arms (for an example see fig. 15.3).[57] When goods were hung from a weighing collar on the shorter arm, a counterpoise weight was moved back and forth along the longer, graduated arm until the beam was horizontal. The weight of the goods was indicated by the position of the counterweight on the graduated scale. Most late antique steelyards were equipped with three (or two) fulcra with suspension hooks, attached on a different side of the four-sided beam at varying distances from the weighing collar. Each fulcrum corresponded to a different calibrated face on the longer beam. The counterpoise weights often take the shape of a sculptured bust made of hollow cast bronze, open at the bottom and filled with lead to obtain the exact weight. More modest examples are of plain lead or lead with a copper-alloy casing and take a globular or oblong shape (fig. 16.5).[58] Symmetrical balances, in contrast, have a slender horizontal beam. A movable suspension device is attached to the center of the beam with a vertical pointer, which was centered between the legs of the suspension device when the two ends of the beam were in equilibrium.[59] Weighing on the balance scale was performed with flat weights of copper alloy, lead, and glass. Glass weights were primarily used for weighing coins.[60]

In order to illustrate the steelyards and balance scales in the context of their use, I have selected

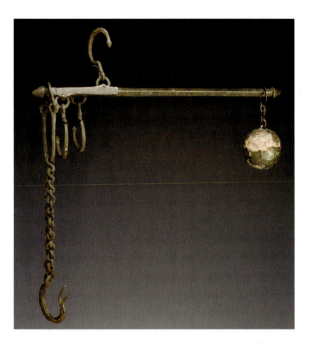

Figure 16.5. Steelyard with globular counterweight, 5th–7th c., Pera Museum, inv. no. PMA 588 (photo courtesy of the Pera Museum)

examples from excavations in the commercial areas of late antique urban centers as well as from shipwrecks. Numerous steelyards and balance scales, used concurrently, were found in seventh-century dye shops and restaurants at Sardis. The catalogued finds include nine steelyards and four accessory pieces of steelyards, eighteen symmetrical balances or parts of balances, and fifteen copper-alloy flat weights. Elaborate sculpted busts are not found among the counterweights, which have simpler globular and pearlike shapes.[61] Further interesting finds are two steelyards inscribed with Greek and Arabic graduation marks from the shops of Bet Shean.[62] A bronze steelyard beam with incised markings indicating weight was found in June 2004 in the excavations of the Agora at Athens. The steelyard comes from fifth- to sixth-century levels and was unearthed in a street lined with shops.[63] Mention should also

---

Oaks, Washington, D.C., ed. A. Kirin, exhibition catalogue (Athens, Ga., 2005), 105.

57   For a synthetic study on steelyards, see J. Garbsch, "Wagen oder Waagen?" *Bayerische Vorgeschichtsblätter* 53 (1988): 191–222. For detailed descriptions of the method of their use, see G. Kenneth Sams, "The Weighing Implements," in *Yassı Ada,* ed. G. F. Bass and F. Van Doorninck Jr., vol. 1, *A Seventh-Century Byzantine Shipwreck* (College Station, Tex., 1982), 221–23; J. C. Waldbaum, *Metalwork from Sardis,* Archaeological Exploration of Sardis 8 (Cambridge, Mass., 1983), 80–81; N. Karydas, "Χάλκινος κάμπανος (καντάρι) από παλαιοχριστιανική επαυλή τής Θεσσαλονίκης/A Bronze Steelyard from an Early Christian Villa in Thessaloniki," *Μουσείο Βυζαντινού Πολιτισμού = Museum of Byzantine Culture* 5 (1998): 36–45 (in Greek and English).

58   See, for example, Istanbul, Pera Museum, inv. no. PMA 588; first published in G. Kürkman, *Suna-İnan Kıraç Akdeniz Medeniyetleri Araştırma Enstitüsü: Anadolu Ağırlık ve Ölçüleri* (Istanbul, 2003), 211, no. 30.

59   See Waldbaum, *Metalwork from Sardis,* 82–83; Davidson, *The Minor Objects,* 216–17; nos. 1671–78, pls. 98–99; R. M. Harrison, *Excavations at Saraçhane in Istanbul,* vol. 1, *The Excavations, Structures, Architectural Decoration, Small Finds, Coins, Bones, and Molluscs* (Princeton, N.J., 1986), 257, nos. 466–68.

60   C. Entwistle, "Byzantine Weights," in *EHB,* 2:612.

61   Crawford, *Byzantine Shops at Sardis,* E7, 61, 64, fig. 306; E14, 86, 88, figs. 468, 476; Waldbaum, *Metalwork from Sardis,* 80–87, pls. 28–30.

62   Y. Tsafrir and G. Foerster, "Bet Shean Excavation Project—1988/1989," *Excavations and Surveys in Israel 1989/1990,* vol. 9 (1991): 127; Khamis, "The Shops of Scythopolis in Context," 458–59, 466–68, figs. 12, 18.

63   J. McKesson Camp II, "Excavations in the Athenian Agora 2002–2007," *Hesp* 76 (2007): 634–35.

be made of the recent excavations at the Theodosian harbor in Yenikapı, Istanbul, which have yielded several implements related to conducting trade. In addition to a counterpoise weight with the bust of Athena and a balance scale with slightly concave pans dated from the fifth to seventh century,[64] the finds also include a wooden box that holds a heavily corroded balance scale and three flat weights. The interior of the box has two circular compartments for the pans of the balance scale and a T-shaped one for its horizontal beam with pointer, while a set of small circular compartments are reserved for the flat weights. The outer surface of the box's sliding lid bears a schematic representation of a building with a triangular roof that shelters a large cross. The background of the lid is covered with punched, concentric circles.[65] This object, dated to the sixth century, has similarities with wooden cases for balance scales from Byzantine Egypt.[66] Finally, most of the numerous weighing instruments and accessories yielded by the Corinth excavations were also probably associated with the exercise of trade. By contrast with the above contexts, which are all from late antiquity, Corinth brings materials covering the whole Byzantine period.[67]

Weighing instruments are common in the catalogues of finds from shipwrecks. The Yassı Ada wreck (625–26) off the southern Aegean coast of Turkey is one of the best-known examples.[68] The weighing instruments all come from the same part of the galley. They include three steelyards, two counterweights, a weighing pan, and a set of eight flat bronze weights that were originally held in a wooden case, as well as a glass pendant weight. With a length of 1.46 meters and a maximum weight capacity of 400 Roman pounds, the longest steelyard is the largest preserved example from antiquity. The fulcrum beam has an animal head on its end, apparently some sort of feline or dog. A punched dot two-line inscription between the two fulcra indicates that its owner, George *presbyteros* and *nauklēros,* was also the captain of the ship. The counterpoise weight of this steelyard takes the shape of a bust of Athena, whereas the smaller one is of simple pyriform shape. A further shipwreck from the same period is Dor G (ca. 600–640), found off the coast of Carmel in Israel.[69] The finds here include two bronze steelyards—a larger one with its weighing collar and suspension chains intact, and a smaller one with only the rod preserved. The fulcrum bars of both steelyards bear punched inscriptions providing the name "Psates of Rhion," who was probably their owner. Other Byzantine objects dated to the seventh century were recovered about 20 meters further south of that shipwreck. These include a counterweight in the form of a bust of an empress, artifacts related to fishing, and Byzantine coins, the latest dating from 659 to 663/64.[70] This rare find is important because it shows that "empress" bust counterweights were produced well into the mid-seventh century.[71] Finally, we should consider two shipwrecks in the western Mediterranean. The finds from the La Palud shipwreck at Port-Cros, Var, France, dated to the second half of the sixth century, include a rectangular wooden case holding a money changer's balance

---

64 *Gün Işığında: Istanbul'un 8000 Yılı: Marmaray, Metro, Sultanahmet Kazıları,* exhibition catalogue (Istanbul, 2007), 258, no. Y14; 261, no. Y18.

65 Istanbul Archaeological Museums, inv. no. MRY 08.9000. See M. Gökçay, "Yenikapı Ahşap Buluntularından Seçmeler/ Selected Wooden Finds from Yenikapı," in *Istanbul Arkeoloji Müzeleri 1. Marmaray-Metro Kurtarma Kazıları Sempozyumu Bildiriler Kitabı 5–6 Mayıs 2008 / Istanbul Archaeological Museums: Proceedings of the 1st Symposium on Marmaray-Metro Salvage Excavations, 5th–6th May 2008,* ed. U. Kocabaş (Istanbul, 2010), 146, no. 12.

66 Parallels from Egypt are discussed below; see 422 and note 147.

67 Davidson, *The Minor Objects,* 206–17, pls. 94–99.

68 Sams, "The Weighing Implements," 202–30.

69 S. A. Kingsley and K. Raveh, *The Ancient Harbour and Anchorage at Dor, Israel: Results of Underwater Surveys 1976–1991,* BAR International Series 626 (Oxford, 1996), 69–72, pl. 71; S. A. Kingsley, *A Sixth-Century AD Shipwreck off the Carmel Coast, Israel: Dor D and Holy Land Wine Trade,* BAR International Series 1065 (Oxford, 2002), 1–5, fig. 10.

70 E. Galili and B. Rosen, "Fishing Gear from a 7th-Century Shipwreck off Dor, Israel," *International Journal of Nautical Archaeology* 37.1 (2008): 67–76 and fig. 3.

71 In his dissertation devoted to the counterweight busts, Norbert Franken suggests a dating from the fourth or the early fifth century to the mid-sixth century for the empress bust counterweights, while his chronology for the Athena busts goes from the early fifth to the early seventh century; see N. Franken, "Aequipondia: Figürliche Laufgewichte römischer und frühbyzantinischer Schnellwaagen" (Ph.D. diss., Rheinisch-Friedrich-Wilhelms-Universität zu Bonn, 1994), 92–95. Another empress bust counterweight retrieved from excavations was found in the Octagon of Philippi (built ca. AD 500): G. Gounaris, "Kupfernes altchristliches 'Stathmion' (Gewicht) aus Philippi," *Makedonika* 20 (1980): 209–17; idem, "Chroniques des fouilles et découvertes archéologiques en Grèce en 1981," *BCH* 106 (1982): 582; Franken, "Aequipondia," 180, no. CA 63, pl. 100; D. Papanikola-Bakirtzi, ed., *Everyday Life in Byzantium* (Athens, 2002), 77, no. 25.

Figure 16.6. Steelyard beam from the 11th-c. Serçe Limanı shipwreck (photo courtesy of INA)

and copper-alloy flat weights; and the mid-seventh-century Byzantine shipwreck Grazel B in Gruissan, near Narbonne, Languedoc-Roussillon, has yielded a steelyard and a small pan that once belonged to a symmetrical balance.[72]

In contrast to the great number of steelyards from the seventh century, few have been found in medieval contexts.[73] For this reason the weighing instruments yielded by the eleventh-century Serçe Limanı shipwreck from the southern coast of Anatolia, opposite Rhodes, are of great interest.[74] The steelyard beam with animal heads on the ends suggests that similar types were maintained throughout the Byzantine period (fig. 16.6), though in later examples the animal heads are less elaborate.[75] The counterpoise found close to the Serçe Limanı steelyard beam has a pear-shaped body. Its upper surface displays a distinctive pattern of tongue-shaped motifs in relief. The U-shaped metal suspension shackle hinged to the fulcrum bar provides further evidence for dating. Comparison with a tenth- to eleventh-century iron steelyard from Pliska,[76] and with a bronze example in the Pera Museum, Istanbul, that may be attributed to eleventh- to twelfth-century Anatolia, indicates that flat and longer shackles, sometimes adorned with moldings and other decorative patterns, were introduced in the medieval period (fig. 16.7).[77] The Serçe Limanı wreck has also yielded three symmetrical balances of various sizes, including a fine example equipped with deep pans, and many disk- and barrel-shaped weights. The decorative moldings on the slender beams of the balance scales (fig. 16.8) provide, once again, evidence for a dating in the medieval period.

Dry and Liquid Measuring Instruments

Commerce in dry and liquid goods required the use of measuring tools in the form of vessels. These were usually named after the unit of measure for which they were intended. But unfortunately, few examples have been identified, either in the archaeological record or in museum collections.

Modios

The standard measure for grain in late antiquity and Byzantium was the *modios*. From the *Parastaseis Syntomoi Chronikai* we learn that a bronze modios was set up in the time of Valentinian (364–75) in a public place on the Mese. Above the modios was a pair of bronze hands fixed on spikes, reminding merchants of the penalty of mutilation prescribed

---

72 L. Long and G. Volpe, "Le chargement de l'épave 1 de la Palud (VIᵉ s.) à Port-Cros (Var): Note préliminaire," in *Fouilles à Marseille: Les mobiliers (Iᵉʳ–VIIᵉ siècles ap. J.-C.)*, ed. M. Bonifay, M.-B. Carre, and Y. Rigoir, Études massaliètes 5, Travaux du Centre Camille-Jullian 22 (Paris, 1998), 339–40, fig. 303; *Les épaves de Gruissan*, ed. Y. Solier, Archaeonautica 3 (Paris, 1981), 28, 30–35.

73 See examples from the Corinth excavations: Davidson, *The Minor Objects*, 216–17, nos. 1662–65, 1668, 1671–74, 1677–78, pls. 98–99.

74 F. Hocker, "Weight, Money, and Weight-Money: The Scales and Weights from Serçe Limanı," *INA Quarterly* 20.4 (1993): 13–21.

75 A steelyard beam with stylized animal-head terminal was found in a ninth-century context in Corinth: Davidson, *The Minor Objects*, 216, no. 1664, pl. 98.

76 The Pliska steelyard comes from the monastery at the Basilica: J. Henning, "Catalogue of Archaeological Finds from Pliska," in Henning, ed., *Post-Roman Towns*, 2:688–89, no. 154, pl. 13.

77 Istanbul, Pera Museum, inv. no. PMA 1348; see Kürkman, *Anadolu Ağırlık ve Ölçüleri*, 37, 211, no. 32. Similar attachment devices for fulcrum hooks are attested on Ottoman steelyards from Anatolia (57, 115, 240, nos. 148–49). The decorative terminal on the beam of the Pera Museum steelyard compares with a steelyard found in Byzantine layers in Corinth; see Davidson, *The Minor Objects*, 216, no. 1662, pl. 98.

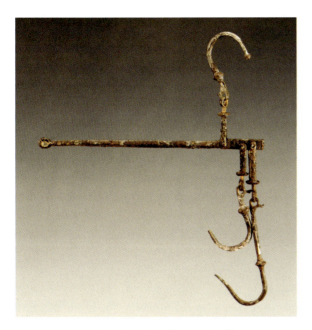

Figure 16.7. Steelyard, medieval Anatolia (?), Pera Museum, inv. no. PMA 1348 (photo courtesy of the Pera Museum)

Figure 16.8. Equal-arm balance scale from the 11th-c. Serçe Limanı shipwreck (photo courtesy of INA)

for fraud.[78] Despite the lack of material evidence, we know the modios from visual sources.[79] In late antique iconography, the modios appears as a standard motif in depictions of Circus games, where it contains the coins to be distributed as prize money to winning horses. Usually cylindrical, the modios is shown as a vessel with straight or flared sides standing on a protruding pedestal, sometimes equipped with two lateral handles.[80]

Measuring Tables or sekomata

Another official measure in antiquity for both dry and liquid goods was the *sekoma*, or *rabo* in Latin.[81] This was a marble block with bowl-shaped cavities lined with metal, either removable or permanently fixed. As illustrated by a recent find from the excavations at Caunos, on the border of Caria and Lycia, the cavities of antique *sekomata* were labeled with

---

78 Originally, the modios was located between the Philadelphion and the Forum Tauri. The mention of a modios in the Amastrianon, in the text of the *Patria*, may suggest that the original modios was moved there: *Constantinople in the Early Eighth Century: The Parastaseis Syntomoi Chronikai*, ed. and trans. Av. Cameron and J. Herrin (Leiden, 1984), 75, chap. 12.

79 An evocative example is found on a black-and-white mosaic pavement from Ostia, dated to the mid-third century, among a vast complex of warehouses. Three men are shown measuring the grain poured into a large cylinder, a modios: G. Becatti, *Scavi di Ostia*, vol. 4, *Mosaici e pavimenti marmorei* (Rome, 1961), 33–36, no. 58, pls. 157–58; Dunbabin, *Mosaics of the Greek and Roman World*, 313–14, fig. 313.

80 See N. Duval, "Les prix du cirque dans l'Antiquité tardive," in *Le cirque et les courses de chars: Rome-Byzance,* ed. C. Landes, exhibition catalogue (Lattes, 1990), 138; idem, "L'introduction des couronnes métalliques et des 'cylindres de prix' en Occident d'après l'Histoire Auguste," in *Historiae Augustae Colloquium Parisinum*, ed. G. Bonamente and N. Duval (Paris, 1991), 171–82. For further discussion, see C. Morrisson, "Le Modiolos: Couronne impériale ou couronne pour l'empereur?" *Mélanges Gilbert Dagron, TM* 14 (2002): 499–510. On mosaic pavements from Tunisia, as in one example found in the private baths of a domain in the region of Bizerte and kept in the Bardo Museum, Tunis, the modios has a yellow color evoking metal and is studded with cabochons. See M. Blanchard-Lemée, M. Ennaïfer, and H. and L. Slim, *Sols de l'Afrique romaine: Mosaïques de Tunisie* (Paris, 1995), 197–98, fig. 145. A modios also appears below the representation of the victorious charioteer on a small group of silk textiles dated to the eighth century, such as the well-known example at the musée de Cluny in Paris. See *Byzance: L'art byzantin dans les collections publiques françaises,* exhibition catalogue (Paris, 1992), 194, no. 129.

81 One example found in the Latin municipality of Choba, on the Mauretanian coast in North Africa, bears an inscription stating that it is the official *rabo* of the municipality (*Rabo publicus municipii Aelii Chobae*). Late second–early third century; capacity 27–28 L; with metal liner, 26 L. See P. Salama, "Recherches sur la notion de 'Rabo'," *Bulletin de la Société des Antiquaires de France* (1993): 190–96.

Figure 16.9. Measuring table or sekoma, episcopal quarter of Byllis, Albania, excavation inv. no. 764 (photo courtesy of Nicolas Beaudry)

Figure 16.10. Sekoma, episcopal quarter of Byllis, Albania, excavation inv. no. 1070 (photo courtesy of Nicolas Beaudry)

inscriptions specifying the measures, while holes at the bottom of each cavity facilitated the filling of a receptacle placed beneath.[82] The sekoma from Caunos was reused for street paving in the sixth century. However, the archaeological record shows that measuring tables continued to be used in later periods. A fragmentary example was found during the excavations of the Agora of Argos in 1967. The object was reemployed in later constructions, but had belonged to the late levels of the Agora.[83] Two sekomata recently found during excavations of the episcopal quarter of Byllis, Albania, attest to their use in the early Christian period. One was retrieved together with numerous limestone furnishings in a room of a large building complex, which included a succession of hearths. The sekoma has a large central cavity and four bowls (fig. 16.9). It was cut out of stones taken from the nearby antique theater, as were also the stone basins, mortars, and pestles found in the same area and used for the processing and preparation of food.[84] A later subdivision of the same room has yielded a second sekoma cut out of a block from the *proskēnion* frieze of the theater. It has two large cavities and four smaller ones (fig. 16.10).[85]

Liquid Measures for Wine and Oil

The standard measure used by the Byzantines for liquids was the *xestēs* (Lat. *sextarius*) and the same word was applied to the measuring instrument itself.[86] The most common type of vessel used for measuring small quantities of liquids was a copper-alloy cylindrical jug equipped with a lateral handle. An engraved inscription providing the unit of measure and sometimes the capacity allow their identification as measuring instruments, but unfortunately very few examples were preserved. Such a find was yielded during the excavations of the fortress of Niš in Serbia in 1972. The associated material makes possible a dating in the second half of

---

82 A. Diler, "Kaunos'tan bir ölçek taşı (Sekoma)," in *Calbis: Baki Öğün'e Armagan: Mélanges offerts à Baki Öğün,* ed. C. Işık, Z. Çizmeli Öğün, and B. Varkıvanç, Türk Tarih Kurumu Yayınları VII-226 (Ankara, 2007), 75–85.

83 J.-P. Sodini and H. Serian, "Argos: Secteur α (Agora)," *BCH* 92 (1968): 1021, fig. 34.

84 Byllis excavations, inv. no. 764. Length 45 cm; width 45 cm; diameter of cavities 13–38 cm. N. Beaudry and I. Tassignon, in N. Beaudry, P. Blanc, Y. Cerova, et al., "Byllis (Albanie)," *BCH* 127 (2003): 628.

85 Byllis excavations, inv. no. 1070. Diameter of cavities 6.0–27.5 cm. N. Beaudry, in P. Chevalier et al., "Byllis," *BCH* 130 (2006): 849, figs. 16–17.

86 See M. Mundell Mango, *Silver from Early Byzantium: The Kaper Koraon and Related Treasures,* ed. G. Vikan (Baltimore, 1986), 107, no. 14, who observes that the word *xestēs* gave birth to the composite word *cherniboxestin* (or *cherniboxeston*), used for the pair formed by the ewer and basin. See also the occurrence of the word ὑελοξέστια, identified as wine or water carafes, in lists of household contents: N. Oikonomides, "The Contents of the Byzantine House from the Eleventh to the Fifteenth Century," *DOP* 44 (1990): 211.

Figure 16.11. "Borchardt measure," sixth century, British Museum, inv. no. 1972,0103.1 (photo courtesy of the British Museum)

the fourth century.[87] The vessel is in the shape of a truncated cone and has a capacity of 0.818 liters. The body is marked with lathe-turned parallel grooves. An engraved inscription ending with a Christogram runs around the rim. It reads "Sex(tarium) I exaggivit (sic) Naissat(ibus) Uran(ius?)." The form *exagivit* is uncommon. The editor of the inscription, Martin Gabričević, stresses its link with the Latin *exagium* and the Greek ἐξαγιάζω. Uranius was probably the official authority who guaranteed the accuracy of the measure for the people of Niš. From the ratio of 1:1.5 between the *sextarius italicus* (0.5436 L) and the *sextarius* of this vessel, Gabričević concludes that the measure used here may be identified as the *sextarius castrensis*.[88] The same author mentions a second copper-alloy measuring tool from Serbia, found in 1966 on the site of the Roman cemetery at Sremska Mitrovica during the construction of a road. The copper-alloy vessel has the shape of a truncated cone and is spouted. The exterior of the body is divided into bands by five pairs of lathe-turned concentric grooves. The section below the rim is inscribed SEX ITAL, "Sex(tarius) Ital(icus)." The vessel has a capacity of 0.645 liters of water and 0.580 liters of oil.[89]

A further example is the sixth-century "Borchardt measure," said to be from Antioch and today in the British Museum (fig. 16.11).[90] This copper-alloy vessel of cylindrical shape was originally equipped with a lateral handle of which only traces remain. It has a capacity of 0.960 liters, or 33.5 fluid ounces. As in the above example, the body is covered with lathe-turned decorative bands. The latter frame an engraved inscription in five lines:

ΕΙΤΑΛΙΚΟC ΤΗC ΔΕCΠΟΤΙΑC
ΤΟΥ ΚΟΜΗΤΟC ΟΥΑΔΙΛΑ ΑΠΟ
ΚΕΛΕΥCΕΩC ΤΟΥ ΑΡΧΩΝΤΟC
ΕΓΡΑΨΑ ΚΑΙ ΕΞΑΓΙΑCΜΕΝΟΝ
ΞΕCΤΙΝ ΑΠΟ ΟΝΟΜΑΤΟC
ΕΟΡΤΑCΙΟΥ ΔΙΚΑΙΟΝ ΟΝΚΙΩΝ
ΙΚΟCΙ ΤΕCΑΡΩΝ CΤΡΑΤΙΟΤΙΚΩΝ.

I, Italikos, of the dominion of Count Wadila, inscribed in accordance with an order of the governor this *xestin*, duly certified under the authority of Heortasios, as a just measure of twenty-four soldier's ounces.

The name Wadila is Germanic. Italikos was perhaps an agent of Wadila in the East, in which case Wadila would have been a western *comes* and is perhaps identical with the Wadila who was *comes* of Sicily

---

87 Height 9.0 cm; diameter (top) 10.4 cm; diameter (bottom) 11.1 cm. M. Gabričević, "A Contribution to Roman Metrology," *Archeologia Iugoslavica* (1974): 42–43.
88 Ibid., 43. For a discussion on the ratio between italic and castrensis measure, see R. P. Duncan-Jones, "The Size of the Modius Castrensis," *ZPE* 21 (1976): 59–61. See also J. Gascou, *Fiscalité et société en Égypte byzantine*, Bilans de Recherche 4 (Paris, 2008), 321.
89 Gabričević, "A Contribution to Roman Metrology," 43–44.
90 London, British Museum, inv. no. 1972,0103.1. Height 132.0 mm; max. diameter 104.8 mm. Borchardt was the first owner of the object. He acquired it in Alexandria, where he was told that it came from Antioch. The British Museum acquired it from K. J. Hewitt in 1972. See L. Borchardt and O. Viedebantt, "Ein spätromisches Massgefäss," *AA* in *JDAI* 38–39 (1923–24): 154–64; W. F. Oakeshott, "The Borchardt Measure," *JHS* 83 (1963): 154–56; Jalabert and Mouterde, *IGLSyr* 3.2:586–87, no. 1073; E. Schilbach, *Byzantinische Metrologie*, HAW 12.4, Byzantinisches Handbuch 4 (Munich, 1970), 110; M. Gabričević, "Ογκία Στρατιοτική," *ZRVI* 19 (1980): 7–15; C. J. S. Entwistle, *A Catalogue of the Late Roman and Byzantine Weights and Measures in the British Museum* (forthcoming), no. 817.

between 507 and 511.⁹¹ The capital iota of KAI preceding the word ΕΞΑΓΙΑϹΜΕΝΟΝ has a short horizontal stroke that creates a cross shape, thereby strengthening the official value of the inscription and placing it under divine protection. Ἀπὸ ὀνόματος is not a common formula. Heortasios, to whom it refers, is a name well attested in the Eastern Empire but not attested in the prosopography of the later Roman Empire.⁹² He was probably the official charged with certifying measures.

In a discussion of the metrology of the Borchardt measure, R. P. Duncan-Jones disputes its earlier identification as a measure of grain for soldiers and argues that it is a measure of oil.⁹³ He points to the fact that the Syriac version of Epiphanius's *Treatise* gives two standards of volume. It first gives the oil weight of the Italian xestēs (*sextarius*) as 22 ounces, while the ratio between the Italic and castrensis measure is about 1:1.5.⁹⁴ In this case, the Borchardt measure would have contained 33 ounces of oil. But elsewhere the *Treatise* says that "the Italian xestēs holds 22 ounces (of oil); the *castrensis* similarly holds 24 ounces more or less."⁹⁵ The alternative ratio of 1:1.375 between the Italic and castrensis standard conforms with the capacity of the Borchardt measure. Another, more recent, interpretation by Constantin Zuckerman suggests that the unit of the Borchardt measure was the xestēs of Gothic soldiers, roughly double the standard xestēs, used to calculate their daily ration of wine.⁹⁶

The measuring of larger quantities of liquids required the use of ceramic amphorae and jars of various sizes. The unit of measure (xestēs) abbreviated in various ways was painted on the shoulder of the vessels. However, the metrological system adopted to indicate the capacity of late antique amphorae is complicated and difficult to understand. The xestēs was subject to change in accordance with the nature of the transported goods, the region, and the period. Very often, attempts to correlate the capacity of late antique amphorae to given standards have failed because during this period different modules coexisted: the standard Roman xestēs (0.539 L),⁹⁷ the Cypriot xestēs (0.546 L), the Syrian xestēs (0.674 L), and the Alexandrine xestēs (0.728 L)⁹⁸ are the most common units. The study of the tituli painted on late antique amphorae found during the excavations of the Agora of Athens has suggested that the Alexandrine xestēs was the most commonly used unit from the third to the fifth–sixth centuries. Recent archaeological research indicates, however, that such general statements may need to be qualified.⁹⁹ In this context we might also note a passage from a letter of Michael Choniates, metropolitan of Athens (1182–1204), who informs his correspondent, kyr Isaiah Antiocheites, that he has sent him oil in a water bag (*askos*) containing 12 Attic *xestai*.¹⁰⁰

Though ceramic jars and amphorae with *tituli* as well as leather bags were more appropriate for transport, in domestic contexts (both private and monastic) marble vessels were also used. A marble jar in the Istanbul Archaeological Museums, said to have been found on the island of Chalke (Heybeliada) in the sea of Marmara, bears such a *titulus* (fig. 16.12).¹⁰¹ This large jar has a globular body resting on a short base. The broad recess around the rim indicates that it was originally equipped with a flat lid. The surface is not polished. An inscription is inserted within a *tabula ansata* carved on the shoulder: Ξ(έσται) ΤΝΕ, "three

---

91   J. R. Martindale, *The Prosopography of the Later Roman Empire*, vol. 2, *AD 395–527* (Cambridge, 1980), 9.

92   One example is a topos inscription on a column base in Aphrodisias, dated to the third–fourth century; *ALA*, no. 195 (Heortasios *koniortos*).

93   Duncan-Jones, "The Size of the Modius Castrensis," 59–61.

94   *Epiphanius' Treatise on Weights and Measures: The Syriac Version,* ed. and trans. J. E. Dean and M. Sprengling, Oriental Institute of the University of Chicago, Studies in Ancient Oriental Civilization 11 (Chicago, 1935), 13–14, chap. 46c.

95   Ibid., 55, chap. 66c.

96   C. Zuckerman, *Du village à l'Empire: Autour du registre fiscal d'Aphroditô (525/526),* Centre de recherche d'histoire et civilisation de Byzance, Monographies 16 (Paris, 2004), 164–65.

97   A slightly different value of 0.547 l is offered by Gascou, *Fiscalité et société,* 321.

98   Ibid., 321, gives the value of 0.716 liters.

99   M. Lang, *Graffiti and Dipinti,* Athenian Agora 21 (Princeton, N.J., 1976), 55–64. See D. Pieri, *Le commerce du vin oriental à l'époque byzantine, V^e–VIIe siècles: Le témoignage des amphores en Gaule,* Bibliothèque archéologique et historique 174 (Beirut, 2005), 79, 136; J.-L. Fournet and D. Pieri, "Les *dipinti* amphoriques d'Antinoopolis," in *Antinoupolis,* ed. R. Pintaudi, Scavi e materiali 1 (Florence, 2008), 175–216. See also the chapter by Pieri in this volume, "Regional and Interregional Exchanges in the Eastern Mediterranean during the Early Byzantine Period: The Evidence of Amphorae."

100 ἀπεστάλη τῇ ἁγιωσύνῃ σου ἔλαιον (ἀσκὸς πλήρης χωρῶν δώδεκα ξέστας ἀττικούς); see *Michaelis Choniatae Epistulae,* ed. F. Kolovou, CFHB 41 (Berlin, 2001), letter 84, l. 15.

101 I am indebted to Denis Feissel, who drew my attention to this object. Istanbul Archaeological Museums, inv. no. 78.102 T. Height 95.0 cm; max. diameter at mouth 37.0 cm; diameter base 30.0 cm; height of the foot 4.3 cm.

Figure 16.12. (a) Marble jar with titulus, late antique, Istanbul Archaeological Museums, inv. no. 78.102 T; (b) titulus, detail (photos courtesy of the Istanbul Archaeological Museums / T. Birgili)

to indicate the quantity of 430 xestai. The unit of measurement is not indicated.[103] Another marble jar of similar shape, approximately half the size of the Istanbul example, is preserved in the Spätantikes Museum in Berlin and bears an engraved inscription identifying it as an oil measure.[104] The inscription reads ΕΛΕΟΥ (for ΕΛΑΙΟΥ) ΞΕΣΤ(ΑΙ) ΝΔ, "54 *xestai* of oil." The vessel has a capacity of 59.6 liters, which gives a module of 1.1 liters for the xestēs. This corresponds to double the standard Italic xestēs (0.539 L). On the basis of the form of the letters and the champlevé ornament around the neck, the object has been attributed to the tenth to eleventh century and is thought to have been intended for liturgical use.

A further unit of measure that the Byzantines used for wine was the *metron*.[105] The British Museum has a copper-alloy jug handle decorated with a punched inscription framed by two crosses. It reads ΜΕΤΡΟΝ ΔΙΚΕΙΝ ΓΕΩΡΓΙΟΥ ΔΙΑΚ(ΟΝΟΥ), "The true measure of George the deacon" (fig. 16.13).[106] The arch-shaped handle with a thumb rest on top has a horseshoe-shaped lateral projection for attachment at the upper part of the neck. This device is well-attested on copper-alloy ewers and *authepsae*, or samovars, dated to the sixth to seventh centuries.[107] As in the case of the Borchardt measure,

hundred and fifty-five *xestai*." The jar can be dated to the fourth to sixth century.[102] A similar large marble storage jar was found in a late Roman house to the northeast of the *tetrapylon* in Aphrodisias. The letters ΥΛ inscribed on the shoulder would appear

102 The use of the letter Ξ as an abbreviation for *xestēs* is attested on the tituli of amphorae, especially on the fourth- to fifth-century LR1 type manufactured on the Cilician coast. See Pieri, *Le commerce du vin oriental*, 78–79, 101.

103 *ALA*, no. 215, pl. 44.
104 Berlin, Staatliche Museen zu Berlin, inv. no. 4696. Height 47.9 cm; max. diameter 50.1 cm; thickness 1.5–2.2 cm. The jar is said to come from the region of Bursa in Anatolia; see L. Wamser, ed., *Die Welt von Byzanz: Europas Östliches Erbe,* exhibition catalogue (Munich, 2004), 356, no. 781; O. Wulff, *Altchristliche und mittelalterliche, byzantinische und italienische Bildwerke,* vol. 1, *Altchristliche Bildwerke* (Berlin, 1909), 23–24, no. 41.
105 See Schilbach, *Byzantinische Metrologie*, 112–14. From the chapter devoted to the tavern keepers in the *Book of the Prefect*, we learn that in tenth-century Constantinople, the μέτρον had to contain 30 liters of wine, and what is called the μίνα, 3 liters: *Eparchenbuch* 19.1.
106 London, British Museum, inv. no. 1986,0703.1. The interior of the handle has a max. diameter of 11 cm; exterior diameter 14 cm; height 13 cm.
107 See B. Pitarakis, "Survivance d'un type de vaisselle antique à Byzance: Les authepsae en cuivre des Ve–VIIe siècles," *Mélanges Jean-Pierre Sodini, TM* 15 (2005): 678–85, figs. 1–2, 5, 8, 12–13; M. Mundell Mango, "Beyond the Amphora: Non-Ceramic Evidence for Late Antique Industry and Trade," in *Economy and Exchange in the East Mediterranean during Late Antiquity: Proceedings of a Conference at Somerville College, Oxford, 29th May, 1999,* ed. S. Kingsley and M. Decker (Oxford, 2001), 100, fig. 5.10 (copper-alloy objects from the Plemmyrion shipwreck near Syracuse, Sicily). Lateral handles with a horseshoe-shaped projection, sometimes enriched with dedicatory inscriptions, are also

Figure 16.13. Bronze handle of a jug that served as a wine measure, 6th–7th c., British Museum, inv. no. 1986,0703.1 (photo courtesy of the British Museum)

the word ΔΙΚΑΙΟΝ, with variations and different spellings, intended to emphasize the accuracy of the measure, are common on various measuring instruments[108] as well as on flat copper-alloy weights.[109] The jug to which this handle belonged was probably intended for liturgical use. This object and the above marble jar from Berlin thus introduce the category of liturgical xestai; and to these, one may add a mid-sixth-century silver ewer from the Hama treasure in the Walters Art Museum.[110] However, in this instance, as in the references to xestai in church inventories on papyri dated to the fifth to sixth centuries,[111] it is unclear whether the word *xestin* refers to the measure or to the ewer itself.

Ethics, Magic, and the Protection of Transactions
Protective Devices against Fraud in the Decoration of Weighing Instruments

"There shall be among you just balances and just weights and a just liquid measure" (Leviticus 19:36). This biblical prescription is beautifully illustrated in the ninth-century manuscript of the Sacra Parallela in Paris (fig. 16.14).[112] Two youths in short tunics hold balances in their left hands. While one of them also carries on his shoulder a cylindrical container, perhaps a *modios* for grain, the other holds a ewer that may be a *xestion* for liquids. The second youth holds with two fingers the cord from which the balance hangs in apparently exemplary fashion, conforming with the principles of honest weighing.[113]

From the prescriptions of the *Book of the Prefect* we learn that in tenth-century Constantinople, weighing instruments and measures had to bear the stamp of the eparch. If the inspector of weights (βουλλωτής) detected the absence of a regulation stamp, the merchant was liable to severe penalties ranging from flogging and shaving to the payment of fines, confiscation, and exile.[114]

---

attested on silver chalices of the fifth and sixth centuries. See I. Kalavrezou, ed., *Byzantine Women and Their World,* exhibition catalogue (New Haven, 2003), 110–11, nos. 49–50.

108 For example, the graffito on the shoulder of a small pottery jug of a mid-third-century type from the Agora of Athens mentions it as an honest wine measure: ο[ἰ]νηρὸς δίκαιο[ς]. The graffito of a further example from the same period reads ξέστης δίκαιος. See Lang, *Graffiti and Dipinti,* 61, nos. Ha 27 and Ha 28.

109 See also a money weight dated to the eleventh–twelfth centuries in the Cabinet des Médailles, Paris, with the inscription ΔΙΚΑΙΟΣ ΣΤΑΘΜΟΣ ΤΟΥ ΤΡΑΧΕΟΣ ΥΠΕΡΠΥΡΟΝ. V. Laurent, "Le 'juste poids' de l'hyperpyron trachy," *Congrès international de numismatique, Paris, 6–11 juillet, 1953,* vol. 2, *Actes* (Paris, 1957), 299–307; discussed in C. Morrisson, "Byzantine Money: Its Production and Circulation," in *EHB* 3:918. Another formula attested on a money weight is Θ(εοτόκε) Β(οήθει) ΔΙΚΕΣΥΝΗ (for ΔΙΚΑΙΟΣΥΝΗ) ΚΑΛΗ: G. Schlumberger, *Mélanges d'archéologie byzantine: Monnaies, médailles, méreaux, jetons, amulettes, bulles d'or et de plomb, poids de verre et de bronze, ivoires, objets d'orfèvrerie, bagues, reliquaires, etc.,* Première série (Paris, 1895), 341. ΔΙΚΕ and ΔΙΚΕΟΝ are found on money weights and commercial weights as well. For the first category, see S. Bendall, *Byzantine Weights: An Introduction* (London, 1996), 42–43, nos. 109–10. A commercial weight in Athens bears the inscription ΔΙΚΕΑ. See B. Basilopoulou, "Βυζαντινά σταθμία του Νομισματικού Μουσείου Αθηνών: Συμβολή στη μελέτη του Βυζαντινού σταθμιτικού συστήματος," *Ἀρχαιολογική Ἐφημερίς* (1983): 255, no. 4.

110 See Mundell Mango, *Silver from Early Byzantium,* 107, no. 14.

111 E.g., *Papyri Graecae Wessely Pragenses (P.Prag. II)*, ed. R. Pintaudi, R. Dostalova, L. Vidman, et al., Papyrologica Florentina 26 (Florence, 1995), 78, 3; Mundell Mango, *Silver from Early Byzantium,* 263–64, no. 91.

112 Sacra Parallela, BnF, Manuscrits, grec 923, fol. 201v; K. Weitzmann, *The Miniatures of the Sacra Parallela, Parisinus Graecus 923,* Studies in Manuscript Illumination 8 (Princeton, N.J., 1979), 58, fig. 67, pl. 18.

113 See the edict of Constantine the Great (305–37): "Now, when gold is paid, it shall be received with level pans and equal weights, in such a fashion that the end of the cord (i.e. the cord from which the balance was suspended) is held with two fingers so as to permit the level and equal movement of the balance." Translation in Hendy, *Studies,* 329. See also Nesbitt, "Steelyards and Weights," 104–5.

114 *Eparchenbuch* 6.4, 11.9, 12.9, 13.2, 16.6, 19.1 and 4.

Figure 16.14. Balances and weights (Leviticus 19:36), Sacra Parallela, BnF, Manuscrits, grec 923, fol. 201v (photo courtesy of the BnF)

The detection of fraud was a crucial concern also reflected in decorative patterns on weighing and measuring instruments. The presence of the imperial image provided a symbolic link to imperial authority ensuring legality and reliable standards. Imperial portraiture was a conventional feature on copper-alloy flat weights in the early Byzantine period.[115] Emperors are also to be found in the iconographic repertory of counterpoise weights. The well-known series of so-called Constantine weights represent a seated emperor holding an orb in his right hand, while his left hand rests on a shield placed at the side of the throne. According to the shape of the orb, the group may be divided into two variants: one with a plain orb and one with a cross on its top. The figure is dressed in a mantle draped diagonally over the left shoulder and arm, leaving the upper body naked. On his head is a gem-studded diadem. The shield has a projecting boss at its center and sometimes a star-like ornament, a staurogram and a motif that recalls the emblem of horns terminating in goats' heads used by the cornuti, a regiment of Teutonic warriors that fought with Constantine at the Battle of the Milvian Bridge in 312.[116] In addition to the ten counterweights already identified in the literature, an unpublished example is to be found in the Pera Museum in Istanbul (fig. 16.15).[117] The deep folds of

---

115 Entwistle, "Byzantine Weights," 613, figs. 8–9; Vikan and Nesbitt, *Security in Byzantium,* 34; Bendall, *Byzantine Weights,* 13, 18–23, 31, 34–39.

116 See Franken, "Aequipondia," 101–2, 192–93, nos. CC1–CC9, pls. 115–17. On this group, see also A. Alföldi and M. C. Ross, "A Teutonic Contingent in the Service of Constantine the Great and Its Decisive Role in the Battle at the Milvian Bridge: With a Discussion of Bronze Statuettes of Constantine the Great," *DOP* 13 (1959): 179–83; *DOCat* 1:60–61, no. 70; *Romans and Barbarians,* exhibition catalogue (Boston, 1976), 122–23, no. 135; S. Ćurčić and A. St. Clair, eds., *Byzantium at Princeton: Byzantine Art and Archaeology at Princeton University,* exhibition catalogue (Princeton, N.J., 1986), 71–72, no. 46. For a reappraisal of the discussion on the Princeton weight, see J. Bardill, *Constantine: Divine Emperor of the Christian Golden Age* (Cambridge, 2012), 164–66; A. Demandt and J. Engemann, eds., *Imperator Flavius Constantinus: Konstantin der Grosse,* exhibition catalogue (Trier, 2007), 375, nos. I.9.24–25 (one of the two examples illustrated here, from an anonymous private collection in Germany, does not appear among the nine pieces published by Franken). For an example found in Rudnik, Bulgaria (Franken, "Aequipondia," no. CC7), see M. Cullin-Mingaud, M. Doncheva, C. Landes, and C. Huguenot, eds., *Des Thraces aux Ottomans: La Bulgarie à travers les collections des musées de Varna,* exhibition catalogue (Montpellier, 2006), 198, no. 283.

117 Istanbul, Pera Museum, inv. no. PMA 3824. Height 105 mm; width 44 mm; weight 440.55 g.

Figure 16.15. Bronze counterweight in the shape of a seated emperor: (a) facing; (b) left side; (c) right side; (d) back; 5th–7th (?) c., Pera Museum, inv. no. PMA 3824 (photos courtesy of the Pera Museum)

the draperies are enhanced with short vertical and oblique hatchings, while punched circles and a pattern of interlocking lozenges ornament the back and right side of the throne. The shield, with a central boss, is covered with punched dots. As is also the case with a similar example in Princeton, the orb has a fragmentary tip thought to represent a cross, though it appears to be oversized. Alternatively, one can also envision a winged Nike in place of the cross. The large cross preserved on the orb of an example at the State Historical Museum in Moscow extends from a similar square block, but instead of being vertical, it leans backward, toward the arm of the seated emperor. It has often been suggested that the prototype for these weights was a monumental statue of Constantine the Great. Similarities with the iconography of Zeus/Jupiter and Roma have also been stressed, although exact parallels are not known. It is perhaps more likely that this type was created by combining elements drawn from various prototypes, including imperial medals and coins.[118] Like the "empress bust" counterweights, the type under discussion may be considered a generic representation—here, of the enthroned emperor. The meaning and function of the imperial figure here may perhaps be better understood in light of the wide group of pseudo-coins bearing a generic imperial portrait or the effigy of an ancient ruler of special holiness of power such as Constantine. These imitation coins set in jewelry mounts were designed to ensure that the wearer would enjoy protection or good luck.[119]

Emperors' busts are also included in the iconographic repertory of bronze counterpoise weights. But their identification is often questionable. A counterpoise weight thought to represent an emperor was found during the excavations in the area of the Western Shops at Old Corinth in 1920. The figure here wears a cuirass and helmet and has a large cross motif in relief on the chest. Though it was first identified as a man, Norbert Franken has recently argued that it depicts the female Athena with her hair characteristically parted in the center of her forehead.[120] A well-known counterweight bust in the British Museum, said to have been found in Haifa, is thought to rep-

---

118 Franken, "Aequipondia," 102.

119 H. Maguire, "Magic and Money in the Early Middle Ages," *Speculum* 72 (1997): 1040; repr. in *Approaches to Early-Medieval Art: For Ernst Kitzinger on His Eighty-Fifth Birthday,* ed. L. Nees, Speculum Book (Cambridge, Mass., 1998), 82, and in H. Maguire, *Image and Imagination in Byzantine Art,* Variorum Collected Studies (Aldershot, 2007), art. V.

120 F. O. Waagé, "Bronze Objects from Old Corinth, Greece," *AJA* 39 (1935): 79–86, pl. 21; Davidson, *The Minor Objects,* 212–13: no. 1638, pl. 96; A. McClanan, *Representations of Early Byzantine Empresses: Image and Empire* (New York, 2002), 62–63; Franken, "Aequipondia," 191, no. CB53, pl. 115.

Figure 16.16. Bronze counterweight in the shape of an imperial bust, 4th–7th c., British Museum, inv. no. 1980,0602.17 (photo courtesy of the British Museum)

resent the emperor Phocas (602–10). The bearded figure wears a gemmed diadem and a *paludamentum* fastened on his right shoulder with a circular *fibula* with three *pendilia*. Weighing 5.4 kilograms, this is also one of the largest and heaviest preserved examples of bronze counterweights.[121] The same collection holds an additional, less elaborate counterweight bust in the form of a beardless male figure dressed in a paludamentum fastened with a circular fibula on the right shoulder (fig. 16.16). The plain band framing his forehead may evoke the diadem of an emperor.[122] However, a very similar bust counterweight in a private collection in Munich was identified as an eparch.[123] And as shown by the male bust counterweight in the Virginia Museum of Fine Arts in Richmond, with its distinctive "pageboy hairstyle," the repertory of male counterweight busts was not restricted to emperors. The Richmond figure, dressed in a mantle fastened with a fibula on his right shoulder, may represent a civil authority, perhaps a city eparch, whose image acted as guarantor of reliable standards and government authority.[124] Indeed, portraits of eparchs have also been identified in the decoration of flat copper-alloy and glass coin weights.[125] The suggested chronology for the group of counterweights in the form of emperors or eparchs (?) goes from the early fourth until the sixth or early seventh century.[126]

Interestingly enough, the busts of empresses are prominent in the repertory of counterpoise weights (fig. 16.17).[127] Their striking importance in the context of trade requires further consideration. The common attributes of these figures are a gem-studded diadem with a jewelry necklace or collar and a cylindrical object held in the right hand. In the left hand they either hold a seam of their outer garment or make a gesture of speech or blessing. On account of this gesture, the cylindrical object is better identified as a scroll than a *mappa*, which is not otherwise attested in the official iconography of the empress. The scroll conveys the notions of learning and wisdom, which, in turn, imply good balance and honest behavior. However, in this context it also recalls a legal document, attesting to the integrity of the weight.[128] As Liz James has recently pointed out,

---

121 London, British Museum, inv. no. 67, 10-5, 1. Height 191 mm; max. width 144.5 mm. See D. Buckton, ed., *Byzantium: Treasures of Byzantine Art and Culture,* exhibition catalogue (London, 1994), 100–101, no. 110; Entwistle, *A Catalogue,* no. 810.

122 London, British Museum, inv. no. 1980,0602.17. Height 109.6 mm; max. width 63.5 mm; weight 1046.99 g. See Franken, "Aequipondia," 194, no. CD2, pl. 118; Entwistle, *A Catalogue,* no. 809.

123 Wamser, *Die Welt von Byzanz,* 358, no. 783.

124 A. Gonosova and C. Kondoleon, *Art of Late Rome and Byzantium in the Virginia Museum of Fine Arts* (Richmond, Va., 1994), 247–49, no. 84; McClanan, *Representations of Early Byzantine Empresses,* 61.

125 See Bendall, *Byzantine Weights,* 46–49, 60–63.

126 Franken, "Aequipondia," 94–95.

127 See, for example, Istanbul, Pera Museum, inv. no. PMA 564; Kürkman, *Anadolu Ağırlık ve Ölçüleri,* 210, no. 25. In his catalogue, published in 1994, Norbert Franken records seventy-two empress counterweights: Franken, "Aequipondia," 173–81, nos. CA1–CA 72, pls. 82–101.

128 Let us note that the scroll in the hand of the seated emperor as consul in coin iconography of the fourth and fifth century is identified as the traditional symbol of the *rector orbis* as civilian lawgiver. See P. Grierson and M. Mays, *Catalogue of Late Roman Coins in the Dumbarton Oaks Collection and in the Whittemore Collection: From Arcadius and Honorius to the Accession of Anastasius* (Washington, D.C., 1992), 75. One may also think of a codicil, or official title of office, as in the representation of Pilate holding a scroll in the representation of the Trial of Christ in the sixth-century Rossano Gospels. See Cavallo, *Codex Purpureus Rossanensis,* 86–87, fol. 8v, fig. 14; W. Loerke, "The Miniatures

the diadem and jewelry collar of these female busts are traditional attributes of various female personifications. Rather than being actual portraits of specific empresses of the fifth century, as has long been accepted,[129] these figures, she argues, may be seen as personifications of the virtues both of imperial authority and of such divinities as Good Fortune, Justice, and Tyche, which would fit well in the context of commercial exchange. The magical and apotropaic powers of such female figures contribute to the divinization of the image of the empress, who consequently joins the realm of goddesses and personifications. As a generic figure with superhuman attributes, the "empress" brings good fortune and wealth to the user.[130] Indeed, confusion of identity between imperial images, ancient gods, and personifications was common among the population of Constantinople and may perhaps reflect the general trend of a superstitious attitude toward ancient statuary.[131] Liz James has drawn attention to the confusion over the identity of a seated female statue in the Hippodrome thought to represent the empress Verina (died 484), wife of Leo the Great, or the goddess Athena in the eighth-century *Parastaseis syntomoi chronikai*.[132] But there are also earlier testimonies from late antiquity. For example, in the sixth century, John of Ephesos says that Constantinopolitans knew, or thought they knew, that the personification

Figure 16.17. Bronze counterweight in the shape of an empress bust, 5th–7th c., Pera Museum, inv. no. PMA 564 (photo courtesy of the Pera Museum)

of Constantinople on the coins in their purses was really Aphrodite.[133] But the most eloquent example is the great bronze statue representing Apollo-Helios that Constantine set up as his own effigy on top of the porphyry column of the Forum in 328.[134]

A peculiar "empress" weight in the British Museum, adorned with a prominent three-lobed diadem, earrings, and a necklace of beads or pearls, stands apart from the above group on account of the cross held before its chest (fig. 16.18).[135] The radiating diadem suggests a dating in the sixth century, while the attribute of the cross may allow identification with the Tyche of Constantinople rather than an empress, although a confusion between the two types is also possible. This unique bust can be associated with three other examples, including the

---

of the Trial in the Rossano Gospels," *ArtB* 43 (1961): 180–81. The codicilli are also illustrated among the insignia of various offices in the *Notitia Dignitatum*: P. Berger, *The Insignia of the Notitia Dignitatum* (New York and London, 1981), 175–83.

129 Following the first identifications by R. Delbrueck, *Spätantike Kaiserporträts* (Berlin, 1933), pls. 122–23.

130 L. James, "Who's That Girl? Personifications of the Byzantine Empress," in *Through a Glass Brightly: Studies in Byzantine and Medieval Art and Archaeology Presented to David Buckton*, ed. C. Entwistle (Oxford, 2003), 51–56. On the prominence of female personifications in late antiquity, see also J. Herrin, "The Imperial Feminine in Byzantium," *Past and Present* 169 (2000): 3–35.

131 On the attitudes of the Byzantines toward ancient statuary, see C. Mango, "Antique Statuary and the Byzantine Beholder," *DOP* 17 (1963): 53–75.

132 Cameron and Herrin, eds., *Parastaseis Syntomoi Chronikai*, 139, chap. 61; James, "Who's That Girl?" 53. This passage from the *Parastaseis* is also discussed in McClanan, *Representations of Early Byzantine Empresses*, 58. Misunderstandings of pagan statues wrongly identified with Byzantine emperors are discussed in H. Saradi-Mendelovici, "Christian Attitudes toward Pagan Monuments in Late Antiquity and Their Legacy in Later Byzantine Centuries," *DOP* 44 (1990): 47–61; L. James, "'Pray Not to Fall into Temptation and Be on Your Guard': Pagan Statues in Christian Constantinople," *Gesta* 35 (1996): 12–20.

133 John of Ephesos, *Historiae ecclesiasticae*, ed. E. W. Brooks, CSCO, Scriptores syri, 106.55 (Louvain, 1964), 3:3.14.

134 For a discussion on the ambiguous identity of this statue, see G. Fowden, "Constantine's Porphyry Column: The Earliest Literary Allusion," *JRS* 81 (1991): 119–31.

135 London, British Museum, inv. no. 1980,0602.16. Height 13.6 cm; max. width 7.4 cm; weight 1776.68 g; see Entwistle, *A Catalogue*, no. 806.

Figure 16.18. Bronze counterweight in the shape of an empress or Tyche, 6th c., British Museum, inv. no. 1980,0602.16 (photo courtesy of the British Museum)

the vast array of monumental statues of goddesses, female allegories, and empresses decorating the city center of Constantinople. Besides Tyche, another monumental statue which dominated the marketplace in the capital was that of Athena.[138] It is no accident that this other city divinity, who was also the goddess of justice, wisdom, and crafts, emerges as the second most prevalent figure in the repertory of counterpoise weights in the sixth and seventh centuries.[139] Like Tyche, Athena was a protectress believed to possess apotropaic powers.[140] On counterweights, her apotropaic *gorgoneion* was sometimes complemented with cross motifs on her body or at the base of the weight and with Christian religious invocations.[141] The dominant role of Athena in the context of commercial transactions in late antiquity was perhaps also reinforced by the iconography of Roma,

one from Corinth mentioned above which Norbert Franken identifies as Athena and on which the cross ornaments the cuirass at the center of the chest.[136] As a symbol of civic guardianship, the Tyche of Constantinople is a perfectly plausible choice for the repertory of bronze counterweights. The attributes of the female bust on another example in the British Museum confirm this identification. The figure wears a high mural crown and holds a cornucopia in her left hand, while with her right hand she waves a torch.[137]

Let us now consider the milieu in which these weights were produced. In all likelihood, the models used by bronze workers were taken from among

---

136 Franken, "Aequipondia," 191, nos. CB52–CB53, pl. 115.

137 London, British Museum, inv. no. GR 1907.10-22.1. See James, "Who's That Girl?" 54, fig. 7.2; Franken, "Aequipondia," 197, no. CE8, pl. 123. For representations of Constantinopolis holding a torch and a cornucopia, see ivory diptychs of the fifth to sixth centuries: K. Weitzmann, ed., *Age of Spirituality: Late Antique and Early Christian Art, Third to Seventh Century*, exhibition catalogue (New York, 1979), 173–75, no. 153; G. Bühl, *Constantinopolis und Roma: Stadtpersonifikationen der Spätantike* (Zurich, 1995), 185–86, fig. 98.

138 A 9-meter-high bronze statue of Athena standing on a column was in the Forum of Constantine (van Dieten, ed., *Nicetae Choniatae Historia*, 558–59). See also discussion in Mango, "Antique Statuary," 62–63; Kalavrezou, *Byzantine Women*, 37–38; R. J. H. Jenkins, "The Bronze Athena at Byzantium," *JHS* 67 (1947): 31–33.

139 In his catalogue published in 1994, Norbert Franken records seventy-two empress and fifty-five Athena-Minerva counterweights: Franken, "Aequipondia," 173–81, nos. CA1–CA72, pls. 82–101, and 181–91, nos. CB1–CB40, pls. 102–13. New examples can regularly be added to the above list. A recent find is an Athena counterweight from the excavations of the Theodosian harbor at Yenikapı in Istanbul (Istanbul Archaeological Museums, inv. MRY'07-4900; *Gün Işığında*, 261, no. Y18). I will also mention one example from the seventh-century Saint-Gervais 2 shipwreck at Fos-sur-Mer, France; see M.-P. Jézégou, "Le mobilier de l'épave Saint-Gervais 2 (VIIᵉ s.) à Fos-sur-Mer (B-du-Rh.)," in *Fouilles à Marseilles: Les mobiliers (Iᵉʳ–VIIᵉ siècles ap. J. C.)*, ed. M. Bonifay, M.-B. Carre, and Y. Rigoir, Études massaliètes 5 (Paris, 1998), 351, no. 28 and fig. 314.

140 The monumental statue of Athena in the forum of Constantinople was associated with magical properties well into the middle Byzantine period. In 1204 a mob destroyed the statue, believing that with her outstretched hand Athena had beckoned the invading crusaders; see Cameron and Herrin, eds., *Parastaseis Syntomoi Chronikai*, 251; van Dieten, ed., *Nicetae Choniatae Historia*, 558–59; *O City of Byzantium: Annals of Niketas Choniatēs*, trans. H. J. Magoulias (Detroit, 1984), 305–6. For a discussion of this passage, see Kalavrezou, *Byzantine Women*, 38. The apotropaic meaning of Athena counterweights is also discussed in J. Russell, "The Archaeological Context of Magic in the Early Byzantine Period," in *Byzantine Magic*, ed. H. Maguire (Washington, D.C., 1995), 48–49, fig. 17.

141 The inscription ΚΥΡΙΕ ΒΟΗΘ(Ε)Ι is engraved on the base of an Athena counterpoise weight in the Metropolitan Museum of Art in New York. Crosses are attested on the body of Athena counterpoise weights in the Virginia Museum of Fine Arts, Richmond. See Gonosova and Kondoleon, *Art of Late Rome and Byzantium*, 242–45, no. 83.

who had taken on the features of Minerva in the iconography of coins of the fifth century.¹⁴² The presence of the Tyche of Constantinople in the repertory of counterpoise weights and the probable allusion to Roma through the resemblance to Athena-Minerva bring consistency to the whole group of early Byzantine weights, including the flat copper-alloy weights for symmetrical balance scales, on which the Tychai of the two cities are also depicted.¹⁴³

There is a considerable discrepancy in the stylistic features and workmanship of the counterweights. The details of the facial features and the garments are not always represented with the same precision. An Athena bust counterweight in the Pera Museum, for example, has a high-crested helmet that ends at the front in a trefoil, and the two diagonal stripes of her breastplate, or *aegis,* appear on the chest, but the gorgoneion is lacking (fig. 16.19).

The securing of divine protection was a constant concern for the Byzantines in all aspects of their lives. The importance of devotional practices in the Byzantine marketplace is beautifully illustrated in the prescription in the *Book of the Prefect* that the counters of the perfumers should be set up between the Milion and the icon of Christ of the Chalke, in order that the sweet perfume might waft upward to the icon and at the same time permeate the vestibule of the imperial palace.¹⁴⁴ In the context of commercial transactions, divine protection was invoked as a guarantee against fraudulent practices. Concerning the official weights and measures used for the payment of taxes, chapter 15 of Justinian's *Novella* 128 stipulates that "the latter are to be kept for safeguarding in the most holy church of each city."¹⁴⁵ The protective presence of God within a church building was transferred to any architectural element bearing religious images and invocations. The cross placed under an arch, for instance, is a standard pattern found on copper-alloy weights

Figure 16.19. Bronze counterweight in the shape of Athena, 5th–7th c., Pera Museum, inv. no. PMA 4004 (photo courtesy of the Pera Museum)

of the early Byzantine period, while more elaborate variants include inscriptions invoking the Grace of God (ΘΕΟΥ ΧΑΡΙC) or the help of the Theotokos (ΑΓΙΑ ΜΑΡΙΑ ΒΟΗΘΙ CON).¹⁴⁶ The composition associating the Grace of God formula with a cross under an arcade was also reproduced on the lids of wooden boxes from Egypt containing the balance scales and weights of money changers.¹⁴⁷

Parallel with religious motifs and inscriptions, there is a range of apotropaic devices attested on both weighing instruments and the boxes intended to hold them. A recurrent device is the animal heads

---

142 See Grierson and Mays, *Catalogue of Late Roman Coins,* 83; McClanan, *Representations of Early Byzantine Empresses,* 50–51.
143 See Buckton, ed., *Byzantium,* 50, no. 33; Weitzmann, *Age of Spirituality,* 343–44, nos. 325–26; Vikan and Nesbitt, *Security in Byzantium,* 34–35.
144 *Eparchenbuch* 10.1.
145 Trans. Vikan and Nesbitt, *Security in Byzantium,* 31. See also the discussion in E. Schilbach, "'Rechtes Maß von Gott gesetzt': Zur Legitimierung von Maßen in Antike und frühem Mittelalter," in *Acta Metrologiae Historicae V: Internationaler Kongreß des Internationalen Komitees für Historische Metrologie,* ed. H. Witthöft (St. Katharinen, 1999), 17–31.

146 See Entwistle, "Byzantine Weights," 613, figs. 8–9. Several other examples are in Bendall, *Byzantine Weights,* 31–2, no. 50; 34–35, no. 63; 36–37, nos. 66, 74; 43–44, no. 111; 54–55, no. 158; Basilopoulou, "Βυζαντινά σταθμία," 257, no. 9; D. Feissel and C. Morrisson, in D. Feissel, C. Morrisson, and J.-C. Cheynet, with B. Pitarakis, *Trois donations byzantines au Cabinet des médailles: Froehner (1925), Schlumberger (1929), Zacos (1998),* exhibition catalogue (Paris, 2001), 14, no. 8; 36, no. 12; Ćurčić and St. Clair, eds., *Byzantium at Princeton,* 73, no. 48. A weight bearing the "Grace of God" legend was found in Amorion in association with the destruction layers dated to the years 829–830/31, thus demonstrating that this category of weights continued to be used after the seventh century. See E. A. Ivison, "Amorium in the Byzantine Dark Ages (Seventh to Ninth Centuries)," in Henning, ed., *Post-Roman Towns,* 51.
147 M.-H. Rutschowscaya, *Catalogue des bois de l'Égypte copte* (Paris, 1986), 78–79, no. 271, inv. AF900/AF 5159. 36, fig. 82; Rutschowscaya and Bénazeth, eds., *L'art Copte en Égypte,* 198, no. 227.

Figure 16.20. Copper-alloy box with a folding equal-arm balance: (a) stylized eagles on the lid; (b) interior with folding equal-arm balance scale, 11th–12th c., British Museum, inv. no. 1983,0501.1 (photos courtesy of the British Museum)

on the ends of steelyards from late antiquity to medieval Byzantium. Besides the usual feline heads, boars and dogs are also found.[148] A similar apotropaic intention might explain the presence of two stylized eagles on the lid of a copper-alloy box of a small folding symmetrical balance, presumably intended for weighing coins, in the British Museum (fig. 16.20). The lid, hinged at the back, was originally fastened with a swivel hasp, now broken. The shape and decoration of the hasp may be paralleled by the fulcrum shackles of medieval steelyards from Anatolia (see fig. 16.7). A suspension loop with a ring is soldered along the middle of the left-hand side. The balance has two circular pans with slightly convex bases.[149] Two other copper-alloy boxes of similar type and size are in private collections in Istanbul. One, which has preserved an intact folding balance, bears a cable motif framed by four compartments and six concentric circles on its lid (fig. 16.21).[150] The second, without its balance, is decorated with two schematic nimbed busts, which are the hallmark of a vast production of bronze crosses dated to the tenth to twelfth centuries, but which are also attested on sealing devices and padlocks of the same period (fig. 16.22).[151] On the crosses these figures are sometimes anonymous, but in most cases they are accompanied by inscriptions identifying saints or the Mother of God; on secular objects they are usually anonymous. They probably had a generic protective significance.

Perceptions of the Swindler in Byzantine Society

Let us now examine the appearance of the swindler in written and iconographical sources. George Koutales, the nine-year-old son of a couple engaged in the business of exchanging gold and bartering, was a reader in the church of John the Baptist in Oxeia in seventh-century Constantinople. The boy was trained by his parents in the precise use of scales and weights. The hagiographer of the *Miracles of St. Artemios,* who reports this story, adds that the child detected their vain and unscrupulous profiteering and tampering with scales and their greedy and

---

148 S. Campbell, *The Malcove Collection: A Catalogue of the Objects in the Lillian Malcove Collection of the University of Toronto* (Toronto, 1985), 73, no. 91 (dog's head terminal).

149 London, British Museum, inv. no. 1983,0501.1. Bought from S. Bendall (1983). Box: 62.9 × 39.9 × 14.3 mm; length of balance 113.2 mm; max. diameter of pans 31.8 mm. See Entwistle, *A Catalogue,* no. 816.

150 Istanbul, Emel Kolaşın Collection, inv. no. 777. Box: 65 × 37.5 × 19 mm; length of balance 108 mm; diameter of pans 29 mm. See G. Kürkman, ed., *Osmanlılarda ölçü ve tartılar/Ottoman Weights and Measures,* exhibition catalogue (Istanbul, 1991), appendix to the catalogue (the box is attributed to the early Islamic period).

151 Istanbul, Halûk Perk Museum, inv. no. M. 2935. 64 × 37 × 10 mm. For the use of similar figures on crosses and other kinds of objects, see B. Pitarakis, *Les croix-reliquaires pectorales byzantines en bronze,* Bibliothèque des Cahiers archéologiques 16 (Paris, 2006), esp. 153–63. See also Vikan and Nesbitt, *Security in Byzantium,* 6, fig. 10.

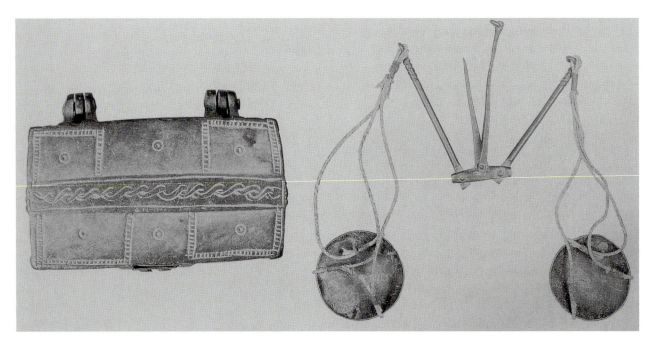

Figure 16.21. Copper-alloy box with a folding equal-arm balance, 11th–12th c., Emel Kolaşan collection, Istanbul (after Kürkman, ed., *Osmanlılarda ölçü ve tartılar,* 95)

Figure 16.22. Copper-alloy balance box: (a) stylized nimbed busts on the lid; (b) interior of the box, 11th–12th c., Halûk Perk Museum, Istanbul, inv. no. M. 2935 (photos by author)

usurious rates of interest.[152] A story in the eighth-century *Parastaseis syntomoi chronikai*—that of Karkinelos, a silversmith who used rigged scales (ζυγοπλάστης)—offers further proof that swindlers were familiar elements of the marketplace in the Byzantine capital.[153] Another evocative testimony is provided by the late eleventh-century *Strategikon* of Kekaumenos. The author states: "Seek no lucrative profession—no matter how clever at it you are—

---

152 V. S. Crisafulli and J. W. Nesbitt, *The Miracles of St. Artemios: A Collection of Miracle Stories by an Anonymous Author of Seventh-Century Byzantium,* Medieval Mediterranean 13 (Leiden, 1997), 198 (Miracle 38).

153 G. Dagron, *Constantinople imaginaire: Études sur le recueil des "Patria"* (Paris, 1984), 43–44, P37; Cameron and Herrin, eds., *Parastaseis Syntomoi Chronikai,* 99–101.

Figure 16.23. (a) Last Judgment scene, Church of St. George, Kalyvia Kouvara, Attica, Greece, second quarter of the 13th c.; (b) the falsifier of weights, detail (photos courtesy of the Byzantine and Christian Museum, BIE [Basiliko Idryma Ereunon] Archives, 72-30, 72-33)

which causes you harm or danger, such as falsifying and clipping pieces off gold coins, drawing up false documents, fabricating seals, and such like."[154]

A strong deterrent against such practices was the inclusion, beginning in the thirteenth century, of the falsifier of weights among the sinners in scenes of the Last Judgment.[155] In the church of St. George in Kalyvia Kouvara, Attica, dated to the second quarter of the thirteenth century, the falsifier of weights is recognizable by the instrument of his vice, a balance scale with small concave pans, hung around his neck (fig. 16.23). On one side of the balance hangs a small bundle. The gravity of his crime is stressed by his association with the figure of Herod, who, in popular tradition, was a symbol of human cruelty. The next sinner in the composition is the greedy archimandrite, depicted with a money bag around his neck.[156] In the narthex program of the Panaghia Mavriotissa in Kastoria, dated to the first half of the thirteenth century, the man who cheats in weighing goods is labeled ὁ παρακανπαιστής (a corrupt form of ὁ παρακαμπανιστής), and is depicted upside down, suspended above the flames, next to the usurer (ὁ τοκηστίς), whose money bag is likewise

---

154 Kekaumenos, *Raccomandazioni e consigli di un galantuomo (Στρατηγικόν)*, ed. M. Dora Spadaro (Alessandria, 1998), 170–71, §122. I am grateful to Michael Featherstone for the English translation of this passage.

155 See M. Garidis, *Études sur le Jugement Dernier Post-Byzantin* (Thessalonike, 1985), 87.

156 D. Mouriki, "An Unusual Representation of the Last Judgement in a Thirteenth Century Fresco at St. George near Kouvaras in Attica," *ΔXAE* 8 (1975–76): 147, 157–58, pls. 76, 86, 88. See also E. Gini-Tsofopoulou, "Late Byzantine Period (13th–15th Century)," in *Mesogaia: History and Culture of Mesogaia in Attica,* ed. G. Aikaterinidis (Athens, 2001), 192–93.

attached to his neck.¹⁵⁷ In a fresco at the Panaghia Phorbiotissa in Asinou, Cyprus, dated 1332–33, the falsifier of weights is identified as both a τοκιστίς, or usurer, and παραζυγιαστής, and is shown with a serpent coiled around his body.¹⁵⁸

* * * * * * * *

Close examination of available visual sources in parallel with texts, archaeological finds, and museum objects brings us closer to everyday life in the marketplace, with emphasis on foodstuffs and drink as essential parts of daily exchange. The study of weighing instruments found in archaeological excavations illustrates their use and function in the exercise of trade. Weighing instruments do not appear to have undergone much change during the eleven centuries of the Byzantine Empire. A more precise understanding of innovations, aside from simplification in the shape of counterweights, would require a greater quantity of dated material from medieval contexts. The measuring instruments for liquids also retain similar shapes throughout the period. It appears, however, that different standards coexisted. Consequently, it is difficult to establish any correlation between a given unit and the actual measure, though it is clear that there were well-established conventions for the use of different standards. Groupings of jugs or ewers of similar size according to their capacity will certainly aid a better understanding of the different standards and practices in various contexts (monasteries, taverns, military expeditions . . .). It is therefore desirable that all future publications of such vessels also mention their capacity.¹⁵⁹ On every occasion, the most important thing was to assure the customer that the measure was "just" and "honest." Official weights and measures used in the payment of taxes were issued by state officials certifying their accuracy. In daily transactions, trust in the accu-

Figure 16.24. Fraudulent tradesman, watercolor, 19th c. (after Kürkman, *Anadolu ağırlık ve ölçüleri*, 149)

racy of the weighing instruments was enhanced by a range of protective devices included in their decoration. The imperial image, religious motifs, and invocations were intended to protect transactions and render them fruitful. Accuracy and fairness are thus the leitmotifs of our study and the motive forces of daily exchange in Byzantium. Nevertheless, despite all the preventive measures, including severe corporal punishment, swindlers were habitués of the marketplace and were thus included among the sinners in scenes of the Last Judgment. As can be seen from a nineteenth-century watercolor of a fraudulent tradesman nailed to a wooden post by his ear, a similar ambience prevailed in late Ottoman Istanbul (fig. 16.24).¹⁶⁰

---

157 N. Moutsopoulos, *Καστοριά: Παναγία Μαυριώτισσα* (Athens, 1967), 39, pl. 53; L. Hadermann-Misguich, "À propos de la Mavriotissa de Castoria: Arguments iconographiques pour le maintien de la datation des peintures dans la première moitié du XIIIᵉ siècle," in *Studia Slavico-Byzantina et Mediaevalia Europensia*, vol. 1, *Studies on the Slavo-Byzantine and West European Middle Ages: In memoriam Ivan Dujčev* (Sofia, 1989), 143–48.

158 A. and J. Stylianou, *Panagia Phorbiotissa, Asinou* (Nicosia, 1973), 66.

159 E.g., an allusion to three-measure pitchers (κουκούμια τριμετραῖα) in the household service that accompanied a military expedition; see Haldon, ed., *Constantine Porphyrogenitus: Three Treatises*, 106–7.

160 Garo Kürkman Collection, Istanbul. See Kürkman, *Anadolu ağırlık ve ölçüleri*, 149.

Conclusion

• SEVENTEEN •

Byzantine Trade
Summary and Prospect

PETER TEMIN

THE SIMPLE SUMMARY OF THIS VOLUME ON Byzantine trade is that it provides a grand, fascinating overview of the sweep of Byzantine trade in a formerly dark age. Cécile Morrisson, the able symposiarch, structured the conference that was its genesis to move from the general to the specific. I follow that pattern in these summary comments and try to make explicit some of the interactions between the original papers that emerged from the discussion.

I hope that my training as an economist will make these comments useful to the historians and archaeologists who attended the conference and will read this book. I start by examining how the discussion of "markets" among ancient and medieval historians relates to the way economists use that term. I then describe how economists test these ideas as a standard against which to evaluate the chapters drawn from this conference. Individual chapters are described along the way as they relate to the question of generalizing about the progress of Byzantine trade. Finally, the contributions are plotted in a figure to indicate how scholarship might progress from here.

Jean-Michel Carrié opened the conference by linking Roman and Byzantine economic studies. He rejected the primitivist position of M. I. Finley in favor of a limited presence of the markets I describe elsewhere.[1] To understand how such a middle position can apply to the study of Byzantine trade, we need to back up a bit and clarify the nature of the debate. Karl Polanyi asserted that "The main forms of integration in the human economy are, as we find them, reciprocity, redistribution, and exchange."[2] These forms describe different ways of organizing the economic functions of any society. *Reciprocity*, as the term suggests, is a system in which people aim at a rough balance between those goods and services they receive and those they give to others. The reciprocal obligations are determined by social obligations and tradition, and they change only slowly. This organization can be used within stable social groups and for limited trade, but it is not flexible or impersonal enough to support extensive trade. *Redistribution* is a system in which goods are collected into one hand and then distributed by virtue of custom, law, or ad hoc central decisions. This system is present in units as small as households, where it is known as householding, as well as in the taxation levied by Roman and Byzantine states. The essential characteristic is that a central authority collects and distributes goods and services. *Exchange* is the familiar economic transaction in which people voluntarily exchange goods for each other or for money.

Frederic Pryor proposed tests that can be used to differentiate Polanyi's forms of integration.[3] Pryor distinguished between what he called exchanges

---

[1] M. I. Finley, *The Ancient Economy* (Berkeley, 1973); P. Temin, "A Market Economy in the Early Roman Empire," *JRS* 91 (2001): 169–81.

[2] K. Polanyi, *The Livelihood of Man* (New York, 1977), 35–36.

[3] F. L. Pryor, *The Origins of the Economy: A Comparative Study of Distribution in Primitive and Peasant Economies* (New York, 1977).

and transfers. Exchanges are balanced transactions: goods or services are exchanged for other goods or services of equal value. This of course is the kind of behavior most often observed in markets. Transfers are one-way transactions in which goods and services are given without a direct return. Grants, tributes, and taxes are all transfers. Pryor excluded invisible or intangible commodities, such as protection from enemies or benefits in another life, from this accounting. Taxes therefore are classified as transfers rather than as exchanges of goods or money in order to purchase social order or military success. This exclusion is necessary because one can always hypothesize an invisible gain that makes all transactions balanced, leaving no way to discriminate between different forms of behavior.

Pryor subdivided exchanges into those in which the ratio of goods or services exchanged can vary and those in which it cannot. The former may or may not involve money; the latter do not. He termed the former "market exchange"; the latter, "reciprocal exchange." The use of money is a good index of this distinction, as are changes in the exchange ratio over time. When money is employed, of course, changes in exchange ratios are expressed as changes in prices.

Finally, Pryor divided transfers into "centric" and "noncentric" ones. Centric transfers are between individuals in a society and "an institution or an individual carrying out a societal-wide role."[4] In the Byzantine context, large-scale centric transfers would be those with the imperial authorities. If the grain to feed Constantinople was provided by taxes or tribute, this transaction would be a centric transfer. If the grain was obtained by being purchased with money, it would be a market exchange.

These categories correspond closely to Polanyi's forms of economic integration. Polanyi's first form, reciprocity, is composed of Pryor's noncentric transfers and reciprocal exchanges. His second form, redistribution, is the same as centric transfers. His third form, exchange, is characterized by what Pryor called market exchange.

This tripartite schema also corresponds to a division within types of individual behavior.[5] Even today, people rely on a mixture of behavioral modes, choosing which one to use in response to internal and external forces, such as their degree of personal autonomy and the rapidity of change in the external environment. When people are less autonomous and change is slow, they typically depend on customary behavior. When change is rapid and personal autonomy is neither very high nor very low, they use command behavior. When personal autonomy is high and the pace of change is moderate, people employ instrumental behavior—that is, they have explicit goals in mind and choose actions that advance their plans. These different modes of behavior correspond to the three types of organization used in economic life. Customary behavior generally is used for noncentric transfers and reciprocal exchanges; command behavior is typical of centric transfers; and instrumental behavior is used in market exchanges.

There consequently are two kinds of tests we can use to discriminate between the various kinds of organizations. Prices are used in market exchanges, but not in noncentric transfers. In addition, in market exchanges people will behave instrumentally, not customarily or by command. Those two modes of behavior are typical of reciprocal and redistributive organizations. Neither prices nor behavior can be clearly discerned from the historical record of Byzantium, but the variety of possible tests enables us to discriminate between alternative categories by reviewing the disparate evidence accumulated.

If we are trying to understand the extent to which markets and market behavior were present, we can look at either aggregate or individual behavior. The two kinds of evidence are very different, and they illuminate different aspects of market behavior. If we see individuals acting in instrumental ways, changing prices or exchanging goods, we can infer that they were acting in a market context. If we observe ships moving in different directions, we can infer that they cannot all be responding to centric transfers or taxes. If the evidence from individual stories and accounts is consistent with those from extensive excavations, the picture becomes clearer. But if it appears to be inconsistent, we need to understand how contemporary people understood a process that looks quite different to us.

Economists look at prices to evaluate markets, examining price fluctuations and comparing prices of buyers and sellers. It is illuminating to bracket the Byzantine period with price observations before and after. A few wheat prices survive from the early

---

4 Ibid., 34.
5 P. Temin, "Modes of Behavior," *Journal of Economic Behavior and Organization* 1 (1980): 175–95.

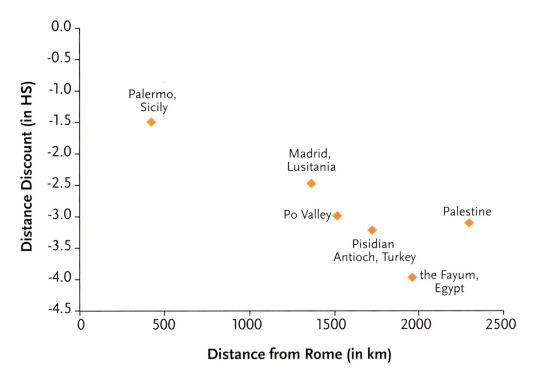

Figure 17.1. Wheat prices across the early Roman Empire (from Kessler and Temin, "Money and Prices in the Early Roman Empire")

Roman Empire.[6] Some of them are arrayed along the horizontal axis of figure 17.1, positioned by their distance from the city of Rome. Prices are indicated by the height of points, expressed as differences between the price in Rome and the local price. This procedure takes into account the increase in prices in Rome over the two centuries represented by these few prices, and it shows the prices as discounts from the Roman price.

Wheat prices from one end to the other of the Mediterranean Sea were quite similar in the late Roman Republic and early Roman Empire. The price in Rome varied between 3 and 6 sesterces (HS) per modius, and between 0.5 and 4 sesterces from one end of the Mediterranean to the other. Such uniformity alone is evidence of extensive market behavior, with common or easily converted monetary systems spread over this large distance. In addition, the prices were not at random levels in different places; they were lower in locations farther from Rome. This relationship between distance and price is highly unlikely to result from any random assignment of prices.[7] It most probably reflects the presence of a wide wheat market in which provincial prices were lower than those in the metropolis. The difference was due to the cost of transporting wheat from the provinces to the city plus a small import duty. Subject to the cost of transport, the so-called law of one price held throughout the Mediterranean Sea.

These observations can be contrasted with those offered by Ibn Baṭṭūṭa, a traveler from the fourteenth century. He noted that Turkish tribes exported horses to India—and the same horse that sold for about 1 dinar in Asia could fetch more than 200 dinars in India.[8] These traders were operating in markets, but the price range in their markets was far larger than in Roman times. Prices differed by two orders of magnitude between Asia and India, but only by insignificant amounts between Syria and Spain. These are extreme examples selected to illustrate a wide range of market conditions.

6   G. Rickman, *The Corn Supply of Ancient Rome* (Oxford, 1980).
7   D. Kessler and P. Temin, "Money and Prices in the Early Roman Empire," in *The Monetary Systems of the Greeks and Romans*, ed. W. V. Harris (Oxford, 2008), 137–59.
8   H. A. R. Gibb, *Ibn Battuta: Travels in Asia and Africa, 1325–1354* (1929; reprint, New Delhi, 1986), 145.

Economists distinguish between these two kinds of markets in two ways. The first way is to distinguish between *perfect* and *imperfect* markets. In a perfect market, the law of one price holds—that is, prices are identical in different stores or locations. The price of gasoline in any single country is a good example of a close to perfect market. Imperfect markets are those in which there are *transactions costs* that prevent prices from approaching this common value. Wheat in Rome may have sold for a single price despite its varied origins, but provincial farmers received only that price less the transport cost. (In modern parlance, this is the difference between the price at a product's destination, known as the c.i.f. price—which includes cost, insurance, and freight—and the price at the product's origin, known as the f.o.b. or "free on board" price.) Horses a millennium later may have sold for one price within either Asia or India, but the cost of transport clearly ensured a large price difference between those two locations.

This can be illustrated in a simple graph. I show in figure 17.2 the classic functions of supply and demand. The quantity of wheat or horses supplied increases with the price, and the supply curve slopes upward. The quantity demanded typically decreases with the price, and the demand curve slopes down. Equilibrium is reached where the curves cross: at that quantity, the price at which sellers want to sell equals the price at which buyers want to buy. If the supply and demand functions do not change, the price and quantity sold will be stable at the quantity marked A in the figure.

What happens if the price paid by the buyer in Rome or India is higher than the price received in the provinces or Asia due to transport costs? Then we have to allow in our graph for the difference between the buying and selling price as the vertical distance between the curves. Equilibrium in this case will be at a quantity like B, where the buying price is higher than the selling price. The difference between the curves was much larger in the fourteenth century than in the first century, but the concept is the same. Economists term these price differences "transactions costs."

Why were the transactions costs so much higher later than earlier? One reason is that horses were transported from Asia to India over land, while wheat was shipped to Rome by sea. Diocletian's Price Edict set the overland transport price as five times

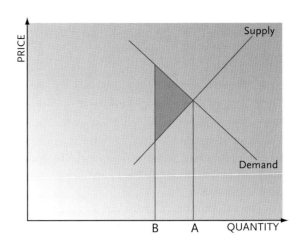

Figure 17.2. Supply and demand curves (drawn by author)

the seaborne price. This is a substantial difference, but it does not seem large enough to explain the great price differential observed in the fourteenth century. There undoubtedly were additional transactions costs in moving horses from Asia to India, despite the obvious fact that horses can move themselves.

Another distinction that economists make is between *thick* and *thin* markets. A thick market is one in which there are many buyers and sellers. Observed prices are likely to be representative of other prices in thick markets. In a thin market, conversely, there are only a few buyers and sellers. Prices may vary in such markets because of information problems as well as those arising from even temporary monopolies. Imperfect markets often are thin markets, and the great price difference between Asia and India may have been due to the thinness of the horse market observed by Ibn Baṭṭūṭa. One or the other of his prices may have been atypical for the area. We cannot always distinguish between price differences caused by transactions costs and those that result from thin markets, but conceptually they are distinct.

In addition to geographical limitations, a market is limited in its internal extent. Even in a market economy, all transactions need not be market exchanges. In fact, it is hard to conceive of an economy composed entirely of market exchanges. A market economy is one in which market exchanges are the most common type of interaction, but even full-blown modern market economies do not channel all transactions through markets. Robert Eisner has calculated that one-third of all economic activity in the United States today takes place within households[9]—that is, in householding or reciprocal activity. Taxes also are substantial in modern societies; in advanced industrial societies, they typically reach one-third of marketed output. Yet these clearly are market economies, a characterization earned not by the universality of market exchanges but by the prominence of market exchanges in transactions between unrelated private people and enterprises and by the importance of these transactions in the economy as a whole.

A story from modern Cuba can be used to illustrate what economic life is like in the absence of markets facilitated by private ownership and the use of money.[10] Cuba today is organized as a socialist economy in which the government owns all houses. People can move, but only if they can trade places with someone else with the approval of the government. A couple in this story wants to downsize, as many elderly couples do routinely in the United States today. Someone offers them an apartment in trade for their house.

But the apartment is not the equal of the house, and the proposed trade will not gain government approval. The proposed trade is actually two apartments for the couple's house. The couple will live in one apartment, while the trader's sister will live in the other. To make this trade, the husband leaving his house must divorce his wife and marry the trader's sister. Once the trade is approved, he can divorce the sister, remarry his wife, and move to her apartment. If all goes well, they will have traded their house for an apartment.

This is a very complex trade, and in this case the couple decided it was too tricky and risky for them. To use the economic terms introduced above, we can say that this difficult transaction illustrates a market with very high transactions costs, typical of non-monetary barter. Since the couple withdrew from the transaction, we can say further that the transactions costs were so high that a reasonable market for dwelling places in Cuba does not exist. If we do not believe there were monetized markets in Byzantium, this is the kind of transaction we are imputing to the historical and archaeological record.

9 R. Eisner, *The Total Incomes System of Accounts* (Chicago, 1989), 26.
10 N. Alonso, *Closed for Repairs* (Willimantic, Conn., 2007), 52–64.

Several chapters in this volume brought evidence to bear on this issue. The most conclusive and arresting finding came from Alan Walmsley, who presented a storekeeper's financial records from eighth-century Syria-Palestine. At the lowest point of the Byzantine economy, in a part of Byzantium already lost to Muslims, Walsmley found evidence that Christian storekeepers were keeping monetary accounts that look like those from eighteenth-century Britain. Customers were listed together with the value of their outstanding consumer credit.

We have to wait for the full publication of this striking finding, but the preliminary presentation provides dramatic evidence that the decline of the Byzantine economy did not result in demonetization. The evidence is oblique, since it comes from outside the Byzantine sphere, but there clearly was no resort to Cuban-style barter. Instead, storekeepers continued to do business as they had done before and would do in more prosperous times. Money was the unit of account, and probably a store of value even in those hard times. Long-distance trade might have been sharply curtailed, but local monetary commerce continued apace.

Dominique Pieri argued that larger amphorae provide evidence of expanding long-distance trade at roughly the same time. However, this suggestion confuses changes in the design and manufacture of amphorae with changes in the volume of trade. An increase in trade could have involved either larger amphorae or more amphorae. Had the increase in trade been substantial, it is hard to imagine that the size of amphorae could have grown sufficiently to ship the larger volume in the same number of containers. If, for example, trade had doubled, it would be strange to discover that it had been carried in the same number of containers—each of which held twice as much. It is more likely that this speculative inference is not warranted by the evidence presented.

Michael McCormick revisited a more popular index of trade, the number of shipwrecks. He argued both that we can identify more shipwrecks than could previous commentators and that changes in technology alter the frequency with which we find ships two thousand years after their sinking. These assertions can be organized by means of an equation. This long equation expresses a tautology, but it is useful nonetheless. It expresses the volume of trade, here labeled simply "Trade," as the product of a series of ratios. Because we can cancel all the magnitudes

$$\text{Trade} = \frac{\text{Trade}}{\text{Voyages}} \times \frac{\text{Voyages}}{\text{Voyages with heavy cargoes}} \times \frac{\text{Voyages with heavy cargoes}}{\text{Shipwrecks}} \times \frac{\text{Shipwrecks}}{\text{Known shipwrecks}} \times \text{Known shipwrecks}$$

that appear in both the denominator and numerator of a ratio, the equation says only that the volume of trade equals the volume of trade. The value of using this long equation is that it directs our attention to three items. First, McCormick is using the number of known shipwrecks as an index of Byzantine trade. Second, this index is a good one only if all the ratios in the equation stay constant. Third, if we think they were not constant, the equation helps us restructure our investigation of changes as we pursue a better index of trade.

Let us examine the ratios in turn. The ratio of trade to voyages varies by the kind of trade being considered. Local trade of the kind discussed by Walmsley did not entail sea voyages, while the long-distance trade discussed by Pieri did. Voyages clearly give an index only of seaborne trade, which typically involves longer distances. It follows that shipwrecks will be a better index of long-distance trade than of local trade.

The ratio of voyages to those with heavy cargoes can change for many reasons. The most obvious is the nature of containers. Amphorae are heavy and durable. Ships containing amphorae will sink, and the amphorae will stay intact even as the ships themselves disappear. Late Romans learned to use barrels instead of amphorae to ship liquids. This was a gain to the porters who carried these containers, but it was a loss to later archaeologists, who could not recover evidence of barrel shipments. A rise in the ratio of total voyages to those containing heavy amphorae will change the ratio of known shipwrecks to the volume of trade. Put differently, a decline in the number of known shipwrecks might be an index of a decline in trade or of progress in technology that reduced the dead weight being carried around in the form of amphorae.

The ratio of voyages with heavy cargoes to shipwrecks is affected by the skill of ship captains. If the captains learned how to improve their navigation or weather prediction, this ratio might have changed. The ratio of shipwrecks to known shipwrecks similarly is affected by the skill of archaeologists in dating shipwrecks. McCormick reported progress in this dimension, arguing that we now can date shipwrecks that previous generations could not.

These essays advance our understanding in Byzantine trade in various ways. They raise the prospect that various kinds of trade did not decline as precipitously in the late Roman and early Byzantine periods as has been thought. The evidence is still sparse, but they suggest the possibility of more evidence to come. The essays also advance our understanding of the methods that can be used to estimate the volume of trade. We gain by clarifying our thought processes as well as by accumulating new evidence. New evidence of course raises new problems of interpretation, and improvements in methodology must accompany advances in the search for archaeological evidence.

It is useful to array the chapters in this volume in a two-dimensional matrix. One dimension is space, and the other is time. Consider space first. Several authors made a tripartite division of trade by distance. Local trade to supply cities and towns was across distances that could be covered in a day or two, said to be up to 50 kilometers. Regional trade entailed distances that could be covered in several days to a week—set by contributors at up to 150 kilometers for land travel and 300 kilometers by sea. Since both of these kinds of trade could go by land or sea, it is clear that shipwrecks are not a good index for their volume and extent. Long-distance trade was for longer distances, and Neville Morley argues that the extent of long-distance trade is a good index of economic prosperity.[11]

The time dimension can be taken from Angeliki Laiou and Cécile Morrisson, who provide a

11 N. Morley, *Trade in Classical Antiquity* (Cambridge, 2007).

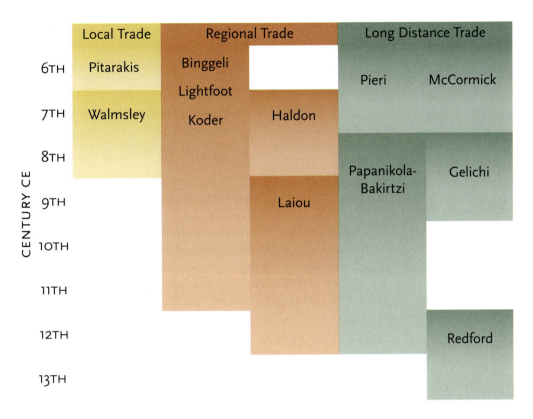

Figure 17.3. The focus of this volume's chapters, by time and distance of trade

summary of our current evidence on the state of the Byzantine economy.[12] Their narrative is structured by century, an approach that provides a simple framework for our analysis. According to Laiou and Morrisson, the sixth and seventh centuries were periods of plague and invasion that decreased the scope of the Byzantine economy. The eighth century witnessed the nadir of the Byzantine economy, while the ninth and tenth centuries contained evidence of economic growth. The eleventh and twelfth centuries were periods of economic prosperity, while the thirteenth and fourteenth centuries were periods of recurrent decline. This simple scheme of down, up, and down again can be used to place evidence of trade into the context of what we think we know about the economy as a whole.

In figure 17.3, I have arrayed, according to these two dimensions, the chapters from this volume that were originally presented at the conference. The rows show the centuries they discuss, and the columns show the type of trade analyzed, as classified by its distance. As the sizable boxes make obvious, many chapters discussed more than one type of trade and ranged over several centuries. I put authors into the columns they discussed most extensively.

Two conclusions emerge from this array. First, most chapters range over multiple centuries. In fact, many of them include several of the periods outlined by Laiou and Morrisson. This is testimony to the scarcity of evidence, forcing scholars to make use of very partial information for any particular period. It also means that these chapters can provide only limited information about the fall, rise, and subsequent fall of the Byzantine economy. The table does not work at all for a broad survey like the one presented by Cécile Morrisson. She discussed the institutions of trade and ranged widely over both time and space. The paper is wonderfully informative about the transactions costs involved in Byzantine trade, but it cannot say much about the extent of that trade. There is some evidence of declining long-distance trade late in the Byzantine period, insofar as different weights and measures appear to have been coming into use.

---

12 A. E. Laiou and C. Morrisson, *The Byzantine Economy* (Cambridge, 2007).

(Morrisson's chapter consequently is not included in figure 17.3; Carrié's is omitted because he did not discuss a particular time or place.)

Second, the entries in the table appear to be concentrated in its upper right portion. Hardly any author analyzed local and regional trade in the later part of the Byzantine period. This may simply reflect who happened to attend a single conference, or it may reveal a topic neglected in the field as a whole. If the latter, then the blank corner of figure 17.3 raises questions to be answered.

I close by making three suggestions for research that I hope will be stimulated by this volume and by the fine conference from which it originated.

First, explore the assumptions underlying any indirect evidence for trade in the Byzantine period. Exposing the logic used in making inferences from archaeological evidence will suggest auxiliary questions that can help interpret this evidence and may provide answers that are interesting and informative in their own right.

Second, document the time pattern of Byzantine trade. The conference provided ample evidence of trade of all sorts, but (as just noted) that trade was seldom tied to specific times. Perhaps data from different chapters can be combined to flesh out our knowledge of changes over time in the prosperity of Byzantine trade.

Third, fill in the empty spaces in figure 17.3. The volume provided little information about local and regional trade in the late Byzantine years. This appears to be an open area for future research.

ABBREVIATIONS

AA	*Archäologischer Anzeiger*
AASOR	*The Annual of the American Schools of Oriental Research*
AASS	*Acta sanctorum* (Paris, 1863–1940)
AB	*Analecta Bollandiana*
AbhGött, Philol.-hist.Kl.	Akademie der Wissenschaften, Göttingen, Philologisch-historische Klasse, Abhandlungen
ActaArchHung	*Acta Archaeologica Academiae Scientiarum Hungaricae*
ADAJ	*Annual of the Department of Antiquities of Jordan*
ADSV	*Antichnaia drevnost' i srednie veka*, Sverdlovsk
AE	*L'Année épigraphique*
AJA	*American Journal of Archaeology*
ALA	C. Roueché, *Aphrodisias in Late Antiquity: The Late Roman and Byzantine Inscriptions*, 2nd ed. (2004), http://insaph.kcl.ac.uk/ala2004
AnatArch	*Anatolian Archaeology. British Institute at Ankara Research Reports*
AnatSt	*Anatolian Studies*
AnnalesESC	*Annales: Economies, sociétés, civilisations*
AnTard	*Antiquité Tardive*
AntJ	*The Antiquaries Journal*
Ἀρχ.Δελτ.	*Ἀρχαιολογικὸν δελτίον*
ArSonTop	*Araştırma Sonuçları Toplantısı*
ArtB	*Art Bulletin*
ASAtene	*Annuario della Scuola archeologica di Atene e delle Missioni italiane in Oriente*
AStIt	*Archivio Storico Italiano*
AttiLinc	*Atti della Accademia nazionale dei Lincei*
BAC	*Bulletin archéologique du Comité des travaux historiques et scientifiques*
BAR	*British Archaeological Reports*
BASOR	*Bulletin of the American Schools of Oriental Research*
BASP	*Bulletin of the American Society of Papyrologists*

BBA	Berliner byzantinistische Arbeiten
BCH	*Bulletin de correspondance hellénique*
BCTH	*Bulletin du Comité des Travaux Historiques*
BEODam	*Bulletin d'études orientales de l'Institut français de Damas*
BHG	*Bibliotheca hagiographica graeca,* 3rd ed., ed. F. Halkin, Subsidia hagiographica 47 (Brussels, 1957; repr. 1969)
BHL	*Bibliotheca hagiographica latina antiquae et mediae aetatis,* Subsidia hagiographica 6 (Brussels, 1898–1911; new suppl. 1986)
BMFD	*Byzantine Monastic Foundation Documents: A Complete Translation of the Surviving Founders' "Typika" and Testaments,* ed. J. Thomas and A. C. Hero (Washington, D.C., 2000)
BMGS	*Byzantine and Modern Greek Studies*
BnF	Bibliothèque nationale de France
BSA	*The Annual of the British School at Athens*
BSl	*Byzantinoslavica*
BSOAS	*Bulletin of the School of Oriental and African Studies*
ByzArch	Byzantinisches Archiv
ByzF	*Byzantinische Forschungen*
ByzVindo	Byzantina Vindobonensia
BZ	*Byzantinische Zeitschrift*
CahArch	*Cahiers Archéologiques*
CCSL	Corpus christianorum, Series latina
CDS	*Codex Diplomaticus Regni Croatiae, Dalmatiae et Slavoniae,* ed. T. Smičiklas (Zagreb, 1904–)
CFHB	Corpus fontium historiae byzantinae
CI	*Codex Iustinianus,* vol. 2 of *Corpus Iuris Civilis,* ed. P. Krüger (Berlin, 1887)
CIC	*Corpus iuris civilis,* ed. P. Krüger et al. (Berlin, 1928–29; repr. 1993)
CIL	*Corpus inscriptionum latinarum* (Berlin, 1862–)
CMG	*Corpus Medicorum Graecorum*
CRAI	*Comptes rendus de l'année de l'Académie des Inscriptions et Belles-Lettres*
CSEL	Corpus scriptorum ecclesiasticorum latinorum
CSHB	Corpus scriptorum historiae byzantinae
CTh	*Theodosiani libri XVI cum constitutionibus Sirmondianis et leges novellae ad Theodosianum pertinentes,* ed. T. Mommsen and P. M. Meyer (Berlin, 1905)
ΔXAE	Δελτίον τῆς Χριστιανικῆς ἀρχαιολογικῆς ἑταιρείας
DCV	R. Morozzo della Rocca and A. Lombardo, eds., *Documenti del commercio veneziano nei secoli XI–XIII,* 2 vols. (Rome, 1940),
DenkWien	Österreichische Akademie der Wissenschaften, Philosophisch-historische Klasse, Denkschriften
DOC	A. R. Bellinger, P. Grierson, and M. F. Hendy, *Catalogue of the Byzantine Coins in the Dumbarton Oaks Collection and in the Whittemore Collection* (Washington, D.C., 1966–99)

DOCat	*Catalogue of the Byzantine and Early Mediaeval Antiquities in the Dumbarton Oaks Collection,* vols. 1–2 by M. C. Ross (Washington, D.C., 1962–65); vol. 3 by K. Weitzmann (1972)
DOP	*Dumbarton Oaks Papers*
DOSeals	N. Oikonomides and J. Nesbitt, eds., *Catalogue of Byzantine Seals at Dumbarton Oaks and in the Fogg Museum of Art* (Washington, D.C., 1991–)
EHB	*The Economic History of Byzantium: From the Seventh through the Fifteenth Century,* ed. A. E. Laiou, Dumbarton Oaks Studies 39, 3 vols. (Washington, D.C., 2002)
EHR	*English Historical Review*
EI²	*Encyclopaedia of Islam,* 2nd ed. (Leiden, 1960–)
Eparchenbuch	*Das Eparchenbuch Leons des Weisen,* ed. J. Koder (Vienna, 1991)
FGH	*Fragmenta historicorum graecorum,* ed. C. Müller (Paris, 1841–70)
GCS	*Die griechischen christlichen Schriftsteller der ersten [drei] Jahrhunderte*
GOTR	*Greek Orthodox Theological Review*
GRBS	*Greek, Roman, and Byzantine Studies*
HAW	*Handbuch der [klassischen] Altertumswissenschaft,* ed. I. Müller; new ed. by W. Otto et al. (Munich, 1923–)
Hesp	*Hesperia*
HZ	*Historische Zeitschrift*
IGLSyr	*Inscriptions grecques et latines de la Syrie,* ed. L. Jalabert, R. Mouterde, and C. Mondésert (Paris, 1929–70)
ILS	*Inscriptiones latinae selectae,* ed. H. Dessau (Berlin, 1892–1916)
INA	Institute of Nautical Archaeology
IstMitt	*Istanbuler Mitteilungen,* Deutsches Archäologisches Institut, Abteilung Istanbul
JAOS	*Journal of the American Oriental Society*
JHS	*Journal of Hellenic Studies*
JMedHist	*Journal of Medieval History*
JÖB	*Jahrbuch der Österreichischen Byzantinistik*
Josh. Styl.	*The Chronicle of Joshua the Stylite: Composed in Syriac A.D. 507,* trans. and ed. W. Wright (Cambridge, 1882)
JRAS	*Journal of the Royal Asiatic Society*
JRS	*Journal of Roman Studies*
KazSonTop	*Kazı Sonuçları Toplantısı*
Lib.ann	*Studium biblicum franciscanum: Liber annuus*
MGH Capit	Monumenta Germaniae historica, Capitularia regum Francorum
MGH Form	Monumenta Germaniae historica, Legum sectio V, Formulae
MGH ScriptRerGerm	Monumenta Germaniae historica, Scriptores rerum Germanicarum
MGH ScriptRerMerov	Monumenta Germaniae historica, Scriptores rerum Merovingicarum
NC	*The Numismatic Chronicle [and Journal of the Royal Numismatic Society]*
NDCV	A. Lombardo and R. Morozzo della Rocca, eds., *Nuovi documenti del commercio veneto dei secoli XI–XIII,* Monumenti storici, n.s., 7 (Venice, 1953)
NZ	*Numismatische Zeitschrift*

ODB	*The Oxford Dictionary of Byzantium,* ed. A. Kazhdan et al. (New York–Oxford, 1991)
ÖJh	*Jahreshefte des Österreichischen Archäologischen Instituts in Wien*
ÖJhBeibl	*Jahreshefte des Österreichischen Archäologischen Instituts in Wien,* Beiblatt
OrChr	*Orientalia christiana*
PBSR	*Papers of the British School at Rome*
PEQ	*Palestine Exploration Quarterly*
PG	Patrologiae cursus completus, Series graeca, ed. J.-P. Migne (Paris, 1857–66)
PL	Patrologiae cursus completus, Series latina, ed. J.-P. Migne (Paris, 1844–80)
PLRE	*The Prosopography of the Later Roman Empire,* vol. 1, ed. A. H. M. Jones, J. R. Martindale, and J. Morris (Cambridge, 1971); vols. 2–3, ed. J. R. Martindale (1980–92)
PO	*Patrologia orientalis*
RBK	*Reallexikon zur byzantinischen Kunst,* ed. K. Wessel (Stuttgart, 1963–)
RBN	*Revue belge de numismatique*
RE	*Paulys Real-Encyclopädie der classischen Altertumswissenschaft,* new rev. ed. by G. Wissowa and W. Kroll (Stuttgart, 1894–1978)
REA	*Revue des études anciennes*
REB	*Revue des études byzantines*
RHC HOcc	Recueils des historiens des Croisades, Historiens occidentaux (Paris, 1844–95)
RIS	*Rerum italicarum scriptores,* ed. L. A. Muratori (Milan, 1723–51)
RN	*Revue numismatique*
RSBN	*Rivista di studi bizantini e neoellenici*
RSBS	*Rivista di Studi bizantini e slavi*
SBMünch	Sitzungsberichte der Bayerischen Akademie der Wissenschaften, Philosophisch-historische Klasse
SC	Sources chrétiennes
SEER	*The Slavonic and East European Review*
SEG	*Supplementum epigraphicum graecum,* ed. P. Roussel et al. (Leiden, 1923–)
SubsHag	Subsidia hagiographica
TAPS	*Transactions of the American Philosophical Society*
TIB	*Tabula imperii byzantini,* ed. H. Hunger (Vienna, 1976–)
TM	*Travaux et mémoires*
VizVrem	*Vizantiiskii vremennik*
Zepos, *Jus*	*Jus graecoromanum,* ed. J. and P. Zepos (Athens, 1931; repr., 1962)
ZPapEpig	*Zeitschrift für Papyrologie und Epigraphik*
ZRVI	*Zbornik radova Vizantološkog instituta, Srpska akademija nauka*

ABOUT THE AUTHORS

ANDRÉ BINGGELI holds a permanent research position in the National Centre for Scientific Research (CNRS) in Paris, in the Institute for Textual Research and History (IRHT). He specializes in Greek, Syriac, and Arabic literature and manuscripts related to Christian-Muslim relations in the first centuries AH. His most recent publication is "Converting the Caliph: A Legendary Motif in Christian Hagiography and Historiography of the Early Islamic Period," in *Writing "True Stories": Historians and Hagiographers in the Late Antique and Medieval Near East*, ed. A. Papaconstantinou et al. (Turnhout, 2010), and he is currently finishing his edition of the *Narrationes* of Anastasius of Sinai.

JEAN-MICHEL CARRIÉ is director of research and teaches late Roman history at EHESS (Paris). He is the editor of the international journal *Antiquité tardive*. His research focuses on the transition from late antiquity to the early Middle Ages in the Germanic West and the early Byzantine East, particularly from the point of view of economic and social history; military, fiscal, and monetary matters; and ancient technology. Among his publications are *L'Empire romain en mutation des Sévères à Constantin, 192–337* (with Aline Rousselle) (Paris, 1999) and contributions to *Mons Claudianus: Survey and Excavation, 1987–1993*, part 2 (Cairo, 2001); *Cambridge Ancient History*, vol. 12 *(A.D. 193–337)*, 2nd ed. (Cambridge, 2005); *Dictionnaire de l'Antiquité* (Paris, 2005); and *La monnaie dévoilée par ses crises*, ed. B. Théret, 2 vols. (Paris, 2007).

ROWAN DORIN is a doctoral candidate at Harvard University. He was introduced to the medieval Mediterranean as an undergraduate by the late Angeliki Laiou, and is currently working on a dissertation on the expulsions of merchants in medieval Europe, under the supervision of Daniel Lord Smail and Michael McCormick.

SAURO GELICHI is professor of medieval archaeology at the University of Ca' Foscari of Venice. His current research focuses on Venice and Adriatic towns during the Middle Ages. Among his more recent publications are *The Archaeology of an Abandoned Town: The 2005 Project in Stari Bar* (Florence, 2006), *A Town through the Ages: The 2006–2007 Archaeological Project in Stari Bar* (Florence, 2008), and *L'isola del vescovo: Gli scavi archeologici intorno alla Cattedrale di Comacchio / The Archaeological Excavations near the Comacchio Cathedral* (Florence, 2009).

JOHN HALDON is professor of history at Princeton University. He studied in the United Kingdom, Greece, and Germany, and is a Senior Fellow at Dumbarton Oaks. His research focuses on the history of the early and middle Byzantine Empire, in particular the seventh to the eleventh century; on state systems and structures across the European and Islamic worlds from late ancient to early modern times; and on the production, distribution, and consumption of resources in the late ancient and medieval world, especially in the context of warfare. His publications include *Byzantium in the Seventh Century* (Cambridge, 1990; rev. 1997); *Three Treatises on Byzantine Imperial Military Expeditions* (Vienna,

1990); *The State and the Tributary Mode of Production* (London–New York, 1993); *Warfare, State, and Society in the Byzantine World, 565–1204* (London, 1999); *Byzantium: A History* (Charleston, 2000); and *The Palgrave Atlas of Byzantine History* (New York, 2005).

JOHANNES KODER is emeritus professor at the Institute for Byzantine and Neohellenic Studies at the University of Vienna, where he was professor and director from 1985 to 2010. His current research focuses on settlement and traffic structures in Byzantium, on the history of Byzantine nutrition, on liturgical hymnography of the fifth and sixth centuries, and on middle Byzantine mystical literature (Symeon Neos Theologos). His publications include two volumes of the *Tabula Imperii Byzantini* and a German translation of the *Kontakia* of Romanos Melodos.

ANGELIKI E. LAIOU (1941–2008) was Dumbarton Oaks Professor of Byzantine History in the Department of History at Harvard University. Her research interests included Byzantine social and economic history, notably trade and manufacturing. She was the editor of *The Economic History of Byzantium* (Washington, D.C., 2002). Her complete bibliography and biography, written by C. Morrisson and A.-M. Talbot, appears in *Dumbarton Oaks Papers* 63 (2009).

LUKE LAVAN is lecturer in archaeology at the University of Kent, Canterbury, where he specializes in the archaeology of late antiquity. His doctorate (2001) considered provincial capitals of late antiquity. He is series editor of the annual *Late Antique Archaeology* and he currently directs excavations at Ostia, the port of Rome, where he focuses on the later development of streets and public space within the city, in partnership with the Humboldt University of Berlin.

CHRIS LIGHTFOOT is a curator in the Department of Greek and Roman Art at The Metropolitan Museum of Art, New York, where he specializes in Roman art and ancient glass. He has been the director of the Amorium Excavations Project since 1993; he is the editor of the Amorium Reports monograph series, and in 2007 he produced a guidebook with versions in English and Turkish titled *Amorium: A Byzantine City in Anatolia*.

MICHAEL MCCORMICK is Goelet Professor of Medieval History and teaches history and archaeology at Harvard University. His current research focuses on the economic and environmental history and archaeology of the late Roman and early medieval period, on computational philology, and on the natural science of the human past. His most recent major works include *The Digital Atlas of Roman and Medieval Civilizations* (2010), http://darmc.harvard.edu/; coedited with Jennifer R. Davis, *The Long Morning of Medieval Europe: New Directions in Early Medieval Studies* (Aldershot, 2008); and *Charlemagne's Survey of the Holy Land* (Washington, D.C., 2011).

CÉCILE MORRISSON is Director of Research Emerita at the Centre national de la recherche scientifique, Paris, and Advisor for Byzantine Numismatics, Dumbarton Oaks. Her research interests lie in Byzantine coins, monetary history, and economic history. She contributed to *The Economic History of Byzantium* (Washington, D.C., 2002), and published with A. Laiou *The Byzantine Economy* (Cambridge, 2007). Of the three volumes of *Le Monde byzantin* (Paris, 2004–11), she edited and co-authored volume one, *L'Empire romain d'Orient (330–641)*, and (with A. E. Laiou) volume 3, *L'Empire grec et ses voisins (1204–1453)*.

DEMETRA PAPANIKOLA-BAKIRTZI is an archaeologist in the Leventis Municipal Museum of Nicosia. She works on aspects of material culture in Byzantium, specializing in Byzantine glazed pottery. Among her publications are *Ceramic Art from Byzantine Serres* (with E. Dauterman-Maguire and H. Maguire) (Urbana, 1992); *Medieval Glazed Pottery of Cyprus: Paphos and Lapithos Ware* (Thessalonike, 1996 [in Greek]); and "Glazed Pottery Workshops in the Byzantine World," in *Proceedings of the 7th International Conference on Medieval Pottery of the Mediterranean, Thessaloniki, 1–16 October 1999* (Athens, 2003), 45–66 (in Greek). She is editor of *Byzantine Glazed Ceramics: The Art of Sgraffito* (Athens, 1999) and *Everyday Life in Byzantium* (Athens, 2002).

DOMINIQUE PIERI teaches late Roman and early Byzantine archaeology at Panthéon-Sorbonne University in Paris. He works on aspects of material culture in the Byzantine Near East, specializing in early Byzantine pottery. He is the author of *Le com-

merce du vin à l'époque byzantine: Le témoignage des amphores en Gaule (Beirut, 2005). He has been the director of the French Beirut Excavations (2000–2004) and has worked since 2007 at St. Symeon Sanctuary in North Syria.

BRIGITTE PITARAKIS is *chargée de recherches* at the CNRS (UMR 8167–"Orient et Méditerranée"). Her main area of research is material culture from late antiquity and Byzantium, with a focus on metalwork. She is author of *Les Croix-reliquaires pectorales byzantines en bronze* (Paris, 2006). Her most recent publication is "The Material Culture of Children in Byzantium," in *Becoming Byzantine: Children and Childhood in Byzantium,* ed. A. Papaconstantinou and A.-M. Talbot (Washington, D.C., 2009). She recently organized an exhibition on the Hippodrome of Constantinople at the Pera Museum in Istanbul and edited its catalogue, *Hippodrome / Atmeydanı: A Stage for Istanbul's History* (Istanbul, 2010).

SCOTT REDFORD is professor in the Department of Archaeology and History of Art and Director of the Research Center for Anatolian Civilizations at Koç University, Istanbul. His areas of research include the archaeology, art history, and history of medieval Anatolia and the eastern Mediterranean. He is publishing the medieval levels of Bilkent University excavations at Kinet Höyük, Hatay, Turkey, directed by Prof. Marie-Henriette Gates of Bilkent. His recent publications include *Victory Inscribed: The Seljuk Fetihname on the Citadel Walls of Antalya, Turkey* (with Gary Leiser) (Istanbul, 2008).

PETER TEMIN is the Gray Professor Emeritus of Economics at the Massachusetts Institute of Technology (MIT). Professor Temin was the Pitt Professor of American History and Institutions at Cambridge University, 1985–86; Head of the Economics Department at MIT, 1990–93; and President of the Economic History Association, 1995–96. Professor Temin's research interests include macroeconomic history, the Great Depression, industry studies in both the nineteenth and twentieth centuries, and ancient Rome. His most recent books are *The World Economy between the World Wars* (Oxford, 2008) and *Reasonable RX: Solving the Drug Price Crisis* (Upper Saddle River, N.J., 2008), both with coauthors. He is the author of "A Market Economy in the Early Roman Empire," *Journal of Roman Studies* 91 (2001).

ALAN WALMSLEY is MSO Professor in Islamic Archaeology and Art at the University of Copenhagen. His research and teaching centers on the archaeology, architecture, art, and numismatics of the Islamic world, with a focus on questions of continuity, resilience, and transformation in Syro-Palestinian society between the fifth and eleventh centuries. He has excavated in the Middle East for thirty-five years and has directed five major field projects, currently at the renowned site of Jarash in Jordan. He is also director of the Materiality in Islam Research Initiative, a research center devoted to investigating new ways of analyzing social trends in Islam by applying critical approaches to the analysis of visual culture. He is the author of *Early Islamic Syria: An Archaeological Assessment* (Duckworth, 2007), in addition to other publications.

INDEX

Page numbers in **bold** indicate illustrative material.

'Abd al-Malik, 287, 320
Abū Nuwās, 289
Abulafia, David, 235–36n4, 248–49n78, 262n175, 269
Abydos, cargo inspectors in, 54, 64–65
accounting practices: shopkeepers' accounts, stone tablet with, 326–29, **329,** 433; Vienna accounting papyri, 22–23
adaeratio, 15
Adamnan, 290n67
Adrianople, 134
Adriatic trade networks in twelfth and thirteenth centuries, 6, 8, 235–79; ceramics, 258, 267n208; coastal geography, tides, currents, and wind factors, 236–40; documentary evidence for, 240–41, 246; extra-Adriatic trade, 263–70, 278; individuals involved in, 270–77, 279; intra-Adriatic trade, non-Venetian, 252–63, 278; lateral versus trans-Adriatic, 256–58, 261; map, **237;** micro-ecological variation, theory of, 239–40, 246, 254, 279; Otranto, Strait of, 236, 265; overland route to Constantinople and, 269–70, 279; pirates and piracy, 262–63; ships sailing Adriatic, 238–39; Venice, Adriatic as *contado* for, 241–52, **243,** 278, 279. *See also specific*

Adriatic coastal settlements and trade goods
Aegean, as shipping zone, 77
Aegean Kapitän amphorae, 6
Aegean Ware, 142n107, 143, 144, 207, 308
Aelianos (Syrian martyr), annual fair associated with, 288, 289
Aetius of Amida, 93n211
African oil gathered for export at Carthage, 53n16, 61, 65
African Red Slip (ARS) Ware, 9, 73, 106, 190, 368, 370, 375, 376
Africana 2D Grande amphorae, 62, **62**
agorai, **343, 344,** 344–46, 348–49, 370–72
agrarian activity: on Adriatic coast, 236–37; in Asia Minor, 155–57, **157, 158;** in Cappadocia, 118; grain supply requirements for nonproducers, 174
Albania, Adriatic trade of. *See* Adriatic trade networks in twelfth and thirteenth centuries
Aldoino, Domenico, 272, 274
Aleppo: annual fair at, 285, 288, 290, 292, 295; Norman Principality of Antioch and, 299, 300n4, 309n29
Alexander of Tralles, 36
Alexandria, 81–82, 284, 359
Alexios I Komnenos (emperor), 132, 137, 145, 180, 264, 270, 299, 392
Alfred the Great (king of Wessex), 58

Alinda, 166n90
almanacs as evidence of Syrian annual fairs in Islamic period, 283–85
Almissan pirates, 263
Almyros, 138, 139
Amastris, 8
Ambrosiani, Björn, 58n40
'Ammān, annual fair at, 286, 288, 289, 290, 292, 293, 314n20
Ammianus Marcellinus, 295n107
Amorion (Amorium), 5, 177–91; Arab sack of 838, recovery following, 179–80, **180;** Army of the Anatolics in, 179; belt buckles from, 118; books and literacy in, **188,** 188–89; as capital of theme of Anatolikon, **178,** 179; ceramic evidence from, 104, 105, 106; ceramics found at, 189, 190, **190;** coin evidence from, 109n39, 110, 180–82, **181;** construction work, artisans and supplies required for, 189–90; de-urbanization of seventh century and, 177, 183–84; documentary evidence on, 117; inland setting, importance of, 177–78, 182–83; Mantzikert, decline after Battle of (1071), 180; maritime trade, distortions caused by focus on, 177, 184, 190; medicinal plants from, 188; metalwork and jewelry found at, 190–91, **191;** new construction in seventh century, 178–79, **179;** regional networks in Asia Minor

445

Amorion, *continued*
and, **168**, 168–69, **169**, 177–78; silk and luxury leather goods found at, 187–88; spolia, use of, 180, 189; weight with protective inscription from, 422n146; wine-making in, 184–87, **185–87**

amphorae, 5–6, 8, 27–49, 60–77; at Amorion, paucity of, 186; barrels versus, 73, 74–76, 91–94, 186; chain of transactions evidenced by, 61; changes in local and regional exchange in seventh and eighth centuries, 107; from church workshops, 45, **46**; from Comacchio and Northern Italy in eighth century, **225**, 228–31, **229**, **230**; as commercial packaging with marketing implications, 43; concept of market economy and evidence from, 19; contents of, 36, 43–44, 61; distribution patterns, economic significance of, 68; diversity and proliferation of different forms, 28–30, **30**, **31**, **34**, 43; Dumbarton Oaks, *cover*, 309; eastern Mediterranean trade dynamism, as evidence of, 28–36, **32–35**; economic significance of specific amphorae and their cargoes, 64–65; as imitative or forged packaging, 47–48, **48**, 69; as liquid measures, 414–16; means and agents of exchange, 39–42; modern economic theory and, 433; operational approach to studying, 61–64, **62**, **63**; overland shipment of, 69–73, **70–72**, 120–21; painted inscriptions on, 40, **41**, **42**, 44, 45, **46**; Persian wars and Arab Muslim conquests affecting production and export of, 31, 32; production of, 45–47; relative values and volumes of contents, assessing, 77; size, shape, capacity, and tare weight, significance of, 8, 32, **34**, 42–45, 61–64, **62**, **63**, 65–68, 91; standardization issues, 42–45; storage, organization, and sale of contents at receiving end, 66–67, **67**, **68**; transfer of contents into, 65–66, 69; typological classification of, 28–29, **29–31**; western centers of production, decline of, 31; wine trade and, 36–39. *See also specific types*

anaglypha asēmia, 196
Anastasius I (emperor), 150
Anastasius Bibliothecarius, 127n14
Anatolia, 177–91; environment of vigorous supply and demand in, 177–78; livestock from, 53, 102, 182–83; manpower, as source of, 182; map, **178**; numismatic evidence from, 110; resilience of, 8; Sagalassos pottery in, 106; urban life, change and continuity in, 99. *See also specific sites*
Anazarbos, 169–71, **170**, 301, 401
Anchialos, 128
Ancona: extra-Adriatic trade, 267–69, 270; identity of traders and naucleri, 271; intra-Adriatic trade, 253, 259, 260, 263, 278; Venice, trade with, 236, 240, 245–46, 248–49, 252
Ancyra, 179
Andrew the Fool, *Life* of, 403–4, 407
Andriake inscription on official weights and measures, 383–85
Andronikos II (emperor), 393, 394–95
Anemourion, 104, 377
'Anjar, 322, 362
Anna Komnena, 162n73, 270
annona, 15, 20, 49, 52, 53n16, 61, 65n76, 96
annual fairs or markets, 116; in Balkans, 137; de Ligt's criteria for classifying, 289–90, 292, 293; at Ephesos, 116, 121; Thessalonike, Demetria in, 208. *See also* Syria, annual fairs in
Anskar (missionary), *Life* of, 78n157
"anti-primitivist" view of Byzantine trade and markets, 13–14
Antinoopolis, amphorae found at, 44–45, **46**
Antioch, city of: physical shops and marketplaces in, 340–42, 348–52, 361, 364; Yakto mosaic depicting daily life in, 340, 349, 350, 353, 357, 359, 360, 402, **403**
Antioch in Pisidia, 358, 359, 360, 361, 383

Antioch, Norman Principality of, 5, 6, 297–309; archaeological evidence of geographic/political disjunction in, 305–9; Byzantine Duchy of Antioch, modeled on, 297; Cilicia rather than southern territories, geographic and economic links to, 5, 6, 297, 299, 300–305; Italian merchants and, 304–9; maps of region, **298**, **299**; port cities of Port Saint Symeon and Laodikeia, 297–99, 300, 304–5; thirteenth-century commercial boom, 305
Antonio de Andriuccio da Saxoferato, 271n241
Apameia, 5, 319, 355, 356, 399n2, 401, 407n50
Aphiona, 105
Aphrodisias, 339, 340–41, **344**, **346–47**, **348**, 352, 353, 355, 357, 359–62, 407
Apollinarios, amphorae of, 41–42, **42**
apothēkai, lead seals of, **112**, 112–14, **113**, 115, 148n9
apotropaic devices on weighing instruments, 422–23, **423**, **424**
Appianus archive, 22
Apulia: extra-Adriatic trade, 263–64, 265–66; intra-Adriatic trade, non-Venetian, 253, 255, 256, 258n142, 263; Venice, trade with, 244n37, 246–47, 249–51
Aqaba, amphorae from, 28, **30**, **46**, 47, 48
Aquileia, 75, 92n208, 93
Arab Muslim conquests: agrarian and pastoral activity, effects on, 118; Amorion, 838 sack of, 179; amphorae, production and export of, 31, 32; dissolution of Mediterranean community and, 148–49; Ḥaṭṭīn, Battle of (1187), 305; Syrian trade networks, shift in, 295–96 (*See also* Syria, annual fairs in; Syria-Palestine, Byzantine and early Islamic, regional exchange in); textual evidence for trade and markets during, 117
Arabic, adoption of, in Syria-Palestine, 328–29
Arabic Gospel of the Infancy of the Savior, 365

Arcadius (emperor), 15, 385, **386**
archaeological sources of information about trade and markets, 5–6
Arculf, 287, 313
Argos, 141
Aristotle, 379
Armenian Cilicia. *See* Cilicia
Army of the Anatolics, in Amorion, 179
Arnobius the Elder, 74n114
ARS (African Red Slip) Ware, 9, 73, 106, 190, 368, 370, 375, 376
Arta, Epiros, Blachernitissa narthex painting, 404–6, **405**
St. Artemios, *Miracles* of, 423–24
Asdracha, C., 133n39
Asia Minor, regional networks in, 8, 147–75; agrarian productivity, 155–57, **157, 158**; central and eastern Asia Minor, **166–70**, 166–71; ceramic evidence of, 104, 105, 107, 108; combining concrete information with theoretical models, 171–73, **172, 173**; documentary evidence of, 117; map, **149**; monetization of economy, 147; names of sites, Byzantine and modern, 175; numismatic evidence of, 109, 110, 111; roads in, 118–19, **120**, 152–55, **153–55**, 157, **162, 167**, 167–68, 171; settlement size, population density, and chronology, 149–51, **151, 152**, 171–73, **173**, 174; western Asia Minor, 158–66, **159–62, 164, 165**. *See also specific sites*
Asinou, Cyprus, Panaghia Phorbiotissa in, 426
Askalon ('Asqalān): amphorae made at, 47; annual fair at, 287, 288, 289, 292, 294; camel-shaped bottle from, 70–71, **71**; shipwrecks off, 81n168; wine from, 36–37
astrological charts and shipwreck evidence, 80
al-Āthār al-Bāqiyya 'an al-Qurūn al-Khāliyya ("Chronology of Ancient Nations" of al-Bīrūnī), 283–84
Athena, weights and statues representing, 418, 420–22, **422**
Athens, 44n40, 110, 111, 138–40, 142, 350

Attaleiates, 391n76, 392
Augenti, Andrea, 66n78
Augustine of Hippo, 76, 78, 350, 352, 364–65
Augustus Caesar (emperor), 383
Aurelius Symmachus, 346
Ausonius, 56
autarkeia or self-sufficiency, 3, 21–22, 24, 122, 138, 147, 148
Autun (Augustodunum), 18
Aylward, William, 159

Badoer, Giancomo, 392–93, 397, 405–6
Bag amphorae, 5, 38, **38**, 44n38, 64
Bahariya, 68
Baḥīra, 291
Baird, Jennifer, 349
balance scales, 382–83, **384**, 407–10, **411**, 416, **417**, **423, 424**
Balard, Michel, 235–36n4, 301n8
Baldini Lippolis, Isabella, 333, 334n8
Balkans, regional networks in, 125–46; Adriatic trade and, 251, 260–62, 268–69, 279; ceramic evidence, 136, 137, **141–45**, 141–46; Constantinople and, 127, 128–29, 136, 140, 146; defining regional and interregional trade, 125–27; Greece and the Peloponnese, 137–45; Gregory Pakourianos, estates of, 130–35, **132**; Macedonia, 127, 129, 135, 137, 145; map of, **131**; maritime trade, 127, 135, 137; metal, ore, and mineral trade, Adriatic, 261–62, 279; monetization of economy, 129; numismatic evidence from, 110, 111, 129, 132–33, 137, 142, 145; patterns of, 145–46; roads and overland transport, 118–19, **119**, 127–28, 135–37; slave trade, 251, 260–61, 279; Slavic robbers, problem of, 127n13, 135; Thessalonike, 127, 129, 135–37; Thrace, 127–35, 145; urban life, change and continuity in, 100; Venetian commercial privileges, **131**, 133, 134–35, 137–41, 145. *See also specific sites*
Ballet, Pascale, 47
Balzaretti, Ross, 220
Bang, Peter, 4, 13
Bari, 258, 263, 266

Barletta, 266
barrels: as bathing vessels, 93; as transport containers, 73, 74–76, 91–94, 186
barter economy, 22–23
Basil I (emperor), 145
Basil II (emperor), 137
basket earrings from Amorion, **191**
Bawit, amphorae from, 47, **48**
Baybars (Mamluk sultan), 306
Baysān. *See* Skythopolis
beach markets, 53, 87–89, **89**
beasts of burden, 120, 151, 313, 401
Beersheba, 69
Beirut: amphorae found in, 5, **30**, 32, **35**, 47; physical shops and marketplaces in, 349, 350, 352, 358, 359
Bell, Gertrude, 313–14
belt buckles, distribution patterns of, 118
Benjamin of Tudela, 137, 139n86, 140, 266, 267, 304n14
Beryozovo, silver bowl from, 196
biblical statements regarding weighing and measuring, 387n42, 416, **417**
Bilād al-Shām, annual fairs of. *See* Syria, annual fairs in
Binggeli, André, 7, 281, **435**, 441
Birka, Sweden, as trading center, 58
Birsama, 69, 72
al-Bīrūnī, 283–86, 289–92, 294
Bisceglie, 257
Bithynia, 117, 118, 162, 184
Blachernitissa narthex painting (Arta, Epiros), 404–6, **405**
black glaze ceramic, 18
black markets, 52, 89
Black Sea: evidence for trade via, 107, 114–15; north-south trade route, 8; sailor-traders of, 276; as shipping zone, 77; slave trade in, 261n170, 302
Blackman, M. James, 213, 308
bladders or skins used for transport of goods, 65, 120, 187, 401
Blanco, Deodatus, 275
Blasios of Amorion, 138n69
Boeotia, 8, 138, 141–42
Boğazköy, 118
Bogomils, as slaves, 261n170
Boncompagno da Signa, 253n107, 268

Index 447

Bonifay, Michel, 62n61, 66n80, 69n85, 73n108, 77n139
Book of the Prefect: Asia Minor, regional networks in, 155–56; Balkans, regional networks in, 126, 128, 129; daily life in the marketplace, 400, 407; evidence of markets and trade in, 52, 87n189; market economy, concept of, 21; physical shops and marketplaces, 333, 349; weighing and measuring, 389, 391, 407, 422
books and literacy in Amorion, **188**, 188–89
Booth, Ian, 152
Borchardt measure, **413**, 413–14
Bosporos (Kerch), 107
Bouras, Charalambos, 142
Brand, Charles, 148
Bresson, Alain, 26
Brindisi, 253, 265, 266, 275
Brskovo, 261
Bruhns, Hinnerk, 24
Bücher, Karl, 13n4
Bulgars and Bulgaria, 110, 114, 126–29, 136–37, 208–9
Burono, Guglielmo, 273
Butler, Thomas, 59n49
Butrint, 8, 105, 108, 122
Byrne, Eugene H., 276n276
Byzantine-Bulgarian treaty of 716, 126, 128, 129
Byzantine coarse ware, 188
Byzantine glazed ceramics, 193–216; common tableware from thirteenth to fourteenth centuries, 205–12, 215–16; from Constantinople, tenth to thirteenth centuries, 194–98, **195–97**, 214; from Constantinople, thirteenth to fourteenth centuries, 207–8; from Corinth, 197–200, **199**, 201, 214; Cypriot tablewares, twelfth to fifteenth centuries, 212–14, **213, 214**, 216; demands of market, meeting, 214–16; elite tableware from tenth to thirteenth centuries, 194–205, 214–15; emergence of lead glazing technique, 194; Italian majolica workshops compared, 215; from Kastellorizo shipwreck, 201–5, **203, 204**, 207, 214; metal vessels, based on, **196**, 196–97, **197, 199**, 200–201, **202**; metal vessels, departure from, 205; from Pelagonnesos-Alonnesos shipwreck, 200–201, **201**, 214; from Pergamon, 211–12; relief decoration on, 195–96, **196**; from Serres, 209–10, **210**, 215; from Thessalonike, **208**, 208–9, **209**, 215; from Thrace, **211, 212**, 215; tripod stilts, use of, 205, 207, 213, 215. *See also specific types and classifications*

Ca' Vendramin Calergi, 231
Çadır Höyük, 105, 106, 185n42
Caesarius of Arles, 76n131
Cairo Genizah, 55, 80, 93, 275–76
camels: as beasts of burden, 120, 151, 313, 401; wine amphorae transported by, 70–72, **71, 72**
Camurlu, cistern at, **167**, 167–68
Capo Granitola 4 wreck, 82n169
Capodistria, 255
Cappadocia, agricultural and pastoral activity in, 118
Caraciacanape, Vitale, 263
Caria, 162, 166n90
Carrié, Jean-Michel, 2, 3, 13, 429, 436, 441
Carthage: olive oil gathered for export at, 53n16, 61, 65, 73n105; physical shops and marketplaces in, 334n8, 350, 352, 353, 362
Casana, J., 303n12
Cassiodorus, 348, 363, 387n42
Cassius Dio, 383n23
Çatal Höyük, 303n12
Cato the Elder, 336
Caunos, *sekoma* from, 411–12
caviar, Byzantine consumption of, 405
Cazichi pirates, 263
Central Greek Painted Ware, 105
Central Place Theory of land use and development, 171
ceramics: Adriatic, 258, 267n208; from Amorion, 189, 190, **190**; in Antioch, 304; Balkans, regional networks in, 136, 137, **141–45**, 141–46; changes in local and regional exchange in seventh and eighth centuries, evidence for, 103–8; Comacchio, unglazed ware from, 227, **228**; comparative find studies, need for, 9; Nonantola, excavation of monastery of, **232**, 233; olive oil trade and, 73; as sources of information about trade and markets, 4, 5–6; Syria-Palestine, Byzantine and early Islamic, regional exchange in, 312n8, 313–17, **314–17**, 321; widespread trade in common wares, 18. *See also* amphorae; Byzantine glazed ceramics; *specific types and classifications*

Cervia, 250–51, 255, 264
Chalkidike, ceramics from, 208, 210
Champlevé Ware, 143–44, **144**, 212
changes in local and regional exchange in seventh and eighth centuries, 99–122; ceramic evidence for, 103–8; demand, 101–3; differentiation in trade activities in different areas, 121–22; documentary evidence of, 114–18; estate economy and, 101–2; lead seals of *kommerkiarioi* and *apothēkai,* **112**, 112–14, **113**, 115; monetization of economy, 99, 102–3, 111–12; numismatic evidence for, 104, 108–12; overland movement of goods, 118–21, **119, 120**; plague, effects of, 101; seasonal fluctuations in trade activity, 121; urban patterns of life, 99–101
Charax, 115
Charlemagne, 59, 74n111
cheating. *See* fraud and cheating
Cherson, 8, 104, 107, 108, 114, 206
Chian amphorae, 61
Chioggia, 241, 250, 255, 256
Chonai, **166**, 166–68
Choniates, Michael, 140, 414
Choniates, Niketas, 139, 166, 170n107, 268n216, 392n78, 407
Choricius of Gaza, 340, 364
Christaller, Walter, 171
Chrysoupolis, 133
church workshops, amphorae from, 45, **46**
Cicero, 17n23
Cilicia: amphorae from, 45–46, 64–65, 69; natural links of Norman Principality of Antioch to, 5, 6, 297, 299, 300–305; thirteenth-century commercial

boom, 305; unitary material culture of, 306
cities. *See* urban areas and trade
civil basilicas, 341–42, **343**, 367–68
Classe, storehouse at, 66–67, **67, 68**
cloth and clothing. *See* textile and clothing production and trade
coins: from Amorion, 180–82, **181**; from Balkans, 110, 111, 129, 132–33, 137, 142, 145; changes in local and regional exchange in seventh and eighth centuries, evidence for, 104, 108–12; from Comacchio, 227, **228**; counterfeiting, 388, 391; as evidence of trade and markets, 6; informal markets, coin finds as markers of, 53n11; monetized versus "natural" or barter economic system and, 22–23; physical shops and markets, evidence of, 326, 327, 330, 336, 360; shipwreck data, combined with, 80; Syria-Palestine, Byzantine and early Islamic, regional exchange in, 317–21, **319–21**, 326, 327, 330; Trier, coins minted in, 56; Veronese currency as standard 12th-c. coinage of Venice, 246n57
colleganza contracts, 240–41, 264, 277
collegia, 21
Comacchio, 5, 8, 222–28; amphorae from, **225**, 228–31, **229, 230**; archaeological evidence from, 224–28, **224–29**; changes in local and regional exchange in seventh and eighth centuries and, 105, 108; destruction of, 245; Liutprand Capitulary and, 220–21, 231; maps, **221, 226**; reconstruction of, **231**; trade relations of, 230–33
commerce. *See* trade and markets in Byzantium
Constance (empress), 258
Constans II (emperor), 110, 180, 227n32
Constantine I (emperor), 383, 416n113, 417, 418, 420
Constantine IV (emperor), 109, 110
Constantine V (emperor), 129

Constantine VII Porphyrogenitus (emperor), 136, 157n50, 166n90, 389n59, 401
Constantine (Cyril, Apostle to the Slavs), 59–60
Constantine weights, 417–19, **418, 419**
Constantinople: amphorae from eastern Mediterranean and rise of, 49; Ancona, trade relationship with, 267–68; Balkans, regional networks in, 127, 128–29, 136, 140, 146; ceramic evidence for trade with, 107, 108; glazed ceramics of tenth to thirteenth centuries from, 194–98, **195–97**, 214; glazed ceramics of thirteenth to fourteenth centuries from, 207–8; Hodegetria icon procession in, Blachernitissa narthex painting of, Arta, Epiros, 404–6, **405**; market buildings in, 341, 342, **344,** 346; overland trade routes from Dalmatian ports to, 269–70, 279; physical shops and shopping in, 349, 350, 352, 353, 355, 361, 362, 364; regulation of public behavior in, 339–40; road network in Asia Minor and, 152, 153, 157; Rome, as separate market from, 59; shipwreck evidence regarding importance relative to Rome, 85–86; short-distance deliveries by ship in and around, 77; street encroachments, removal of, 336; as supermarket, 53; Venetian trade with, 264–65; water supply of, 54n21; wine consumption in, 54
Constantinopolitan Glazed White Ware, 104, 106, 107, 136–37, 141, 146, 194–98, **195**, 200
Constantinopolitan Petal Ware, **190**
Constantinopolitan Polychrome Ware, 136–37, **141,** 146, 196–97, **197**, 198
consumer cities versus producer cities, as historiographical concept, 24
Corfu, 238n11, 239, 265n192, 267
Corinth: Balkans, regional networks in, 127, 138–45; Byzantine glazed ceramics from, 197–200,

199, 201, 214; changes in local and regional exchange in seventh and eighth centuries, 104, 110, 111; physical shops and marketplaces, 346; weighing instruments and weights from, 409, 418, 421
Corippus (Flavius Cresconius Corippus), 37, 54n17, 387
Corner, Domenico, 272
Cosyns, Peter, 336
cotton trade in Adriatic, 249–50, 260
Cotyaeum, 184
counterfeiting coins, 388, 391
craft associations, Roman versus medieval, 21
credit and credit instruments, 102, 112, 327
Cretan merchants, 276
Crimean transport amphorae, 8
Crnomir of Bosnia, 261
Crow, James, 54n21
Crusades: First Crusade, 134, 304n14, 305, 308n27; Second Crusade, 134, 298; Third Crusade, 130n28, 132, 134, 301; Fourth Crusade, 243, 264, 265, 270, 421n140; Almissan pirates, preaching of crusade against, 263; Antioch, Norman Principality of, 298–300, 301, 304–6, 308n27; Asia Minor, regional networks in, 149; Byzantine glazed ceramics and, 212, 213, 214, 216; distinctive material culture, crusader states' lack of, 306; Ḥaṭṭīn, Battle of (1187), 305; Syrian annual fairs and, 286, 291
Cuba, non-market economy in, 433
currency. *See* monetization of economy; coins
Cyprus: amphorae from, 46; Byzantine glazed ceramics from, 212–14, **213, 214,** 216; changes in local and regional exchange in seventh and eighth centuries, 8, 105, 108, 111, 116; Red Slip Ware, Cypriot, 104, 105, 107; weighing and measuring in, 394
Cyrene, **343**, 344, 350
Cyril (Constantine), Apostle to the Slavs, 59–60

Dagron, Gilbert, 54n21
daily life in the marketplace, 399–426; pictorial evidence of, 340, 359, 360, 364–65, 402–7, **403, 405, 406**; shopping, as social and daily life in the marketplace, *continued*
    cultural experience, 362–65. *See also* physical shops and marketplaces; transport of goods; weighing and measuring
Dalmatia, Adriatic trade of. *See* Adriatic trade networks in twelfth and thirteenth centuries
Damascus, annual fairs at, 289, 292, 293, 294
Dandolo, Andrea, 246n53–54
Dark-on-Light Slip-Painted Ware, 198, **199**
de Ligt, Luuk, 4, 126n6, 289, 292
De velitatione, 166n91
Decker, Michael, 1, 44, 125
demand: "abundance" and "dearth" in Byzantine writings as proxies for concept of, 57; Anatolia, environment of vigorous supply and demand in, 177–78; Byzantine glazed ceramics meeting market demand, 214–16; changes in local and regional exchange in seventh and eighth centuries, 101–3; in Greece and the Peloponnese, 138, 142–43; modern economic theory, supply and demand in, **432**; regular trade of goods, incentives for, 147–48
Demetrias, 135, 138
Derardo, Giuliano, 274
Develtos, 128
Diaporit, 105
Didymoteichon, 134
"Digenes and the Girl" Champlevé plate, 144, **144**
Diocletian (emperor), Price Edict of, 23, 69, 71, 77
Divine Institutes (Lactantius), 365
documentary evidence, 6–7; for Adriatic trade networks in twelfth and thirteenth centuries, 240–41, 246; almanacs as evidence of Syrian annual fairs in Islamic period, 283–85; of changes in local and regional exchange in seventh and eighth centuries, 114–18; on Northern Italy in eighth century, 220–22, **223**; of physical shops and marketplaces, 340. *See also specific texts and documents*
dolia, 74, 76, 358, 374
Domenico of Chioggia, 251
Domergue, Claude, 17
Domitian (emperor), 336
Donatus of Uzalis, 57–58, 76n131
Dor G shipwreck, 409
Dorin, Rowan W., 5, 6, 235, 441
Doughty, C. M., 313
Dramont E wreck, 42, 43n34
Dressel 20 amphorae, 67, 91n203
Ducellier, Alain, 274n262
Dūmat al-Jandal, annual fair of, 281
Dumbarton Oaks amphora, 309
Duncan-Jones, Richard P., 414
Dunn, Archibald, 140
Dura-Europos, 349
Durak, Koray, 126
Durazzo: extra-Adriatic trade, 264, 269, 270; intra-Adriatic trade, 253n109, 254–55, 256, 259, 278; Venice and, 243, 247, 270, 274
Durliat, Jean, 20

Eberulf of Tours, 37
economic concepts of trade and markets, 429–36
economy, Byzantine. *See* market economy, concept of; trade and markets in Byzantium
Edessa, 340
Edwards, Robert, 301n7, 306n21
Egypt: Adriatic trade with, 266, 267n207; Antioch's economic links to, 300; imitative amphorae from, 47–48, **48**; Serapeion, official weights and measures kept in, 383
Eirene (empress), 117, 127–28
Eisner, Robert, 432–33
El Mahrine, 73n105, 73n109
Elaborate Incised Ware, 207–8, **208**, 215
Elaiussa Sebaste, 345
Eleutheropolis, 286, 293, 294
Elousa, 69, 72
Emesa, 339, 340, 341, 349, 351, 355, 357, 360, 362
Empereur, Jean-Yves, 46
emperors and empresses, weights in shape of busts of, 417–21, **418–21**
Das Eparchenbuch, 87–88n189, 390n65, 391
Ephesos: annual fair at, 116, 121; city walls, 162–63n81; physical shops and marketplaces, 353, **354,** 355, 356, 358, 359, 361; road network in Asia Minor and, 152, 153, 157
Epiphanios of Salamis, 286, 287n40, 293, 414
Epiros: Despotate, in Adriatic trade, 254, 255n121, 267, 269–70; monastery of Molyvdoskepasti at, 210; procession of Hodegetria icon in Constantinople, Blachernitissa narthex painting of, Arta, 404–6, **405**. *See also* Durazzo
Erdkamp, Paul, 24
ergastēria, 347–50
Eski Manyas, 161, 162
estate economy and market economy, 21–23, 102–3
Euchaita, 105, 106, 116, 121, 185n42
Euripos, 139, 140, 141
evidence for trade and markets in Byzantium, 5–7, 51–98; amphorae, 60–77 (*See also* amphorae); archaeological sources, 5–6; barrels as transport containers, 73, 74–76, 91–94, 186; ceramics (*See* ceramics); documentation (*See* documentary evidence); "market," polysemantic meanings of, 51–54, 97; mental disposition towards markets and modes of economic behavior, 54–60; ships and shipwrecks, 77–97 (*See also* maritime trade; shipwrecks)
exchange, as economic function, 429–30
Expositio totius mundi, 56–57, 64n70, 87
Expulsion of the Merchants from the Temple, depictions of, **406**, 406–7

fairs. *See* annual fairs or markets; Syria, annual fairs in
Fano, 244–45, 252n105, 271
Farmer's Law, 93
Fazio, Bartolomeo, 275
Fees, Irmgard, 273n253
Fermo, 248, 254, 259

Filasṭīn, 7, 285–87, 290–94, 296, 319, **321**
Filippo di Albiola, 270
Fine Sgraffito Ware, 142, *142*, 143, 144, **145**, 198–99, **199**, 200, **201**, 207, 212
Finley, Moses, 3, 13, 17, 24, 125, 429
First Crusade, 134, 304n14, 305, 308n27
Fiumicino 12 wreck, 90n200
flat-bottomed amphorae, 43n35
Flavios Eutolmios, 384
Flavius Cresconius Corippus, 37, 54n17, 387
Flexo, Ingo de, 273
fora, shops associated with, 336, 341, 342, 345–46, 347, 351, 352, 370–72
Formulae Salzburgenses, 59n48
forum rerum venalium, 15, 17
Forum Ware, 227n30
Fos-sur-Mer, 75
foundax of Rodosto (Raidestos), 391–92
Fourth Crusade, 243, 264, 265, 270, 421n140
François, Véronique, 205–6, 207–8
Franken, Norbert, 409n71, 418, 421
fraud and cheating: biblical statements regarding, 387n42, 416, **417**; counterfeiting coins, 388, 391; perception of swindlers, 423–26, **425**, **426**; practice, detection, and punishment of, 387–91, **390**, 410–11, 416–17; protective devices against, in decoration of weighing instruments, 416–23, **418–24**
Frederick Barbarossa, 130n28, 132, 134, 268
Frederick II of Sicily, 247, 249, 263, 266
Frontinus, 76
Fulford, Michael, 9
fullonicae, 339, 350, 352, 357, 358

Gabričević, Martin, 413
garbellatura, 396
Gardiki, 140
Garnier, N., 62n61, 66n80, 73n108
Gates, Marie-Henriette, 305
Gaul: barrels from, 93; *Expositio totius mundi* on prices in, 56; Gaza wine imported to, 37,

68n83, 69n93, 77, 87; political situation and economic demand in, 87
Gaza: fairs at, 291, 294, 340; North Syrian (Gaza wine) amphorae, 5, 34, 67–68, 68n83, 69, 326; physical shops, 340, 341; wine from, 5, 36–38, 53–54, 64–65, 77, 87
Gelichi, Sauro, 5, 219, 435, 441
Genoa, 206, 261n170, 273, 276, 307, 393
Geoponica, 169
St. George, annual fairs in Syria on feast day of, 286, 287
Gerasa. *See* Jarash/Gerasa
Gering, Axel, 346
Gesta apud Zenophilum, 76n132
Ghaly, Holeil, 47
Giros, Christophe, 383n24, 391n76, 396
glass: in Antioch, 304; China, Roman exports to, 104–5n22; Corinth as production center for, 143; physical shops dealing in, 350, 357, 357n140, 359, 365; raw materials, trade in, 17–18
globular amphorae, 6, 228n33
gods, goddesses, and personifications, weights in shape of, 420–22, **421**, **422**
Goitein, Shelomo D., 276n279
Göksu (Kalykadnos) Valley, 107
gold currency market, 16
Gradenigo, Domenico, 272, 273
grain supply: *annona,* 15, 20, 49, 52, 53n16, 61, 65n76, 96; nonproducers, requirements for, 174; Rome, wheat prices and distance from, 430–32, **431**
Gratian (emperor), 385
Gratianou ceramics, 211, **212**
Graufesenque, la, 18
Grazel B shipwreck, 410
Green and Brown Painted Ware, 142, 143, 144, 203, 212
Greene, Kevin, 17
Gregoras, Nikephoros, 394
Gregory I the Great (pope), 387n42
Gregory the Decapolite, 127n13, 135
Gregory of Nazianzus, 407n2
Gregory of Tours, 36, 37, 69n93, 290n67
Grierson, Philip, 3

Günsenin 3/Saraçhane 61 type amphorae, 138
Günsenin, Nergis, 73, 77–78n144

Hadrian (emperor), 383
Hadrumetum, **62**, 357
ḥajj and annual fairs in Syria, 281
Haldon, John, 6, 99, 126, **435**, 441
Halmyros, 8, 138
Hama treasure, 416
harbors, silting of, 91
Harris, Anthea, 349, 359
Hārūn al-Rashīd, 59, 292
Ḥaṭṭīn, Battle of (1187), 305
Hayes, John W., 194, 229
Heliopolis, 93
Henchir Ech Chkaf, amphorae from, 47
Hendy, Michael, 3, 132, 133n37, 137, 145
Henry VI Hohenstaufen, 266
Heraclius (emperor), 65, 109, 110, 111
Herakleia, 129, 134
Hero of Alexandria, 76, 93
Herodian, 75n126
Heroninos archive, 21
Hesiod, 78
Heyd, Wilhelm, 6, 302n9
Hierokles, 158
Hilarion of Gaza, 341
Hishām (caliph), 314n19, 321, 322, 326
Hodges, Richard, 235
Honorius (emperor), 15, 385, **386**
Honorius II (pope), 263
Hopkins, Keith, 3
Horden, Peregrine, 2, 239–40
horreiarioi, lead seals of, 129
horse prices, Ibn Baṭṭūṭa on, 431–32
Hugh of Provence, 227n32

al-Iāṭakhrī, 292
Ibn al-Athīr, 302n11
Ibn Bahlūl, 283–89, 290n68–70
Ibn Baṭṭūṭa, 302n11, 431, 432
Ibn Buṭlān, 303
Ibn Ḥabīb, 281n2
Ibn Ḥawqal, 292, 303
Ibn Hishām, 291n75
Ibn al-Iskandar, 276
Ibn Khurradādhbih, 296n109
Ibn Māsawayh, 283–87, 294
Ibn Saʿīd, 300n6

al-Idrīsī, 133, 134, 137n66, 139, 260n161, 266, 268, 269, 303–4
Ignatios the Deacon, 102n12, 115
imperfect and perfect markets, 432
Incised Sgraffito Ware, 142, 143, 144, **144**, **203**, 203–4, **204**, 212, **213**
Incised Ware, 143
informal markets and market events, 53, 87–89
Innocent IV (pope), 253
instrumental mode of economic behavior, 55, 57, 59, 60, 78, 97
international exchange differentiated from regional and interregional trade, 125–26
interregional exchange: defining, 4, 5, 99, 125, 126, 147, 434; fairs, interregional, 290, 293; scholarly interest in, 311–12
Iol Caesarea, 336, 360
Isidore of Seville, 29, 36
Isis shipwreck, 81–82n169
Iskandil Burnu 1 wreck, 82n170
Islam: Seljuk Turks, arrival of, 149, 180. *See also* Arab Muslim conquests
Israel, Y., 69n88
Istria, Adriatic trade of. *See* Adriatic trade networks in twelfth and thirteenth centuries
Italian majolica workshops compared to Byzantine glazed ceramics, 215
Italian merchants: Norman Principality of Antioch and, 304–9; weighing and measuring, international trade affecting, 392–94. *See also* Adriatic trade networks in twelfth and thirteenth centuries; Northern Italy in eighth century; *specific cities in Italy*

Jacoby, David, 308
James, Liz, 419–20
Jarash/Gerasa: coins and ceramic finds, 314–18, 320, 322; Jerash Bowls, 4, **314**, 314–15, 316, 317; physical shops and marketplaces, 7, 326–29, **327–28**, 334, 342, 358, 362
Jazīra, annual fairs of. *See* Syria, annual fairs in

Jerash Bowls, 4, **314**, 314–15, 316, 317
Jerusalem: annual fair in, 287, 291, 292, 294; shops in, 334
jewelry found at Amorion, 190–91, **191**
Jews: Cairo Genizah documents, 55, 80, 93, 275–76; as coppersmiths, 352, 356; at fairs, 287n50, 294; as glassmakers, 304, 363, 365; in maritime trade, 41, 296n109; as shopkeepers and artisans generally, 363; travel limitations, 314; wine intended for Jewish communities, 38
John the Almsgiver, 37, 40, 54n17, 87n189, 386
John Chrysostom, 60n52, 78, 340, 350, 355, 356, 363, 364, 365, 379, 388n48
John of Damascus, 78, 79n153
John of Ephesos, 54n18, 420
John of Jerusalem, 88n189
John Malalas, 93, 342
John Mauropous, 148n43
Jones, Hugo, 3
Julian the Apostate (emperor), 37, 339, 340, 383n24
Julian of Askalon, 335, 339, 351, 357
Justin I (emperor), 318
Justin II (emperor), 37, 39, 54n18, 162n81, 318, 320
Justinian I (emperor), 37, 96n227, 150, 318, 364, 385, 422
Justinianic Code, 335

Kaisaropolis, 130
Kalenderhane, 109
Kalykadnos (Göksu) Valley, 107
Kalyvia Kouvara, Attica, Last Judgment scenes from Church of St. George in, **425**
Kameniates, 136n56, 136n59
Kapitän 2 amphorae, **62**, 62–63, **63**
Karkinelos, 387–88, 424
Kastamonu, 190
Kastellorizo shipwreck, 144, **144**, 201–5, **203**, **204**, 207, 214
Kastoria, Panaghia Mavriotissa in, 425–26
Kastron Mefaʿa (Umm al-Raṣāṣ), 7, 322–25, **324**, **325**
Kaupang, Norway, beach market in, 53n11

Keay type amphorae, 42, 66, 77n139
Kekaumenos, 138, 148, 387, 424–25
Kellia, amphorae from, 47, **48**
Kellis, 22
Kennedy, Hugh, 333
Khirbat Susiyah, 324
Kılıç Arslan (sultan), 407
Kilistra, **167**, 168
Kinet, 305, 307, 308–9
Kingsley, Sean, 1, 125
Kinnamos, John, 268
Kissufim mosaic pavement, 71–72, **72**
Kitāb ʿAjāʾib al-Makhlūqāt ("Cosmography" of al-Qazwīnī), 284–86
Kitāb al-Azmina ("Book of Times" of Ibn Māsawayh), 283
Kitāb al-Azmina wa-l-Amkina ("Book of Times and Places" of al-Marzūqī), 283
Kitāb al-Dalāʾil ("Book of Signs" of Ibn Bahlūl), 283
Knights Templar, 301, 302n11, 305, 306, 308
Koder, Johannes, 1, 5, 147, 389n62, 391, **435**, 442
Kolossai, 166
Komani-Kruja culture, 119
kommerkiarioi, lead seals of, **112**, 112–14, 115, 128, 148n9, 150, 189
kommerkion (tax), 392, 395
Konstantinos Alanos treasure, **199**, 201
Kotor, 258, 261
Koutales, George, 387, 423–24
Kruit, Nico, 69n86
Kubitschek, Wilhelm, 385
Kyzikos, 159, 162

Lactantius, 365
Laiou, Angeliki, ix, 2, 3, 6, 8, 13, 125, 129n26, 148, 236n4, 392n80, 434, **435**, 442
Lake of Nicaea, agrarian productivity of land around, 156–57
Lake Tatta, agrarian nonproductivity of land around, 156–57, **158**
Lane, Arthur, 299–300n4, 306
Lane, Frederic C., 277n285
Lang, Mabel, 44n40
Laodikeia, 167, 297–99, 304–5, 333

Last Judgment scenes, swindlers portrayed in, 425–26
Late Roman (LR) 1 amphorae, 19, 29, **29, 31,** 32, 41, **41,** 42, 45–46, **46,** 47–48, **48,** 64–65, 66n78, 68n82, 77n139, 80n163, 82n170
Late Roman (LR) 2 amphorae, 19, **29,** 34, 66n78, 68n82, 96, 97n230, 228n33
Late Roman (LR) 3 amphorae, **29,** 34n12, 77n131
Late Roman (LR) 4 amphorae, 19, **29,** 32, **34,** 42, 47, 64, 68n82–83, 69n88, 71, 77n139
Late Roman (LR) 7 amphorae, **29,** 45, 46, 48
Late Roman (LR) 9 amphorae, 6, 63
Late Roman (LR) 13 amphorae, 65n76
Late Roman Coarse Wares (LRCW), 4
Lavan, Luke, 7, 333, 442
Lazaros of Galesion, 187n46
lead glazing technique in Byzantium, emergence of, 194
lead seals. *See* seals
Lefort, Jacques, 148
Lemerle, Paul, 133n37
Leo III (emperor), 110, 117
Leo IV (emperor), 156n48
Leo VI the Wise (emperor), 21, 391
Leo of Synada, 53n15, 184
Leontius of Neapolis, 87–88n189, 364, 365, 386n39, 391n69, 401n15
St. Leucius, *Vita* of, 253n106
Levanto, Ugolino da, 276
Levi, Doro, 402
Lex Rhodia (Rhodian Sea Law), 94, 96, 276
Libanius, 340, 341, 348, 353, 359, 363, 364, 402
Liber Comunis, 247, 250n88–90
Liber Syro-Romanus, 335
Licinius (emperor), 93
Lightfoot, Christopher, 5, 6, 109n39, 177, **435,** 442
Limestone massif, villages of, 5
Limyra, 107, 163n88
Lipefina, Manolesso, 275
literacy and books in Amorion, **188,** 188–89
liturgical wine, 37, 415, 416
Liutprand Capitulary, 220–21, 231

local exchange: changes in seventh and eighth centuries, 99–122 (*See also* changes in local and regional exchange in seventh and eighth centuries); defining, 4–5, 99, 147, 434; fairs, local, 289
Location Theory of land use and development, 171
Longobards in Northern Italy. *See* Northern Italy in eighth century
Lopadion, 161, **161**
Louis the Pious (Frankish ruler), 58, 227n32
Low-ring Base Ware, 205
Lower Po Valley. *See* Northern Italy in eighth century
LR amphorae. *See entries at* Late Roman
Lunt, Horace, 59n49
Luzzatto, Gino, 244

macella, 342–44, **343, 345,** 346
Magdalino, Paul, 391n76
majolica workshops of Italy compared to Byzantine glazed ceramics, 215
Malatesta family, 271, 276
Manfred of Sicily, 246, 249, 250, 251, 259, 260
Manganaro, Giacomo, 385
Mango, Marlia Mundell, 148, 333
Mantzikert, Battle of (1071), 149, 180
Manuel I Komnenos (emperor), 264, 268, 407
Mar Saba, 78
Marcello, Filippo, 273
Marcus Aurelius (emperor), 355
Marignoni, Gabriele, 272
maritime trade: antique connection between commerce and the sea, 78–79; in Balkans, 127, 135, 137; distortions caused by overemphasis of, 177, 184, 190; heterogeneity of cargo, 80; importance of, 177; overall economic networks, relationship of sea routes to, 85–87; regional/interregional distinction blurred in, 5; short-distance deliveries by ship, 77–78. *See also* Adriatic trade networks in twelfth and thirteenth centuries; shipwrecks

Mark the Deacon, 53n16
market economy, concept of, 2–4, 13–26; conceptual awareness of market prices and economic processes, 15–17, 54–60; criteria for, 14–15; economic life in absence of, 433; estate economy and, 21–23; low-cost artifacts and raw materials, trade in, 17–19; modern economic theory and, 429–30; "modernist," "primitivist," and "anti-primitivist" views of, 2–3, 13–14, 125, 429; monetized versus "natural" or barter system, 22–23; moral restraints on commerce, absence of, 17; professional craft associations, Roman versus medieval, 21; state intervention in economy, 20–21; technological innovation for commercial purposes, existence of, 17–19; unified currency market and regionally integrated commercial markets, 16; world-empire versus world-economy, 14, 21
marketplaces. *See* agorai, physical shops and marketplaces
St. Markianos, *Life* of, 387
Marlière, Élise, 74n118
Marmara Coast, wines of, 73, 77
Marseille, 30–31, 77, 87
Martin, J.-M., 266n197
al-Marzūqī, 283–88, 290n68
Maslama, 163
Maurice, *Strategikon,* 76
Mauricius Tiberius (emperor), 227n32
Mauss, Marcel, 3
Maximian (emperor), 23
Maximinus (emperor), 75
Maximus of Hispania (usurper), 380
Mayer, Hans Eberhard, 299n4
McCormick, Michael, 2, 6, 8, 51, 219, 235, 251n97, 433–34, **435,** 442
Measles Ware, 143, **143**
measuring goods. *See* weighing and measuring
Mecca, 281
medicine: Amorion, medicinal plants from, 188; wine, medicinal use of, 36–37

Mefalsim, 69
Megalopsychia Hunt, Yakto mosaic depicting, 340, 349, 350, 353, 357, 359, 360, 402, **403**
Megaw, A. H. S., 205
Melenikon, 210
Melitoupolis, 162
Mesembria, 110, 126, 128
metal, ore, and mineral trade, Adriatic, 261–62, 279
metalwork: Amorion, found at, 190–91, **191**; Byzantine glazed ceramics based on, **196**, 196–97,
metalwork, *continued*
  197, 199, 200–201, **202**; Byzantine glazed ceramics departing from, 205
Metcalf, Michael, 305, 318
Methone, T'ang marbled ware vessel found at, 102
metron, 415–16, **416**
Meyer, Eduard, 13n4
Michael III (emperor), 179, 180–82n13
Michael IV (emperor), 129
Michael VII (emperor), 391
Michael VIII (emperor), 396–97, 396n108
Michael Psellos, 156n47
Michiel, Vitale II (doge of Venice), 246
micro-ecological variation in Adriatic coastline, 239–40, 246, 254, 279
Migeotte, Léopold, 26
Mijušković, Slavko, 258n141
Mikro Pisto ceramics, **211**, 215
Miletos, 162, 163–66, **165**
Milvian Bridge, Battle of (312), 417
mining activities: in Balkans, 261–62, 279; fuel and mining in Cilicia, relationship between, 300
Miracles of St. Stephen, 57n37
Mirnik, I., 130n26
"modernist" view of Byzantine trade and markets, 2–3, 13–14
modios, 410–11, 416, **417**
Mokisos, 150–51, **151, 152**
Molfetta, 257, 258, 259
Molin, Pietro da, 270, 274
Monemvasia, 127
monetization of economy, 22–23; Asia Minor, regional networks in, 147; Balkans, regional networks in, 129; changes in local and regional exchange in seventh and eighth centuries, 22–23
money. *See* coins
money changers, 387, 391, 406–7
Monica (mother of Augustine of Hippo), 76
Monochrome Glazed Ware, 231n41, 304n14
Monopoli, 258
Monte Testaccio, Rome, amphora dump at, 67
Morel, Jean-Paul, 18, 25
Morelli, Federico, 22, 26
Morgan, Charles H., II, 143
Morley, Neville, 3, 434
Morosini, Pietro, 270
Morrisson, Cécile, ix, 9, 379, 429, 434–36, 442
Moselle Valley, wines of, 73
Mosynopolis, 130, 133, 211, **212**
Mouchasos the camel driver, 401
Mount Athos, Protaton church, Expulsion of the Merchants from the Temple, **406**
Mount Ganos, 73, 77
muda, 249
Muḥammad's encounter with Baḥīra at Syrian fair, 291
al-Muqaddasī, 292, 293, 294
murex shells, 140
Muslims: Seljuk Turks, arrival of, 149, 180. *See also* Arab Muslim conquests
Mysia, **159,** 159–61

Nag Hammadi, camel-shaped bottle from, 70–71, **71**
Naḥal Bohu, 69
Narentari pirates, 263
"natural" or barter economy, 22–23
Neapolis, 68
Nessana papyri, 316n27
Nicaea, Lake of, agrarian productivity of land around, 156–57
Nicaea, Second Council of (787), 115–16
Nicholas, "*metrētēs* of the Phylax," 389
Nicolo da Lacroma of Ragusa, 271
Niewöhner, Philipp, 151n28, 163, 173
Nikephoros I (emperor), 115, 292
Nikephoros II Phokas (emperor), 180
Nikephoros (patriarch of Constantinople), 163
Niš, *xestēs* from, 412–13
Nonantola, excavation of monastery of, **232,** 233
Normans, in Mediterranean, 137, 246, 265, 397. *See also* Antioch, Norman Principality of; Sicily
North Syrian (Gaza wine) amphorae, 5, 34, 67–68, 68n83, 69, 326
Northern Italy in eighth century, 219–33; amphorae, **225,** 228–31, **229, 230**; documentary and archaeological evidence regarding, 220–22, **223**; Nonantola, excavation of monastery of, **232,** 233; trade relations of, 220–22, 230–33; Venice, eventual flourishing of, 219–20, 231, 232–33. *See also* Comacchio
Notker the Stammerer, 60n53
numismatics. *See* coins

Odo of Cluny, 59n44
Odoacer (king of Italy), 66
Ohthere (Scandinavian trader), 58n38
Oikonomides, Nicolas, 128n18, 148n9, 389n56, 395, 405
oil. *See* olive oil
Olbia ships, 84n176
Old English Orosius, 58n38–39
olive oil: African oil gathered for export at Carthage, 53n16, 61, 65; in bladders, 65, 120; ceramic industries and production of, 73; Chian amphorae, flavored oils transported in, 61; liquid measures for, 412–16, **413, 415, 416**; from Sparta, 138, 139, 143
Orbikon the camel driver, Kissufim mosaic pavement, 71–72, **72**
Oribasius, 37
Orseolo, Pietro II (doge of Venice), 263
Ostia: *modios,* depiction of, 411n79; physical shops and marketplaces, 334, 342, **345,** 346, 349, 353, 357, 358, 359, 361, 362, 364; wine amphorae, decline in, 92
Otranto, 105, 253, 266
Otranto, Strait of, 236, 265
overland trade: amphorae, shipment of, 69–73, **70–72,** 120–21; in Bal-

kans, 118–19, **119,** 127–28, 135–37; changes in local and regional exchange in seventh and eighth centuries, 118–21, **119, 120;** Constantinople, overland route from Dalmatian ports to, 269–70, 279; inland sites, importance of, 177–78, 182–83; pack animals and wheeled vehicles, 120, 155, 313, 401. *See also* roads

Oxyrhynchos papyri, 16, 19, 55

Pacatus, 380
pack animals, 120, 151, 313, 401
Pag, island of, 251, 255
Painted Fine Sgraffito Ware, 142, **142,** 200
Pakourianos, Gregory, estates of, 130–35, **132**
Palace Ware, **316,** 316–17
Palaia, 162
Palestine. *See* Syria-Palestine
Palestinian Fine Ware, 4, **315,** 315–16
Palladas, 379
Palmyra, 7, 322, 336, 362
Palud, La, shipwreck, 409–10
Panella, Clementina, 9
Panidos, 134
Papanikola-Bakirtzi, Demetra, 5, 8, 144, 193, **435,** 442
Paphlagonia, 8, 107, 115, 171, **173,** 190
Parastaseis syntomoi chronikai, 387–88, 410, 424
Parion, 159
Parker, Anthony J., 8, 39, 79, 81, 84, 90n197
Patara, 353, **354,** 362
Patlagean, Évelyne, 3, 333
Patria, 352, 388n46, 411n78
Paul of Aegina, 36
Pefkos wreck, 82n170
Pegai, 159–60, **160**
Pegolotti, Francesco Balducci, 379, 392, 395n107, 396
Pelagonisi shipwreck, 144, **145**
Pelagonnesos-Alonnesos shipwreck, glazed ceramics from, 200–201, **201,** 214
Pella, 7, **316,** 318, 320, 322, 326
perfect and imperfect markets, 432
Pergamon, 162–63, **164,** 166, 211–12, 215

Perge, 339, 353
Peritheorion, 130, 133, 134
Persian wars: amphorae, production and export of, 31, 32; dissolution of Mediterranean community and, 148–49
Pesaro, 245
Peschlow, Urs, 194
Phaselis, 345
Philagrius, 363
Philippikos (emperor), 110
Philippopolis, 128, 129, 130, 133, 134, 135, 136
Philotheos, 389
Phocas (emperor), 110, 419
Photius (patriarch of Constantinople), 60, 78
physical shops and marketplaces, 7, 333–77; accounting practices, 326–29, **329,** 433; amphorae, storage, organization, and sale of contents from, 66–67, **67, 68;** archaeological evidence, appendix of, 366–77; architecture of, 353–55, **354;** building and repair of, 361–62, 366–68, 372–75; coin evidence of, 326, 327, 330, 336, 360; commercialization of city centers, 7, 333–36; decoration of, 355–56; documentary evidence of, 340; evidence for, 52–53; goods and services sold in, 325–26, 340–41, 350–51; as houses, 359–60; internal organization of, 356–59; laws and regulations regarding, 334, 335–36, 351, 357, 361–62, 364, 366; location and distribution in urban settings, 351–52; market buildings, 335, 341–47, **343–45, 347,** 366–69; objects from, 325–26, 359–60; permanent retail establishments, defining and identifying, 347–50, **348, 354,** 360; pictorial evidence of, 340, 359, 360, 364–65, 402–7, **403, 405, 406;** portico mosaics, 356, 360; regulated market stalls, 336–41, **337,** 407; restaurants, 357, 364; shopkeepers, 362–63; shopping, as social and cultural experience, 362–65; street and industrial encroachments, 333–36, 357, 362, 375–77; Syria-Palestine, Byzantine and early Islamic,

regional exchange in, 321–29, **324, 325, 327–29;** *topos* inscriptions, 334, 338–40
Piccolpasso, Cipriano, 214
Picon, Maurice, 18, 25, 46
Pieri, Dominique, 5–6, 27, 62–63, 64, 91n203, 433, **435,** 442–43
Pietro of Bari, 260–61
pirates and piracy, Adriatic, 262–63
Pirenne, Henri, 3, 6, 87, 219, 235, 294–95n100
Pisa, 267, 269
Pisidian Antioch, 358, 359, 360, 361, 383
Pitarakis, Brigitte, 7, 379, 383, 389, 398, 399, **435,** 443
pithoi, 76, 186
plague: fourteenth century, 84, 89, 90; Justinianic, 8, 73n100, 90, 101, 151, 158, 169
Plain-Glazed Ware, 212
Plain-Sgraffito Ware, 212
Po Valley plain. *See* Northern Italy in eighth century
Poimanenon, 161–62, **162**
Polanyi, Karl, 3, 429, 430
Pompeii, 75, 336, 341
population density in Asia Minor, 149–51, **151, 152,** 171–73, **173,** 174
Porphyrius of Gaza, 53n16
Port Saint Symeon, 297–99, 300, 304, 305, 309
Port Saint Symeon Ware, 6, 214, 216, 304n15, 306–9
post markets, 53–54
Potter, Timothy W., 336
pottery. *See* ceramics
Preslav, 129
Presthlavitza, 129
prices and pricing: conceptual awareness of market prices in Roman world, 15–17, 58–59, 430; Diocletian, Price Edict of, 23, 69, 71, 77; *Expositio totius mundi* on, 56–57; increases and decreases in, 52; modern economic theory and, 430–32, **431;** price controls, Roman efforts at, 23
Prilongion, 130, 133
"primitivist" view of Byzantine trade and markets, 2–3, 13–14, 125, 429
Pringle, Denys, 213, 306
Procopius, 118n79

producer cities versus consumer cities, as historiographical concept, 24
professional craft associations, Roman versus medieval, 21
prostitution, association of taverns with, 364
Protaton church, Mount Athos, Expulsion of the Merchants from the Temple, **406**
Pryor, Frederic, 2, 429–30
Psellos, 380
Pseudo-Fulgentius of Ruspe, 53n13
Pseudo-Lucian, 137n67
Pseudo-Macarius/Symeon, 52n35
Ptochoprodromos, 405n41
Puglia, 249
Purcell, Nicholas, 2, 239–40

al-Qazwīnī, 284, 285, 286

Ragusa: extra-Adriatic trade, 264, 266–67, 269, 270; inter-Adriatic trade, non-Venetian, 254–63 *passim*, 278; Venice, trade with, 239, 240
Raidestos (Rodosto), 128, 130, 134, 391–92
Rathbone, Dominic, 21–22
Ravenna, 66, 117, 239–40, 248, 251, 253, 258, 259
Recanati, 248
reciprocity, as economic function, 24–25, 429, 430
Red Painted Ware, 4, **316**, 316–17, **317**
Red Sgraffito Ware, 144n122
Red Slip Ware: African (ARS), 9, 73, 106, 190, 368, 370, 375, 376; Cypriot, 104, 105, 107
Redford, Scott, 5, 213, 297, **435**, 443
redistribution, as economic function, 429, 430
regional exchange: Adriatic trade networks, 6, 8, 235–79 (*See also* Adriatic trade networks in twelfth and thirteenth centuries); in Asia Minor, 8, 147–75 (*See also* Asia Minor, regional networks in); in Balkans, 8, 125–46 (*See also* Balkans, regional networks in); changes in seventh and eighth centuries, 99–122 (*See also* changes in local and regional exchange in seventh and eighth centuries); defining, 4, 5, 125–27, 147, 434; fairs, regional, 289–90, 293; scholastic interest in, 235–36; in Syria-Palestine, 311–30 (*See also* Syria-Palestine, Byzantine and early Islamic, regional exchange in); value of studying, 311–12
Reidt, Klaus, 163
restaurants, 357, 364, 402
retail shops. *See* physical shops and marketplaces
Rhodes, wrecks off, 81, 83
Rhodian Sea Law (*Lex Rhodia*), 94, 96, 276
Rhosos (Cilicia), amphorae produced at, 46
Ribe, Denmark, beach market in, 53n11
Rice, David Talbot, 194
Riley, John A., 28, **29**
Riley-Smith, Jonathan, 305, 306
roads: in Asia Minor, 118–19, **120**, 152–55, **153–55**, 157, **162**, **167**, 167–68, 171; in Balkans, 127–28; changes in local and regional exchange in seventh and eighth centuries, 118–21, **119**, **120**. *See also entries at* Via
Rodosto (Raidestos), 128, 130, 134, 391–92
Roger II of Sicily, 139, 246, 266, 303
Rome: barrels used for maritime imports to, 75–76, 92; Constantinople, as separate market from, 59; Ephesos as traditional connector to, 152; official weights and measures kept in temples of, 383; physical shops and marketplaces in, 341, 342, 350, 351, 355; shipwreck evidence regarding importance relative to Constantinople, 85–86; wheat prices and distance from, 430–32, **431**
Rossano Gospels, 340, 419–20n128
Rostovtzeff, Michael, 2–3
Roueché, Charlotte, 333, 339
Rovinj, 257, 258
Ruṣāfa (Sergiopolis), 5, 7, 289n61, 304, 321, 322
Russell, James, 174
Russo, Giovanni, 275

Sabbato of Split, 260
Sacra Parallela manuscript (Paris. gr. 923), 416, **417**
Sagalassos: continuation of monumentalized main avenues in, 334; decline in seventh century, 151n28, 183; local semifine and coarse kitchen wares, 8, 106, 108; physical shops and marketplaces in, 336–39, **337**, 342, 349, 351–53, 355, 357, 359–62
sailor-trader, combined occupation of, 275–77
Saint-Gervais 2 wreck, 96
Saliou, Catherine, 335, 340
salt trade, Adriatic, 220, 239, 241, 250–51, 255–56, 259, 260, 271
Salvo of Savona, 276
San Salvatore a Brescia, 220
Sanders, Guy D. R., 143
Santamaria, Claude, 43n34
Saqqara, amphorae from, 47, **48**
Saraçhane, 108, 111, 229
Saraçhane 61/Günsenin 3 type amphorae, 138
Saradi, Helen, 333, 335
Sardinia, wrecks off, 83, 84n176
Sardis: amphorae from, 34n12; inscription at, 21; physical shops at, 353, 355–58, 402n29, 408
Sasanids. *See* Persian wars
Sauvaget, Jean, 333
Scala, Giacomo della, 251
Schiavone, Aldo, 18
seals: of *horreiarioi*, 129; of *kommerkiarioi* and *apothēkai*, **112**, 112–14, **113**, 115, 128, 148n9, 150, 189; on weighing instruments, 389–90
Second Crusade, 134, 298
sekomata (measuring tables), 411–12, **412**
Seleukeia Pieria, amphorae produced at, 46
self-sufficiency or *autarkeia*, 3, 21–22, 24, 122, 138, 147, 148
Seljuk Turks, arrival of, 149, 180
Selymbria, 134
Serapeion, 383
Serçe Limanı wreck, 80n163, 95, **410**
Sergiopolis (Ruṣāfa), 5, 7, 289n61, 304, 321, 322

Serres, Byzantine glazed ceramics from, 209–10, **210**, 215
Severian of Gabala, 78
Sgraffito Ware: from Antioch, 304n14; Fine, 142, **142**, 143, 144, **145**, 198–99, **199**, 200, **201**, 207, 212; Incised, 142, 143, 144, **144**, **203**, 203–4, **204**, 212, **213**; locally made, 143; Painted Fine, 142, **142**, 200; Plain-Sgraffito Ware, 212; Red, 144n122
Shatzman, I., 72n104
shipbuilding industry, Adriatic, 260
shipwrecks, 77–97; amphorae found in, 36; barrel remains found in, 75; cargo visibility, problem of, 94, 96–97; drop in number over time, 9, 39, **40**, **84**, 84–85, 90; future studies of, 8–9, 89–90; geodatabase study of, 80–89, **82–84, 86**; independent sources, relating data to, 79–80; limitations of evidence from, 89–97; modern economic theory and, 433, 434, **434**; new discoveries, value of, 79; raw materials and low-cost goods, evidence of trade in, 17, 19; sinking rate and age of ships, 94–96, **95**; sizes and capacities of ships, inferences drawn from, 90–92, 93–94
Shivta/Subaytah, 7, 69, 323–24
shopkeepers' accounts, stone tablet with, 326–29, **329**, 433
shopping, as social and cultural experience, 362–65
shops. *See* physical shops and marketplaces
Sicily: Adriatic trade and Kingdom of, 246–47, 249, 252, 253, 262, 264–65, 266; coin evidence from, 110–11; wrecks off, 81–83, 86
Sidonius Apollinaris, 36
sigillata, 18
sigillography. *See* seals
sigma plazas, 346–47, **347**, 361, 368–69
silk textiles, 139–40, 187, 259, 270, 304
Simeticulo, Leonardo, 263
Sinope: amphorae from, 28, **30**, 47, 48; as commercial center, 115

Sirkeci railway station, Istanbul, Byzantine glazed ceramic finds from, 194, 207, 208, 209
skins or bladders used for transport of goods, 65, 120, 187, 401
Skopelos bowls, 204n55
Skopelos shipwreck, 144
Skuldelev vessels, 95, **95**
Skylitzes, John, 129n22, 389n61, **390**
Skythopolis (Baysān): annual fair, 294; coins and ceramic finds, 314, 315, 318, 320, 321; physical shops and marketplaces, 7, 322, 325, 326, 328, 334, **344**, 346, 349, 350, 355–57, 359, 360, 361, 364
slave trade: Adriatic, 251–52, 260–61; in eastern Mediterranean, 261n170, 302
Slavic robbers in the Balkans, 127n13, 135
Slip-Painted Ware, 142, 143, 203, 212
Smith, Adam, 2, 379
Sofia, 128, 134
Sokoloff, Michael, 72n103
Sombart, Werner, 24
Sparta, 138, 139, 141, 143, 144, 200
spatheia, 42, 43n34
spindle-shaped amphorae, 47
Split, 258, 259, 263, 267n209
spolia, use of: in Amorion, 180, 189; in Asia Minor, 151, 162n74, 168n99
Spufford, Peter, 379
Sravikion, 130, 133
Saint-Bertrand-de-Comminges, 346
Stagnario, Giovanni, 247
Stagnario, Pietro, 251
Standing Caliph coins, **320**
state intervention in economy, 20–21
staterae, 382
steelyards, 381–82, 407–10; amphorae, weighing of, 45, 87; with apotropaic devices, **423**; as archaeological finds, 408–10; beachside markets, use at, 53, 87–89; defined and described, 407–8; illustrations of, **381, 382, 408, 410, 411**; shipboard use of, 87–89
Stenimachos, 130, 133
Stephanos Byzantinos, 162n73
Stephen, St., *Miracles* of, 57n37

Stephen of Dioclea, 129n26
Stern, Edna, 213
stillaturae, 15
Subaytah/Shivta, 7, 69, 323–24
Sulaymān b. ʿAbd al-Malik, 286
Sullecthum, 68
superregional exchange. *See* interregional exchange
supply and demand. *See* demand
Svetoslav (Russian prince), 129
swindlers. *See* fraud and cheating
Symeon (tsar), 129
Symeon the Fool, *Life* of, 339, 341, 356, 357, 360, 363, 365, 391n69, 401, 402
Symeon Stylites, 355
Synesius, 81n168
Syria, annual fairs in, 6–7, 281–96; almanacs as evidence of fairs in Islamic period, 283–85; Christian saints' days and festivals, origins in, 286, 287–89; commodities exchanged at, 292; *ḥajj* and, 281; list of, 285–87; map of antique and medieval fairs, **282**; Muḥammad's encounter with Baḥīra at, 291; pre-Islamic cycle of, 281–83, 284; range, scope, timing, and duration, 289–93; timing of, 290; trade networks and, 293–96. *See also specific towns and fairs*
Syria-Palestine, Byzantine and early Islamic, regional exchange in, 311–30; Arabic language, adoption of, 328–29; ceramics, 312n8, 313–17, **314–17**, 321; coins, 312n8, 317–21, **319–21**, 326, 327, 330; map of area, **313**; operation of shops, 325–29, **329**; physical shops and markets, 321–29, **324, 325, 327, 328**

tabernae, 347–50
Tadić, Jorjo, 264n187, 267n209
Tafur, Pero, 404
T'ang marbled ware vessel found at Methone, 102
taverns, 7, 350, 357, 359, 364, 402–4
taxation: border duties, 313n11; in cash rather than kind, 129; fairs, abolition of taxes during, 290; private collection system, 22;

taxation *(continued)*
professional craft associations and, 21; sales process, taxes associated with, 392, 394–97; of salt, 220, 250; surplus production and, 148; tax offices, 351n96

Tchernia, André, 72n104, 86n183, 92

Temin, Peter, 2, 9, 13, 26, 55, 57, 59, 60, 78, 97, 429, 443

Terlizzi, 258

Termoli, 254, 257

Teutonic Knights, 266, 301

textile and clothing production and trade: in Adriatic, 249–50, 259–60, 279; Antioch and Cilicia, 302, 304; market prices, concept of, 58–59; silk, 139–40, 187, 259, 270, 304; technological innovation in, 18–19; value of studying, 25; wool and cotton, 249–50, 260

textual evidence. *See* documentary evidence

Thamugadi, 335n15, 341, 342, 349, 358

Thebes, 138–42, 145, 270

Theoderic (king of Italy), 66

Theodore of Sykeon, 117

Theodoret of Cyrrhus, 78–79n153, 294, 295n104, 355

Theodoros Stoudites, 60, 155n41

Theodosian Code, 334, 335, 361, 386–87

Theodosius I (emperor), 15

Theodosius II (emperor), 169, 352, 385, **386**

Theophanes the Confessor, 116, 126n8, 129n21

Theophanes Continuatus, 52n4, 114n56, 116, 129n22

Theophilos (emperor), 52, 109, 180, **181**, **390**

Theosebius of Skythopolis, 350

Thessalonike: Balkans, regional networks in, 127, 129, 135–37; Byzantine glazed ceramics from, **208**, 208–9, **209**; changes in local and regional exchange in seventh and eighth centuries, 8, 109; Demetria (annual fair), 208; Serres ceramics found at, 210

thick and thin markets, 432

Thietmar, 291, 292

Thignica, 346

Third Crusade, 130n28, 134, 301

Thrace: Balkans, regional networks in, 127–35, 145; Byzantine glazed ceramics from, **211, 212,** 215

Tiberias Hoard, 191

Tiepolo, Marco, 272

timber and wood: Adriatic timber trade, 256, 260; Asia Minor, wood trade in, 147–48; mining and wood fuel in Cilicia, relationship between, 300

Tommaso de Drogasse of Zara, 271

Topkapli, Roman road near, **154, 155, 155**

topos inscriptions, 334, 338–40

Tor, Deborah, 72n103

Touratsoglou, Ioannis, 137

towns. *See* urban areas and trade

Trajan (emperor), 267, 293

Tralleis, 349, 350, 353

Trani, 246, 265, 266, 275

transfer, as economic function, 430

transmarini negotiatores, 41–42

transport of goods, 401; barrels, 73, 74–76, 91–94, 186; bladders or skins used for, 65, 120, 187, 401; pack animals, 120, 151, 313, 401; wheeled vehicles, 120, 151, 313, 401. *See also* amphorae; maritime trade; overland trade

transregional exchange. *See* interregional exchange

Tremiti islands, monks of, 253, 271

tria augustia (standard weights with busts of emperors), 385, **386**

Trier, 56, 87

tripod stilts used in making glazed ceramics, 205, 207, 213, 215

Triscina 3 wreck, 82n169

Trogir, 258, 259, 270

Tyche of Constantinople, weights possibly in shape of, 420–22, **421**

Tzetzes, John, 391

ʿUkāẓ, fair of, 281, 290n67

Ulpian, 74n114, 75n125

Umm al-Jimāl, 324–25

Umm al-Raṣāṣ (Kastron Mefaʿa), 7, 322–25, **324, 325**

urban areas and trade: Asia Minor, settlement size, population density, and chronology in, 149–51, **151, 152,** 171–73, **173,** 174; change and continuity in urban patterns of life, seventh to eighth centuries, 99–101; commercialization of city centers, 7, 333–36; common relationship between, 7, 8; consumer cities versus producer cities, as historiographical concept, 24; country and town, interplay of, 23–26; de-urbanization attributed to seventh century, 99, 171–73, **173,** 177, 183–84; grain supply requirements for nonproducers, 174; location and distribution of shops, 351–52. *See also specific cities and towns*

Uyun Musa, amphorae from, 47, **48**

Uzalis, wine from, 57–58, 76n131

Valens (emperor), 15, 342, 385

Valentinian I (emperor), 15, 385, 388, 410

Valentinian III (emperor), 53n12, 75, 89

van Alfen, Peter G., 44, 65n76, 80n163

van Doorninck, Fred Jr., 65n76, 74n118, 80n163, 81n168, 96n223, 184n37

Van Minnen, Peter, 19

Vandals, 66, 83, 86, 334n8, 362, 376

Venantius Fortunatus, 37

Venice: Adriatic trade networks and supply of, 241–52, **243,** 278, 279; Balkans, commercial privileges in, **131,** 133, 134–35, 137–41, 145; *colleganza* contracts, 240–41, 264, 277; Constantinople, trade with, 264–65; documentary evidence of new settlements of seventh and eighth centuries in Venetian lagoon plexus, 221–22, **223**; Durazzo, Venetian colony in, 270, 274; extra-Adriatic trade, 263–70; famine of 1224–27, 243, 244, 247, 263; identity of traders and naucleri, 271–77; Northern Italy in eighth century and, 219–20, 231, 232–33; pirates and piracy, 263; shipping losses in, 94; slaves and slave trade, 251–52; Thessalonike, glazed ceramics from, 208, 209; Veronese currency as standard coinage of, 246n57; Zeuxippus Ware and, 206

Vera, Domenico, 20
Verina (empress), 420
Veroe, 128, 130
Veronese currency as standard coinage of Venice, 246n57
Via Egnatia, 118n79, 119, 127, 211, 269
Via Militaris/Via Regia, 127, 128, 133
Via Nova, 293
Via Sebaste, **167,** 167–68
Viadro, Tommaso, and Viadro family, 273–75, **275,** 279
Vienna accounting papyri, 22–23
Vienna Dioscurides, 359
vinum populi Romani, 15
Vitruvius, 341, 349
von Thuenen, Johann Heinrich, 171
Vorderstrasse, Tasha, 303n12, 305
Vroom, Joanita, 142
Vryonis, Speros, 21
Waelkens, Marc, 336
Waksman, Sylvie-Yona, 205–6, 213
al-Walīd I (caliph), 322
Wallerstein, Immanuel, 13n4, 14
Walmsley, Alan, 4, 7, 73n109, 311, 433, 434, **435,** 443
Ward-Perkins, Bryan, 333
Wartburg, Marie-Louise, 213
water power, 17, 130, 303, 304n14
wax seals. *See* seals
Weber, Max, 24
weighing and measuring, 7, 379–98, 407–26; amphorae and jars used for, 414–16, **415, 416;** balance scales, 382–83, **384,** 407–10, **411,** 416, **417, 423, 424;** biblical statements regarding, 387n42, 416, **417;** counterfeiting coins, 388, 391; decoration of weighing instruments, 416–23, **418–24;** dry and liquid measures, 410–16; in early Byzantine period (fourth to sixth centuries), 380–89; fraudulent (*See* fraud and cheating); international trade affecting, 392–94; in late Byzantine period, 392–97; *metron,* 415–16, **416;** in middle Byzantine period (Leo VI to twelfth century), 389–92; *modios,* 410–11, 416, **417;** money changers, 387, 391, 406–7; official controls on, 383–87, 389–91, 394; *sekomata* (measuring tables), 411–12, **412;** *staterae,* 382; taxes associated with, 392, 394–97; in traditional images of merchants, 379, **380;** *tria augustia* (standard weights with busts of emperors), 385, **386;** weighing instruments, 381–83, 407–10 (*See also* steelyards); wine and oil, liquid measures for, 412–16, **413, 415, 416;** *xestai,* **41,** 54n21, 64, 384, 412–16, **417**
wheeled vehicles, 120, 151, 313, 401
Whitehouse, David, 4
Wickham, Chris, 2, 233, 235, 311
Wikander, Örjan, 17
Wilkinson, Tony J., 303n12
William I of Sicily, 266
William II of Sicily, 246
William of Tyre, 302n9, 304n14
Wilson, Andrew, 341
wine: Adriatic trade in, 259; aged wines, market for, 57n36; Amorion, winemaking in, 184–87, **185–87;** amphorae mainly used for, 36–39 (*See also* amphorae); in bladders or skins, 65, 120, 187, 401; from Gaza, 5, 36–38, 53–54, 64–65, 77, 87; liquid measures for, 412–16, **413, 415, 416;** liturgical, 37, 415, 416; port markets for, 53–54
winepresses, 69, 73, 184, **185**
wood. *See* timber and wood
wool trade in Adriatic, 249–50
Woolf, Gregg, 13n4, 14, 20–21
Woolley, Sir Leonard, 306
world-empire versus world-economy, 14, 21
Worp, Klaas, 69n86

Xanthe, 130, 133
Xanthos, 358
xestai, **41,** 54n21, 64, 384, 412–16, **417**

Yakto mosaic, 340, 349, 350, 353, 357, 359, 360, 402, **403**
al-Yaʿqūbī, 281n2
Yassı Ada shipwreck, 65, 79, 80n163, 85, 90, 96n223, 228n33, 381, 409
Yenikapı, ships found at, 77, 79, 84n176, 91n202, 409, 421n139

Zaccaria, Giacomo, 274
Zara, 240, 251, 258, 259, 265, 269, 270
Zeno, Rainier (doge of Venice), 245n44, 276–77
Zeugma, 5
Zeuxippus Ware, 142n107, 205–7, **206,** 211, 212
Ziani family, 273
Ziani, Pietro (doge of Venice), 273
Zimolo, 268n217
Zonaras, John, 389n61
Zorzi, Pietro, 274n259
Zuckerman, Constantin, 414
zygostatai, 383, 386, 389